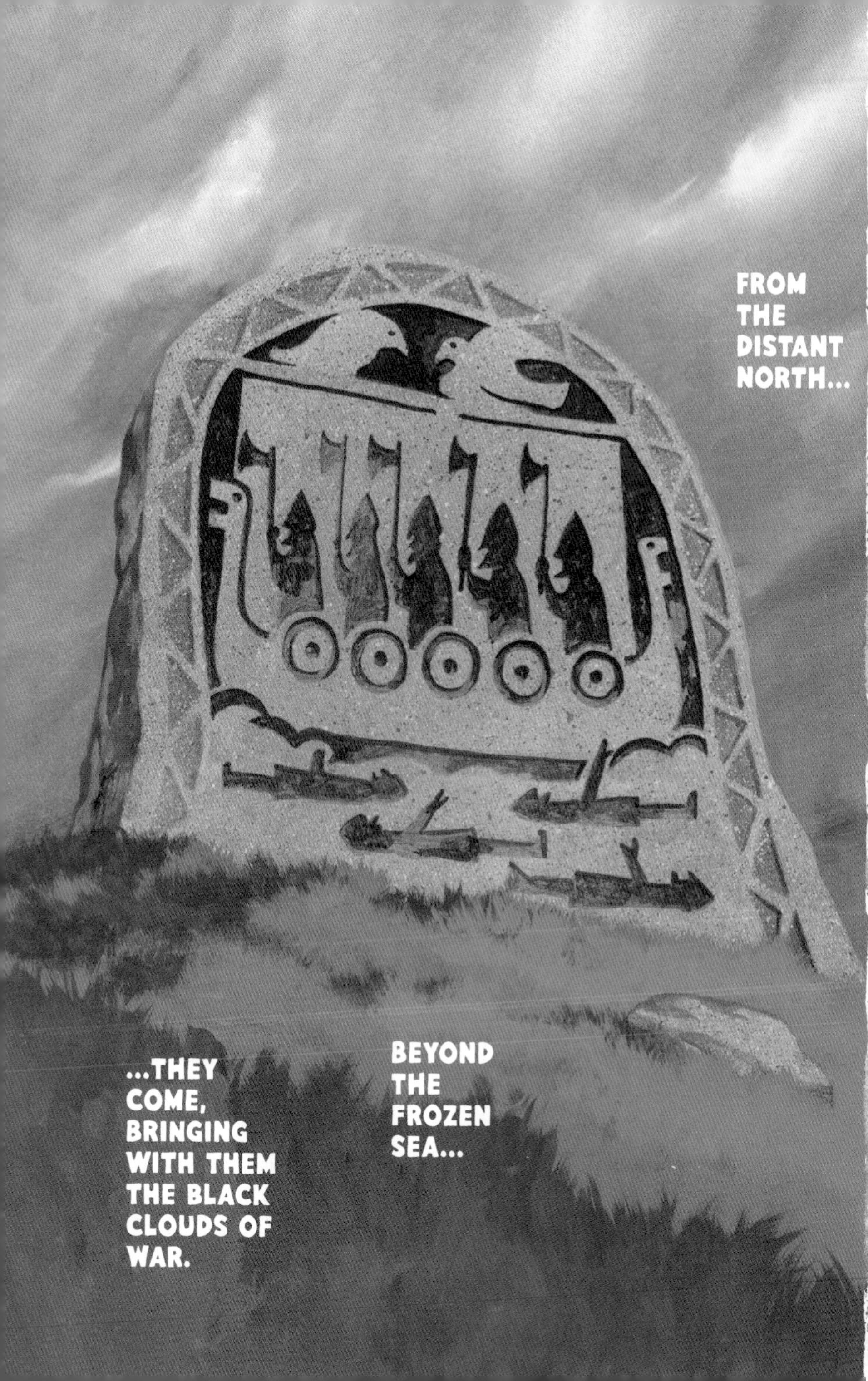
FROM THE DISTANT NORTH...
BEYOND THE FROZEN SEA...
...THEY COME, BRINGING WITH THEM THE BLACK CLOUDS OF WAR.

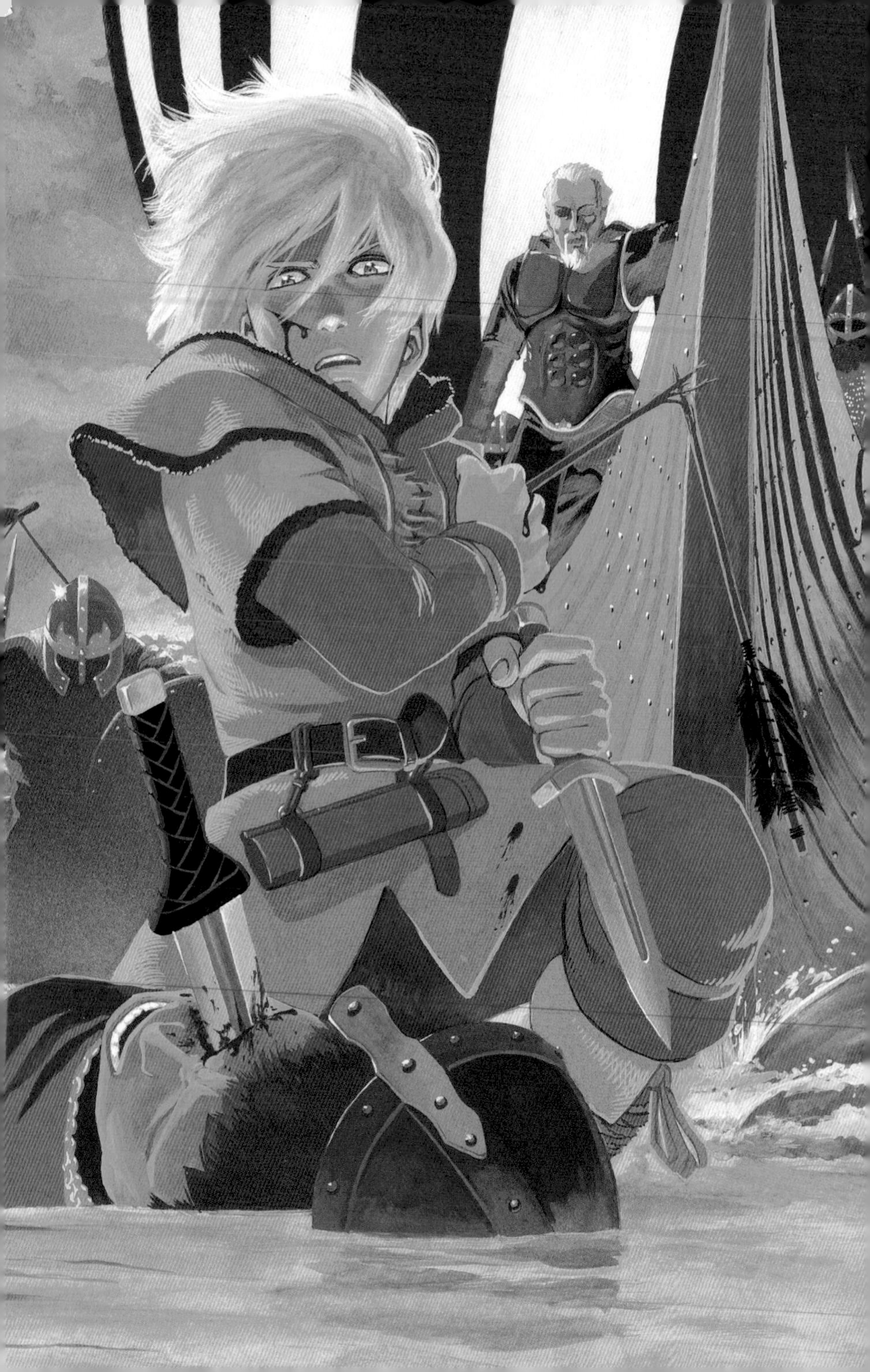

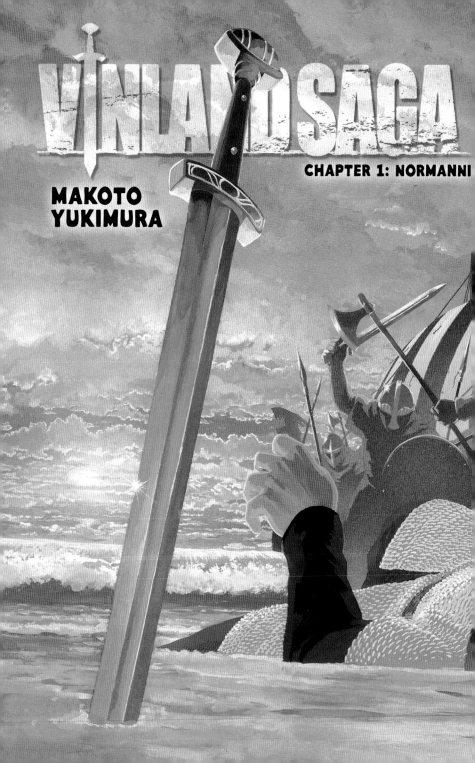

VINLAND SAGA

CHAPTER 1: NORMANNI

MAKOTO YUKIMURA

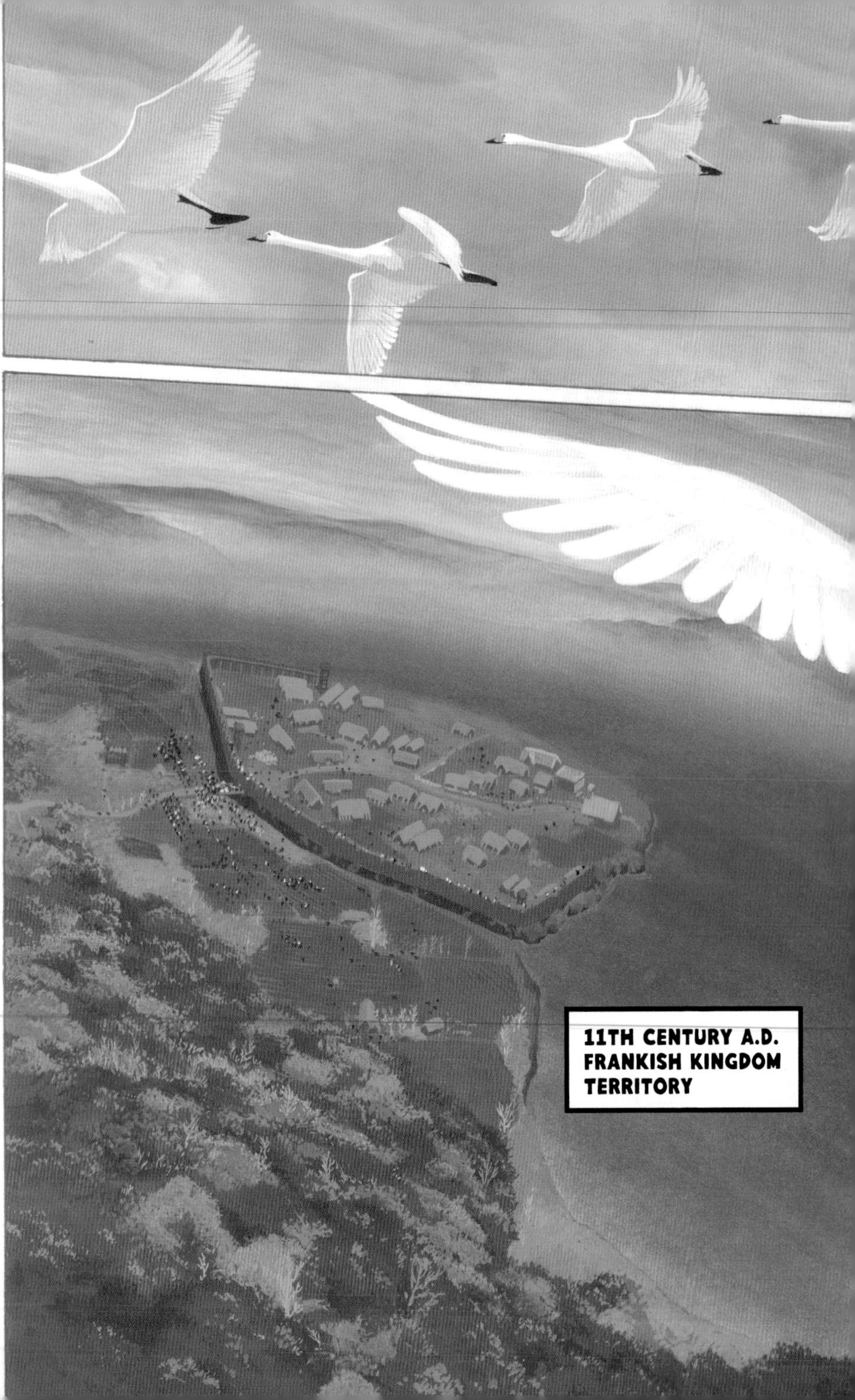
11TH CENTURY A.D.
FRANKISH KINGDOM
TERRITORY

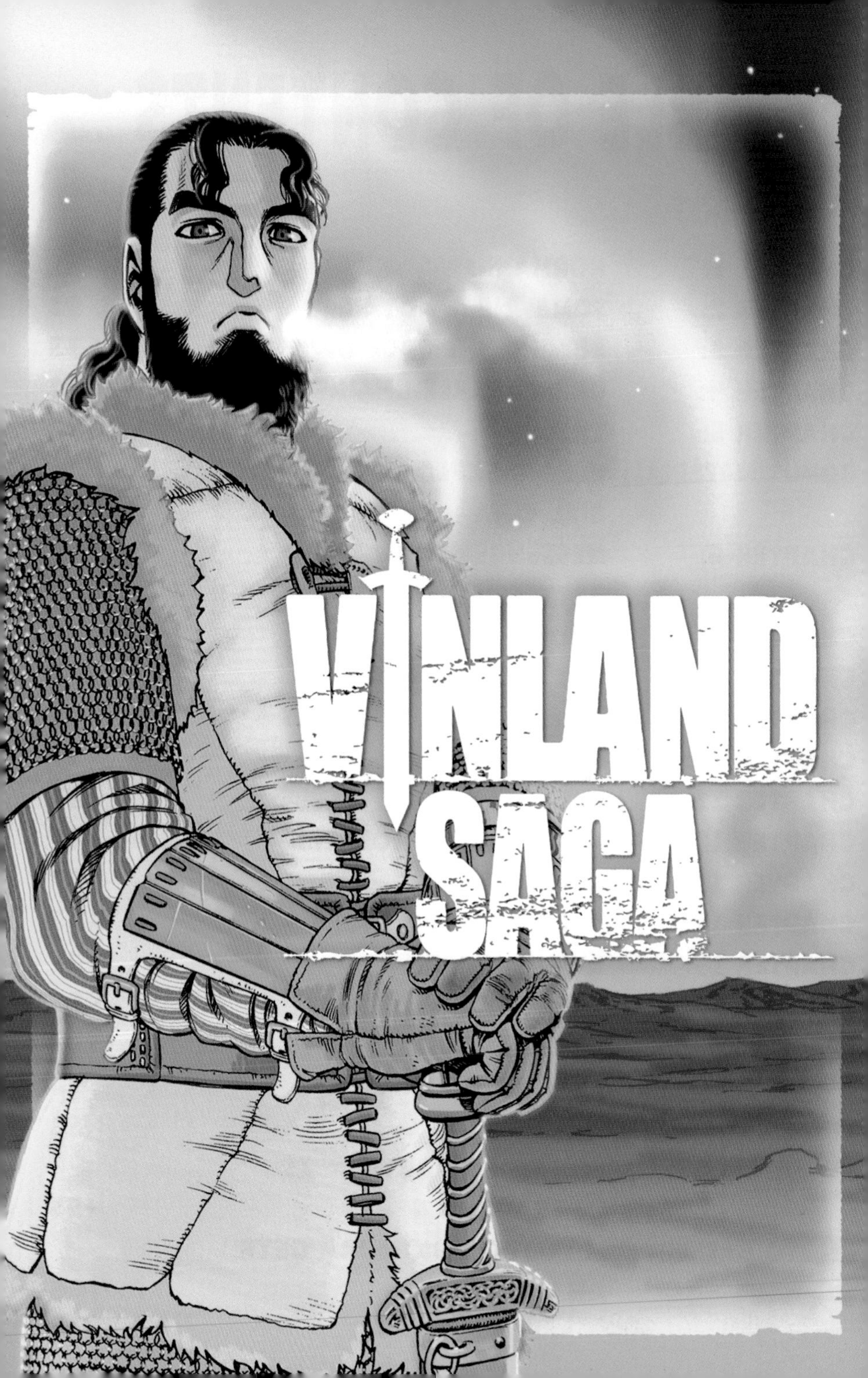
VINLAND
SAGA

TABLE OF CONTENTS

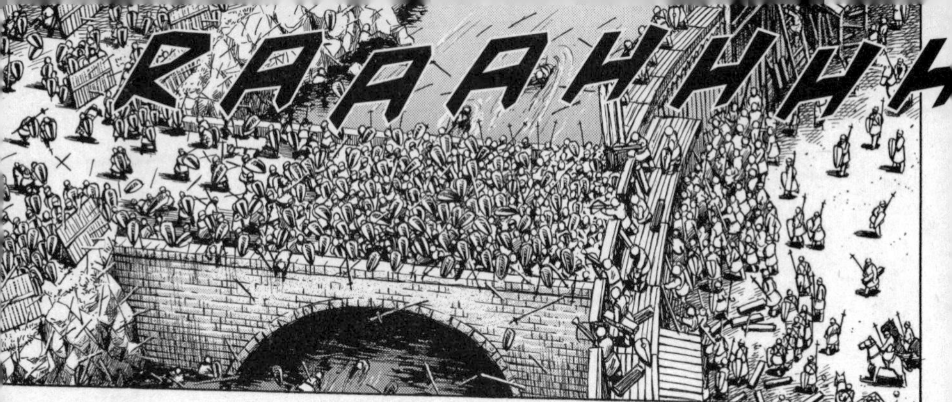
RAAAHHHH

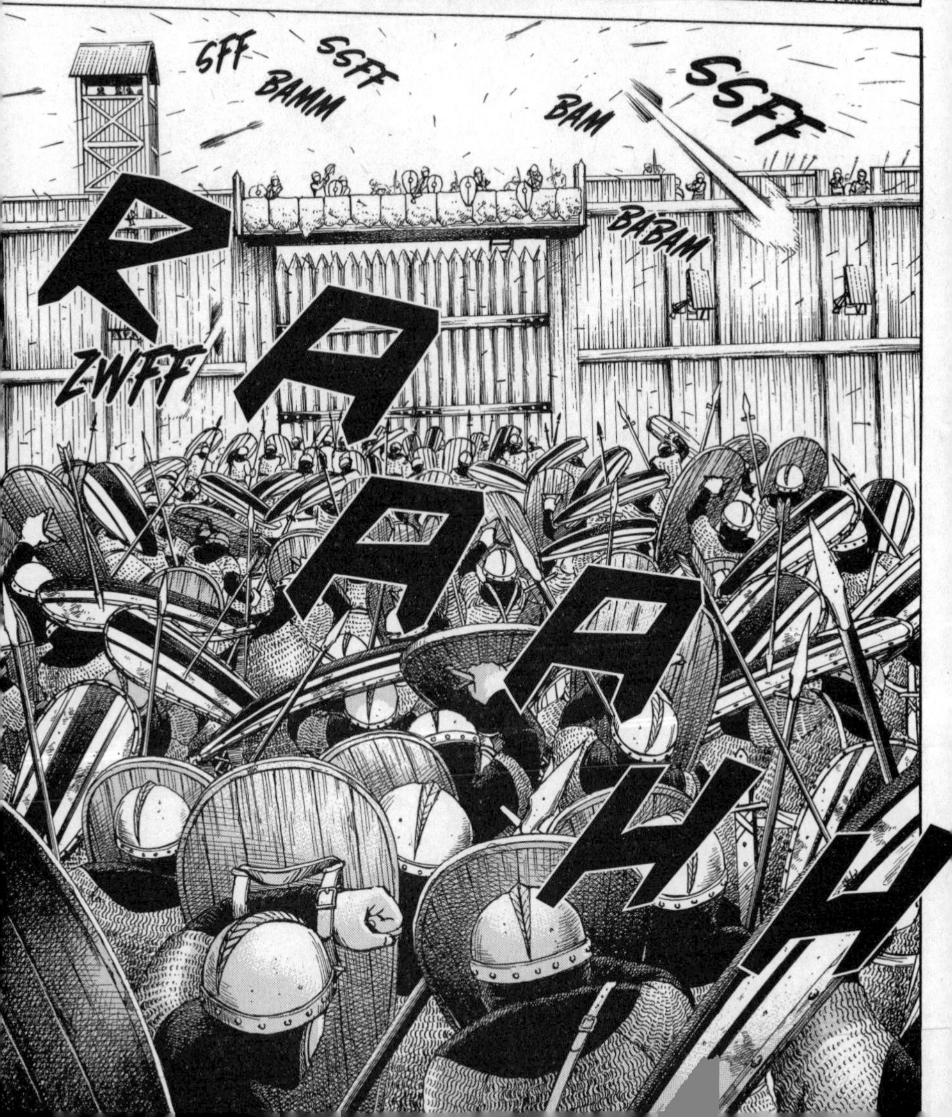
SSFF
BAM
BABAM
SSFF
SFF
BAMM
ZWFF
RAAAHHH

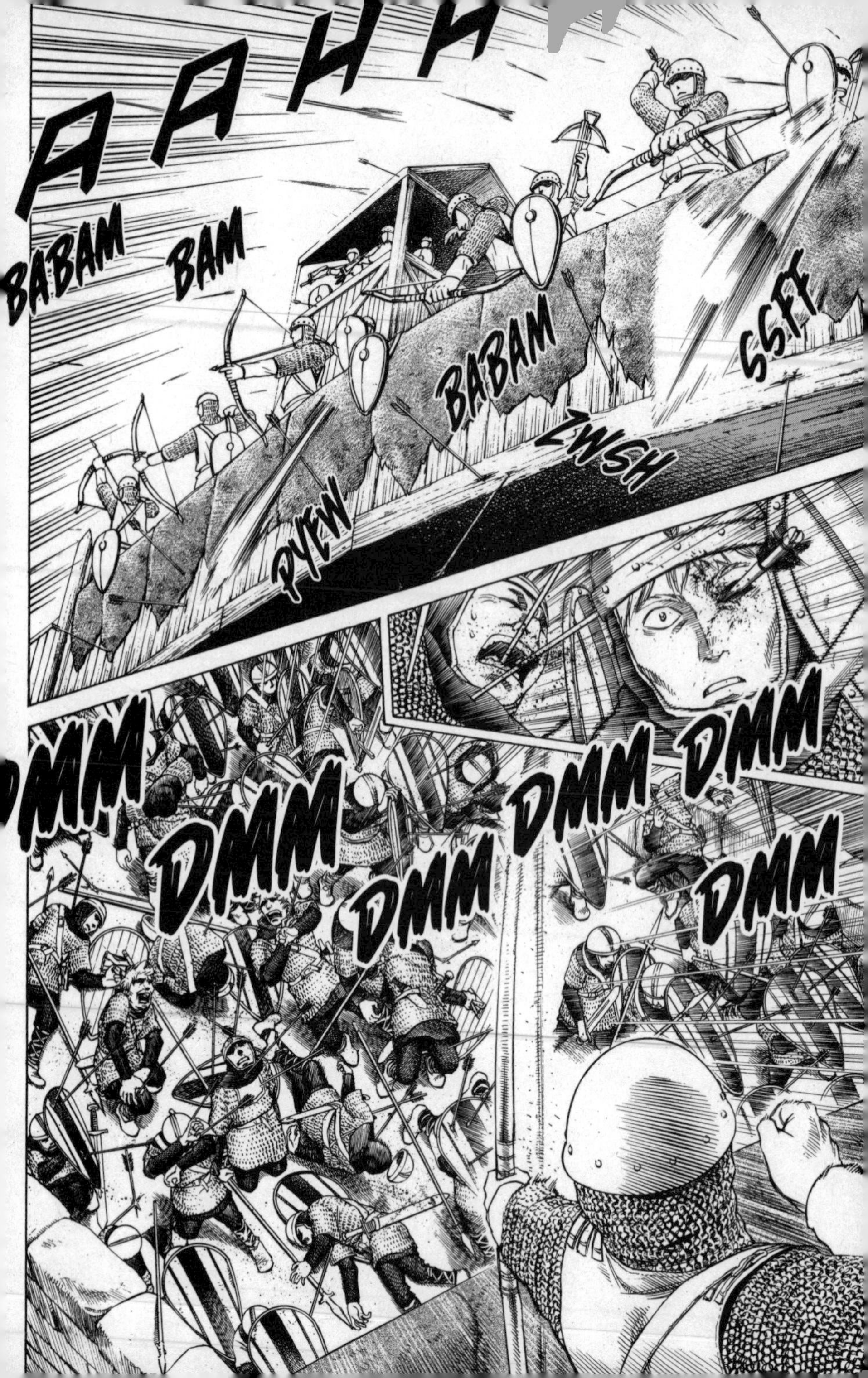
AAHH
SSFF
BABAM
ZWSH
PYEW
BAM
BABAM
DMM
DMM
DMM
DMM
DMM
DMM

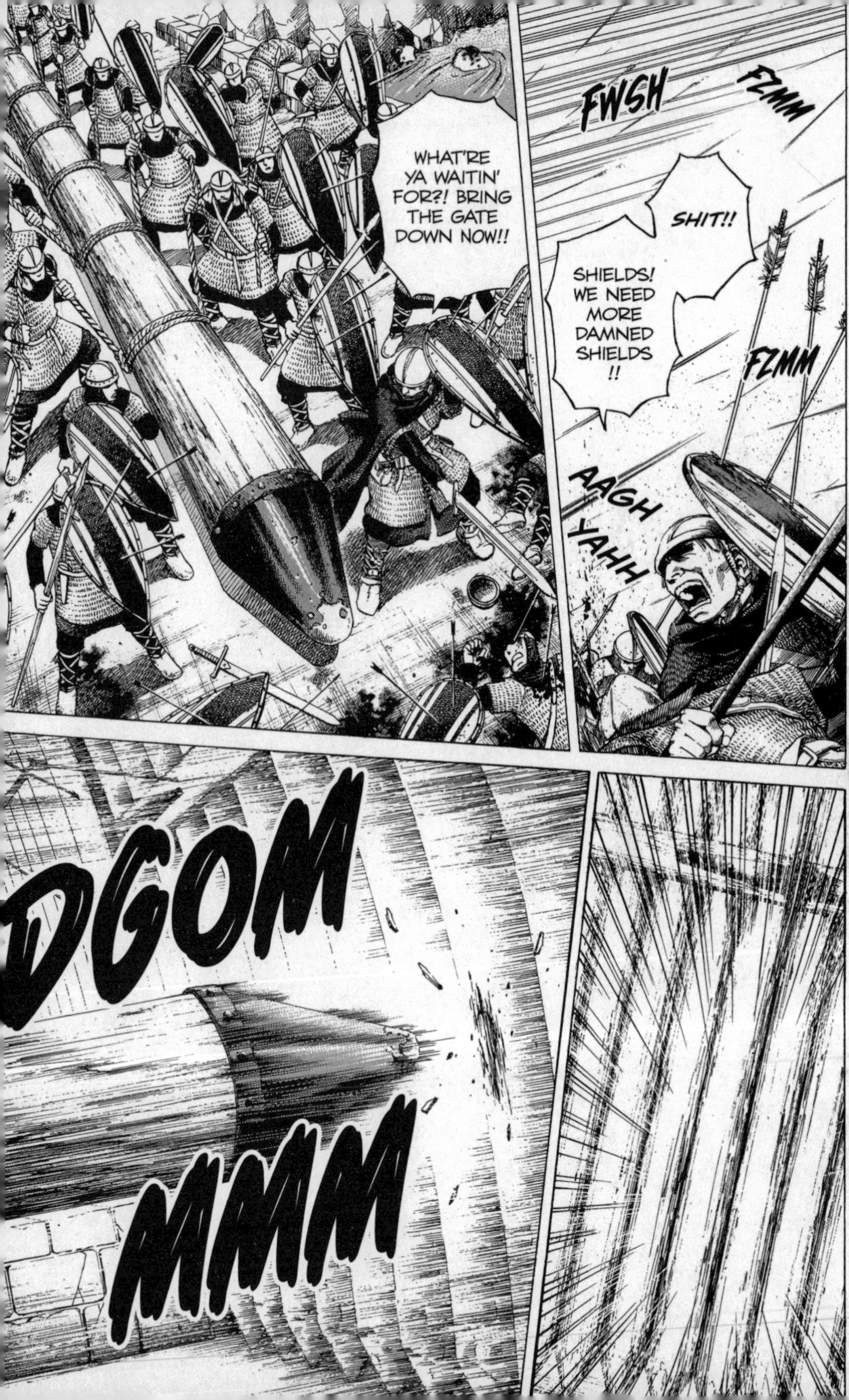
FZMM
FWSH
SHIT!!
SHIELDS! WE NEED MORE DAMNED SHIELDS!!
FZMM
AAGH
YAHH
WHAT'RE YA WAITIN' FOR?! BRING THE GATE DOWN NOW!!
DGOM
MMMM

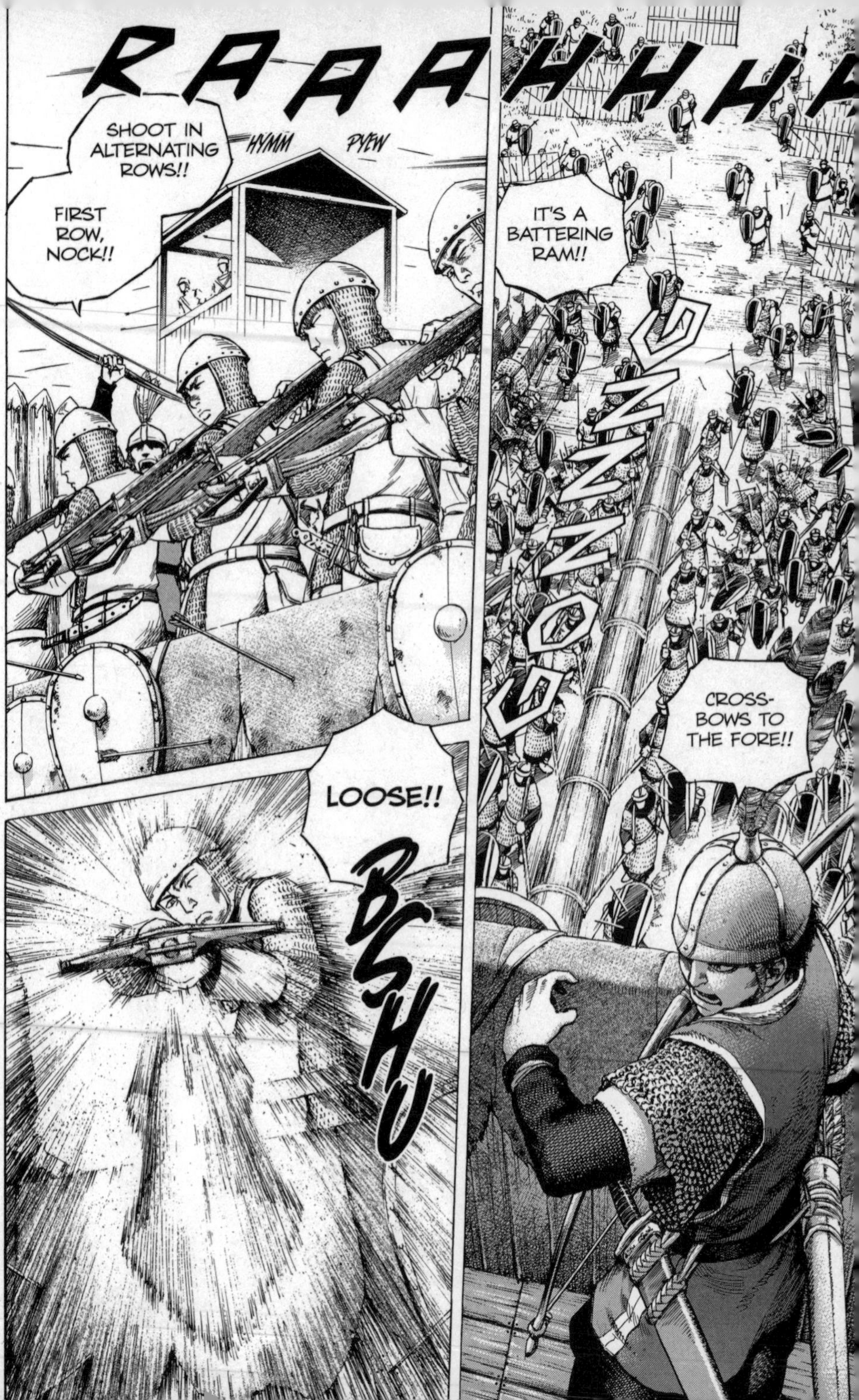
RAAAAHHHHA
IT'S A BATTERING RAM!!
CROSS-BOWS TO THE FORE!!
SHOOT IN ALTERNATING ROWS!!
FIRST ROW, NOCK!!
HYMM
PYEW
LOOSE!!
BSHU

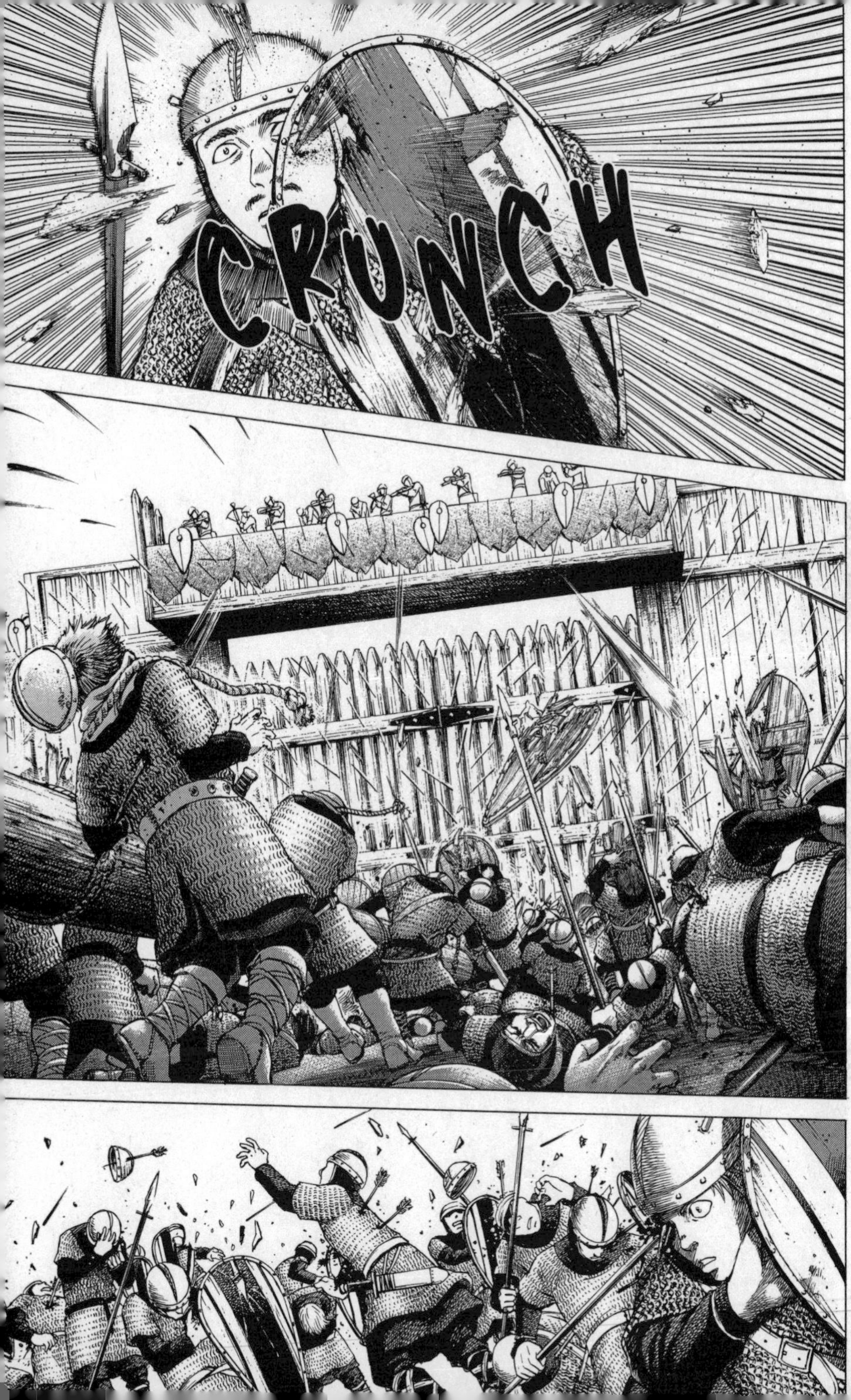
CRUNCH

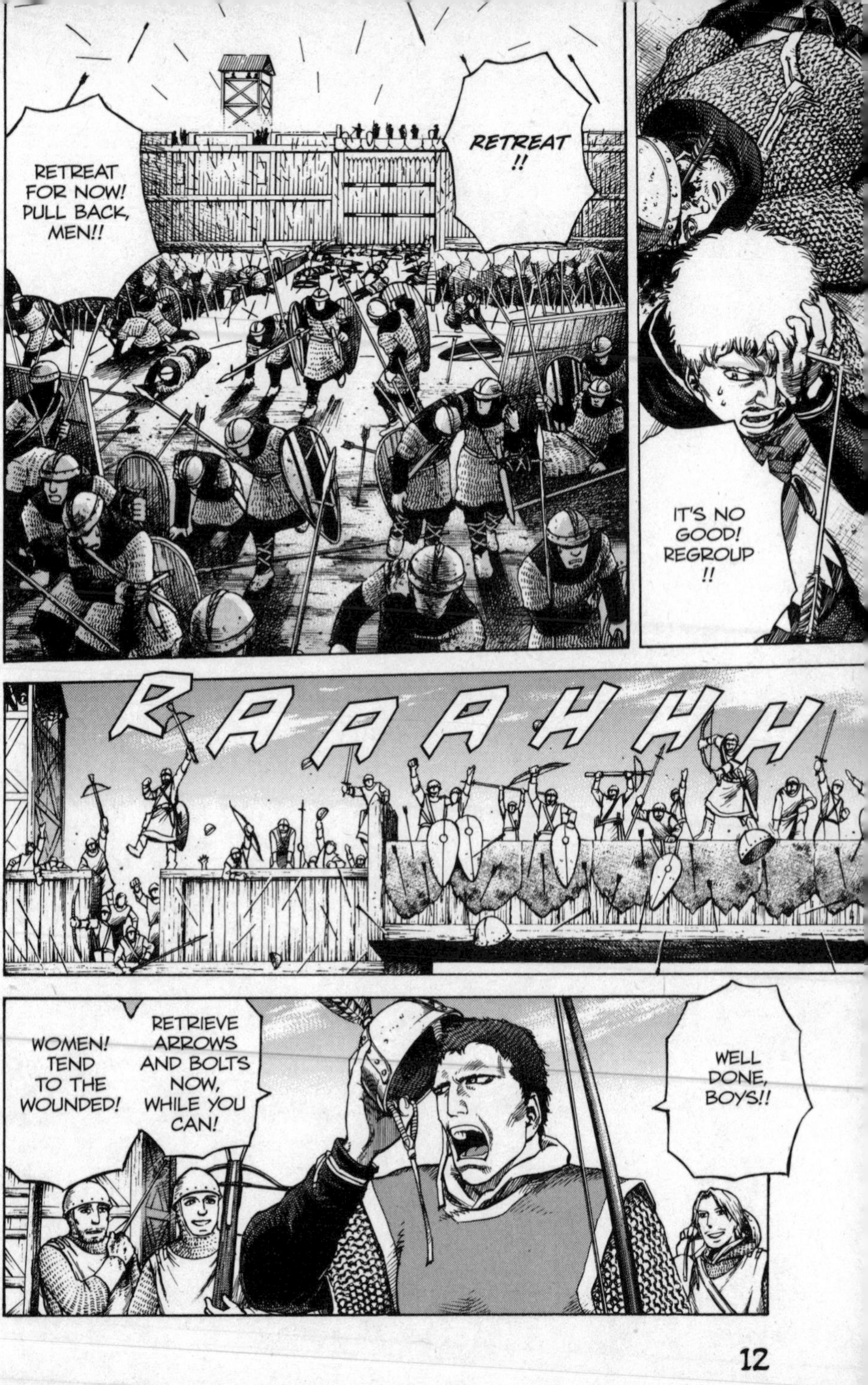
IT'S NO GOOD! REGROUP!!
RETREAT!!
RETREAT FOR NOW! PULL BACK, MEN!!
RAAAHHH
WELL DONE, BOYS!!
RETRIEVE ARROWS AND BOLTS NOW, WHILE YOU CAN!
WOMEN! TEND TO THE WOUNDED!

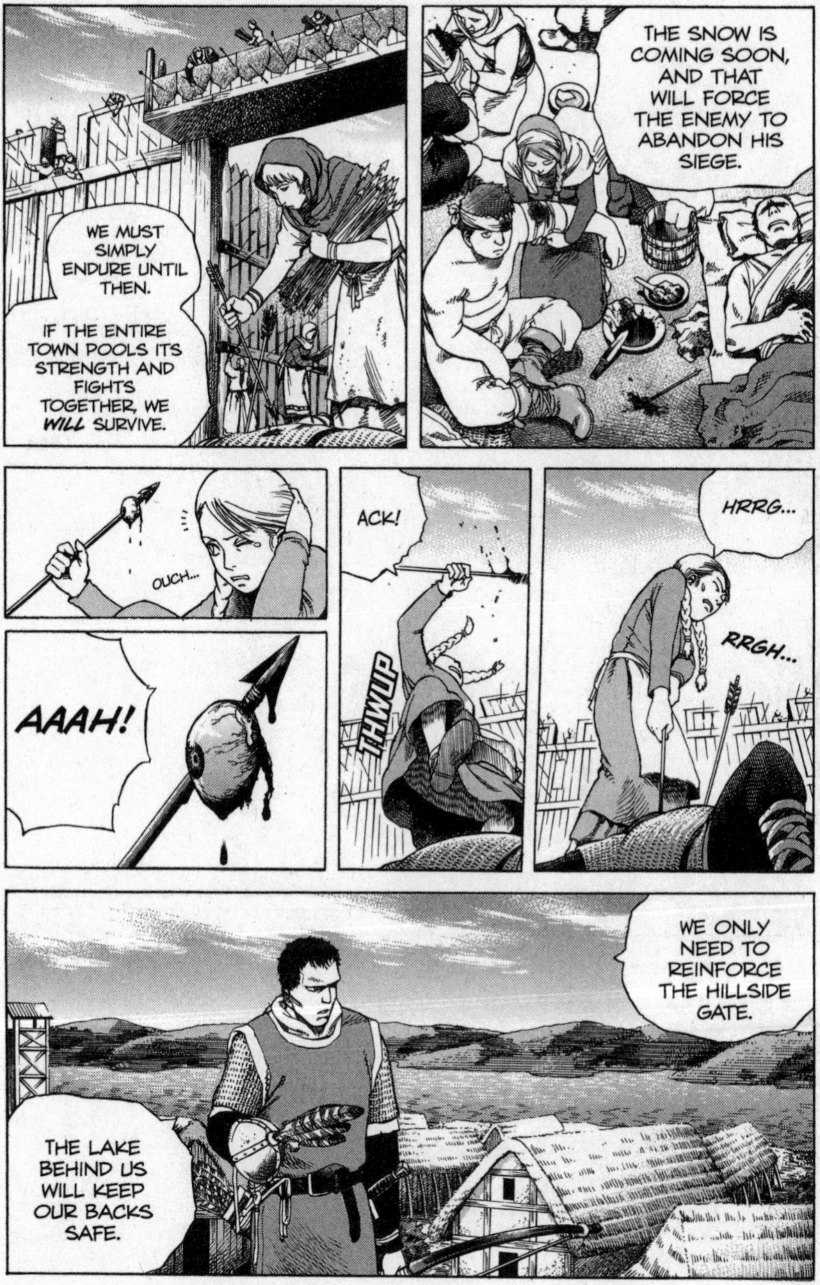
THE SNOW IS COMING SOON, AND THAT WILL FORCE THE ENEMY TO ABANDON HIS SIEGE.
WE MUST SIMPLY ENDURE UNTIL THEN.
IF THE ENTIRE TOWN POOLS ITS STRENGTH AND FIGHTS TOGETHER, WE *WILL* SURVIVE.
HRRG...
RRGH...
ACK!
THWUP
OUCH...
AAAH!
WE ONLY NEED TO REINFORCE THE HILLSIDE GATE.
THE LAKE BEHIND US WILL KEEP OUR BACKS SAFE.

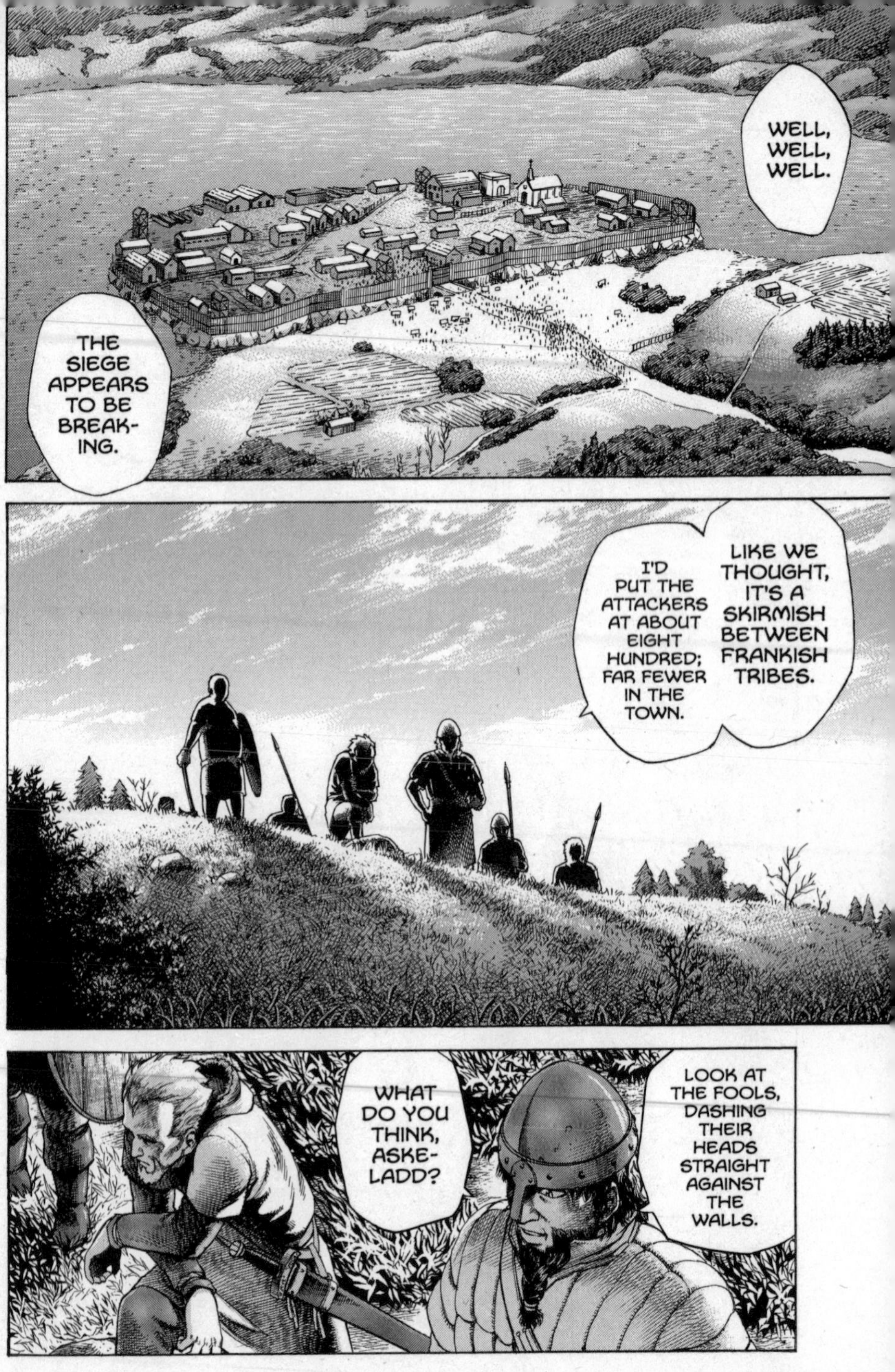
WELL, WELL, WELL.
THE SIEGE APPEARS TO BE BREAKING.
LIKE WE THOUGHT, IT'S A SKIRMISH BETWEEN FRANKISH TRIBES.
I'D PUT THE ATTACKERS AT ABOUT EIGHT HUNDRED; FAR FEWER IN THE TOWN.
LOOK AT THE FOOLS, DASHING THEIR HEADS STRAIGHT AGAINST THE WALLS.
WHAT DO YOU THINK, ASKELADD?

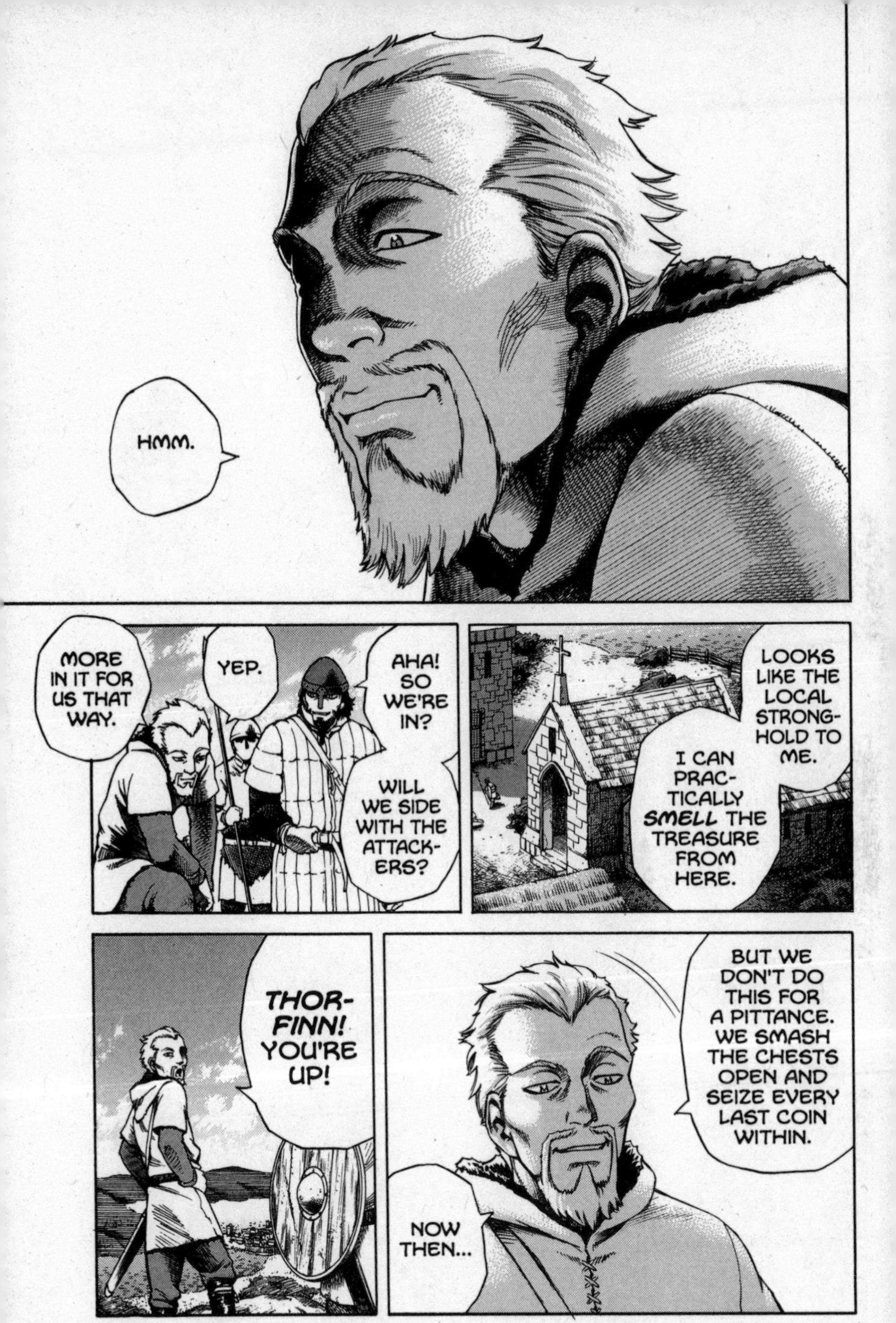
HMM.
LOOKS LIKE THE LOCAL STRONG-HOLD TO ME.
I CAN PRAC-TICALLY *SMELL* THE TREASURE FROM HERE.
AHA! SO WE'RE IN?
WILL WE SIDE WITH THE ATTACK-ERS?
YEP.
MORE IN IT FOR US THAT WAY.
BUT WE DON'T DO THIS FOR A PITTANCE. WE SMASH THE CHESTS OPEN AND SEIZE EVERY LAST COIN WITHIN.
NOW THEN...
THOR-FINN! YOU'RE UP!

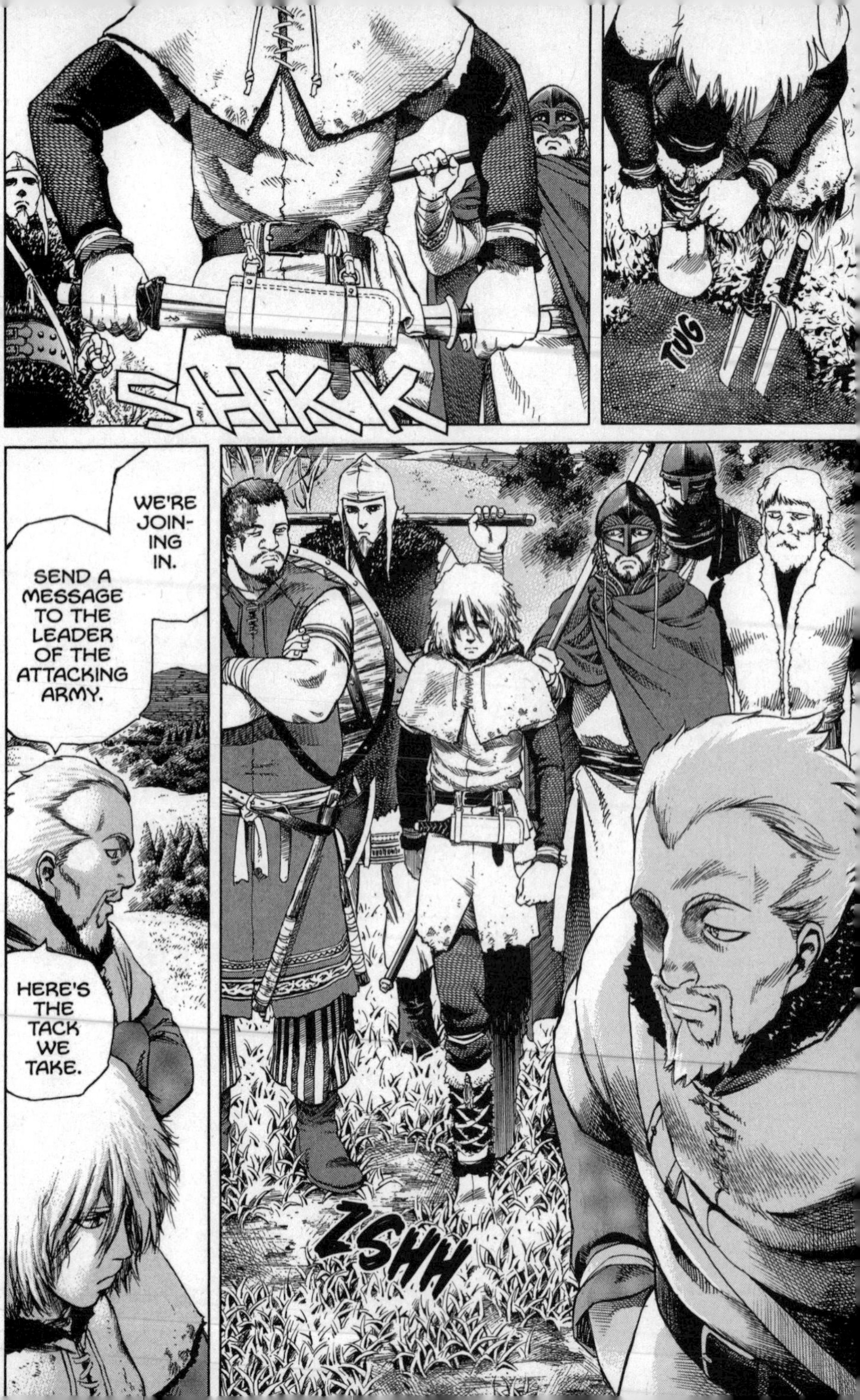
TUG
SHKK
ZSHH
WE'RE JOINING IN.
SEND A MESSAGE TO THE LEADER OF THE ATTACKING ARMY.
HERE'S THE TACK WE TAKE.

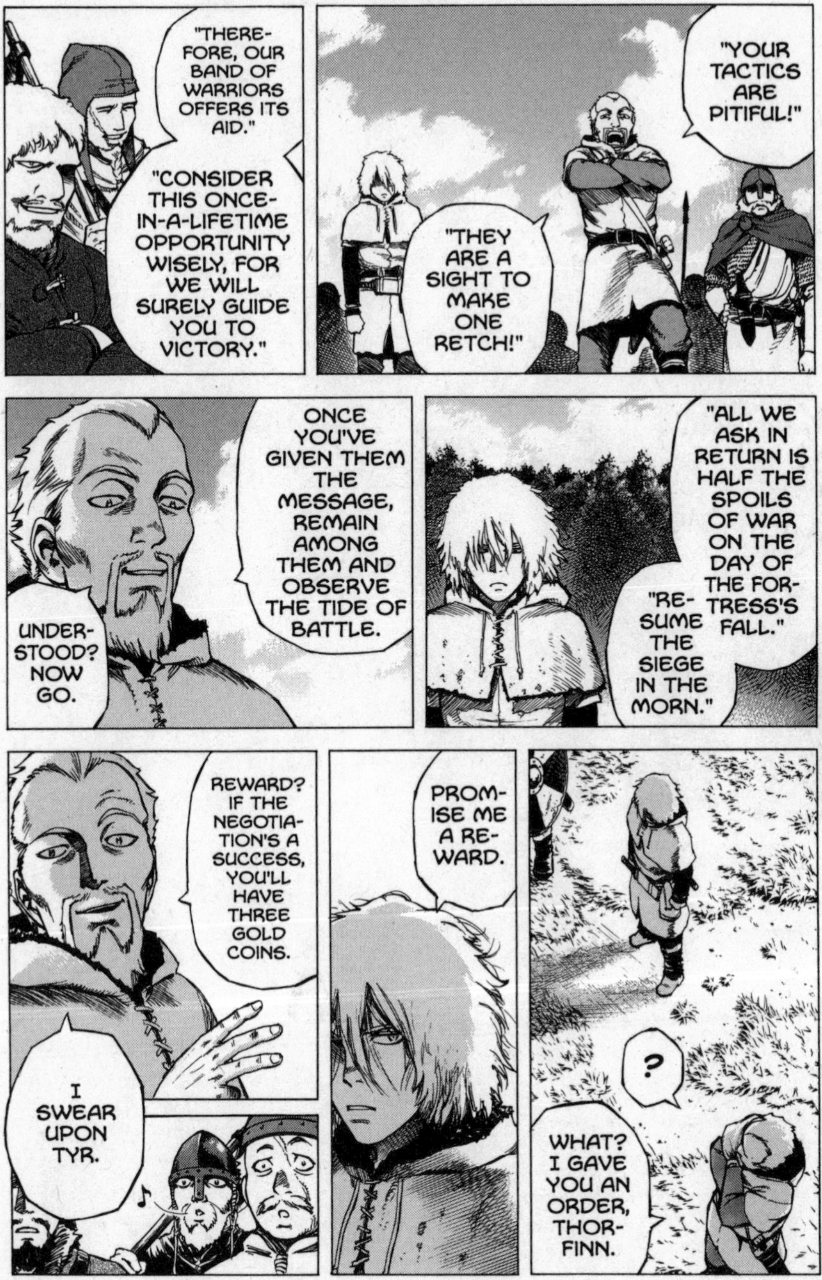
"YOUR TACTICS ARE PITIFUL!"
"THEY ARE A SIGHT TO MAKE ONE RETCH!"
"THERE-FORE, OUR BAND OF WARRIORS OFFERS ITS AID."
"CONSIDER THIS ONCE-IN-A-LIFETIME OPPORTUNITY WISELY, FOR WE WILL SURELY GUIDE YOU TO VICTORY."
"ALL WE ASK IN RETURN IS HALF THE SPOILS OF WAR ON THE DAY OF THE FOR-TRESS'S FALL."
"RE-SUME THE SIEGE IN THE MORN."
ONCE YOU'VE GIVEN THEM THE MESSAGE, REMAIN AMONG THEM AND OBSERVE THE TIDE OF BATTLE.
UNDER-STOOD? NOW GO.
?
WHAT? I GAVE YOU AN ORDER, THORFINN.
PROM-ISE ME A RE-WARD.
REWARD? IF THE NEGOTIA-TION'S A SUCCESS, YOU'LL HAVE THREE GOLD COINS.
I SWEAR UPON TYR.
♪

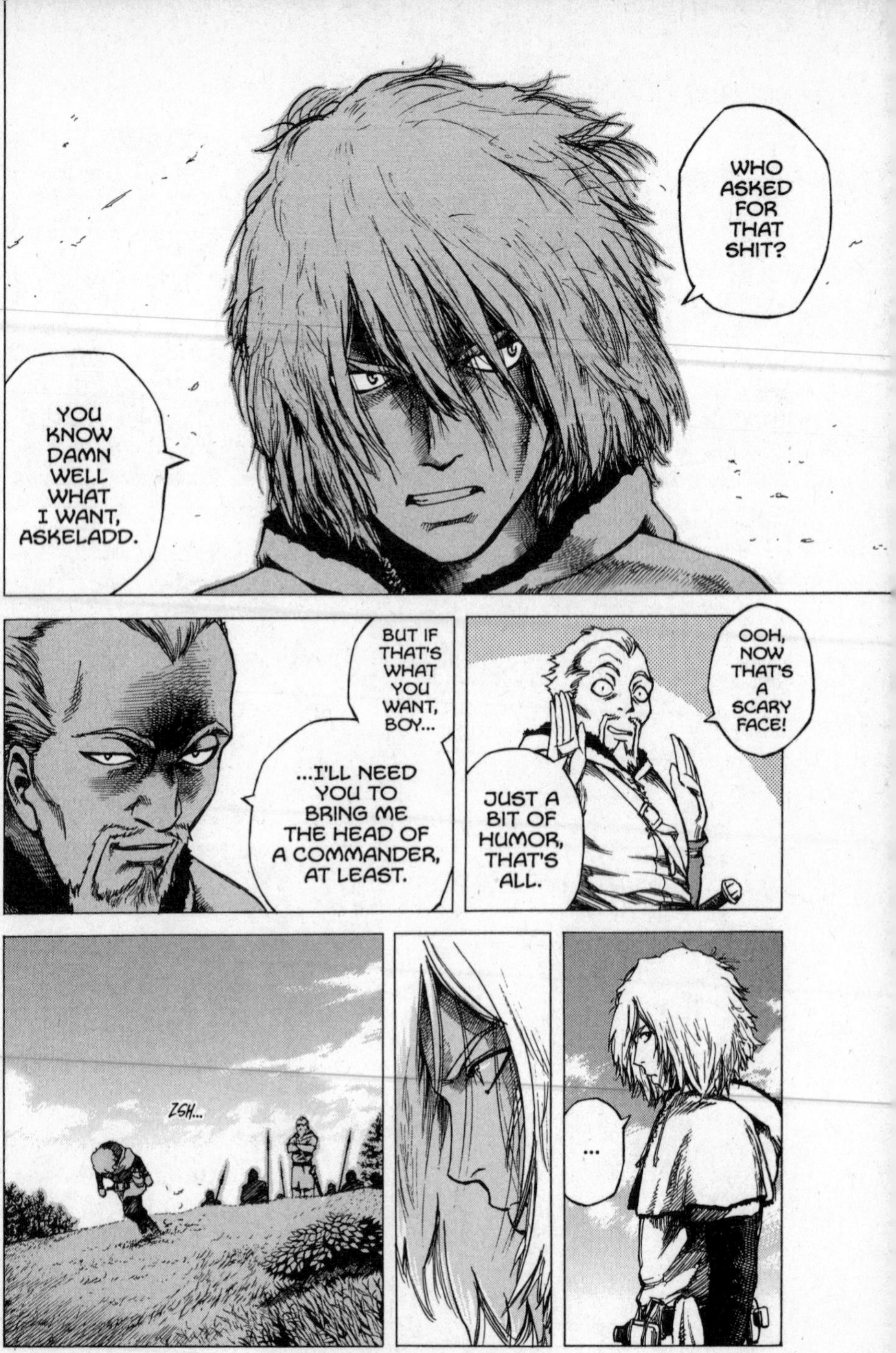
WHO ASKED FOR THAT SHIT?
YOU KNOW DAMN WELL WHAT I WANT, ASKELADD.
OOH, NOW THAT'S A SCARY FACE!
JUST A BIT OF HUMOR, THAT'S ALL.
BUT IF THAT'S WHAT YOU WANT, BOY...
...I'LL NEED YOU TO BRING ME THE HEAD OF A COMMANDER, AT LEAST.
...
ZSH...

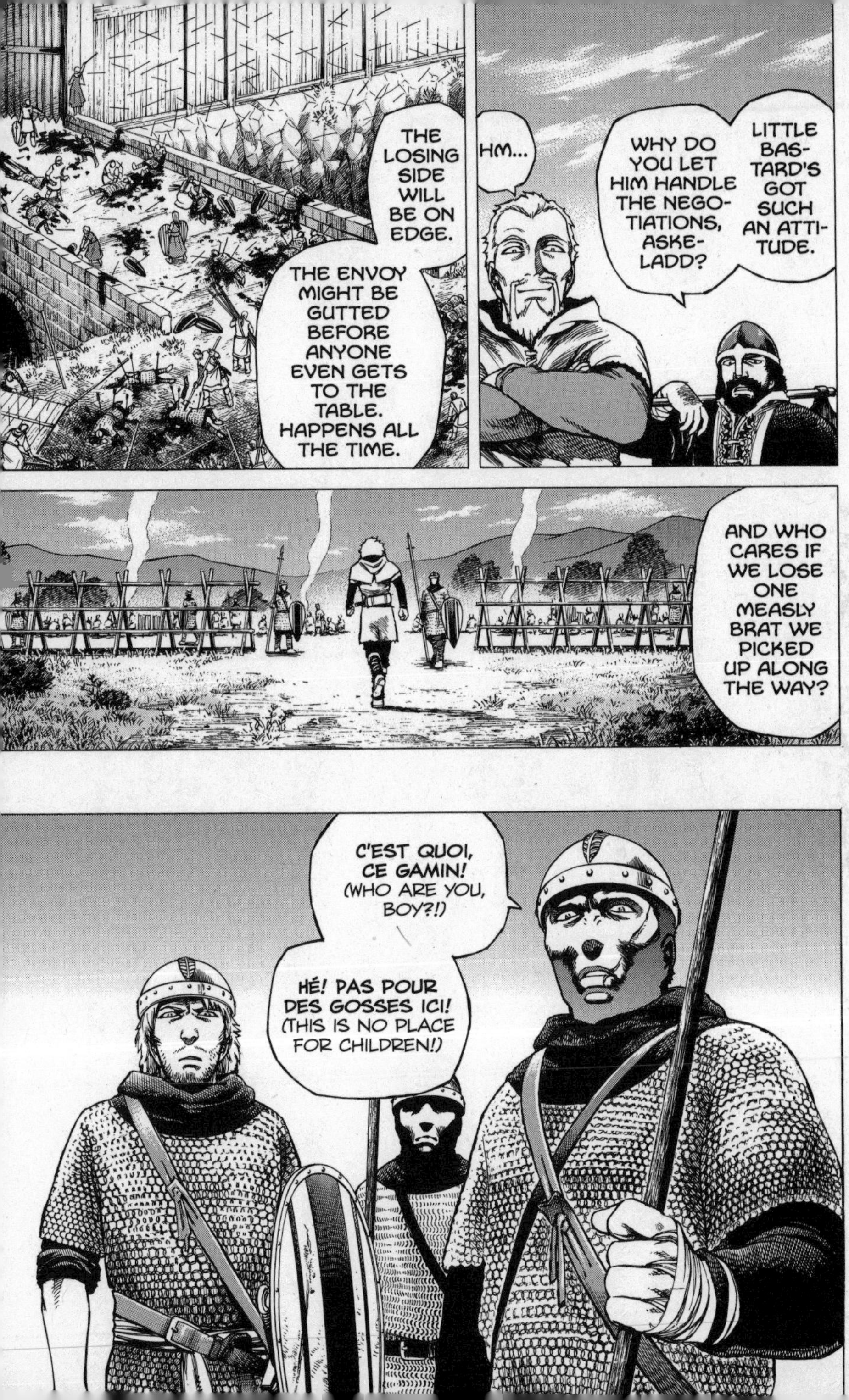
LITTLE BASTARD'S GOT SUCH AN ATTITUDE.
WHY DO YOU LET HIM HANDLE THE NEGOTIATIONS, ASKELADD?
HM...
THE LOSING SIDE WILL BE ON EDGE.
THE ENVOY MIGHT BE GUTTED BEFORE ANYONE EVEN GETS TO THE TABLE. HAPPENS ALL THE TIME.
AND WHO CARES IF WE LOSE ONE MEASLY BRAT WE PICKED UP ALONG THE WAY?
C'EST QUOI, CE GAMIN! (WHO ARE YOU, BOY?!)
HÉ! PAS POUR DES GOSSES ICI! (THIS IS NO PLACE FOR CHILDREN!)

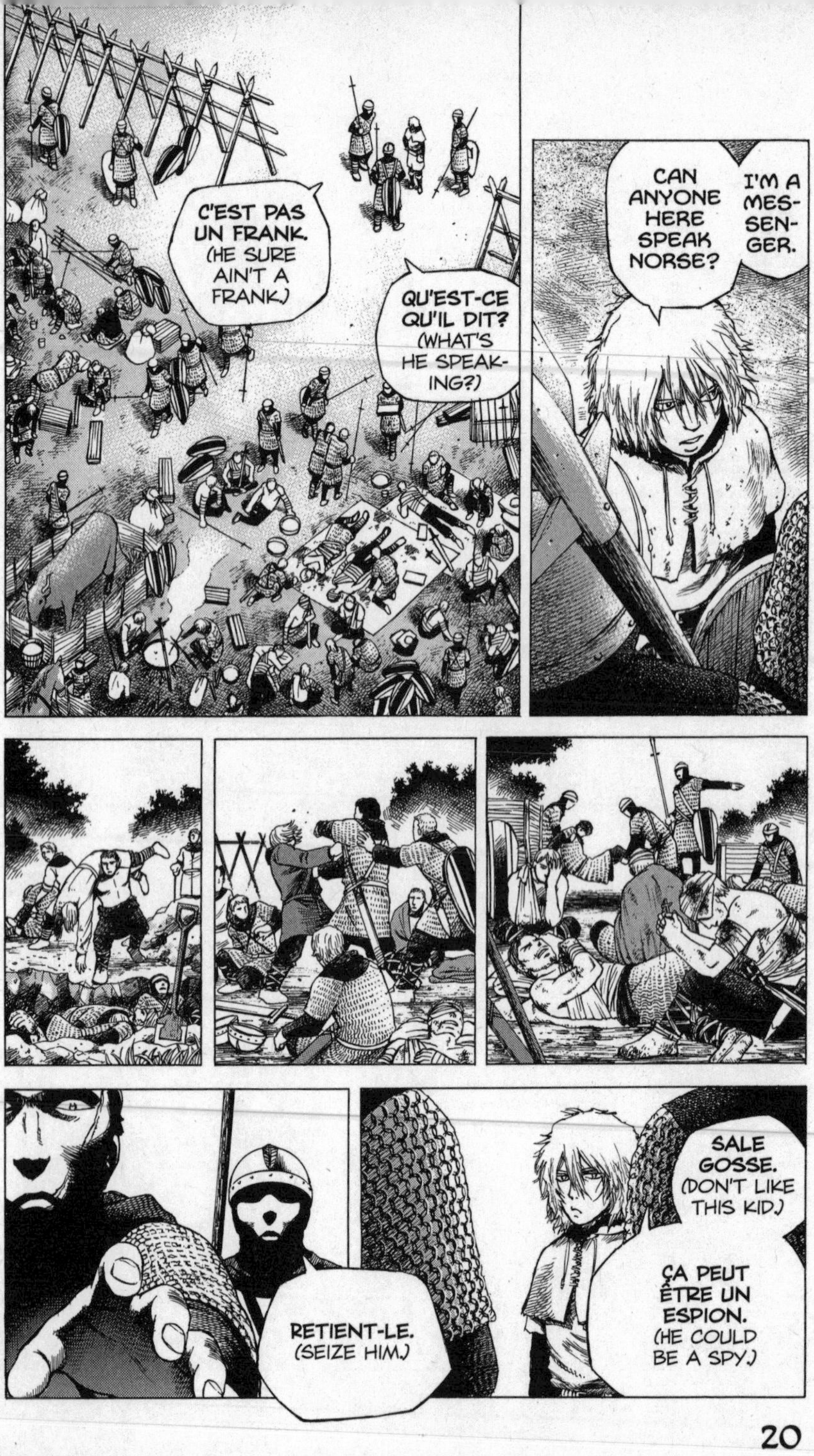
I'M A MES-SEN-GER.
CAN ANYONE HERE SPEAK NORSE?
QU'EST-CE QU'IL DIT? (WHAT'S HE SPEAK-ING?)
C'EST PAS UN FRANK. (HE SURE AIN'T A FRANK.)
SALE GOSSE. (DON'T LIKE THIS KID.)
ÇA PEUT ÊTRE UN ESPION. (HE COULD BE A SPY.)
RETIENT-LE. (SEIZE HIM.)

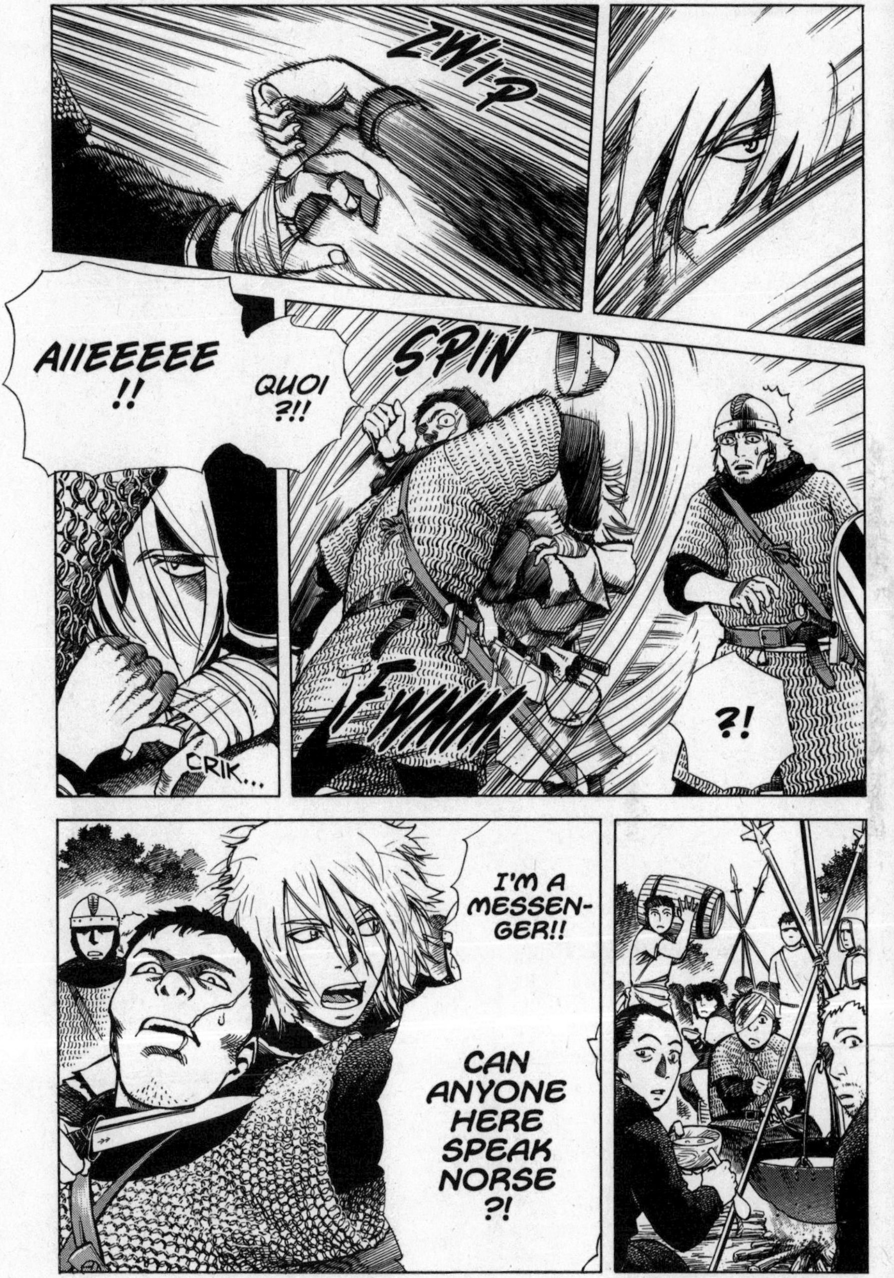
ZWIP
SPIN
?!
QUOI ?!!
AIIEEEEE !!
CRIK...
I'M A MESSENGER!!
CAN ANYONE HERE SPEAK NORSE ?!

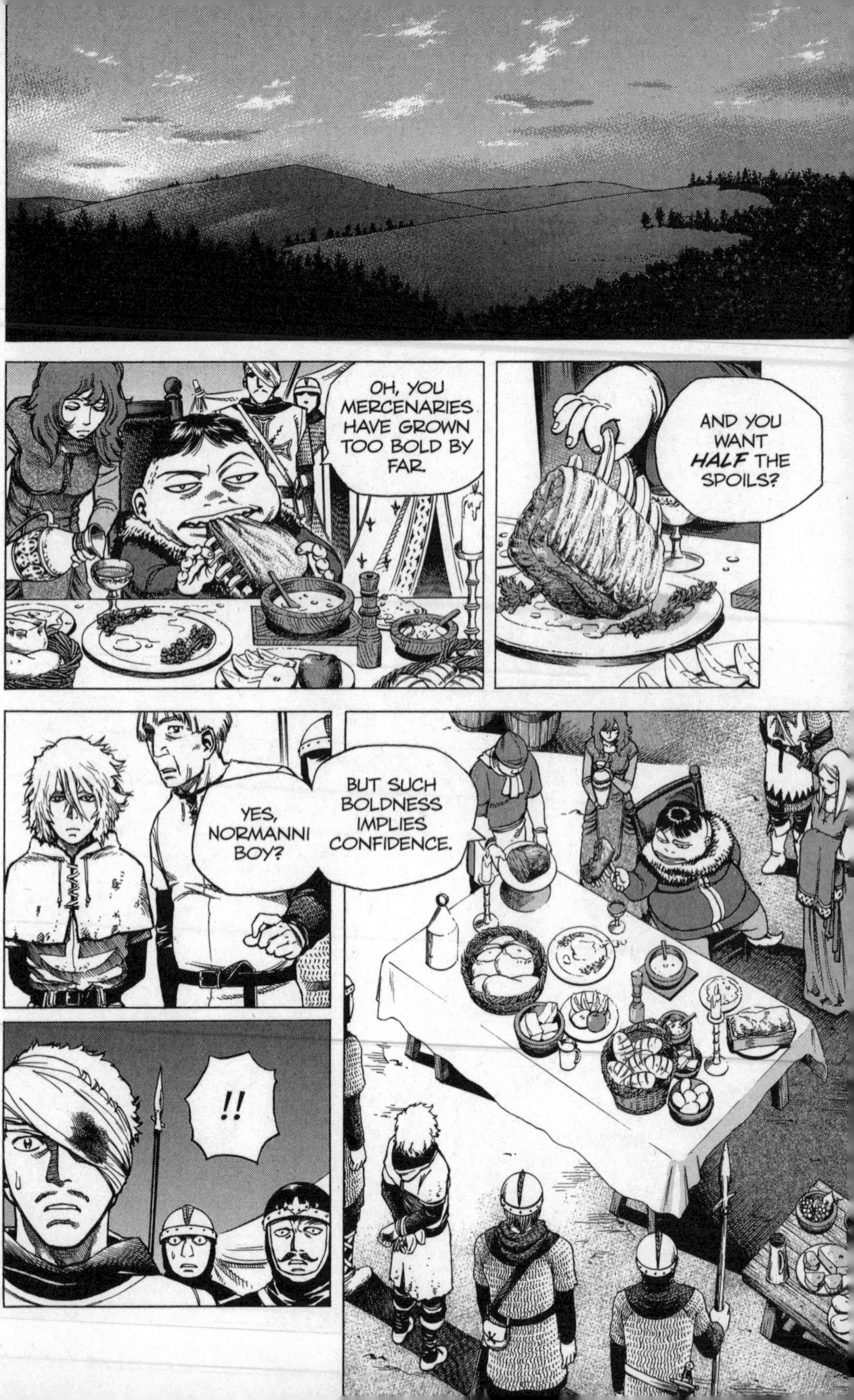
AND YOU WANT HALF THE SPOILS?
OH, YOU MERCENARIES HAVE GROWN TOO BOLD BY FAR.
BUT SUCH BOLDNESS IMPLIES CONFIDENCE.
YES, NORMANNI BOY?
!!

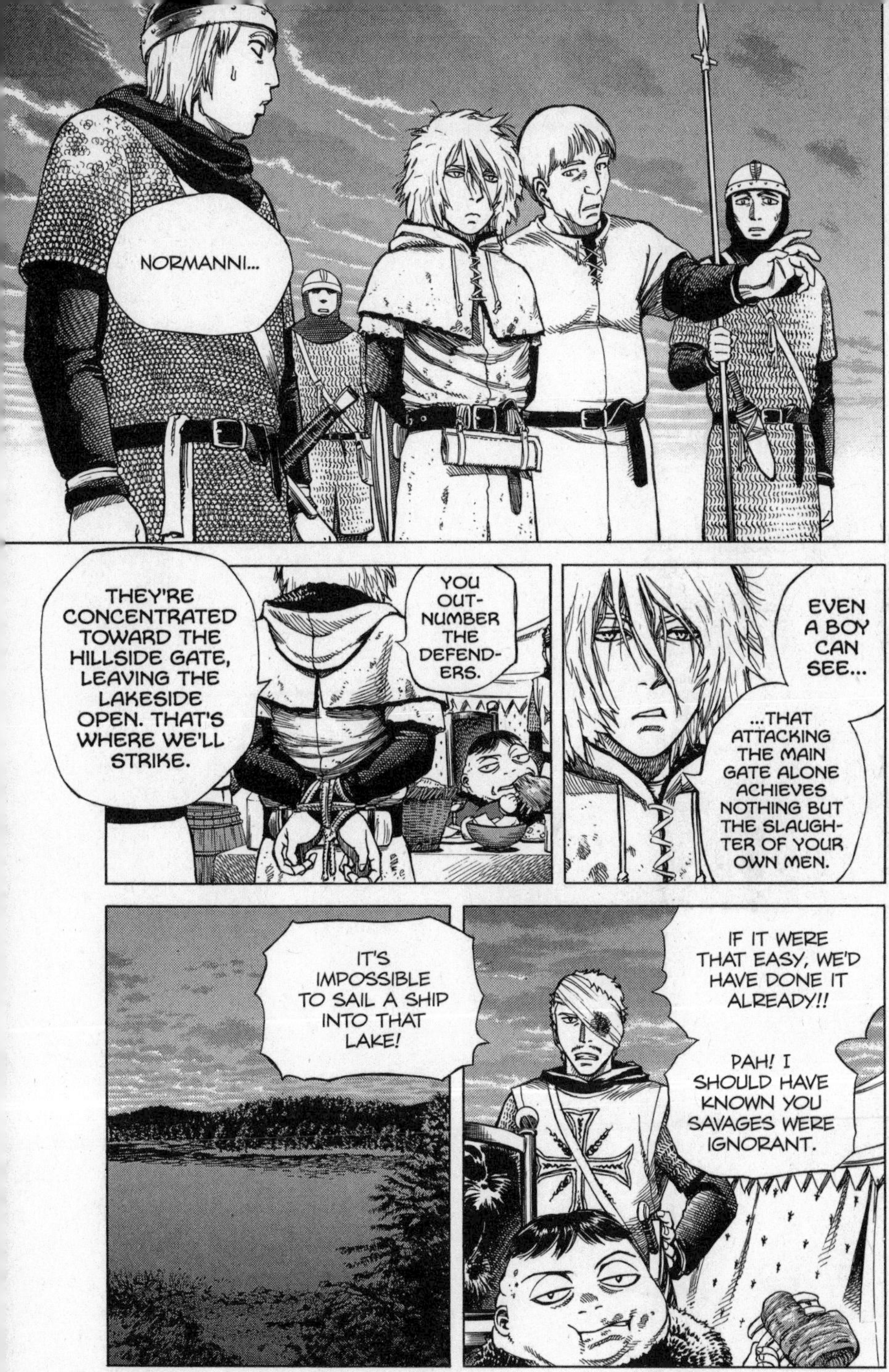
NORMANNI...
EVEN A BOY CAN SEE...
...THAT ATTACKING THE MAIN GATE ALONE ACHIEVES NOTHING BUT THE SLAUGHTER OF YOUR OWN MEN.
YOU OUTNUMBER THE DEFENDERS.
THEY'RE CONCENTRATED TOWARD THE HILLSIDE GATE, LEAVING THE LAKESIDE OPEN. THAT'S WHERE WE'LL STRIKE.
IF IT WERE THAT EASY, WE'D HAVE DONE IT ALREADY!!
PAH! I SHOULD HAVE KNOWN YOU SAVAGES WERE IGNORANT.
IT'S IMPOSSIBLE TO SAIL A SHIP INTO THAT LAKE!

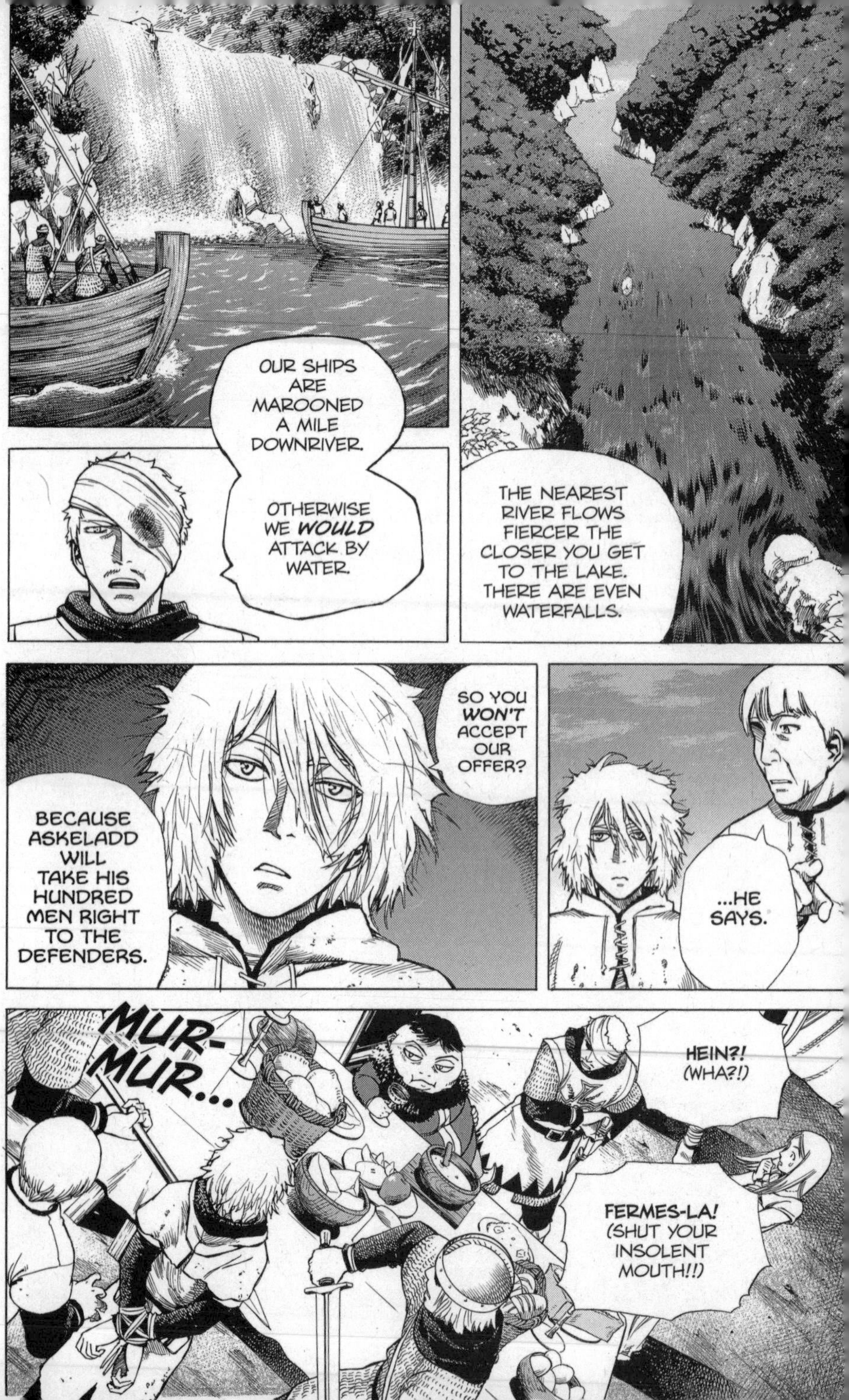
THE NEAREST RIVER FLOWS FIERCER THE CLOSER YOU GET TO THE LAKE. THERE ARE EVEN WATERFALLS.
OUR SHIPS ARE MAROONED A MILE DOWNRIVER.
OTHERWISE WE ***WOULD*** ATTACK BY WATER.
...HE SAYS.
SO YOU ***WON'T*** ACCEPT OUR OFFER?
BECAUSE ASKELADD WILL TAKE HIS HUNDRED MEN RIGHT TO THE DEFENDERS.
HEIN?! (WHA?!)
FERMES-LA! (SHUT YOUR INSOLENT MOUTH!!)
MUR-MUR...

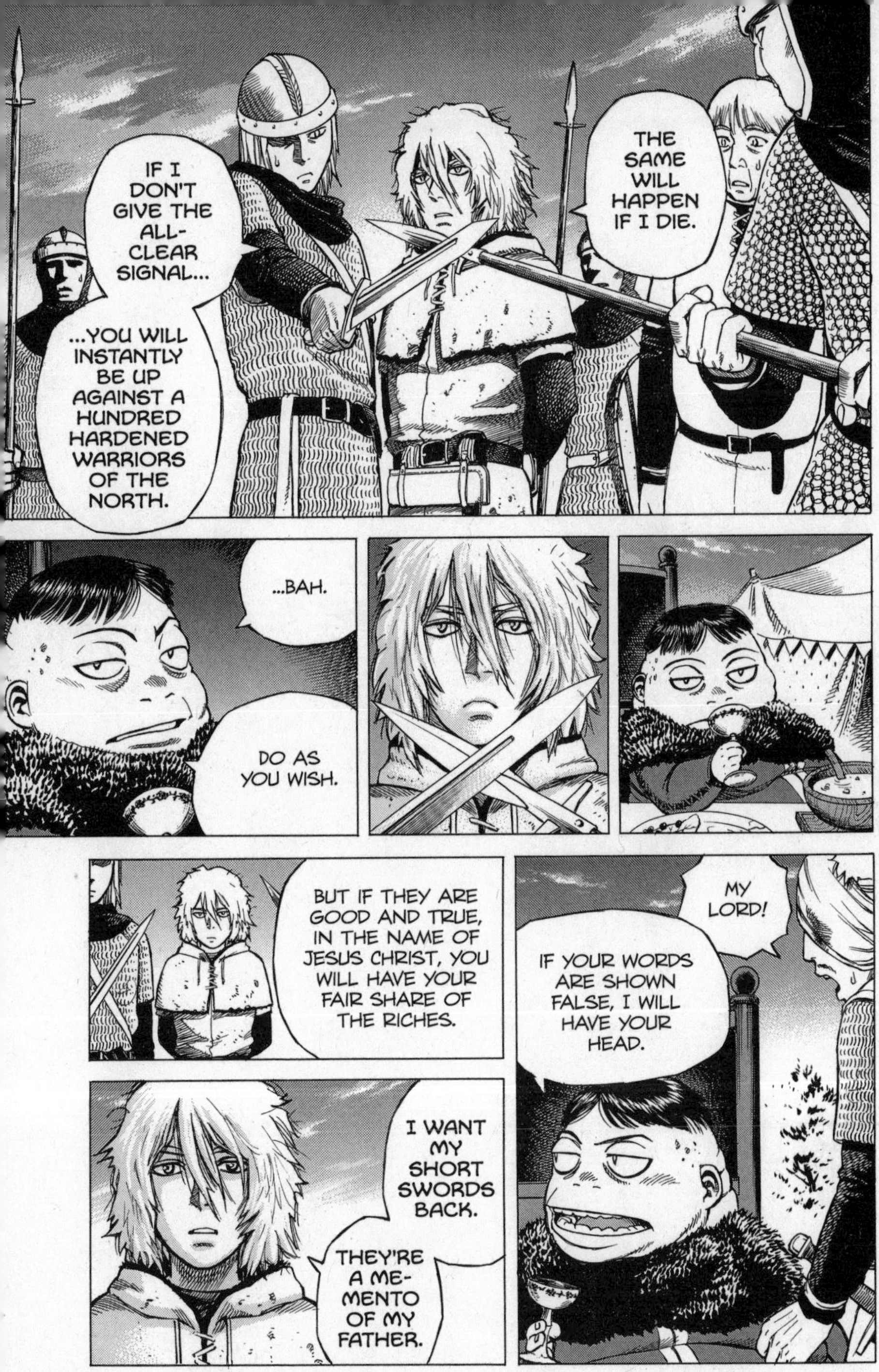
IF I DON'T GIVE THE ALL-CLEAR SIGNAL...
...YOU WILL INSTANTLY BE UP AGAINST A HUNDRED HARDENED WARRIORS OF THE NORTH.
THE SAME WILL HAPPEN IF I DIE.
...BAH.
DO AS YOU WISH.
MY LORD!
IF YOUR WORDS ARE SHOWN FALSE, I WILL HAVE YOUR HEAD.
BUT IF THEY ARE GOOD AND TRUE, IN THE NAME OF JESUS CHRIST, YOU WILL HAVE YOUR FAIR SHARE OF THE RICHES.
I WANT MY SHORT SWORDS BACK.
THEY'RE A MEMENTO OF MY FATHER.

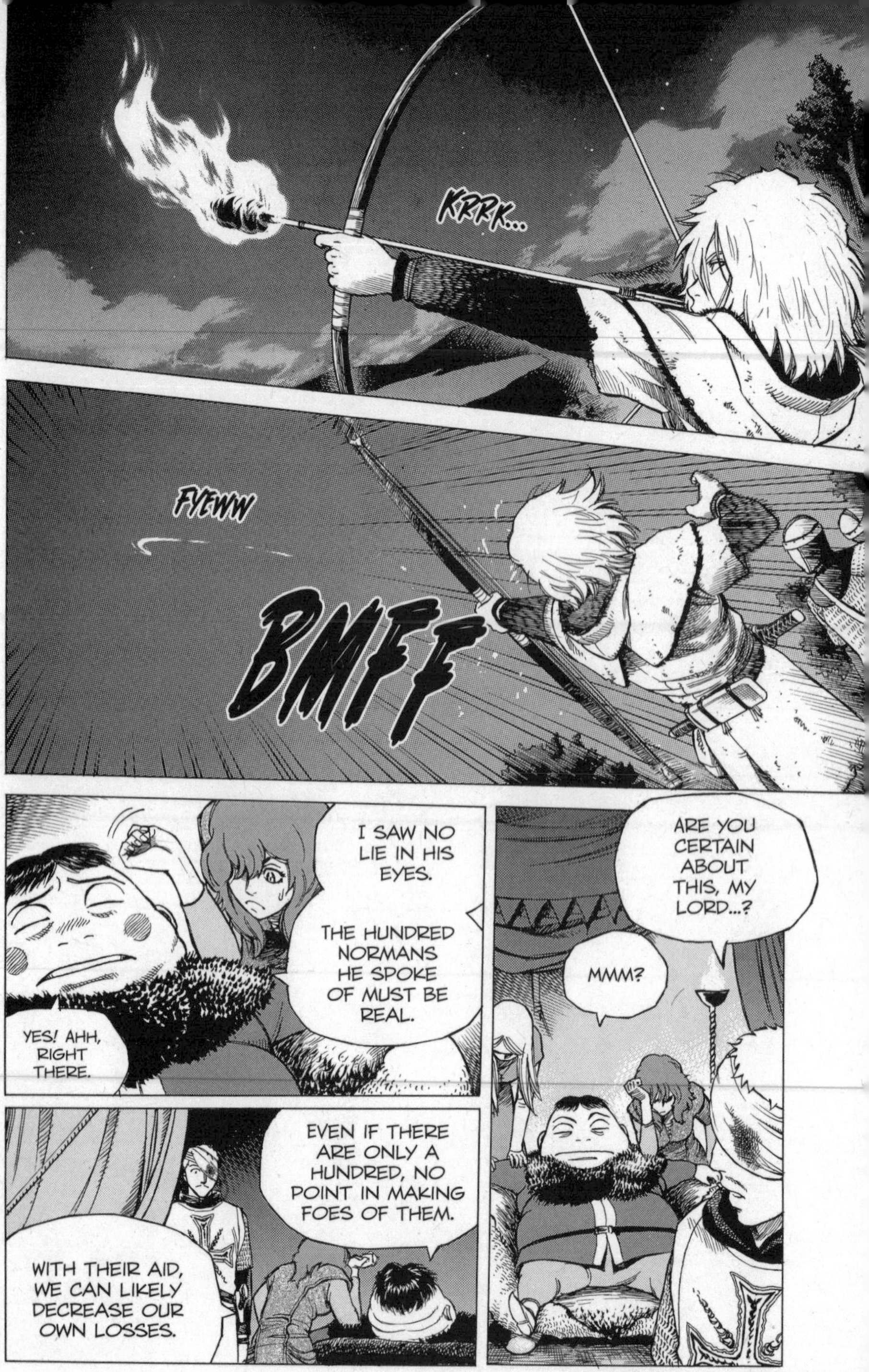
KRRK...
FYEWW
BMFF
ARE YOU CERTAIN ABOUT THIS, MY LORD...?
MMM?
I SAW NO LIE IN HIS EYES.
THE HUNDRED NORMANS HE SPOKE OF MUST BE REAL.
YES! AHH, RIGHT THERE.
EVEN IF THERE ARE ONLY A HUNDRED, NO POINT IN MAKING FOES OF THEM.
WITH THEIR AID, WE CAN LIKELY DECREASE OUR OWN LOSSES.

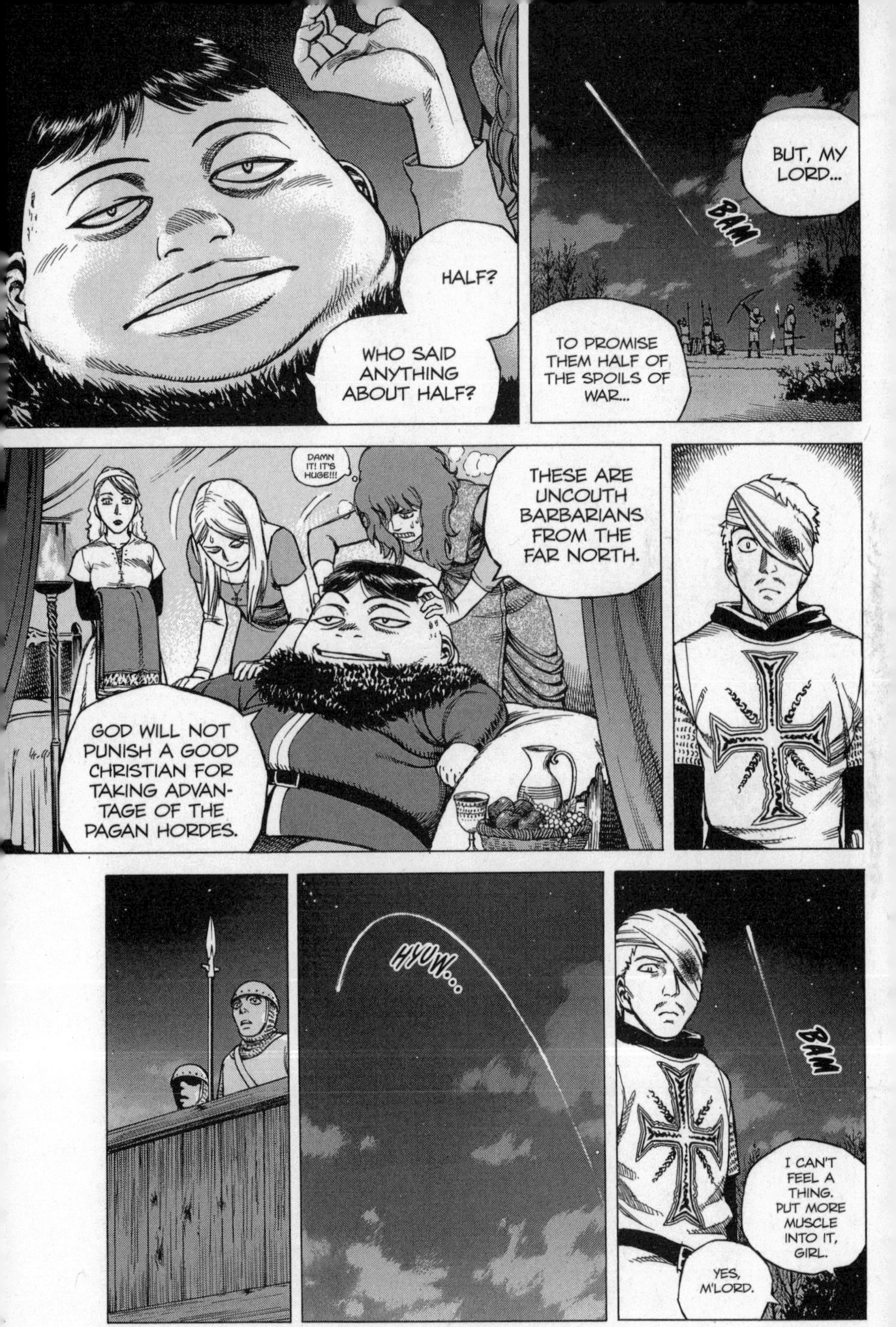
BUT, MY LORD...
BAM
TO PROMISE THEM HALF OF THE SPOILS OF WAR...
HALF?
WHO SAID ANYTHING ABOUT HALF?
THESE ARE UNCOUTH BARBARIANS FROM THE FAR NORTH.
DAMN IT! IT'S HUGE!!!
GOD WILL NOT PUNISH A GOOD CHRISTIAN FOR TAKING ADVAN-TAGE OF THE PAGAN HORDES.
BAM
I CAN'T FEEL A THING. PUT MORE MUSCLE INTO IT, GIRL.
YES, M'LORD.
HYUW...

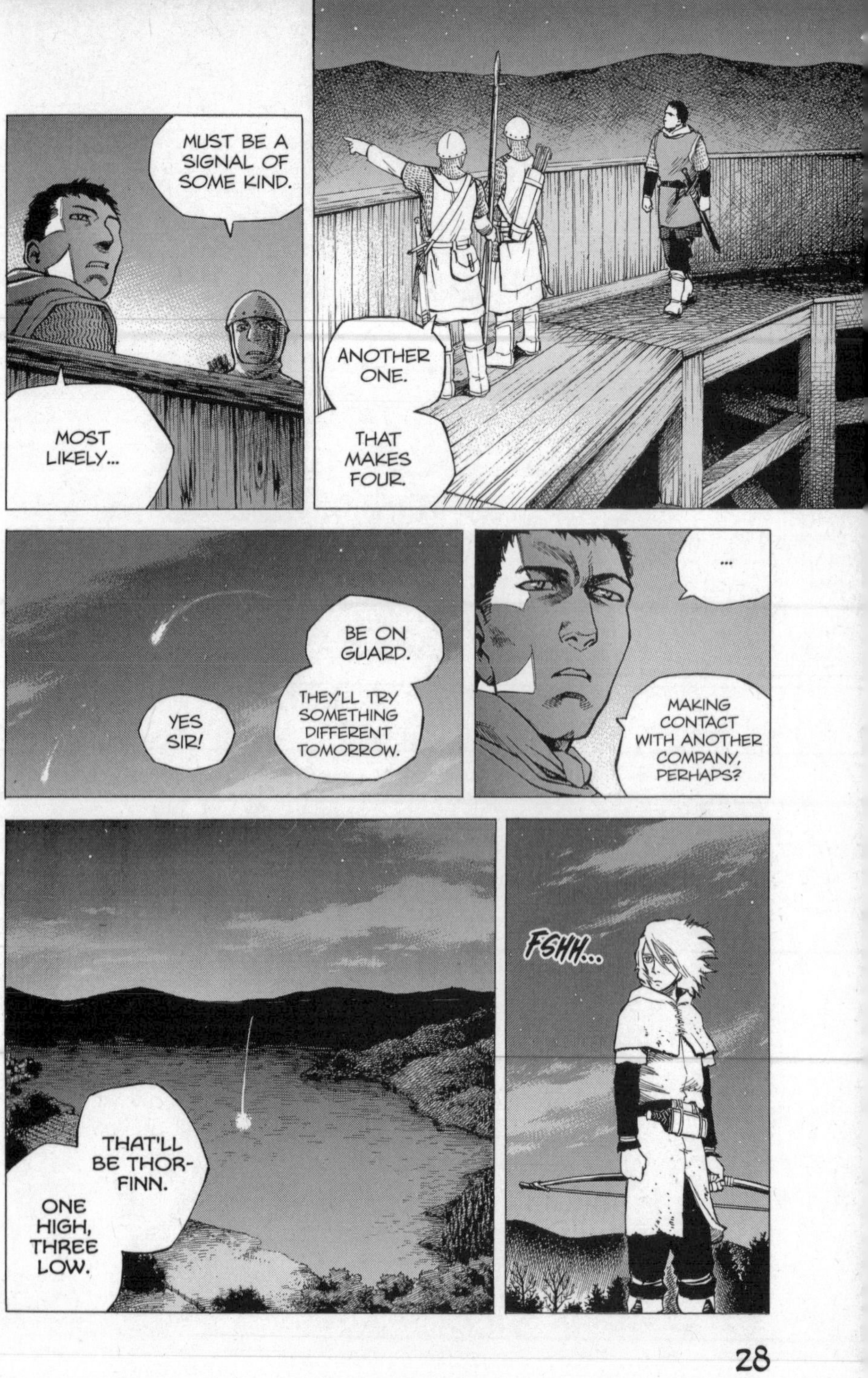
ANOTHER ONE.
THAT MAKES FOUR.
MUST BE A SIGNAL OF SOME KIND.
MOST LIKELY...
...
MAKING CONTACT WITH ANOTHER COMPANY, PERHAPS?
BE ON GUARD.
THEY'LL TRY SOMETHING DIFFERENT TOMORROW.
YES SIR!
FSHH...
THAT'LL BE THOR-FINN.
ONE HIGH, THREE LOW.

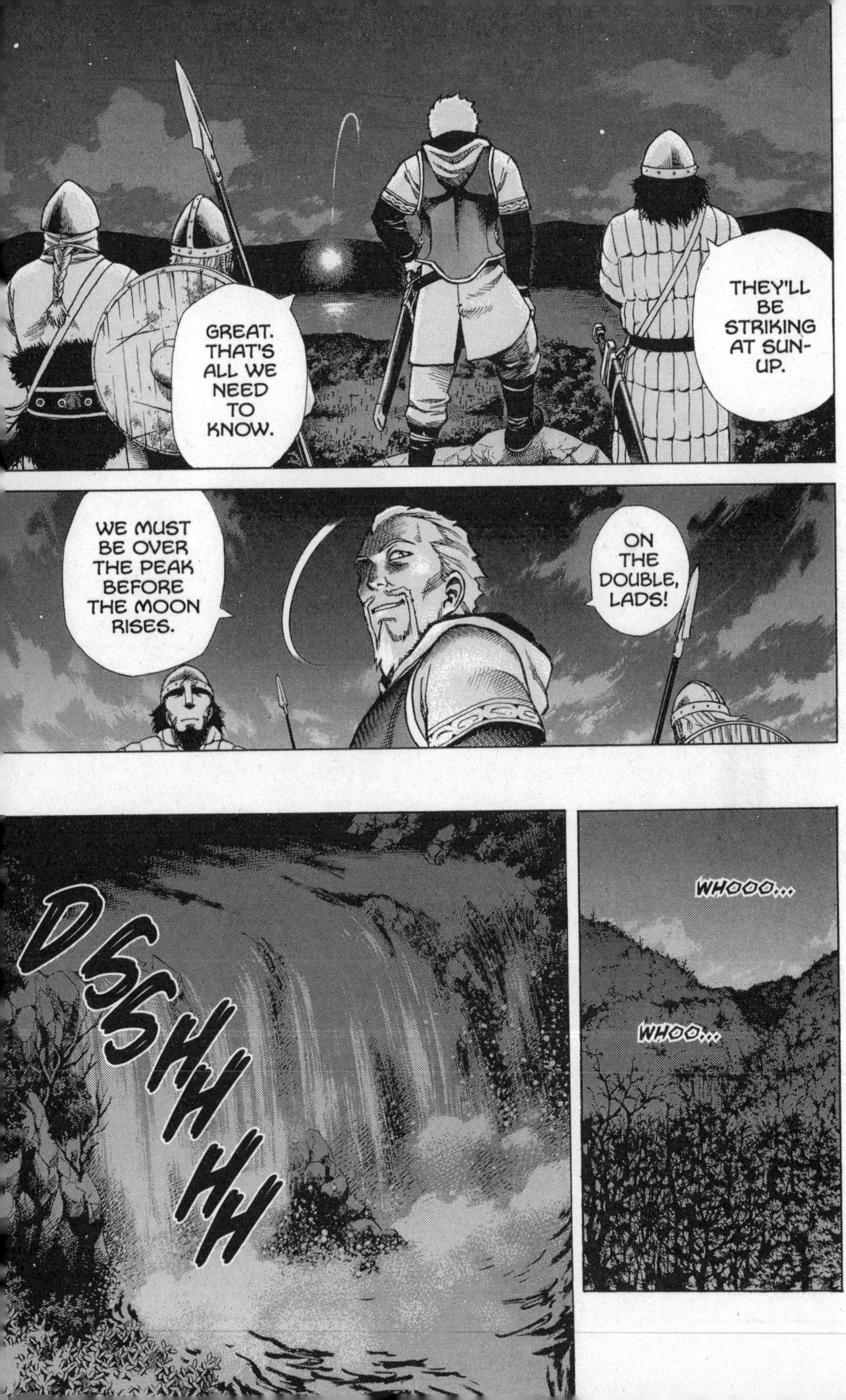
THEY'LL BE STRIKING AT SUN-UP.
GREAT. THAT'S ALL WE NEED TO KNOW.
ON THE DOUBLE, LADS!
WE MUST BE OVER THE PEAK BEFORE THE MOON RISES.
WHOOO...
WHOO...
DSSHHHH

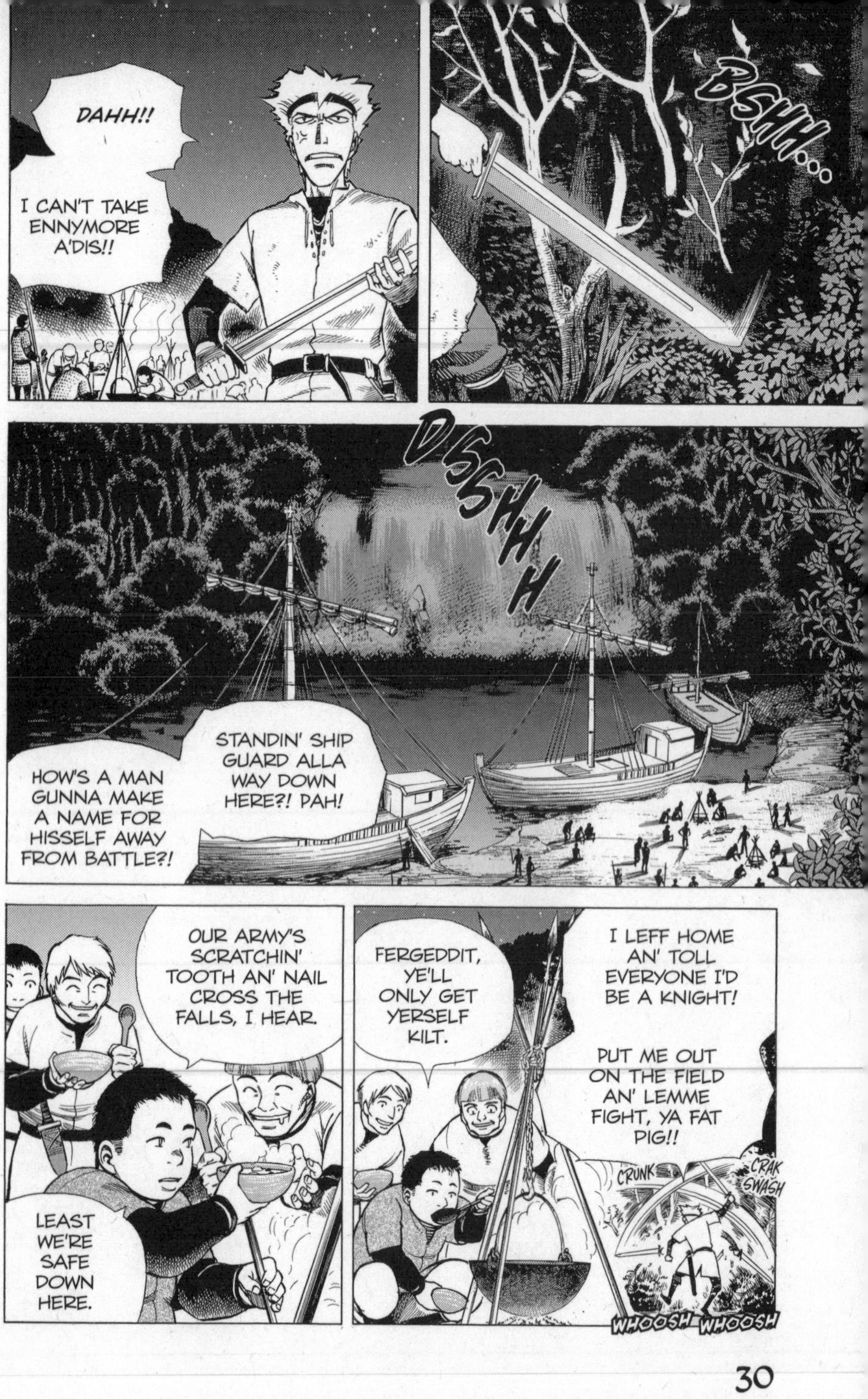

BSHH...
DAHH!!
I CAN'T TAKE ENNYMORE A'DIS!!
DISSHHH
STANDIN' SHIP GUARD ALLA WAY DOWN HERE?! PAH!
HOW'S A MAN GUNNA MAKE A NAME FOR HISSELF AWAY FROM BATTLE?!
I LEFF HOME AN' TOLL EVERYONE I'D BE A KNIGHT!
FERGEDDIT, YE'LL ONLY GET YERSELF KILT.
PUT ME OUT ON THE FIELD AN' LEMME FIGHT, YA FAT PIG!!
CRAK SWASH
CRUNK
WHOOSH WHOOSH
OUR ARMY'S SCRATCHIN' TOOTH AN' NAIL CROSS THE FALLS, I HEAR.
LEAST WE'RE SAFE DOWN HERE.

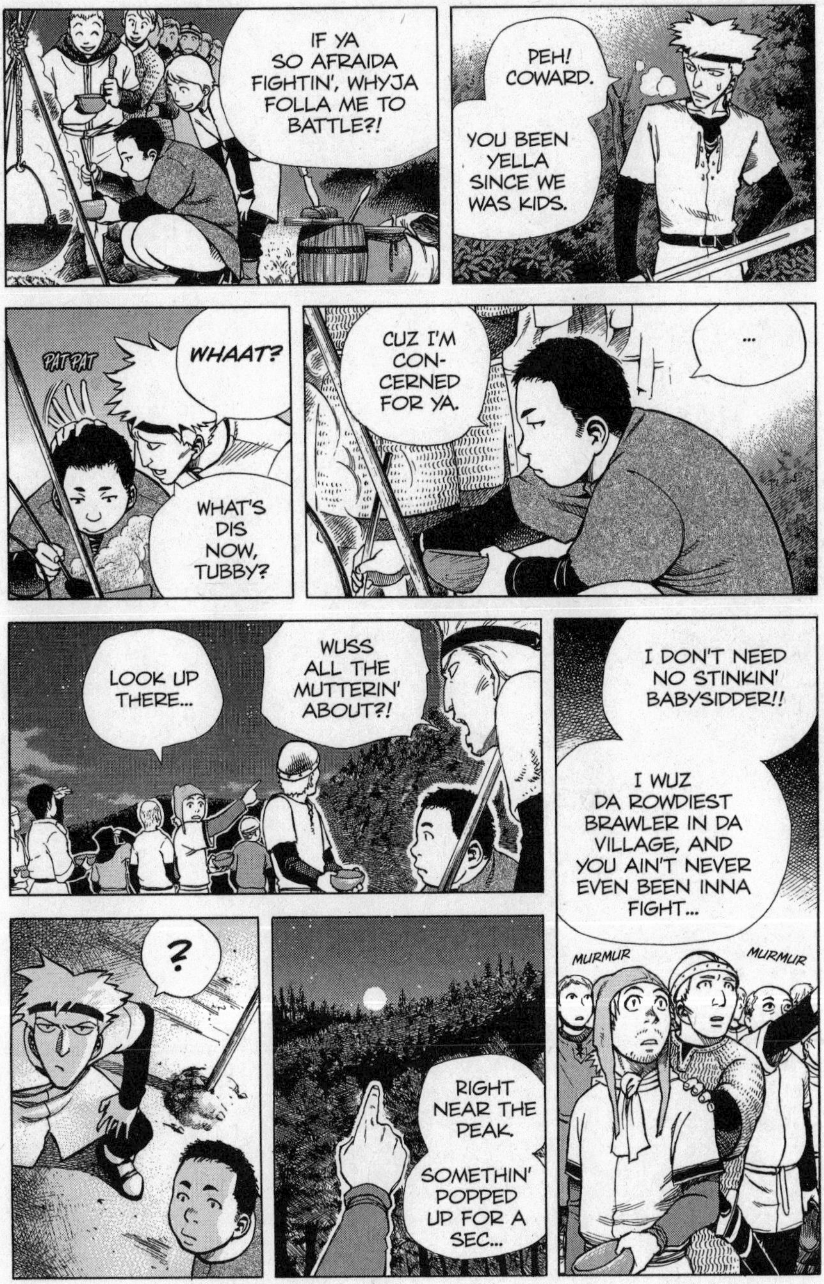
PEH! COWARD.
YOU BEEN YELLA SINCE WE WAS KIDS.
IF YA SO AFRAIDA FIGHTIN', WHYJA FOLLA ME TO BATTLE?!
...
CUZ I'M CON-CERNED FOR YA.
WHAAT?
PAT PAT
WHAT'S DIS NOW, TUBBY?
I DON'T NEED NO STINKIN' BABYSIDDER!!
I WUZ DA ROWDIEST BRAWLER IN DA VILLAGE, AND YOU AIN'T NEVER EVEN BEEN INNA FIGHT...
MURMUR
MURMUR
WUSS ALL THE MUTTERIN' ABOUT?!
LOOK UP THERE...
RIGHT NEAR THE PEAK.
SOMETHIN' POPPED UP FOR A SEC...
?

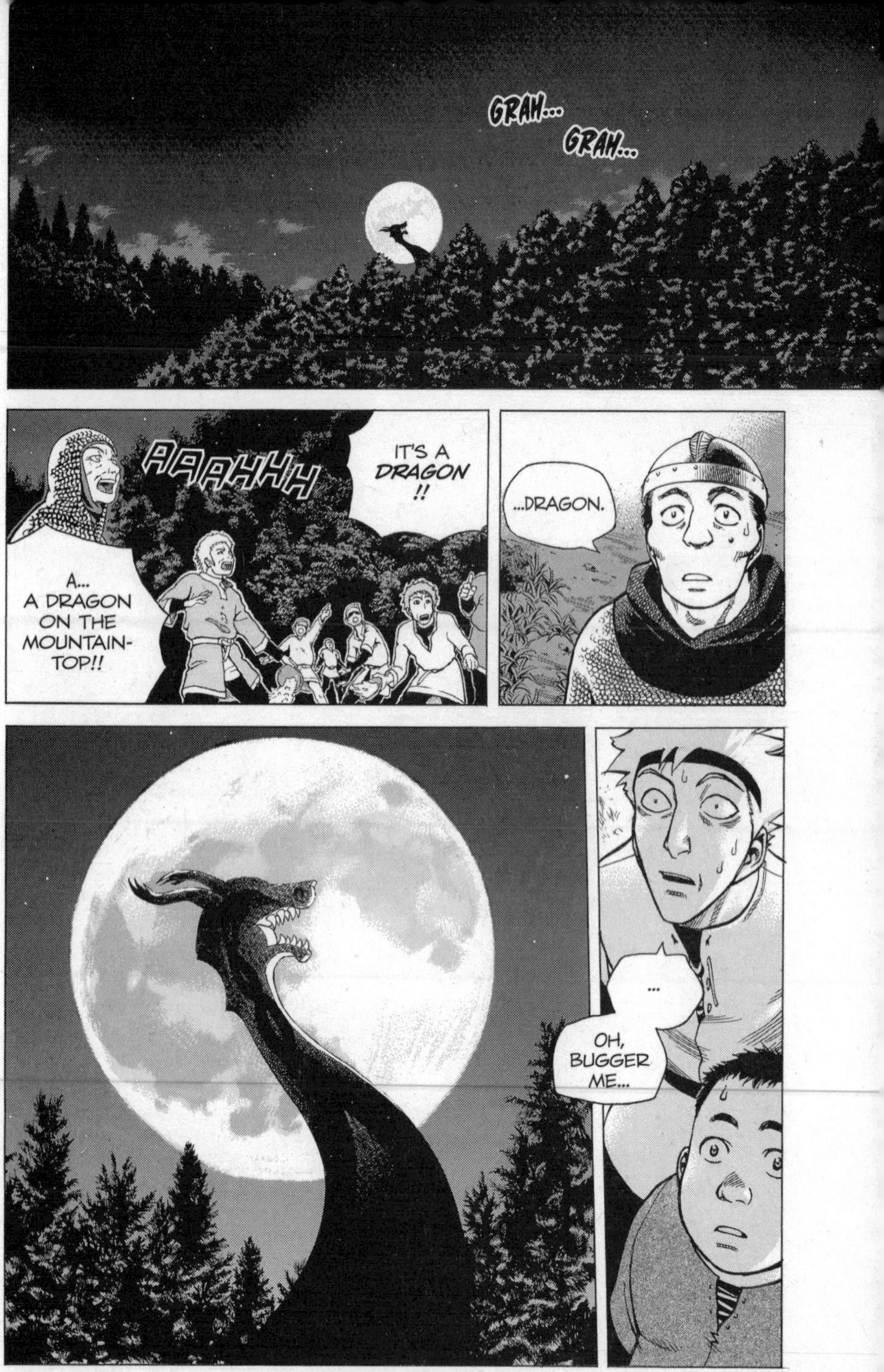
GRAH...
GRAH...
...DRAGON.
IT'S A DRAGON!!
AAAHHH
A... A DRAGON ON THE MOUNTAIN-TOP!!
...
OH, BUGGER ME...

CHIP...

CHRRP...

ZMM ZMM ZMM ZMM ZMM

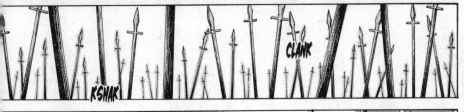

CLANK

KSHAK

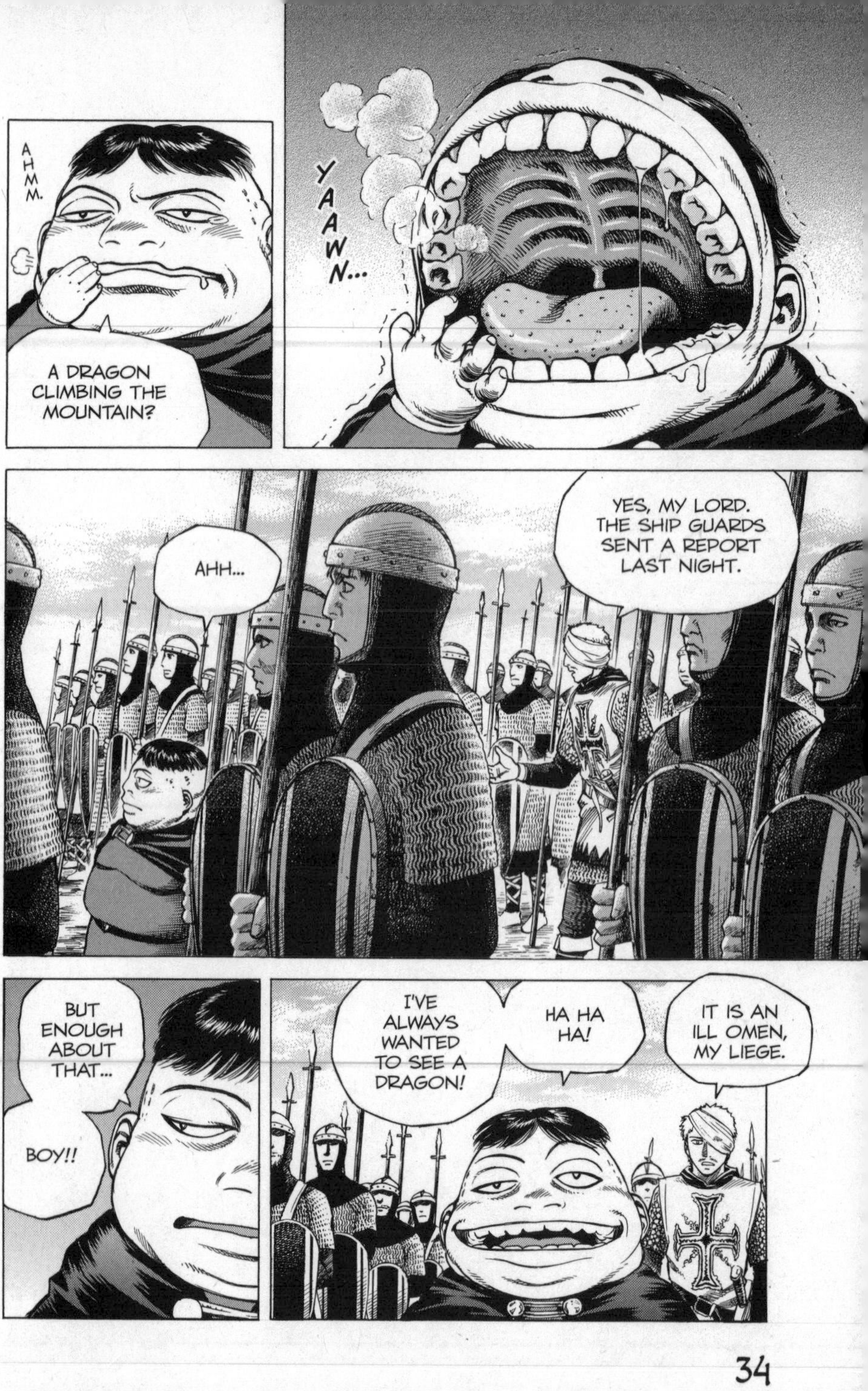
YAAWN...
AHMM.
A DRAGON CLIMBING THE MOUNTAIN?
YES, MY LORD. THE SHIP GUARDS SENT A REPORT LAST NIGHT.
AHH...
IT IS AN ILL OMEN, MY LIEGE.
HA HA HA!
I'VE ALWAYS WANTED TO SEE A DRAGON!
BUT ENOUGH ABOUT THAT...
BOY!!

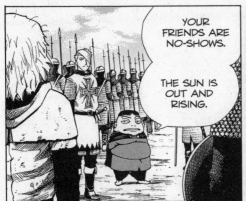

YOUR FRIENDS ARE NO-SHOWS.
THE SUN IS OUT AND RISING.
JUST GET ON WITH THE ATTACK, FAT-ASS.
YOU'LL SEE SOON ENOUGH.
YOU JUST INSULTED ME, DIDN'T YOU?
I'VE AN EAR FOR THESE THINGS.
CHEEKY WHELP...
IT SEEMS YOUR HEAD WILL BE THE CENTER-PIECE OF OUR VICTORY FEAST TONIGHT, BOY!!
PREPARE TO ATTACK!!

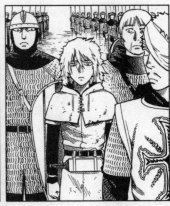

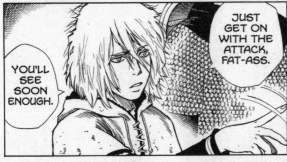

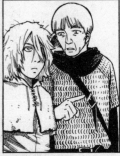

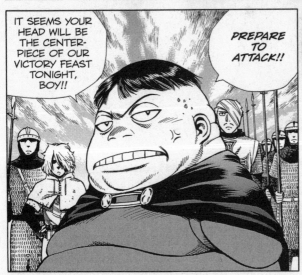

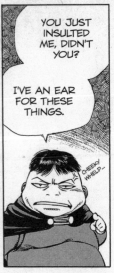

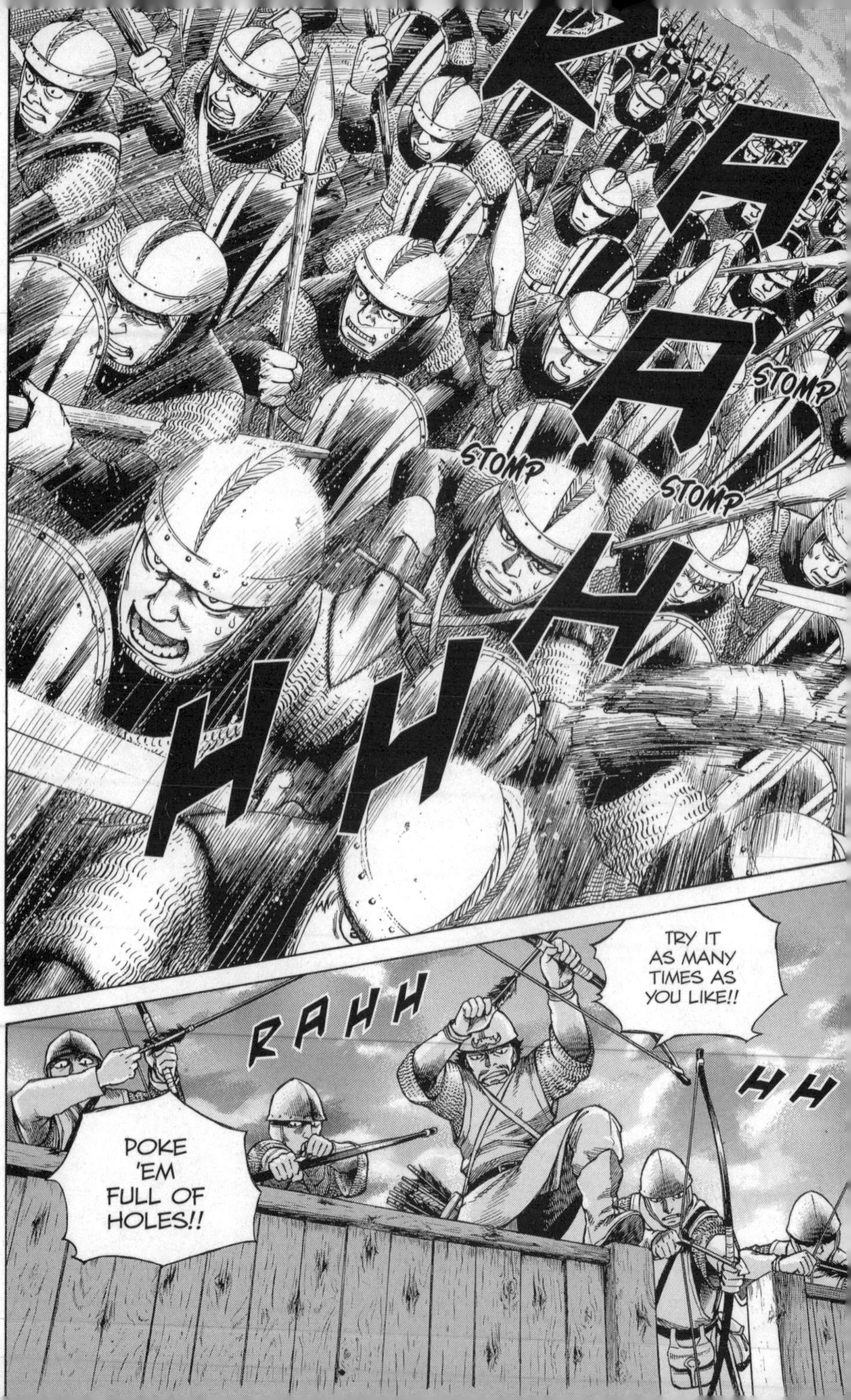
STOMP
STOMP
STOMP
TRY IT AS MANY TIMES AS YOU LIKE!!
RAHH HH
POKE 'EM FULL OF HOLES!!

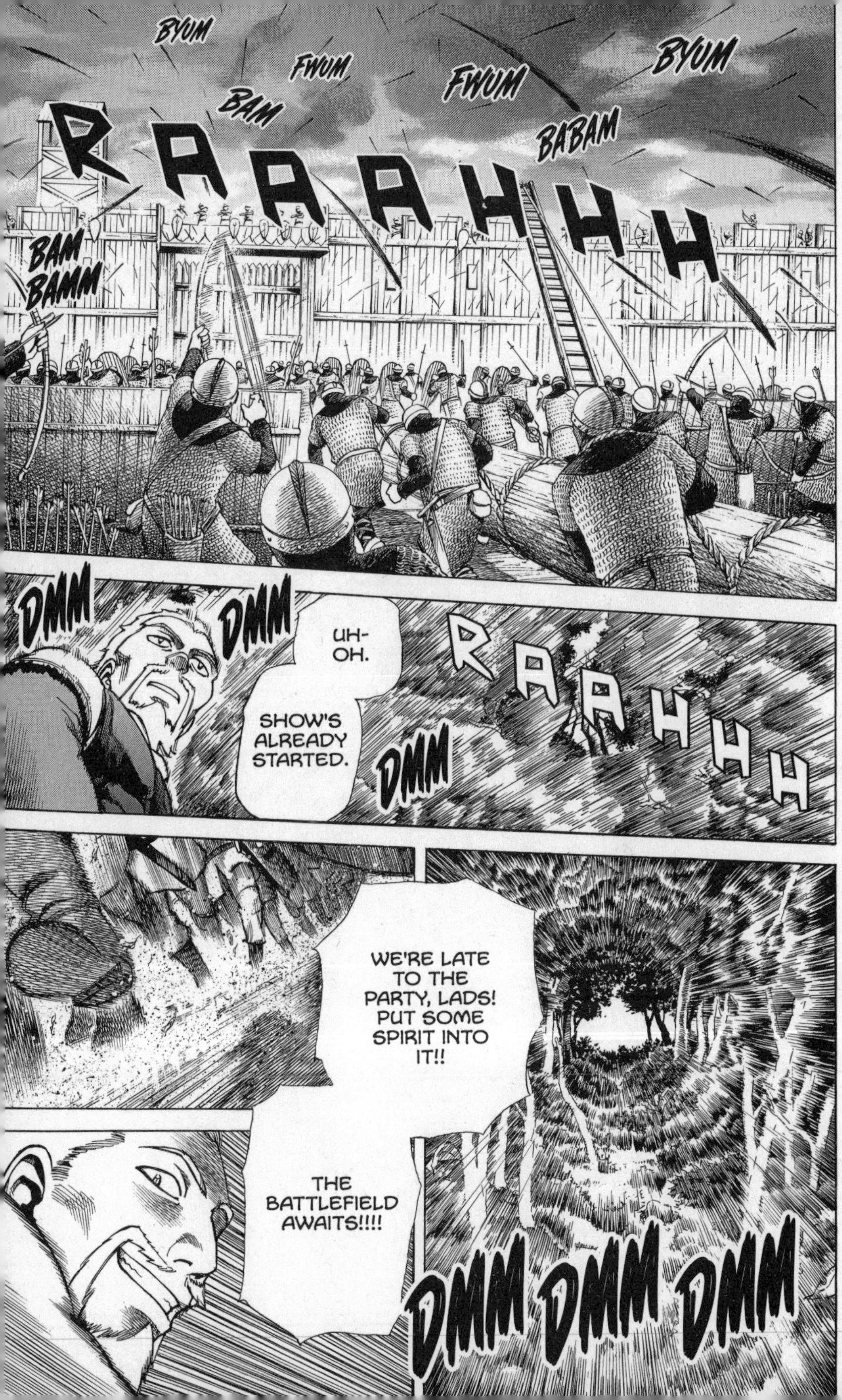
BYUM
BABAM
FWUM
FWUM
BAM
BYUM
RAAAHHHH
BAM BAMM
DMM
UH-OH.
SHOW'S ALREADY STARTED.
RAAAHHHH
DMM
DMM
WE'RE LATE TO THE PARTY, LADS! PUT SOME SPIRIT INTO IT!!
THE BATTLEFIELD AWAITS!!!!
DMM DMM DMM

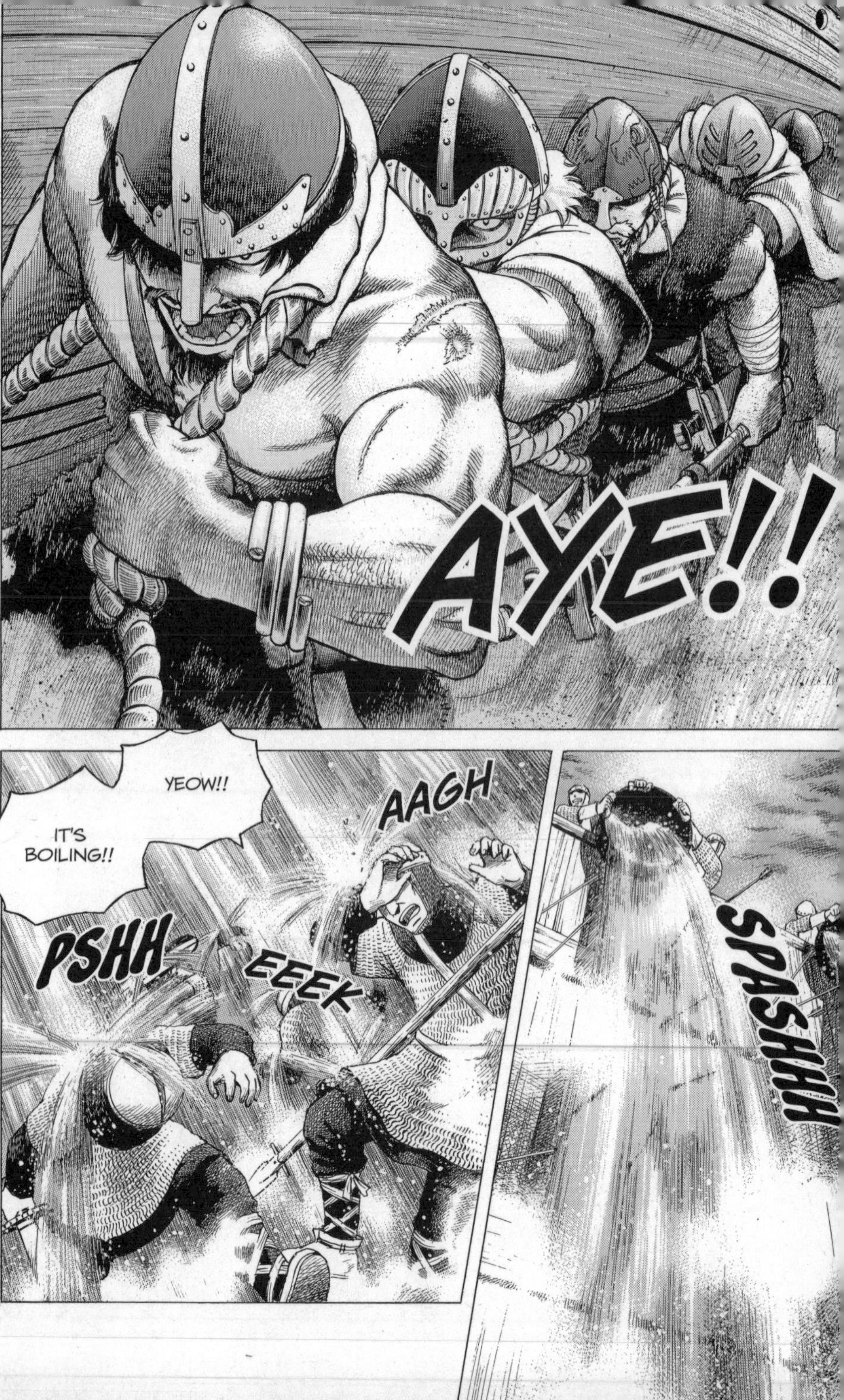
AYE!!
SPASHHH
AAGH
YEOW!! IT'S BOILING!!
EEEK
PSHH

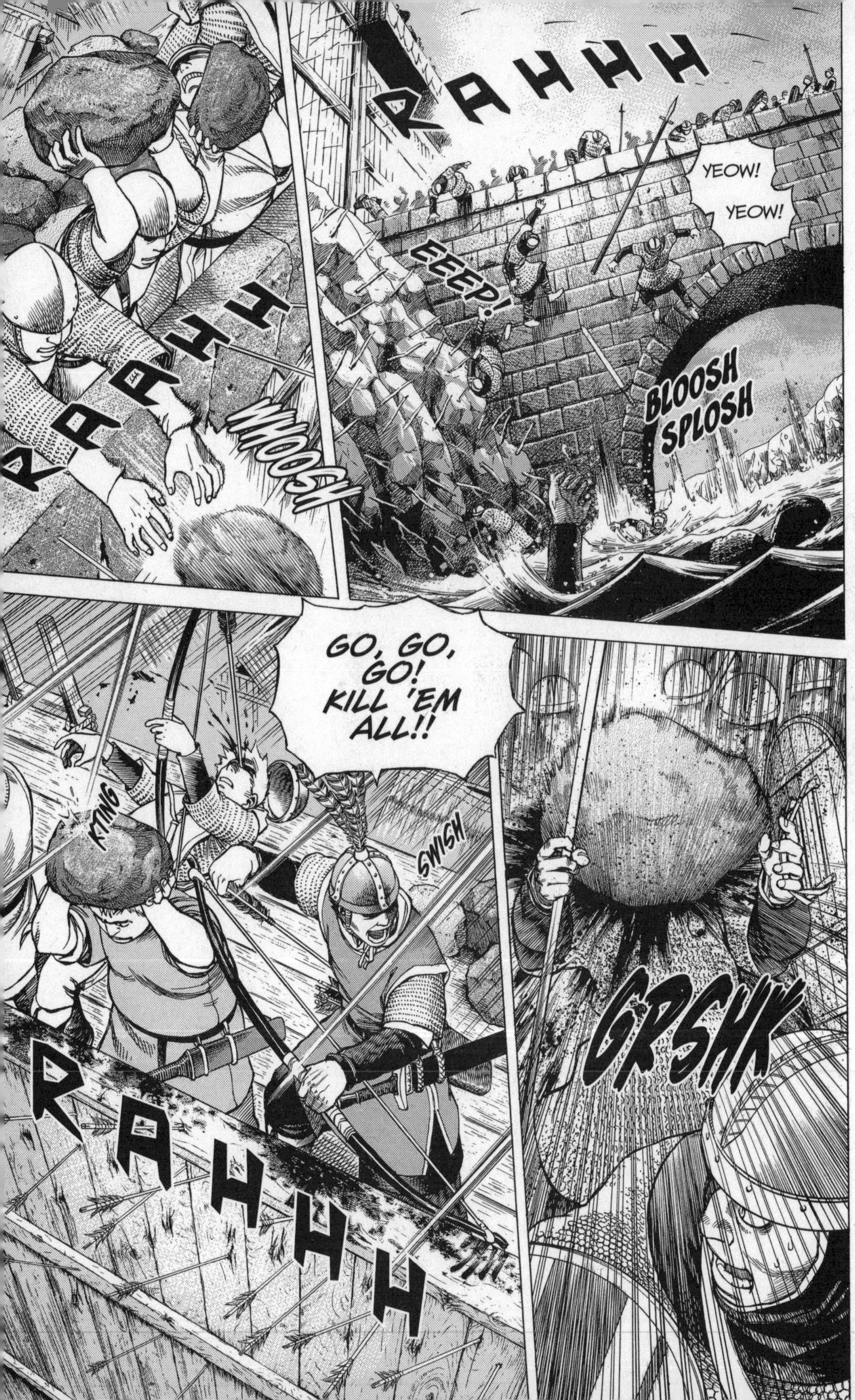
RAHHH
YEOW!
YEOW!
EEEEP!
BLOOSH SPLOSH
RAAHH
WHOOSH
GRSHK
GO, GO, GO! KILL 'EM ALL!!
KTING
SWISH
RAHHHH

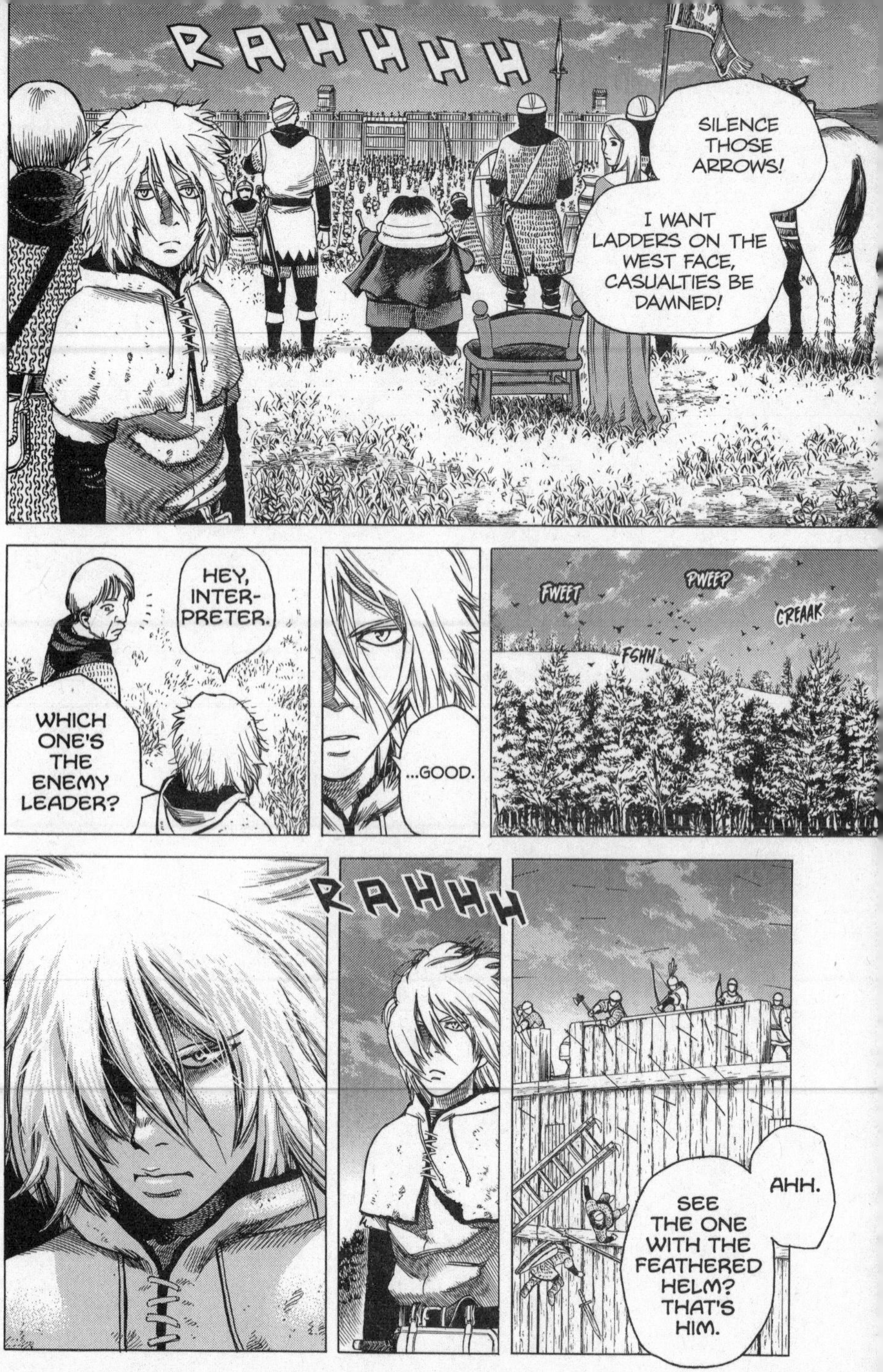
RAHHHH
SILENCE THOSE ARROWS!
I WANT LADDERS ON THE WEST FACE, CASUALTIES BE DAMNED!
FWEET
PWEEP
CREAAK
FSHH
...GOOD.
HEY, INTER-PRETER.
WHICH ONE'S THE ENEMY LEADER?
AHH.
SEE THE ONE WITH THE FEATHERED HELM? THAT'S HIM.
RAHHHH

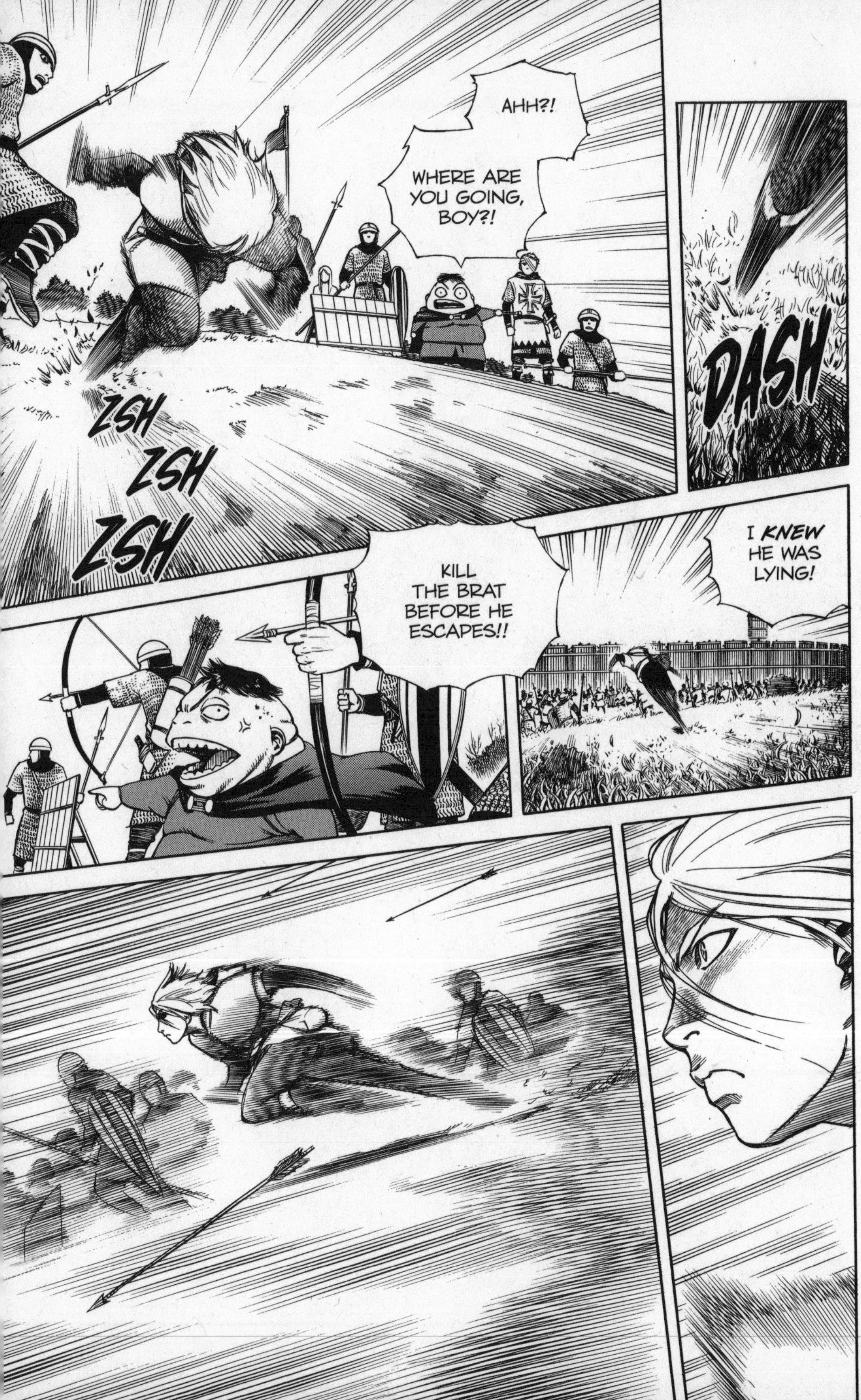
DASH
AHH?!
WHERE ARE YOU GOING, BOY?!
ZSH ZSH ZSH
I KNEW HE WAS LYING!
KILL THE BRAT BEFORE HE ESCAPES!!

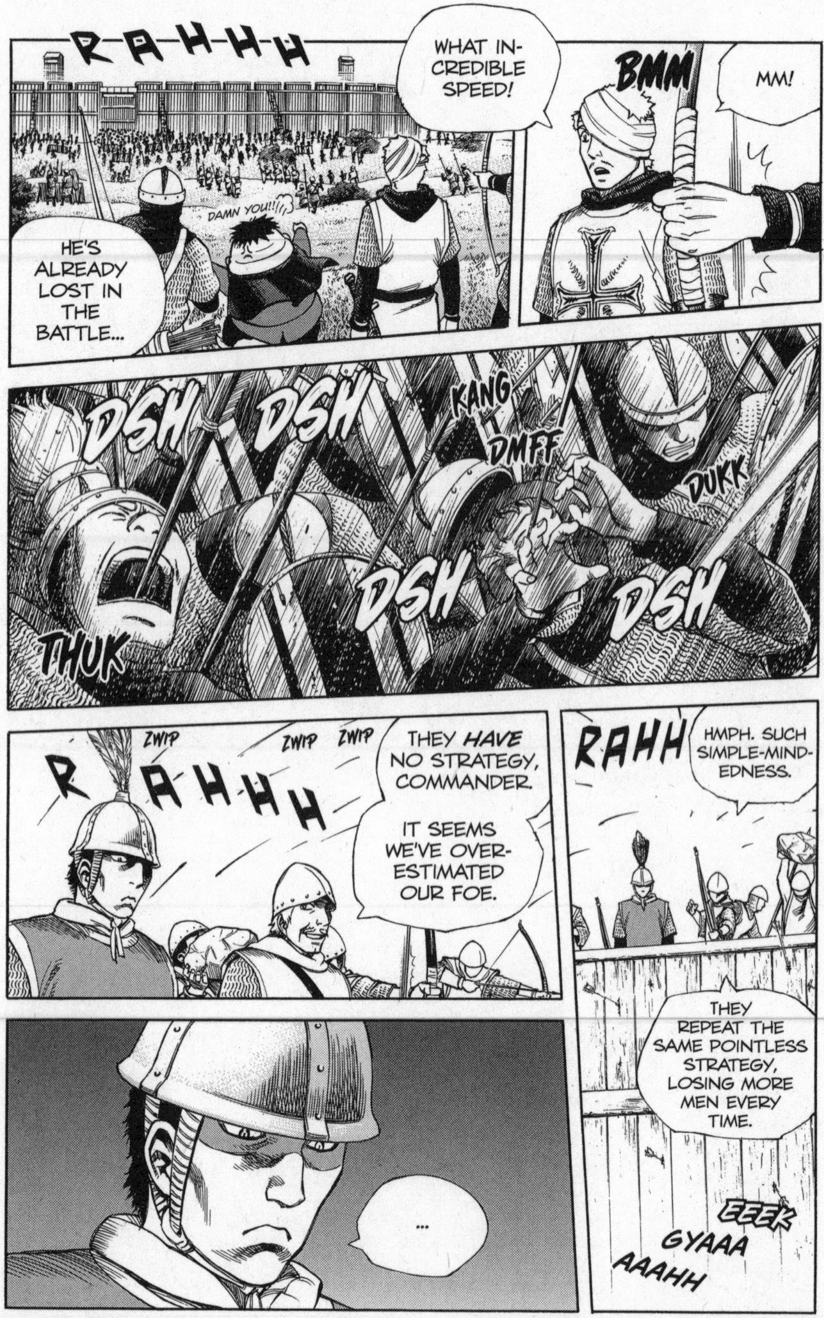
BMM
MM!
WHAT IN-CREDIBLE SPEED!
RAHHHH
DAMN YOU!!
HE'S ALREADY LOST IN THE BATTLE...
DSH DSH
KANG
DMFF
DUKK
DSH DSH
THUK
RAHH
HMPH. SUCH SIMPLE-MIND-EDNESS.
THEY REPEAT THE SAME POINTLESS STRATEGY, LOSING MORE MEN EVERY TIME.
EEEK
GYAAA AAAHH
ZWIP ZWIP ZWIP
THEY *HAVE* NO STRATEGY, COMMANDER.
IT SEEMS WE'VE OVER-ESTIMATED OUR FOE.
RAHHHH
...

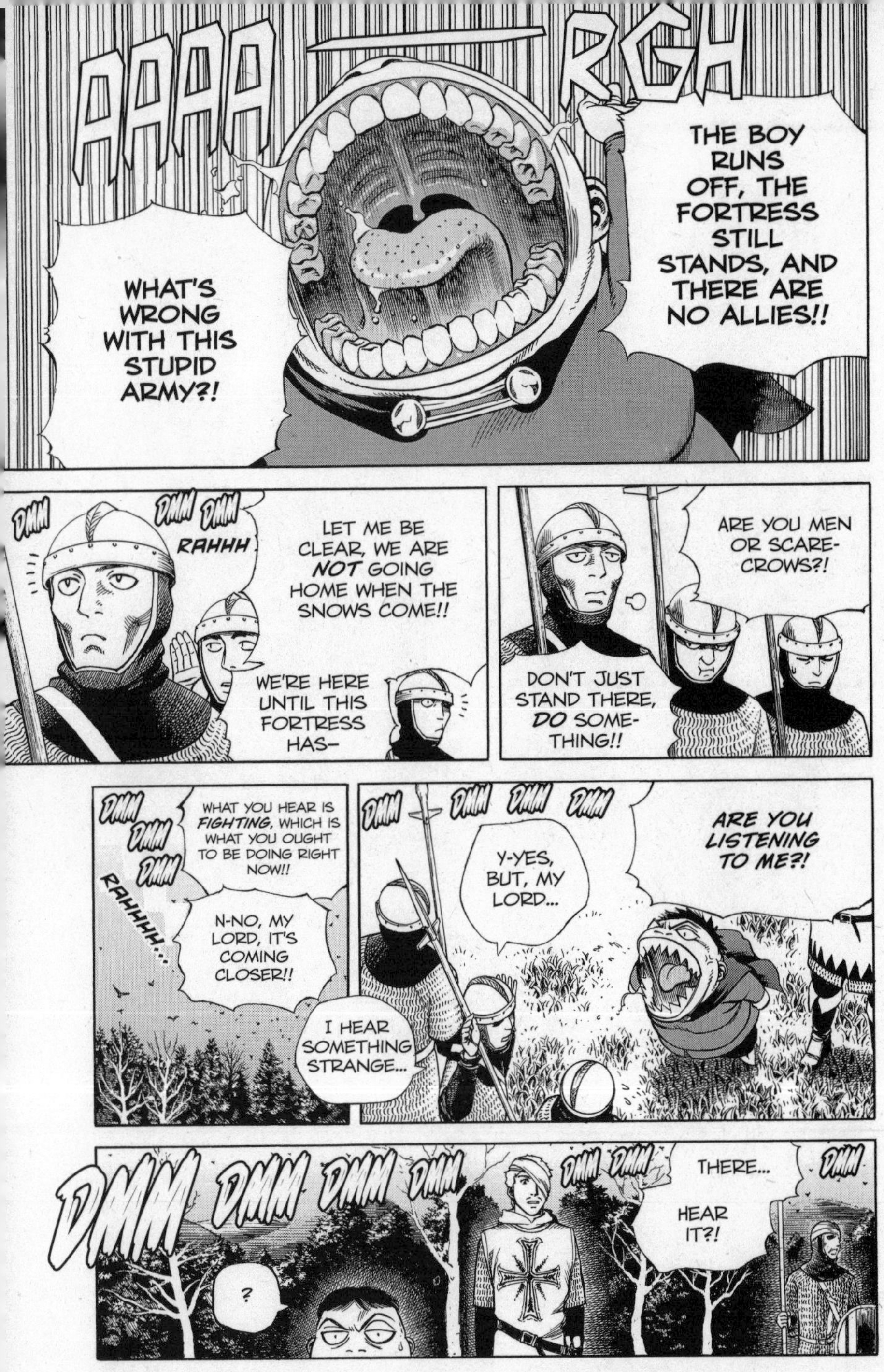
AAAA—RGH
THE BOY RUNS OFF, THE FORTRESS STILL STANDS, AND THERE ARE NO ALLIES!!
WHAT'S WRONG WITH THIS STUPID ARMY?!
ARE YOU MEN OR SCARE-CROWS?!
DON'T JUST STAND THERE, DO SOMETHING!!
DMM DMM
DMM
RAHHH
LET ME BE CLEAR, WE ARE NOT GOING HOME WHEN THE SNOWS COME!!
WE'RE HERE UNTIL THIS FORTRESS HAS–
DMM DMM DMM DMM
ARE YOU LISTENING TO ME?!
Y-YES, BUT, MY LORD...
I HEAR SOMETHING STRANGE...
WHAT YOU HEAR IS FIGHTING, WHICH IS WHAT YOU OUGHT TO BE DOING RIGHT NOW!!
DMM DMM DMM
RAHHHH...
N-NO, MY LORD, IT'S COMING CLOSER!!
DMM
DMM DMM
THERE...
HEAR IT?!
DMM DMM DMM DMM
?

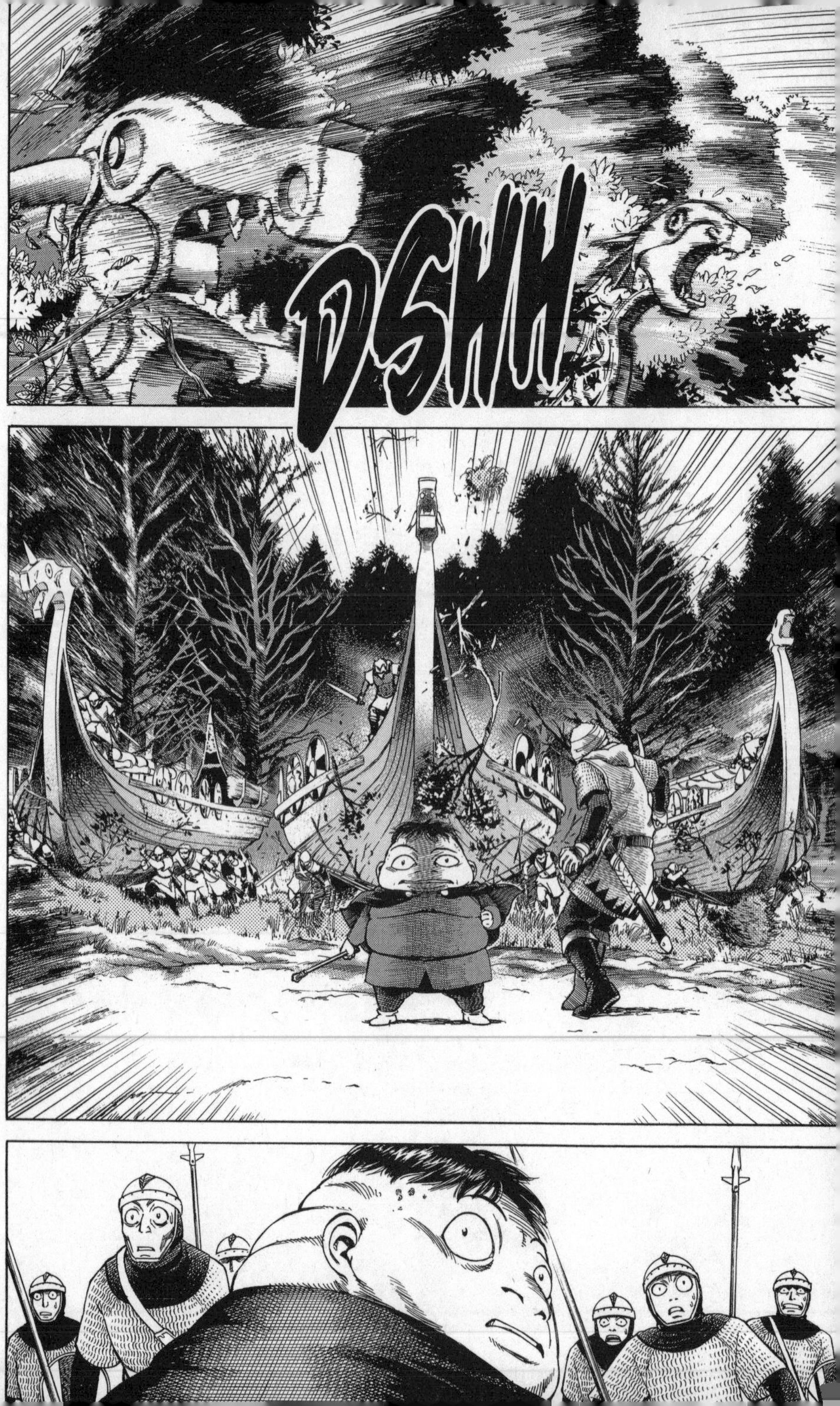
DSHH

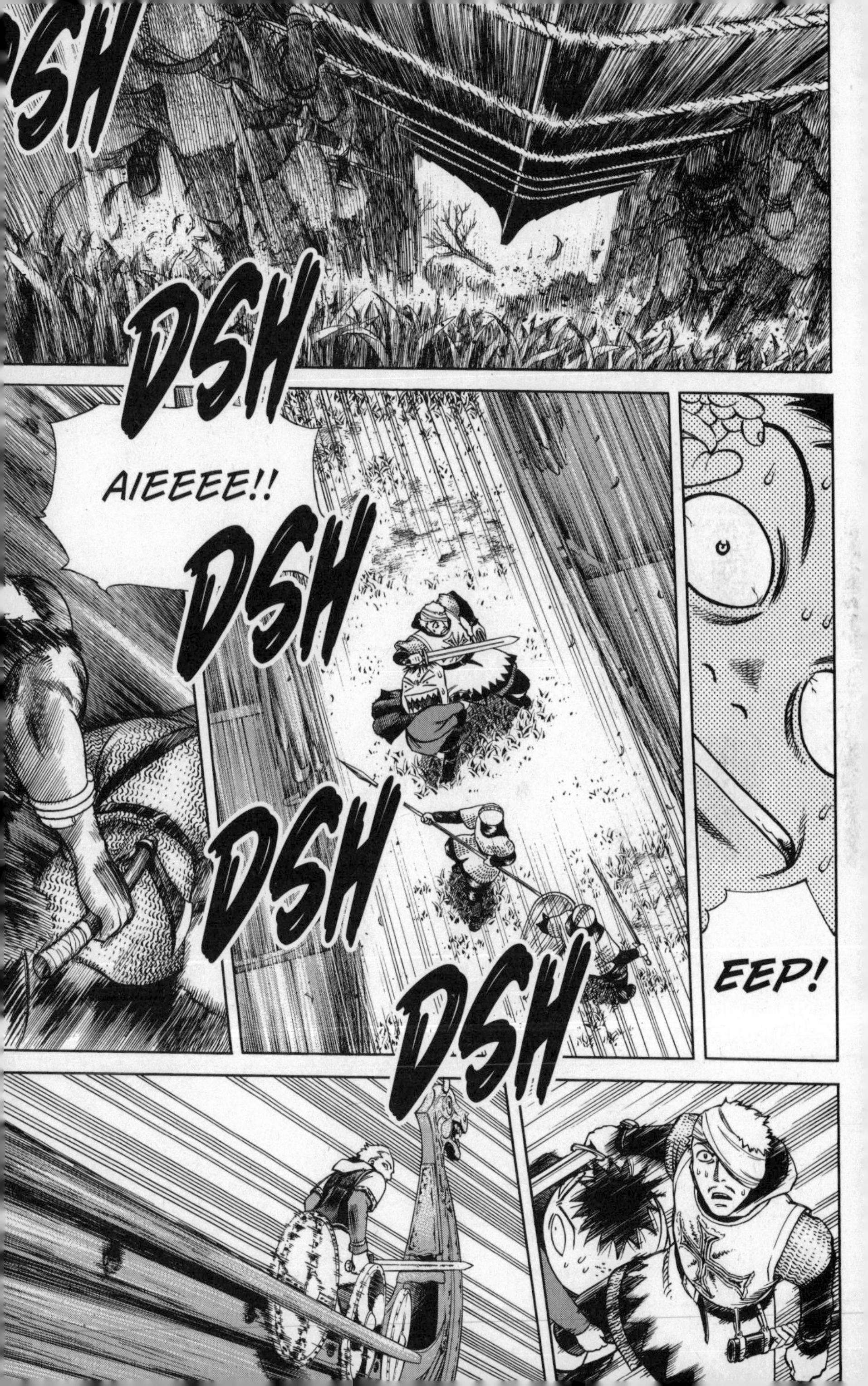

DSH
DSH
EEP!
DSH
DSH
DSH
AIEEEE!!

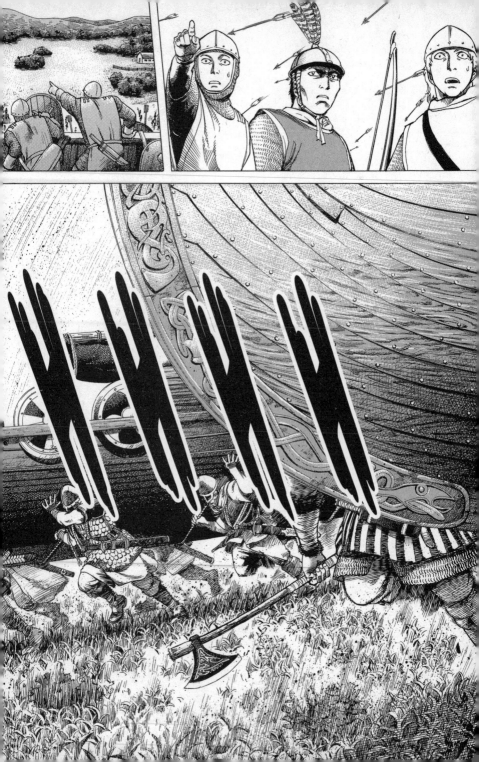

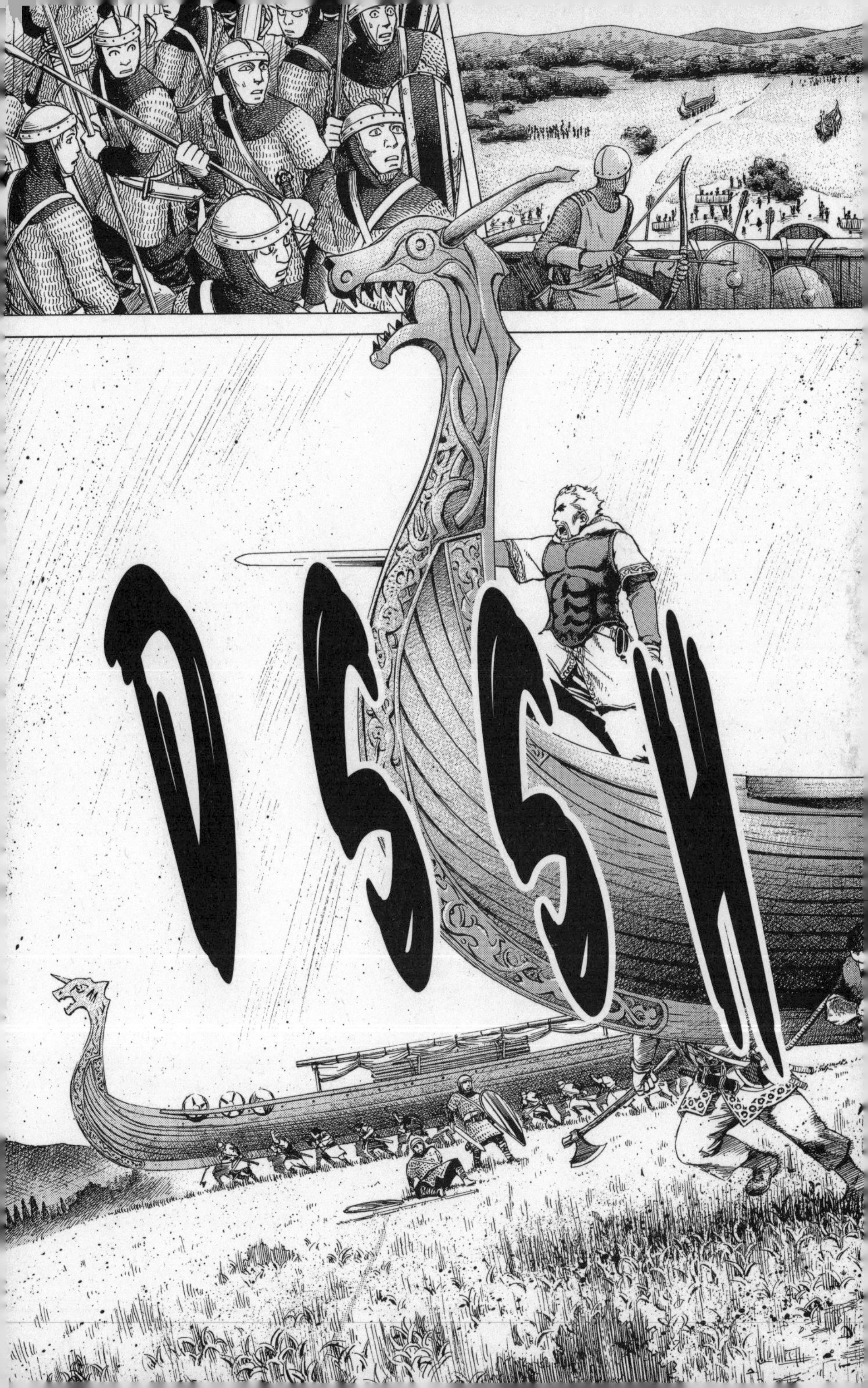
DSSH

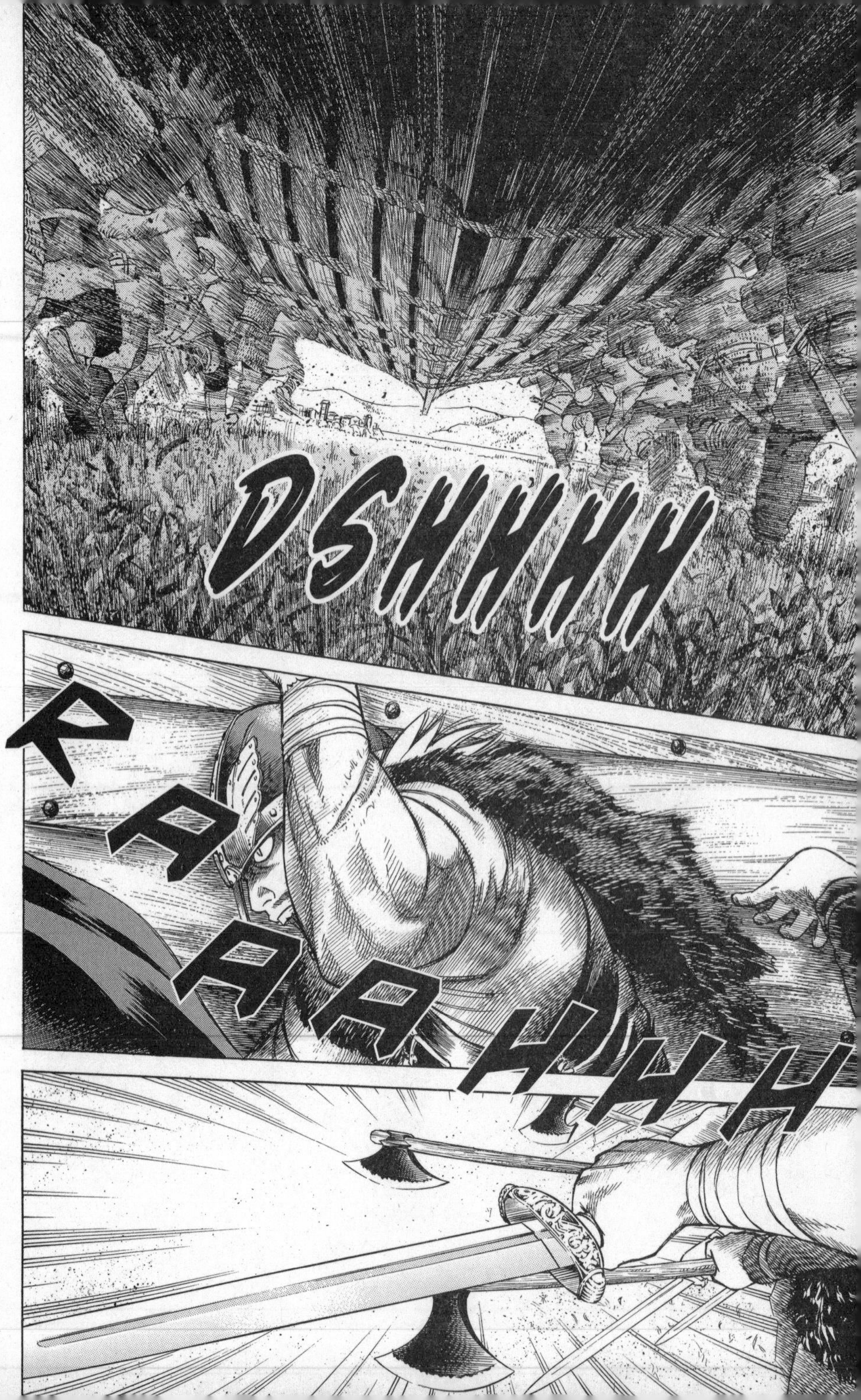
DSHHHH
RAAAAHHHH

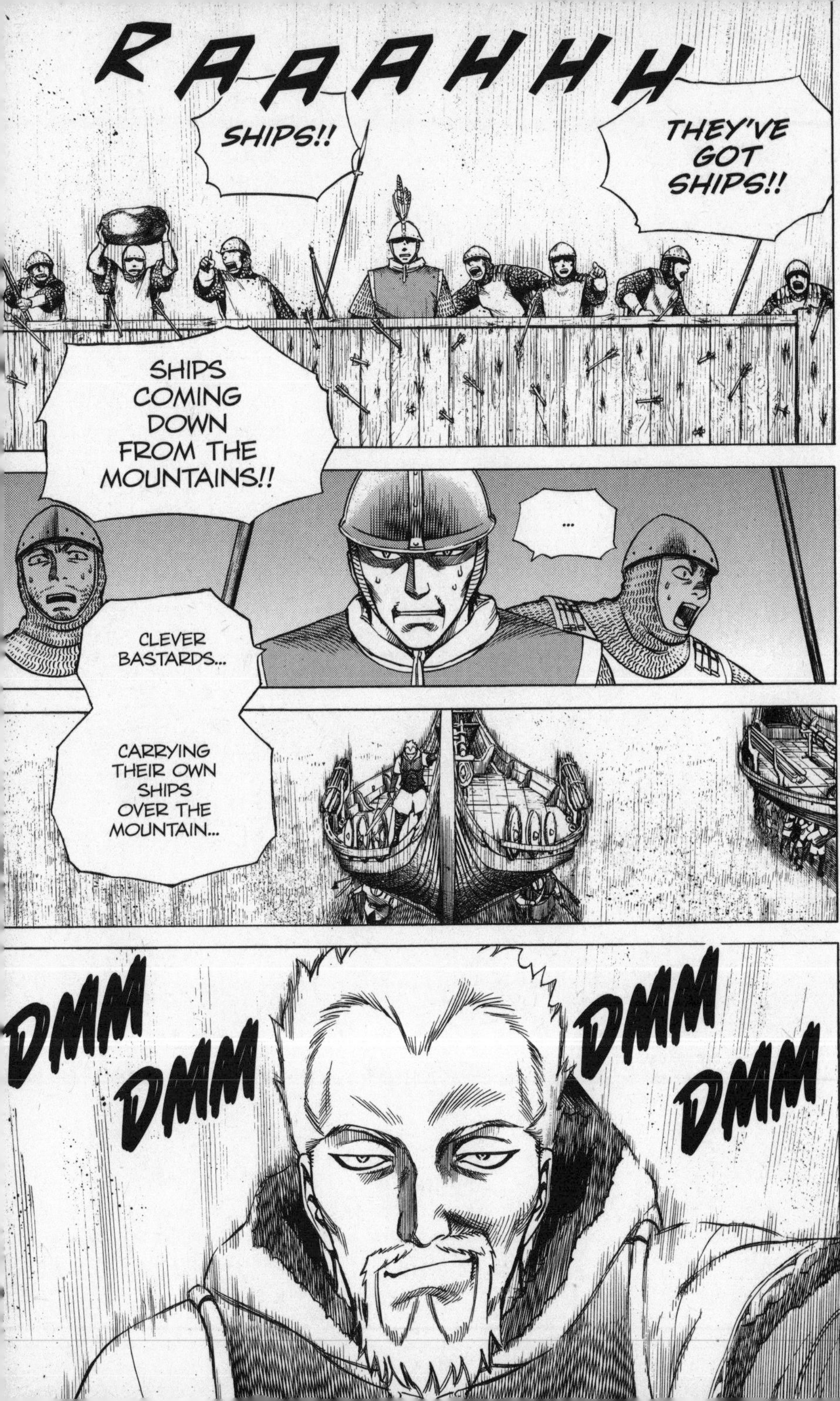
RAAAHHH
THEY'VE GOT SHIPS!!
SHIPS!!
SHIPS COMING DOWN FROM THE MOUNTAINS!!
...
CLEVER BASTARDS...
CARRYING THEIR OWN SHIPS OVER THE MOUNTAIN...
DMM DMM
DMM DMM

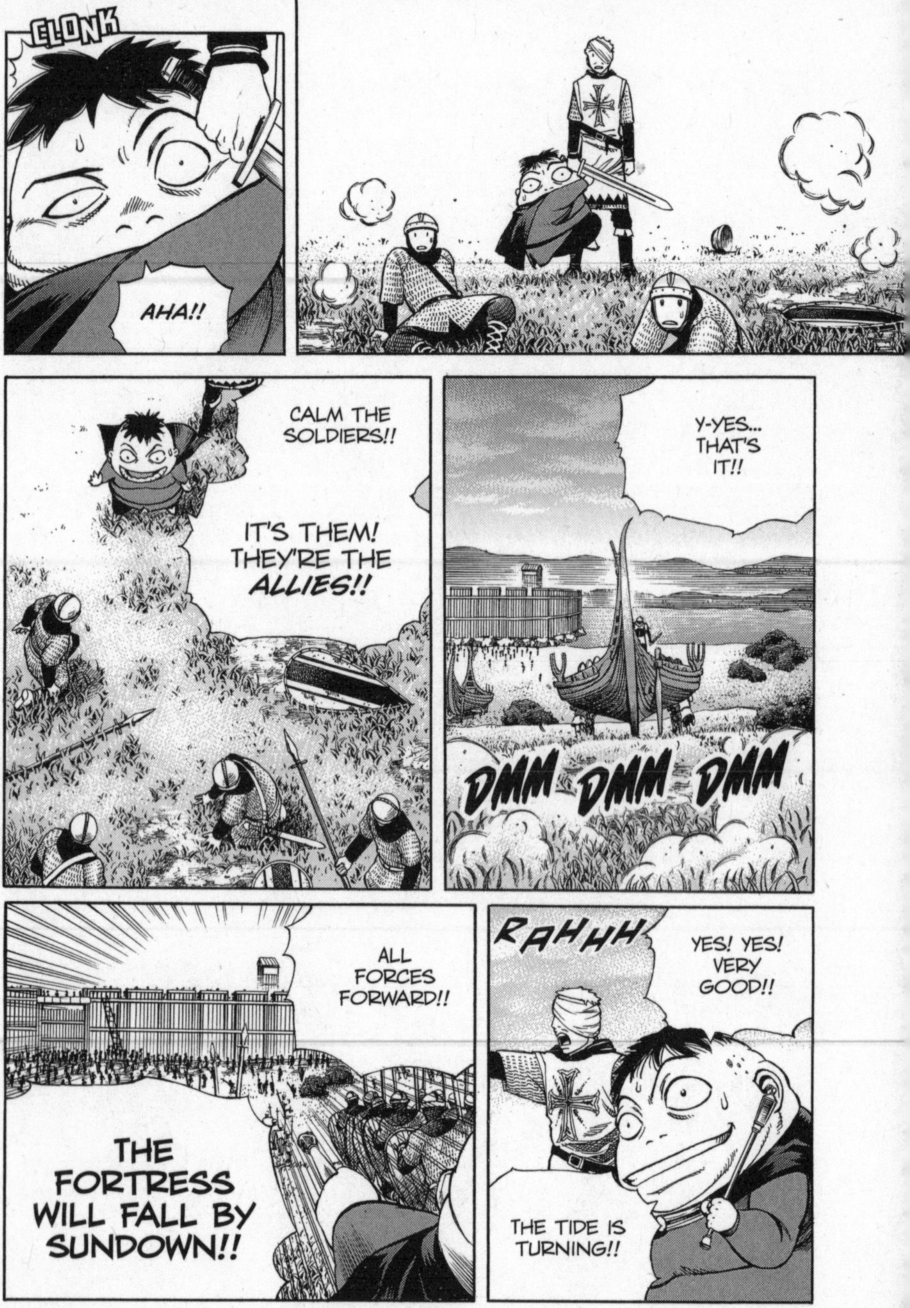
CLONK
AHA!!
Y-YES... THAT'S IT!!
DMM DMM DMM
CALM THE SOLDIERS!!
IT'S THEM! THEY'RE THE ALLIES!!
RAHHH
YES! YES! VERY GOOD!!
THE TIDE IS TURNING!!
ALL FORCES FORWARD!!
THE FORTRESS WILL FALL BY SUNDOWN!!

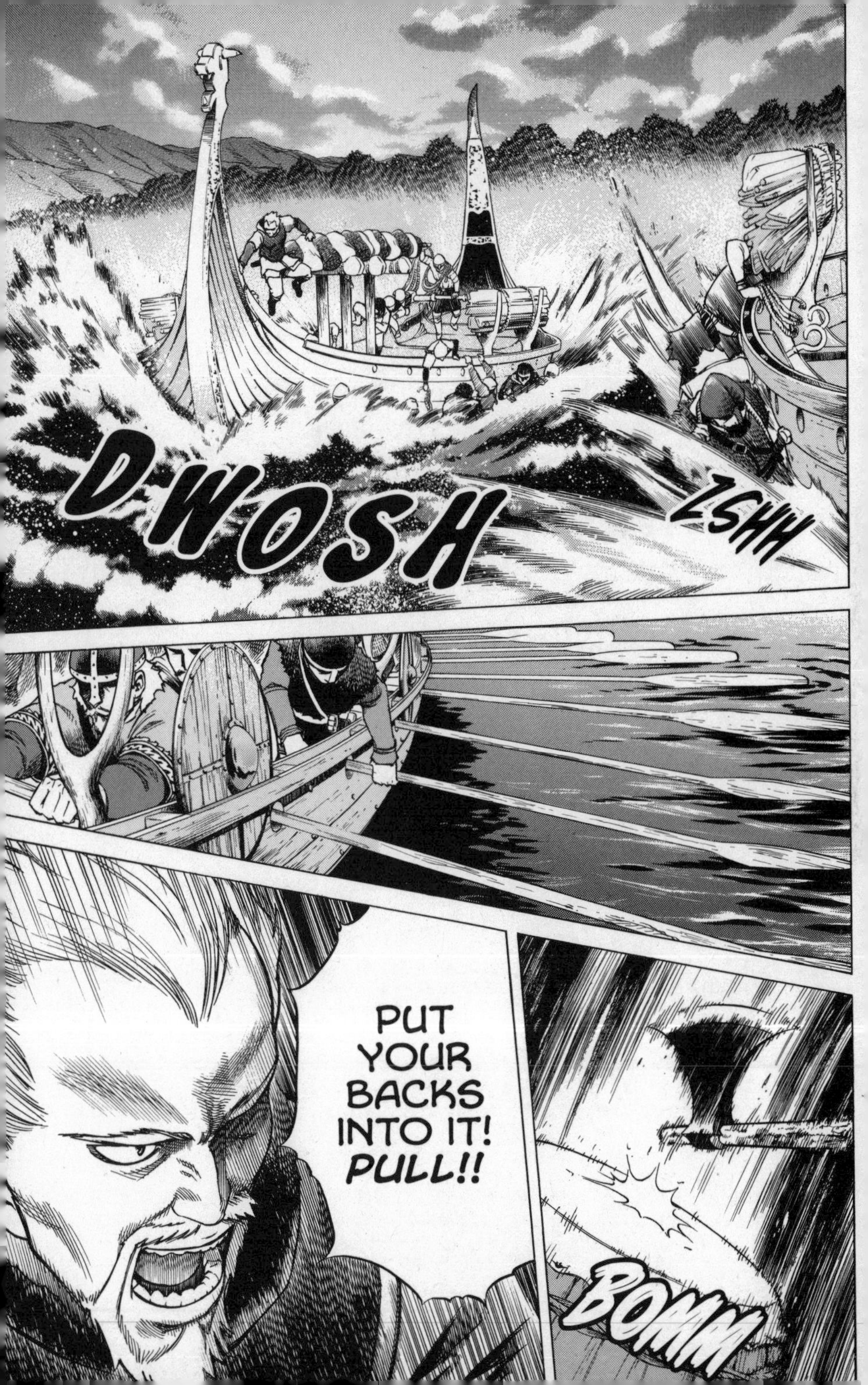
ZSHH
DWOSH
BOMM
PUT YOUR BACKS INTO IT! *PULL!!*

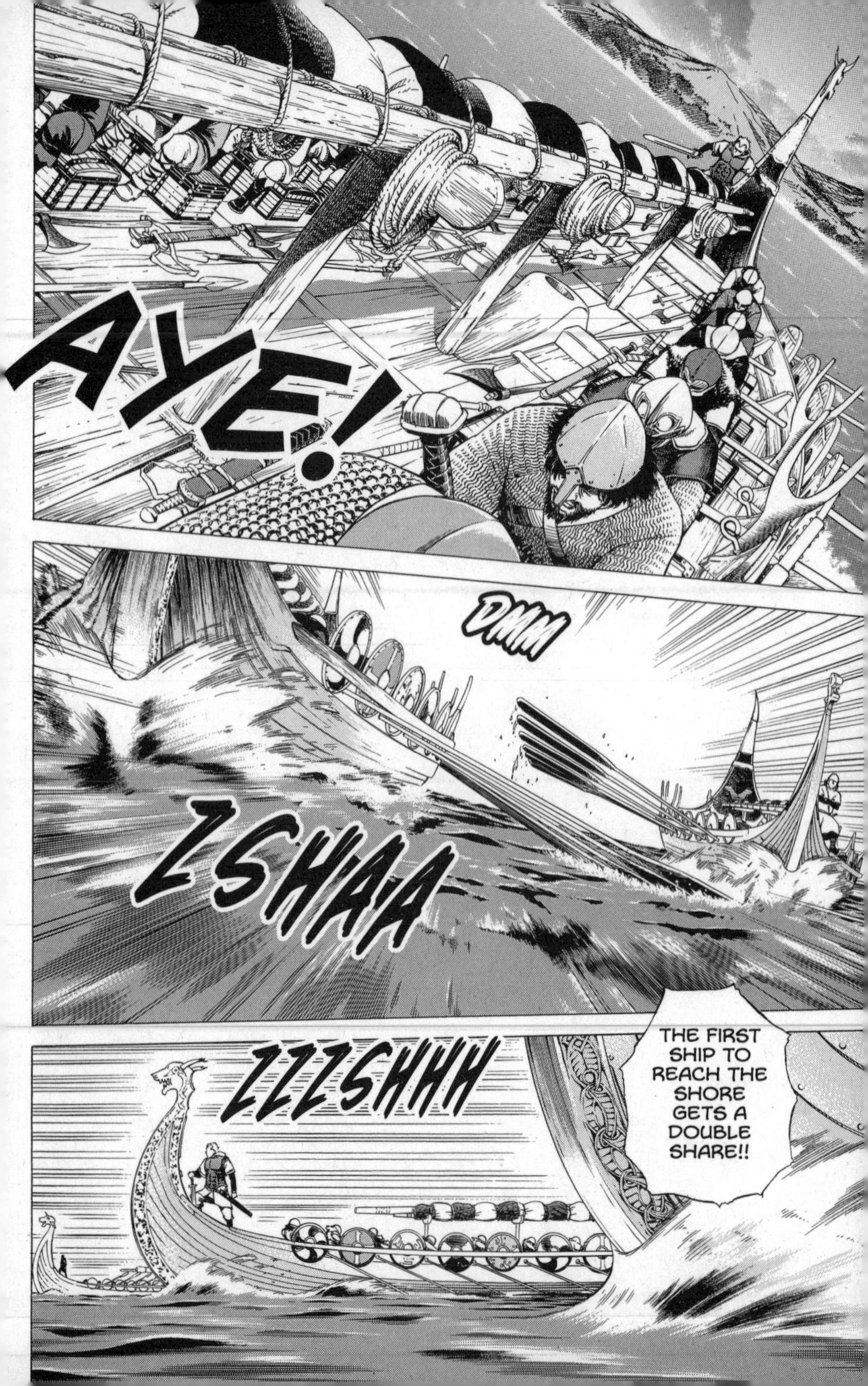
AYE!
DMM
ZSHAA
THE FIRST SHIP TO REACH THE SHORE GETS A DOUBLE SHARE!!
ZZZSHHH

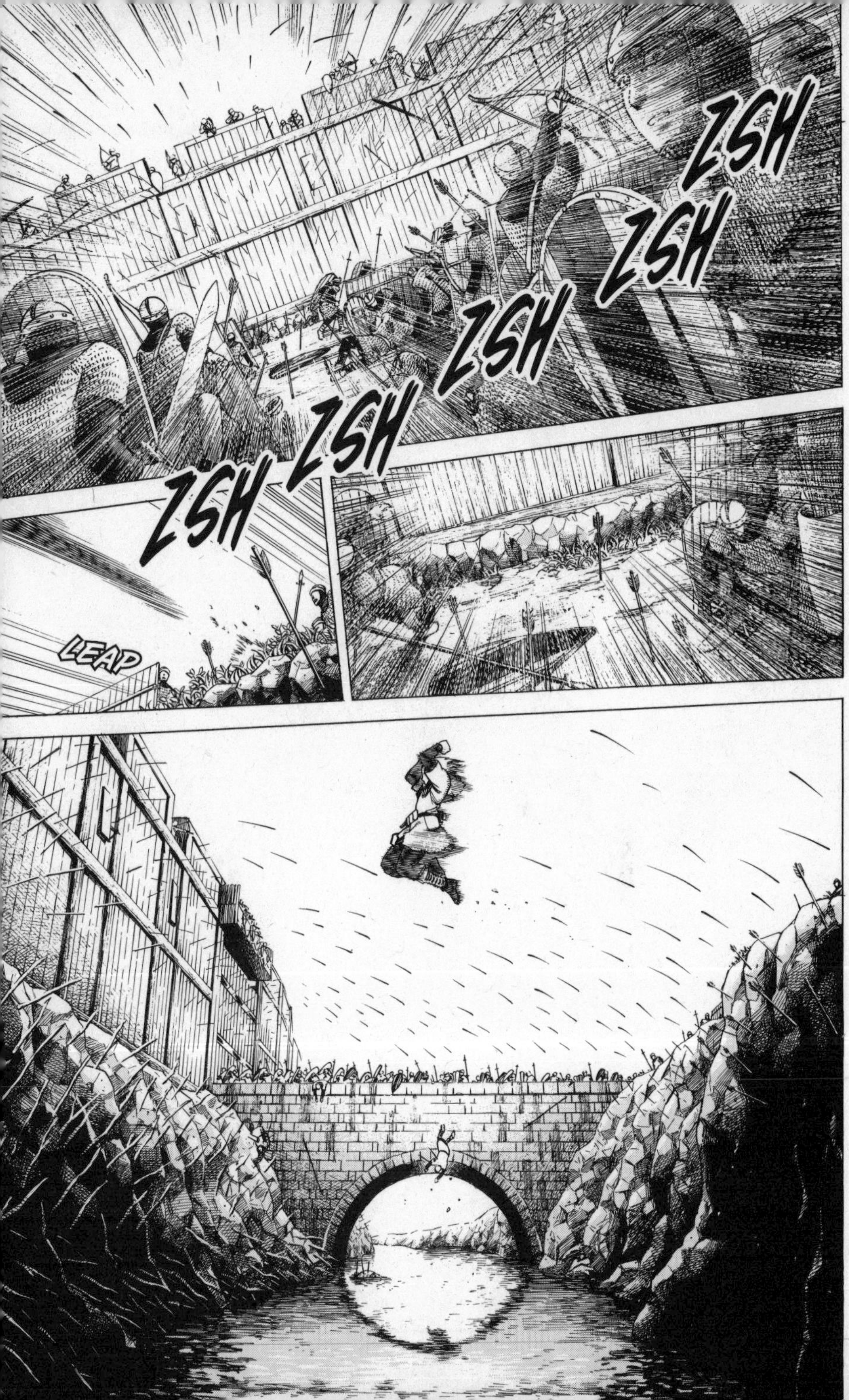
ZSH
ZSH
ZSH
ZSH
ZSH
LEAP

SH KAA

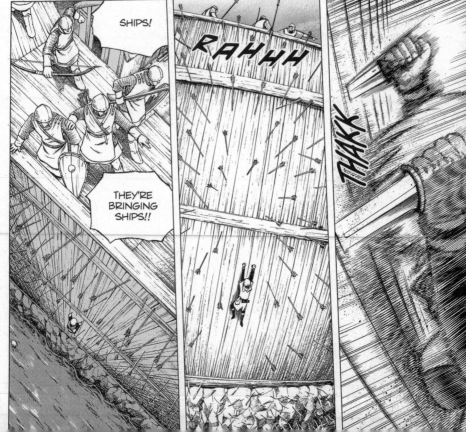

SHIPS!

RAHHH

THAKK

THEY'RE BRINGING SHIPS!!

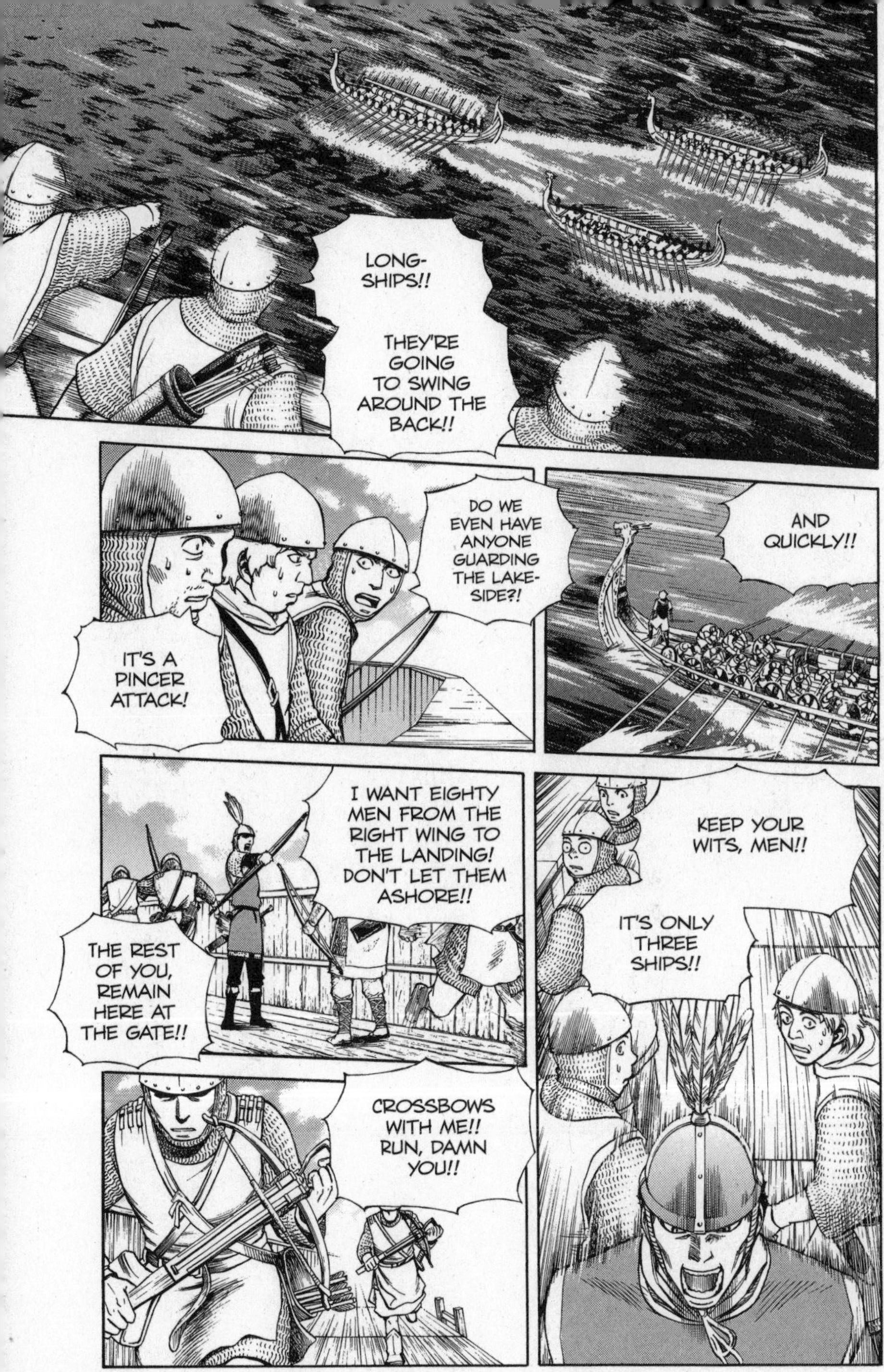
LONG-SHIPS!!
THEY'RE GOING TO SWING AROUND THE BACK!!
AND QUICKLY!!
DO WE EVEN HAVE ANYONE GUARDING THE LAKE-SIDE?!
IT'S A PINCER ATTACK!
KEEP YOUR WITS, MEN!!
IT'S ONLY THREE SHIPS!!
I WANT EIGHTY MEN FROM THE RIGHT WING TO THE LANDING! DON'T LET THEM ASHORE!!
THE REST OF YOU, REMAIN HERE AT THE GATE!!
CROSSBOWS WITH ME!! RUN, DAMN YOU!!

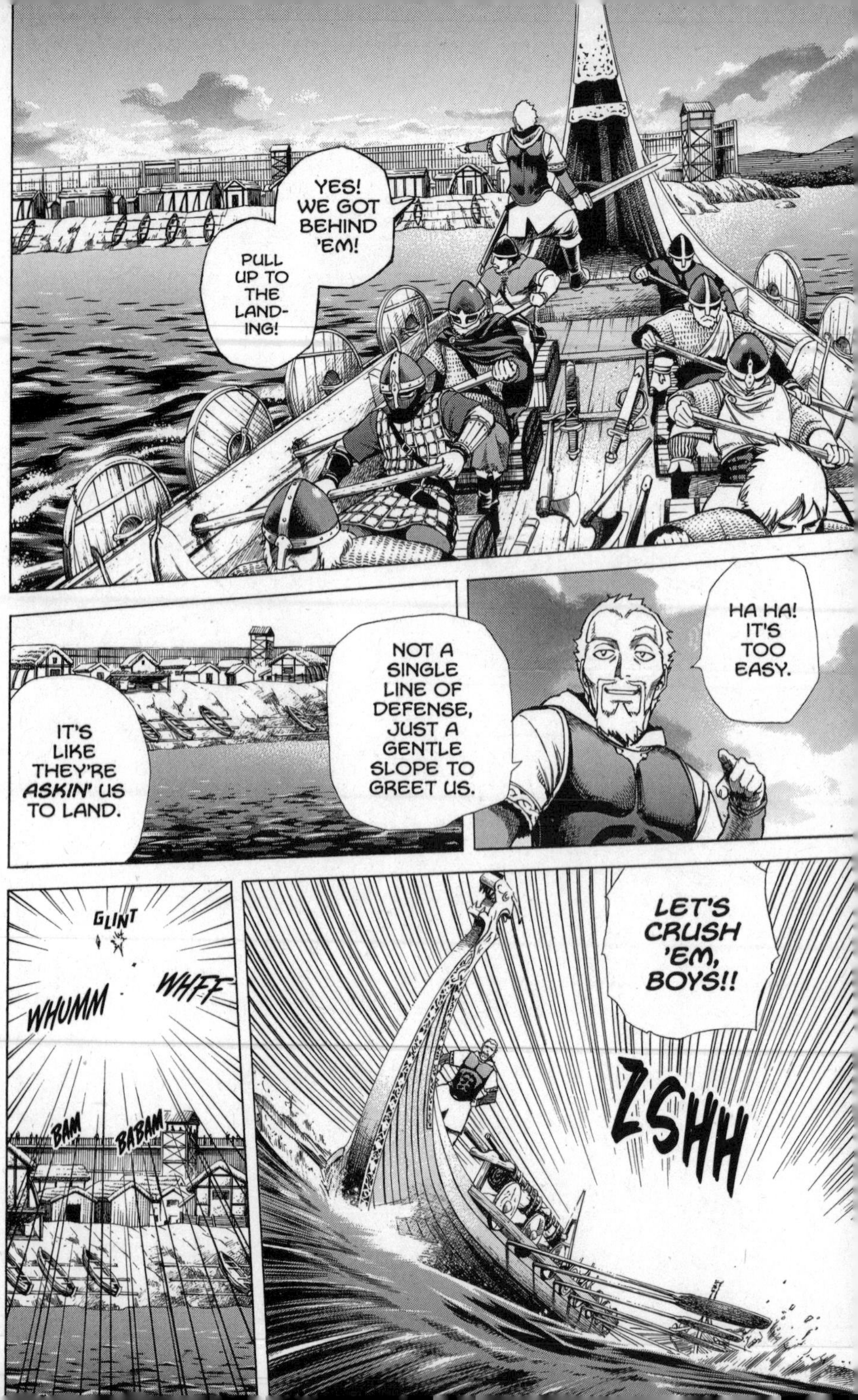
YES! WE GOT BEHIND 'EM!
PULL UP TO THE LAND-ING!
HA HA! IT'S TOO EASY.
NOT A SINGLE LINE OF DEFENSE, JUST A GENTLE SLOPE TO GREET US.
IT'S LIKE THEY'RE *ASKIN'* US TO LAND.
LET'S CRUSH 'EM, BOYS!!
ZSHH
GLINT
WHFF
WHUMM
BAM
BABAM

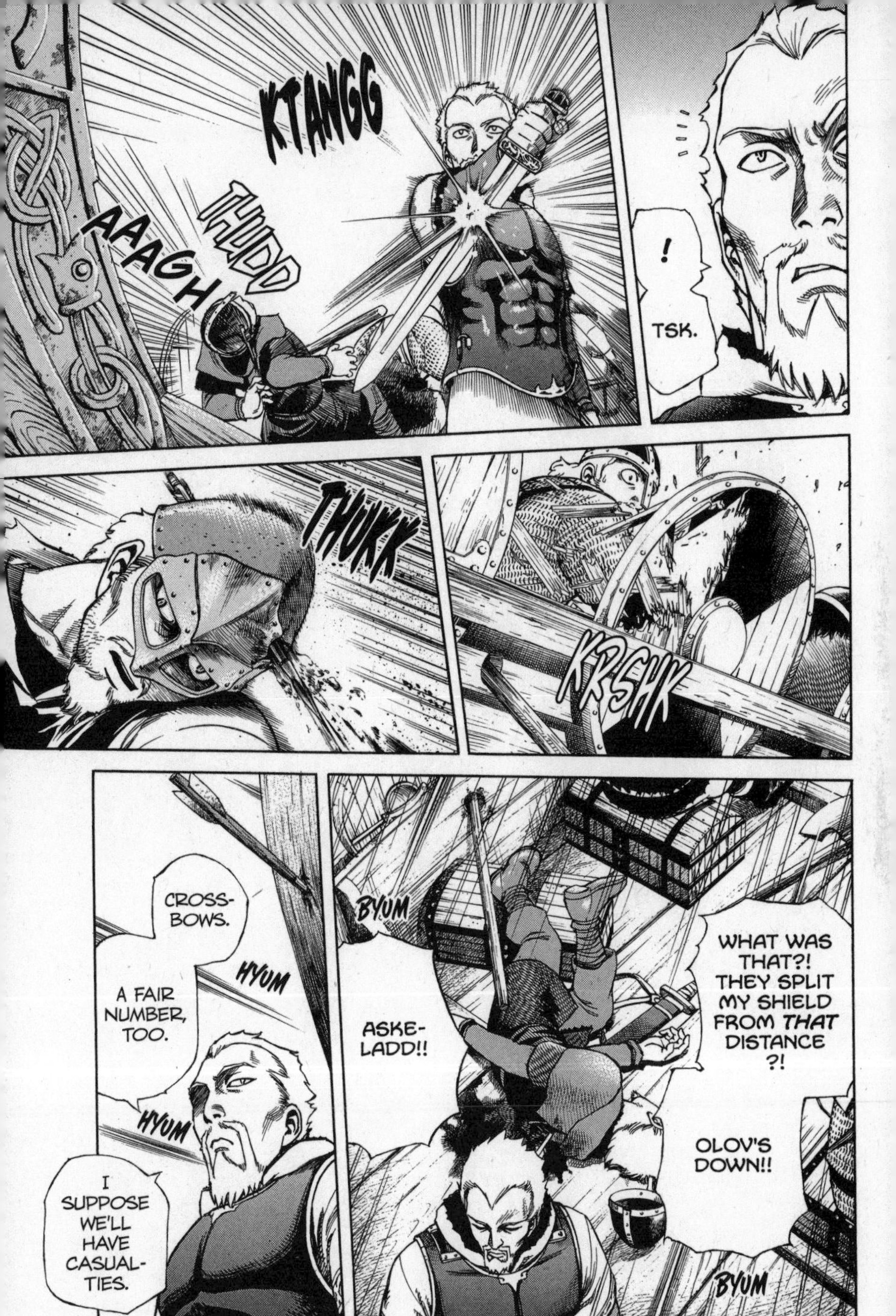
!
TSK.
KTANGG
THUDD
AAAGH
KRSHK
THUKK
WHAT WAS THAT?! THEY SPLIT MY SHIELD FROM *THAT* DISTANCE?!
BYUM
ASKE-LADD!!
OLOV'S DOWN!!
BYUM
CROSS-BOWS.
HYUM
A FAIR NUMBER, TOO.
HYUM
I SUPPOSE WE'LL HAVE CASUAL-TIES.

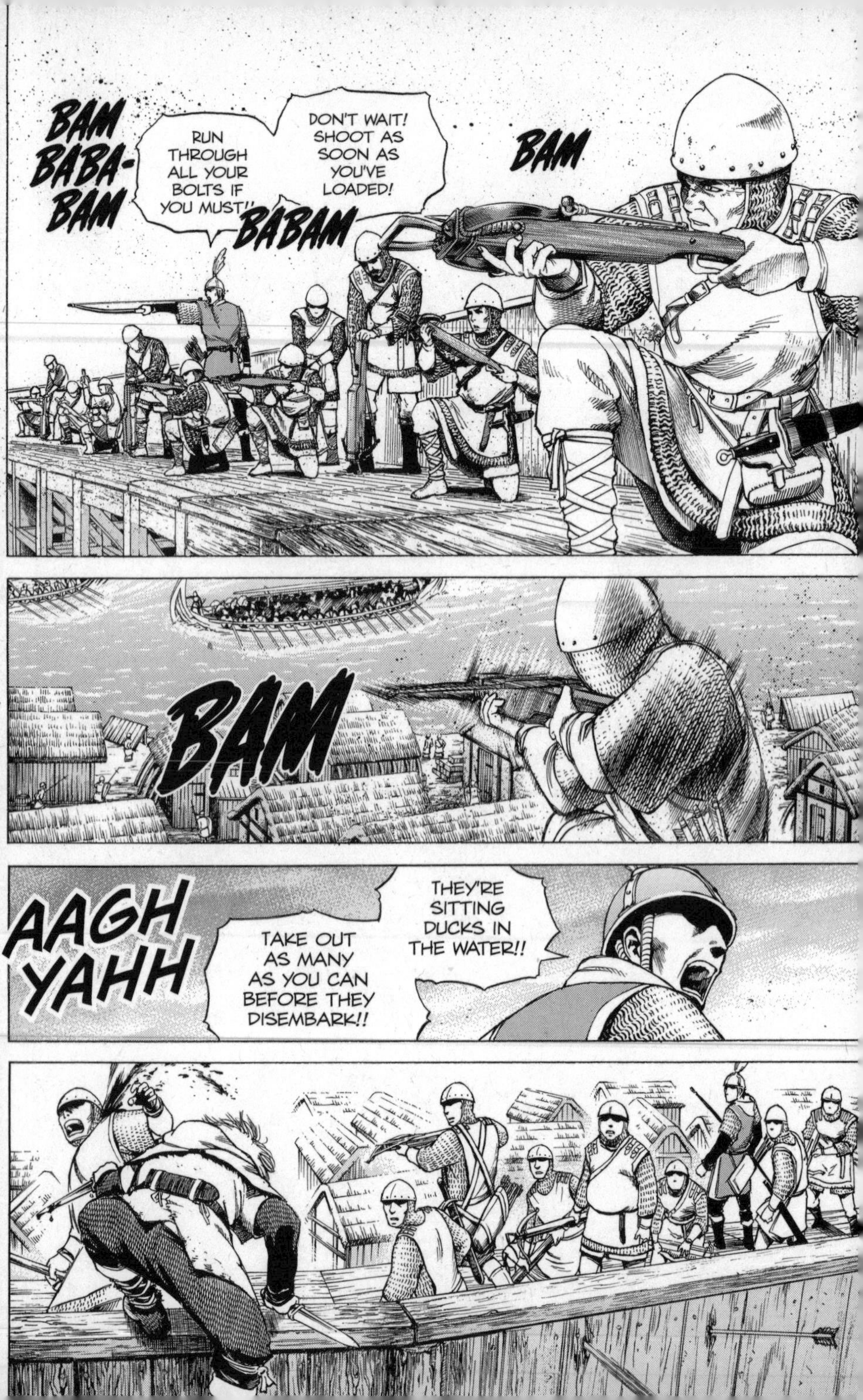
BAM
DON'T WAIT! SHOOT AS SOON AS YOU'VE LOADED!
BAM BABA-BAM
RUN THROUGH ALL YOUR BOLTS IF YOU MUST!!
BABAM
BAM
THEY'RE SITTING DUCKS IN THE WATER!!
TAKE OUT AS MANY AS YOU CAN BEFORE THEY DISEMBARK!!
AAGH YAHH

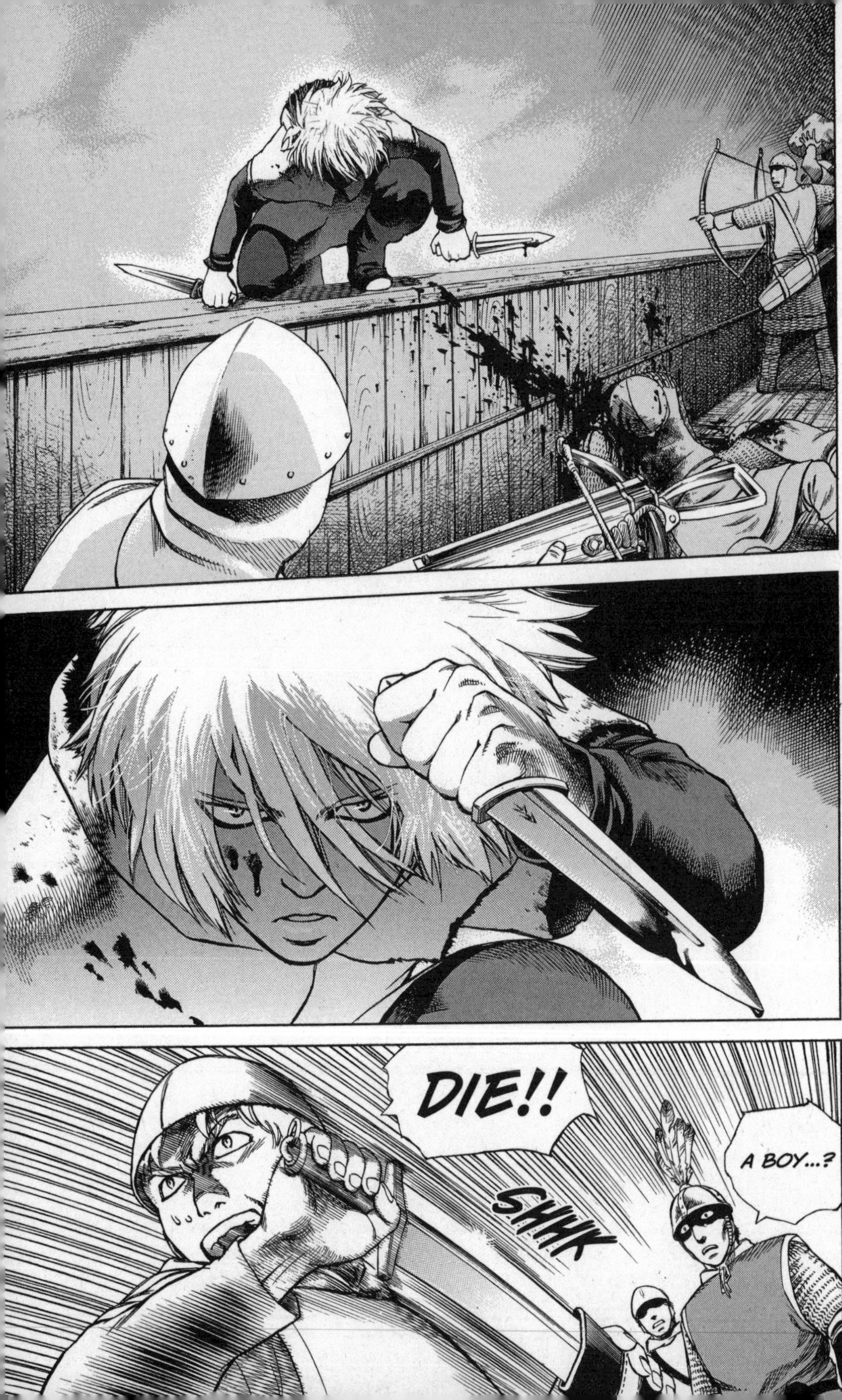
A BOY...?
DIE!!
SHHK

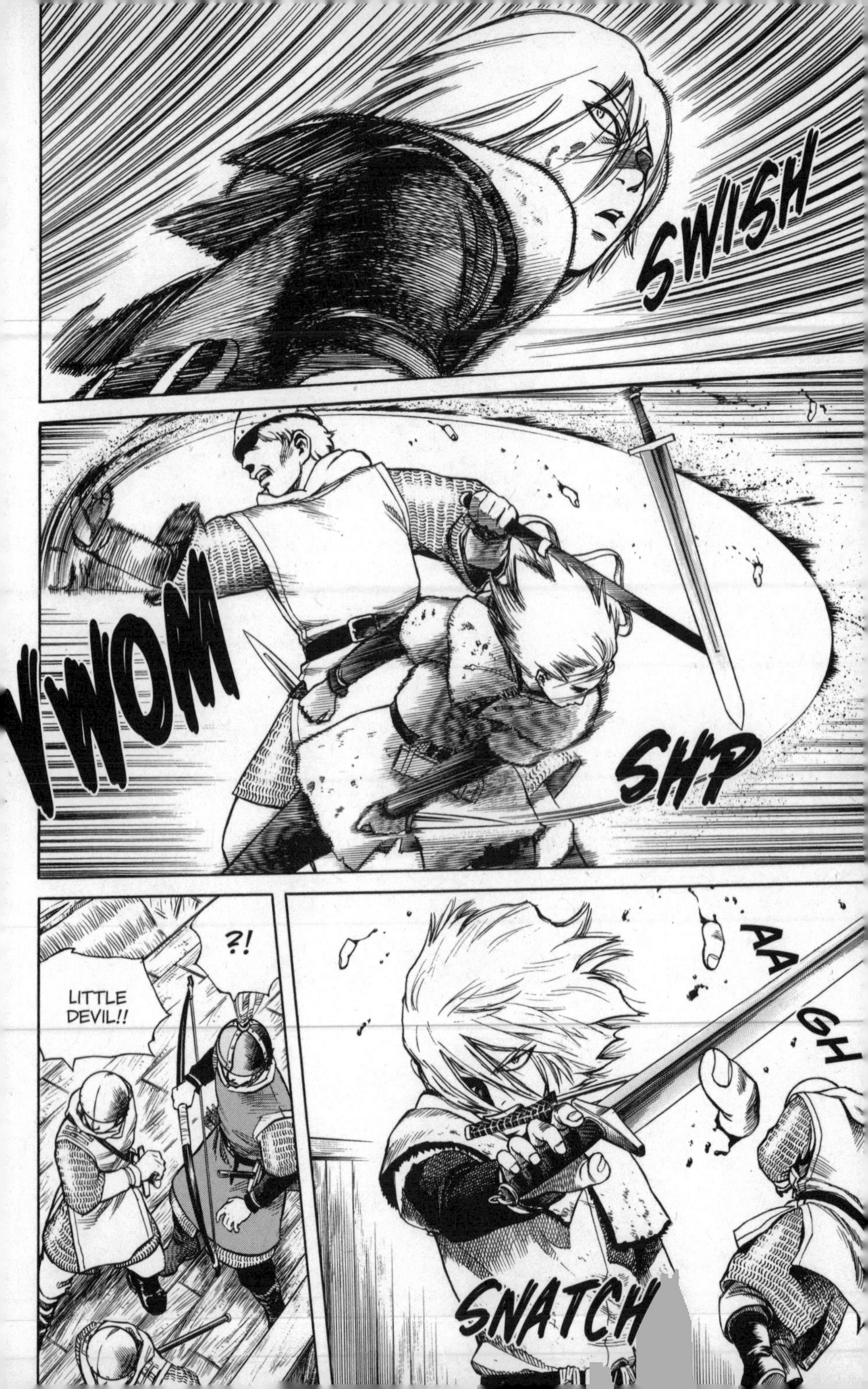
SWISH
SHP
VWOM
AAGH
SNATCH
?!
LITTLE DEVIL!!

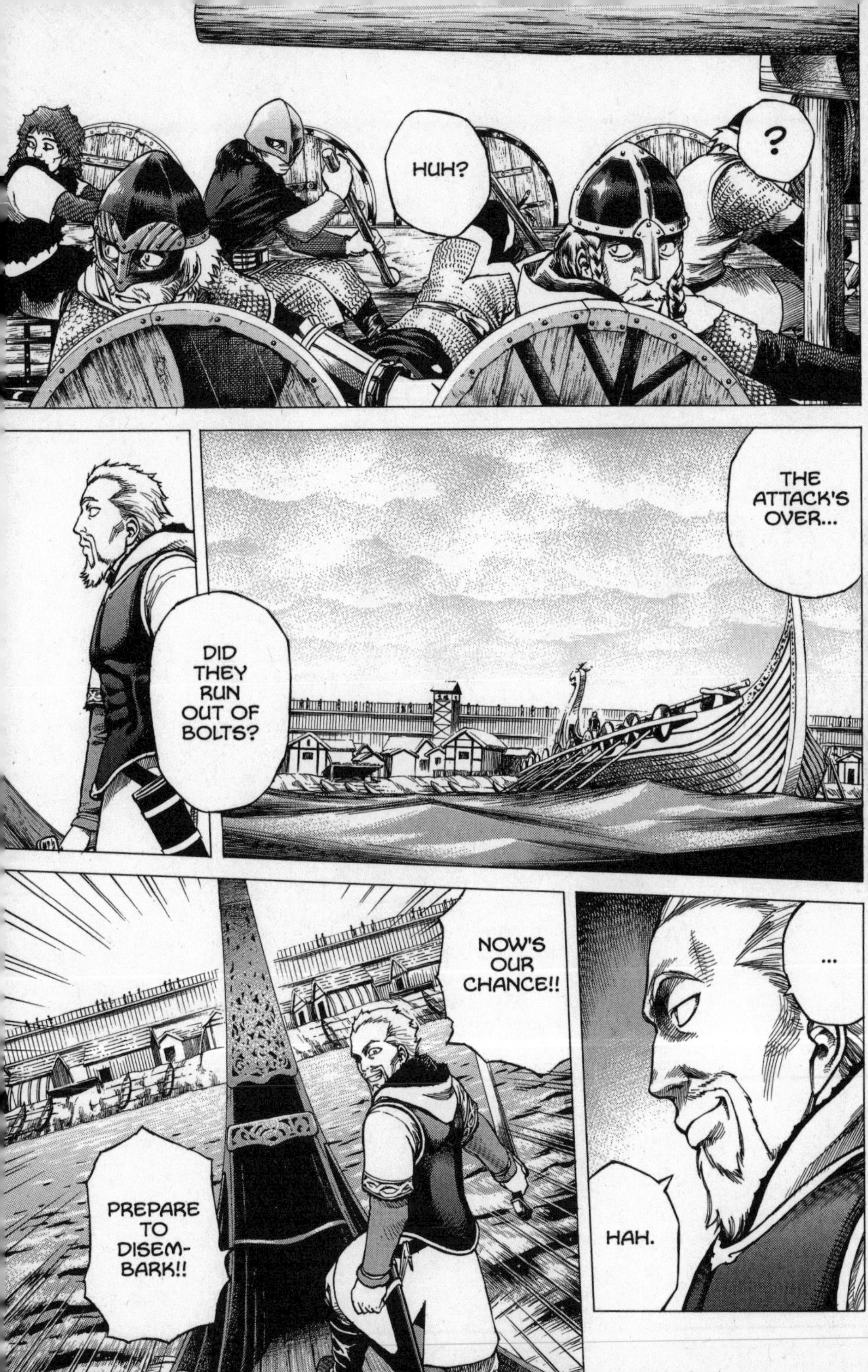
?
HUH?
THE ATTACK'S OVER...
DID THEY RUN OUT OF BOLTS?
...
HAH.
NOW'S OUR CHANCE!!
PREPARE TO DISEM-BARK!!

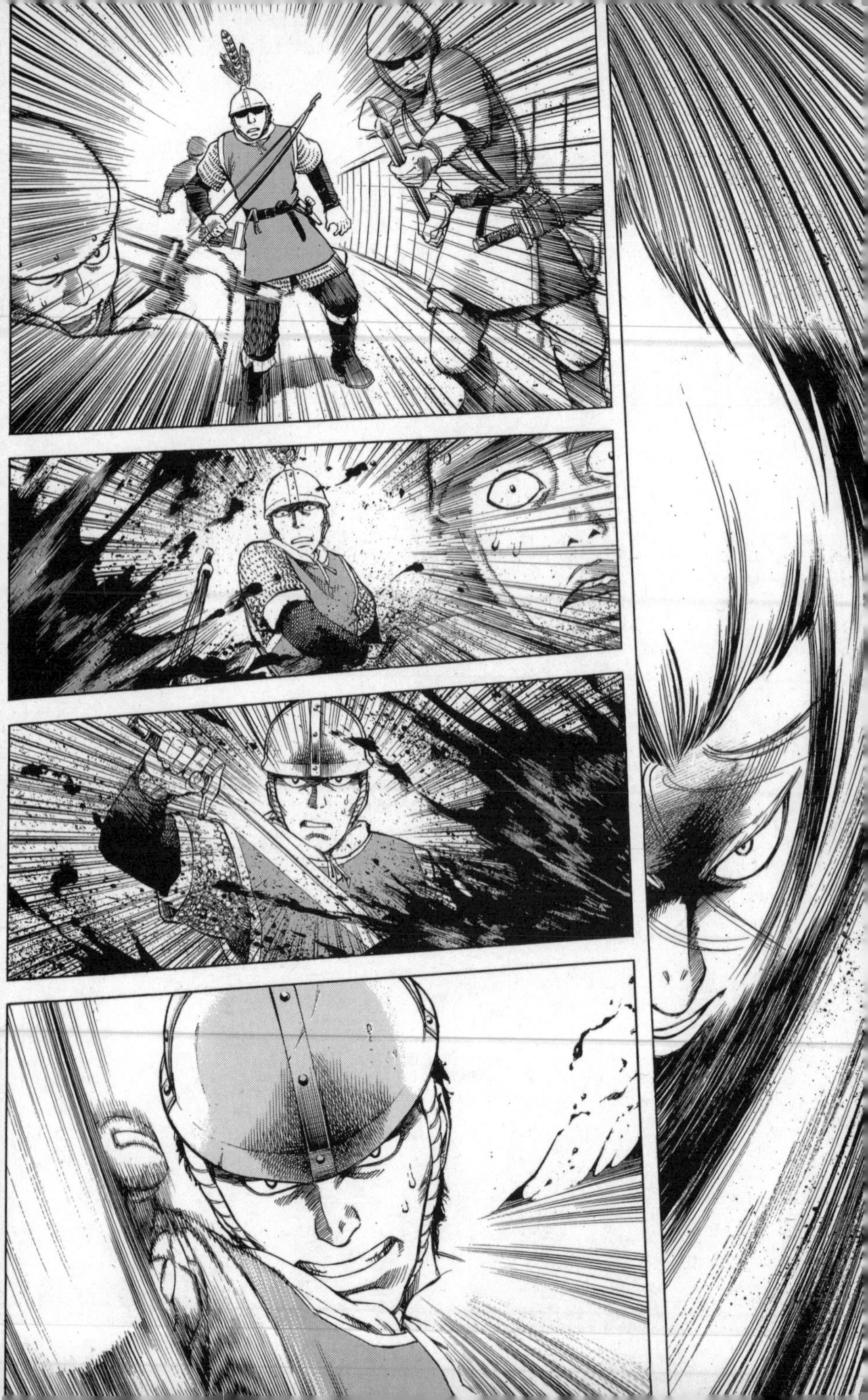

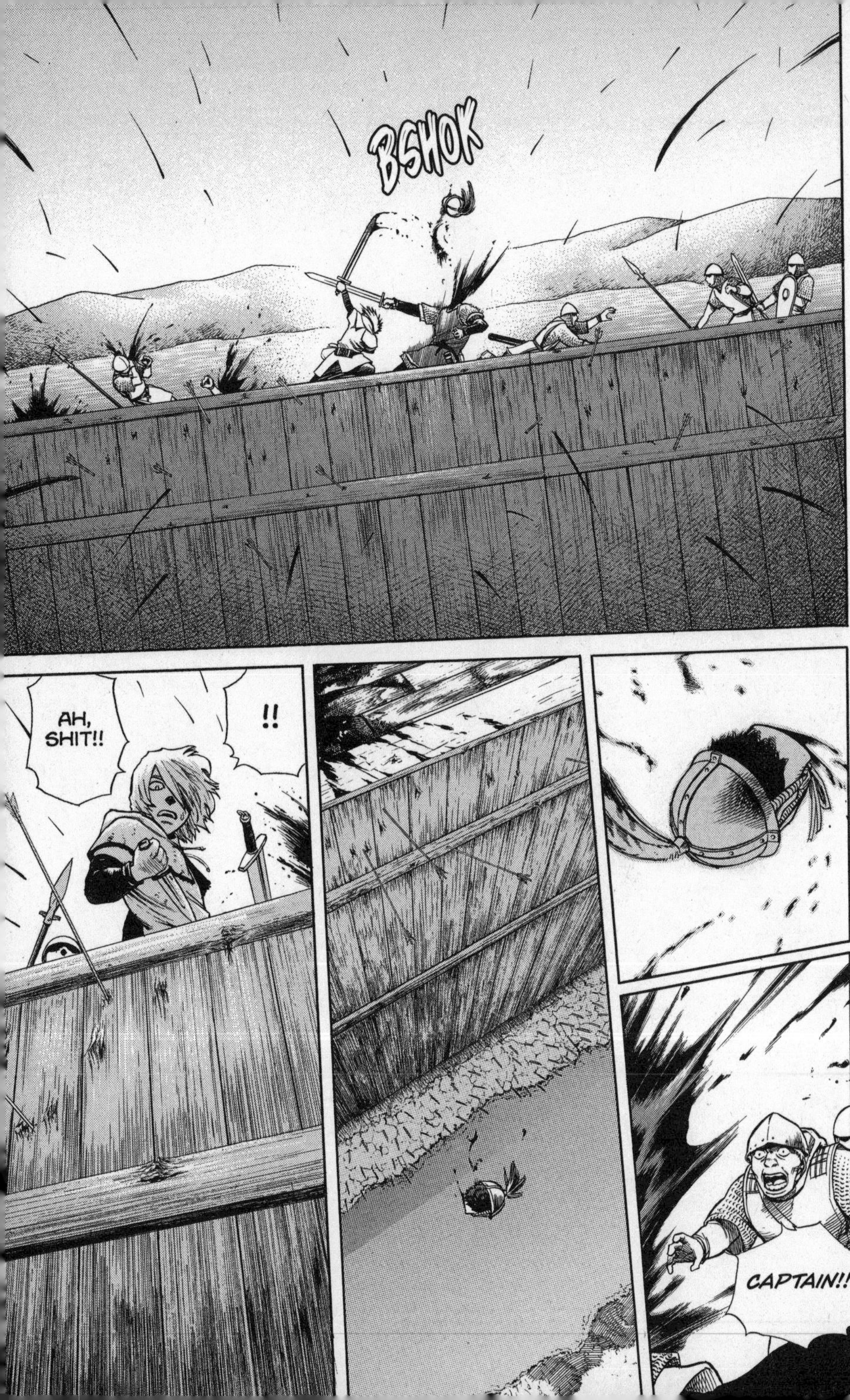
BSHOK
CAPTAIN!!
!!
AH, SHIT!!

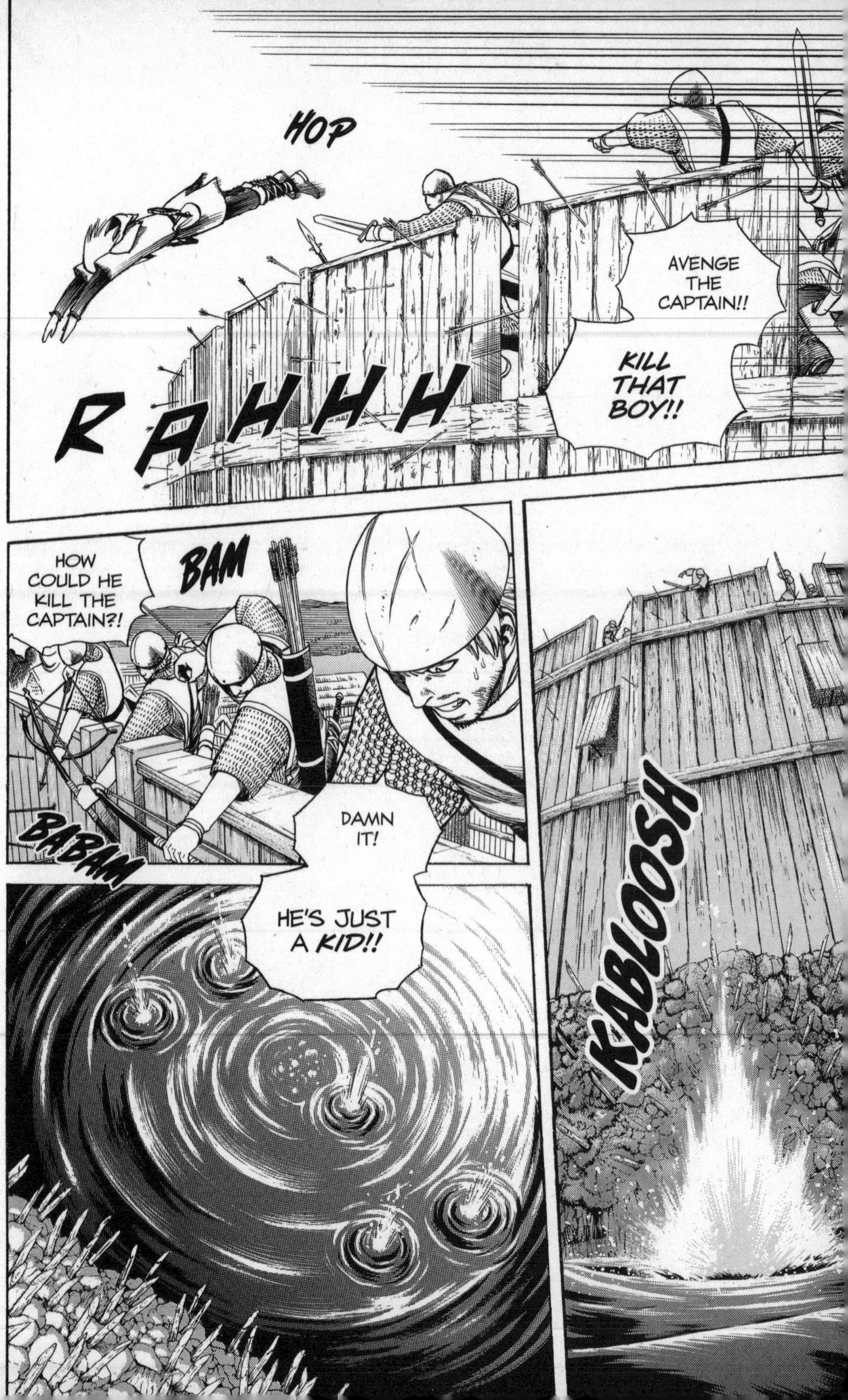
AVENGE THE CAPTAIN!!
KILL THAT BOY!!
HOP
RAHHH
KABLOOSH
BAM
HOW COULD HE KILL THE CAPTAIN?!
DAMN IT!
BABAMM
HE'S JUST A *KID!!*

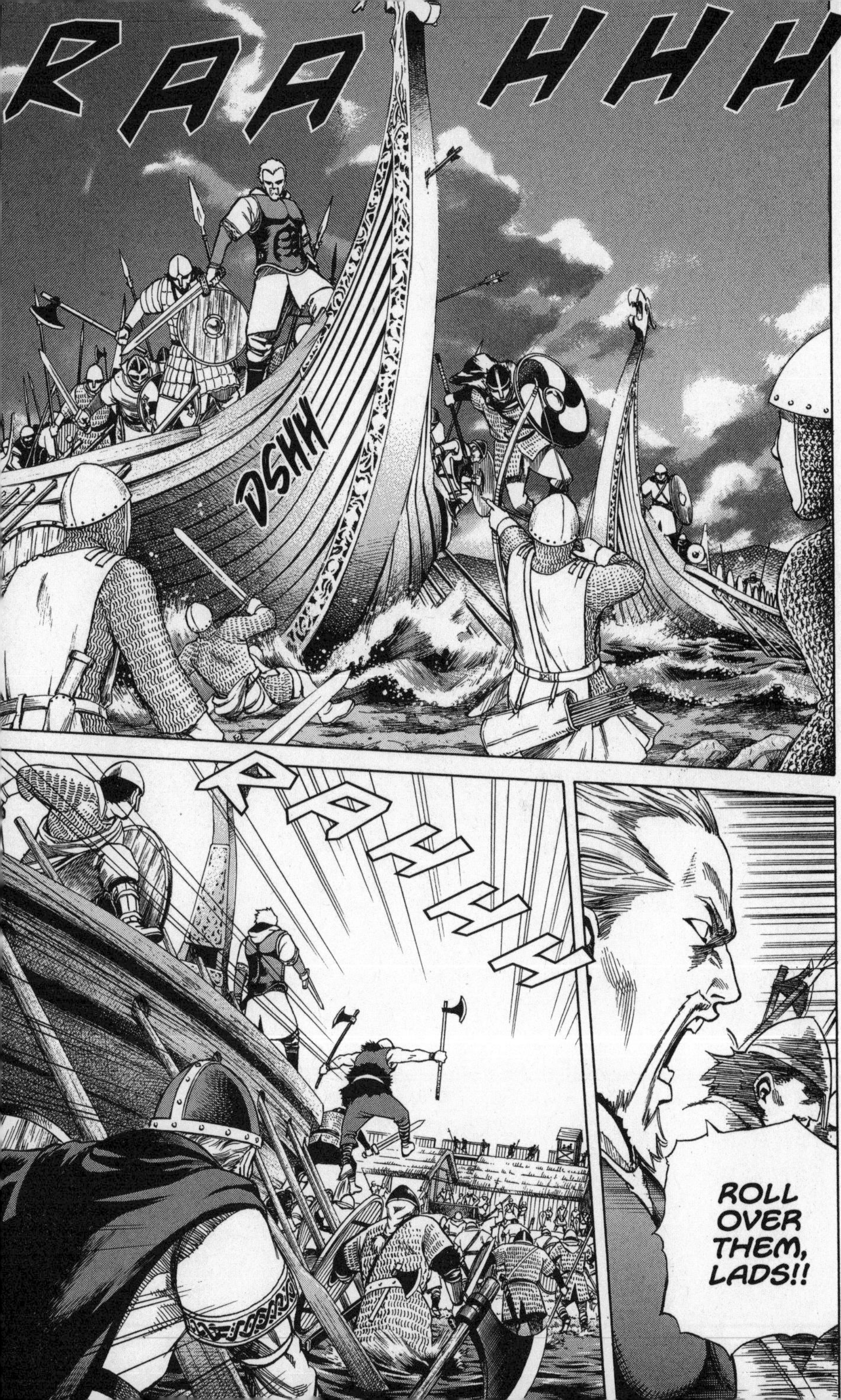
RAAHHH
DSHH
ROLL OVER THEM, LADS!!
RAHHHH

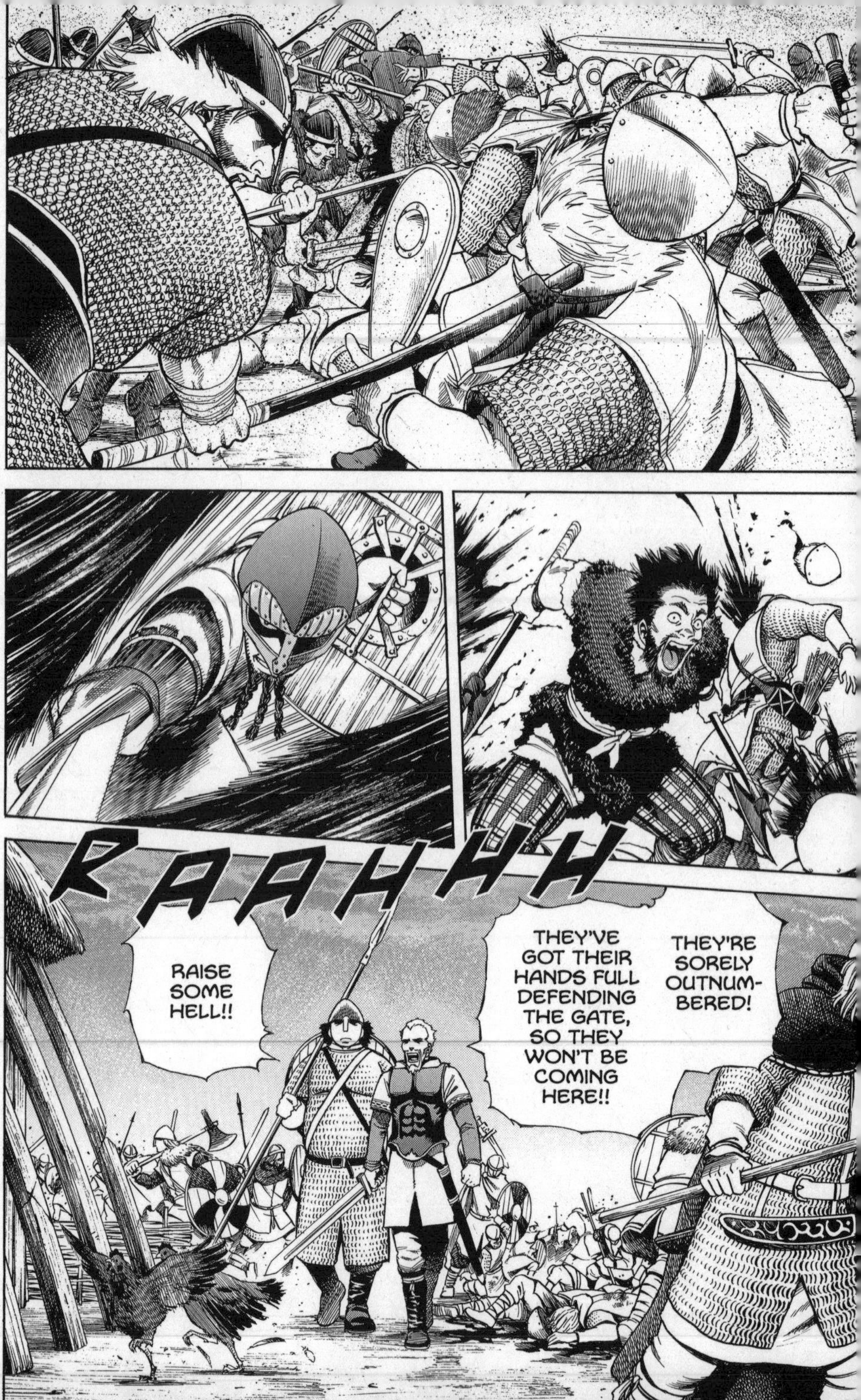
RAAHHH
THEY'RE SORELY OUTNUMBERED!
THEY'VE GOT THEIR HANDS FULL DEFENDING THE GATE, SO THEY WON'T BE COMING HERE!!
RAISE SOME HELL!!

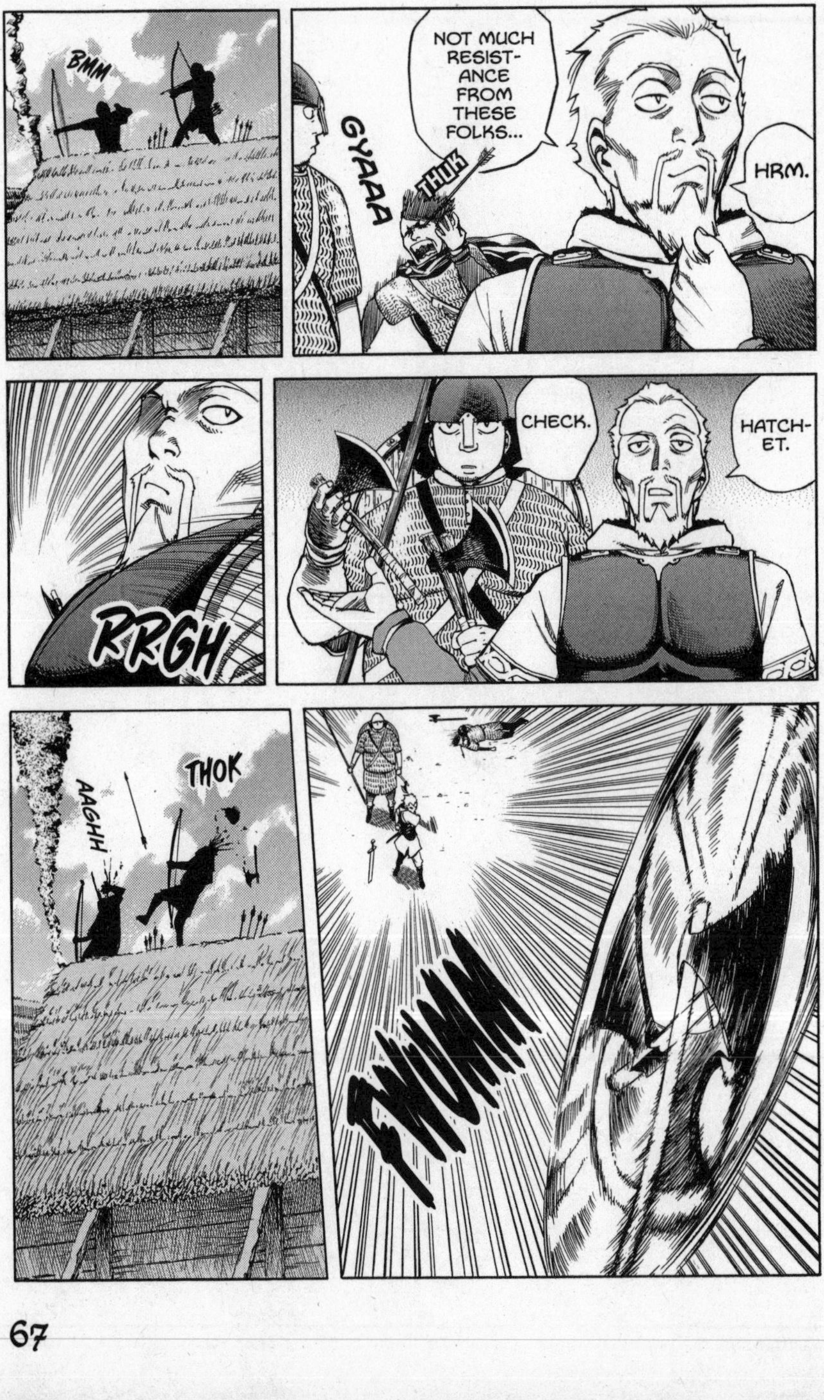

NOT MUCH RESIST-ANCE FROM THESE FOLKS...
HRM.
GYAAA
THUK
BMM
HATCH-ET.
CHECK.
RRGH
FWUMM
THOK
AAGHH

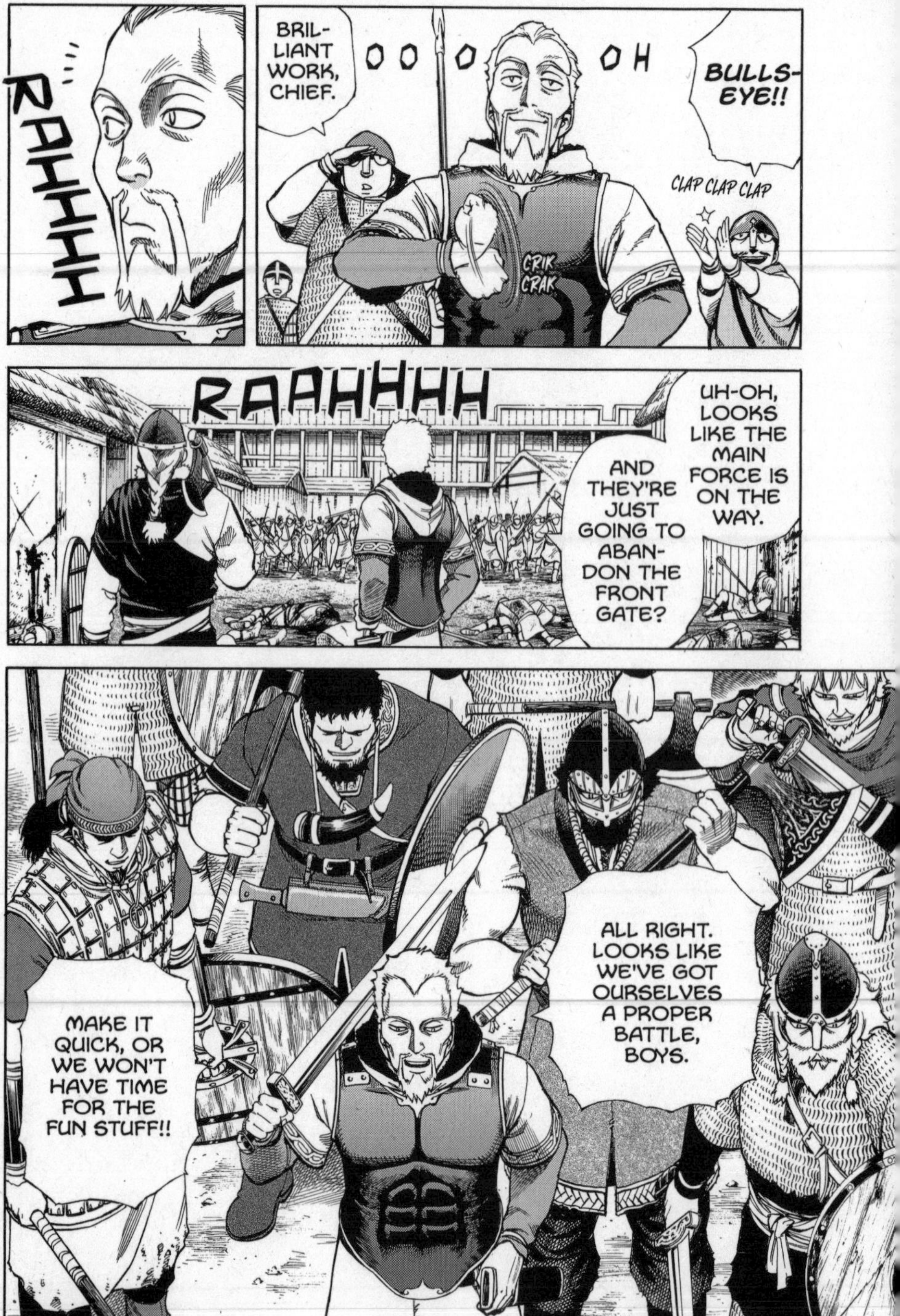
BULLS-EYE!!
OOOOH
CLAP CLAP CLAP
BRIL-LIANT WORK, CHIEF.
CRIK CRAK
RAHHHHH
RAAHHHH
UH-OH, LOOKS LIKE THE MAIN FORCE IS ON THE WAY.
AND THEY'RE JUST GOING TO ABAN-DON THE FRONT GATE?
ALL RIGHT. LOOKS LIKE WE'VE GOT OURSELVES A PROPER BATTLE, BOYS.
MAKE IT QUICK, OR WE WON'T HAVE TIME FOR THE FUN STUFF!!

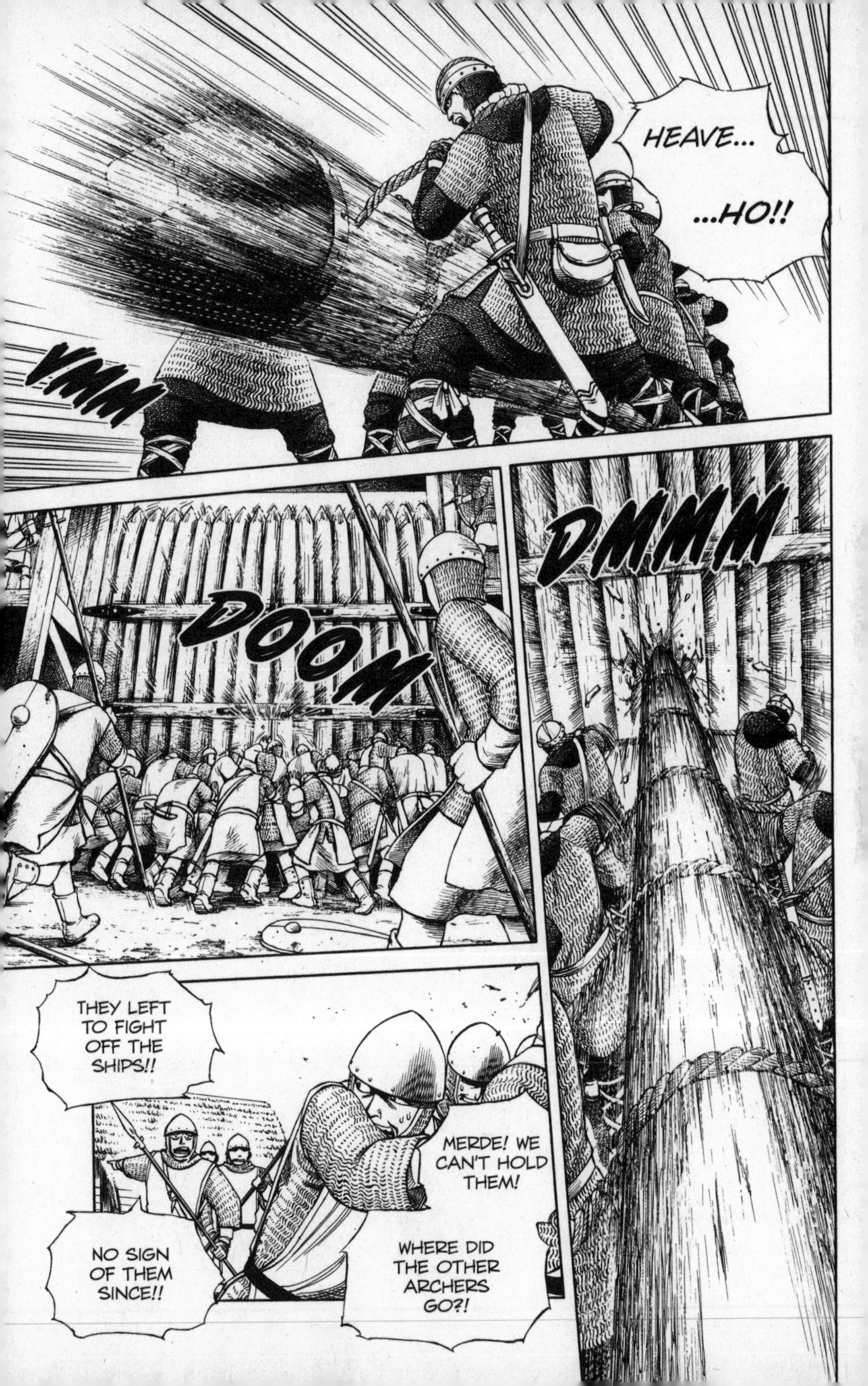
HEAVE...
...HO!!
VMMM
DMMMM
DOOM
MERDE! WE CAN'T HOLD THEM!
WHERE DID THE OTHER ARCHERS GO?!
THEY LEFT TO FIGHT OFF THE SHIPS!!
NO SIGN OF THEM SINCE!!

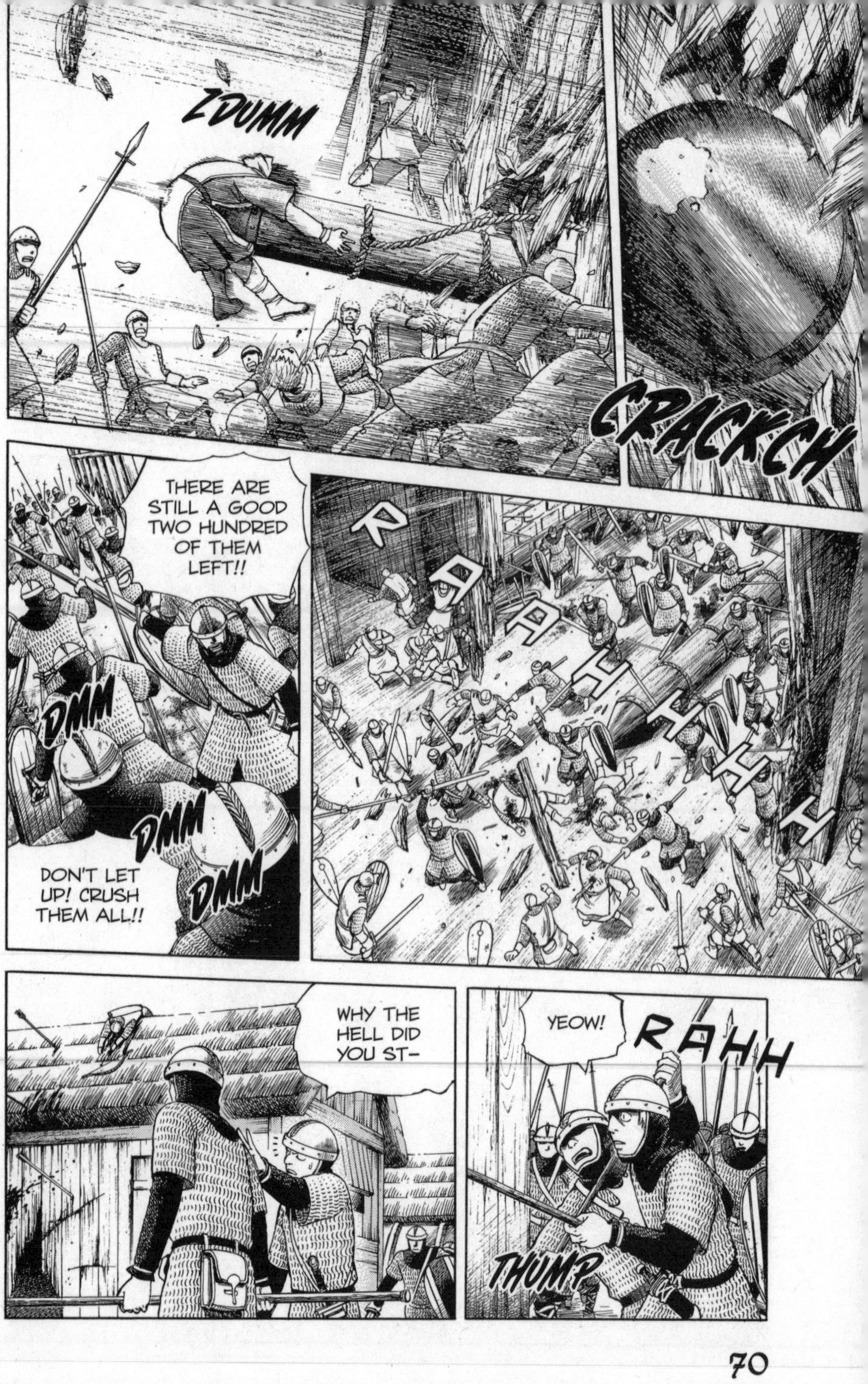
CRACKCH
Z'DUMM
RAAHHHHH
THERE ARE STILL A GOOD TWO HUNDRED OF THEM LEFT!!
DMM
DMM
DMM
DON'T LET UP! CRUSH THEM ALL!!
YEOW!
RAHH
THUMP
WHY THE HELL DID YOU ST-

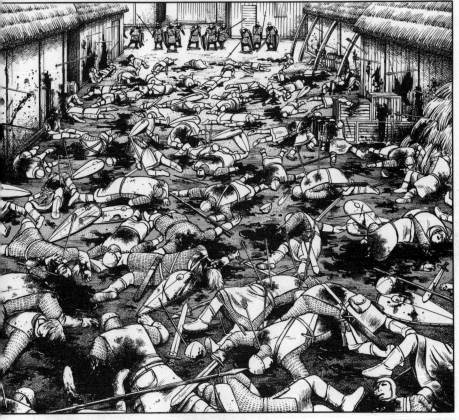

MON DIEU...

THESE NORMANNI...

...

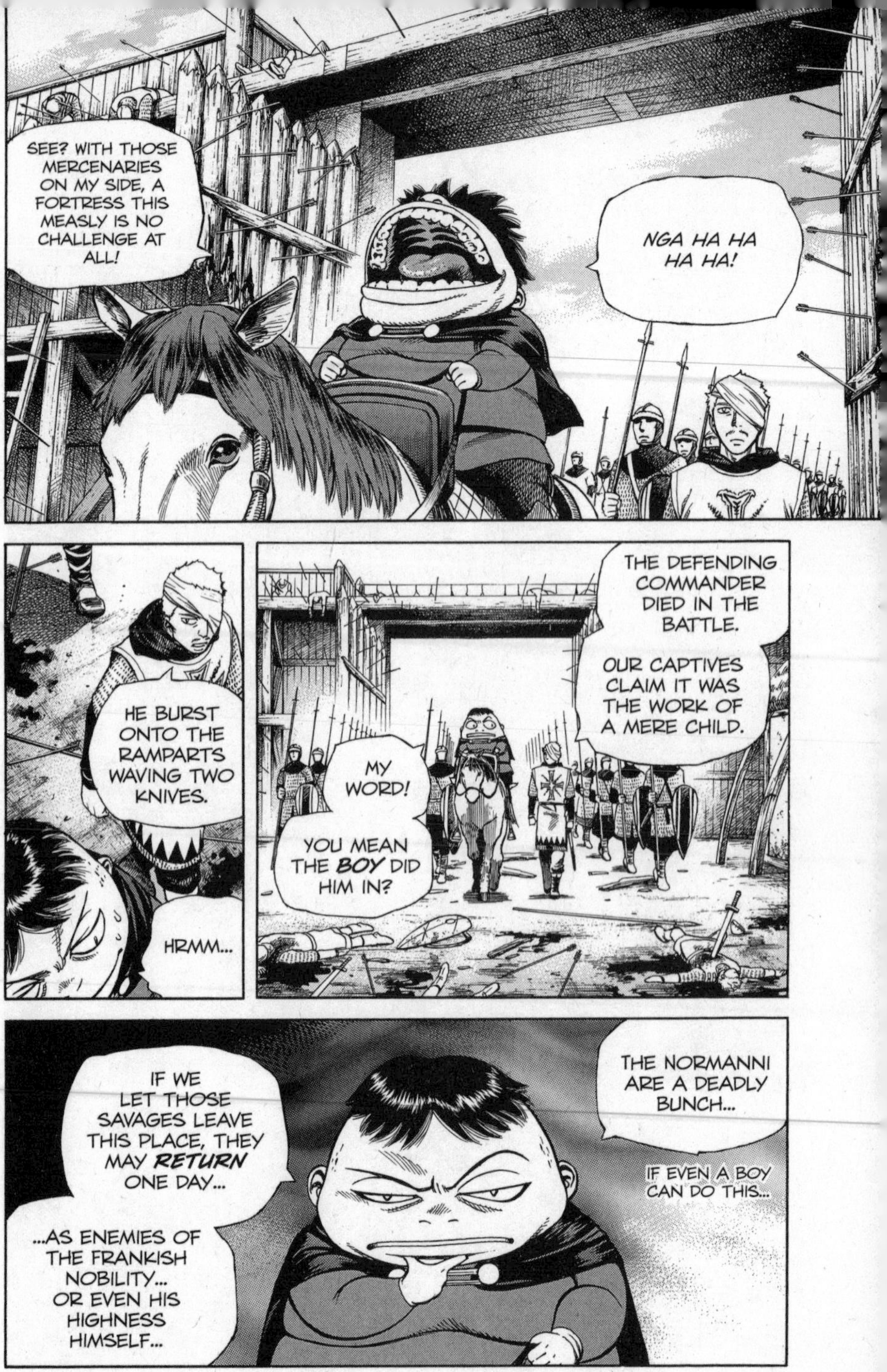
SEE? WITH THOSE MERCENARIES ON MY SIDE, A FORTRESS THIS MEASLY IS NO CHALLENGE AT ALL!
NGA HA HA HA HA!
THE DEFENDING COMMANDER DIED IN THE BATTLE.
OUR CAPTIVES CLAIM IT WAS THE WORK OF A MERE CHILD.
MY WORD!
YOU MEAN THE ***BOY*** DID HIM IN?
HE BURST ONTO THE RAMPARTS WAVING TWO KNIVES.
HRMM...
THE NORMANNI ARE A DEADLY BUNCH...
IF EVEN A BOY CAN DO THIS...
IF WE LET THOSE SAVAGES LEAVE THIS PLACE, THEY MAY ***RETURN*** ONE DAY...
...AS ENEMIES OF THE FRANKISH NOBILITY... OR EVEN HIS HIGHNESS HIMSELF...

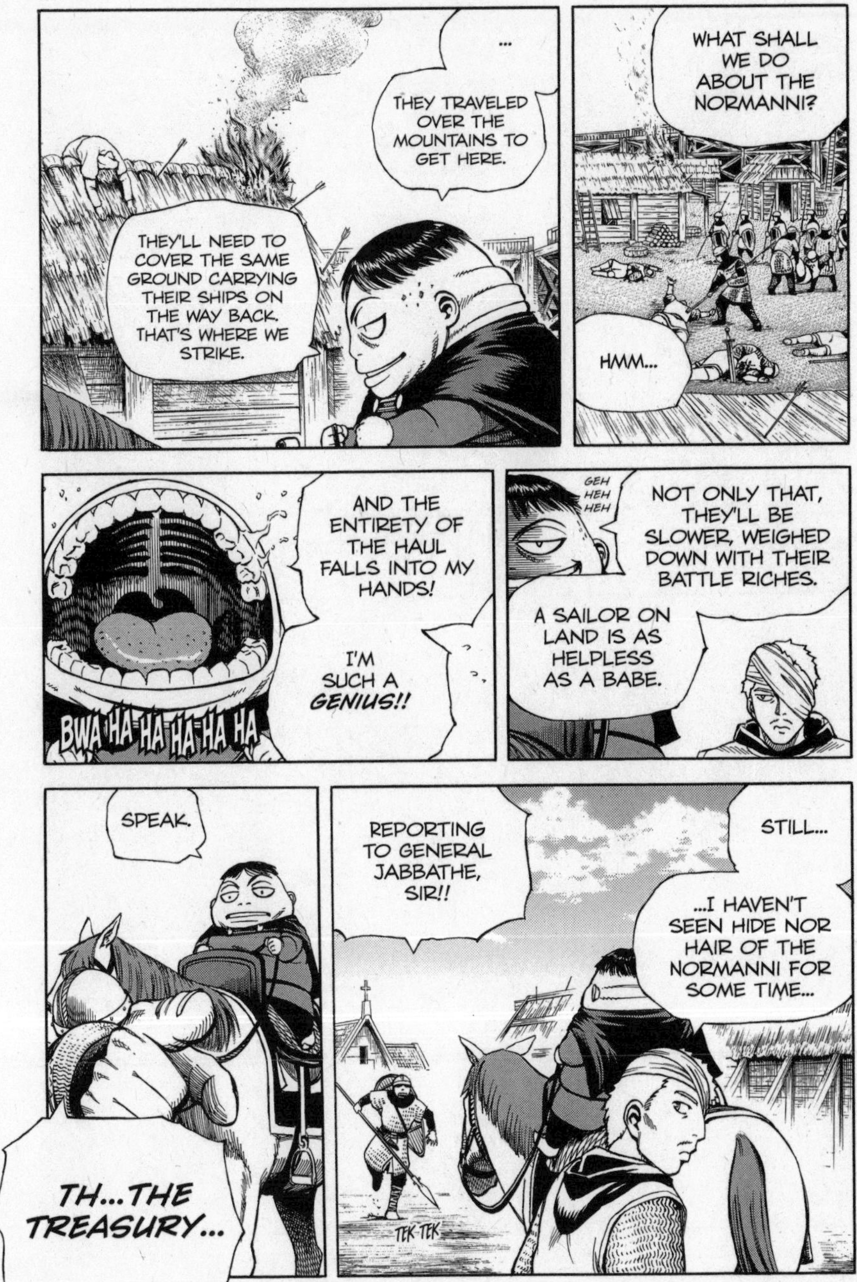
WHAT SHALL WE DO ABOUT THE NORMANNI?
HMM...
...
THEY TRAVELED OVER THE MOUNTAINS TO GET HERE.
THEY'LL NEED TO COVER THE SAME GROUND CARRYING THEIR SHIPS ON THE WAY BACK. THAT'S WHERE WE STRIKE.
GEH HEH HEH
NOT ONLY THAT, THEY'LL BE SLOWER, WEIGHED DOWN WITH THEIR BATTLE RICHES.
A SAILOR ON LAND IS AS HELPLESS AS A BABE.
AND THE ENTIRETY OF THE HAUL FALLS INTO MY HANDS!
I'M SUCH A *GENIUS!!*
BWA HA HA HA HA HA
STILL...
...I HAVEN'T SEEN HIDE NOR HAIR OF THE NORMANNI FOR SOME TIME...
REPORTING TO GENERAL JABBATHE, SIR!!
TEK TEK
SPEAK.
TH...THE TREASURY...

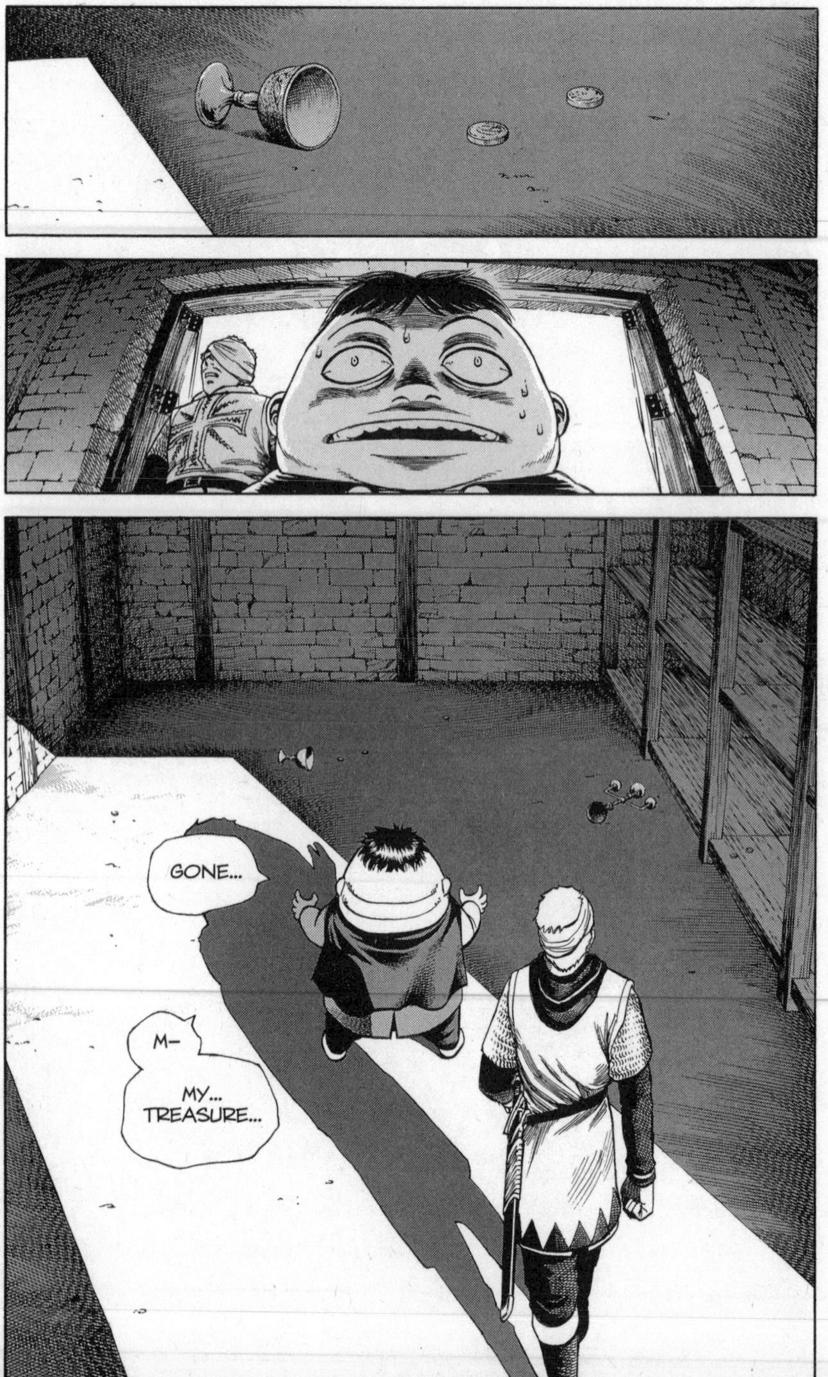
GONE...
M–
MY... TREASURE...

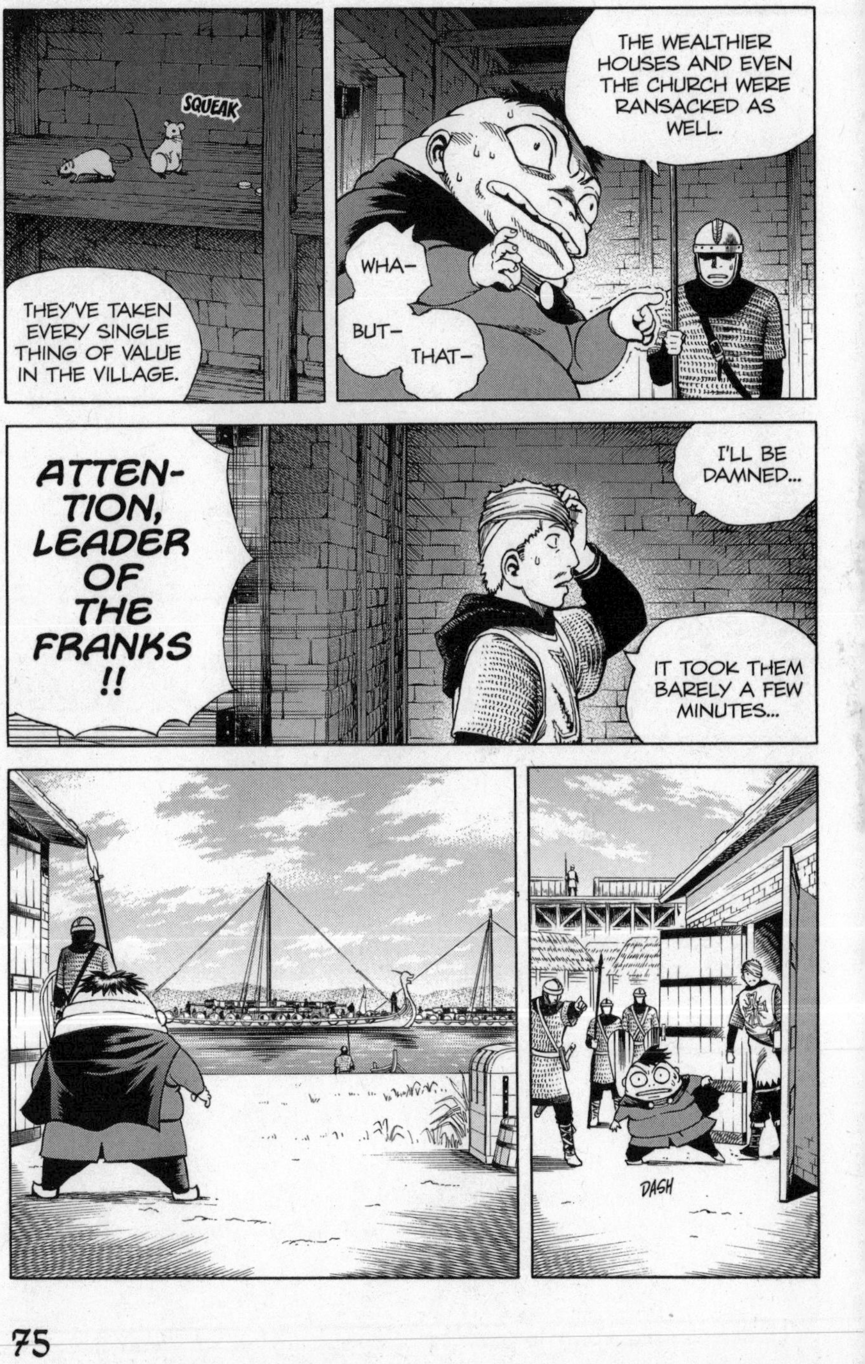
THE WEALTHIER HOUSES AND EVEN THE CHURCH WERE RANSACKED AS WELL.
WHA-
BUT-
THAT-
SQUEAK
THEY'VE TAKEN EVERY SINGLE THING OF VALUE IN THE VILLAGE.
I'LL BE DAMNED...
IT TOOK THEM BARELY A FEW MINUTES...
ATTEN-TION, LEADER OF THE FRANKS !!
DASH

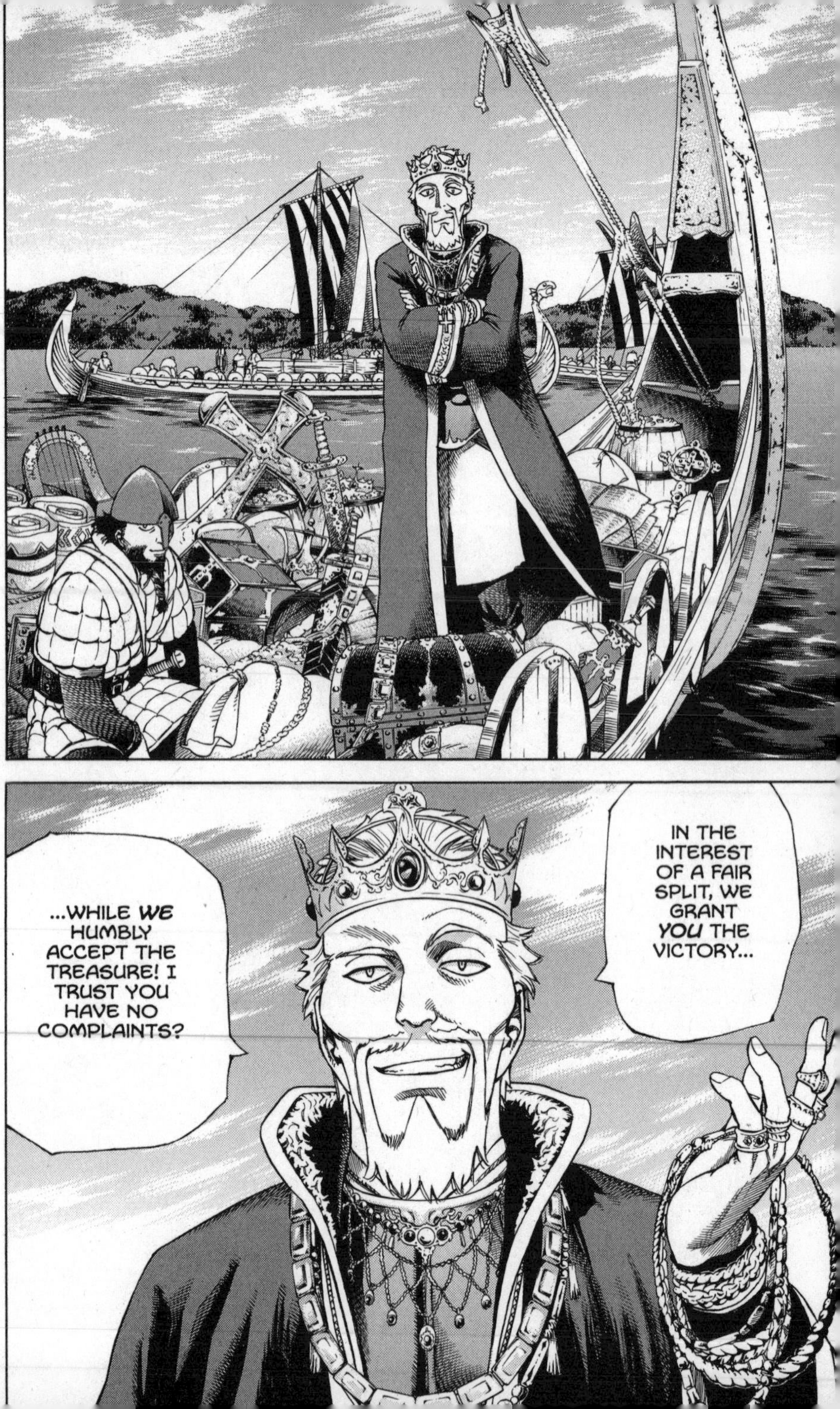
IN THE INTEREST OF A FAIR SPLIT, WE GRANT *YOU* THE VICTORY...
...WHILE *WE* HUMBLY ACCEPT THE TREASURE! I TRUST YOU HAVE NO COMPLAINTS?

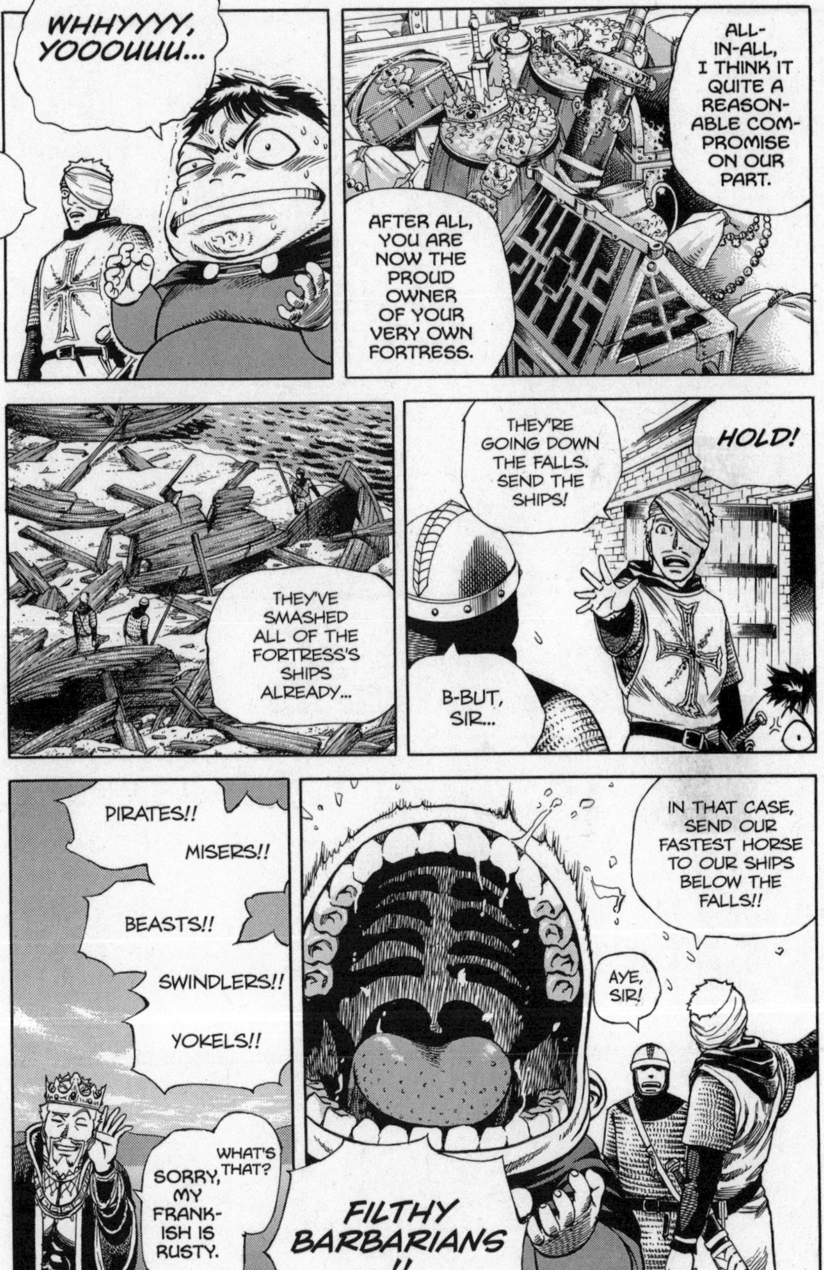
ALL-IN-ALL, I THINK IT QUITE A REASONABLE COMPROMISE ON OUR PART.
AFTER ALL, YOU ARE NOW THE PROUD OWNER OF YOUR VERY OWN FORTRESS.
WHHYYYY, YOOOUUU...
!!
HOLD!
THEY'RE GOING DOWN THE FALLS. SEND THE SHIPS!
B-BUT, SIR...
THEY'VE SMASHED ALL OF THE FORTRESS'S SHIPS ALREADY...
IN THAT CASE, SEND OUR FASTEST HORSE TO OUR SHIPS BELOW THE FALLS!!
AYE, SIR!
FILTHY BARBARIANS !!
PIRATES!!
MISERS!!
BEASTS!!
SWINDLERS!!
YOKELS!!
WHAT'S THAT?
SORRY, MY FRANK-ISH IS RUSTY.

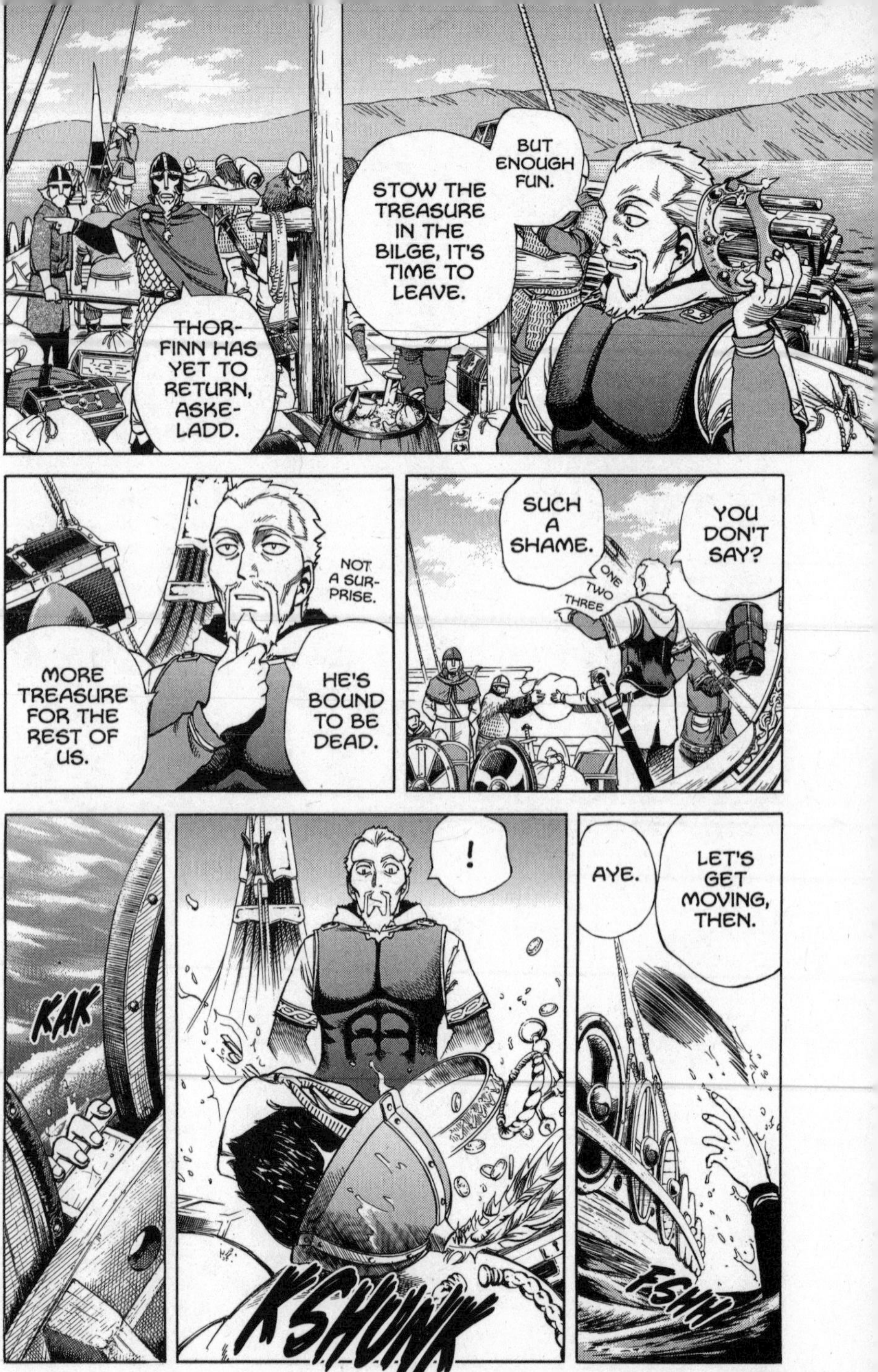
BUT ENOUGH FUN.
STOW THE TREASURE IN THE BILGE, IT'S TIME TO LEAVE.
THORFINN HAS YET TO RETURN, ASKELADD.
YOU DON'T SAY?
SUCH A SHAME.
ONE TWO THREE
NOT A SURPRISE.
HE'S BOUND TO BE DEAD.
MORE TREASURE FOR THE REST OF US.
LET'S GET MOVING, THEN.
AYE.
FSHH
!
K'SHUNK
KAK

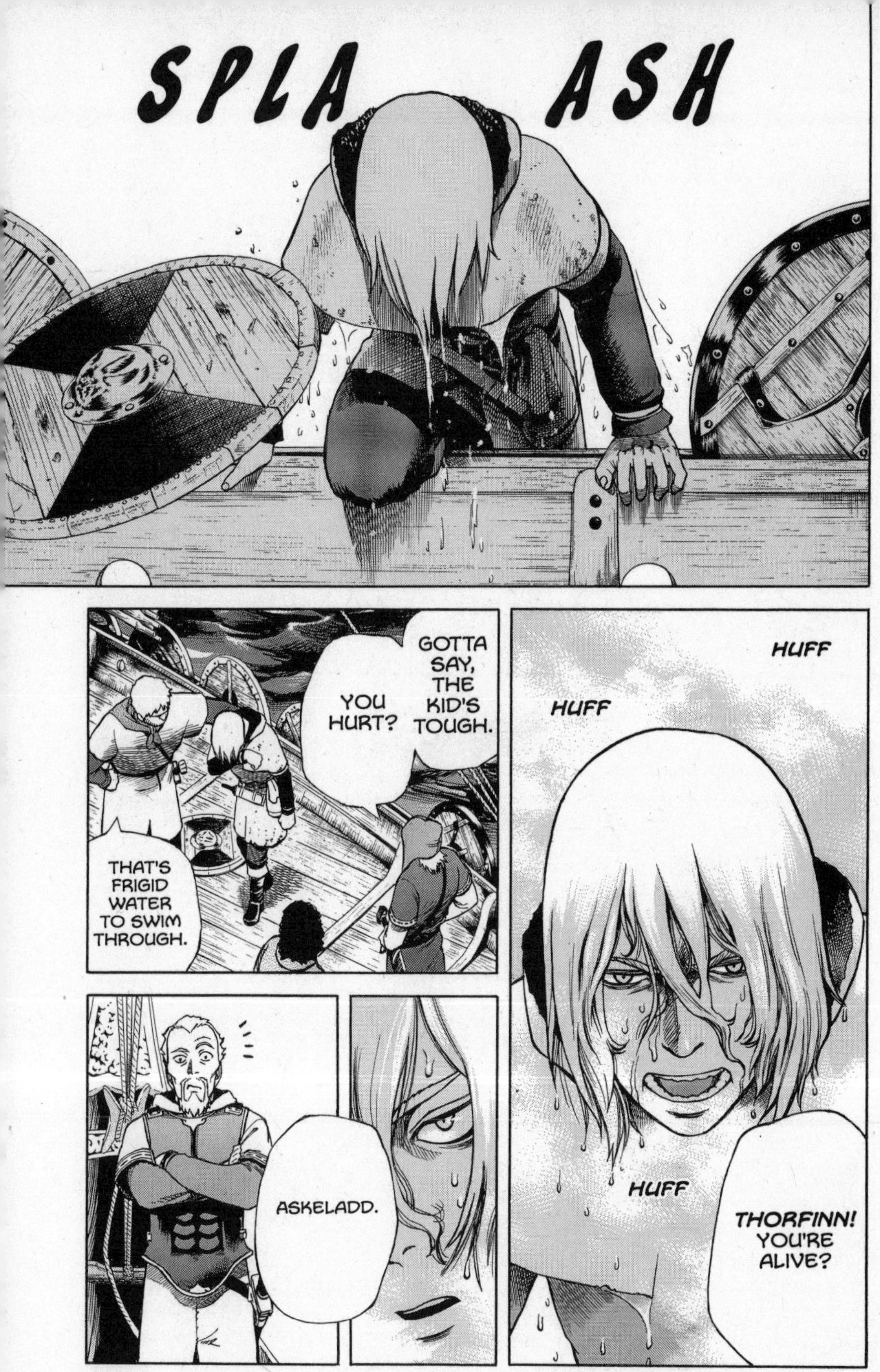
SPLA ASH
HUFF
HUFF
HUFF
THORFINN! YOU'RE ALIVE?
GOTTA SAY, THE KID'S TOUGH.
YOU HURT?
THAT'S FRIGID WATER TO SWIM THROUGH.
ASKELADD.

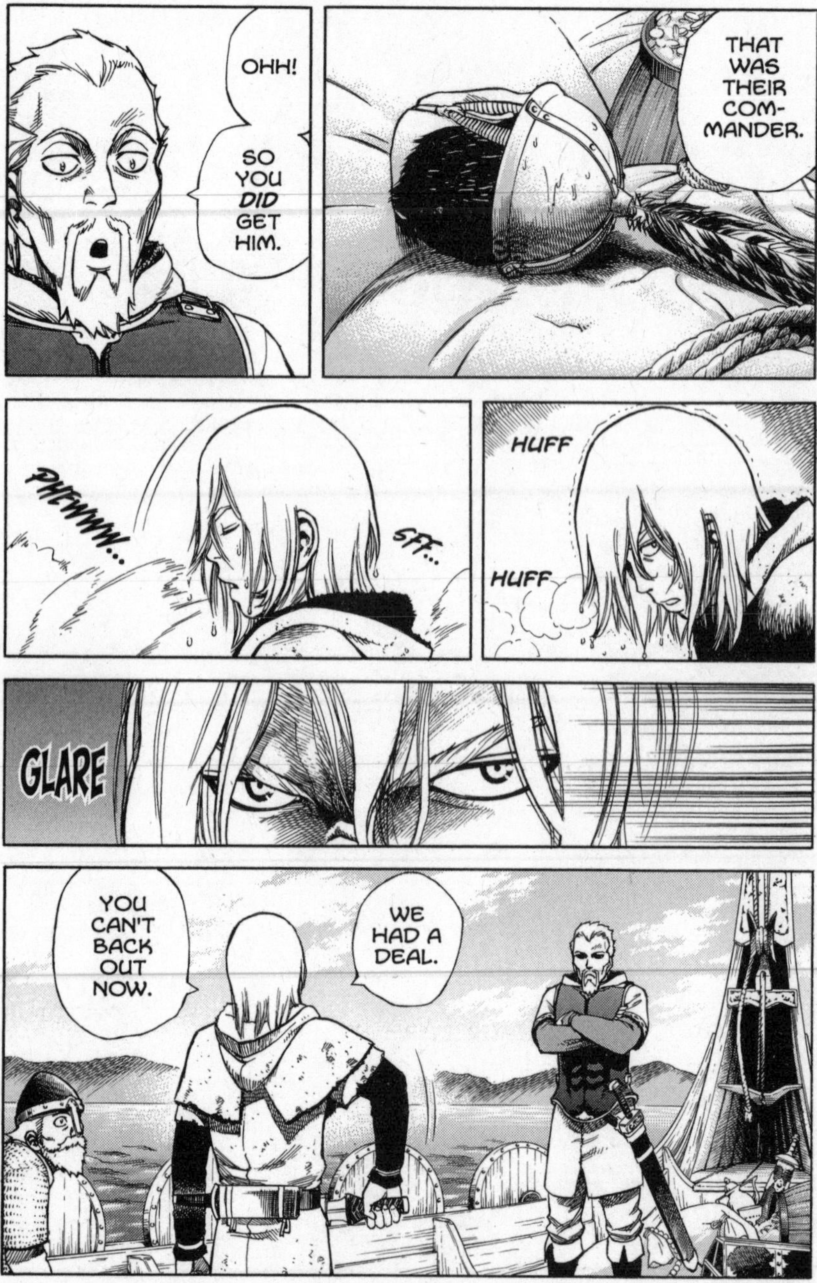
THAT WAS THEIR COM-MANDER.
OHH!
SO YOU *DID* GET HIM.
HUFF
HUFF
SFF...
PHEWWW...
GLARE
WE HAD A DEAL.
YOU CAN'T BACK OUT NOW.

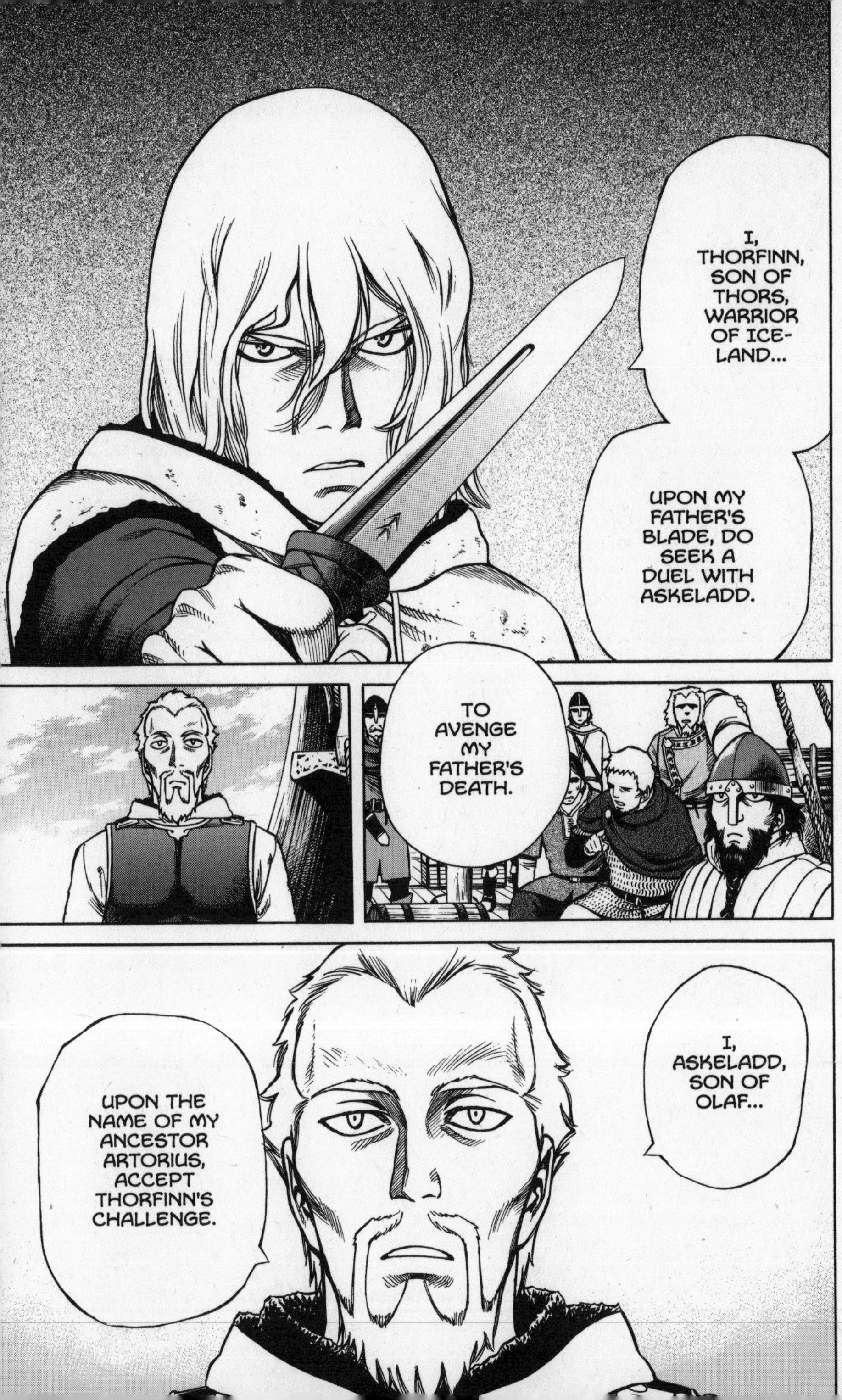
I, THORFINN, SON OF THORS, WARRIOR OF ICE-LAND...
UPON MY FATHER'S BLADE, DO SEEK A DUEL WITH ASKELADD.
TO AVENGE MY FATHER'S DEATH.
I, ASKELADD, SON OF OLAF...
UPON THE NAME OF MY ANCESTOR ARTORIUS, ACCEPT THORFINN'S CHALLENGE.

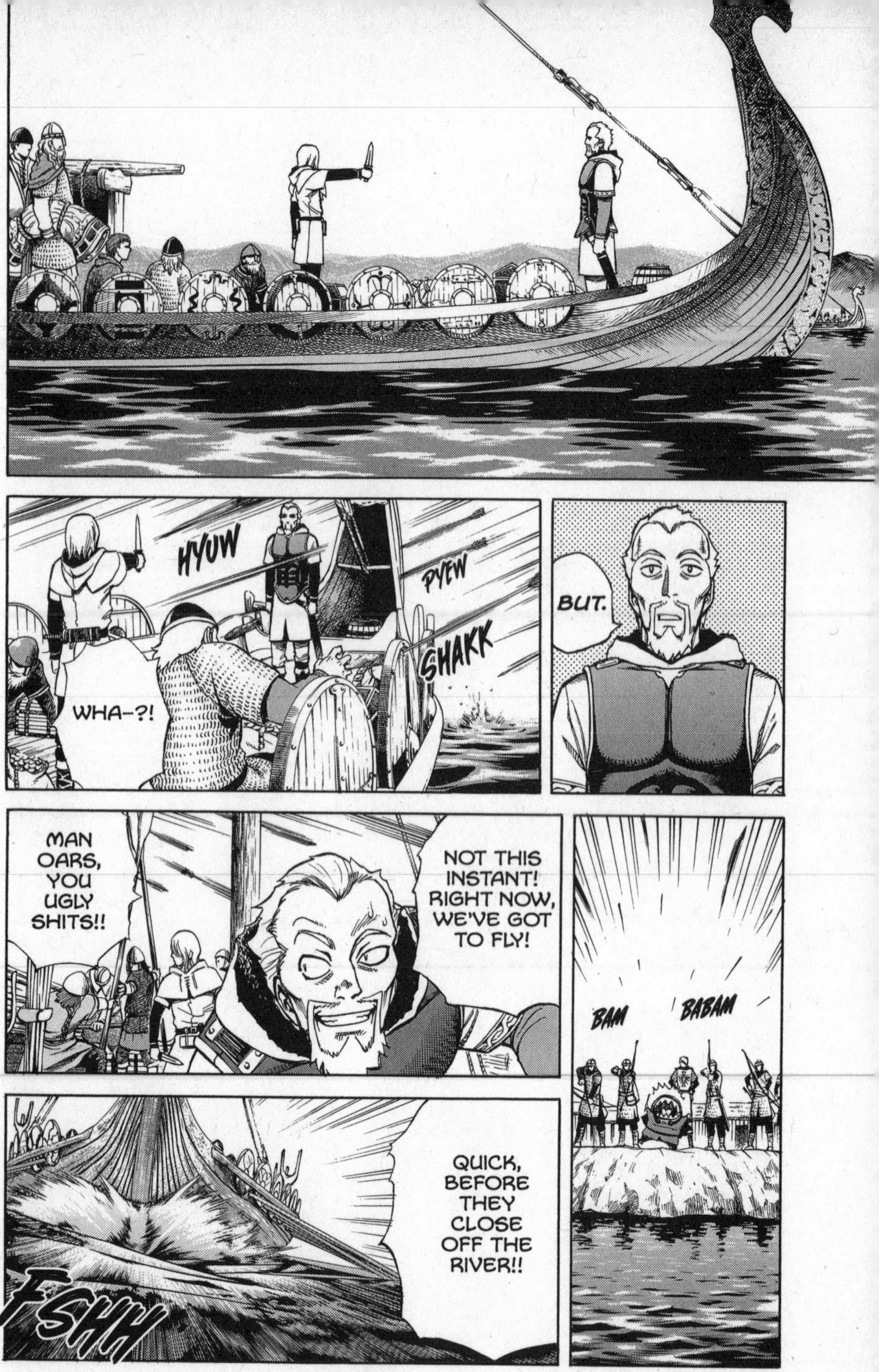
BUT.
PYEW
HYUW
SHAKK
WHA-?!
BABAM
BAM
NOT THIS INSTANT! RIGHT NOW, WE'VE GOT TO FLY!
MAN OARS, YOU UGLY SHITS!!
QUICK, BEFORE THEY CLOSE OFF THE RIVER!!
FSHH

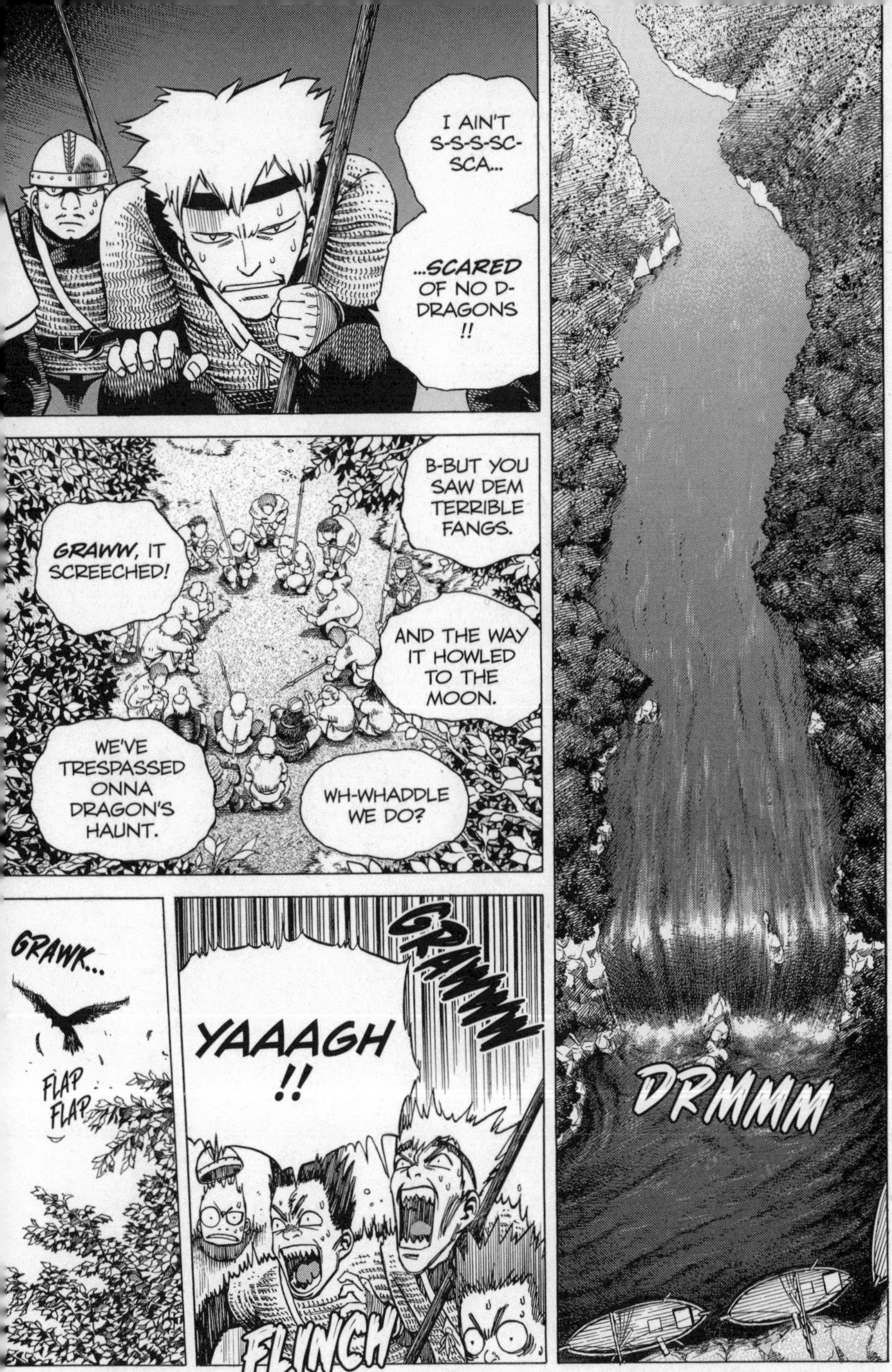
DRMMM
I AIN'T S-S-S-SC-SCA...
...SCARED OF NO D-DRAGONS !!
B-BUT YOU SAW DEM TERRIBLE FANGS.
GRAWW, IT SCREECHED!
AND THE WAY IT HOWLED TO THE MOON.
WE'VE TRESPASSED ONNA DRAGON'S HAUNT.
WH-WHADDLE WE DO?
GRAWWW
YAAAGH !!
FLINCH
GRAWK...
FLAP FLAP

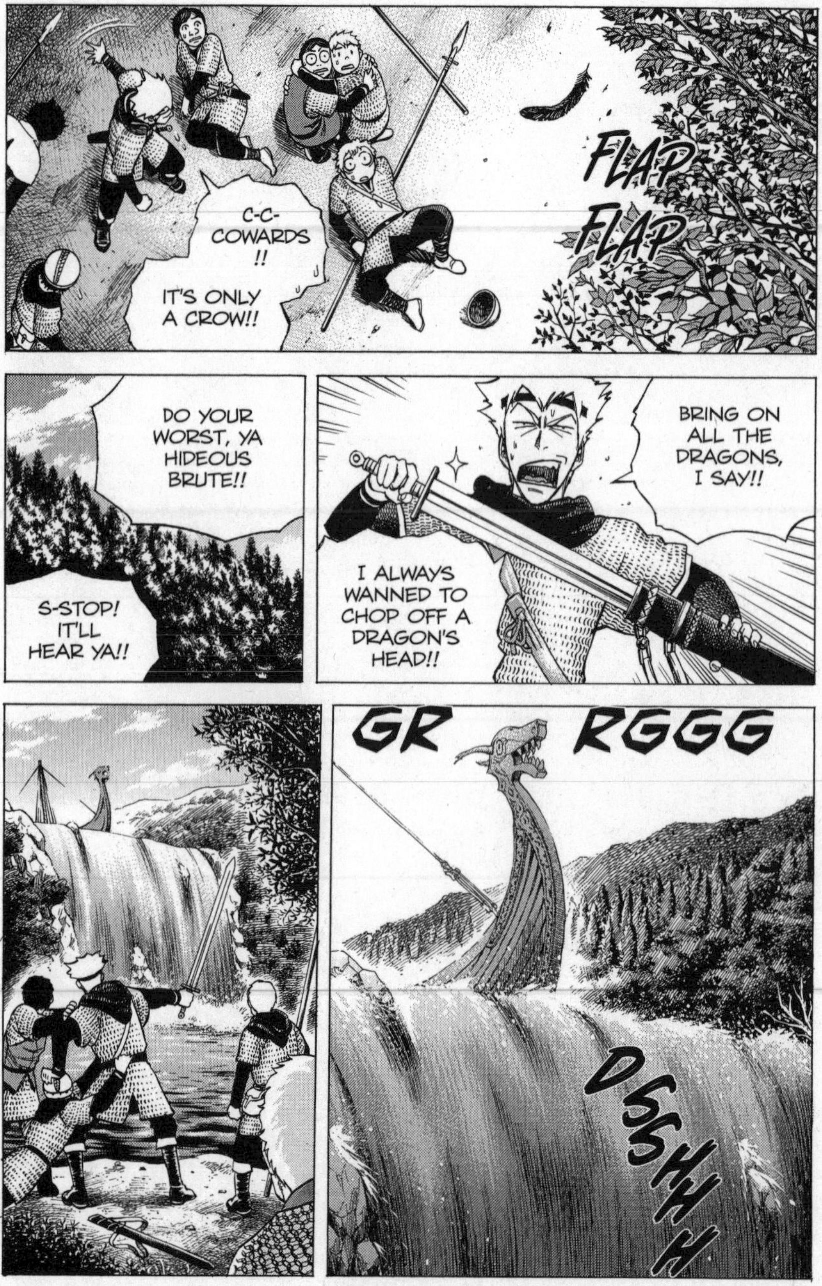
FLAP FLAP
C-C-COWARDS!!
IT'S ONLY A CROW!!
BRING ON ALL THE DRAGONS, I SAY!!
I ALWAYS WANNED TO CHOP OFF A DRAGON'S HEAD!!
DO YOUR WORST, YA HIDEOUS BRUTE!!
S-STOP! IT'LL HEAR YA!!
GR RGGG
DSSHHH

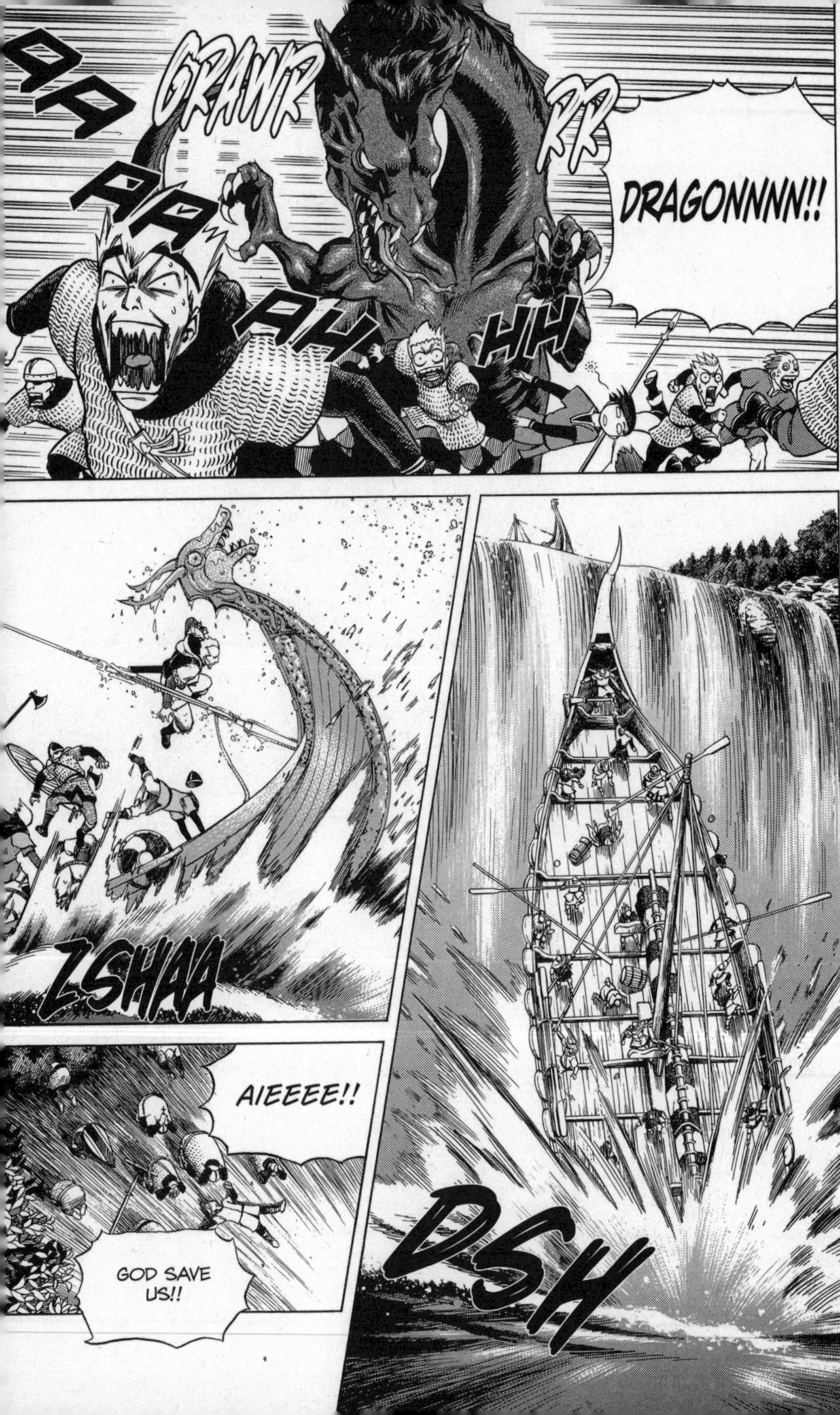
DRAGONNNN!!
GRAWRRR
AAAAAHHH
DSH
ZSHAA
AIEEEE!!
GOD SAVE US!!

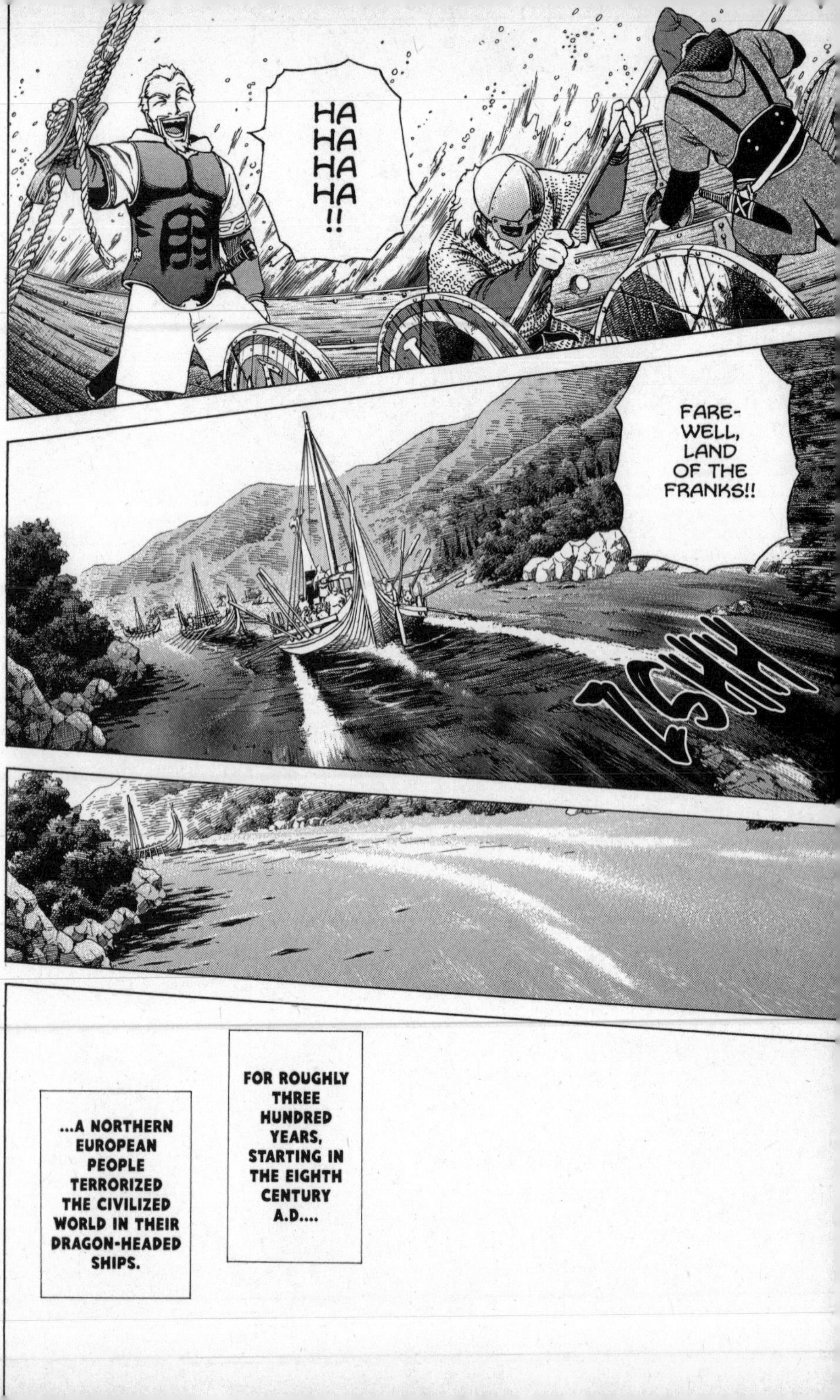
HA HA HA HA!!
FARE-WELL, LAND OF THE FRANKS!!
ZGSHH
FOR ROUGHLY THREE HUNDRED YEARS, STARTING IN THE EIGHTH CENTURY A.D....
...A NORTHERN EUROPEAN PEOPLE TERRORIZED THE CIVILIZED WORLD IN THEIR DRAGON-HEADED SHIPS.

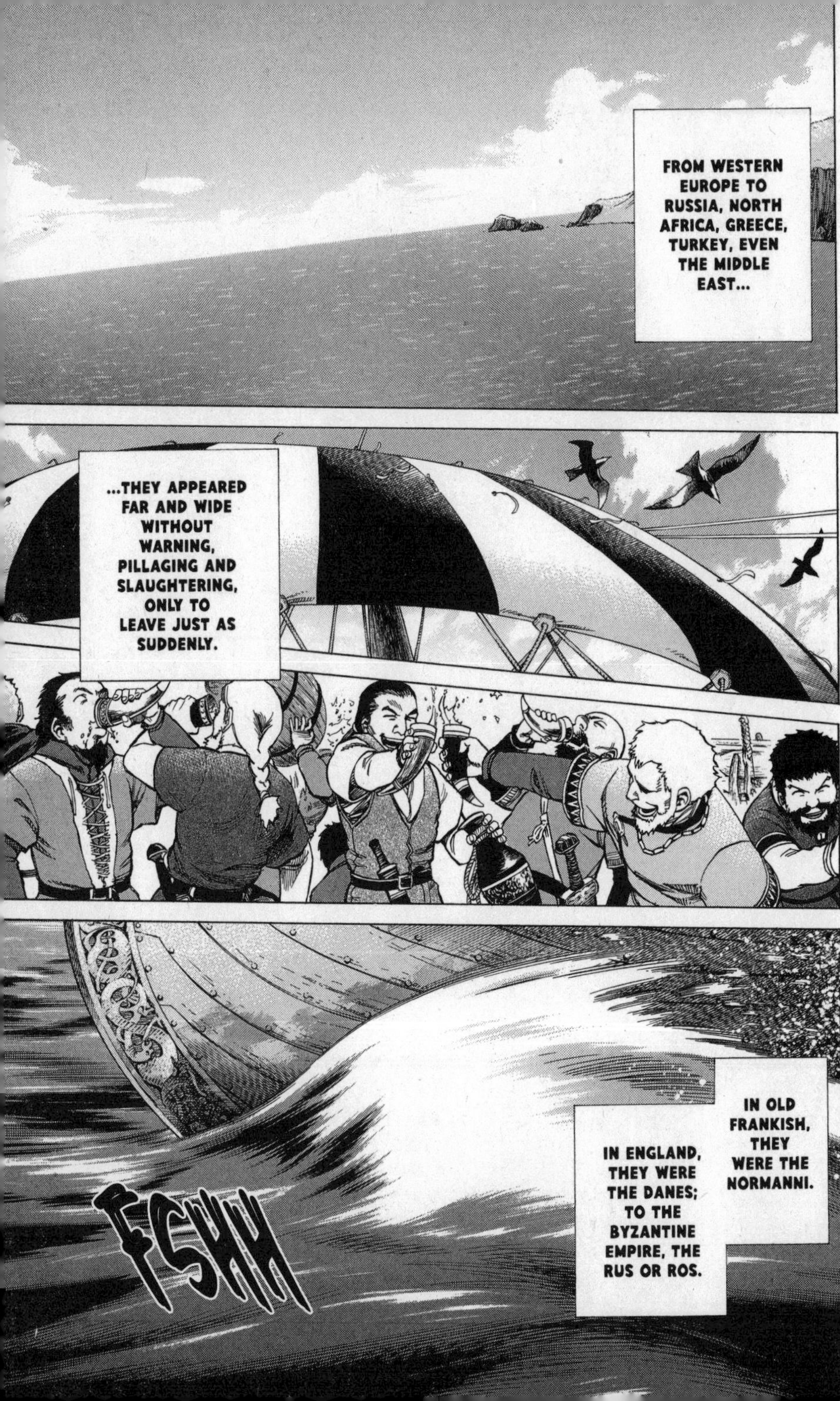
FROM WESTERN EUROPE TO RUSSIA, NORTH AFRICA, GREECE, TURKEY, EVEN THE MIDDLE EAST...
...THEY APPEARED FAR AND WIDE WITHOUT WARNING, PILLAGING AND SLAUGHTERING, ONLY TO LEAVE JUST AS SUDDENLY.
IN OLD FRANKISH, THEY WERE THE NORMANNI.
IN ENGLAND, THEY WERE THE DANES; TO THE BYZANTINE EMPIRE, THE RUS OR ROS.
FSHH

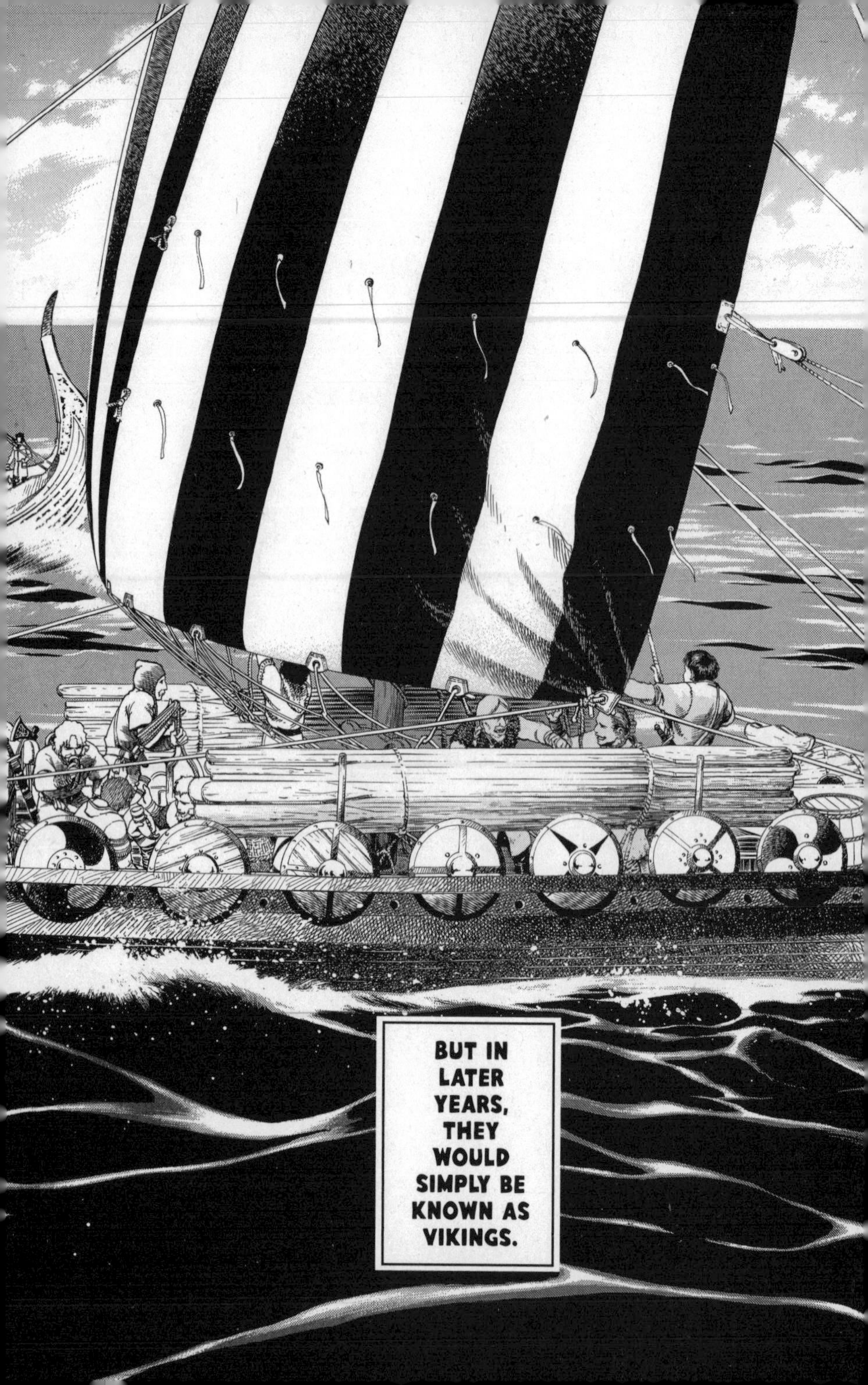
BUT IN LATER YEARS, THEY WOULD SIMPLY BE KNOWN AS VIKINGS.

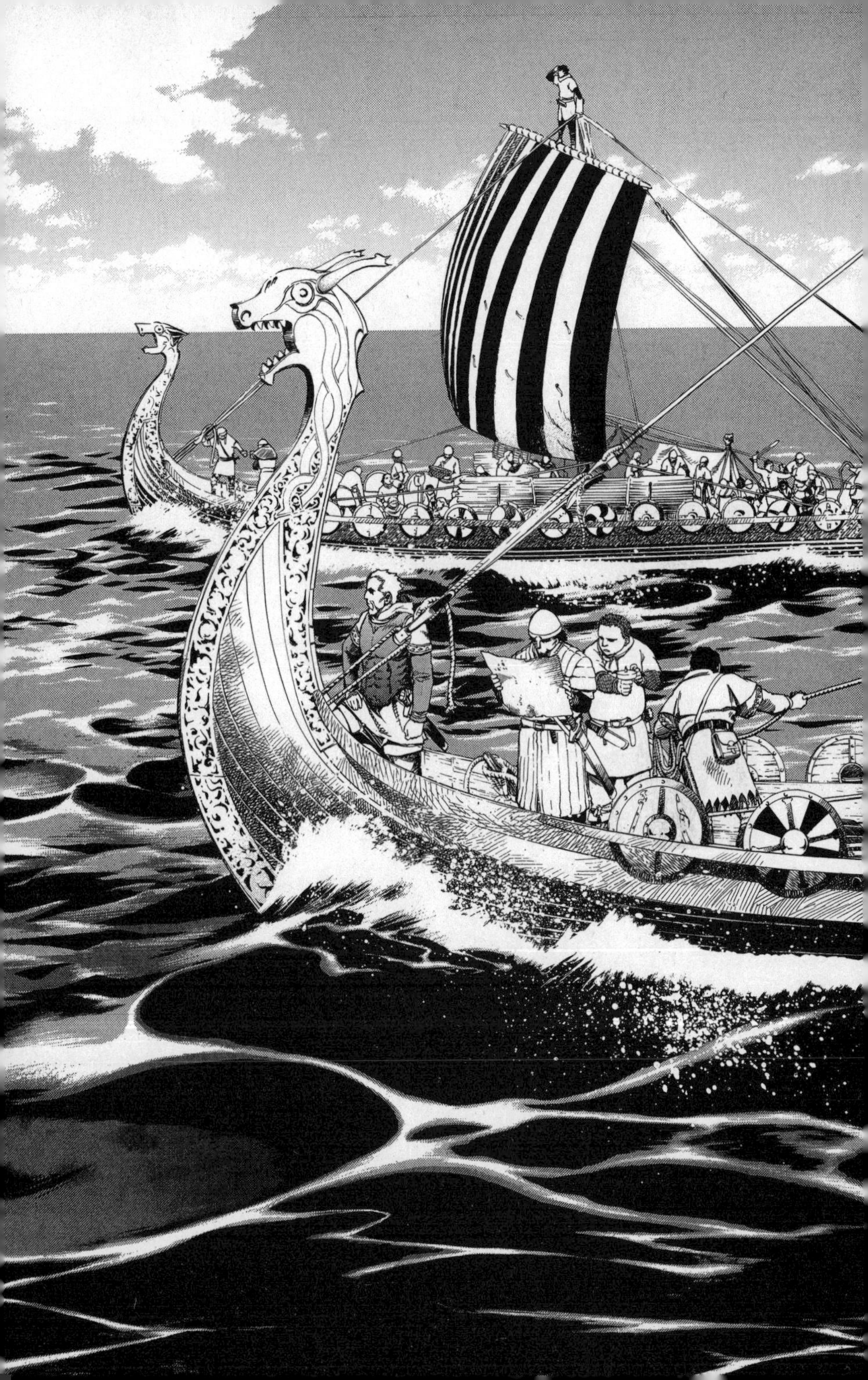

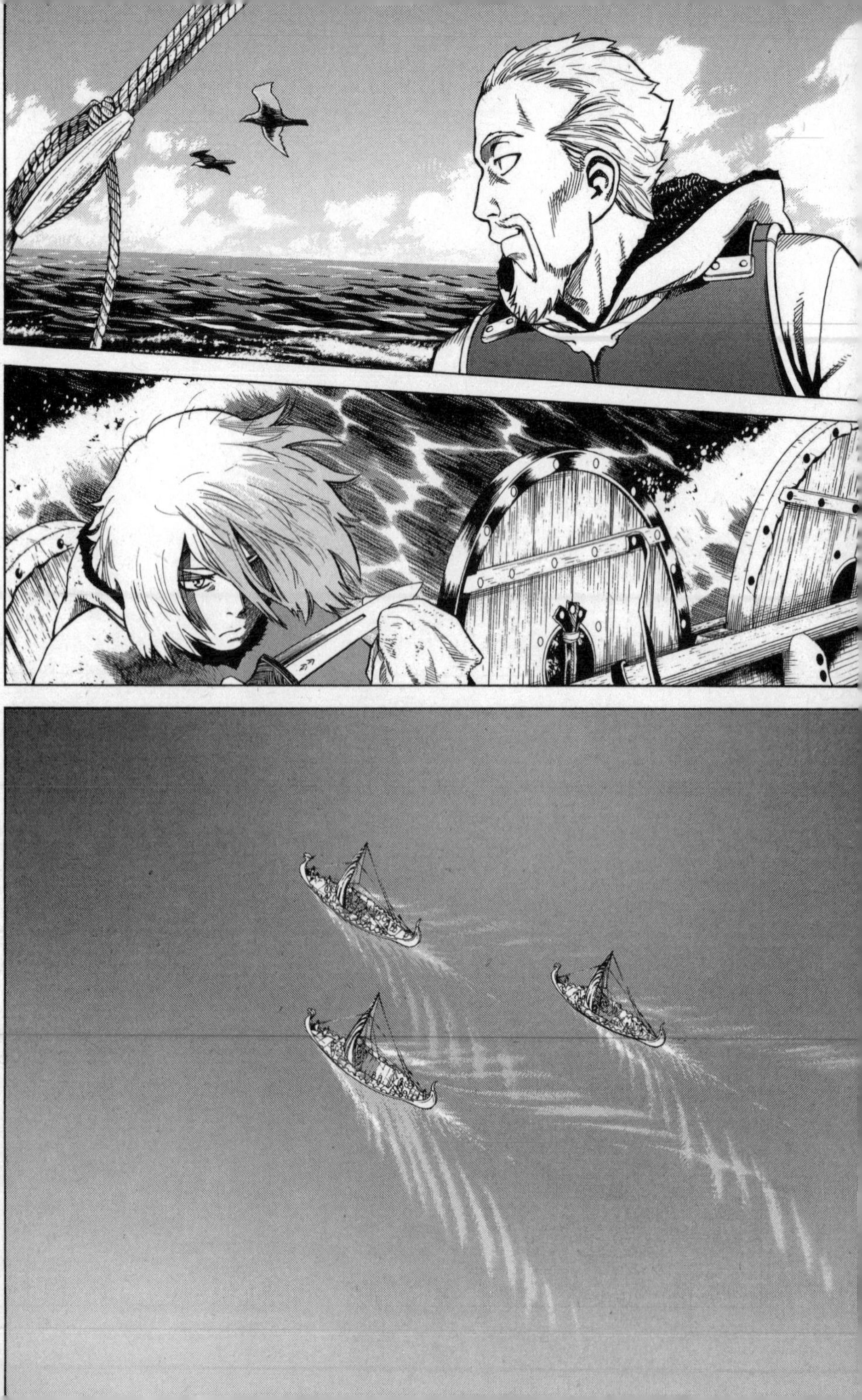

CHAPTER 1 · END

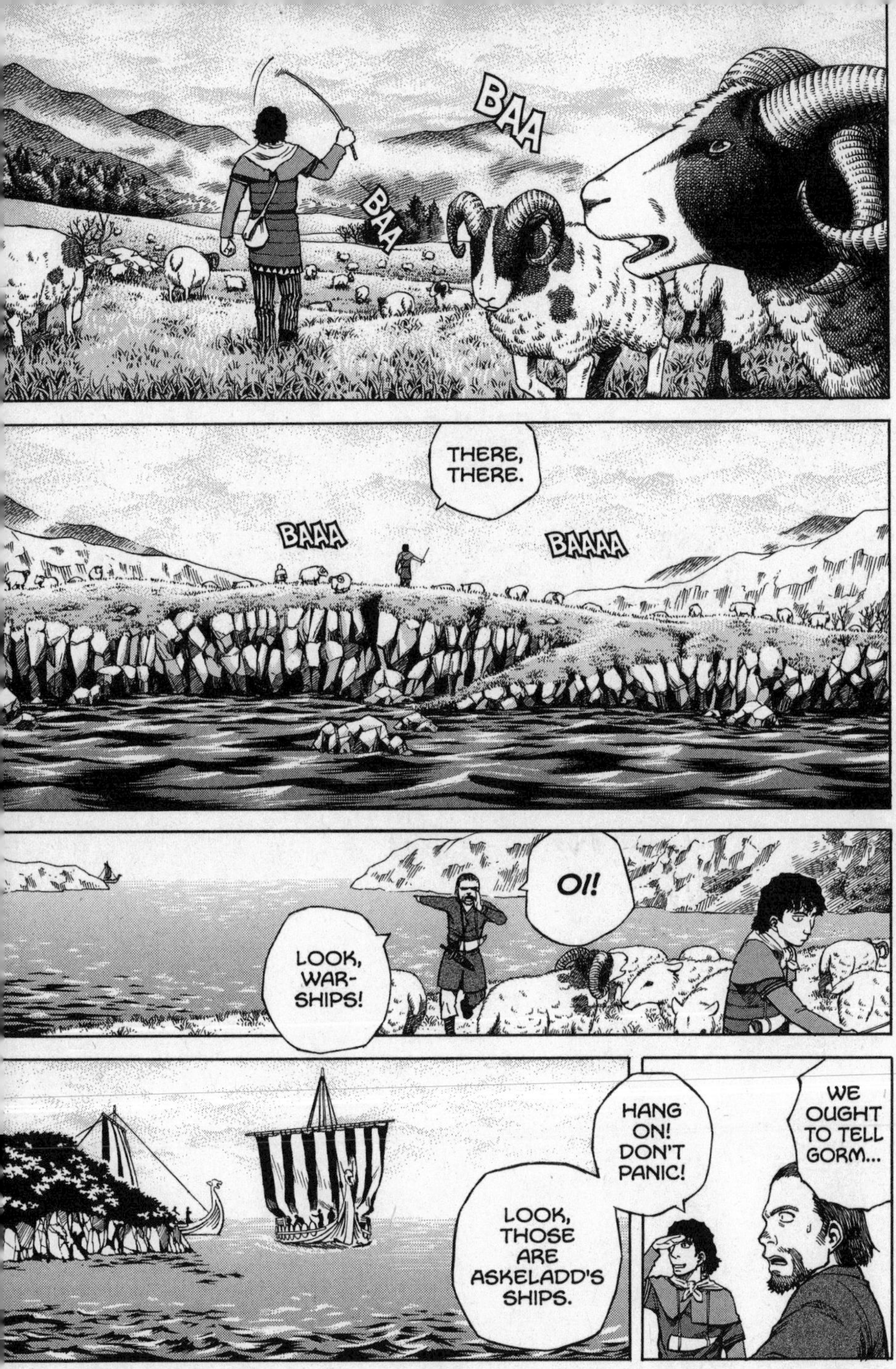
BAA
BAA
THERE, THERE.
BAAAA
BAAA
OI!
LOOK, WAR-SHIPS!
WE OUGHT TO TELL GORM...
HANG ON! DON'T PANIC!
LOOK, THOSE ARE ASKELADD'S SHIPS.

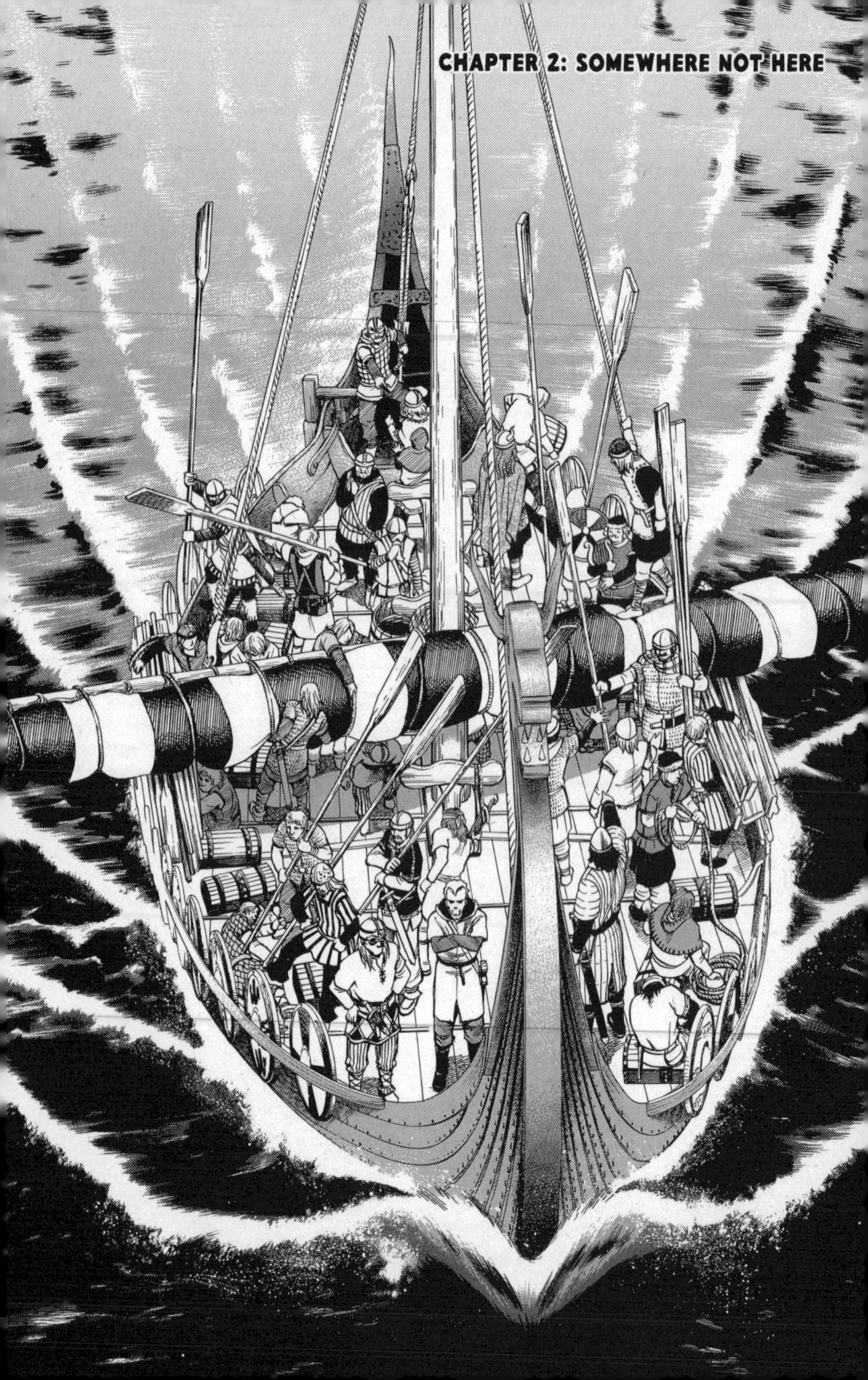
CHAPTER 2: SOMEWHERE NOT HERE

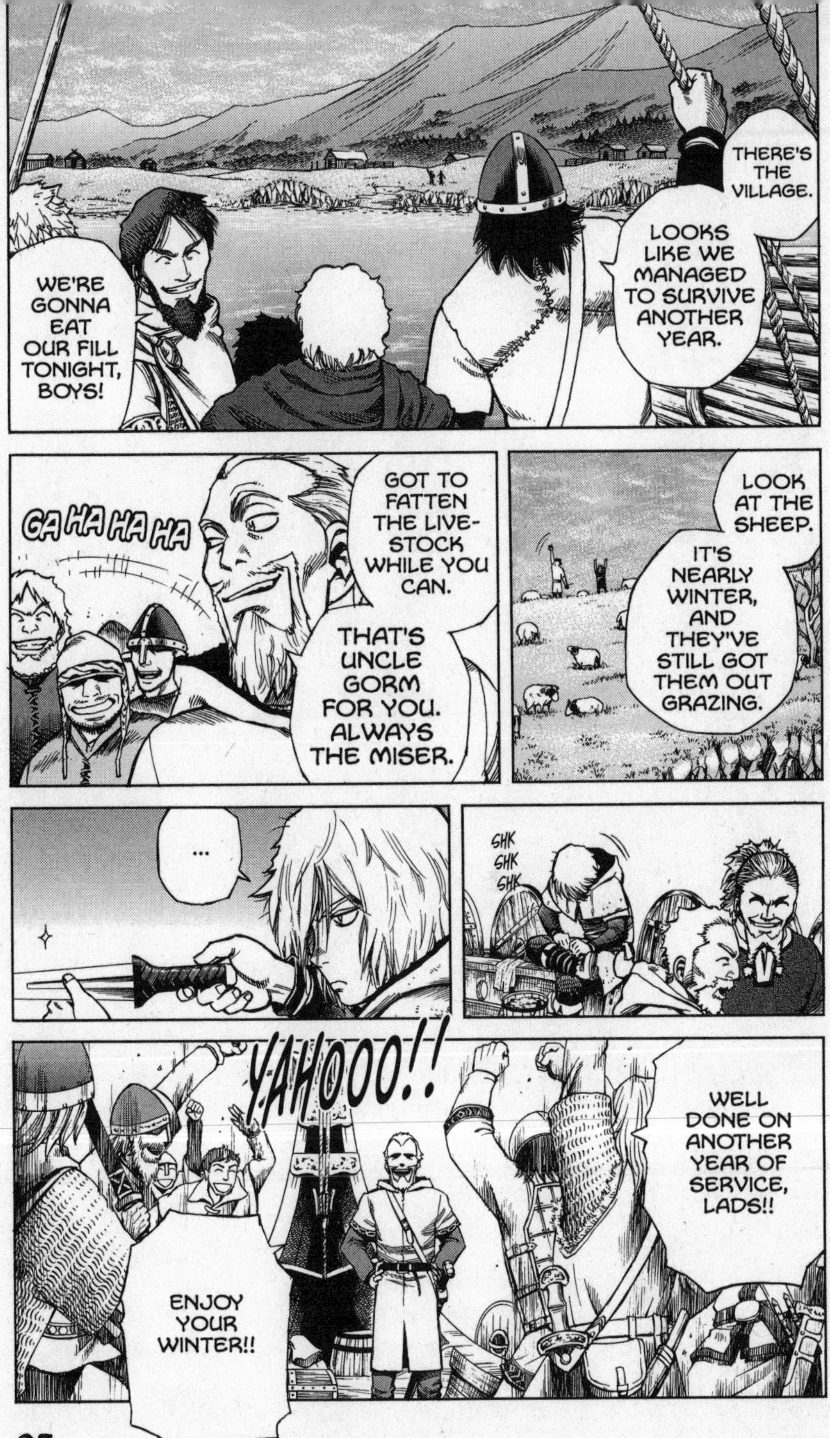
THERE'S THE VILLAGE.
LOOKS LIKE WE MANAGED TO SURVIVE ANOTHER YEAR.
WE'RE GONNA EAT OUR FILL TONIGHT, BOYS!
LOOK AT THE SHEEP.
IT'S NEARLY WINTER, AND THEY'VE STILL GOT THEM OUT GRAZING.
GA HA HA HA
GOT TO FATTEN THE LIVE-STOCK WHILE YOU CAN.
THAT'S UNCLE GORM FOR YOU. ALWAYS THE MISER.
SHK SHK SHK
...
YAHOOO!!
WELL DONE ON ANOTHER YEAR OF SERVICE, LADS!!
ENJOY YOUR WINTER!!

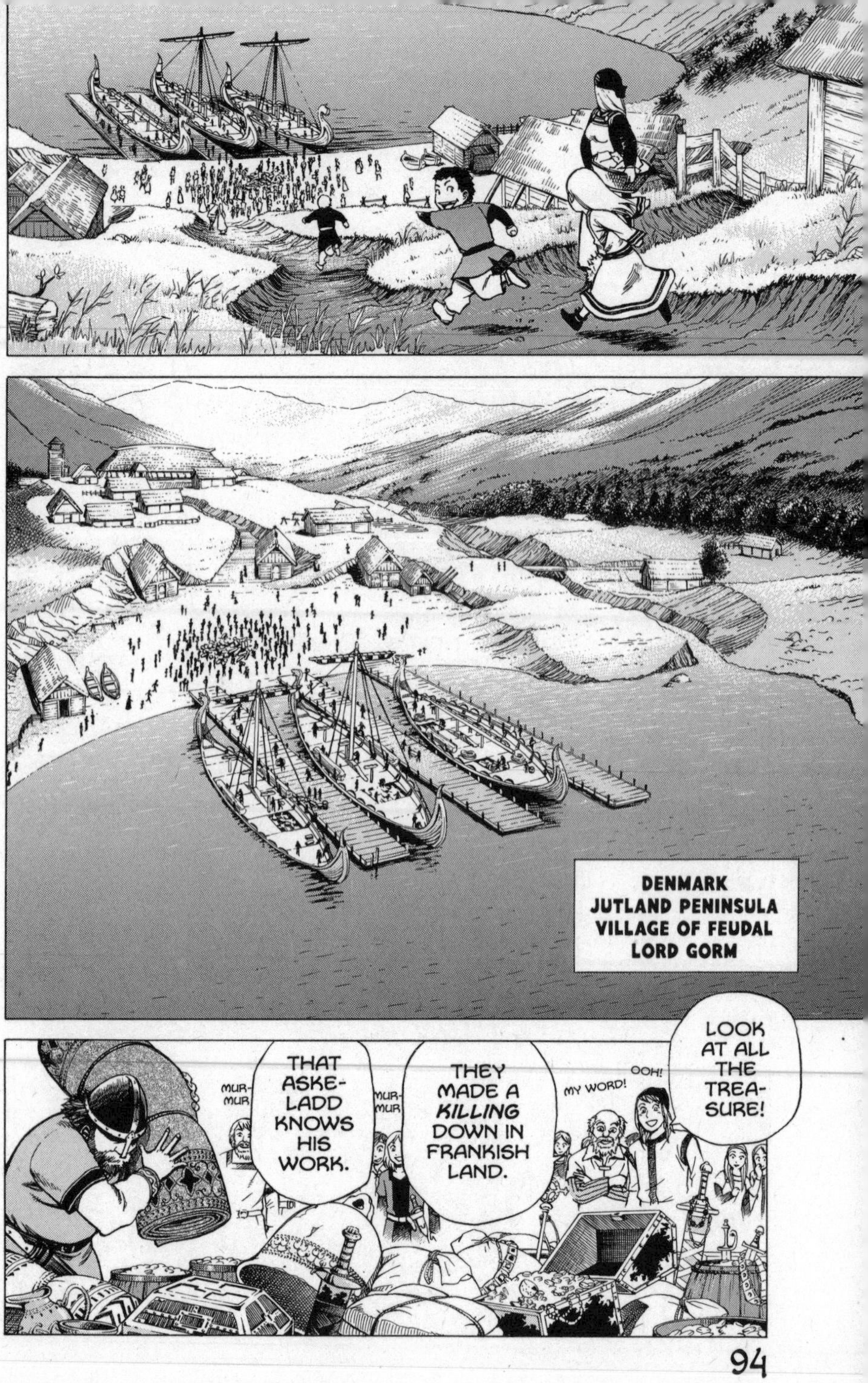
DENMARK JUTLAND PENINSULA VILLAGE OF FEUDAL LORD GORM
LOOK AT ALL THE TREA-SURE!
OOH!
MY WORD!
THEY MADE A *KILLING* DOWN IN FRANKISH LAND.
MUR-MUR
THAT ASKE-LADD KNOWS HIS WORK.
MUR-MUR

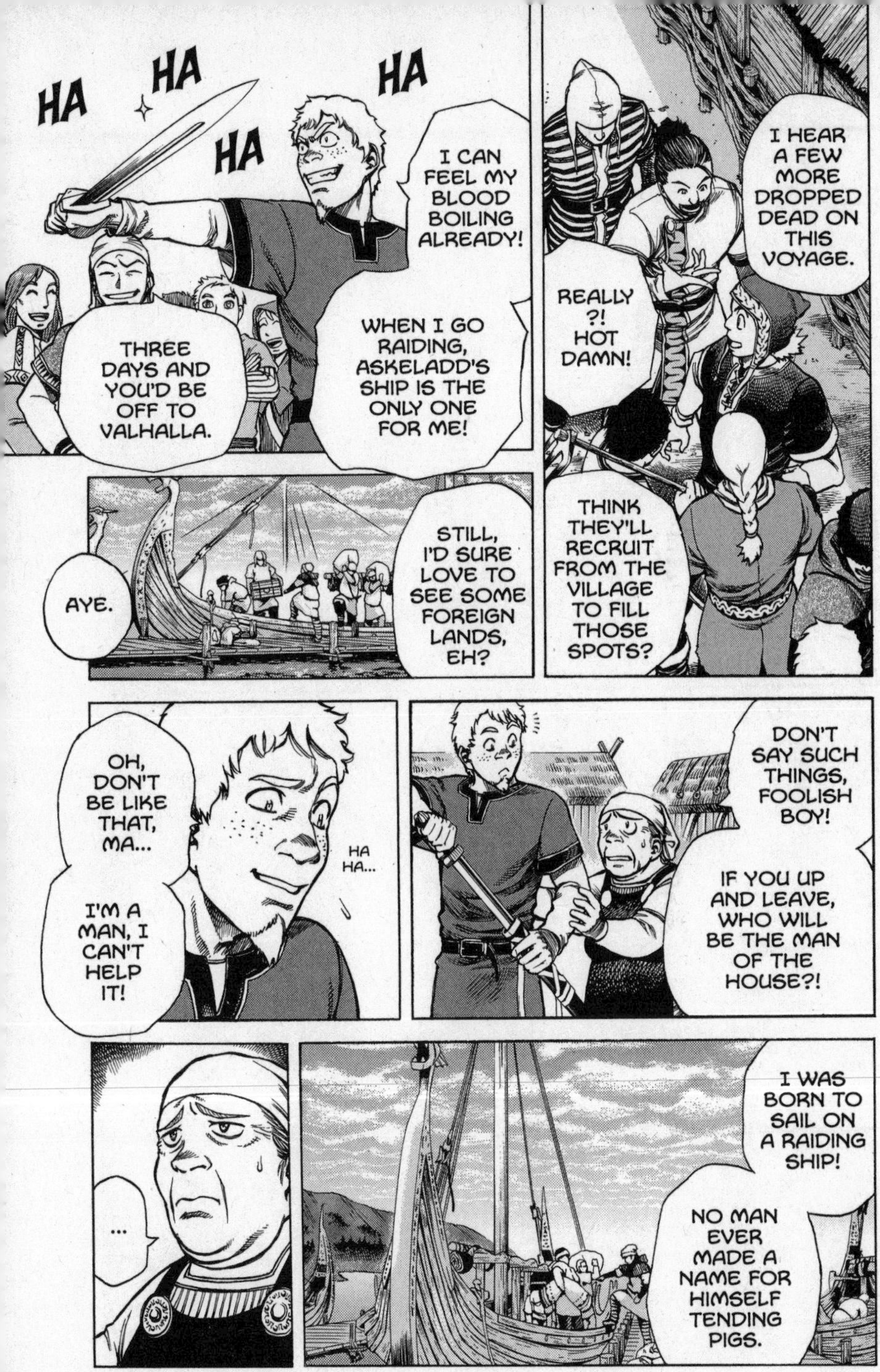
I HEAR A FEW MORE DROPPED DEAD ON THIS VOYAGE.
REALLY?! HOT DAMN!
THINK THEY'LL RECRUIT FROM THE VILLAGE TO FILL THOSE SPOTS?
HA HA HA HA
I CAN FEEL MY BLOOD BOILING ALREADY!
WHEN I GO RAIDING, ASKELADD'S SHIP IS THE ONLY ONE FOR ME!
THREE DAYS AND YOU'D BE OFF TO VALHALLA.
STILL, I'D SURE LOVE TO SEE SOME FOREIGN LANDS, EH?
AYE.
DON'T SAY SUCH THINGS, FOOLISH BOY!
IF YOU UP AND LEAVE, WHO WILL BE THE MAN OF THE HOUSE?!
OH, DON'T BE LIKE THAT, MA...
HA HA...
I'M A MAN, I CAN'T HELP IT!
I WAS BORN TO SAIL ON A RAIDING SHIP!
NO MAN EVER MADE A NAME FOR HIMSELF TENDING PIGS.
...

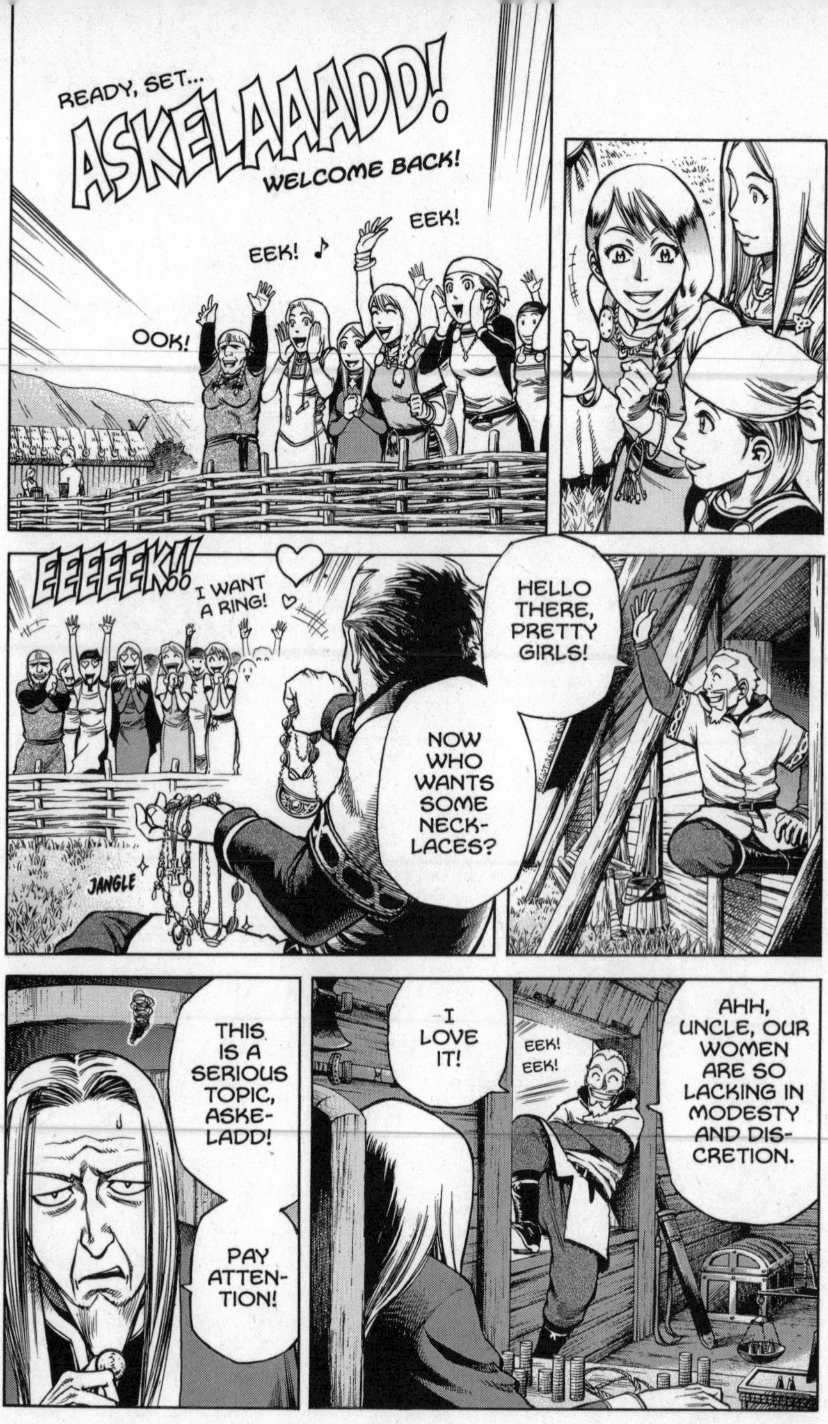
READY, SET...
ASKELAAADD!
WELCOME BACK!
EEK!
EEK! ♪
OOK!
HELLO THERE, PRETTY GIRLS!
NOW WHO WANTS SOME NECK-LACES?
EEEEEK!!
I WANT A RING!
JANGLE
AHH, UNCLE, OUR WOMEN ARE SO LACKING IN MODESTY AND DIS-CRETION.
EEK! EEK!
I LOVE IT!
THIS IS A SERIOUS TOPIC, ASKE-LADD!
PAY ATTEN-TION!

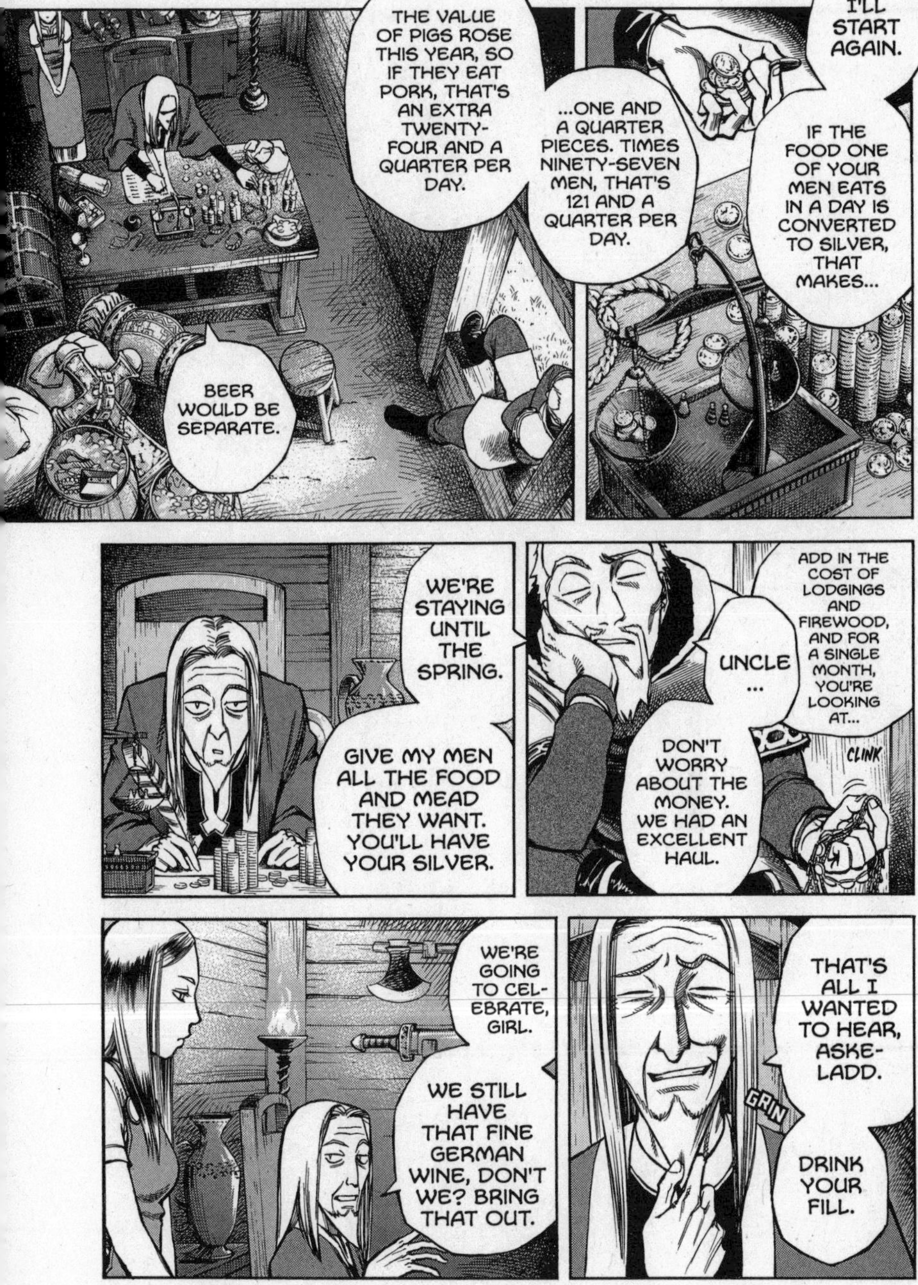
I'LL START AGAIN.
IF THE FOOD ONE OF YOUR MEN EATS IN A DAY IS CONVERTED TO SILVER, THAT MAKES...
...ONE AND A QUARTER PIECES. TIMES NINETY-SEVEN MEN, THAT'S 121 AND A QUARTER PER DAY.
THE VALUE OF PIGS ROSE THIS YEAR, SO IF THEY EAT PORK, THAT'S AN EXTRA TWENTY-FOUR AND A QUARTER PER DAY.
BEER WOULD BE SEPARATE.
ADD IN THE COST OF LODGINGS AND FIREWOOD, AND FOR A SINGLE MONTH, YOU'RE LOOKING AT...
UNCLE ...
DON'T WORRY ABOUT THE MONEY. WE HAD AN EXCELLENT HAUL.
CLINK
WE'RE STAYING UNTIL THE SPRING.
GIVE MY MEN ALL THE FOOD AND MEAD THEY WANT. YOU'LL HAVE YOUR SILVER.
THAT'S ALL I WANTED TO HEAR, ASKE-LADD.
GRIN
DRINK YOUR FILL.
WE'RE GOING TO CEL-EBRATE, GIRL.
WE STILL HAVE THAT FINE GERMAN WINE, DON'T WE? BRING THAT OUT.

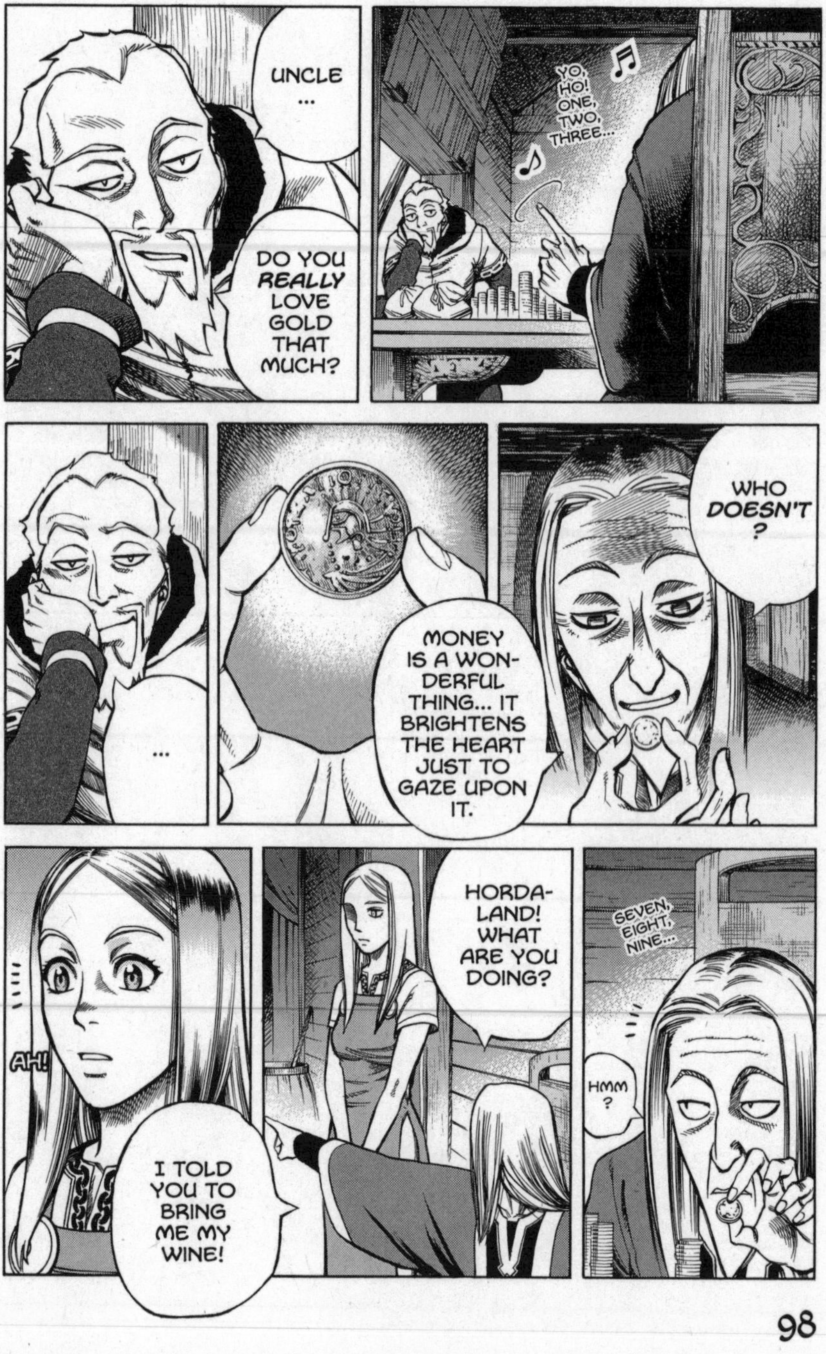
YO, HO! ONE, TWO, THREE...
UNCLE ...
DO YOU *REALLY* LOVE GOLD THAT MUCH?
WHO *DOESN'T* ?
MONEY IS A WONDERFUL THING... IT BRIGHTENS THE HEART JUST TO GAZE UPON IT.
...
SEVEN, EIGHT, NINE...
HMM ?
HORDALAND! WHAT ARE YOU DOING?
I TOLD YOU TO BRING ME MY WINE!
AH!

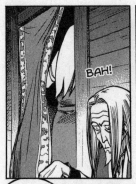

...
...YES, SIR...
BAH!
STRANGE NAME THAT SLAVE'S GOT.
HORDA-LAND. LIKE THE PLACE IN NORWAY?
MM?
YES.
I BOUGHT HER EARLIER THIS YEAR.
APPARENTLY FROM THE BLOODLINE OF SOME LORD IN THAT AREA.
THEY LOST A WAR, AND THE FAMILY WENT INTO RUIN OR SOME SUCH.
SHE COST SOLID COIN FOR THOSE PRETTY LOOKS...
...BUT SHE'S A DREADFUL SLAVE. STILL GOT THE NOBLE AIRS.
WHISPER...
ZSHH

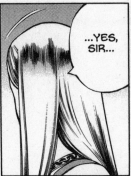

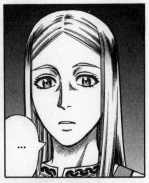

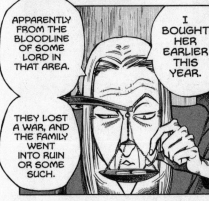

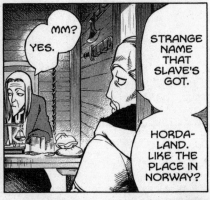

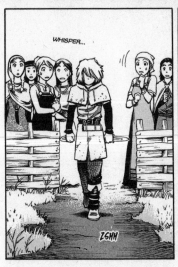

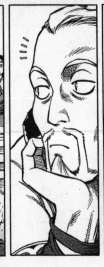

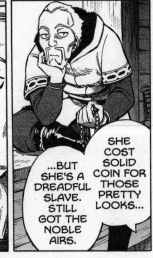

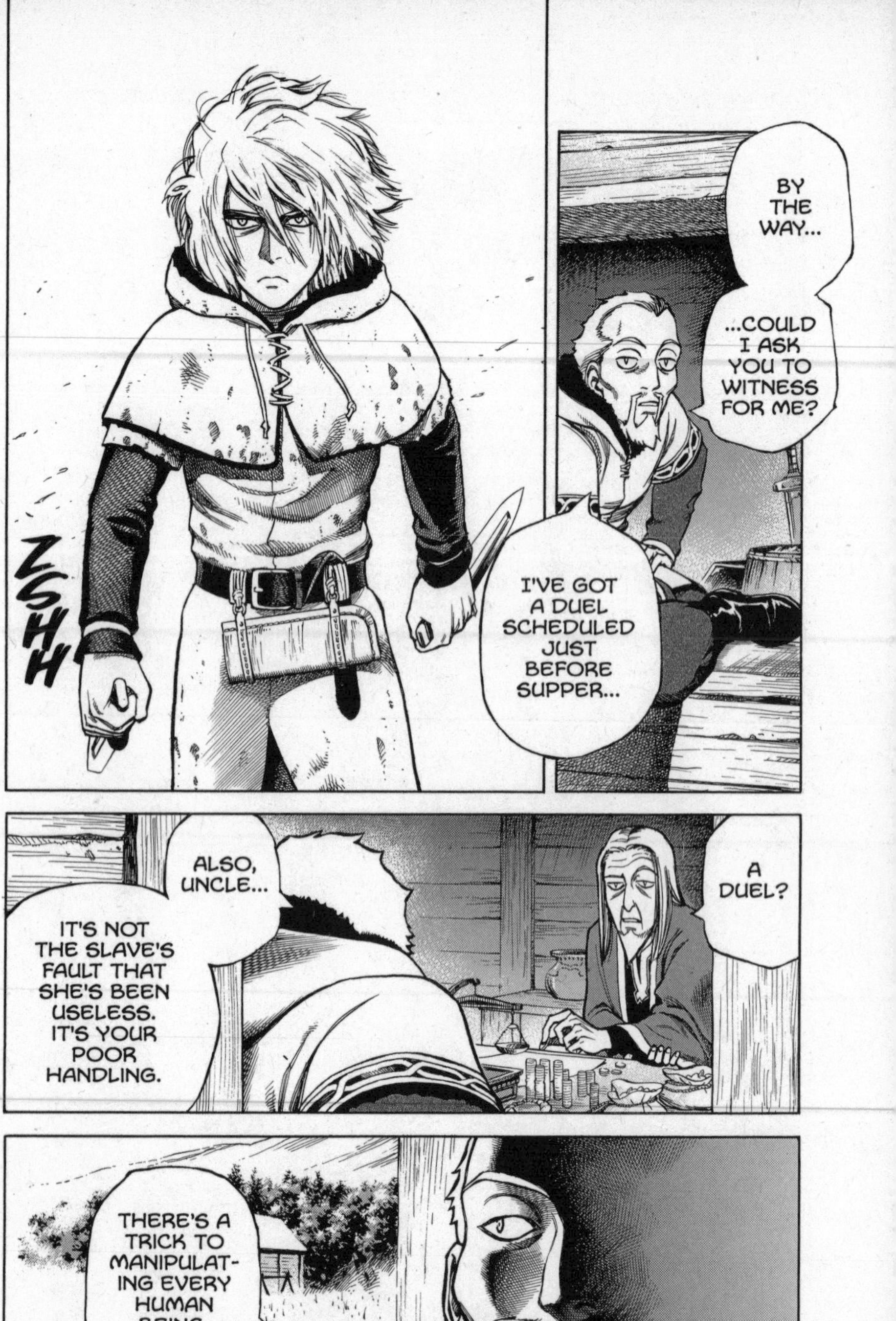
BY THE WAY...
...COULD I ASK YOU TO WITNESS FOR ME?
I'VE GOT A DUEL SCHEDULED JUST BEFORE SUPPER...
ZSHH
A DUEL?
ALSO, UNCLE...
IT'S NOT THE SLAVE'S FAULT THAT SHE'S BEEN USELESS. IT'S YOUR POOR HANDLING.
THERE'S A TRICK TO MANIPULATING EVERY HUMAN BEING.

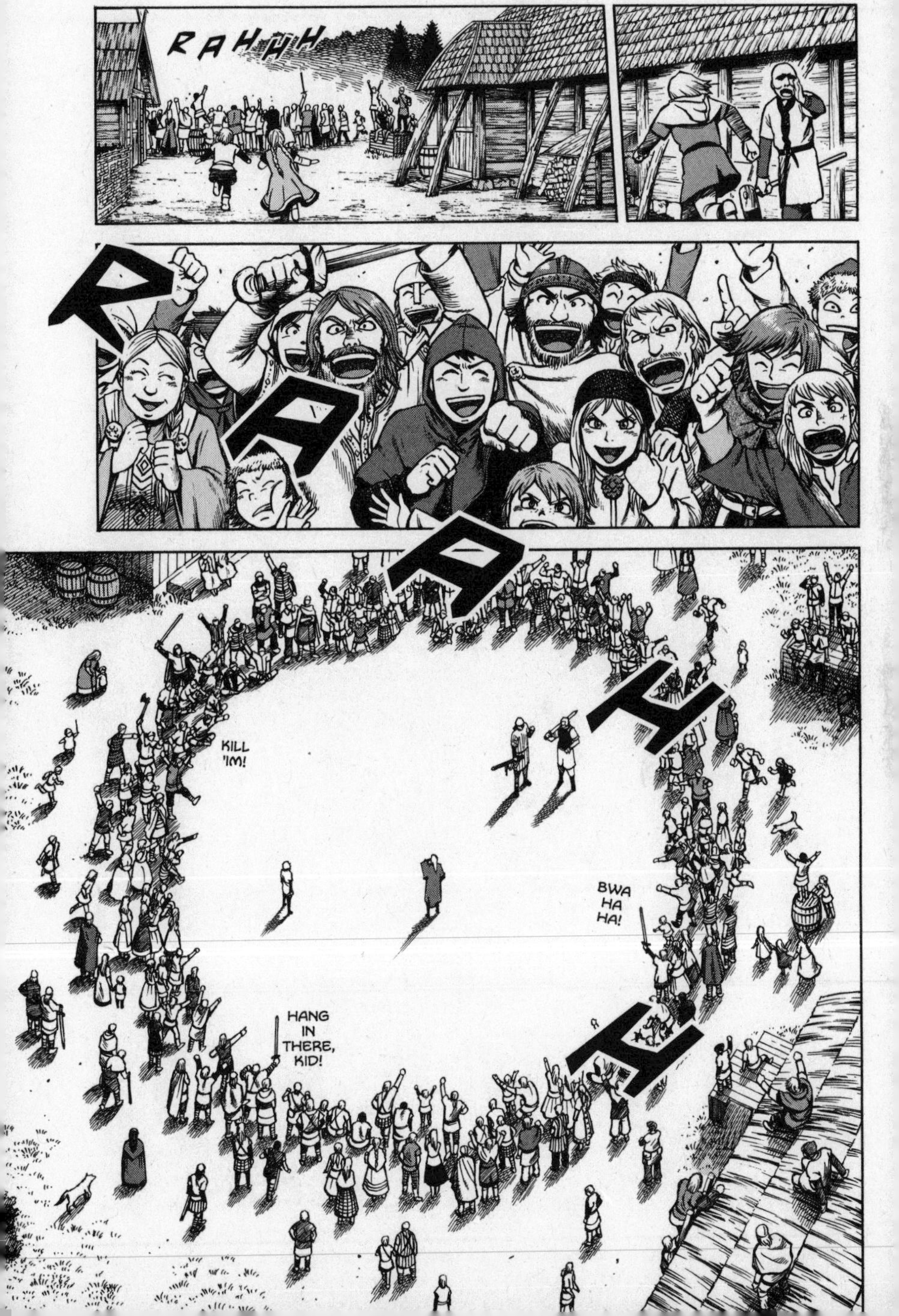
RAHHH
RAAAHH
KILL 'IM!
BWA HA HA!
HANG IN THERE, KID!

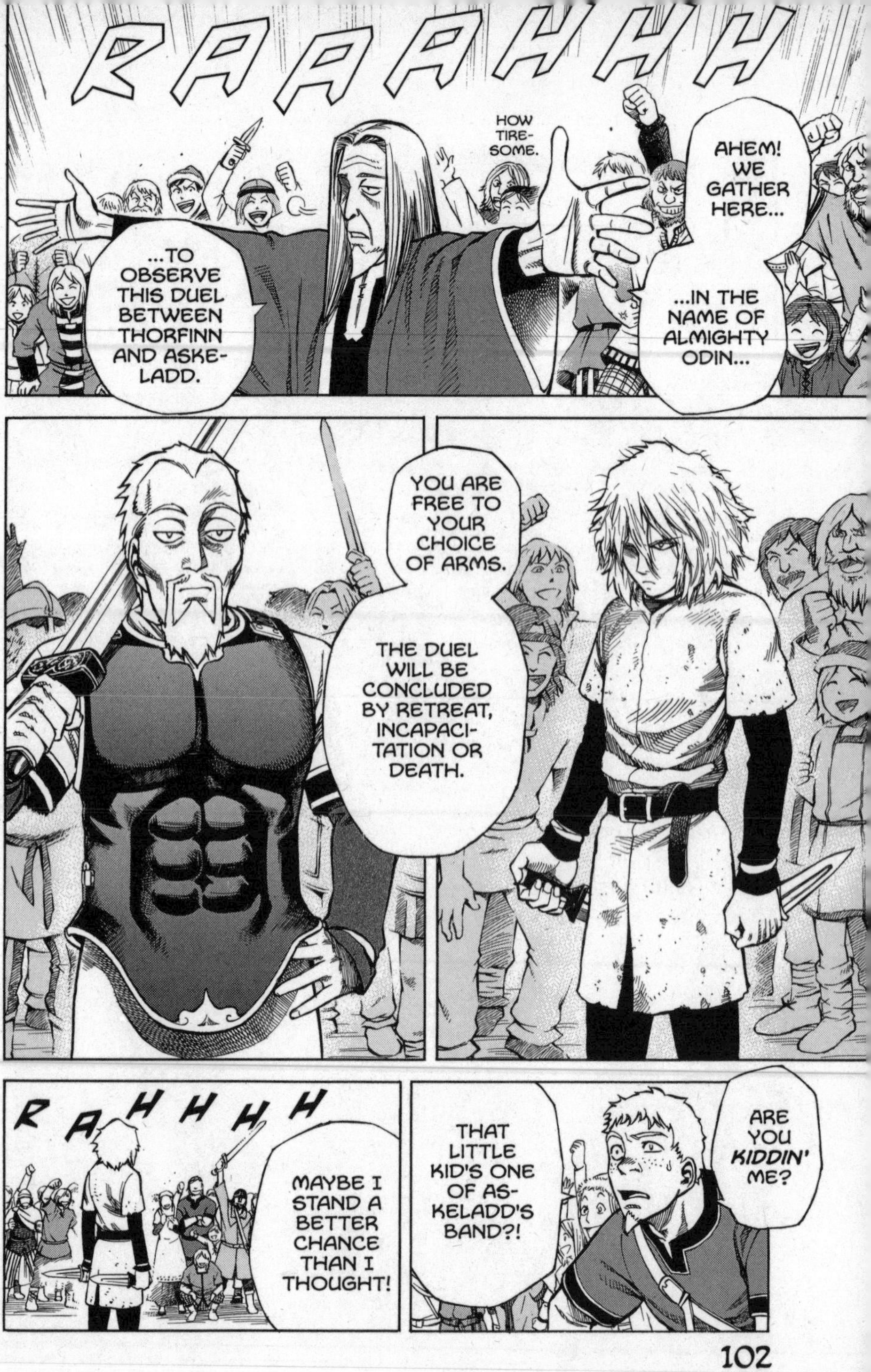
RAAAHHH
AHEM! WE GATHER HERE...
...IN THE NAME OF ALMIGHTY ODIN...
HOW TIRESOME.
...TO OBSERVE THIS DUEL BETWEEN THORFINN AND ASKELADD.
YOU ARE FREE TO YOUR CHOICE OF ARMS.
THE DUEL WILL BE CONCLUDED BY RETREAT, INCAPACITATION OR DEATH.
ARE YOU *KIDDIN'* ME?
THAT LITTLE KID'S ONE OF ASKELADD'S BAND?!
RAHHHH
MAYBE I STAND A BETTER CHANCE THAN I THOUGHT!

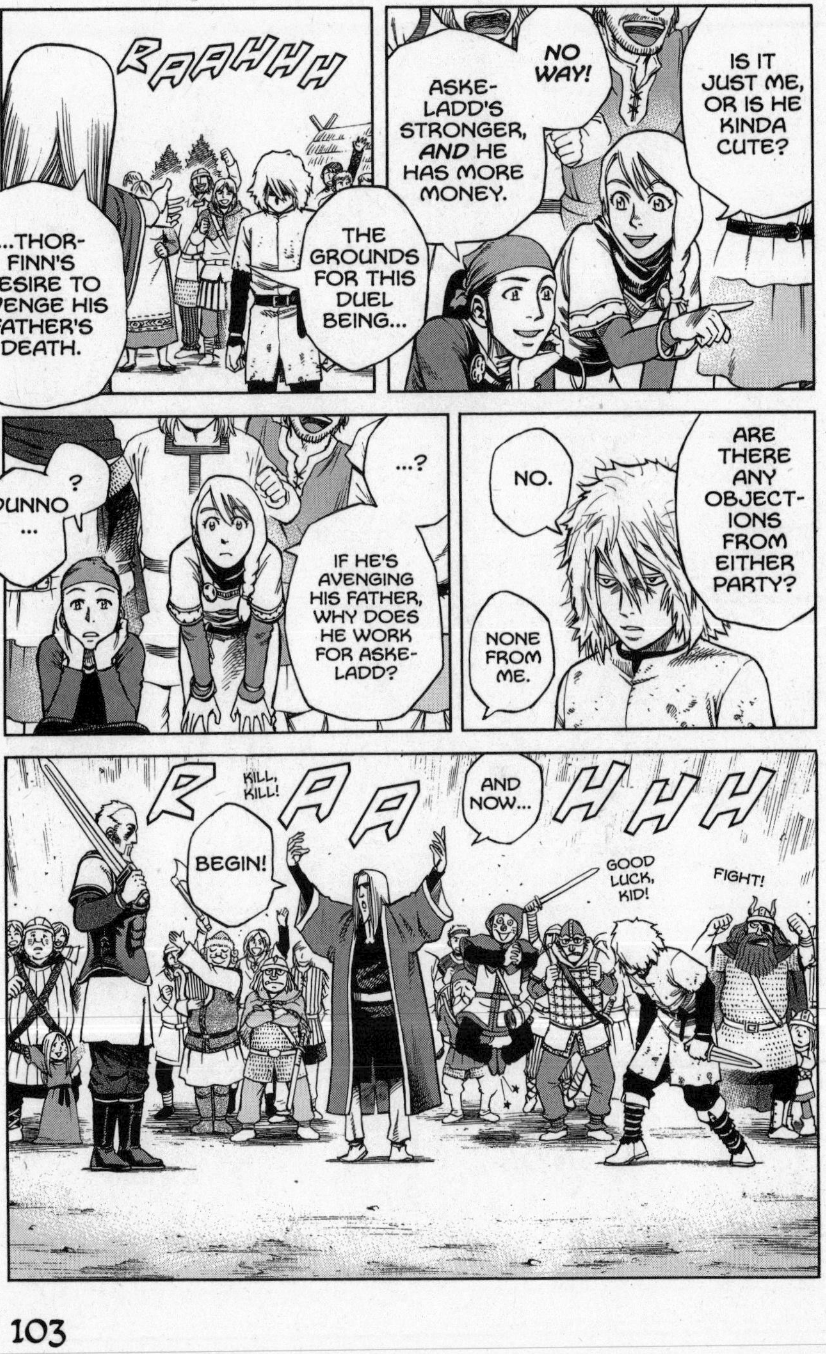
IS IT JUST ME, OR IS HE KINDA CUTE?
NO WAY!
ASKE-LADD'S STRONGER, AND HE HAS MORE MONEY.
RAAHHH
THE GROUNDS FOR THIS DUEL BEING...
...THORFINN'S DESIRE TO AVENGE HIS FATHER'S DEATH.
ARE THERE ANY OBJECTIONS FROM EITHER PARTY?
NO.
NONE FROM ME.
...?
IF HE'S AVENGING HIS FATHER, WHY DOES HE WORK FOR ASKE-LADD?
? DUNNO...
RAAHHH
AND NOW...
KILL, KILL!
FIGHT!
GOOD LUCK, KID!
BEGIN!

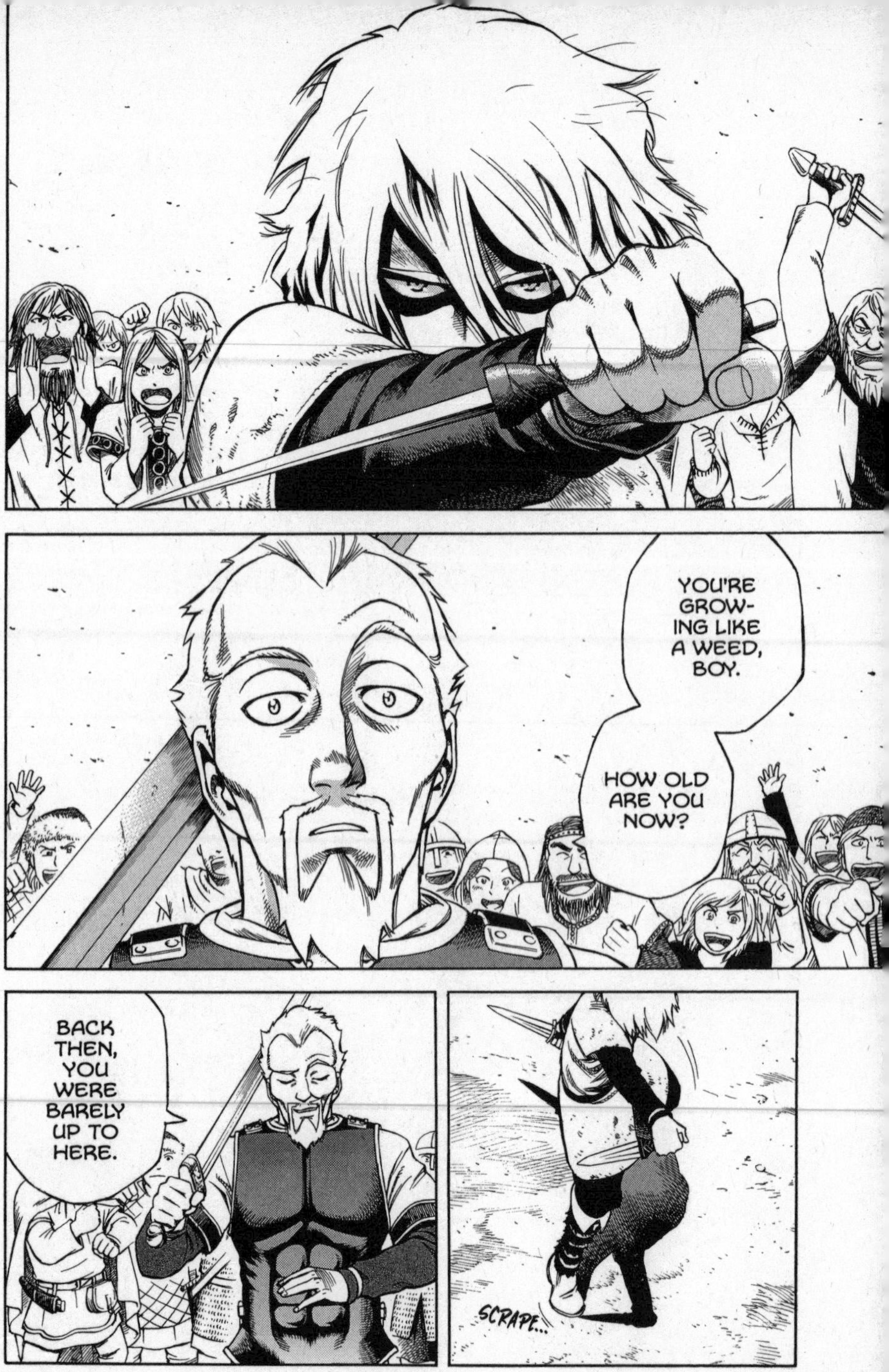
YOU'RE GROWING LIKE A WEED, BOY.
HOW OLD ARE YOU NOW?
SCRAPE...
BACK THEN, YOU WERE BARELY UP TO HERE.

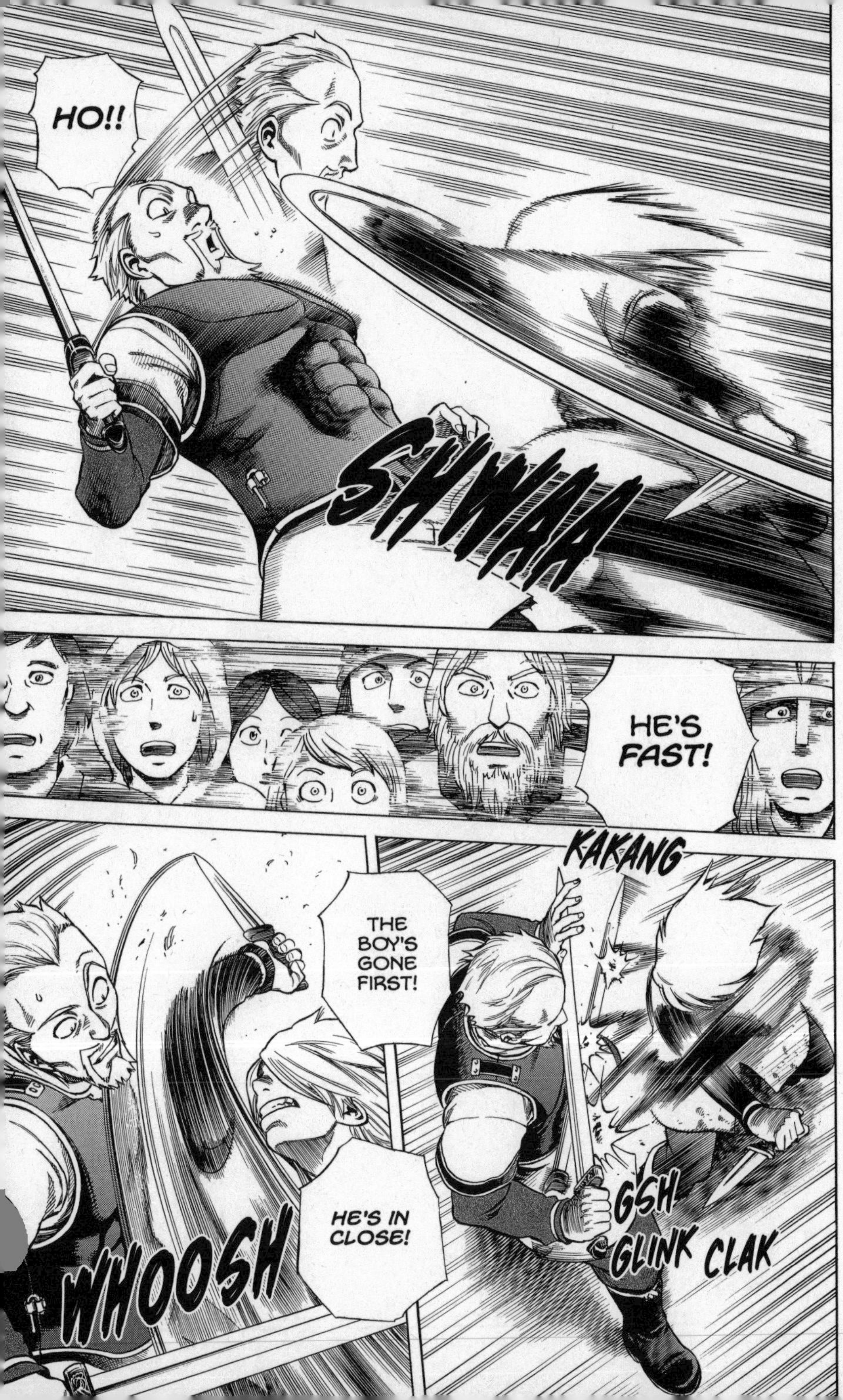
HO!!
SHWAA
HE'S FAST!
KAKANG
GSH
GLINK
CLAK
THE BOY'S GONE FIRST!
HE'S IN CLOSE!
WHOOSH

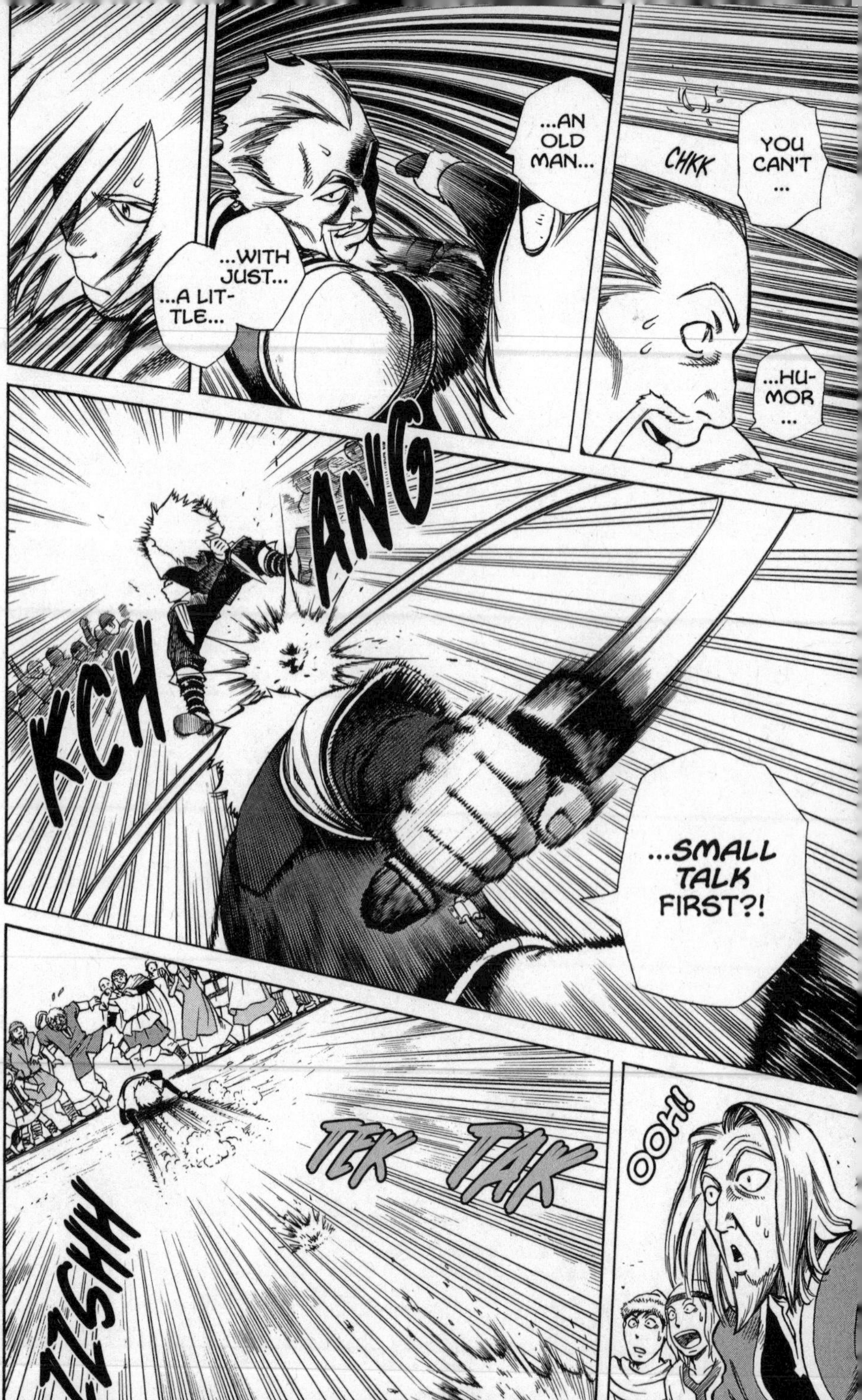
YOU CAN'T ...
CHKK
...HU-MOR ...
...AN OLD MAN...
...WITH JUST... ...A LIT-TLE...
...SMALL TALK FIRST?!
KCH ANG
OOH!
TEK TAK
ZZSHH

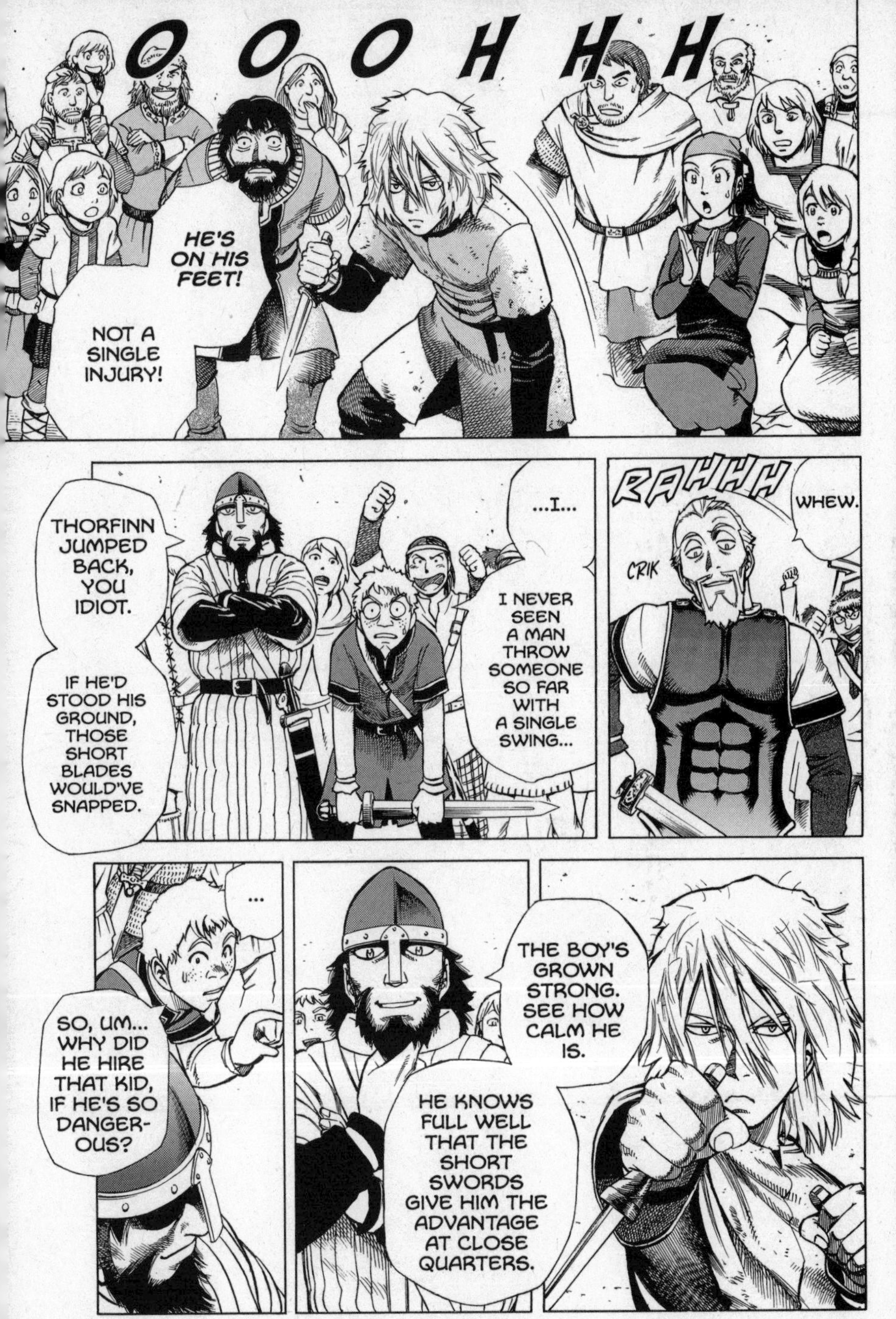
OOOOHHH
HE'S ON HIS FEET!
NOT A SINGLE INJURY!
RAHHHH
WHEW.
CRIK
...I...
I NEVER SEEN A MAN THROW SOMEONE SO FAR WITH A SINGLE SWING...
THORFINN JUMPED BACK, YOU IDIOT.
IF HE'D STOOD HIS GROUND, THOSE SHORT BLADES WOULD'VE SNAPPED.
THE BOY'S GROWN STRONG. SEE HOW CALM HE IS.
HE KNOWS FULL WELL THAT THE SHORT SWORDS GIVE HIM THE ADVANTAGE AT CLOSE QUARTERS.
...
SO, UM... WHY DID HE HIRE THAT KID, IF HE'S SO DANGER-OUS?

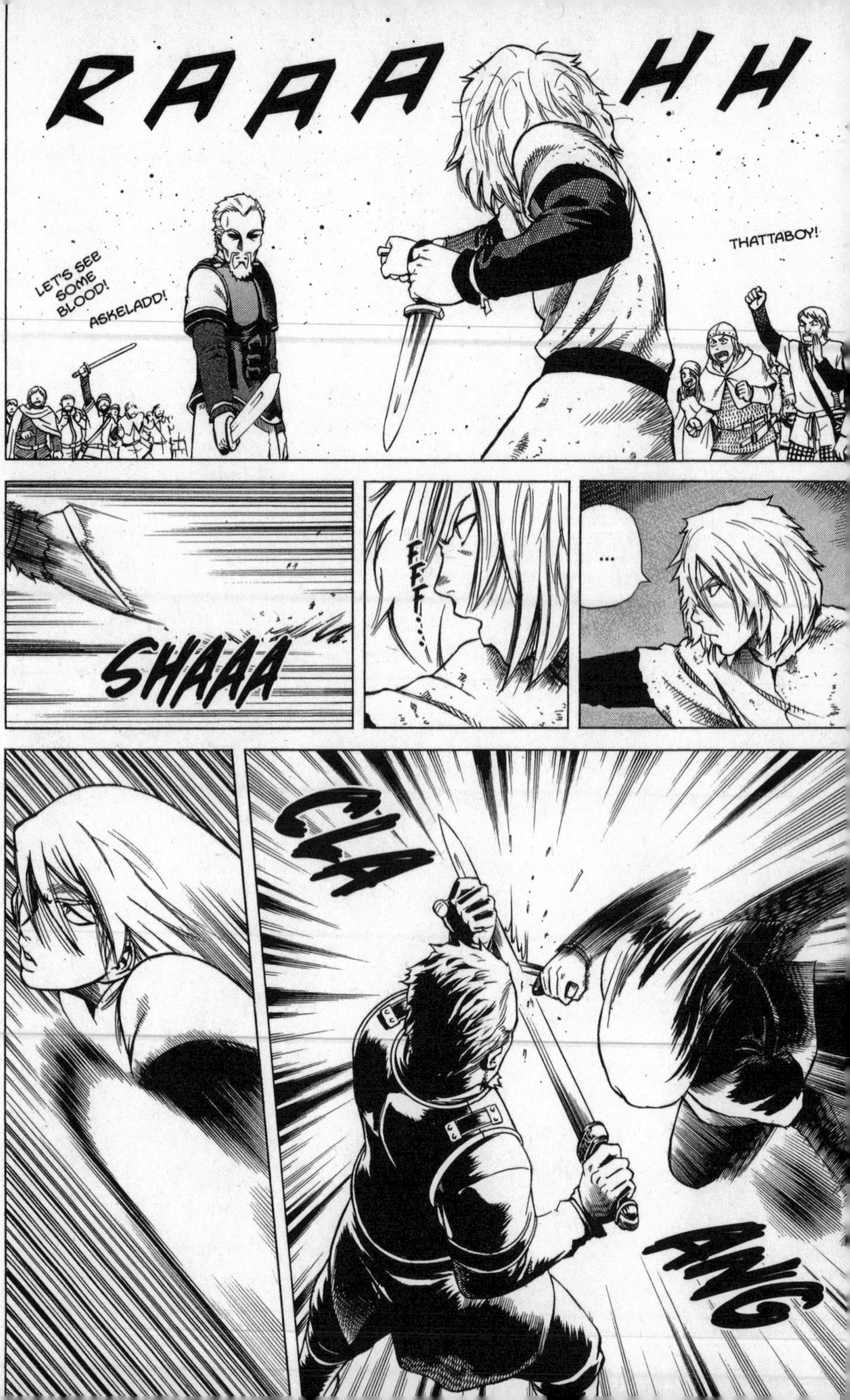
RAAAHH
THATTABOY!
LET'S SEE SOME BLOOD!
ASKELADD!
...
FFF...
SHAAA
CLA
ANG

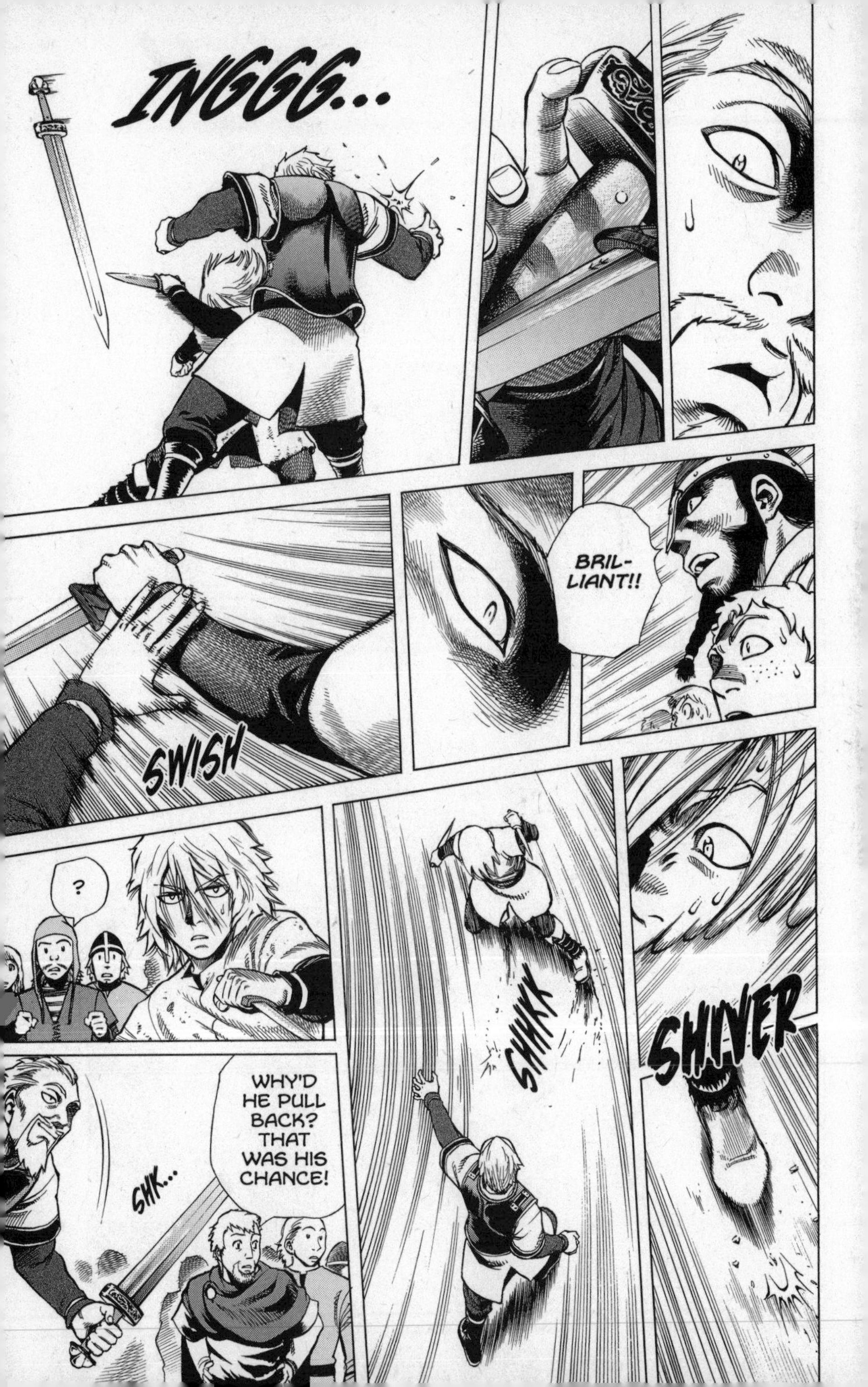
INGGG...
BRIL-LIANT!!
SWISH
SHIVER
SHHK
?
WHY'D HE PULL BACK? THAT WAS HIS CHANCE!
SHK...

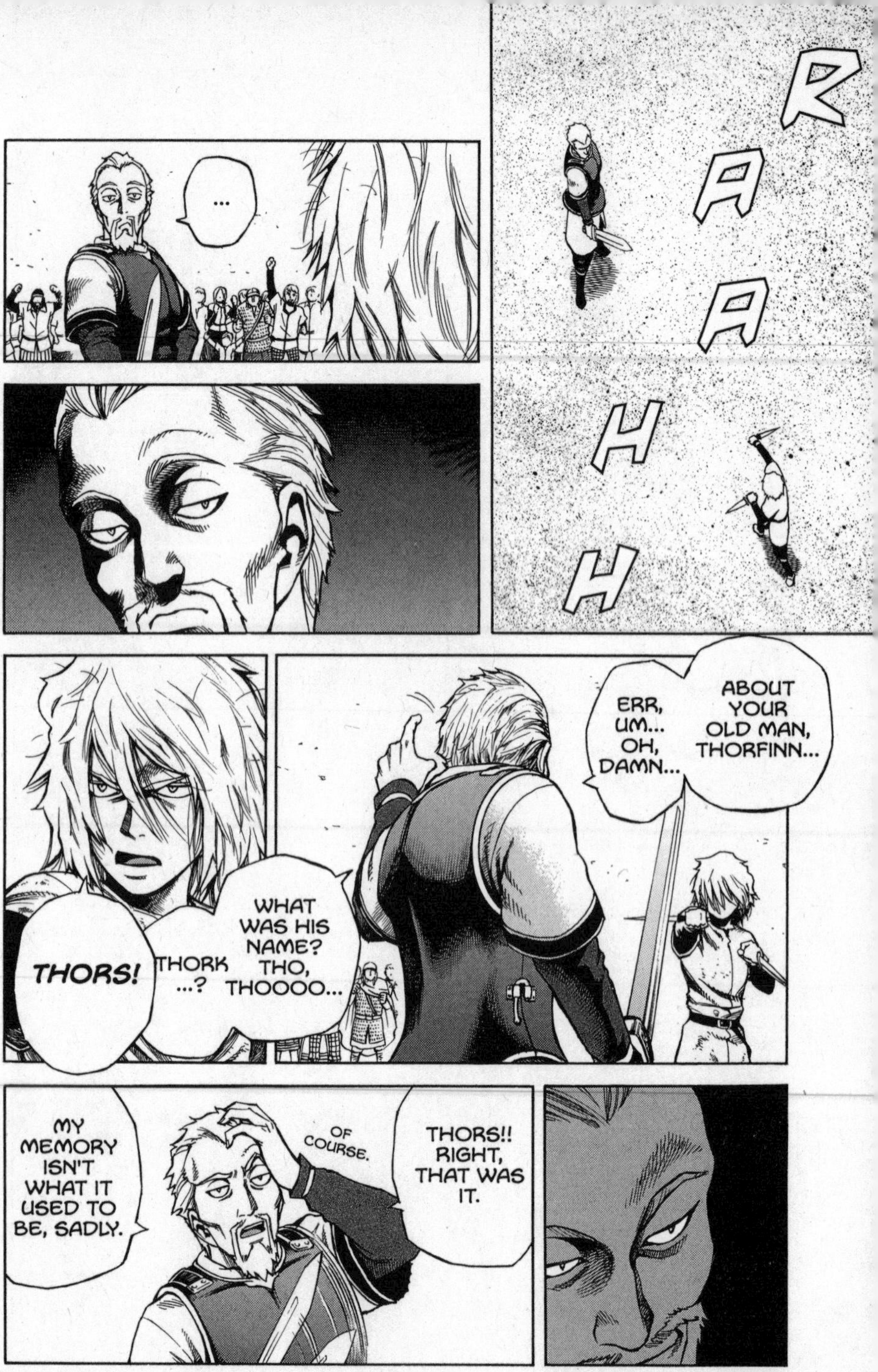
RAAHHH
...
ABOUT YOUR OLD MAN, THORFINN...
ERR, UM... OH, DAMN...
WHAT WAS HIS NAME? THO, THOOOO...
THORK ...?
THORS!
THORS!! RIGHT, THAT WAS IT.
OF COURSE.
MY MEMORY ISN'T WHAT IT USED TO BE, SADLY.

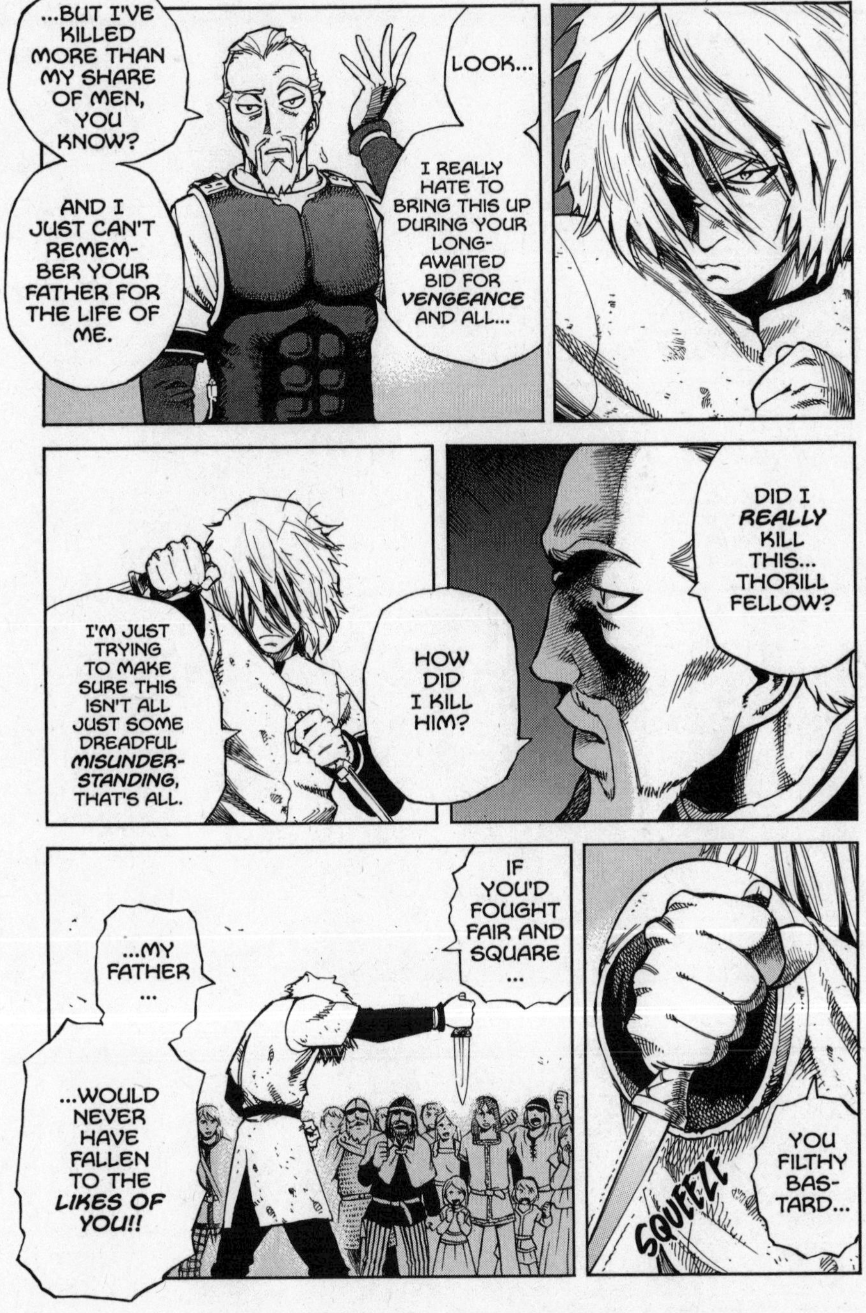

LOOK...
I REALLY HATE TO BRING THIS UP DURING YOUR LONG-AWAITED BID FOR *VENGEANCE* AND ALL...
...BUT I'VE KILLED MORE THAN MY SHARE OF MEN, YOU KNOW?
AND I JUST CAN'T REMEM-BER YOUR FATHER FOR THE LIFE OF ME.
DID I *REALLY* KILL THIS... THORILL FELLOW?
HOW DID I KILL HIM?
I'M JUST TRYING TO MAKE SURE THIS ISN'T ALL JUST SOME DREADFUL *MISUNDER-STANDING*, THAT'S ALL.
YOU FILTHY BAS-TARD...
SQUEEZE
IF YOU'D FOUGHT FAIR AND SQUARE ...
...MY FATHER ...
...WOULD NEVER HAVE FALLEN TO THE *LIKES OF YOU!!*

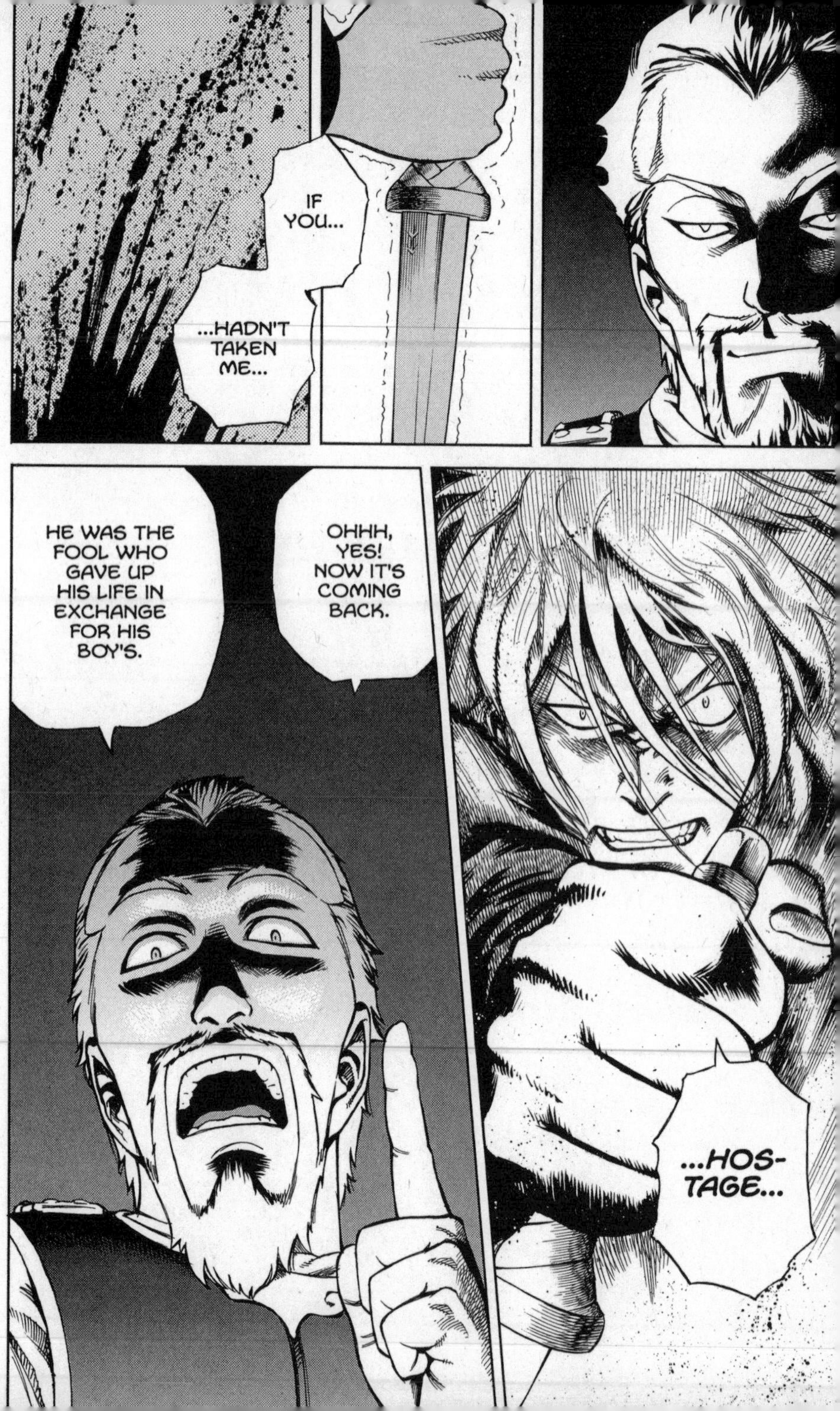
IF YOU...
...HADN'T TAKEN ME...
...HOS-TAGE...
OHHH, YES! NOW IT'S COMING BACK.
HE WAS THE FOOL WHO GAVE UP HIS LIFE IN EXCHANGE FOR HIS BOY'S.

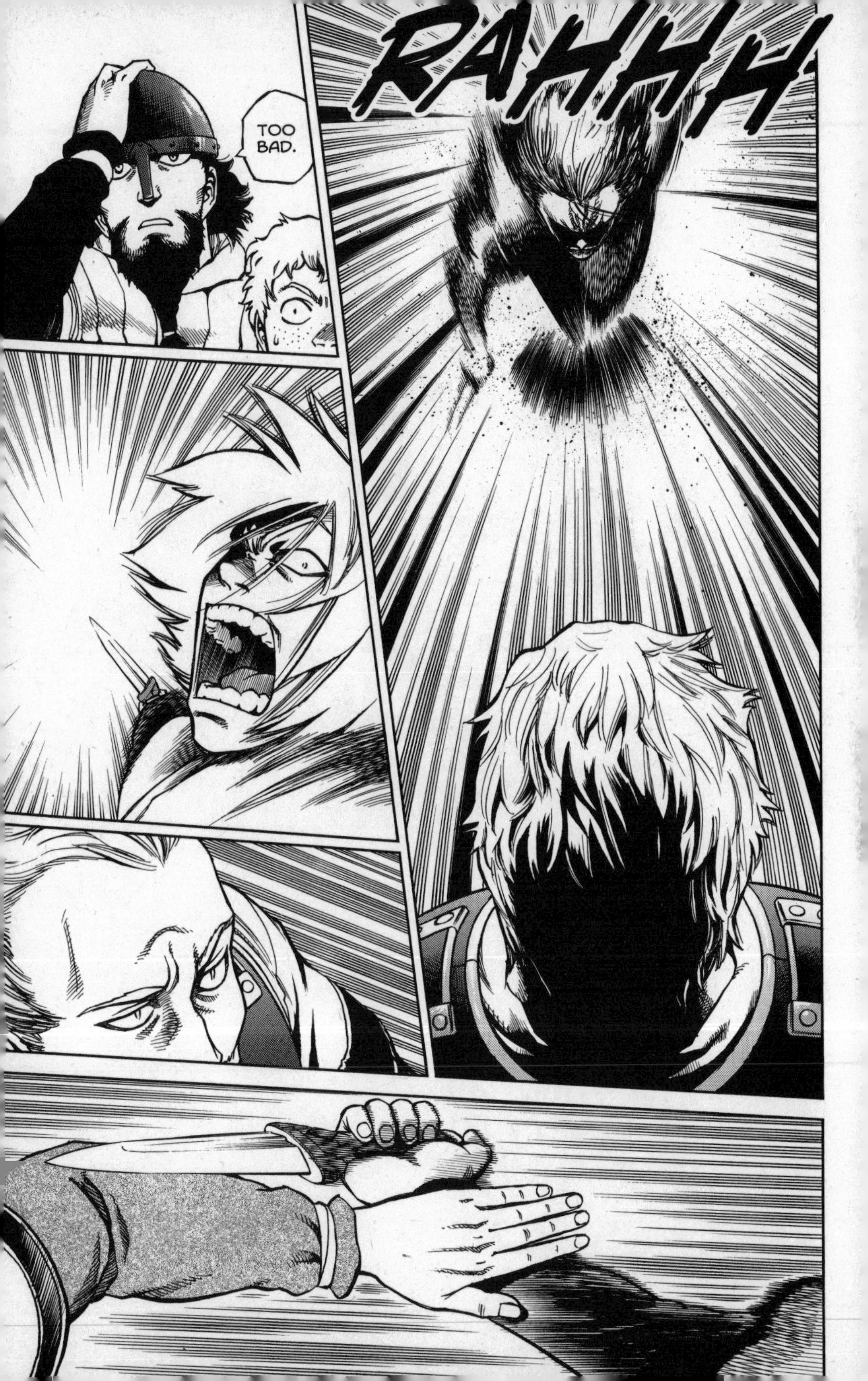
RAHHH
TOO BAD.

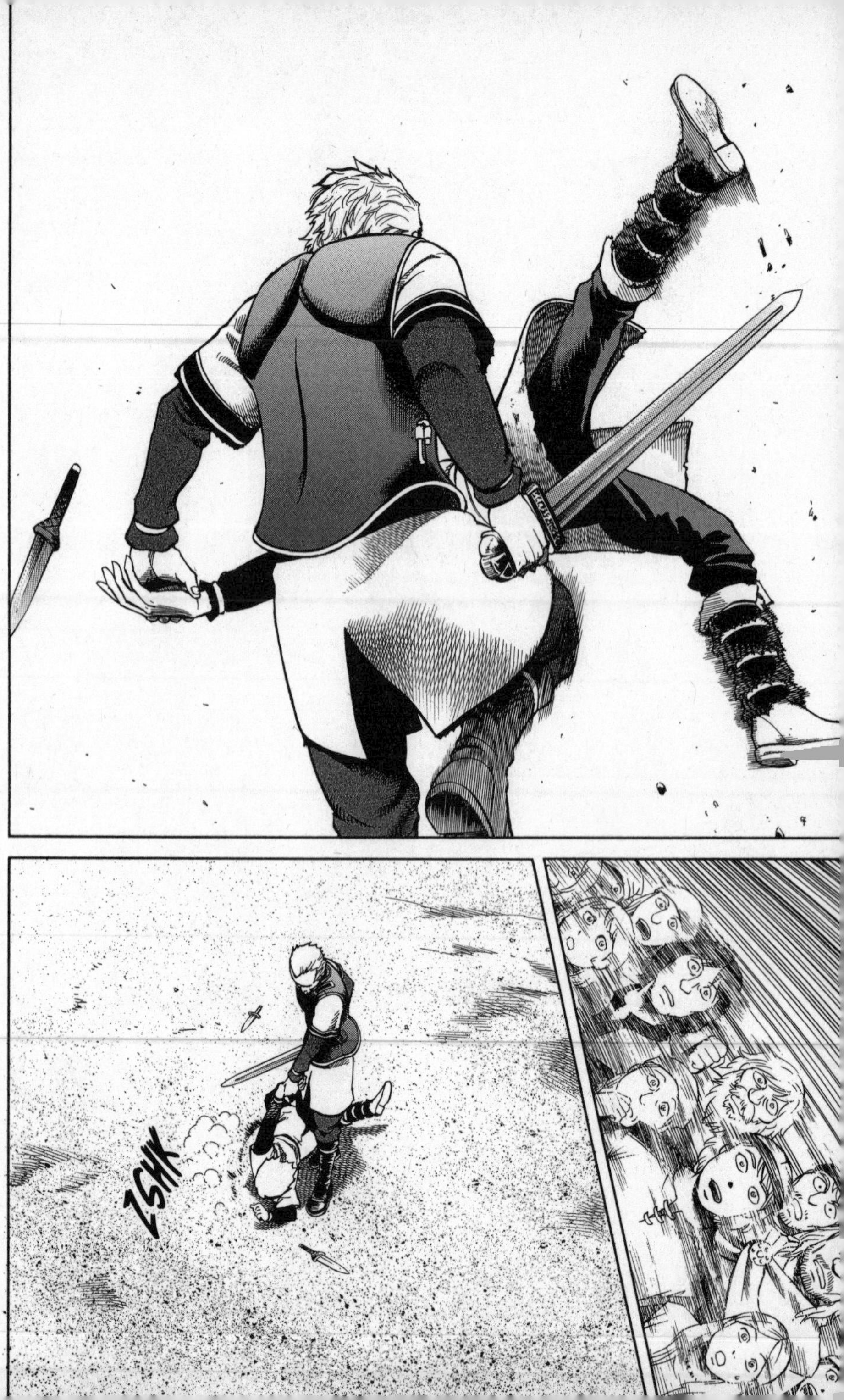
ZSHK

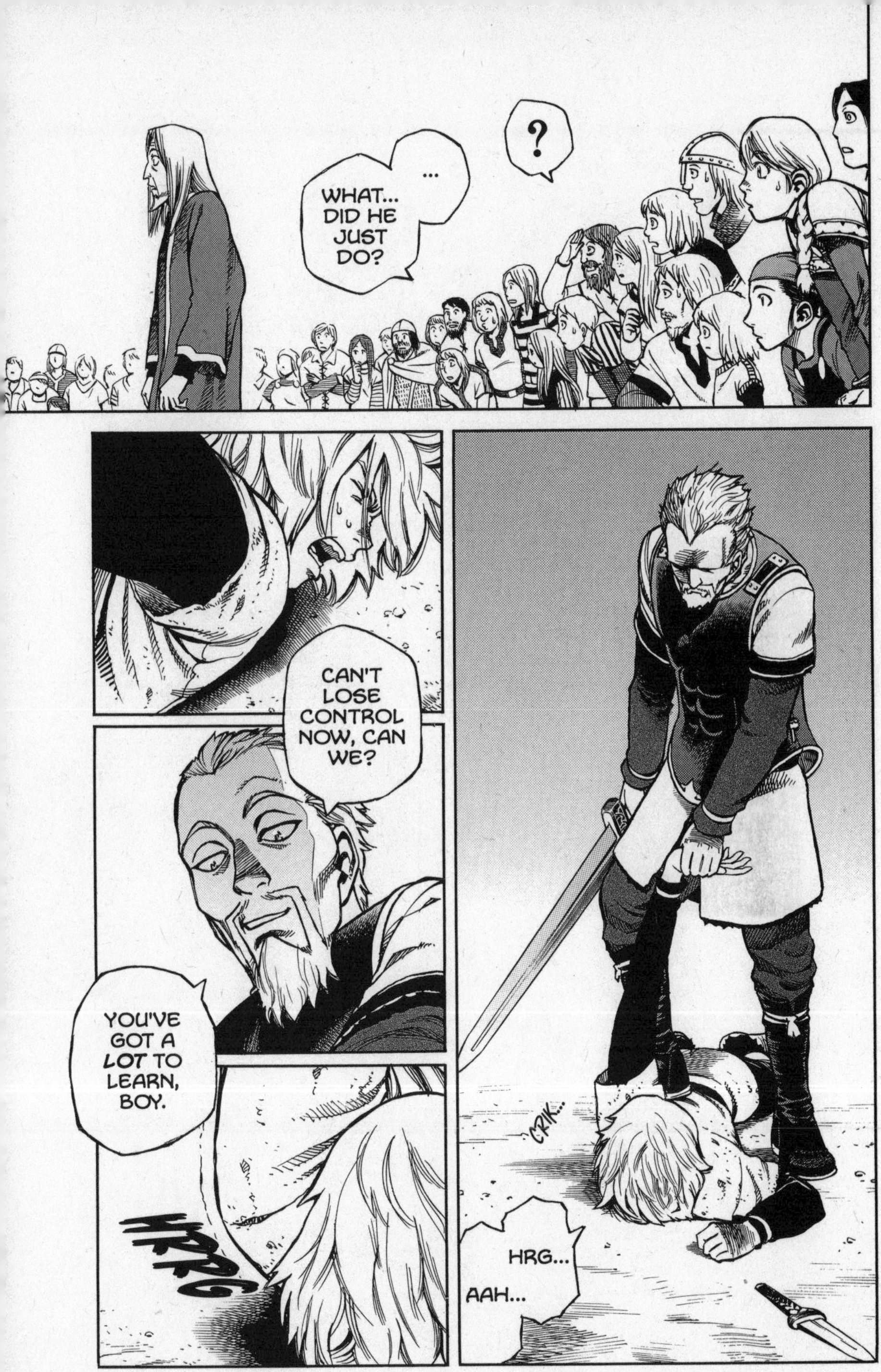
?
...
WHAT... DID HE JUST DO?
CRIK...
HRG...
AAH...
CAN'T LOSE CONTROL NOW, CAN WE?
YOU'VE GOT A *LOT* TO LEARN, BOY.
HRRG

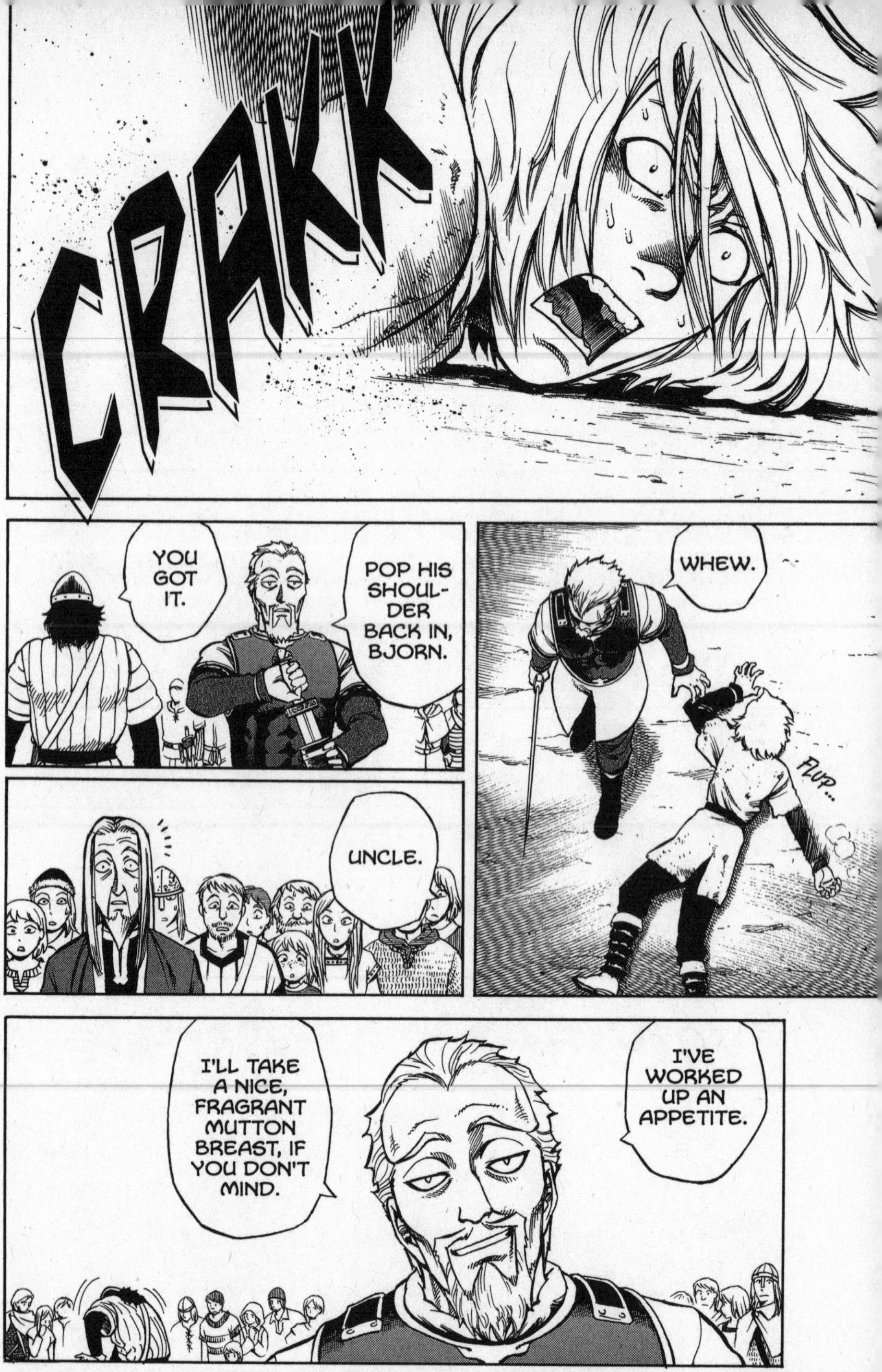
CRAKK
WHEW.
FLUP...
POP HIS SHOULDER BACK IN, BJORN.
YOU GOT IT.
UNCLE.
I'VE WORKED UP AN APPETITE.
I'LL TAKE A NICE, FRAGRANT MUTTON BREAST, IF YOU DON'T MIND.

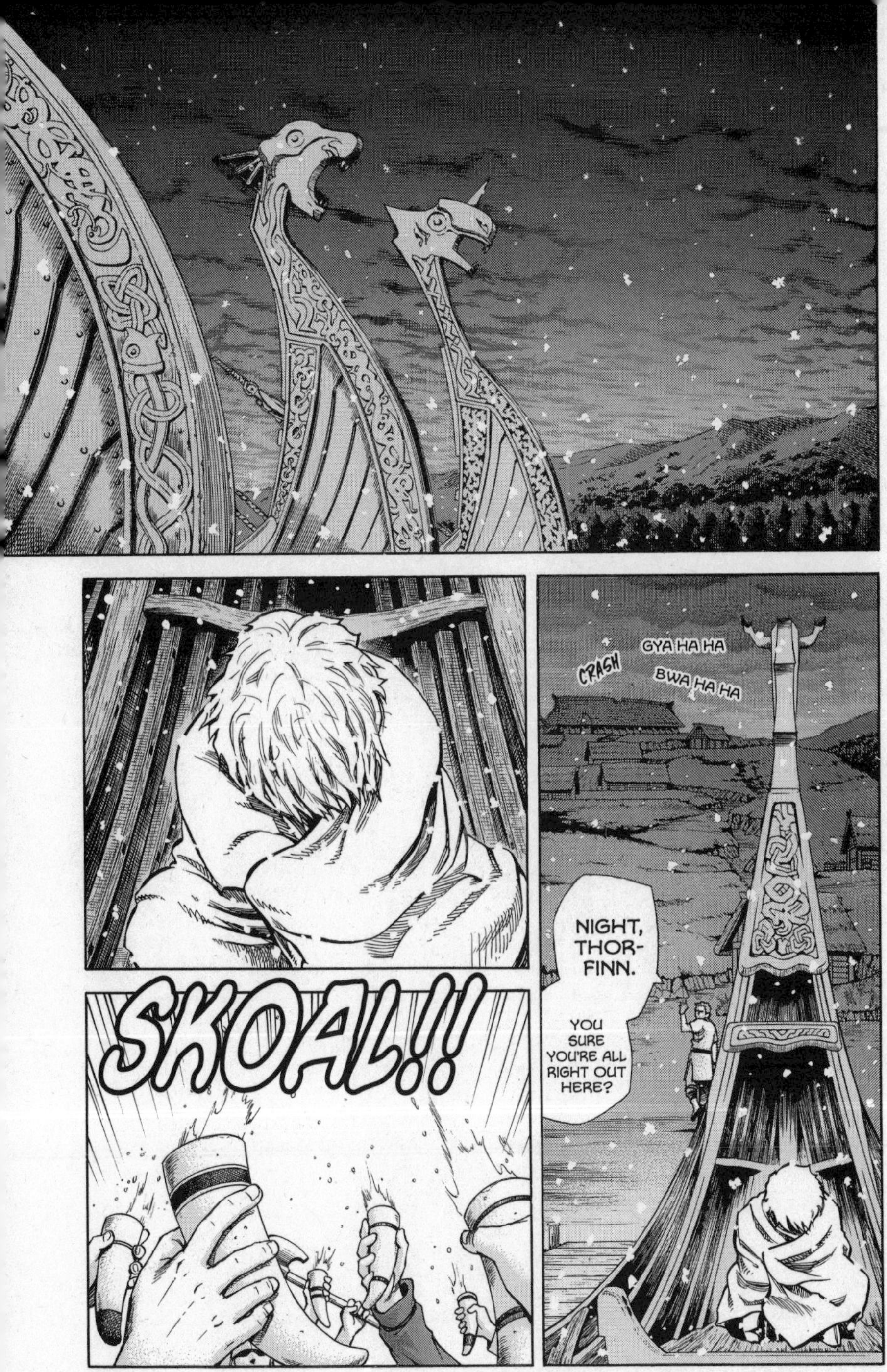
GYA HA HA
CRASH
BWA HA HA
NIGHT, THOR-FINN.
YOU SURE YOU'RE ALL RIGHT OUT HERE?
SKOAL!!

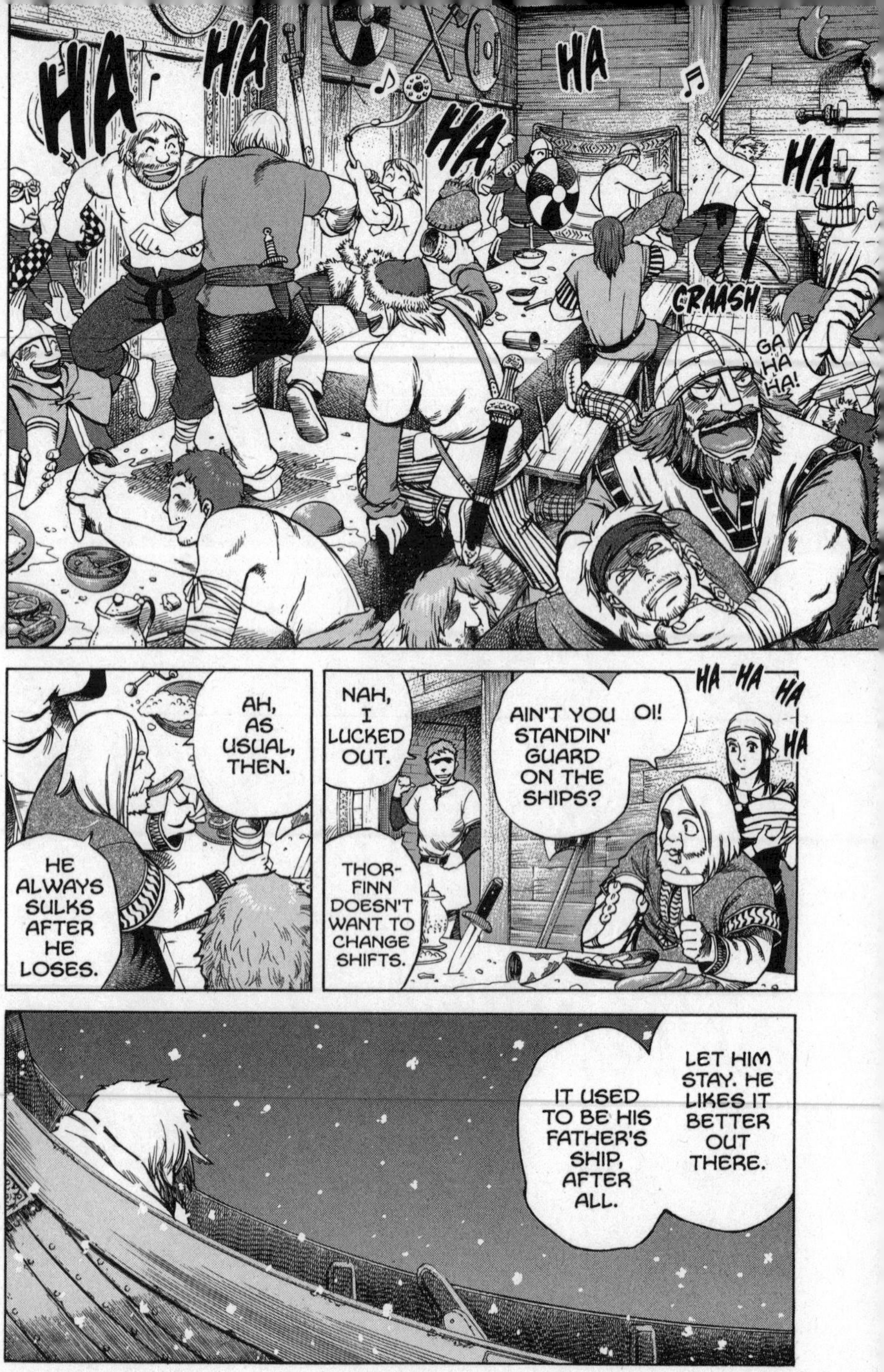
HA
HA
HA
HA
HA
CRAASH
GA HA HA!
HA HA HA HA
OI!
AIN'T YOU STANDIN' GUARD ON THE SHIPS?
NAH, I LUCKED OUT.
THOR-FINN DOESN'T WANT TO CHANGE SHIFTS.
AH, AS USUAL, THEN.
HE ALWAYS SULKS AFTER HE LOSES.
LET HIM STAY. HE LIKES IT BETTER OUT THERE.
IT USED TO BE HIS FATHER'S SHIP, AFTER ALL.

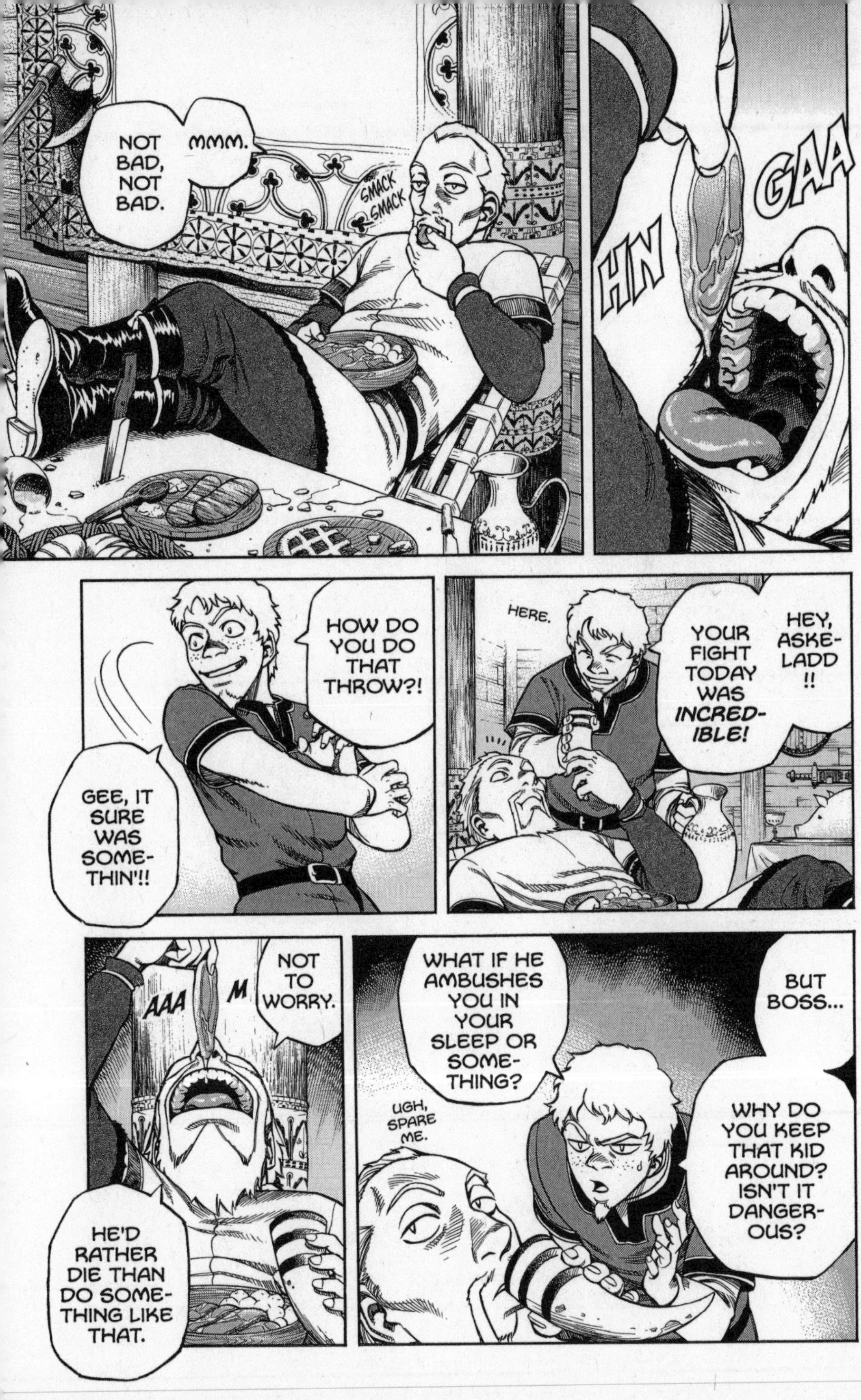
HN GAA
SMACK SMACK
MMM.
NOT BAD, NOT BAD.
HEY, ASKE-LADD!!
YOUR FIGHT TODAY WAS INCRED-IBLE!
HERE.
HOW DO YOU DO THAT THROW?!
GEE, IT SURE WAS SOME-THIN'!!
BUT BOSS...
WHY DO YOU KEEP THAT KID AROUND? ISN'T IT DANGER-OUS?
WHAT IF HE AMBUSHES YOU IN YOUR SLEEP OR SOME-THING?
UGH, SPARE ME.
NOT TO WORRY.
AAA M
HE'D RATHER DIE THAN DO SOME-THING LIKE THAT.

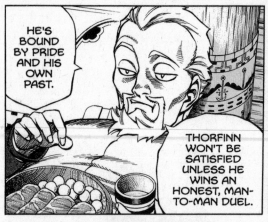

HOW COME?
HOW COME? WELL, HE'S A WARRIOR, FOR ONE THING.
THORFINN WON'T BE SATISFIED UNLESS HE WINS AN HONEST, MAN-TO-MAN DUEL.
HE'S BOUND BY PRIDE AND HIS OWN PAST.
HUH... PRIDE?
CRAAASH
NOT YOU AGAIN, HORDA-LAND!
DO YOU HAVE ANY IDEA WHAT THAT PLATTER OF FOOD COSTS?! DO YOU?!
YOUR DAYS AS A LADY ARE LONG PAST, GIRL!
YOU'RE A SLAVE, AND YOU'LL LEARN TO ACT LIKE ONE!
I DON'T KNOW MUCH ABOUT SUCH THINGS...
...BUT IF I HAD TO LIVE WITHOUT PRIDE, I RECKON I'D RATHER KILL MYSELF.
HEH HEH.
WHAT A SHAME.

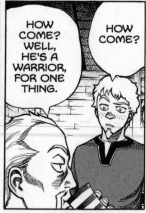

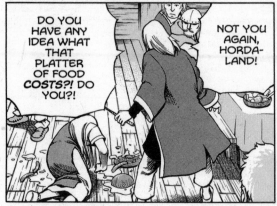

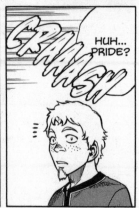

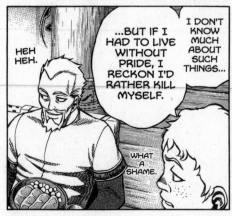

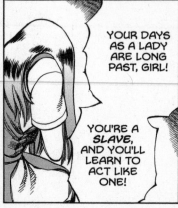

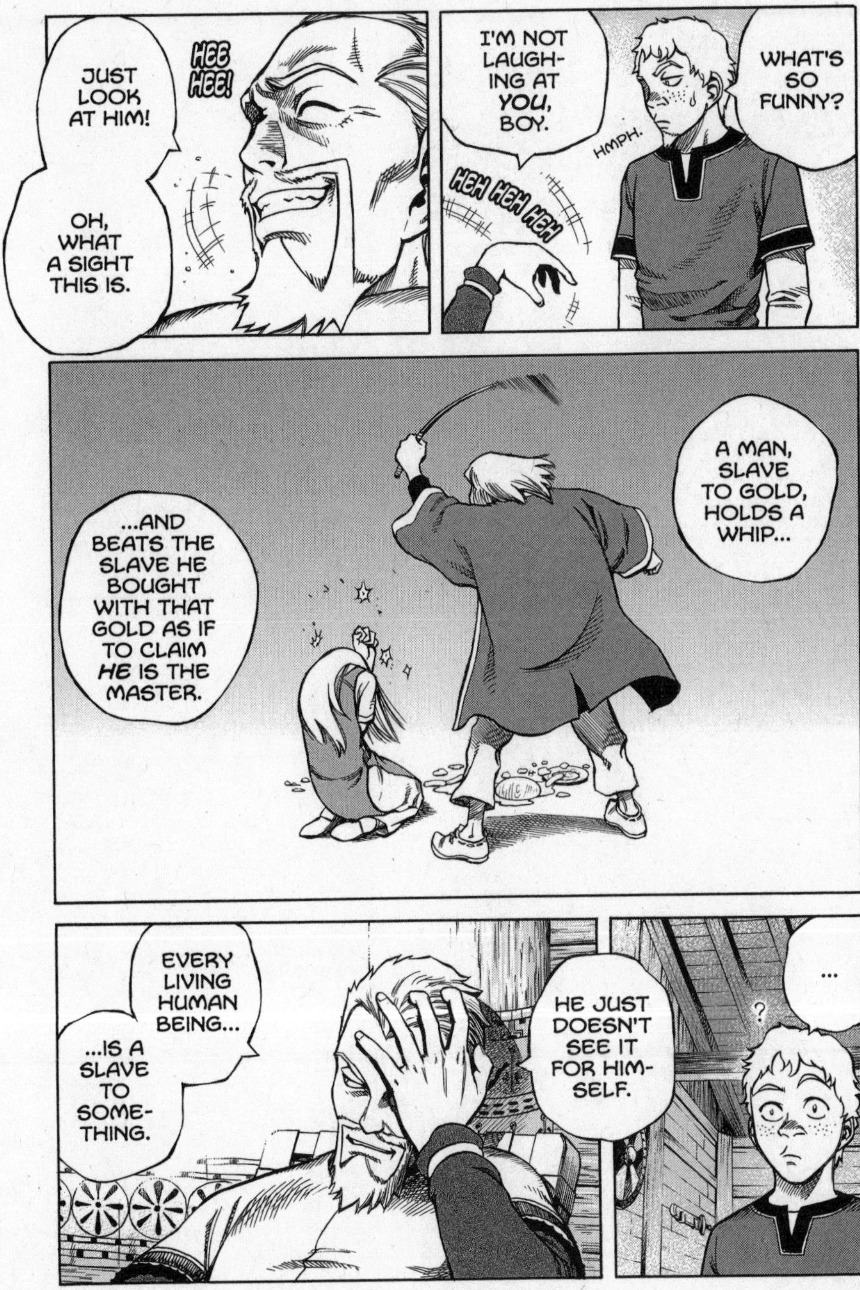
WHAT'S SO FUNNY?
I'M NOT LAUGHING AT YOU, BOY.
HMPH.
HEH HEH HEH HEH
HEE HEE!
JUST LOOK AT HIM!
OH, WHAT A SIGHT THIS IS.
A MAN, SLAVE TO GOLD, HOLDS A WHIP...
...AND BEATS THE SLAVE HE BOUGHT WITH THAT GOLD AS IF TO CLAIM *HE* IS THE MASTER.
...
?
HE JUST DOESN'T SEE IT FOR HIMSELF.
EVERY LIVING HUMAN BEING...
...IS A SLAVE TO SOMETHING.

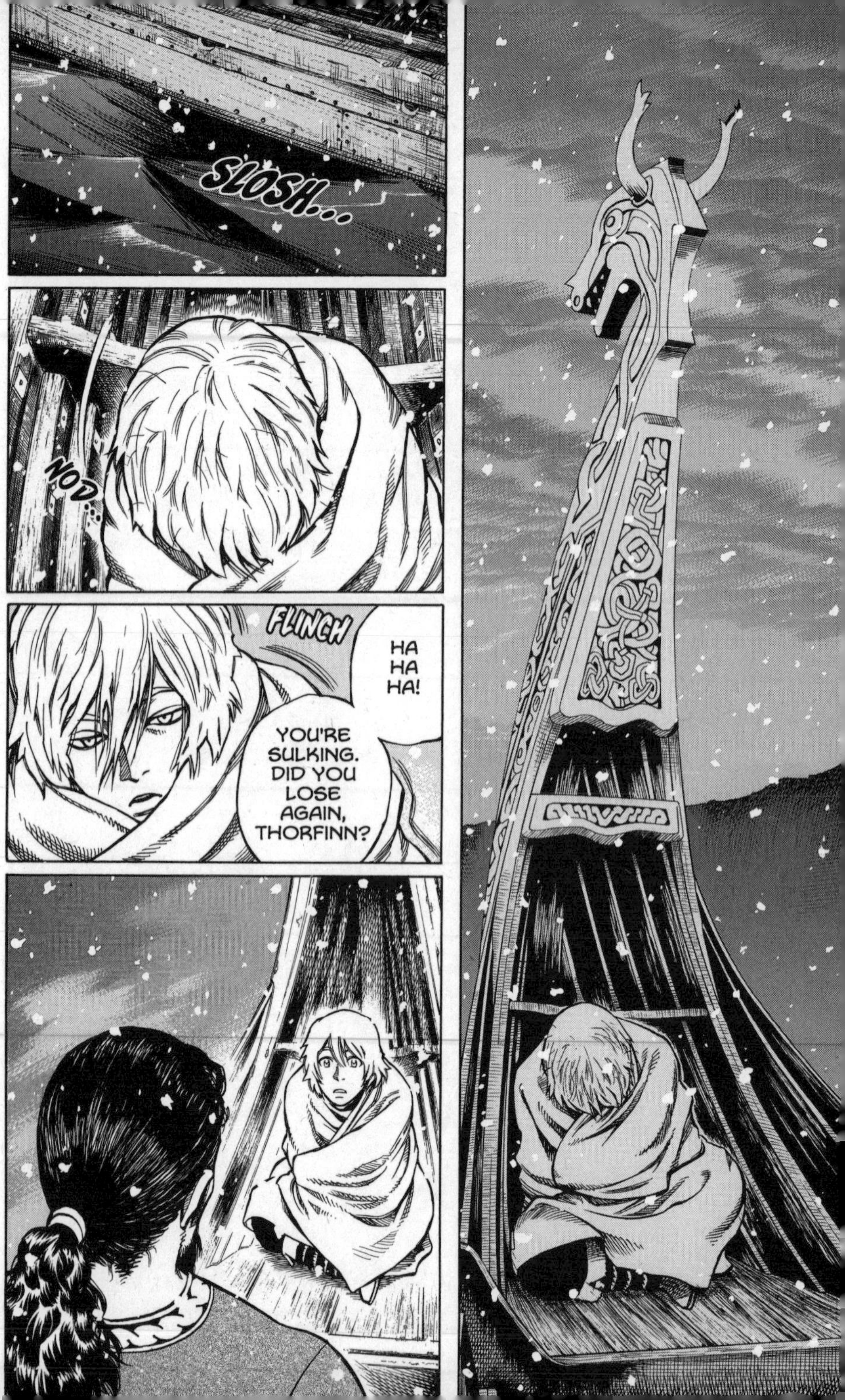
SLOSH...
NOD...
FLINCH
HA HA HA!
YOU'RE SULKING. DID YOU LOSE AGAIN, THORFINN?

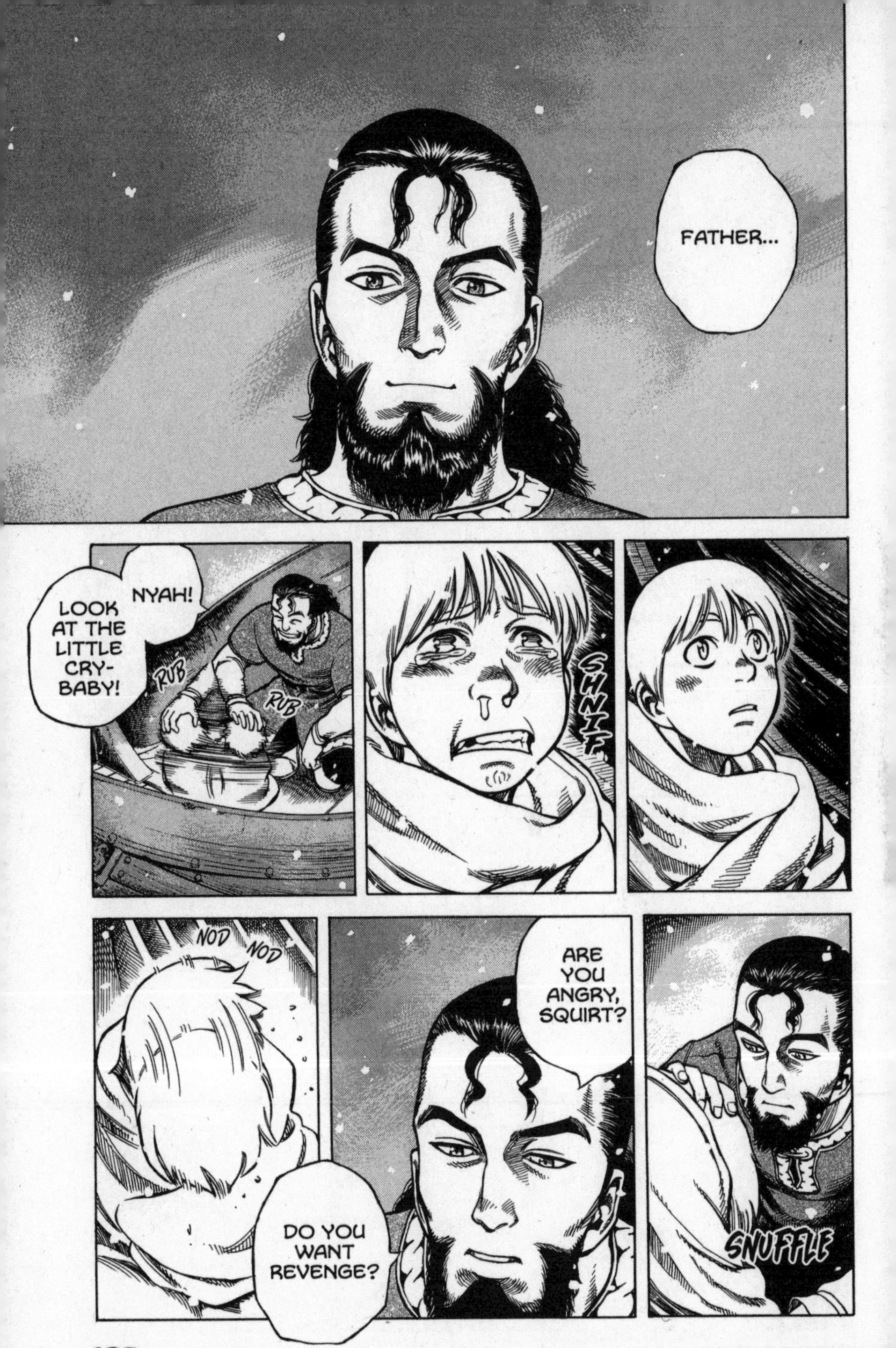
FATHER...
SHNIF
NYAH!
LOOK AT THE LITTLE CRY-BABY!
RUB
RUB
SNUFFLE
ARE YOU ANGRY, SQUIRT?
NOD
NOD
DO YOU WANT REVENGE?

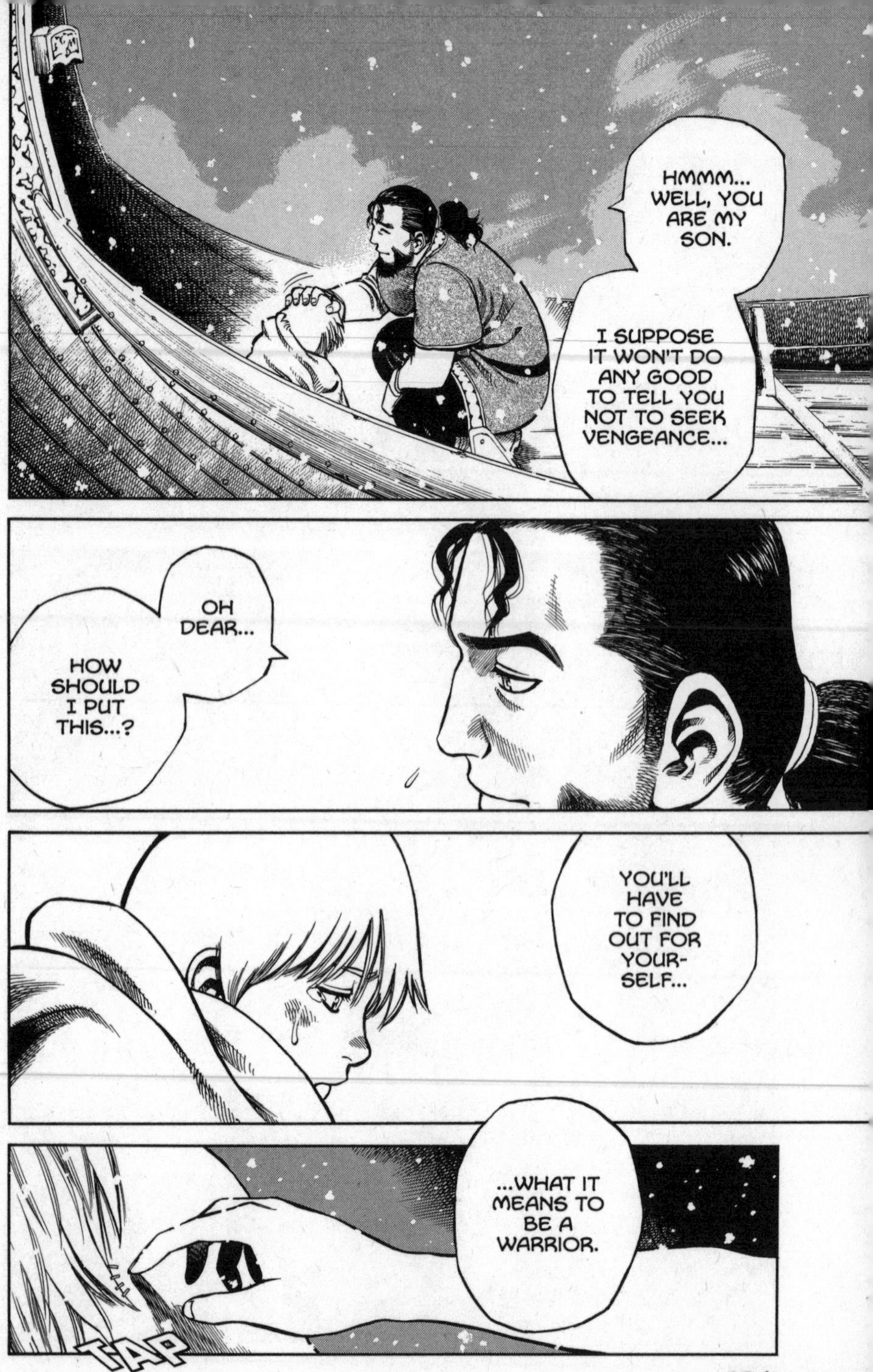
HMMM... WELL, YOU ARE MY SON.
I SUPPOSE IT WON'T DO ANY GOOD TO TELL YOU NOT TO SEEK VENGEANCE...
OH DEAR...
HOW SHOULD I PUT THIS...?
YOU'LL HAVE TO FIND OUT FOR YOUR-SELF...
...WHAT IT MEANS TO BE A WARRIOR.
TAP

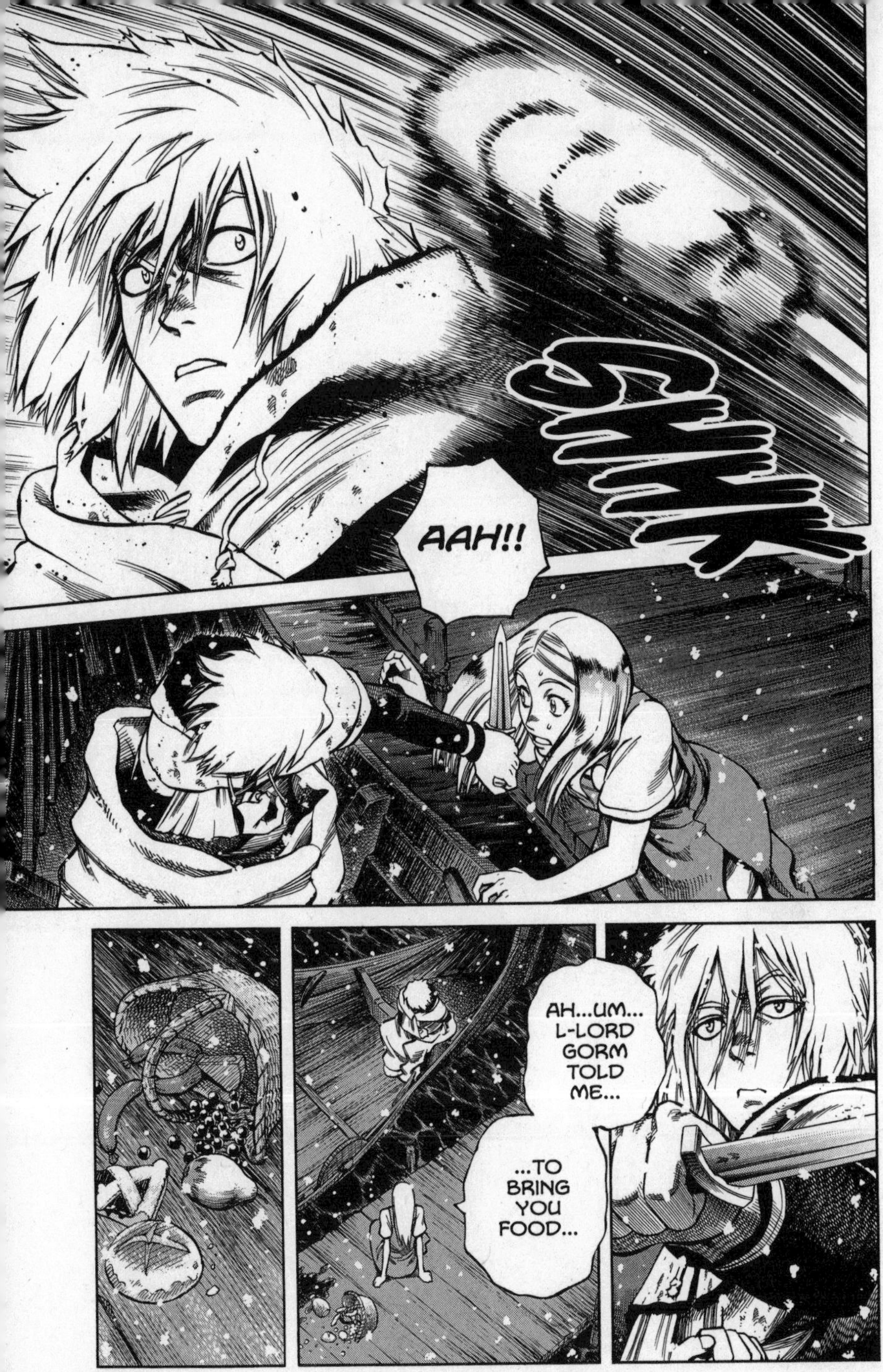
SHNK
AAH!!
AH...UM... L-LORD GORM TOLD ME...
...TO BRING YOU FOOD...

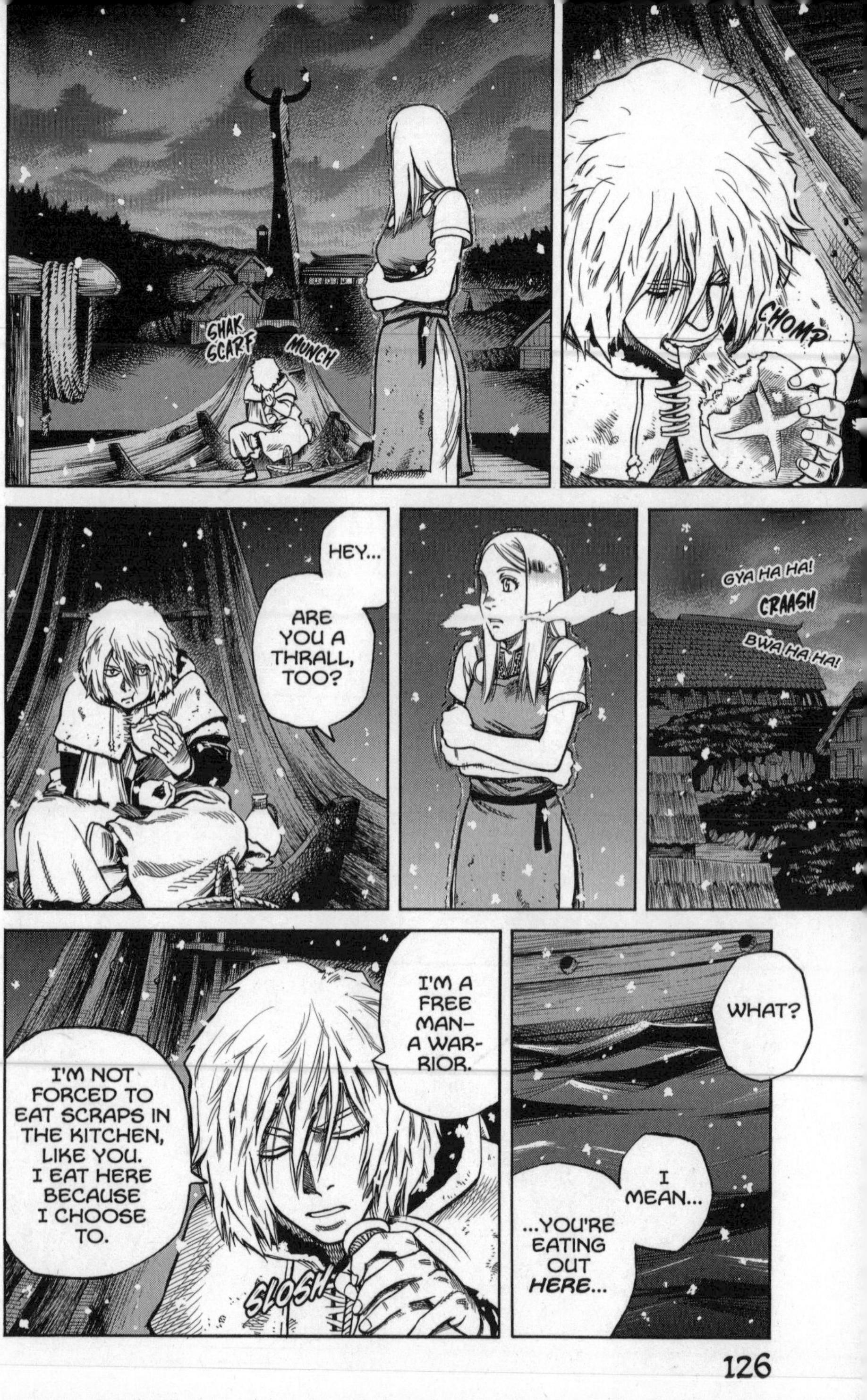
CHOMP
SHAK SCARF
MUNCH
GYA HA HA!
CRAASH
BWA HA HA!
HEY...
ARE YOU A THRALL, TOO?
WHAT?
I MEAN...
...YOU'RE EATING OUT HERE...
I'M A FREE MAN– A WAR-RIOR.
I'M NOT FORCED TO EAT SCRAPS IN THE KITCHEN, LIKE YOU. I EAT HERE BECAUSE I CHOOSE TO.
SLOSH

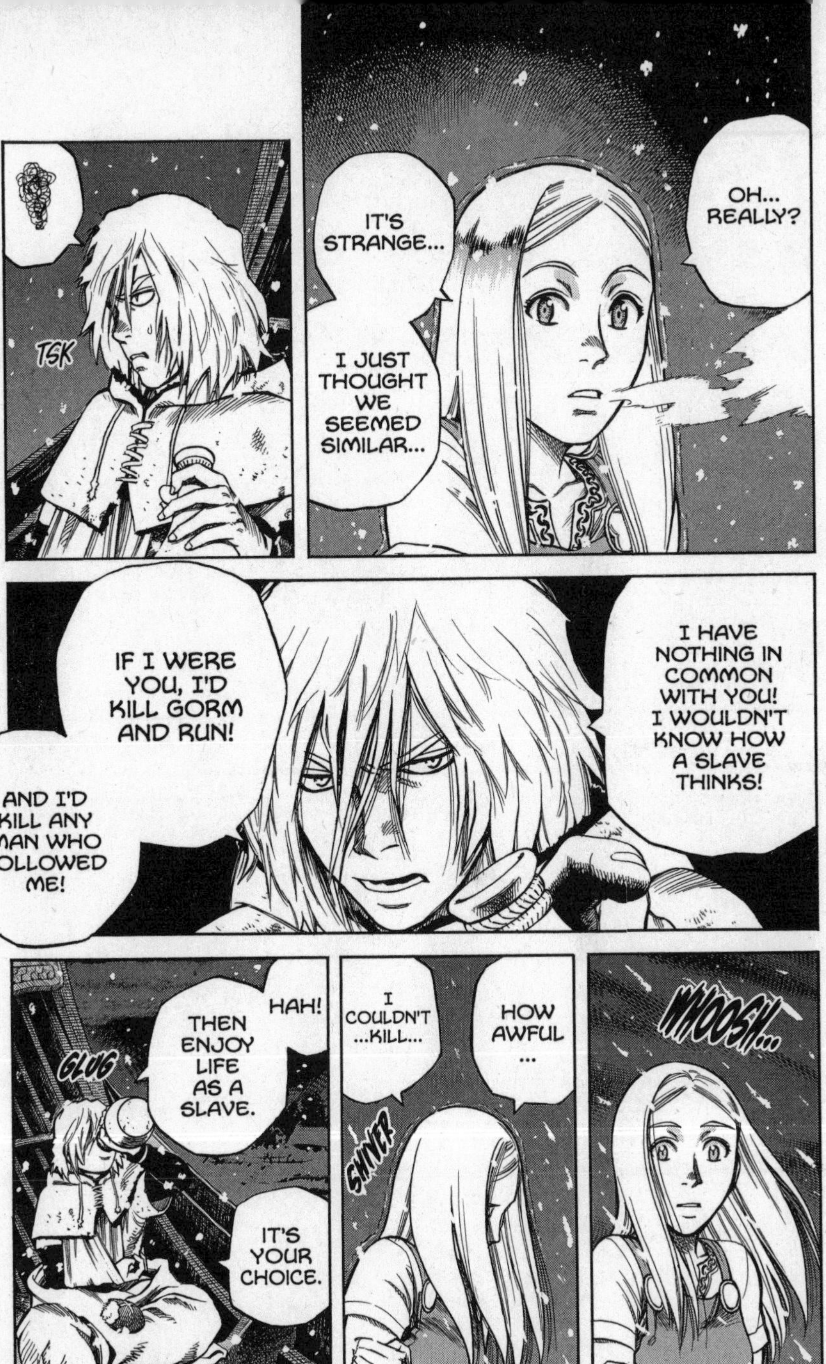
OH... REALLY?
IT'S STRANGE...
I JUST THOUGHT WE SEEMED SIMILAR...
TSK
I HAVE NOTHING IN COMMON WITH YOU! I WOULDN'T KNOW HOW A SLAVE THINKS!
IF I WERE YOU, I'D KILL GORM AND RUN!
AND I'D KILL ANY MAN WHO FOLLOWED ME!
WHOOSH...
HOW AWFUL ...
I COULDN'T ...KILL...
SHIVER
HAH!
THEN ENJOY LIFE AS A SLAVE.
GLUG
IT'S YOUR CHOICE.

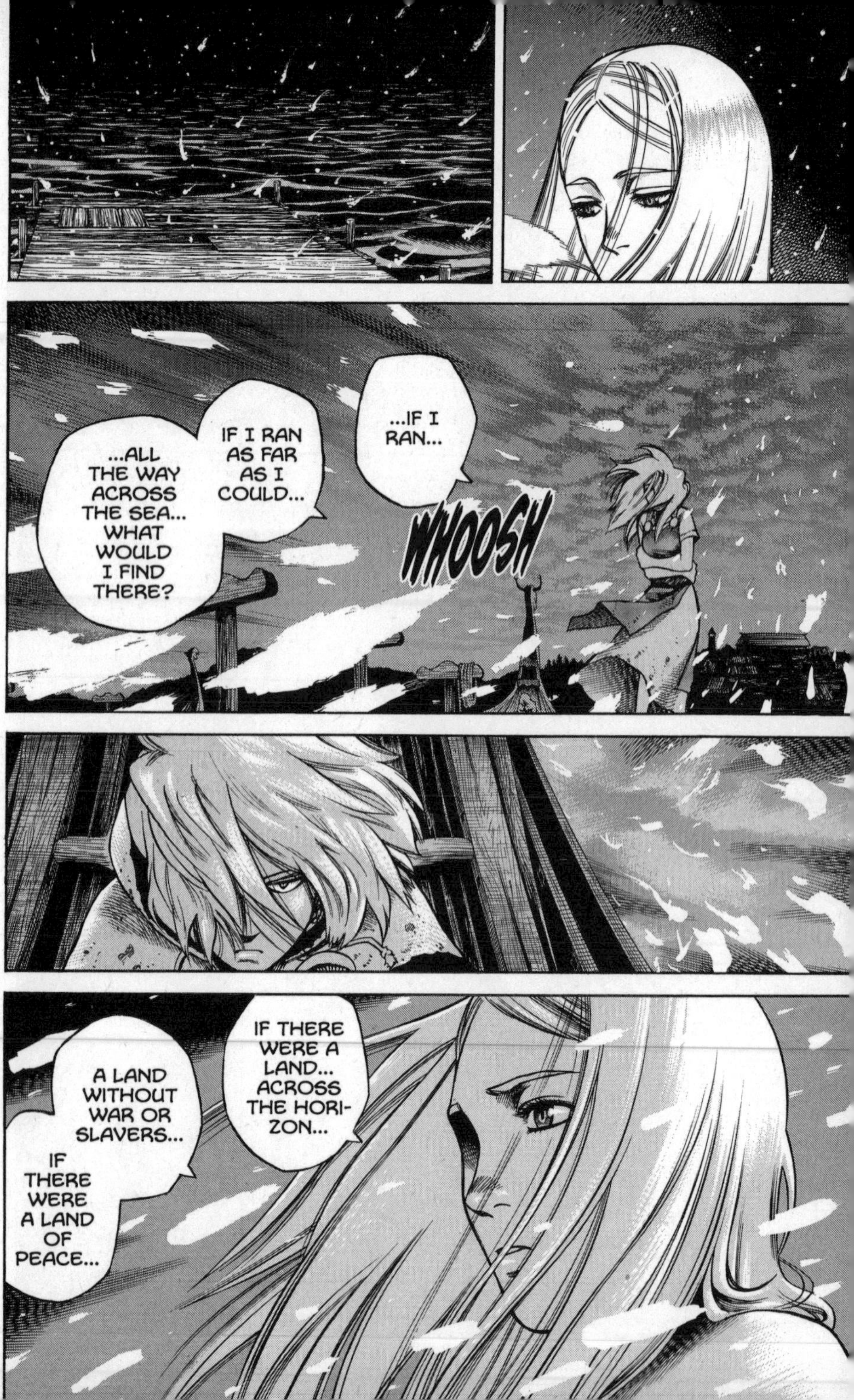
...IF I RAN...
IF I RAN AS FAR AS I COULD...
...ALL THE WAY ACROSS THE SEA... WHAT WOULD I FIND THERE?
WHOOSH
IF THERE WERE A LAND... ACROSS THE HORI-ZON...
A LAND WITHOUT WAR OR SLAVERS...
IF THERE WERE A LAND OF PEACE...

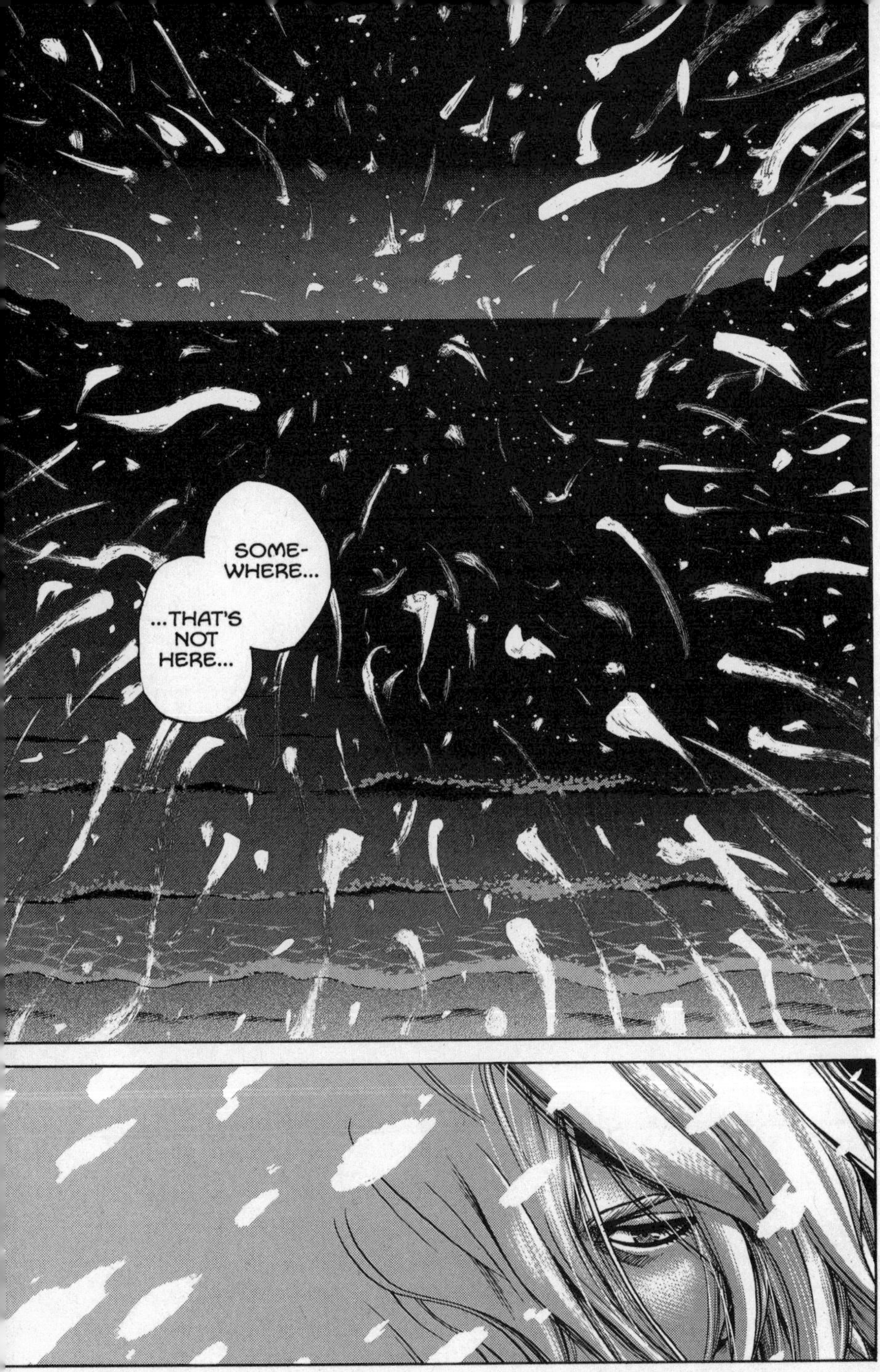
SOME-WHERE...
...THAT'S NOT HERE...

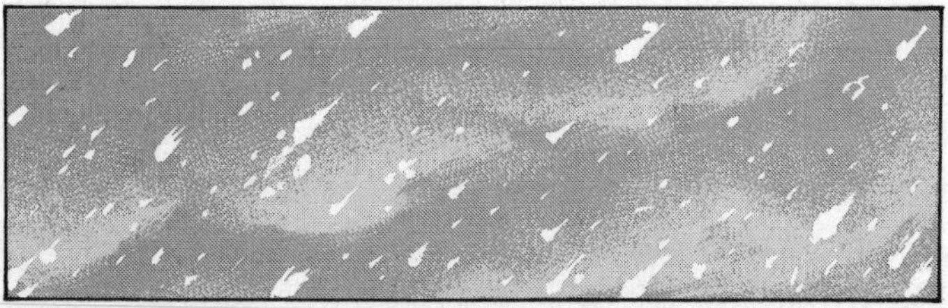
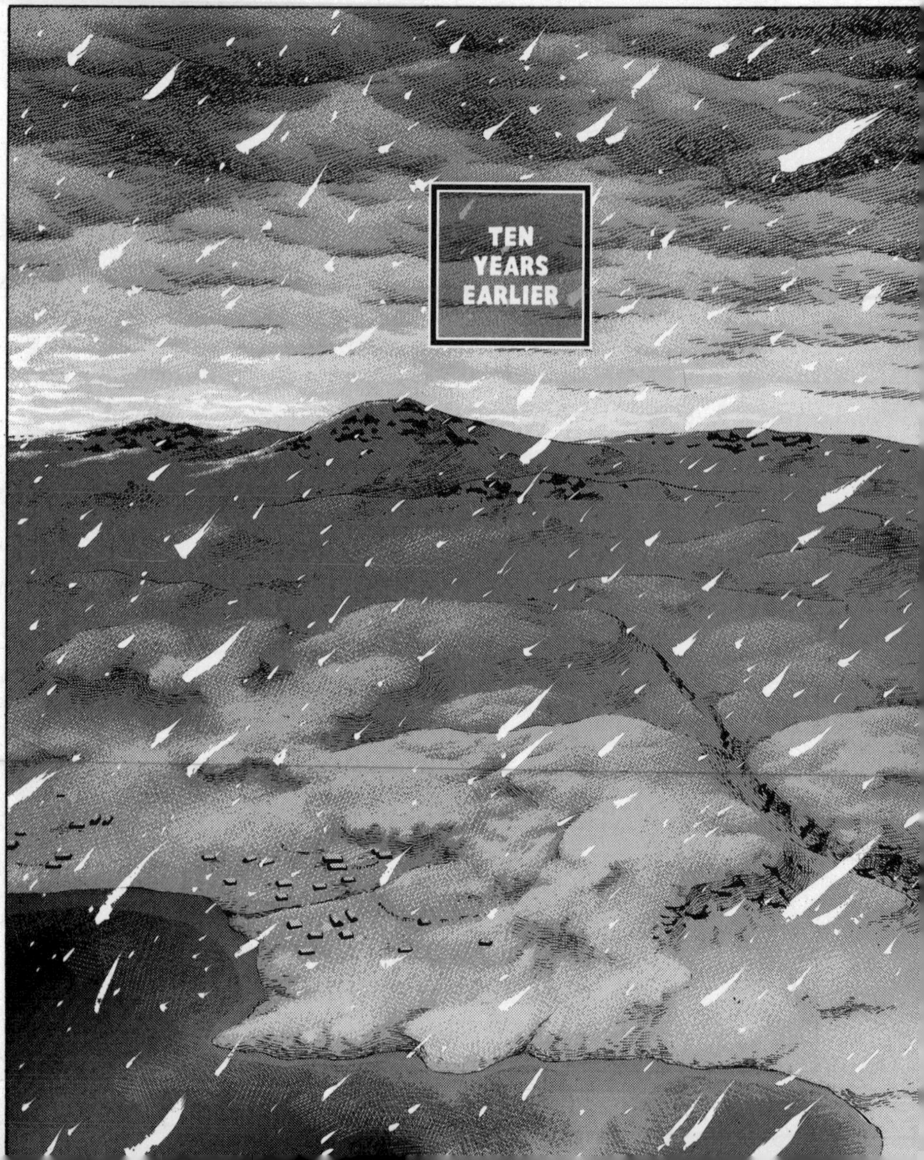
TEN
YEARS
EARLIER

PFFF———...

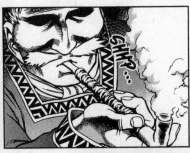

SHH?...

THEN WE LEFT MARK-LAND...

...AND OUR SHIP CHARTED A COURSE FURTHER SOUTH.

POP...

"THERE'S A LAND FAR RICHER AND MORE FERTILE TO THE SOUTH."

THAT'S WHAT THE WIND WAS TELLING US.

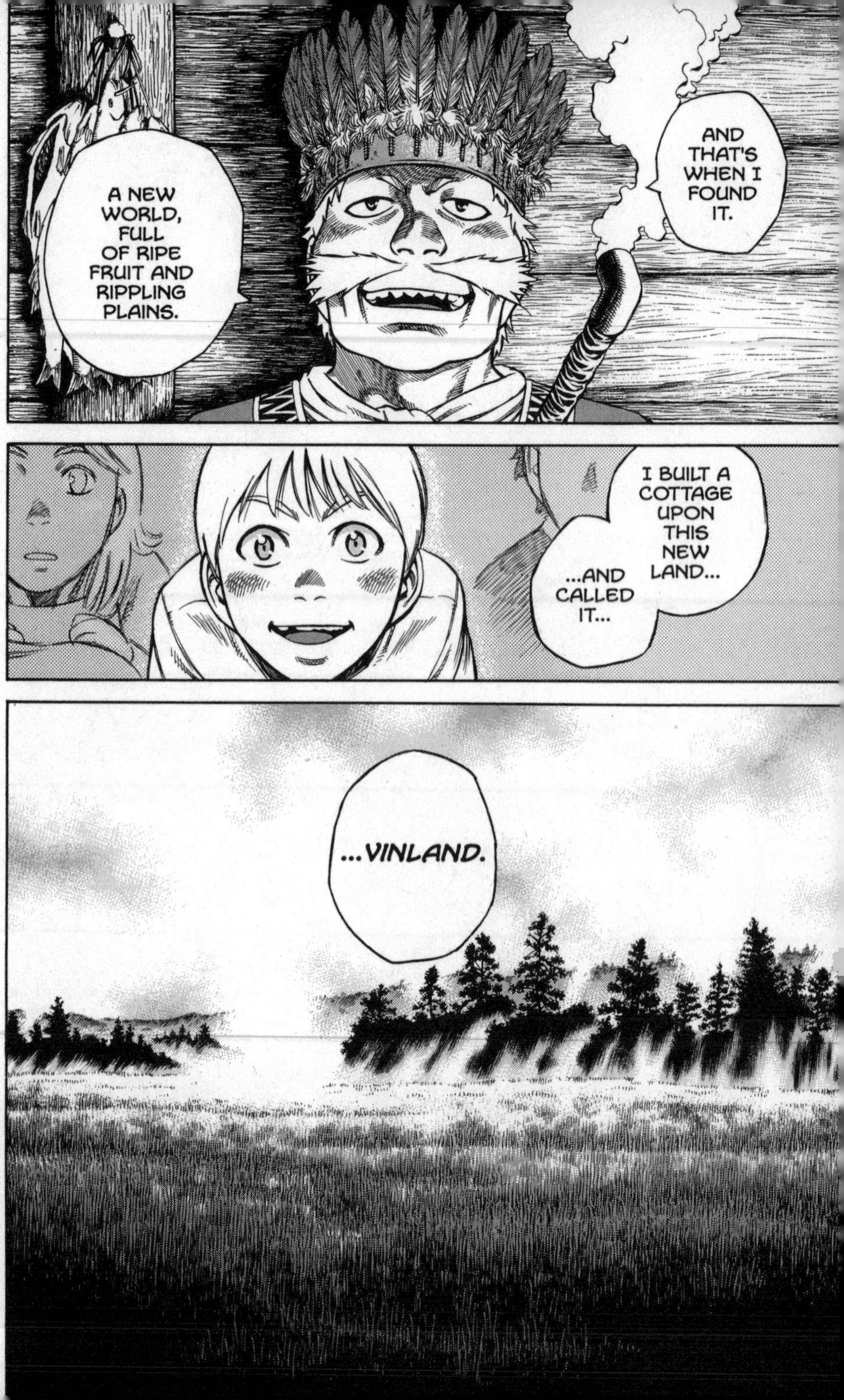
AND THAT'S WHEN I FOUND IT.
A NEW WORLD, FULL OF RIPE FRUIT AND RIPPLING PLAINS.
I BUILT A COTTAGE UPON THIS NEW LAND...
...AND CALLED IT...
...VINLAND.

CHAPTER 2 - END

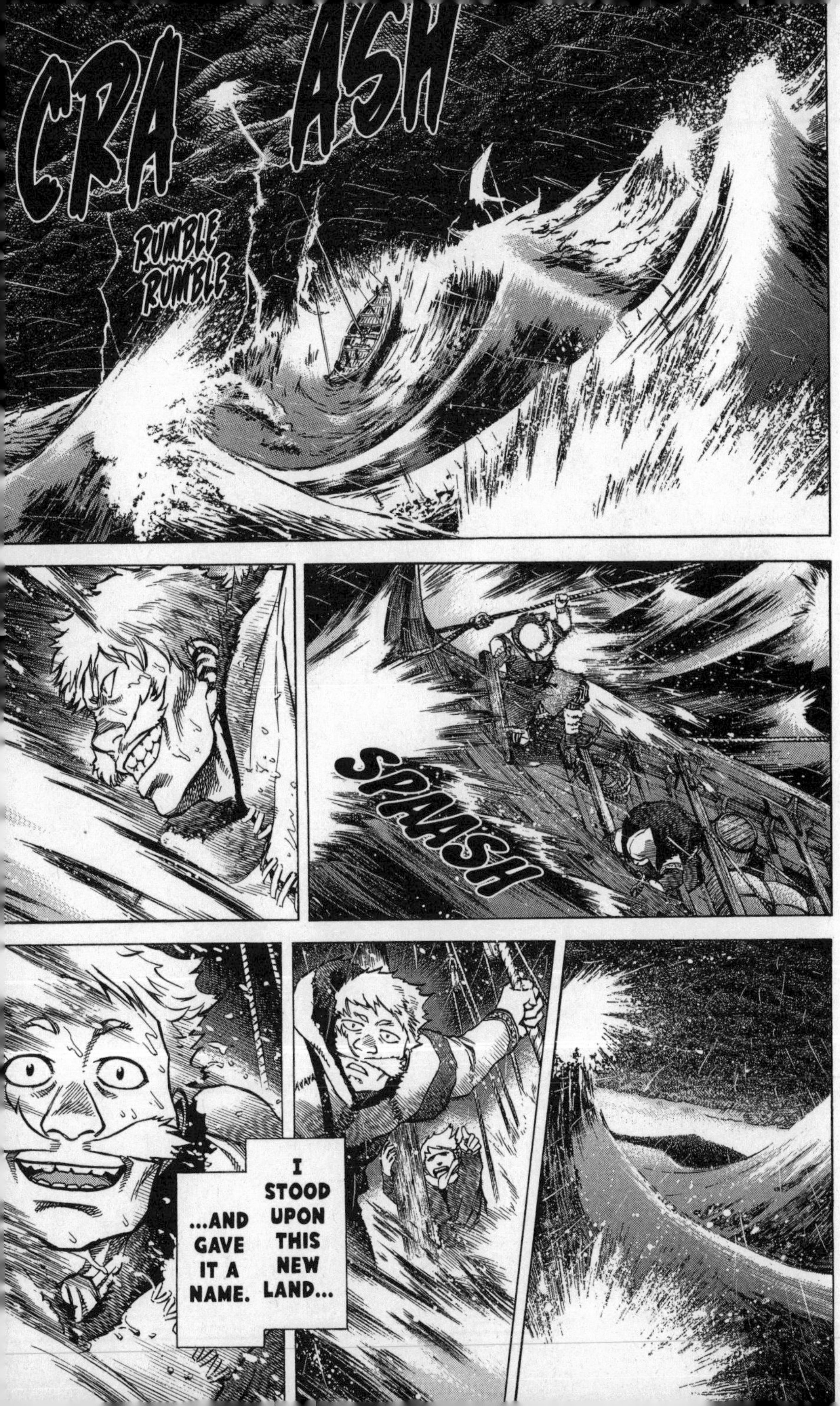
CRA ASH
RUMBLE RUMBLE
SPLASH
I STOOD UPON THIS NEW LAND...
...AND GAVE IT A NAME.

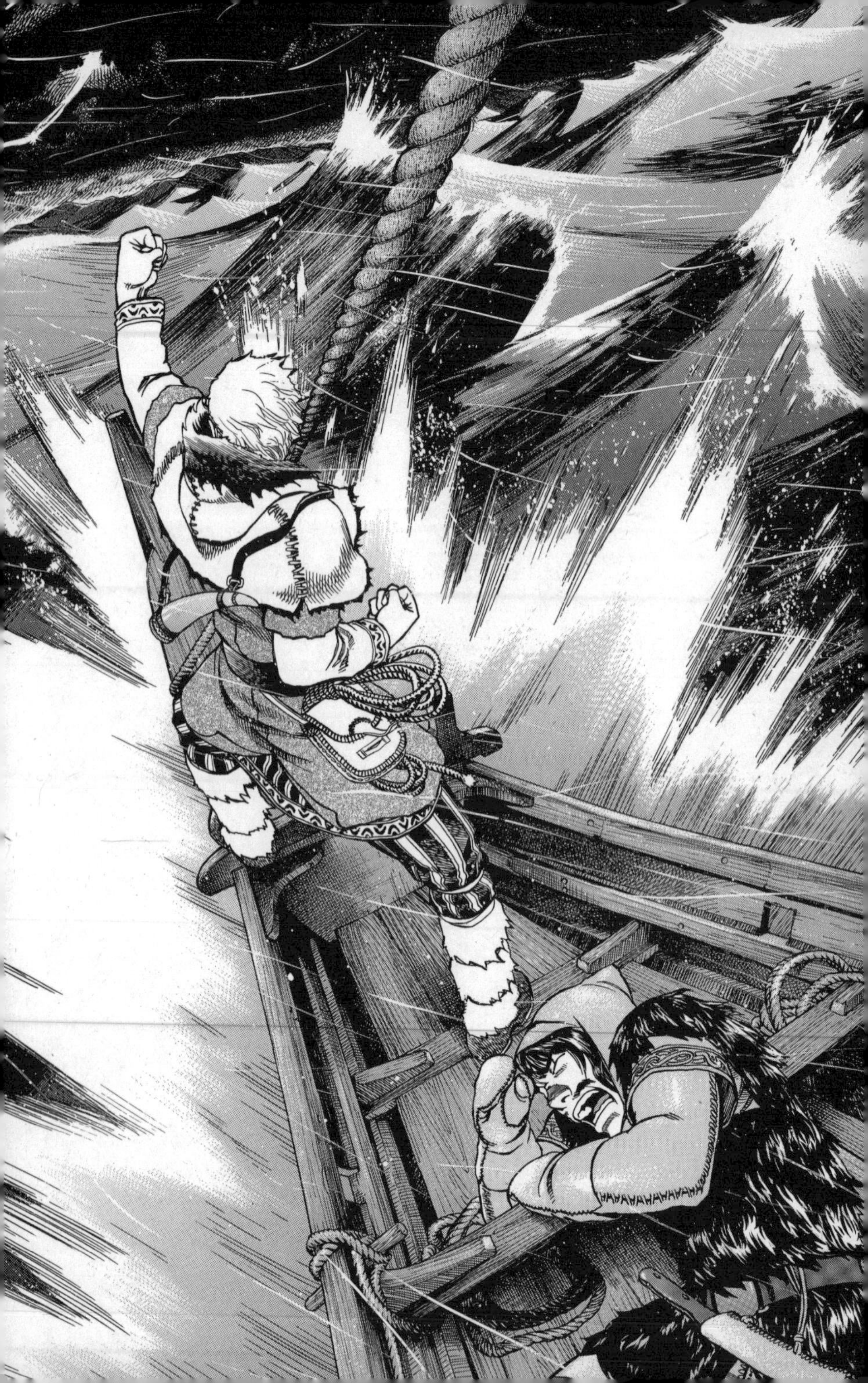

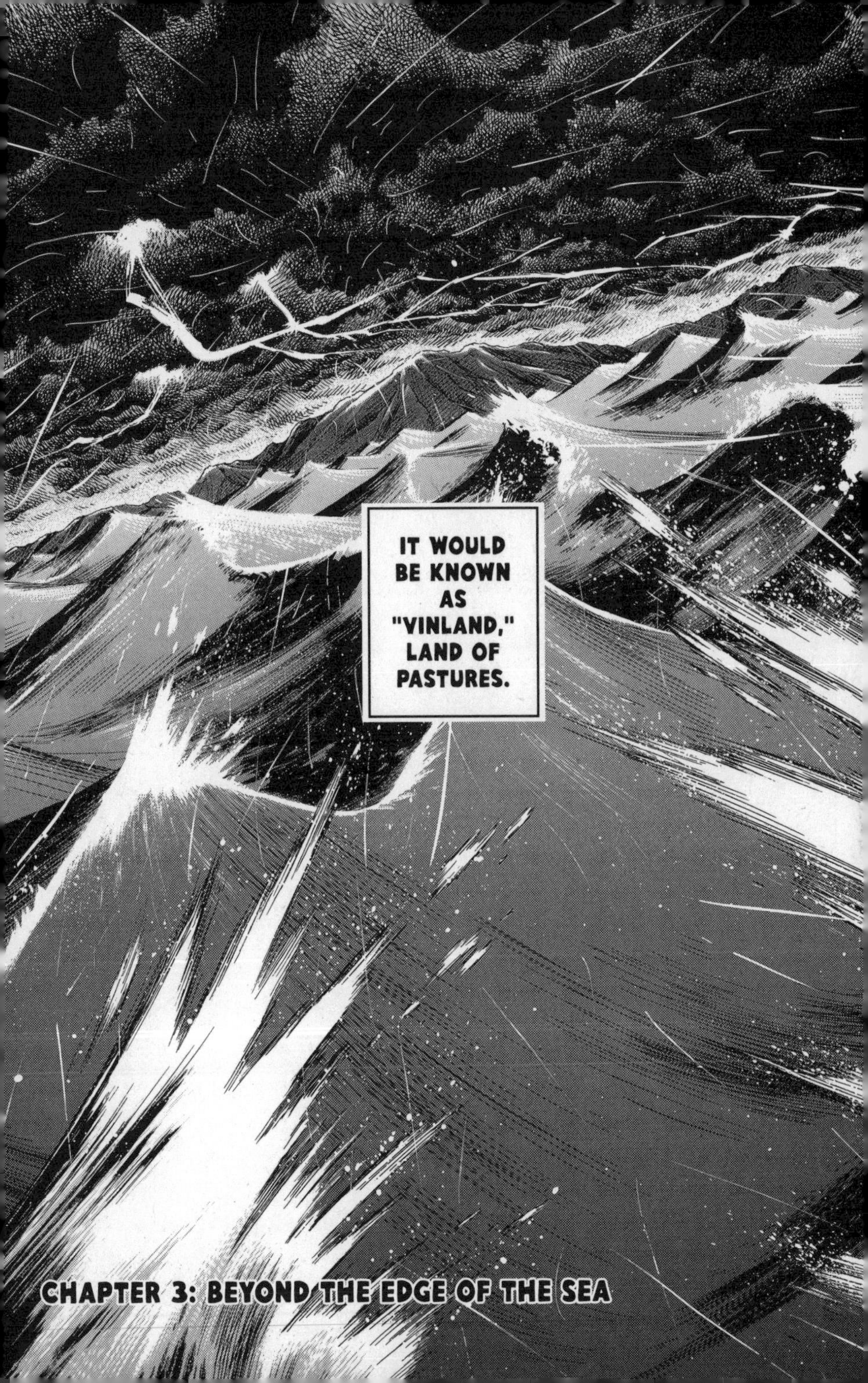
IT WOULD BE KNOWN AS "VINLAND," LAND OF PASTURES.
CHAPTER 3: BEYOND THE EDGE OF THE SEA

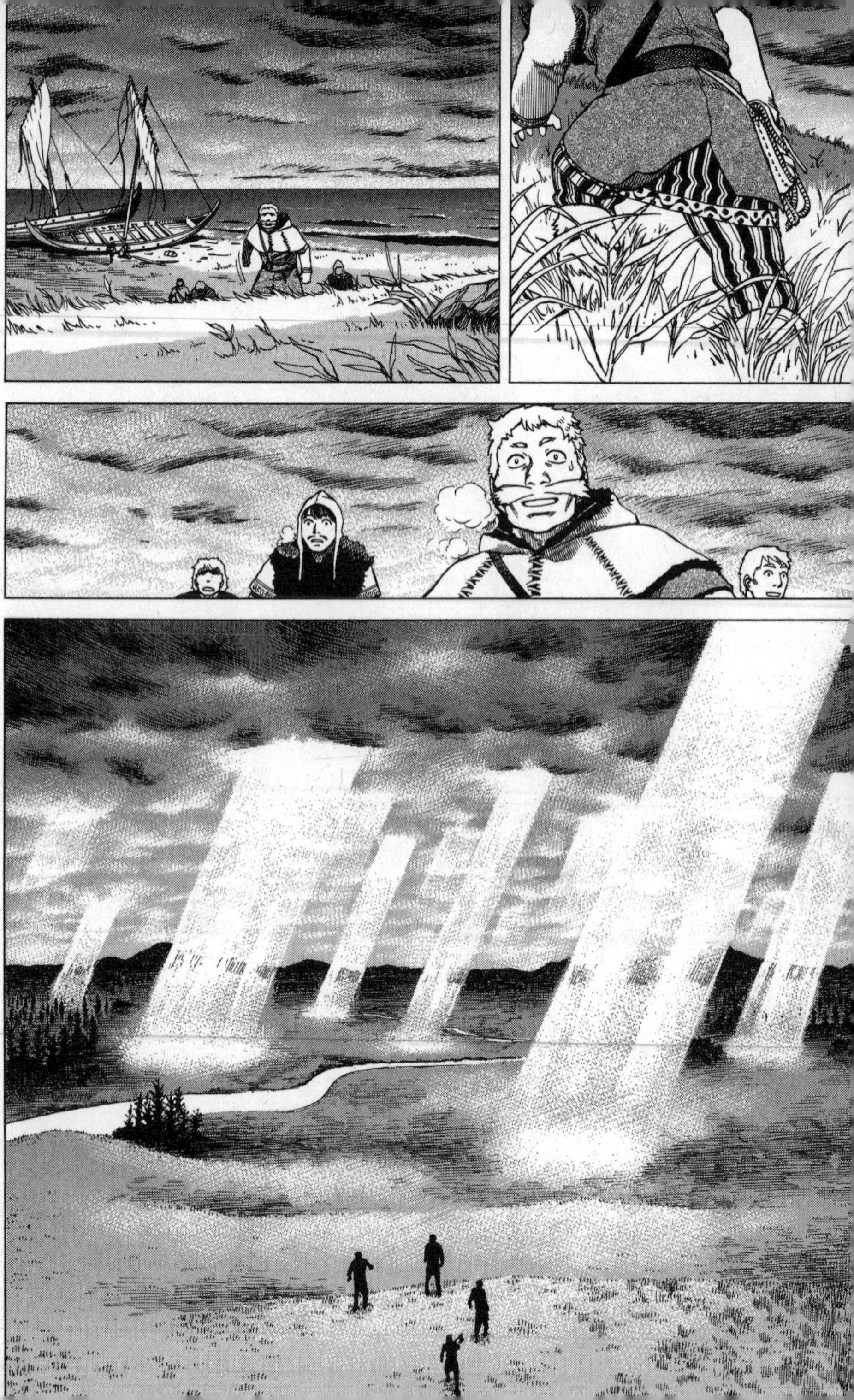

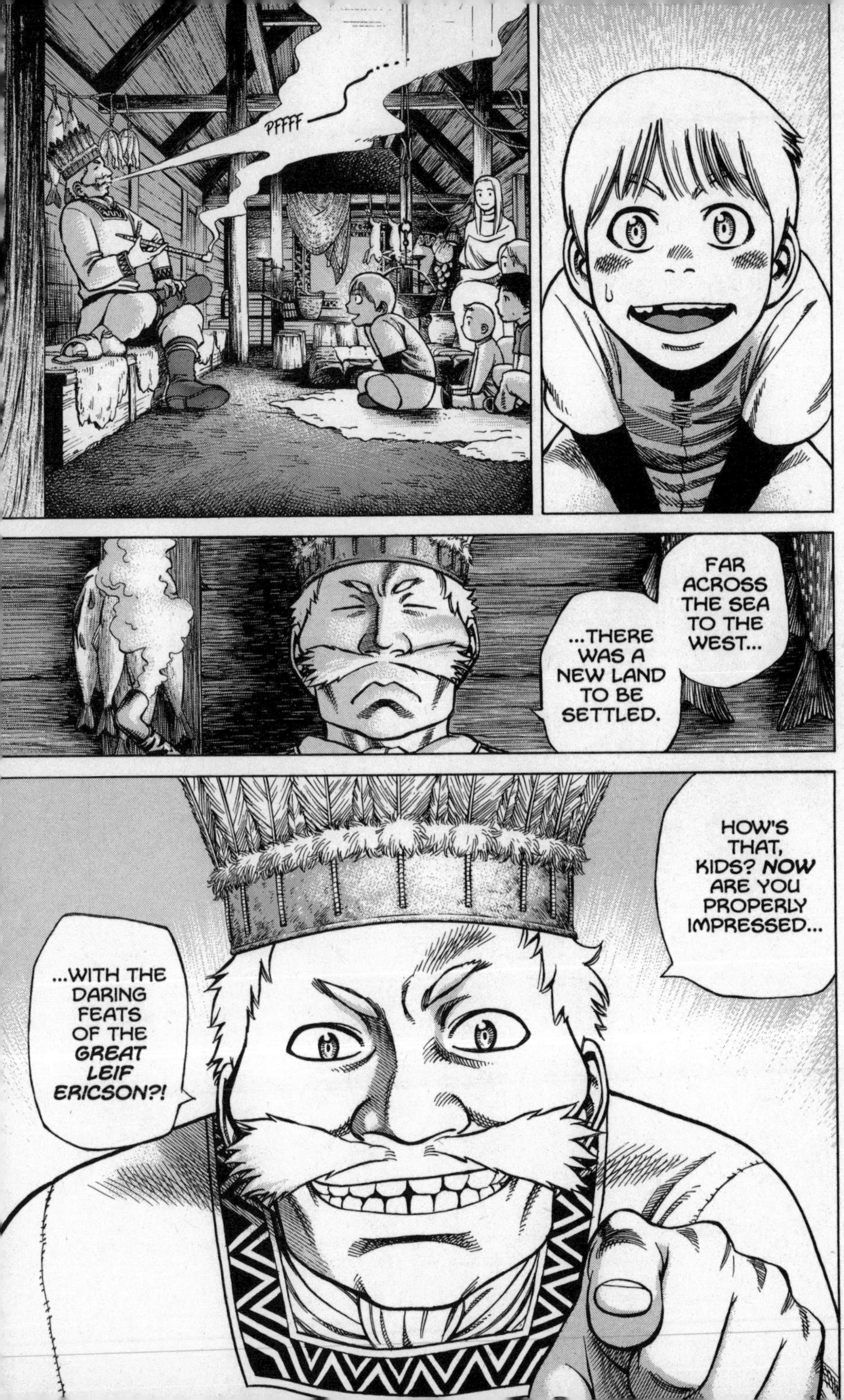
PFFFF
FAR ACROSS THE SEA TO THE WEST...
...THERE WAS A NEW LAND TO BE SETTLED.
HOW'S THAT, KIDS? *NOW* ARE YOU PROPERLY IMPRESSED...
...WITH THE DARING FEATS OF THE *GREAT LEIF ERICSON*?!

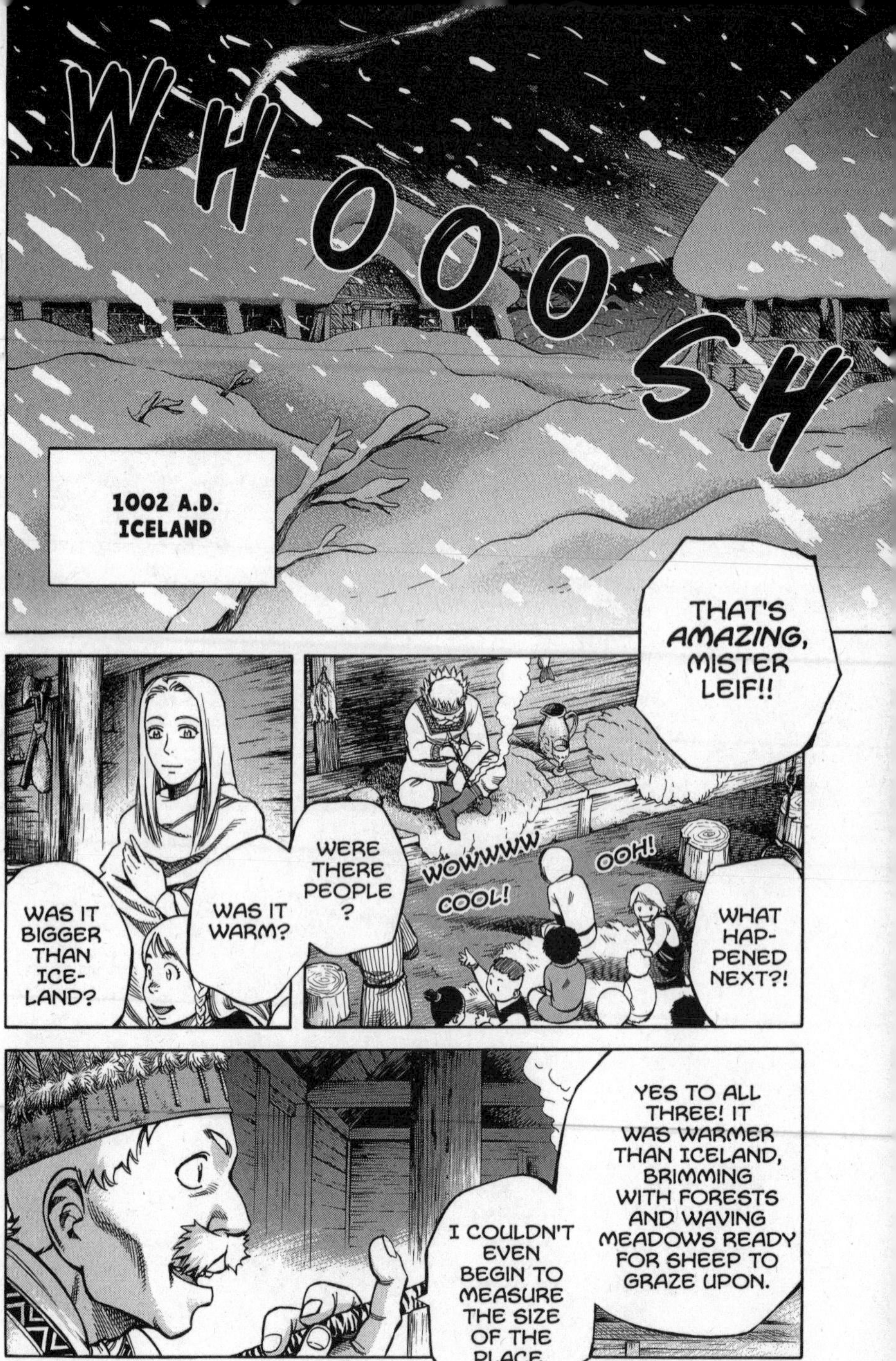
WHOOOOSH
1002 A.D. ICELAND
THAT'S AMAZING, MISTER LEIF!!
WHAT HAPPENED NEXT?!
OOH!
WOWWWW
COOL!
WERE THERE PEOPLE?
WAS IT WARM?
WAS IT BIGGER THAN ICELAND?
YES TO ALL THREE! IT WAS WARMER THAN ICELAND, BRIMMING WITH FORESTS AND WAVING MEADOWS READY FOR SHEEP TO GRAZE UPON.
I COULDN'T EVEN BEGIN TO MEASURE THE SIZE OF THE PLACE.

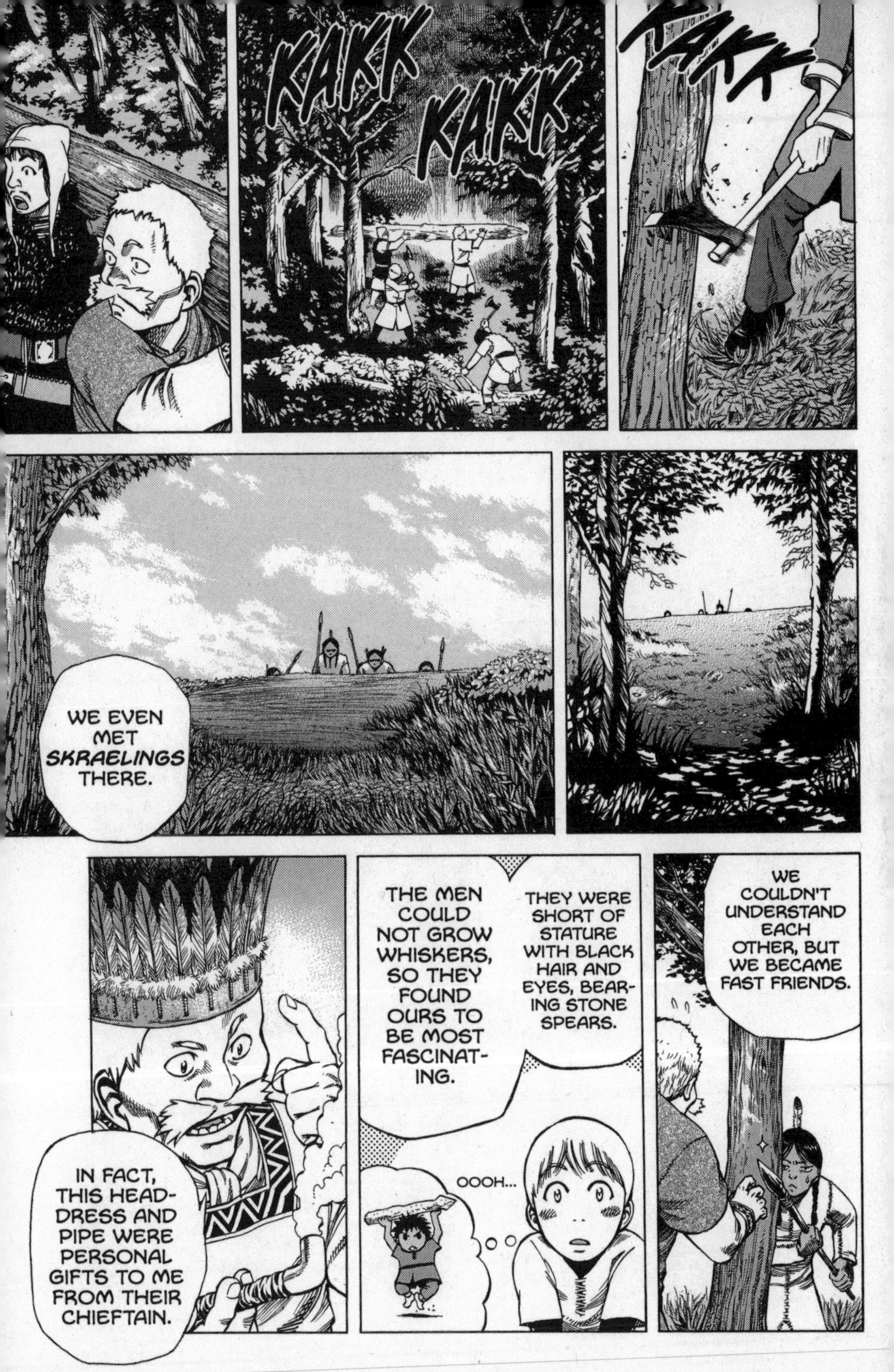
KAKK
KAKK
KAKK
WE EVEN MET SKRAELINGS THERE.
WE COULDN'T UNDERSTAND EACH OTHER, BUT WE BECAME FAST FRIENDS.
THEY WERE SHORT OF STATURE WITH BLACK HAIR AND EYES, BEAR-ING STONE SPEARS.
THE MEN COULD NOT GROW WHISKERS, SO THEY FOUND OURS TO BE MOST FASCINAT-ING.
OOOH...
IN FACT, THIS HEAD-DRESS AND PIPE WERE PERSONAL GIFTS TO ME FROM THEIR CHIEFTAIN.

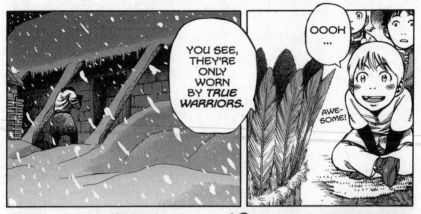

OOOH ...
AWE-SOME!
YOU SEE, THEY'RE ONLY WORN BY TRUE WARRIORS.
WHOOSH
THUMP
WHEW.
PAT PAT
HA HA HA HA
WHAT'S THIS?
THE CHILDREN ARE STILL AWAKE?
I'M SORRY, THORS.
I WANTED TO LET THEM HEAR LEIF'S STORIES...

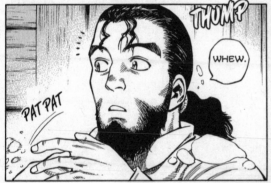

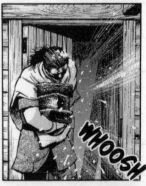

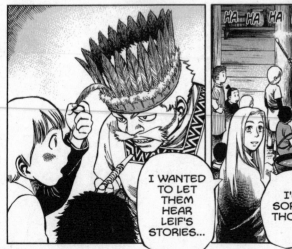

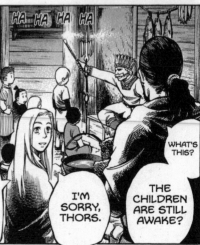

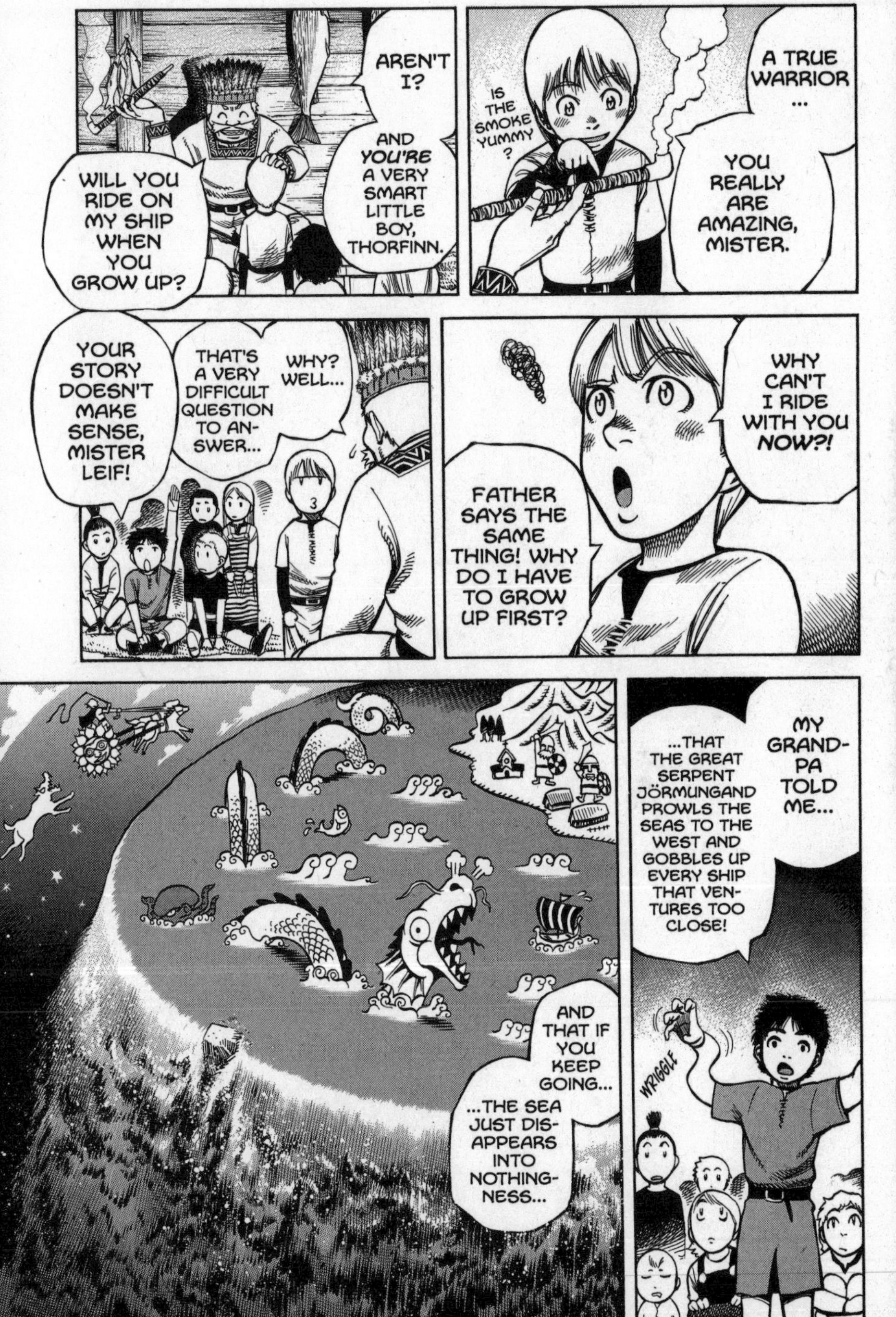
A TRUE WARRIOR ...
YOU REALLY ARE AMAZING, MISTER.
IS THE SMOKE YUMMY?
AREN'T I?
AND *YOU'RE* A VERY SMART LITTLE BOY, THORFINN.
WILL YOU RIDE ON MY SHIP WHEN YOU GROW UP?
WHY CAN'T I RIDE WITH YOU *NOW?!*
FATHER SAYS THE SAME THING! WHY DO I HAVE TO GROW UP FIRST?
WHY? WELL...
THAT'S A VERY DIFFICULT QUESTION TO ANSWER...
YOUR STORY DOESN'T MAKE SENSE, MISTER LEIF!
MY GRANDPA TOLD ME...
...THAT THE GREAT SERPENT JÖRMUNGAND PROWLS THE SEAS TO THE WEST AND GOBBLES UP EVERY SHIP THAT VENTURES TOO CLOSE!
WRIGGLE
AND THAT IF YOU KEEP GOING...
...THE SEA JUST DISAPPEARS INTO NOTHINGNESS...

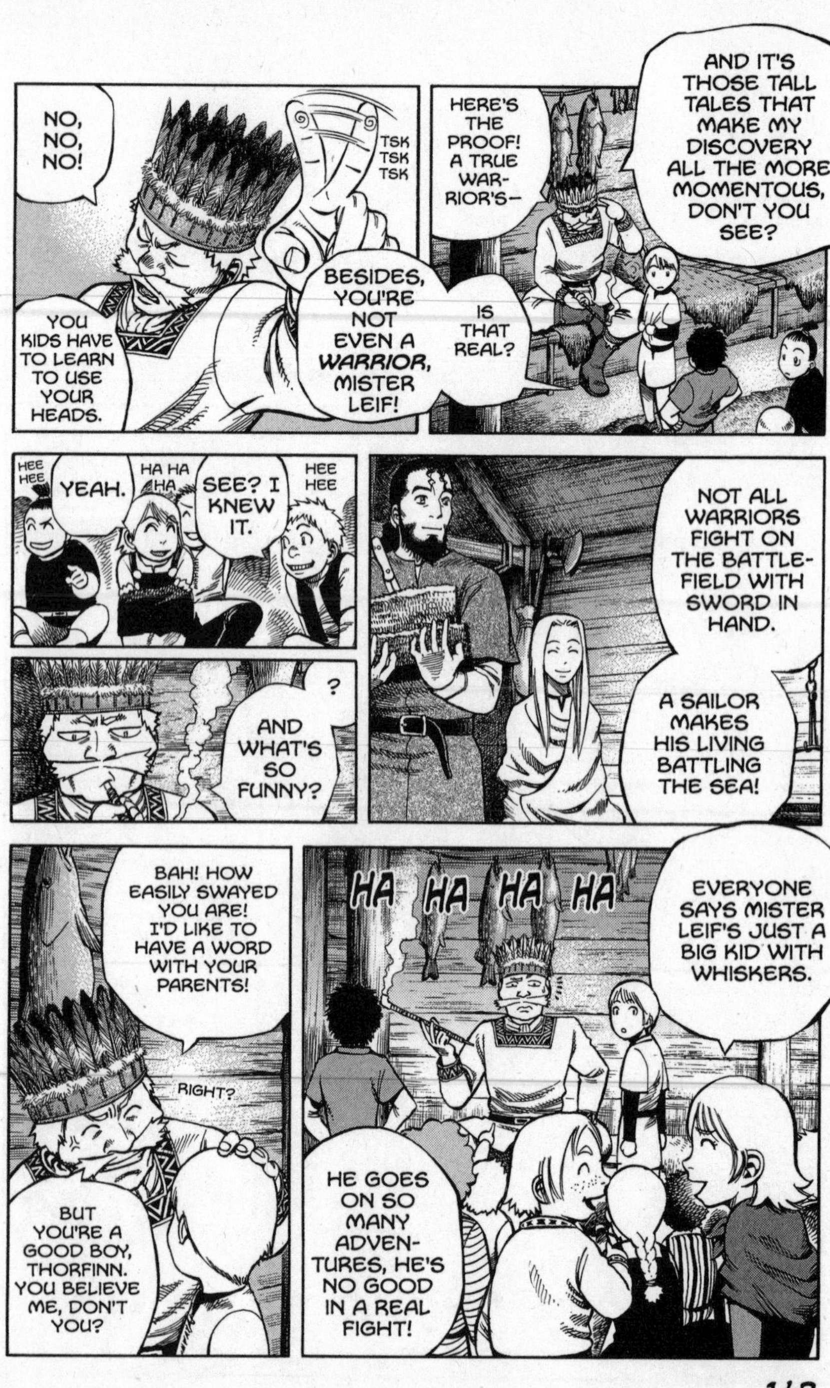
AND IT'S THOSE TALL TALES THAT MAKE MY DISCOVERY ALL THE MORE MOMENTOUS, DON'T YOU SEE?
HERE'S THE PROOF! A TRUE WAR-RIOR'S—
IS THAT REAL?
BESIDES, YOU'RE NOT EVEN A *WARRIOR*, MISTER LEIF!
TSK TSK TSK
NO, NO, NO!
YOU KIDS HAVE TO LEARN TO USE YOUR HEADS.
NOT ALL WARRIORS FIGHT ON THE BATTLE-FIELD WITH SWORD IN HAND.
A SAILOR MAKES HIS LIVING BATTLING THE SEA!
HEE HEE
SEE? I KNEW IT.
HA HA HA
YEAH.
HEE HEE
?
AND WHAT'S SO FUNNY?
EVERYONE SAYS MISTER LEIF'S JUST A BIG KID WITH WHISKERS.
HA HA HA HA
HE GOES ON SO MANY ADVEN-TURES, HE'S NO GOOD IN A REAL FIGHT!
BAH! HOW EASILY SWAYED YOU ARE! I'D LIKE TO HAVE A WORD WITH YOUR PARENTS!
RIGHT?
BUT YOU'RE A GOOD BOY, THORFINN. YOU BELIEVE ME, DON'T YOU?

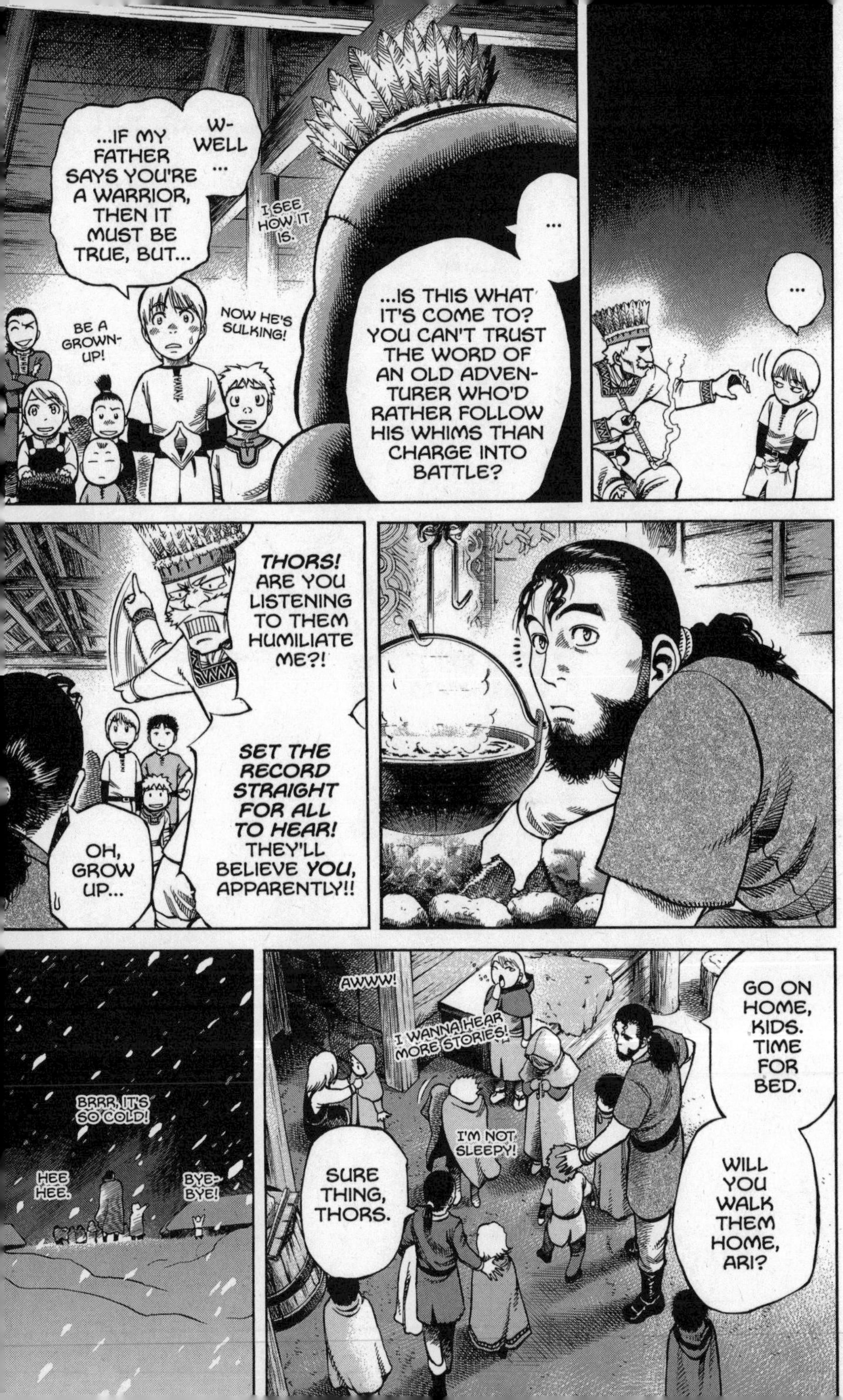
...
...
...IS THIS WHAT IT'S COME TO? YOU CAN'T TRUST THE WORD OF AN OLD ADVENTURER WHO'D RATHER FOLLOW HIS WHIMS THAN CHARGE INTO BATTLE?
I SEE HOW IT IS.
W- WELL ...
...IF MY FATHER SAYS YOU'RE A WARRIOR, THEN IT MUST BE TRUE, BUT...
NOW HE'S SULKING!
BE A GROWN-UP!
THORS! ARE YOU LISTENING TO THEM HUMILIATE ME?!
SET THE RECORD STRAIGHT FOR ALL TO HEAR! THEY'LL BELIEVE YOU, APPARENTLY!!
OH, GROW UP...
GO ON HOME, KIDS. TIME FOR BED.
AWWW!
I WANNA HEAR MORE STORIES!
WILL YOU WALK THEM HOME, ARI?
I'M NOT SLEEPY!
SURE THING, THORS.
BRRR, IT'S SO COLD!
BYE-BYE!
HEE HEE.

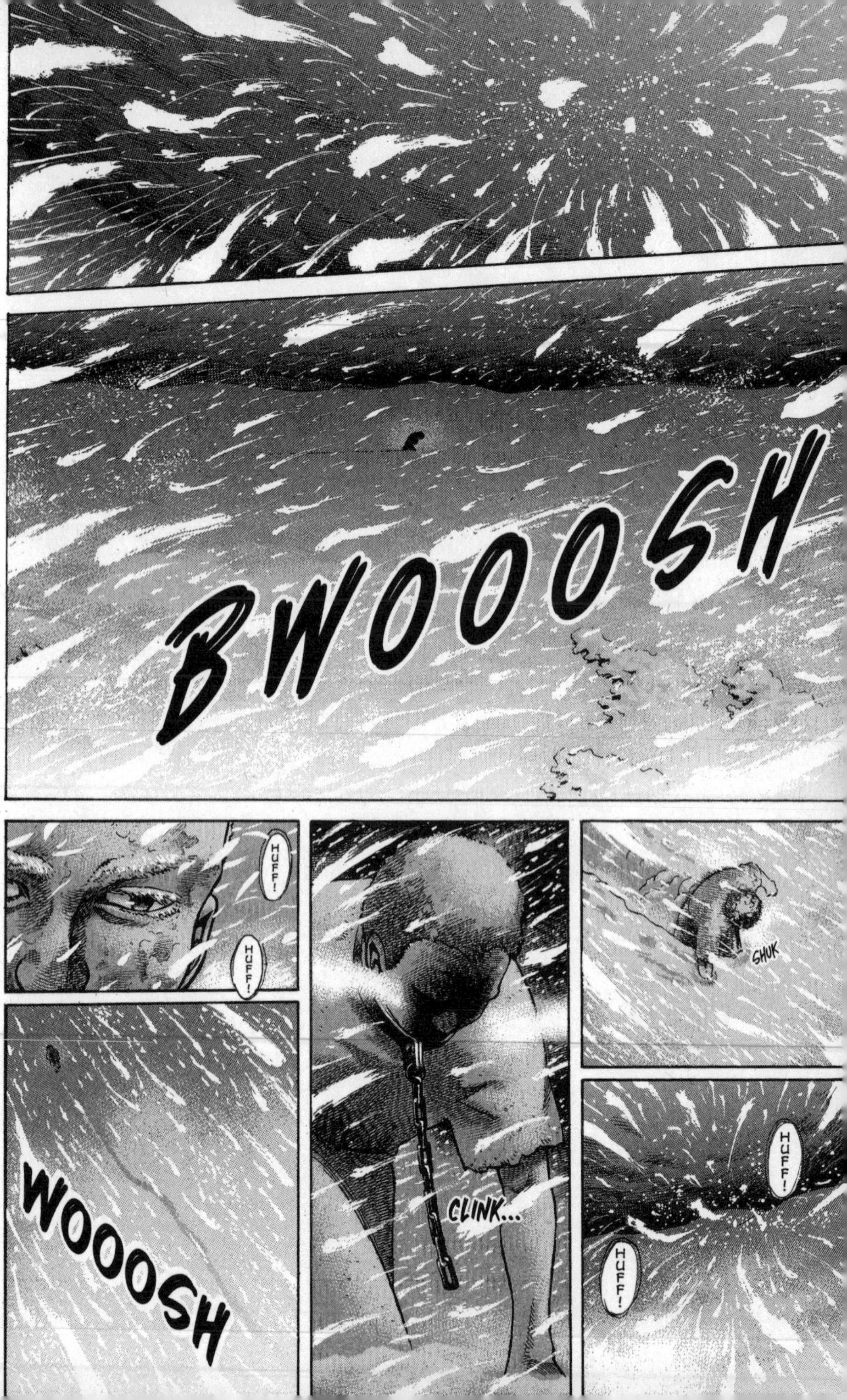
BWOOOSH
SHUK
HUFF!
HUFF!
CLINK...
HUFF!
HUFF!
WOOOSH

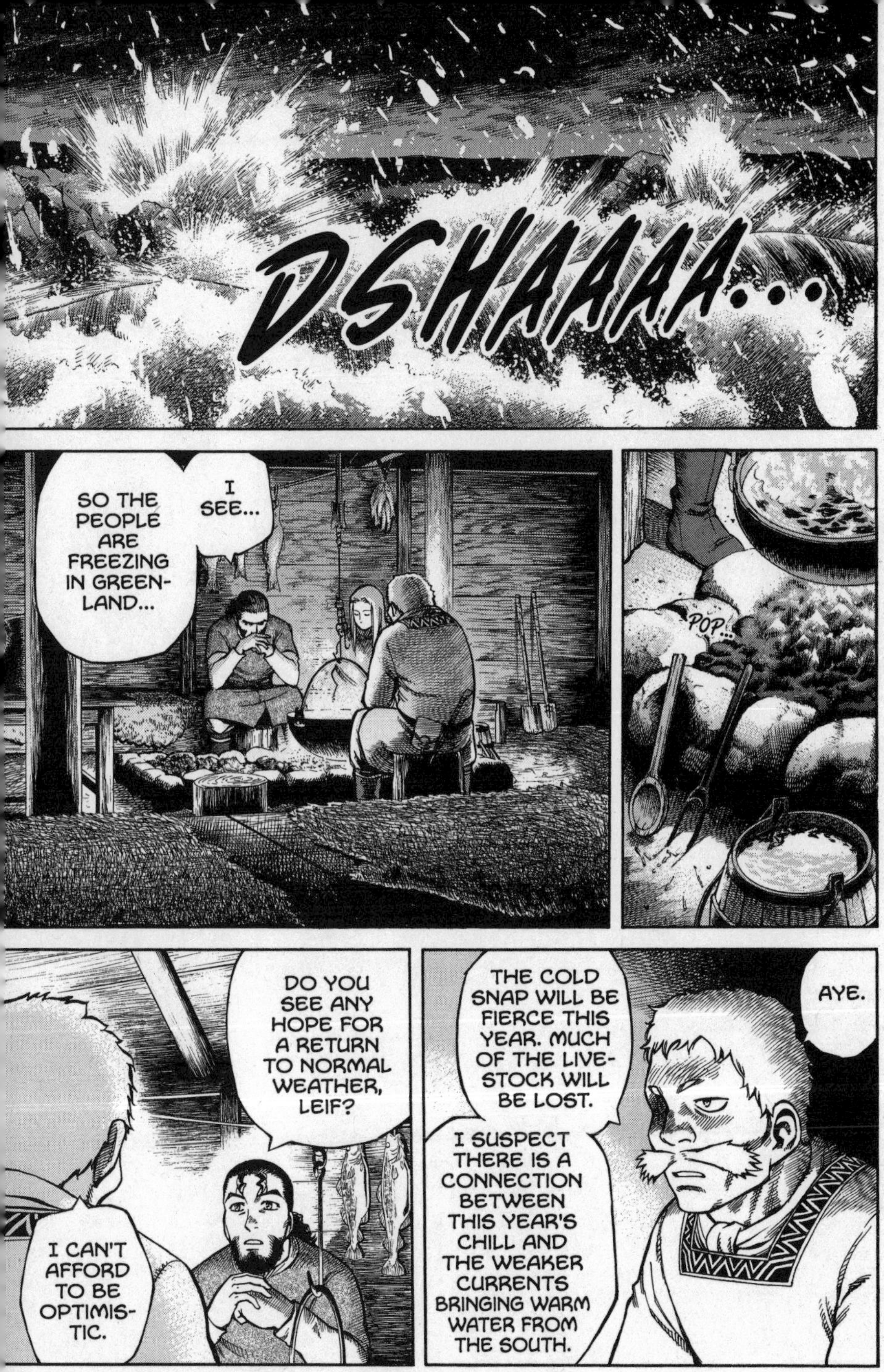
DSHAAAA...
SO THE PEOPLE ARE FREEZING IN GREENLAND...
I SEE...
POP...
DO YOU SEE ANY HOPE FOR A RETURN TO NORMAL WEATHER, LEIF?
I CAN'T AFFORD TO BE OPTIMISTIC.
THE COLD SNAP WILL BE FIERCE THIS YEAR. MUCH OF THE LIVESTOCK WILL BE LOST.
AYE.
I SUSPECT THERE IS A CONNECTION BETWEEN THIS YEAR'S CHILL AND THE WEAKER CURRENTS BRINGING WARM WATER FROM THE SOUTH.

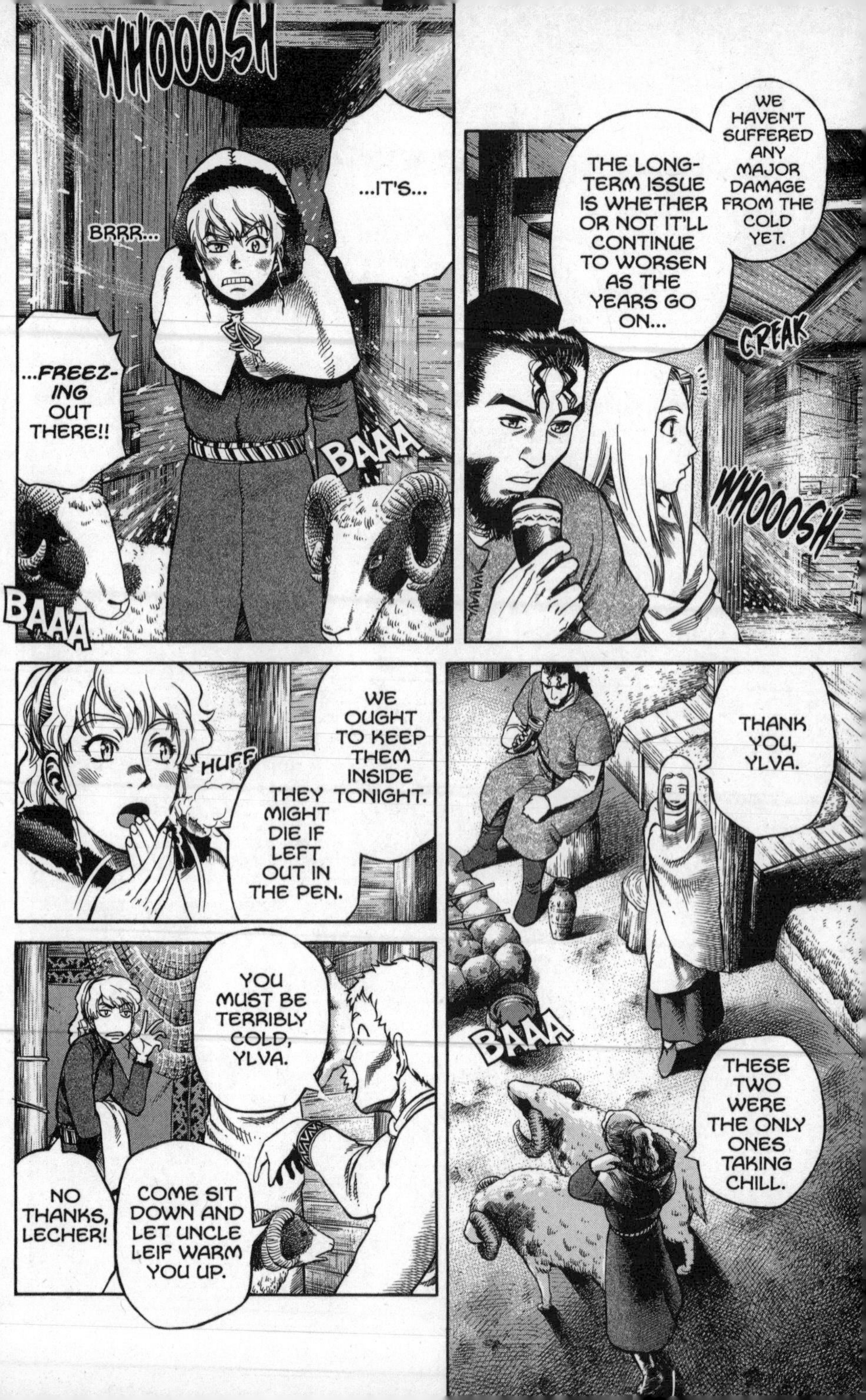
WE HAVEN'T SUFFERED ANY MAJOR DAMAGE FROM THE COLD YET.
THE LONG-TERM ISSUE IS WHETHER OR NOT IT'LL CONTINUE TO WORSEN AS THE YEARS GO ON...
CREAK
WHOOOSH
WHOOOSH
...IT'S...
BRRR...
...FREEZING OUT THERE!!
BAAA
BAAA
THANK YOU, YLVA.
BAAA
THESE TWO WERE THE ONLY ONES TAKING CHILL.
WE OUGHT TO KEEP THEM INSIDE TONIGHT.
THEY MIGHT DIE IF LEFT OUT IN THE PEN.
HUFF
YOU MUST BE TERRIBLY COLD, YLVA.
COME SIT DOWN AND LET UNCLE LEIF WARM YOU UP.
NO THANKS, LECHER!

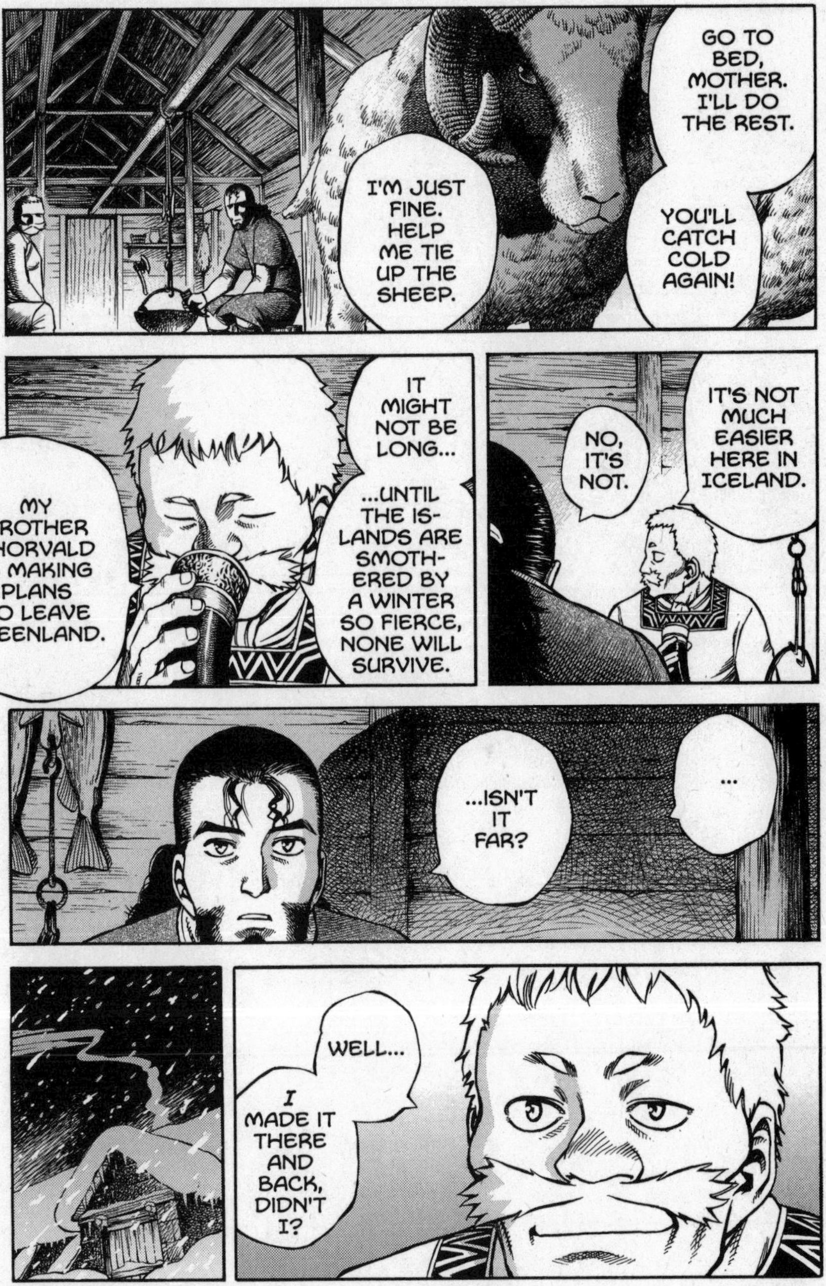
GO TO BED, MOTHER. I'LL DO THE REST.
YOU'LL CATCH COLD AGAIN!
I'M JUST FINE. HELP ME TIE UP THE SHEEP.
IT'S NOT MUCH EASIER HERE IN ICELAND.
NO, IT'S NOT.
IT MIGHT NOT BE LONG...
...UNTIL THE IS- LANDS ARE SMOTH- ERED BY A WINTER SO FIERCE, NONE WILL SURVIVE.
MY BROTHER THORVALD IS MAKING PLANS TO LEAVE GREENLAND.
...
...ISN'T IT FAR?
WELL...
I MADE IT THERE AND BACK, DIDN'T I?

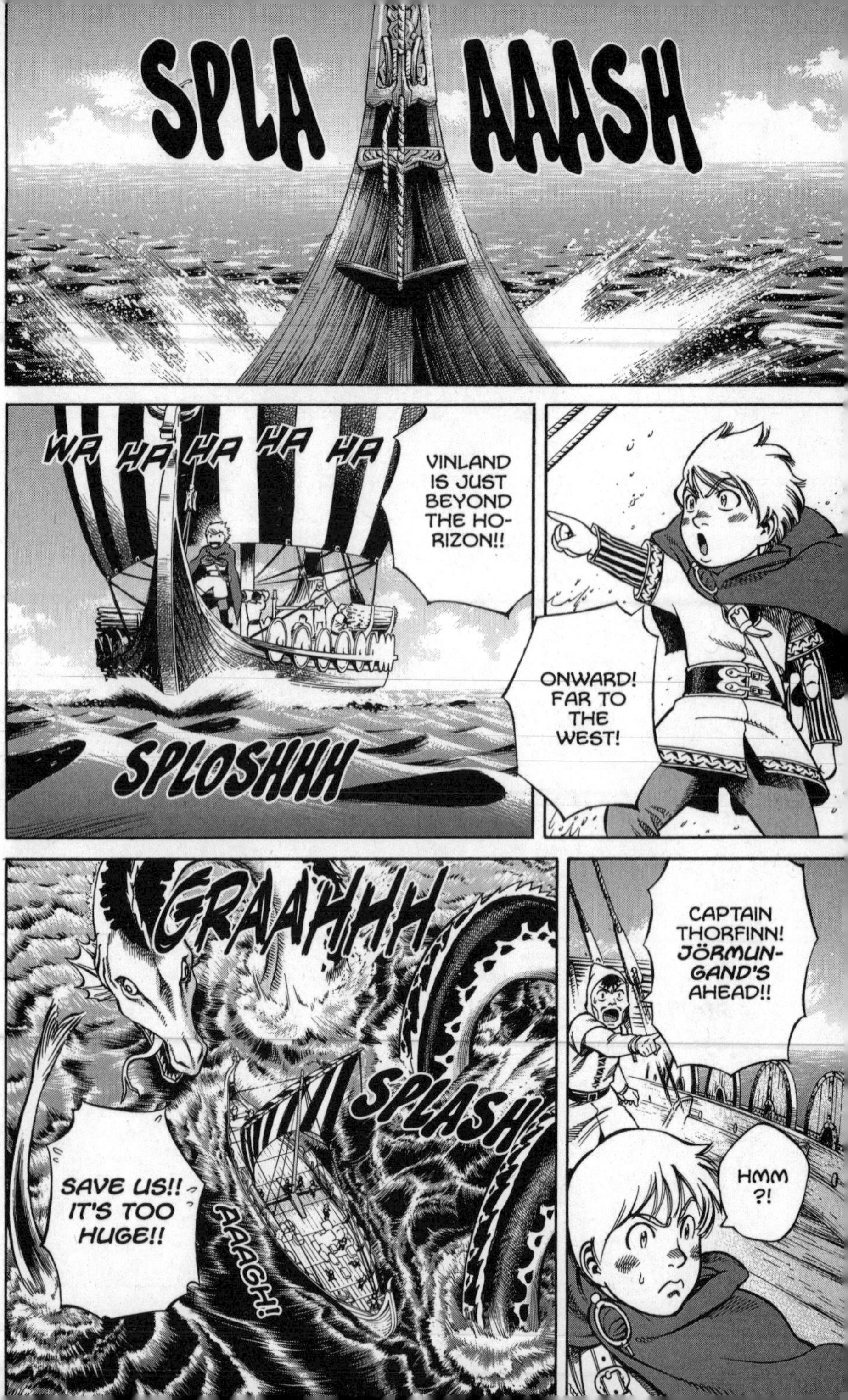
SPLA AAASH
VINLAND IS JUST BEYOND THE HO-RIZON!!
ONWARD! FAR TO THE WEST!
WA HA HA HA HA
SPLOSHHH
CAPTAIN THORFINN! JÖRMUN-GAND'S AHEAD!!
HMM ?!
GRAAHHH
SPLASH
SAVE US!! IT'S TOO HUGE!!
AAAGH!

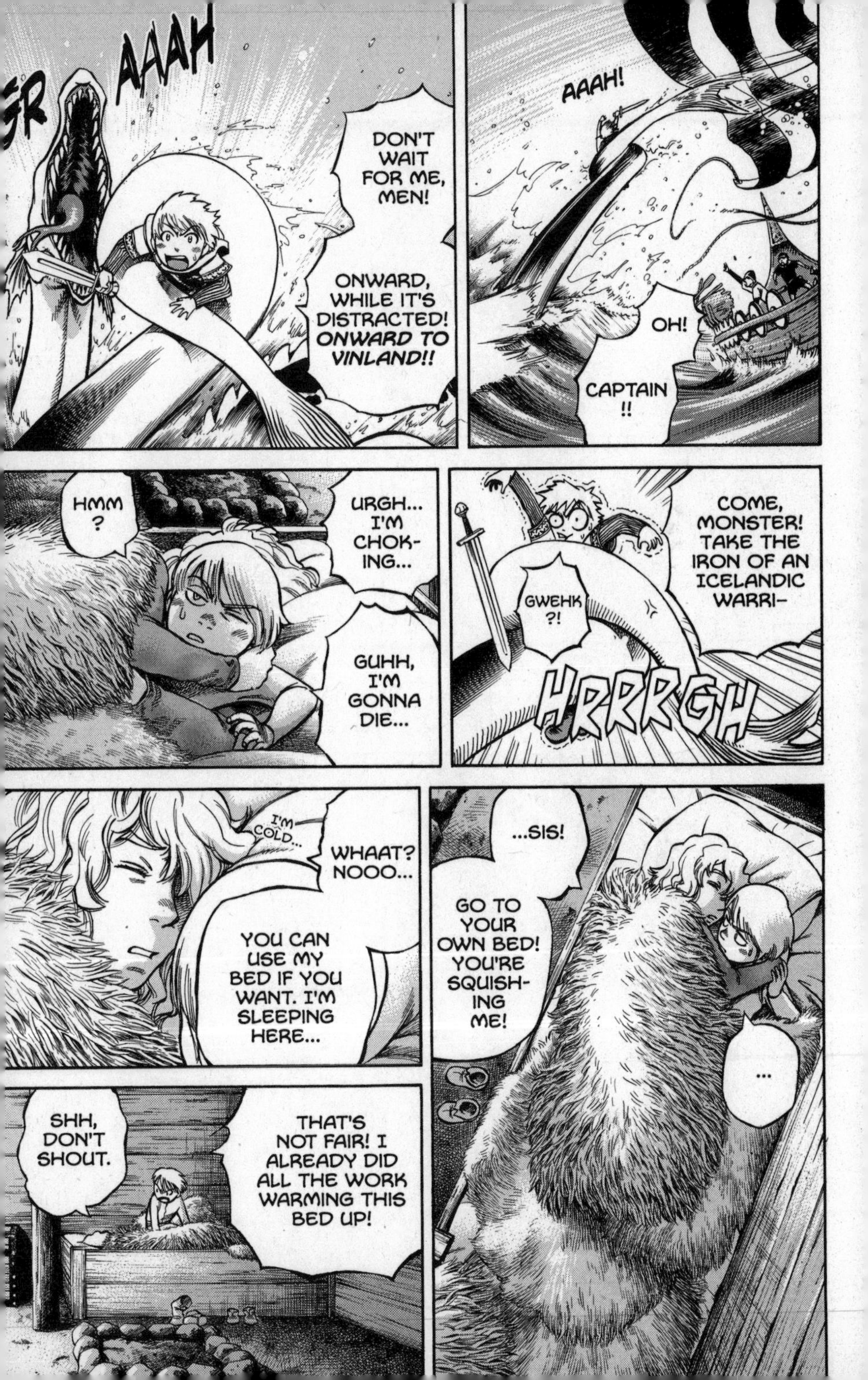
AAAH!
OH!
CAPTAIN !!
GR AAAH
DON'T WAIT FOR ME, MEN!
ONWARD, WHILE IT'S DISTRACTED! ONWARD TO VINLAND!!
COME, MONSTER! TAKE THE IRON OF AN ICELANDIC WARRI-
GWEHK ?!
HRRRGH
URGH... I'M CHOK-ING...
HMM ?
GUHH, I'M GONNA DIE...
...SIS!
GO TO YOUR OWN BED! YOU'RE SQUISH-ING ME!
...
WHAAT? NOOO...
I'M COLD...
YOU CAN USE MY BED IF YOU WANT. I'M SLEEPING HERE...
THAT'S NOT FAIR! I ALREADY DID ALL THE WORK WARMING THIS BED UP!
SHH, DON'T SHOUT.

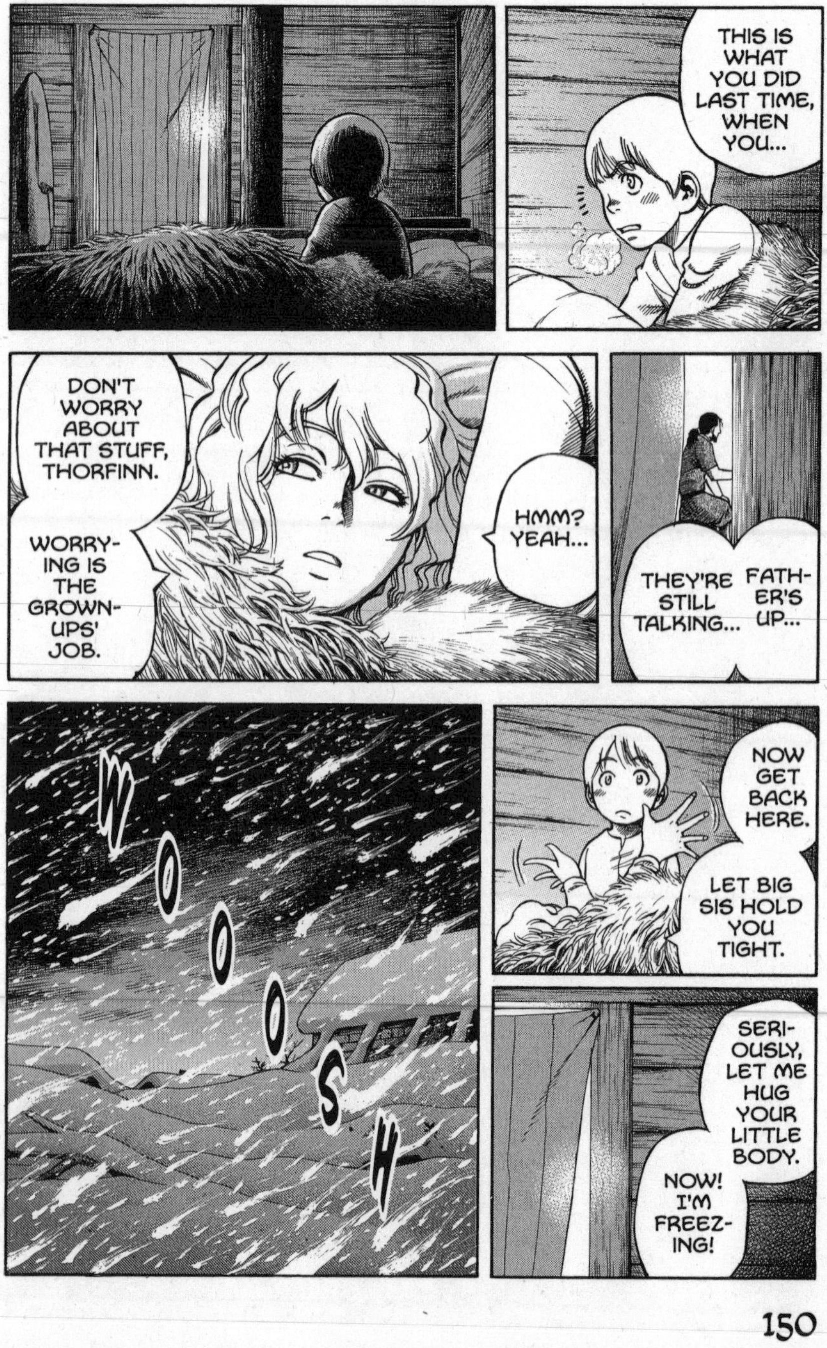
THIS IS WHAT YOU DID LAST TIME, WHEN YOU...
FATHER'S UP...
THEY'RE STILL TALKING...
HMM? YEAH...
DON'T WORRY ABOUT THAT STUFF, THORFINN.
WORRYING IS THE GROWN-UPS' JOB.
NOW GET BACK HERE.
LET BIG SIS HOLD YOU TIGHT.
SERIOUSLY, LET ME HUG YOUR LITTLE BODY.
NOW! I'M FREEZING!
WOOOOSH

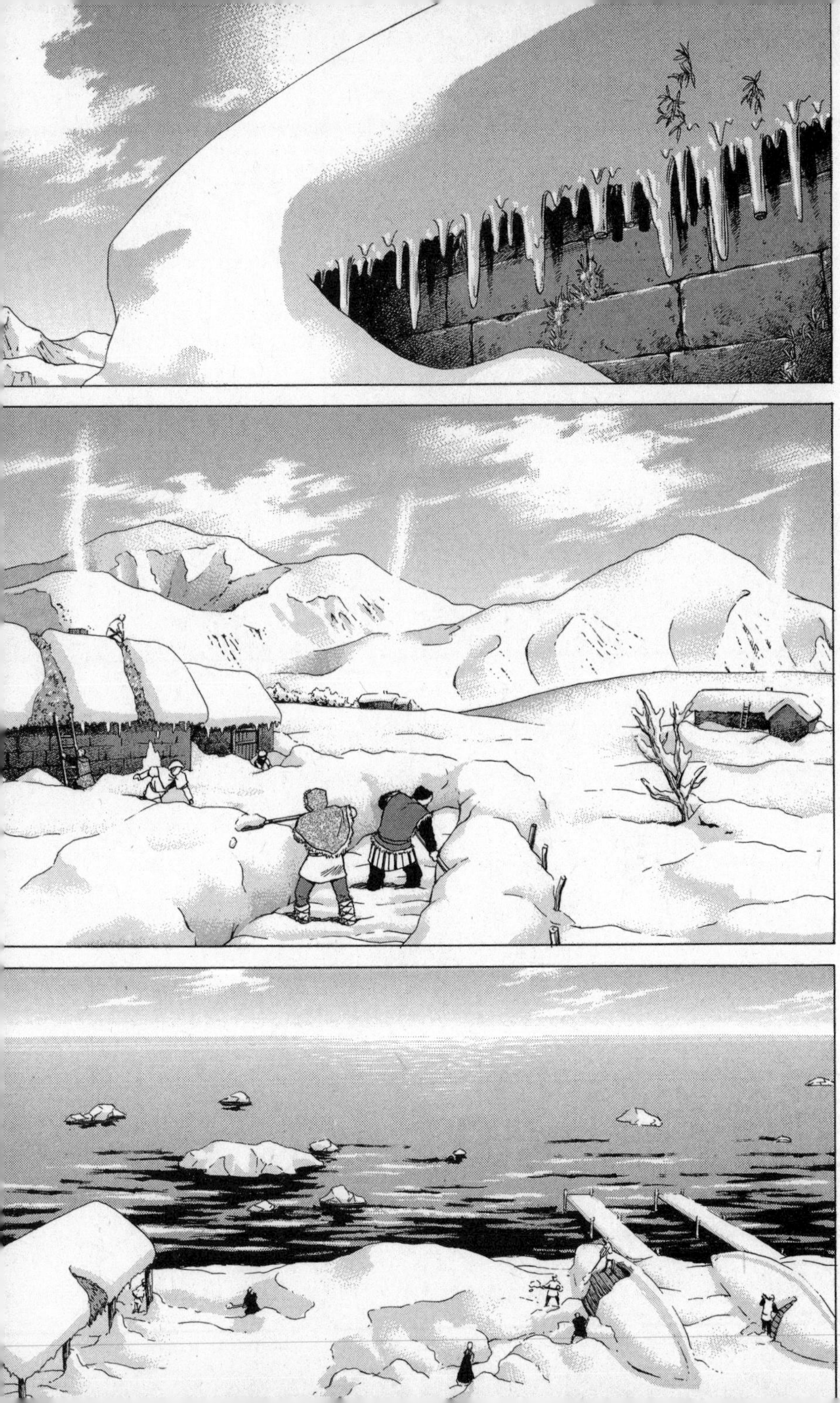

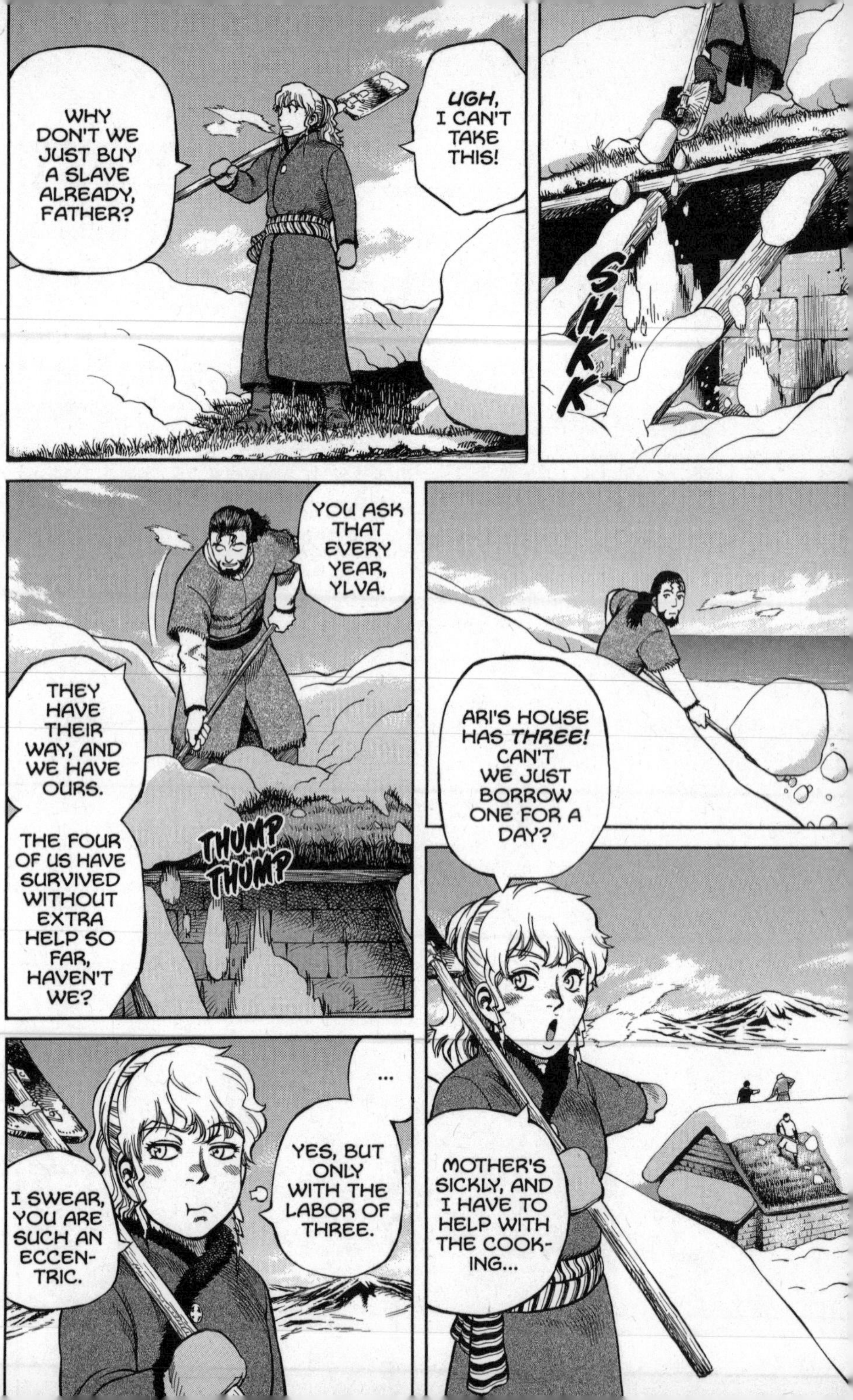
SHKK
UGH, I CAN'T TAKE THIS!
WHY DON'T WE JUST BUY A SLAVE ALREADY, FATHER?
YOU ASK THAT EVERY YEAR, YLVA.
ARI'S HOUSE HAS THREE! CAN'T WE JUST BORROW ONE FOR A DAY?
THEY HAVE THEIR WAY, AND WE HAVE OURS.
THUMP THUMP
THE FOUR OF US HAVE SURVIVED WITHOUT EXTRA HELP SO FAR, HAVEN'T WE?
MOTHER'S SICKLY, AND I HAVE TO HELP WITH THE COOK-ING...
...
YES, BUT ONLY WITH THE LABOR OF THREE.
I SWEAR, YOU ARE SUCH AN ECCEN-TRIC.

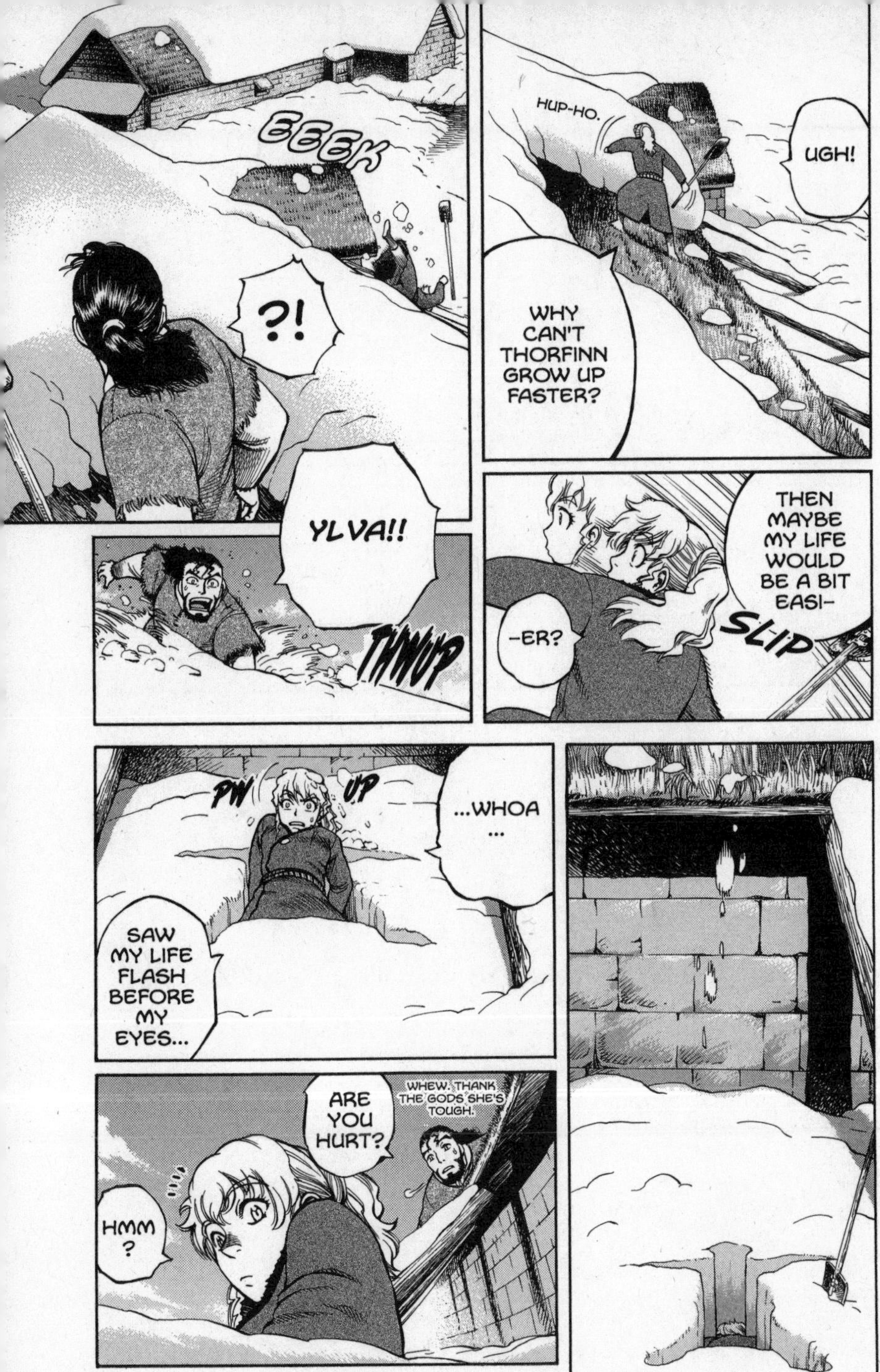
UGH!
HUP-HO.
WHY CAN'T THORFINN GROW UP FASTER?
THEN MAYBE MY LIFE WOULD BE A BIT EASI-
SLIP
-ER?
EEEK
?!
YLVA!!
THWUP
PW UP
...WHOA ...
SAW MY LIFE FLASH BEFORE MY EYES...
ARE YOU HURT?
WHEW. THANK THE GODS SHE'S TOUGH.
HMM ?

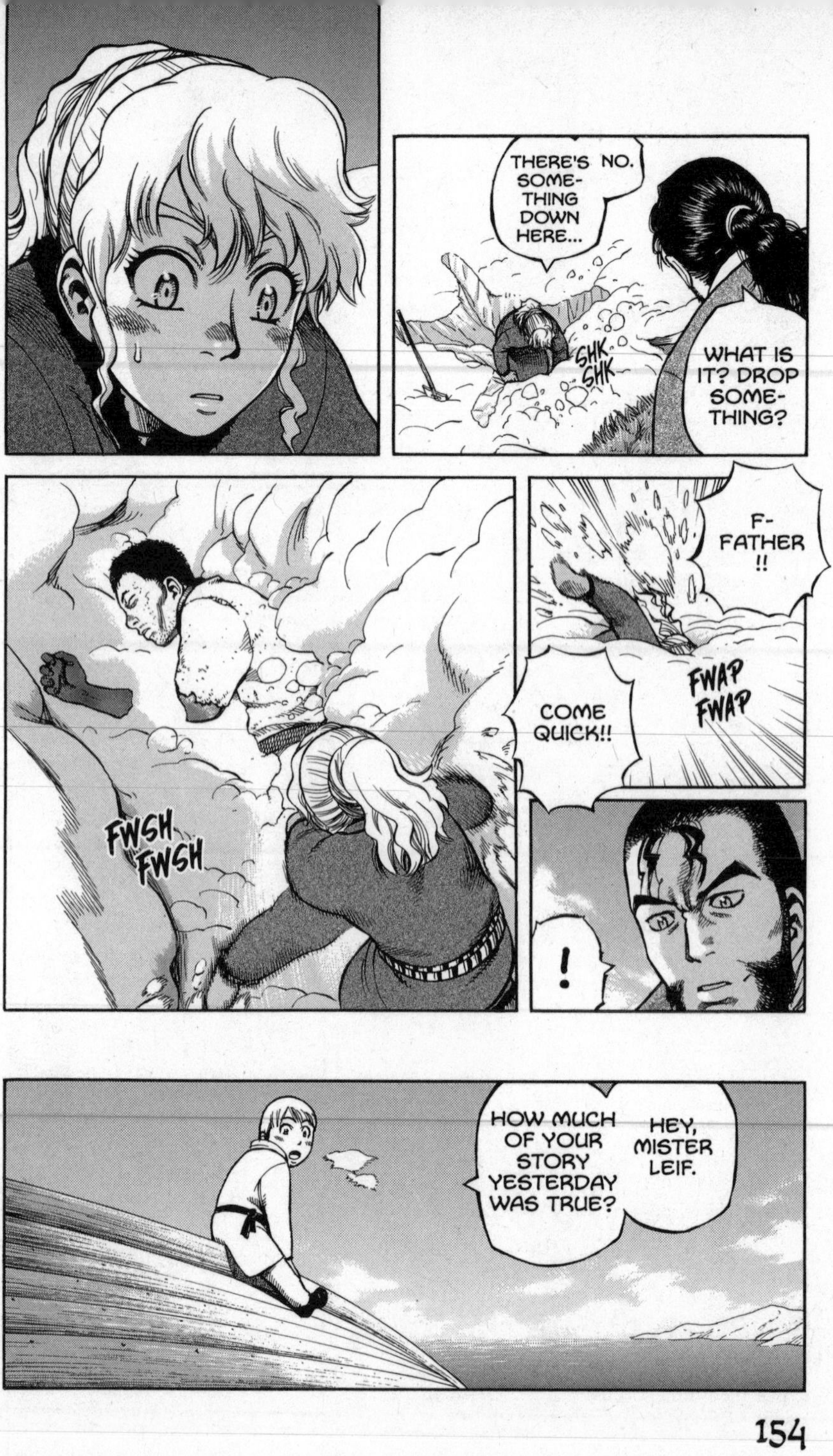
NO.
THERE'S SOMETHING DOWN HERE...
SHK SHK
WHAT IS IT? DROP SOMETHING?
F-FATHER!!
FWAP FWAP
COME QUICK!!
!
FWSH FWSH
HEY, MISTER LEIF.
HOW MUCH OF YOUR STORY YESTERDAY WAS TRUE?

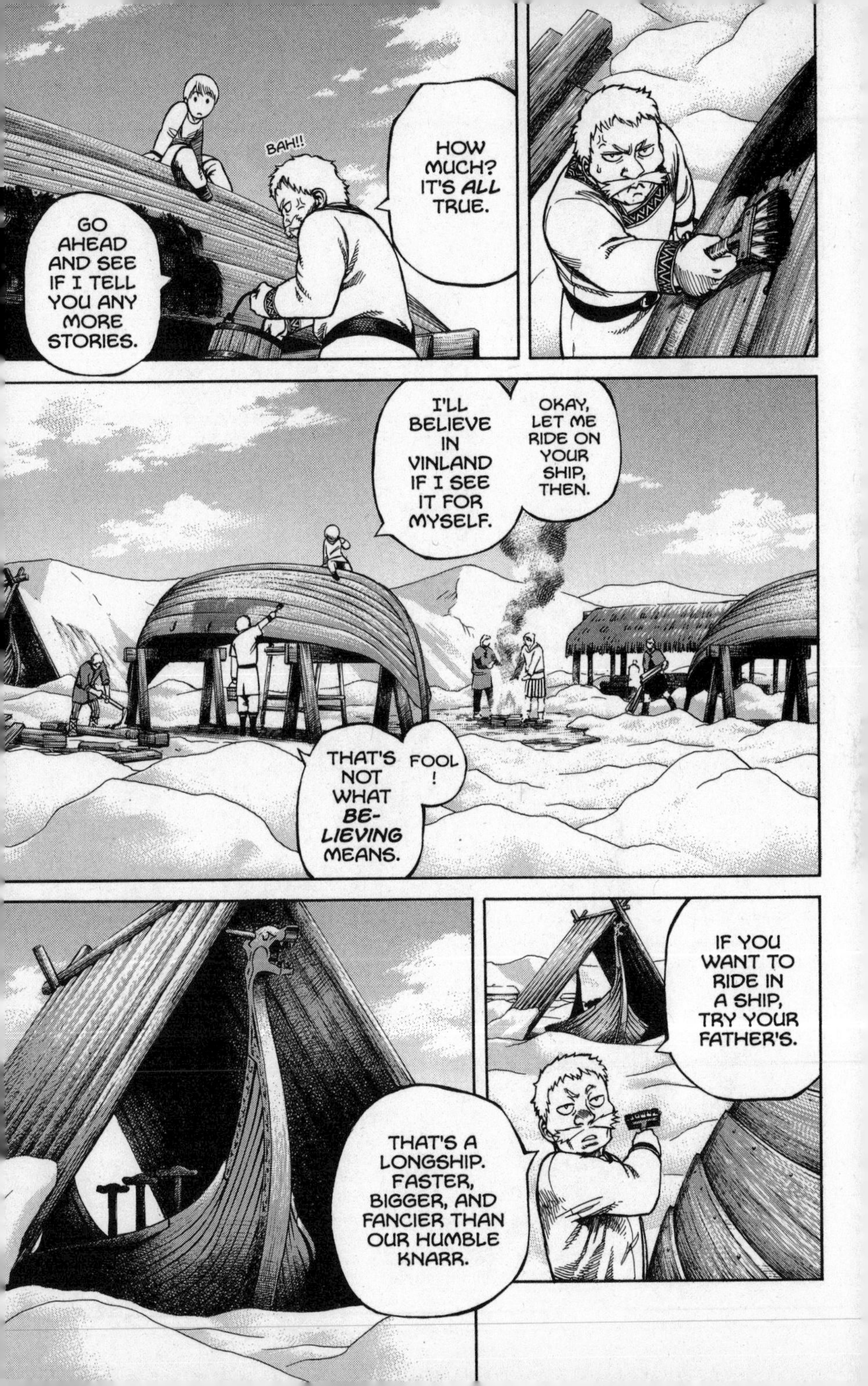
HOW MUCH? IT'S ALL TRUE.
BAH!!
GO AHEAD AND SEE IF I TELL YOU ANY MORE STORIES.
OKAY, LET ME RIDE ON YOUR SHIP, THEN.
I'LL BELIEVE IN VINLAND IF I SEE IT FOR MYSELF.
FOOL!
THAT'S NOT WHAT BE-LIEVING MEANS.
IF YOU WANT TO RIDE IN A SHIP, TRY YOUR FATHER'S.
THAT'S A LONGSHIP. FASTER, BIGGER, AND FANCIER THAN OUR HUMBLE KNARR.

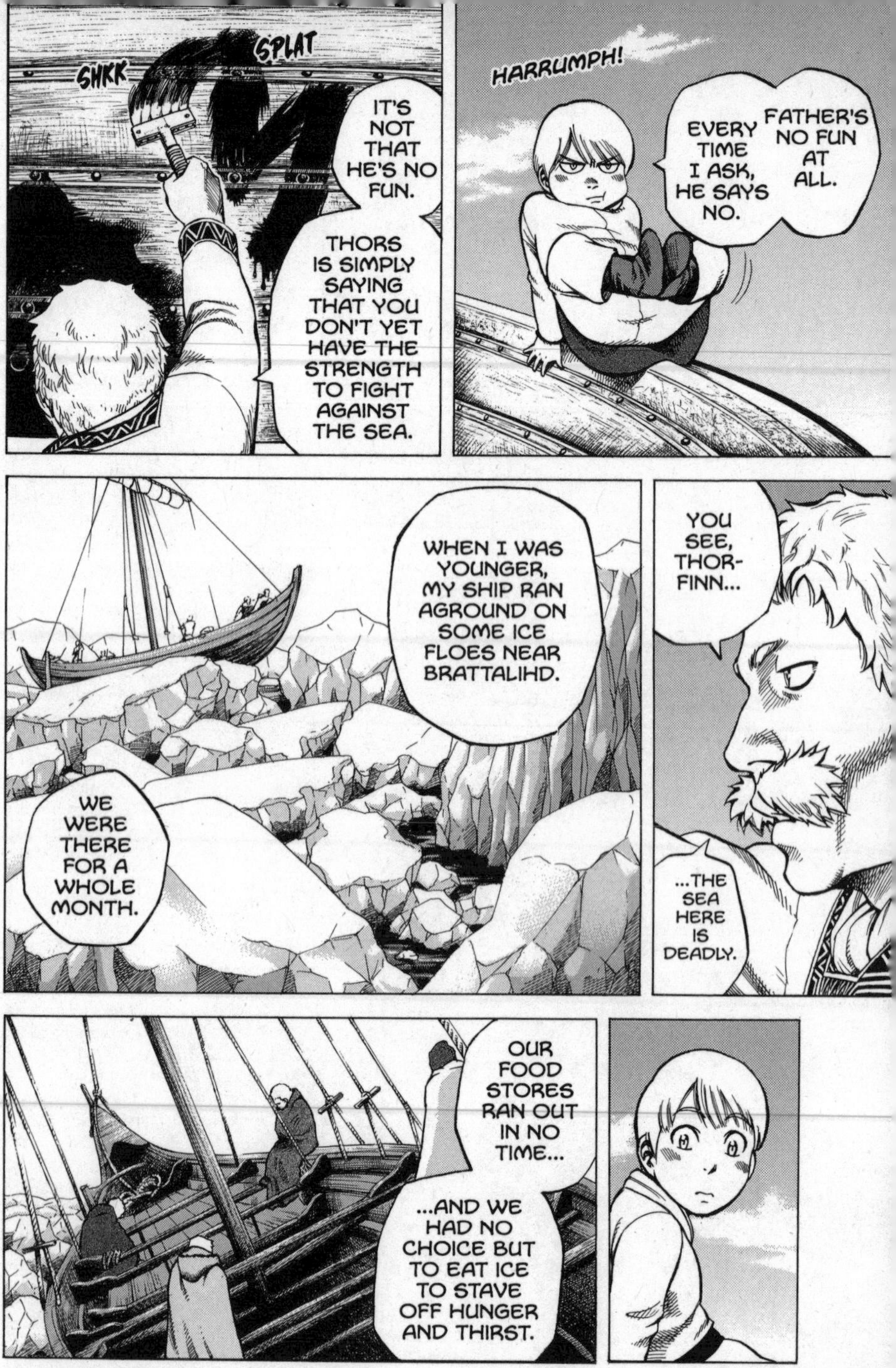
HARRUMPH!
FATHER'S NO FUN AT ALL.
EVERY TIME I ASK, HE SAYS NO.
SHKK
SPLAT
IT'S NOT THAT HE'S NO FUN.
THORS IS SIMPLY SAYING THAT YOU DON'T YET HAVE THE STRENGTH TO FIGHT AGAINST THE SEA.
YOU SEE, THOR-FINN...
...THE SEA HERE IS DEADLY.
WHEN I WAS YOUNGER, MY SHIP RAN AGROUND ON SOME ICE FLOES NEAR BRATTALIHD.
WE WERE THERE FOR A WHOLE MONTH.
OUR FOOD STORES RAN OUT IN NO TIME...
...AND WE HAD NO CHOICE BUT TO EAT ICE TO STAVE OFF HUNGER AND THIRST.

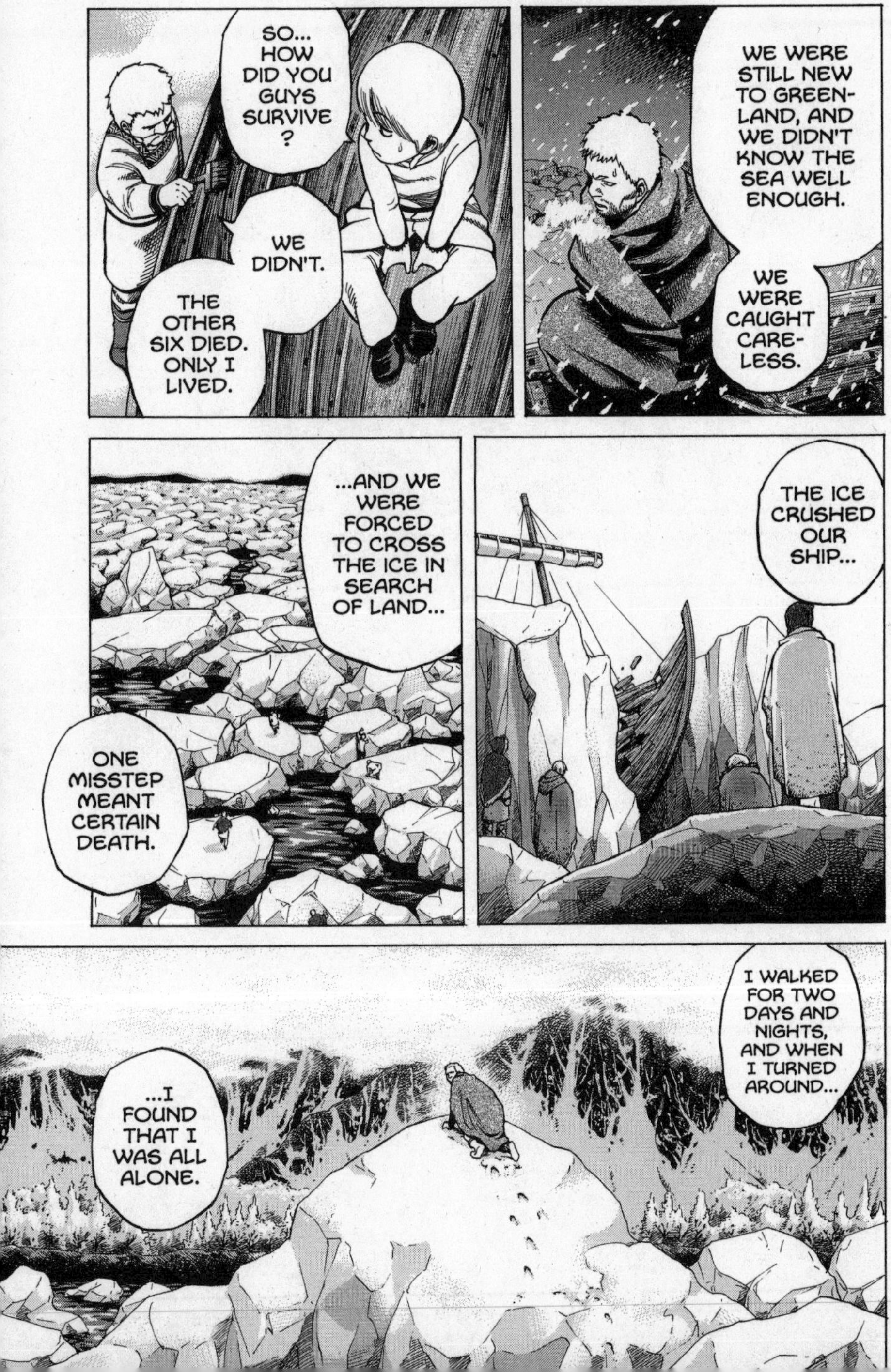
WE WERE STILL NEW TO GREEN-LAND, AND WE DIDN'T KNOW THE SEA WELL ENOUGH.
WE WERE CAUGHT CARE-LESS.
SO... HOW DID YOU GUYS SURVIVE?
WE DIDN'T.
THE OTHER SIX DIED. ONLY I LIVED.
THE ICE CRUSHED OUR SHIP...
...AND WE WERE FORCED TO CROSS THE ICE IN SEARCH OF LAND...
ONE MISSTEP MEANT CERTAIN DEATH.
I WALKED FOR TWO DAYS AND NIGHTS, AND WHEN I TURNED AROUND...
...I FOUND THAT I WAS ALL ALONE.

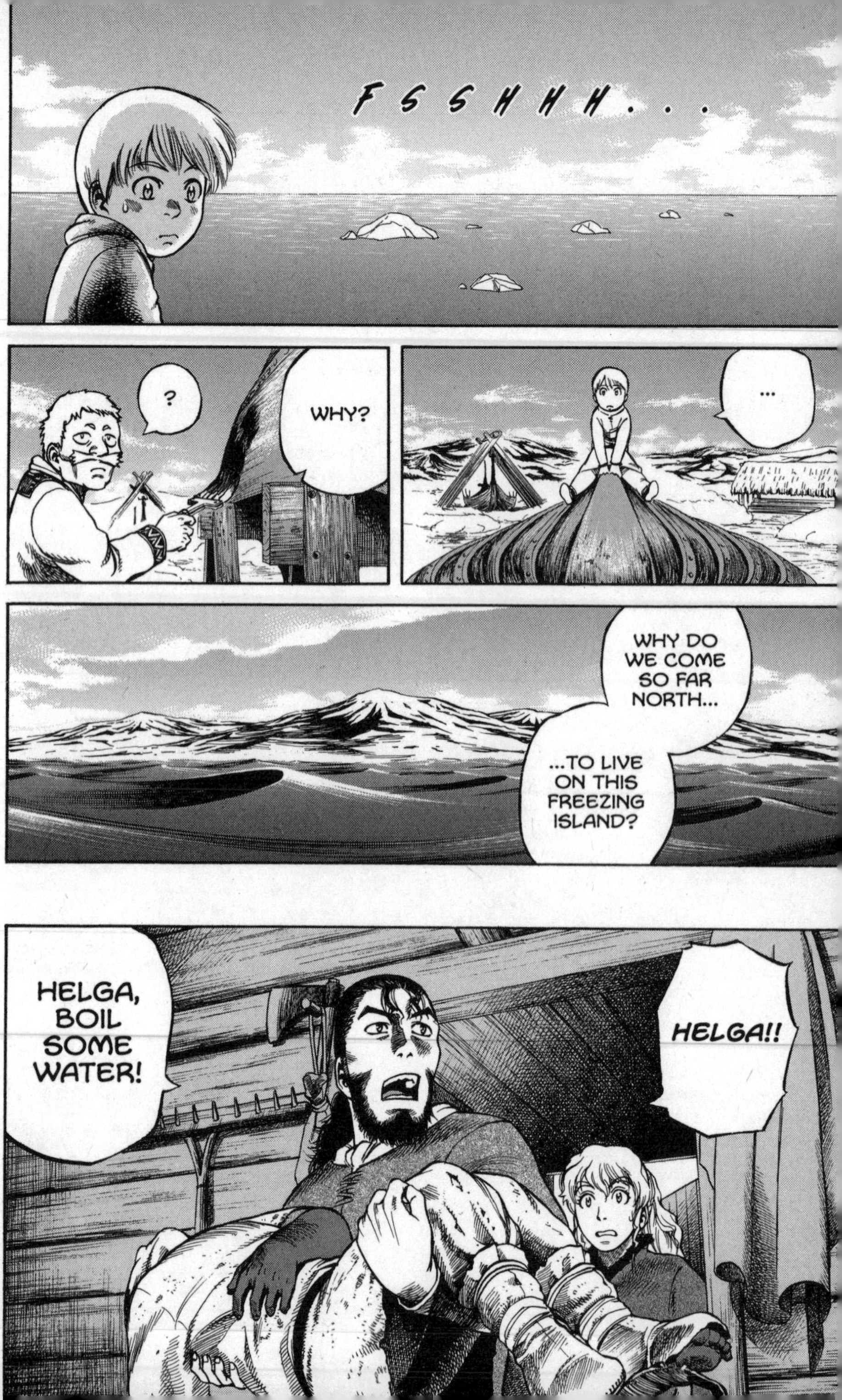
FSSHHH...
...
WHY?
?
WHY DO WE COME SO FAR NORTH...
...TO LIVE ON THIS FREEZING ISLAND?
HELGA!!
HELGA, BOIL SOME WATER!

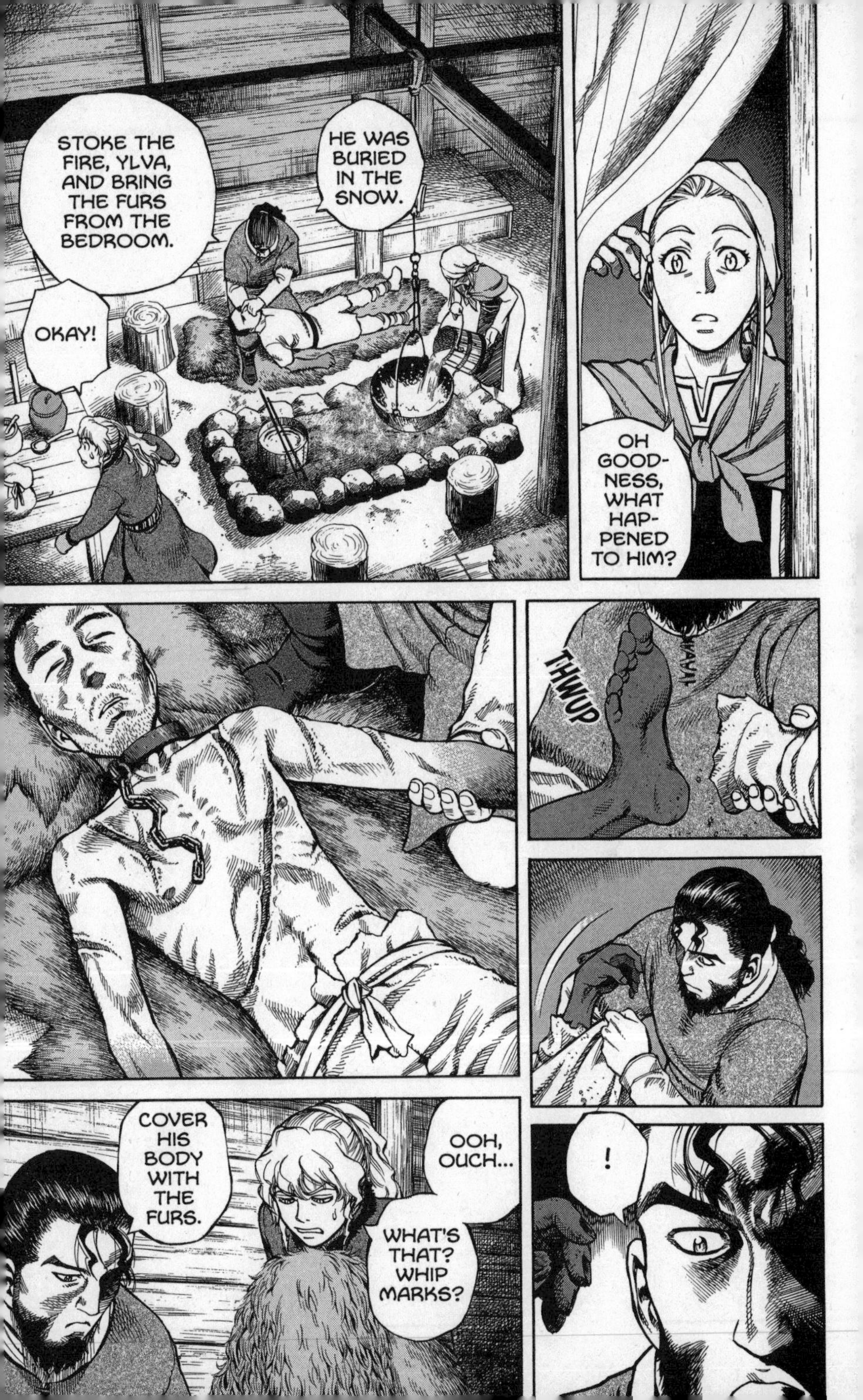
OH GOODNESS, WHAT HAPPENED TO HIM?
HE WAS BURIED IN THE SNOW.
STOKE THE FIRE, YLVA, AND BRING THE FURS FROM THE BEDROOM.
OKAY!
THWUP
!
COVER HIS BODY WITH THE FURS.
OOH, OUCH...
WHAT'S THAT? WHIP MARKS?

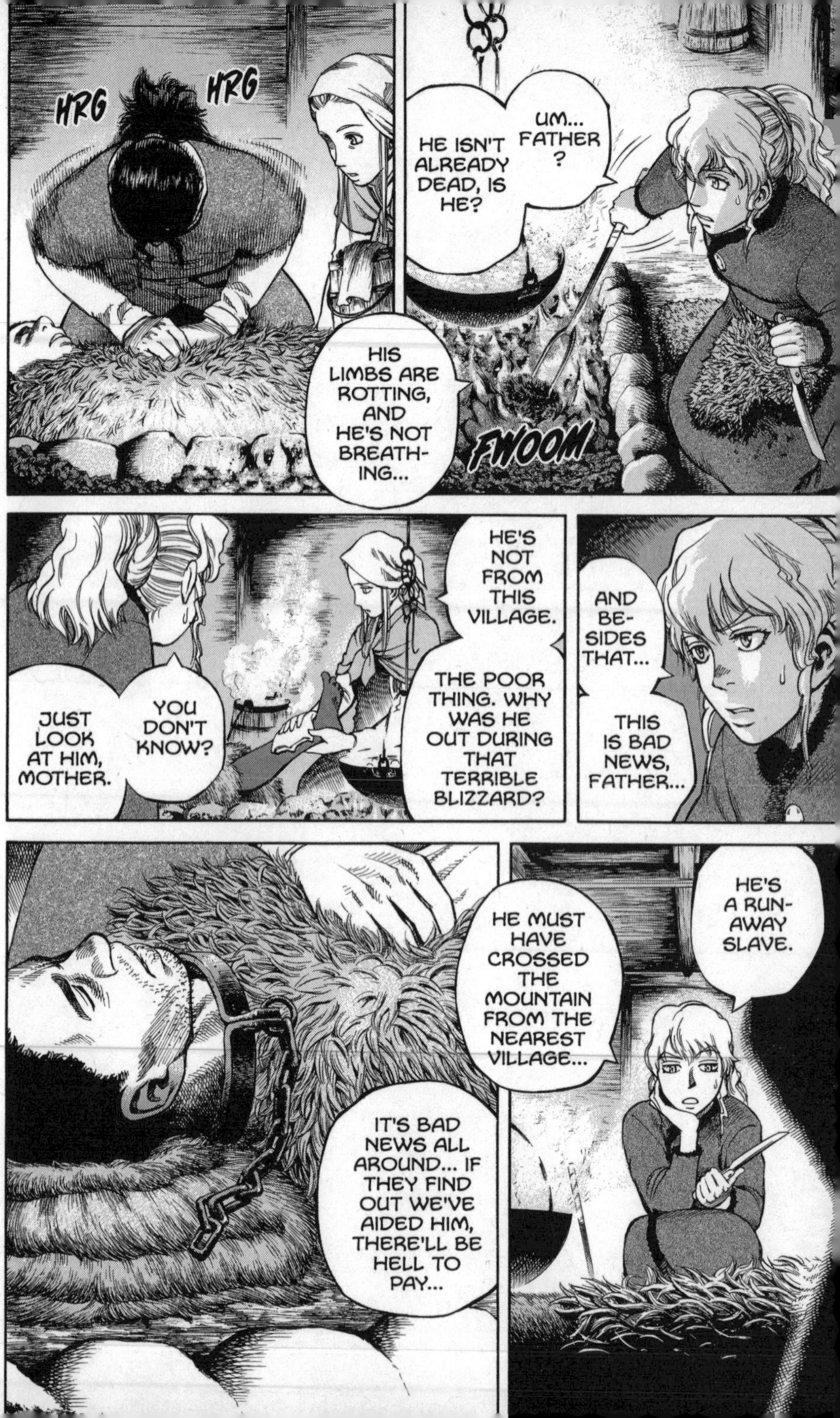
UM... FATHER?
HE ISN'T ALREADY DEAD, IS HE?
HIS LIMBS ARE ROTTING, AND HE'S NOT BREATHING...
FWOOM
HRG
HRG
AND BESIDES THAT...
THIS IS BAD NEWS, FATHER...
HE'S NOT FROM THIS VILLAGE.
THE POOR THING. WHY WAS HE OUT DURING THAT TERRIBLE BLIZZARD?
YOU DON'T KNOW?
JUST LOOK AT HIM, MOTHER.
HE'S A RUNAWAY SLAVE.
HE MUST HAVE CROSSED THE MOUNTAIN FROM THE NEAREST VILLAGE...
IT'S BAD NEWS ALL AROUND... IF THEY FIND OUT WE'VE AIDED HIM, THERE'LL BE HELL TO PAY...

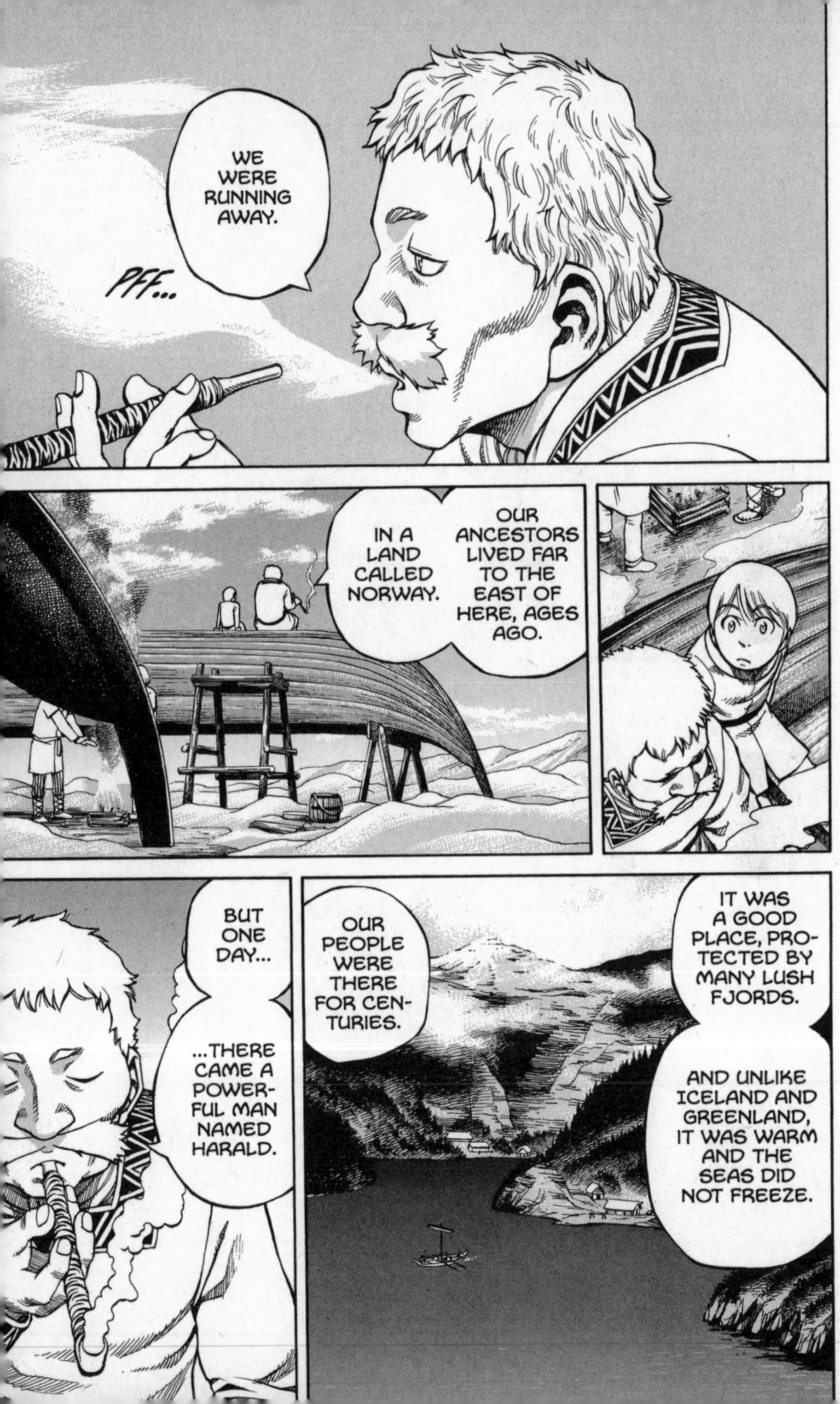
WE WERE RUNNING AWAY.
PFF...
OUR ANCESTORS LIVED FAR TO THE EAST OF HERE, AGES AGO.
IN A LAND CALLED NORWAY.
IT WAS A GOOD PLACE, PROTECTED BY MANY LUSH FJORDS.
AND UNLIKE ICELAND AND GREENLAND, IT WAS WARM AND THE SEAS DID NOT FREEZE.
OUR PEOPLE WERE THERE FOR CENTURIES.
BUT ONE DAY...
...THERE CAME A POWERFUL MAN NAMED HARALD.

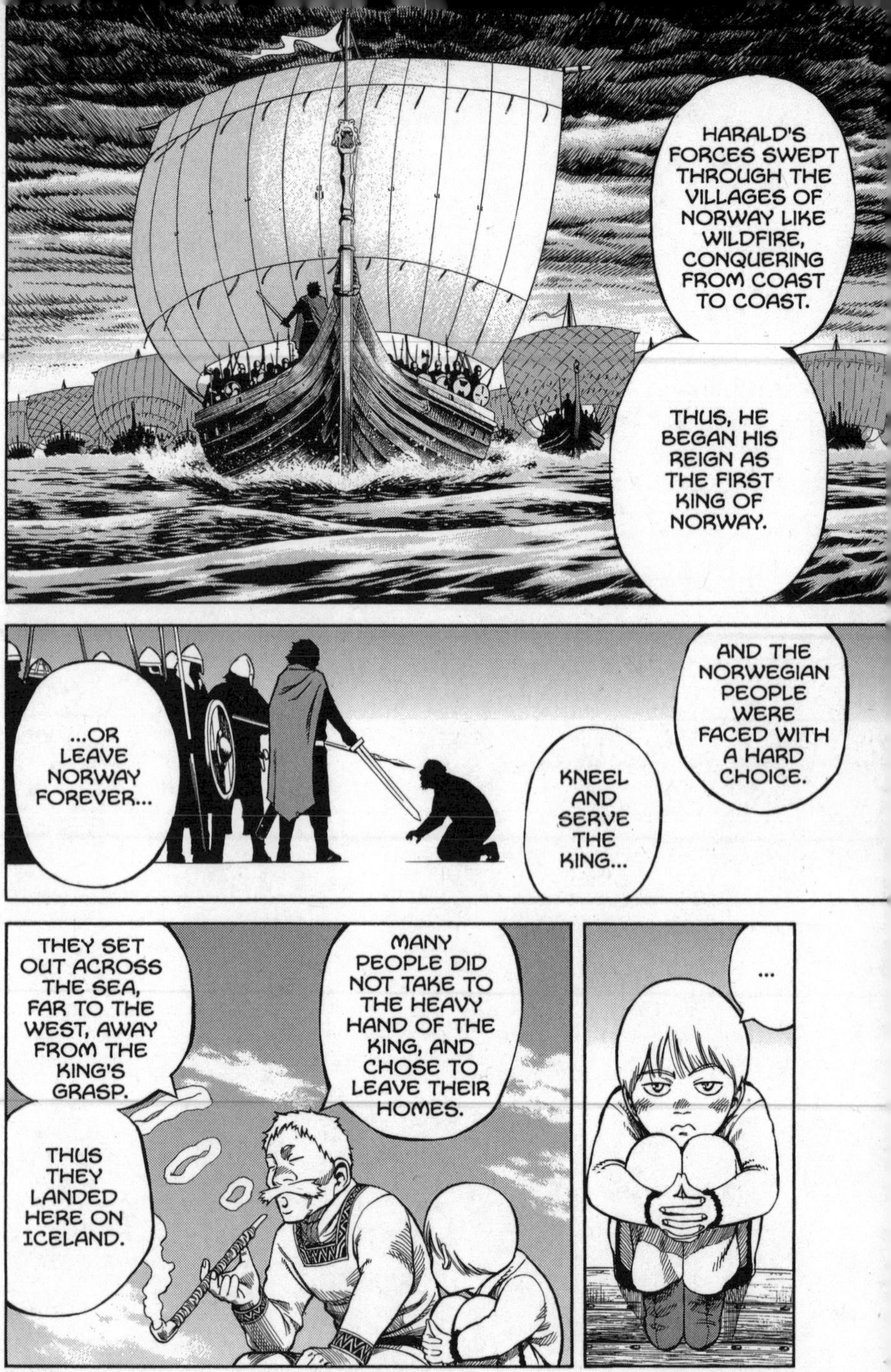
HARALD'S FORCES SWEPT THROUGH THE VILLAGES OF NORWAY LIKE WILDFIRE, CONQUERING FROM COAST TO COAST.
THUS, HE BEGAN HIS REIGN AS THE FIRST KING OF NORWAY.
AND THE NORWEGIAN PEOPLE WERE FACED WITH A HARD CHOICE.
KNEEL AND SERVE THE KING...
...OR LEAVE NORWAY FOREVER...
...
MANY PEOPLE DID NOT TAKE TO THE HEAVY HAND OF THE KING, AND CHOSE TO LEAVE THEIR HOMES.
THEY SET OUT ACROSS THE SEA, FAR TO THE WEST, AWAY FROM THE KING'S GRASP.
THUS THEY LANDED HERE ON ICELAND.

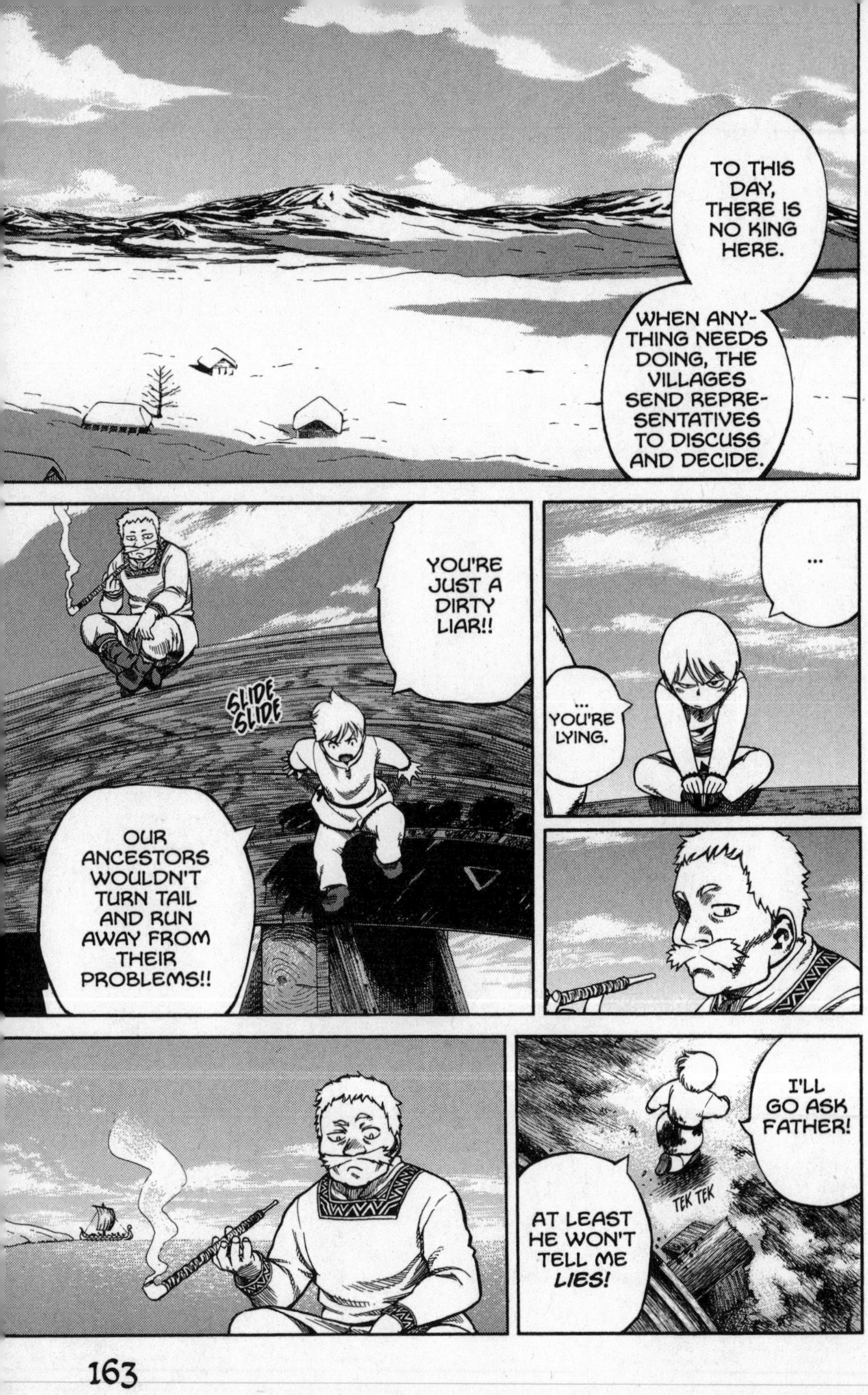
TO THIS DAY, THERE IS NO KING HERE.
WHEN ANYTHING NEEDS DOING, THE VILLAGES SEND REPRESENTATIVES TO DISCUSS AND DECIDE.
...
... YOU'RE LYING.
YOU'RE JUST A DIRTY LIAR!!
SLIDE SLIDE
OUR ANCESTORS WOULDN'T TURN TAIL AND RUN AWAY FROM THEIR PROBLEMS!!
I'LL GO ASK FATHER!
TEK TEK
AT LEAST HE WON'T TELL ME *LIES!*

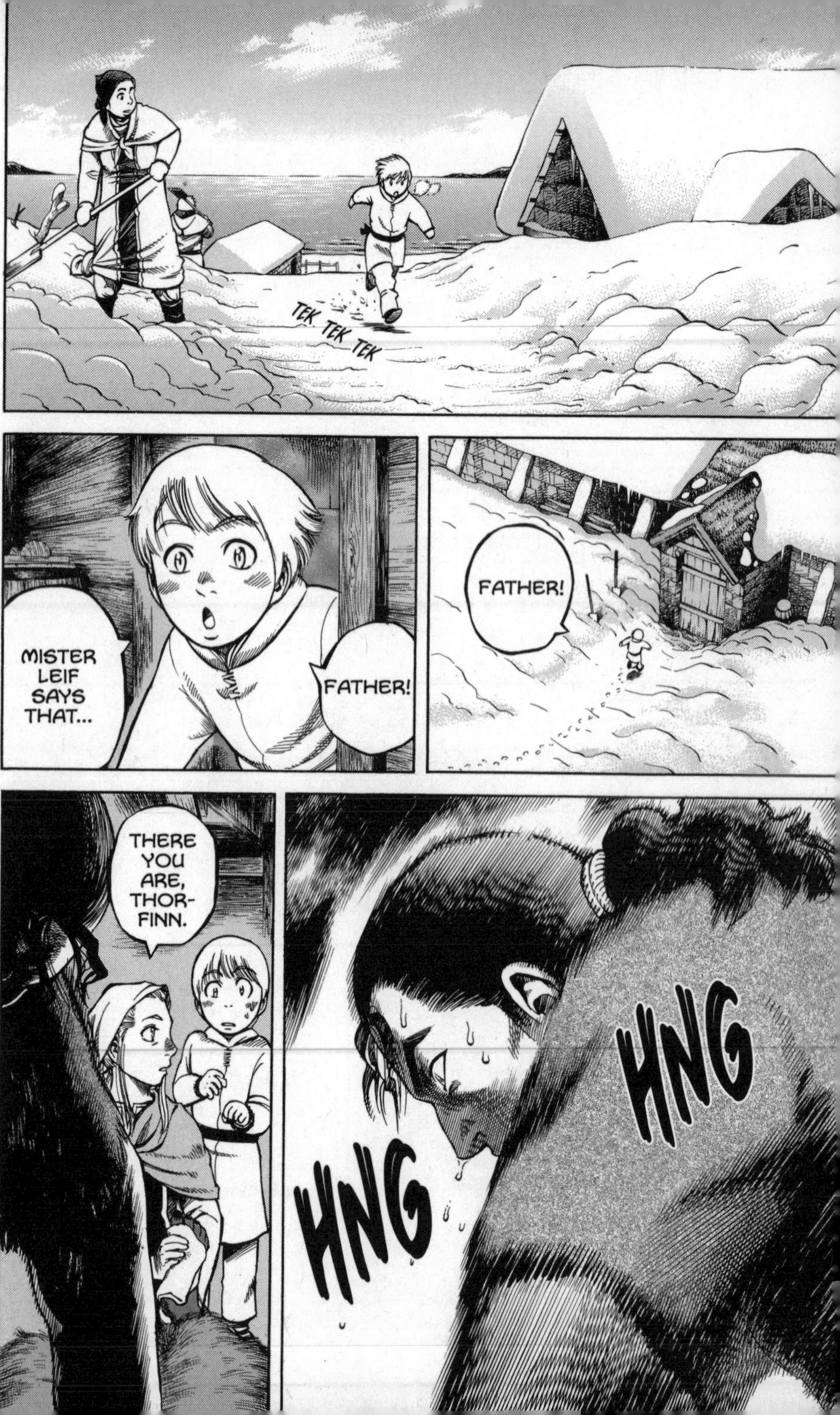
TEK TEK TEK
FATHER!
FATHER!
MISTER LEIF SAYS THAT...
HNG
HNG
THERE YOU ARE, THORFINN.

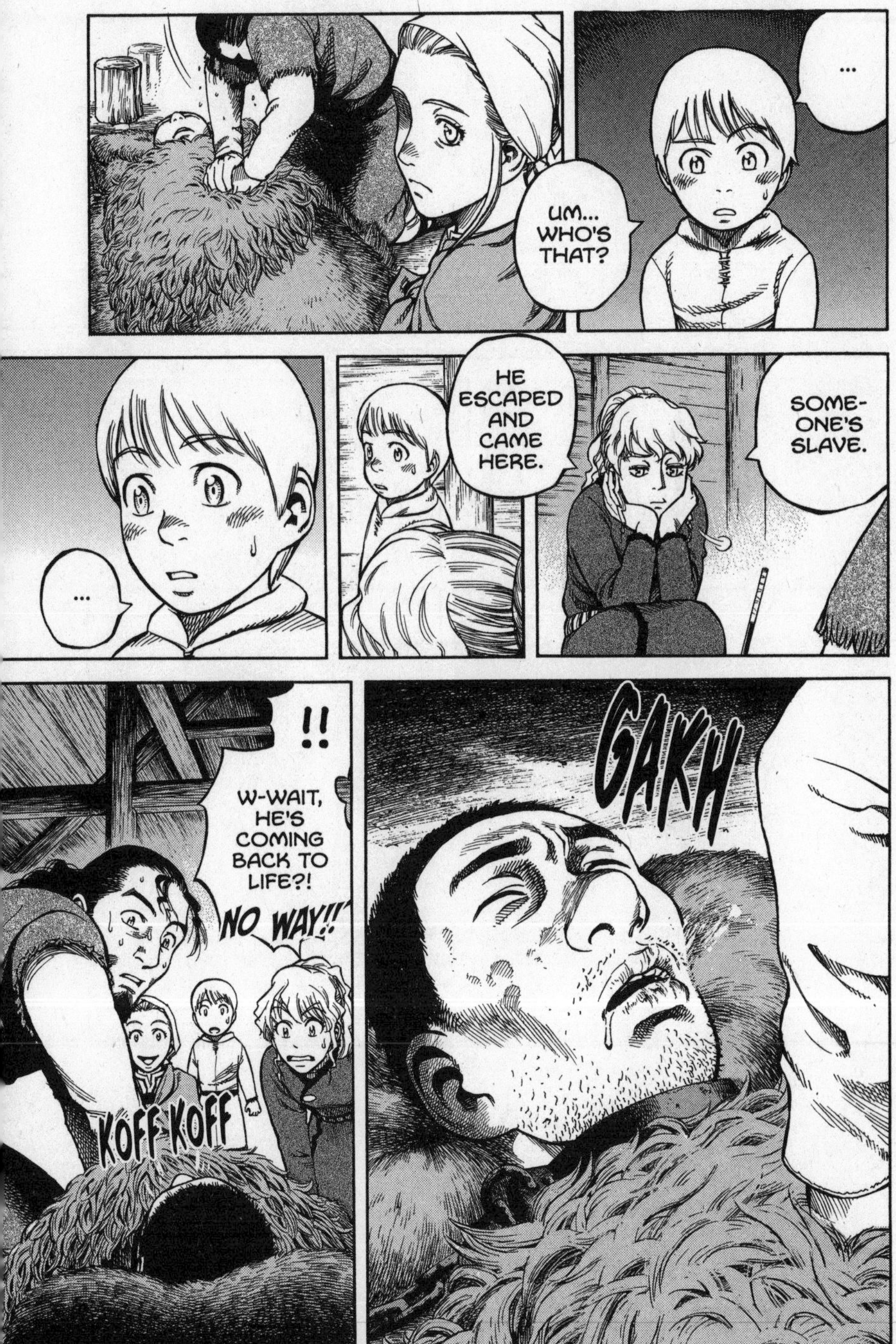
...
UM... WHO'S THAT?
SOME-ONE'S SLAVE.
HE ESCAPED AND CAME HERE.
...
GAKH
!!
W-WAIT, HE'S COMING BACK TO LIFE?!
NO WAY!!
KOFF KOFF

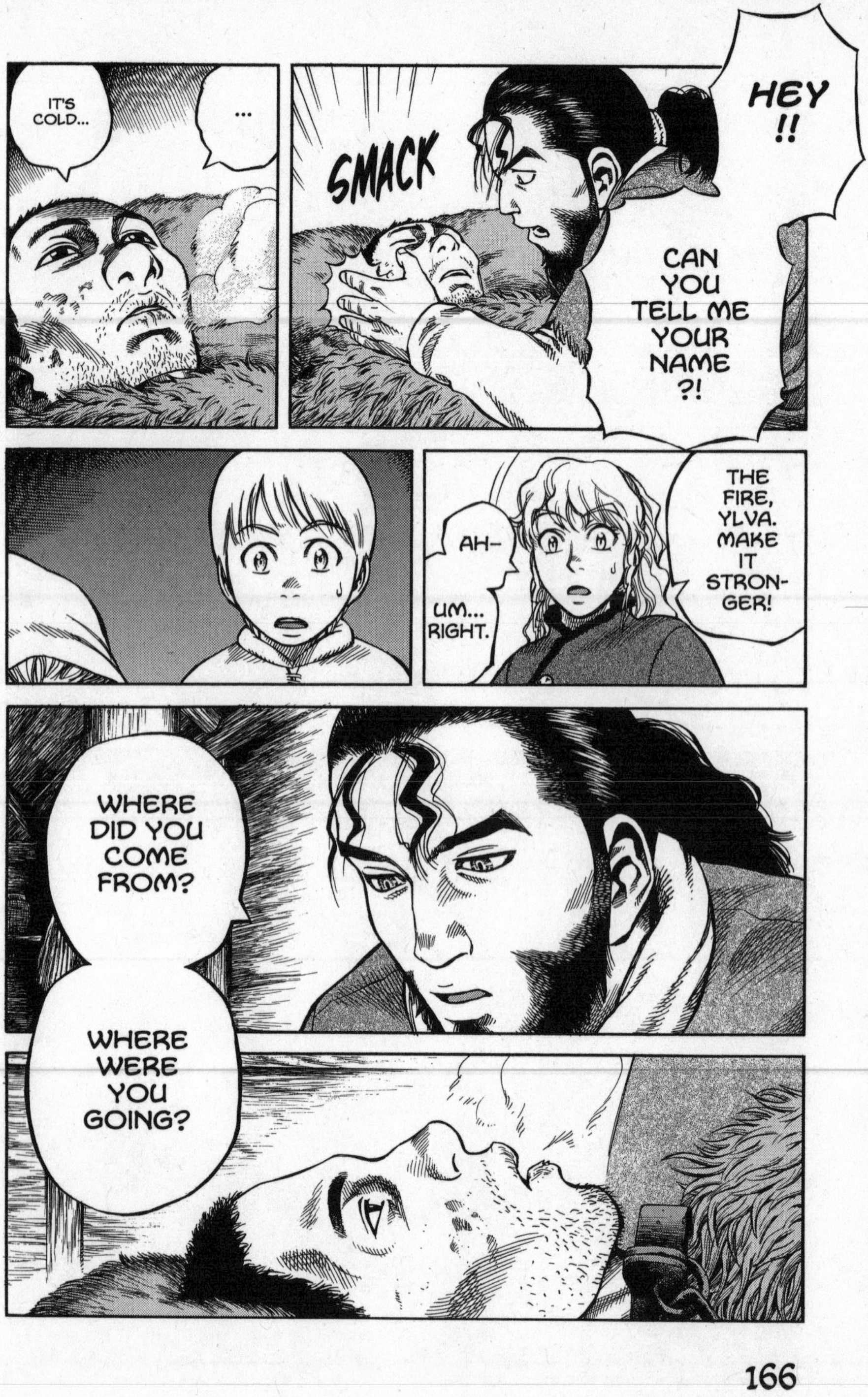
HEY !!
SMACK
CAN YOU TELL ME YOUR NAME ?!
...
IT'S COLD...
THE FIRE, YLVA. MAKE IT STRONGER!
AH— UM... RIGHT.
WHERE DID YOU COME FROM?
WHERE WERE YOU GOING?

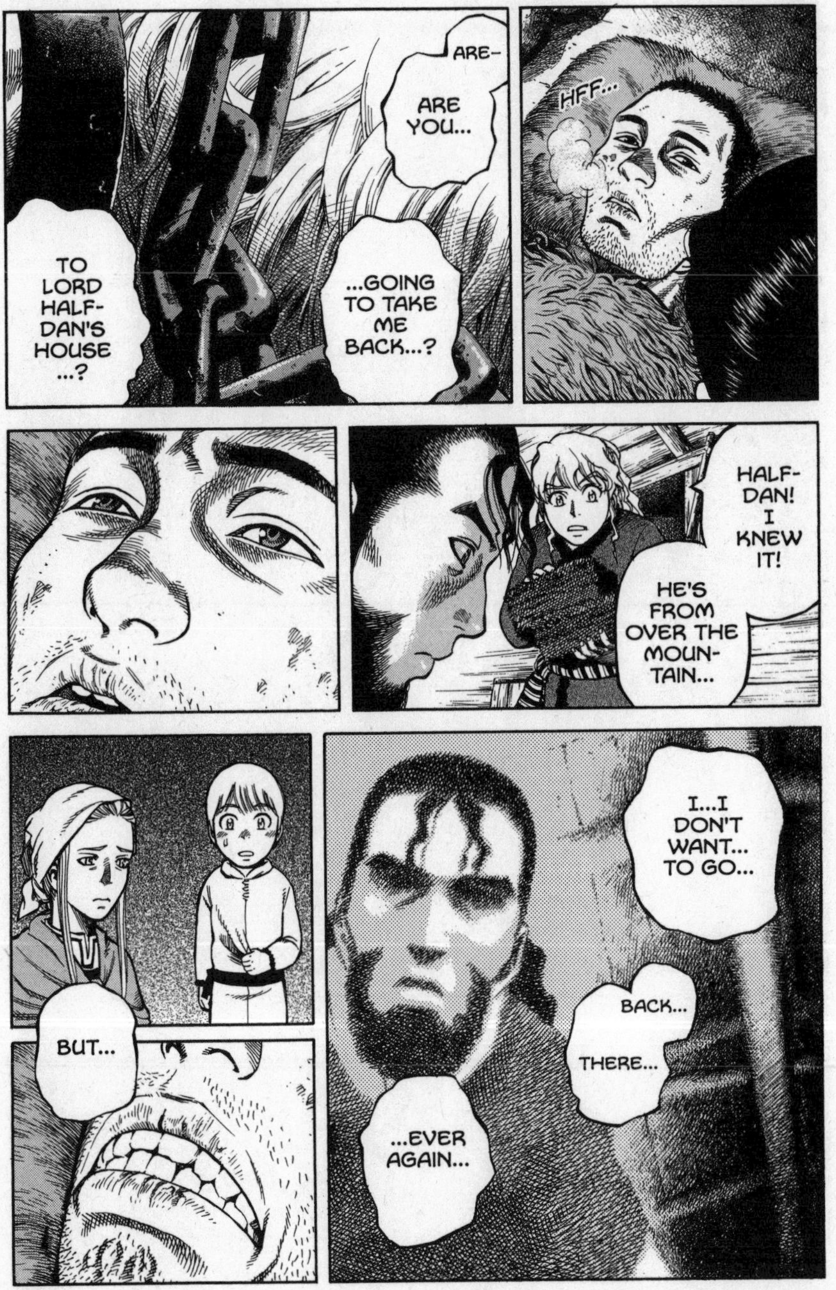
HFF...
ARE-
ARE YOU...
...GOING TO TAKE ME BACK...?
TO LORD HALF-DAN'S HOUSE...?
HALF-DAN! I KNEW IT!
HE'S FROM OVER THE MOUN-TAIN...
I...I DON'T WANT... TO GO...
BACK...
THERE...
...EVER AGAIN...
BUT...

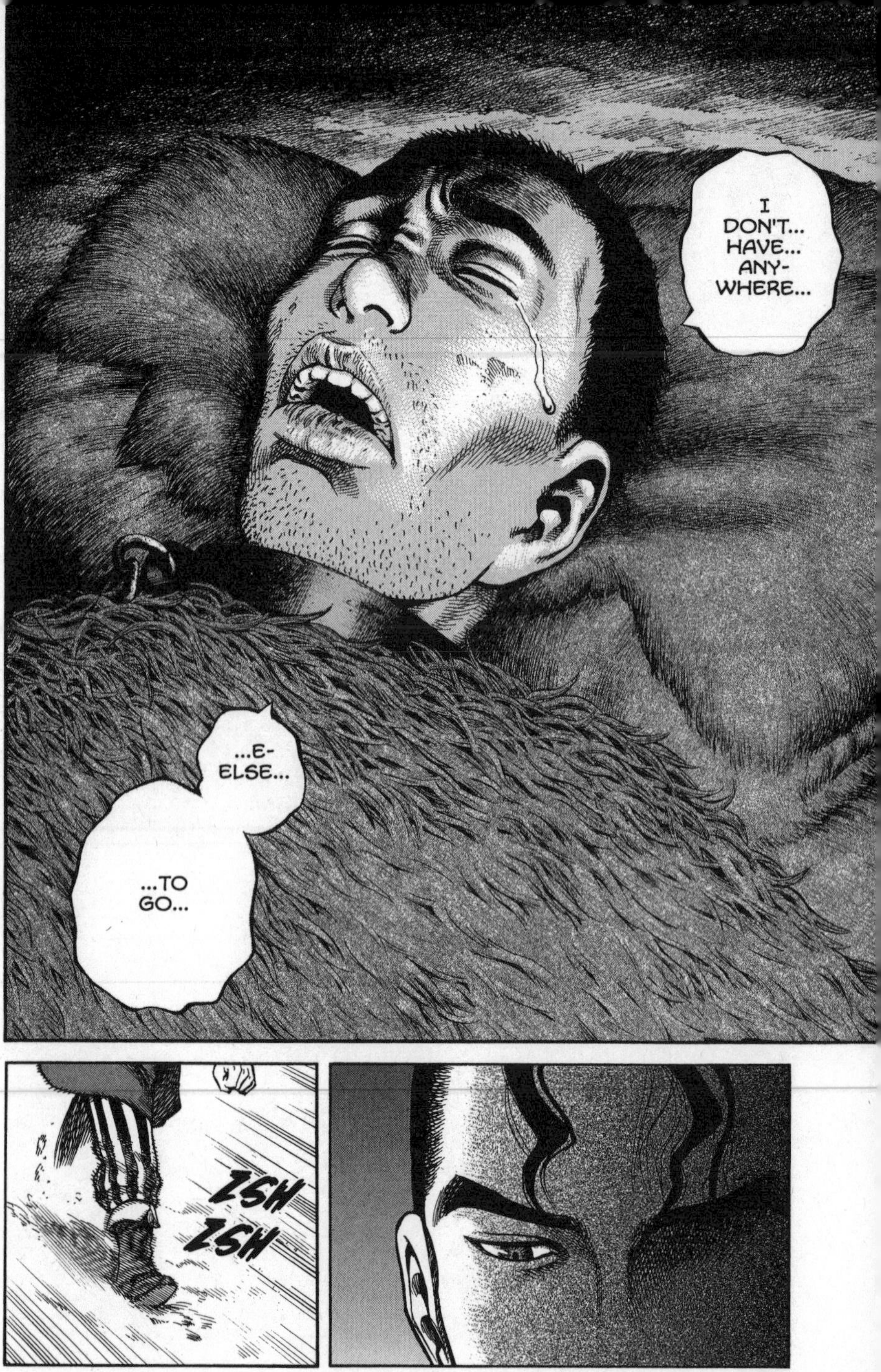
I DON'T... HAVE... ANY-WHERE...
...E-ELSE...
...TO GO...
ZSH ZSH

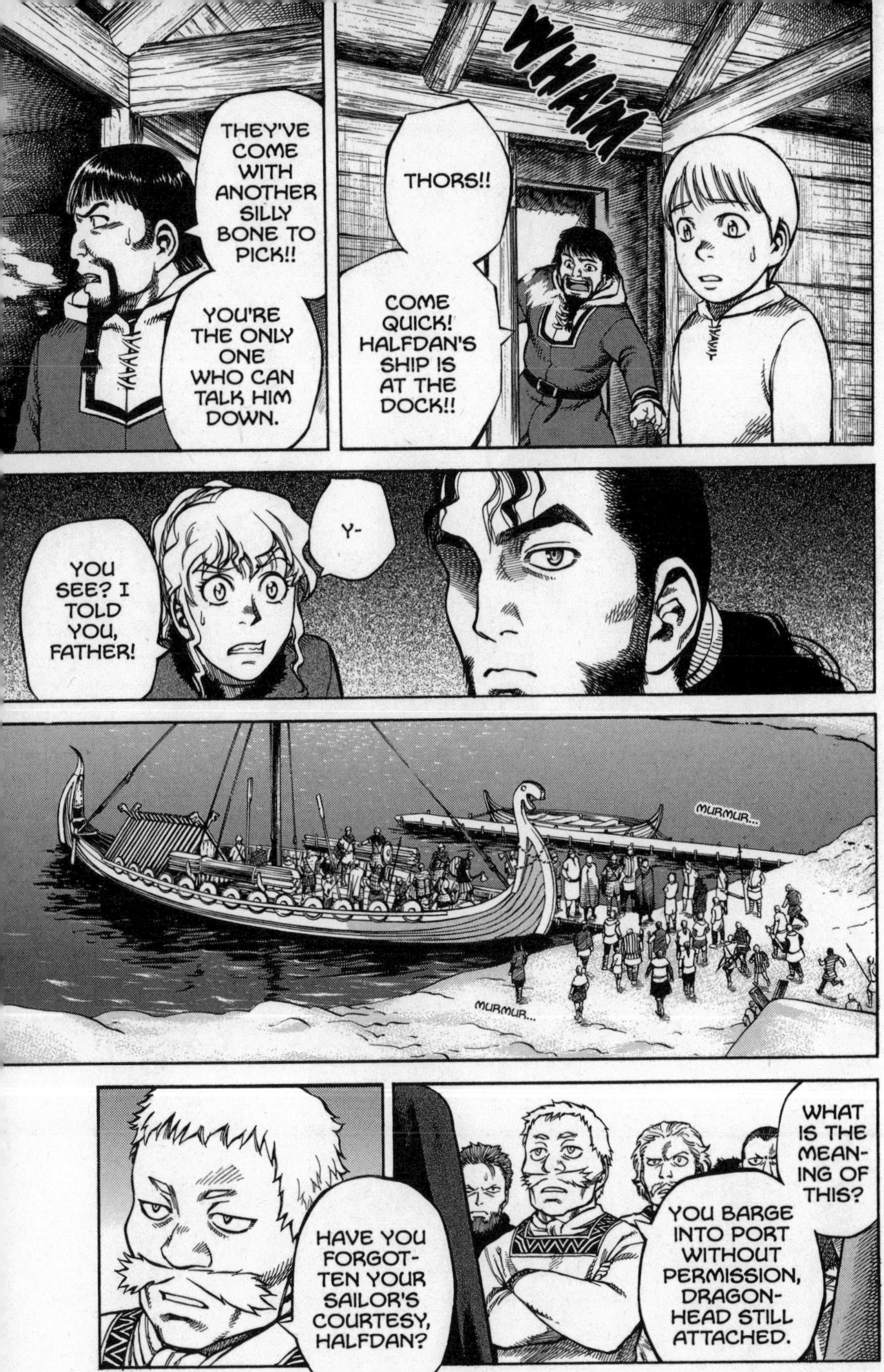
WHAM
THORS!!
COME QUICK! HALFDAN'S SHIP IS AT THE DOCK!!
THEY'VE COME WITH ANOTHER SILLY BONE TO PICK!!
YOU'RE THE ONLY ONE WHO CAN TALK HIM DOWN.
Y-
YOU SEE? I TOLD YOU, FATHER!
MURMUR...
MURMUR...
WHAT IS THE MEAN-ING OF THIS?
YOU BARGE INTO PORT WITHOUT PERMISSION, DRAGON-HEAD STILL ATTACHED.
HAVE YOU FORGOT-TEN YOUR SAILOR'S COURTESY, HALFDAN?

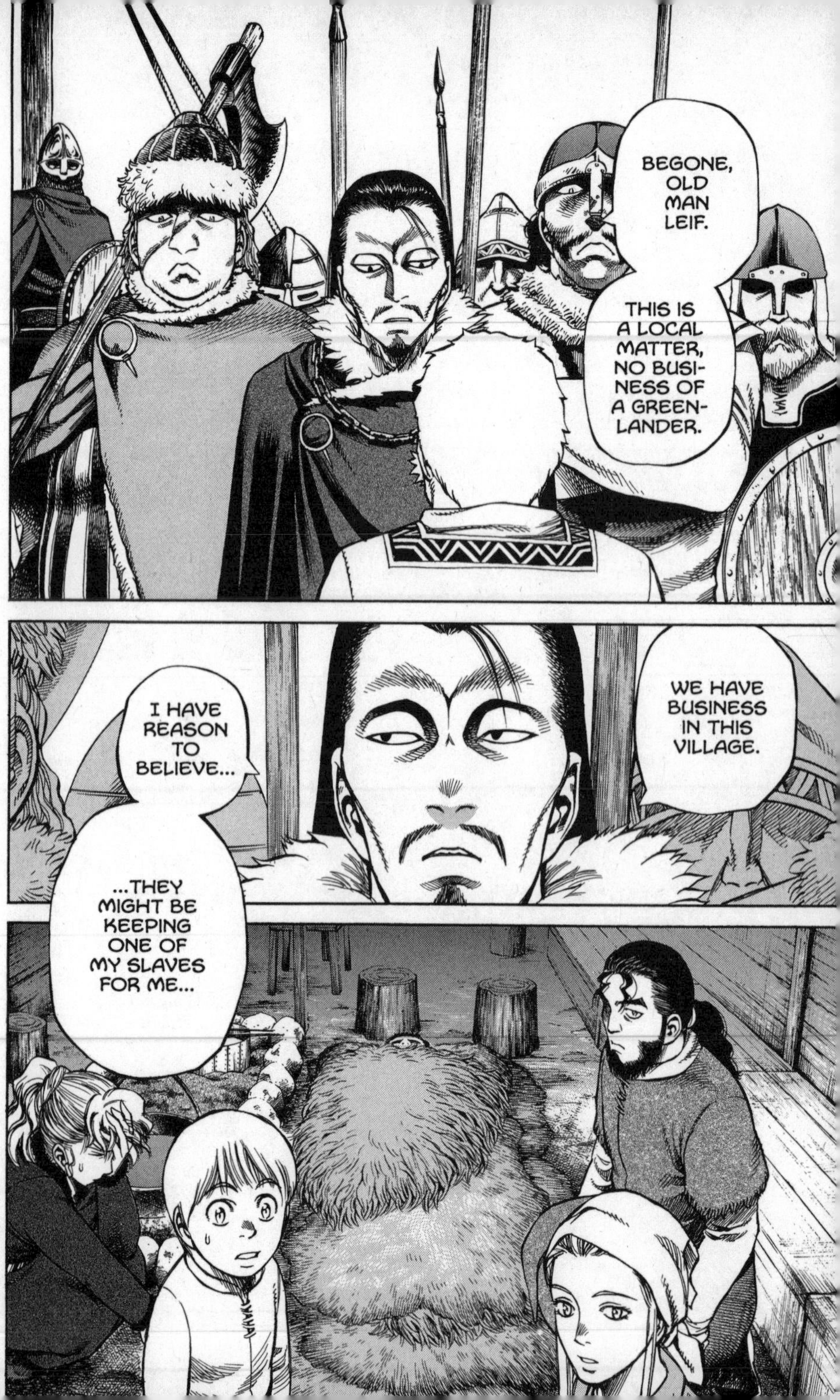
BEGONE, OLD MAN LEIF.
THIS IS A LOCAL MATTER, NO BUSINESS OF A GREENLANDER.
WE HAVE BUSINESS IN THIS VILLAGE.
I HAVE REASON TO BELIEVE...
...THEY MIGHT BE KEEPING ONE OF MY SLAVES FOR ME...

CHAPTER 3 - END

CHAPTER 4: UNBREAKABLE CHAINS

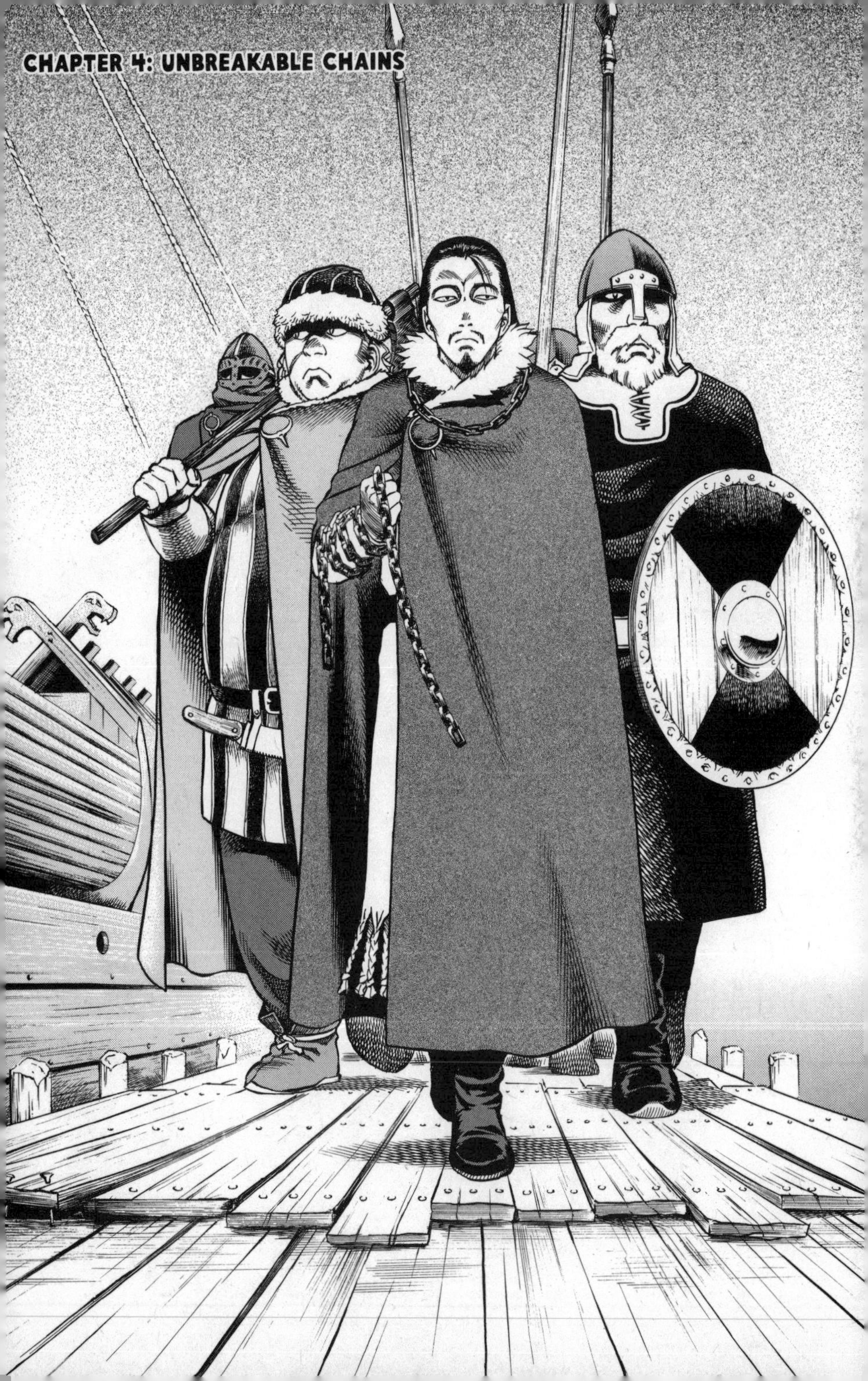

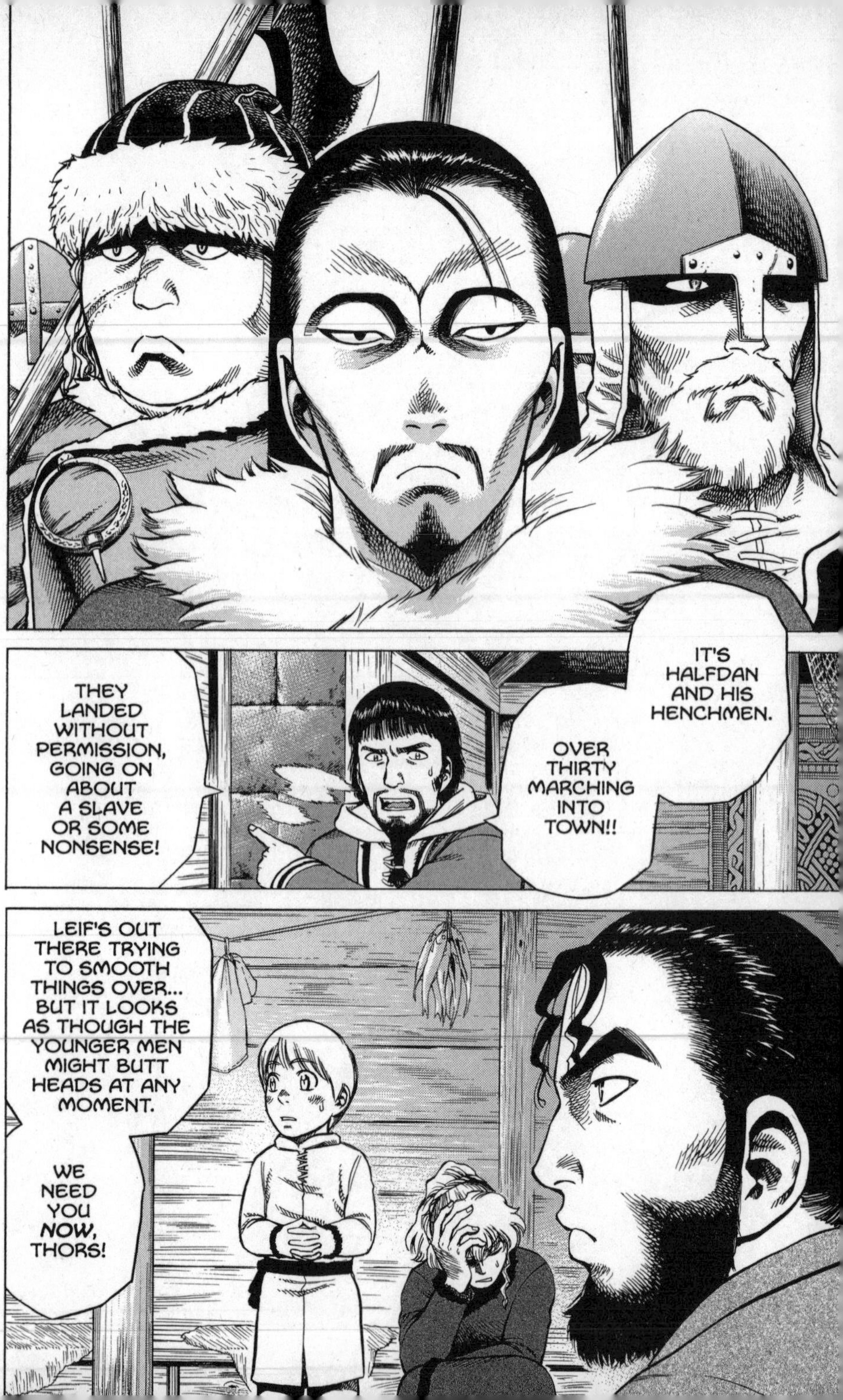
IT'S HALFDAN AND HIS HENCHMEN.
OVER THIRTY MARCHING INTO TOWN!!
THEY LANDED WITHOUT PERMISSION, GOING ON ABOUT A SLAVE OR SOME NONSENSE!
LEIF'S OUT THERE TRYING TO SMOOTH THINGS OVER... BUT IT LOOKS AS THOUGH THE YOUNGER MEN MIGHT BUTT HEADS AT ANY MOMENT.
WE NEED YOU *NOW*, THORS!

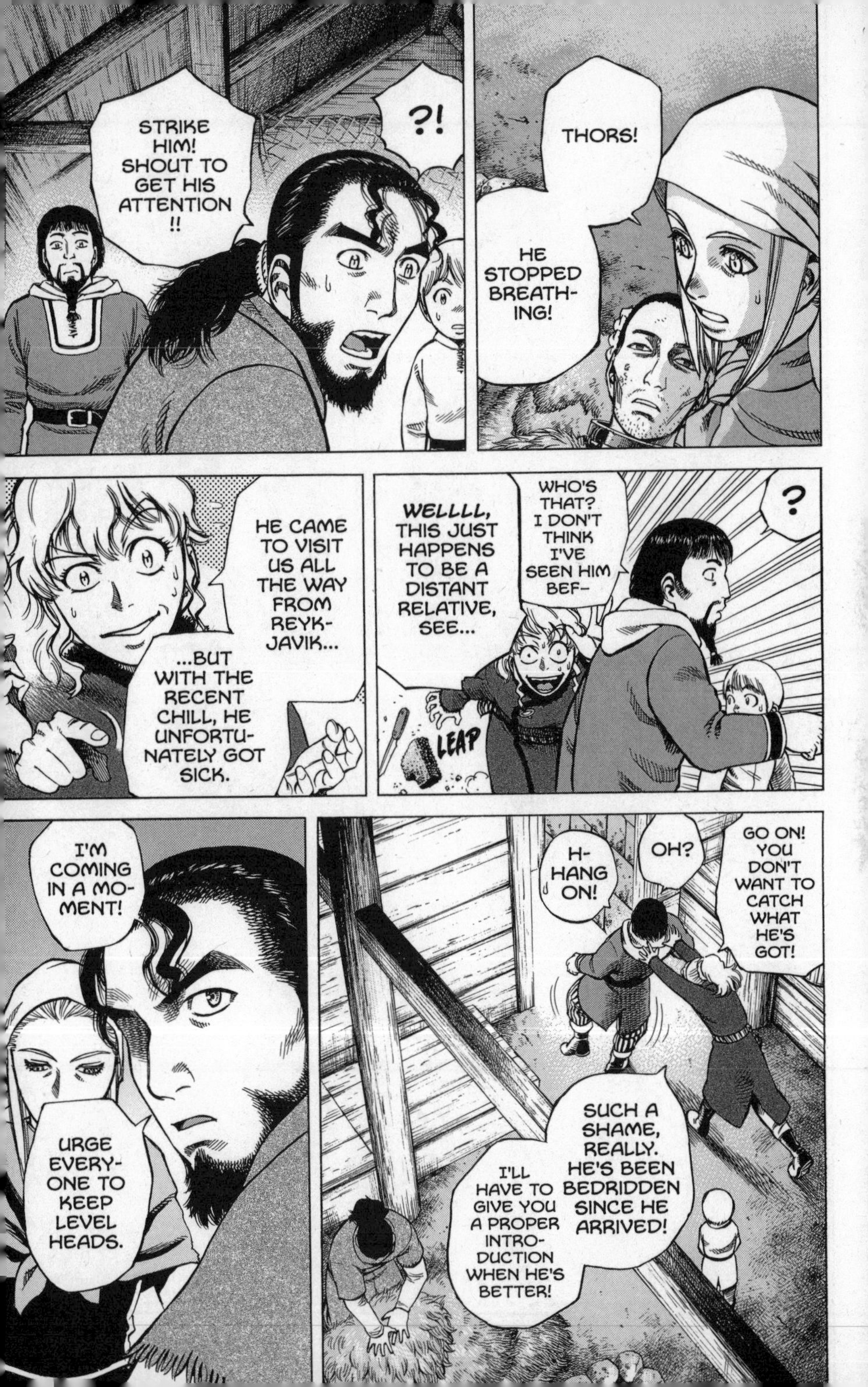
THORS!
HE STOPPED BREATHING!
?!
STRIKE HIM! SHOUT TO GET HIS ATTENTION!!
?
WHO'S THAT? I DON'T THINK I'VE SEEN HIM BEF-
WELLLL, THIS JUST HAPPENS TO BE A DISTANT RELATIVE, SEE...
LEAP
HE CAME TO VISIT US ALL THE WAY FROM REYKJAVIK...
...BUT WITH THE RECENT CHILL, HE UNFORTUNATELY GOT SICK.
GO ON! YOU DON'T WANT TO CATCH WHAT HE'S GOT!
OH?
H-HANG ON!
SUCH A SHAME, REALLY. HE'S BEEN BEDRIDDEN SINCE HE ARRIVED!
I'LL HAVE TO GIVE YOU A PROPER INTRODUCTION WHEN HE'S BETTER!
I'M COMING IN A MOMENT!
URGE EVERYONE TO KEEP LEVEL HEADS.

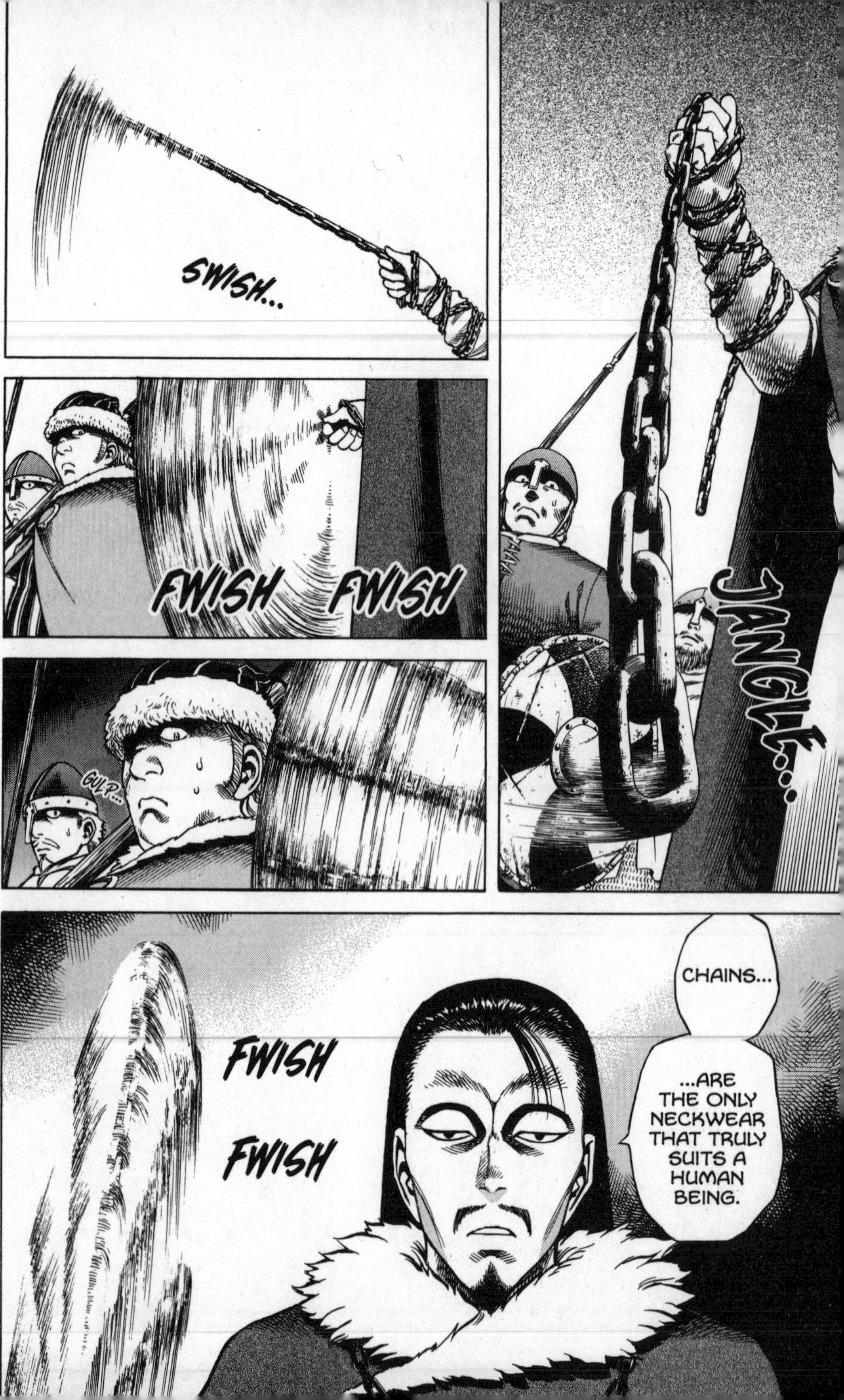
JANGLE...
SWISH...
FWISH FWISH
GULP...
CHAINS...
...ARE THE ONLY NECKWEAR THAT TRULY SUITS A HUMAN BEING.
FWISH
FWISH

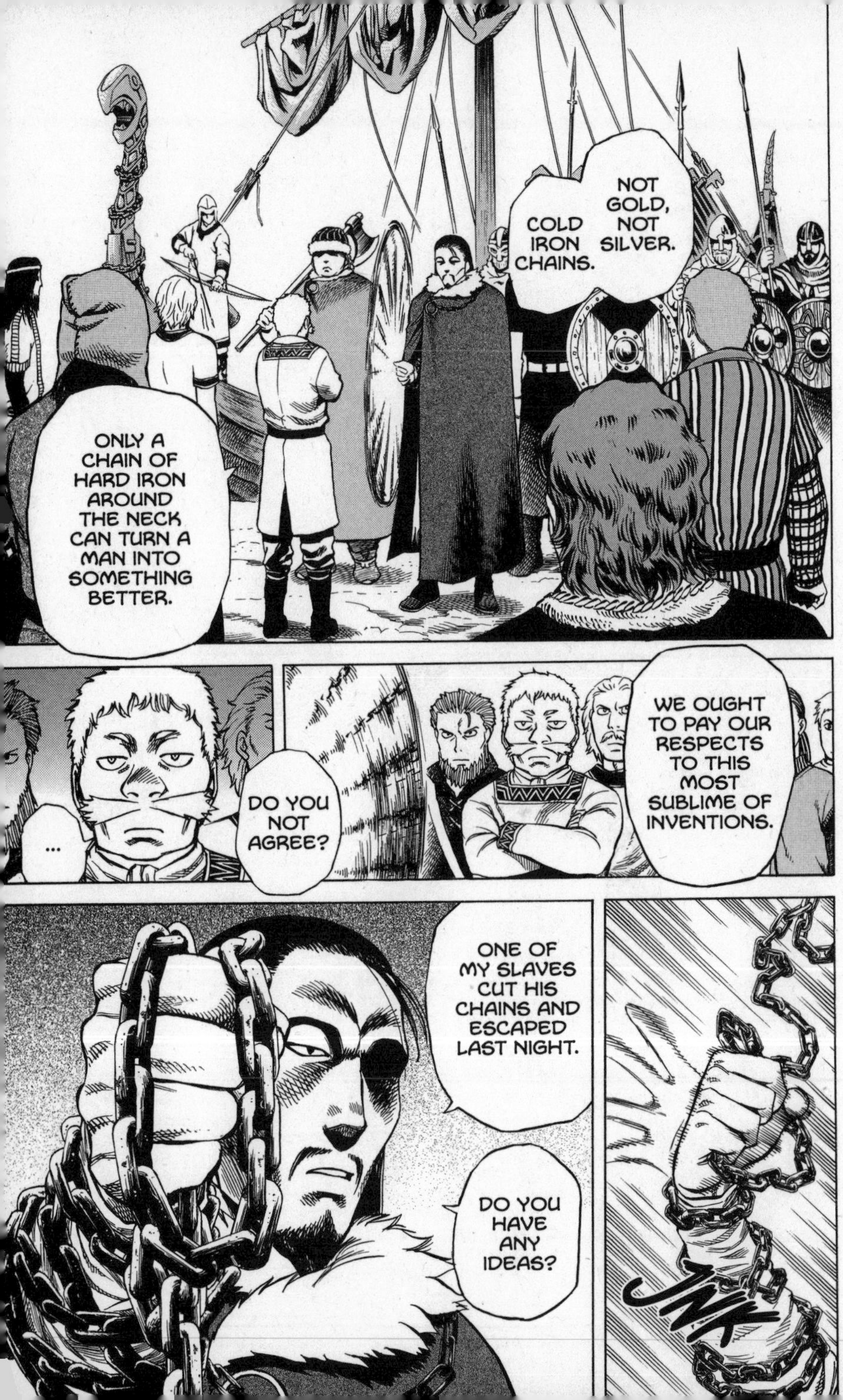
NOT GOLD, NOT SILVER.
COLD IRON CHAINS.
ONLY A CHAIN OF HARD IRON AROUND THE NECK CAN TURN A MAN INTO SOMETHING BETTER.
WE OUGHT TO PAY OUR RESPECTS TO THIS MOST SUBLIME OF INVENTIONS.
DO YOU NOT AGREE?
...
JINK
ONE OF MY SLAVES CUT HIS CHAINS AND ESCAPED LAST NIGHT.
DO YOU HAVE ANY IDEAS?

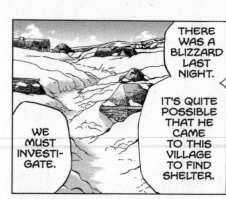

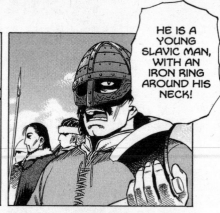

HE IS A YOUNG SLAVIC MAN, WITH AN IRON RING AROUND HIS NECK!
THERE WAS A BLIZZARD LAST NIGHT.
IT'S QUITE POSSIBLE THAT HE CAME TO THIS VILLAGE TO FIND SHELTER.
WE MUST INVESTIGATE.
KEEP YOUR FLIMSY EXCUSES, HALFDAN!!
THIS IS JUST YOUR CHANCE TO SETTLE OUR OLD SCORE, ISN'T IT?!
WHAT'S THE STORY HERE?
WE'VE HAD SEVERAL SQUABBLES OVER THE BOUNDARIES OF GRAZING LAND BETWEEN OUR VILLAGE AND HIS.
THEY LIKE TO BARGE ONTO OUR TERRITORY AND HARVEST OUR GRASS FOR THEIR WINTER STOCK.
WHIS-PER
PEOPLE ON BOTH SIDES WERE GETTING HURT, SO WE JUST HAD IT SETTLED AT THE LAST THING.*

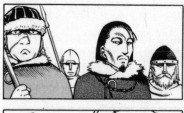

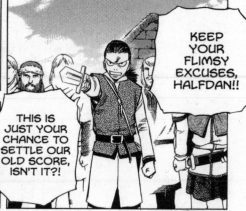

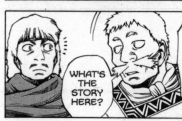

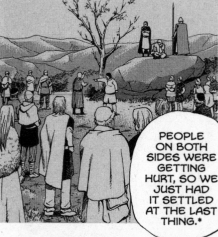

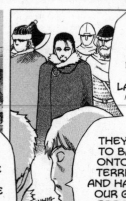

*A "THING" IS A VIKING ASSEMBLY.

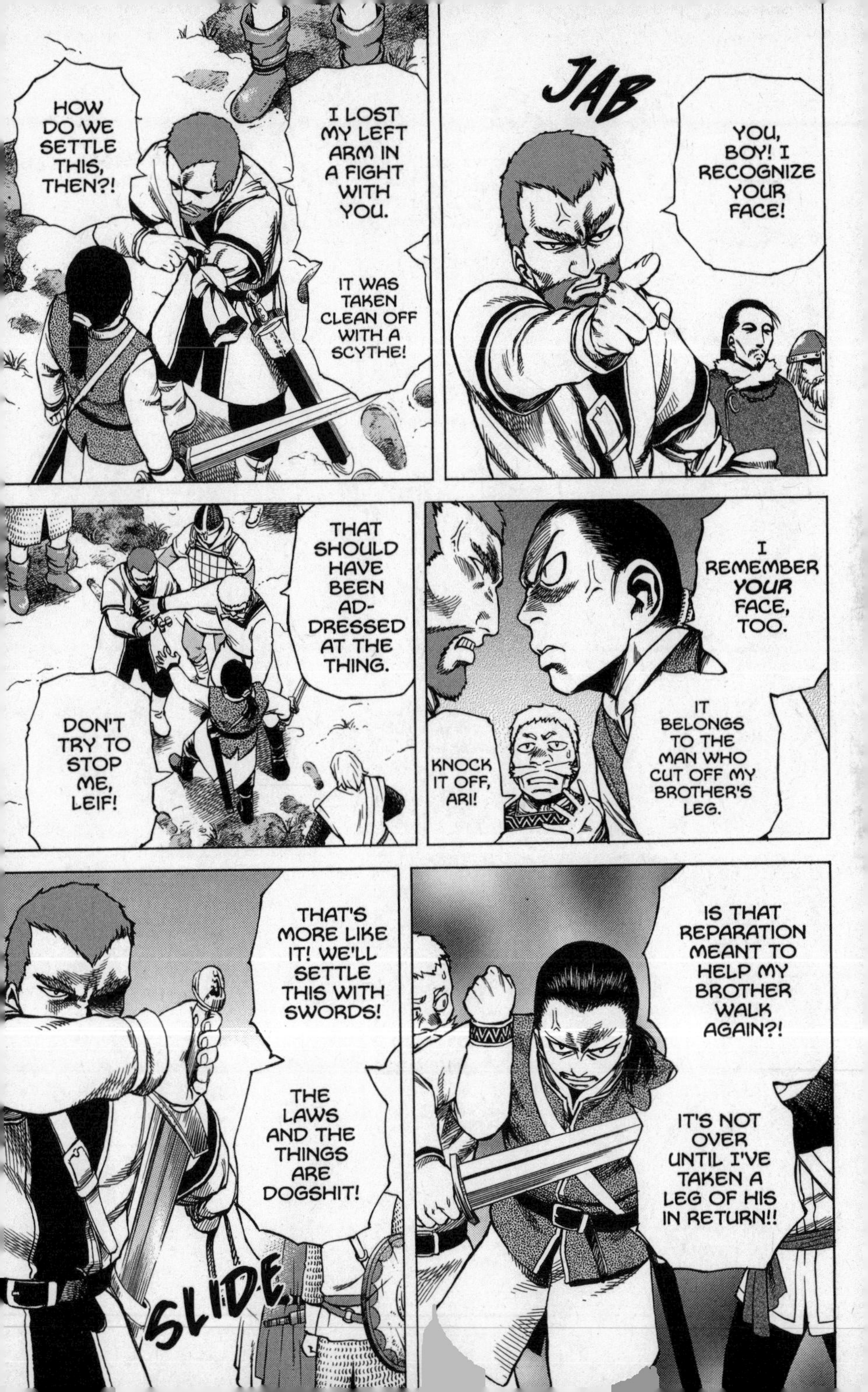
JAB
YOU, BOY! I RECOGNIZE YOUR FACE!
I LOST MY LEFT ARM IN A FIGHT WITH YOU.
IT WAS TAKEN CLEAN OFF WITH A SCYTHE!
HOW DO WE SETTLE THIS, THEN?!
I REMEMBER *YOUR* FACE, TOO.
IT BELONGS TO THE MAN WHO CUT OFF MY BROTHER'S LEG.
KNOCK IT OFF, ARI!
THAT SHOULD HAVE BEEN ADDRESSED AT THE THING.
DON'T TRY TO STOP ME, LEIF!
IS THAT REPARATION MEANT TO HELP MY BROTHER WALK AGAIN?!
IT'S NOT OVER UNTIL I'VE TAKEN A LEG OF HIS IN RETURN!!
THAT'S MORE LIKE IT! WE'LL SETTLE THIS WITH SWORDS!
THE LAWS AND THE THINGS ARE DOGSHIT!
SLIDE

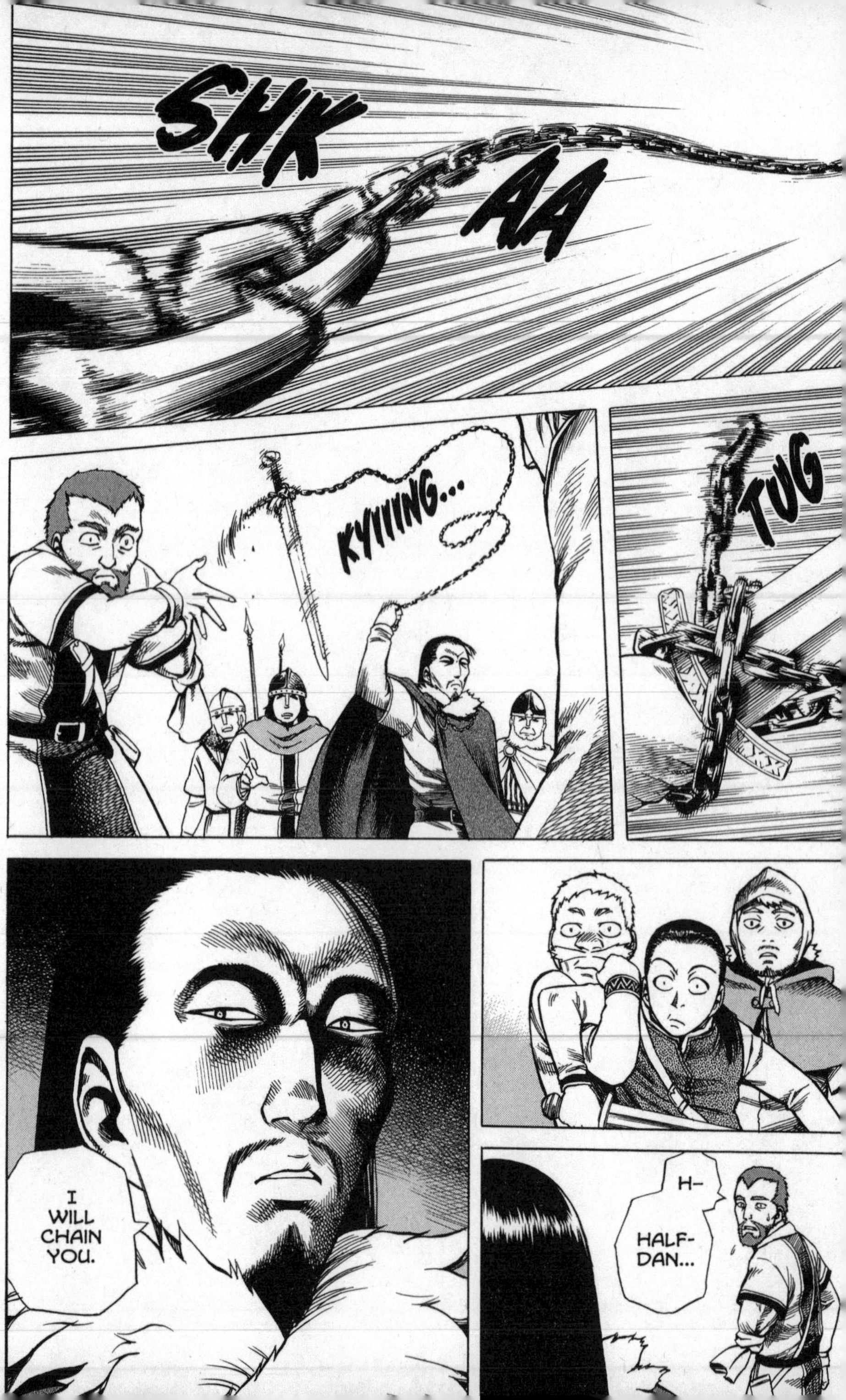
SHK
AA
TUG
KYIIIING...
H-
HALF-DAN...
I WILL CHAIN YOU.

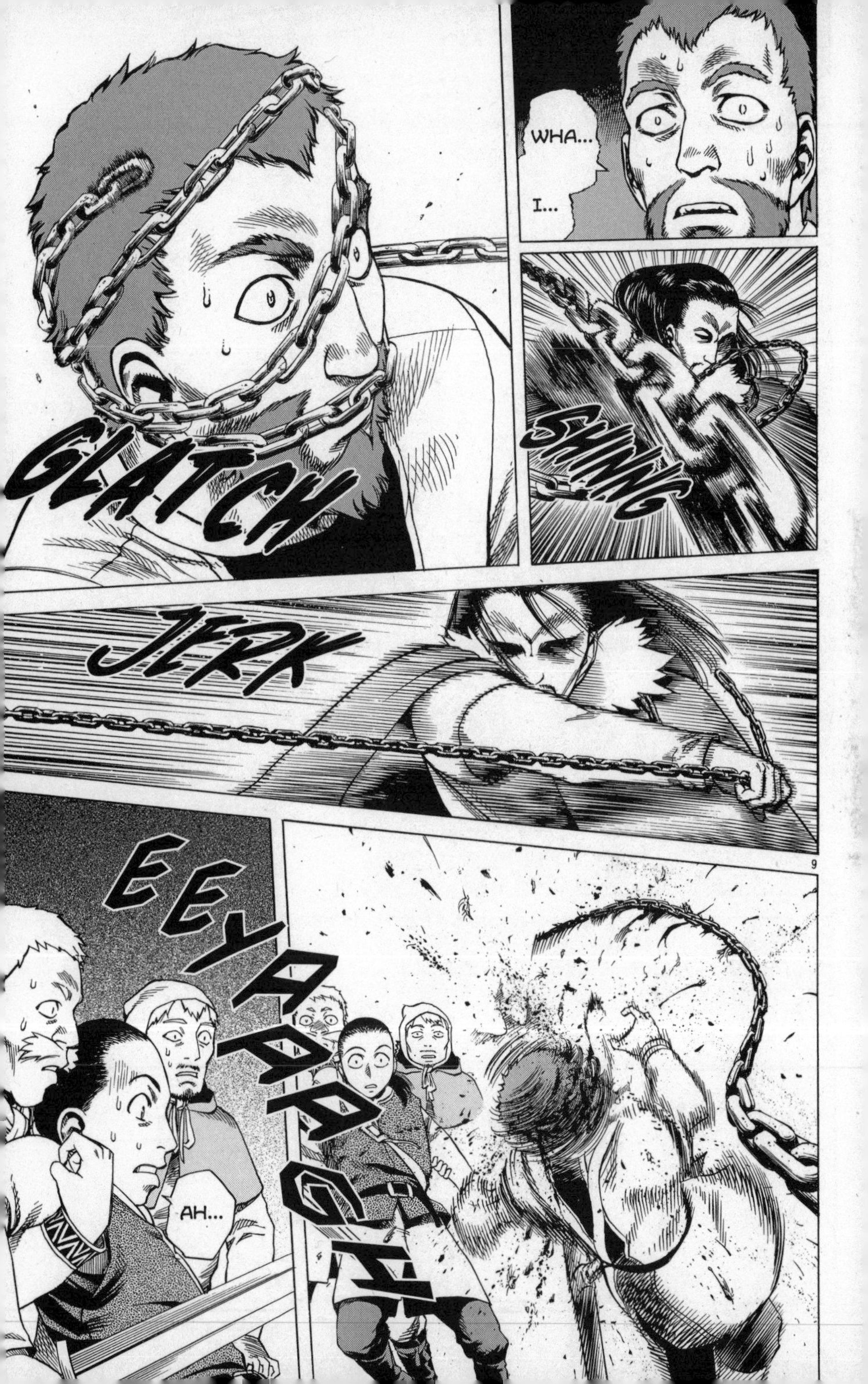

WHA...
I...
SHING
GLATCH
JERK
EEYAAAGH
AH...

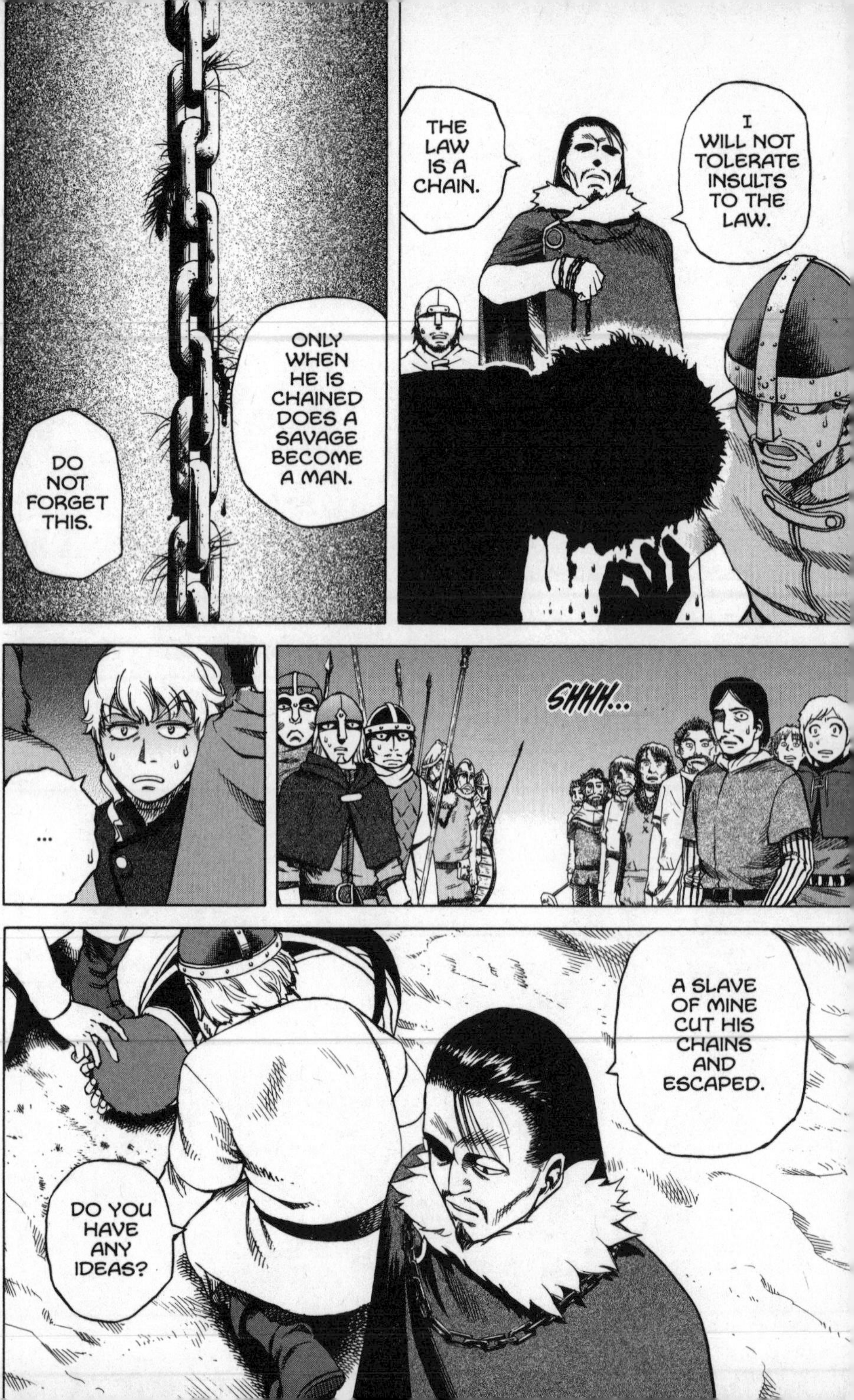
I WILL NOT TOLERATE INSULTS TO THE LAW.
THE LAW IS A CHAIN.
ONLY WHEN HE IS CHAINED DOES A SAVAGE BECOME A MAN.
DO NOT FORGET THIS.
SHHH...
...
A SLAVE OF MINE CUT HIS CHAINS AND ESCAPED.
DO YOU HAVE ANY IDEAS?

I THOUGHT I WAS IN ICELAND...

WHERE... AM I...?

...

GAHHK...

CAWW...

I'VE NEVER BEEN SO AT PEACE...

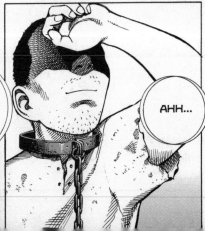

AHH...

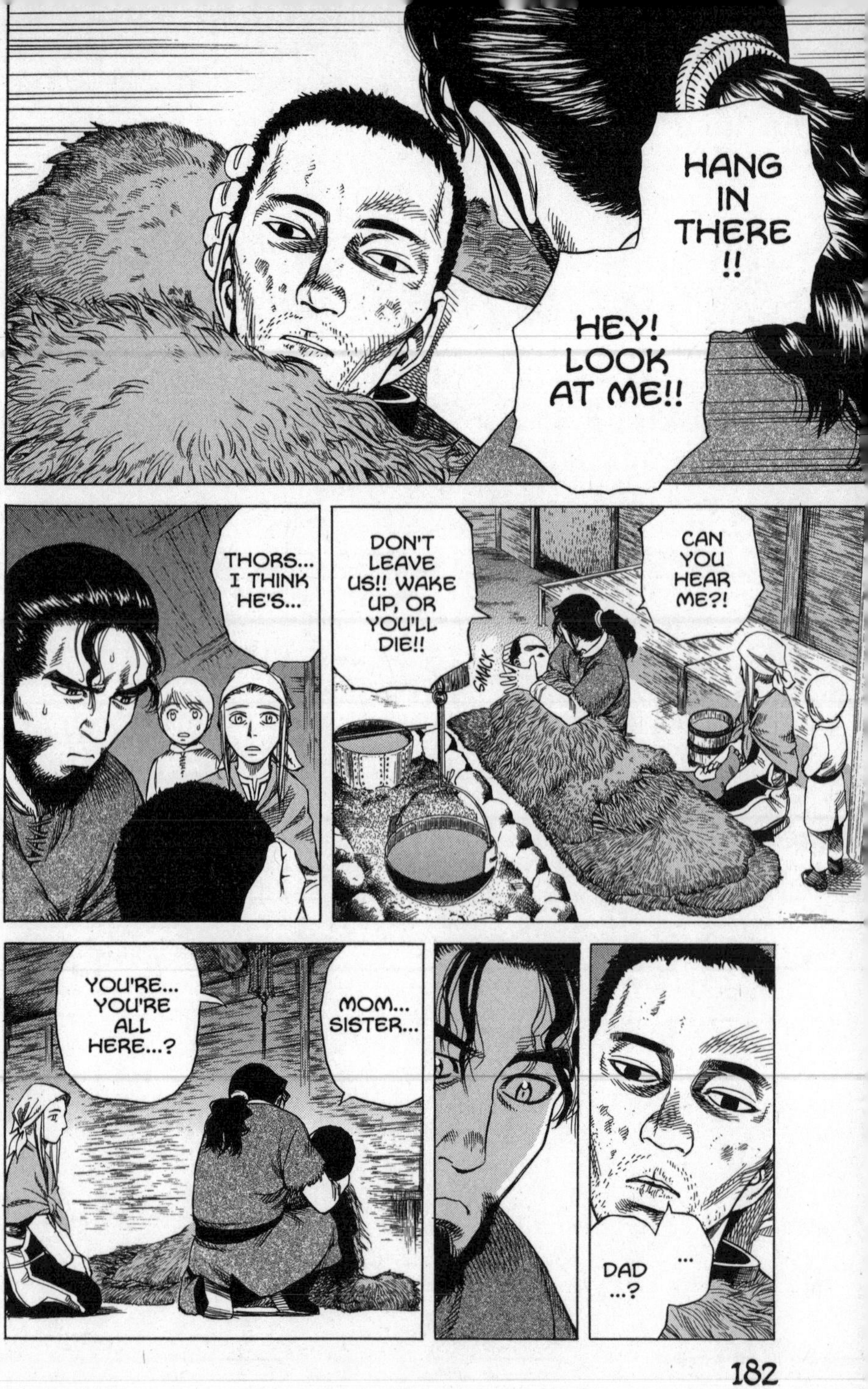
HANG IN THERE !!
HEY! LOOK AT ME!!
CAN YOU HEAR ME?!
DON'T LEAVE US!! WAKE UP, OR YOU'LL DIE!!
SMACK
THORS... I THINK HE'S...
...
DAD ...?
MOM... SISTER...
YOU'RE... YOU'RE ALL HERE...?

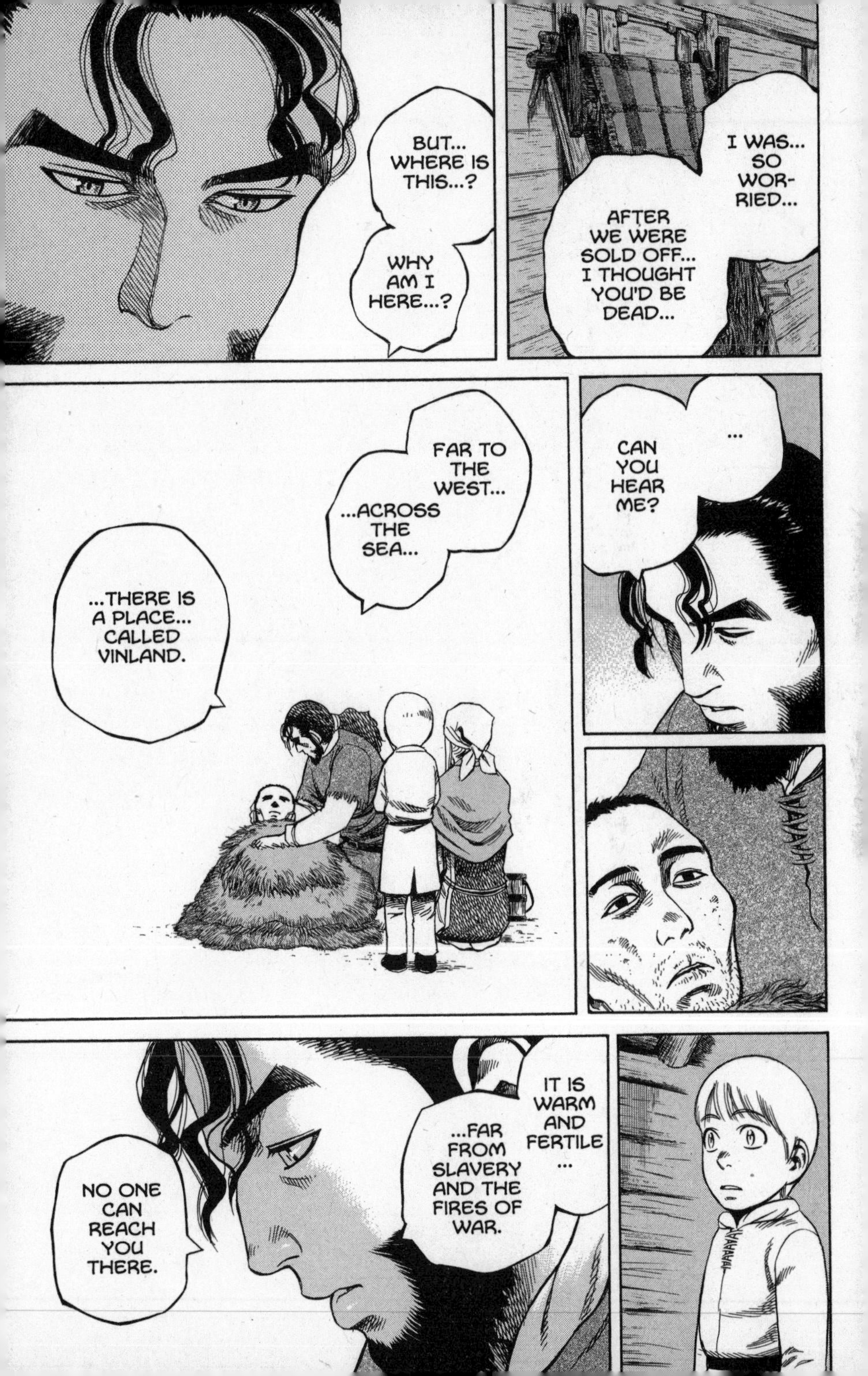
I WAS... SO WOR-RIED...
AFTER WE WERE SOLD OFF... I THOUGHT YOU'D BE DEAD...
BUT... WHERE IS THIS...?
WHY AM I HERE...?
...
CAN YOU HEAR ME?
FAR TO THE WEST...
...ACROSS THE SEA...
...THERE IS A PLACE... CALLED VINLAND.
IT IS WARM AND FERTILE ...
...FAR FROM SLAVERY AND THE FIRES OF WAR.
NO ONE CAN REACH YOU THERE.

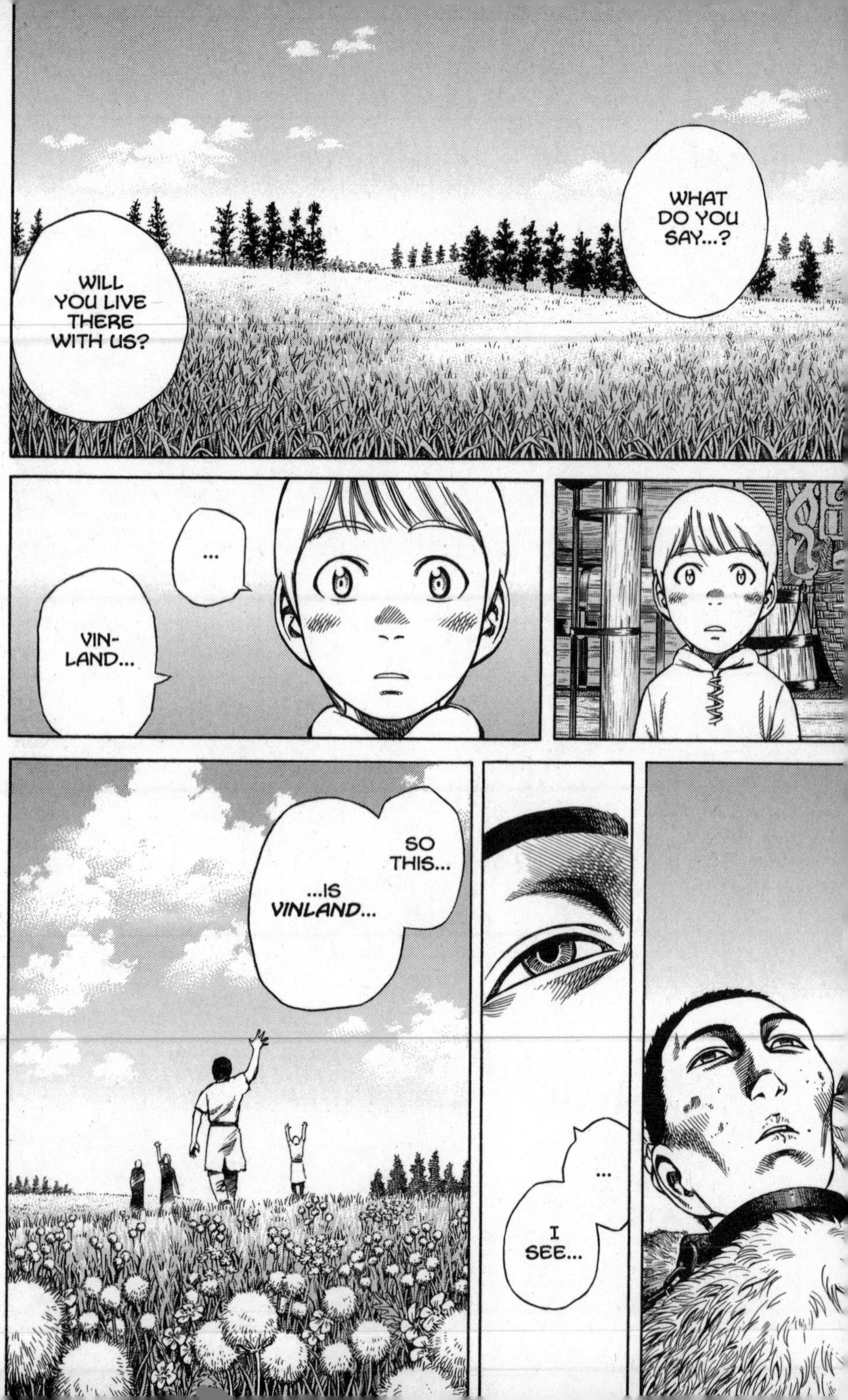
WHAT DO YOU SAY...?
WILL YOU LIVE THERE WITH US?
...
VIN-LAND...
...
I SEE...
SO THIS...
...IS VINLAND...

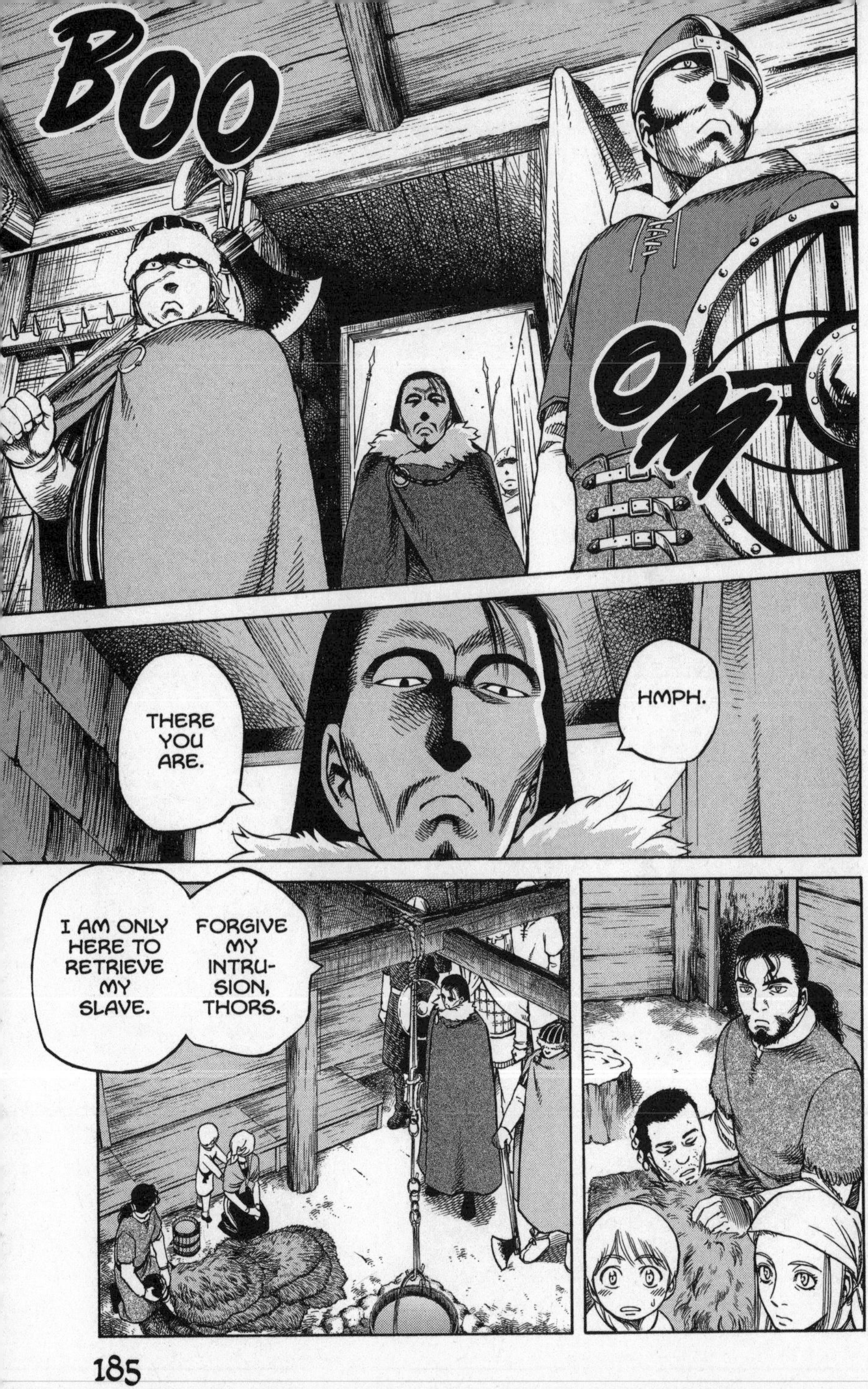
BOOOM
HMPH.
THERE YOU ARE.
FORGIVE MY INTRU-SION, THORS.
I AM ONLY HERE TO RETRIEVE MY SLAVE.

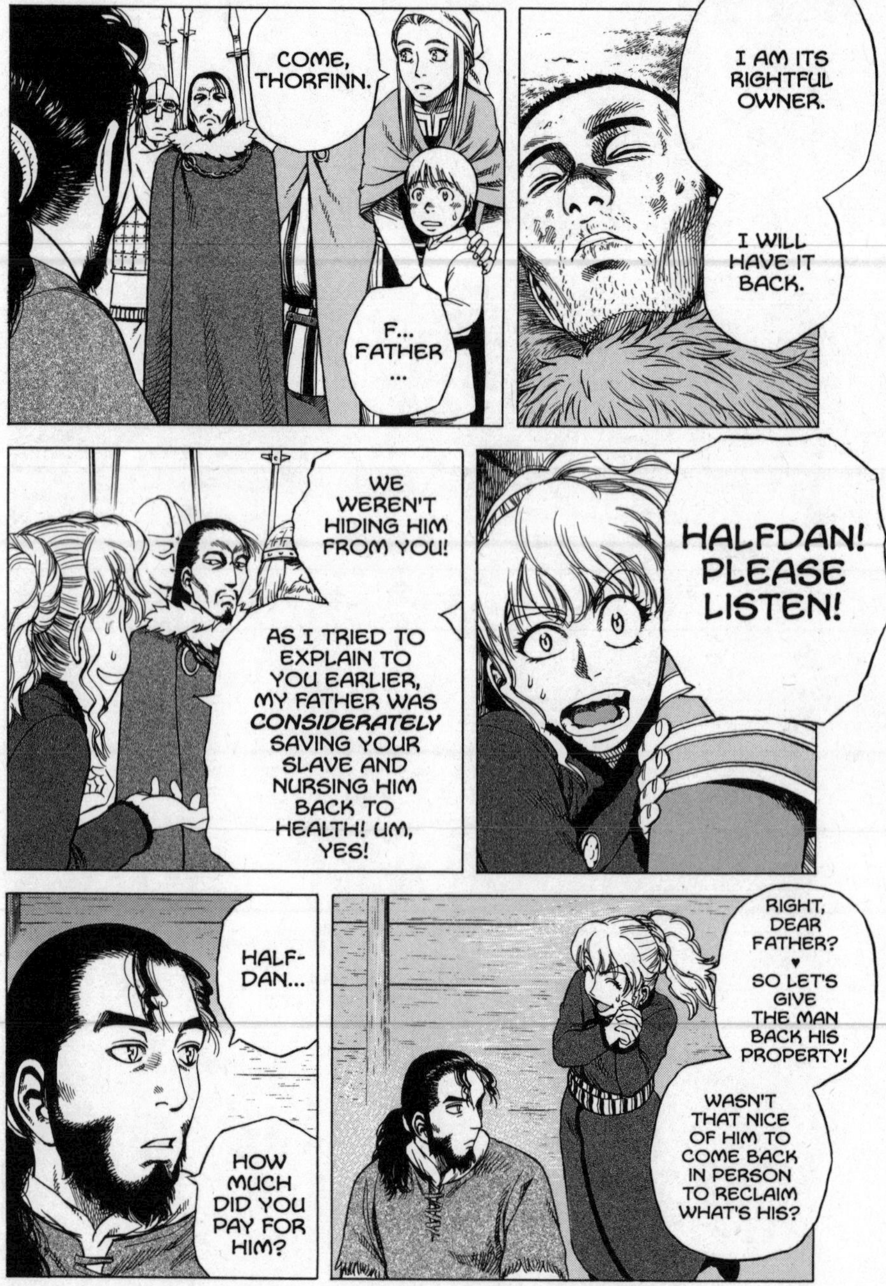
I AM ITS RIGHTFUL OWNER.
I WILL HAVE IT BACK.
COME, THORFINN.
F... FATHER ...
HALFDAN! PLEASE LISTEN!
WE WEREN'T HIDING HIM FROM YOU!
AS I TRIED TO EXPLAIN TO YOU EARLIER, MY FATHER WAS *CONSIDERATELY* SAVING YOUR SLAVE AND NURSING HIM BACK TO HEALTH! UM, YES!
RIGHT, DEAR FATHER? ♥ SO LET'S GIVE THE MAN BACK HIS PROPERTY!
WASN'T THAT NICE OF HIM TO COME BACK IN PERSON TO RECLAIM WHAT'S HIS?
HALF-DAN...
HOW MUCH DID YOU PAY FOR HIM?

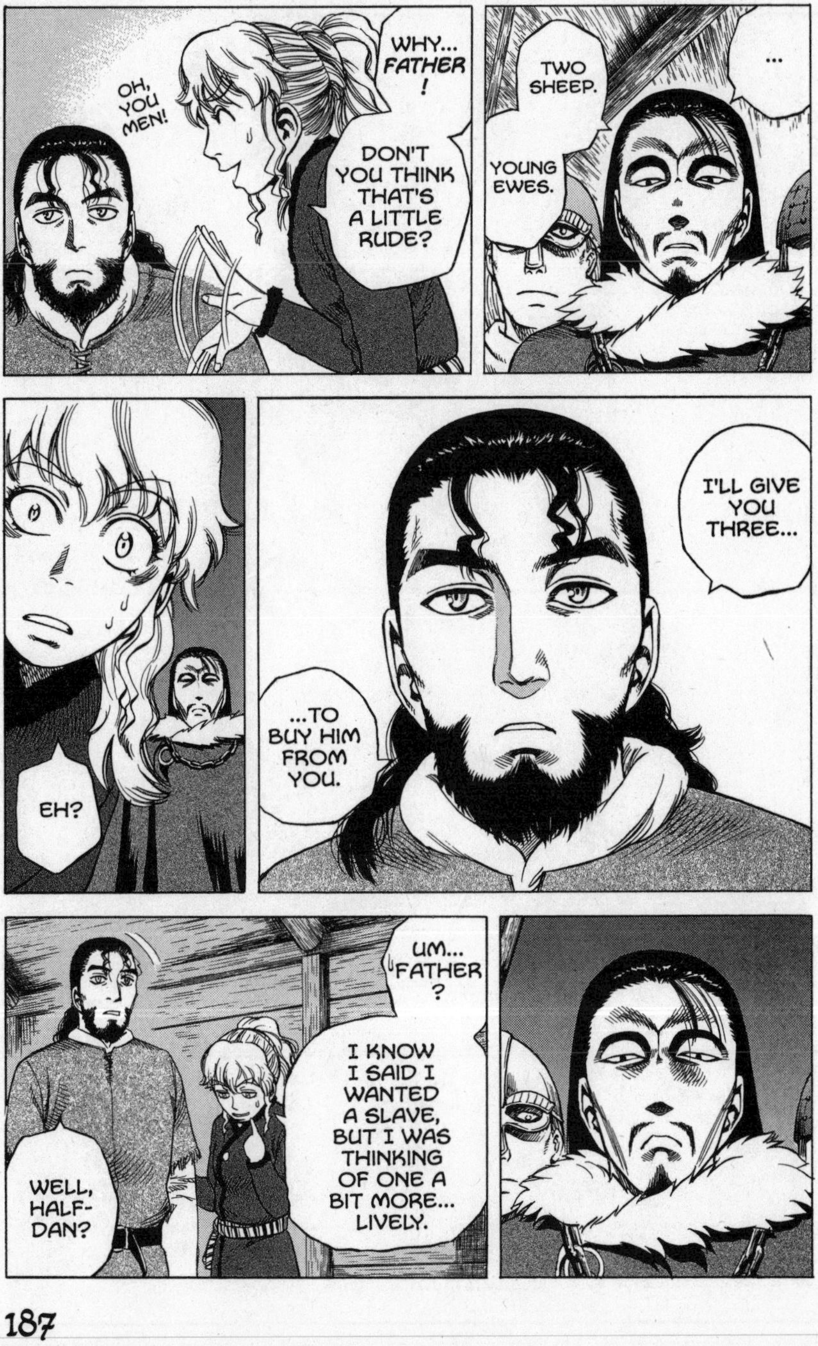
...
TWO SHEEP.
YOUNG EWES.
WHY... FATHER!
OH, YOU MEN!
DON'T YOU THINK THAT'S A LITTLE RUDE?
I'LL GIVE YOU THREE...
...TO BUY HIM FROM YOU.
EH?
UM... FATHER?
I KNOW I SAID I WANTED A SLAVE, BUT I WAS THINKING OF ONE A BIT MORE... LIVELY.
WELL, HALF-DAN?

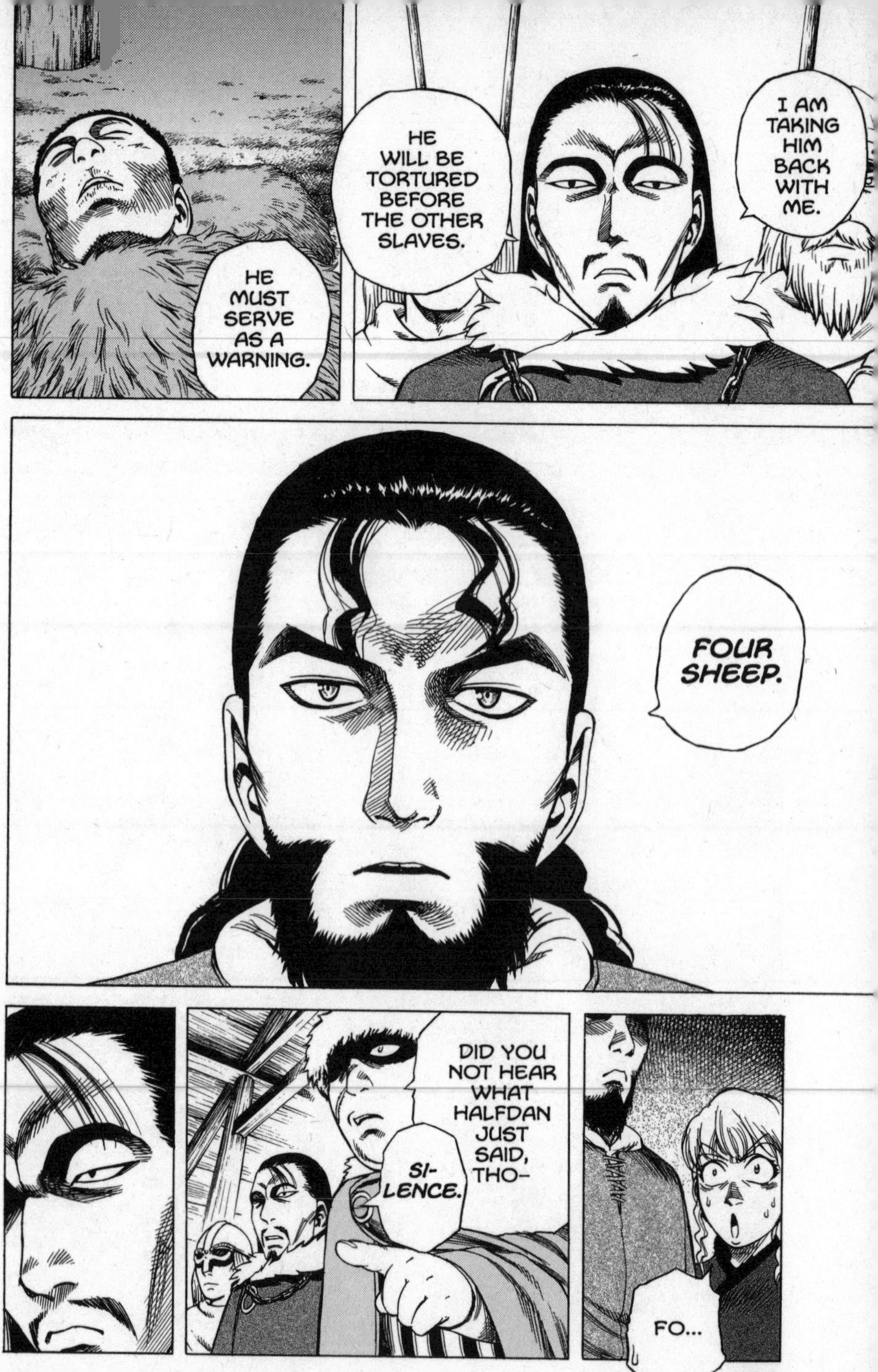
I AM TAKING HIM BACK WITH ME.
HE WILL BE TORTURED BEFORE THE OTHER SLAVES.
HE MUST SERVE AS A WARNING.
FOUR SHEEP.
FO...
DID YOU NOT HEAR WHAT HALFDAN JUST SAID, THO-
SI-LENCE.

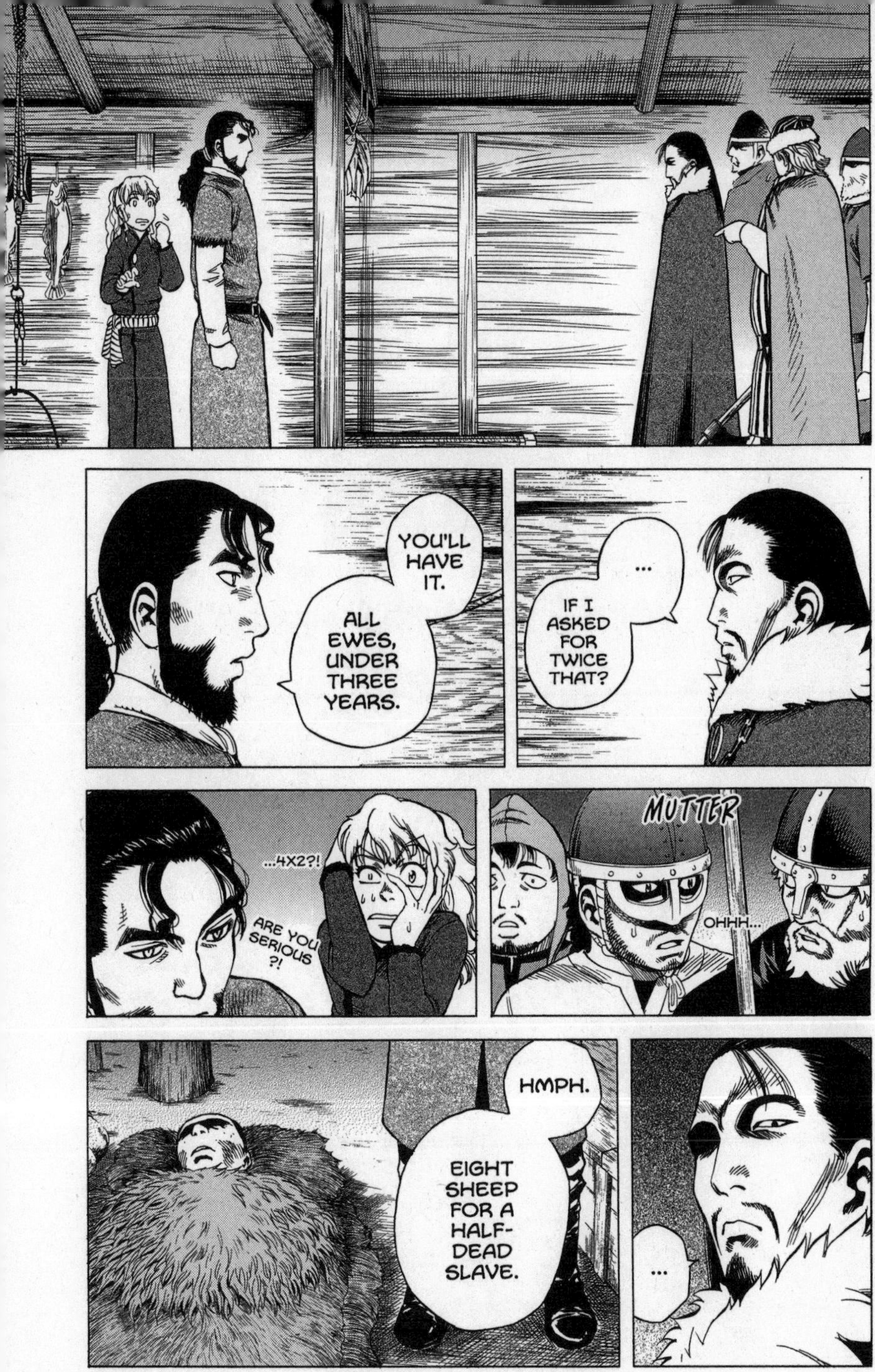
...
IF I ASKED FOR TWICE THAT?
YOU'LL HAVE IT.
ALL EWES, UNDER THREE YEARS.
MUTTER
OHHH...
...4X2?!
ARE YOU SERIOUS?!
...
HMPH.
EIGHT SHEEP FOR A HALF-DEAD SLAVE.

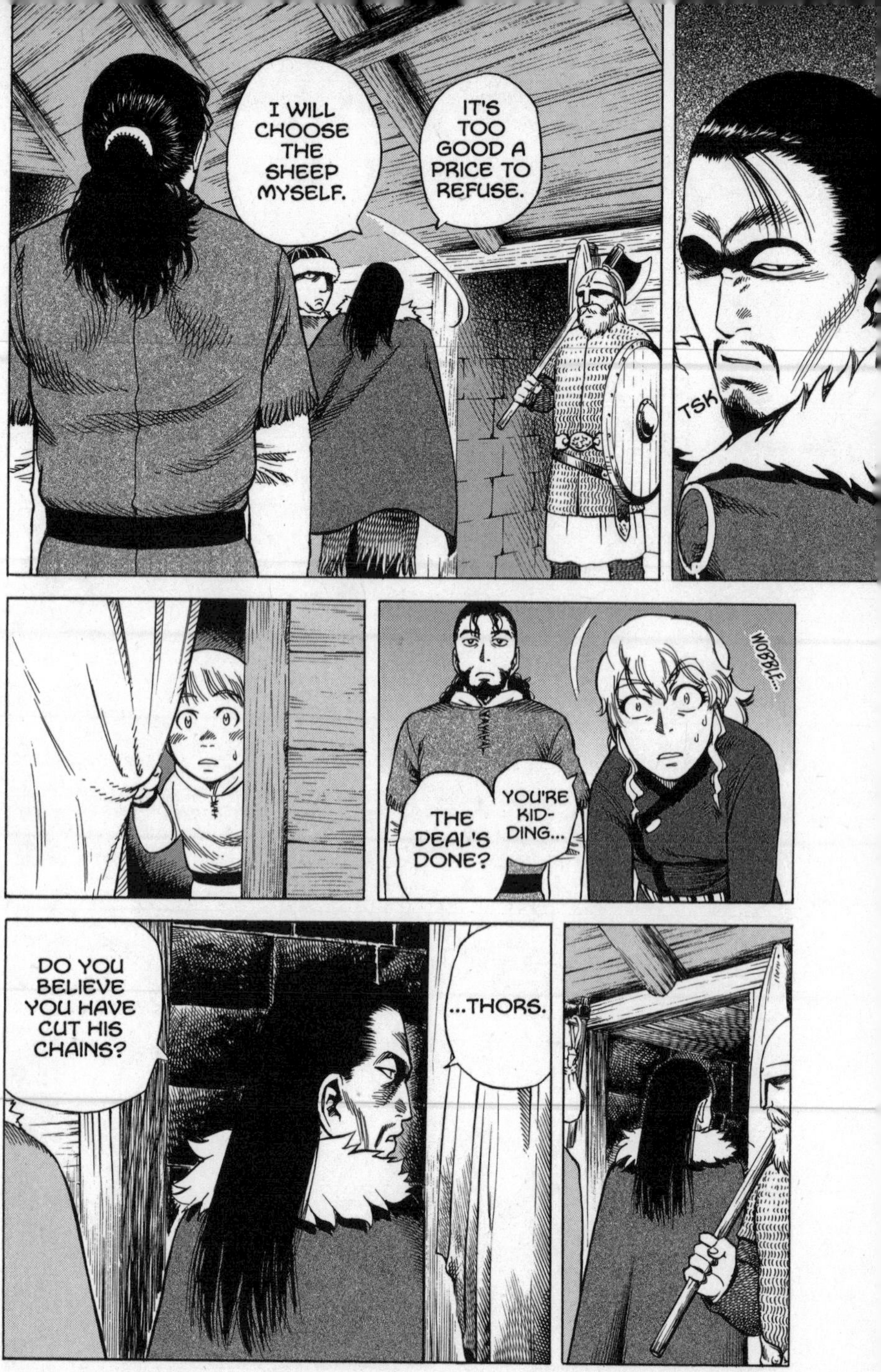
TSK
IT'S TOO GOOD A PRICE TO REFUSE.
I WILL CHOOSE THE SHEEP MYSELF.
WOBBLE...
YOU'RE KID-DING...
THE DEAL'S DONE?
...THORS.
DO YOU BELIEVE YOU HAVE CUT HIS CHAINS?

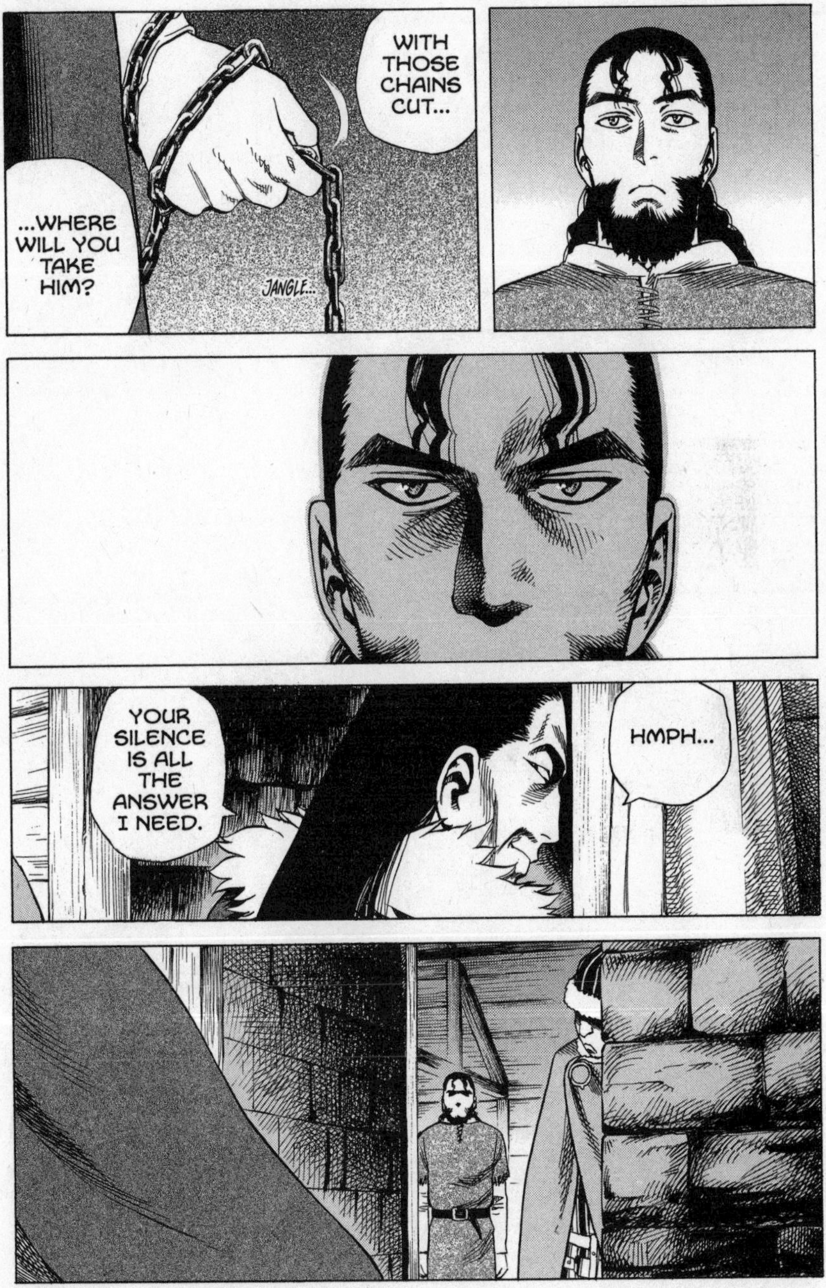
WITH THOSE CHAINS CUT...
...WHERE WILL YOU TAKE HIM?
JANGLE...
HMPH...
YOUR SILENCE IS ALL THE ANSWER I NEED.

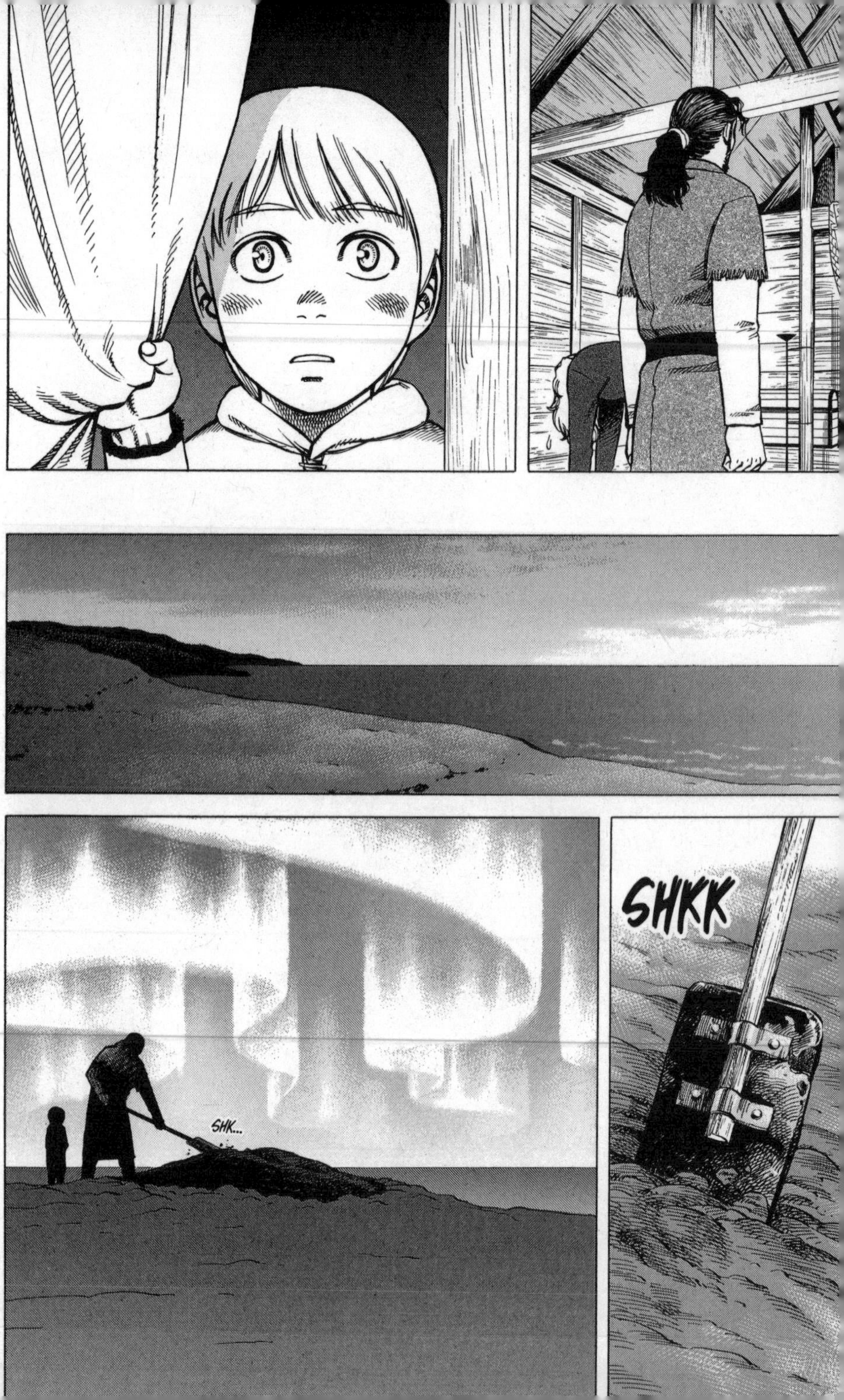
SHKK
SHK...

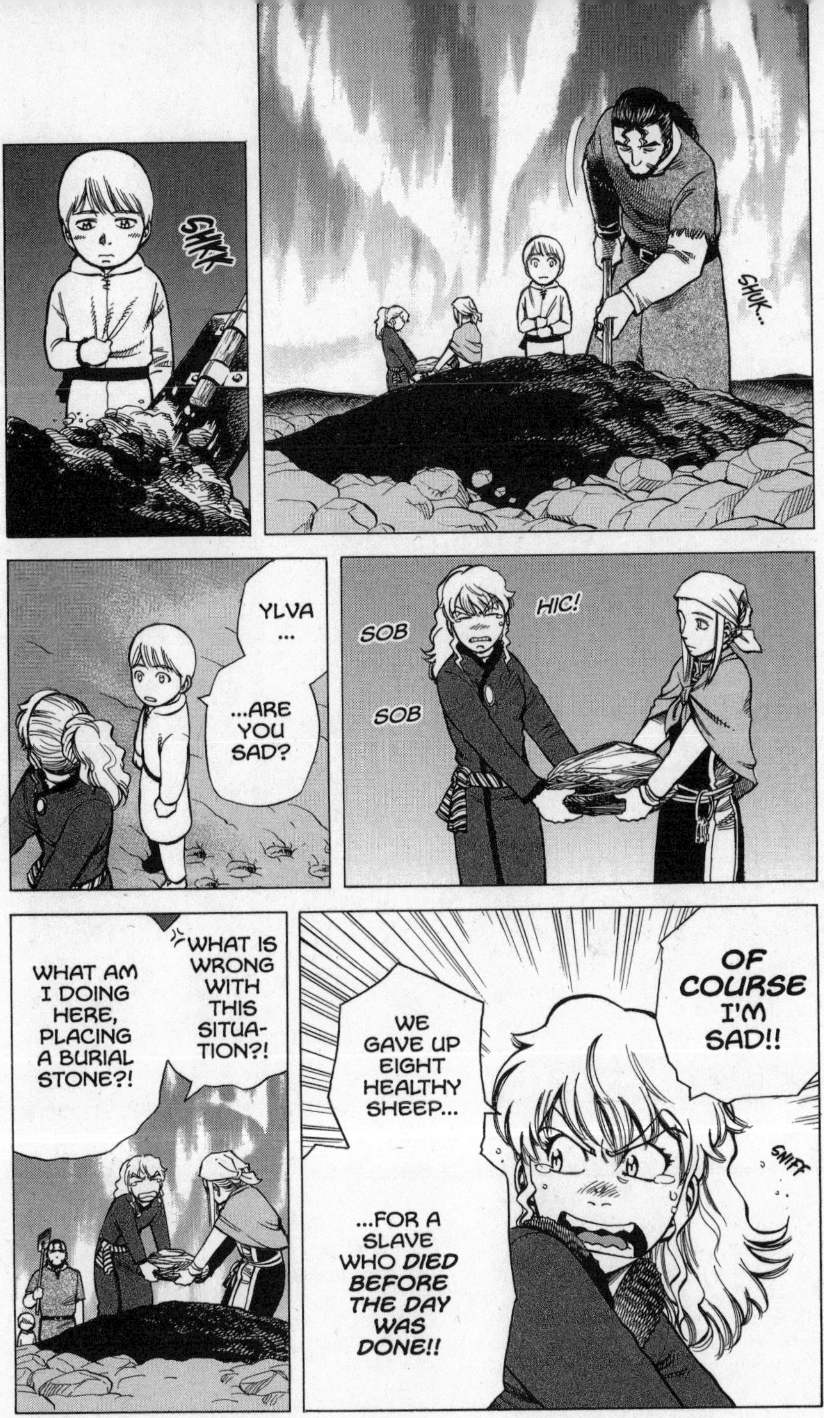
SHUK...
SHKK
SOB
HIC!
SOB
YLVA ...
...ARE YOU SAD?
OF COURSE I'M SAD!!
WE GAVE UP EIGHT HEALTHY SHEEP...
...FOR A SLAVE WHO *DIED* BEFORE THE DAY WAS DONE!!
SNIFF
WHAT IS WRONG WITH THIS SITUATION?!
WHAT AM I DOING HERE, PLACING A BURIAL STONE?!

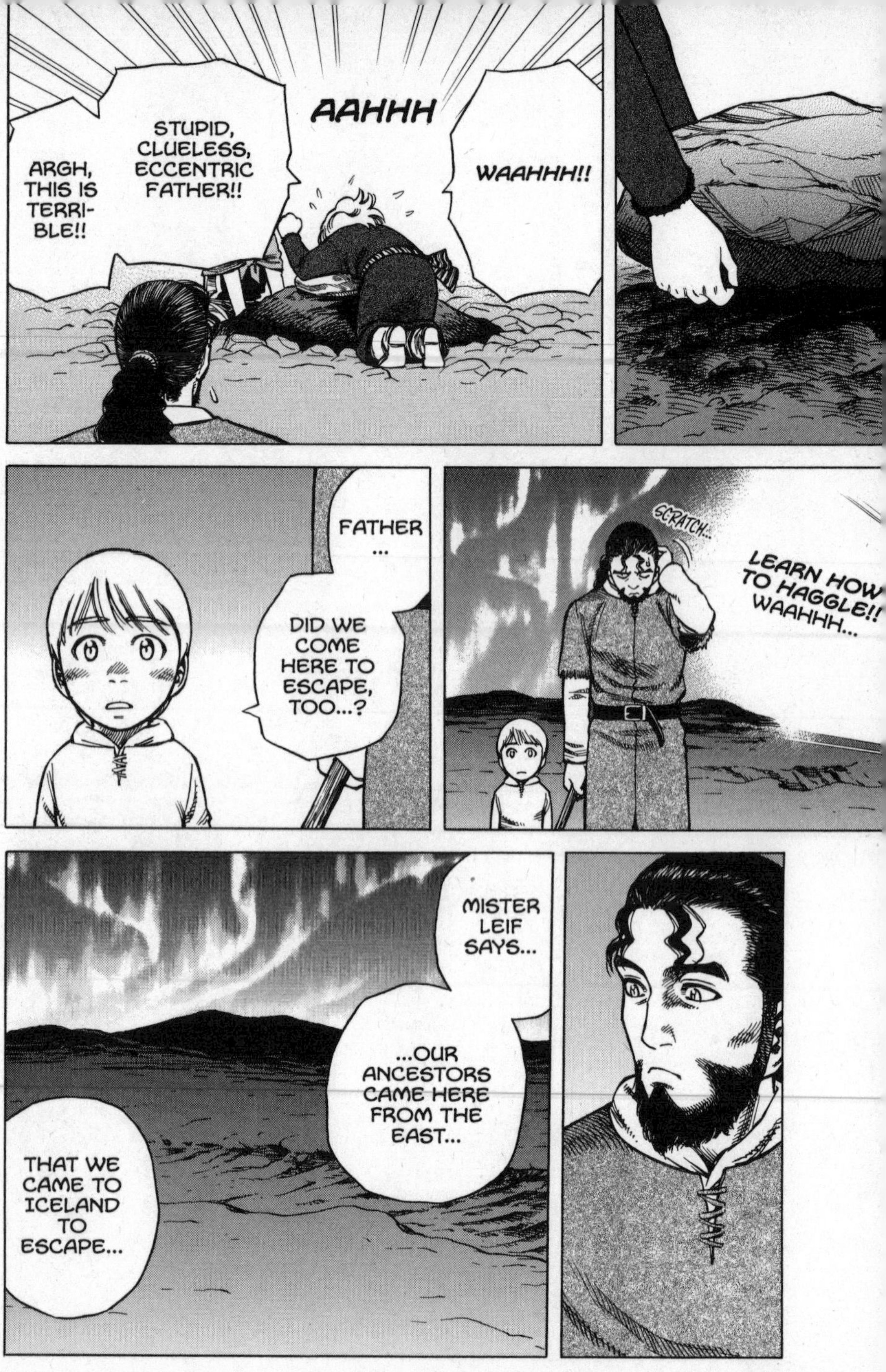
WAAHHH!!
AAHHH
STUPID, CLUELESS, ECCENTRIC FATHER!!
ARGH, THIS IS TERRIBLE!!
LEARN HOW TO HAGGLE!! WAAHHH...
SCRATCH...
FATHER ...
DID WE COME HERE TO ESCAPE, TOO...?
MISTER LEIF SAYS...
...OUR ANCESTORS CAME HERE FROM THE EAST...
THAT WE CAME TO ICELAND TO ESCAPE...

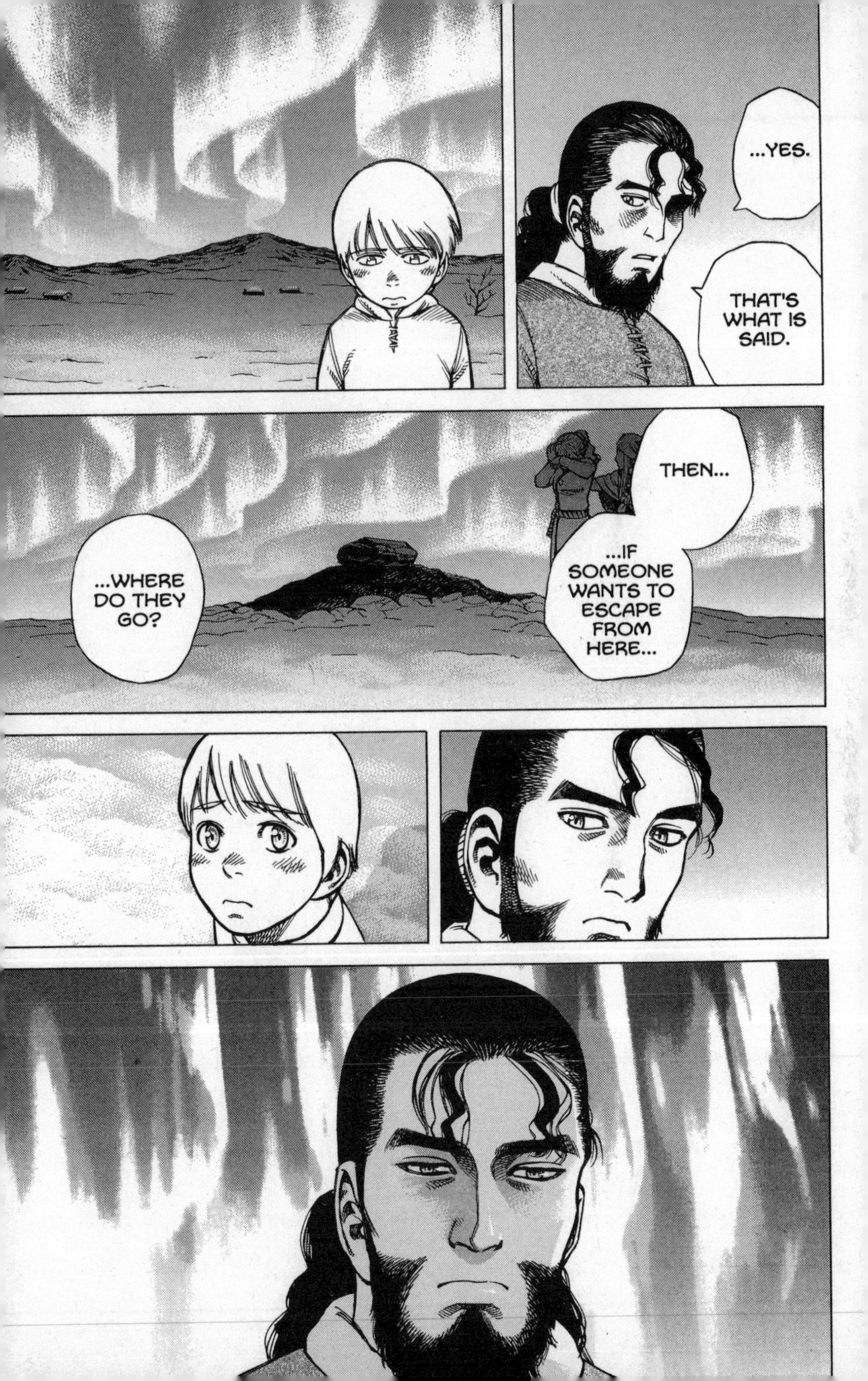
...YES.
THAT'S WHAT IS SAID.
THEN...
...IF SOMEONE WANTS TO ESCAPE FROM HERE...
...WHERE DO THEY GO?

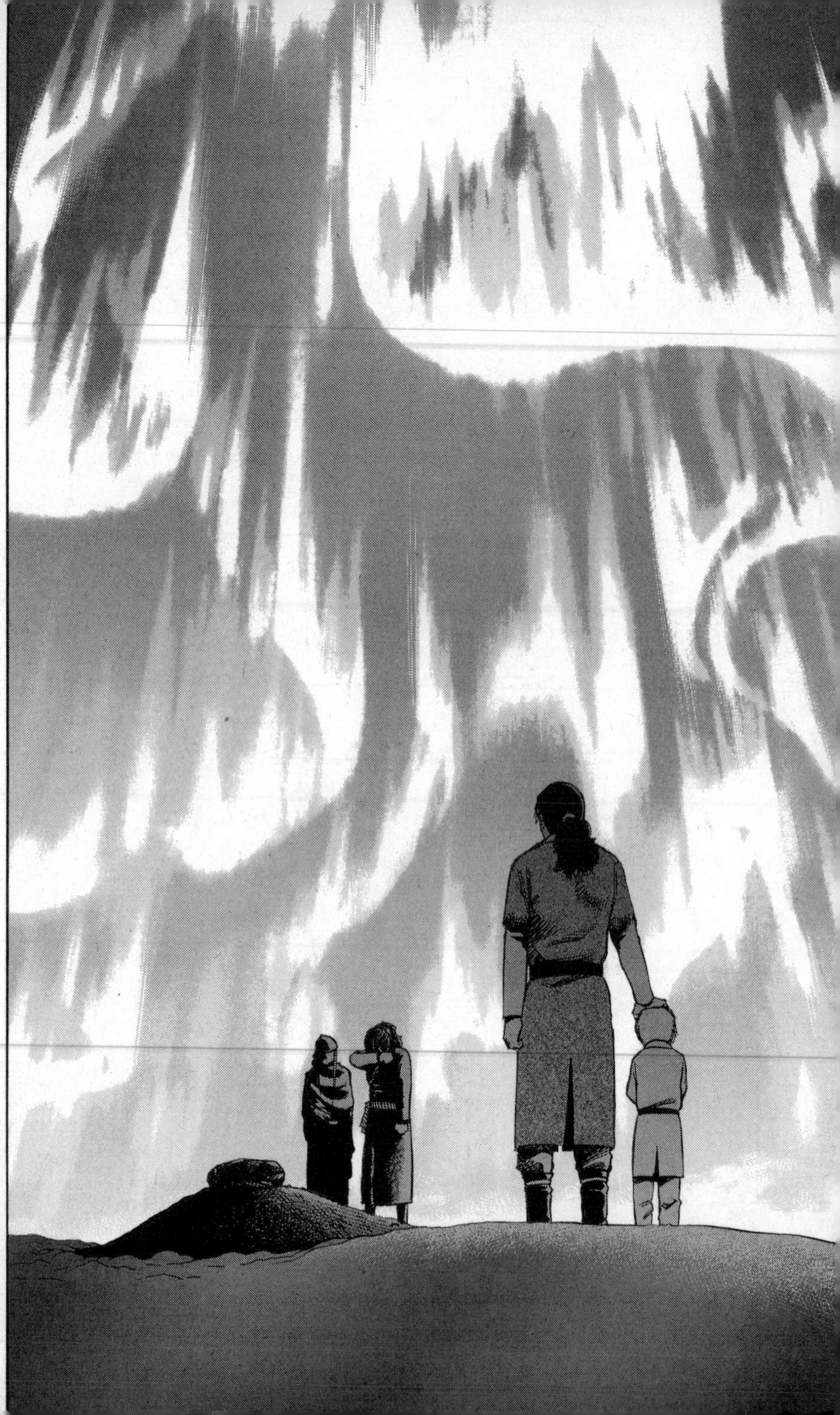

CHAPTER 4 - END

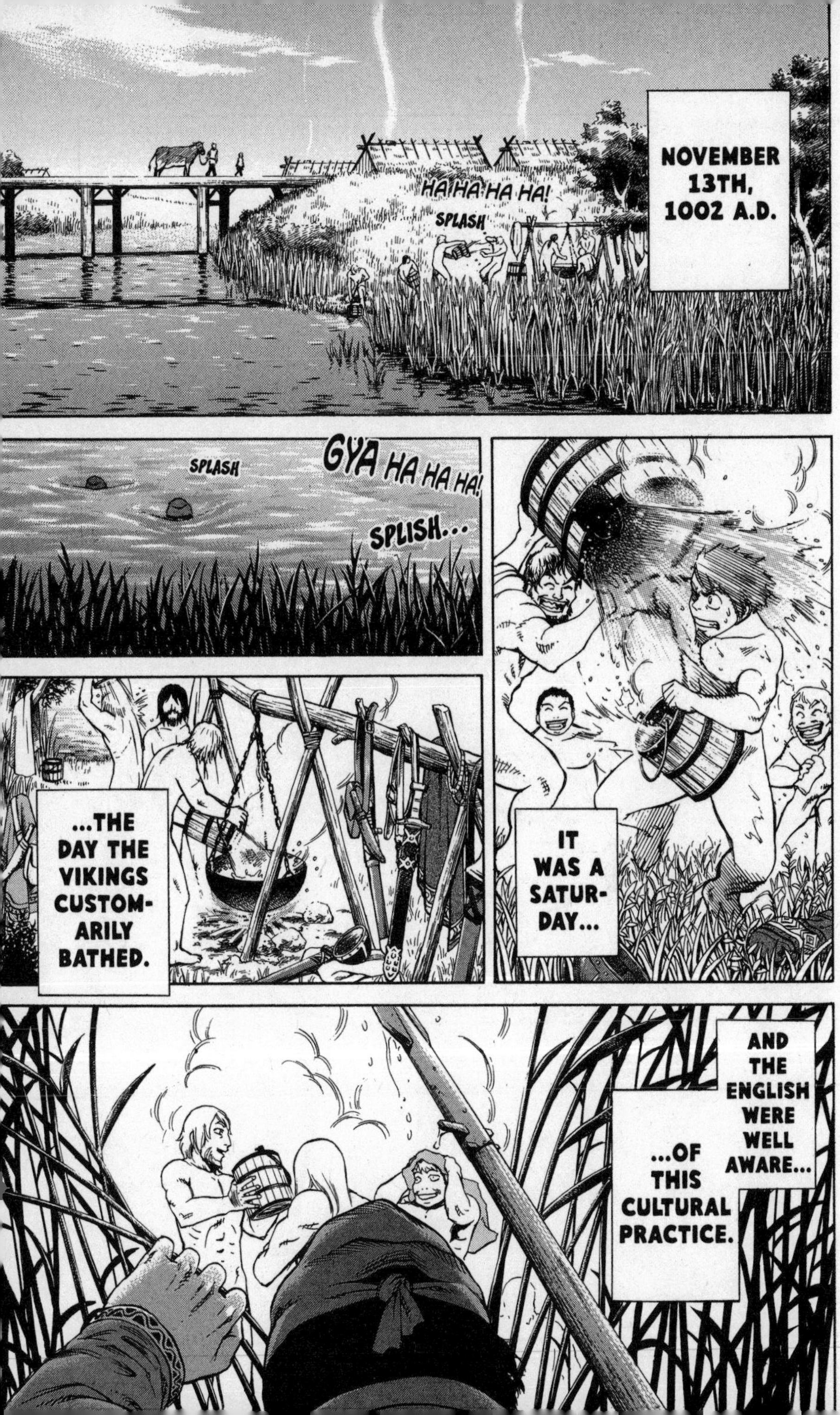
NOVEMBER 13TH, 1002 A.D.
HA HA HA HA!
SPLASH
IT WAS A SATURDAY...
GYA HA HA HA!
SPLASH
SPLISH...
...THE DAY THE VIKINGS CUSTOMARILY BATHED.
AND THE ENGLISH WERE WELL AWARE...
...OF THIS CULTURAL PRACTICE.

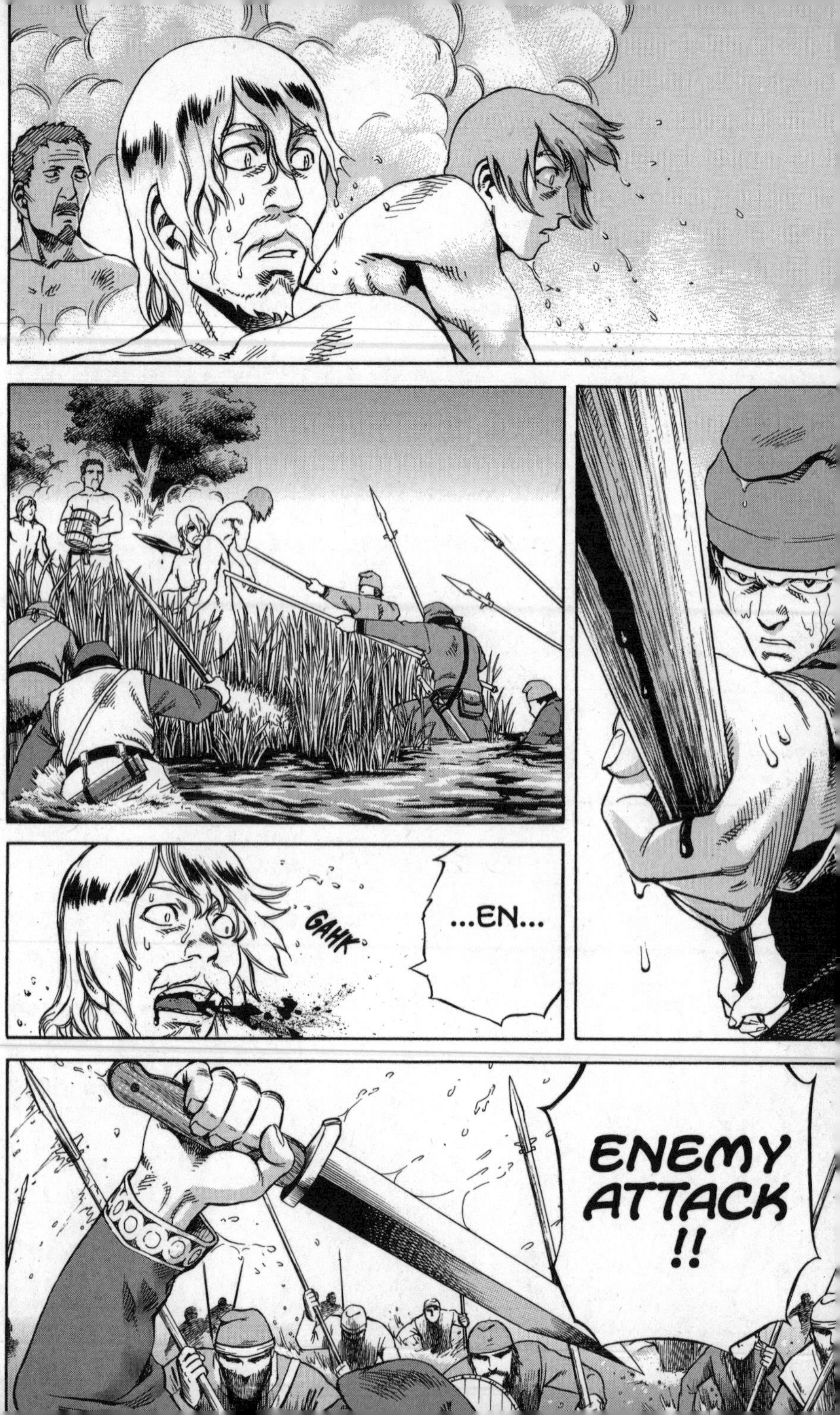
...EN...
GAHK
ENEMY ATTACK !!

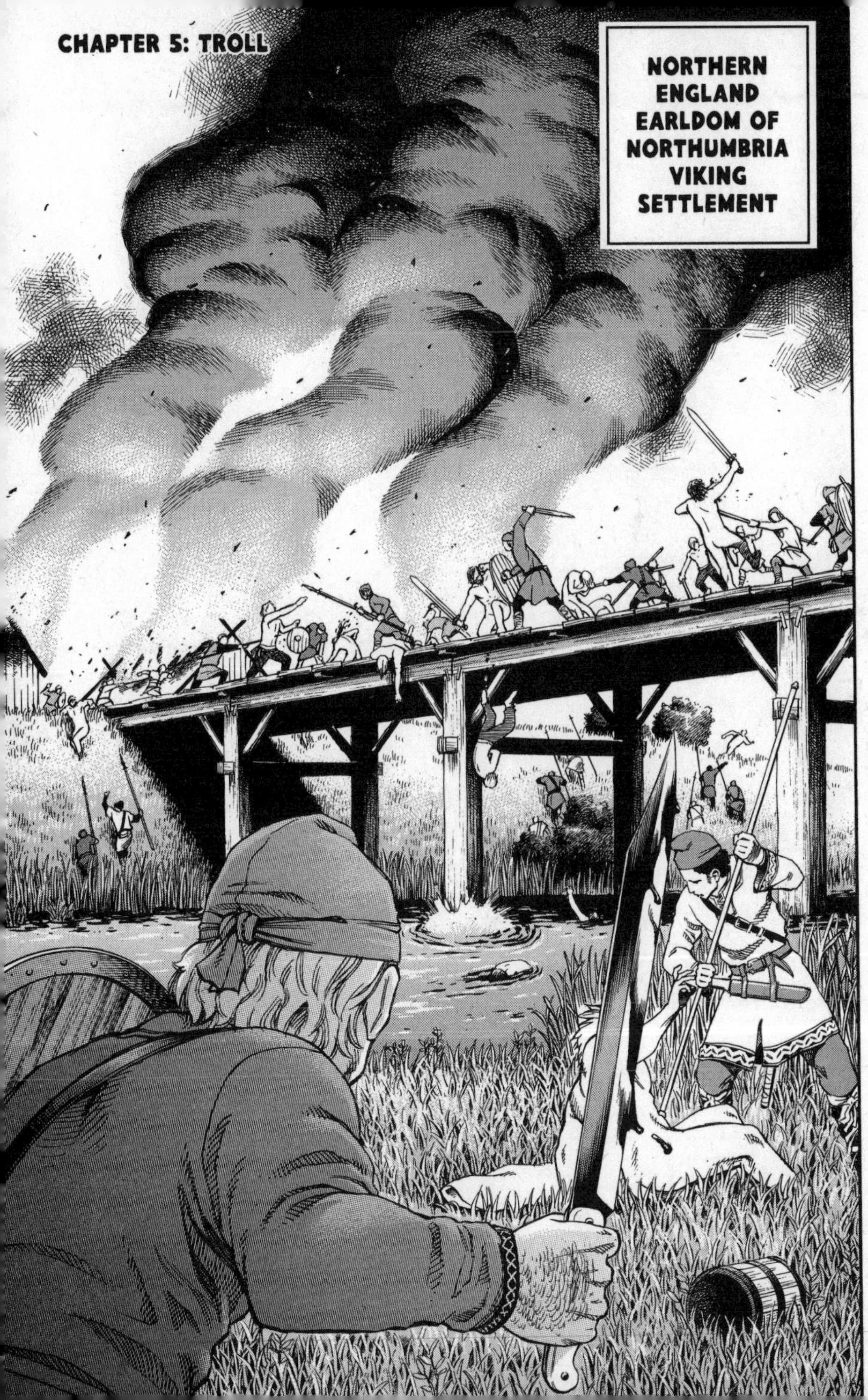
CHAPTER 5: TROLL
NORTHERN ENGLAND EARLDOM OF NORTHUMBRIA VIKING SETTLEMENT

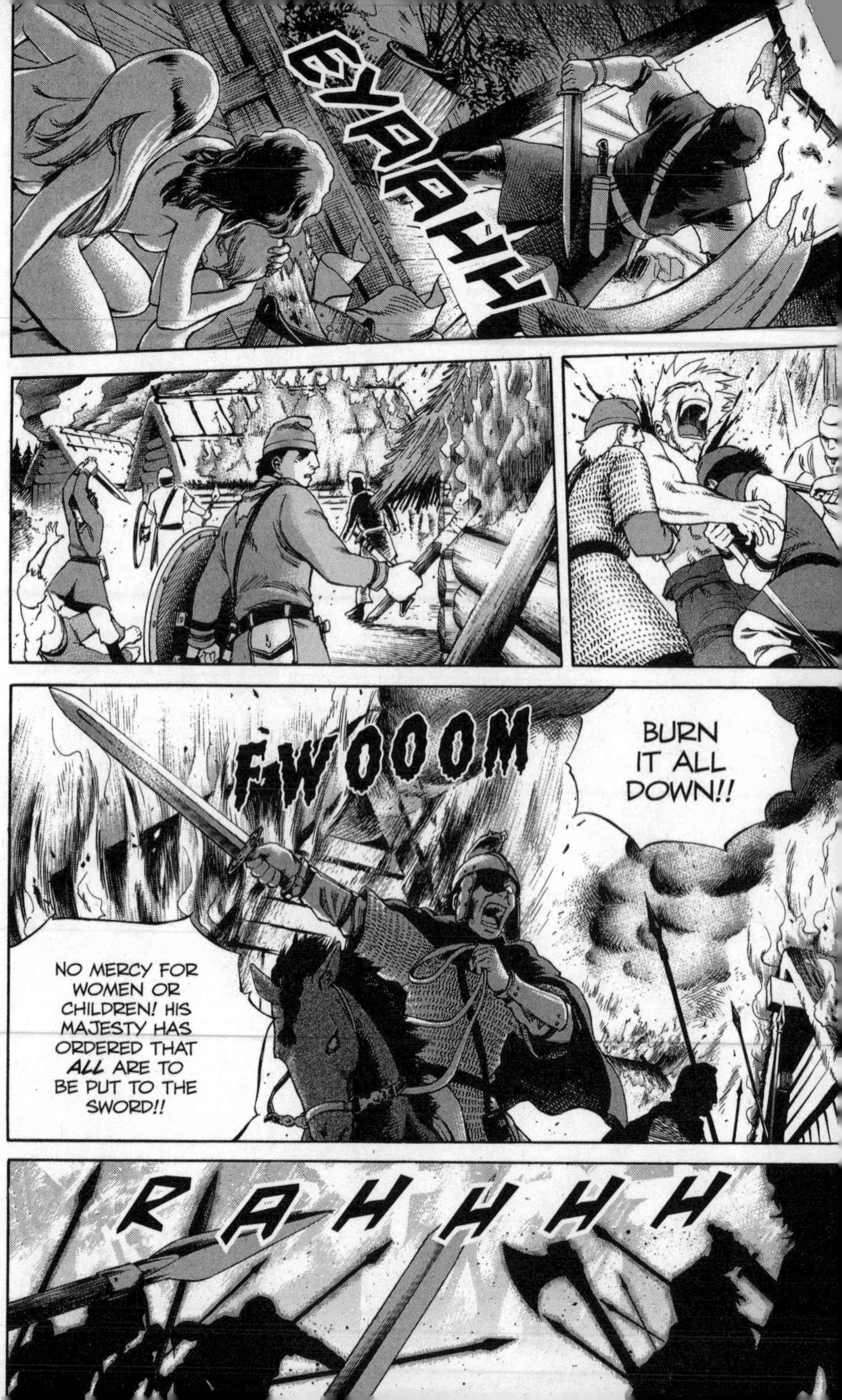
EYAAHH
BURN IT ALL DOWN!!
FWOOOM
NO MERCY FOR WOMEN OR CHILDREN! HIS MAJESTY HAS ORDERED THAT ALL ARE TO BE PUT TO THE SWORD!!
RAHHHH

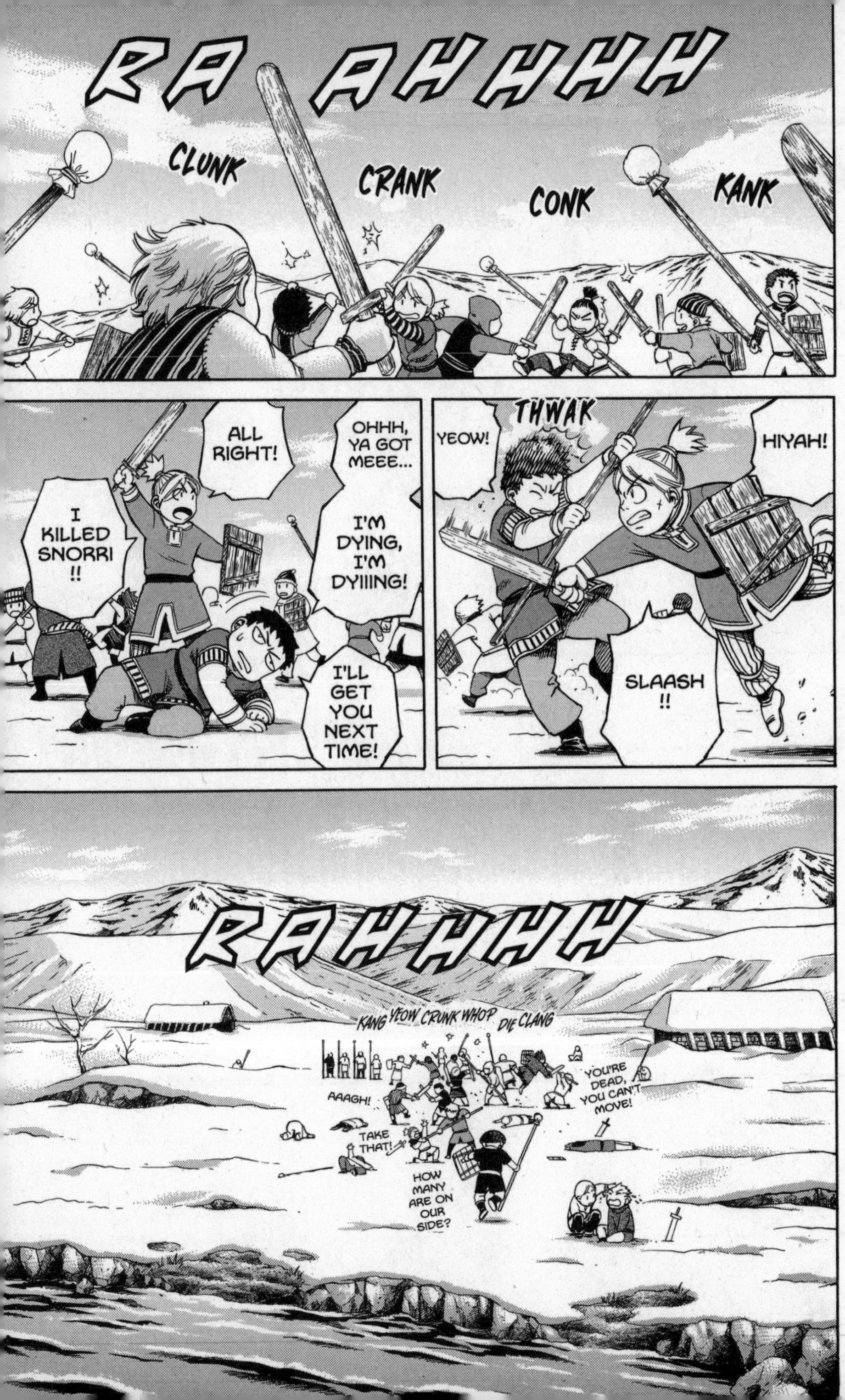
RAAHHHH
KANK
CONK
CRANK
CLUNK
HIYAH!
THWAK
YEOW!
SLAASH!!
OHHH, YA GOT MEEE...
I'M DYING, I'M DYIIING!
ALL RIGHT!
I KILLED SNORRI!!
I'LL GET YOU NEXT TIME!
RAHHHHH
KANG YEOW CRUNK WHOP DIE CLANG
YOU'RE DEAD, YOU CAN'T MOVE!
AAAGH!
TAKE THAT!
HOW MANY ARE ON OUR SIDE?

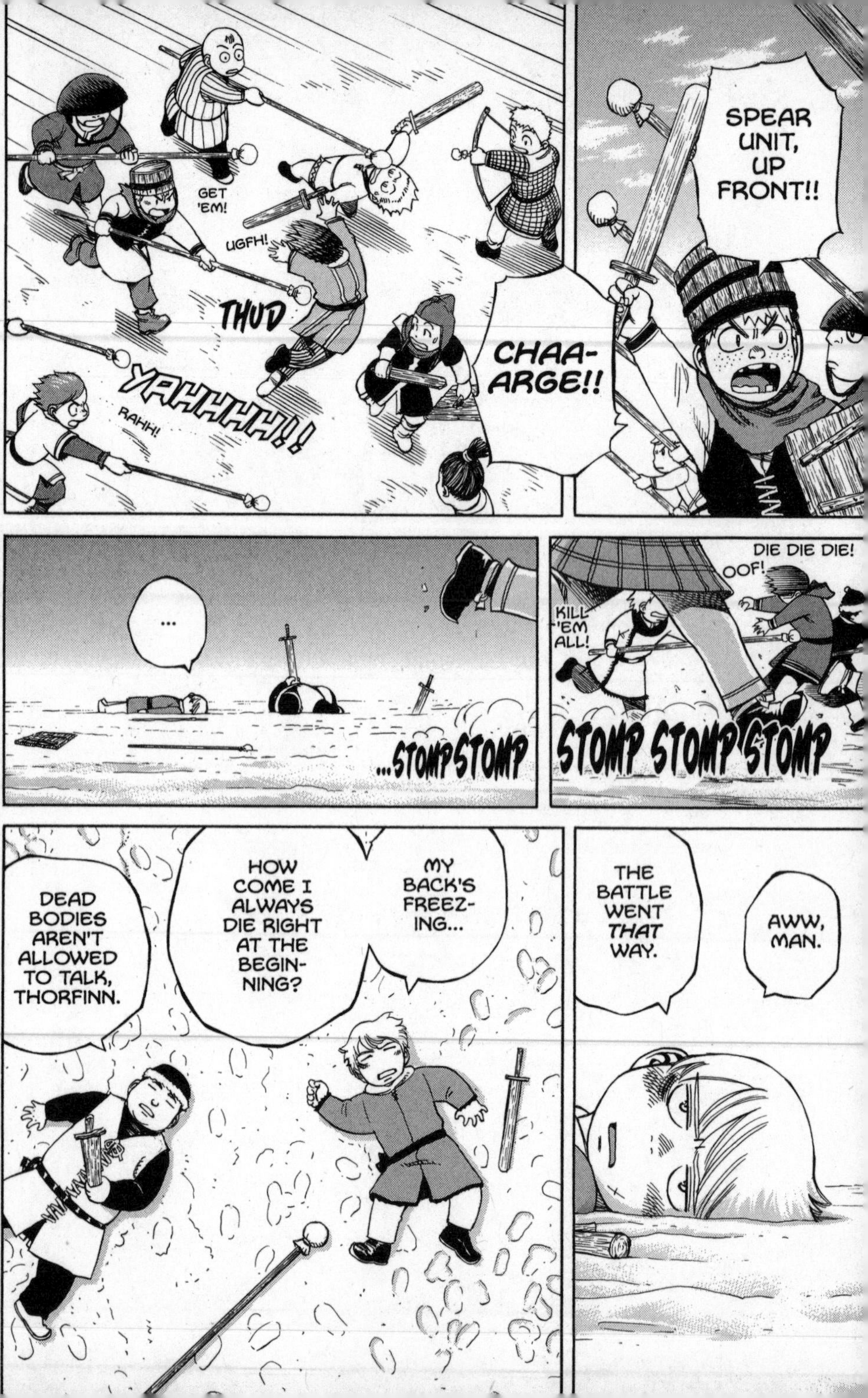
SPEAR UNIT, UP FRONT!!
CHAA-ARGE!!
GET 'EM!
UGFH!
THUD
YAHHHH!!
RAHH!
DIE DIE DIE!
OOF!
KILL 'EM ALL!
STOMP STOMP STOMP
...
...STOMP STOMP
THE BATTLE WENT THAT WAY.
AWW, MAN.
MY BACK'S FREEZ-ING...
HOW COME I ALWAYS DIE RIGHT AT THE BEGIN-NING?
DEAD BODIES AREN'T ALLOWED TO TALK, THORFINN.

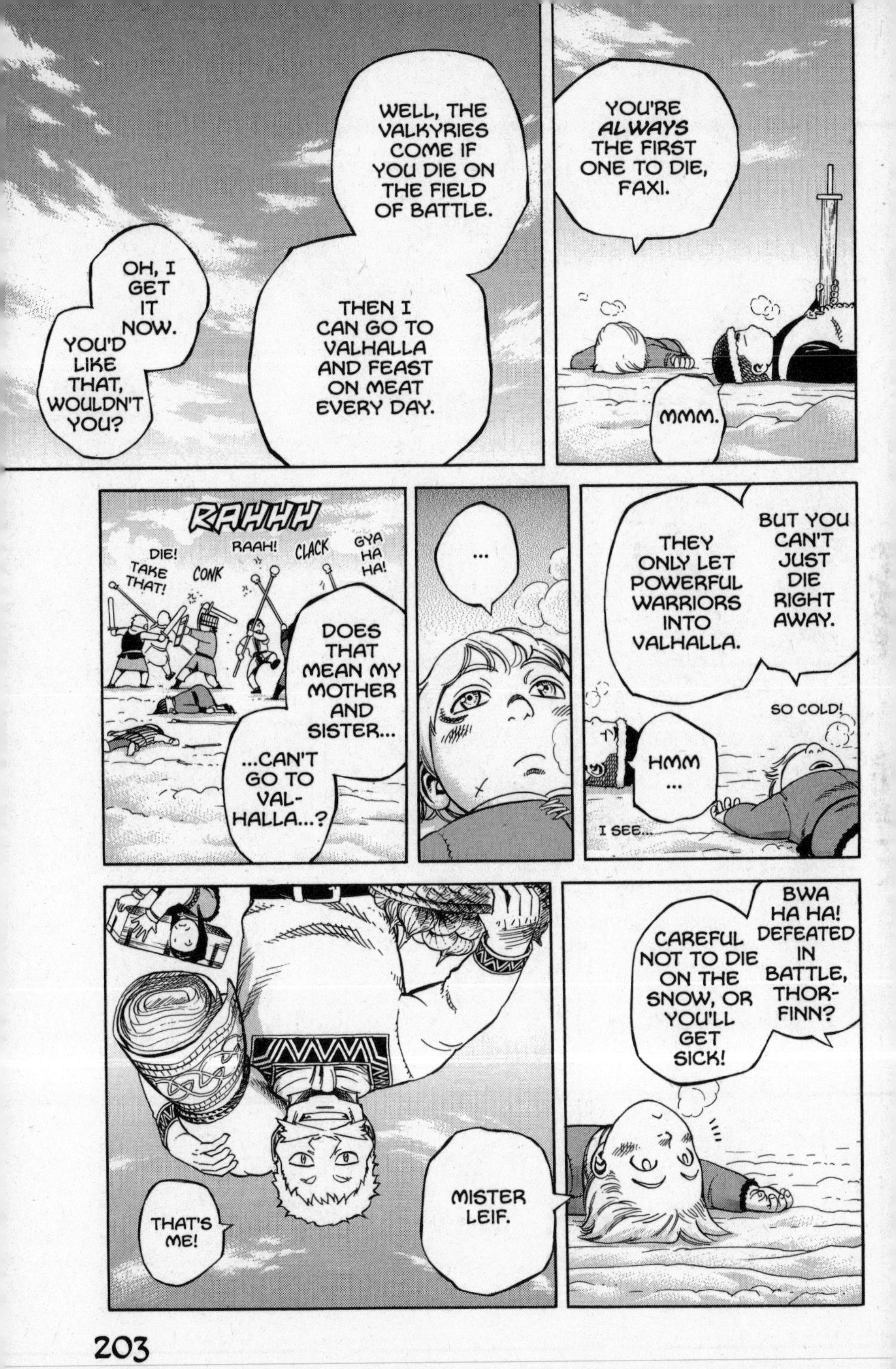
YOU'RE ALWAYS THE FIRST ONE TO DIE, FAXI.
MMM.
WELL, THE VALKYRIES COME IF YOU DIE ON THE FIELD OF BATTLE.
THEN I CAN GO TO VALHALLA AND FEAST ON MEAT EVERY DAY.
OH, I GET IT NOW.
YOU'D LIKE THAT, WOULDN'T YOU?
BUT YOU CAN'T JUST DIE RIGHT AWAY.
THEY ONLY LET POWERFUL WARRIORS INTO VALHALLA.
SO COLD!
HMM ...
I SEE...
...
RAHHH
GYA HA HA!
CLACK
RAAH!
CONK
DIE!
TAKE THAT!
DOES THAT MEAN MY MOTHER AND SISTER...
...CAN'T GO TO VAL-HALLA...?
BWA HA HA! DEFEATED IN BATTLE, THORFINN?
CAREFUL NOT TO DIE ON THE SNOW, OR YOU'LL GET SICK!
MISTER LEIF.
THAT'S ME!

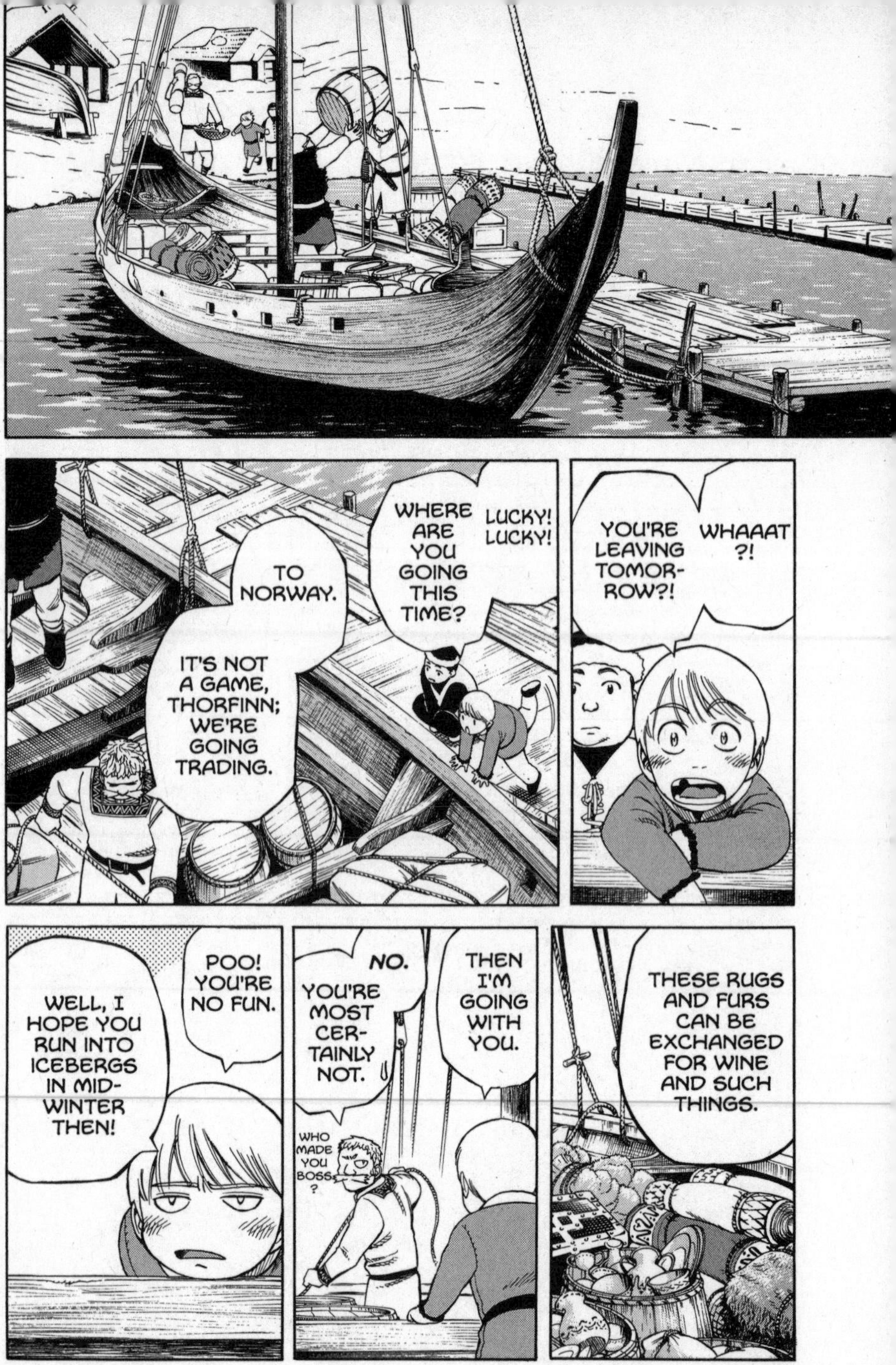
WHAAAT ?!
YOU'RE LEAVING TOMORROW?!
LUCKY! LUCKY!
WHERE ARE YOU GOING THIS TIME?
TO NORWAY.
IT'S NOT A GAME, THORFINN; WE'RE GOING TRADING.
THESE RUGS AND FURS CAN BE EXCHANGED FOR WINE AND SUCH THINGS.
THEN I'M GOING WITH YOU.
NO.
YOU'RE MOST CERTAINLY NOT.
WHO MADE YOU BOSS?
POO! YOU'RE NO FUN.
WELL, I HOPE YOU RUN INTO ICEBERGS IN MIDWINTER THEN!

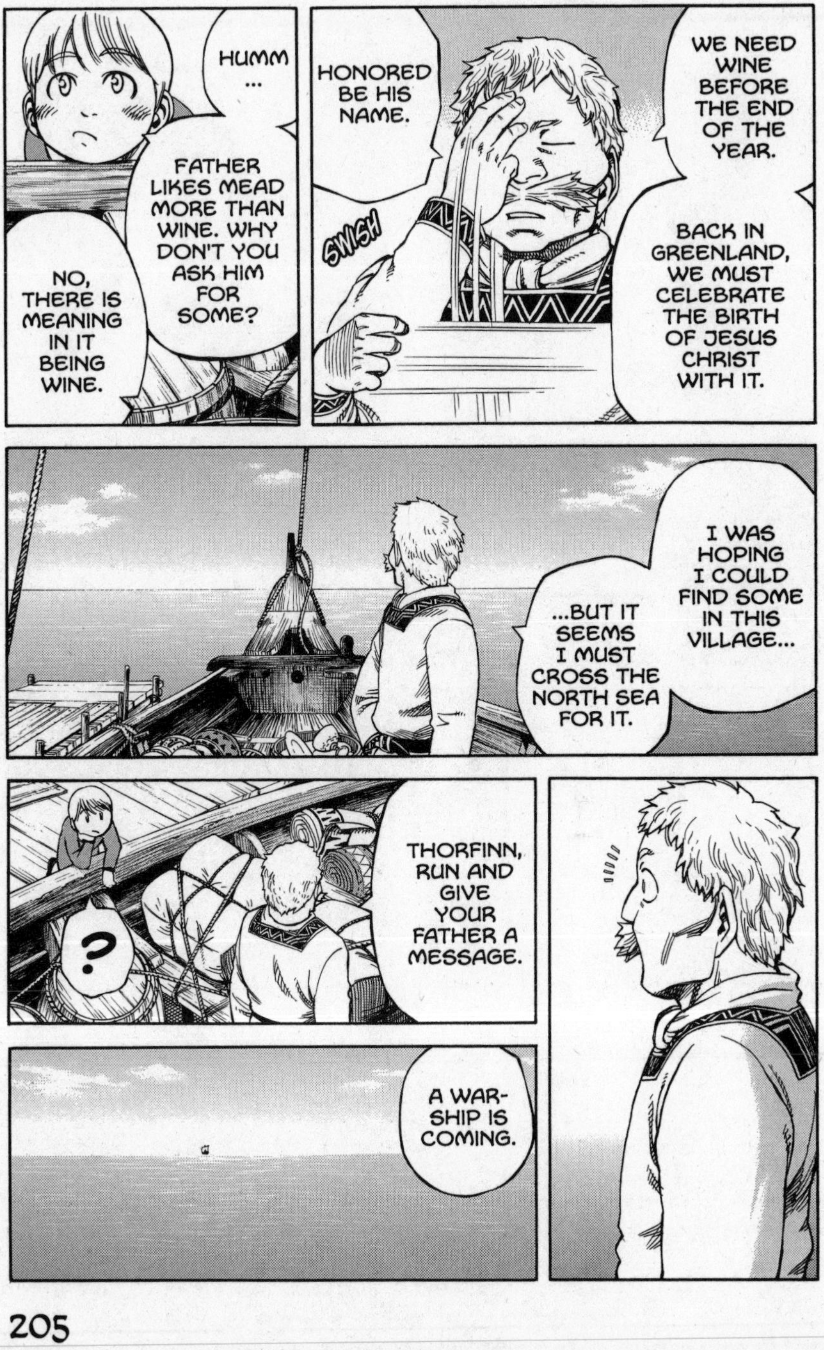
WE NEED WINE BEFORE THE END OF THE YEAR.
BACK IN GREENLAND, WE MUST CELEBRATE THE BIRTH OF JESUS CHRIST WITH IT.
HONORED BE HIS NAME.
SWISH
HUMM ...
FATHER LIKES MEAD MORE THAN WINE. WHY DON'T YOU ASK HIM FOR SOME?
NO, THERE IS MEANING IN IT BEING WINE.
I WAS HOPING I COULD FIND SOME IN THIS VILLAGE...
...BUT IT SEEMS I MUST CROSS THE NORTH SEA FOR IT.
THORFINN, RUN AND GIVE YOUR FATHER A MESSAGE.
?
A WAR-SHIP IS COMING.

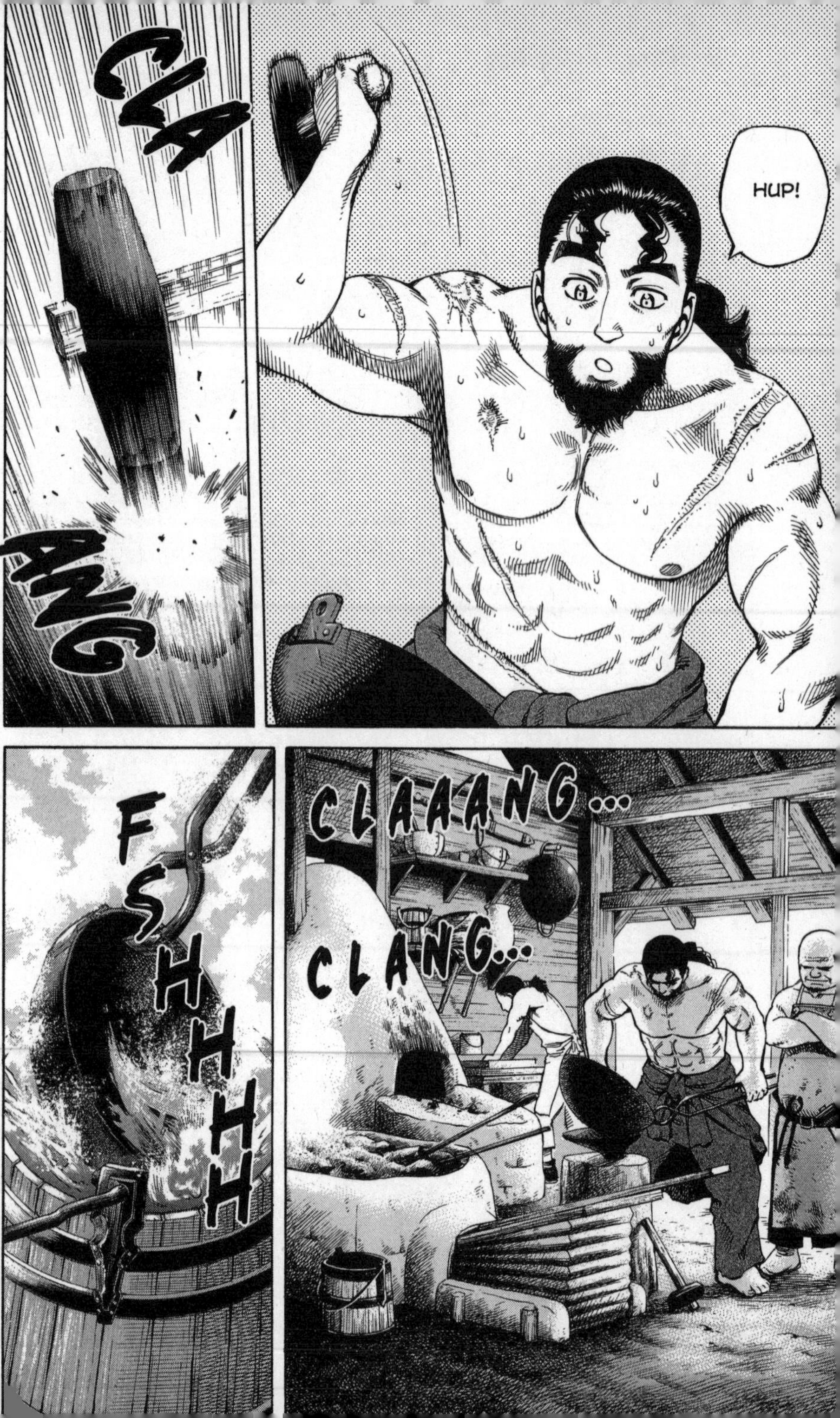
HUP!
CLA
ANG
CLAAANG...
CLANG...
FSHHHH

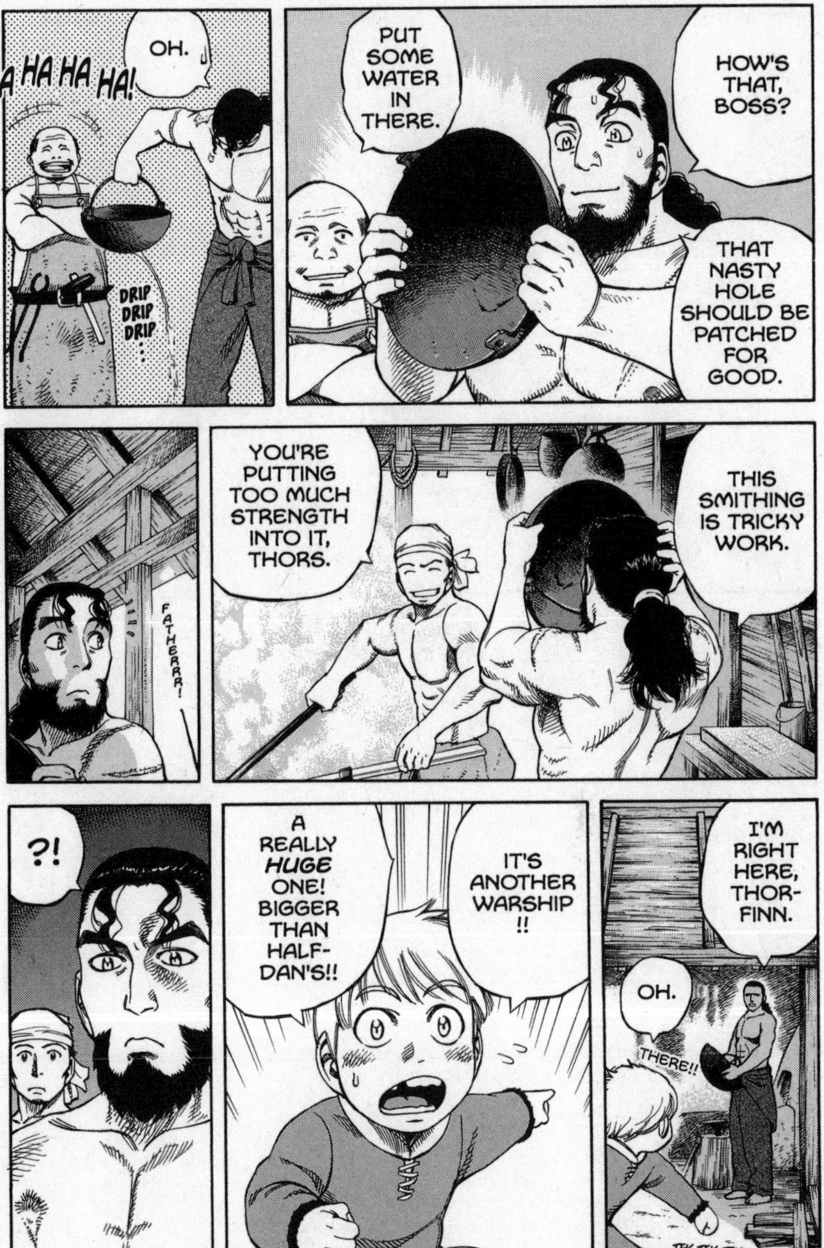
HOW'S THAT, BOSS?
THAT NASTY HOLE SHOULD BE PATCHED FOR GOOD.
PUT SOME WATER IN THERE.
OH.
GA HA HA HA!
DRIP DRIP DRIP...
THIS SMITHING IS TRICKY WORK.
YOU'RE PUTTING TOO MUCH STRENGTH INTO IT, THORS.
FATHERRR!
I'M RIGHT HERE, THOR-FINN.
OH.
THERE!!
TEK TEK TEK
IT'S ANOTHER WARSHIP!!
A REALLY HUGE ONE! BIGGER THAN HALF-DAN'S!!
?!

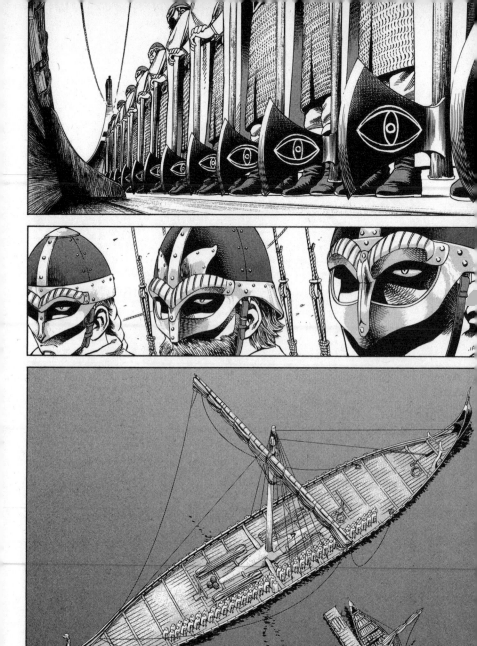

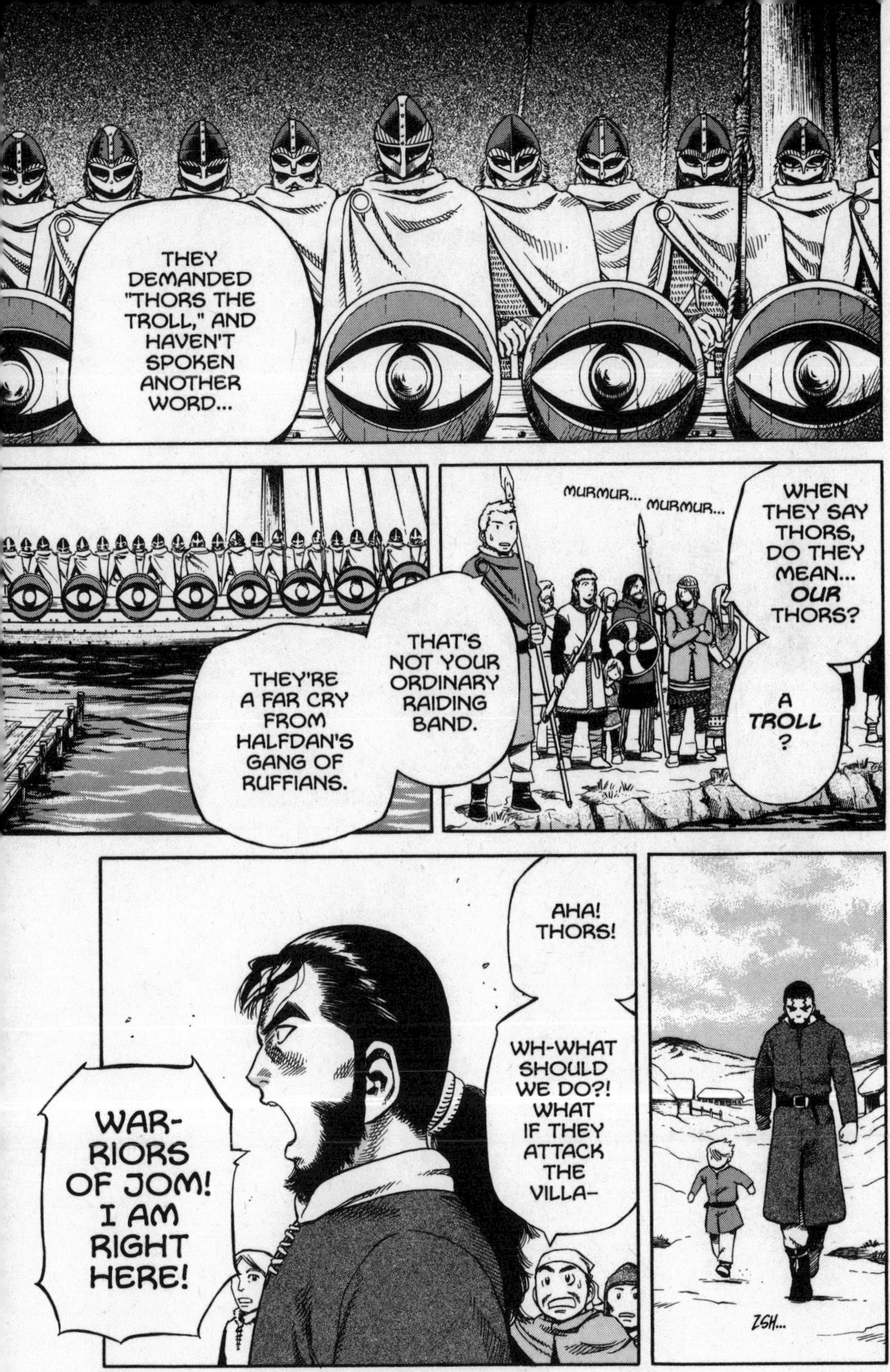
THEY DEMANDED "THORS THE TROLL," AND HAVEN'T SPOKEN ANOTHER WORD...
MURMUR... MURMUR...
WHEN THEY SAY THORS, DO THEY MEAN... OUR THORS?
A TROLL?
THAT'S NOT YOUR ORDINARY RAIDING BAND.
THEY'RE A FAR CRY FROM HALFDAN'S GANG OF RUFFIANS.
ZSH...
AHA! THORS!
WH-WHAT SHOULD WE DO?! WHAT IF THEY ATTACK THE VILLA-
WAR-RIORS OF JOM! I AM RIGHT HERE!

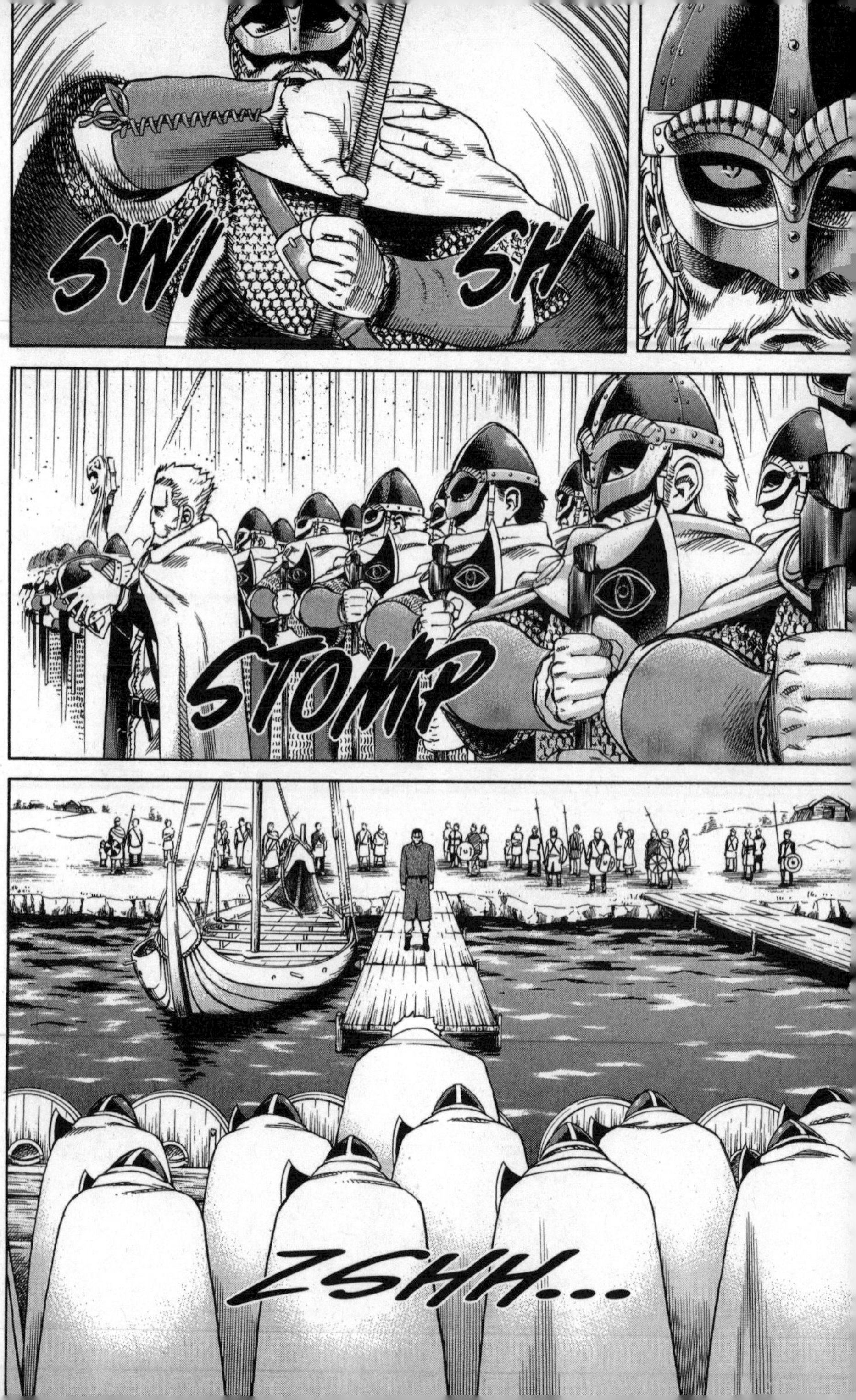
SWISH
STOMP
ZSHH...

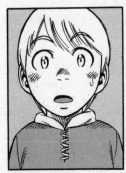

OO
HH
OO
HH
WHOA.
THEY BOWED TO THORS...
MURMUR
...
I NEVER THOUGHT YOU'D FOLLOW ME ALL THE WAY TO ICELAND...
...FLOKI.
I HAVEN'T SEEN YOU SINCE THAT NORWEGIAN EXPEDITION, THORS.
IT'S HARD TO IMAGINE...
...A MAN LIKE YOU, HIDING AT THE ENDS OF THE EARTH HERE...
STATE YOUR BUSINESS, FLOKI.
...
IN THAT CASE...
...FIRST, PERMISSION TO DISEMBARK.

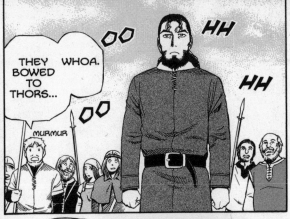

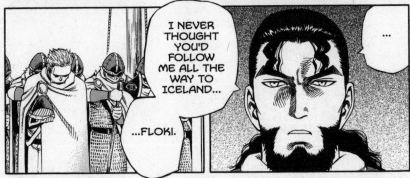

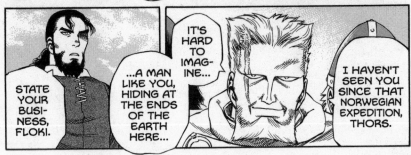

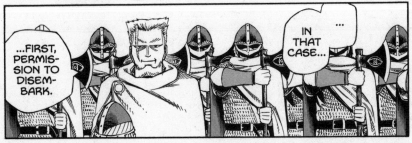

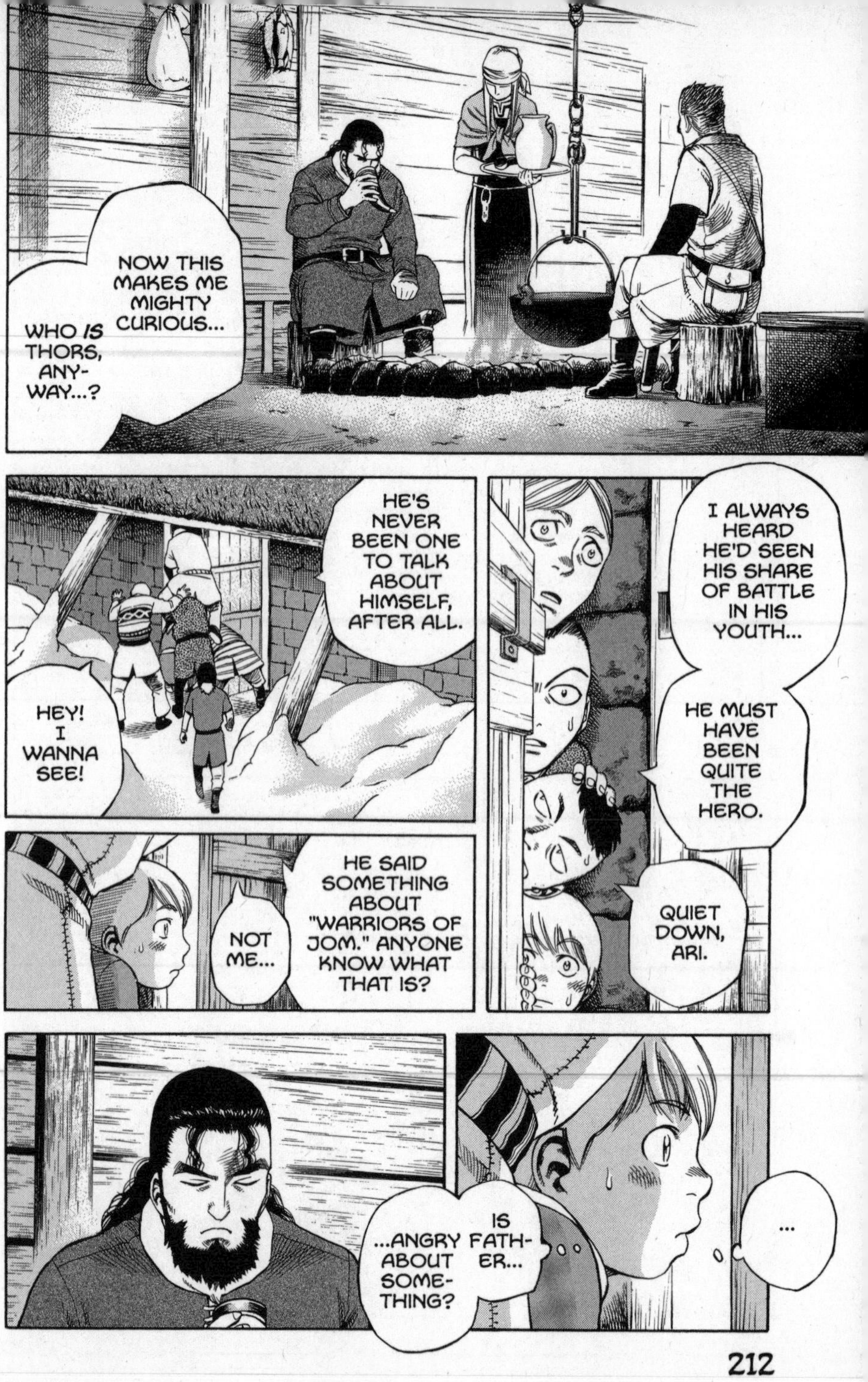
NOW THIS MAKES ME MIGHTY CURIOUS...
WHO *IS* THORS, ANYWAY...?
I ALWAYS HEARD HE'D SEEN HIS SHARE OF BATTLE IN HIS YOUTH...
HE MUST HAVE BEEN QUITE THE HERO.
QUIET DOWN, ARI.
HE'S NEVER BEEN ONE TO TALK ABOUT HIMSELF, AFTER ALL.
HEY! I WANNA SEE!
HE SAID SOMETHING ABOUT "WARRIORS OF JOM." ANYONE KNOW WHAT THAT IS?
NOT ME...
...
IS FATHER...
...ANGRY ABOUT SOMETHING?

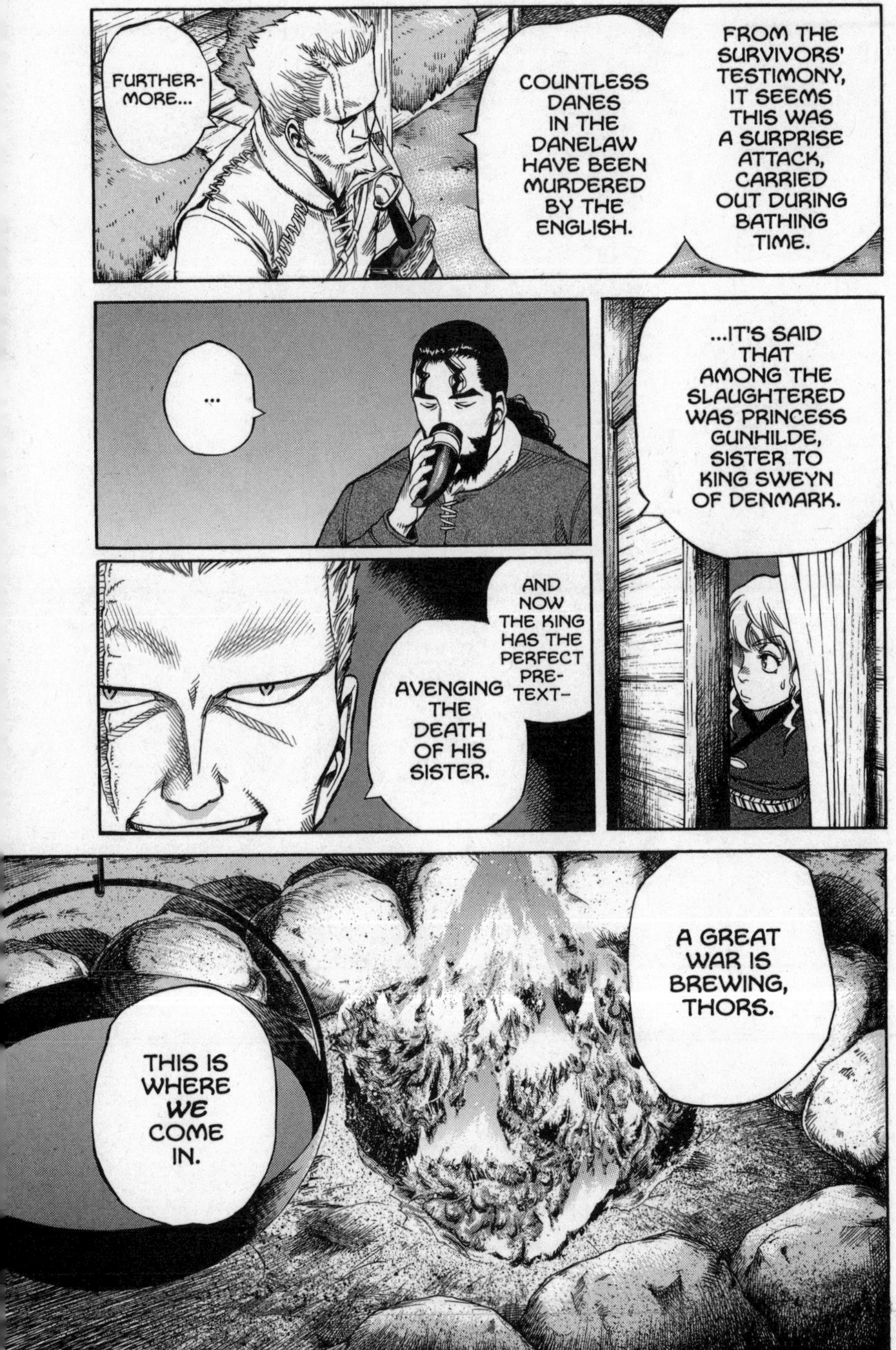
FROM THE SURVIVORS' TESTIMONY, IT SEEMS THIS WAS A SURPRISE ATTACK, CARRIED OUT DURING BATHING TIME.
COUNTLESS DANES IN THE DANELAW HAVE BEEN MURDERED BY THE ENGLISH.
FURTHER-MORE...
...IT'S SAID THAT AMONG THE SLAUGHTERED WAS PRINCESS GUNHILDE, SISTER TO KING SWEYN OF DENMARK.
...
AND NOW THE KING HAS THE PERFECT PRE-TEXT—
AVENGING THE DEATH OF HIS SISTER.
A GREAT WAR IS BREWING, THORS.
THIS IS WHERE *WE* COME IN.

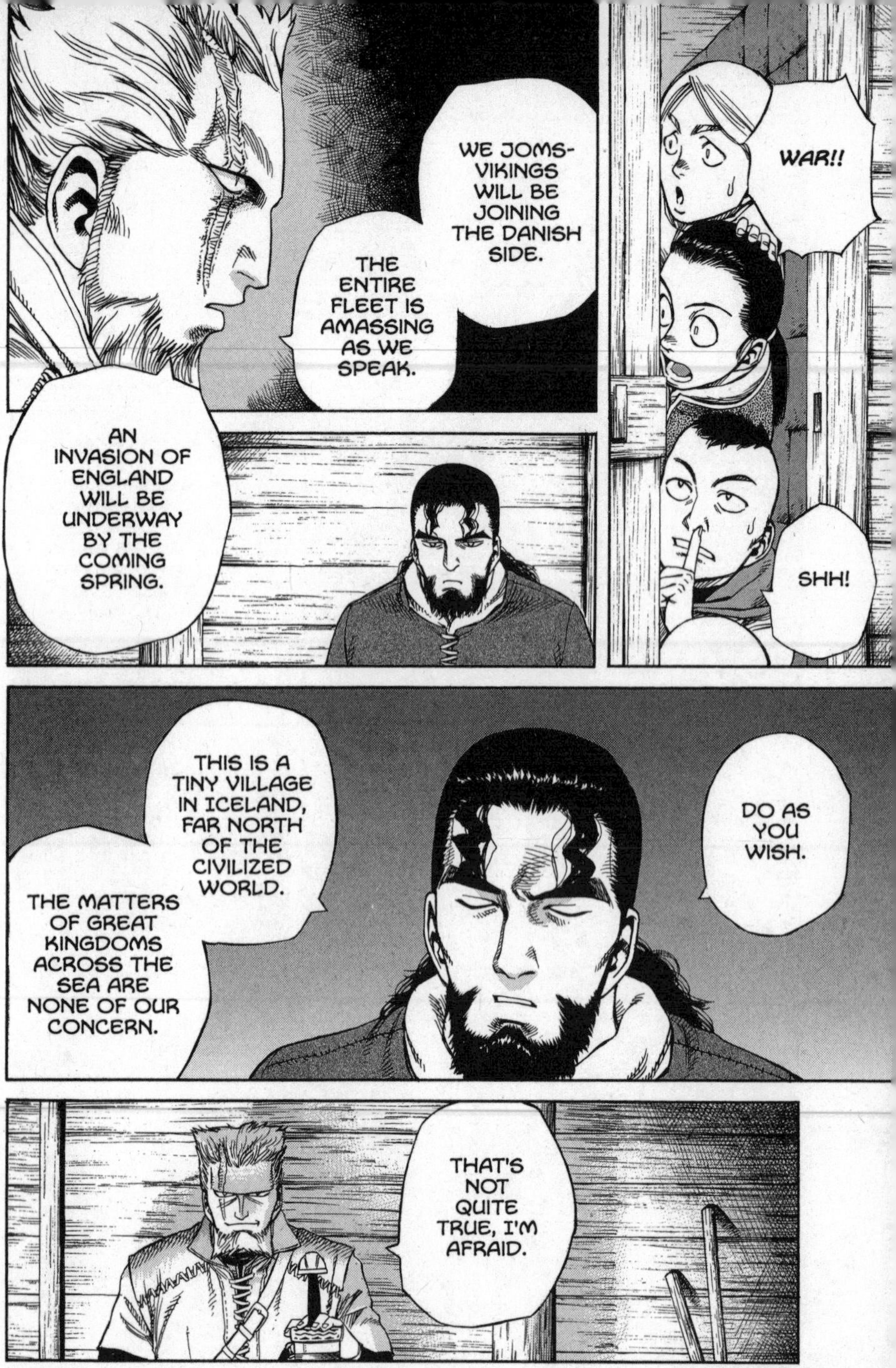
WAR!!
SHH!
WE JOMS-VIKINGS WILL BE JOINING THE DANISH SIDE.
THE ENTIRE FLEET IS AMASSING AS WE SPEAK.
AN INVASION OF ENGLAND WILL BE UNDERWAY BY THE COMING SPRING.
DO AS YOU WISH.
THIS IS A TINY VILLAGE IN ICELAND, FAR NORTH OF THE CIVILIZED WORLD.
THE MATTERS OF GREAT KINGDOMS ACROSS THE SEA ARE NONE OF OUR CONCERN.
THAT'S NOT QUITE TRUE, I'M AFRAID.

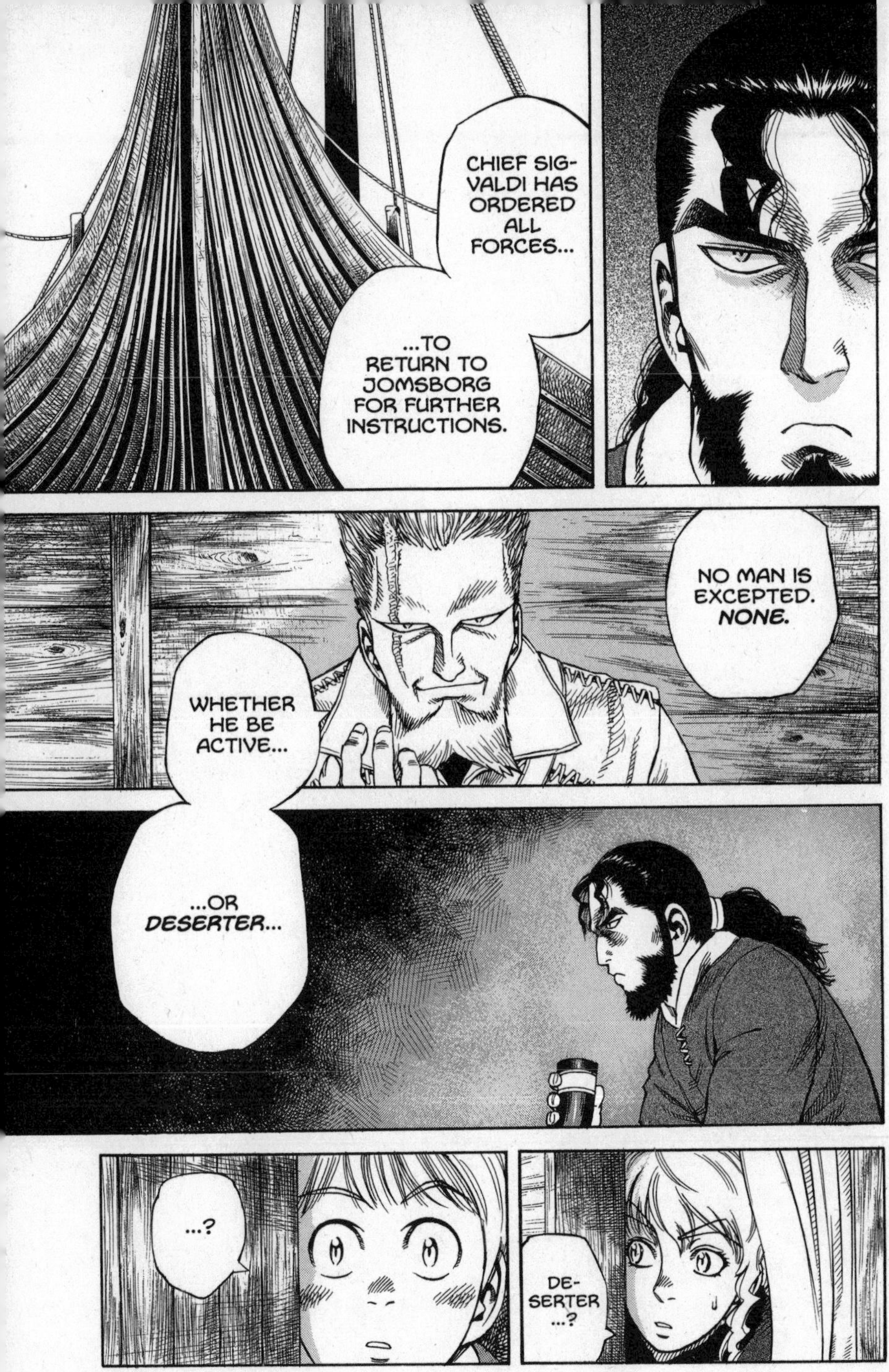
CHIEF SIG-VALDI HAS ORDERED ALL FORCES...
...TO RETURN TO JOMSBORG FOR FURTHER INSTRUCTIONS.
NO MAN IS EXCEPTED. *NONE.*
WHETHER HE BE ACTIVE...
...OR *DESERTER...*
DE-SERTER ...?
...?

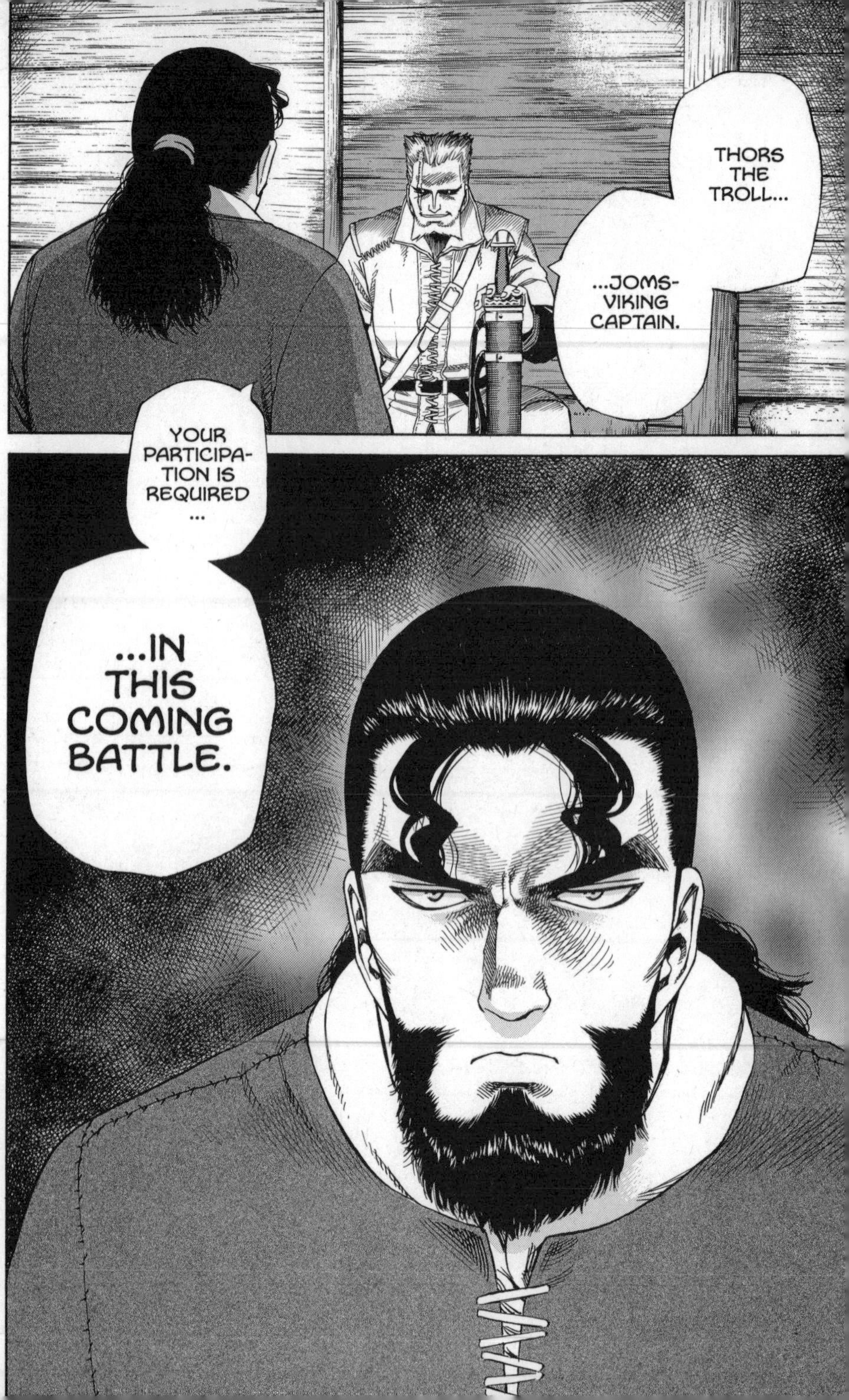

CHAPTER 5 - END

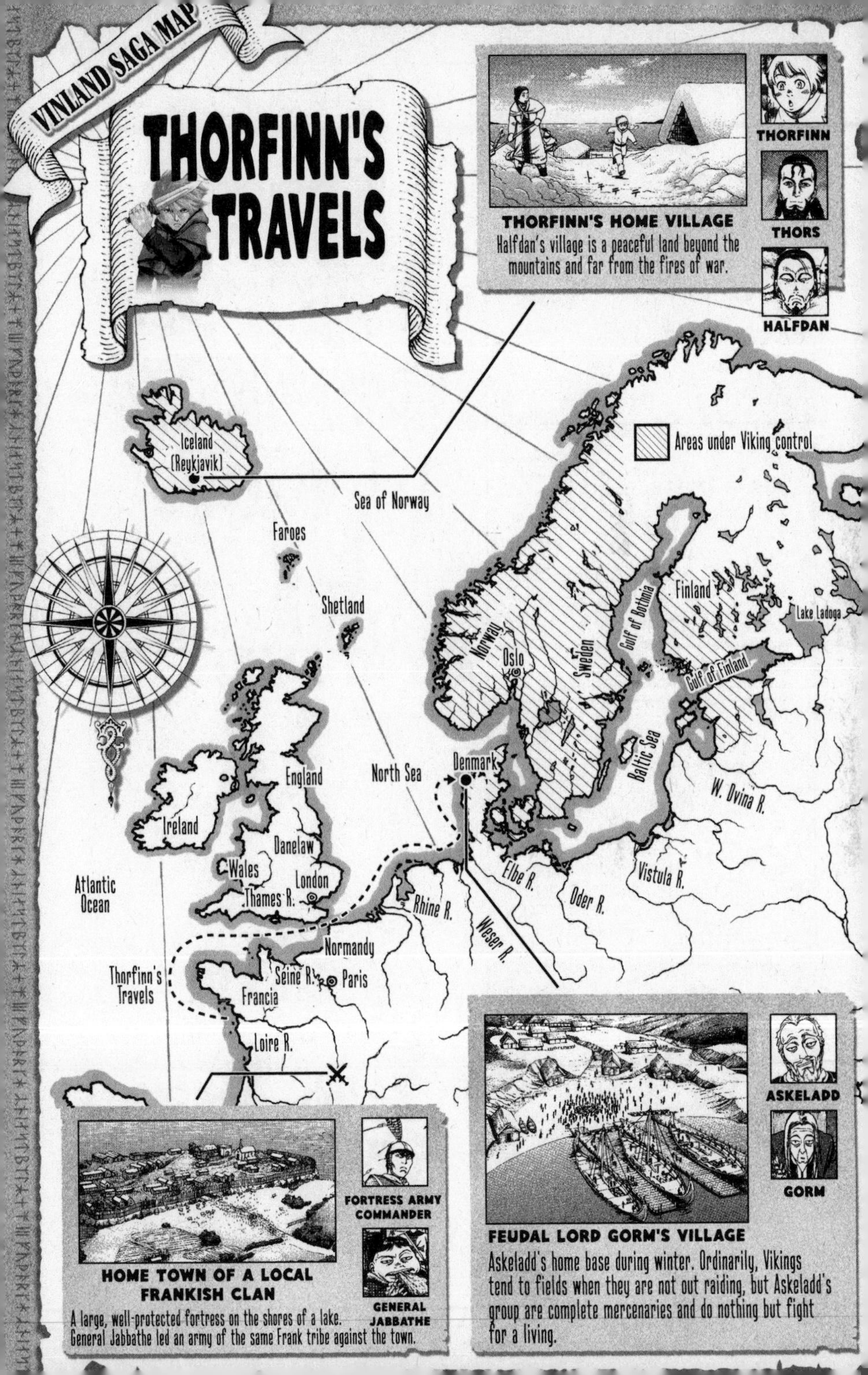

VINLAND SAGA MAP
THORFINN'S TRAVELS
THORFINN'S HOME VILLAGE
Halfdan's village is a peaceful land beyond the mountains and far from the fires of war.
THORFINN
THORS
HALFDAN
Areas under Viking control
Iceland (Reykjavik)
Sea of Norway
Faroes
Shetland
Norway
Oslo
Sweden
Gulf of Bothnia
Finland
Lake Ladoga
Gulf of Finland
Baltic Sea
W. Dvina R.
Denmark
North Sea
England
Ireland
Danelaw
Wales
London
Thames R.
Atlantic Ocean
Elbe R.
Oder R.
Vistula R.
Rhine R.
Weser R.
Normandy
Seine R.
Paris
Thorfinn's Travels
Francia
Loire R.
HOME TOWN OF A LOCAL FRANKISH CLAN
A large, well-protected fortress on the shores of a lake. General Jabbathe led an army of the same Frank tribe against the town.
FORTRESS ARMY COMMANDER
GENERAL JABBATHE
FEUDAL LORD GORM'S VILLAGE
Askeladd's home base during winter. Ordinarily, Vikings tend to fields when they are not out raiding, but Askeladd's group are complete mercenaries and do nothing but fight for a living.
ASKELADD
GORM

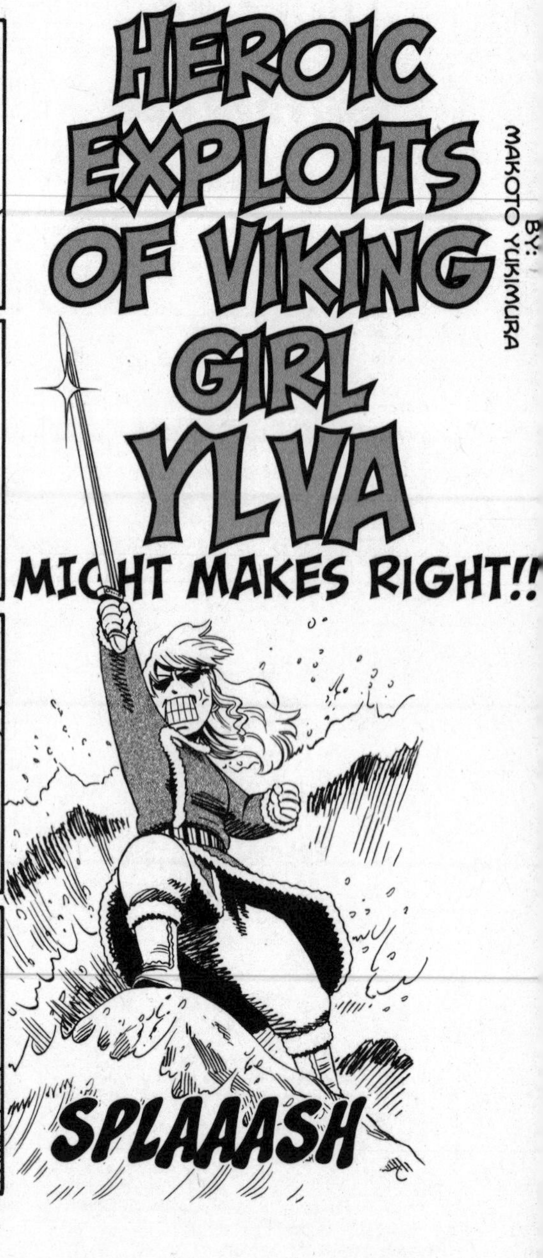
HEROIC EXPLOITS OF VIKING GIRL YLVA
BY: MAKOTO YUKIMURA
MIGHT MAKES RIGHT!!
SPLAAASH

MATH TIME

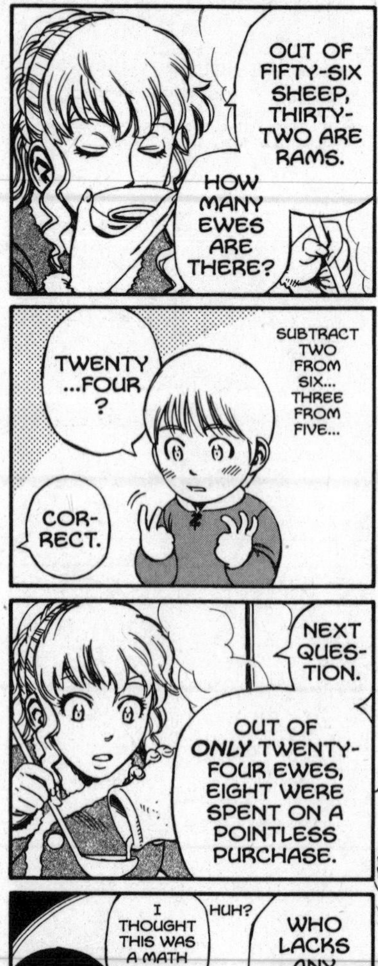
OUT OF FIFTY-SIX SHEEP, THIRTY-TWO ARE RAMS.
HOW MANY EWES ARE THERE?
SUBTRACT TWO FROM SIX... THREE FROM FIVE...
TWENTY ...FOUR ?
COR-RECT.
NEXT QUES-TION.
OUT OF ONLY TWENTY-FOUR EWES, EIGHT WERE SPENT ON A POINTLESS PURCHASE.
WHO LACKS ANY KIND OF FINANCIAL SENSE?
HUH?
I THOUGHT THIS WAS A MATH LESSON.
...
OH, GIVE IT A REST.

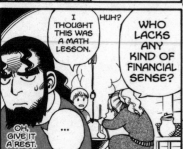

I'M A VIKING, AFTER ALL

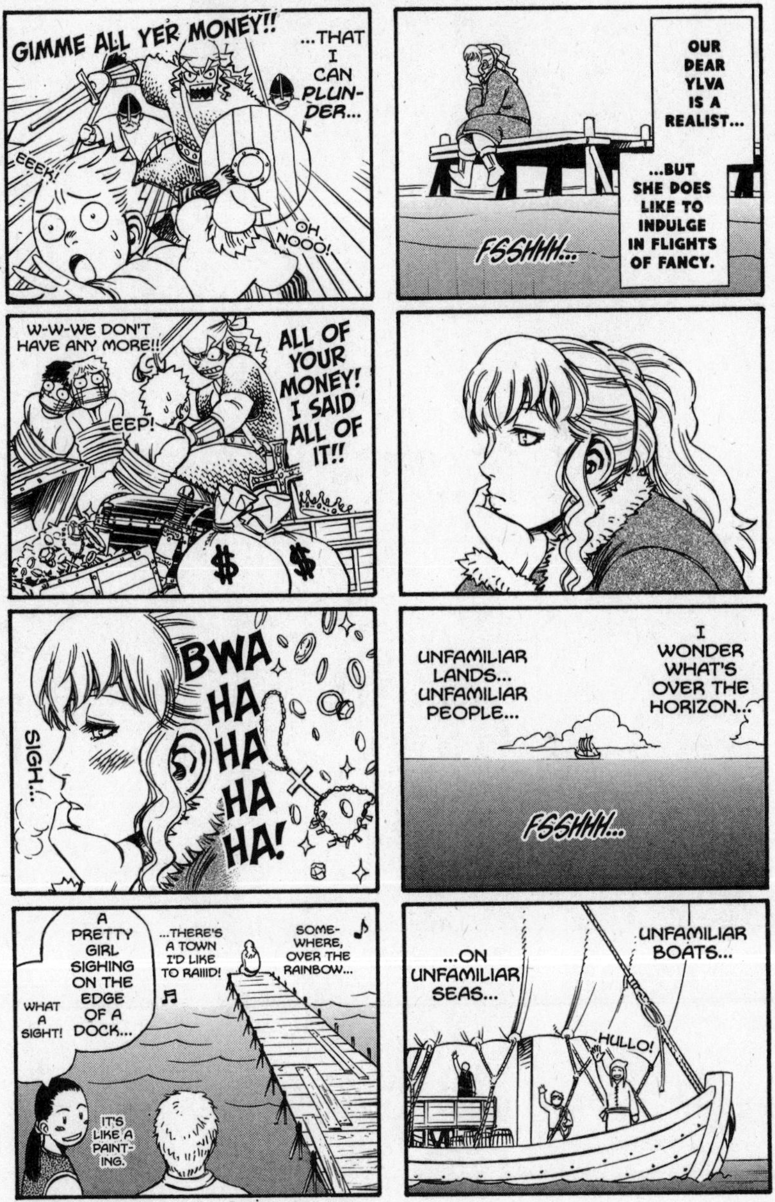
OUR DEAR YLVA IS A REALIST...
...BUT SHE DOES LIKE TO INDULGE IN FLIGHTS OF FANCY.
FSSHHH...
I WONDER WHAT'S OVER THE HORIZON...
UNFAMILIAR LANDS... UNFAMILIAR PEOPLE...
FSSHHH...
UNFAMILIAR BOATS...
...ON UNFAMILIAR SEAS...
HULLO!
GIMME ALL YER MONEY!!
...THAT I CAN PLUNDER...
EEEK!
OH, NOOO!
ALL OF YOUR MONEY! I SAID ALL OF IT!!
W-W-WE DON'T HAVE ANY MORE!!
EEP!
BWA HA HA HA HA HA!
SIGH...
SOME-WHERE, OVER THE RAINBOW...
...THERE'S A TOWN I'D LIKE TO RAIIID!
A PRETTY GIRL SIGHING ON THE EDGE OF A DOCK...
WHAT A SIGHT!
IT'S LIKE A PAINT-ING.

I HAVE A NEWFOUND RESPECT FOR FOUR-PANEL ARTISTS...

THOR'S HOME

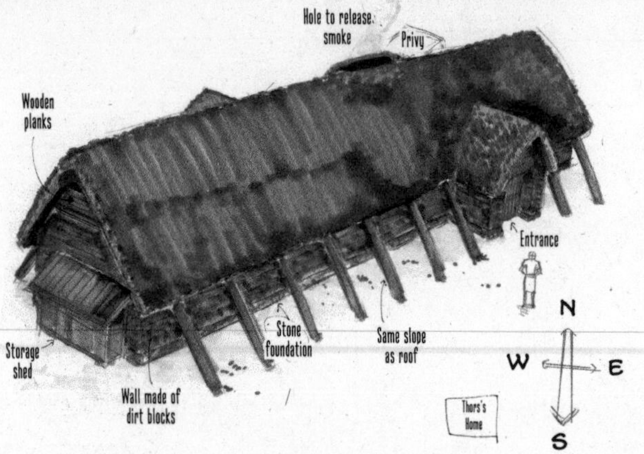
Hole to release smoke
Privy
Wooden planks
Entrance
N
W
E
S
Storage shed
Stone foundation
Same slope as roof
Wall made of dirt blocks
Thors's Home

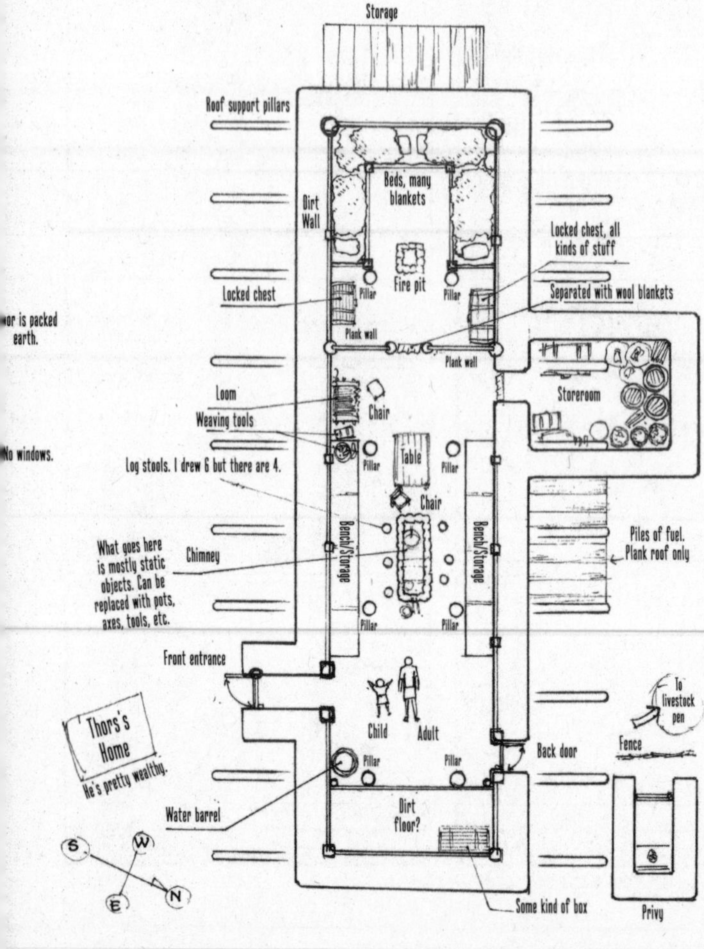
Storage
Roof support pillars
Beds, many blankets
Dirt Wall
Locked chest, all kinds of stuff
Fire pit
Pillar
Pillar
Locked chest
Separated with wool blankets
or is packed earth.
Plank wall
Plank wall
Storeroom
Loom
Chair
Weaving tools
No windows.
Table
Pillar
Pillar
Log stools. I drew 6 but there are 4.
Chair
Bench/Storage
Bench/Storage
Piles of fuel. Plank roof only
What goes here is mostly static objects. Can be replaced with pots, axes, tools, etc.
Chimney
Pillar
Pillar
Front entrance
To livestock pen
Thors's Home
He's pretty wealthy.
Child
Adult
Back door
Fence
Pillar
Pillar
Water barrel
Dirt floor?
S
W
E
N
Some kind of box
Privy

AFTERWORD

We don't truly know the full etymology of the name "viking."
It's said the base of the word is "vik," which means inlet.
They used inlets as natural ports; building villages within them;
raising sheep and pigs; cultivating small amounts of land;
fashioning tools; eating barley, herrings, whales and seals;
drinking beer; crying; laughing; and falling in love. Their piratical
image tends to precede them, but I would like to continue
studying them and portraying them in various other ways.

**MAKOTO
YUKIMURA**

**VINLAND
SAGA**

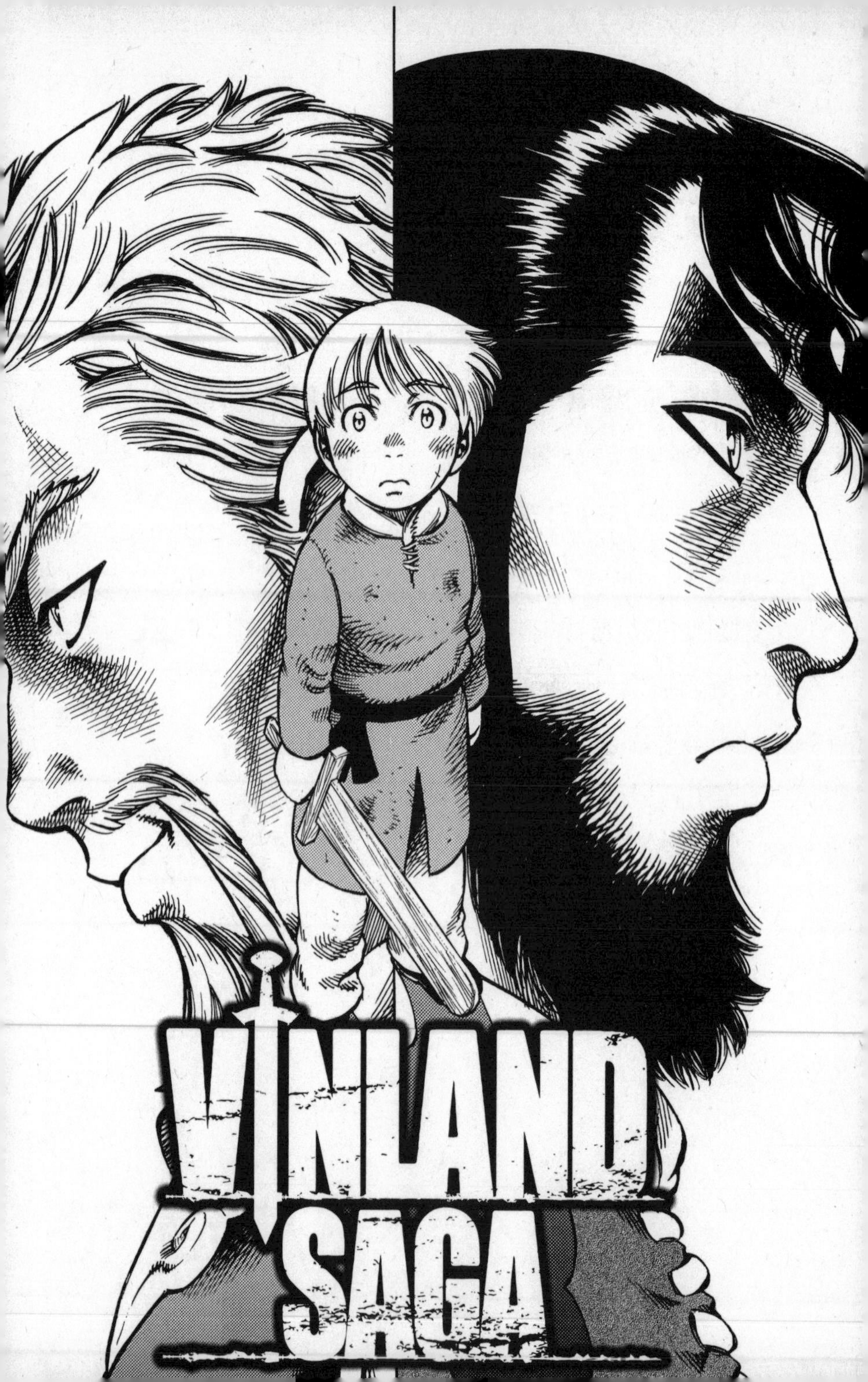
VINLAND SAGA

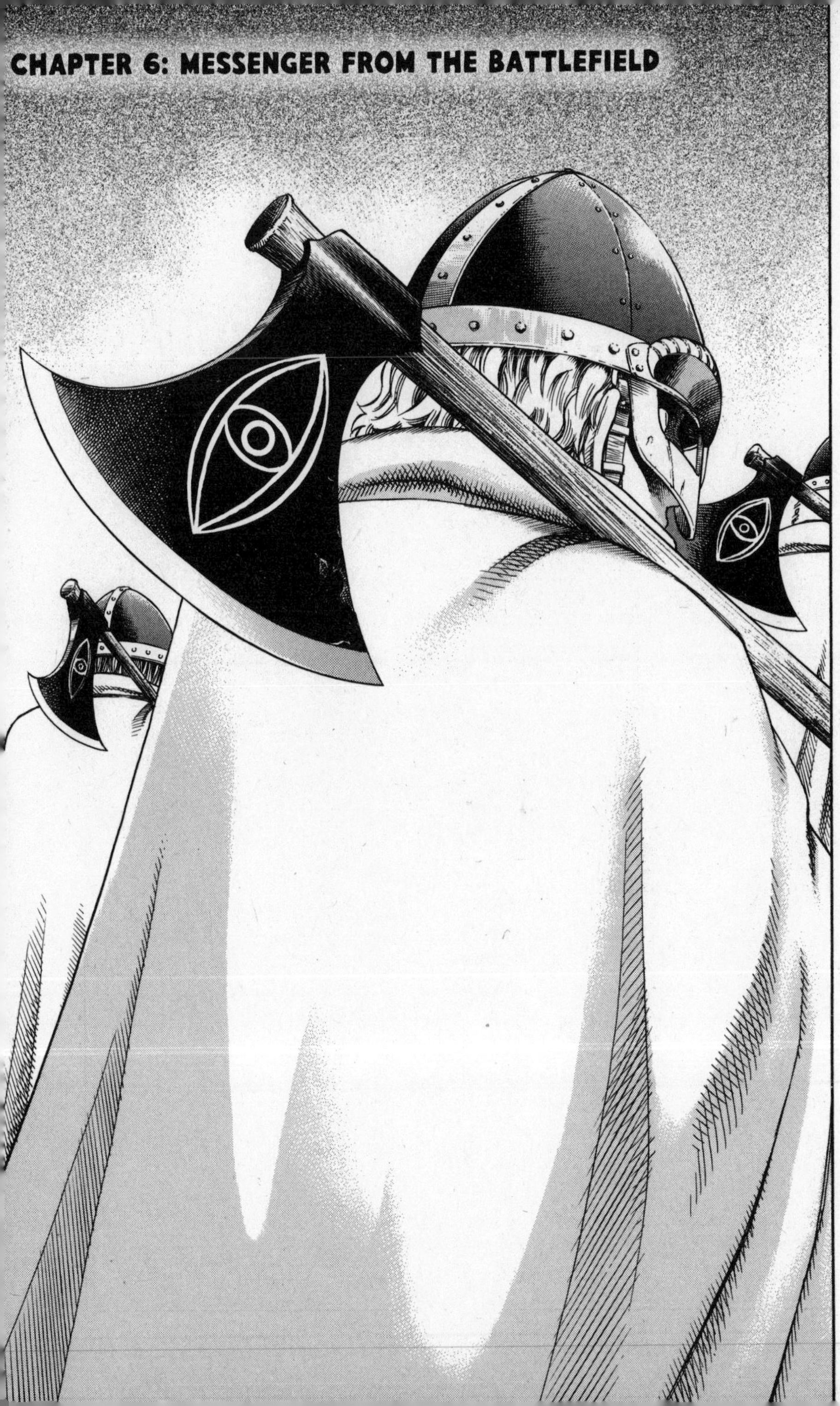
CHAPTER 6: MESSENGER FROM THE BATTLEFIELD

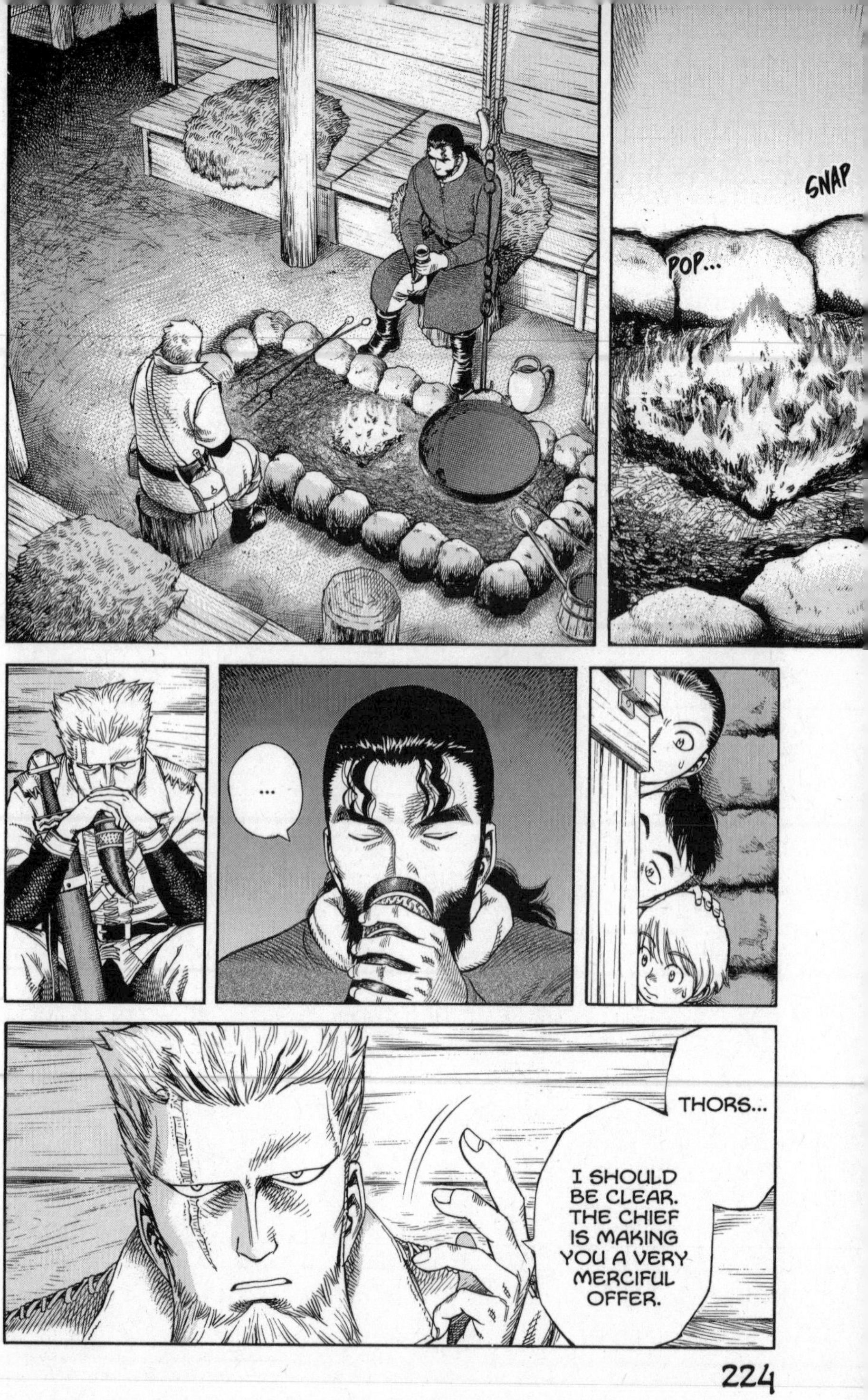
SNAP
POP...
...
THORS...
I SHOULD BE CLEAR. THE CHIEF IS MAKING YOU A VERY MERCIFUL OFFER.

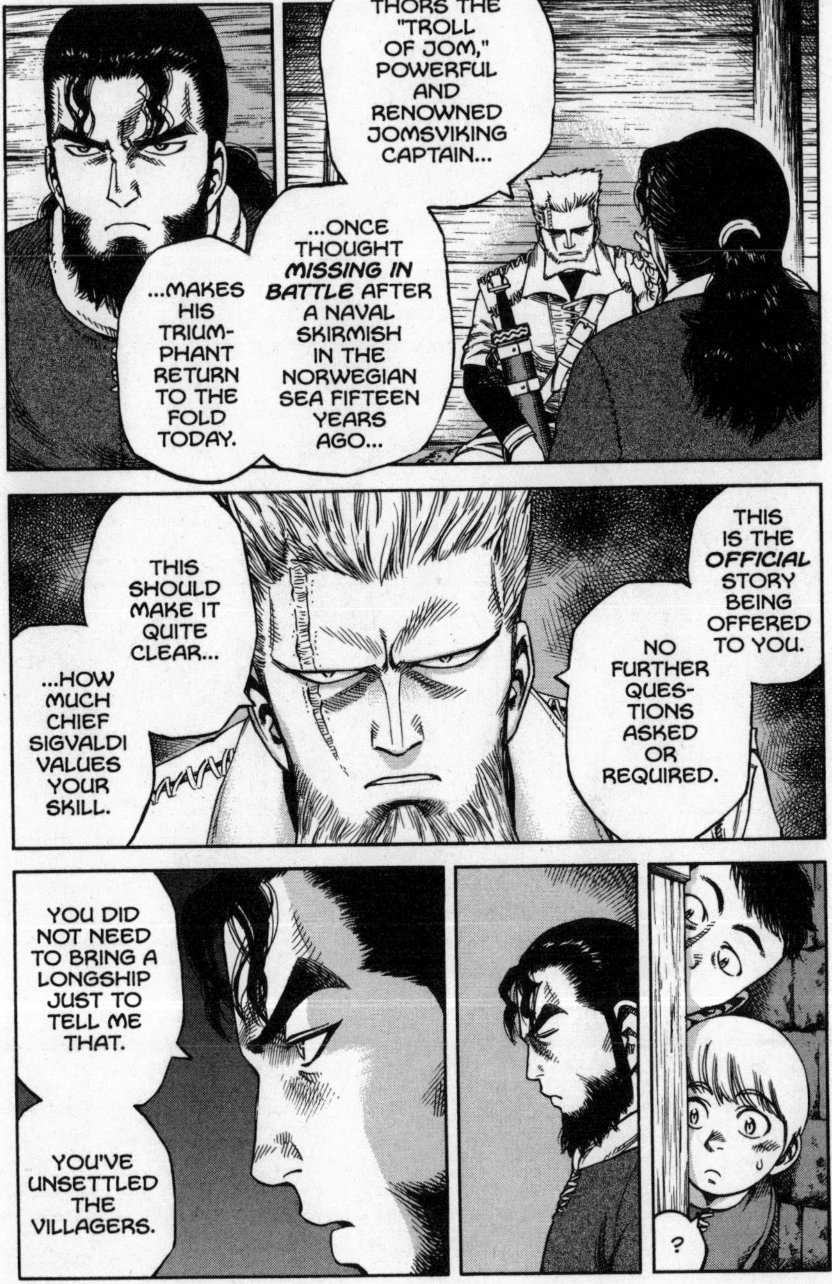
THORS THE "TROLL OF JOM," POWERFUL AND RENOWNED JOMSVIKING CAPTAIN...
...ONCE THOUGHT *MISSING IN BATTLE* AFTER A NAVAL SKIRMISH IN THE NORWEGIAN SEA FIFTEEN YEARS AGO...
...MAKES HIS TRIUMPHANT RETURN TO THE FOLD TODAY.
THIS IS THE *OFFICIAL* STORY BEING OFFERED TO YOU.
NO FURTHER QUESTIONS ASKED OR REQUIRED.
THIS SHOULD MAKE IT QUITE CLEAR...
...HOW MUCH CHIEF SIGVALDI VALUES YOUR SKILL.
?
YOU DID NOT NEED TO BRING A LONGSHIP JUST TO TELL ME THAT.
YOU'VE UNSETTLED THE VILLAGERS.

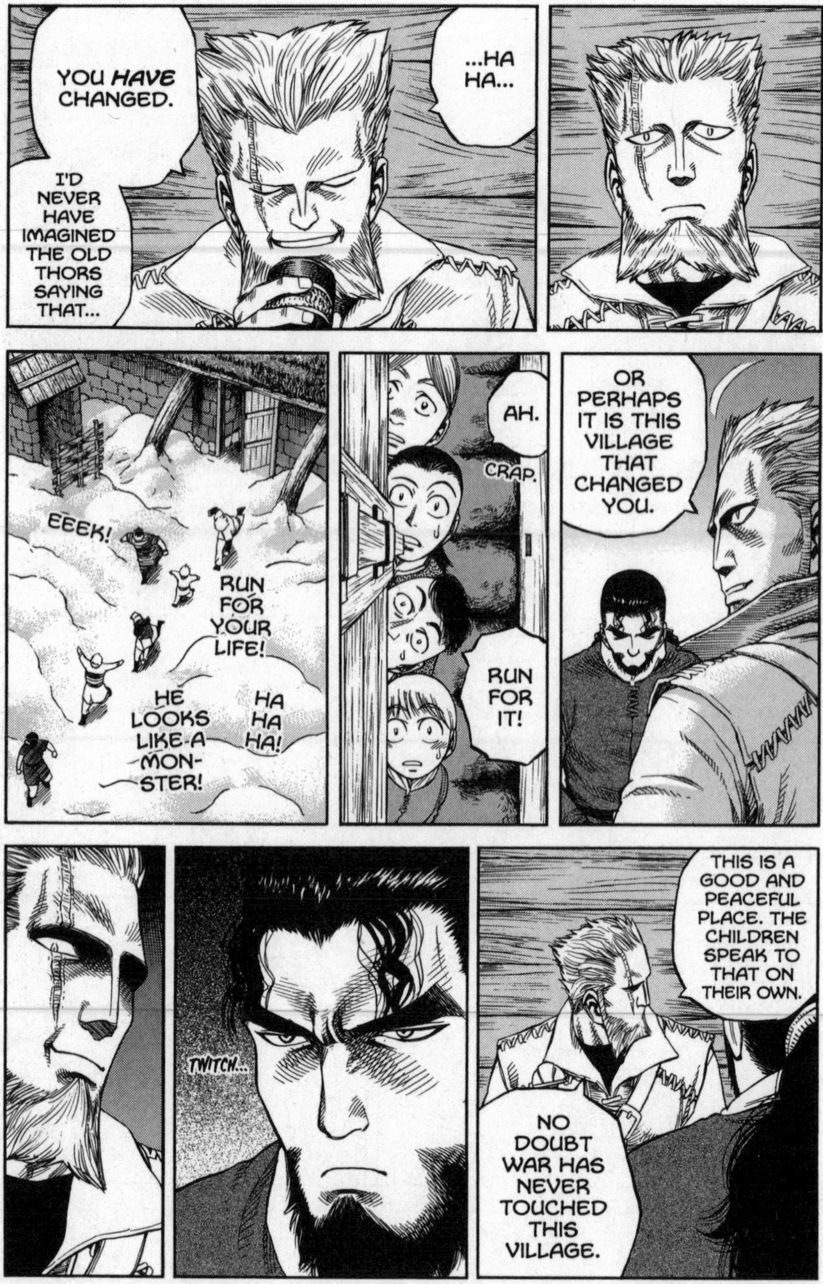
...HA HA...
YOU HAVE CHANGED.
I'D NEVER HAVE IMAGINED THE OLD THORS SAYING THAT...
OR PERHAPS IT IS THIS VILLAGE THAT CHANGED YOU.
AH.
CRAP.
RUN FOR IT!
EEEK!
RUN FOR YOUR LIFE!
HA HA HA!
HE LOOKS LIKE A MON-STER!
THIS IS A GOOD AND PEACEFUL PLACE. THE CHILDREN SPEAK TO THAT ON THEIR OWN.
NO DOUBT WAR HAS NEVER TOUCHED THIS VILLAGE.
TWITCH...

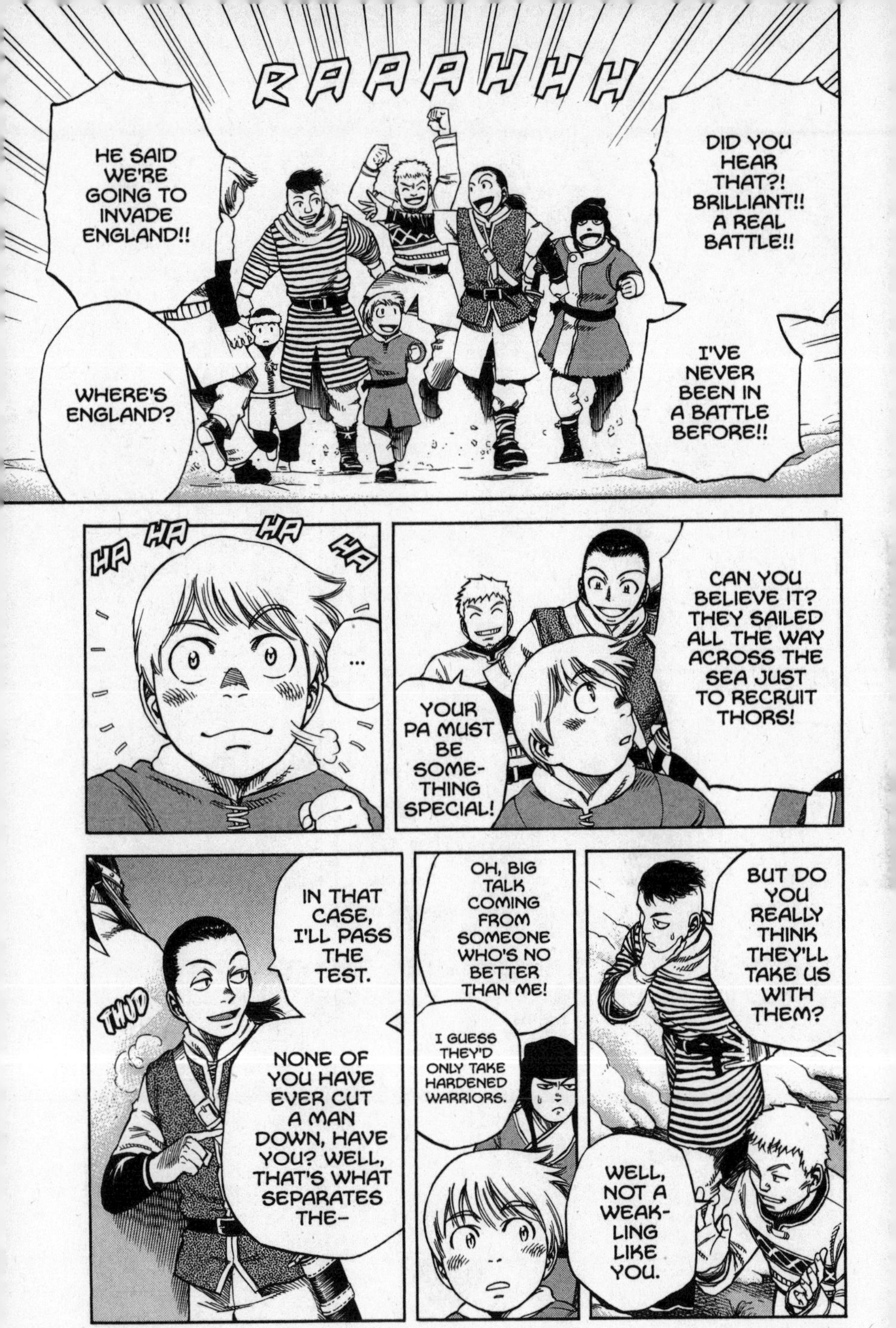
RAAAHHH
DID YOU HEAR THAT?! BRILLIANT!! A REAL BATTLE!!
I'VE NEVER BEEN IN A BATTLE BEFORE!!
HE SAID WE'RE GOING TO INVADE ENGLAND!!
WHERE'S ENGLAND?
CAN YOU BELIEVE IT? THEY SAILED ALL THE WAY ACROSS THE SEA JUST TO RECRUIT THORS!
YOUR PA MUST BE SOME-THING SPECIAL!
HA HA HA HA
...
BUT DO YOU REALLY THINK THEY'LL TAKE US WITH THEM?
WELL, NOT A WEAK-LING LIKE YOU.
OH, BIG TALK COMING FROM SOMEONE WHO'S NO BETTER THAN ME!
I GUESS THEY'D ONLY TAKE HARDENED WARRIORS.
IN THAT CASE, I'LL PASS THE TEST.
THUD
NONE OF YOU HAVE EVER CUT A MAN DOWN, HAVE YOU? WELL, THAT'S WHAT SEPARATES THE-

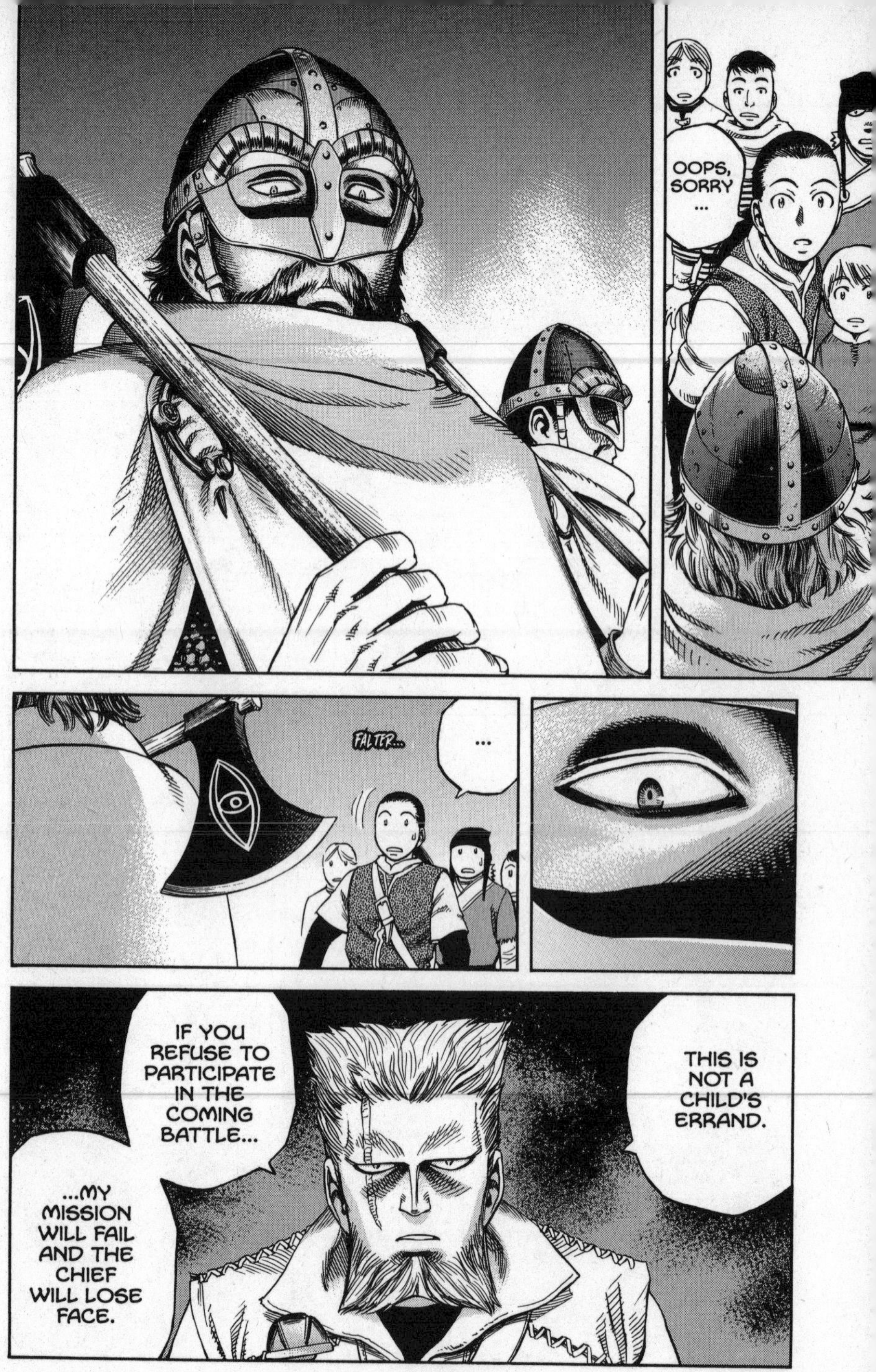
OOPS, SORRY ...
FALTER...
...
THIS IS NOT A CHILD'S ERRAND.
IF YOU REFUSE TO PARTICIPATE IN THE COMING BATTLE...
...MY MISSION WILL FAIL AND THE CHIEF WILL LOSE FACE.

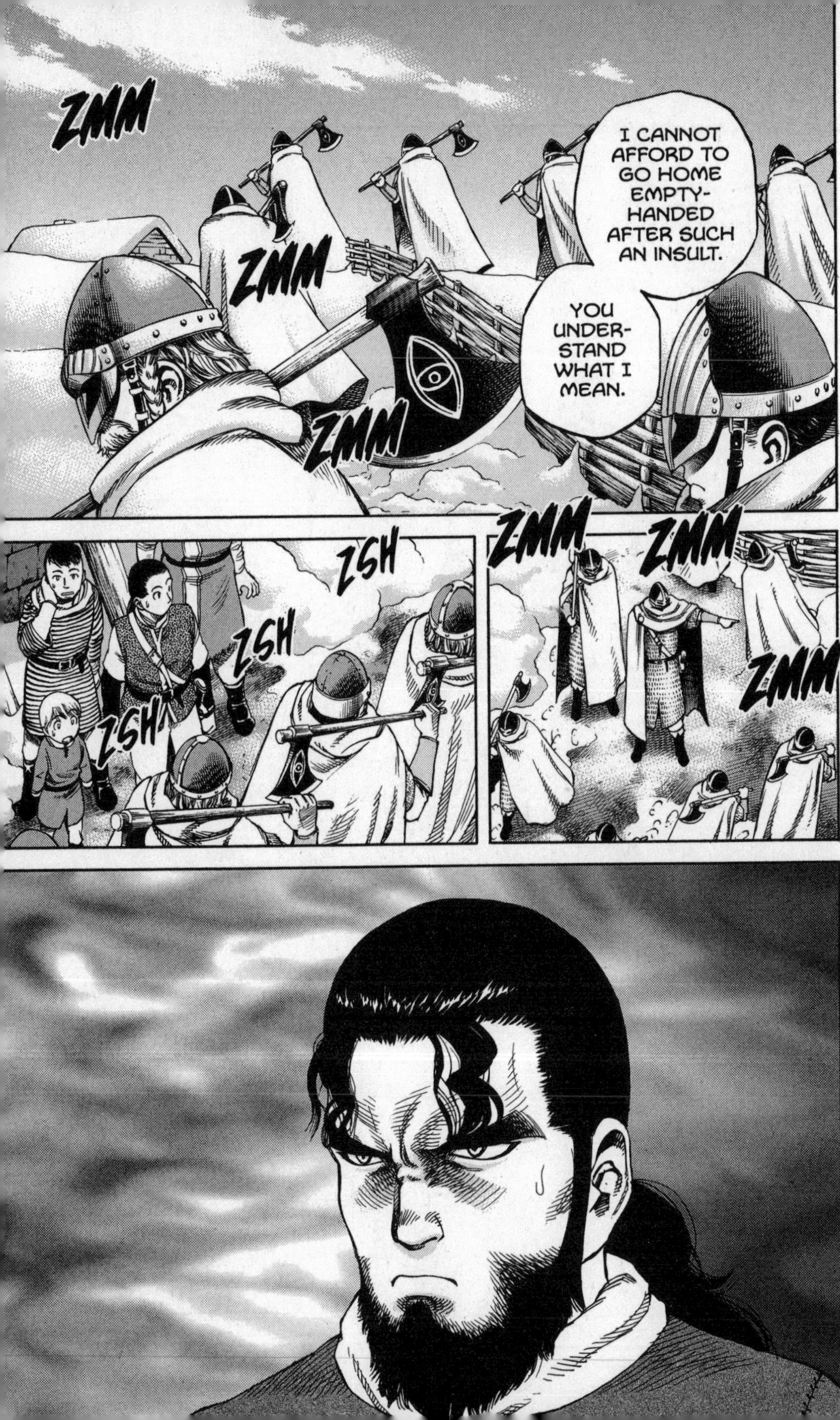
I CANNOT AFFORD TO GO HOME EMPTY-HANDED AFTER SUCH AN INSULT.
YOU UNDER-STAND WHAT I MEAN.
ZMM
ZMM
ZMM
ZMM
ZMM
ZMM
ZMM
ZSH
ZSH
ZSH

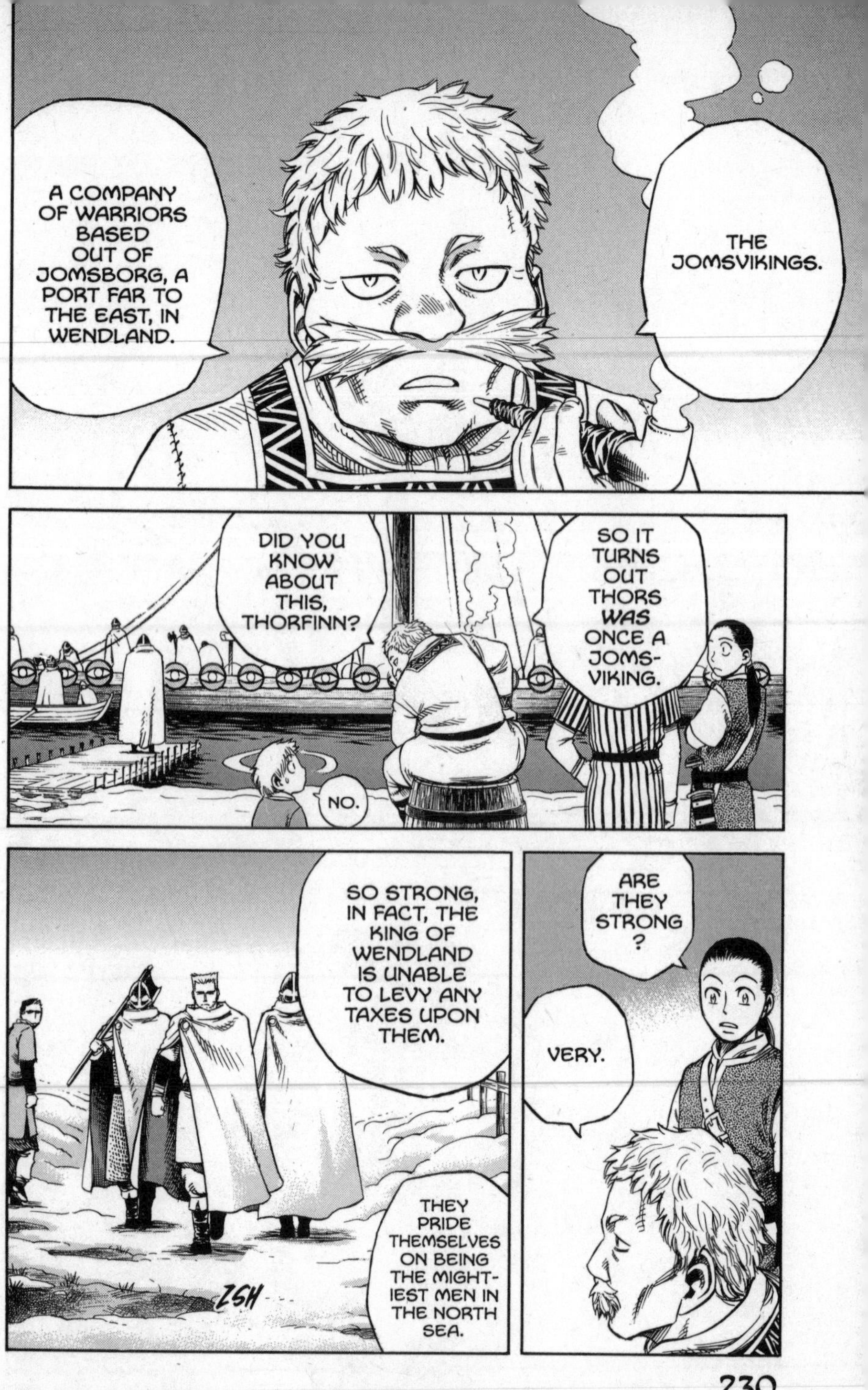
THE JOMSVIKINGS.
A COMPANY OF WARRIORS BASED OUT OF JOMSBORG, A PORT FAR TO THE EAST, IN WENDLAND.
SO IT TURNS OUT THORS *WAS* ONCE A JOMS-VIKING.
DID YOU KNOW ABOUT THIS, THORFINN?
NO.
ARE THEY STRONG?
VERY.
SO STRONG, IN FACT, THE KING OF WENDLAND IS UNABLE TO LEVY ANY TAXES UPON THEM.
THEY PRIDE THEMSELVES ON BEING THE MIGHT-IEST MEN IN THE NORTH SEA.
ZSH

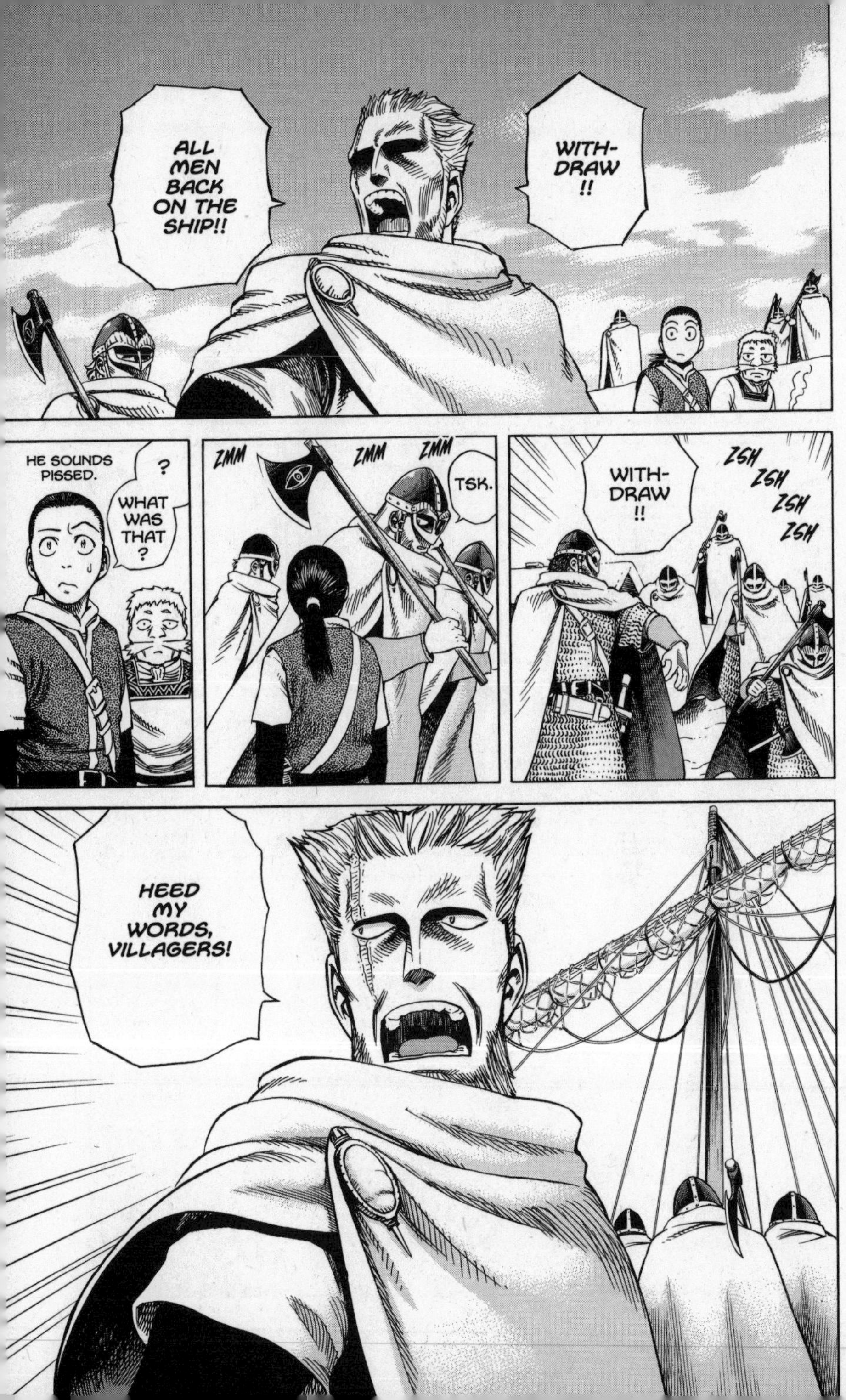
WITH-DRAW!!
ALL MEN BACK ON THE SHIP!!
WITH-DRAW!!
ZSH ZSH ZSH ZSH
ZMM ZMM ZMM
TSK.
?
WHAT WAS THAT?
HE SOUNDS PISSED.
HEED MY WORDS, VILLAGERS!

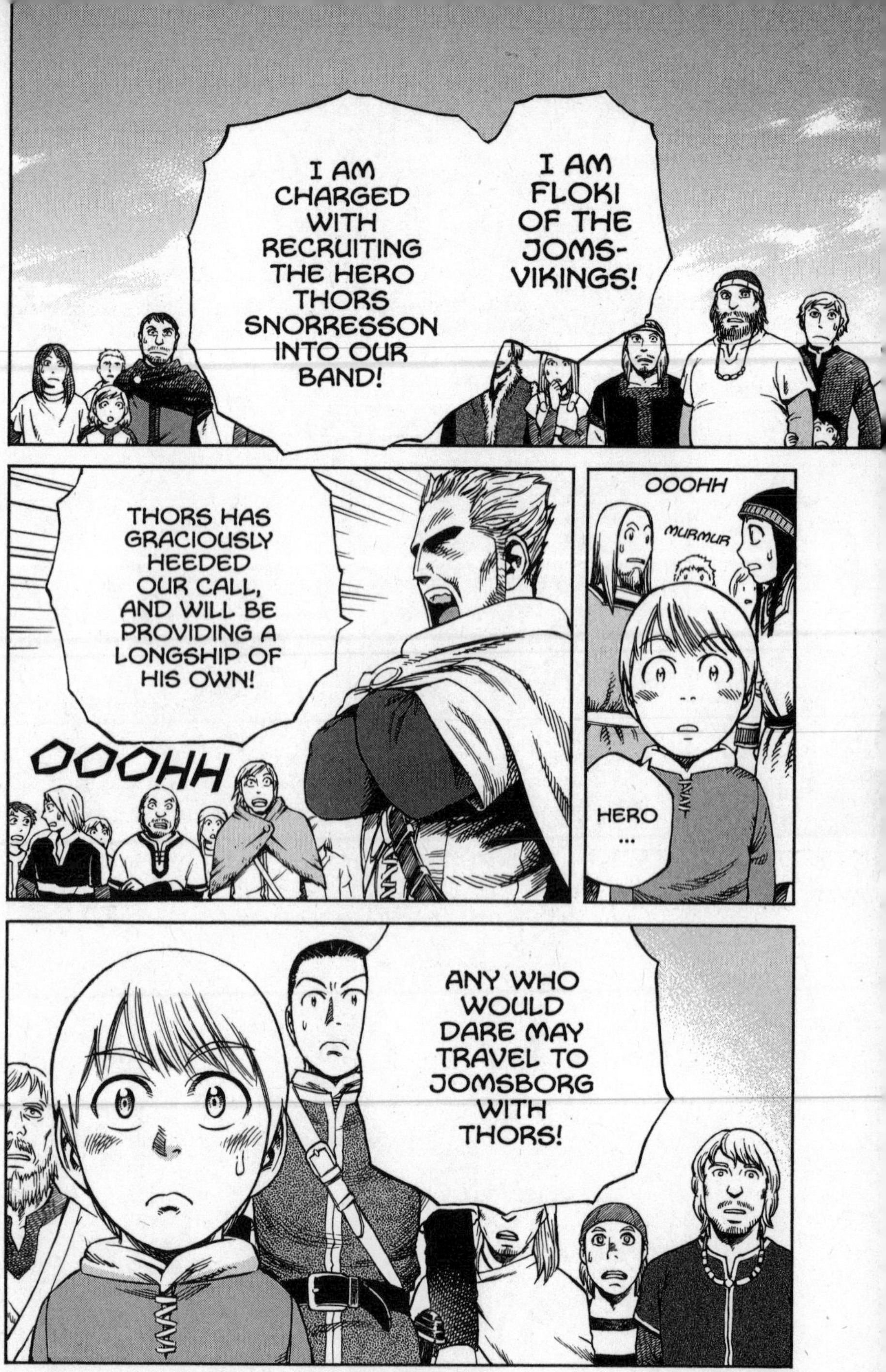
I AM FLOKI OF THE JOMS-VIKINGS!
I AM CHARGED WITH RECRUITING THE HERO THORS SNORRESSON INTO OUR BAND!
OOOHH
MURMUR
HERO ...
THORS HAS GRACIOUSLY HEEDED OUR CALL, AND WILL BE PROVIDING A LONGSHIP OF HIS OWN!
OOOHH
ANY WHO WOULD DARE MAY TRAVEL TO JOMSBORG WITH THORS!

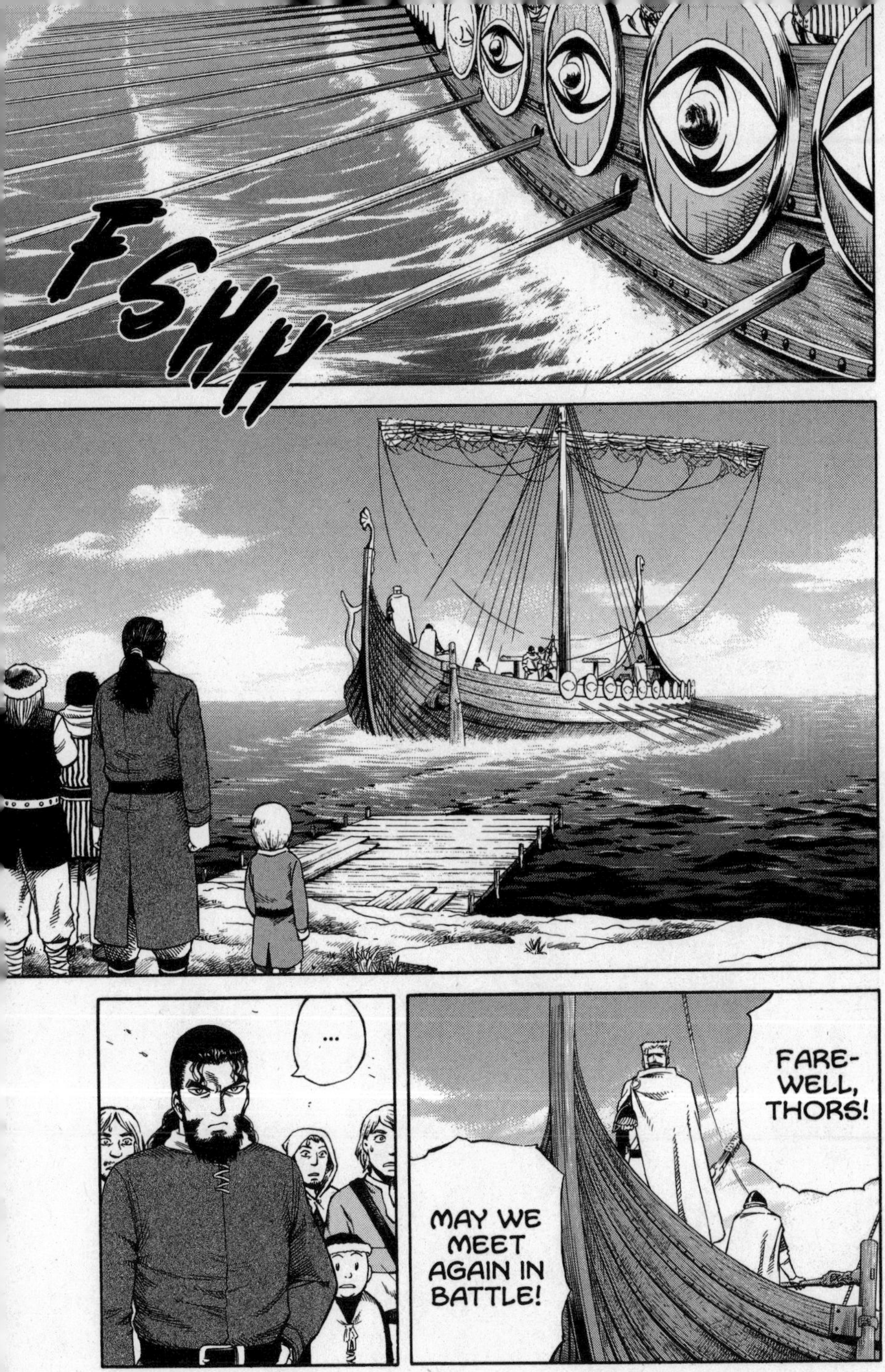
FSHH
FARE-WELL, THORS!
MAY WE MEET AGAIN IN BATTLE!
...

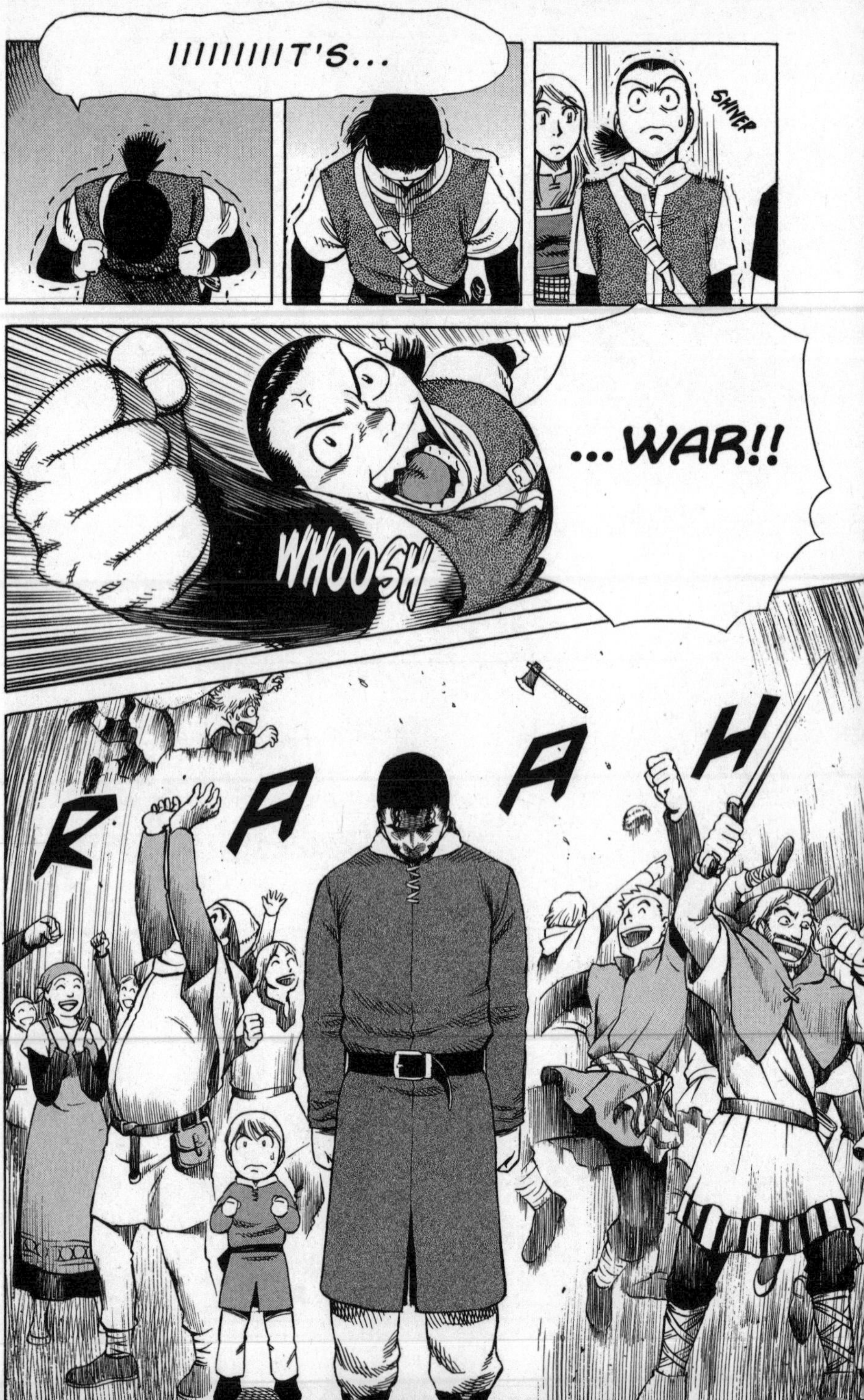
SHIVER
IIIIIIIIIT'S...
...WAR!!
WHOOSH
RAAAH

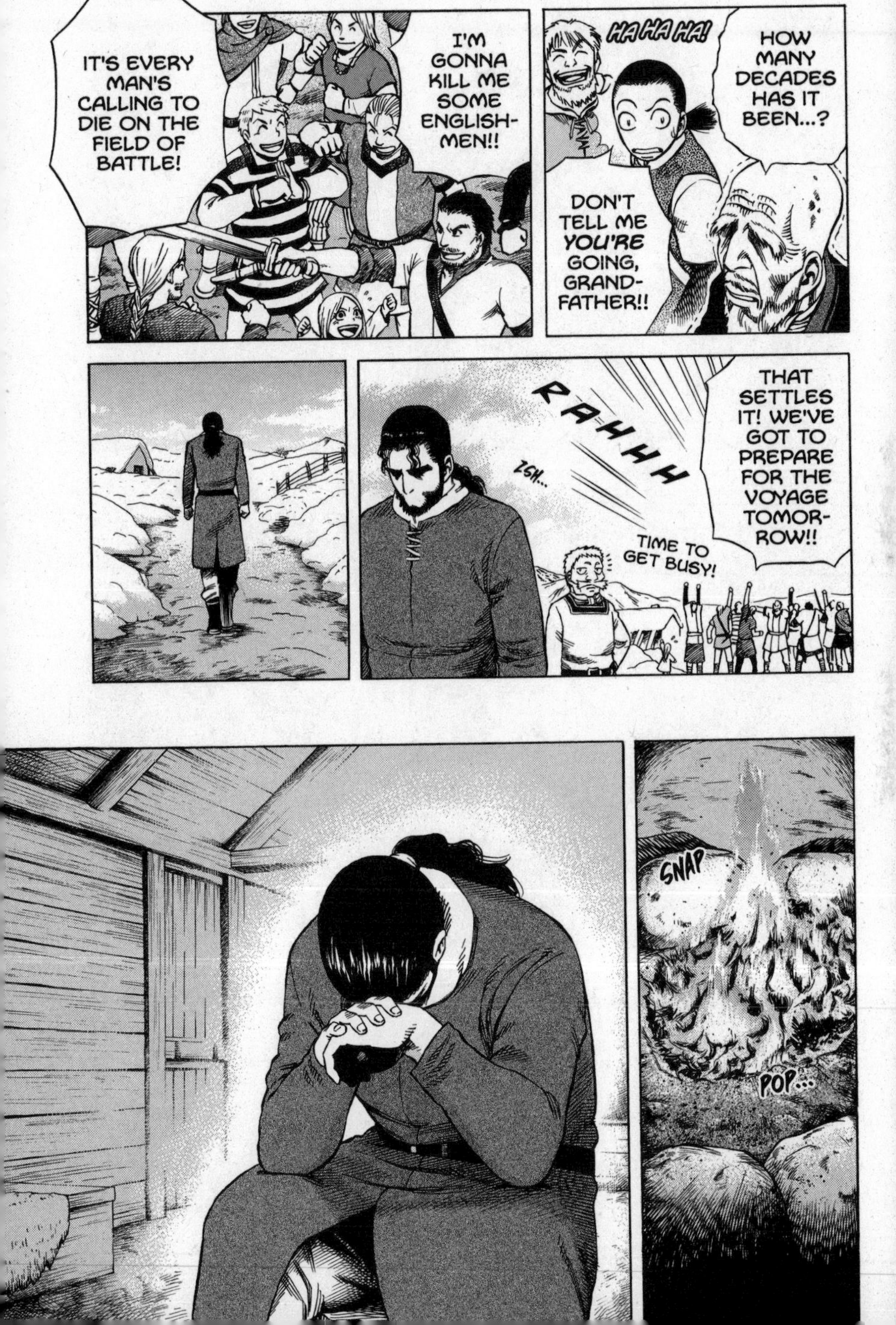
HOW MANY DECADES HAS IT BEEN...?
HA HA HA!
DON'T TELL ME *YOU'RE* GOING, GRANDFATHER!!
I'M GONNA KILL ME SOME ENGLISHMEN!!
IT'S EVERY MAN'S CALLING TO DIE ON THE FIELD OF BATTLE!
THAT SETTLES IT! WE'VE GOT TO PREPARE FOR THE VOYAGE TOMORROW!!
RAHHH
ZSH...
TIME TO GET BUSY!
SNAP
POP...

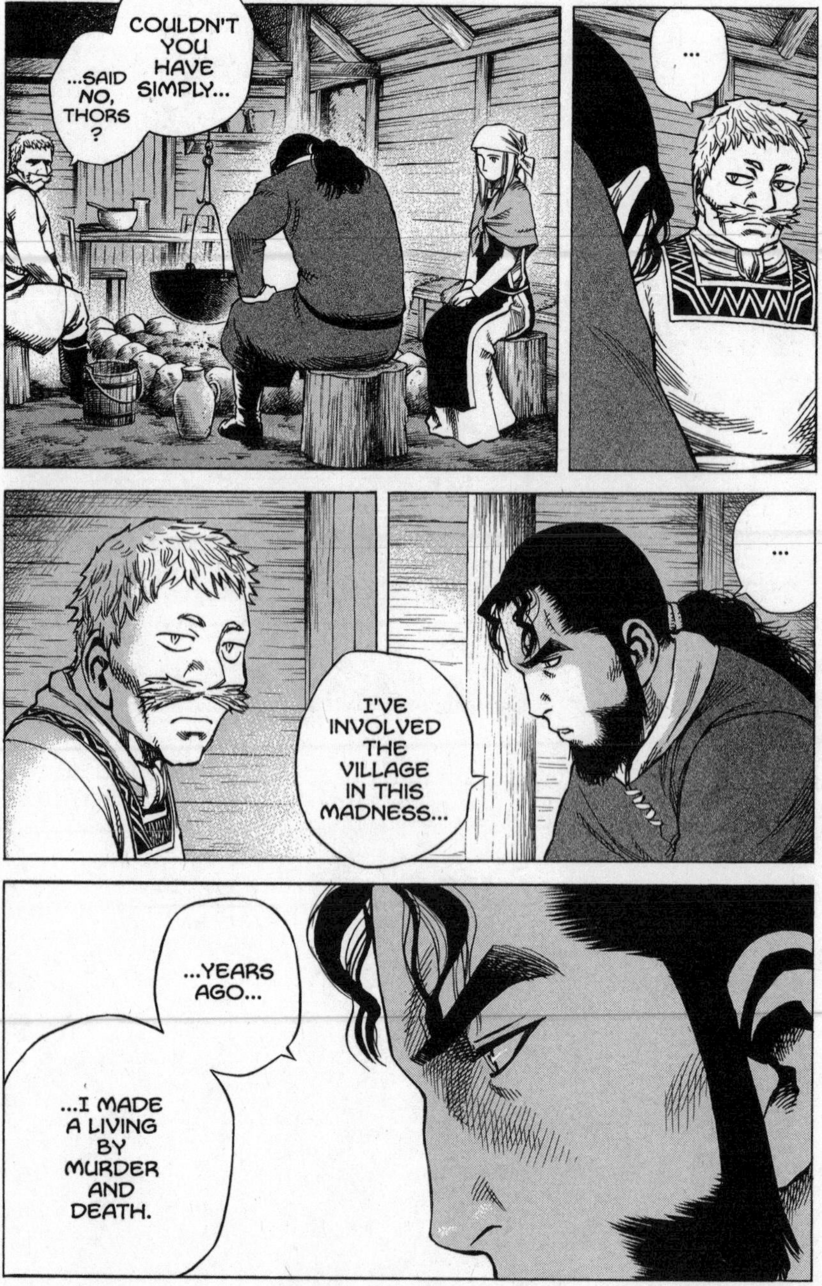
...
COULDN'T YOU HAVE SIMPLY...
...SAID NO, THORS?
...
I'VE INVOLVED THE VILLAGE IN THIS MADNESS...
...YEARS AGO...
...I MADE A LIVING BY MURDER AND DEATH.

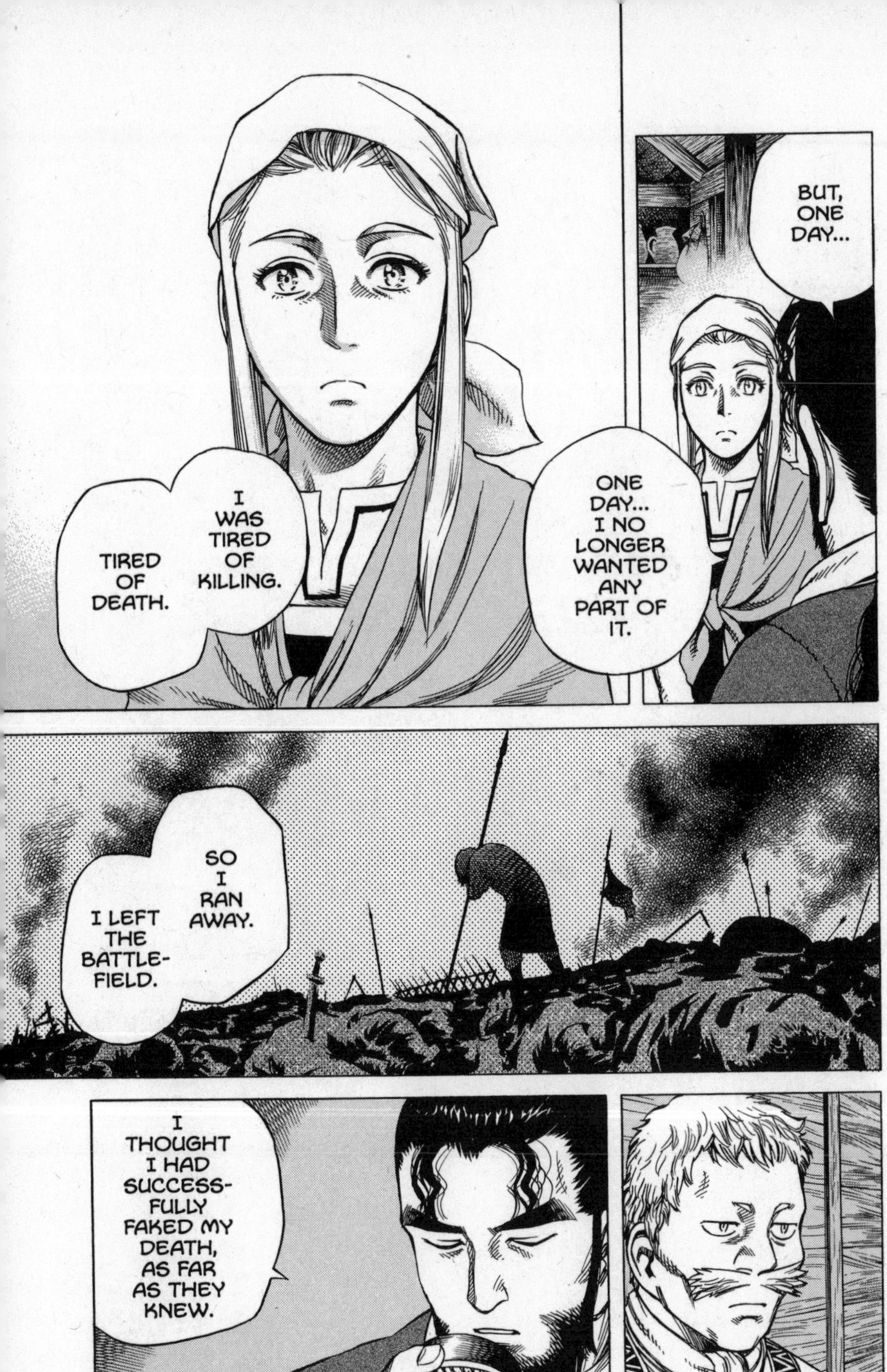
BUT, ONE DAY...
ONE DAY... I NO LONGER WANTED ANY PART OF IT.
I WAS TIRED OF KILLING.
TIRED OF DEATH.
SO I RAN AWAY.
I LEFT THE BATTLE-FIELD.
I THOUGHT I HAD SUCCESS-FULLY FAKED MY DEATH, AS FAR AS THEY KNEW.

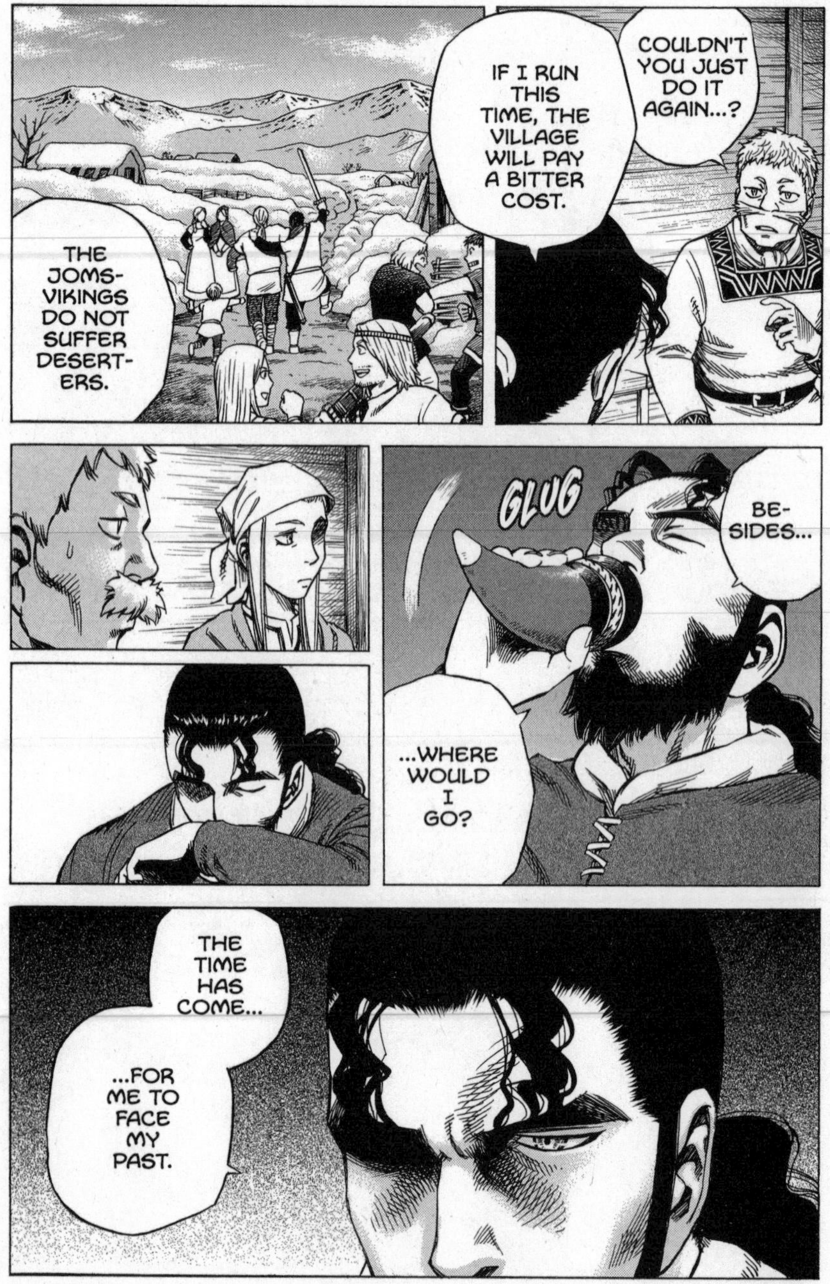
COULDN'T YOU JUST DO IT AGAIN...?
IF I RUN THIS TIME, THE VILLAGE WILL PAY A BITTER COST.
THE JOMS-VIKINGS DO NOT SUFFER DESERTERS.
BE-SIDES...
GLUG
...WHERE WOULD I GO?
THE TIME HAS COME...
...FOR ME TO FACE MY PAST.

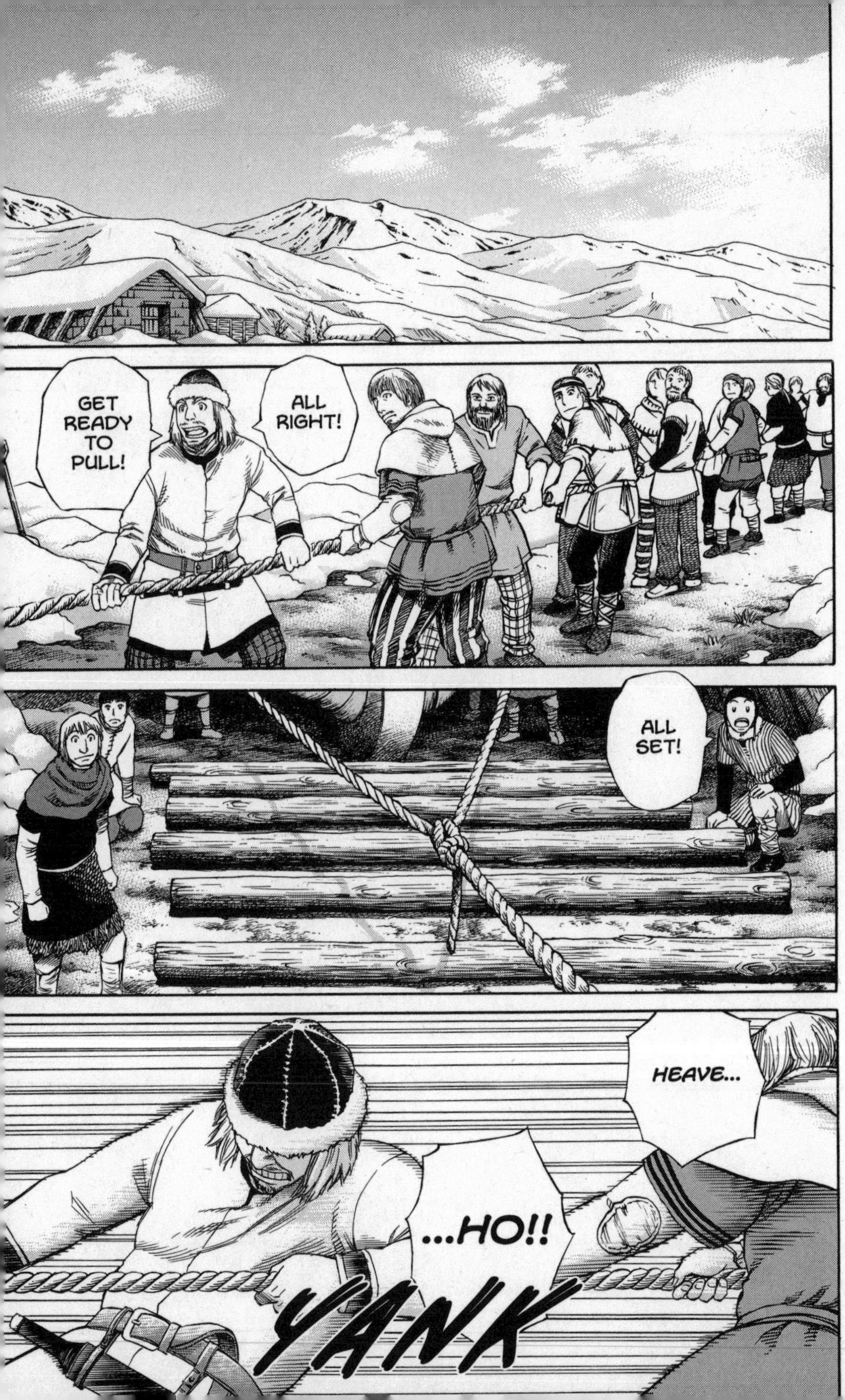
ALL RIGHT!
GET READY TO PULL!
ALL SET!
HEAVE...
...HO!!
YANK

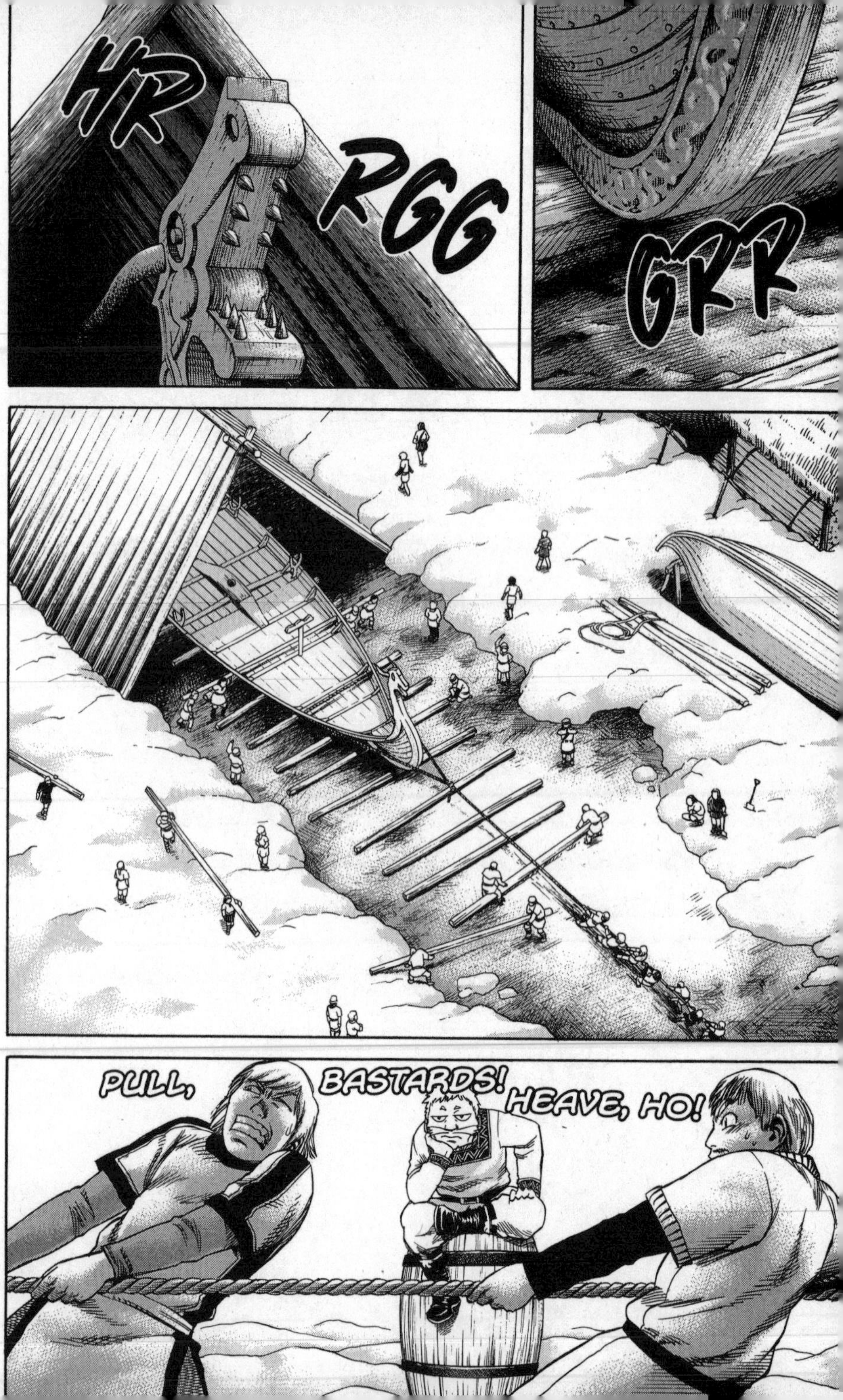
GRR
HR RGG
PULL, BASTARDS! HEAVE, HO!

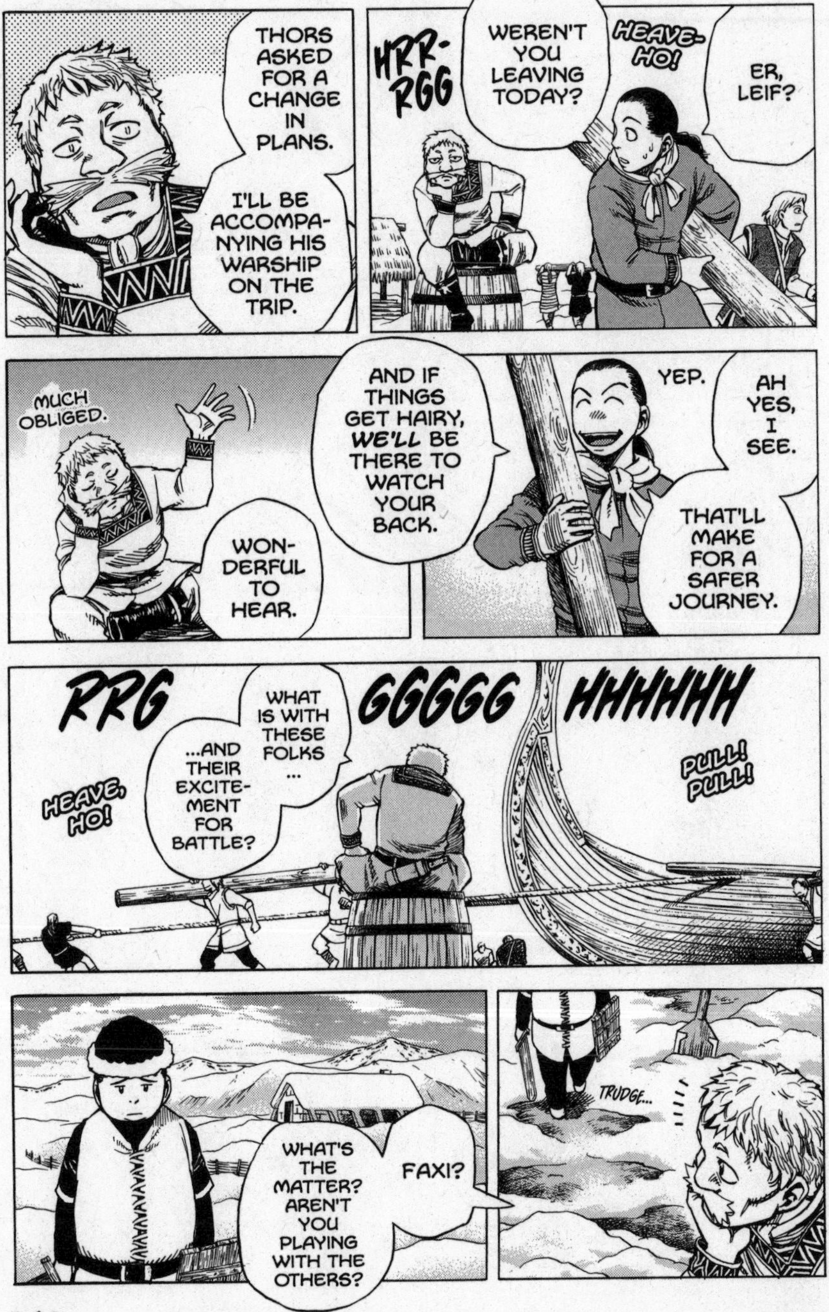
ER, LEIF?
HEAVE-HO!
WEREN'T YOU LEAVING TODAY?
HRR-RGG
THORS ASKED FOR A CHANGE IN PLANS.
I'LL BE ACCOMPANYING HIS WARSHIP ON THE TRIP.
AH YES, I SEE.
THAT'LL MAKE FOR A SAFER JOURNEY.
YEP.
AND IF THINGS GET HAIRY, *WE'LL* BE THERE TO WATCH YOUR BACK.
MUCH OBLIGED.
WONDERFUL TO HEAR.
RRG GGGGG HHHHHH
PULL! PULL!
WHAT IS WITH THESE FOLKS...
...AND THEIR EXCITEMENT FOR BATTLE?
HEAVE, HO!
TRUDGE...
FAXI?
WHAT'S THE MATTER? AREN'T YOU PLAYING WITH THE OTHERS?

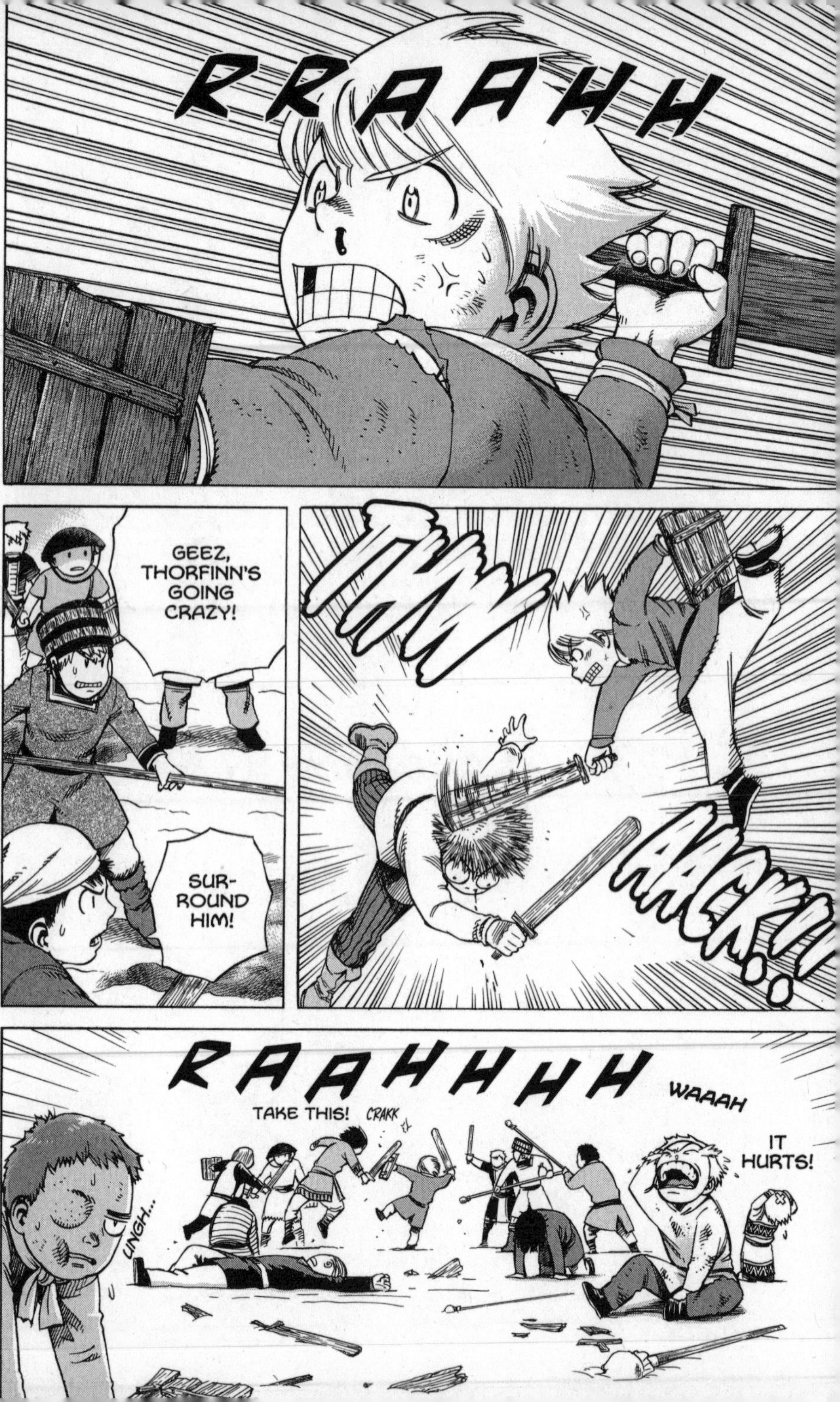
RRAAHH
GEEZ, THORFINN'S GOING CRAZY!
SUR-ROUND HIM!
RAAHHHH
WAAAH
IT HURTS!
CRAKK
TAKE THIS!
UNGH...

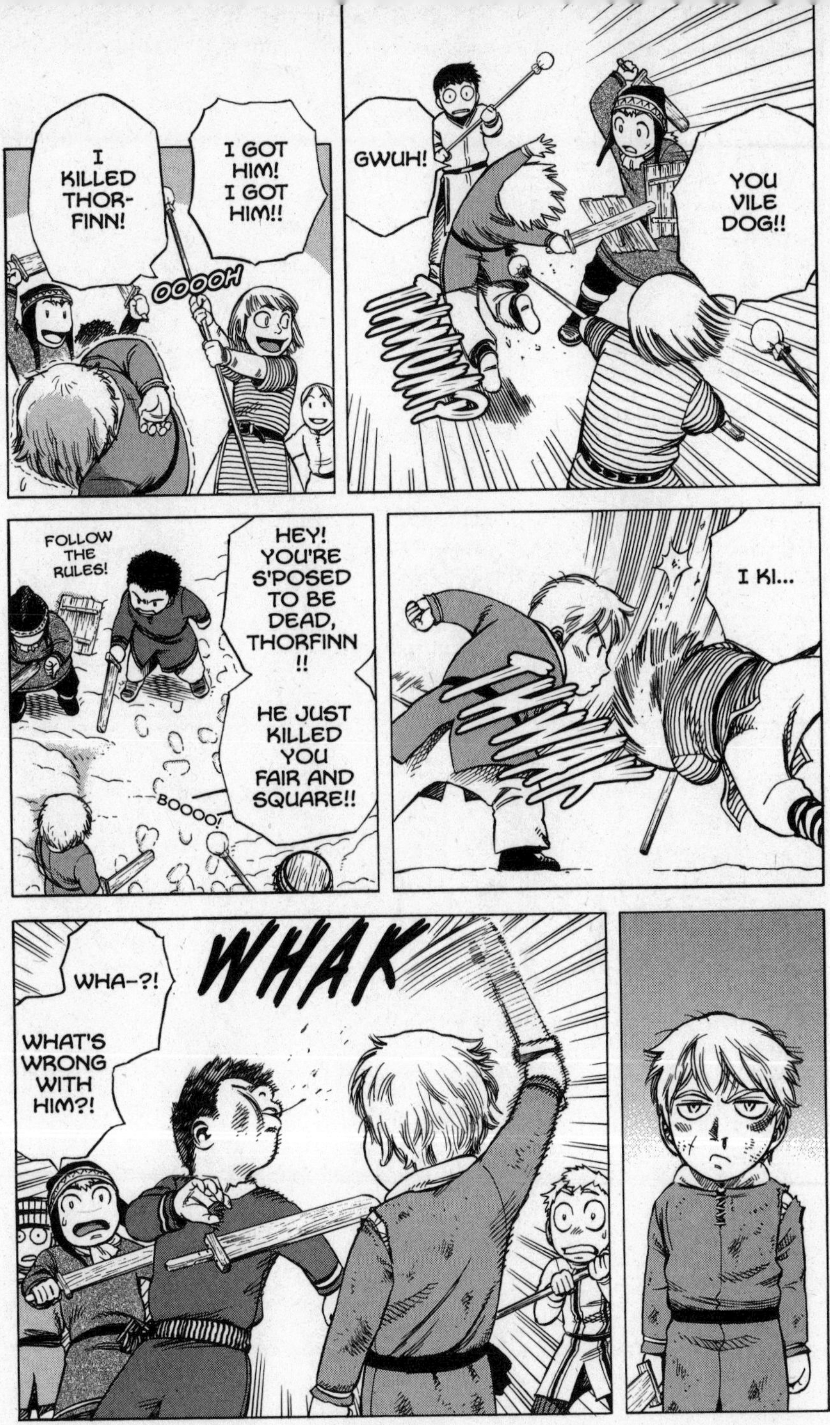
YOU VILE DOG!!
GWUH!
I GOT HIM! I GOT HIM!!
I KILLED THOR-FINN!
OOOOH
I KI...
HEY! YOU'RE S'POSED TO BE DEAD, THORFINN!!
HE JUST KILLED YOU FAIR AND SQUARE!!
FOLLOW THE RULES!
BOOOO!
WHAK
WHA-?!
WHAT'S WRONG WITH HIM?!

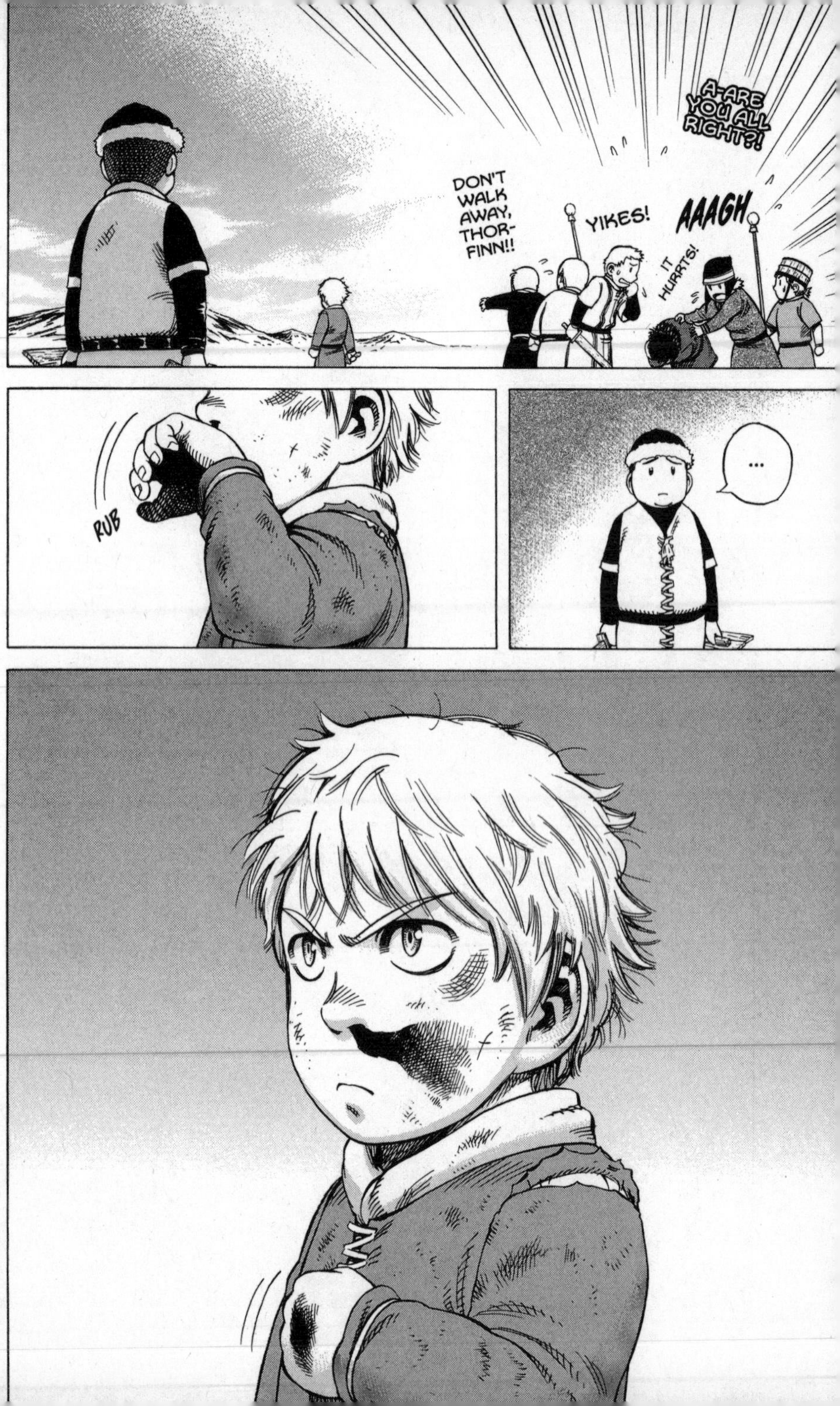
A-ARE YOU ALL RIGHT?!
AAAGH
IT HURRTS!
YIKES!
DON'T WALK AWAY, THOR-FINN!!
...
RUB

CHAPTER 6 - END

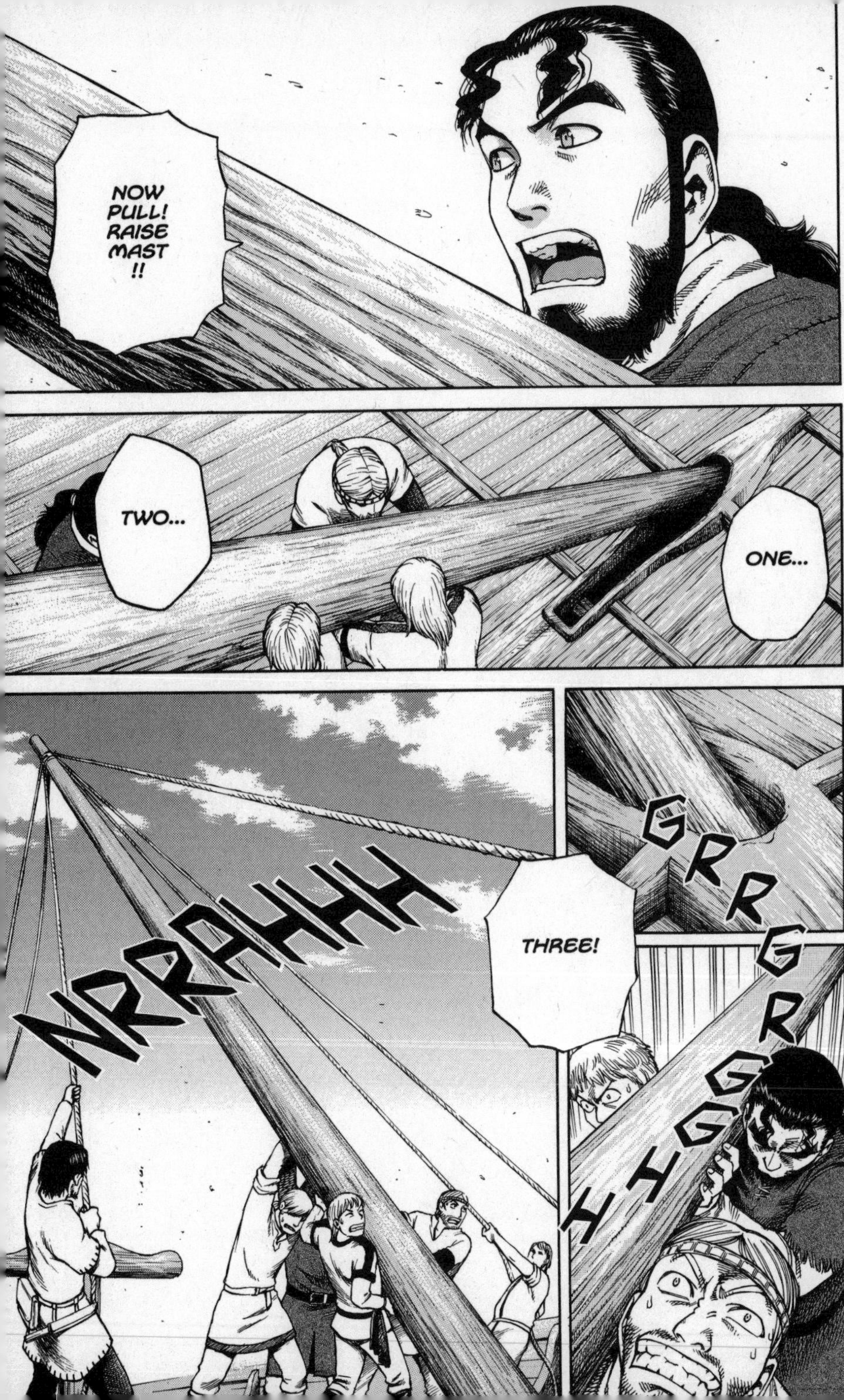
NOW PULL! RAISE MAST !!
ONE...
TWO...
GRRGRGGHHH
THREE!
NRRAHHH

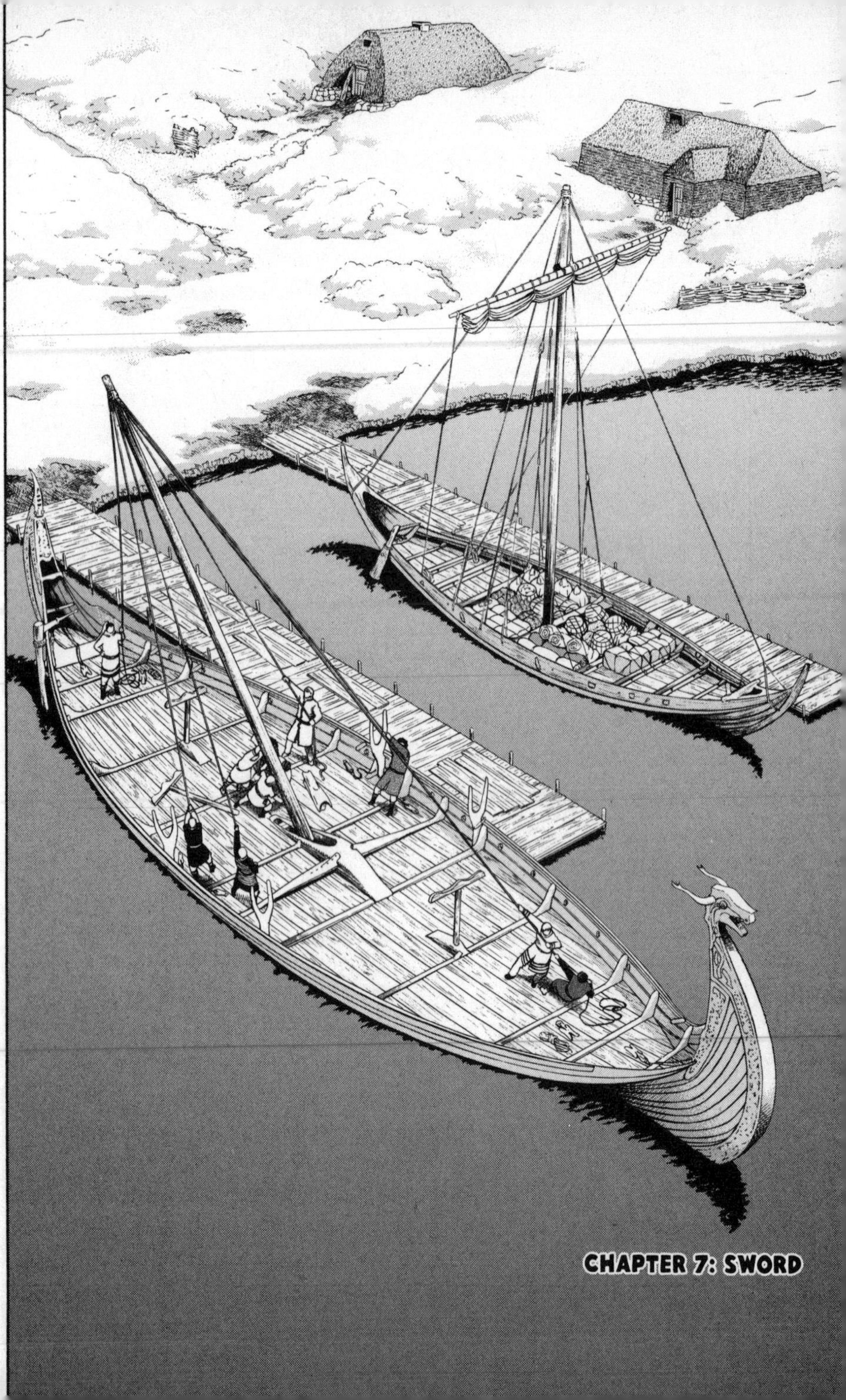
CHAPTER 7: SWORD

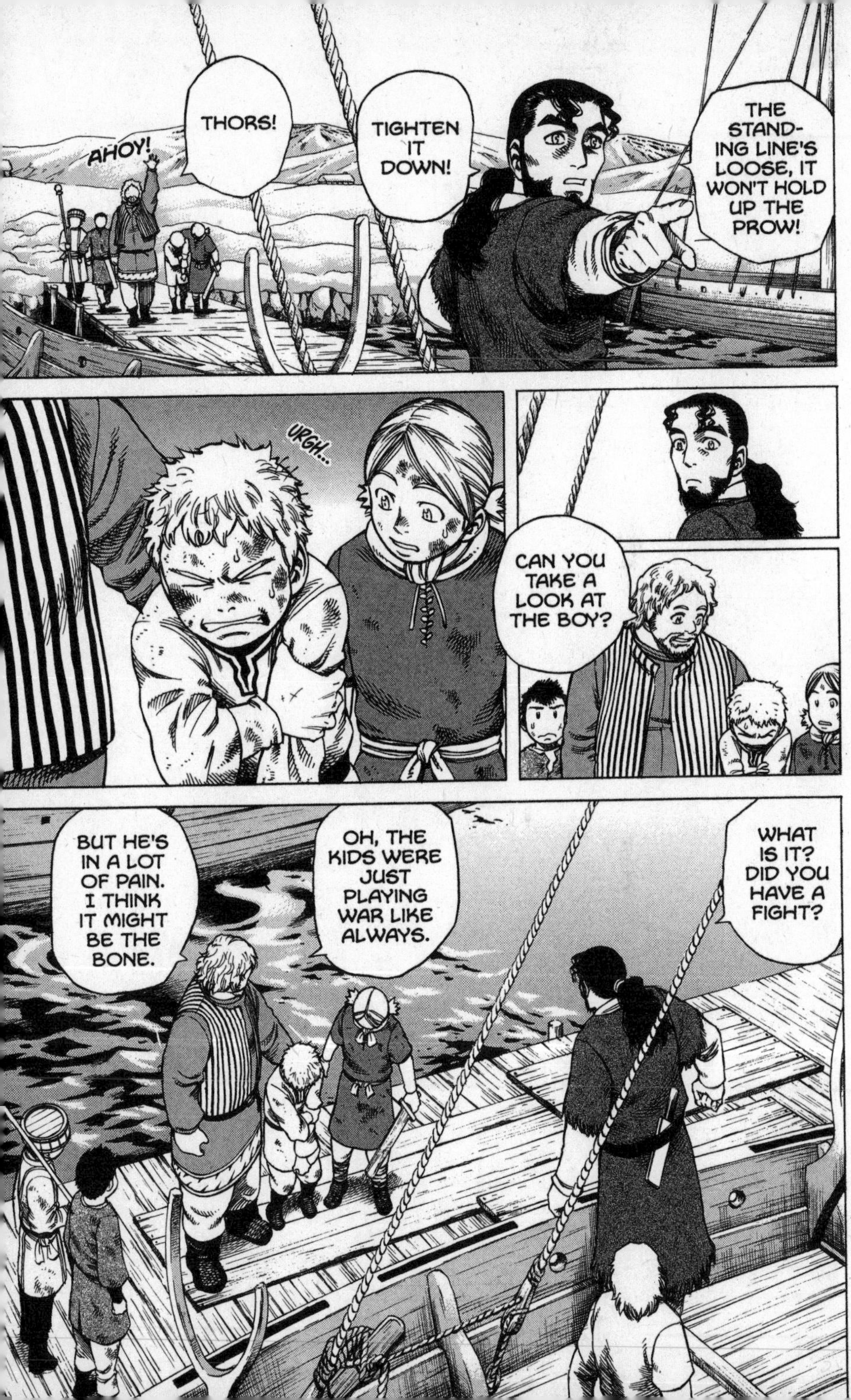
THE STANDING-LINE'S LOOSE, IT WON'T HOLD UP THE PROW!
TIGHTEN IT DOWN!
THORS!
AHOY!
CAN YOU TAKE A LOOK AT THE BOY?
URGH...
WHAT IS IT? DID YOU HAVE A FIGHT?
OH, THE KIDS WERE JUST PLAYING WAR LIKE ALWAYS.
BUT HE'S IN A LOT OF PAIN. I THINK IT MIGHT BE THE BONE.

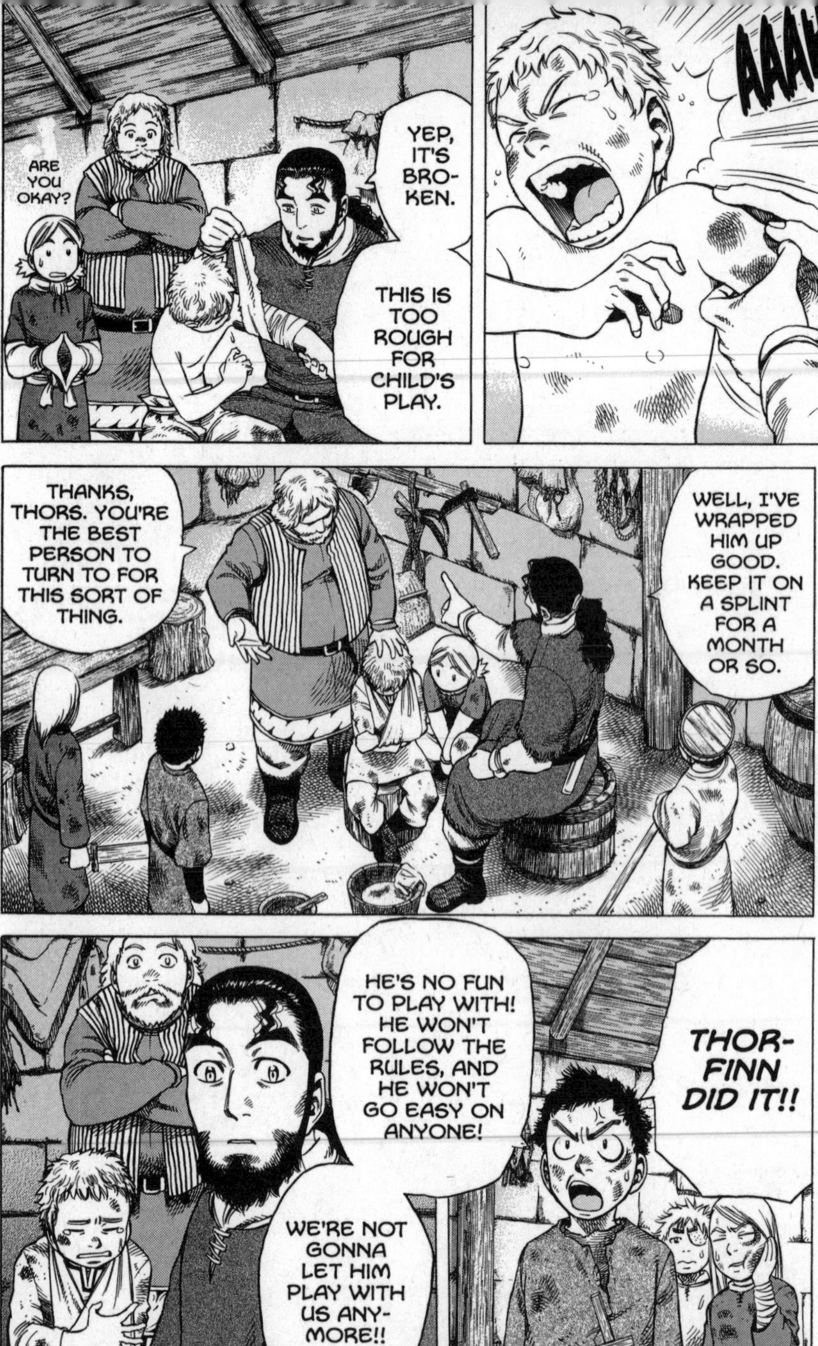
AAAH!!
YEP, IT'S BROKEN.
THIS IS TOO ROUGH FOR CHILD'S PLAY.
ARE YOU OKAY?
WELL, I'VE WRAPPED HIM UP GOOD. KEEP IT ON A SPLINT FOR A MONTH OR SO.
THANKS, THORS. YOU'RE THE BEST PERSON TO TURN TO FOR THIS SORT OF THING.
THORFINN DID IT!!
HE'S NO FUN TO PLAY WITH! HE WON'T FOLLOW THE RULES, AND HE WON'T GO EASY ON ANYONE!
WE'RE NOT GONNA LET HIM PLAY WITH US ANYMORE!!

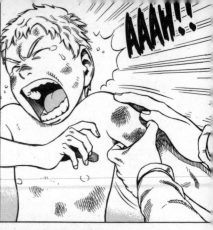

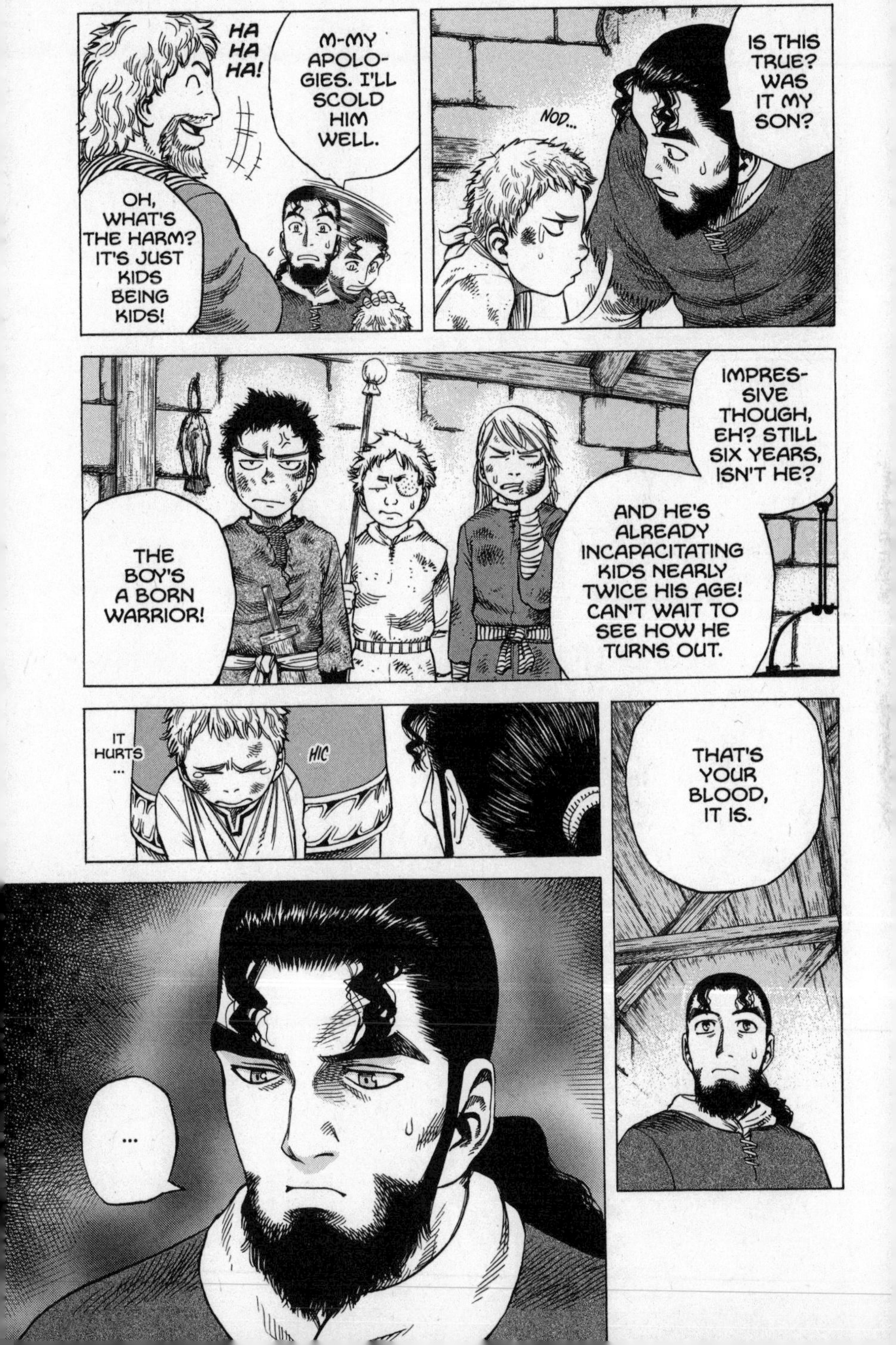
IS THIS TRUE? WAS IT MY SON?
NOD...
M-MY APOLOGIES. I'LL SCOLD HIM WELL.
HA HA HA!
OH, WHAT'S THE HARM? IT'S JUST KIDS BEING KIDS!
IMPRES-SIVE THOUGH, EH? STILL SIX YEARS, ISN'T HE?
AND HE'S ALREADY INCAPACITATING KIDS NEARLY TWICE HIS AGE! CAN'T WAIT TO SEE HOW HE TURNS OUT.
THE BOY'S A BORN WARRIOR!
THAT'S YOUR BLOOD, IT IS.
HIC
IT HURTS ...
...

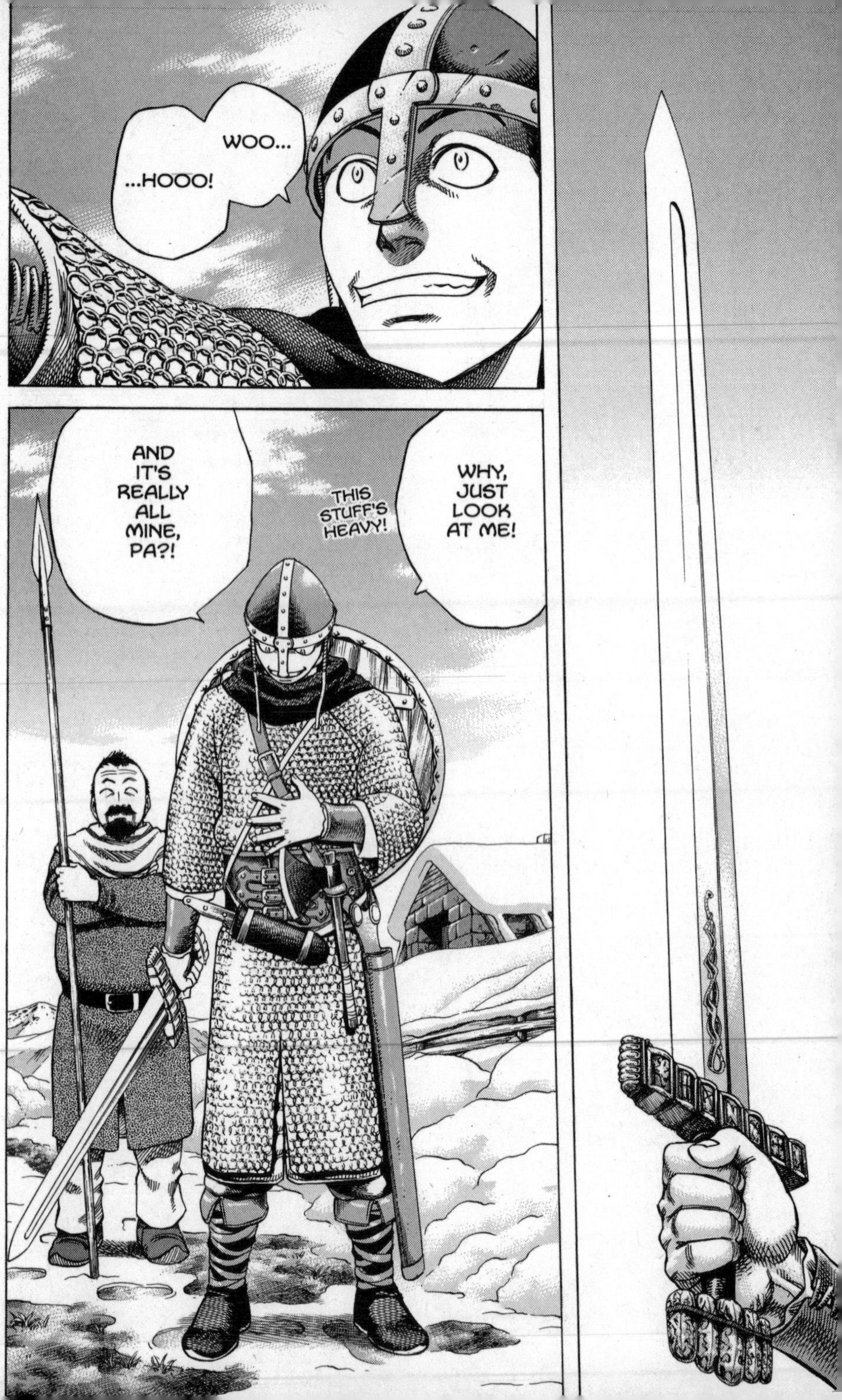
WOO...
...HOOO!
WHY, JUST LOOK AT ME!
THIS STUFF'S HEAVY!
AND IT'S REALLY ALL MINE, PA?!

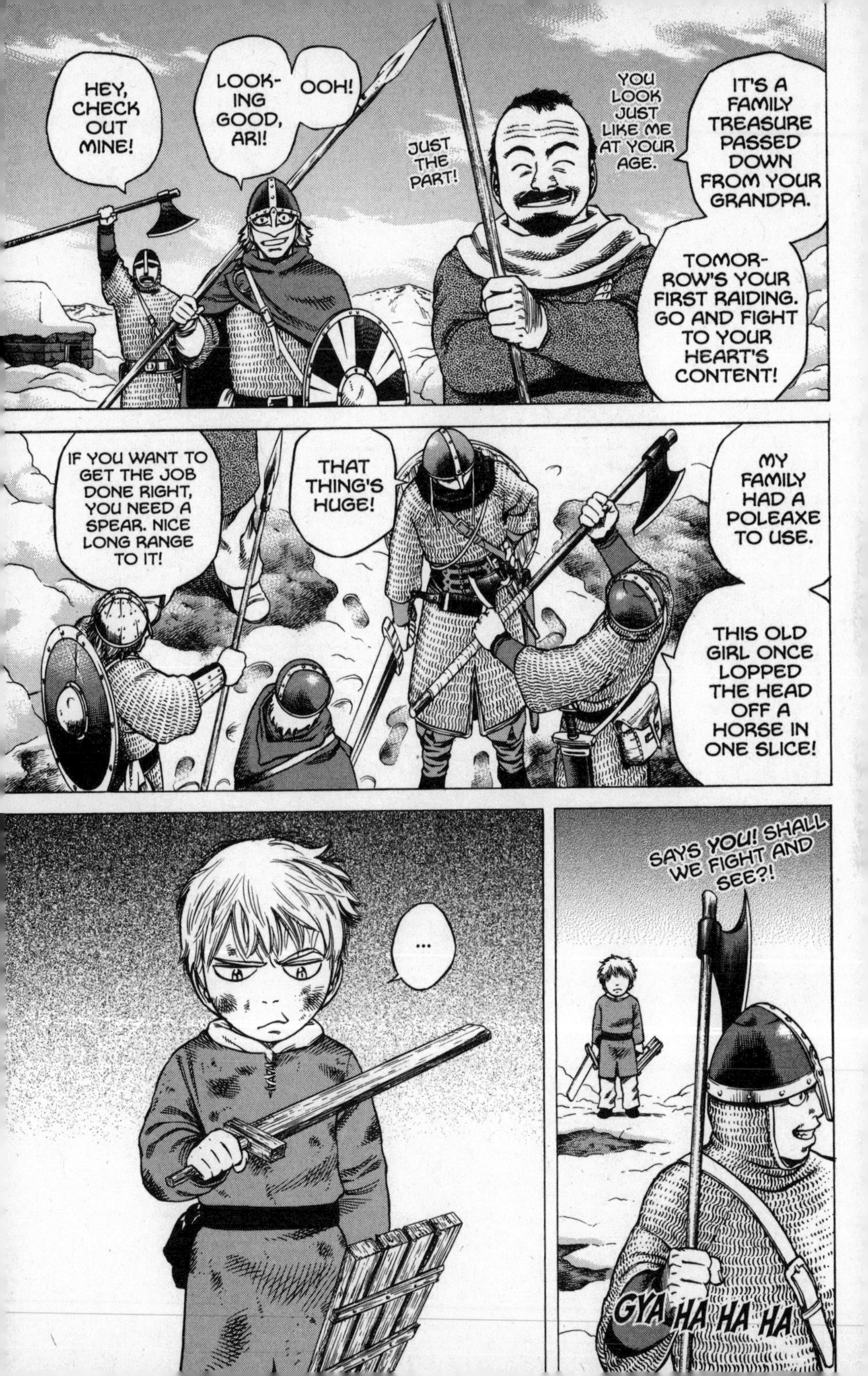
IT'S A FAMILY TREASURE PASSED DOWN FROM YOUR GRANDPA.
YOU LOOK JUST LIKE ME AT YOUR AGE.
JUST THE PART!
TOMOR-ROW'S YOUR FIRST RAIDING. GO AND FIGHT TO YOUR HEART'S CONTENT!
OOH!
LOOK-ING GOOD, ARI!
HEY, CHECK OUT MINE!
MY FAMILY HAD A POLEAXE TO USE.
THIS OLD GIRL ONCE LOPPED THE HEAD OFF A HORSE IN ONE SLICE!
THAT THING'S HUGE!
IF YOU WANT TO GET THE JOB DONE RIGHT, YOU NEED A SPEAR. NICE LONG RANGE TO IT!
SAYS YOU! SHALL WE FIGHT AND SEE?!
GYA HA HA HA
...

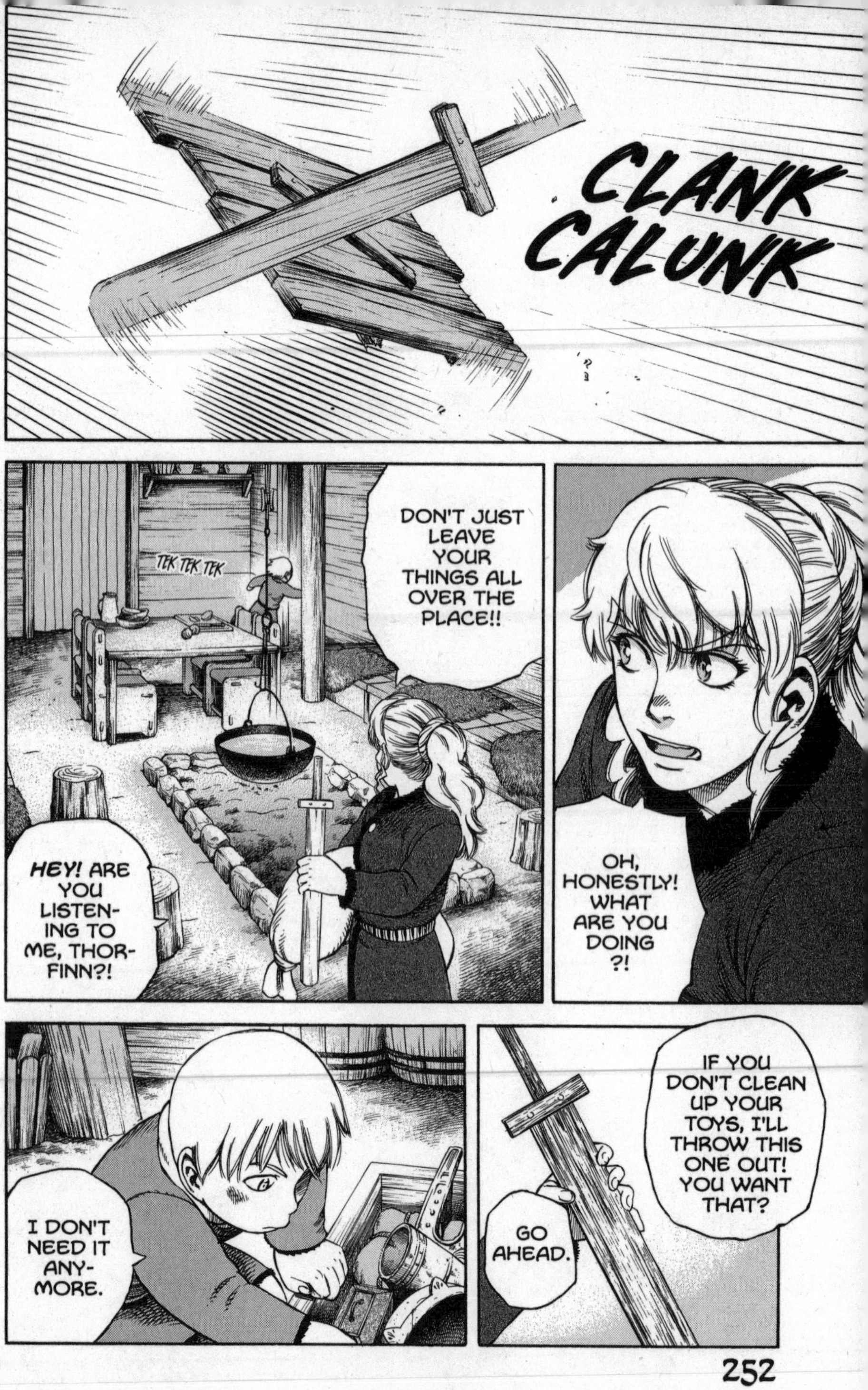
CLANK CALUNK
OH, HONESTLY! WHAT ARE YOU DOING?!
DON'T JUST LEAVE YOUR THINGS ALL OVER THE PLACE!!
TEK TEK TEK
HEY! ARE YOU LISTEN-ING TO ME, THOR-FINN?!
IF YOU DON'T CLEAN UP YOUR TOYS, I'LL THROW THIS ONE OUT! YOU WANT THAT?
GO AHEAD.
I DON'T NEED IT ANY-MORE.

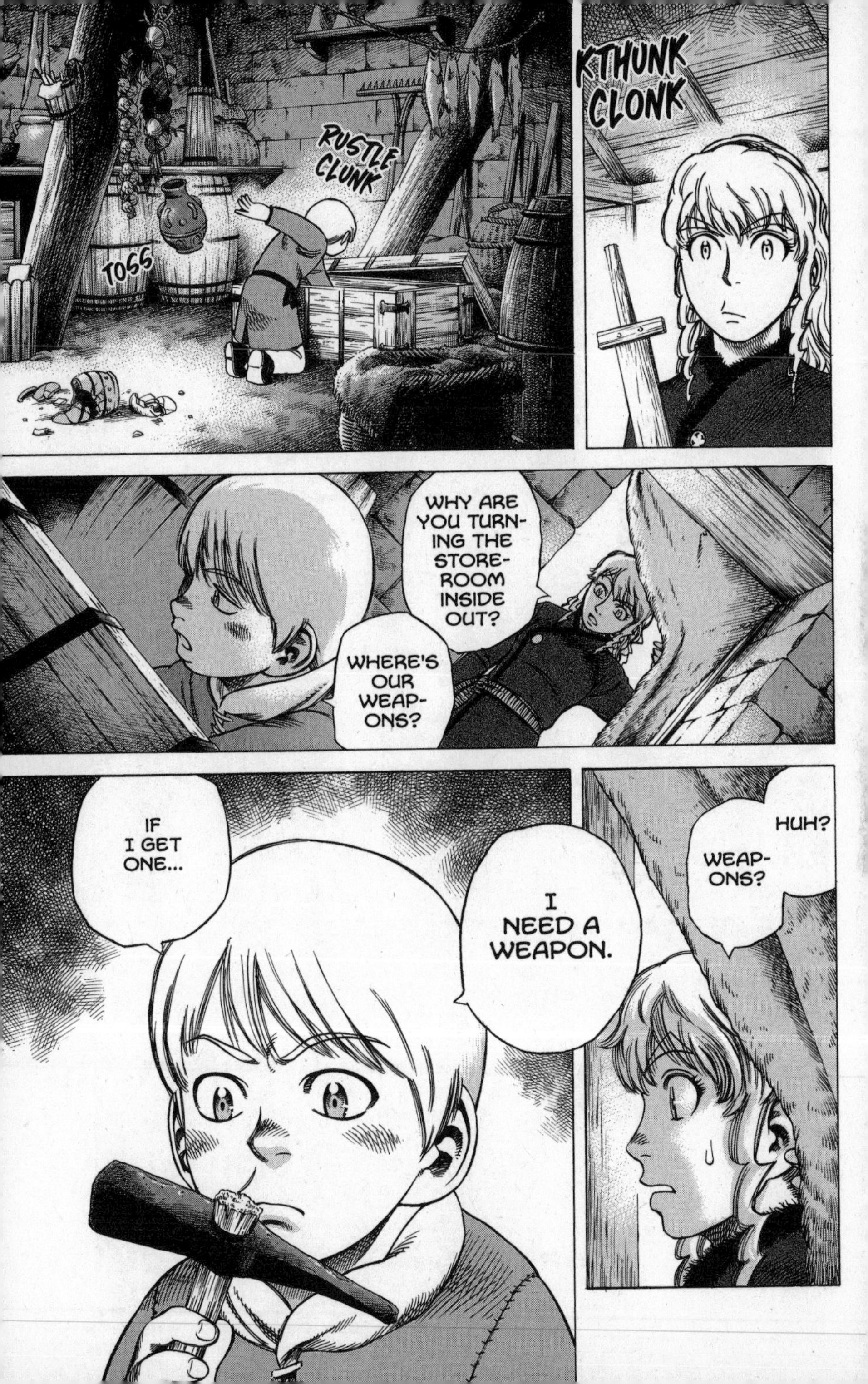
KTHUNK CLONK
RUSTLE CLUNK
TOSS
WHY ARE YOU TURNING THE STORE-ROOM INSIDE OUT?
WHERE'S OUR WEAPONS?
HUH?
WEAPONS?
I NEED A WEAPON.
IF I GET ONE...

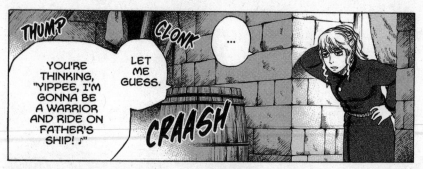

...
CLONK
LET ME GUESS.
THUMP
YOU'RE THINKING, "YIPPEE, I'M GONNA BE A WARRIOR AND RIDE ON FATHER'S SHIP! ♪"
CRAASH
DON'T WASTE YOUR TIME.
YOU'RE JUST A LITTLE BOY. NO AMOUNT OF PLEADING OR SHOWING OFF IS GOING TO CHANGE THE FACTS.
RUSTLE
CREAK
CR RR RK

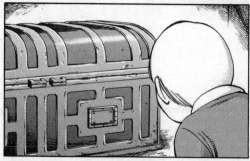

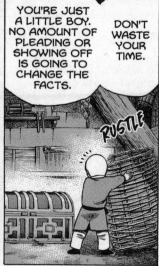

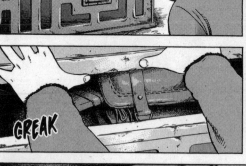

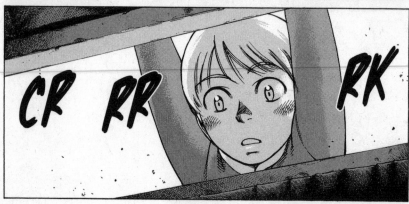

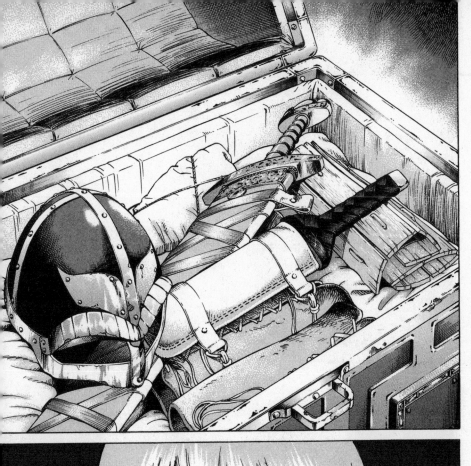

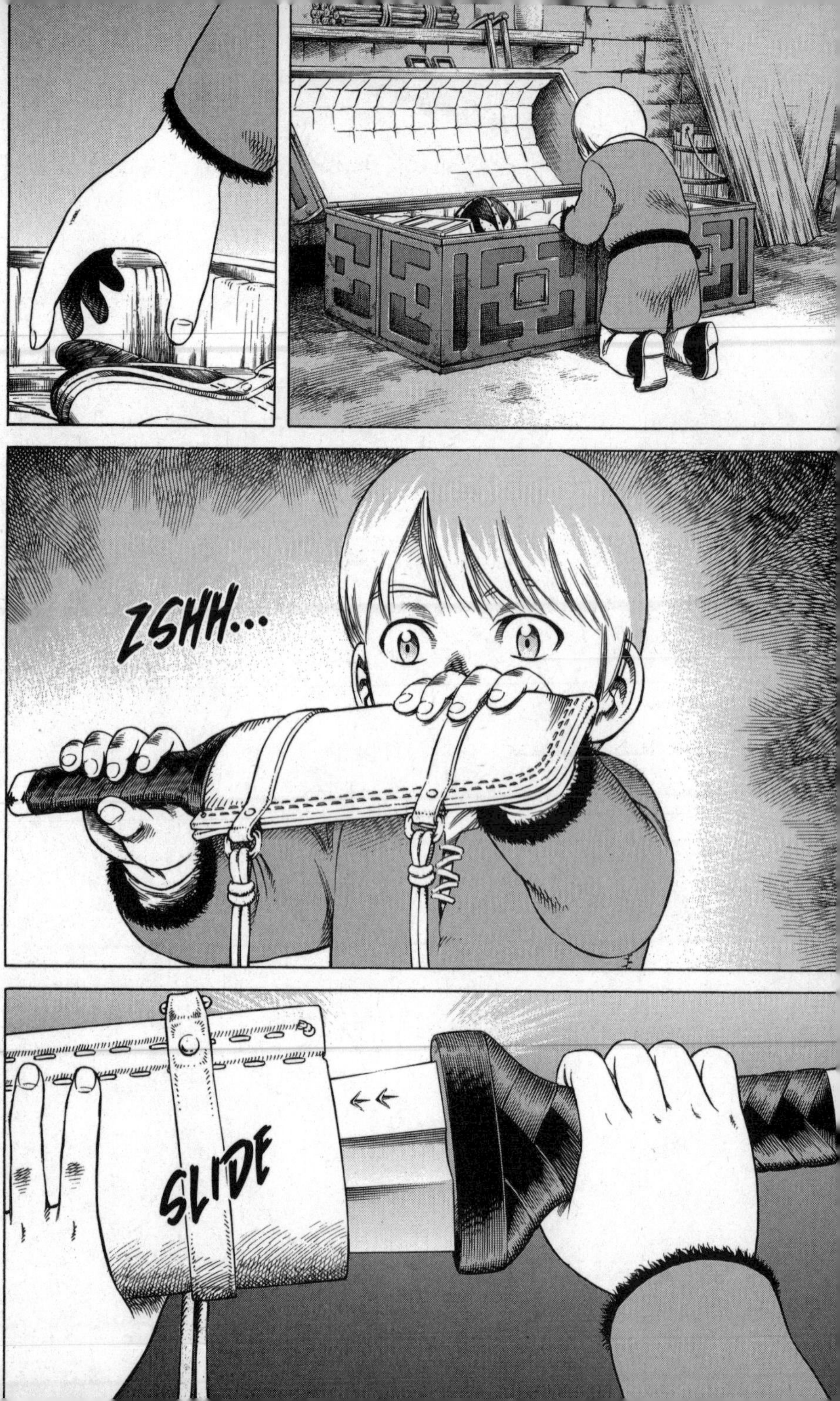
ZSHH...
SLIDE

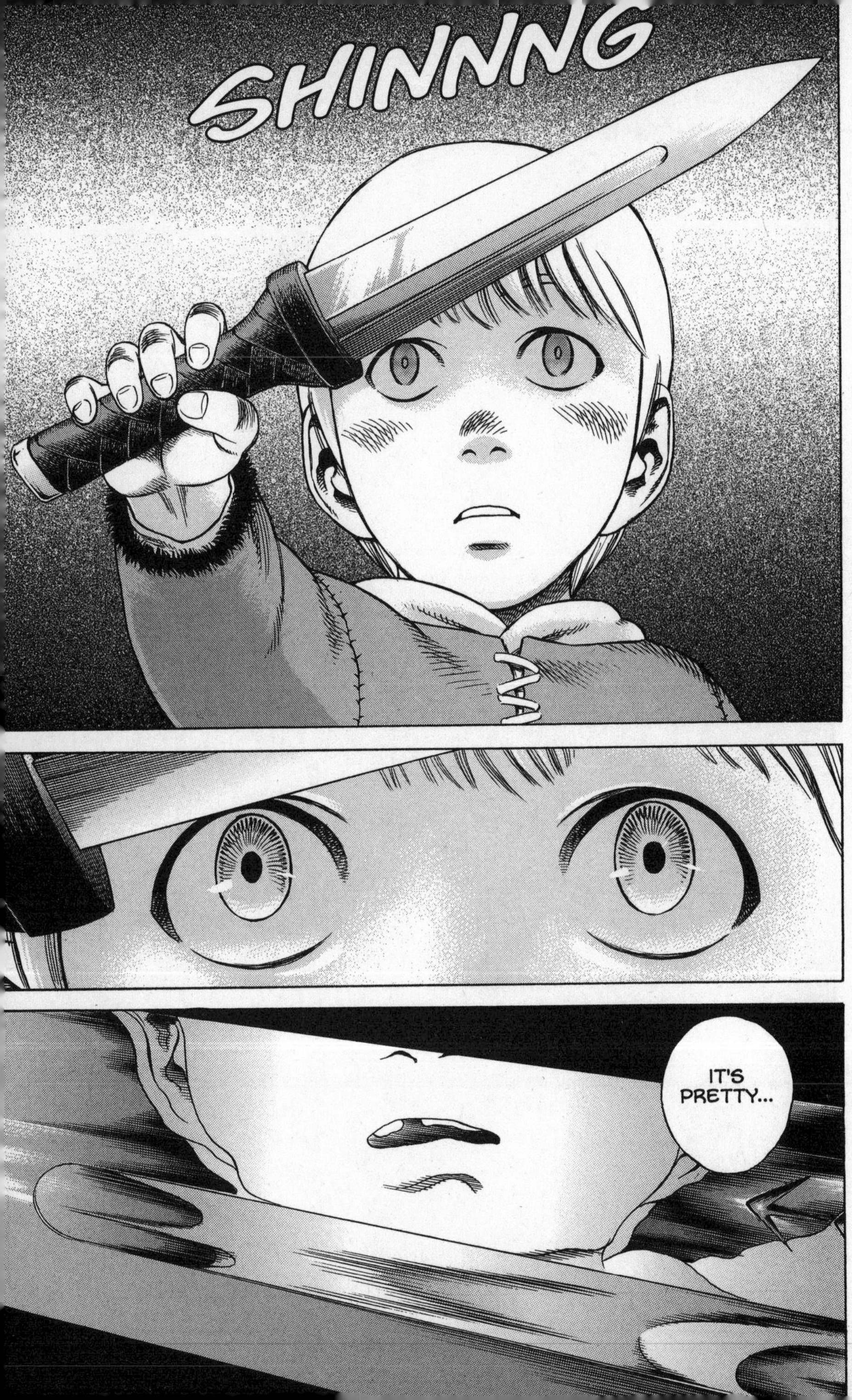
SHINNNG
IT'S PRETTY...

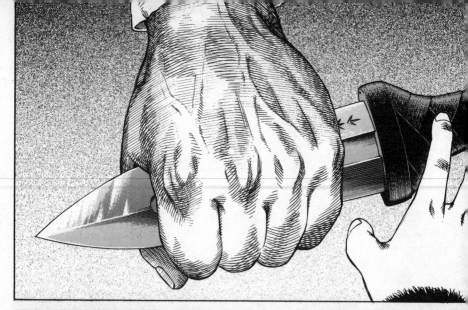

AH...

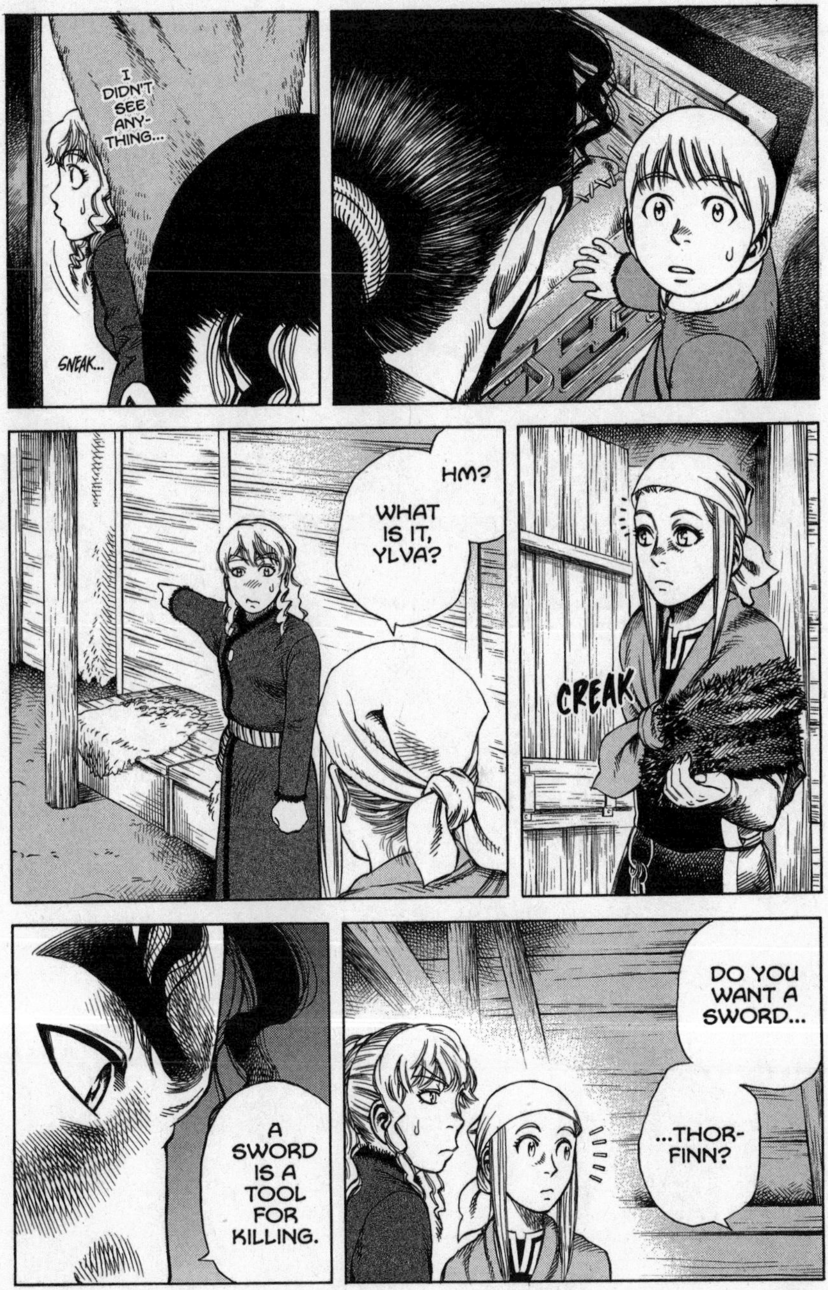
I DIDN'T SEE ANY- THING...
SNEAK...
CREAK
HM?
WHAT IS IT, YLVA?
DO YOU WANT A SWORD...
...THOR- FINN?
A SWORD IS A TOOL FOR KILLING.

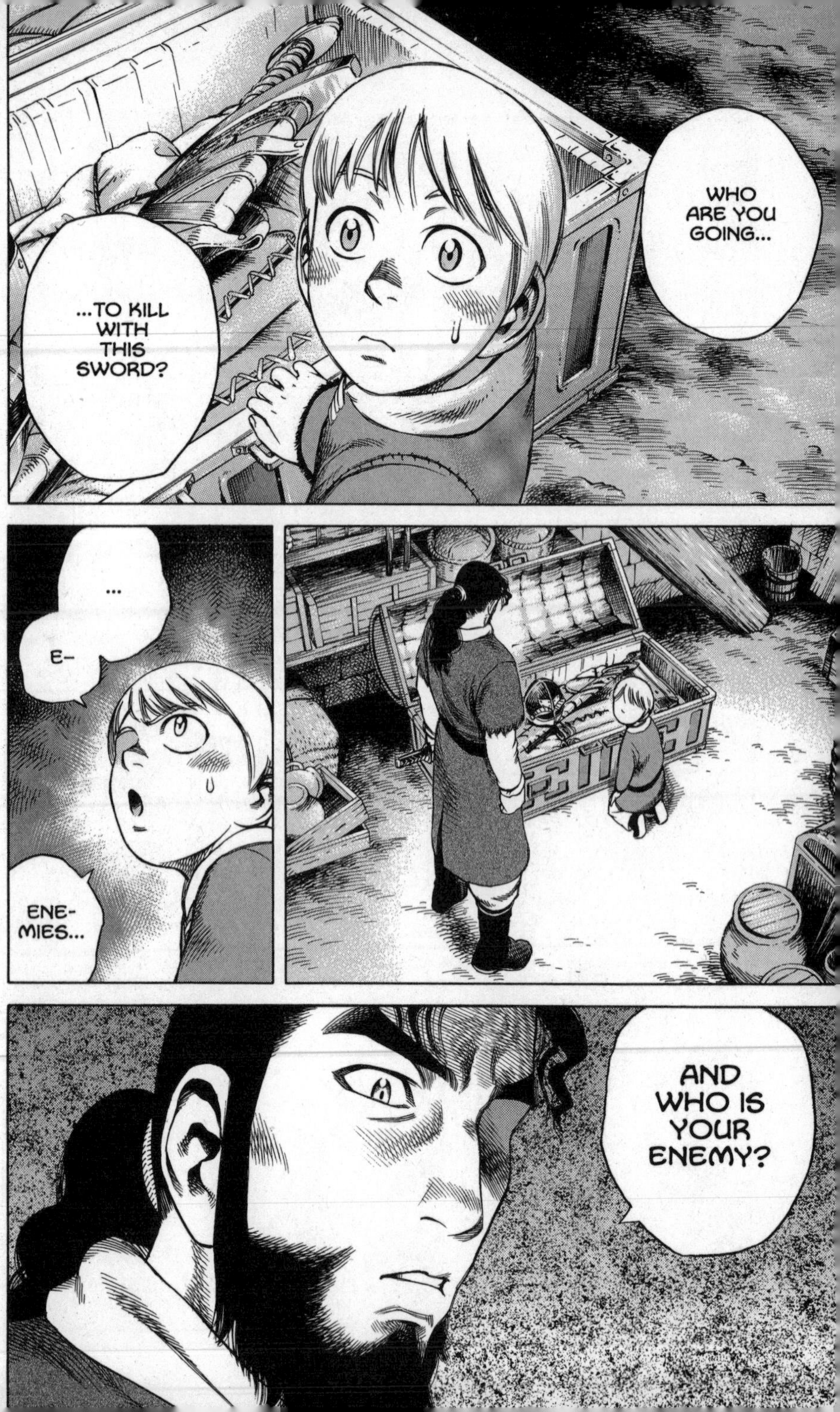
WHO ARE YOU GOING...
...TO KILL WITH THIS SWORD?
...
E-
ENE-MIES...
AND WHO IS YOUR ENEMY?

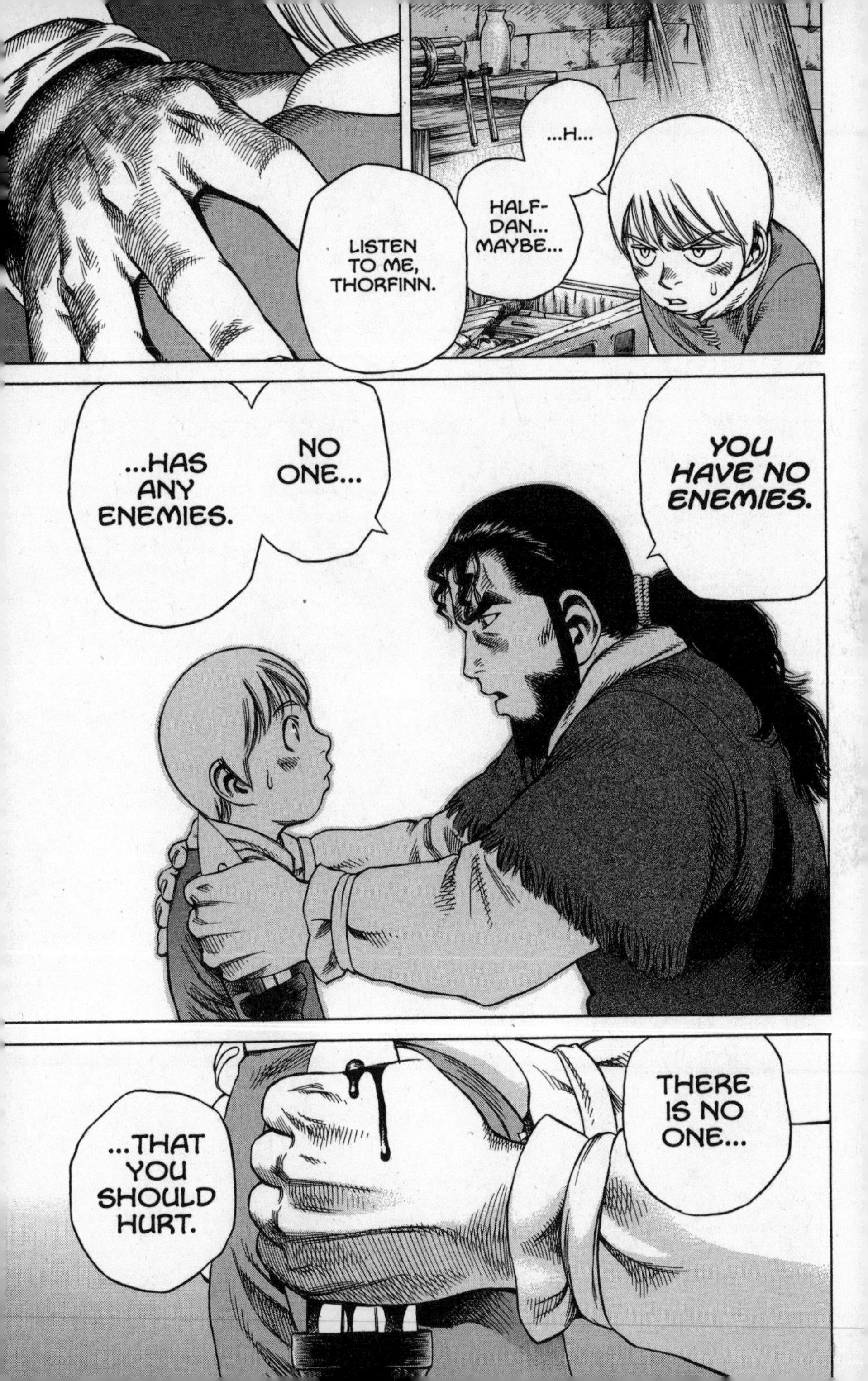
...H...
HALF-DAN... MAYBE...
LISTEN TO ME, THORFINN.
YOU HAVE NO ENEMIES.
NO ONE...
...HAS ANY ENEMIES.
THERE IS NO ONE...
...THAT YOU SHOULD HURT.

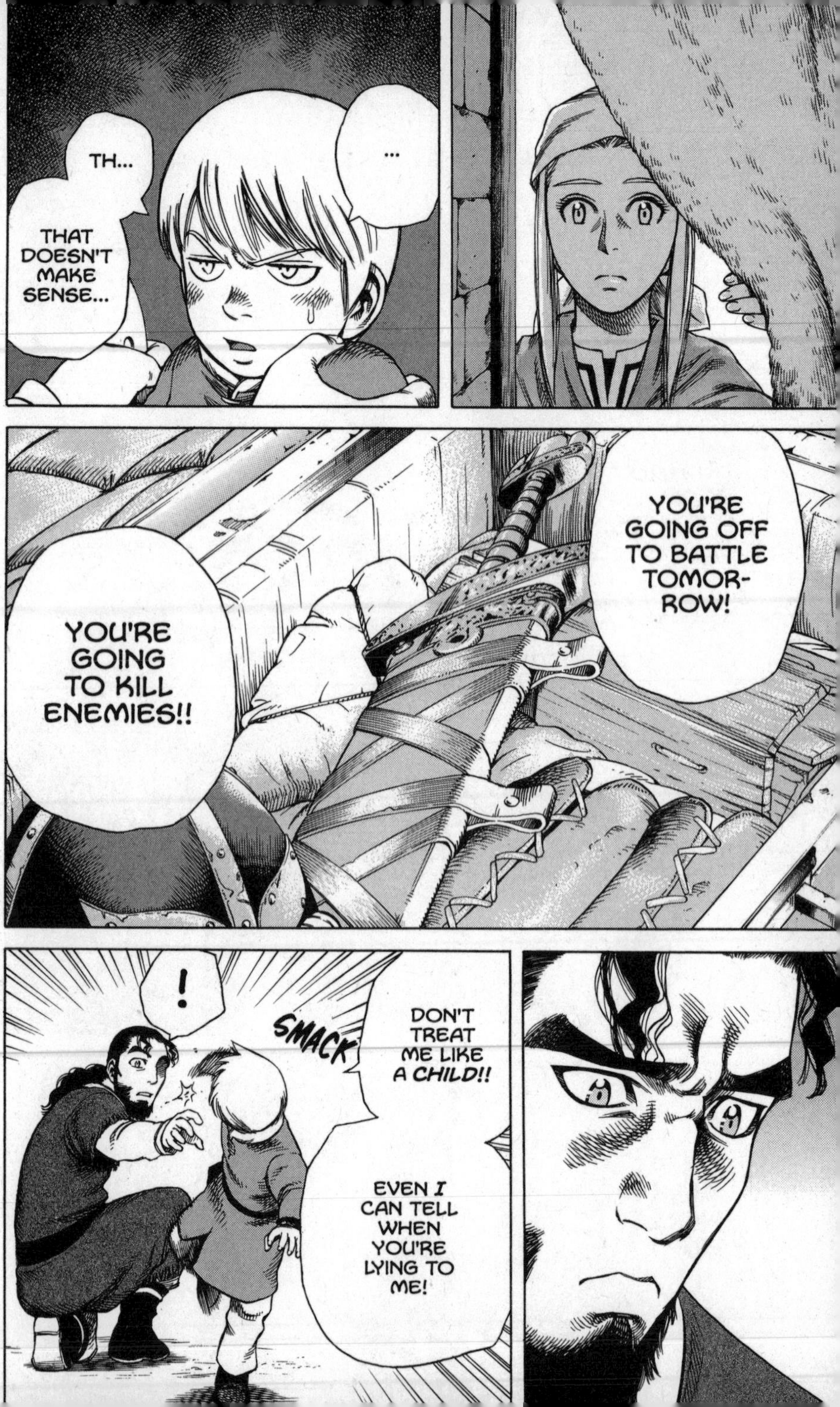
...
TH...
THAT DOESN'T MAKE SENSE...
YOU'RE GOING OFF TO BATTLE TOMOR-ROW!
YOU'RE GOING TO KILL ENEMIES!!
DON'T TREAT ME LIKE A *CHILD*!!
SMACK
!
EVEN *I* CAN TELL WHEN YOU'RE LYING TO ME!

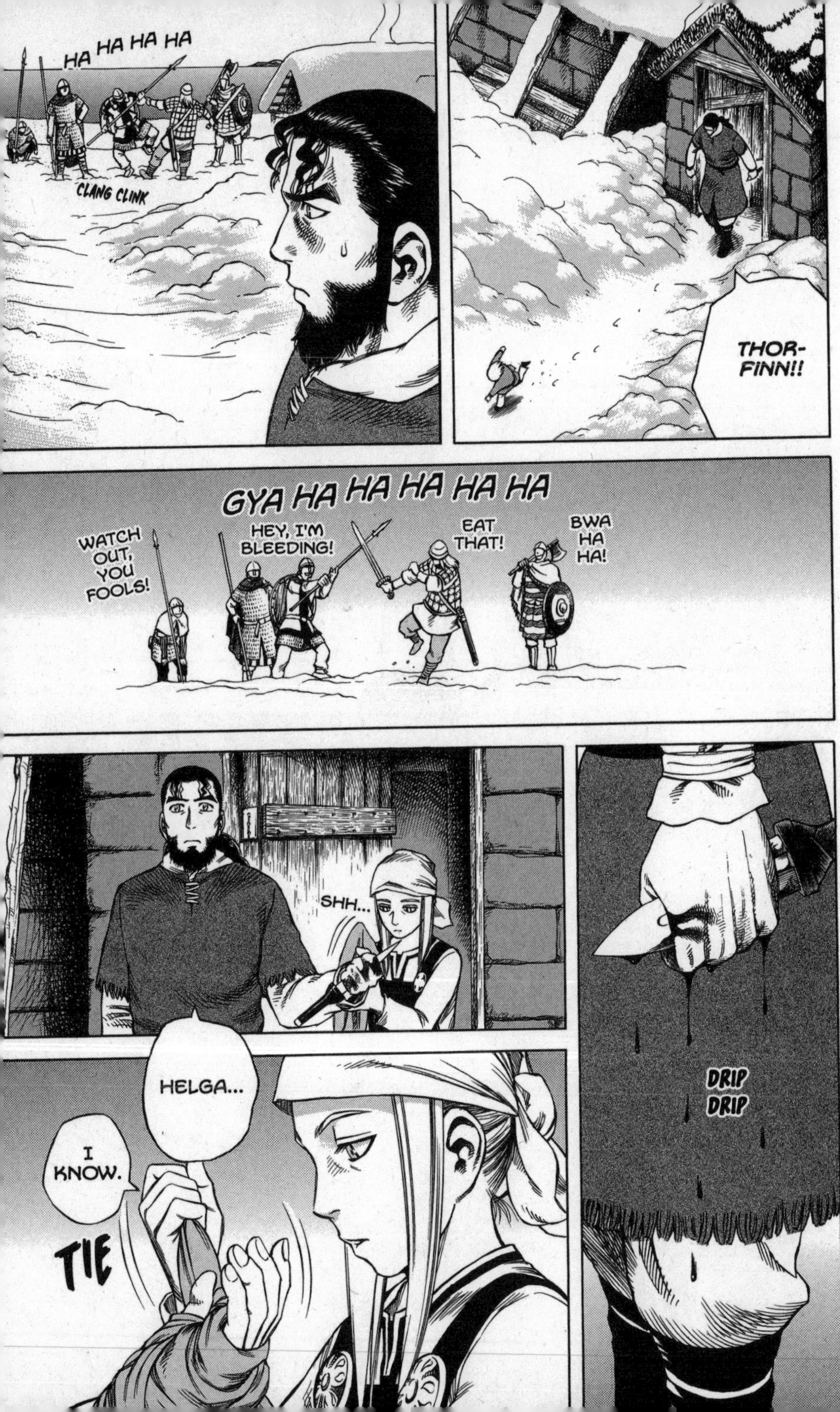
THOR-FINN!!
HA HA HA HA
CLANG CLINK
GYA HA HA HA HA HA
BWA HA HA!
EAT THAT!
HEY, I'M BLEEDING!
WATCH OUT, YOU FOOLS!
DRIP DRIP
SHH...
HELGA...
I KNOW.
TIE

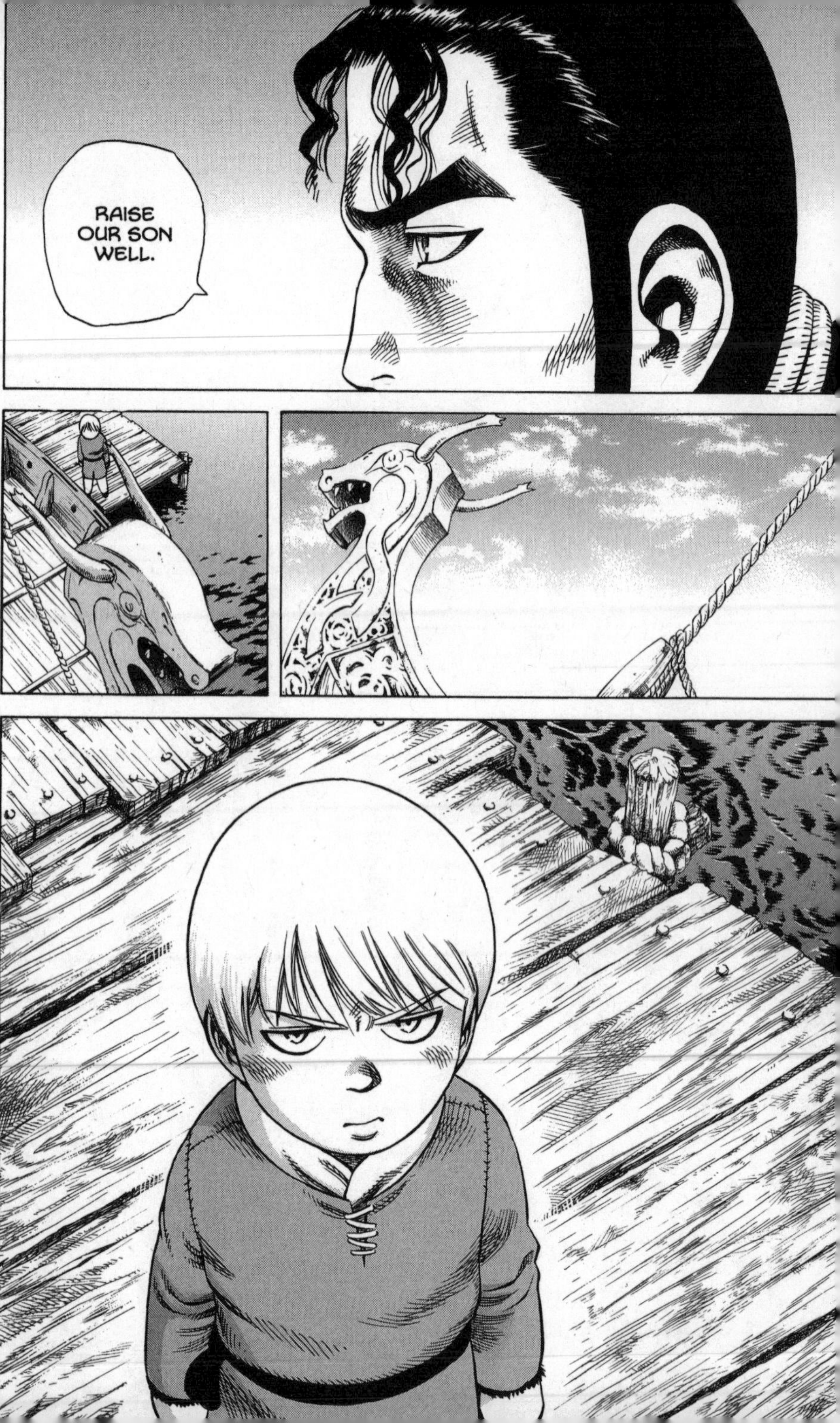
RAISE OUR SON WELL.

CHAPTER 7 - END

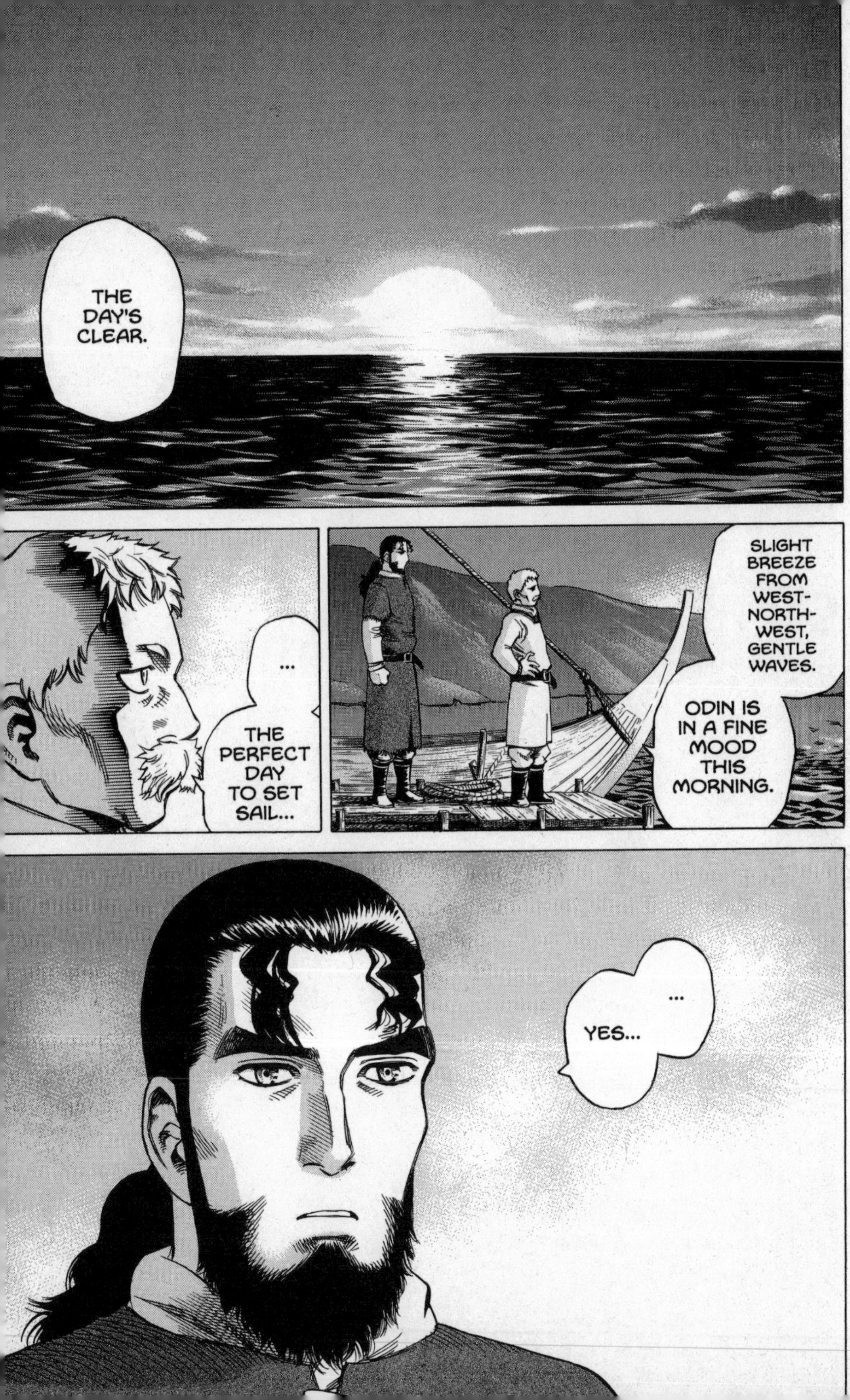
THE DAY'S CLEAR.
SLIGHT BREEZE FROM WEST-NORTH-WEST, GENTLE WAVES.
ODIN IS IN A FINE MOOD THIS MORNING.
...
THE PERFECT DAY TO SET SAIL...
...
YES...

CHAPTER 8: THE JOURNEY BEGINS

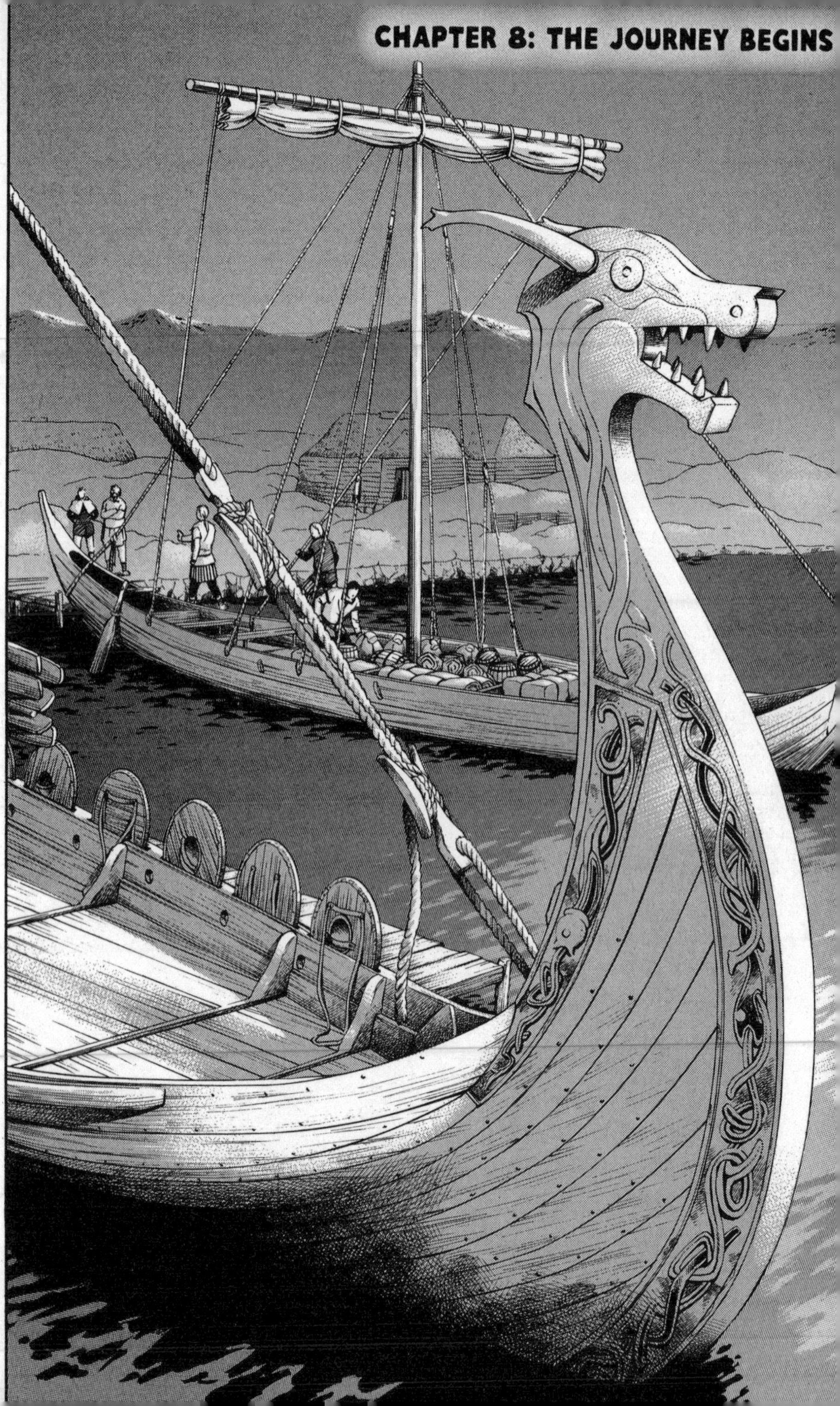

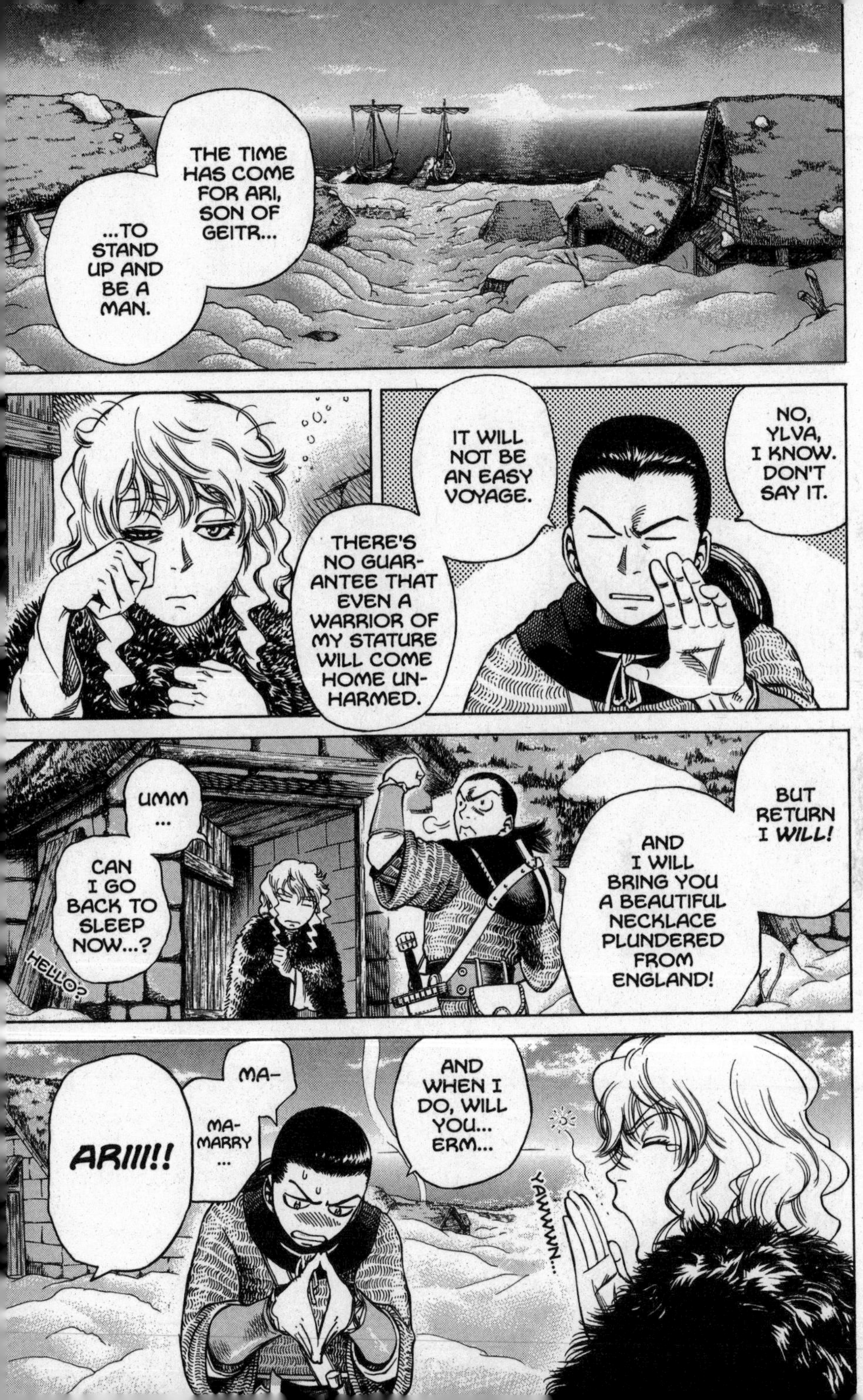
THE TIME HAS COME FOR ARI, SON OF GEITR...
...TO STAND UP AND BE A MAN.
NO, YLVA, I KNOW. DON'T SAY IT.
IT WILL NOT BE AN EASY VOYAGE.
THERE'S NO GUARANTEE THAT EVEN A WARRIOR OF MY STATURE WILL COME HOME UNHARMED.
BUT RETURN I WILL!
AND I WILL BRING YOU A BEAUTIFUL NECKLACE PLUNDERED FROM ENGLAND!
UMM ...
CAN I GO BACK TO SLEEP NOW...?
HELLO?
YAWWWN...
AND WHEN I DO, WILL YOU... ERM...
MA-
MA-MARRY ...
ARIIII!!

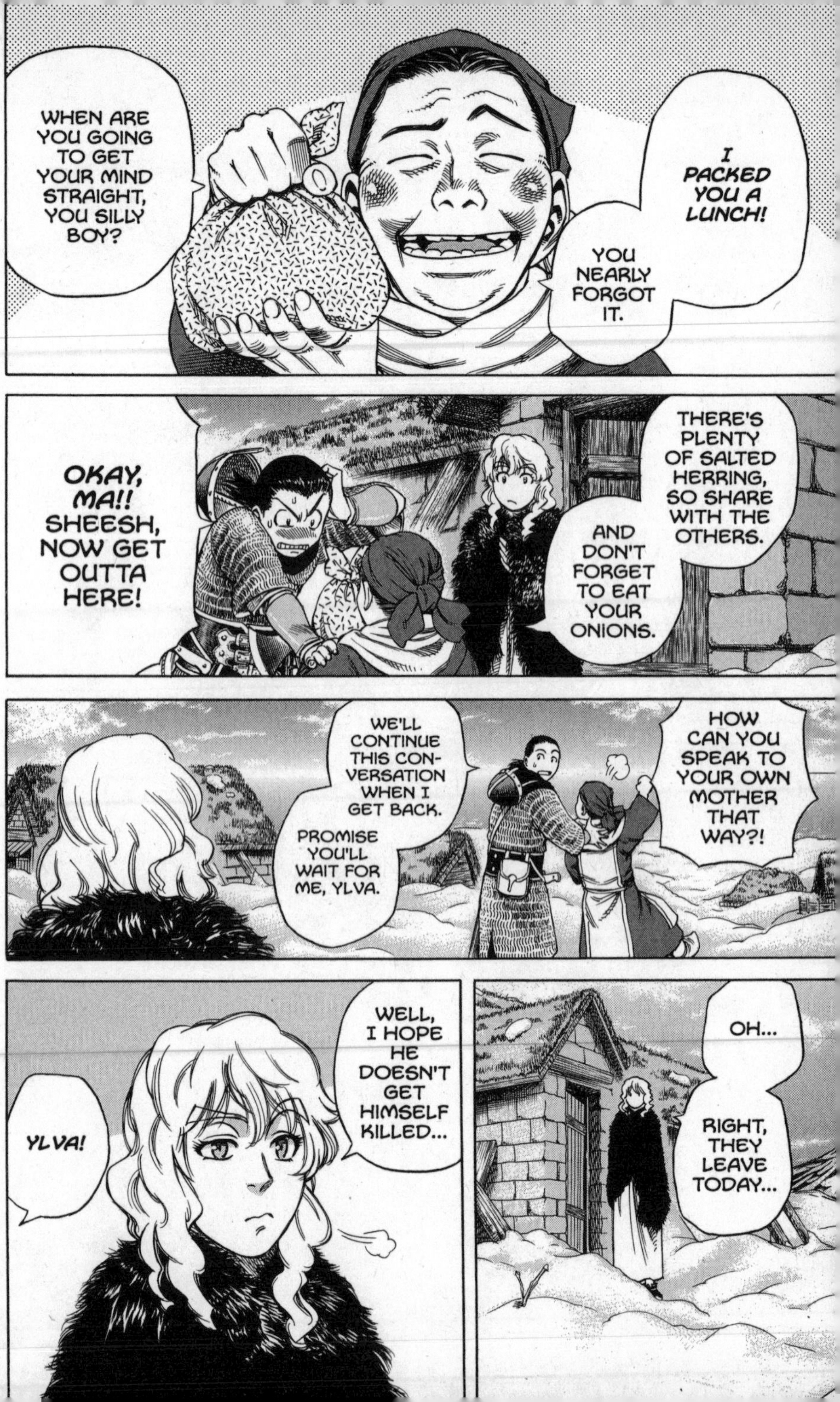
I PACKED YOU A LUNCH!
YOU NEARLY FORGOT IT.
WHEN ARE YOU GOING TO GET YOUR MIND STRAIGHT, YOU SILLY BOY?
THERE'S PLENTY OF SALTED HERRING, SO SHARE WITH THE OTHERS.
AND DON'T FORGET TO EAT YOUR ONIONS.
OKAY, MA!! SHEESH, NOW GET OUTTA HERE!
HOW CAN YOU SPEAK TO YOUR OWN MOTHER THAT WAY?!
WE'LL CONTINUE THIS CON-VERSATION WHEN I GET BACK.
PROMISE YOU'LL WAIT FOR ME, YLVA.
OH...
RIGHT, THEY LEAVE TODAY...
WELL, I HOPE HE DOESN'T GET HIMSELF KILLED...
YLVA!

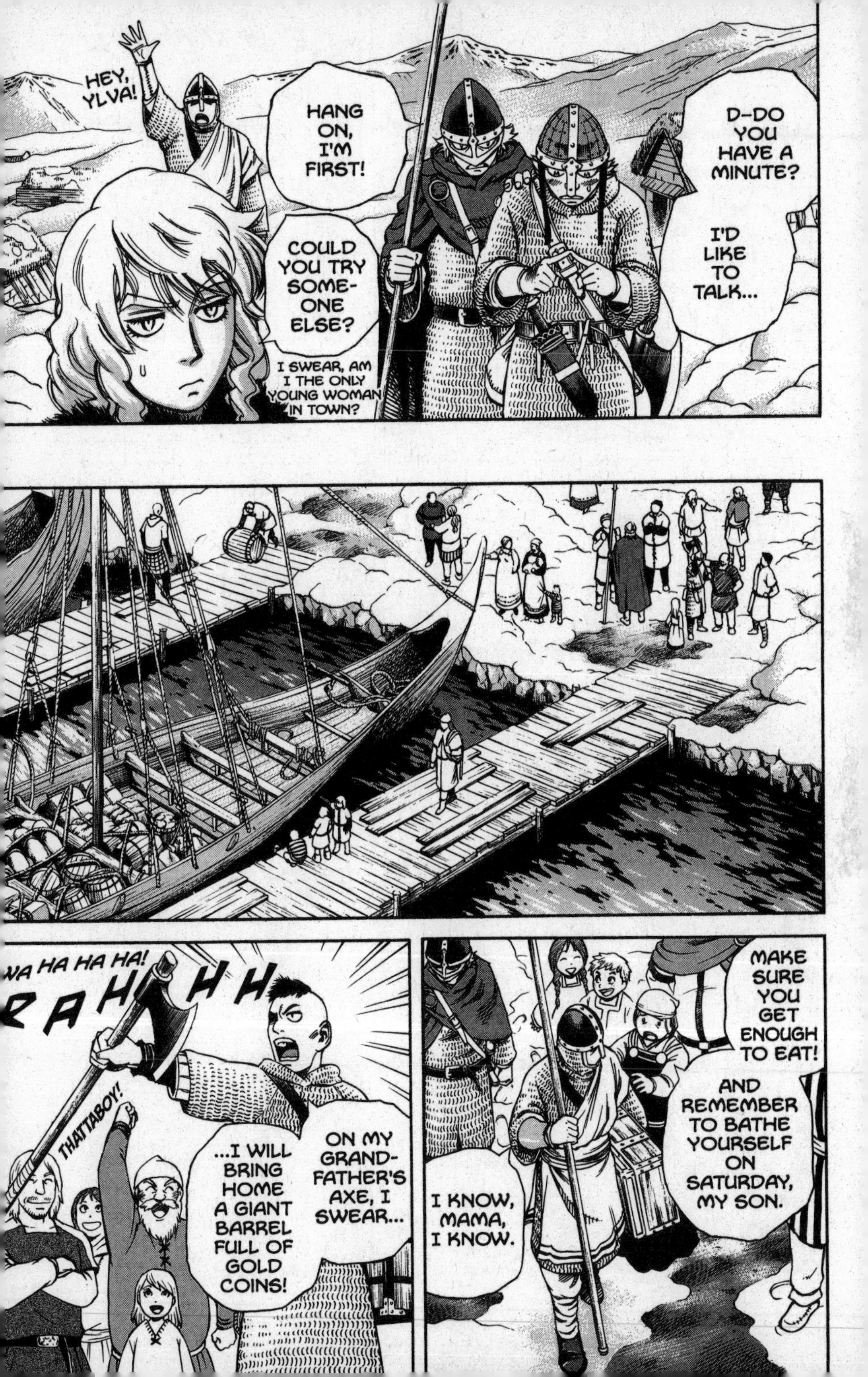

D-DO YOU HAVE A MINUTE?
I'D LIKE TO TALK...
HANG ON, I'M FIRST!
HEY, YLVA!
COULD YOU TRY SOME-ONE ELSE?
I SWEAR, AM I THE ONLY YOUNG WOMAN IN TOWN?
MAKE SURE YOU GET ENOUGH TO EAT!
AND REMEMBER TO BATHE YOURSELF ON SATURDAY, MY SON.
I KNOW, MAMA, I KNOW.
WA HA HA HA!
RAHHH
ON MY GRAND-FATHER'S AXE, I SWEAR...
...I WILL BRING HOME A GIANT BARREL FULL OF GOLD COINS!
THATTABOY!

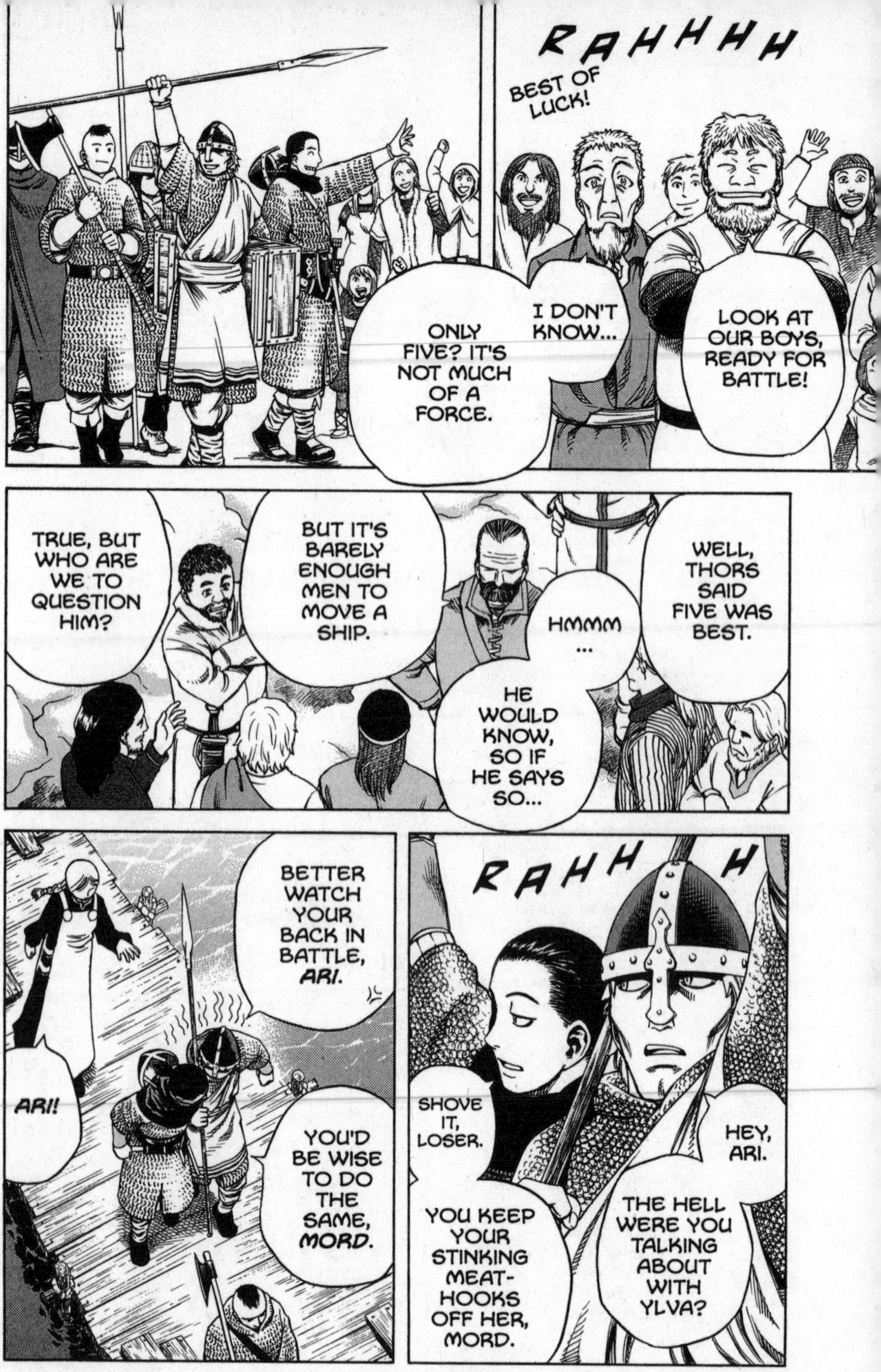
RAHHHH
BEST OF LUCK!
LOOK AT OUR BOYS, READY FOR BATTLE!
I DON'T KNOW...
ONLY FIVE? IT'S NOT MUCH OF A FORCE.
WELL, THORS SAID FIVE WAS BEST.
HMMM...
HE WOULD KNOW, SO IF HE SAYS SO...
BUT IT'S BARELY ENOUGH MEN TO MOVE A SHIP.
TRUE, BUT WHO ARE WE TO QUESTION HIM?
RAHH H
HEY, ARI.
THE HELL WERE YOU TALKING ABOUT WITH YLVA?
SHOVE IT, LOSER.
YOU KEEP YOUR STINKING MEAT-HOOKS OFF HER, MORD.
BETTER WATCH YOUR BACK IN BATTLE, *ARI*.
ARI!
YOU'D BE WISE TO DO THE SAME, *MORD*.

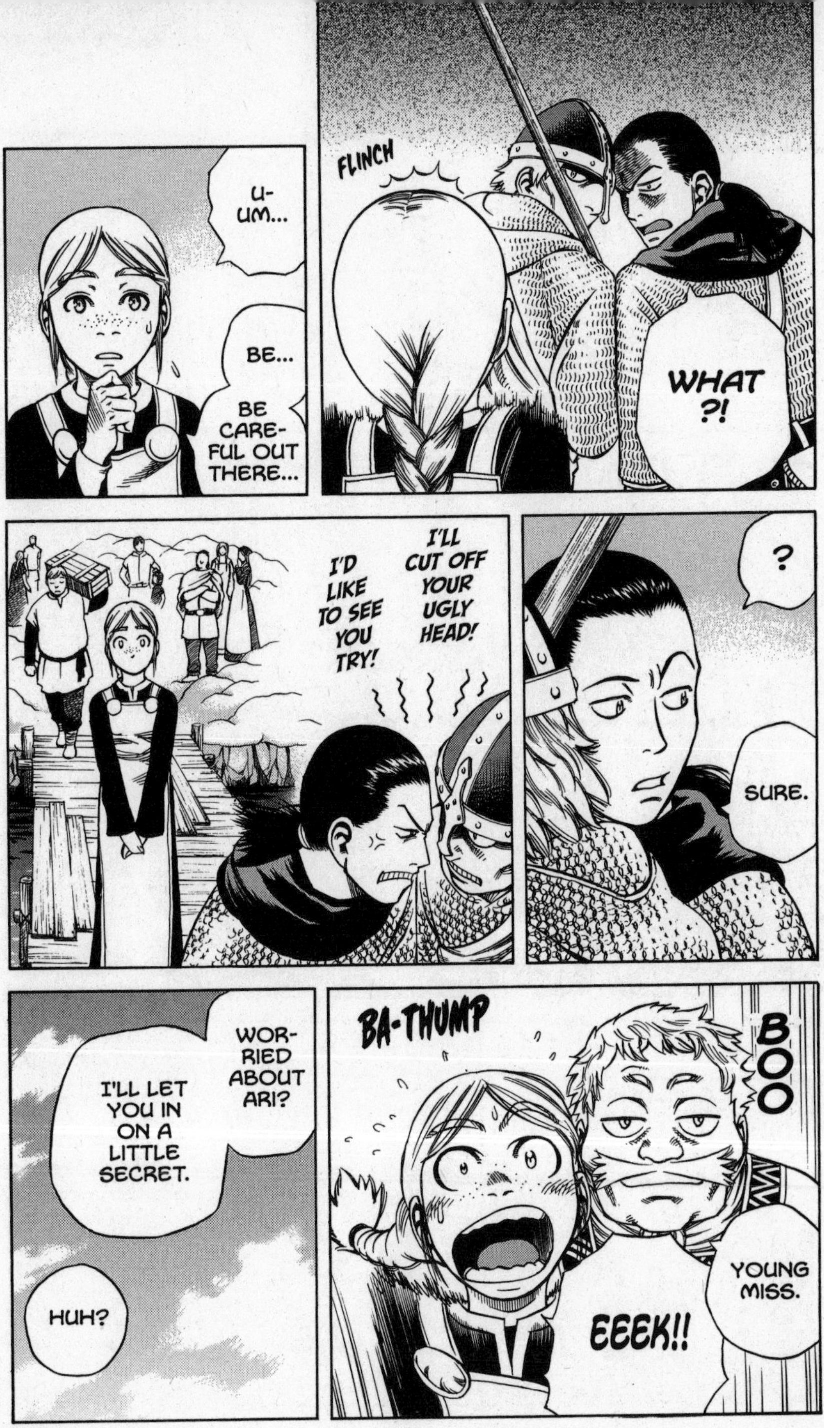
FLINCH
WHAT?!
U-UM...
BE...
BE CAREFUL OUT THERE...
?
SURE.
I'LL CUT OFF YOUR UGLY HEAD!
I'D LIKE TO SEE YOU TRY!
BOO
BA-THUMP
YOUNG MISS.
EEEK!!
WORRIED ABOUT ARI?
I'LL LET YOU IN ON A LITTLE SECRET.
HUH?

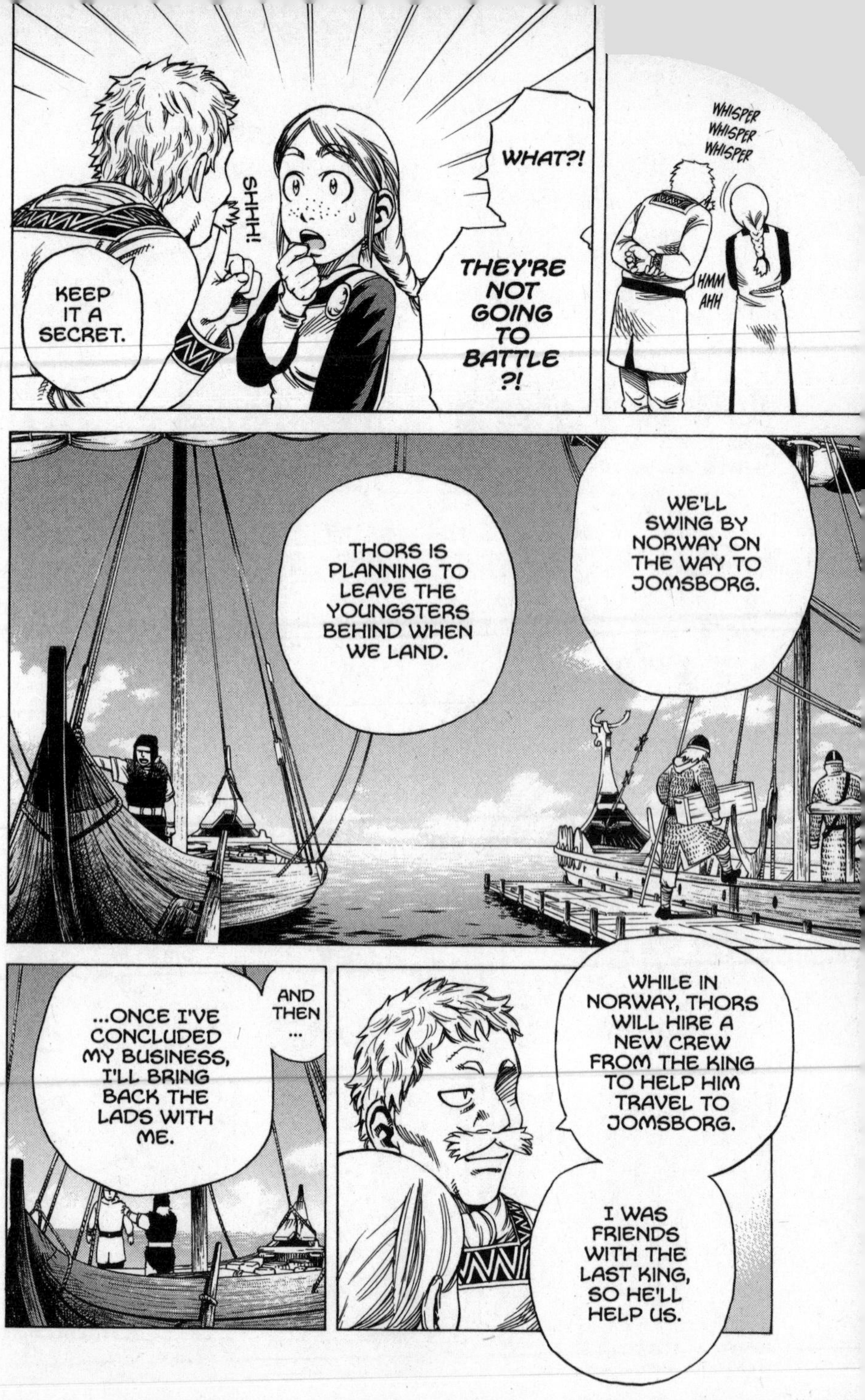
WHISPER WHISPER WHISPER
HMM AHH
WHAT?!
THEY'RE NOT GOING TO BATTLE ?!
SHHH!
KEEP IT A SECRET.
WE'LL SWING BY NORWAY ON THE WAY TO JOMSBORG.
THORS IS PLANNING TO LEAVE THE YOUNGSTERS BEHIND WHEN WE LAND.
WHILE IN NORWAY, THORS WILL HIRE A NEW CREW FROM THE KING TO HELP HIM TRAVEL TO JOMSBORG.
I WAS FRIENDS WITH THE LAST KING, SO HE'LL HELP US.
AND THEN ...
...ONCE I'VE CONCLUDED MY BUSINESS, I'LL BRING BACK THE LADS WITH ME.

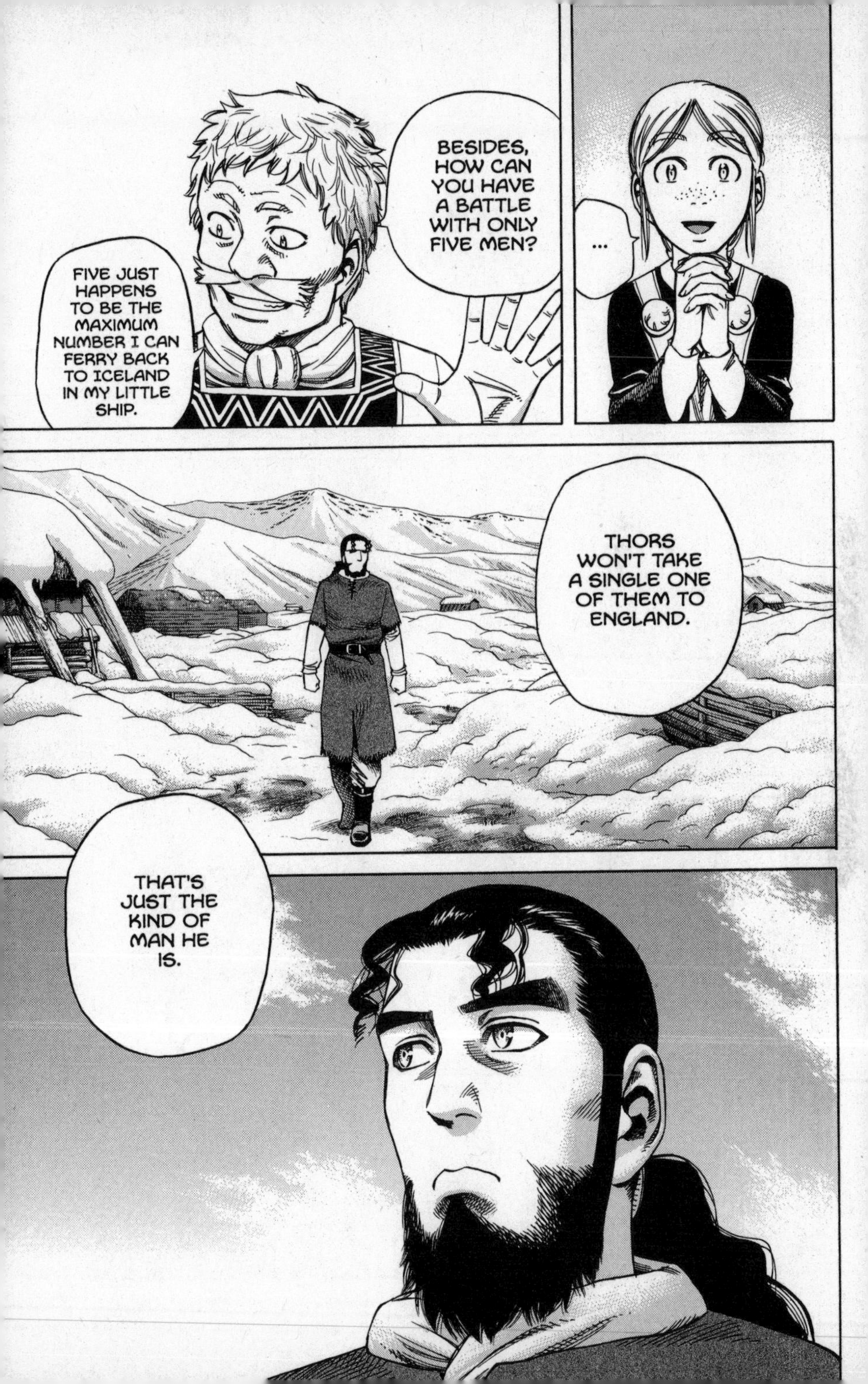
...
BESIDES, HOW CAN YOU HAVE A BATTLE WITH ONLY FIVE MEN?
FIVE JUST HAPPENS TO BE THE MAXIMUM NUMBER I CAN FERRY BACK TO ICELAND IN MY LITTLE SHIP.
THORS WON'T TAKE A SINGLE ONE OF THEM TO ENGLAND.
THAT'S JUST THE KIND OF MAN HE IS.

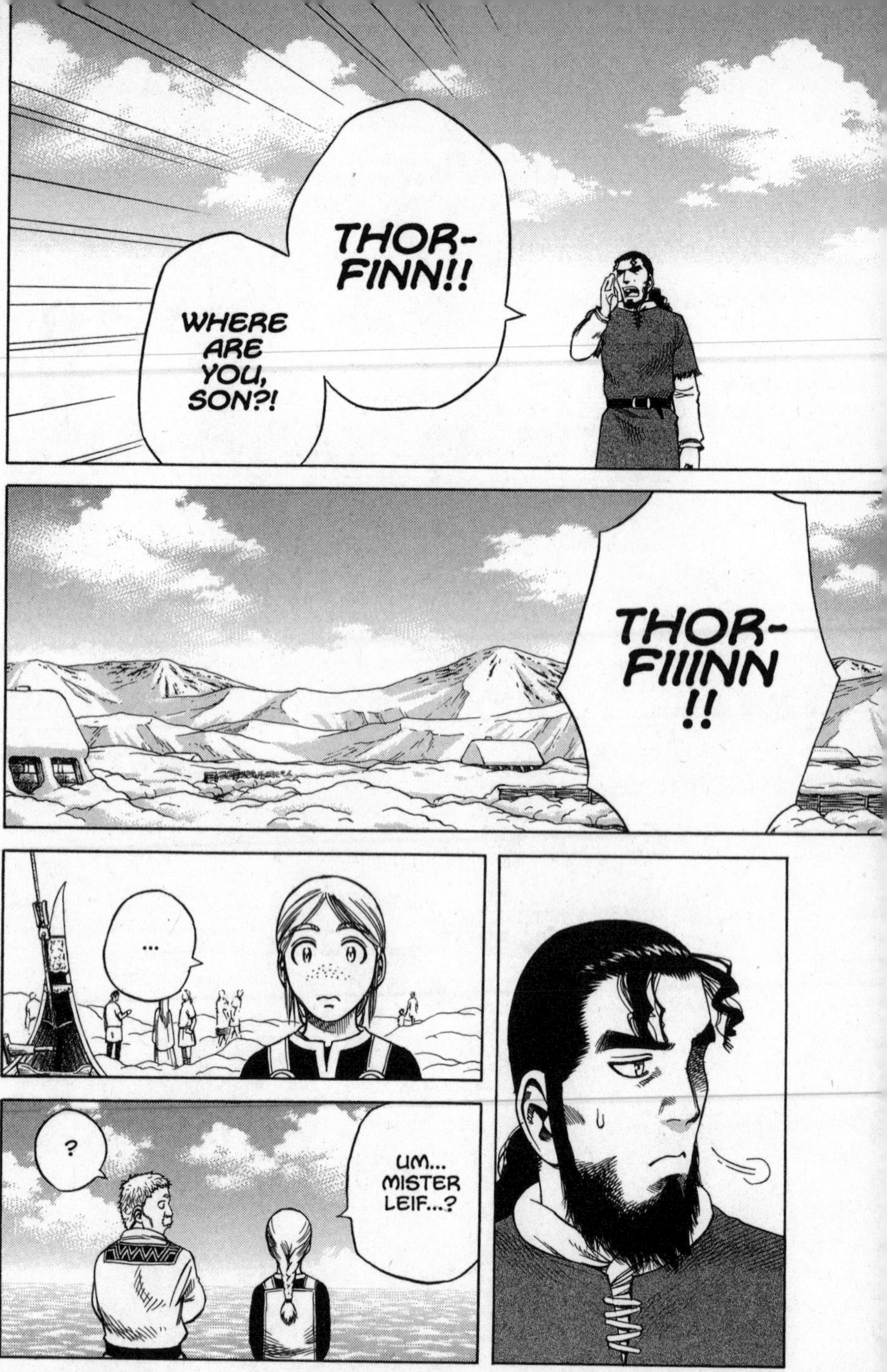
THOR-FINN!!
WHERE ARE YOU, SON?!
THOR-FIIINN !!
...
UM... MISTER LEIF...?
?

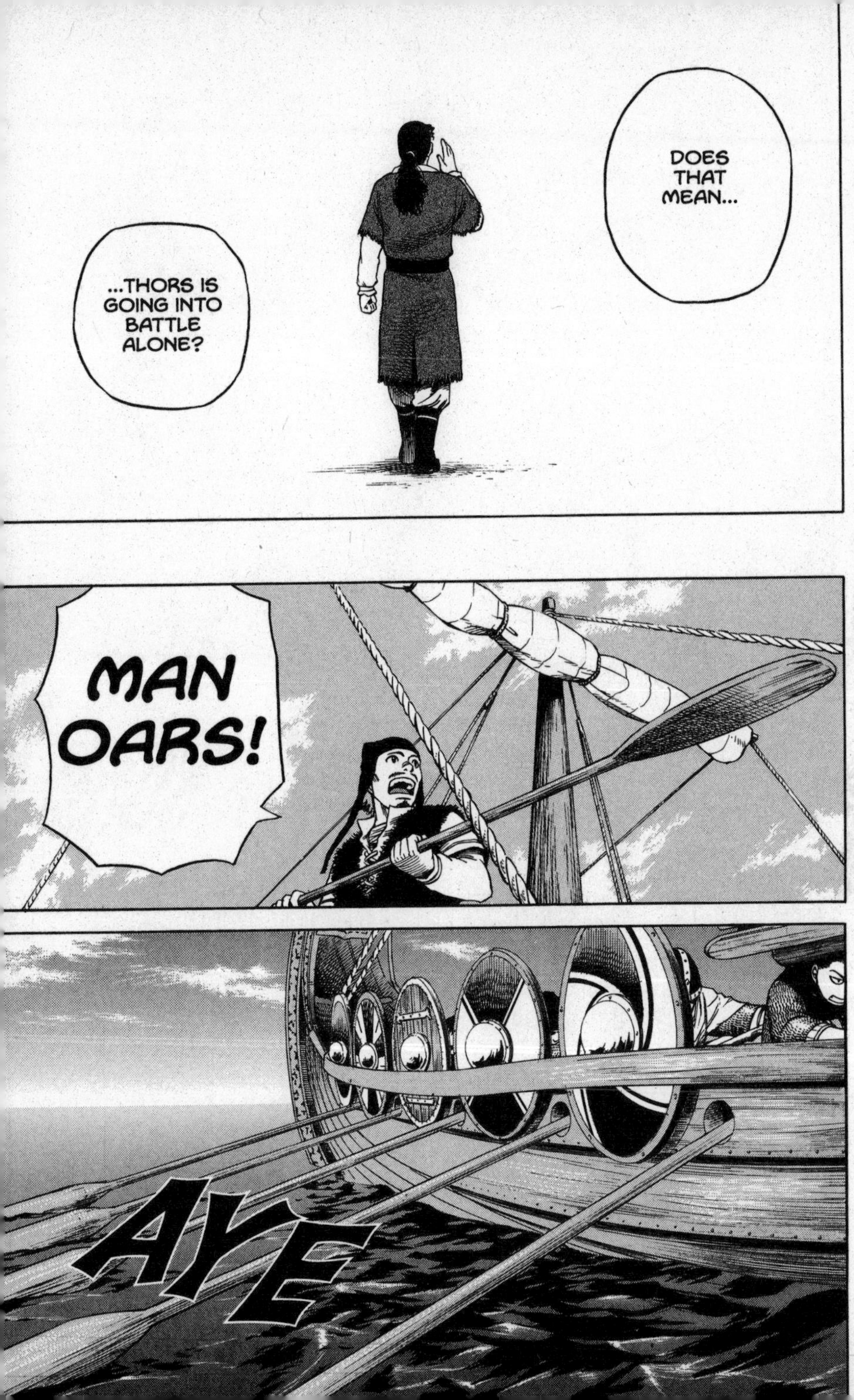
DOES THAT MEAN...
...THORS IS GOING INTO BATTLE ALONE?
MAN OARS!
AYE

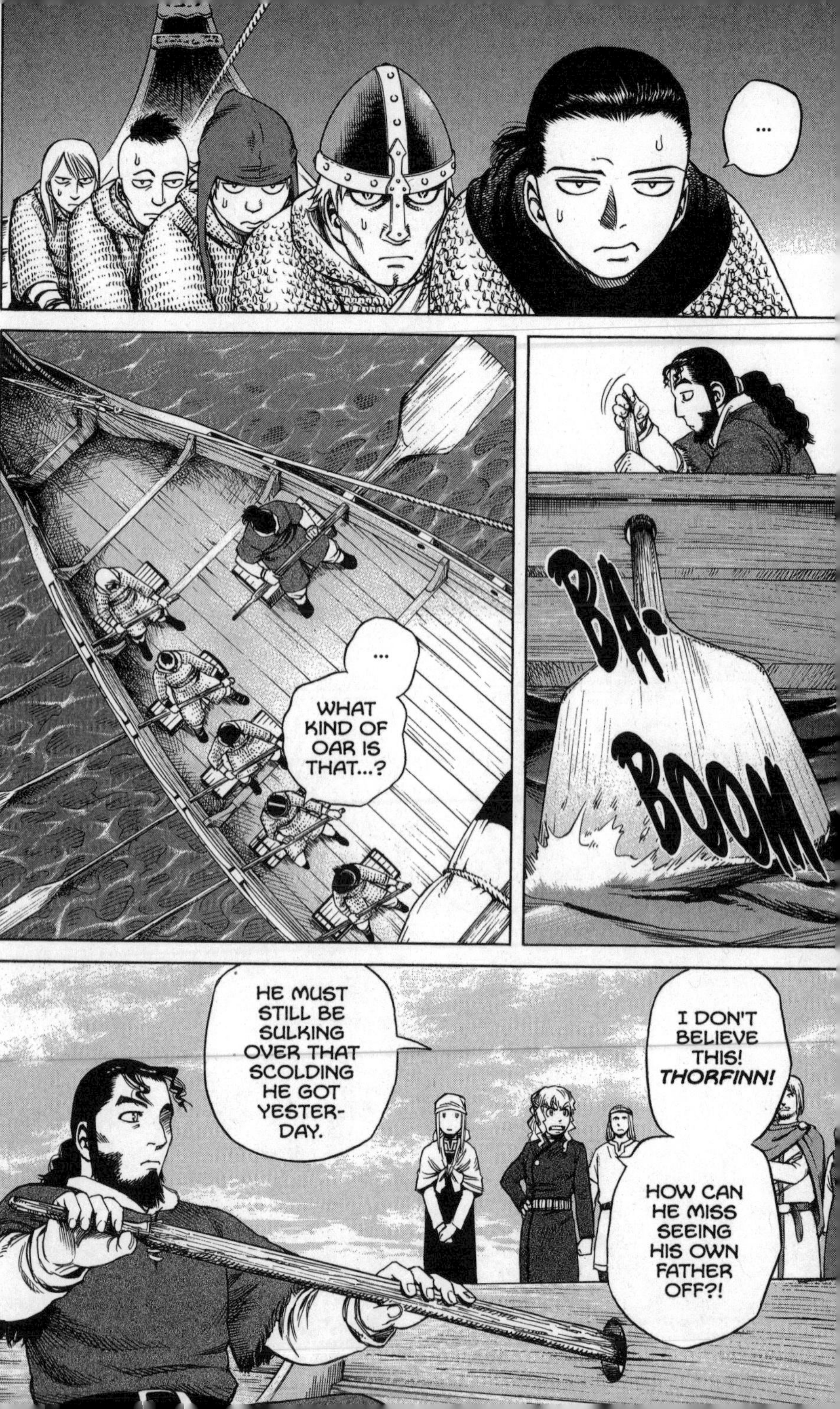
...
BA-BOOM
...
WHAT KIND OF OAR IS THAT...?
I DON'T BELIEVE THIS! *THORFINN!*
HOW CAN HE MISS SEEING HIS OWN FATHER OFF?!
HE MUST STILL BE SULKING OVER THAT SCOLDING HE GOT YESTER-DAY.

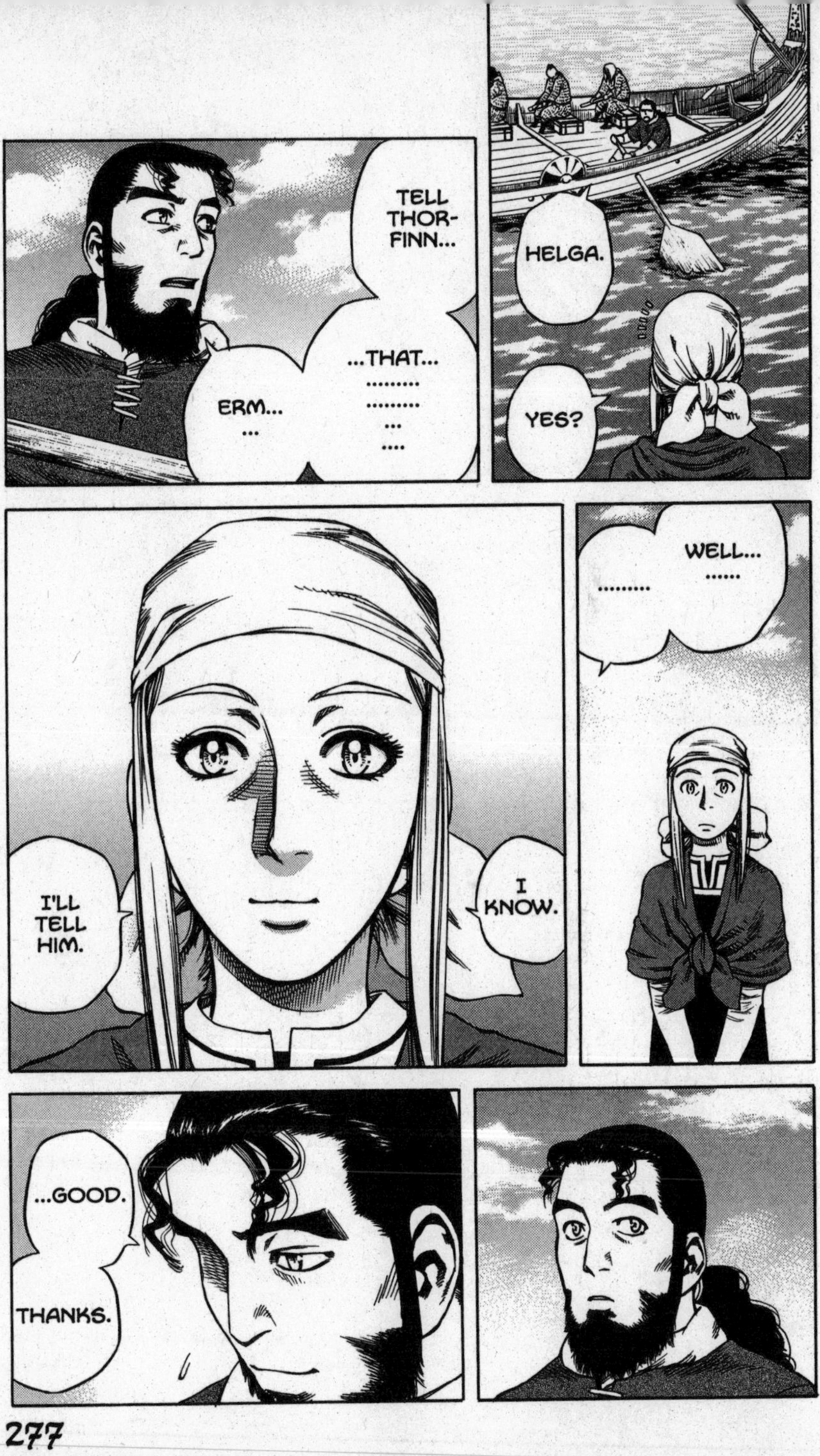
HELGA.
YES?
TELL THORFINN...
...THAT... ....
ERM... ...
WELL... ....
I KNOW.
I'LL TELL HIM.
...GOOD.
THANKS.

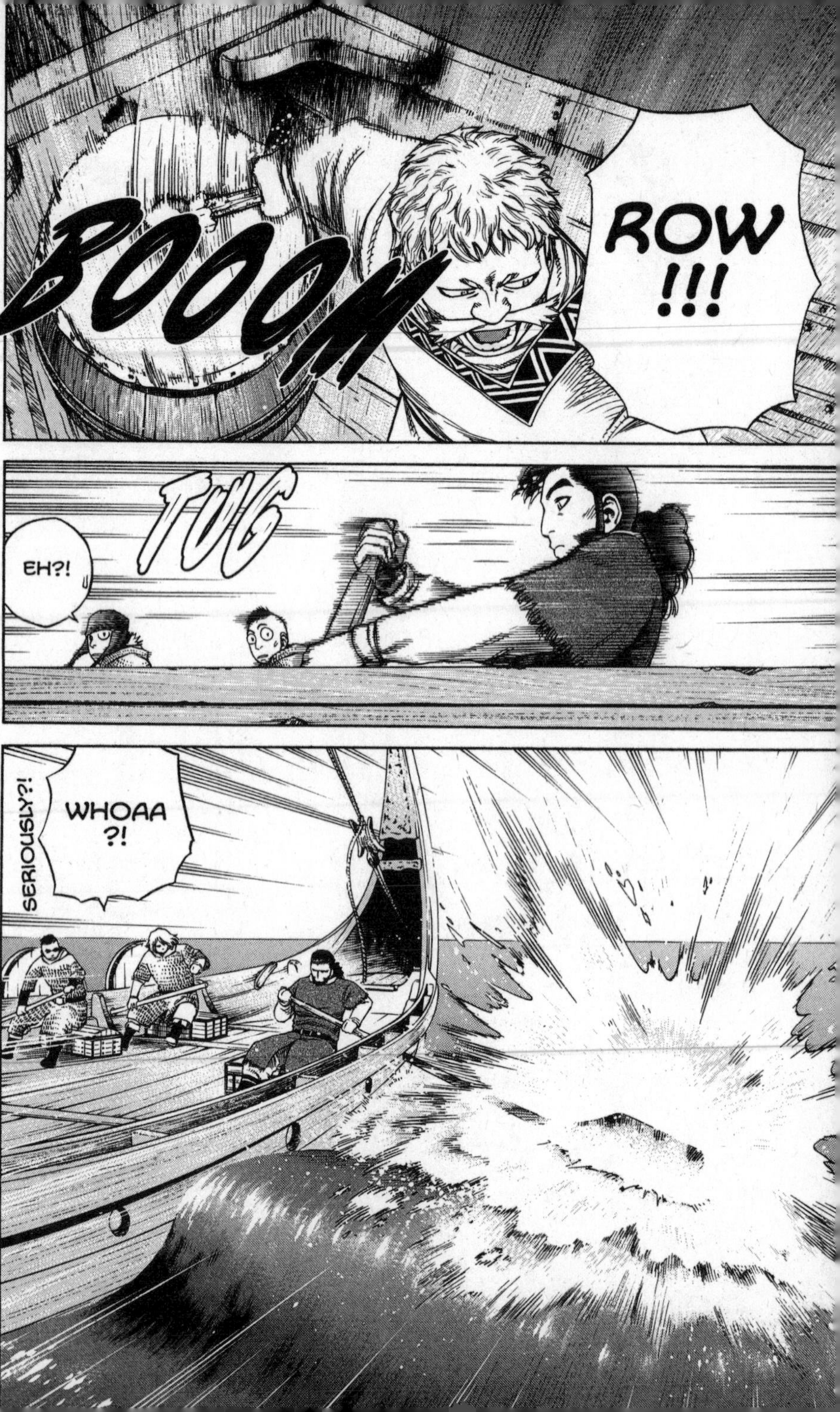
ROW !!!
BOOOM
TUG
EH?!
WHOAA ?!
SERIOUSLY?!

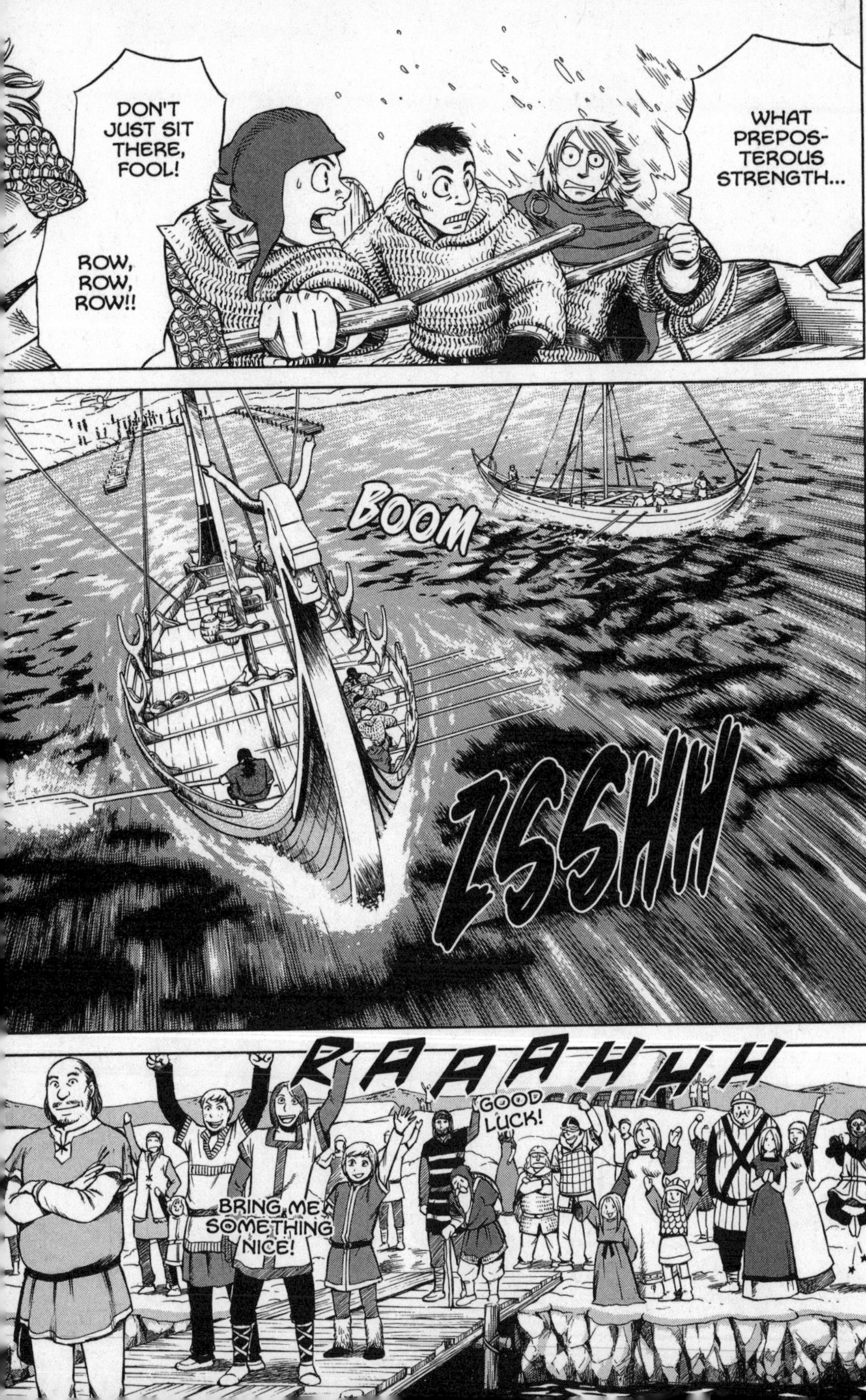
WHAT PREPOSTEROUS STRENGTH...
DON'T JUST SIT THERE, FOOL!
ROW, ROW, ROW!!
BOOM
ZSSHH
RAAAHHHH
GOOD LUCK!
BRING ME SOMETHING NICE!

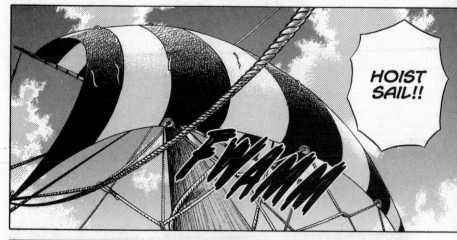

HOIST
SAIL!!

FWAMM

=BLURCH=

=HURRF=

=WHEEZE=

SLUMP....

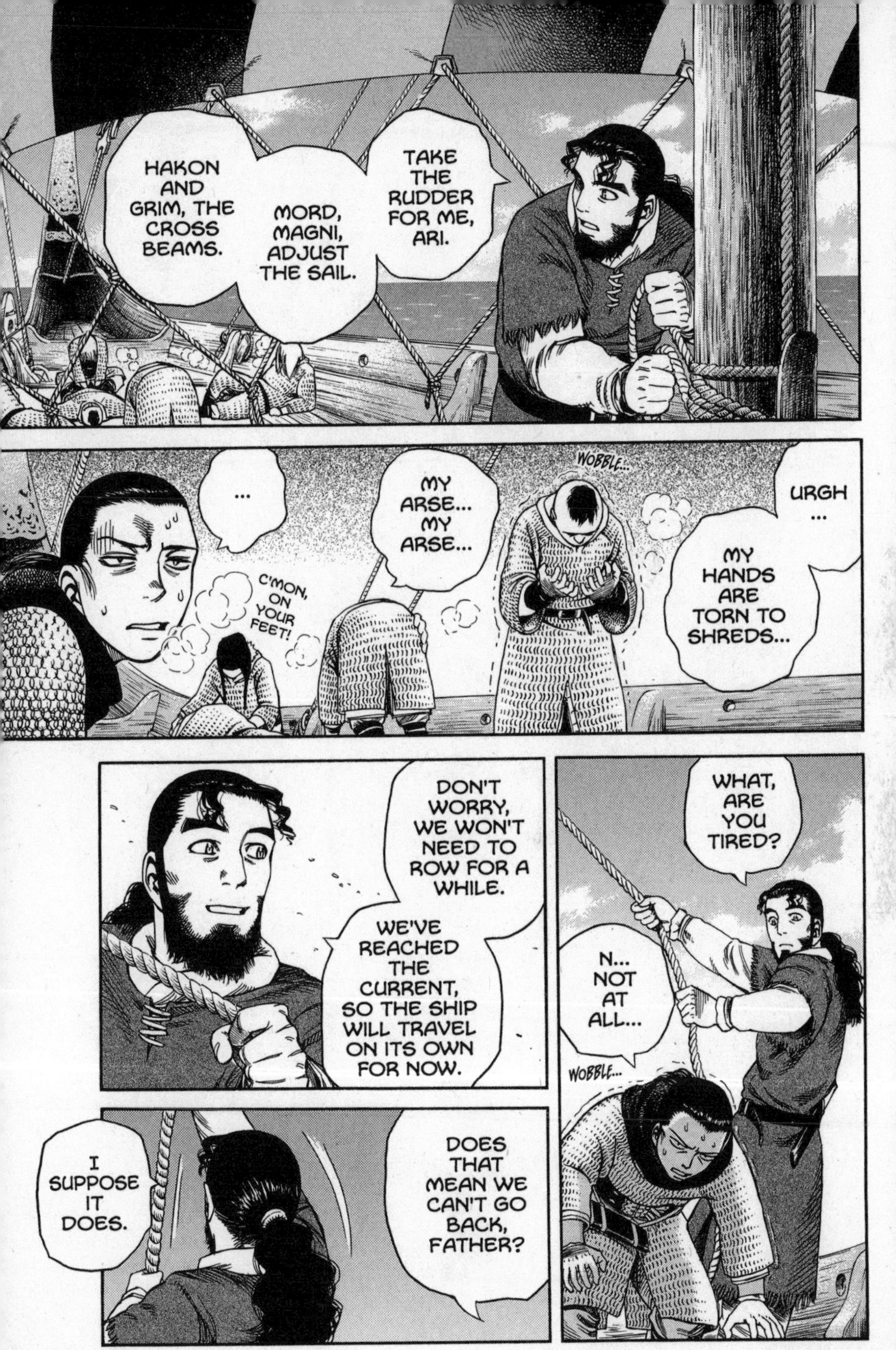
TAKE THE RUDDER FOR ME, ARI.
MORD, MAGNI, ADJUST THE SAIL.
HAKON AND GRIM, THE CROSS BEAMS.
URGH ...
MY HANDS ARE TORN TO SHREDS...
WOBBLE...
MY ARSE... MY ARSE...
C'MON, ON YOUR FEET!
...
WHAT, ARE YOU TIRED?
N... NOT AT ALL...
WOBBLE...
DON'T WORRY, WE WON'T NEED TO ROW FOR A WHILE.
WE'VE REACHED THE CURRENT, SO THE SHIP WILL TRAVEL ON ITS OWN FOR NOW.
DOES THAT MEAN WE CAN'T GO BACK, FATHER?
I SUPPOSE IT DOES.

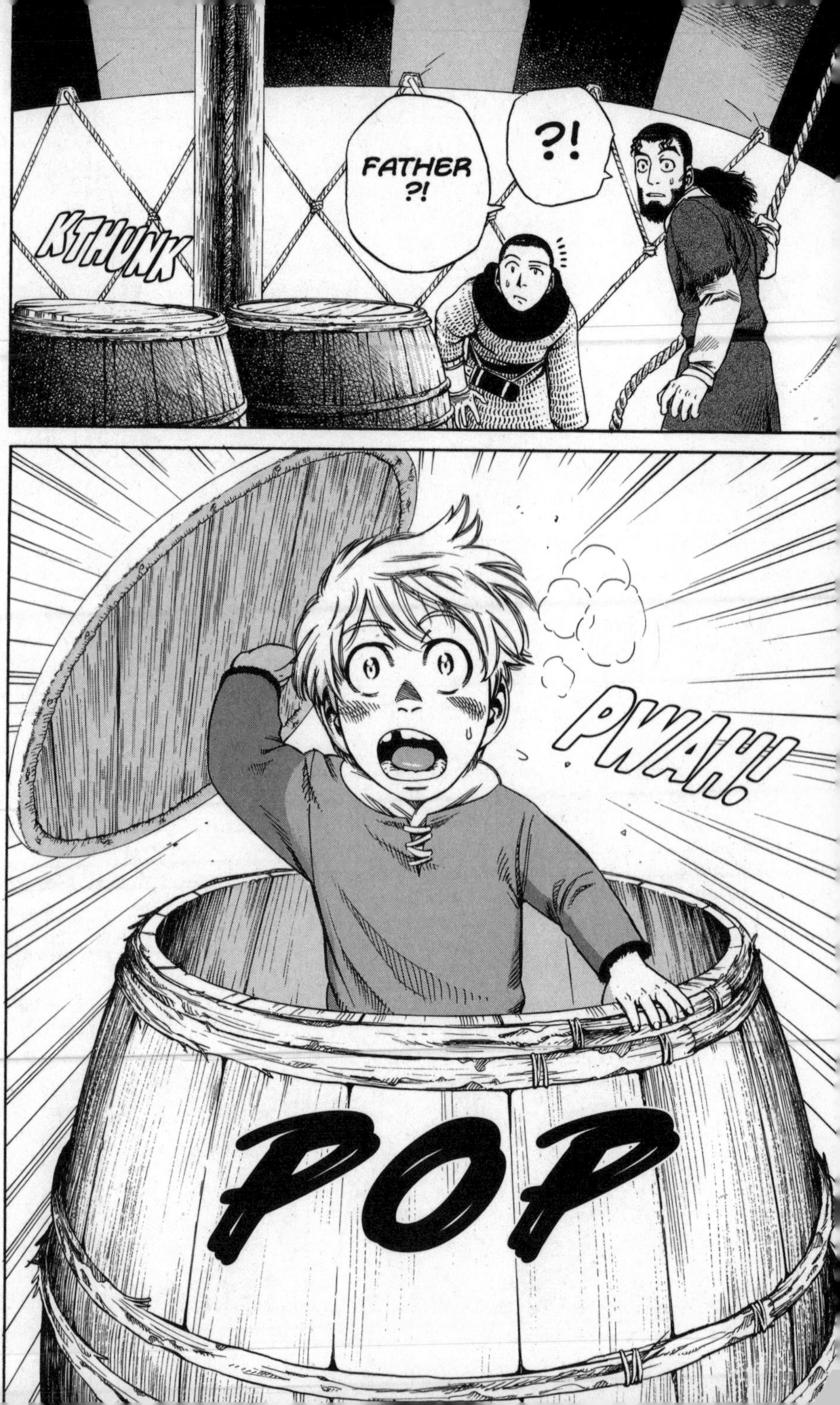
?!
FATHER ?!
KTHUNK
PWAH!
POP

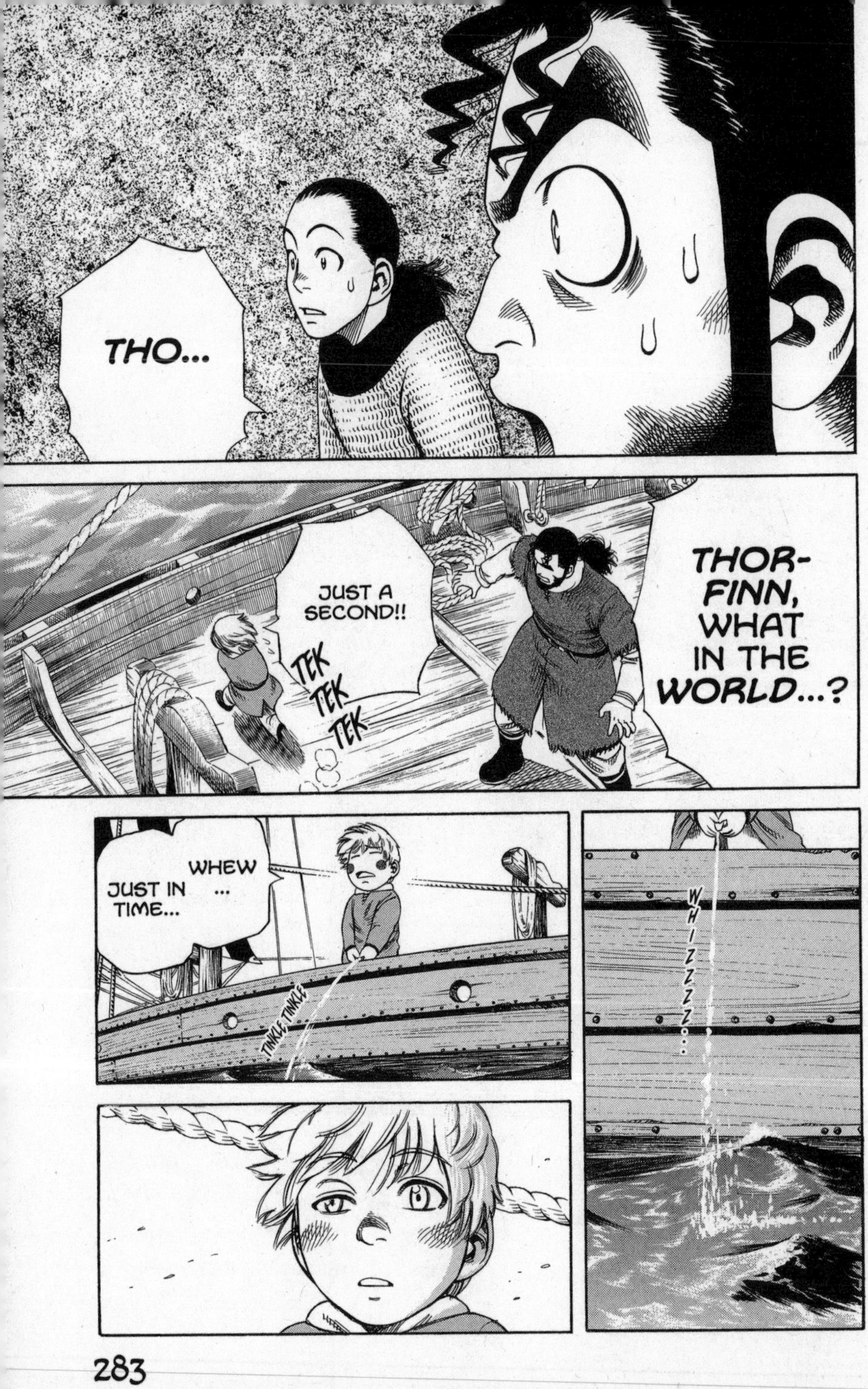
THO...
THOR-FINN, WHAT IN THE WORLD...?
JUST A SECOND!!
TEK TEK TEK
WHIZZZZZ...
WHEW ... JUST IN TIME...
TINKLE TINKLE

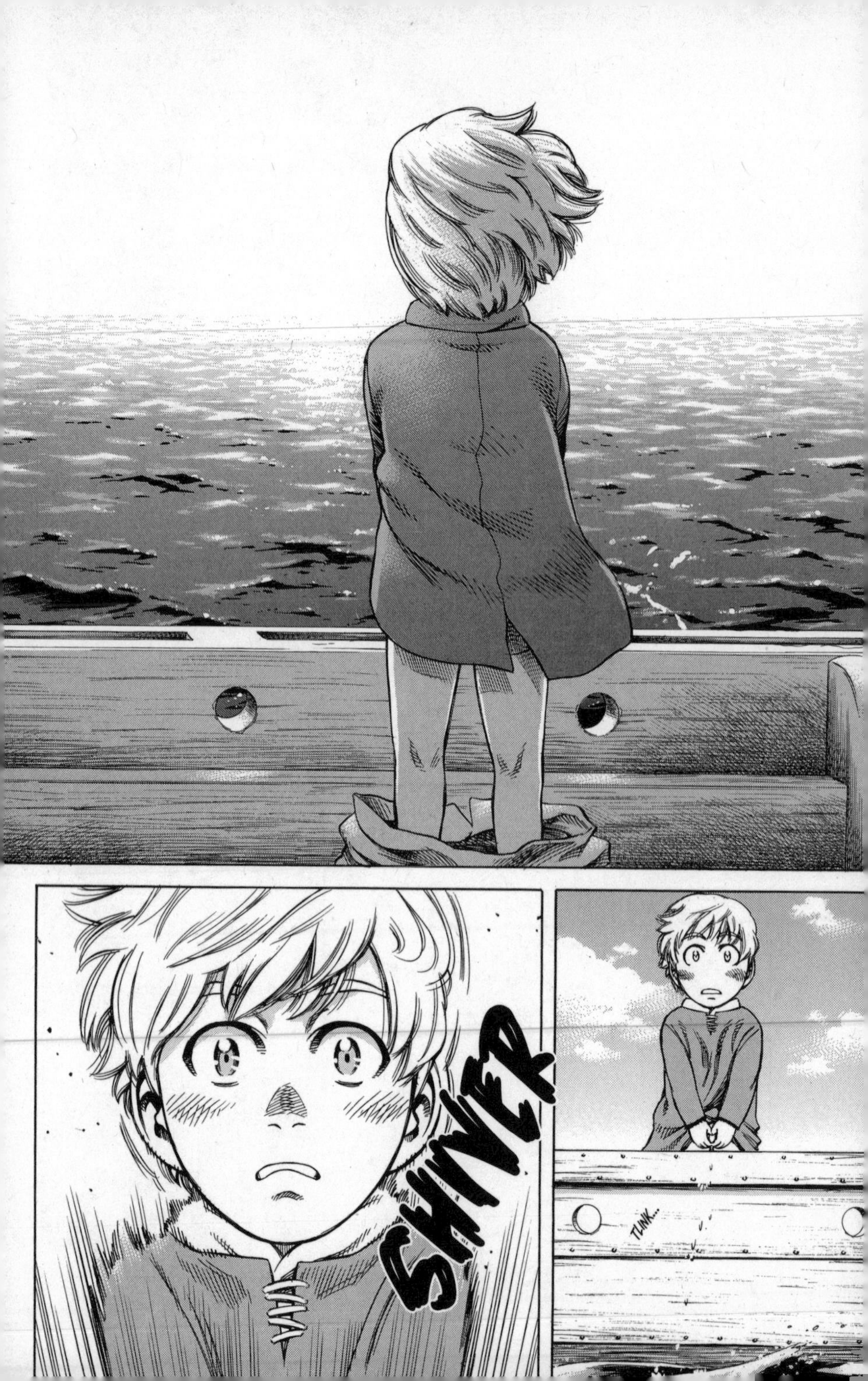
TLINK...
SHIVER

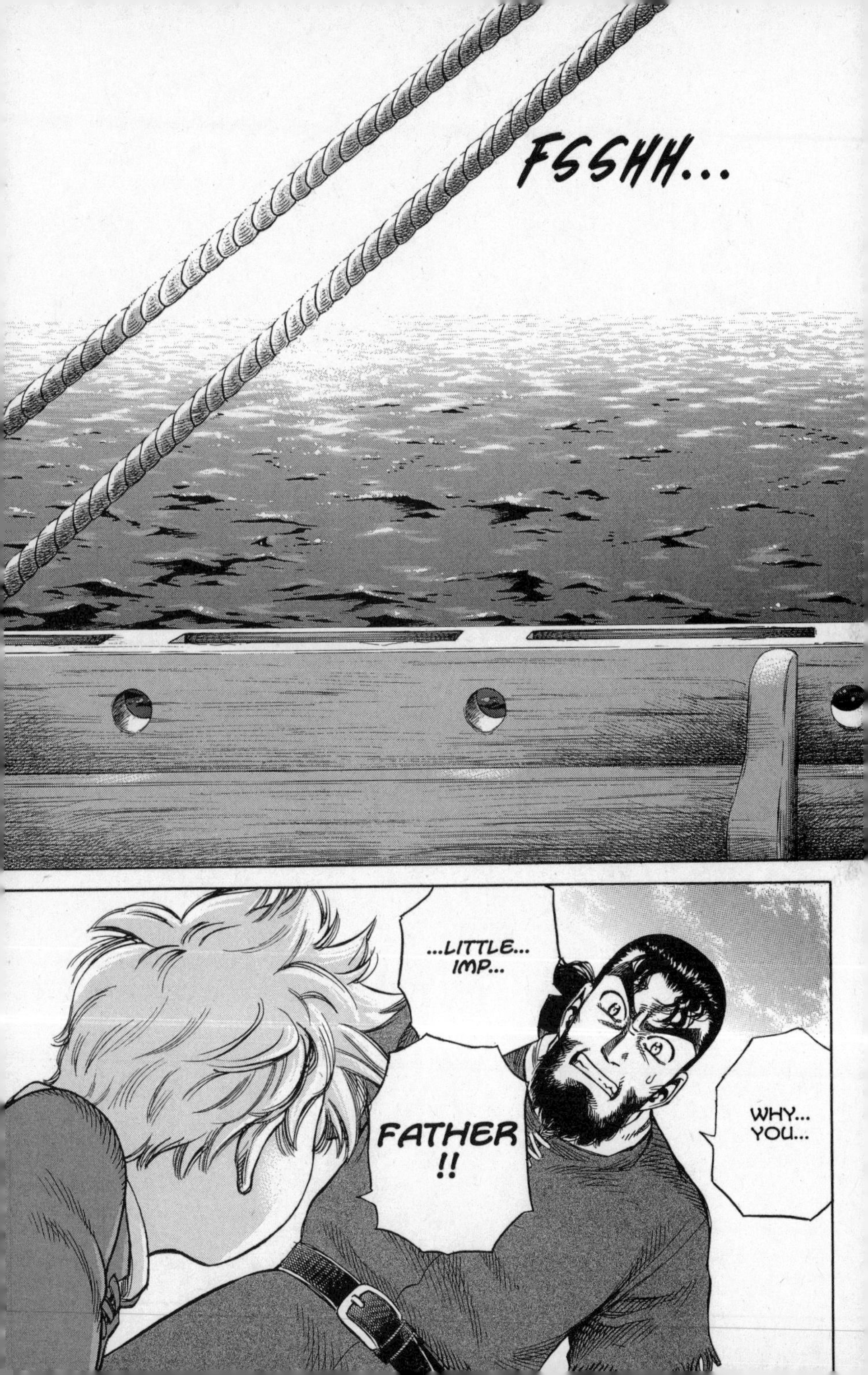
FSSHH...
...LITTLE... IMP...
WHY... YOU...
FATHER !!

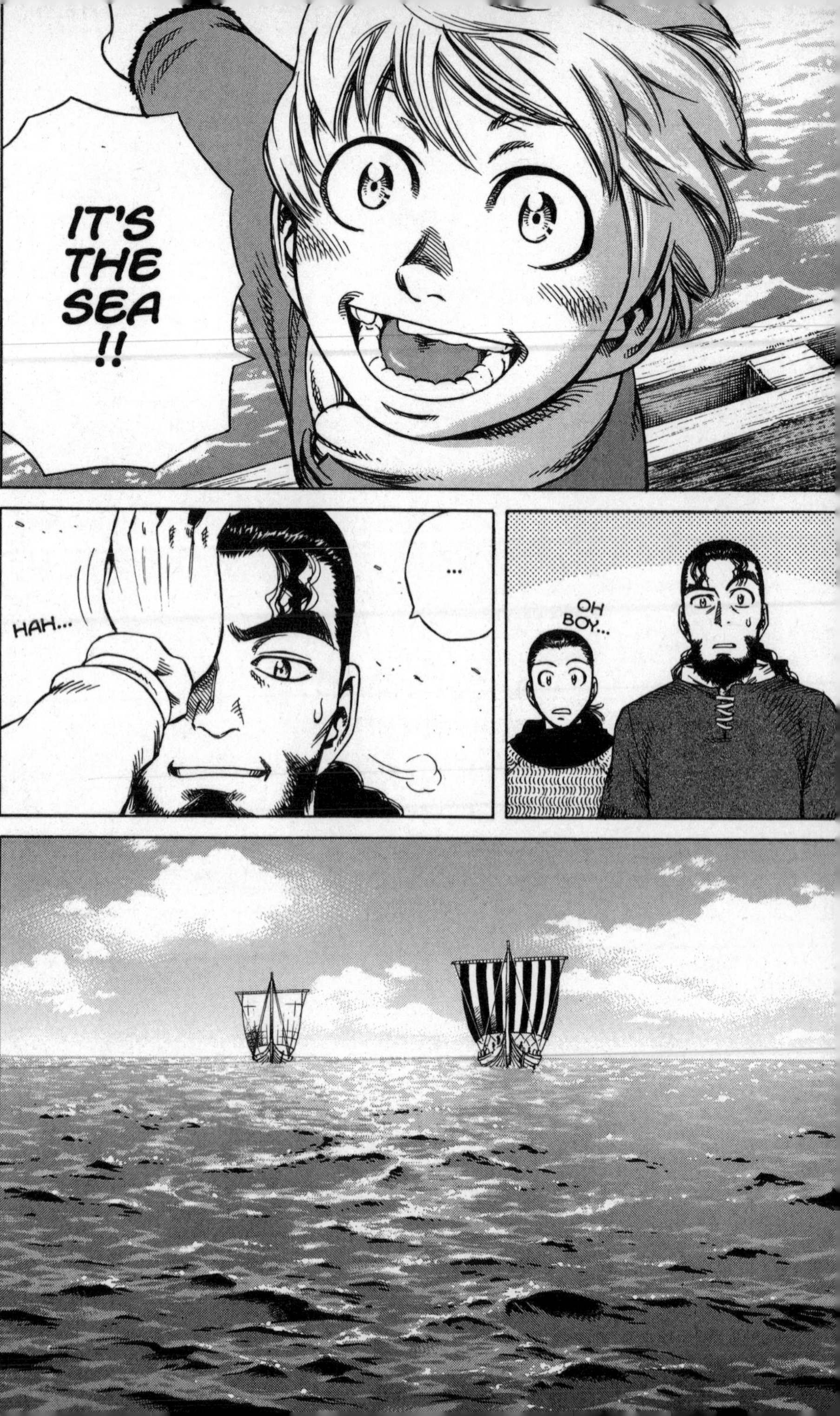
IT'S THE SEA !!
OH BOY...
...
HAH...

CHAPTER 8 - END

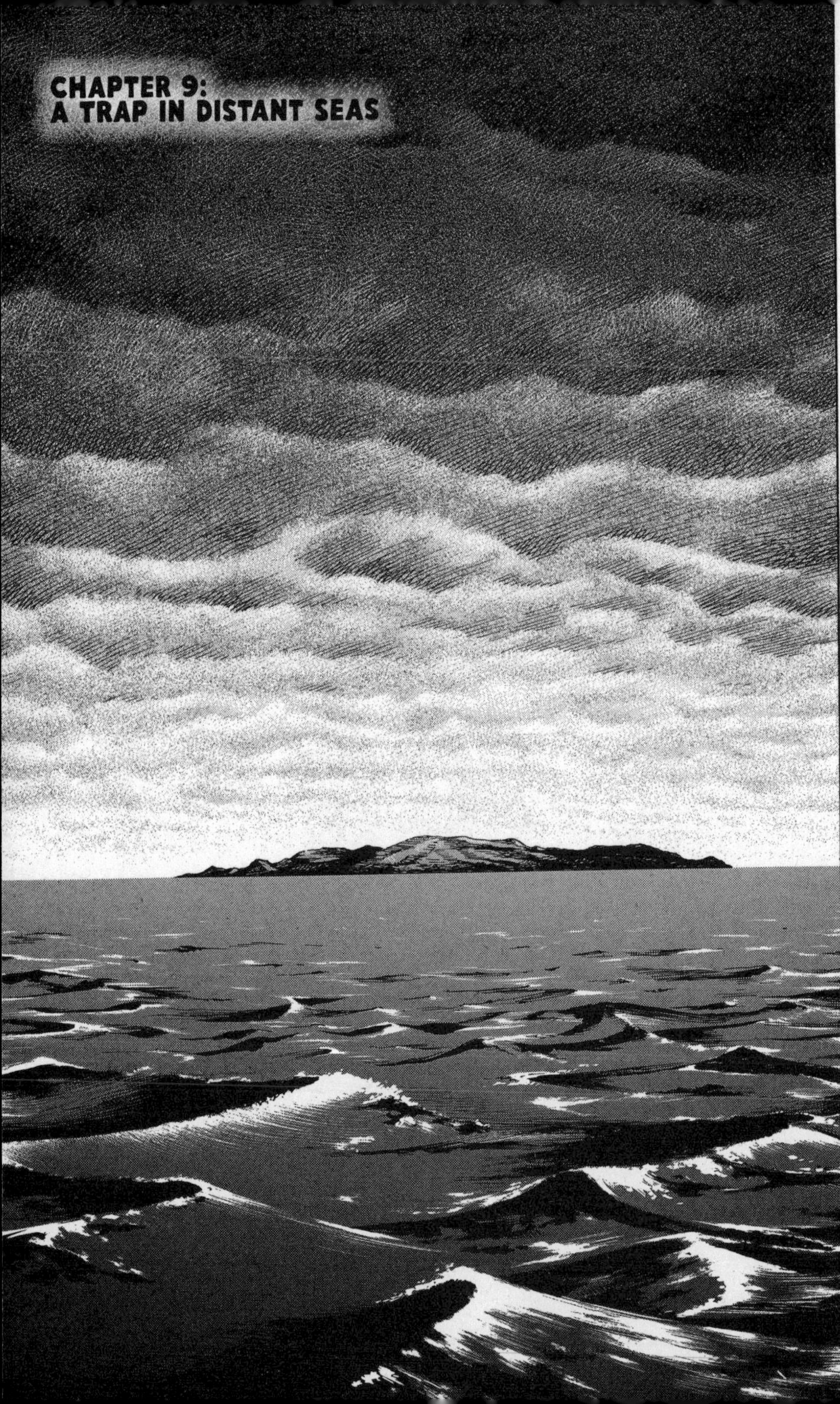
CHAPTER 9:
A TRAP IN DISTANT SEAS

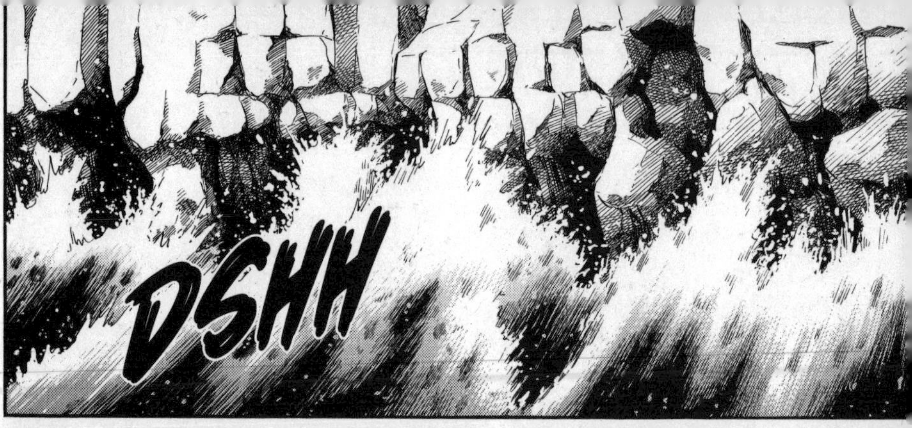
DSHH

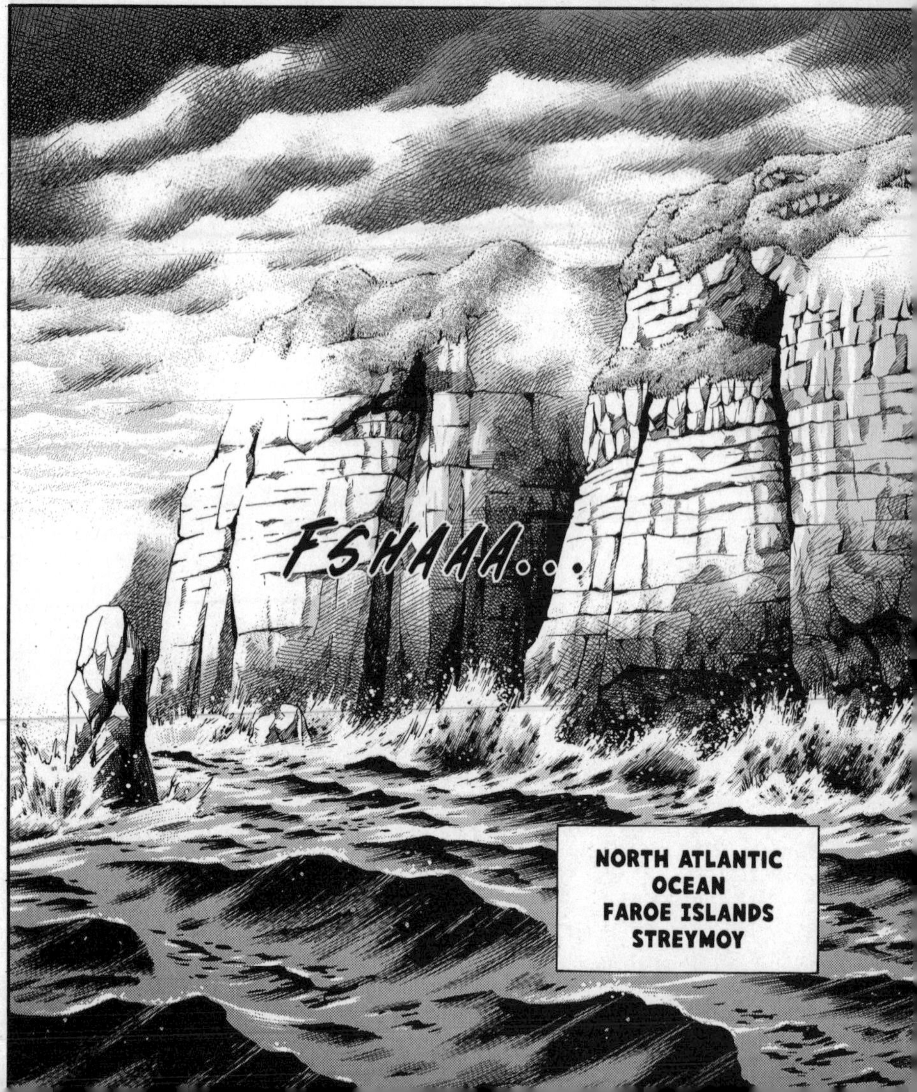
FSHAAA...
NORTH ATLANTIC OCEAN
FAROE ISLANDS
STREYMOY

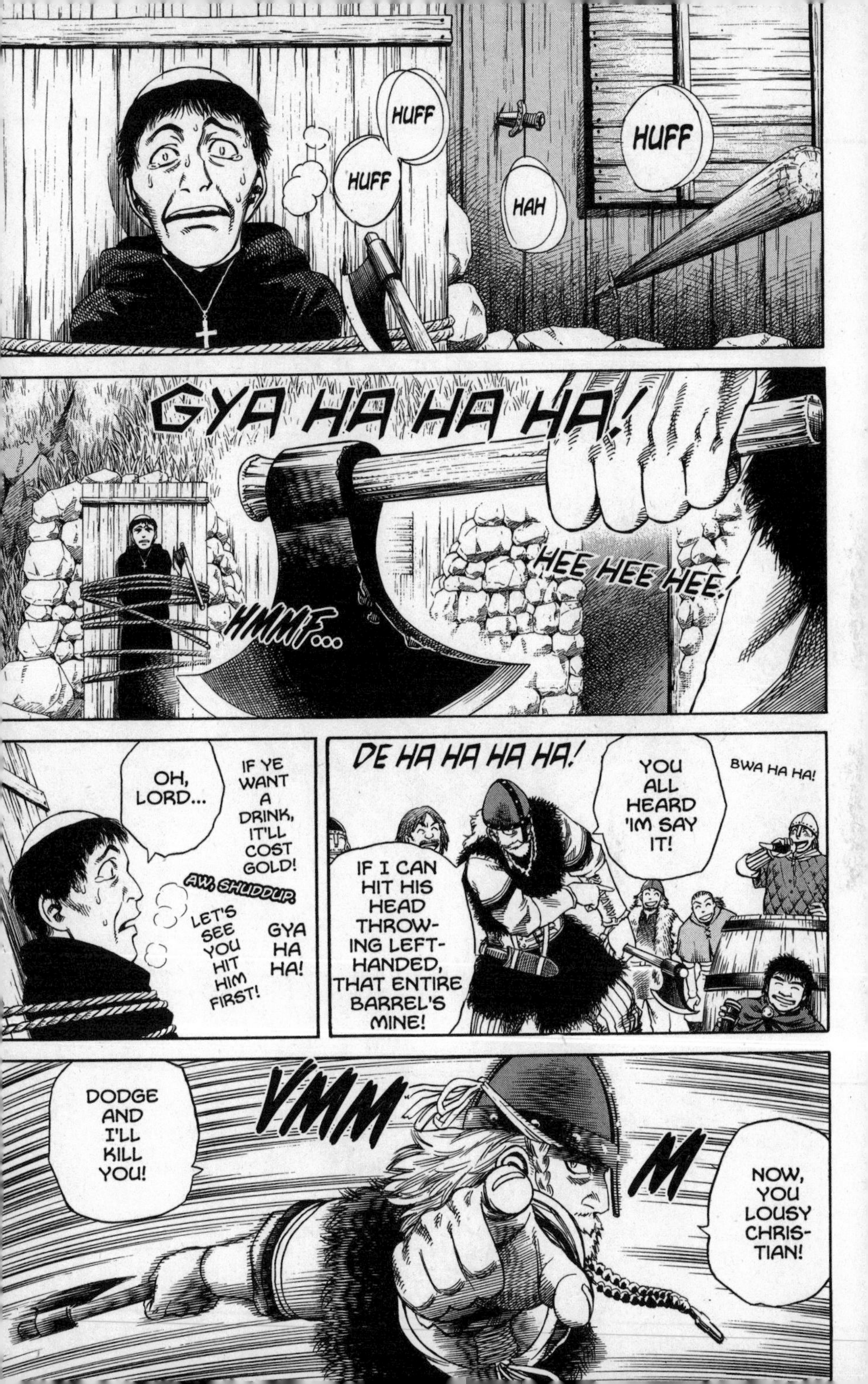
HUFF
HAH
HUFF
HUFF
GYA HA HA HA HA!
HEE HEE HEE!
HMMF...
BWA HA HA!
YOU ALL HEARD 'IM SAY IT!
DE HA HA HA HA!
IF I CAN HIT HIS HEAD THROWING LEFT-HANDED, THAT ENTIRE BARREL'S MINE!
IF YE WANT A DRINK, IT'LL COST GOLD!
OH, LORD...
AW, SHUDDUP.
GYA HA HA!
LET'S SEE YOU HIT HIM FIRST!
NOW, YOU LOUSY CHRISTIAN!
VMMM
DODGE AND I'LL KILL YOU!

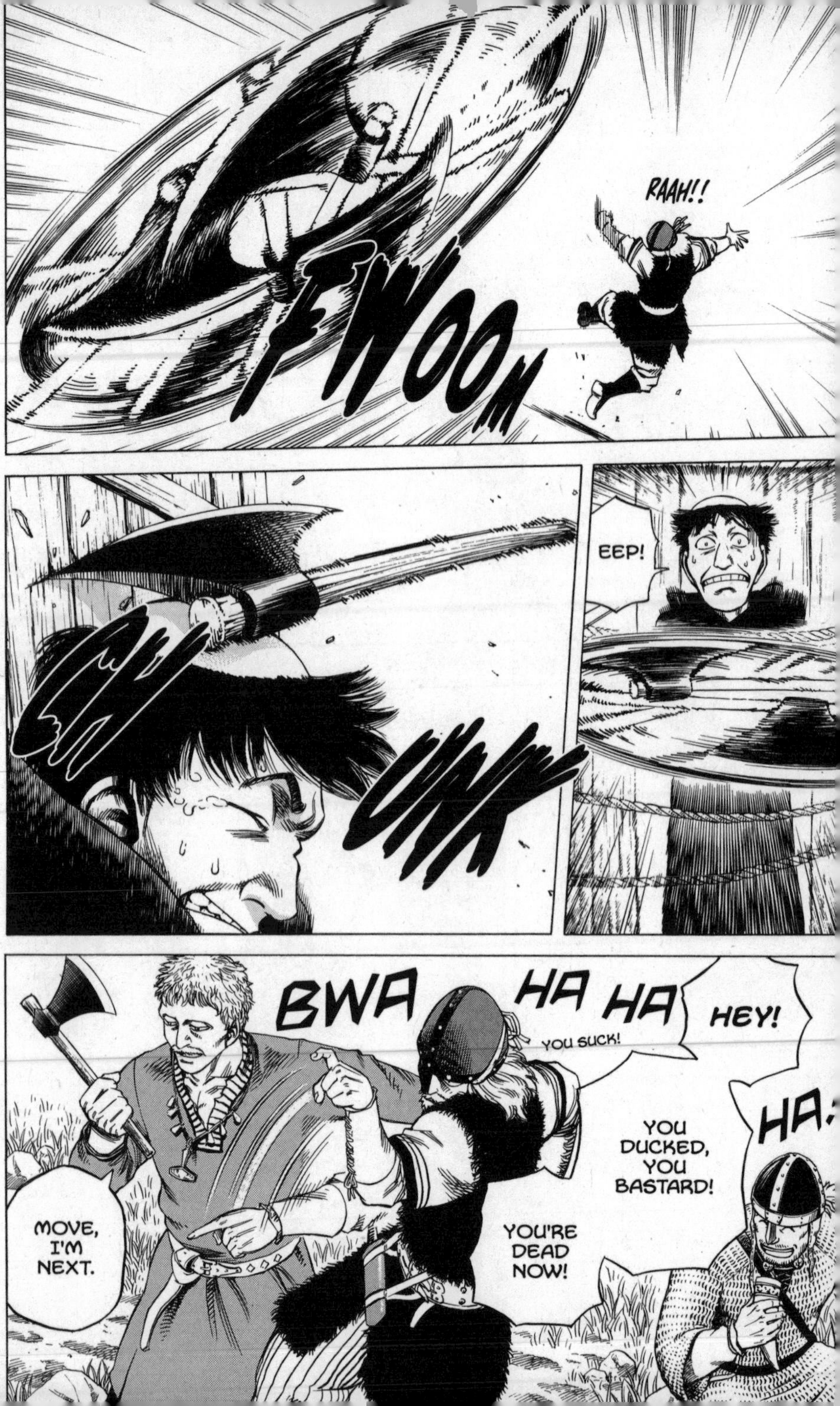
RAAH!!
FWOOM
EEP!
CHUNK
HEY!
HA!
YOU DUCKED, YOU BASTARD!
BWA HA HA
YOU SUCK!
YOU'RE DEAD NOW!
MOVE, I'M NEXT.

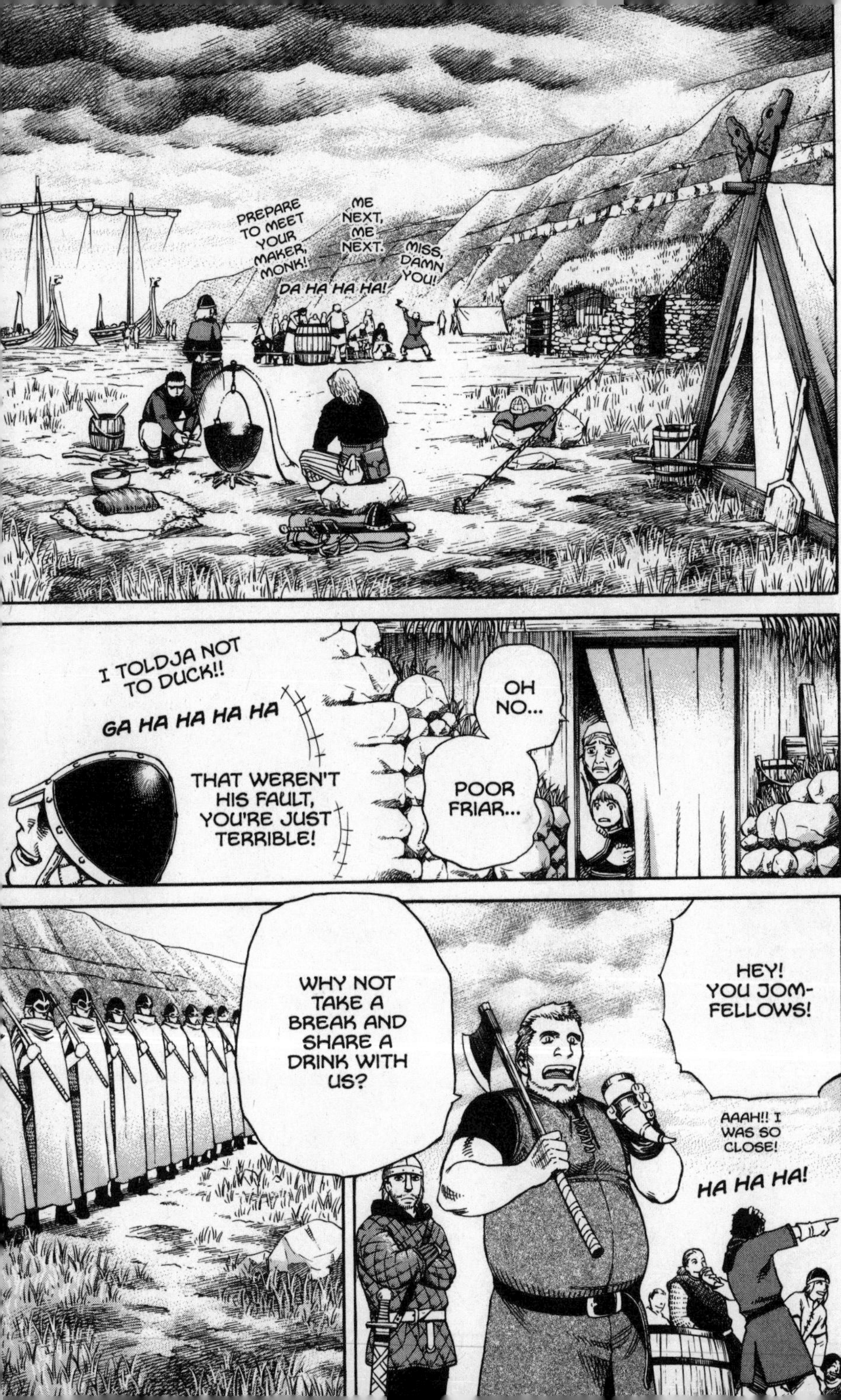
MISS, DAMN YOU!
ME NEXT, ME NEXT.
PREPARE TO MEET YOUR MAKER, MONK!
DA HA HA HA!
OH NO...
POOR FRIAR...
I TOLDJA NOT TO DUCK!!
GA HA HA HA HA
THAT WEREN'T HIS FAULT, YOU'RE JUST TERRIBLE!
HEY! YOU JOM-FELLOWS!
AAAH!! I WAS SO CLOSE!
HA HA HA!
WHY NOT TAKE A BREAK AND SHARE A DRINK WITH US?

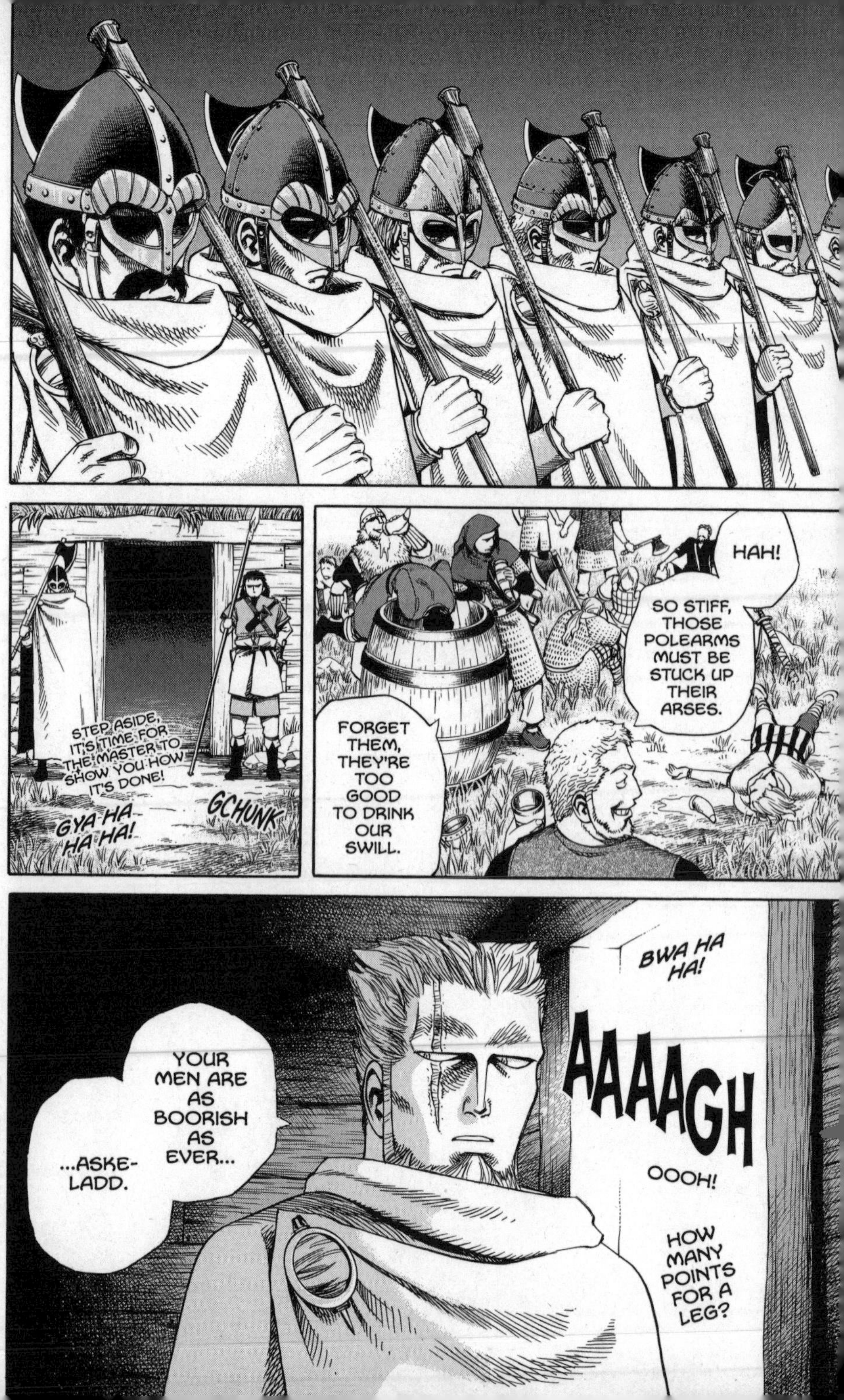
HAH!
SO STIFF, THOSE POLEARMS MUST BE STUCK UP THEIR ARSES.
FORGET THEM, THEY'RE TOO GOOD TO DRINK OUR SWILL.
STEP ASIDE, IT'S TIME FOR THE MASTER TO SHOW YOU HOW IT'S DONE!
GCHUNK
GYA HA HA HA!
BWA HA HA!
AAAAGH
OOOH!
HOW MANY POINTS FOR A LEG?
YOUR MEN ARE AS BOORISH AS EVER...
...ASKE-LADD.

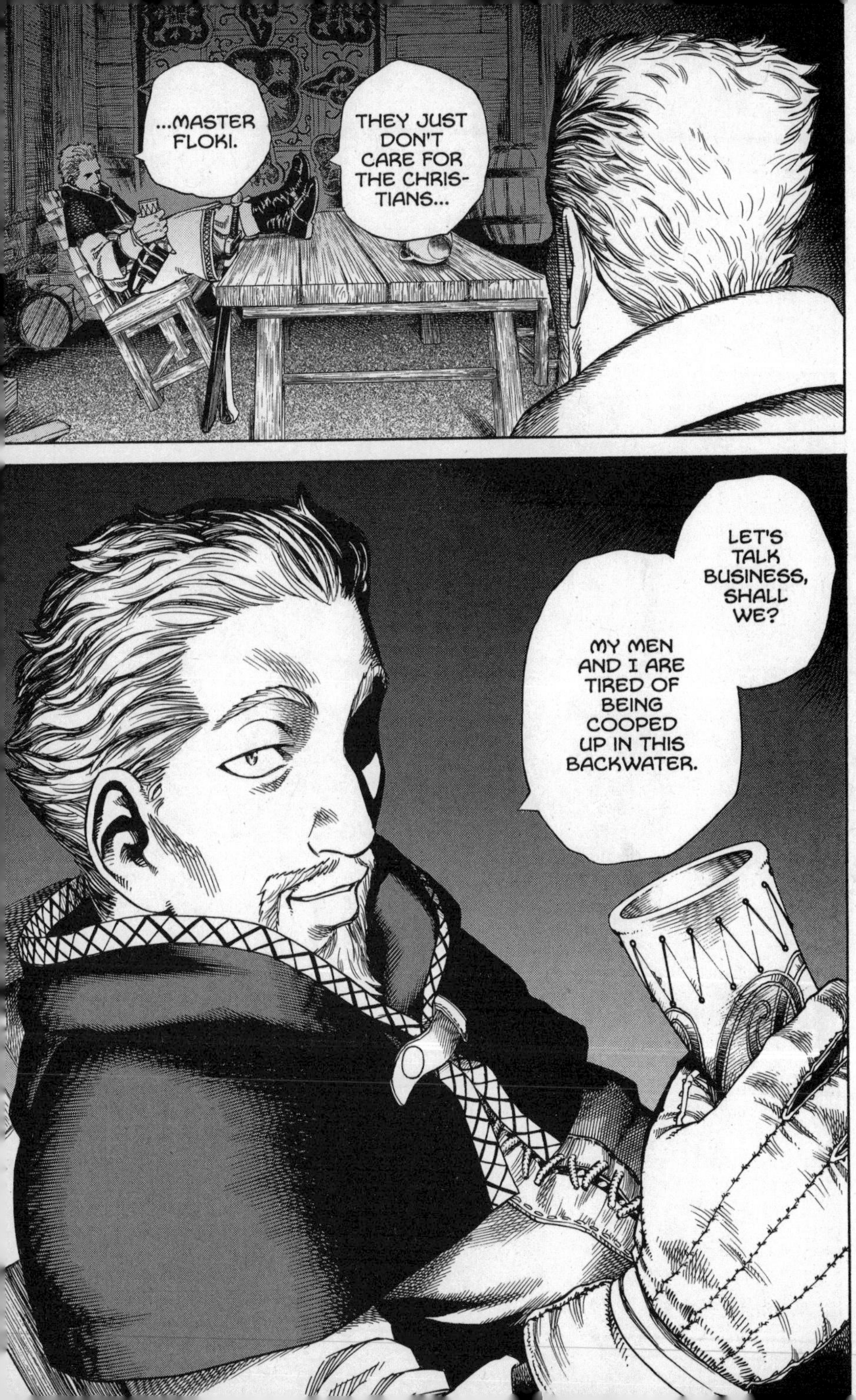
THEY JUST DON'T CARE FOR THE CHRIS-TIANS...
...MASTER FLOKI.
LET'S TALK BUSINESS, SHALL WE?
MY MEN AND I ARE TIRED OF BEING COOPED UP IN THIS BACKWATER.

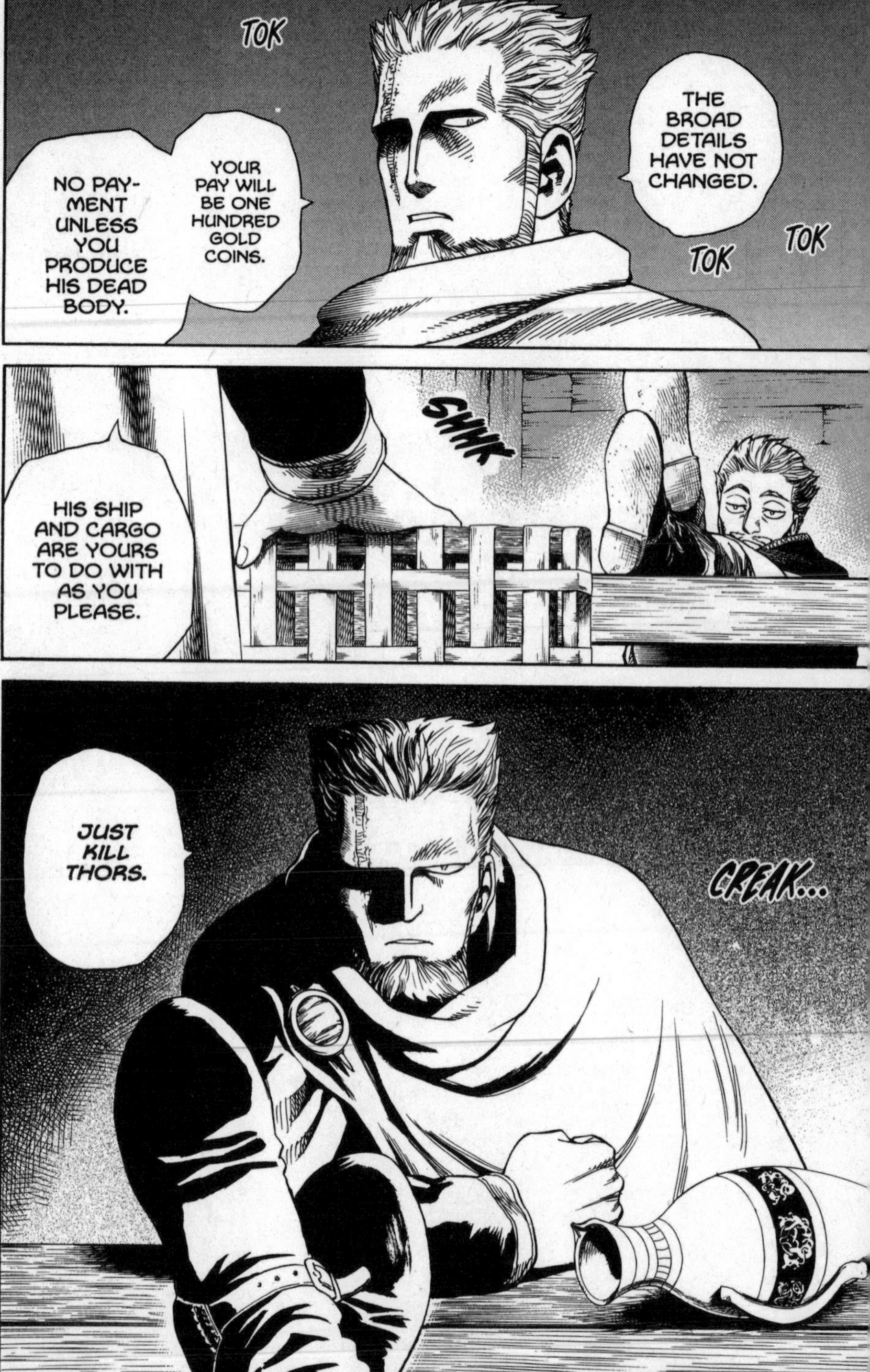
THE BROAD DETAILS HAVE NOT CHANGED.
TOK
TOK
TOK
YOUR PAY WILL BE ONE HUNDRED GOLD COINS.
NO PAY-MENT UNLESS YOU PRODUCE HIS DEAD BODY.
SHHK
HIS SHIP AND CARGO ARE YOURS TO DO WITH AS YOU PLEASE.
CREAK...
JUST KILL THORS.

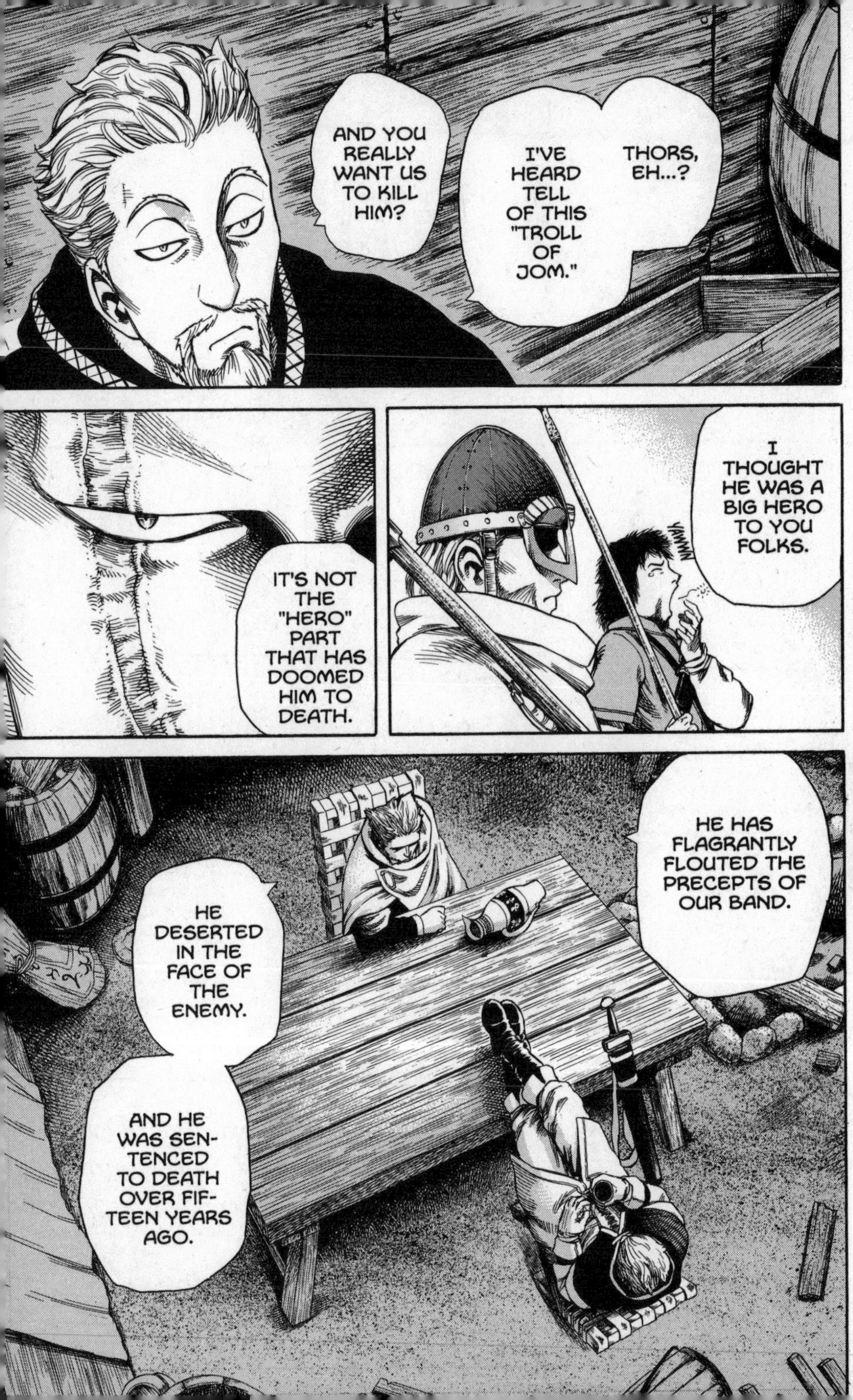
THORS, EH...?
I'VE HEARD TELL OF THIS "TROLL OF JOM."
AND YOU REALLY WANT US TO KILL HIM?
I THOUGHT HE WAS A BIG HERO TO YOU FOLKS.
YAWWN
IT'S NOT THE "HERO" PART THAT HAS DOOMED HIM TO DEATH.
HE HAS FLAGRANTLY FLOUTED THE PRECEPTS OF OUR BAND.
HE DESERTED IN THE FACE OF THE ENEMY.
AND HE WAS SENTENCED TO DEATH OVER FIFTEEN YEARS AGO.

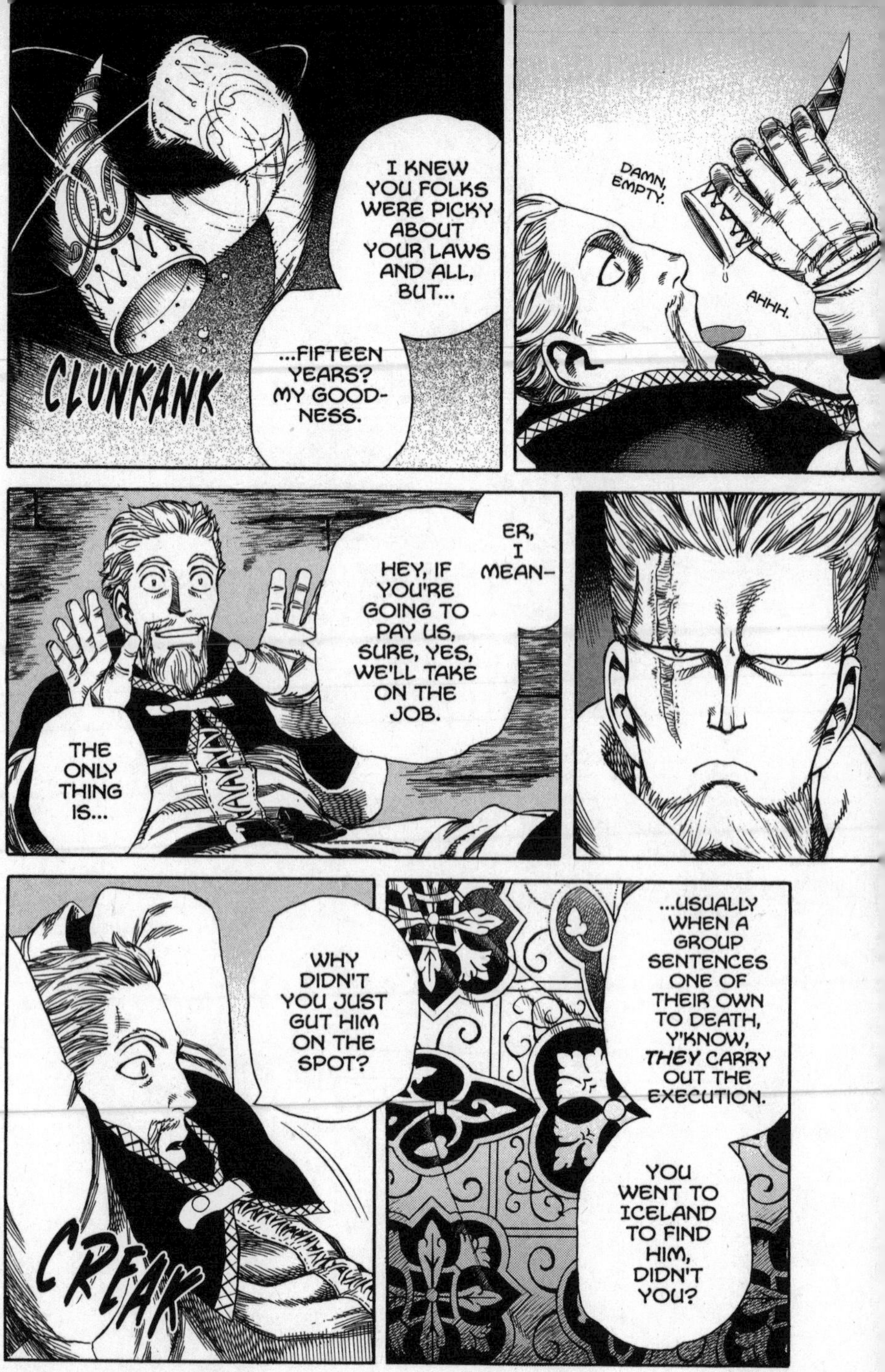
DAMN, EMPTY.
AHHH.
I KNEW YOU FOLKS WERE PICKY ABOUT YOUR LAWS AND ALL, BUT...
...FIFTEEN YEARS? MY GOOD-NESS.
CLUNKANK
ER, I MEAN-
HEY, IF YOU'RE GOING TO PAY US, SURE, YES, WE'LL TAKE ON THE JOB.
THE ONLY THING IS...
...USUALLY WHEN A GROUP SENTENCES ONE OF THEIR OWN TO DEATH, Y'KNOW, *THEY* CARRY OUT THE EXECUTION.
YOU WENT TO ICELAND TO FIND HIM, DIDN'T YOU?
WHY DIDN'T YOU JUST GUT HIM ON THE SPOT?
CREAK

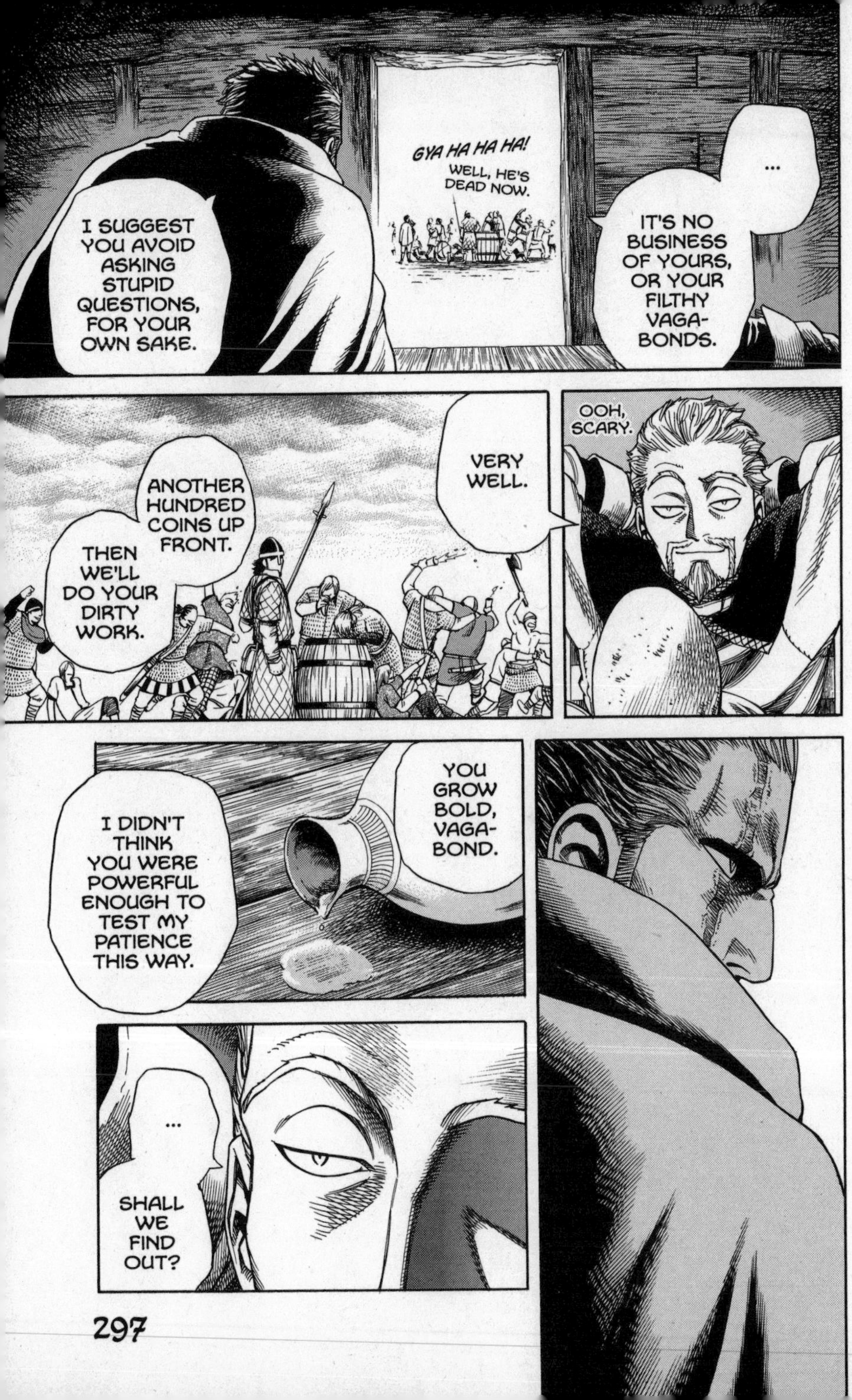
...
IT'S NO BUSINESS OF YOURS, OR YOUR FILTHY VAGABONDS.
GYA HA HA HA!
WELL, HE'S DEAD NOW.
I SUGGEST YOU AVOID ASKING STUPID QUESTIONS, FOR YOUR OWN SAKE.
OOH, SCARY.
VERY WELL.
ANOTHER HUNDRED COINS UP FRONT.
THEN WE'LL DO YOUR DIRTY WORK.
YOU GROW BOLD, VAGABOND.
I DIDN'T THINK YOU WERE POWERFUL ENOUGH TO TEST MY PATIENCE THIS WAY.
...
SHALL WE FIND OUT?

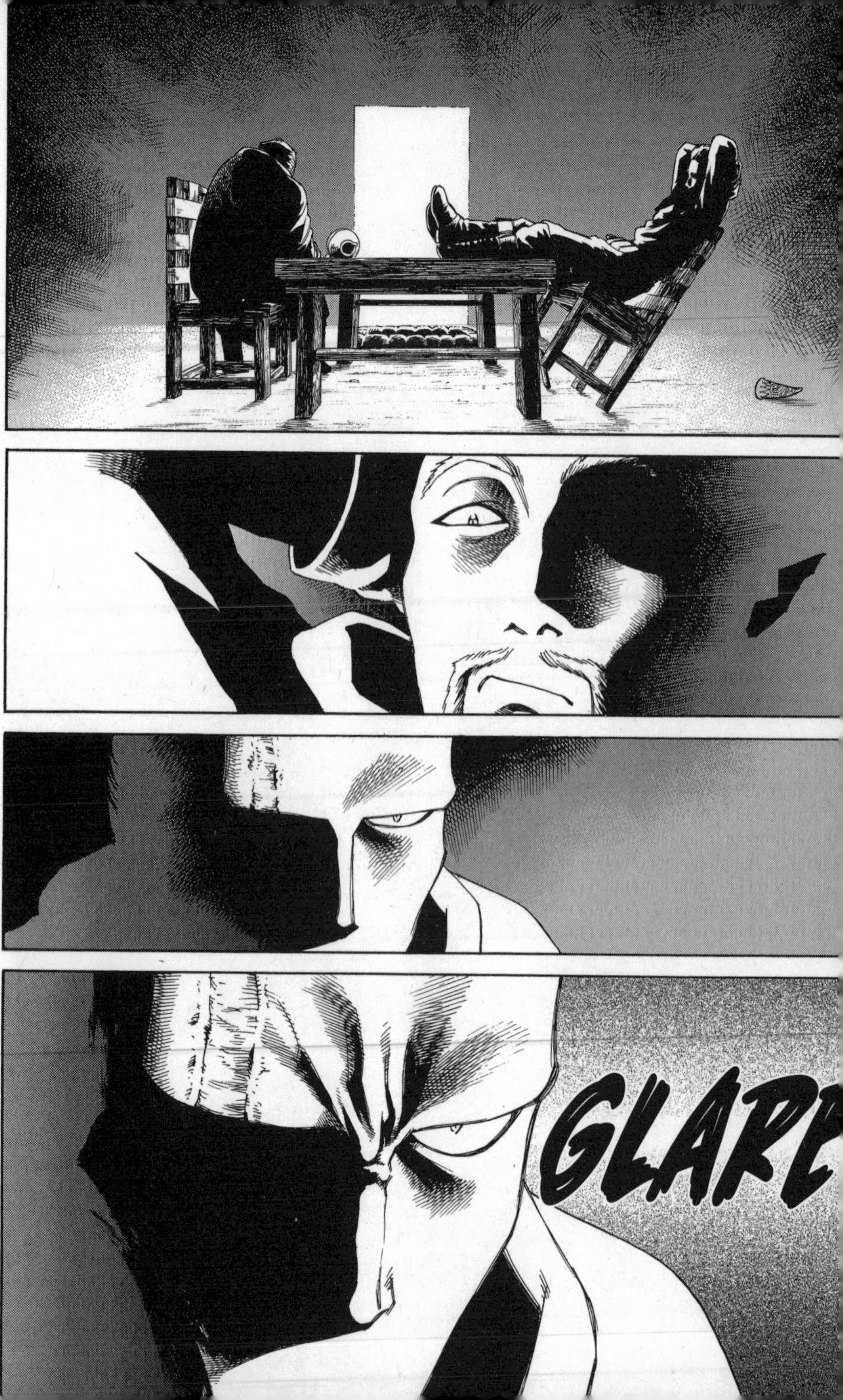
GLARE

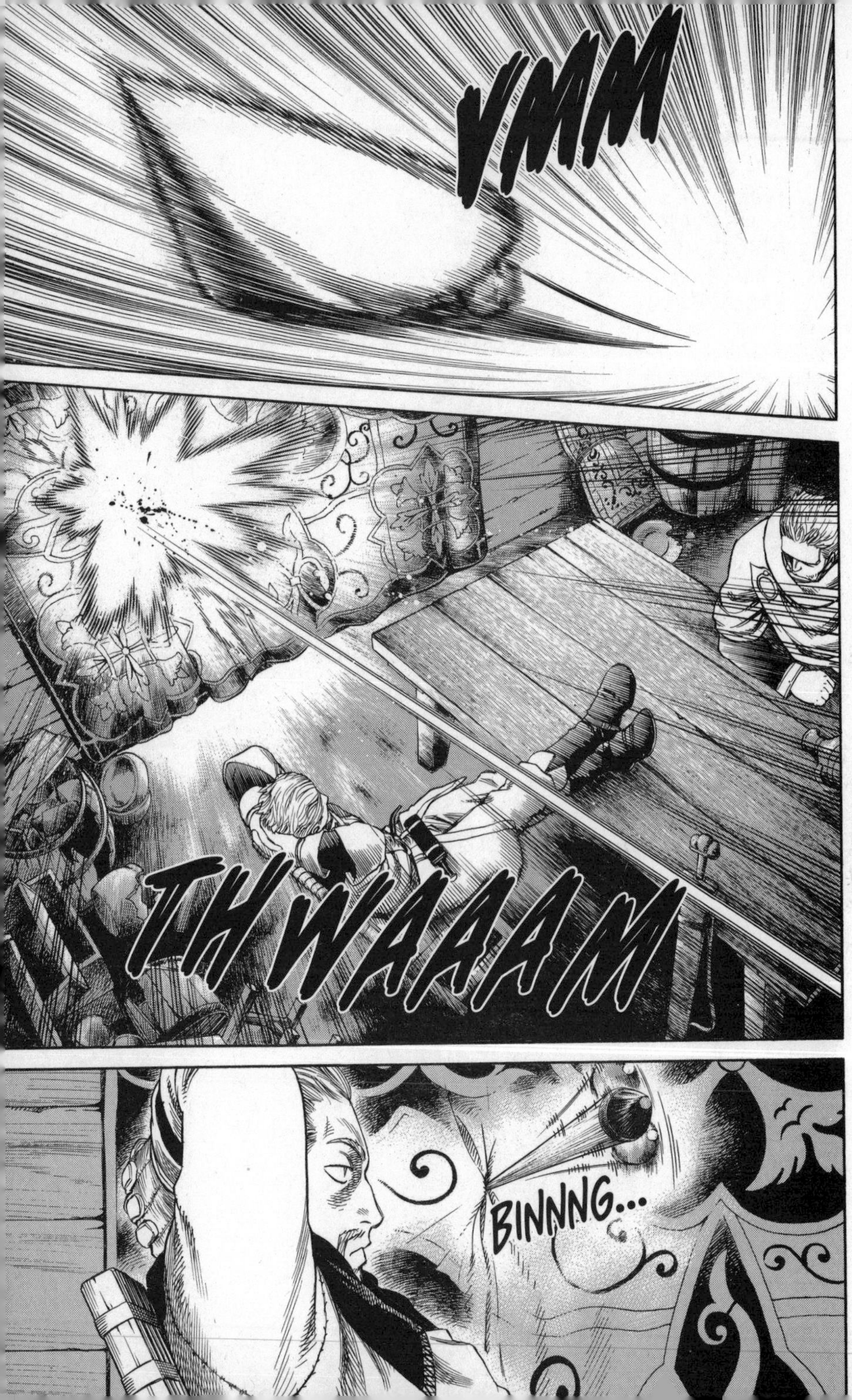
VMM
THWAAAM
BINNNG...

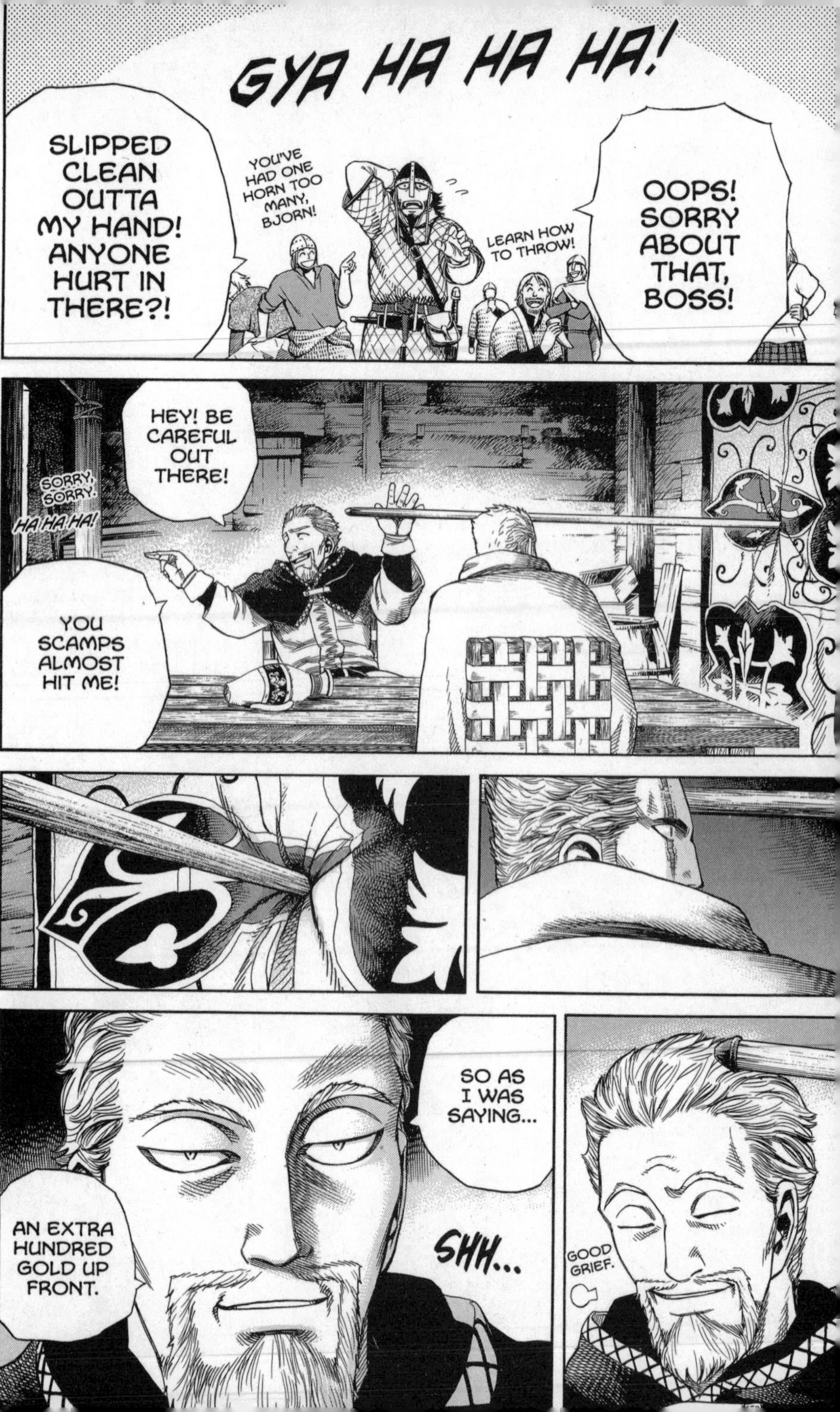
GYA HA HA HA!
OOPS! SORRY ABOUT THAT, BOSS!
LEARN HOW TO THROW!
YOU'VE HAD ONE HORN TOO MANY, BJORN!
SLIPPED CLEAN OUTTA MY HAND! ANYONE HURT IN THERE?!
HEY! BE CAREFUL OUT THERE!
SORRY, SORRY.
HA HA HA!
YOU SCAMPS ALMOST HIT ME!
GOOD GRIEF.
SO AS I WAS SAYING...
SHH...
AN EXTRA HUNDRED GOLD UP FRONT.

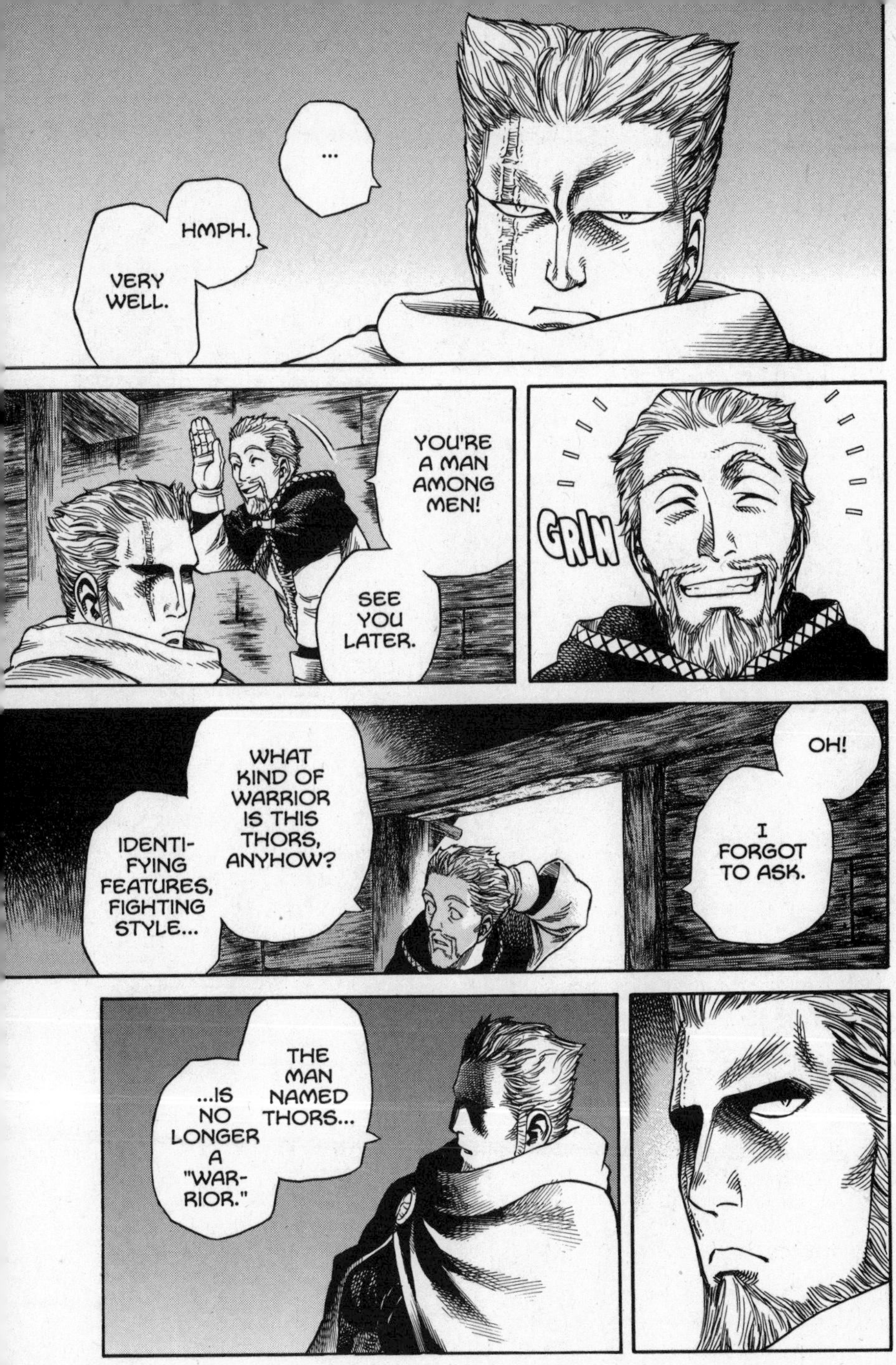
...
HMPH.
VERY WELL.
GRIN
YOU'RE A MAN AMONG MEN!
SEE YOU LATER.
OH!
I FORGOT TO ASK.
WHAT KIND OF WARRIOR IS THIS THORS, ANYHOW?
IDENTI-FYING FEATURES, FIGHTING STYLE...
THE MAN NAMED THORS...
...IS NO LONGER A "WAR-RIOR."

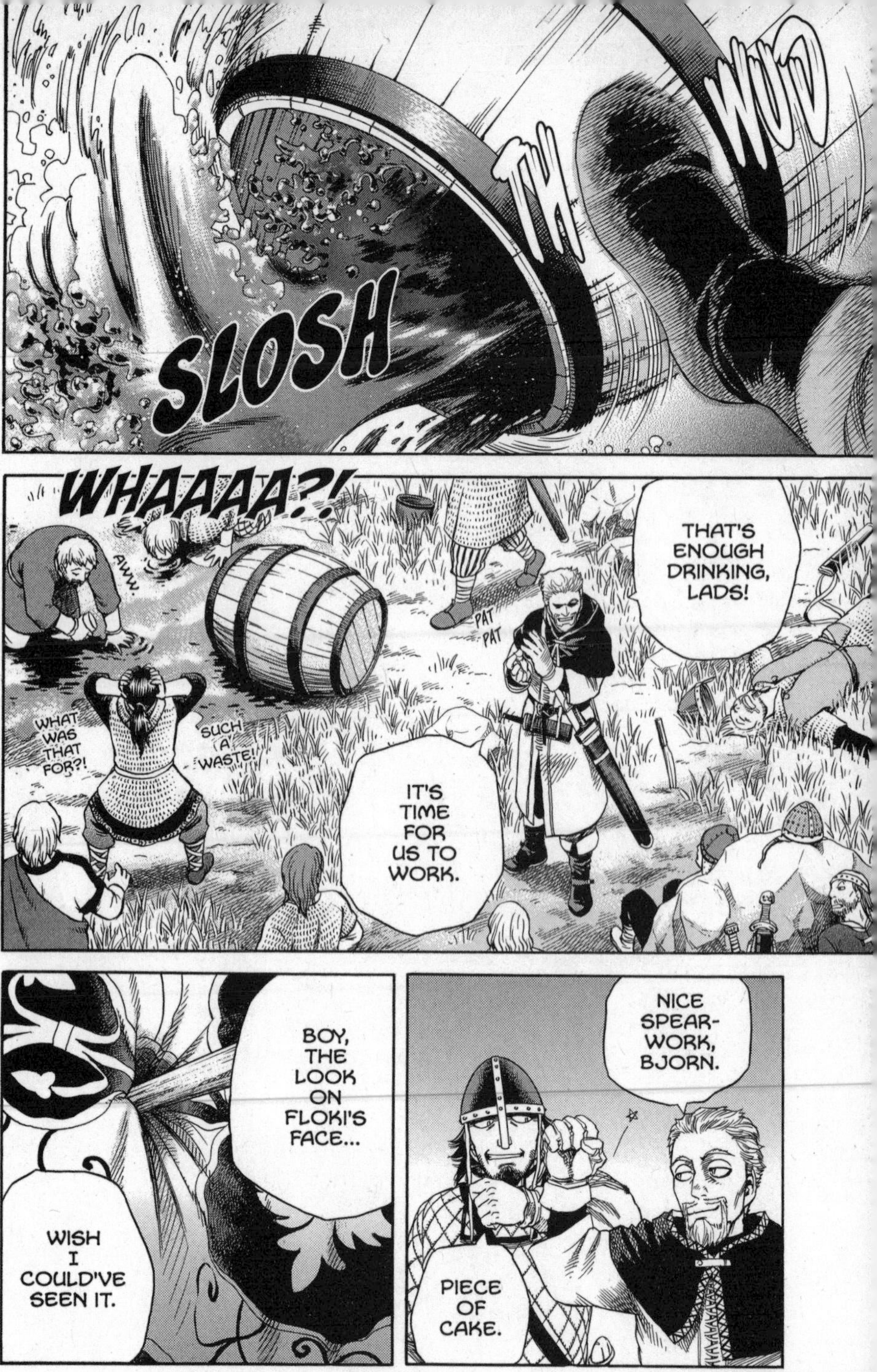
THWUD
SLOSH
THAT'S ENOUGH DRINKING, LADS!
PAT PAT
IT'S TIME FOR US TO WORK.
WHAAAA?!
SUCH A WASTE!
WHAT WAS THAT FOR?!
AWW.
NICE SPEAR-WORK, BJORN.
PIECE OF CAKE.
BOY, THE LOOK ON FLOKI'S FACE...
WISH I COULD'VE SEEN IT.

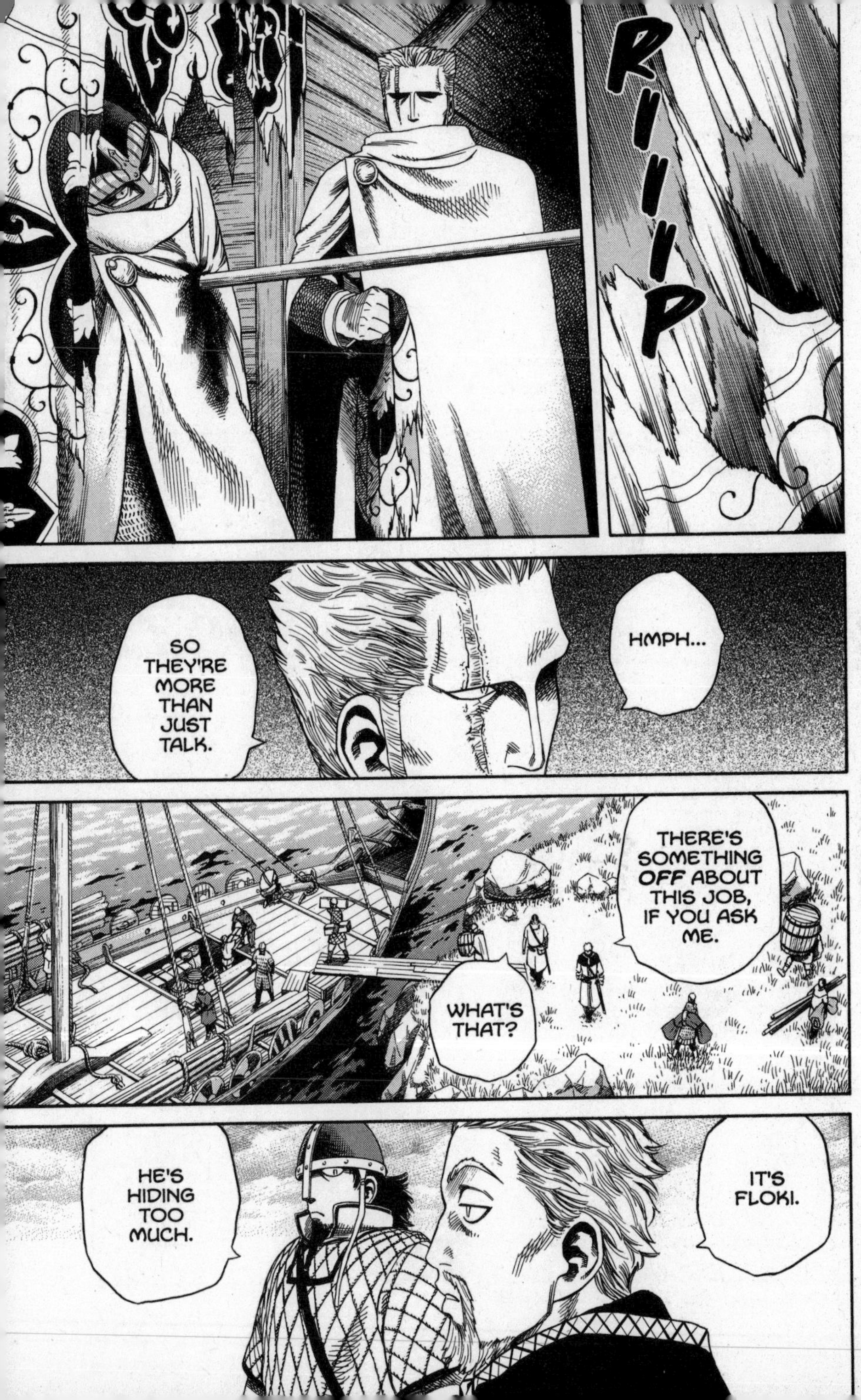
RIIIIP
HMPH...
SO THEY'RE MORE THAN JUST TALK.
THERE'S SOMETHING *OFF* ABOUT THIS JOB, IF YOU ASK ME.
WHAT'S THAT?
IT'S FLOKI.
HE'S HIDING TOO MUCH.

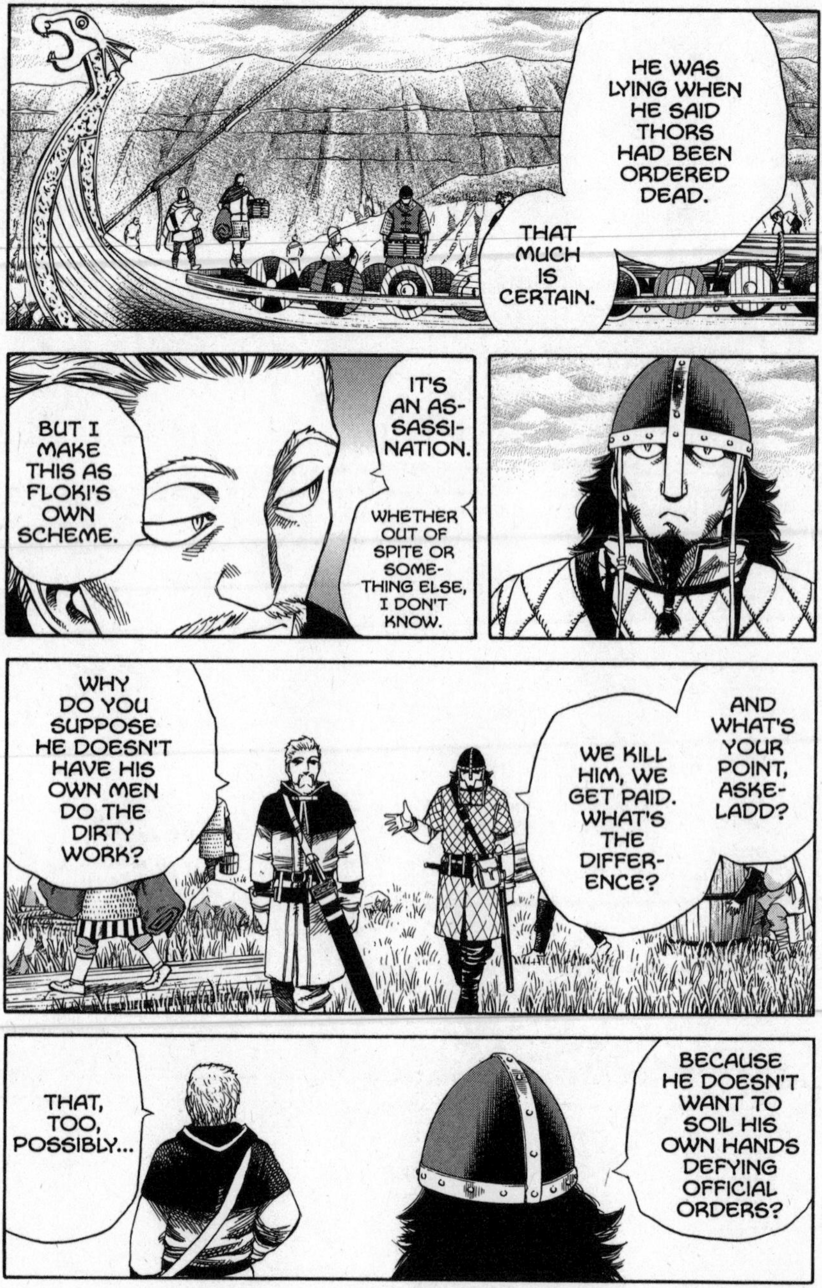
HE WAS LYING WHEN HE SAID THORS HAD BEEN ORDERED DEAD.
THAT MUCH IS CERTAIN.
IT'S AN ASSASSINATION.
BUT I MAKE THIS AS FLOKI'S OWN SCHEME.
WHETHER OUT OF SPITE OR SOMETHING ELSE, I DON'T KNOW.
AND WHAT'S YOUR POINT, ASKELADD?
WE KILL HIM, WE GET PAID. WHAT'S THE DIFFERENCE?
WHY DO YOU SUPPOSE HE DOESN'T HAVE HIS OWN MEN DO THE DIRTY WORK?
BECAUSE HE DOESN'T WANT TO SOIL HIS OWN HANDS DEFYING OFFICIAL ORDERS?
THAT, TOO, POSSIBLY...

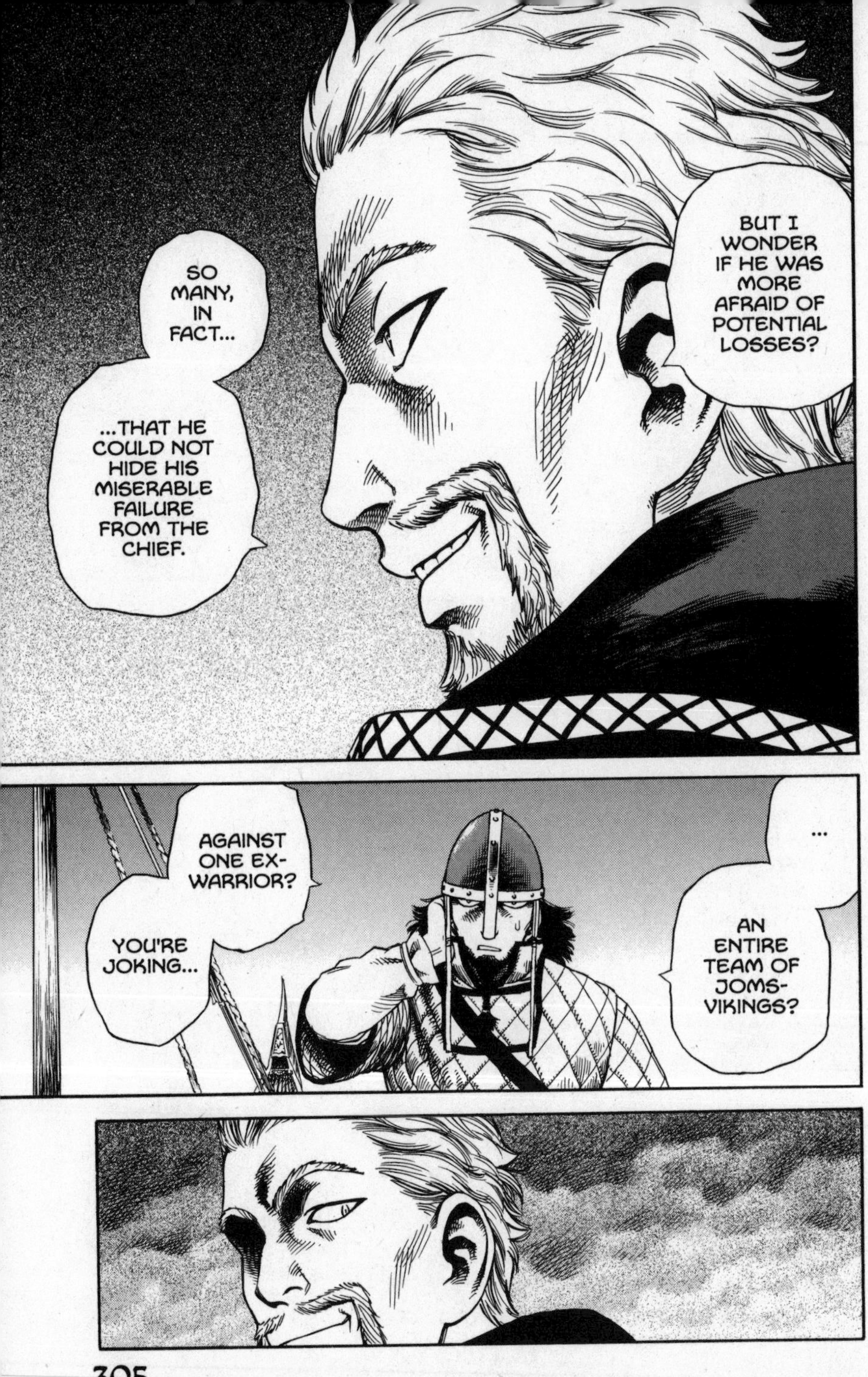
BUT I WONDER IF HE WAS MORE AFRAID OF POTENTIAL LOSSES?
SO MANY, IN FACT...
...THAT HE COULD NOT HIDE HIS MISERABLE FAILURE FROM THE CHIEF.
...
AN ENTIRE TEAM OF JOMS-VIKINGS?
AGAINST ONE EX-WARRIOR?
YOU'RE JOKING...

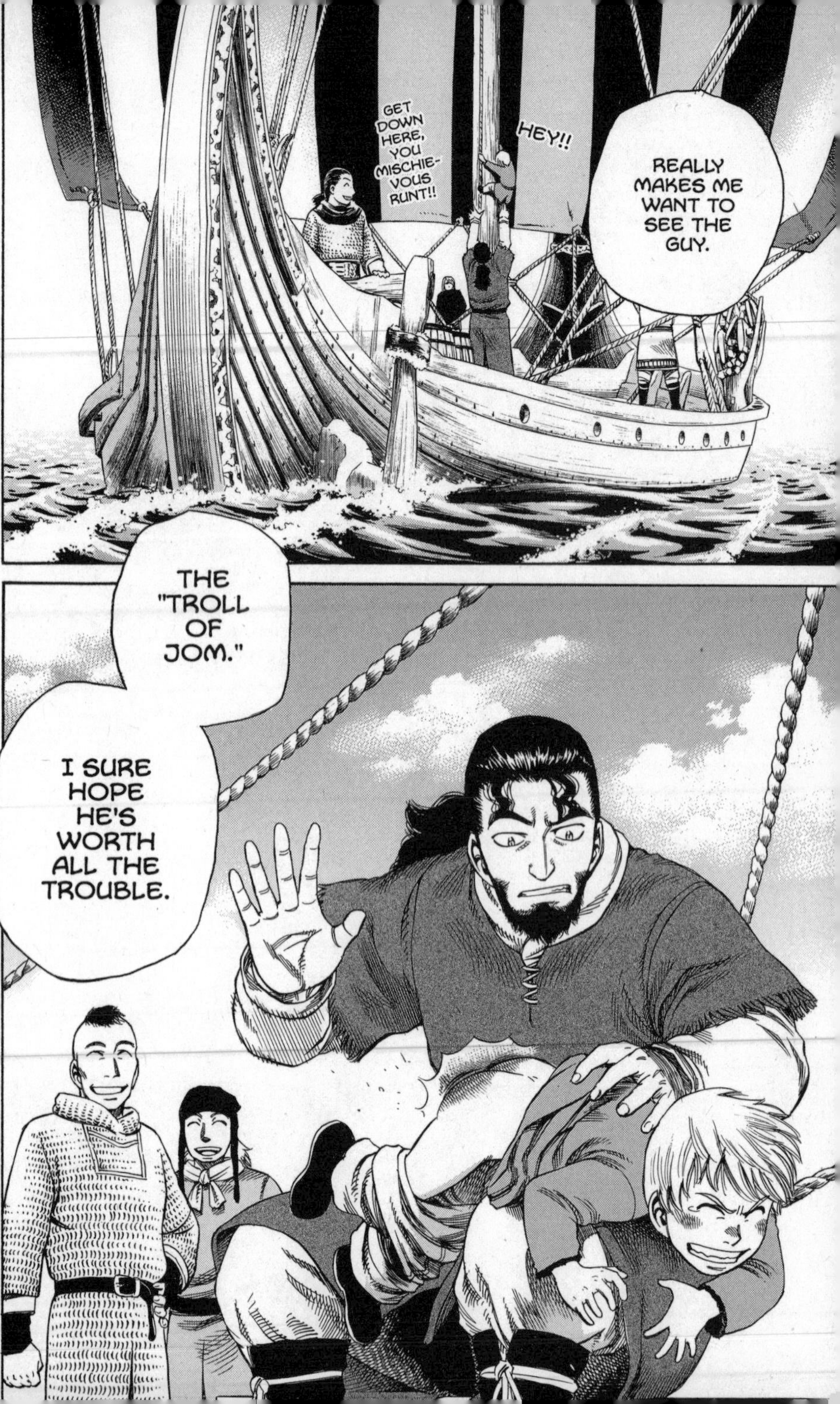
REALLY MAKES ME WANT TO SEE THE GUY.
HEY!!
GET DOWN HERE, YOU MISCHIE-VOUS RUNT!!
THE "TROLL OF JOM."
I SURE HOPE HE'S WORTH ALL THE TROUBLE.

CHAPTER 9 - END

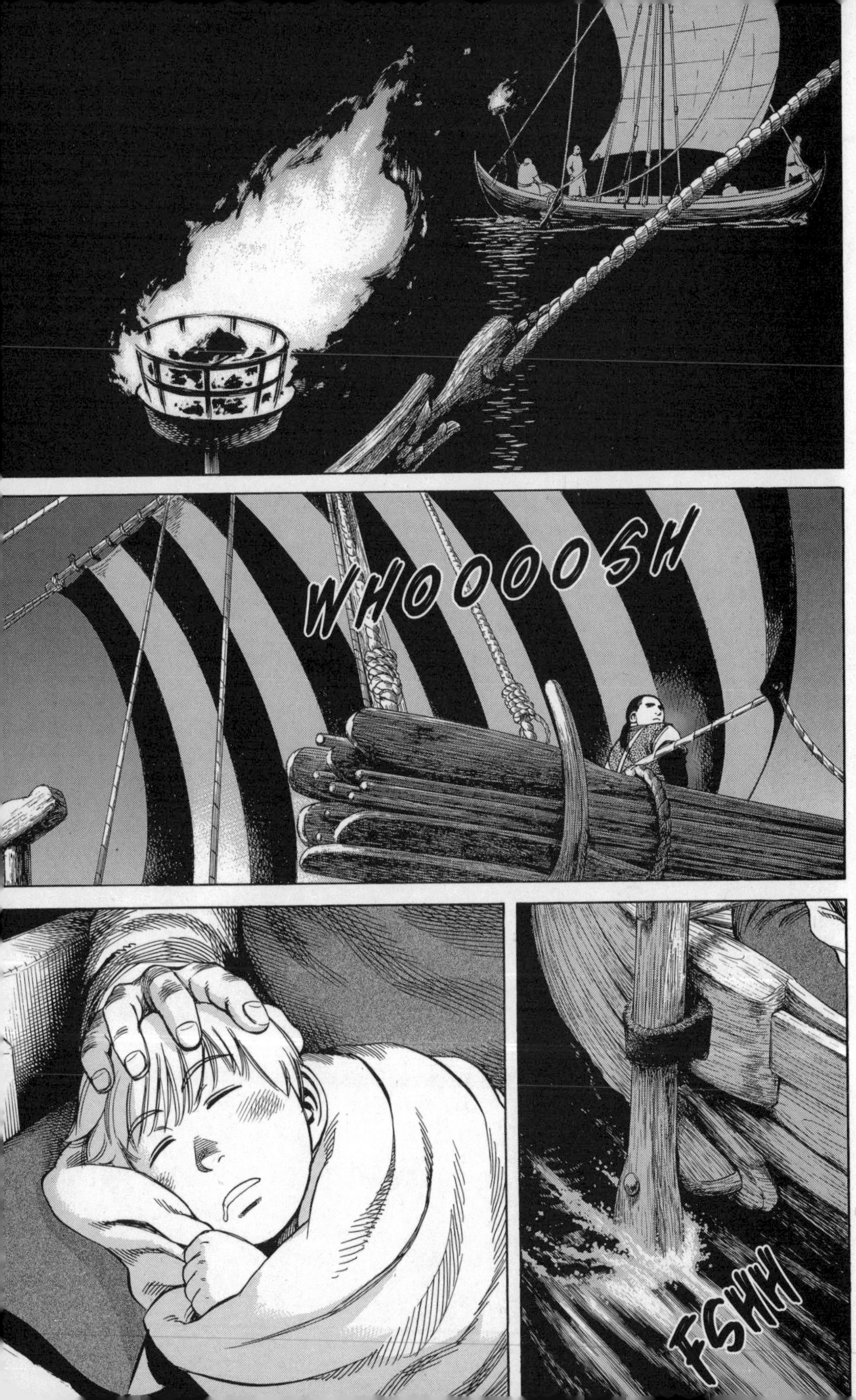
WHOOOOOSH
FSHH

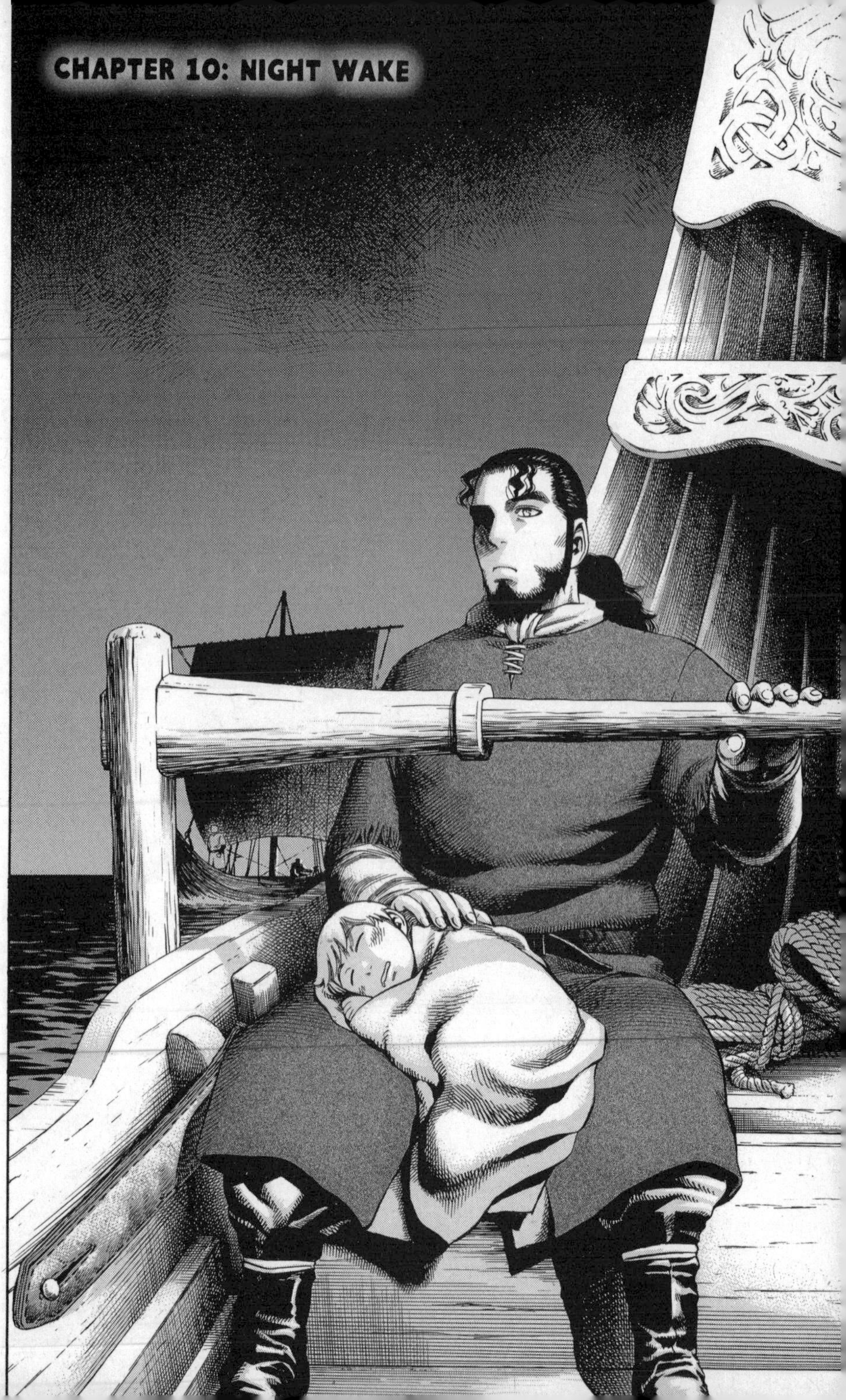
CHAPTER 10: NIGHT WAKE

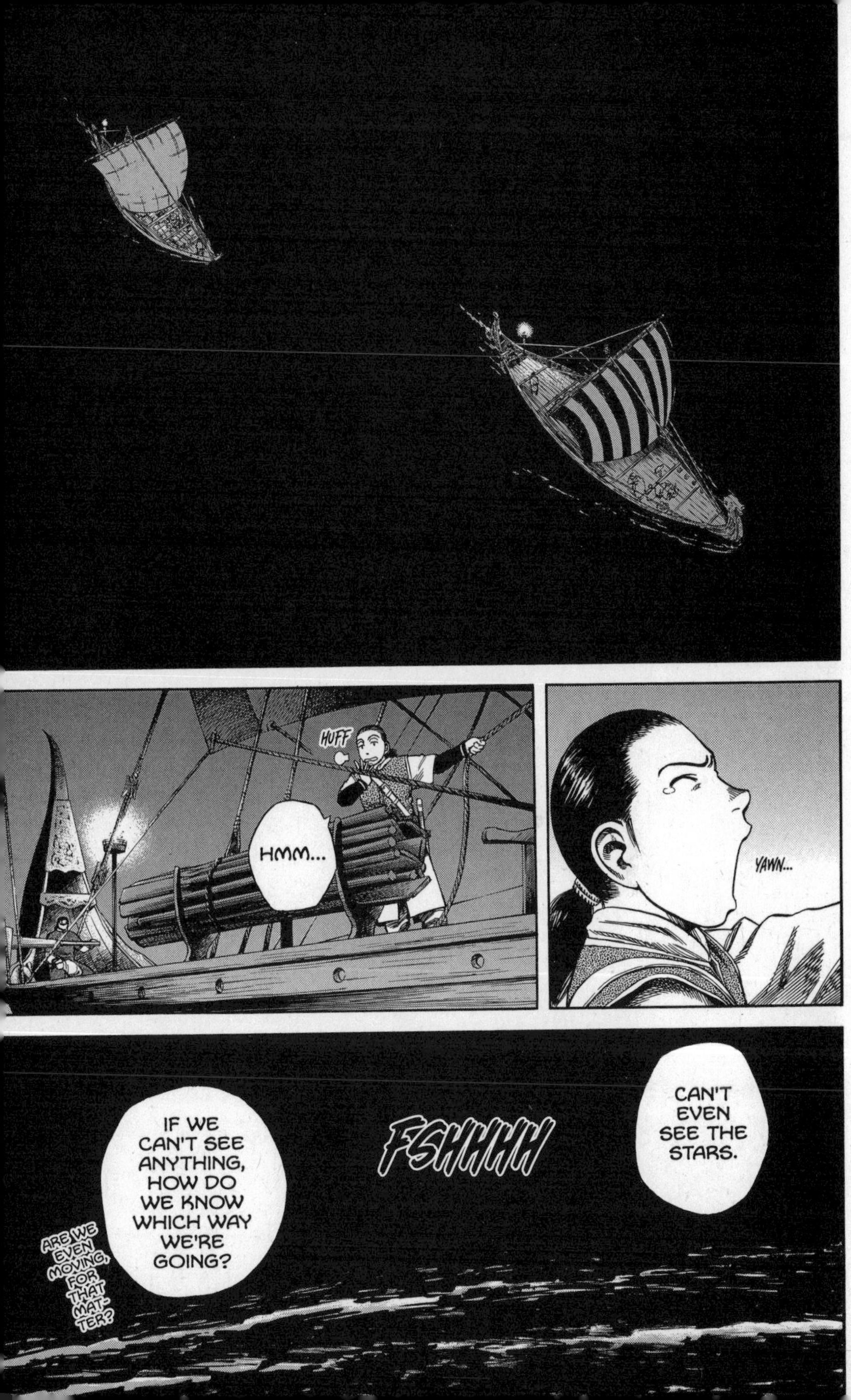
YAWN...
HUFF
HMM...
CAN'T EVEN SEE THE STARS.
FSHHHHH
IF WE CAN'T SEE ANYTHING, HOW DO WE KNOW WHICH WAY WE'RE GOING?
ARE WE EVEN MOVING, FOR THAT MAT-TER?

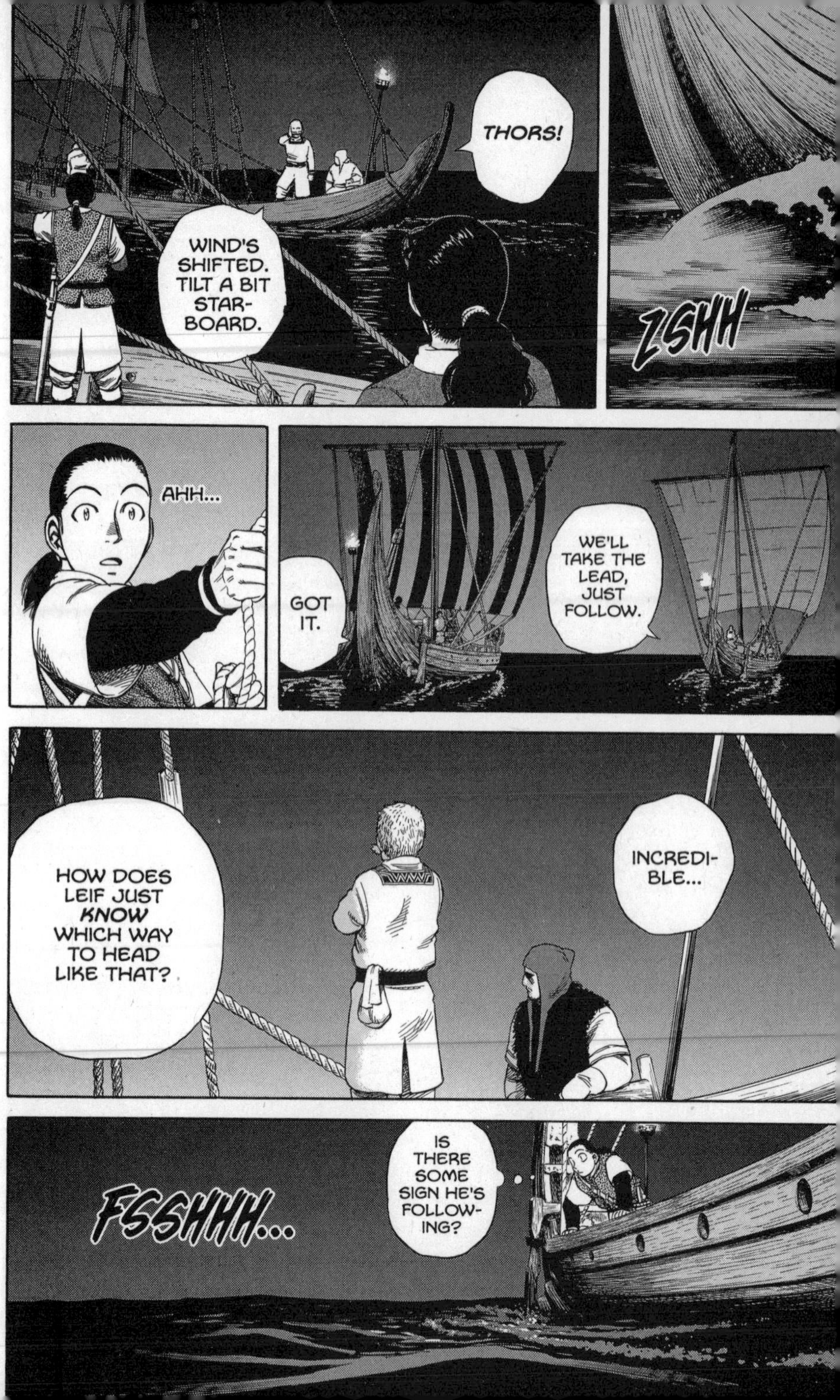
ZSHH
THORS!
WIND'S SHIFTED. TILT A BIT STAR-BOARD.
WE'LL TAKE THE LEAD, JUST FOLLOW.
GOT IT.
AHH...
INCREDI-BLE...
HOW DOES LEIF JUST **KNOW** WHICH WAY TO HEAD LIKE THAT?
IS THERE SOME SIGN HE'S FOLLOW-ING?
FSSHHH...

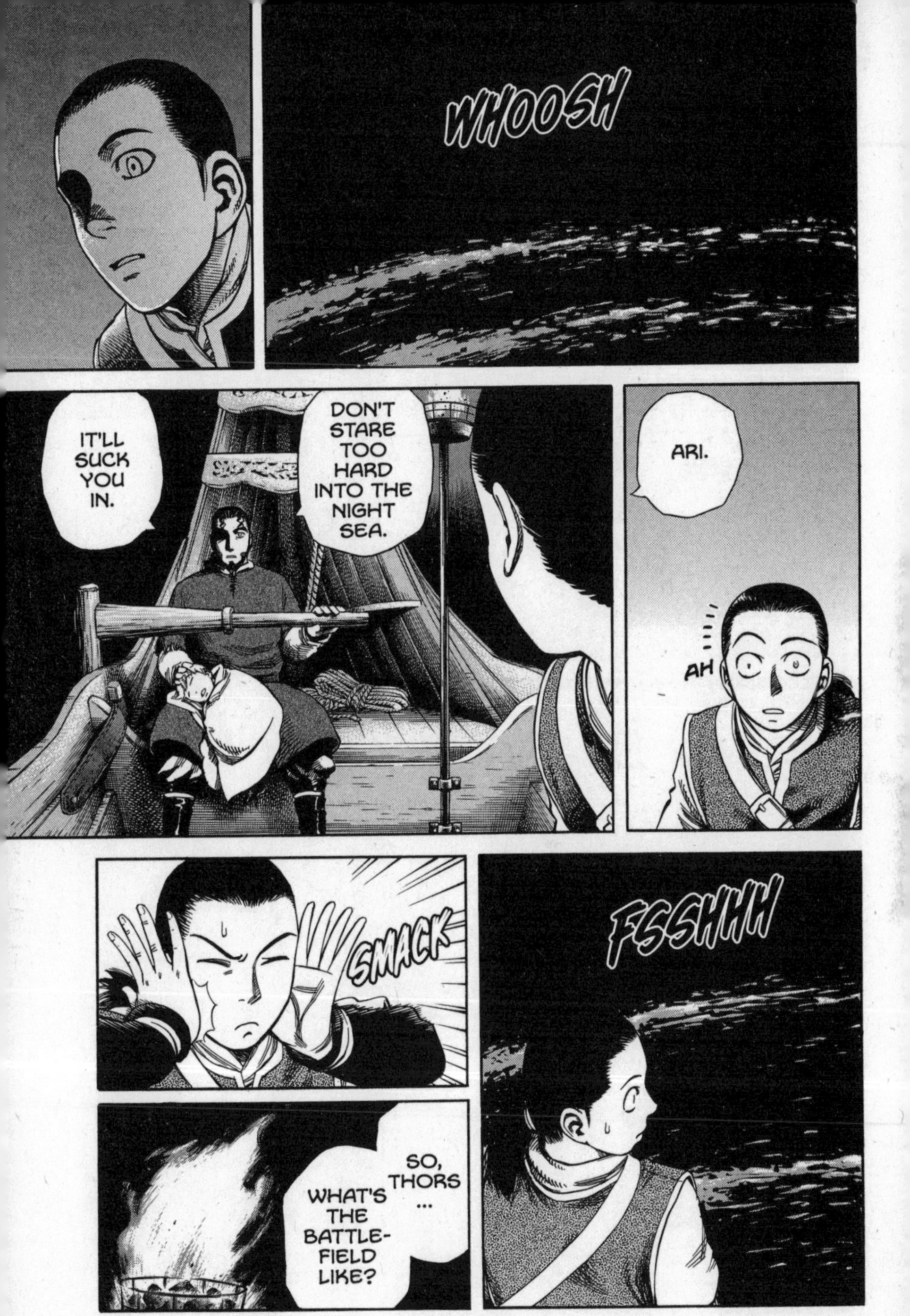
WHOOSH
ARI.
AH
DON'T STARE TOO HARD INTO THE NIGHT SEA.
IT'LL SUCK YOU IN.
FSSHHH
SMACK
SO, THORS...
WHAT'S THE BATTLE-FIELD LIKE?

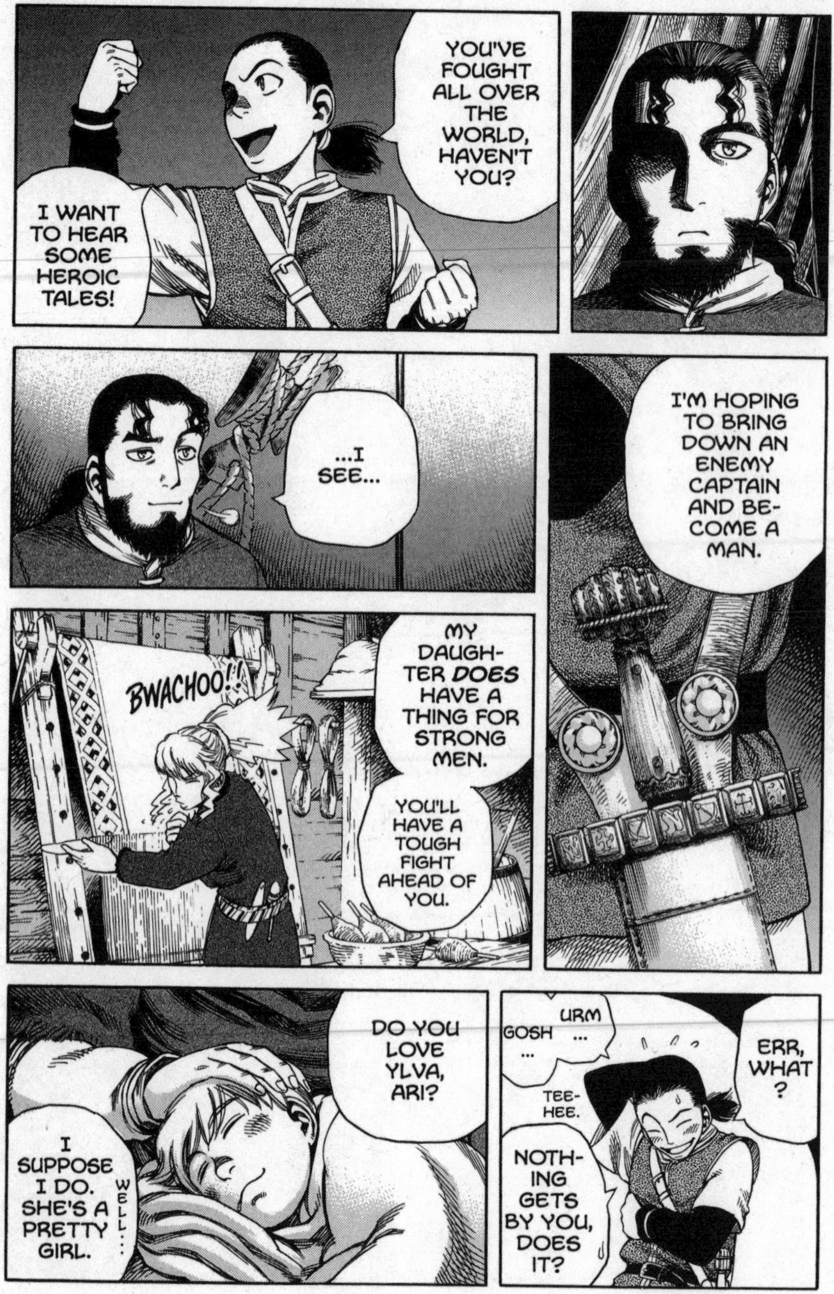
YOU'VE FOUGHT ALL OVER THE WORLD, HAVEN'T YOU?
I WANT TO HEAR SOME HEROIC TALES!
I'M HOPING TO BRING DOWN AN ENEMY CAPTAIN AND BE-COME A MAN.
...I SEE...
MY DAUGH-TER *DOES* HAVE A THING FOR STRONG MEN.
BWACHOO!!
YOU'LL HAVE A TOUGH FIGHT AHEAD OF YOU.
ERR, WHAT?
URM...
GOSH...
TEE-HEE.
NOTH-ING GETS BY YOU, DOES IT?
DO YOU LOVE YLVA, ARI?
WELL...
I SUPPOSE I DO. SHE'S A PRETTY GIRL.

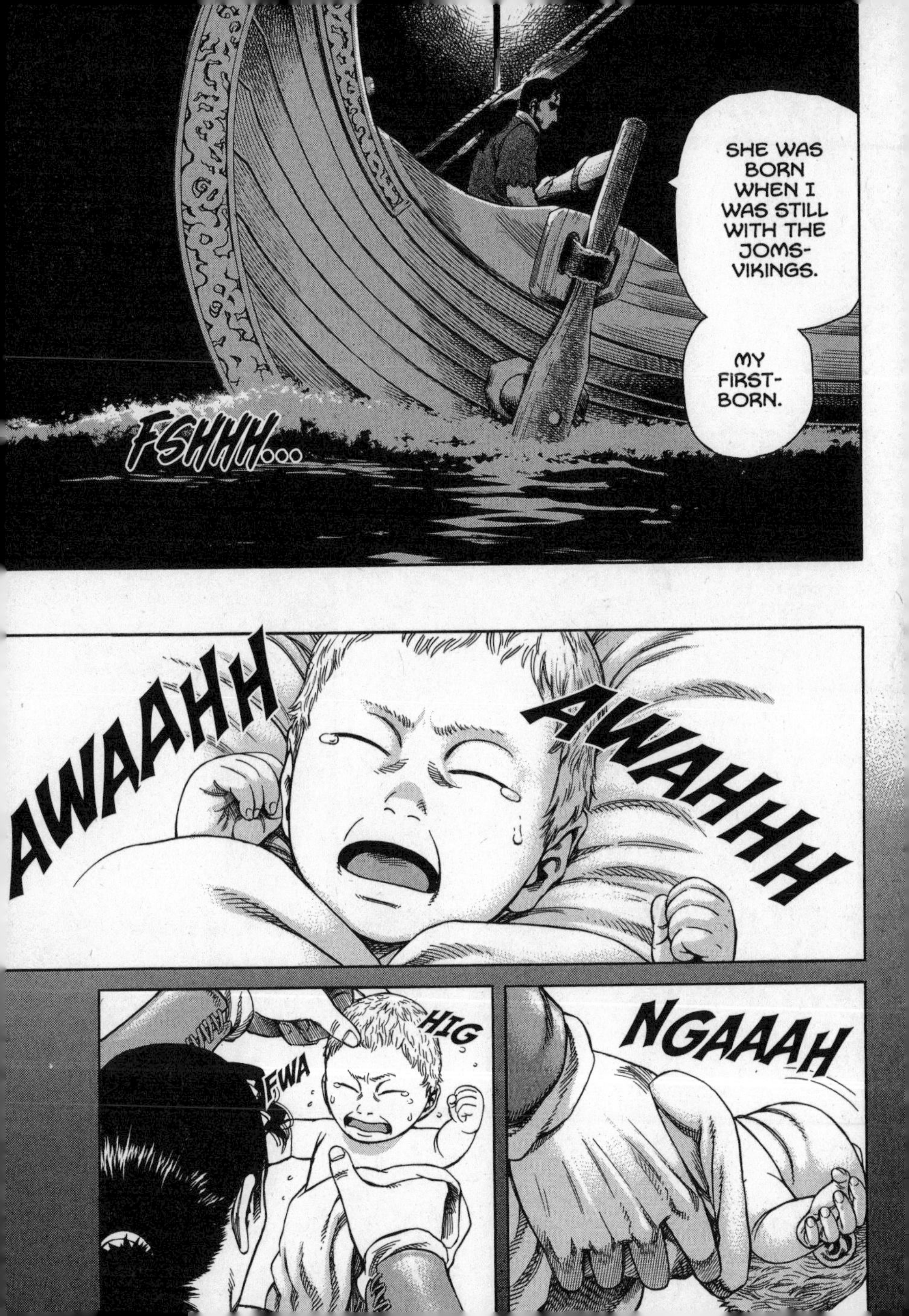
SHE WAS BORN WHEN I WAS STILL WITH THE JOMS-VIKINGS.
MY FIRST-BORN.
FSHHH...
AWAHHH
AWAAHH
NGAAAH
HIG
FWA

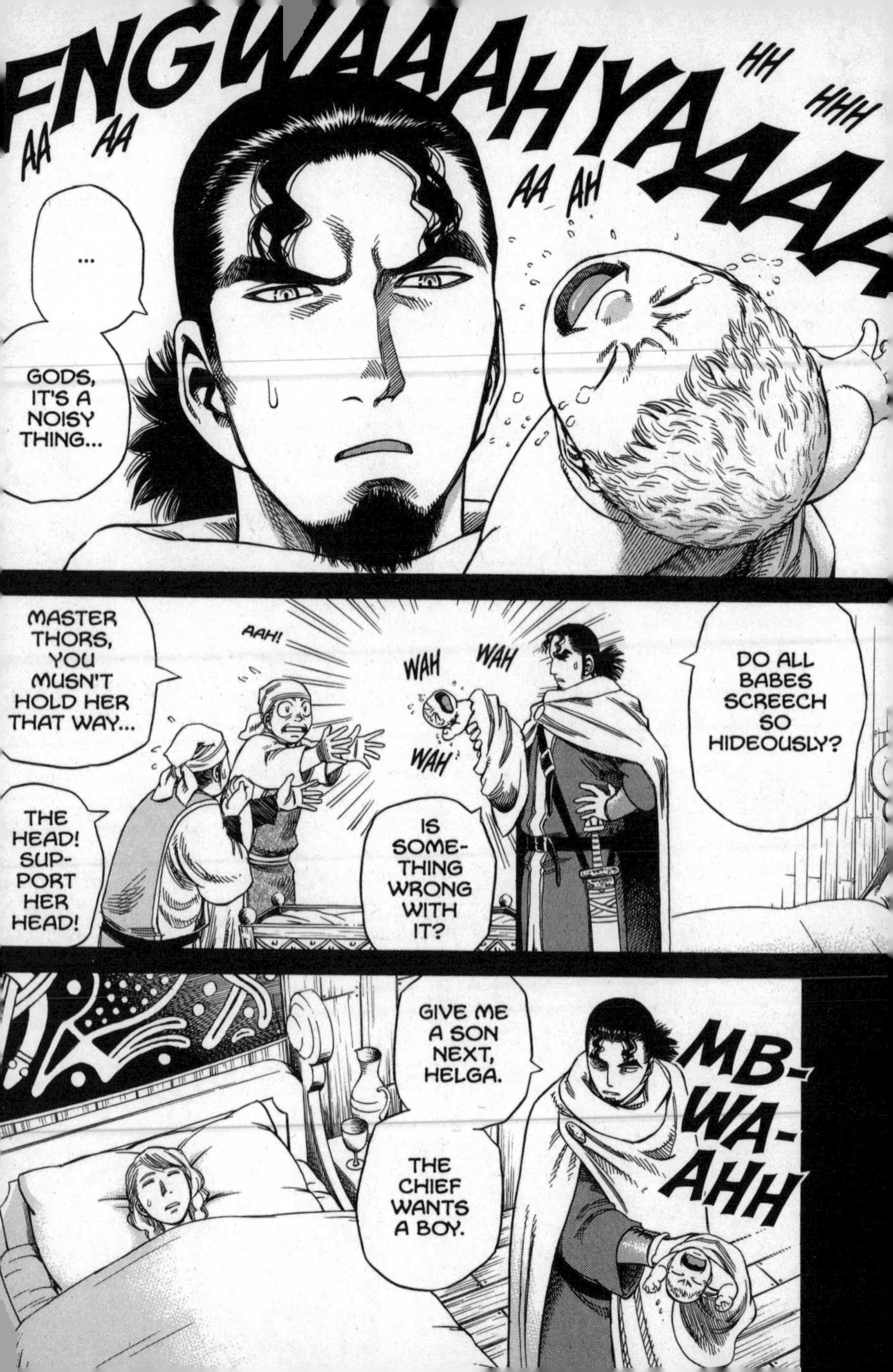
FNGWAAAAHYAAA
HH HHH
AA AH
AA AA
...
GODS, IT'S A NOISY THING...
DO ALL BABES SCREECH SO HIDEOUSLY?
WAH WAH
WAH
IS SOME-THING WRONG WITH IT?
AAH!
MASTER THORS, YOU MUSN'T HOLD HER THAT WAY...
THE HEAD! SUP-PORT HER HEAD!
MB-WA-AHH
GIVE ME A SON NEXT, HELGA.
THE CHIEF WANTS A BOY.

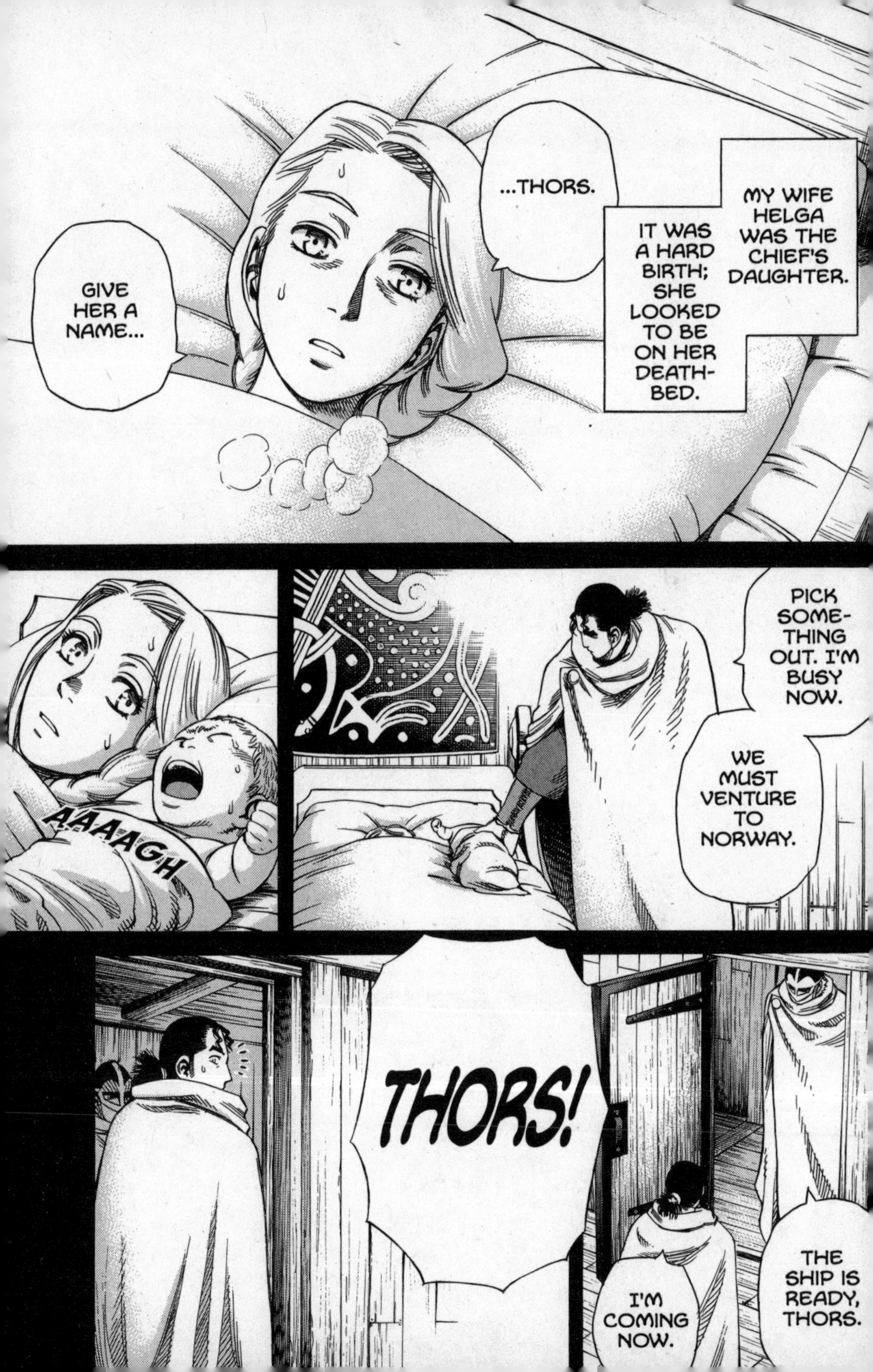

MY WIFE HELGA WAS THE CHIEF'S DAUGHTER.
IT WAS A HARD BIRTH; SHE LOOKED TO BE ON HER DEATHBED.
...THORS.
GIVE HER A NAME...
PICK SOMETHING OUT. I'M BUSY NOW.
WE MUST VENTURE TO NORWAY.
AAAAGH
THE SHIP IS READY, THORS.
I'M COMING NOW.
THORS!

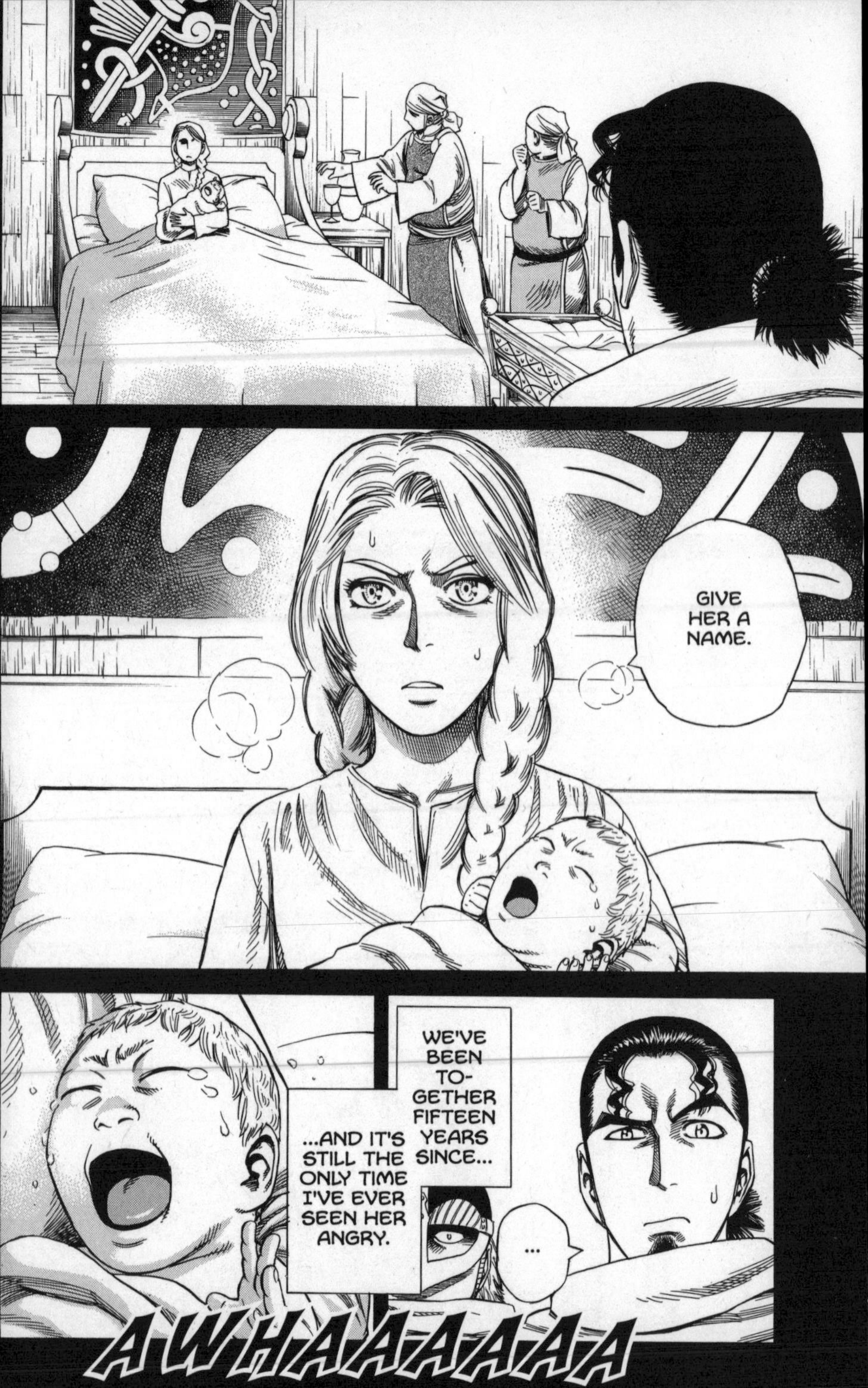
GIVE HER A NAME.
WE'VE BEEN TO-GETHER FIFTEEN YEARS SINCE...
...AND IT'S STILL THE ONLY TIME I'VE EVER SEEN HER ANGRY.
...
AWHAAAAAAA

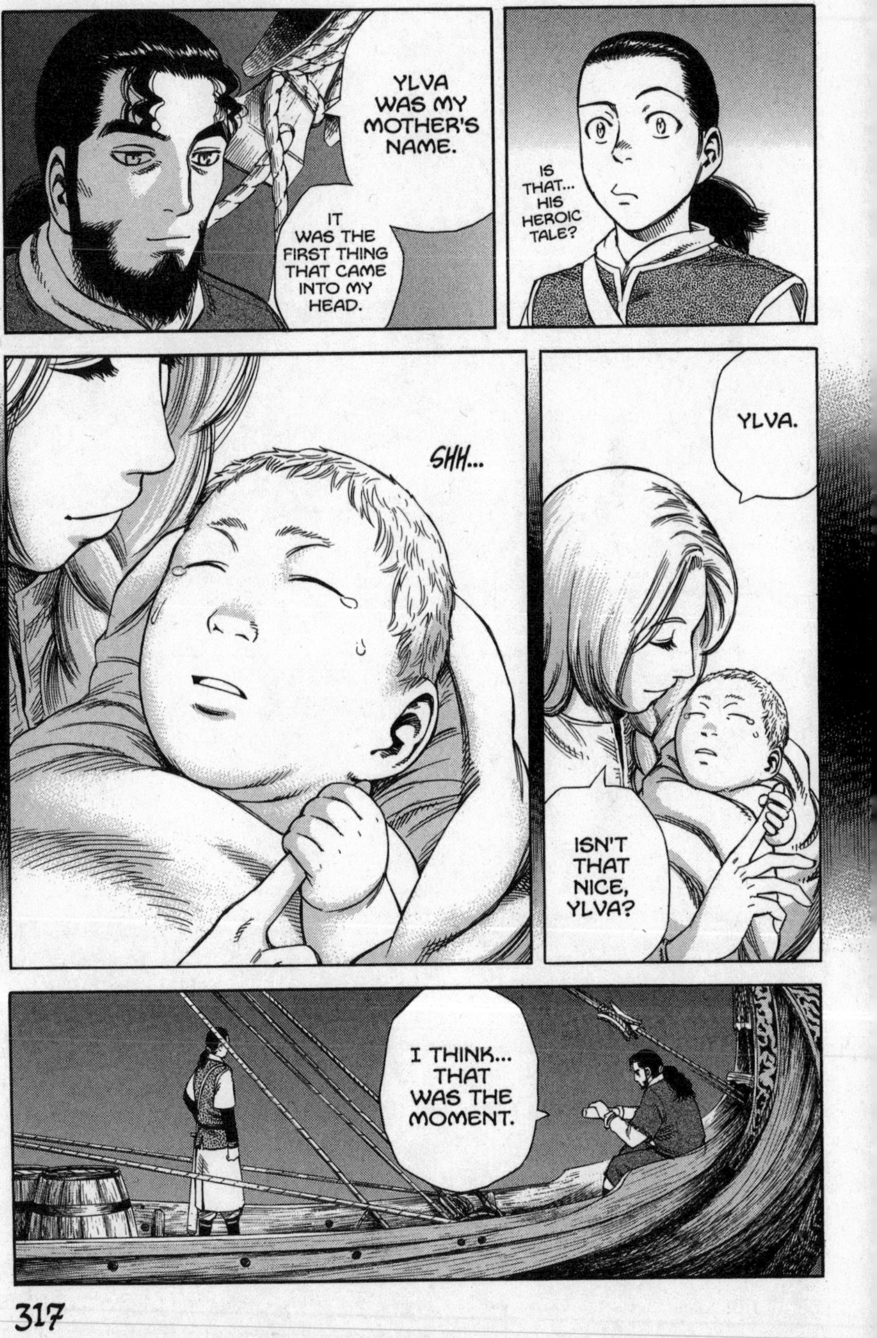
IS THAT... HIS HEROIC TALE?
YLVA WAS MY MOTHER'S NAME.
IT WAS THE FIRST THING THAT CAME INTO MY HEAD.
YLVA.
ISN'T THAT NICE, YLVA?
SHH...
I THINK... THAT WAS THE MOMENT.

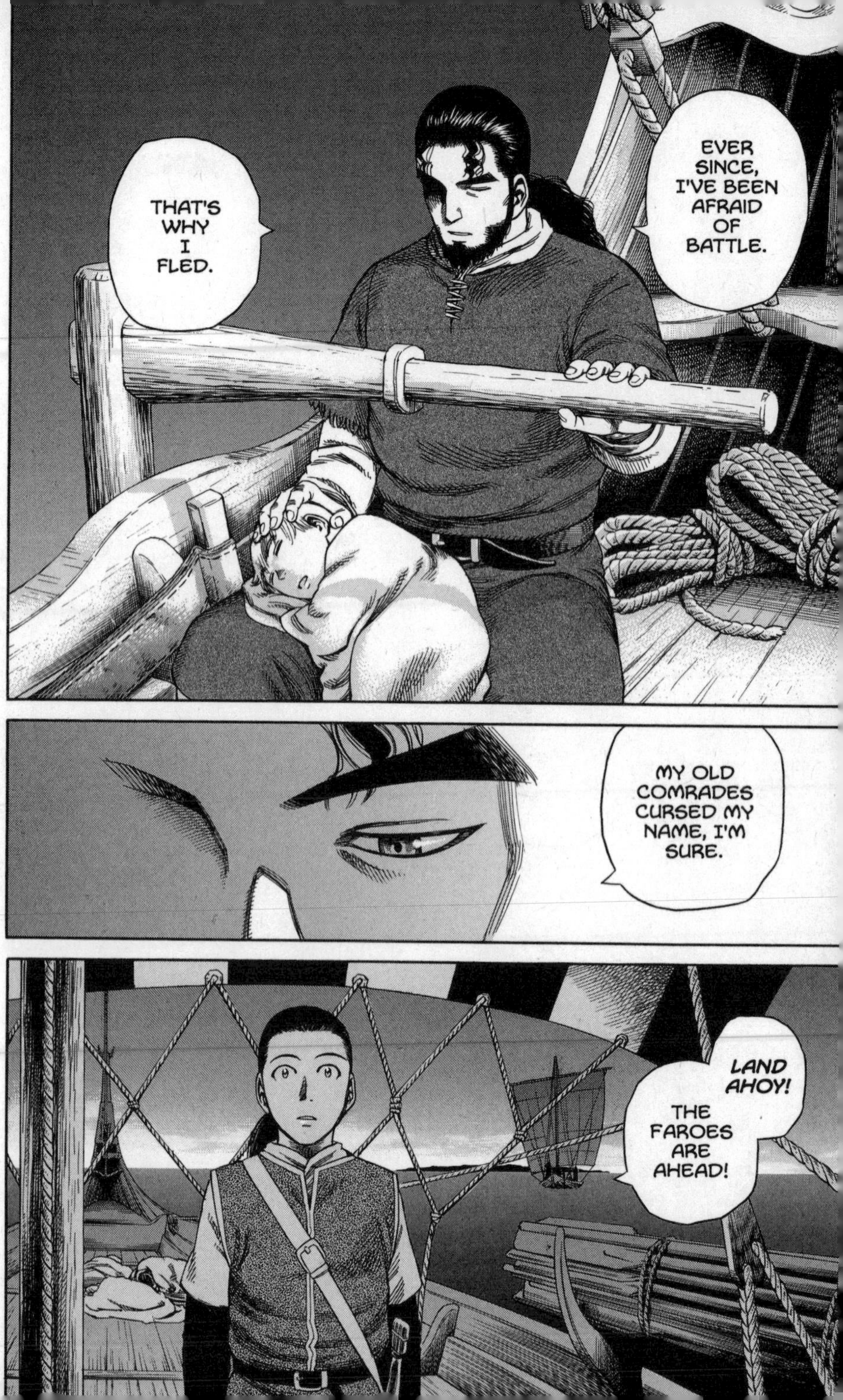
EVER SINCE, I'VE BEEN AFRAID OF BATTLE.
THAT'S WHY I FLED.
MY OLD COMRADES CURSED MY NAME, I'M SURE.
LAND AHOY!
THE FAROES ARE AHEAD!

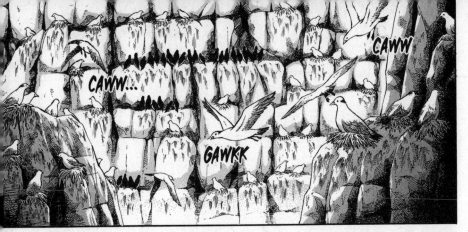

CAWW...

CAWW

GAWKK

CAWW...

CAWW

CAWW

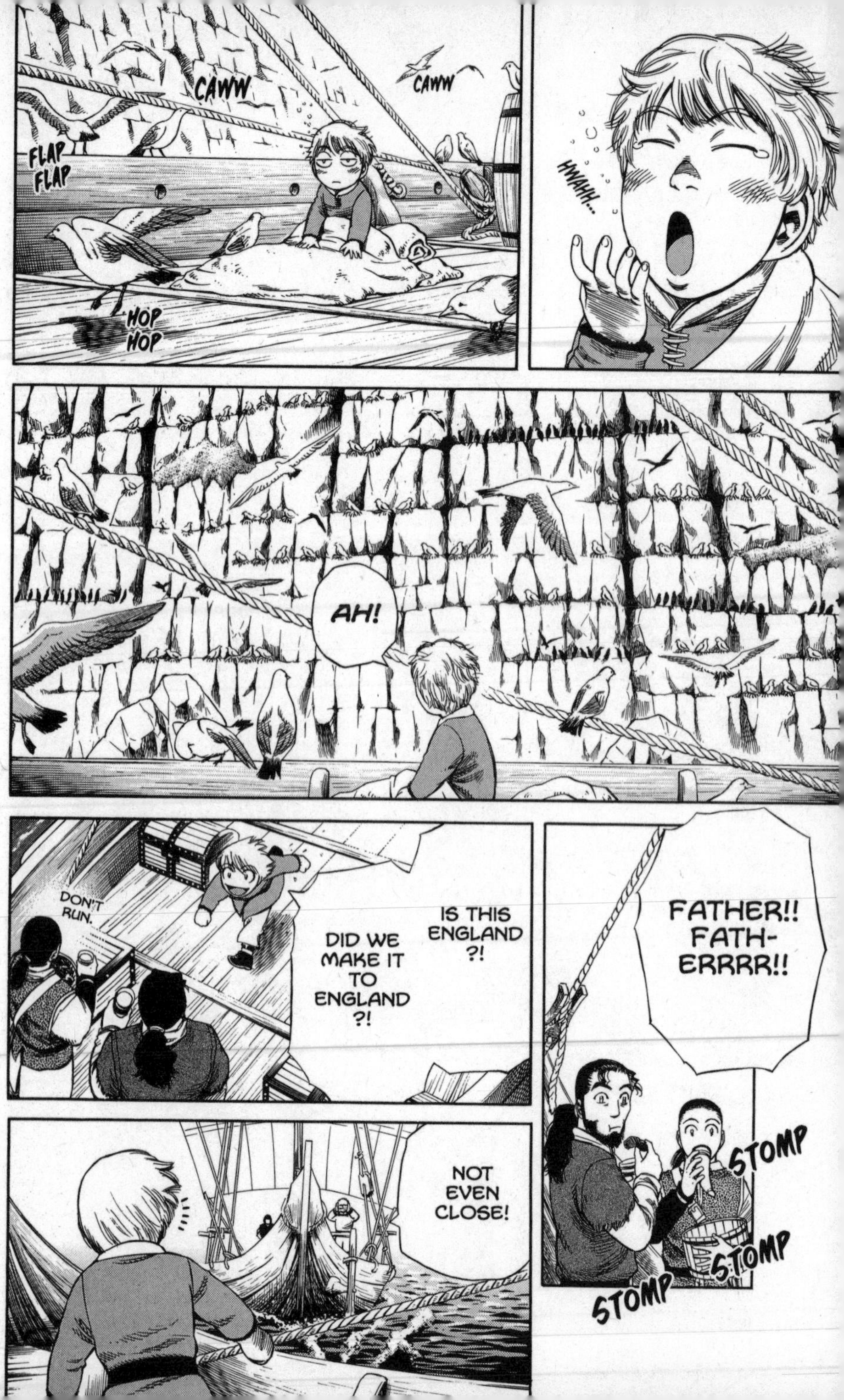
HWAHH...
CAWW
CAWW
FLAP FLAP
HOP HOP
AH!
FATHER!! FATH-ERRRR!!
STOMP
STOMP
STOMP
IS THIS ENGLAND ?!
DID WE MAKE IT TO ENGLAND ?!
DON'T RUN.
NOT EVEN CLOSE!

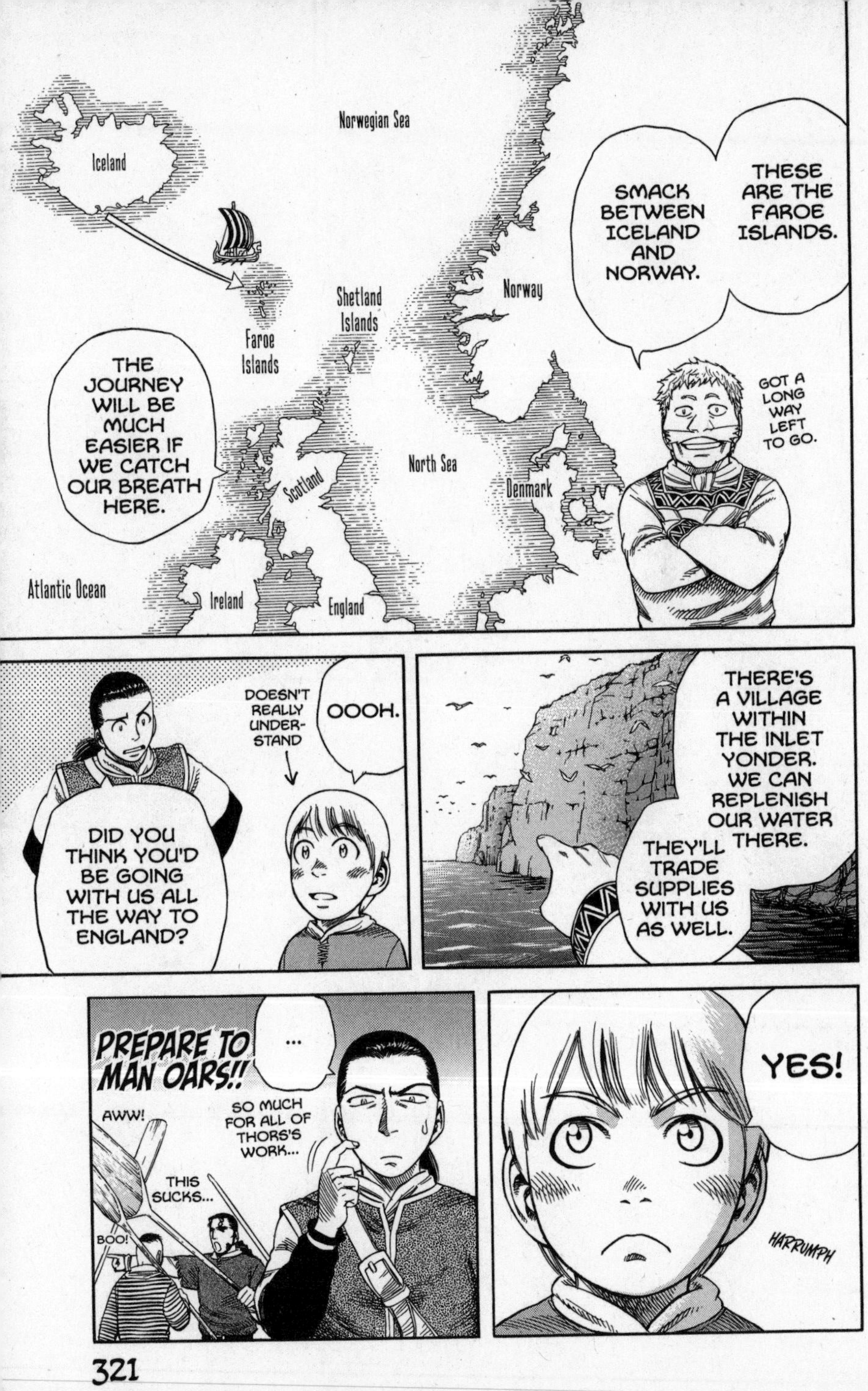
THESE ARE THE FAROE ISLANDS.
SMACK BETWEEN ICELAND AND NORWAY.
GOT A LONG WAY LEFT TO GO.
Norwegian Sea
Iceland
Norway
Shetland Islands
Faroe Islands
North Sea
Denmark
Scotland
Atlantic Ocean
Ireland
England
THE JOURNEY WILL BE MUCH EASIER IF WE CATCH OUR BREATH HERE.
THERE'S A VILLAGE WITHIN THE INLET YONDER. WE CAN REPLENISH OUR WATER THERE.
THEY'LL TRADE SUPPLIES WITH US AS WELL.
OOOH.
DOESN'T REALLY UNDER-STAND
DID YOU THINK YOU'D BE GOING WITH US ALL THE WAY TO ENGLAND?
YES!
HARRUMPH
...
PREPARE TO MAN OARS!!
SO MUCH FOR ALL OF THORS'S WORK...
AWW!
THIS SUCKS...
BOO!

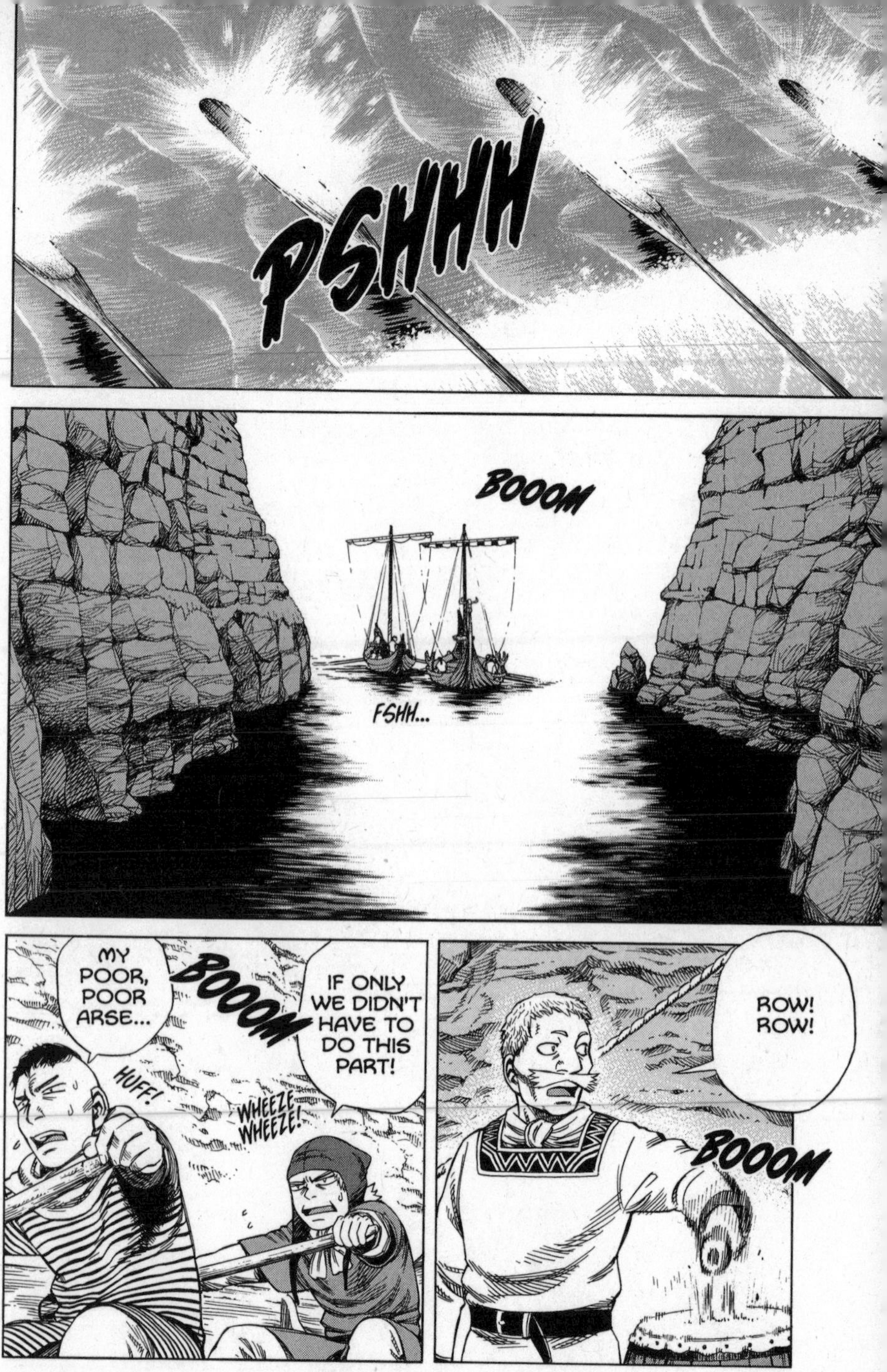
PSHHH
BOOOM
FSHH...
ROW! ROW!
BOOOM
IF ONLY WE DIDN'T HAVE TO DO THIS PART!
BOOOM
MY POOR, POOR ARSE...
WHEEZE WHEEZE!
HUFF!

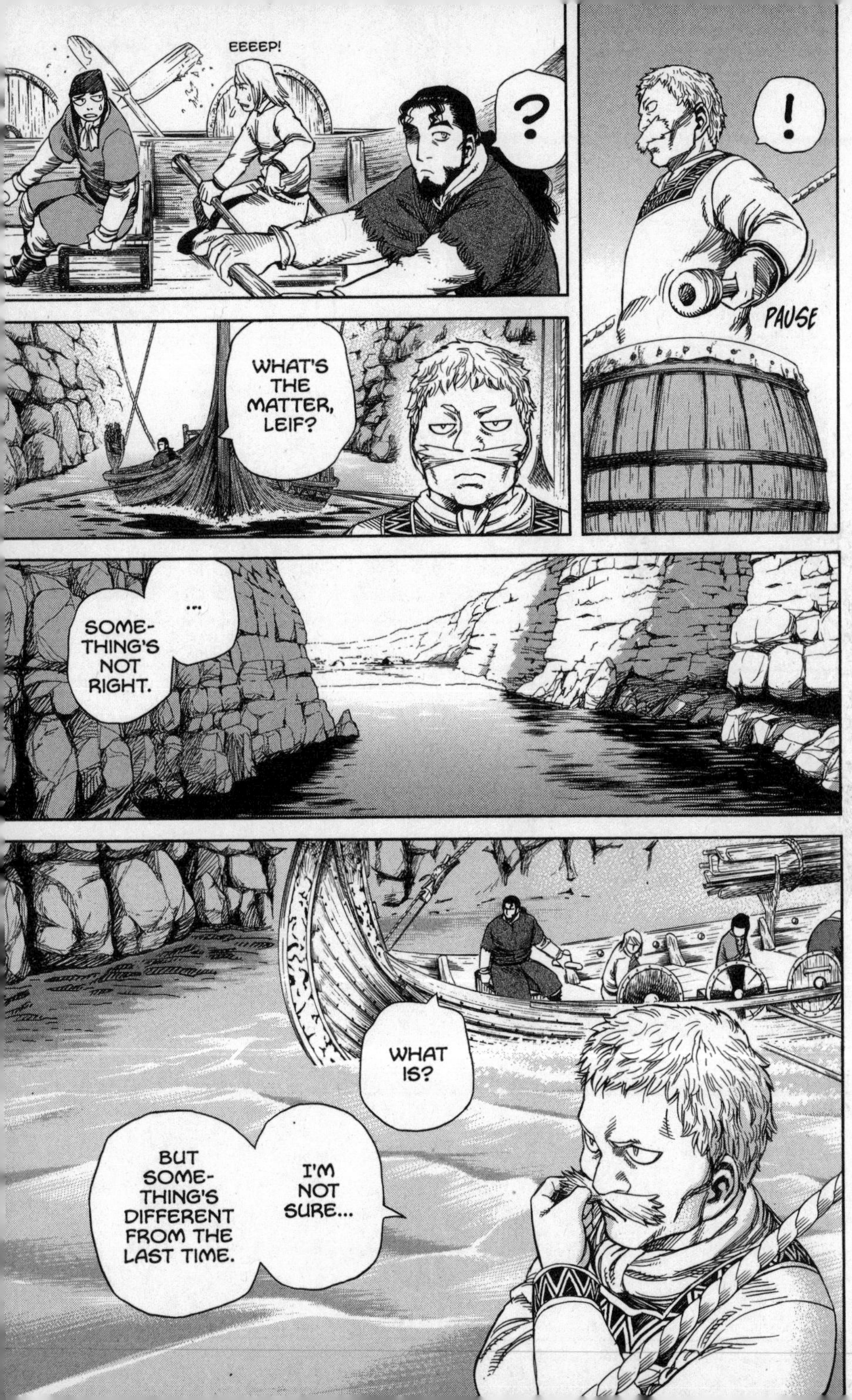
!
PAUSE
?
EEEEP!
WHAT'S THE MATTER, LEIF?
...
SOME-THING'S NOT RIGHT.
WHAT IS?
I'M NOT SURE...
BUT SOME-THING'S DIFFERENT FROM THE LAST TIME.

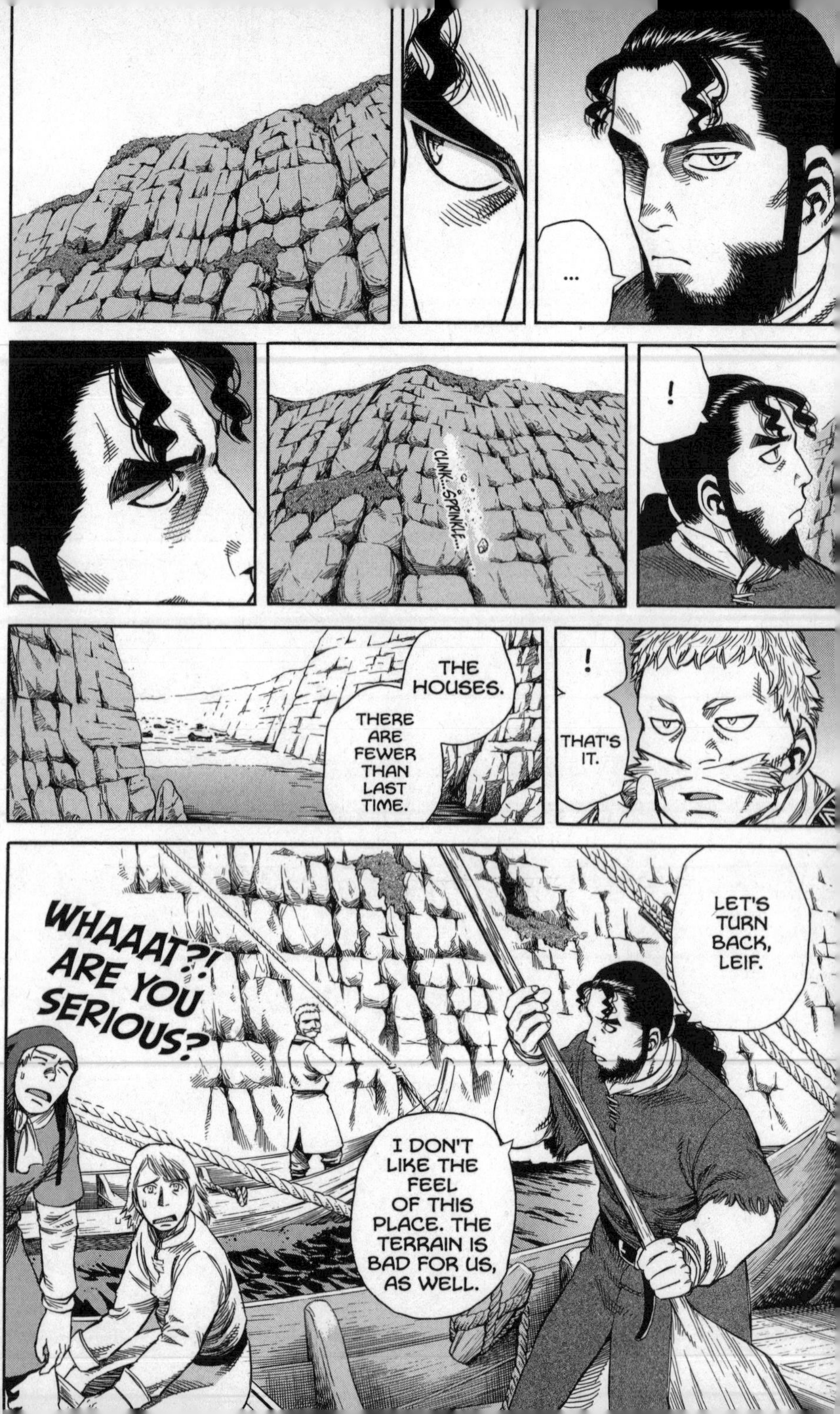
...
!
CLINK... SPRINKLE...
!
THAT'S IT.
THE HOUSES.
THERE ARE FEWER THAN LAST TIME.
LET'S TURN BACK, LEIF.
I DON'T LIKE THE FEEL OF THIS PLACE. THE TERRAIN IS BAD FOR US, AS WELL.
WHAAAT?! ARE YOU SERIOUS?

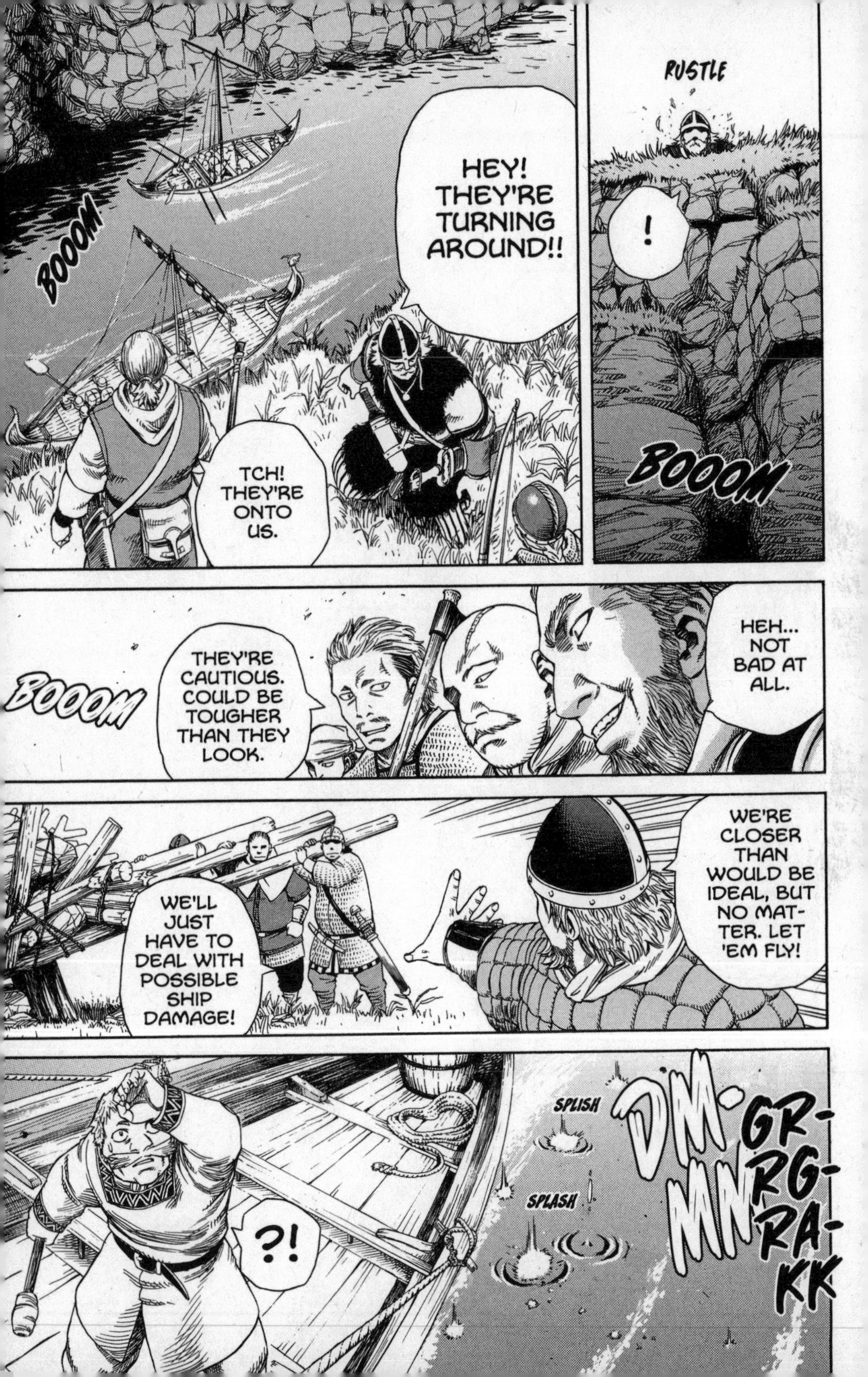
RUSTLE
!
BOOOM
HEY! THEY'RE TURNING AROUND!!
BOOOM
TCH! THEY'RE ONTO US.
HEH... NOT BAD AT ALL.
THEY'RE CAUTIOUS. COULD BE TOUGHER THAN THEY LOOK.
BOOOM
WE'RE CLOSER THAN WOULD BE IDEAL, BUT NO MATTER. LET 'EM FLY!
WE'LL JUST HAVE TO DEAL WITH POSSIBLE SHIP DAMAGE!
DM-MN
GR-RG-RA-KK
SPLISH
SPLASH
?!

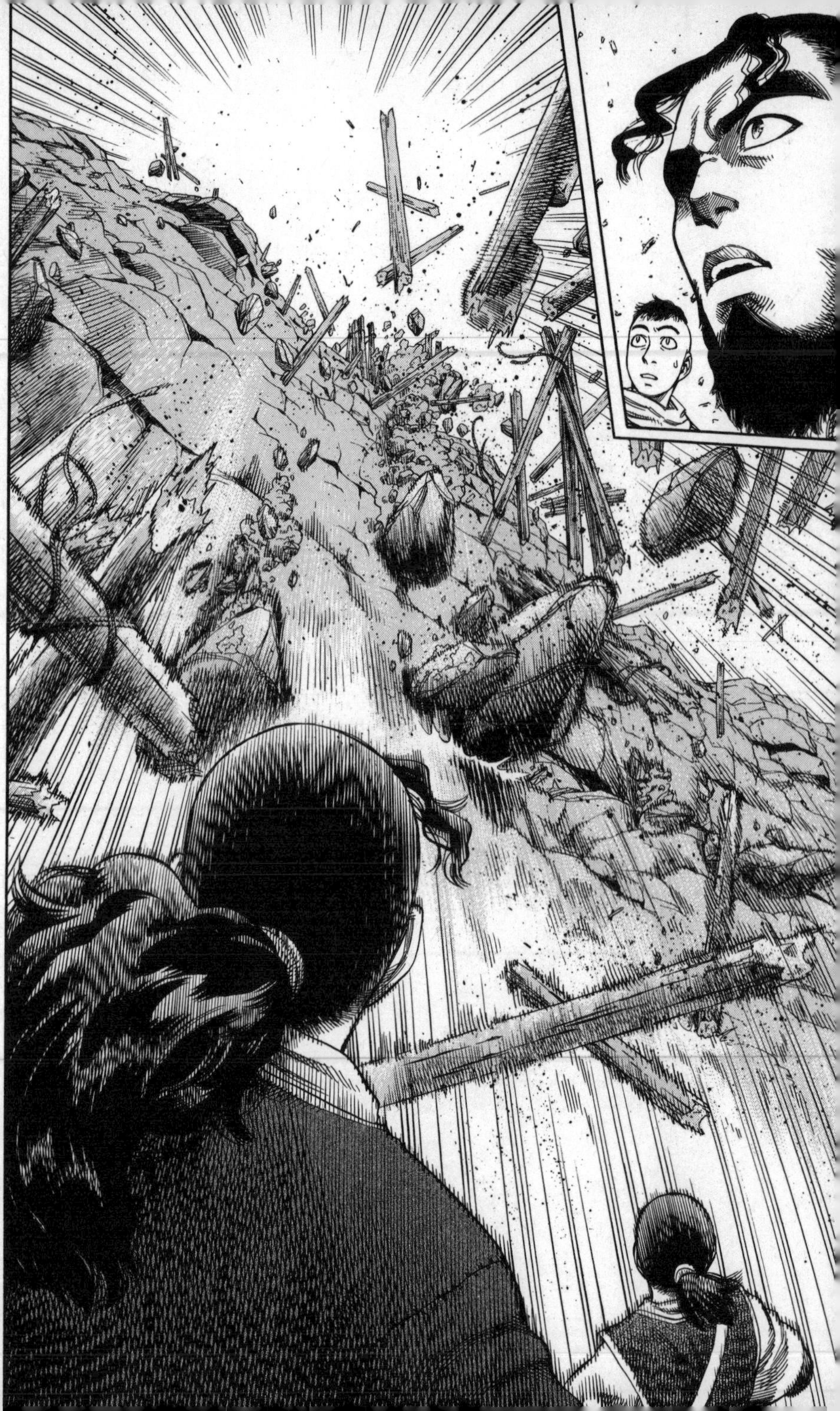

CHAPTER 10 - END

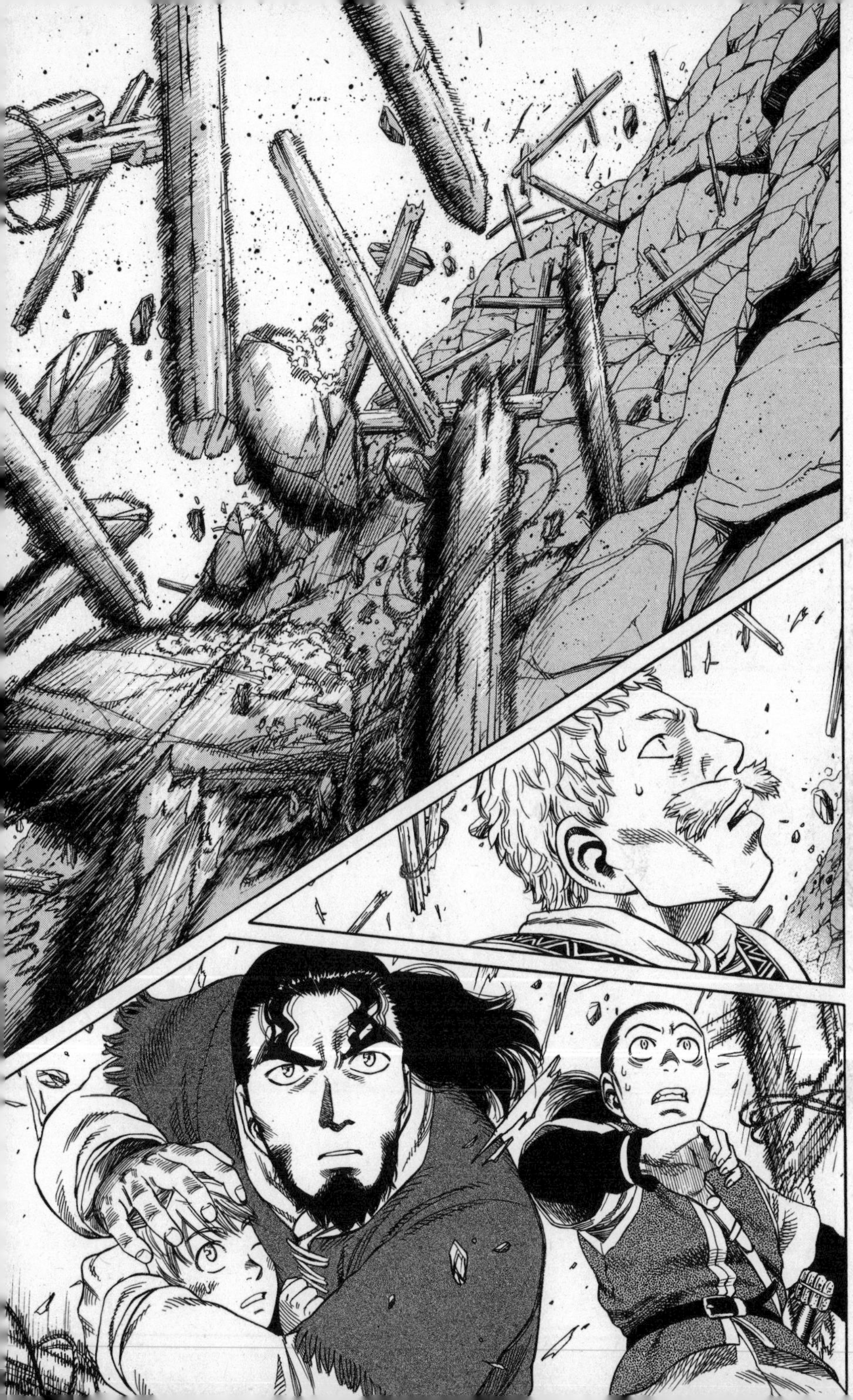

CHAPTER 11: CAGE

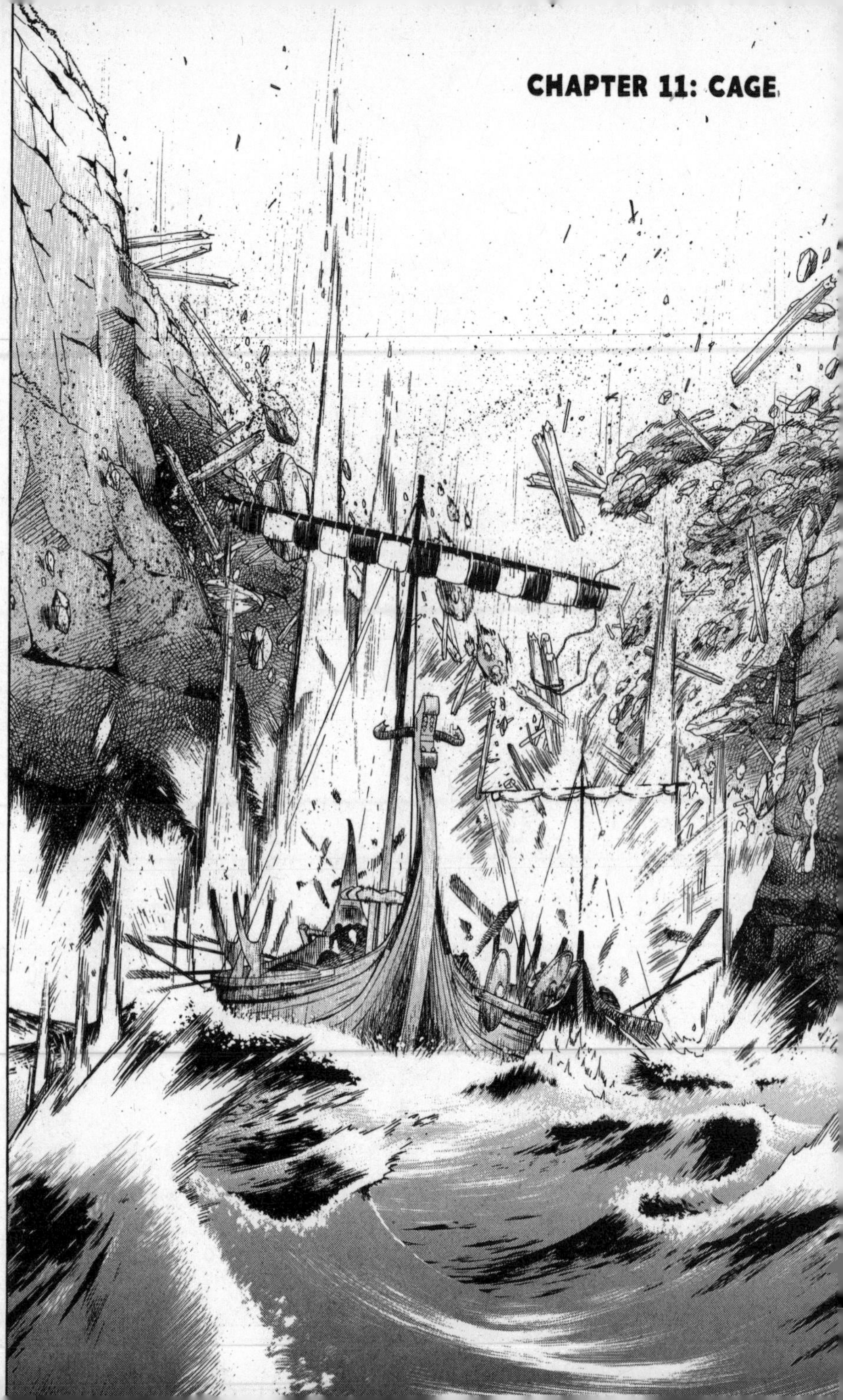

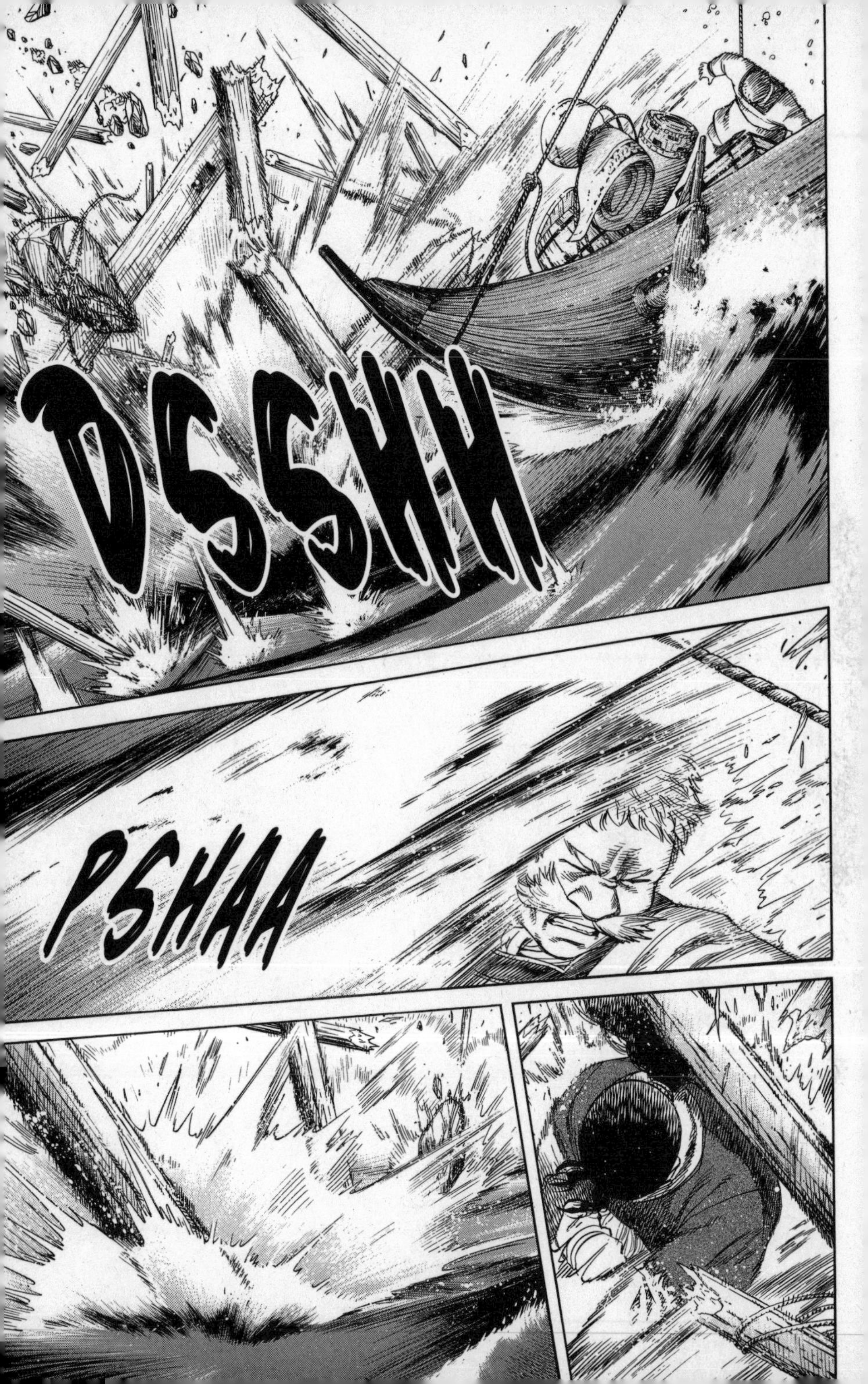
DSSHH
PSHAA

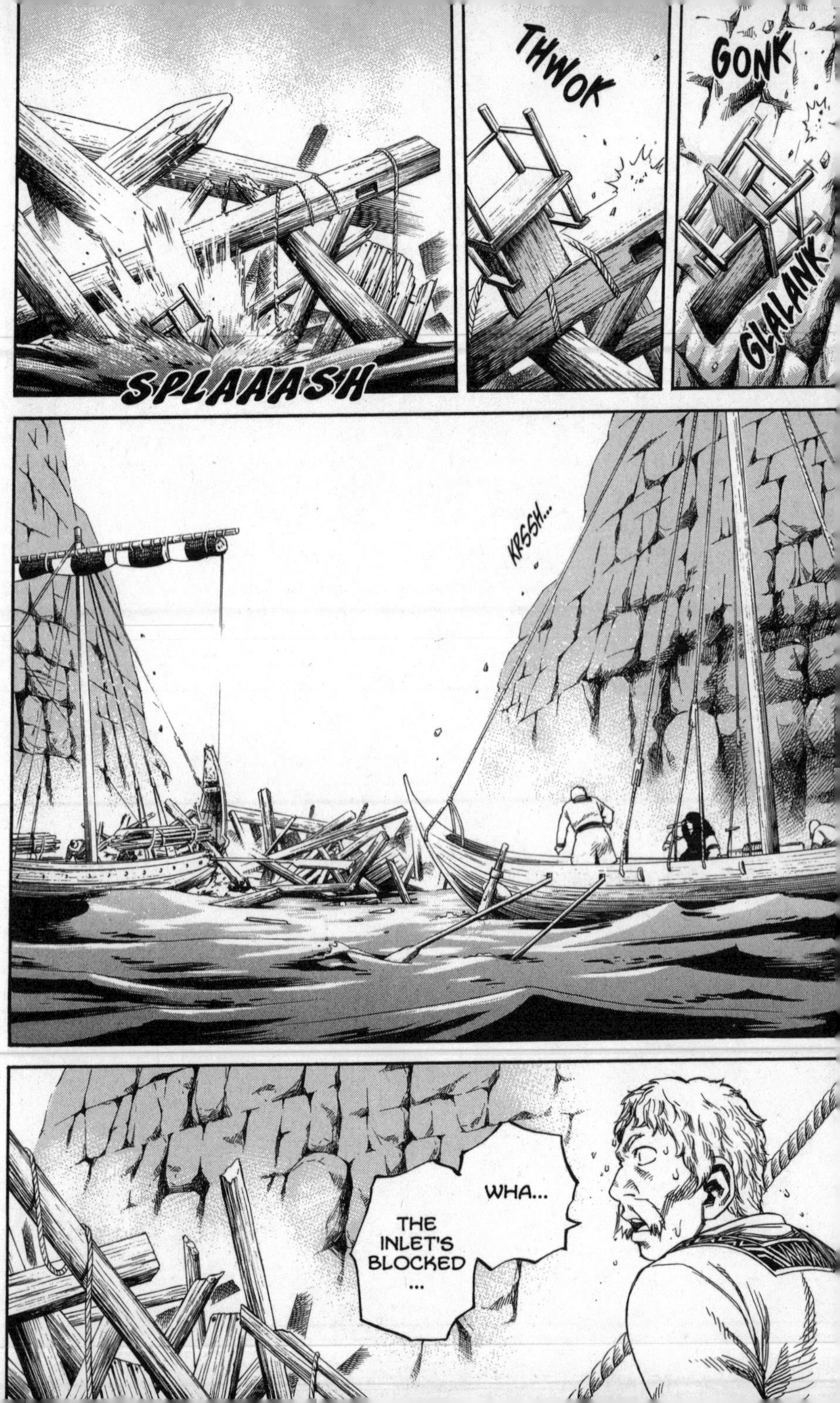
GONK
GLALANK
THWOK
SPLAAASH
KRSSH...
WHA...
THE INLET'S BLOCKED ...

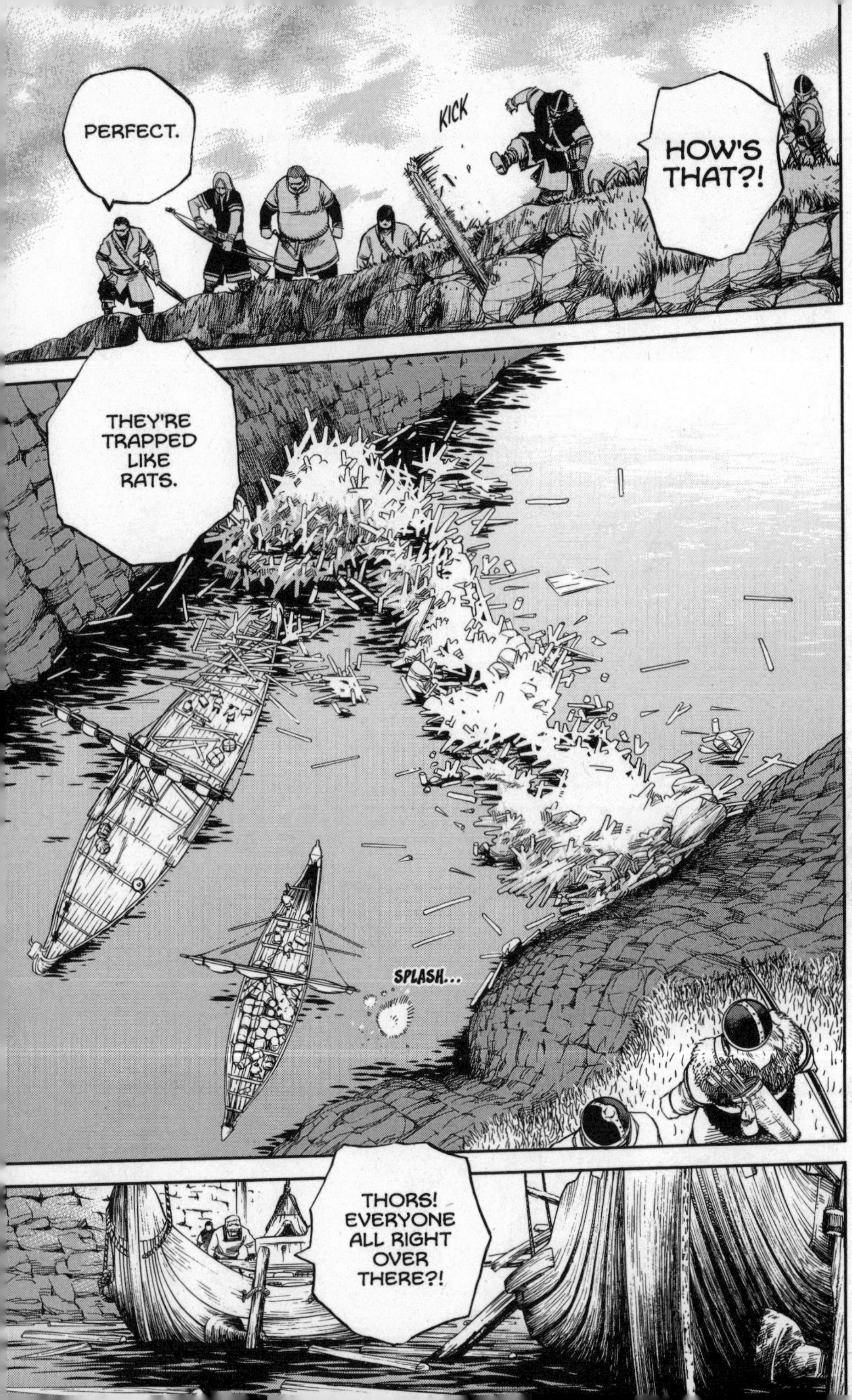
HOW'S THAT?!
KICK
PERFECT.
THEY'RE TRAPPED LIKE RATS.
SPLASH...
THORS! EVERYONE ALL RIGHT OVER THERE?!

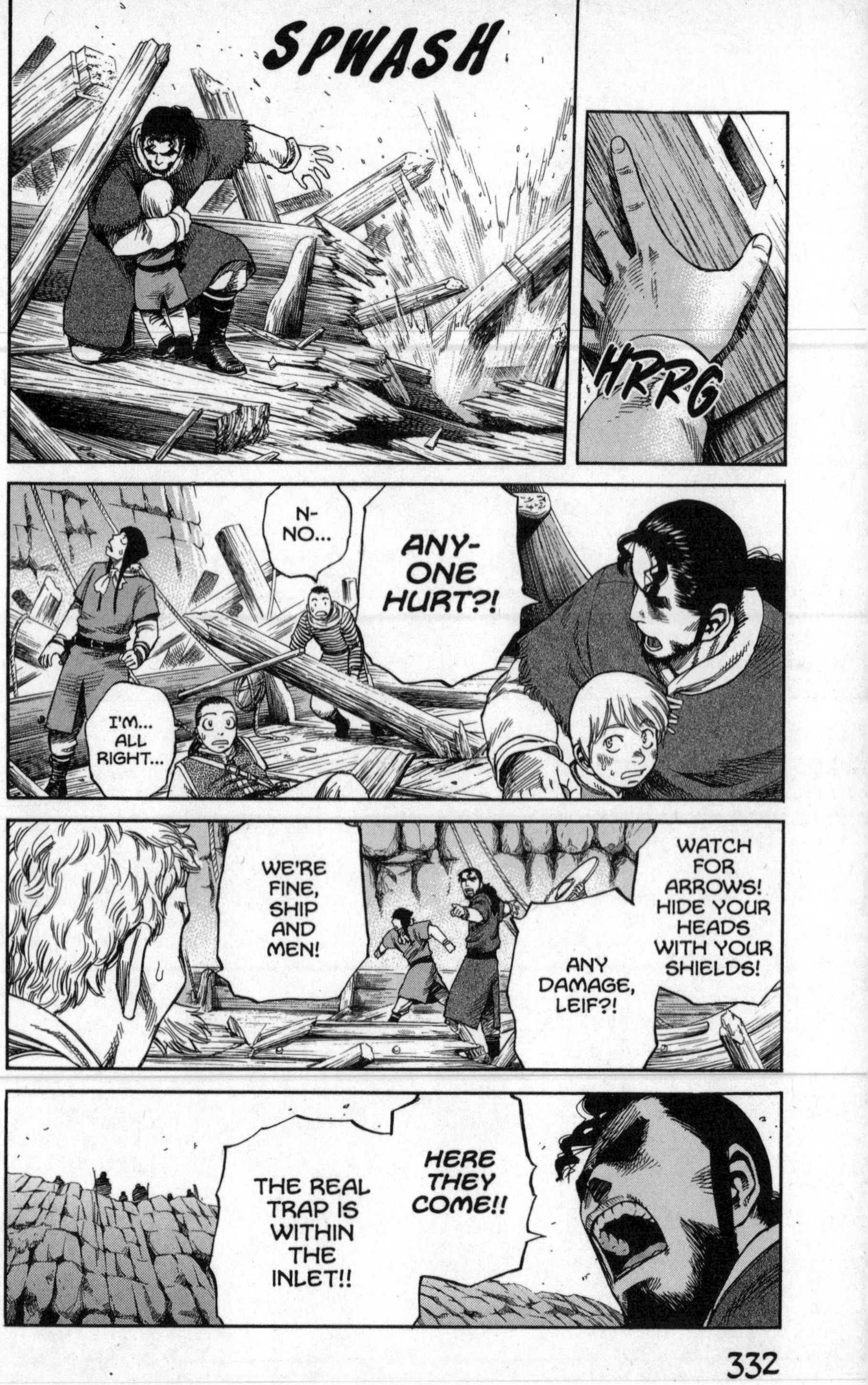
HRRG
SPWASH
ANY-ONE HURT?!
N-NO...
I'M... ALL RIGHT...
WATCH FOR ARROWS! HIDE YOUR HEADS WITH YOUR SHIELDS!
ANY DAMAGE, LEIF?!
WE'RE FINE, SHIP AND MEN!
HERE THEY COME!!
THE REAL TRAP IS WITHIN THE INLET!!

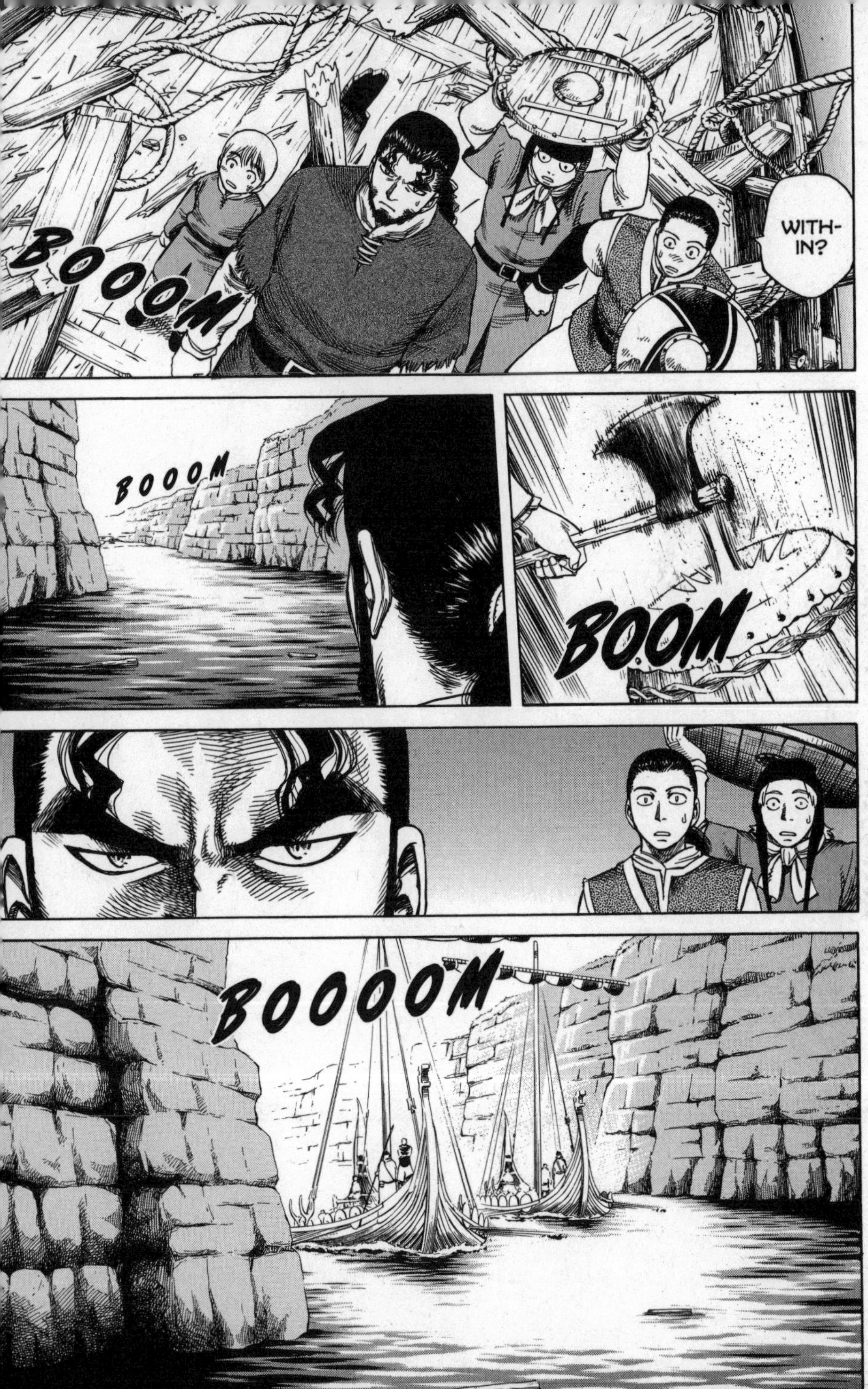
WITH-IN?
BOOOM
BOOM
BOOOM
BOOOOM

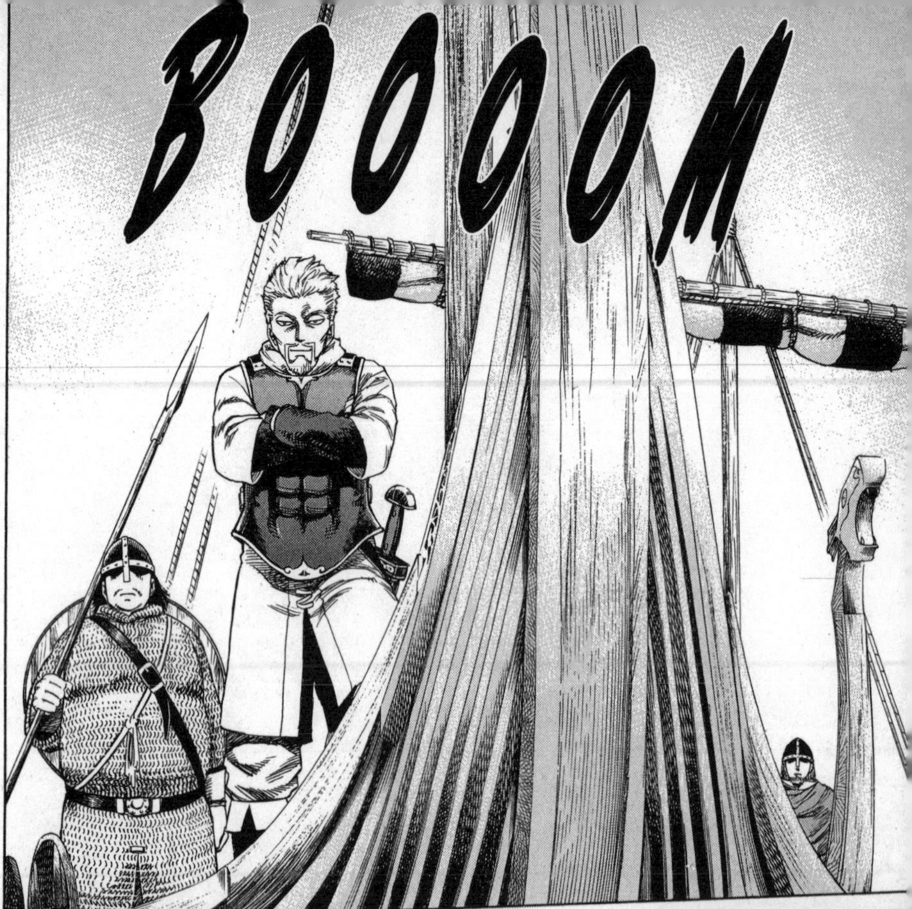
BOOOOM
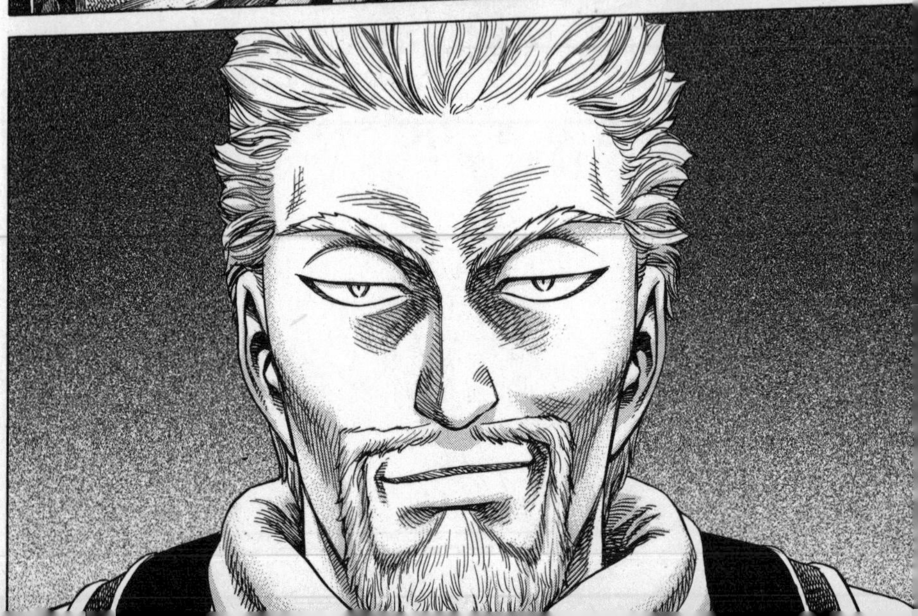

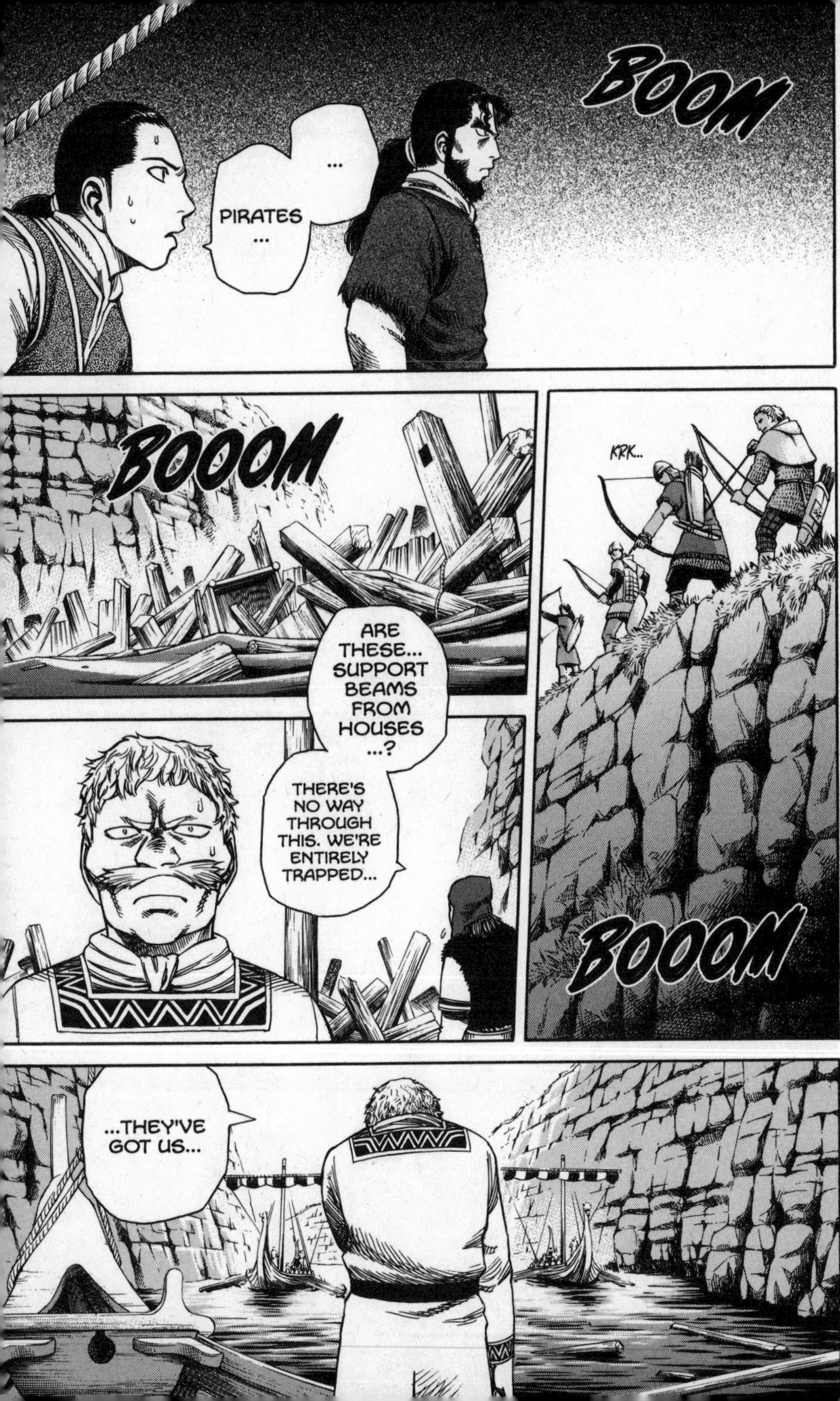
BOOM
...
PIRATES ...
KRK...
BOOOM
BOOOM
ARE THESE... SUPPORT BEAMS FROM HOUSES ...?
THERE'S NO WAY THROUGH THIS. WE'RE ENTIRELY TRAPPED...
...THEY'VE GOT US...

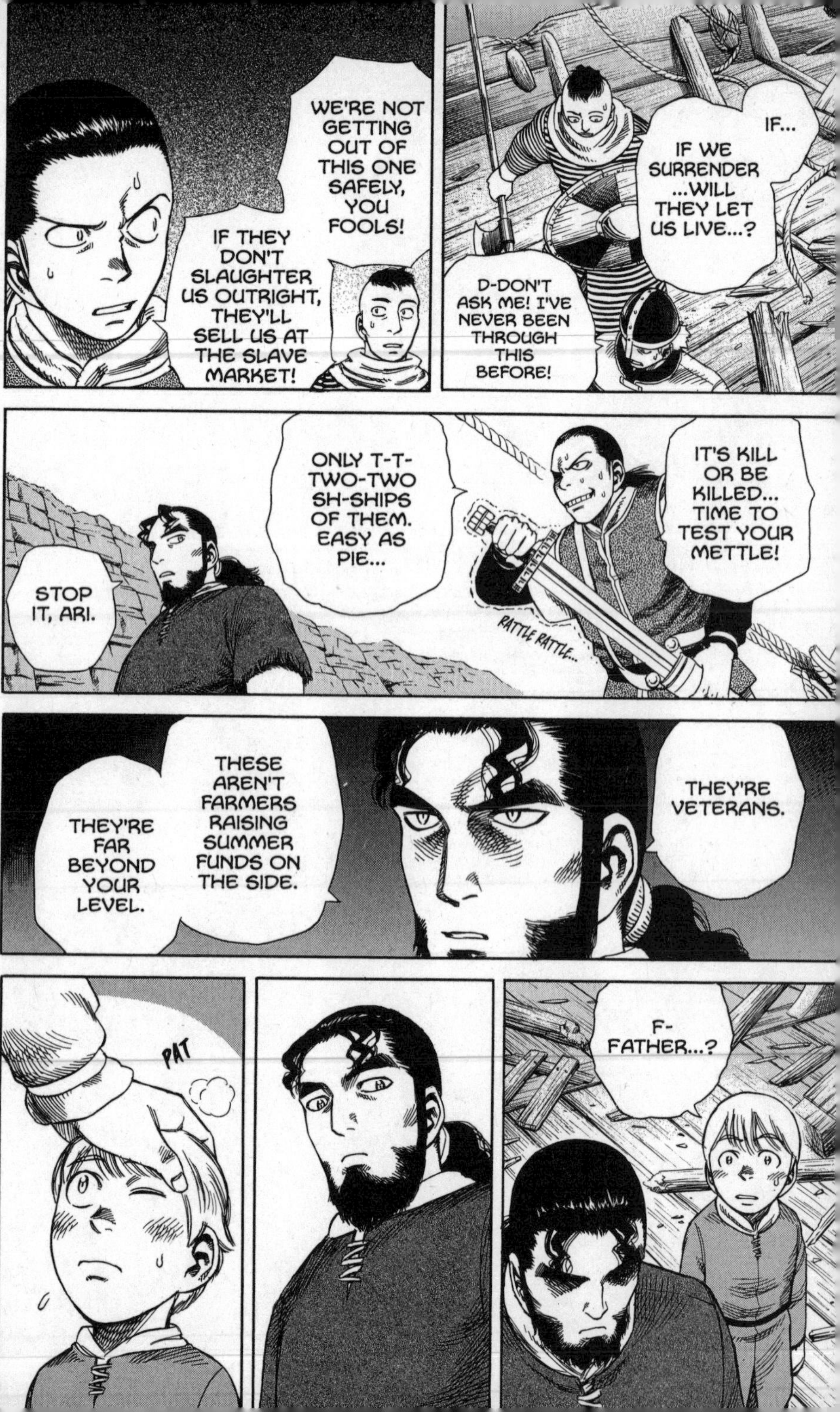
IF...
IF WE SURRENDER ...WILL THEY LET US LIVE...?
D-DON'T ASK ME! I'VE NEVER BEEN THROUGH THIS BEFORE!
WE'RE NOT GETTING OUT OF THIS ONE SAFELY, YOU FOOLS!
IF THEY DON'T SLAUGHTER US OUTRIGHT, THEY'LL SELL US AT THE SLAVE MARKET!
IT'S KILL OR BE KILLED... TIME TO TEST YOUR METTLE!
ONLY T-T-TWO-TWO SH-SHIPS OF THEM. EASY AS PIE...
RATTLE RATTLE...
STOP IT, ARI.
THEY'RE VETERANS.
THESE AREN'T FARMERS RAISING SUMMER FUNDS ON THE SIDE.
THEY'RE FAR BEYOND YOUR LEVEL.
F-FATHER...?
PAT

PFFF...

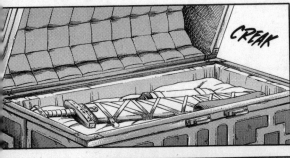

CREAK

UM,
THORS?

?

PLOD...

KCHAK...

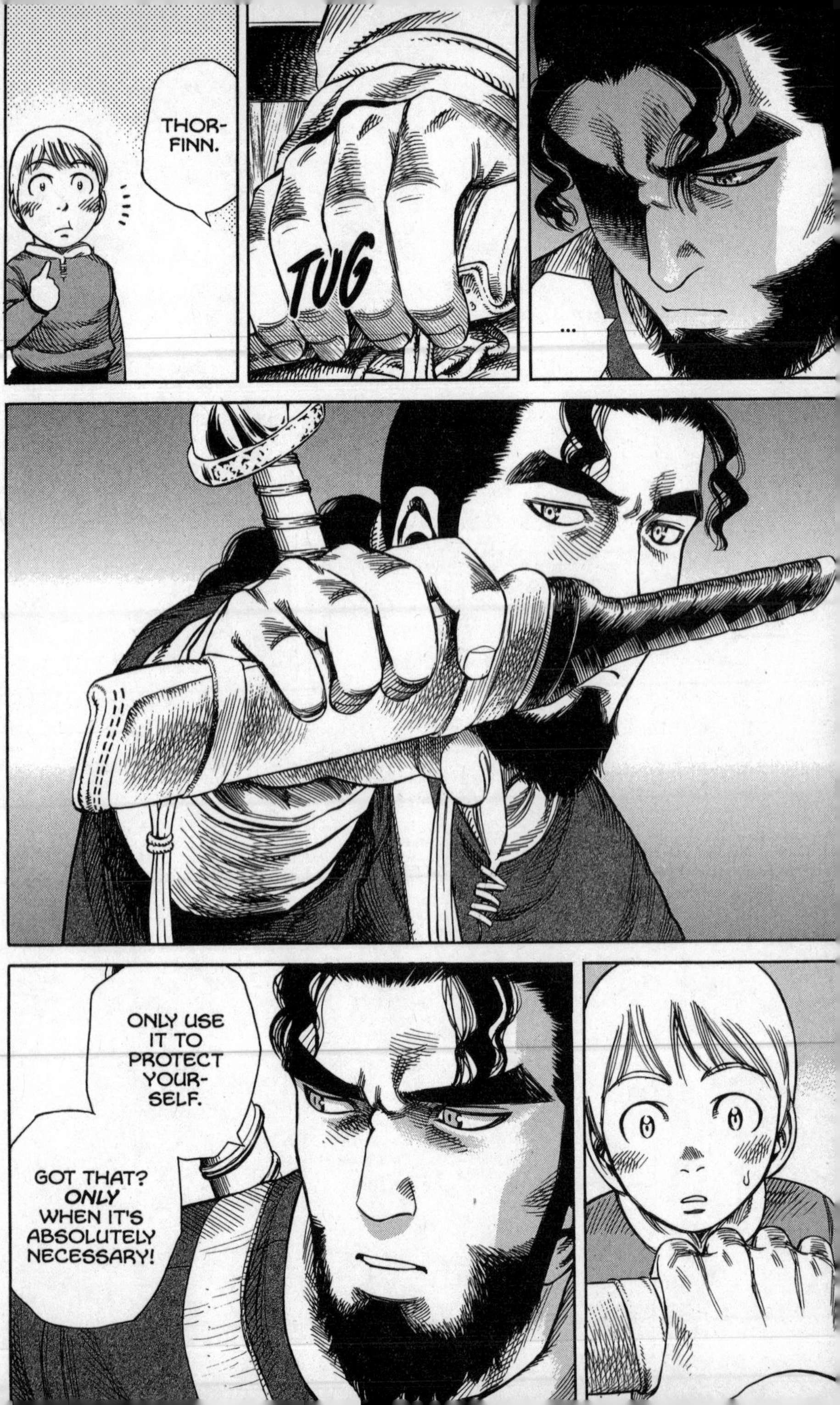
...
TUG
THOR-FINN.
ONLY USE IT TO PROTECT YOUR-SELF.
GOT THAT? *ONLY* WHEN IT'S ABSOLUTELY NECESSARY!

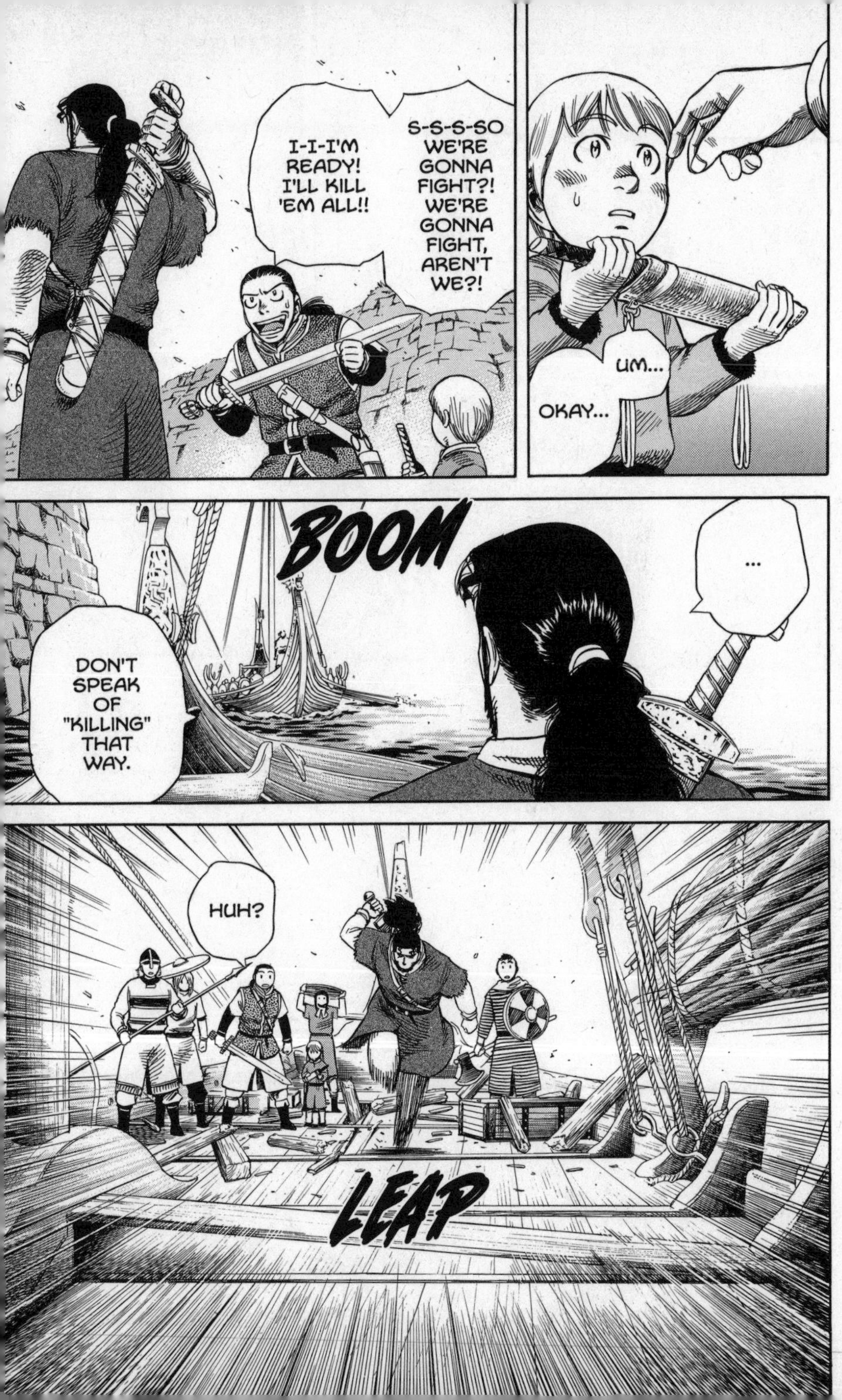
UM...
OKAY...
S-S-S-SO WE'RE GONNA FIGHT?! WE'RE GONNA FIGHT, AREN'T WE?!
I-I-I'M READY! I'LL KILL 'EM ALL!!
...
BOOM
DON'T SPEAK OF "KILLING" THAT WAY.
HUH?
LEAP

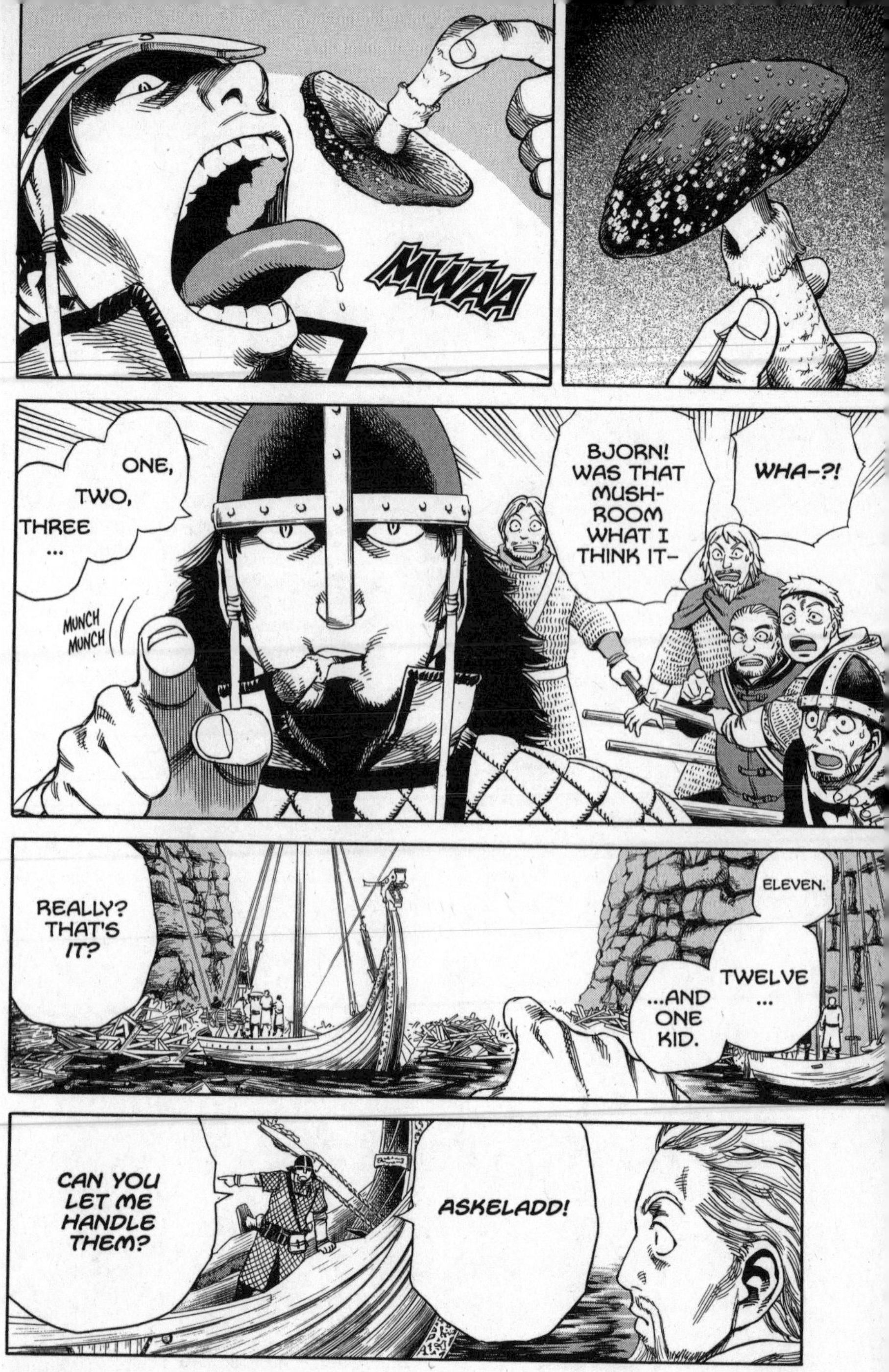

MWAA
WHA-?!
BJORN! WAS THAT MUSH-ROOM WHAT I THINK IT-
ONE, TWO, THREE ...
MUNCH MUNCH
ELEVEN.
TWELVE ...
...AND ONE KID.
REALLY? THAT'S IT?
ASKELADD!
CAN YOU LET ME HANDLE THEM?

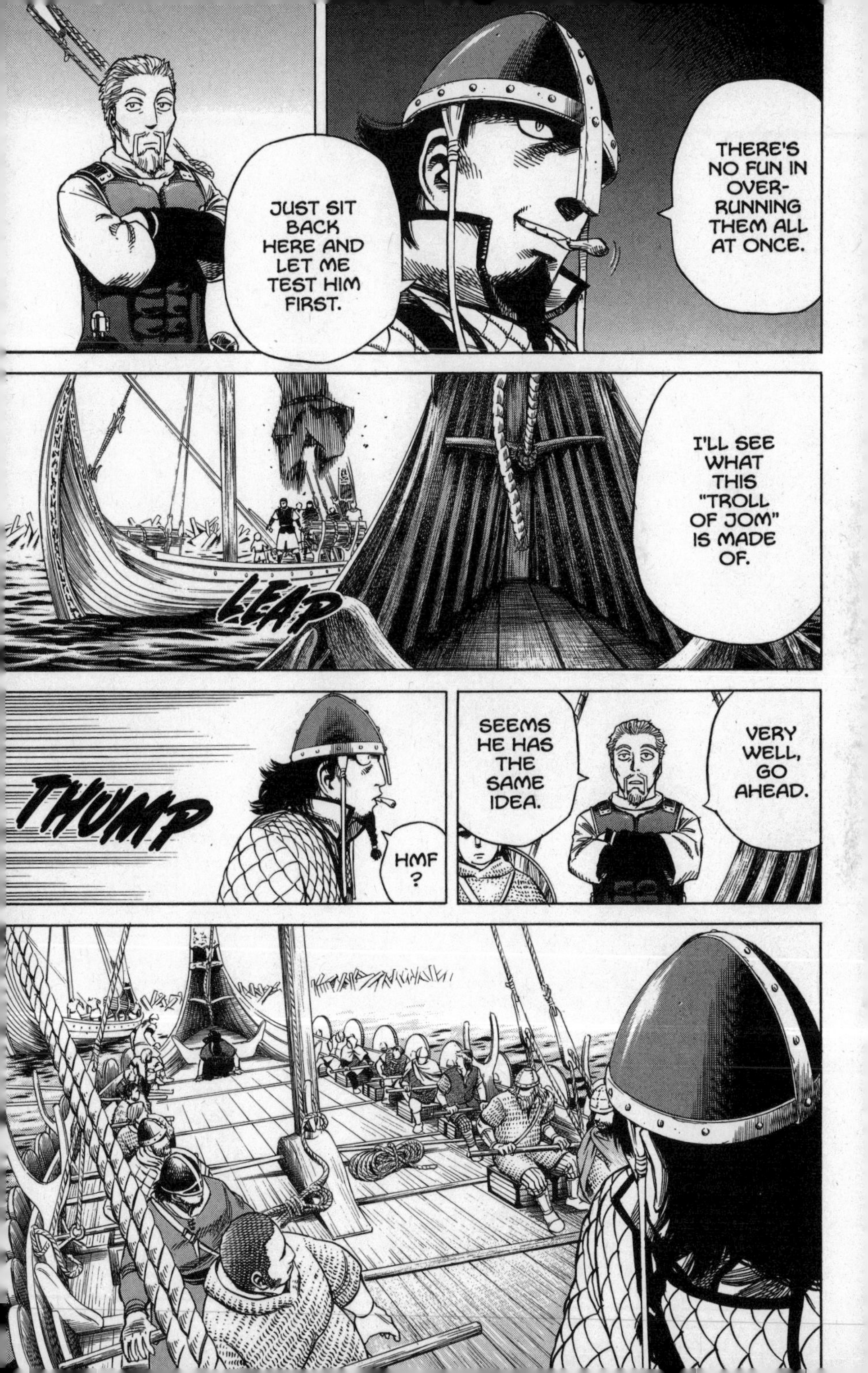
THERE'S NO FUN IN OVER-RUNNING THEM ALL AT ONCE.
JUST SIT BACK HERE AND LET ME TEST HIM FIRST.
I'LL SEE WHAT THIS "TROLL OF JOM" IS MADE OF.
LEAP
VERY WELL, GO AHEAD.
SEEMS HE HAS THE SAME IDEA.
THUMP
HMF ?

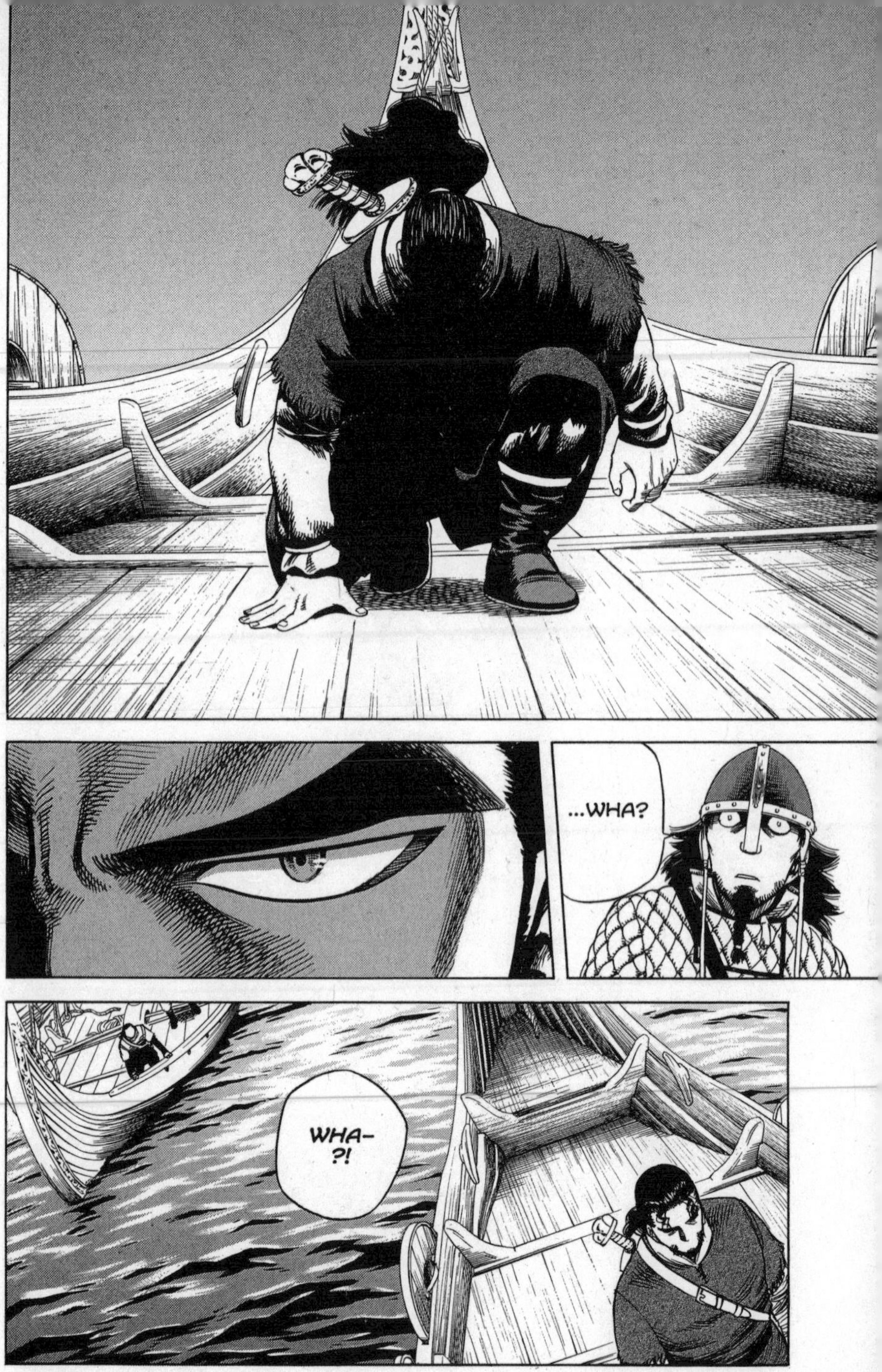
...WHA?
WHA-
?!

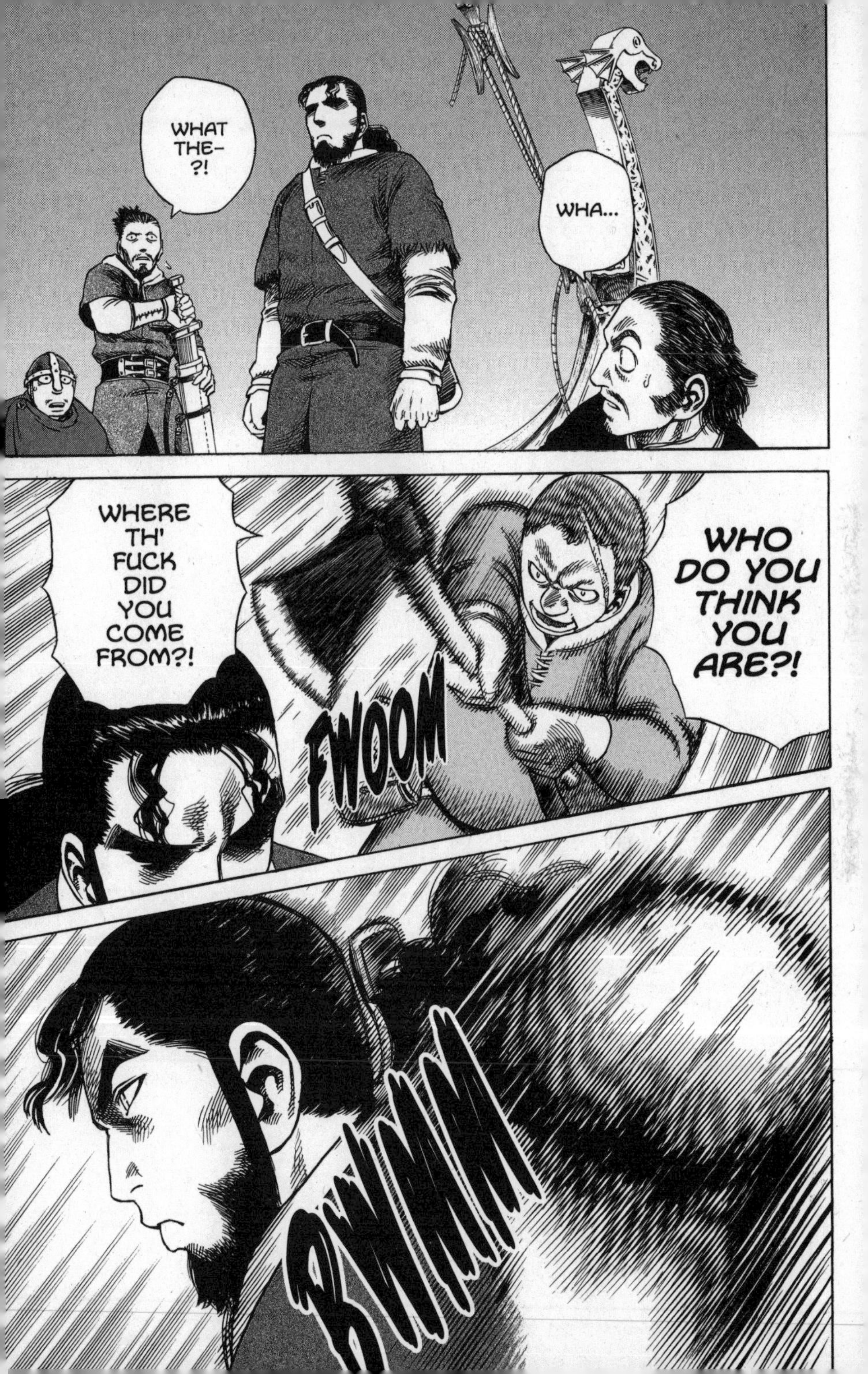
WHA...
WHAT THE- ?!
WHO DO YOU THINK YOU ARE?!
WHERE TH' FUCK DID YOU COME FROM?!
FWOOM

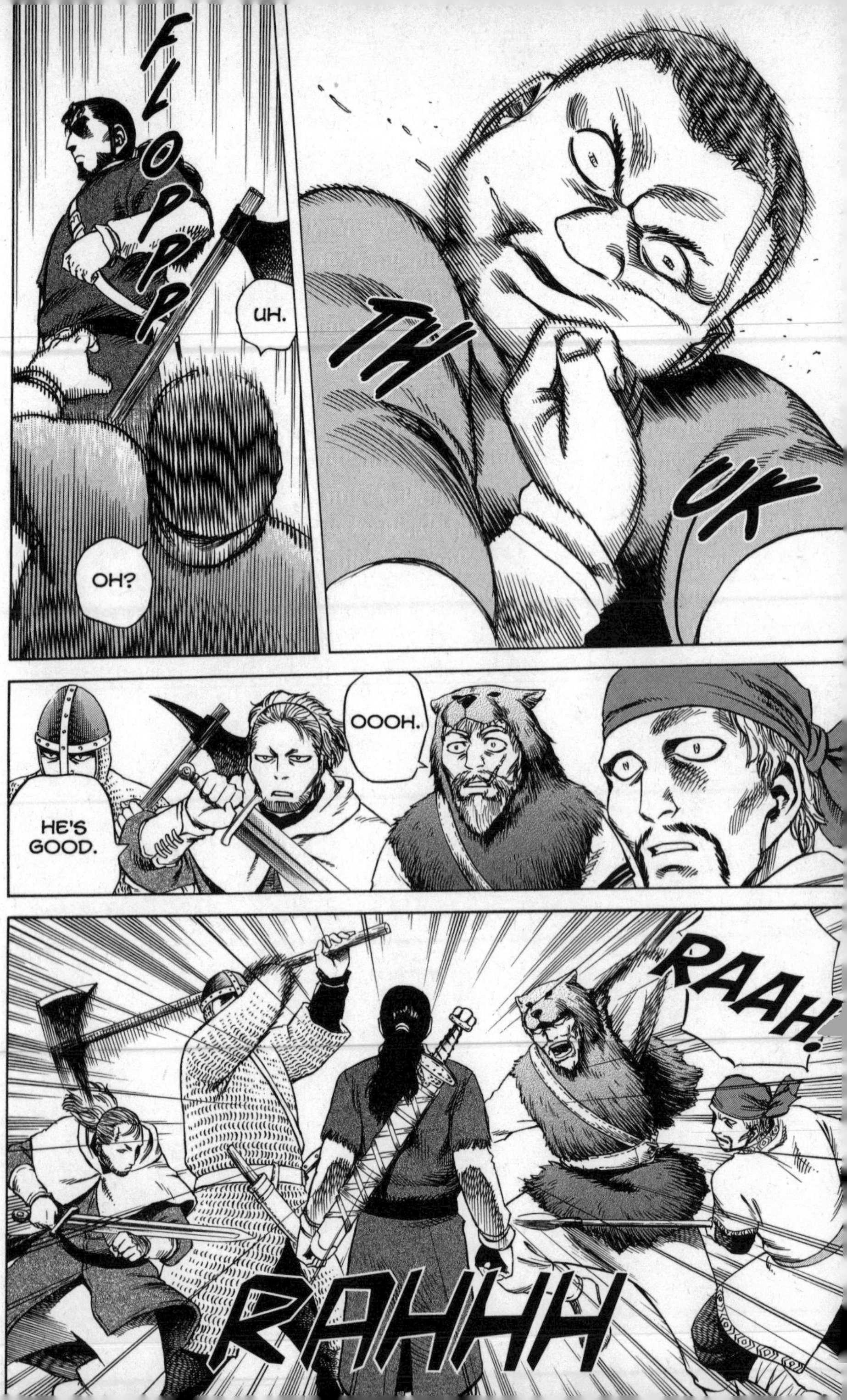
TH
UK
FLOPPP
UH.
OH?
OOOH.
HE'S GOOD.
RAAH!
RAHHH

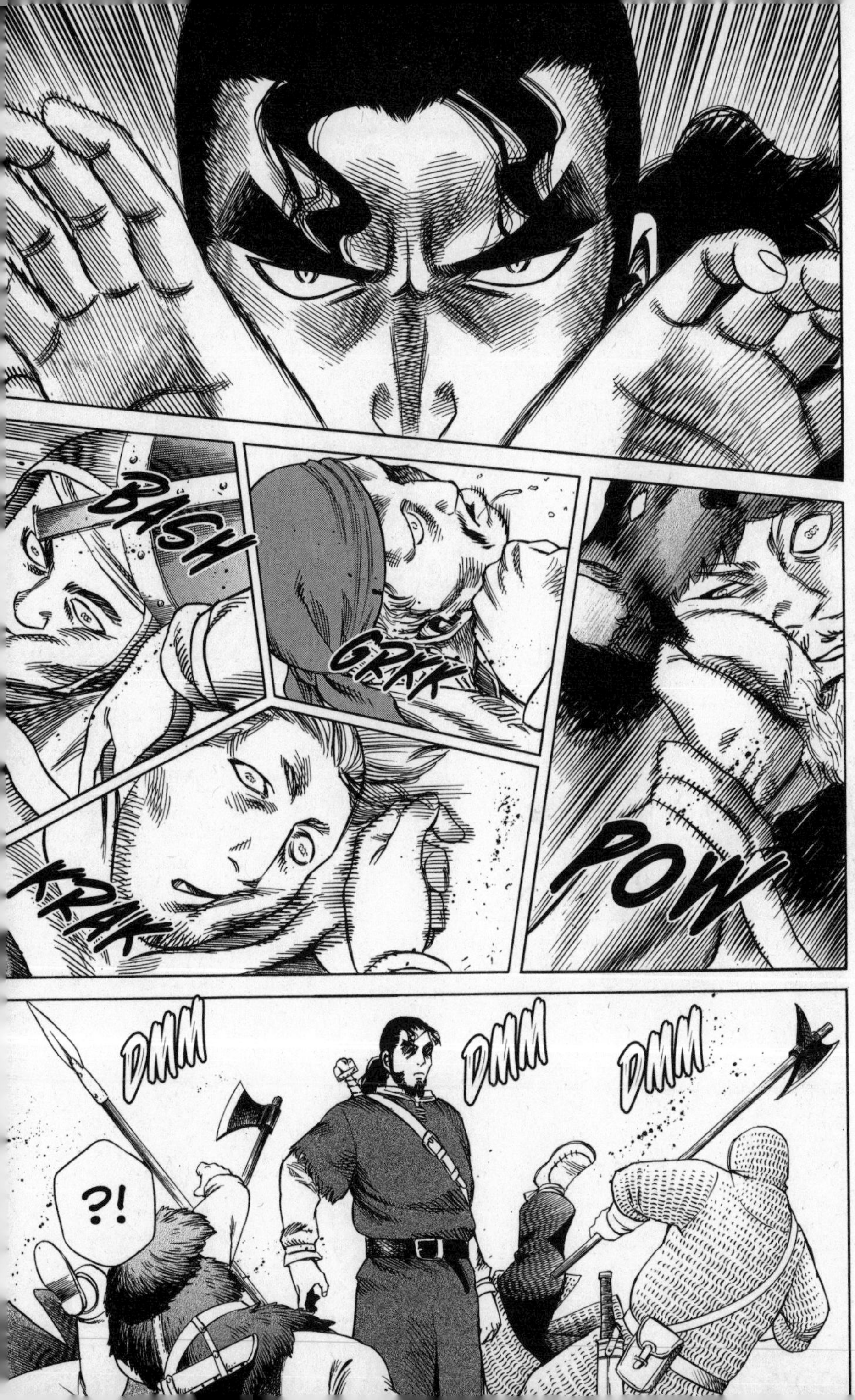
POW
GRKK
BASH
KRAK
DMM
DMM
DMM
?!

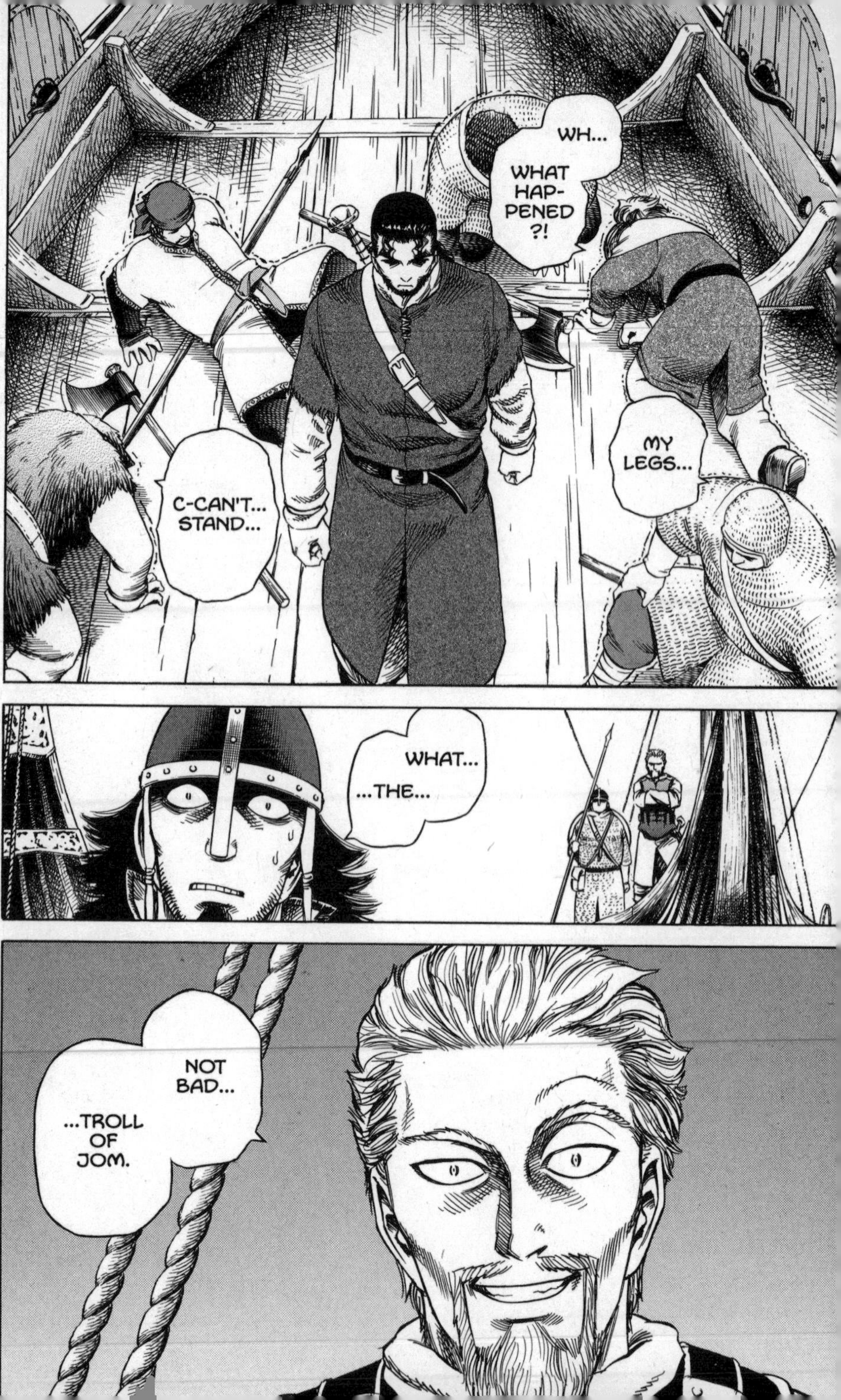
WH... WHAT HAP-PENED?!
MY LEGS...
C-CAN'T... STAND...
WHAT... ...THE...
NOT BAD... ...TROLL OF JOM.

CHAPTER 11 - END

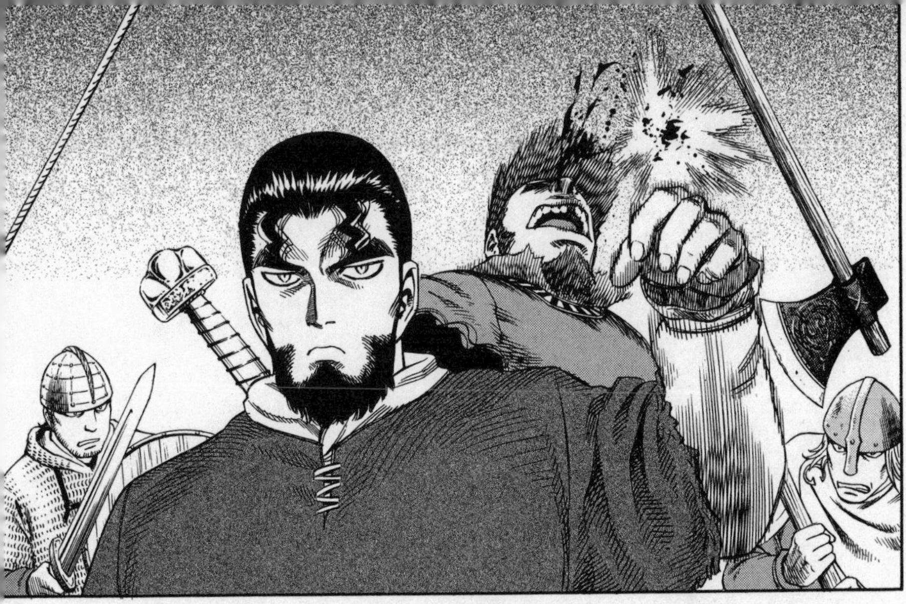

CHAPTER 12: MORE THAN A MONSTER

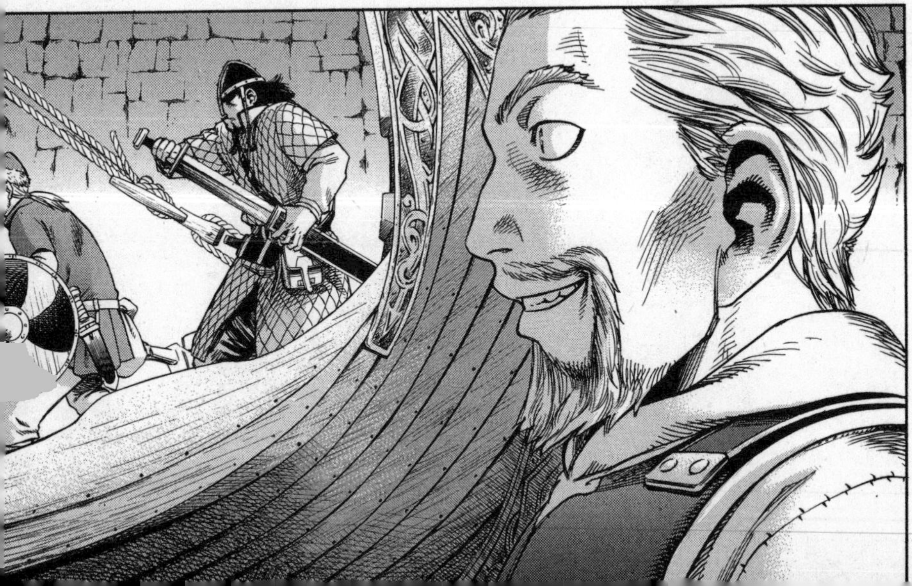

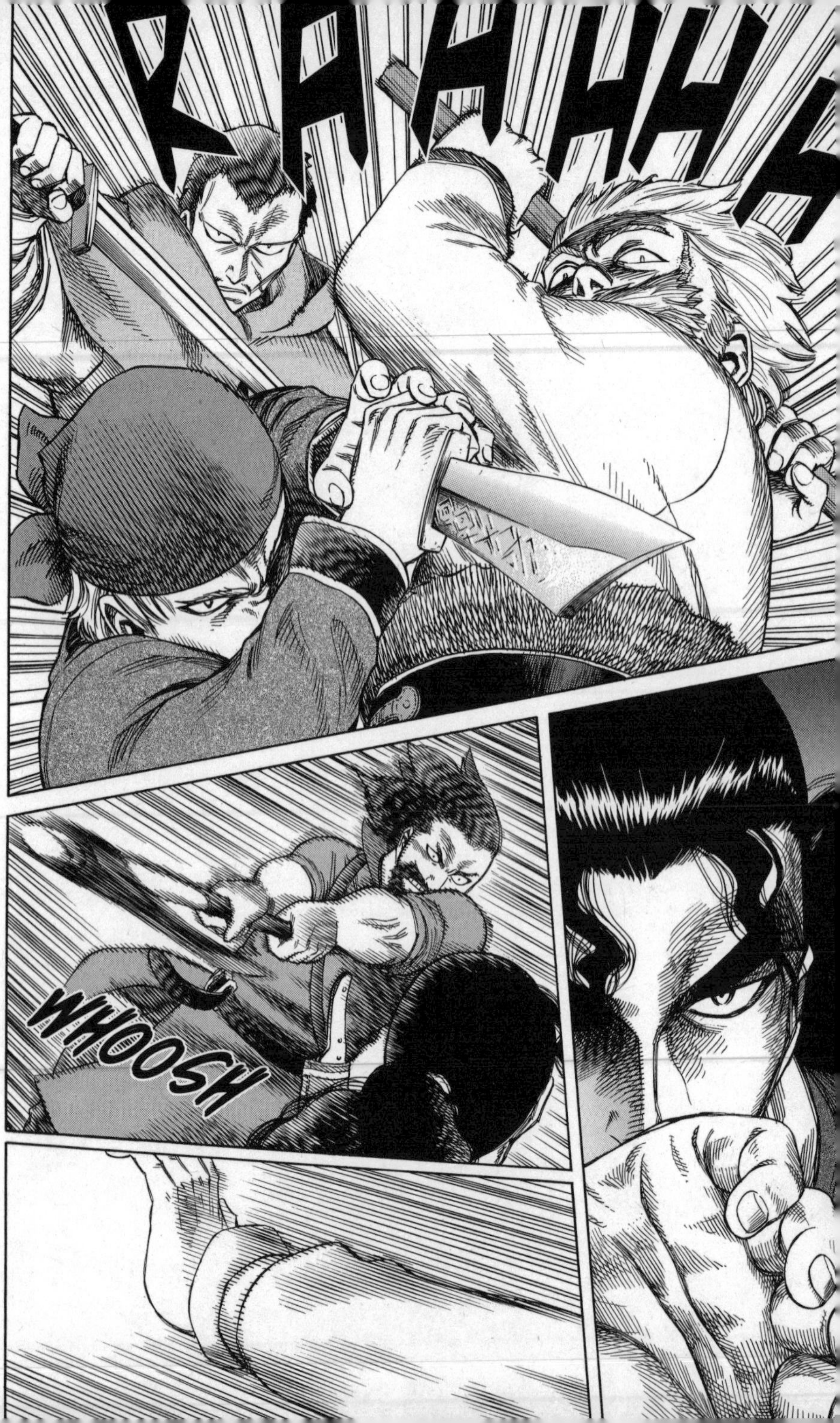
RAAAAH
WHOOSH

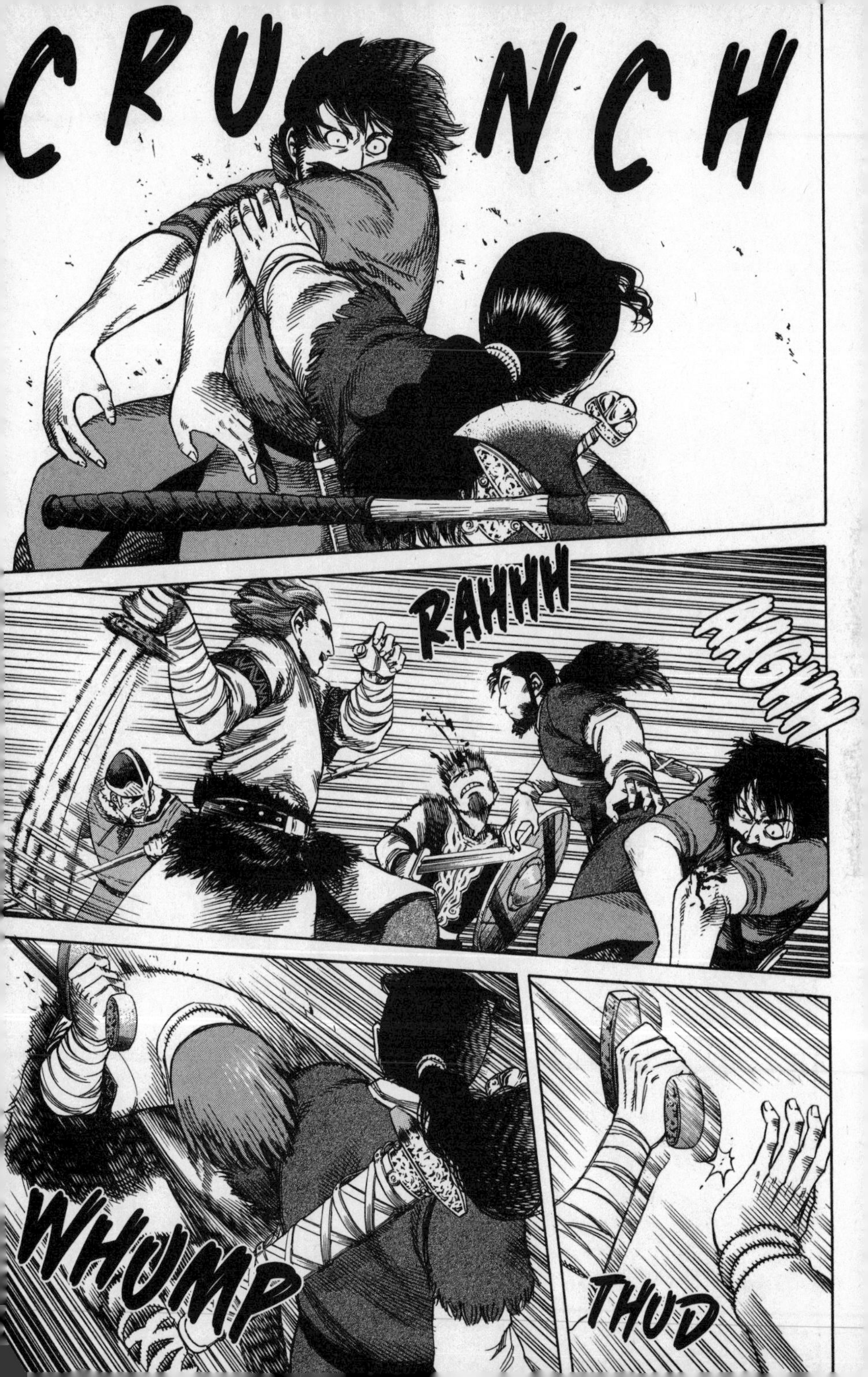
CRUNCH
AAGHH
RAHHH
THUD
WHUMP

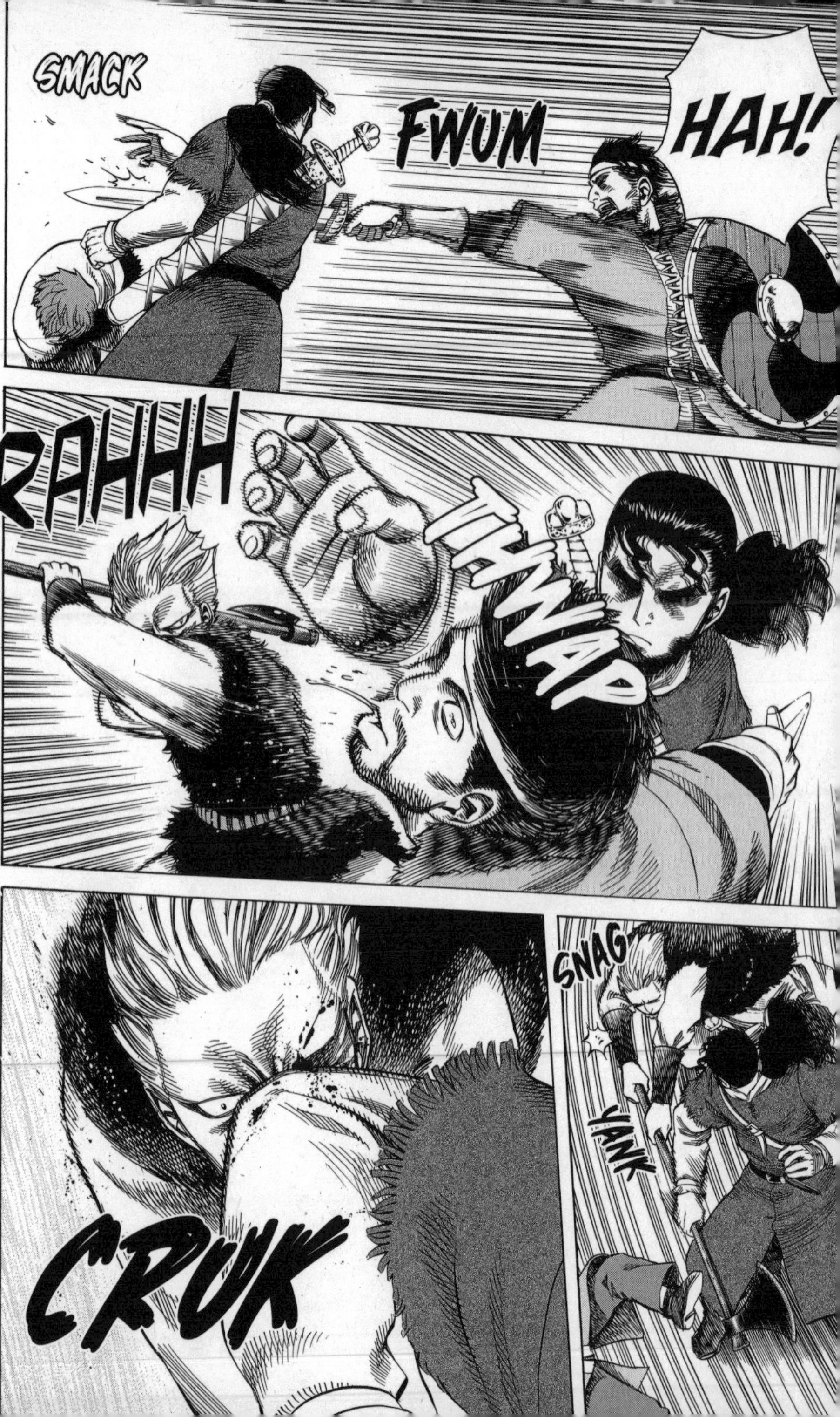
HAH!
FWUM
SMACK
THWAP
RAHHH
SNAG
YANK
CRUK

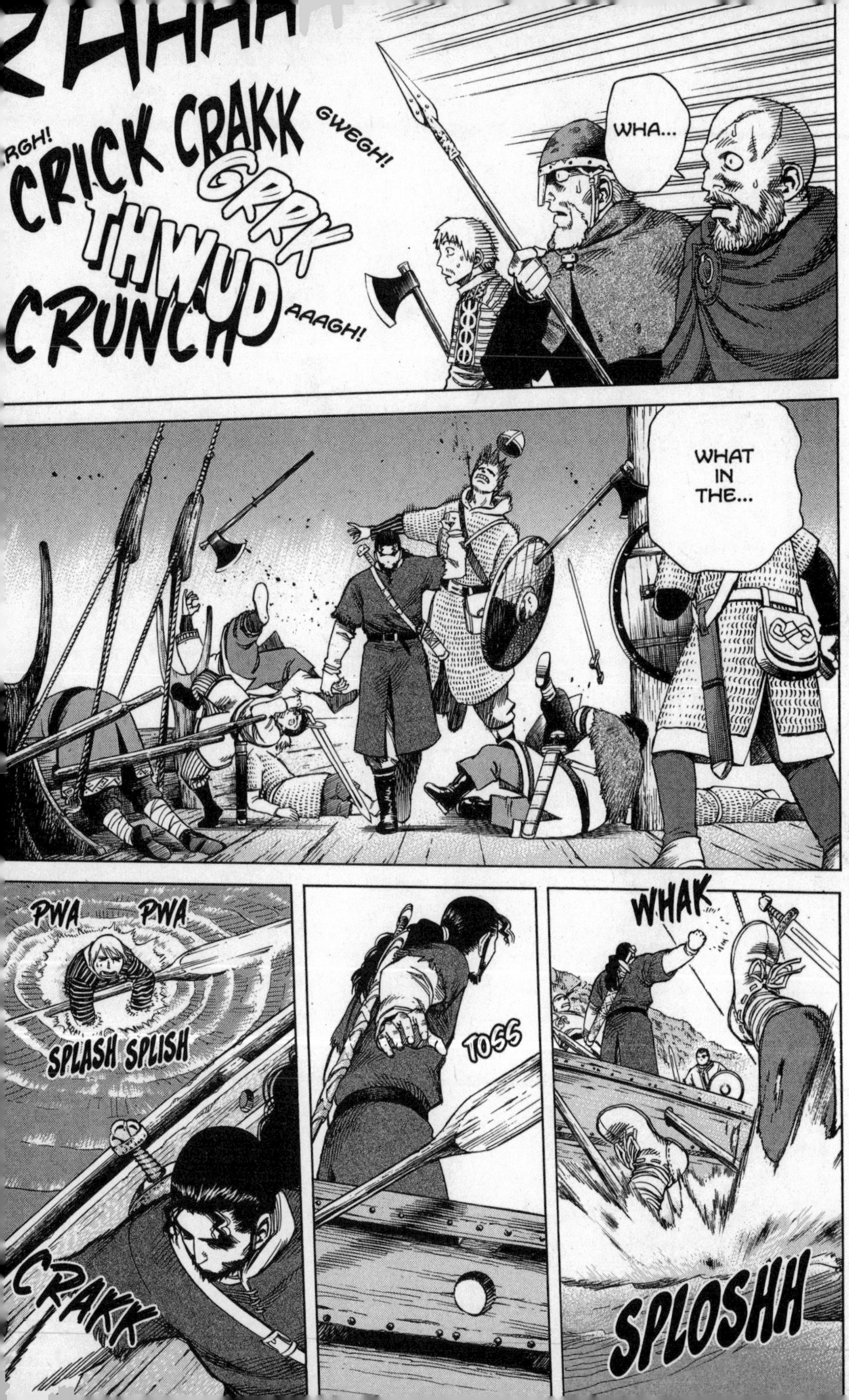
WHA...
GWEGH!
CRICK CRAKK
GRRK
THWUD
CRUNCH
AAAGH!
WHAT IN THE...
WHAK
SPLOSHH
TOSS
PWA PWA
SPLASH SPLISH
CRAKK

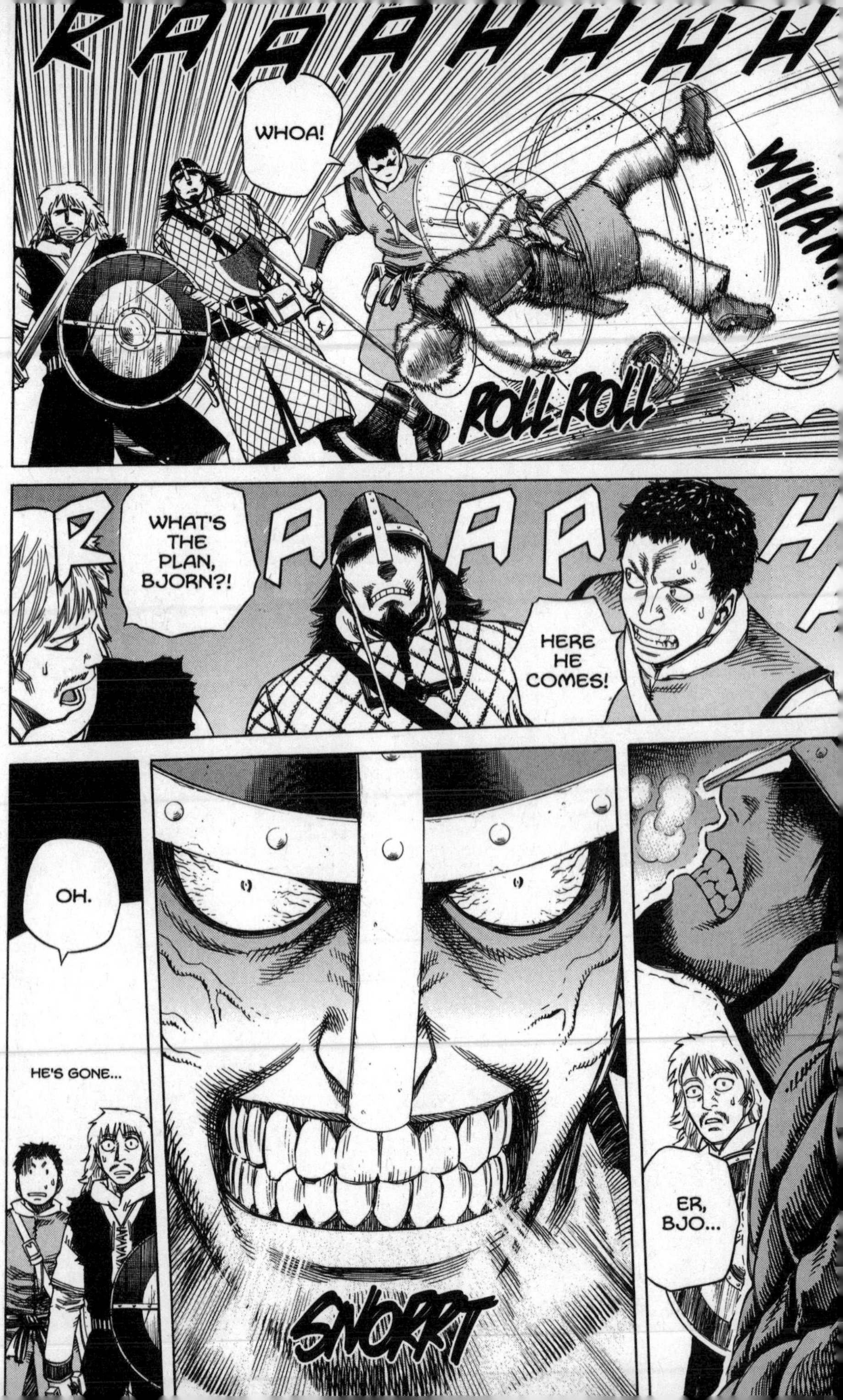
RAAAHHHH
WHAM
WHOA!
ROLL ROLL
RAAAH
HERE HE COMES!
WHAT'S THE PLAN, BJORN?!
ER, BJO...
SNORRT
OH.
HE'S GONE...

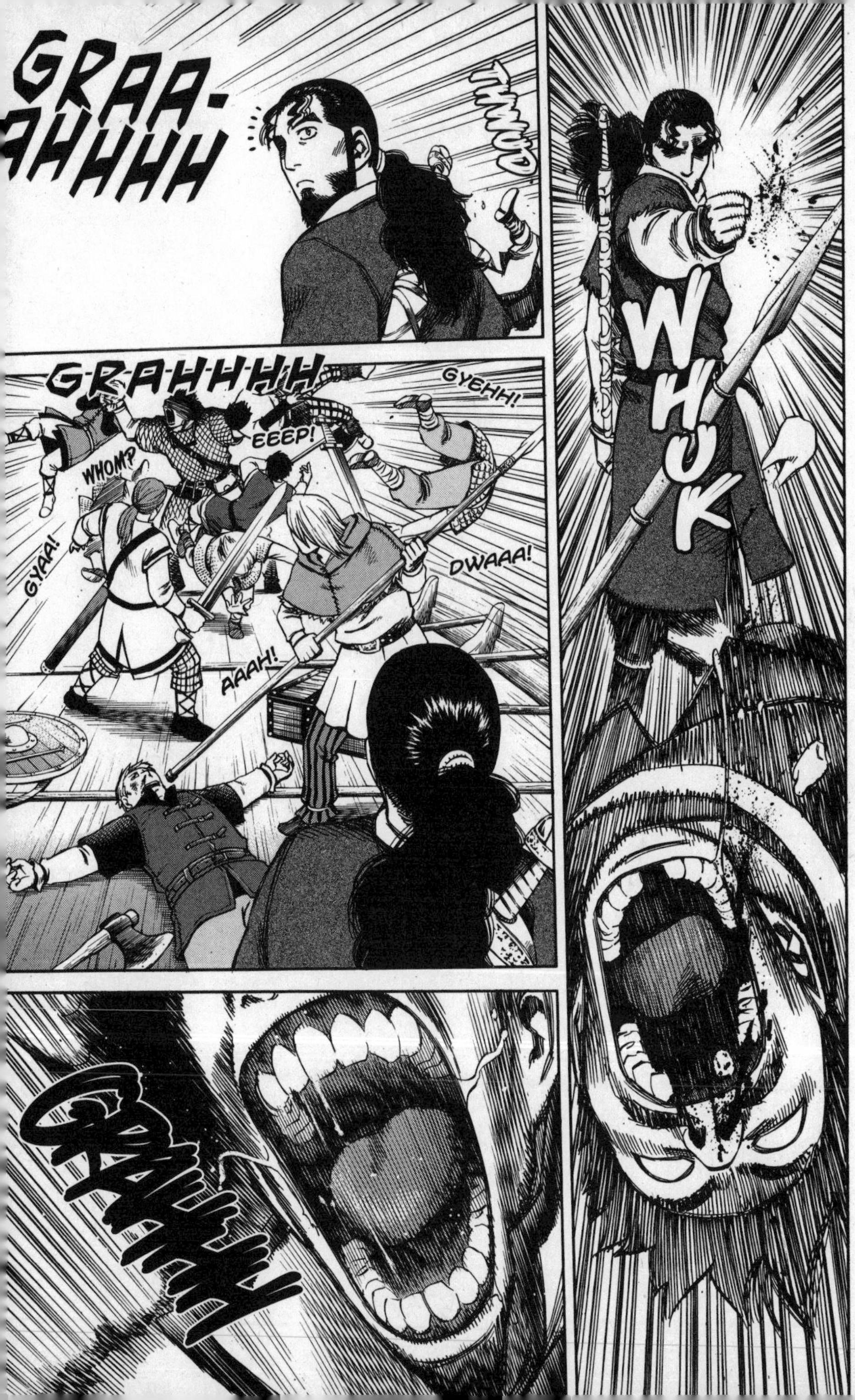
WHUK
GRAA-AHHHH
THWUD
G-R-A-H-H-H-H
GYEHH!
EEEP!
WHOMP
DWAAA!
GYAA!
AAAH!
GRAHHHH!

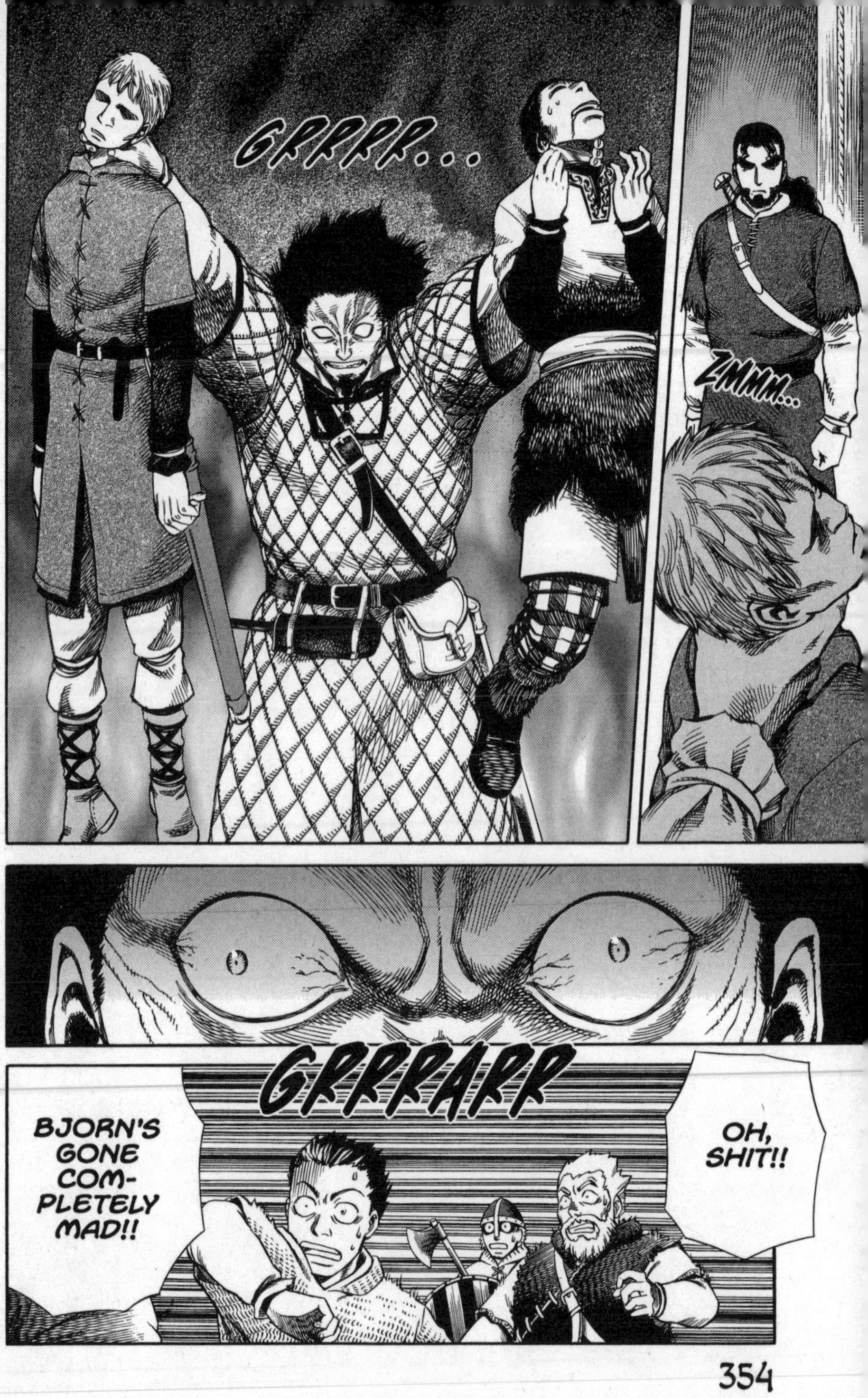
ZMMM...
GRRRR...
GRRRARR
OH, SHIT!!
BJORN'S GONE COM-PLETELY MAD!!

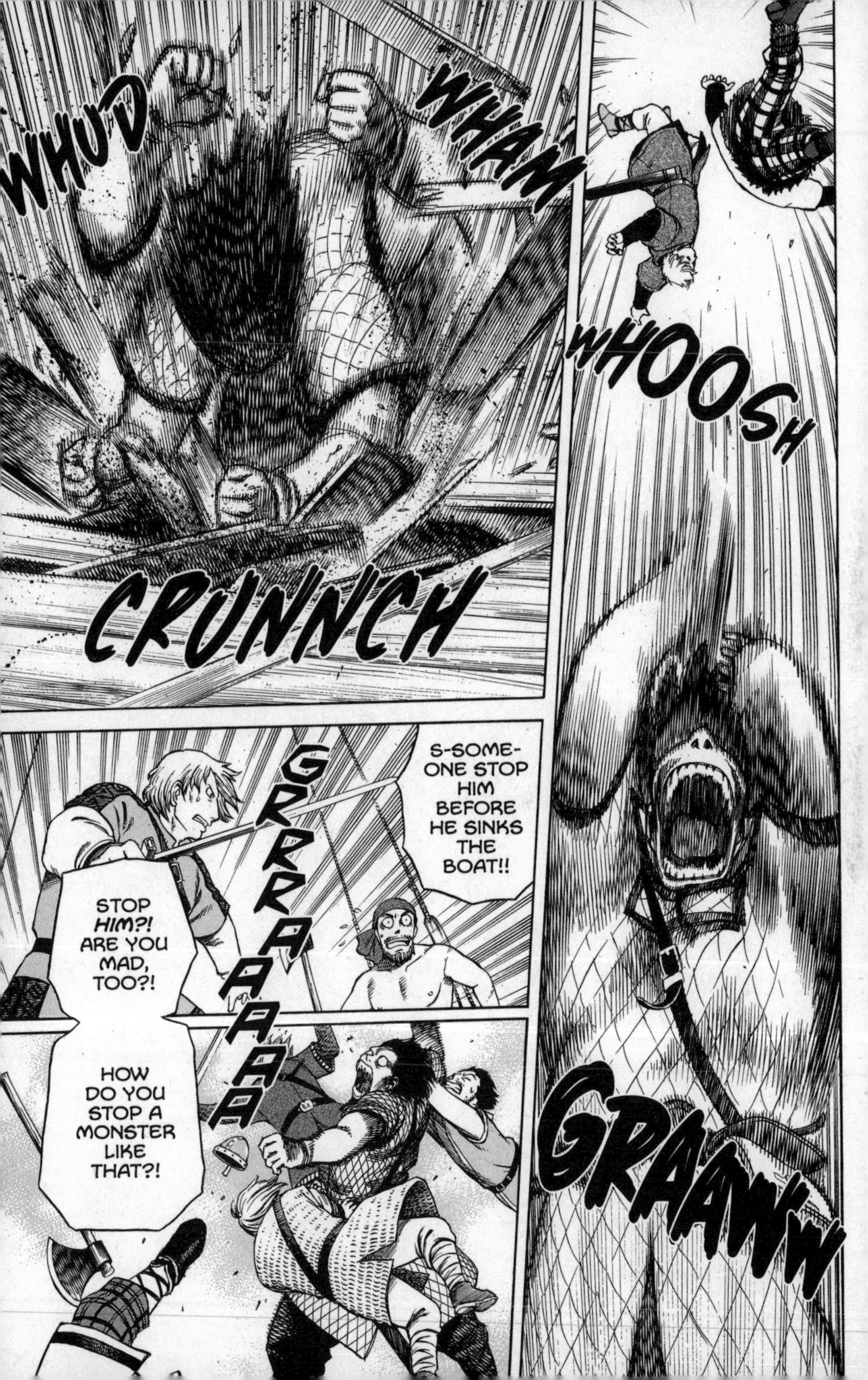
WHOOSH
GRAAWW
WHAM
WHUD
CRUNNCH
S-SOME-ONE STOP HIM BEFORE HE SINKS THE BOAT!!
GRRRAAAAAA
STOP *HIM*?! ARE YOU MAD, TOO?!
HOW DO YOU STOP A MONSTER LIKE THAT?!

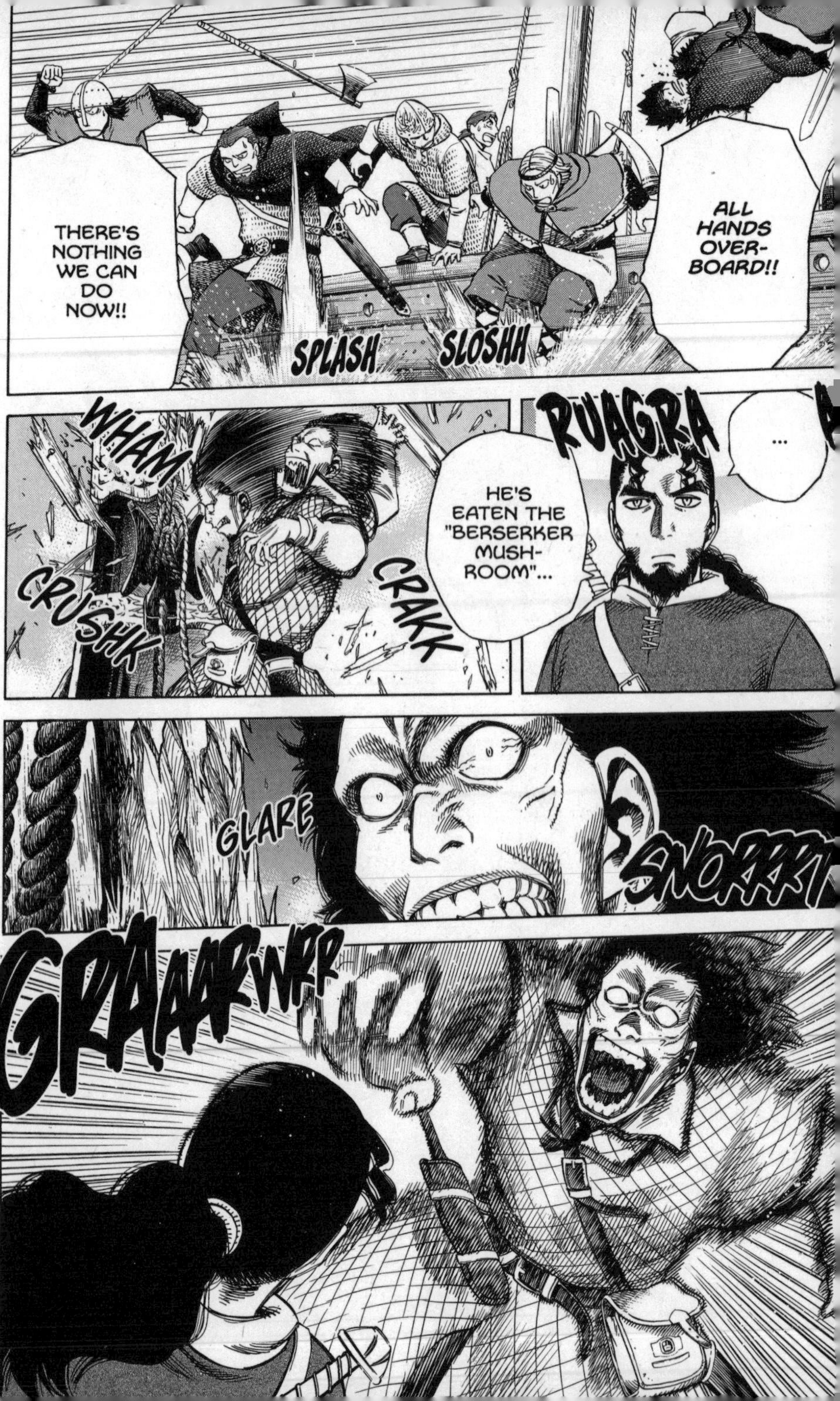
ALL HANDS OVER-BOARD!!
THERE'S NOTHING WE CAN DO NOW!!
SLOSHH
SPLASH
RUAGRA
...
HE'S EATEN THE "BERSERKER MUSH-ROOM"...
CRAKK
WHAM
CRUSHK
SNORRRT
GLARE
GRAAARWRR

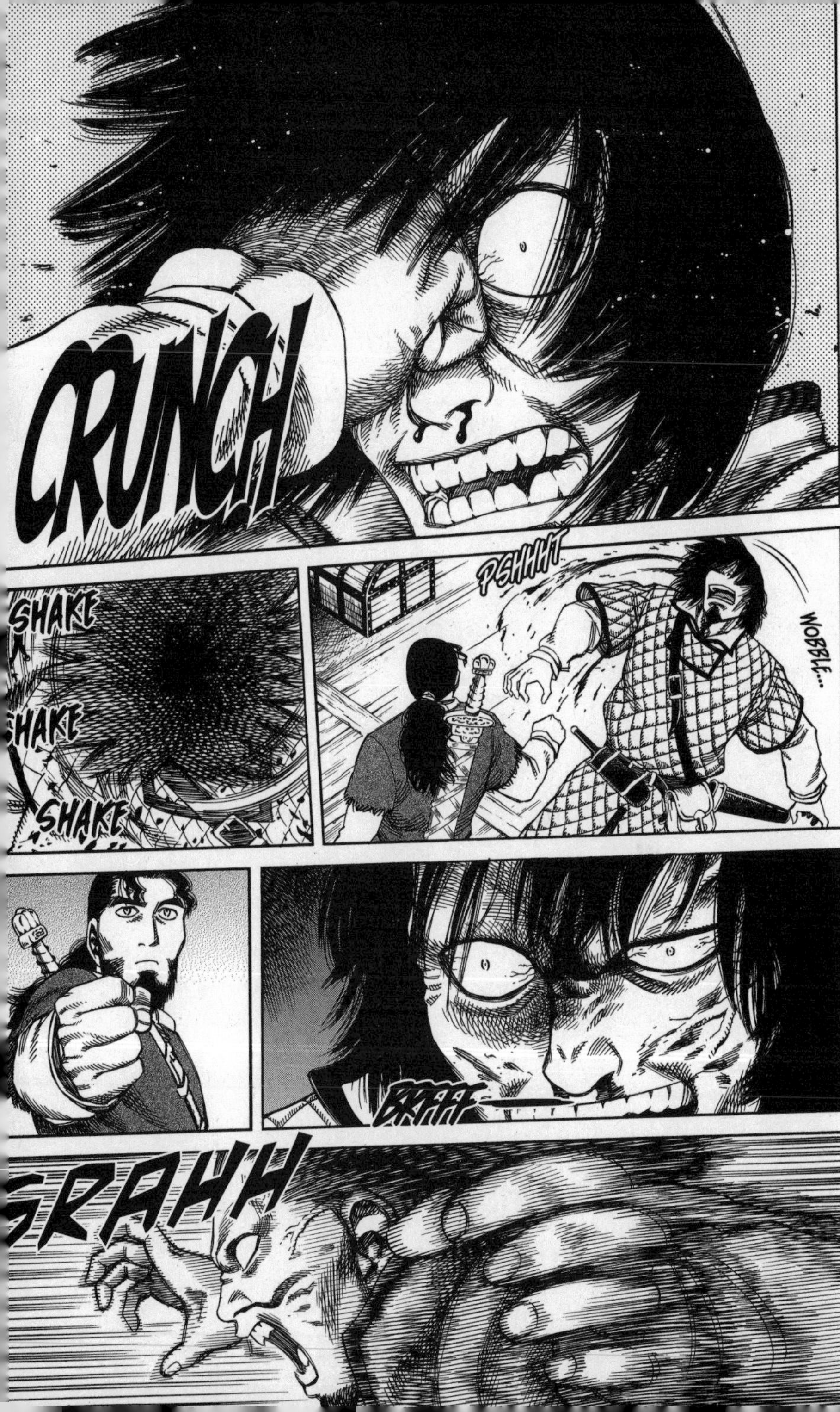
CRUNCH
PSHHHT
WOBBLE...
SHAKE
SHAKE
SHAKE
SRAHH

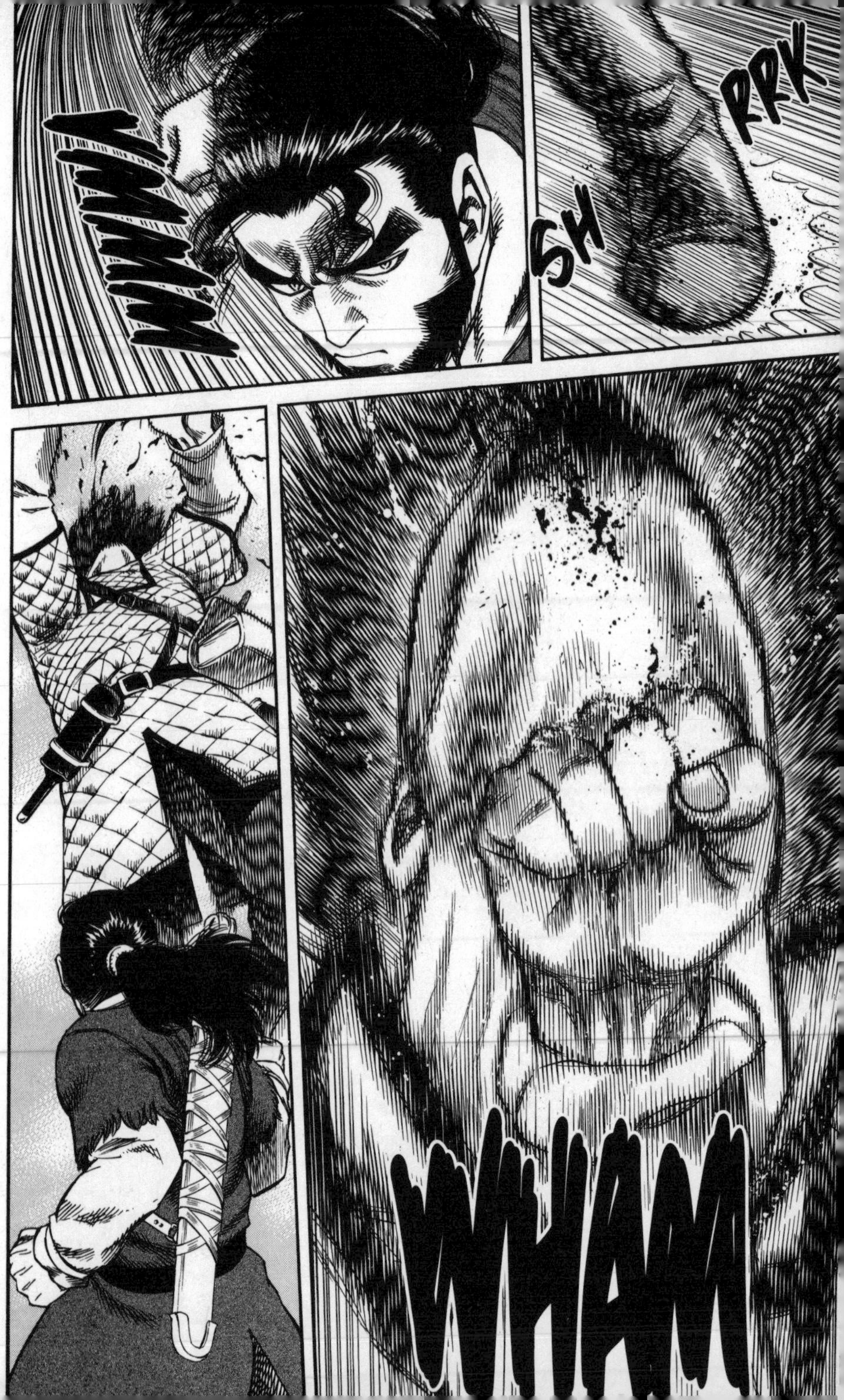
SH RRK
WHAM

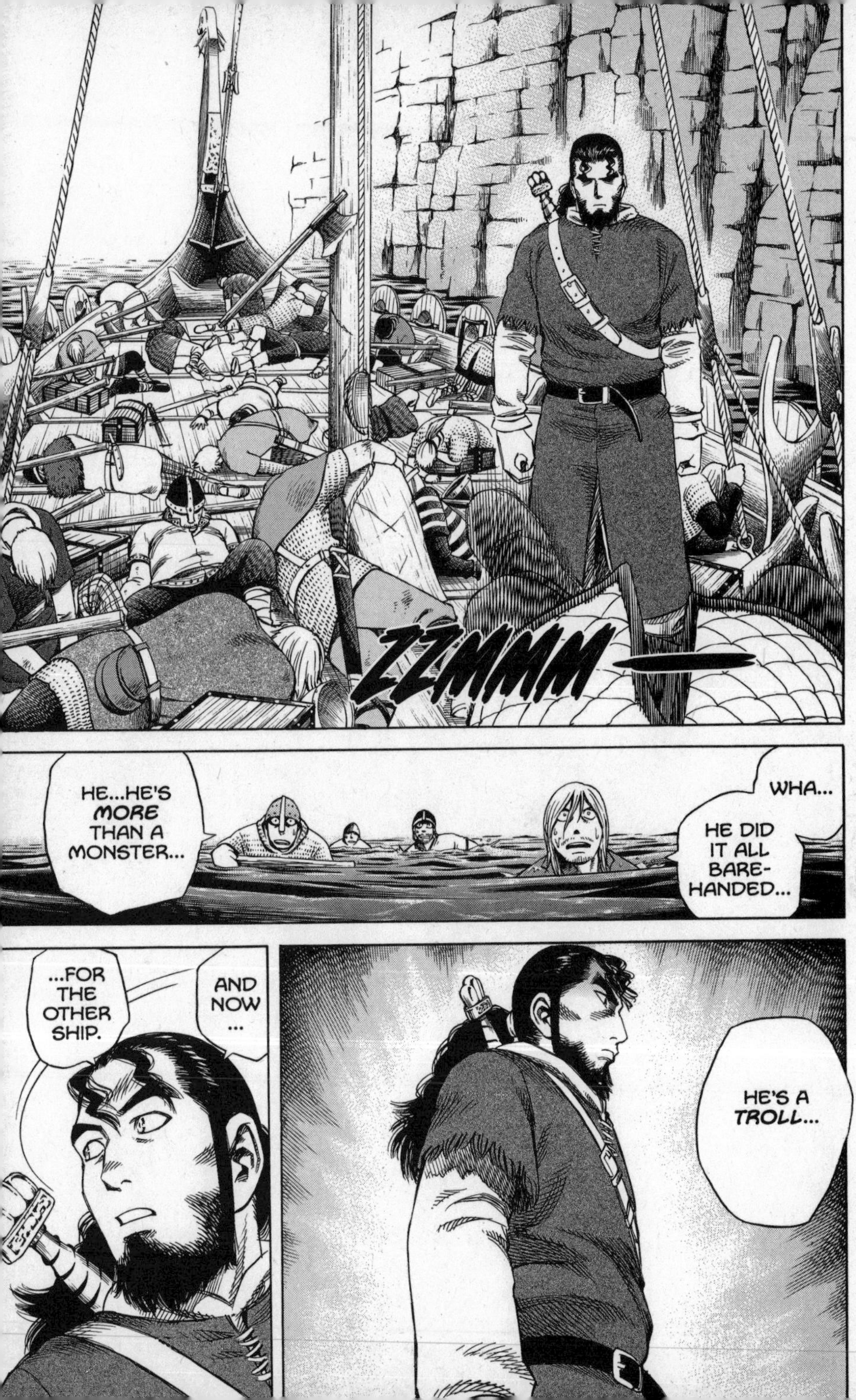
ZZMMMM
WHA...
HE DID IT ALL BARE-HANDED...
HE...HE'S MORE THAN A MONSTER...
HE'S A TROLL...
AND NOW ...
...FOR THE OTHER SHIP.

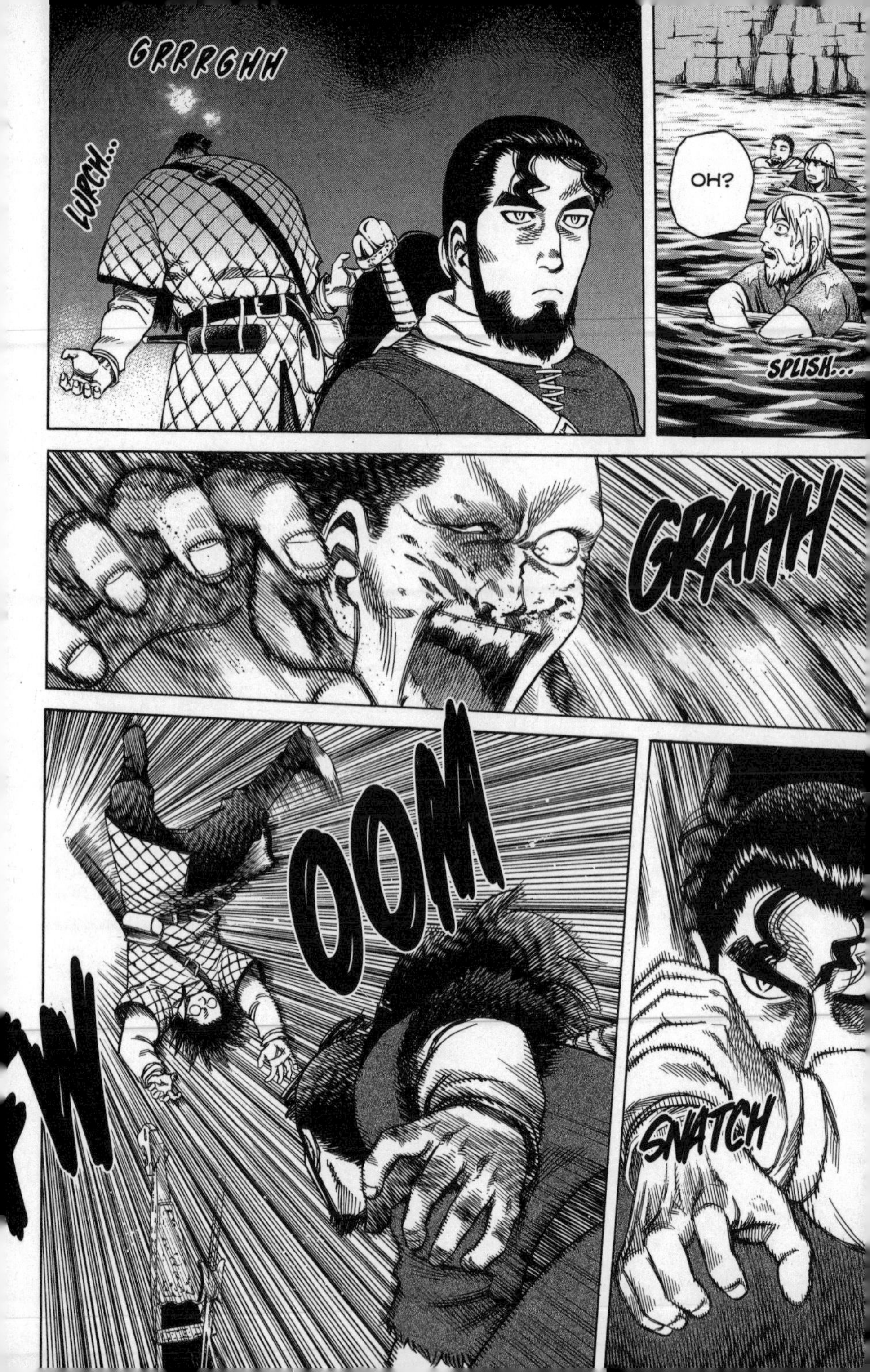
OH?
SPLISH...
GRRRGHH
LURCH...
GRAHH
SNATCH
OOM

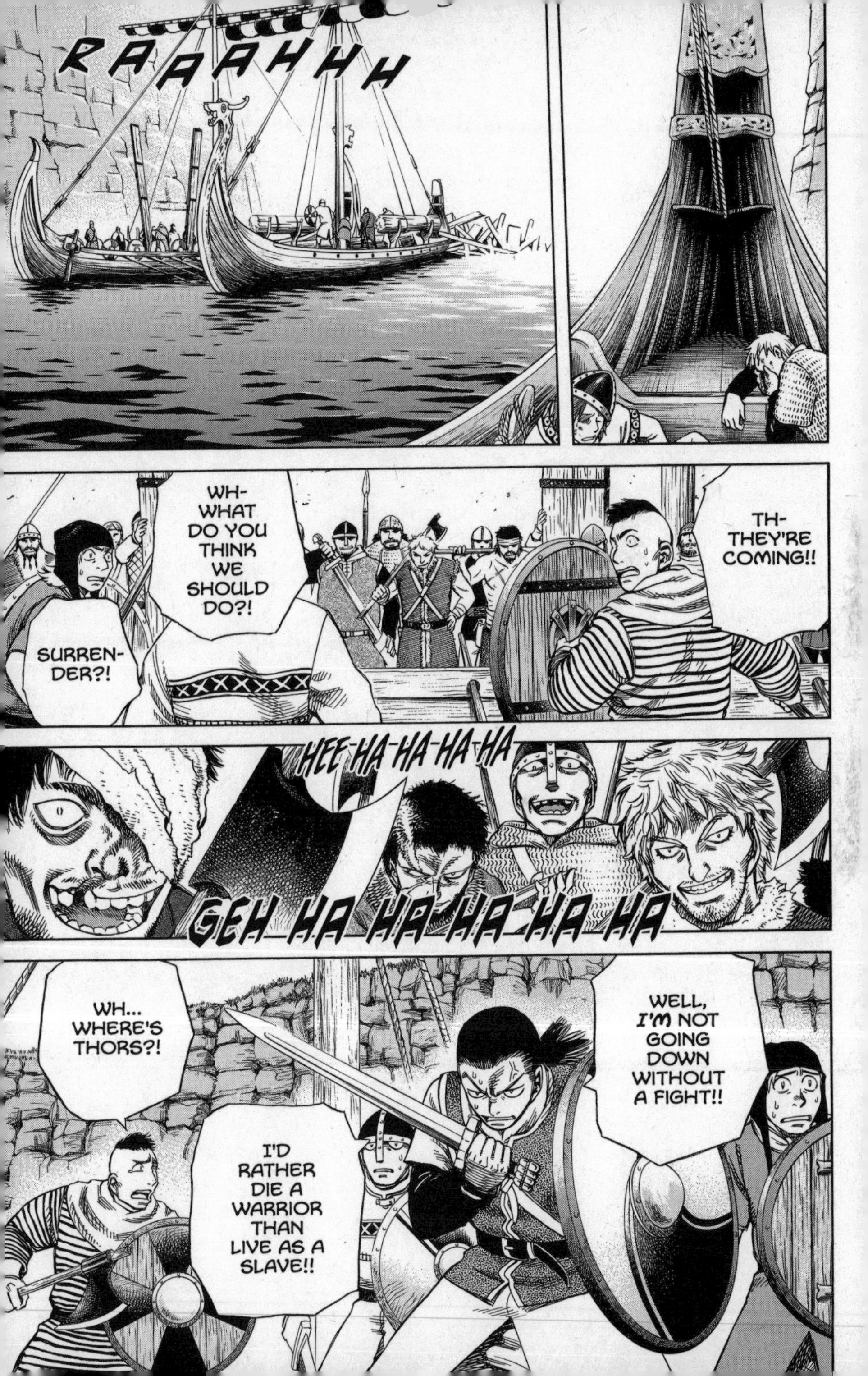
RAAAHHH
TH- THEY'RE COMING!!
WH- WHAT DO YOU THINK WE SHOULD DO?!
SURREN- DER?!
HEE-HA-HA-HA-HA
GEH HA HA HA HA HA
WELL, I'M NOT GOING DOWN WITHOUT A FIGHT!!
WH... WHERE'S THORS?!
I'D RATHER DIE A WARRIOR THAN LIVE AS A SLAVE!!

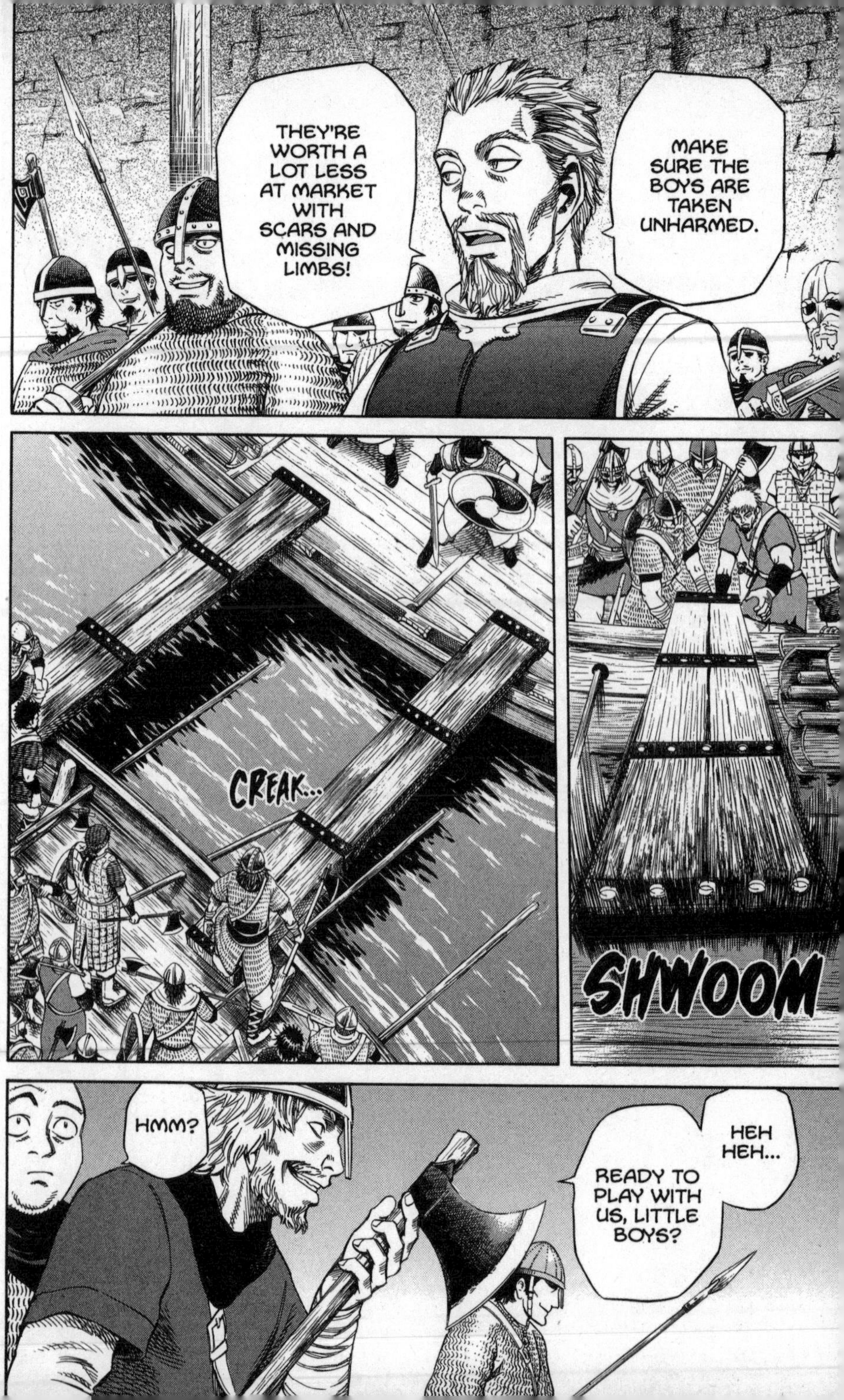
MAKE SURE THE BOYS ARE TAKEN UNHARMED.
THEY'RE WORTH A LOT LESS AT MARKET WITH SCARS AND MISSING LIMBS!
SHWOOM
CREAK...
HEH HEH... READY TO PLAY WITH US, LITTLE BOYS?
HMM?

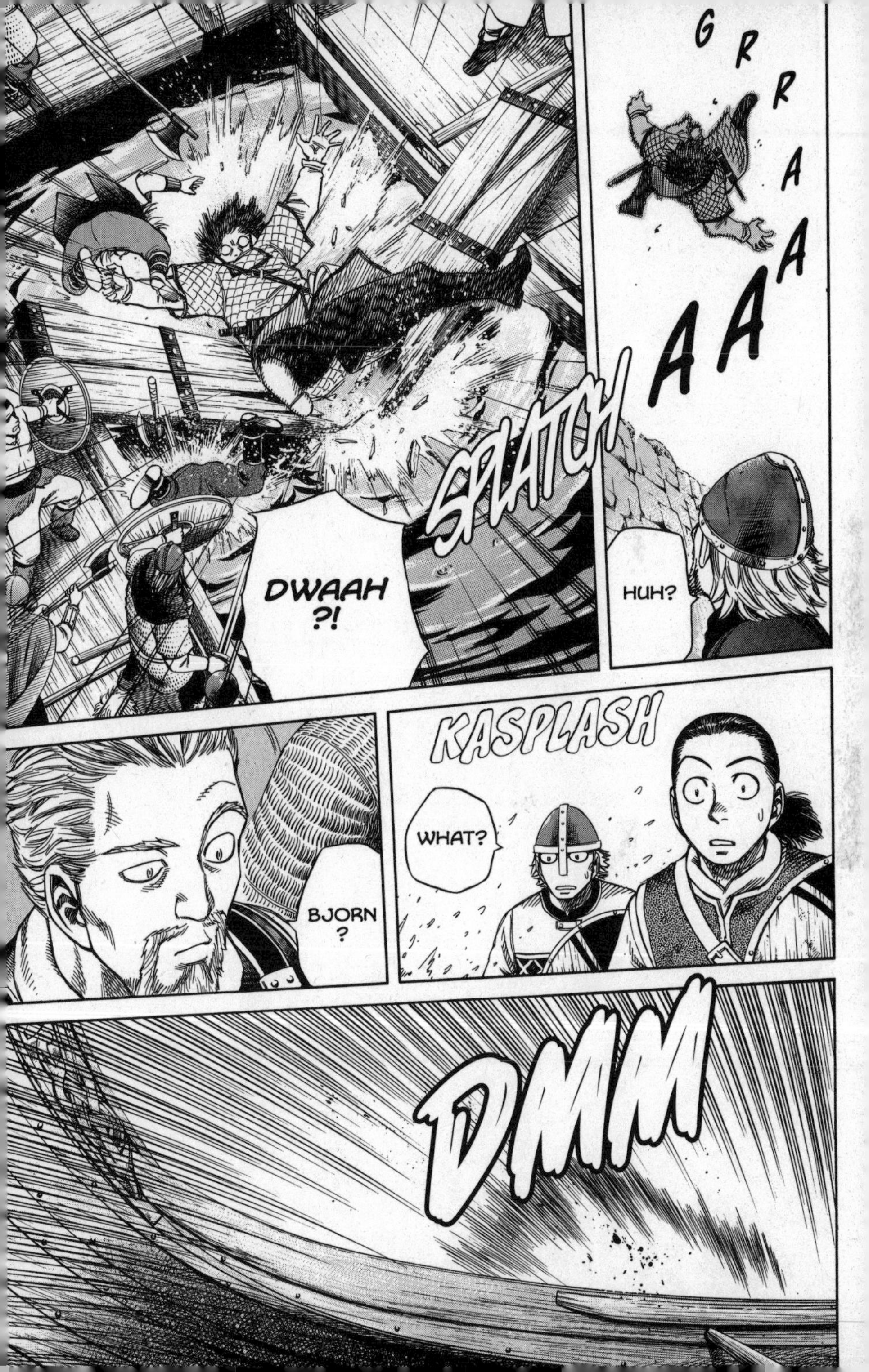
GRRAAAAA
HUH?
SPLATCH
DWAAH ?!
KASPLASH
WHAT?
BJORN ?
DMM

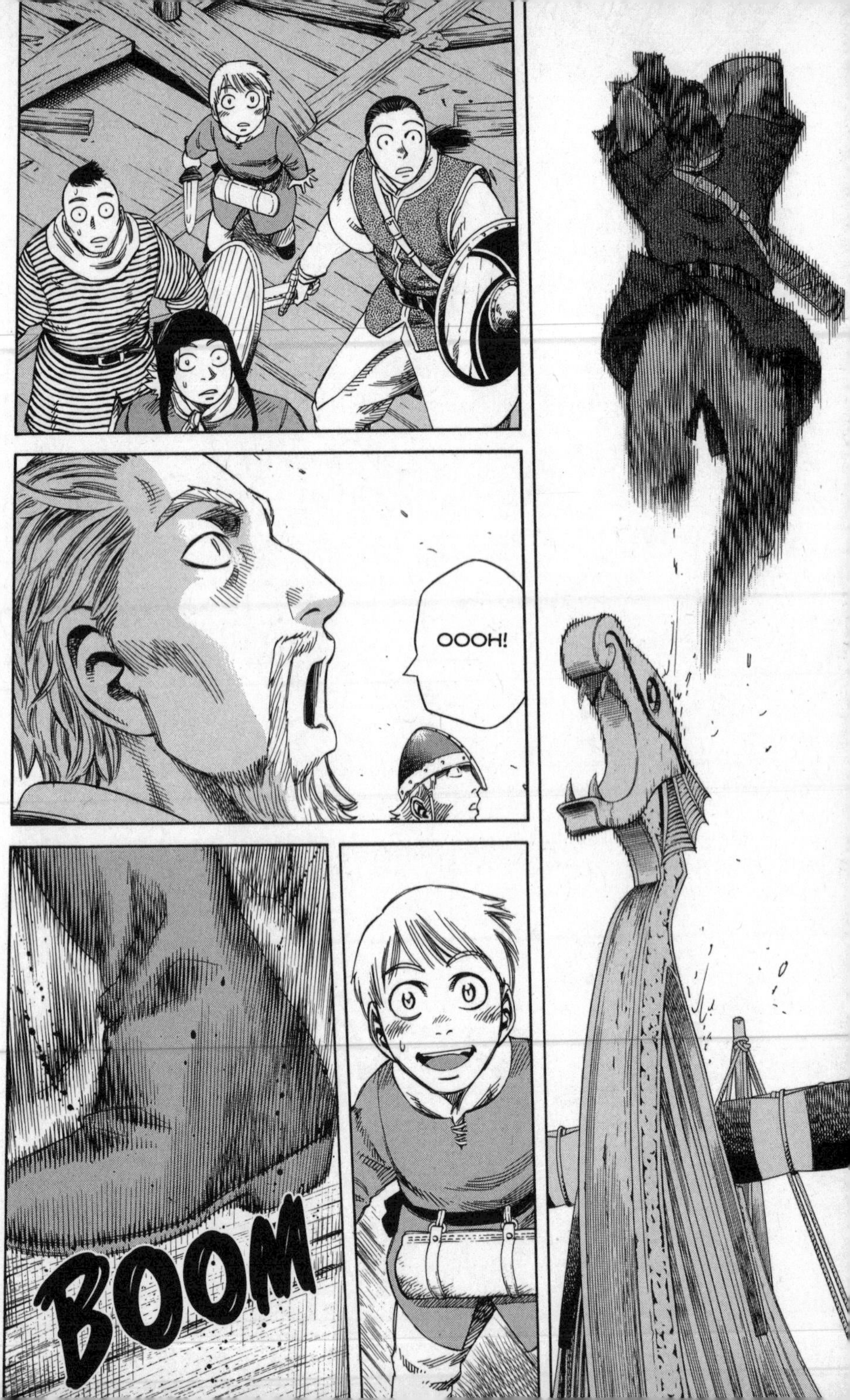
OOOH!
BOOM

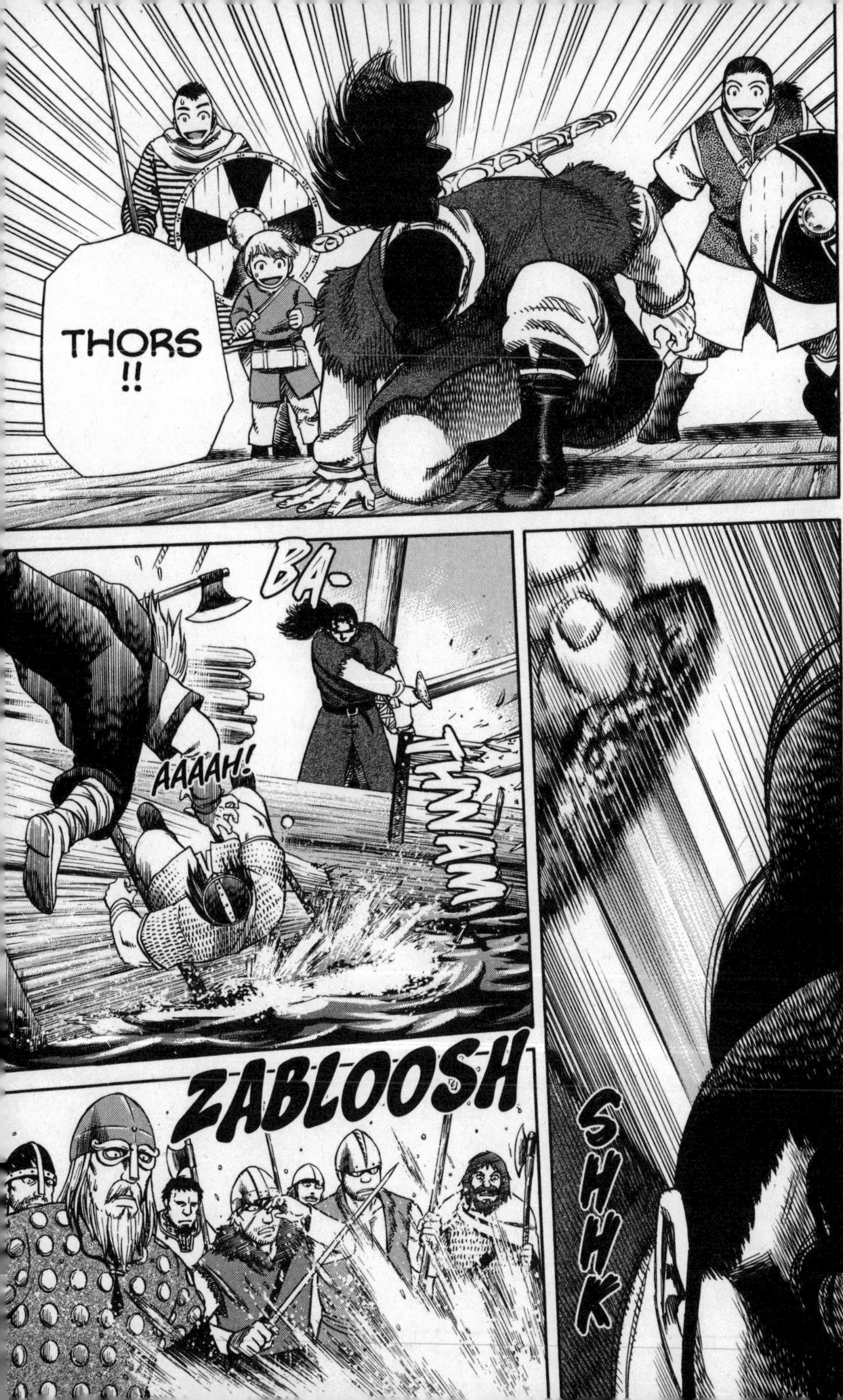
THORS !!
SHHK
BA-
THWAM
AAAAH!
ZABLOOSH

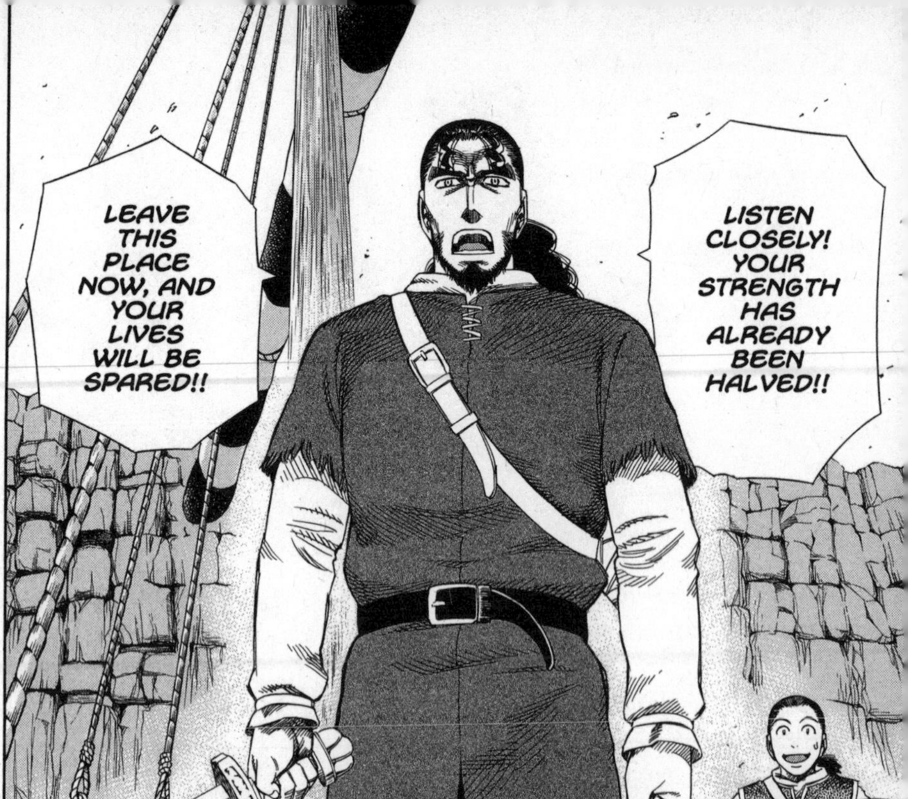
LISTEN CLOSELY! YOUR STRENGTH HAS ALREADY BEEN HALVED!!
LEAVE THIS PLACE NOW, AND YOUR LIVES WILL BE SPARED!!

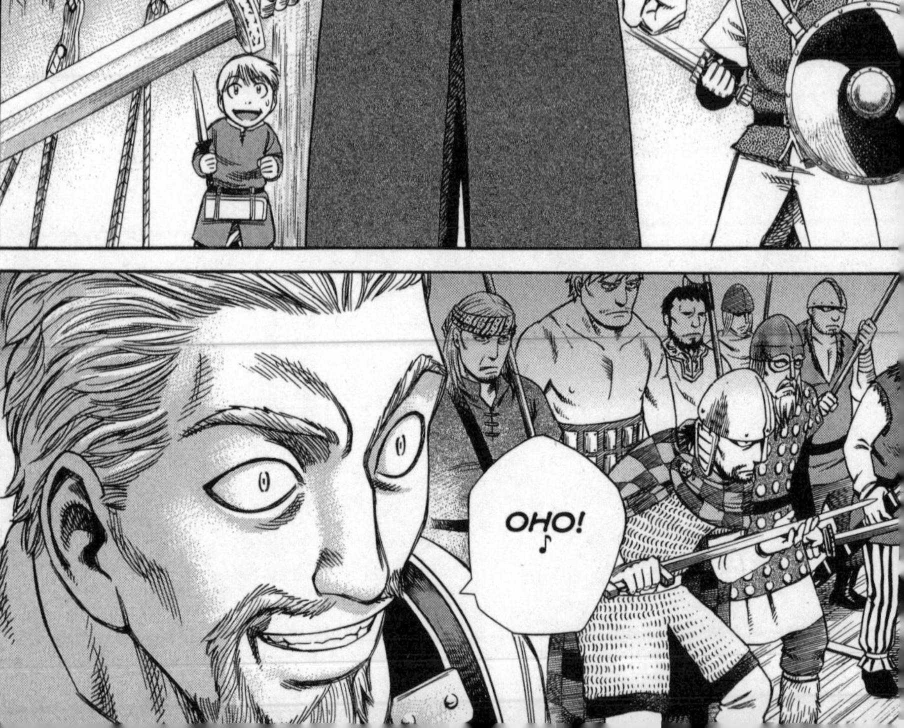
OHO! ♪

CHAPTER 12 - END

CHAPTER 13: SMELL

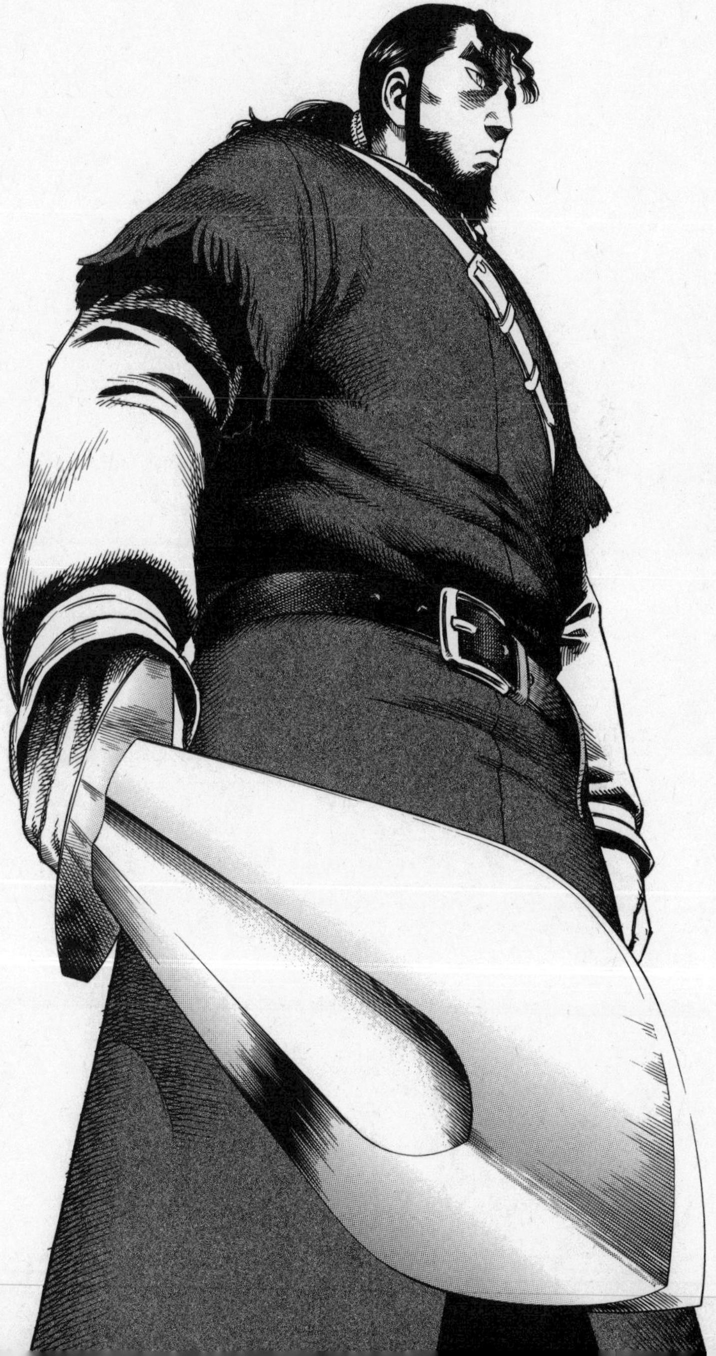

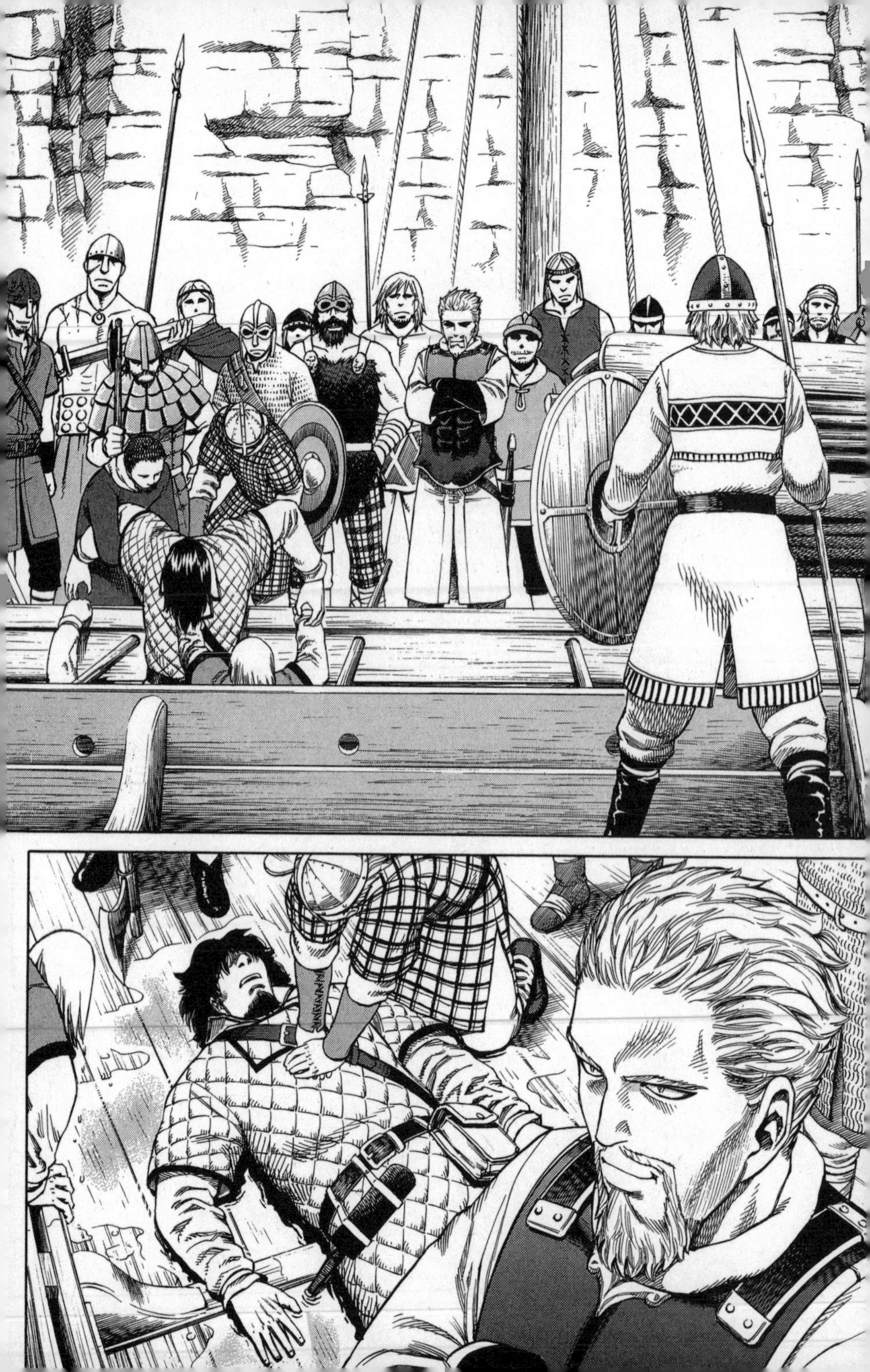

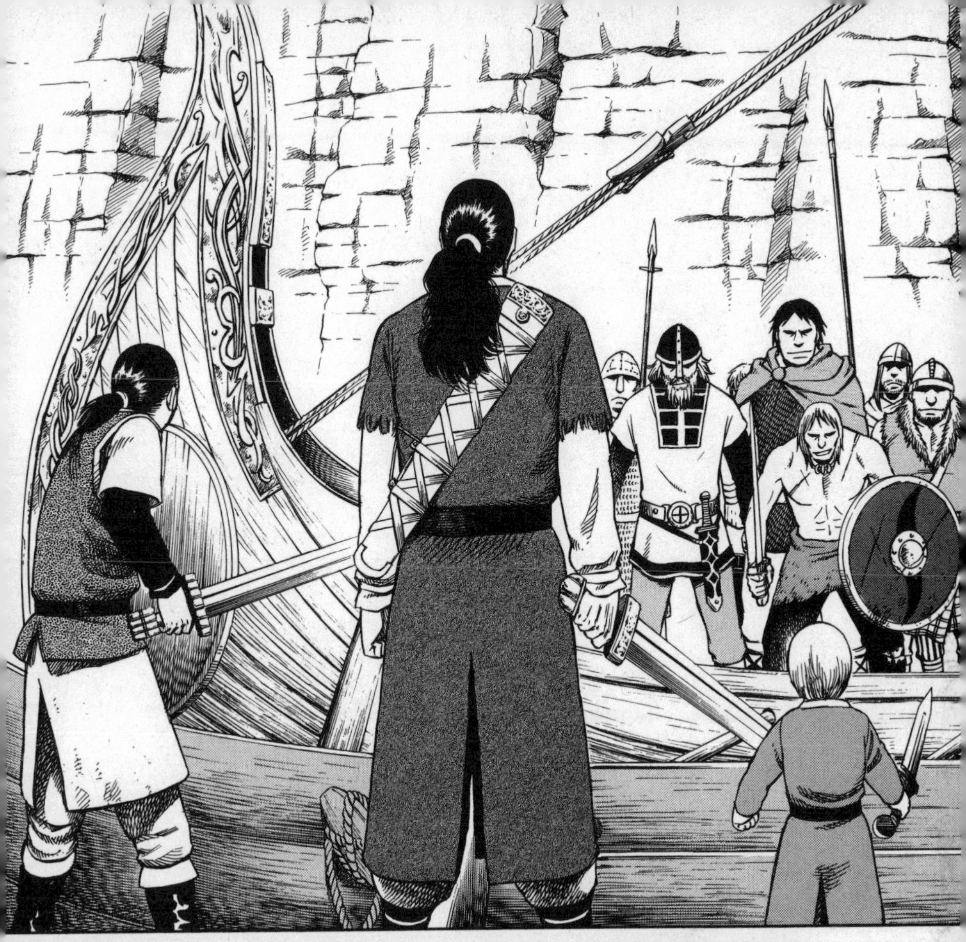

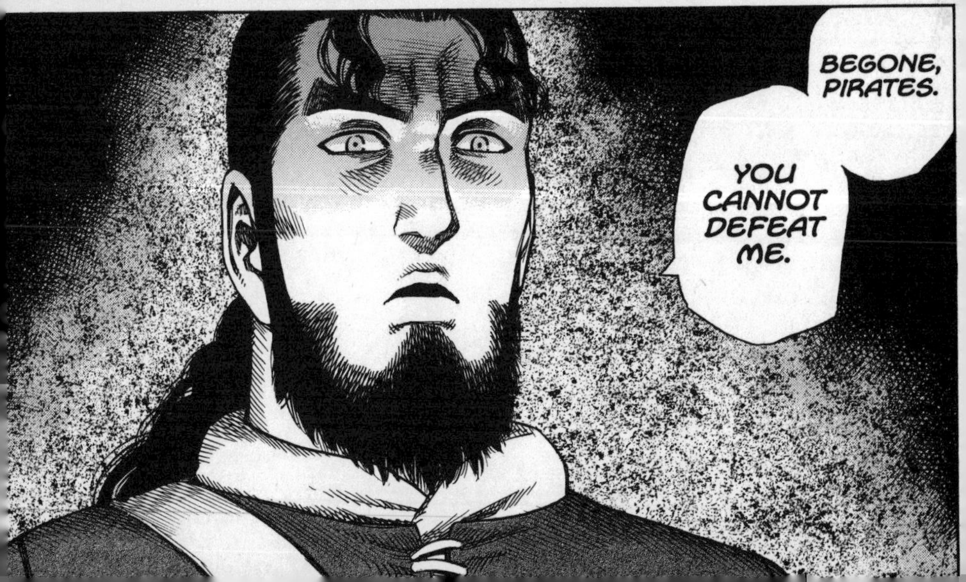
BEGONE, PIRATES.
YOU CANNOT DEFEAT ME.

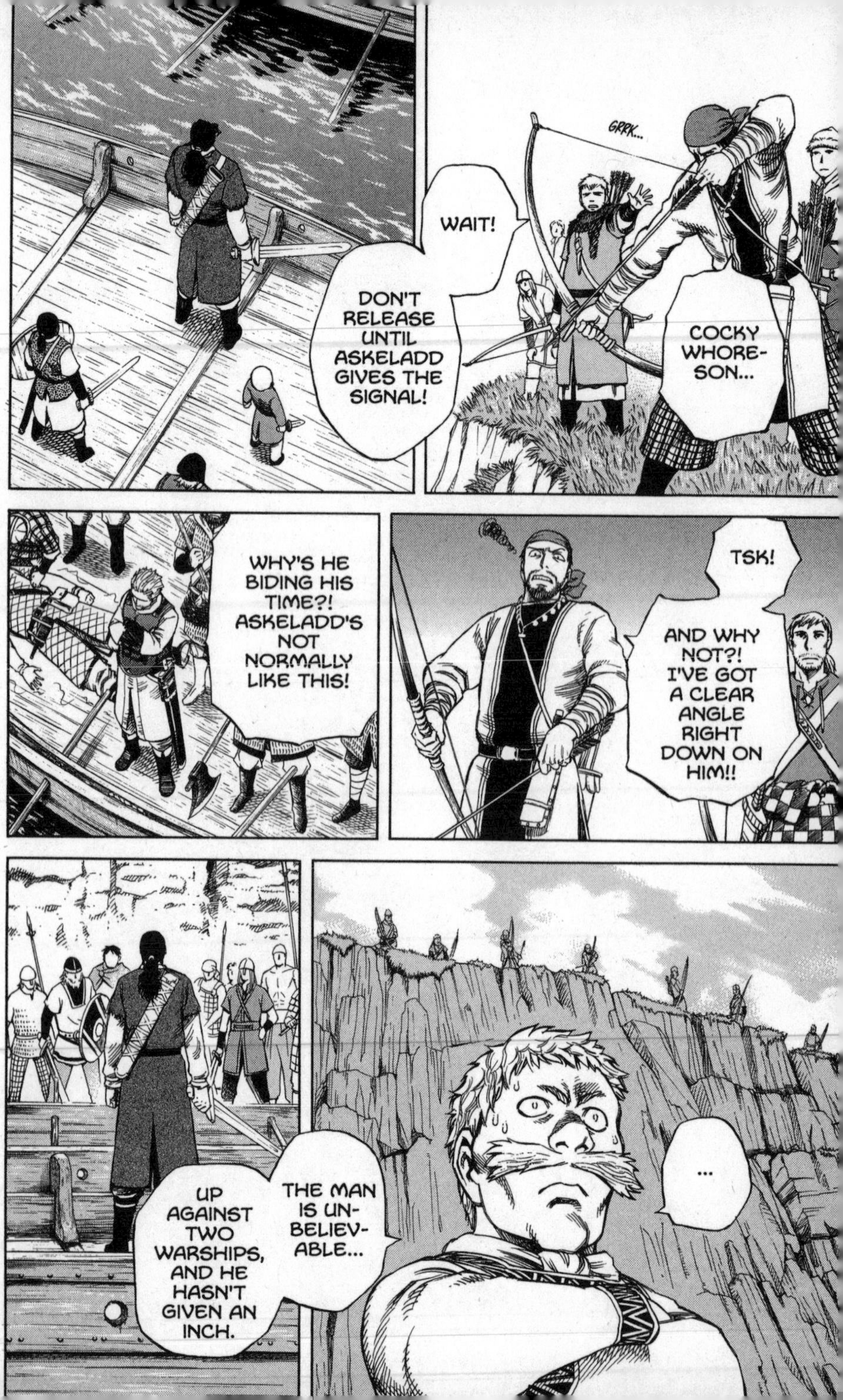
GRRK...
COCKY WHORE-SON...
WAIT!
DON'T RELEASE UNTIL ASKELADD GIVES THE SIGNAL!
TSK!
AND WHY NOT?! I'VE GOT A CLEAR ANGLE RIGHT DOWN ON HIM!!
WHY'S HE BIDING HIS TIME?! ASKELADD'S NOT NORMALLY LIKE THIS!
...
THE MAN IS UN-BELIEV-ABLE...
UP AGAINST TWO WARSHIPS, AND HE HASN'T GIVEN AN INCH.

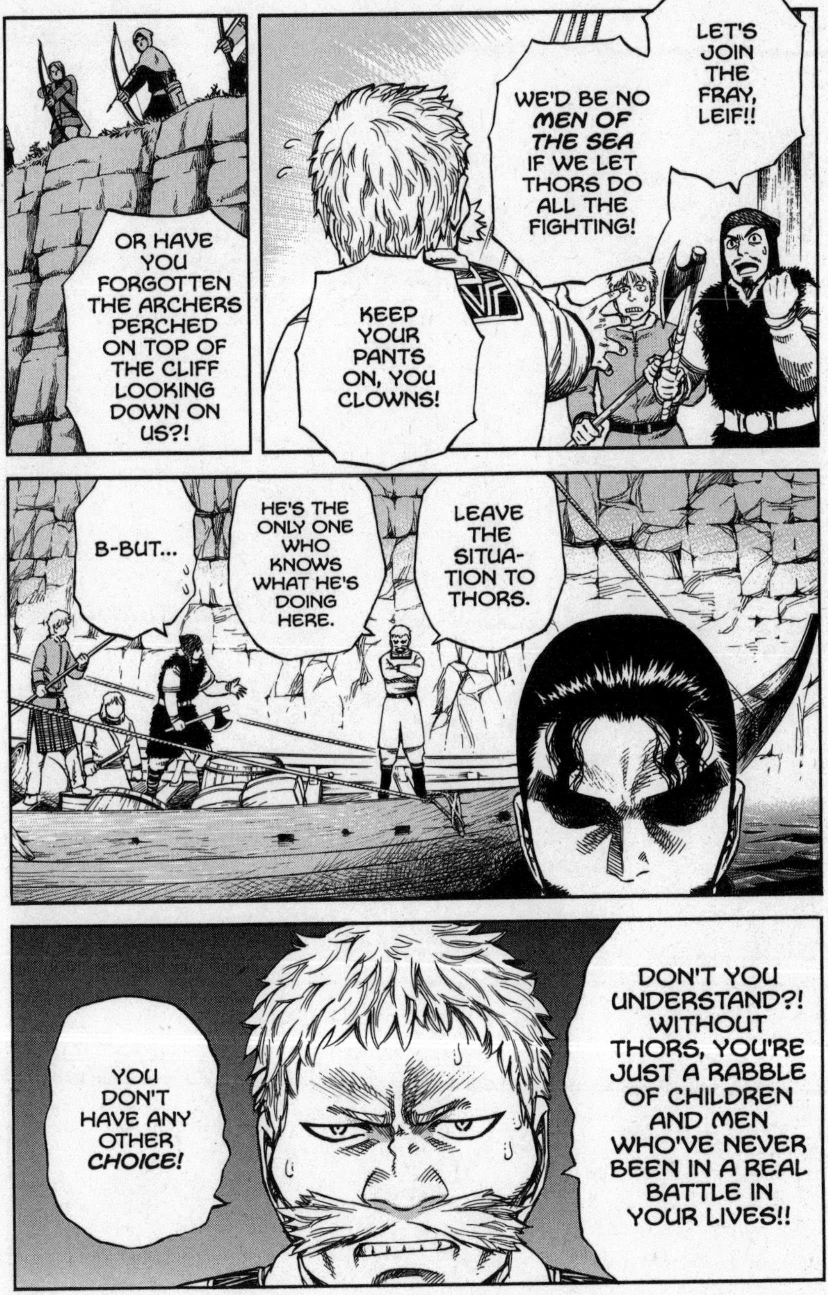
LET'S JOIN THE FRAY, LEIF!!
WE'D BE NO *MEN OF THE SEA* IF WE LET THORS DO ALL THE FIGHTING!
KEEP YOUR PANTS ON, YOU CLOWNS!
OR HAVE YOU FORGOTTEN THE ARCHERS PERCHED ON TOP OF THE CLIFF LOOKING DOWN ON US?!
LEAVE THE SITUA-TION TO THORS.
HE'S THE ONLY ONE WHO KNOWS WHAT HE'S DOING HERE.
B-BUT...
DON'T YOU UNDERSTAND?! WITHOUT THORS, YOU'RE JUST A RABBLE OF CHILDREN AND MEN WHO'VE NEVER BEEN IN A REAL BATTLE IN YOUR LIVES!!
YOU DON'T HAVE ANY OTHER *CHOICE!*

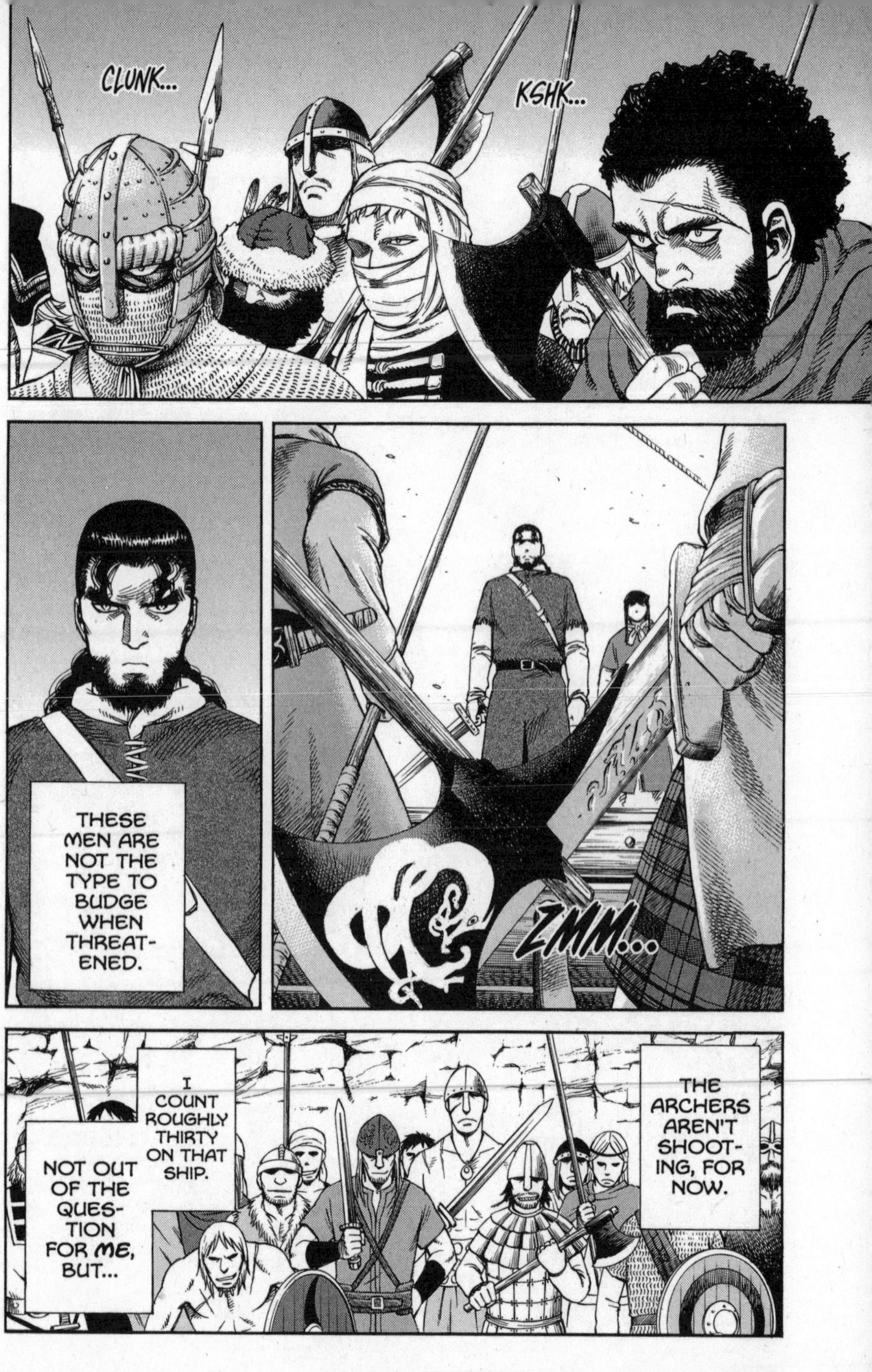
KSHK...
CLUNK...
ZMM...
THESE MEN ARE NOT THE TYPE TO BUDGE WHEN THREAT-ENED.
THE ARCHERS AREN'T SHOOT-ING, FOR NOW.
I COUNT ROUGHLY THIRTY ON THAT SHIP.
NOT OUT OF THE QUES-TION FOR *ME*, BUT...

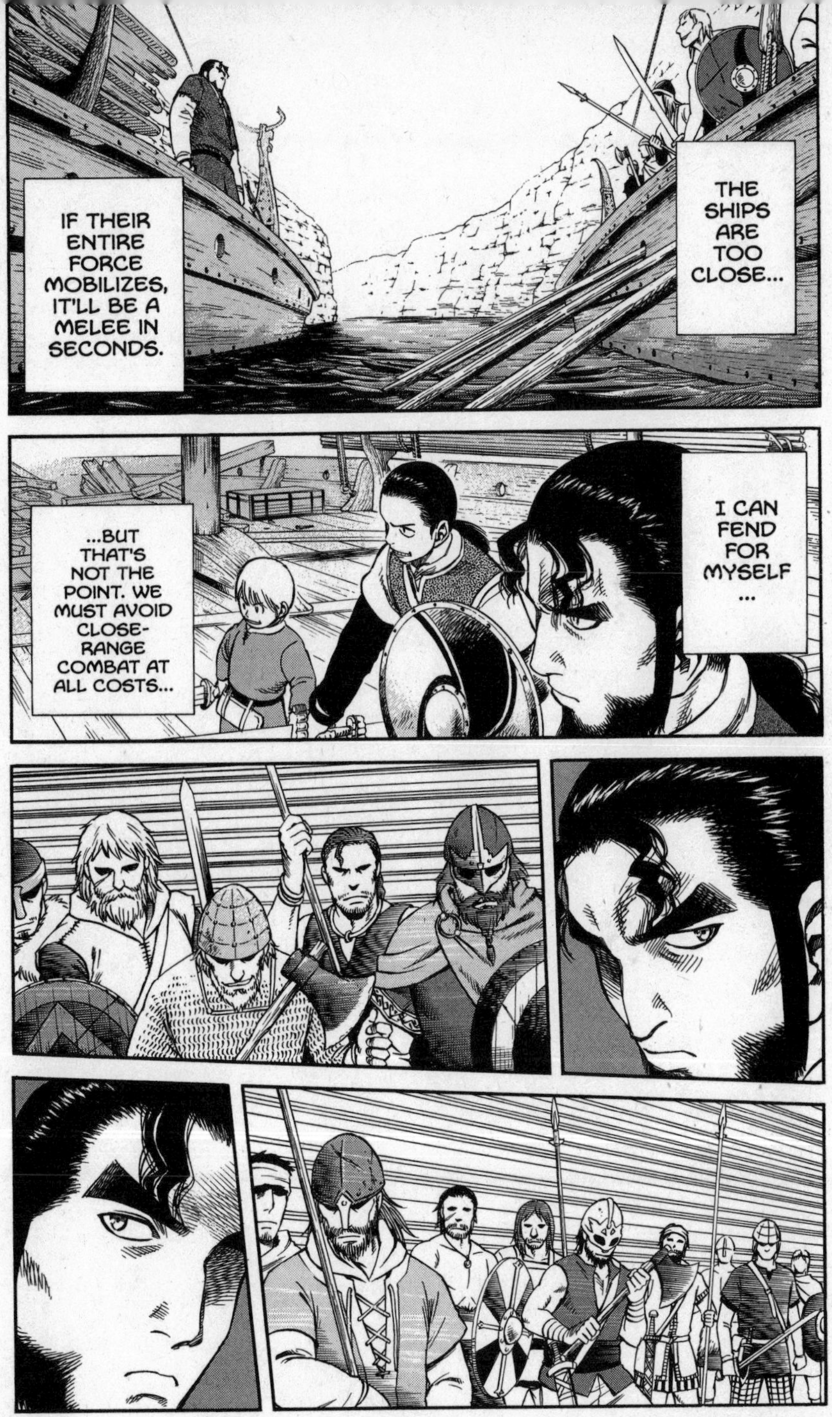
THE SHIPS ARE TOO CLOSE...
IF THEIR ENTIRE FORCE MOBILIZES, IT'LL BE A MELEE IN SECONDS.
I CAN FEND FOR MYSELF ...
...BUT THAT'S NOT THE POINT. WE MUST AVOID CLOSE-RANGE COMBAT AT ALL COSTS...

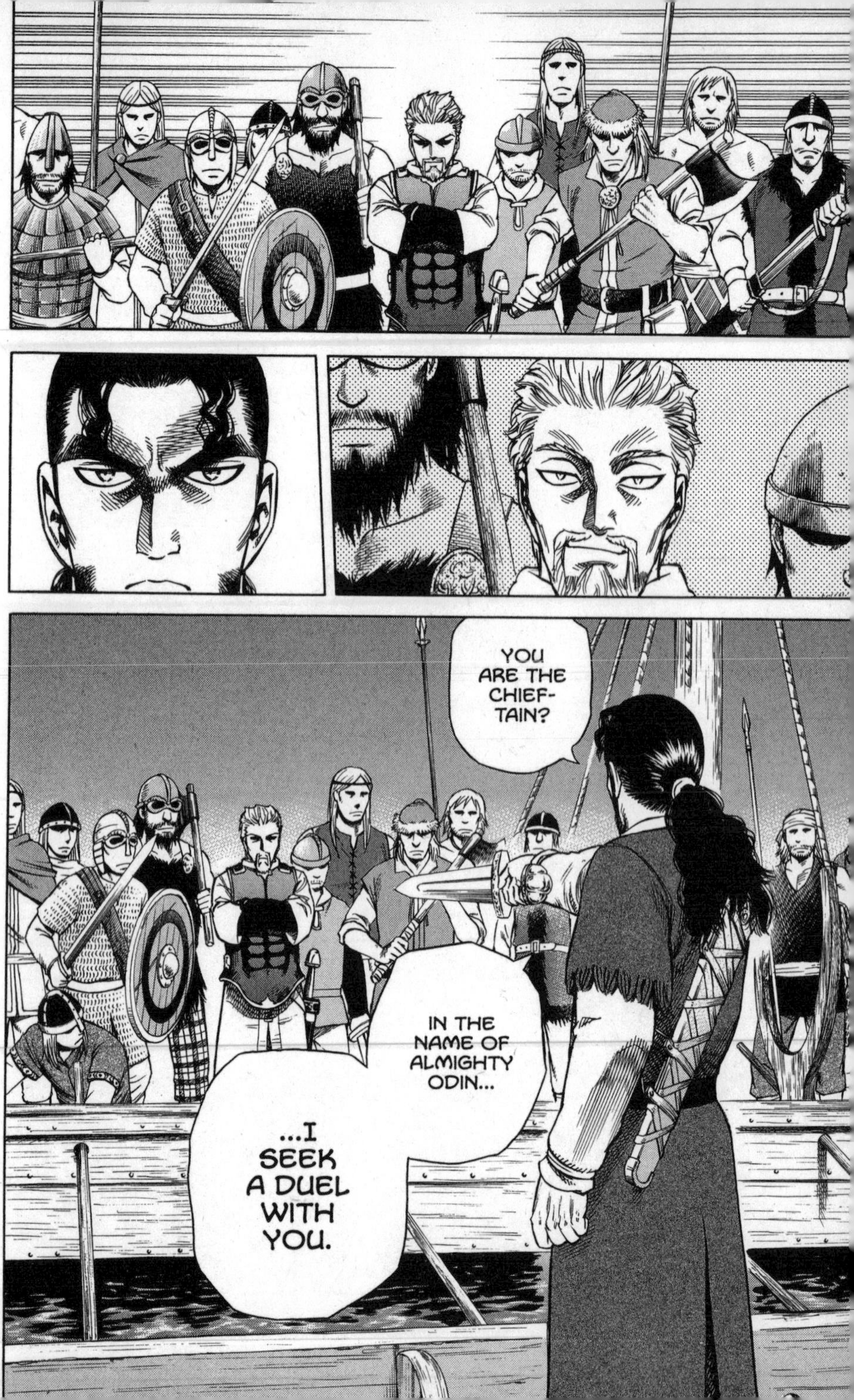
YOU ARE THE CHIEFTAIN?
IN THE NAME OF ALMIGHTY ODIN...
...I SEEK A DUEL WITH YOU.

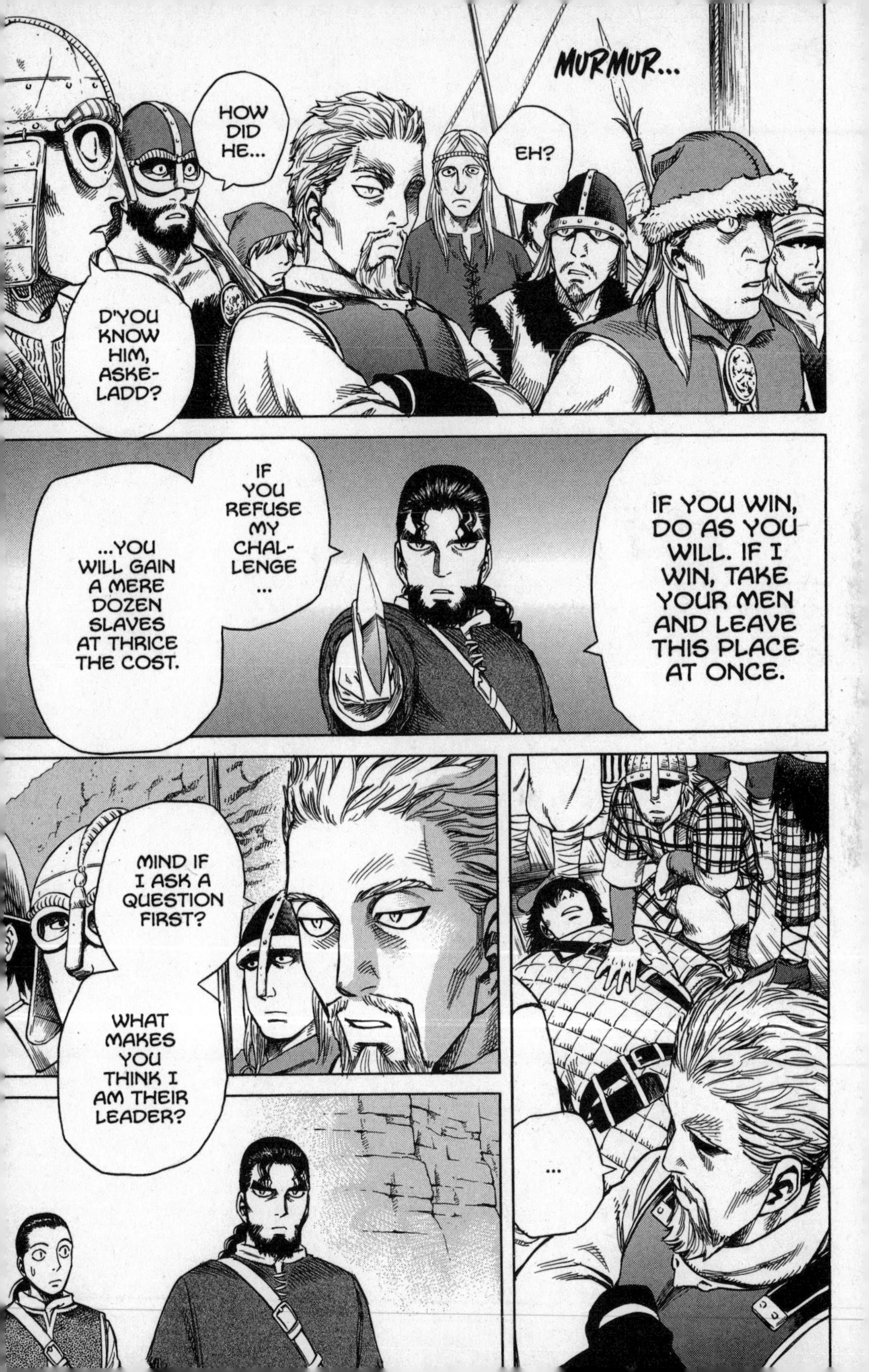
MURMUR...
EH?
HOW DID HE...
D'YOU KNOW HIM, ASKE-LADD?
IF YOU WIN, DO AS YOU WILL. IF I WIN, TAKE YOUR MEN AND LEAVE THIS PLACE AT ONCE.
IF YOU REFUSE MY CHALLENGE...
...YOU WILL GAIN A MERE DOZEN SLAVES AT THRICE THE COST.
...
MIND IF I ASK A QUESTION FIRST?
WHAT MAKES YOU THINK I AM THEIR LEADER?

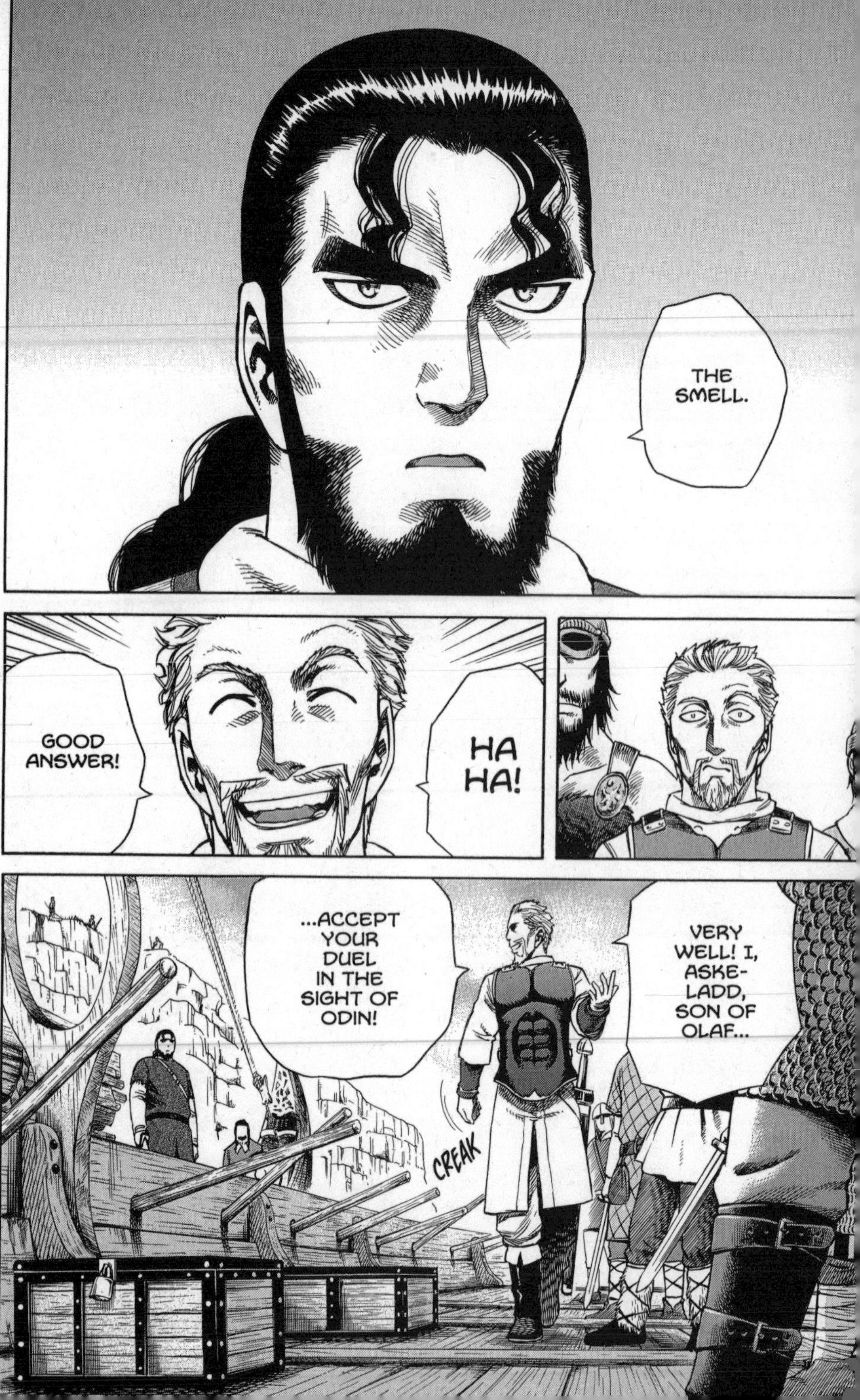
THE SMELL.
HA HA!
GOOD ANSWER!
VERY WELL! I, ASKE-LADD, SON OF OLAF...
...ACCEPT YOUR DUEL IN THE SIGHT OF ODIN!
CREAK

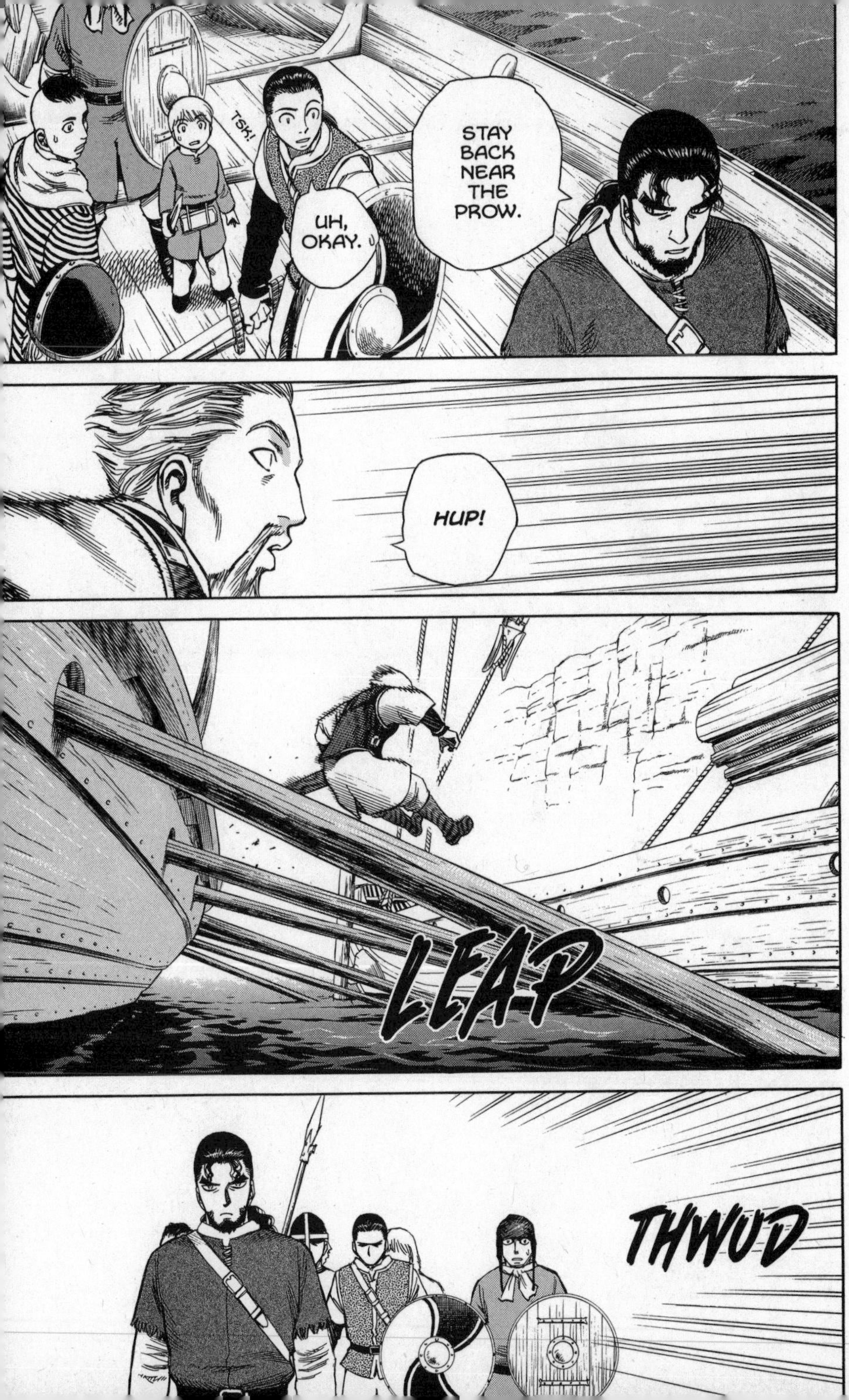
STAY BACK NEAR THE PROW.
UH, OKAY.
TSK!
HUP!
LEAP
THWUD

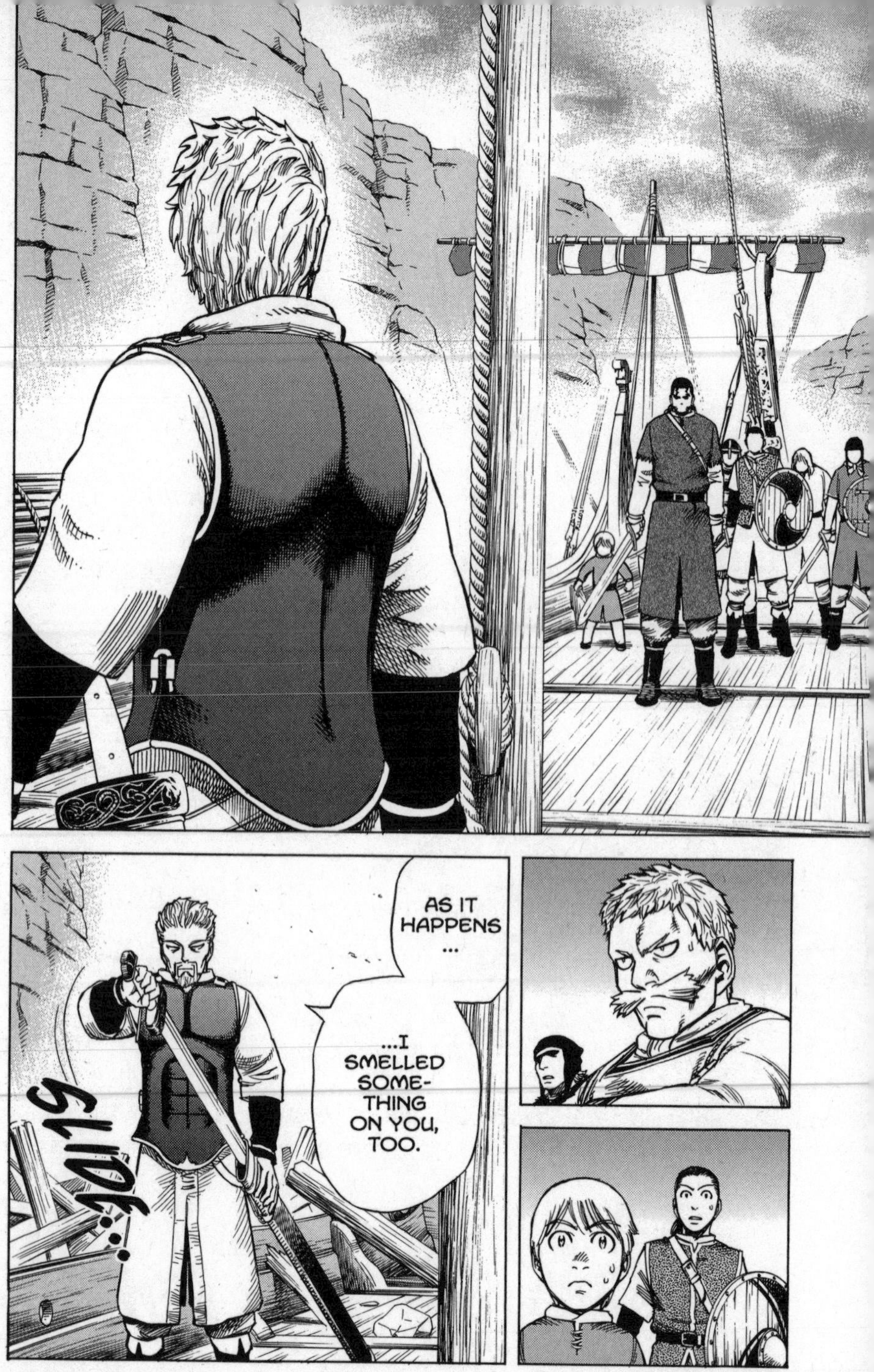
AS IT HAPPENS ...
...I SMELLED SOME-THING ON YOU, TOO.

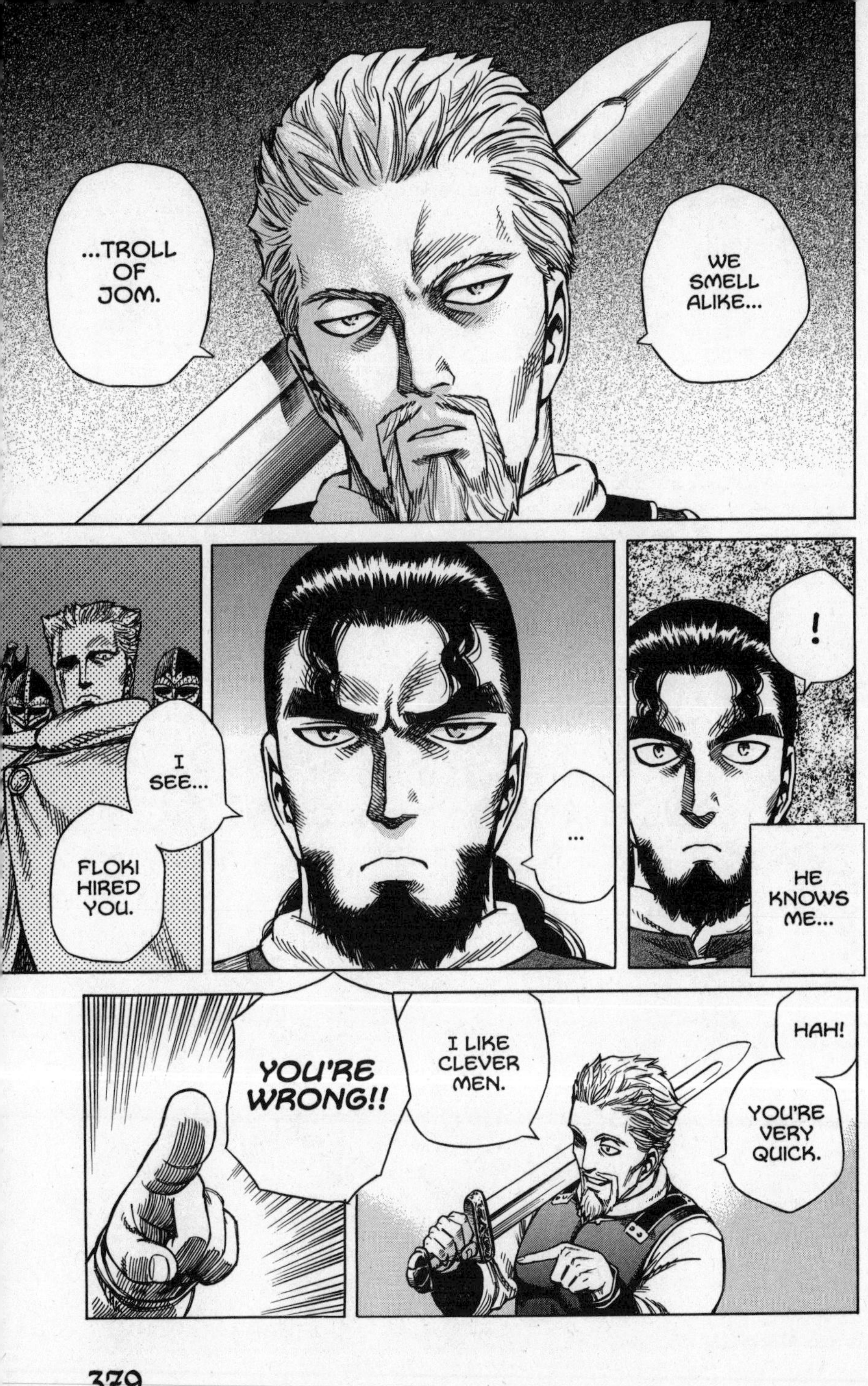
WE SMELL ALIKE...
...TROLL OF JOM.
!
HE KNOWS ME...
...
I SEE...
FLOKI HIRED YOU.
HAH!
YOU'RE VERY QUICK.
I LIKE CLEVER MEN.
YOU'RE WRONG!!

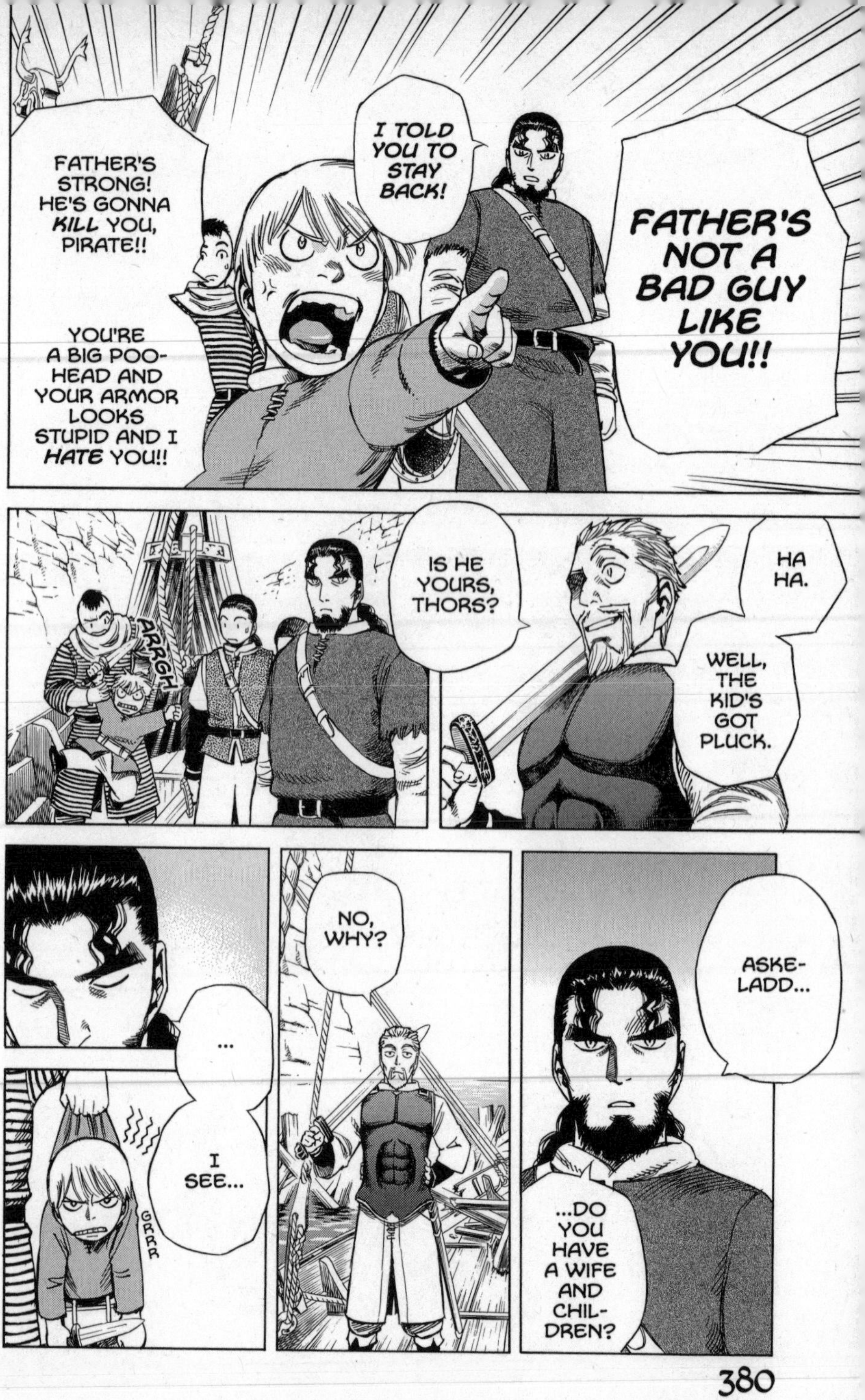
FATHER'S NOT A BAD GUY LIKE YOU!!
I TOLD YOU TO STAY BACK!
FATHER'S STRONG! HE'S GONNA KILL YOU, PIRATE!!
YOU'RE A BIG POO-HEAD AND YOUR ARMOR LOOKS STUPID AND I HATE YOU!!
HA HA.
WELL, THE KID'S GOT PLUCK.
IS HE YOURS, THORS?
ARRGH
ASKE-LADD...
...DO YOU HAVE A WIFE AND CHIL-DREN?
NO, WHY?
...
I SEE...
GRRR

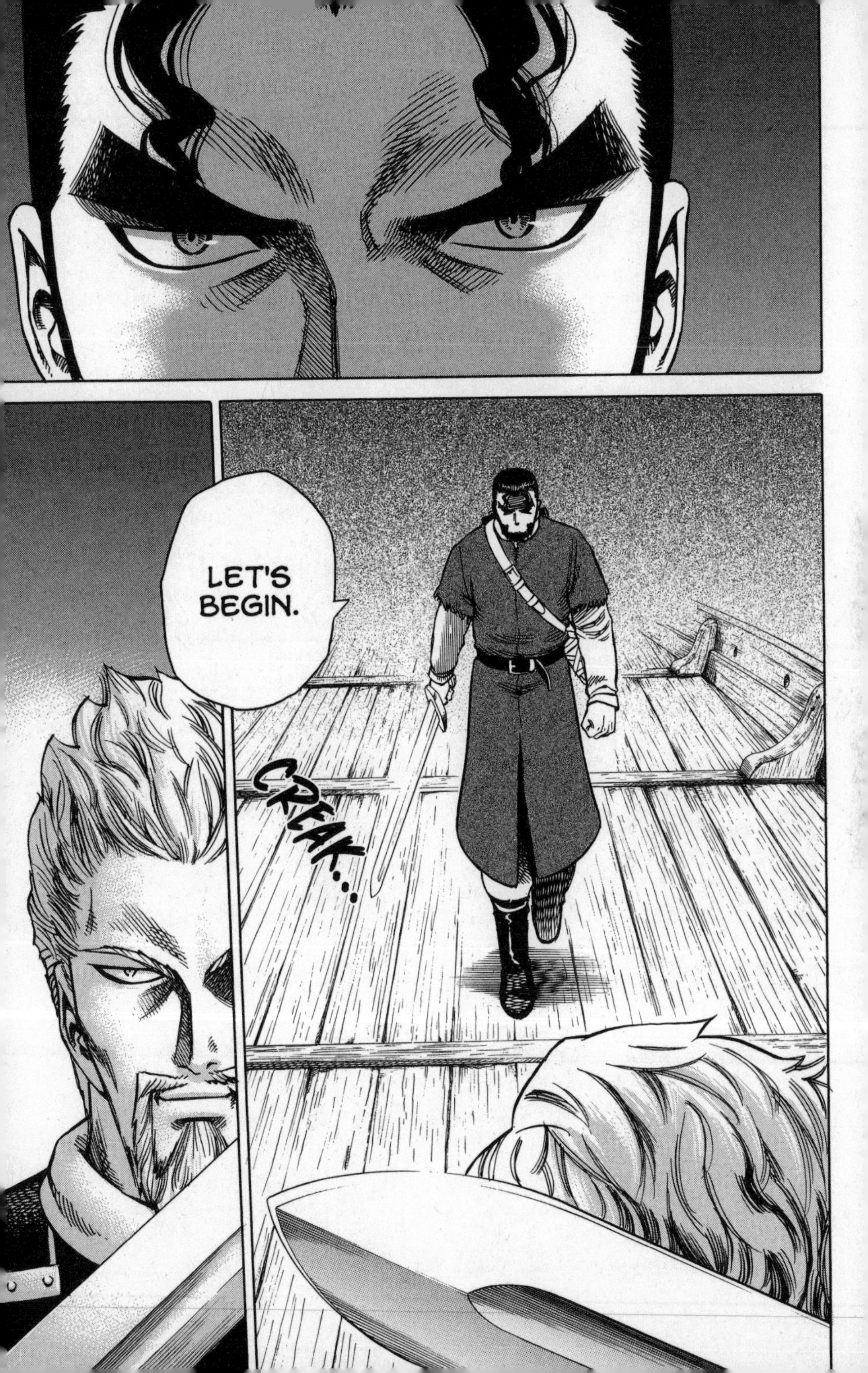
LET'S BEGIN.
CREAK...

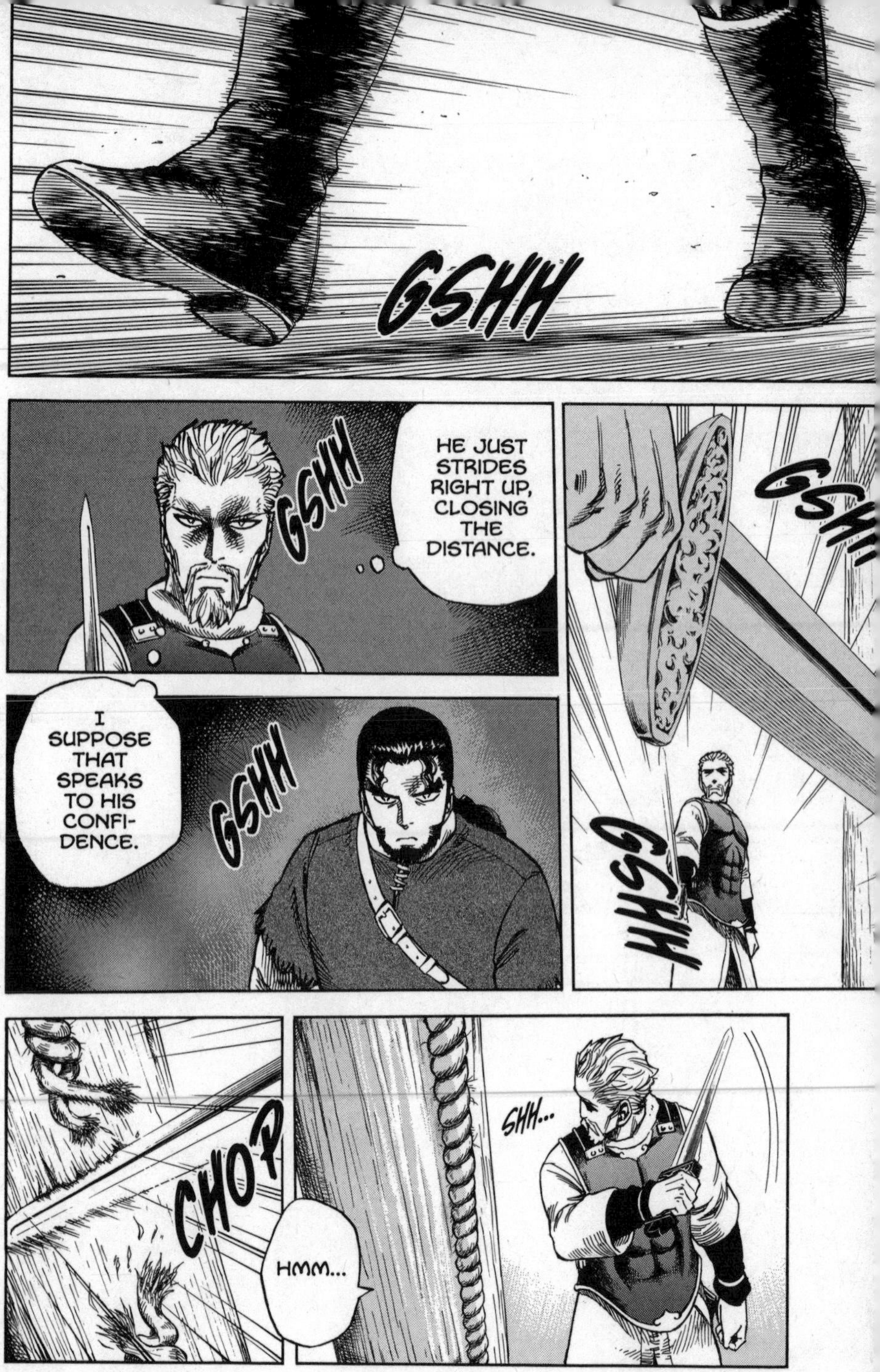
GSHH
GSHH
GSHH
GSHH
HE JUST STRIDES RIGHT UP, CLOSING THE DISTANCE.
GSHH
I SUPPOSE THAT SPEAKS TO HIS CONFIDENCE.
SHH...
HMM...
CHOP

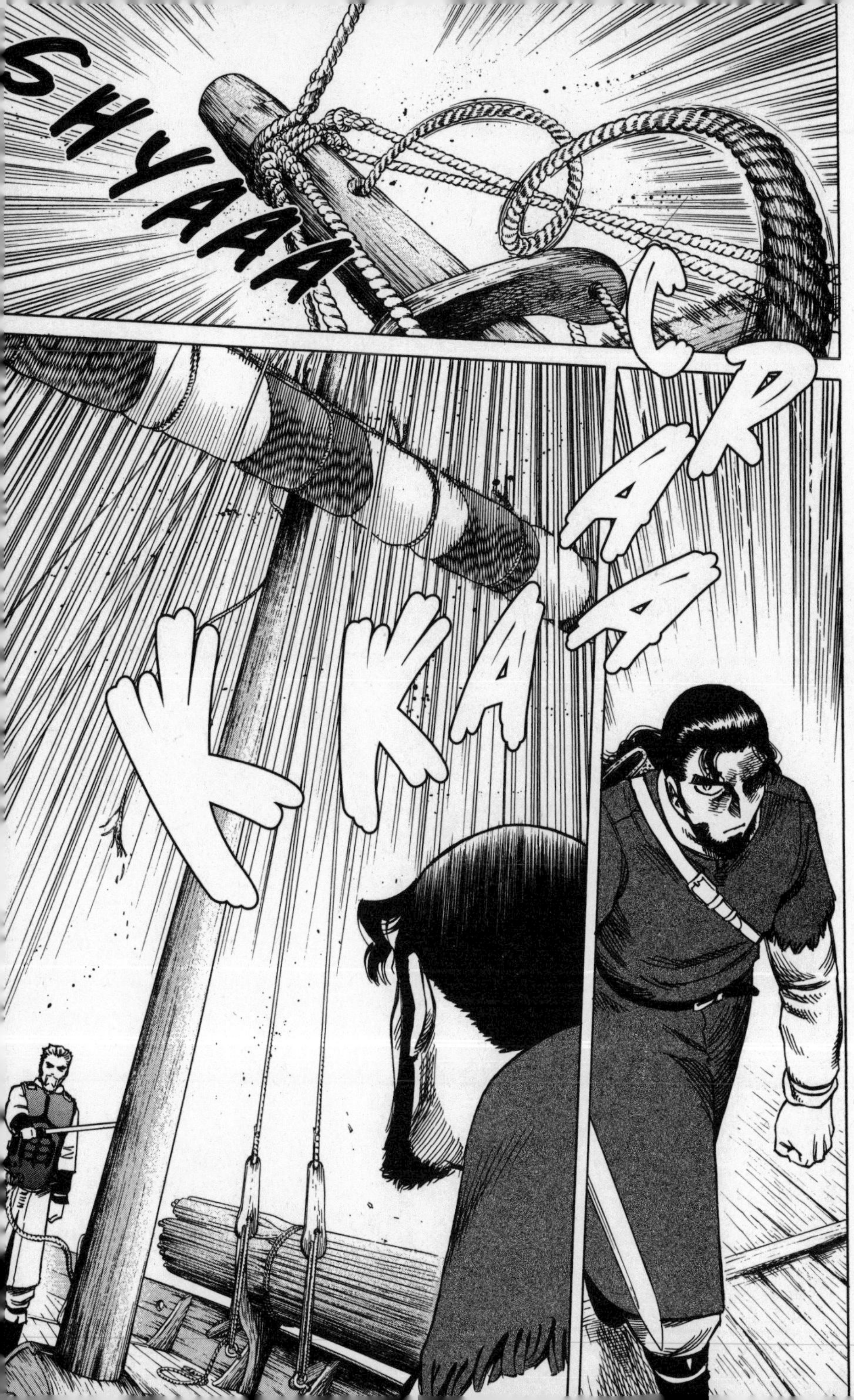
SHYAAA
CRAAA
KKA

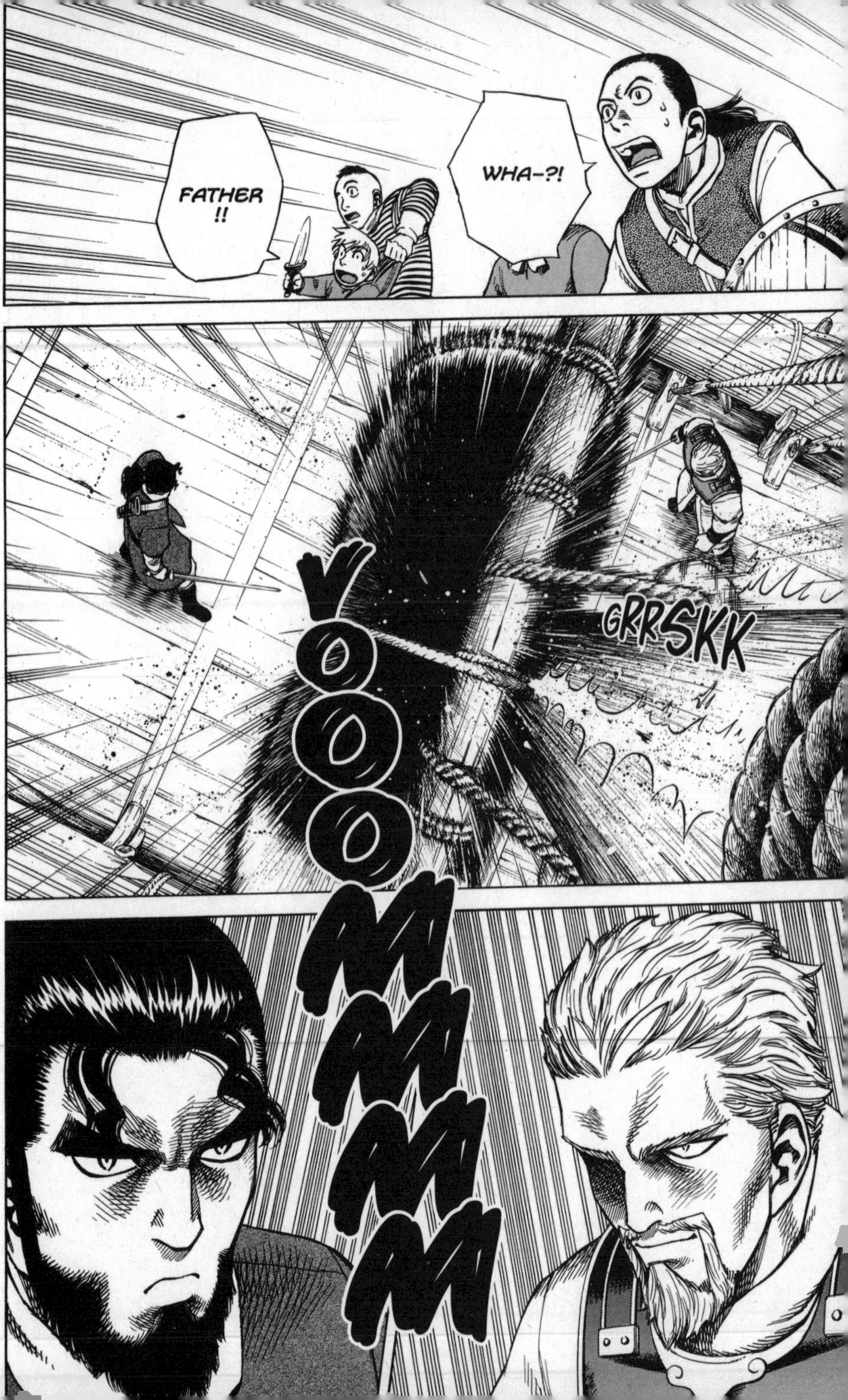
WHA-?!
FATHER !!
GRRSKK

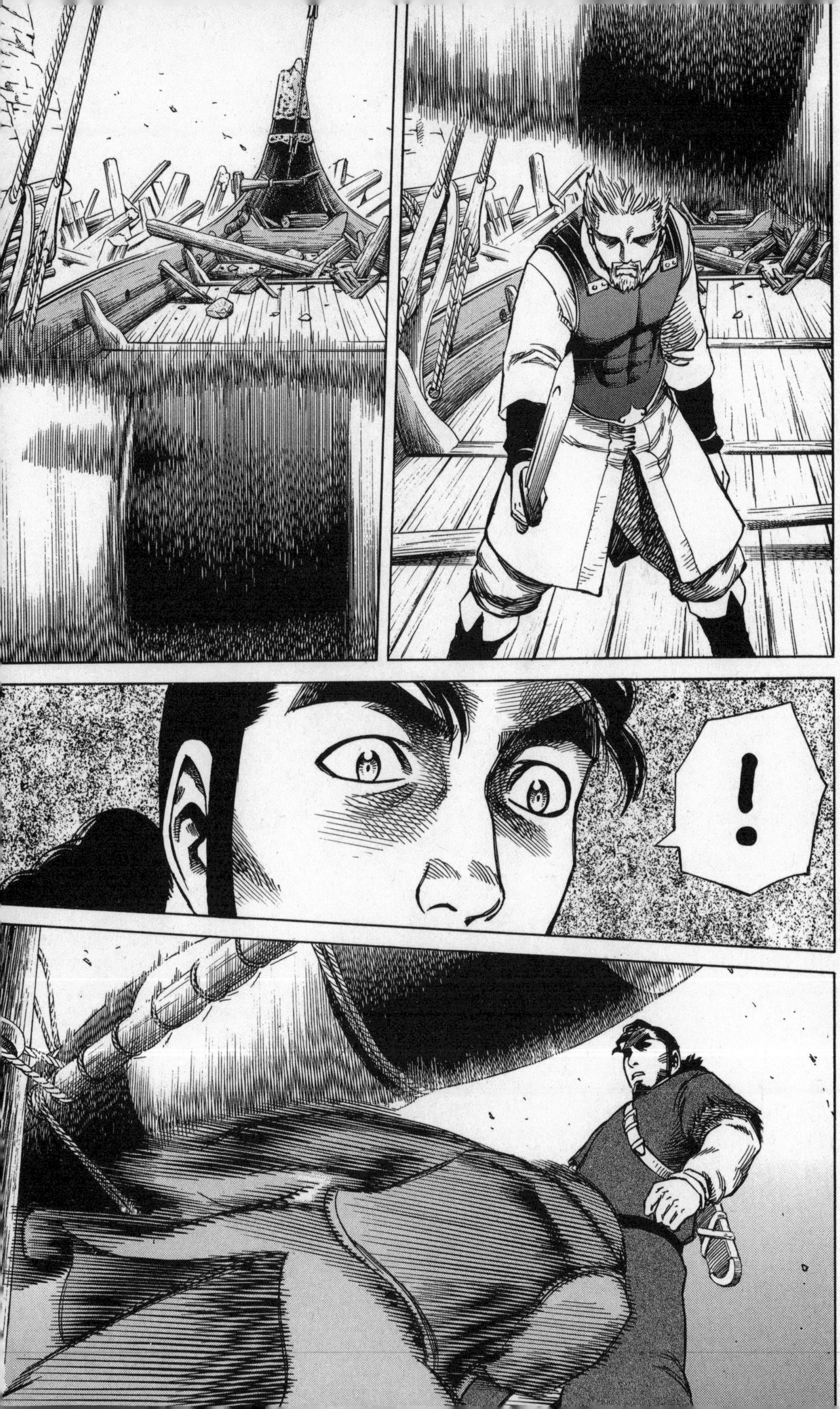
!

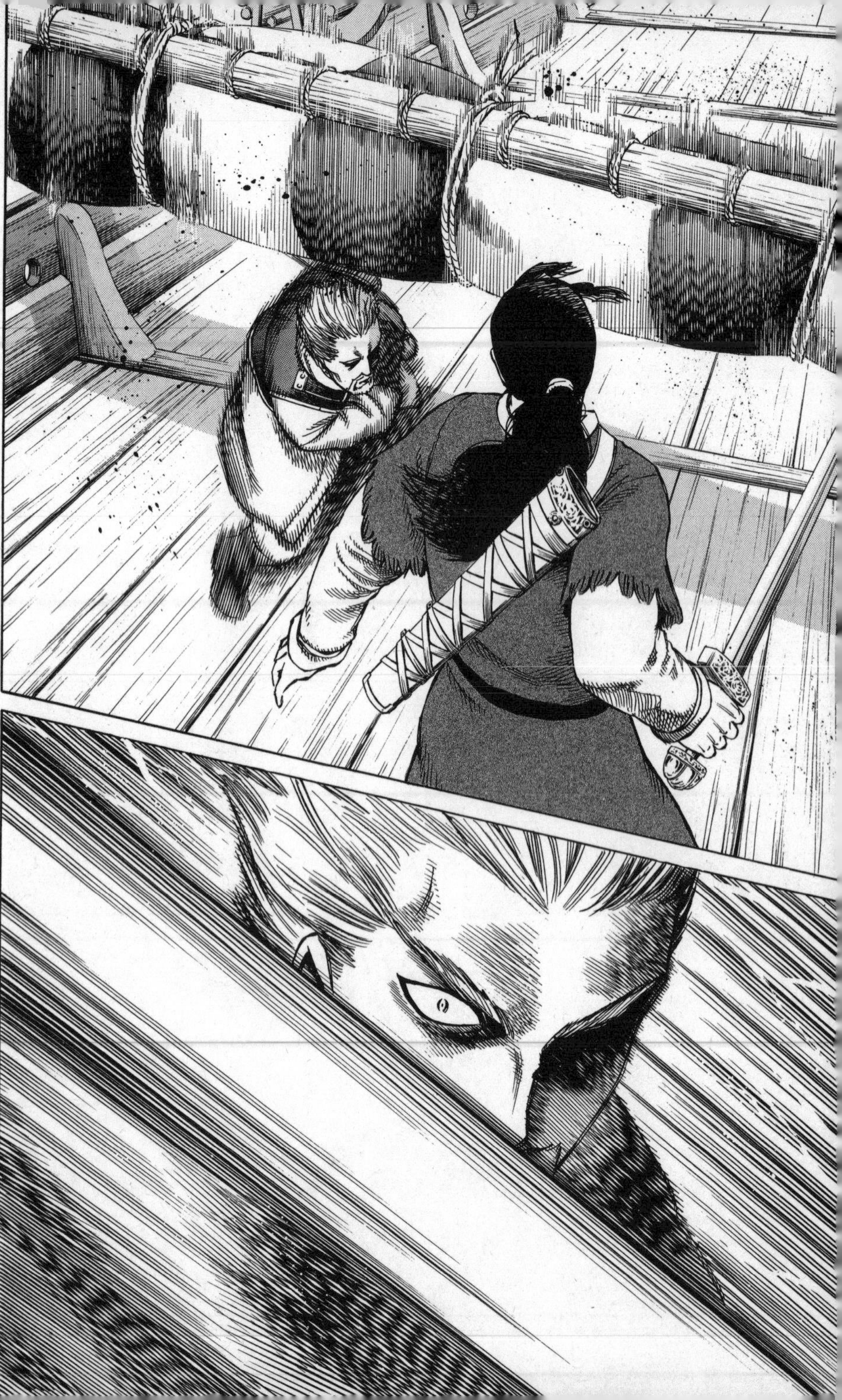

CHAPTER 13 - END

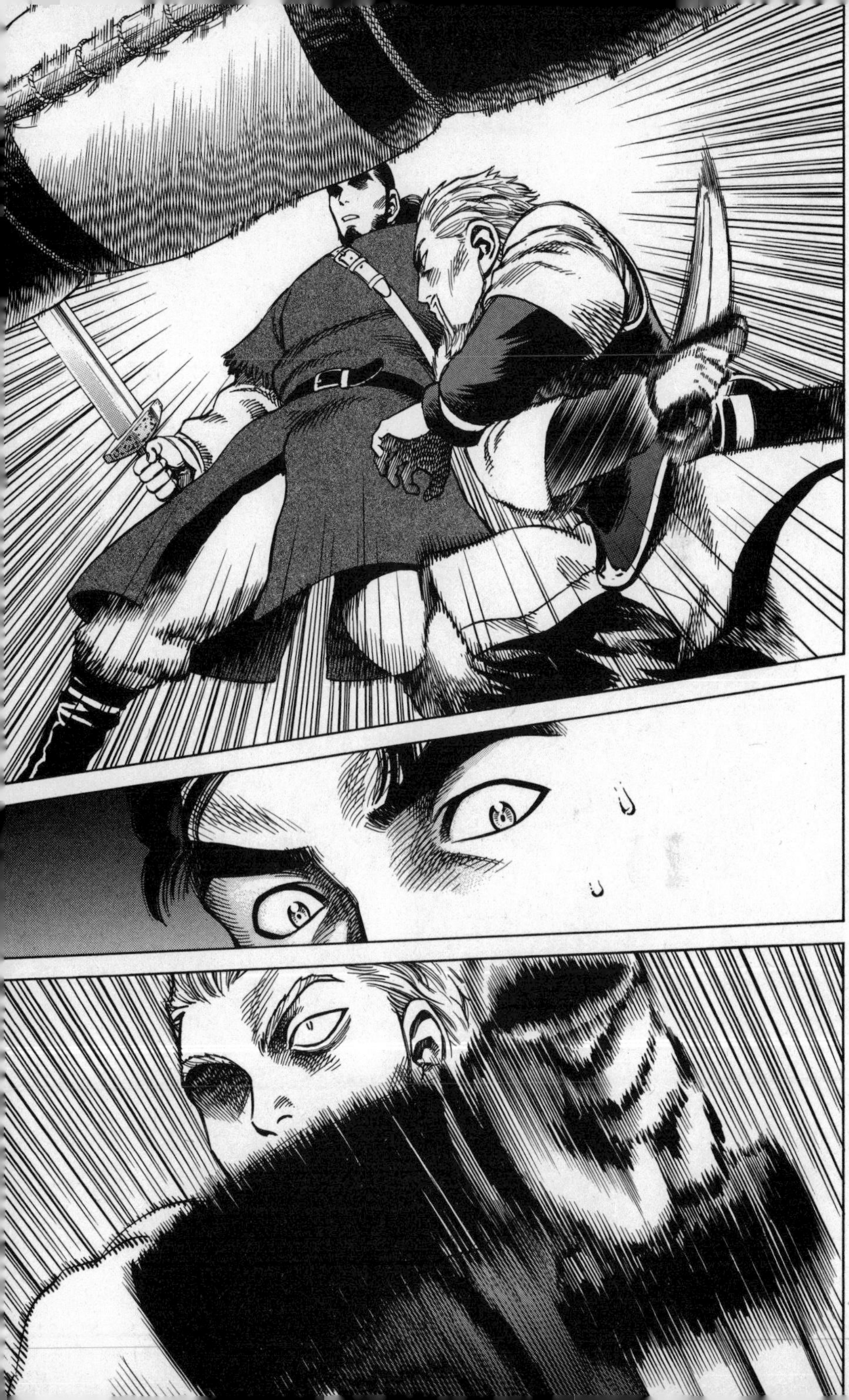

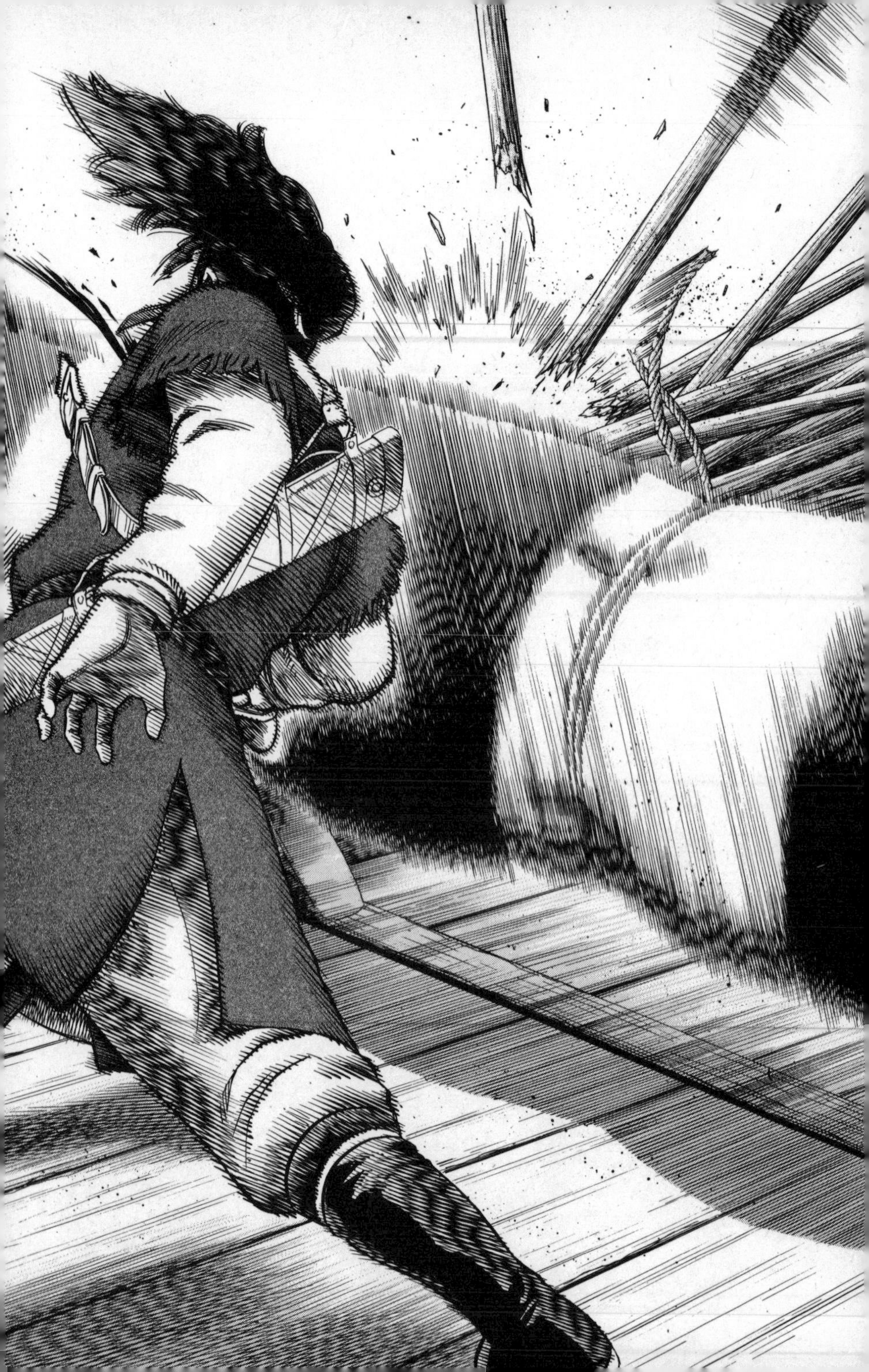

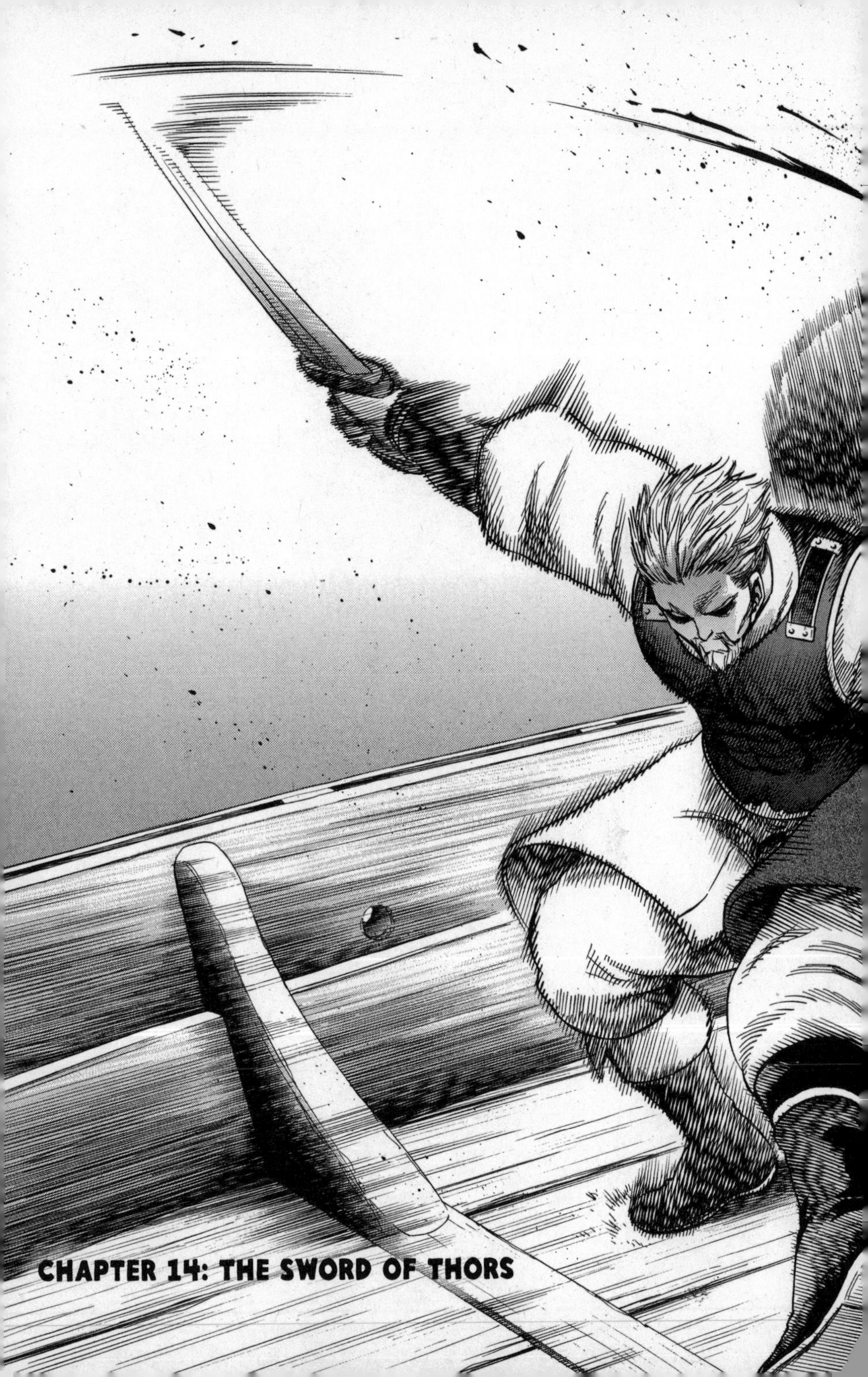
CHAPTER 14: THE SWORD OF THORS

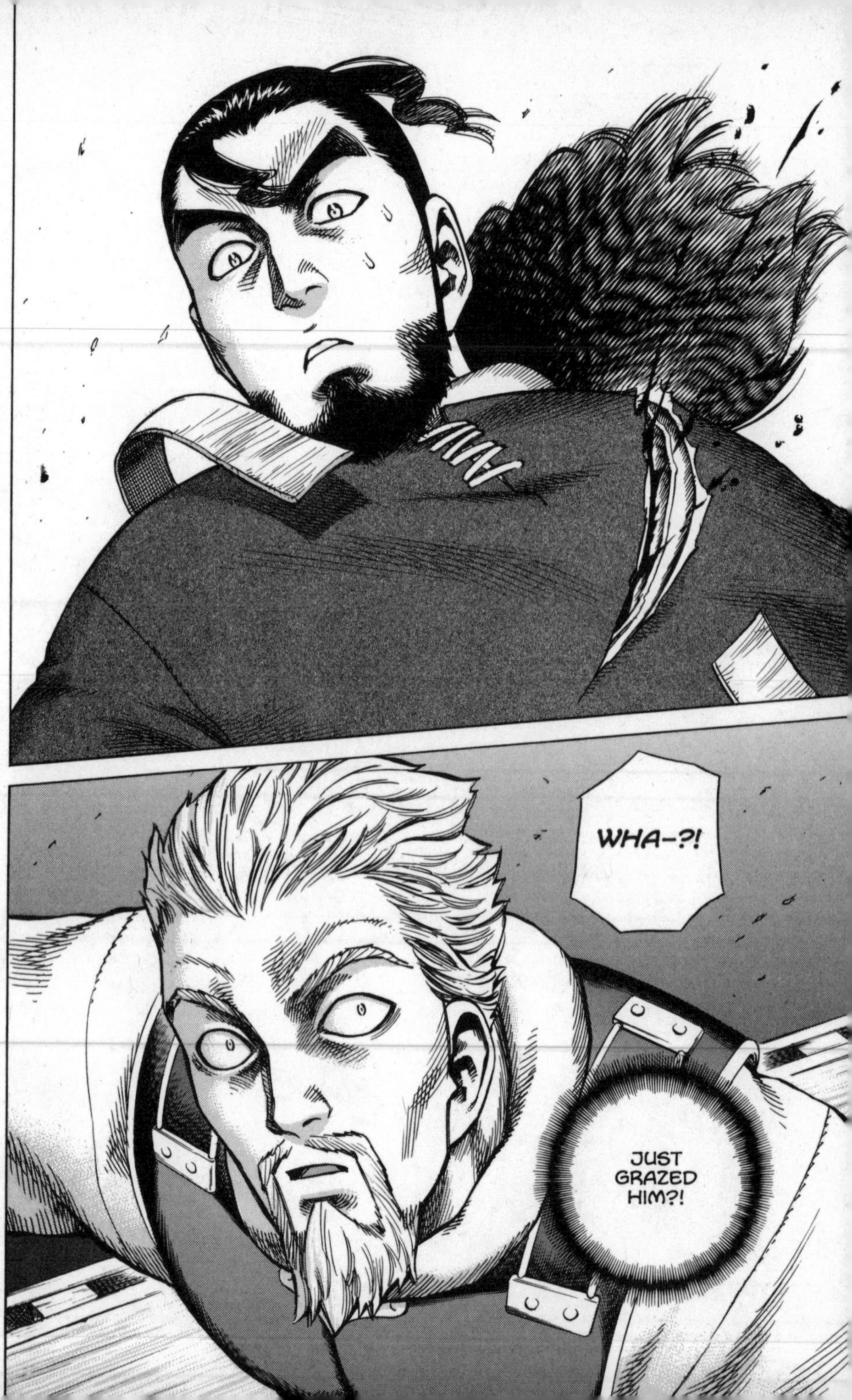
WHA-?!
JUST GRAZED HIM?!

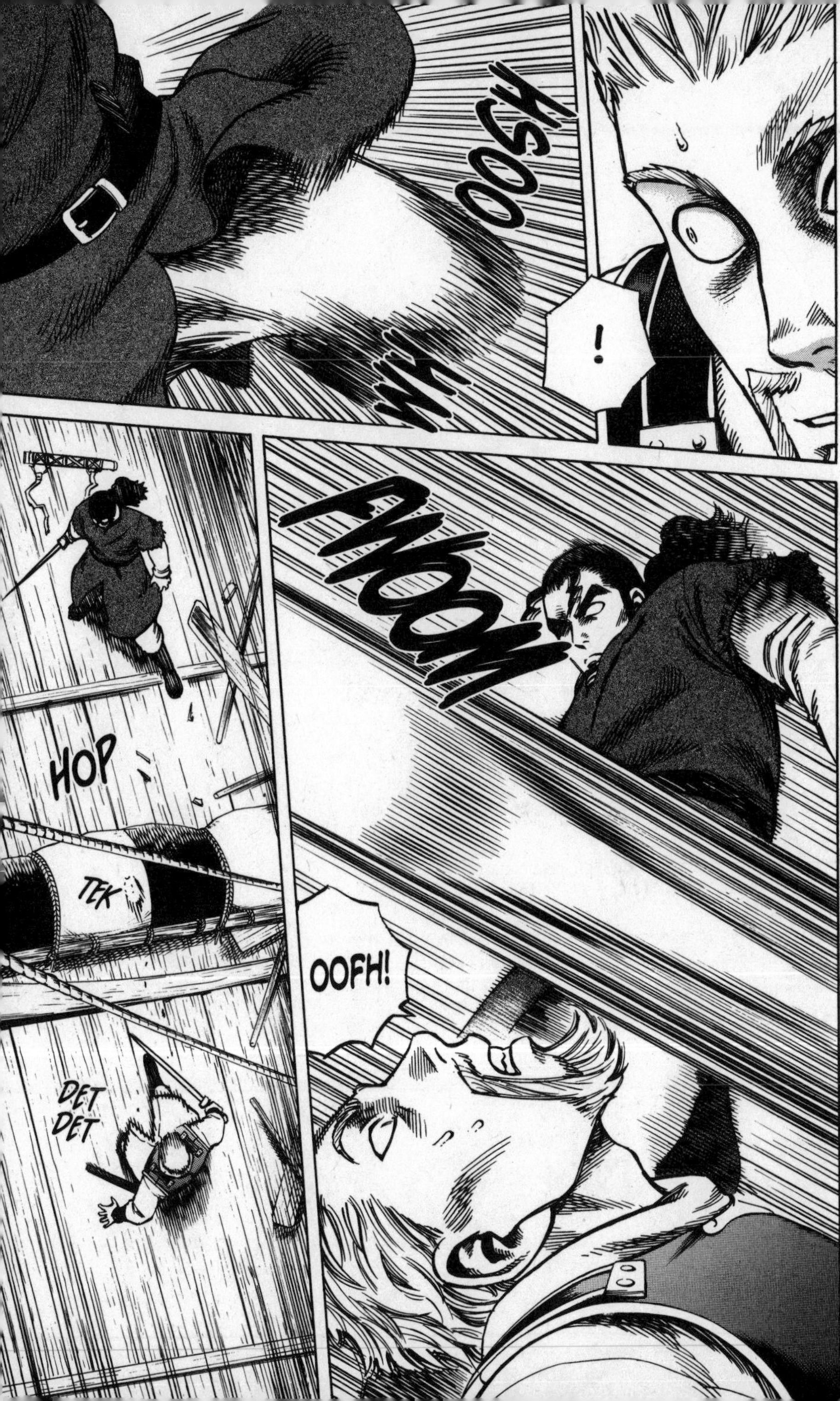
!
WHOOSH
FWOOM
OOFH!
HOP
TEK
DET DET

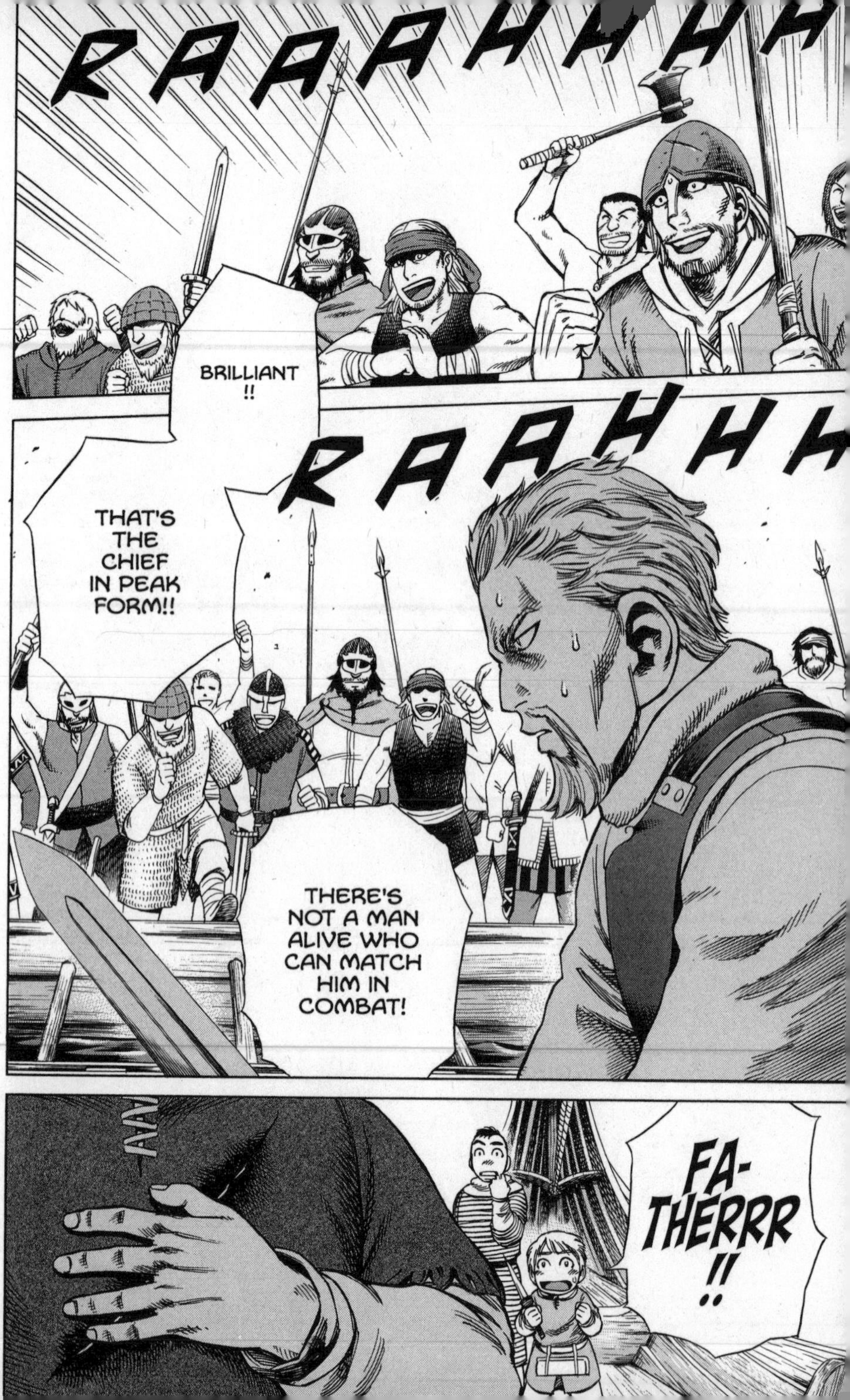
RAAAHHHH
BRILLIANT!!
RAAHHH
THAT'S THE CHIEF IN PEAK FORM!!
THERE'S NOT A MAN ALIVE WHO CAN MATCH HIM IN COMBAT!
FA-THERRR!!

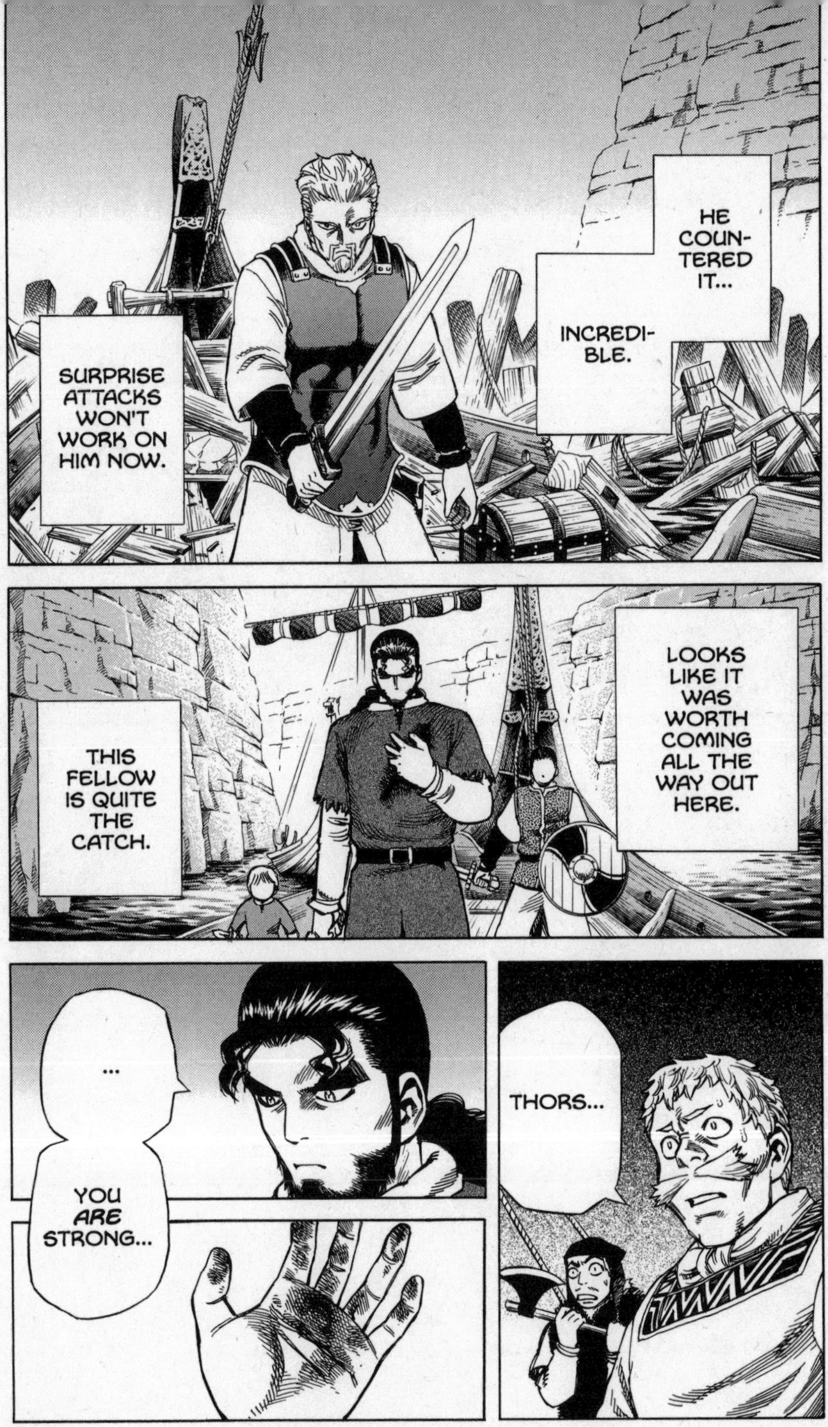
HE COUNTERED IT...
INCREDIBLE.
SURPRISE ATTACKS WON'T WORK ON HIM NOW.
LOOKS LIKE IT WAS WORTH COMING ALL THE WAY OUT HERE.
THIS FELLOW IS QUITE THE CATCH.
THORS...
...
YOU *ARE* STRONG...

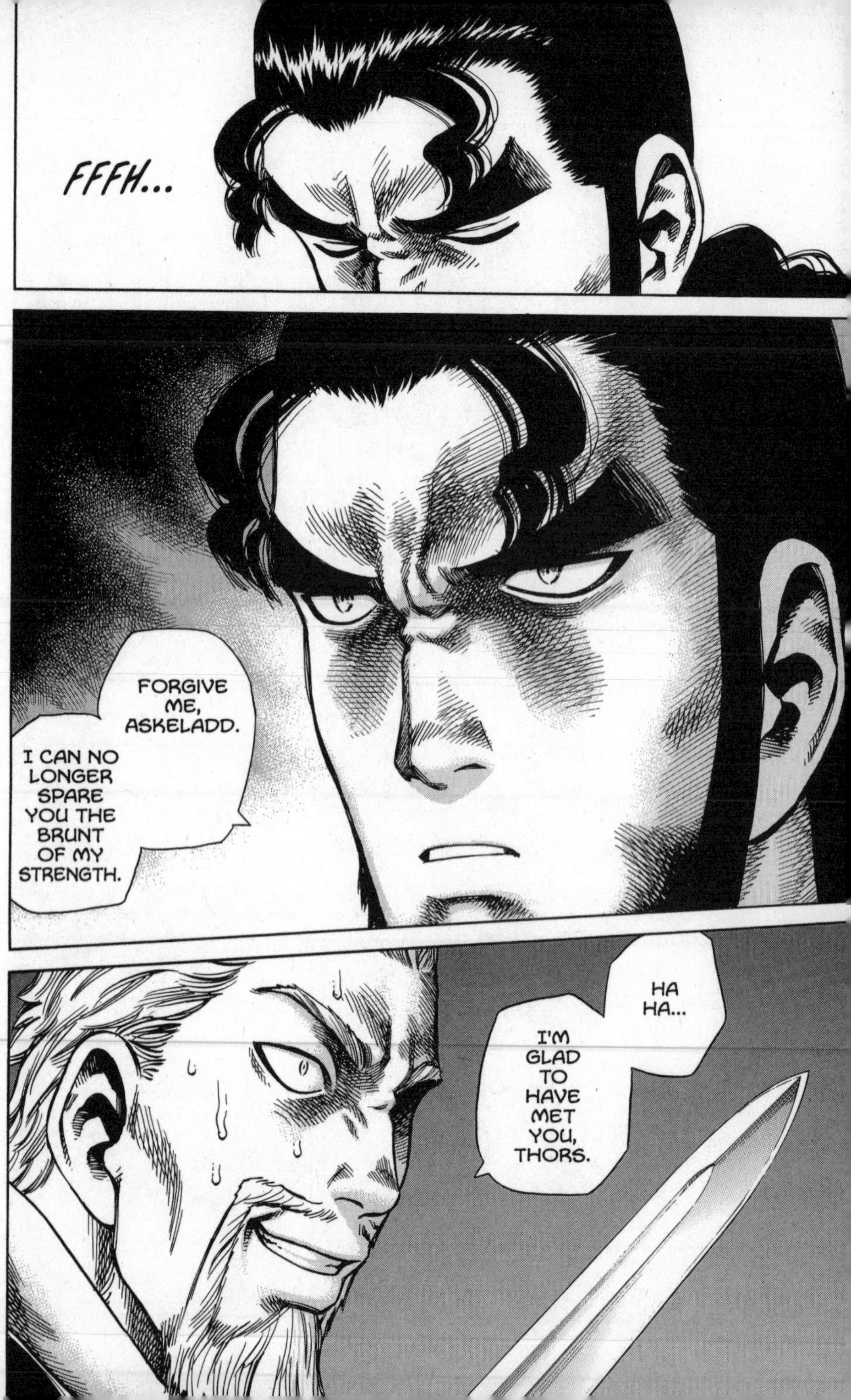
FFFH...
FORGIVE ME, ASKELADD.
I CAN NO LONGER SPARE YOU THE BRUNT OF MY STRENGTH.
HA HA...
I'M GLAD TO HAVE MET YOU, THORS.

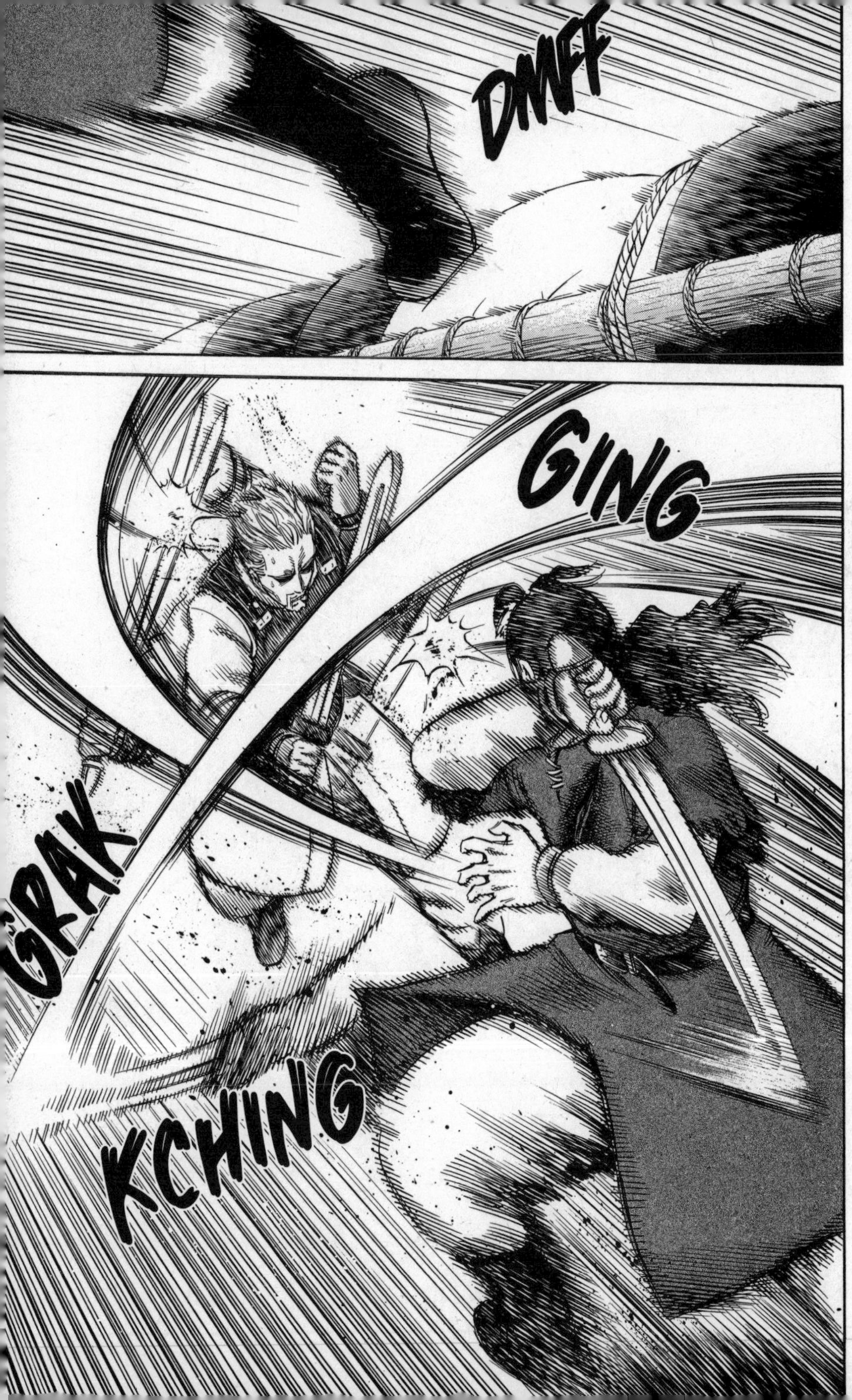
DMFF
GING
GRAK
KCHING

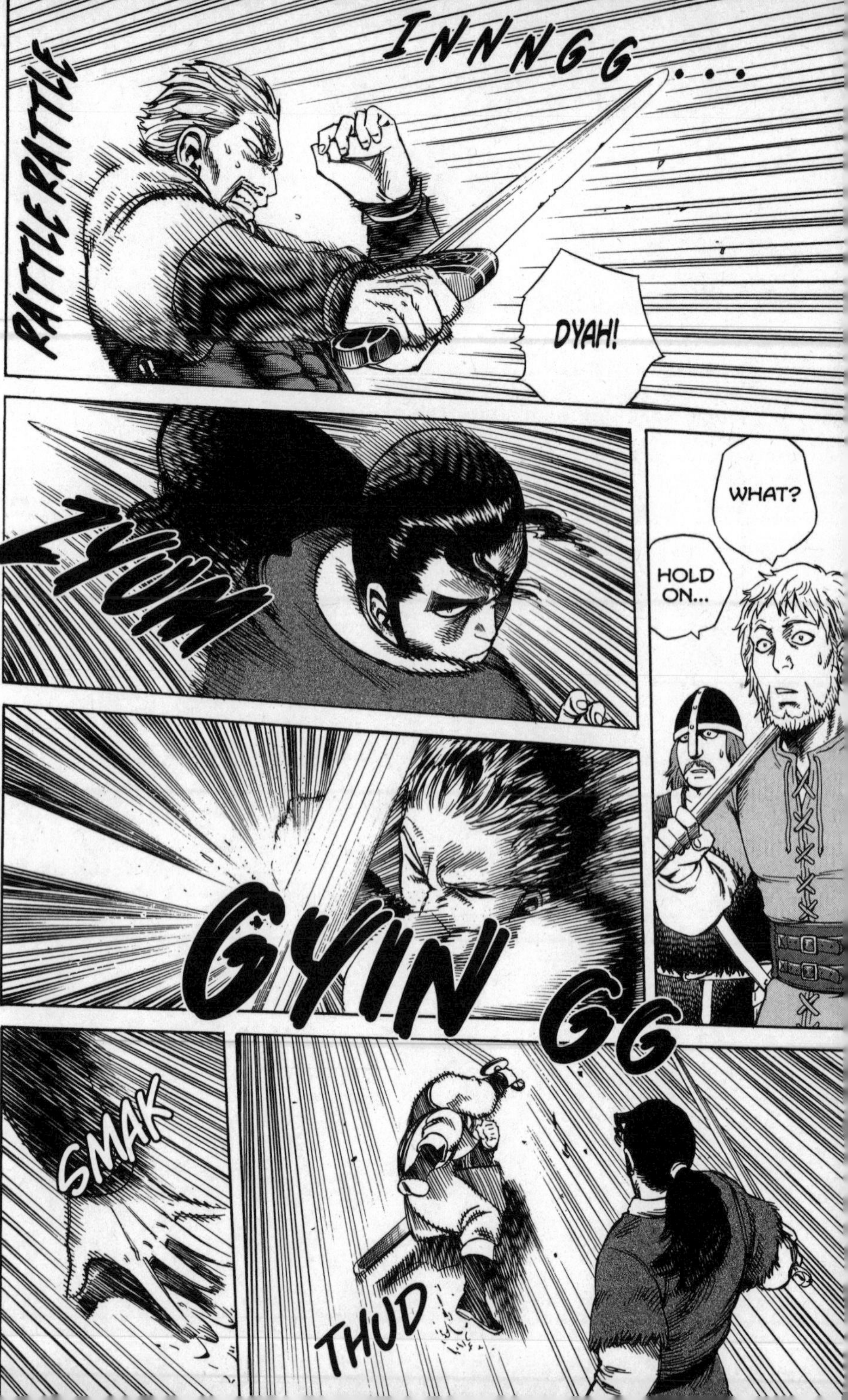
INNNGG...
DYAH!
RATTLE RATTLE
WHAT?
HOLD ON...
ZYUM
GYIN GG
THUD
SMAK

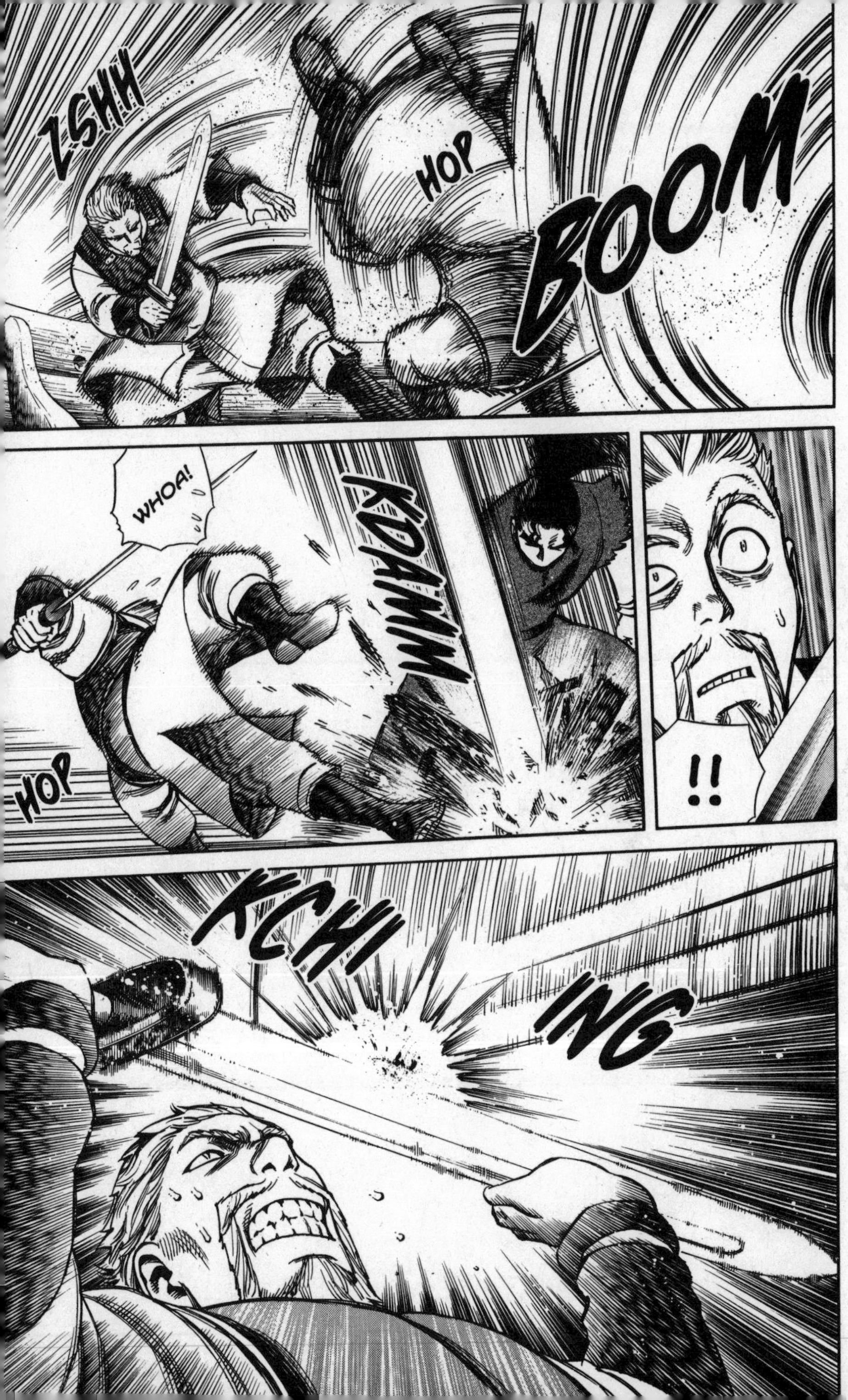
BOOM
HOP
ZSHH
!!
KDAMM
WHOA!
HOP
KCHI
ING

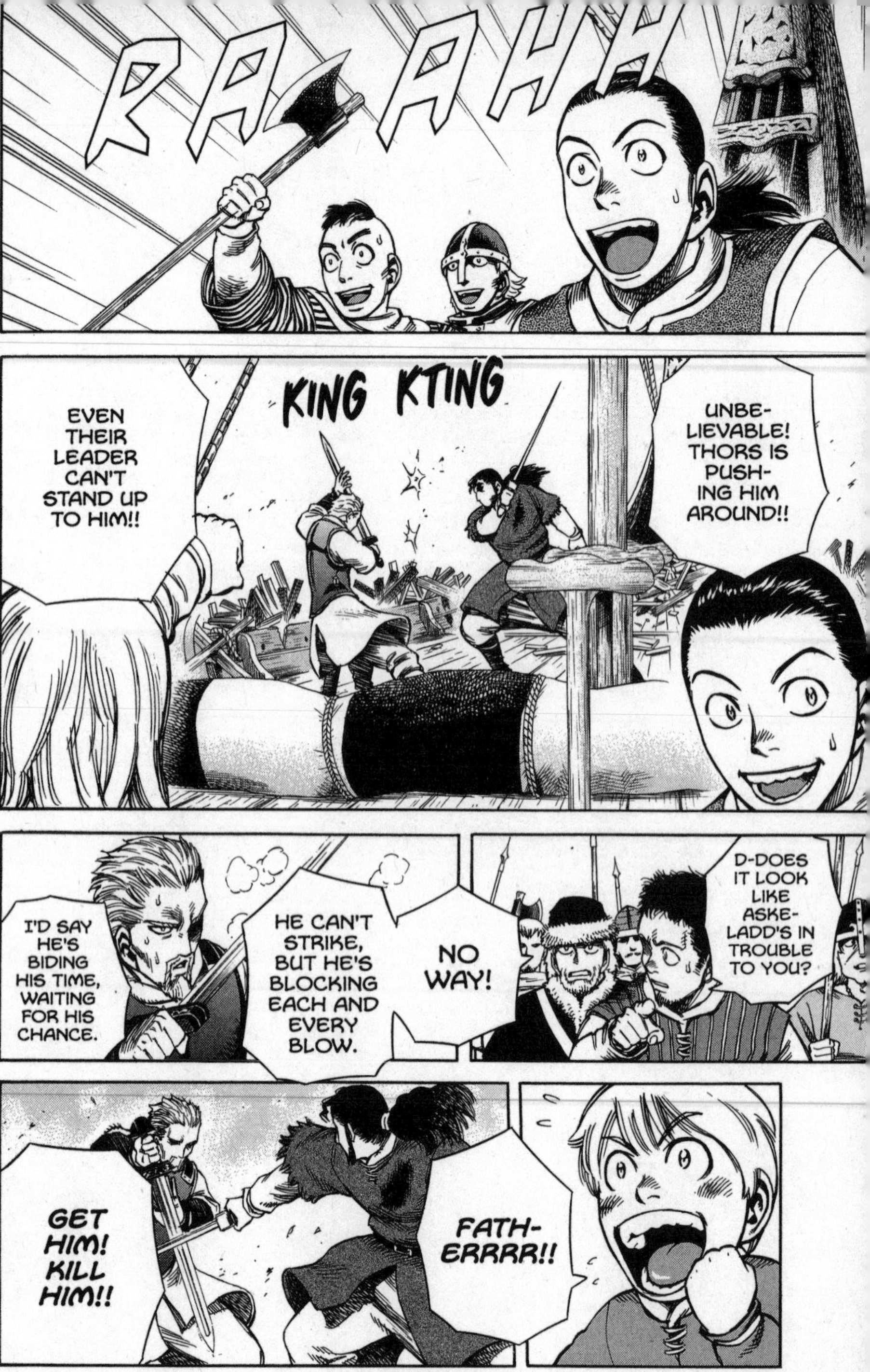
RAAHH
UNBE-LIEVABLE! THORS IS PUSH-ING HIM AROUND!!
KING KTING
EVEN THEIR LEADER CAN'T STAND UP TO HIM!!
D-DOES IT LOOK LIKE ASKE-LADD'S IN TROUBLE TO YOU?
NO WAY!
HE CAN'T STRIKE, BUT HE'S BLOCKING EACH AND EVERY BLOW.
I'D SAY HE'S BIDING HIS TIME, WAITING FOR HIS CHANCE.
FATH-ERRRR!!
GET HIM! KILL HIM!!

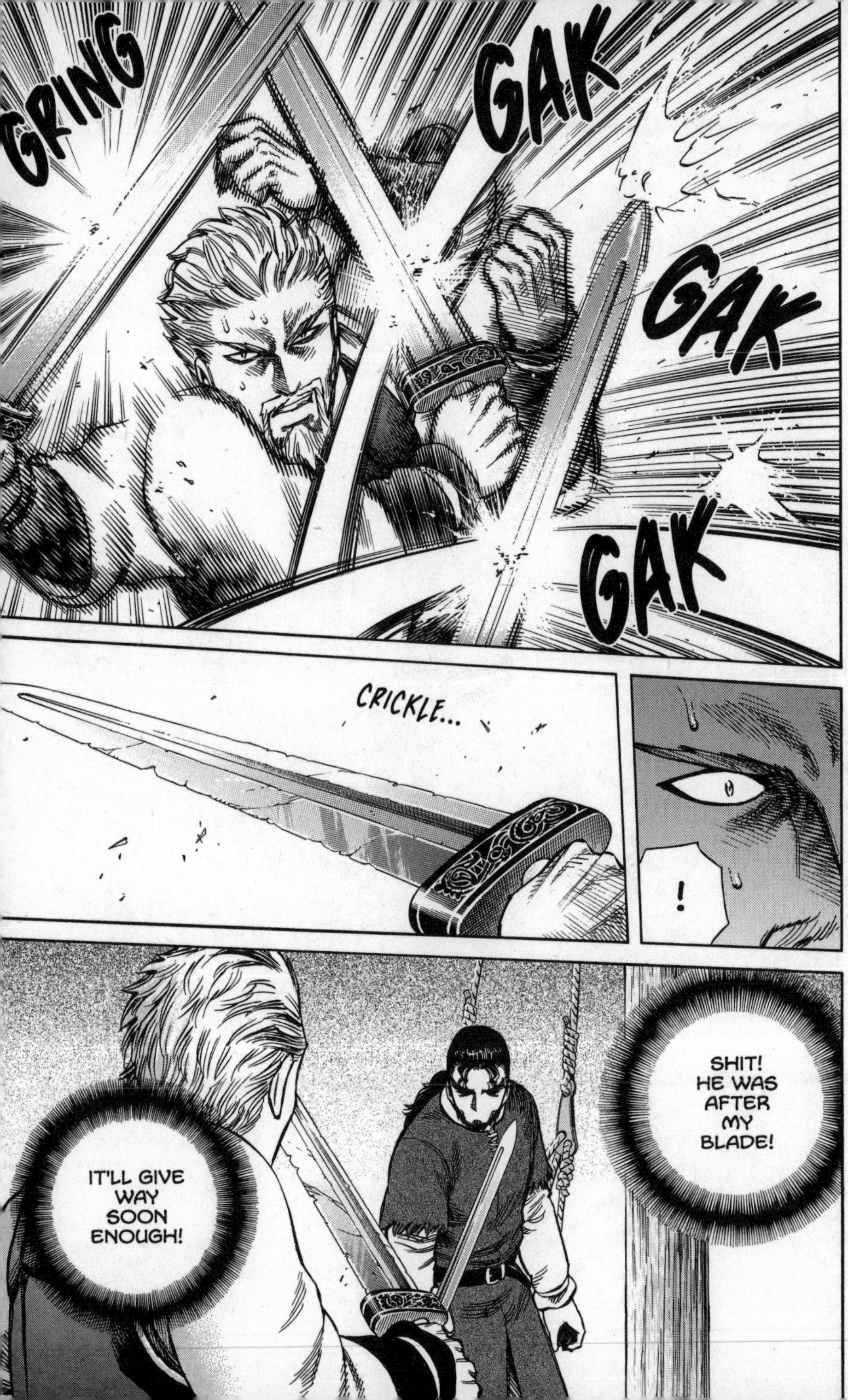
GAK
GAK
GAK
GRING
!
CRICKLE...
SHIT! HE WAS AFTER MY BLADE!
IT'LL GIVE WAY SOON ENOUGH!

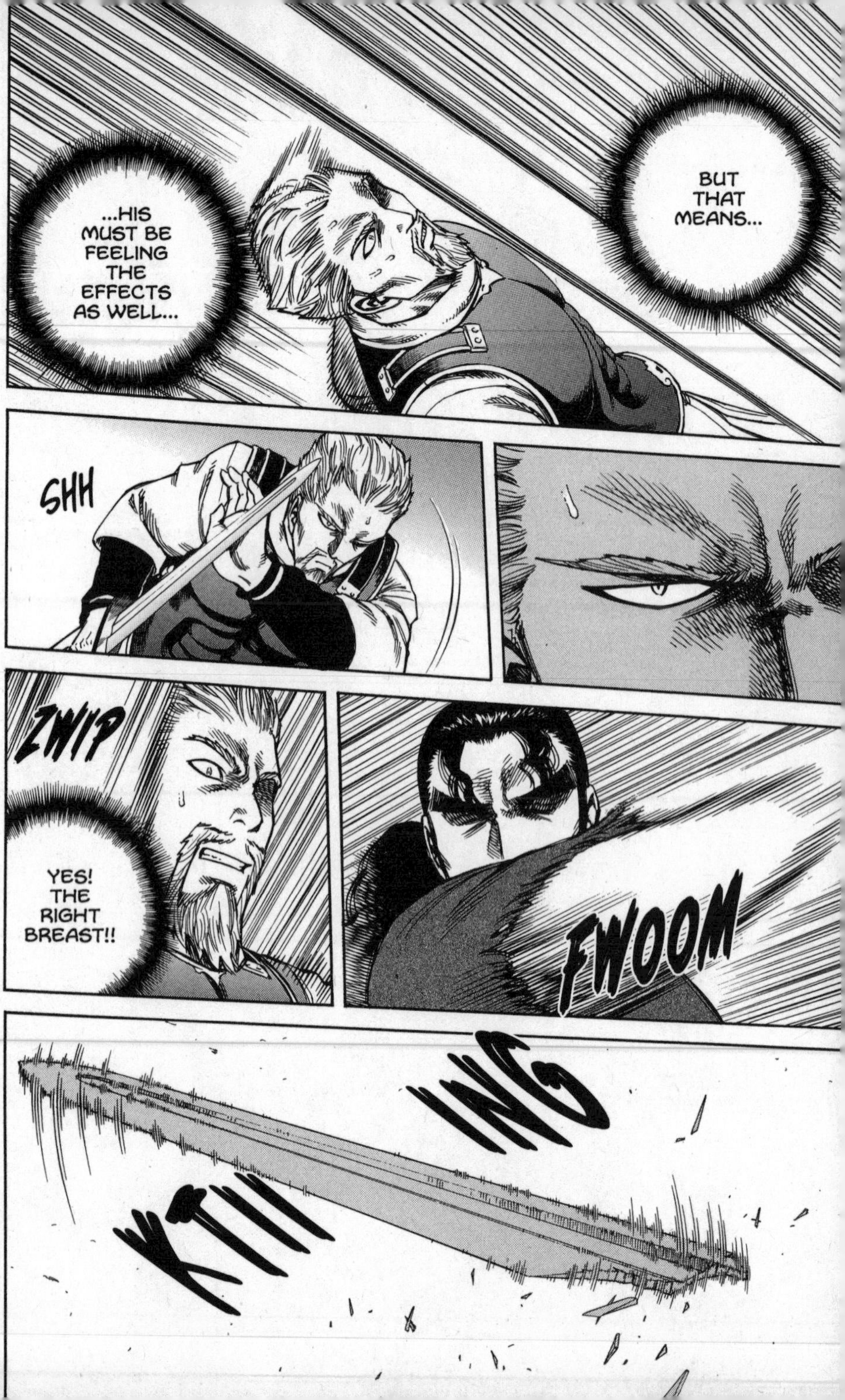
BUT THAT MEANS...
...HIS MUST BE FEELING THE EFFECTS AS WELL...
SHH
FWOOM
ZWIP
YES! THE RIGHT BREAST!!
KTIIIING

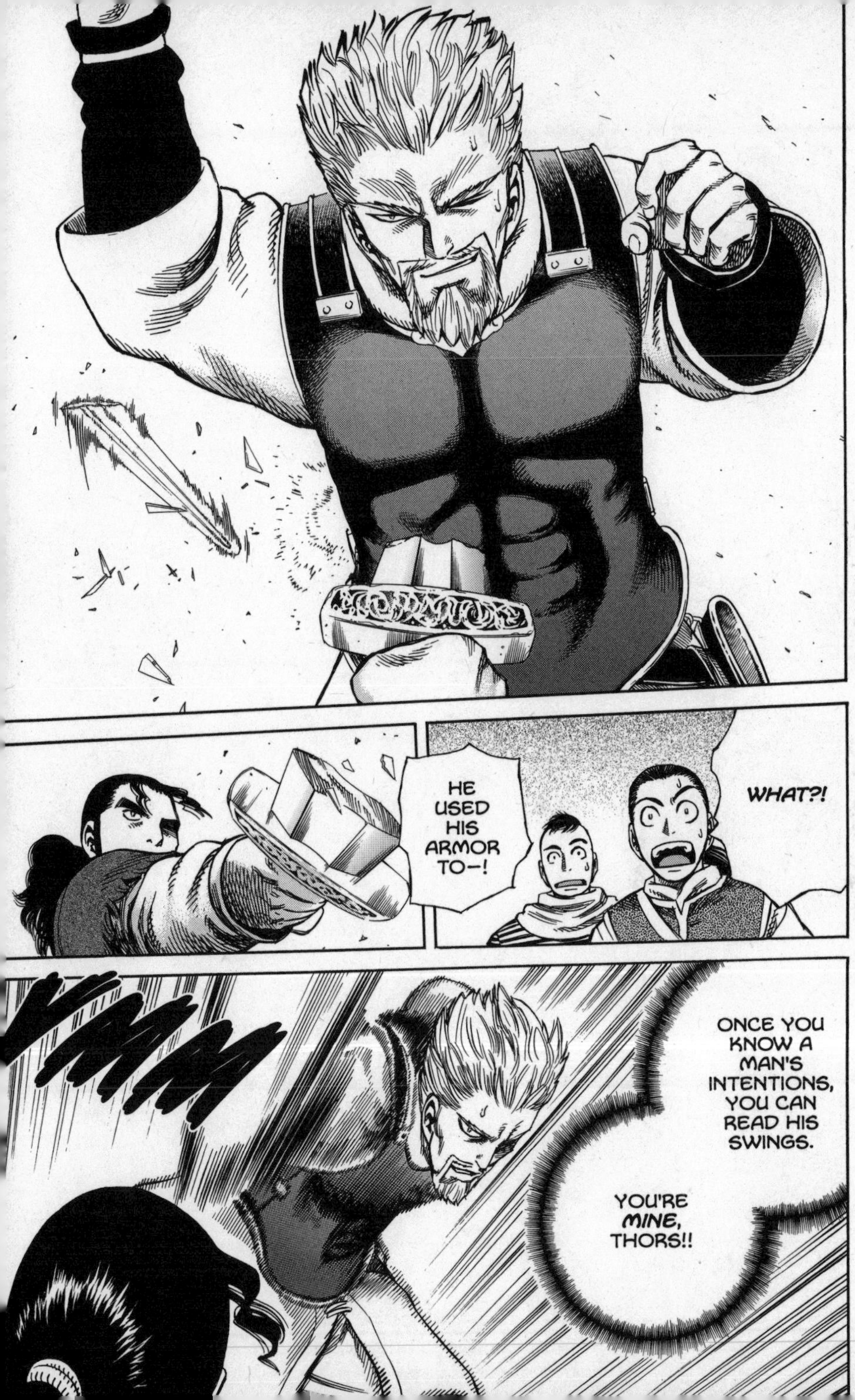
HE USED HIS ARMOR TO-!
WHAT?!
ONCE YOU KNOW A MAN'S INTENTIONS, YOU CAN READ HIS SWINGS.
YOU'RE *MINE*, THORS!!

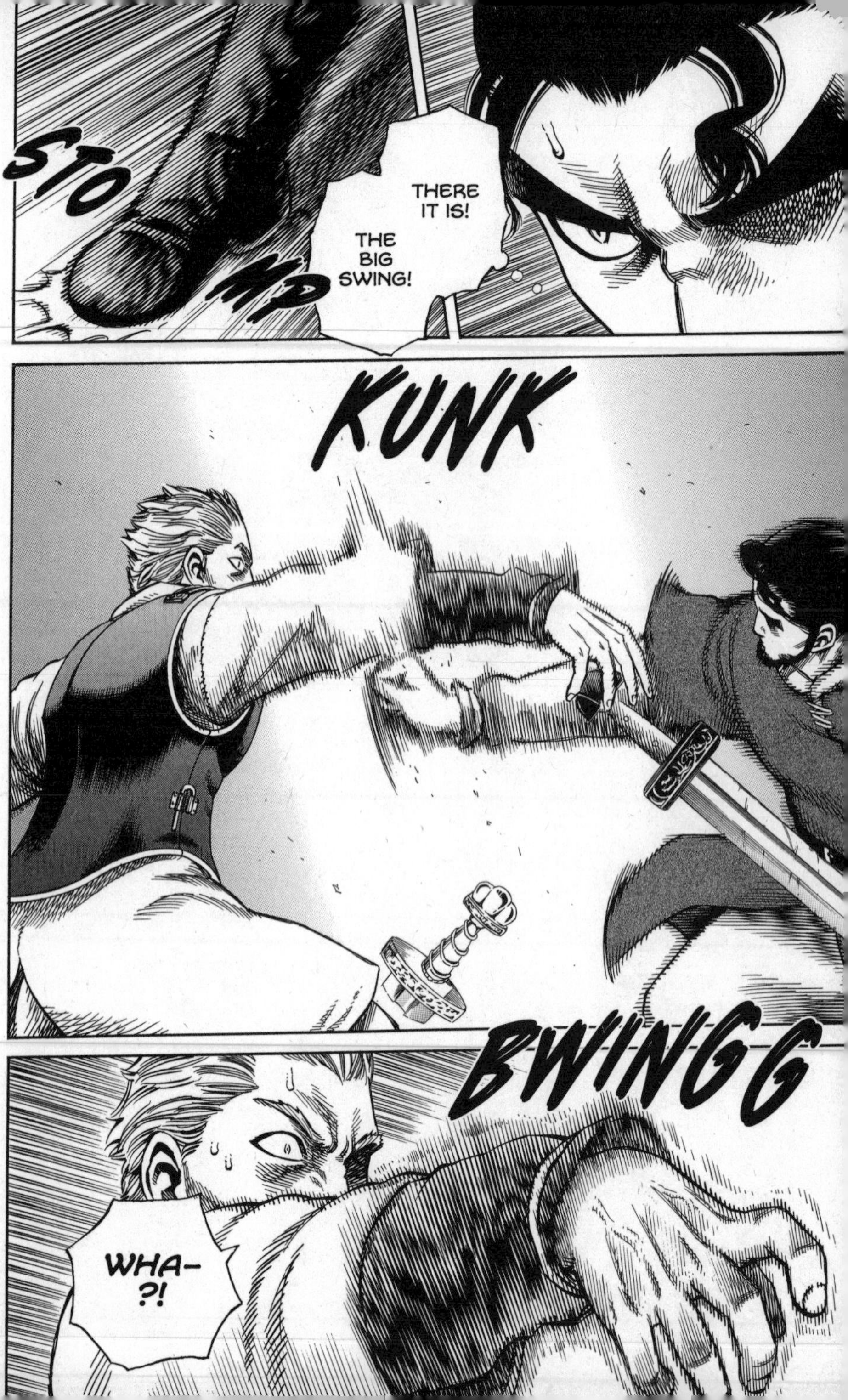
STOMP
THERE IT IS!
THE BIG SWING!
KUNK
BWINGG
WHA-?!

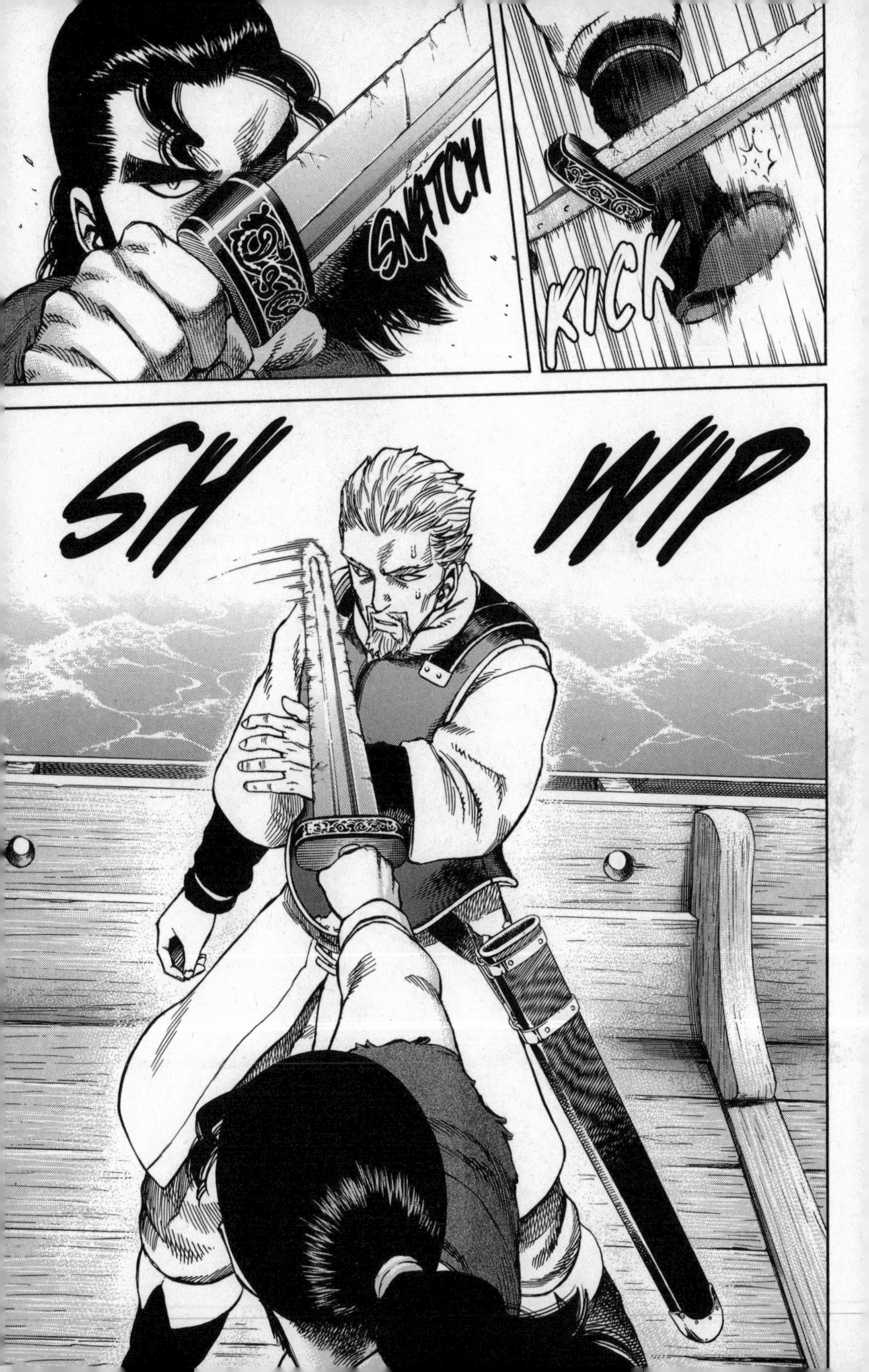
KICK
SNATCH
SH WIP

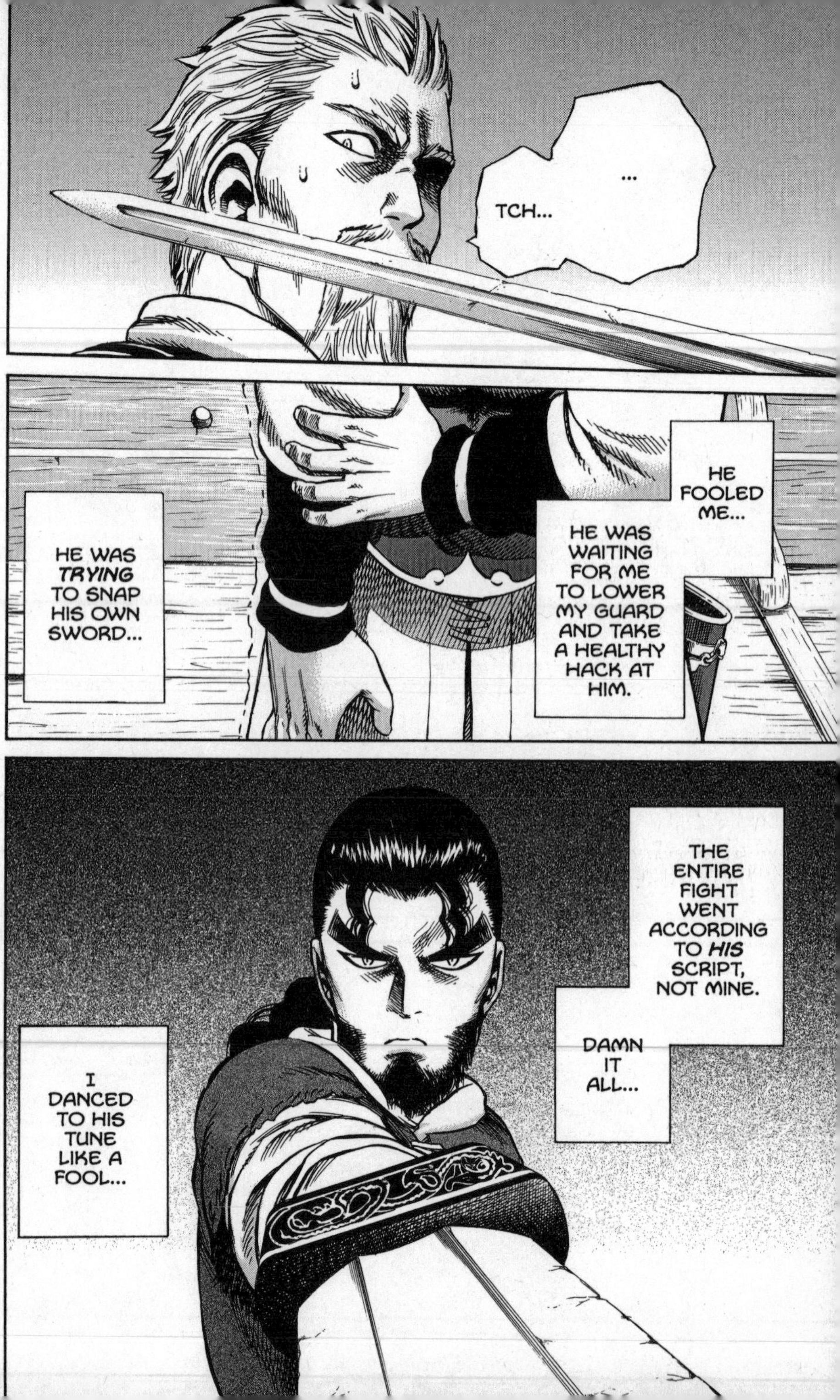
...
TCH...
HE FOOLED ME...
HE WAS WAITING FOR ME TO LOWER MY GUARD AND TAKE A HEALTHY HACK AT HIM.
HE WAS *TRYING* TO SNAP HIS OWN SWORD...
THE ENTIRE FIGHT WENT ACCORDING TO *HIS* SCRIPT, NOT MINE.
DAMN IT ALL...
I DANCED TO HIS TUNE LIKE A FOOL...

CHAPTER 15: A TRUE WARRIOR

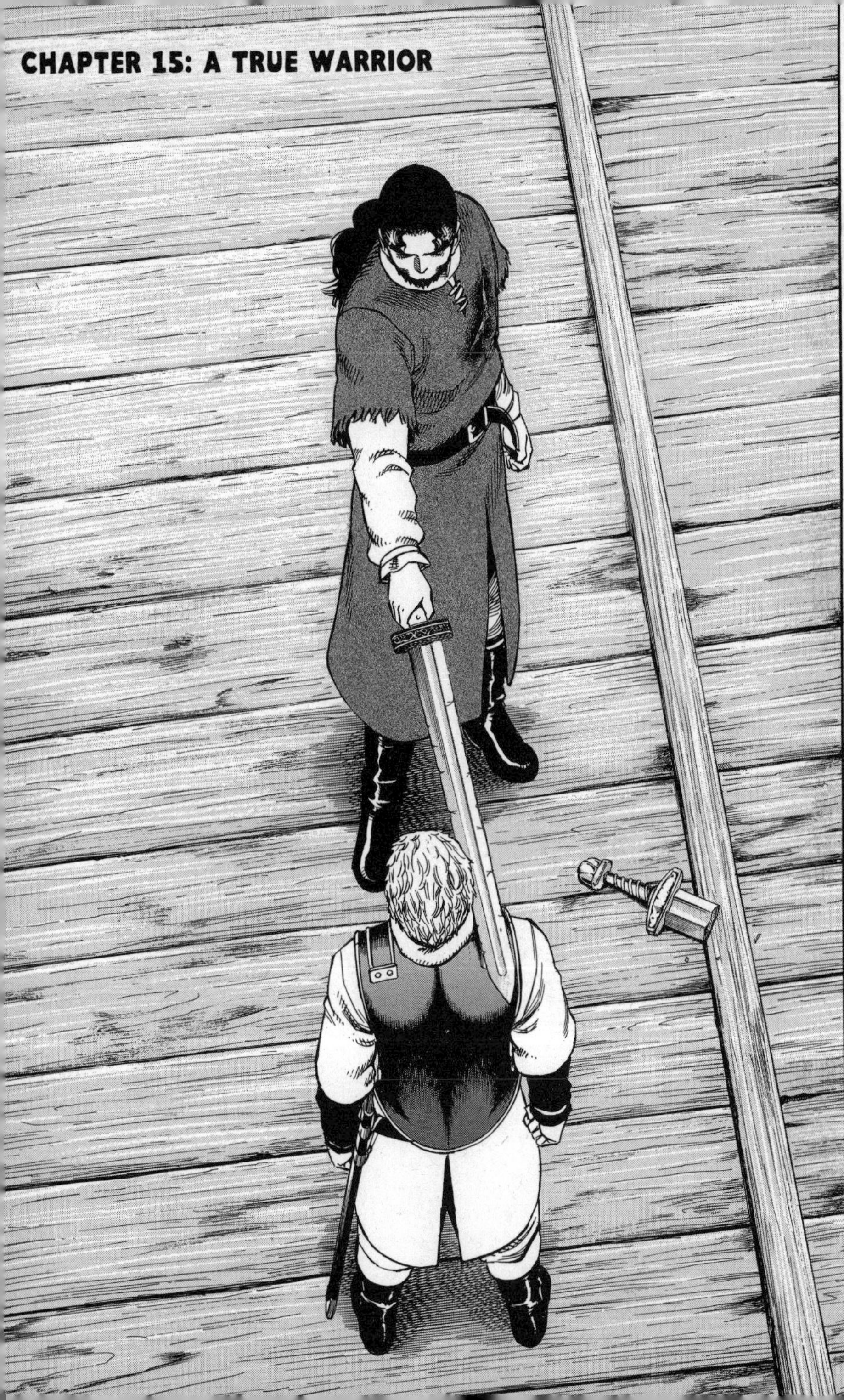

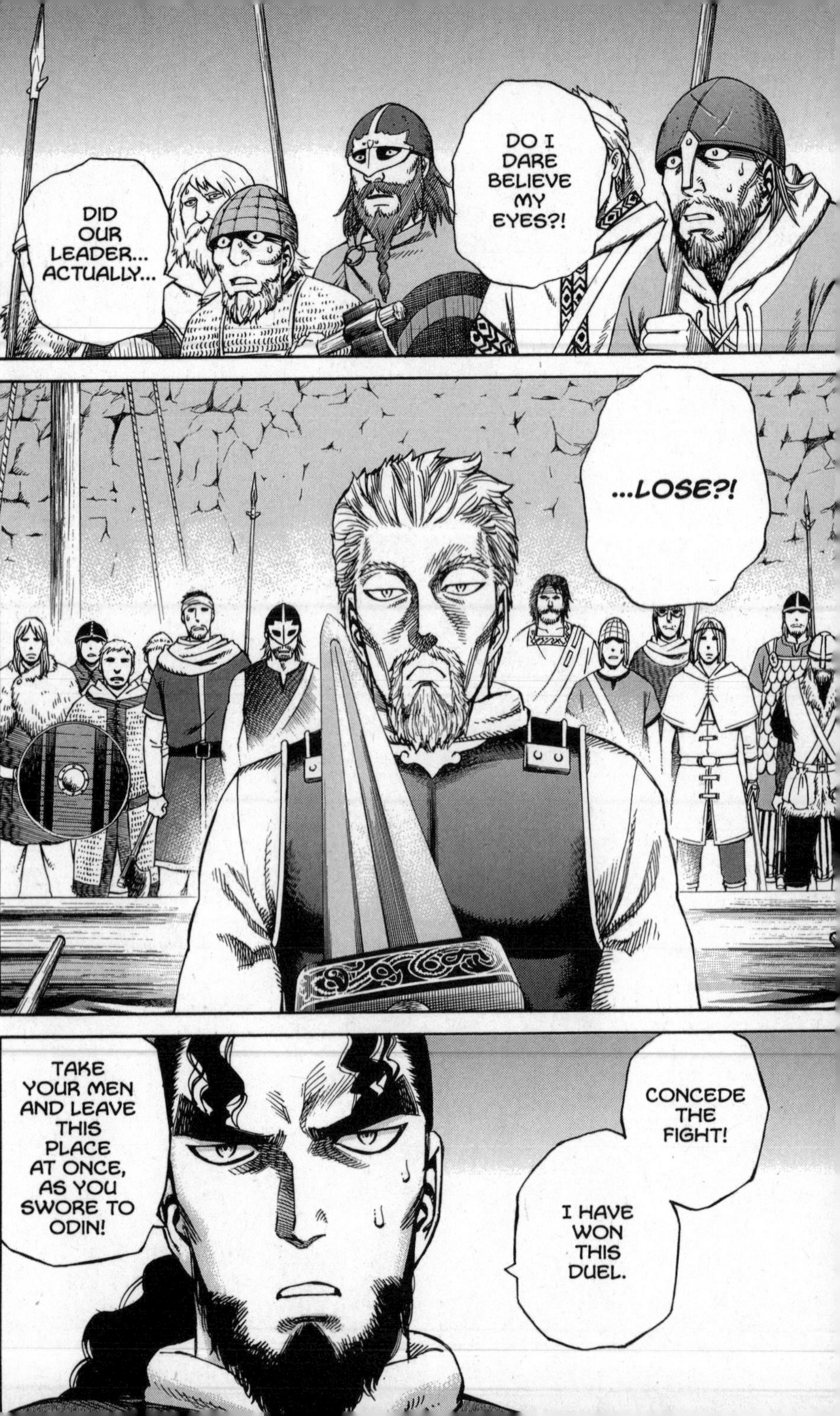
DO I DARE BELIEVE MY EYES?!
DID OUR LEADER... ACTUALLY...
...LOSE?!
CONCEDE THE FIGHT!
I HAVE WON THIS DUEL.
TAKE YOUR MEN AND LEAVE THIS PLACE AT ONCE, AS YOU SWORE TO ODIN!

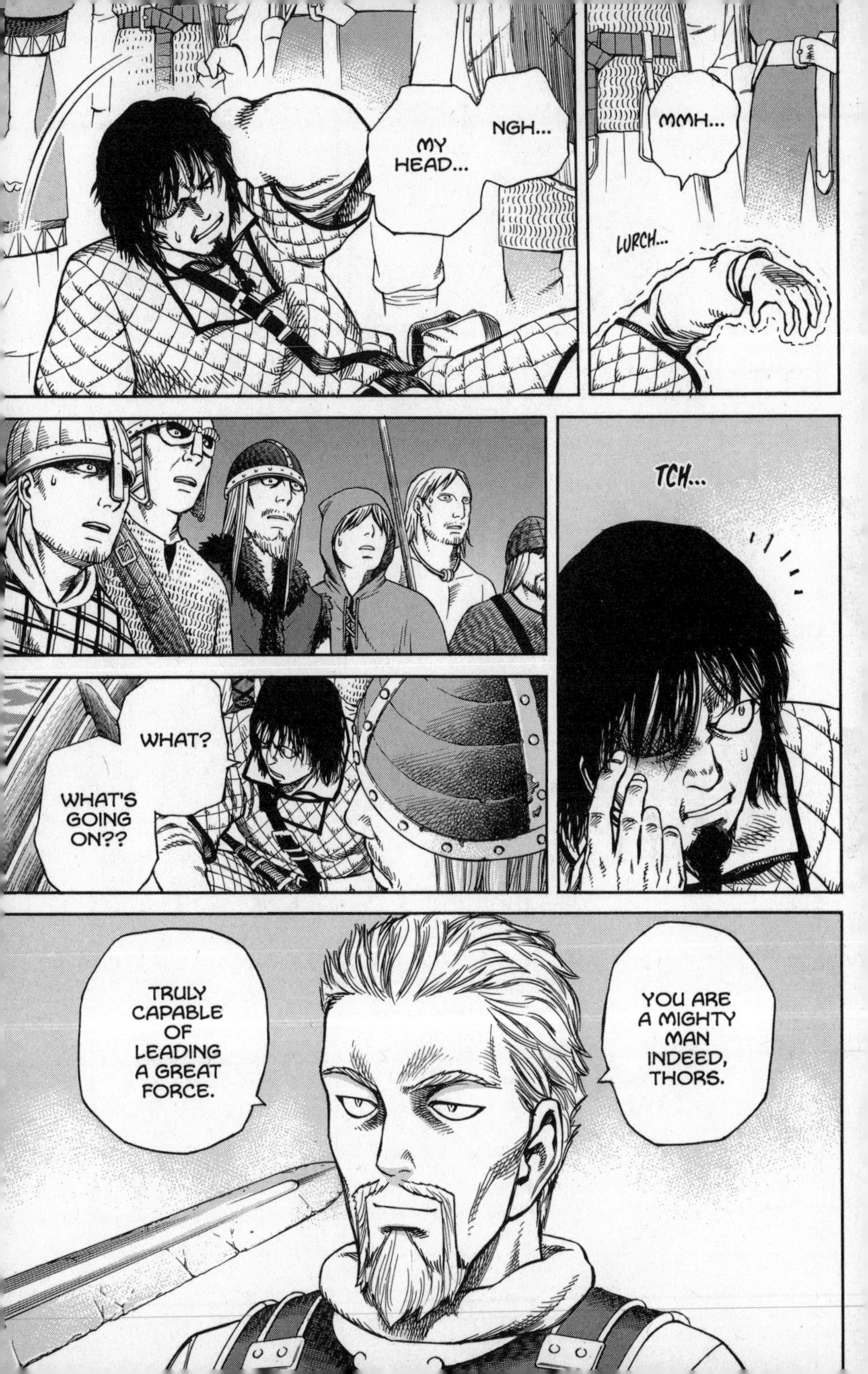
MMH...
LURCH...
NGH... MY HEAD...
TCH...
WHAT?
WHAT'S GOING ON??
YOU ARE A MIGHTY MAN INDEED, THORS.
TRULY CAPABLE OF LEADING A GREAT FORCE.

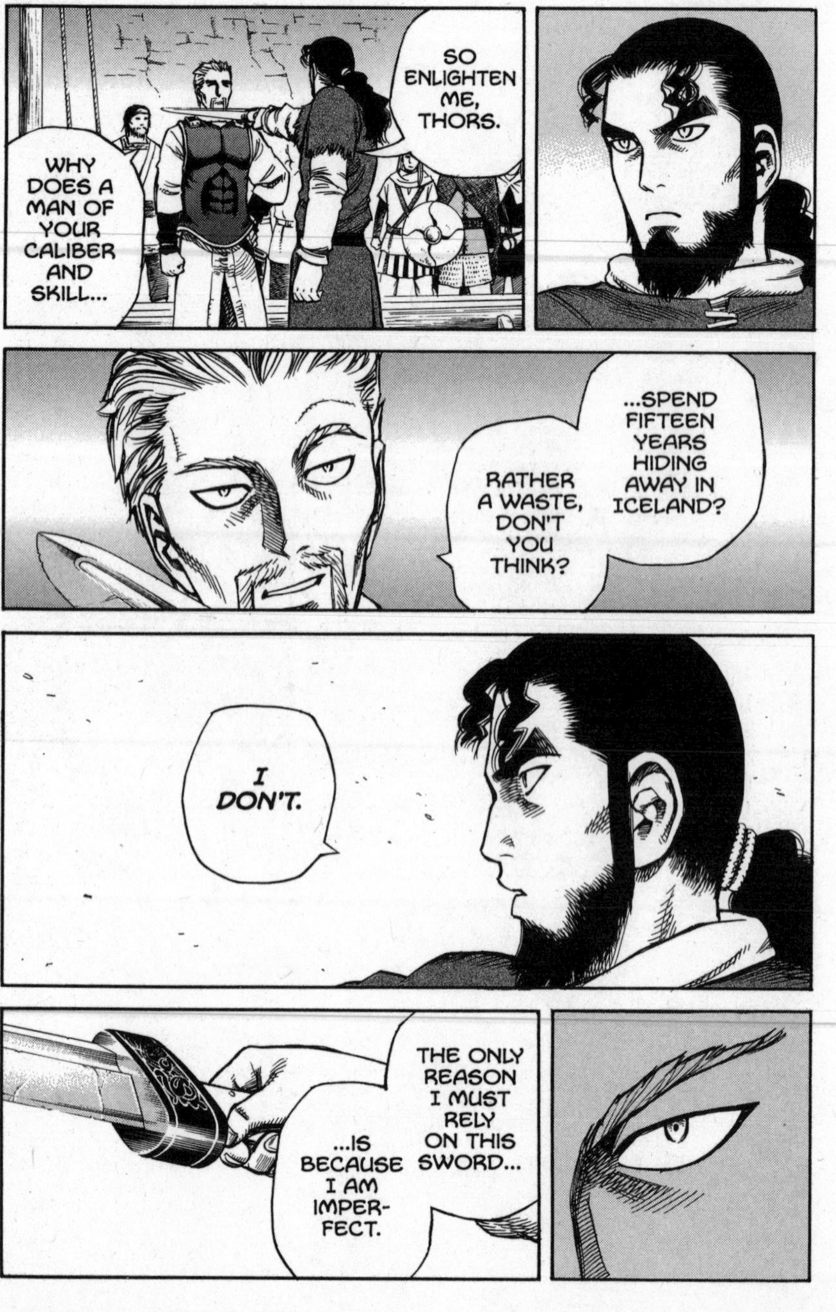
SO ENLIGHTEN ME, THORS.
WHY DOES A MAN OF YOUR CALIBER AND SKILL...
...SPEND FIFTEEN YEARS HIDING AWAY IN ICELAND?
RATHER A WASTE, DON'T YOU THINK?
I DON'T.
THE ONLY REASON I MUST RELY ON THIS SWORD...
...IS BECAUSE I AM IMPERFECT.

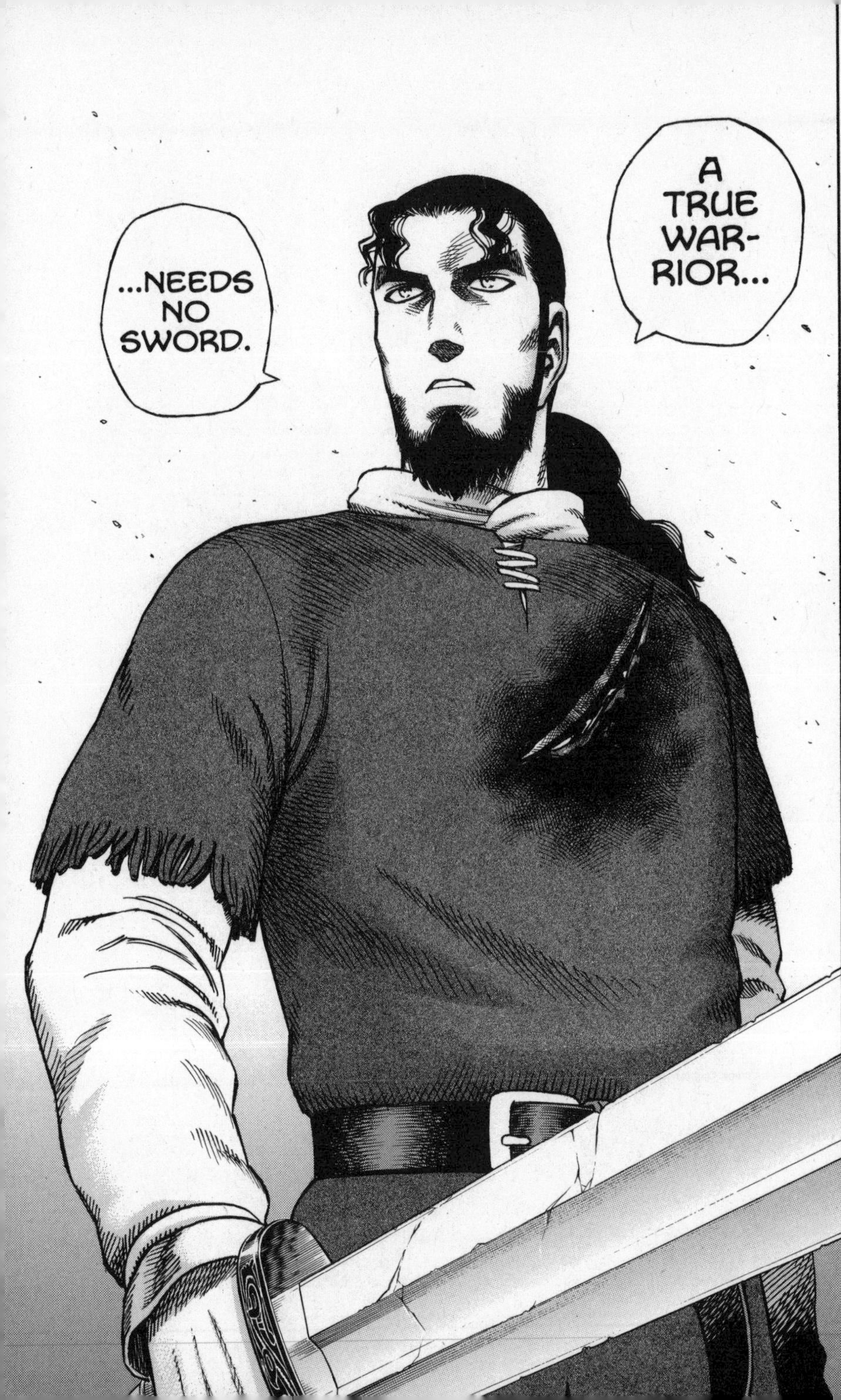
A TRUE WAR-RIOR...
...NEEDS NO SWORD.

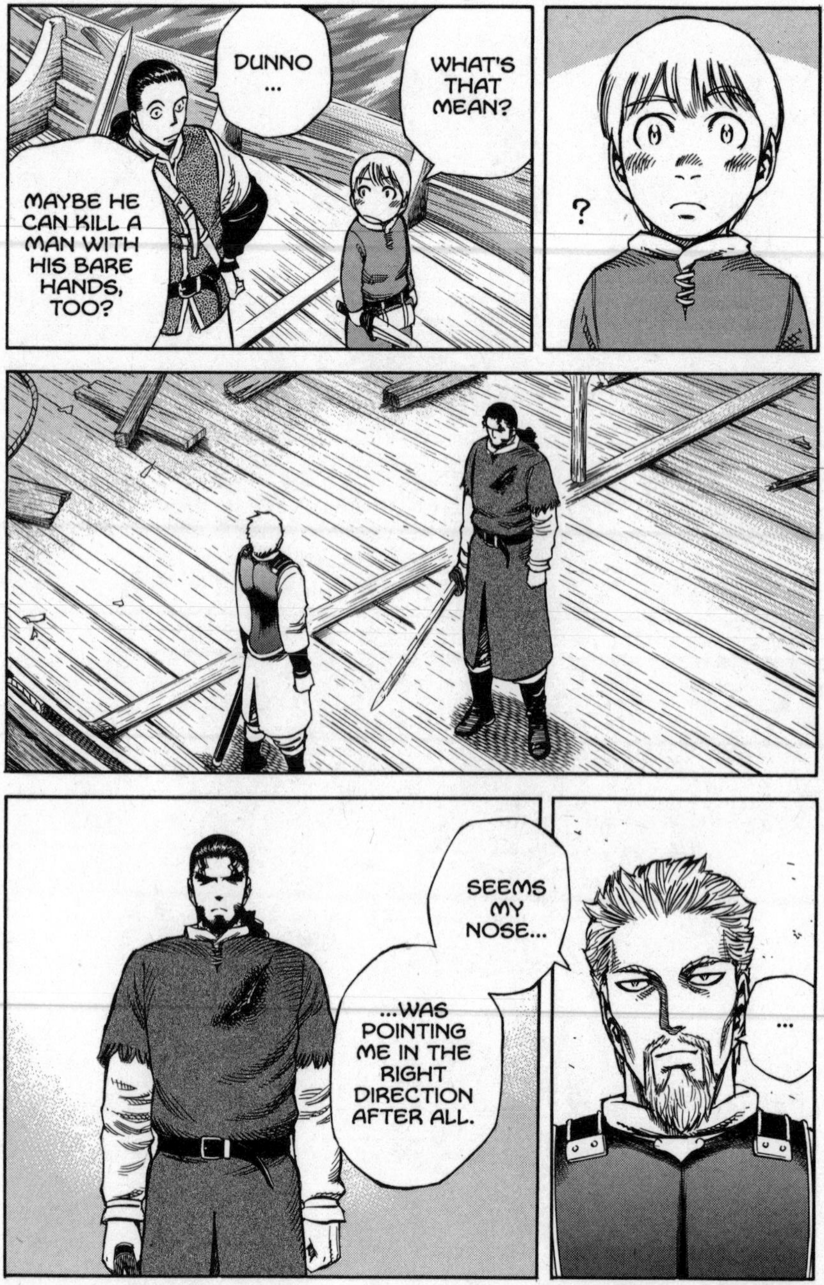
?
WHAT'S THAT MEAN?
DUNNO ...
MAYBE HE CAN KILL A MAN WITH HIS BARE HANDS, TOO?
...
SEEMS MY NOSE...
...WAS POINTING ME IN THE RIGHT DIRECTION AFTER ALL.

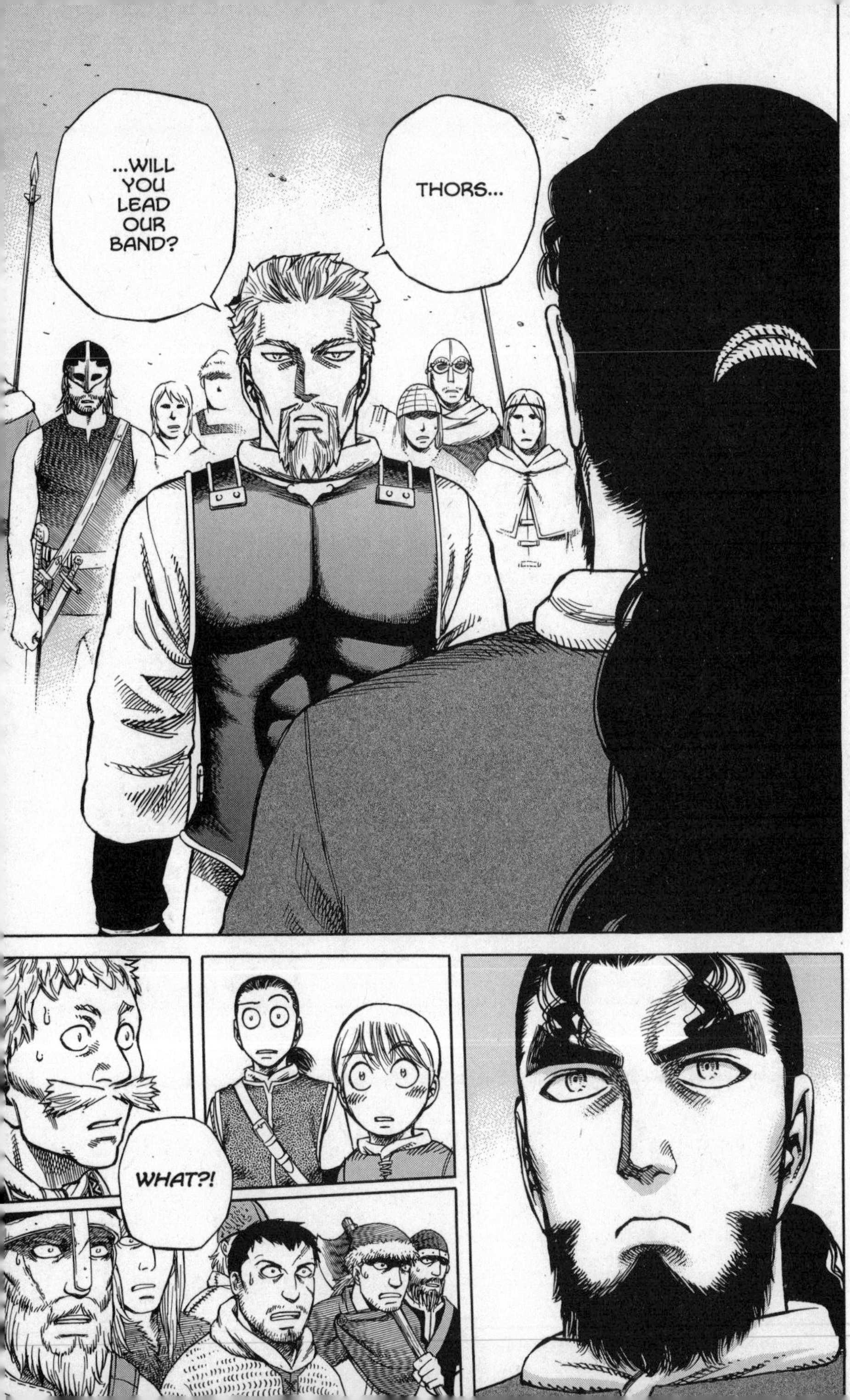

THORS...
...WILL YOU LEAD OUR BAND?
WHAT?!

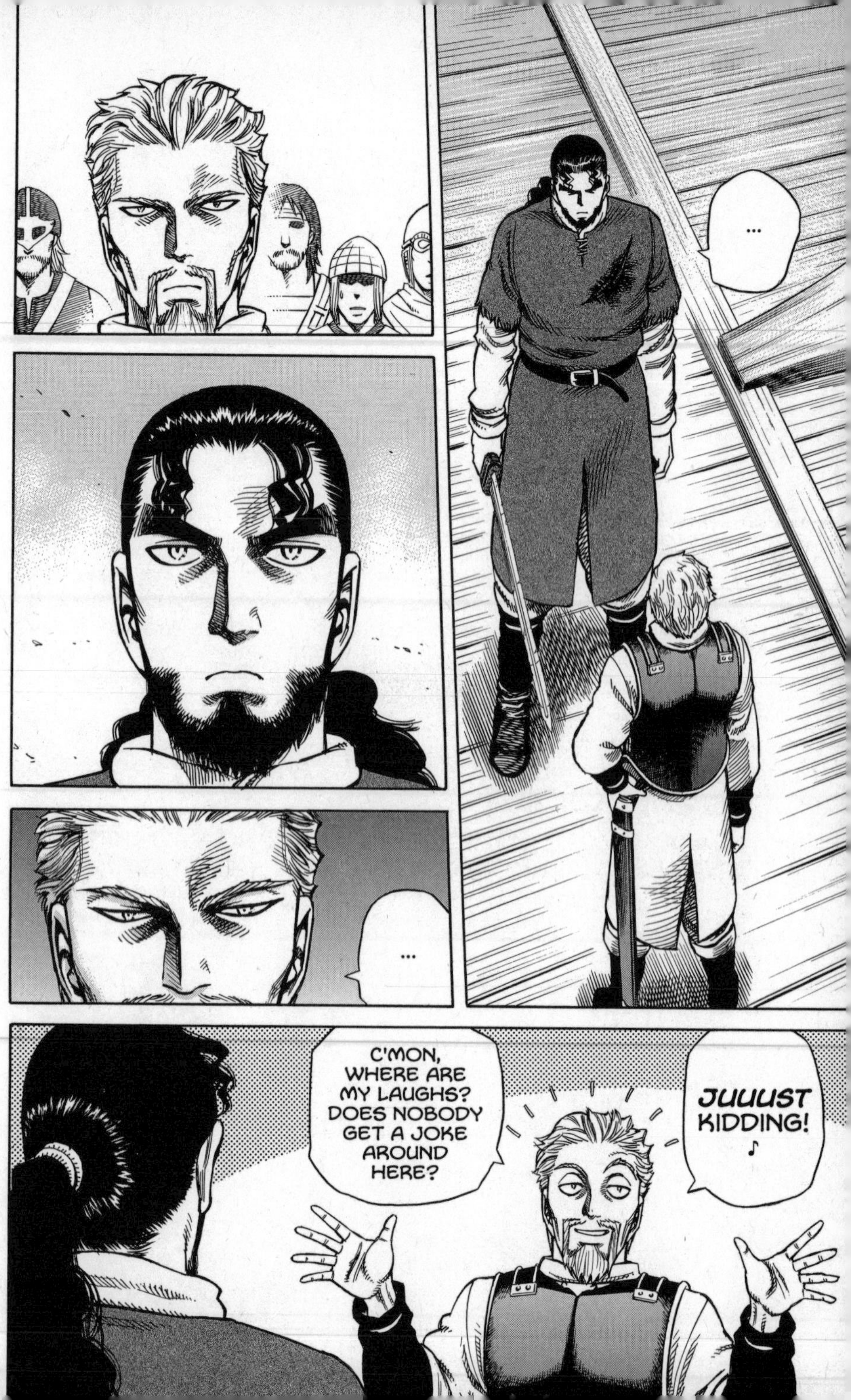
...
...
JUUUST KIDDING! ♪
C'MON, WHERE ARE MY LAUGHS? DOES NOBODY GET A JOKE AROUND HERE?

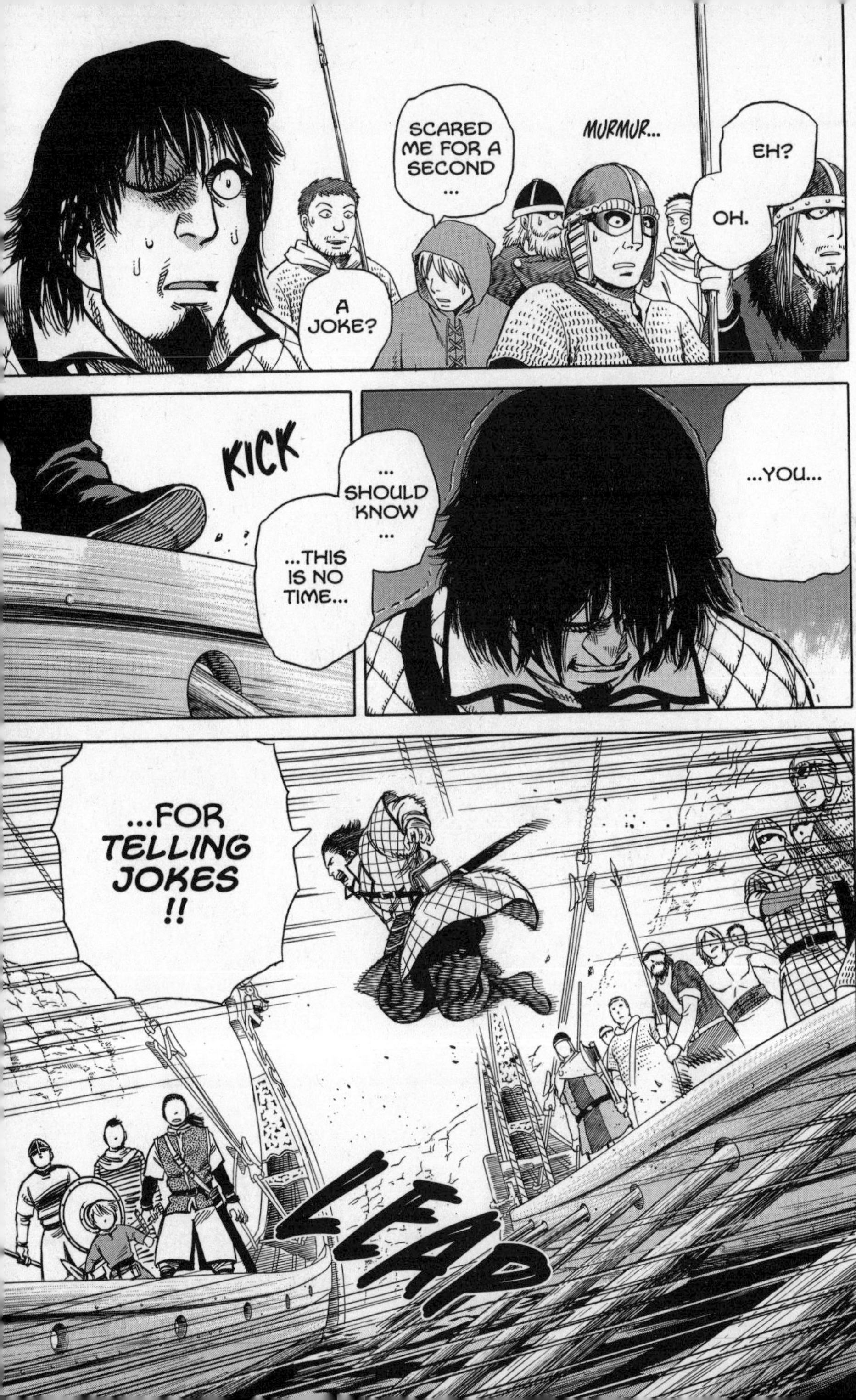
EH?
MURMUR...
OH.
SCARED ME FOR A SECOND ...
A JOKE?
...YOU...
... SHOULD KNOW ...
...THIS IS NO TIME...
KICK
...FOR TELLING JOKES !!
LEAP

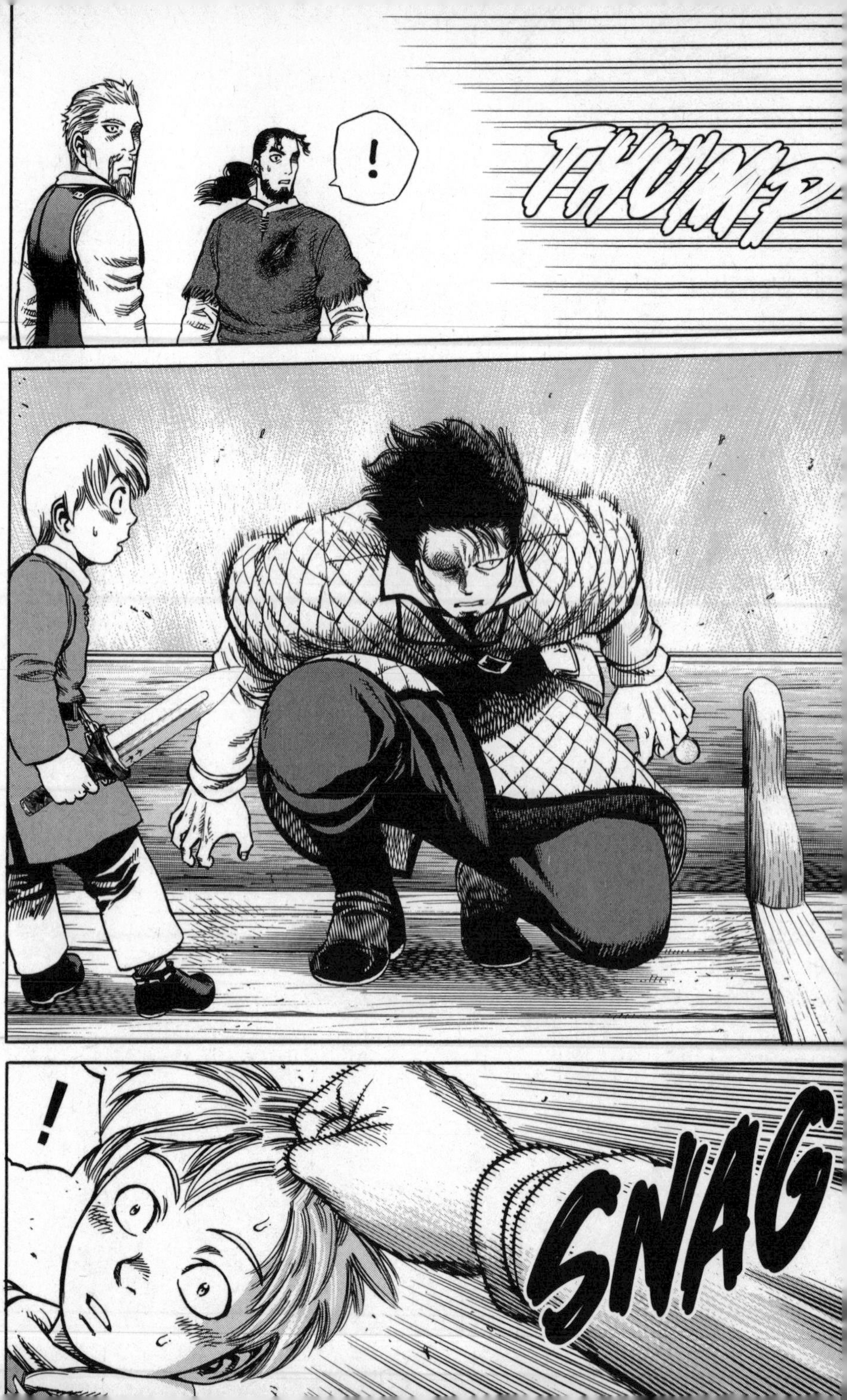
THUMP
!
!
SNAG

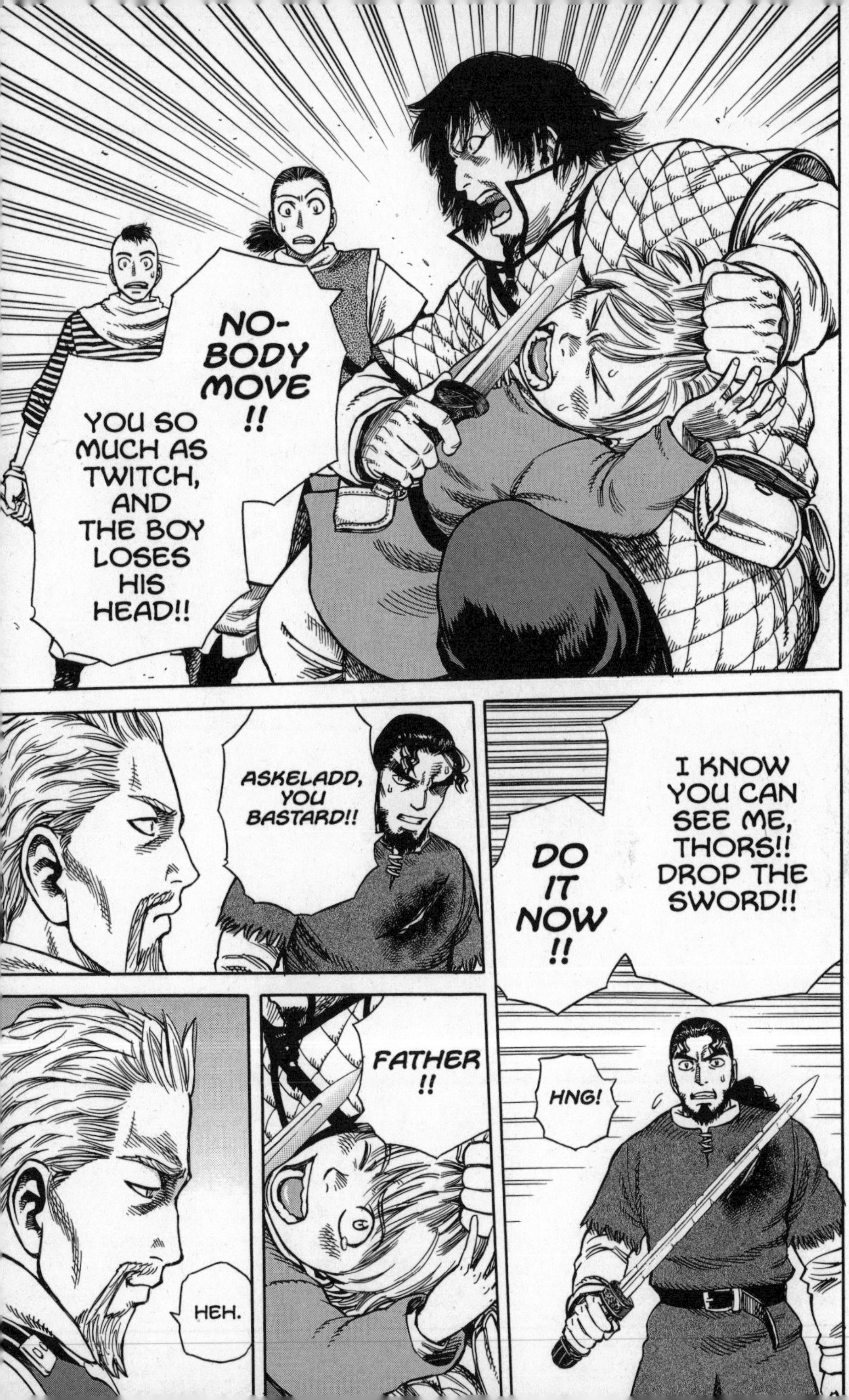
NO-BODY MOVE!!
YOU SO MUCH AS TWITCH, AND THE BOY LOSES HIS HEAD!!
I KNOW YOU CAN SEE ME, THORS!! DROP THE SWORD!!
DO IT NOW!!
HNG!
ASKELADD, YOU BASTARD!!
FATHER!!
HEH.

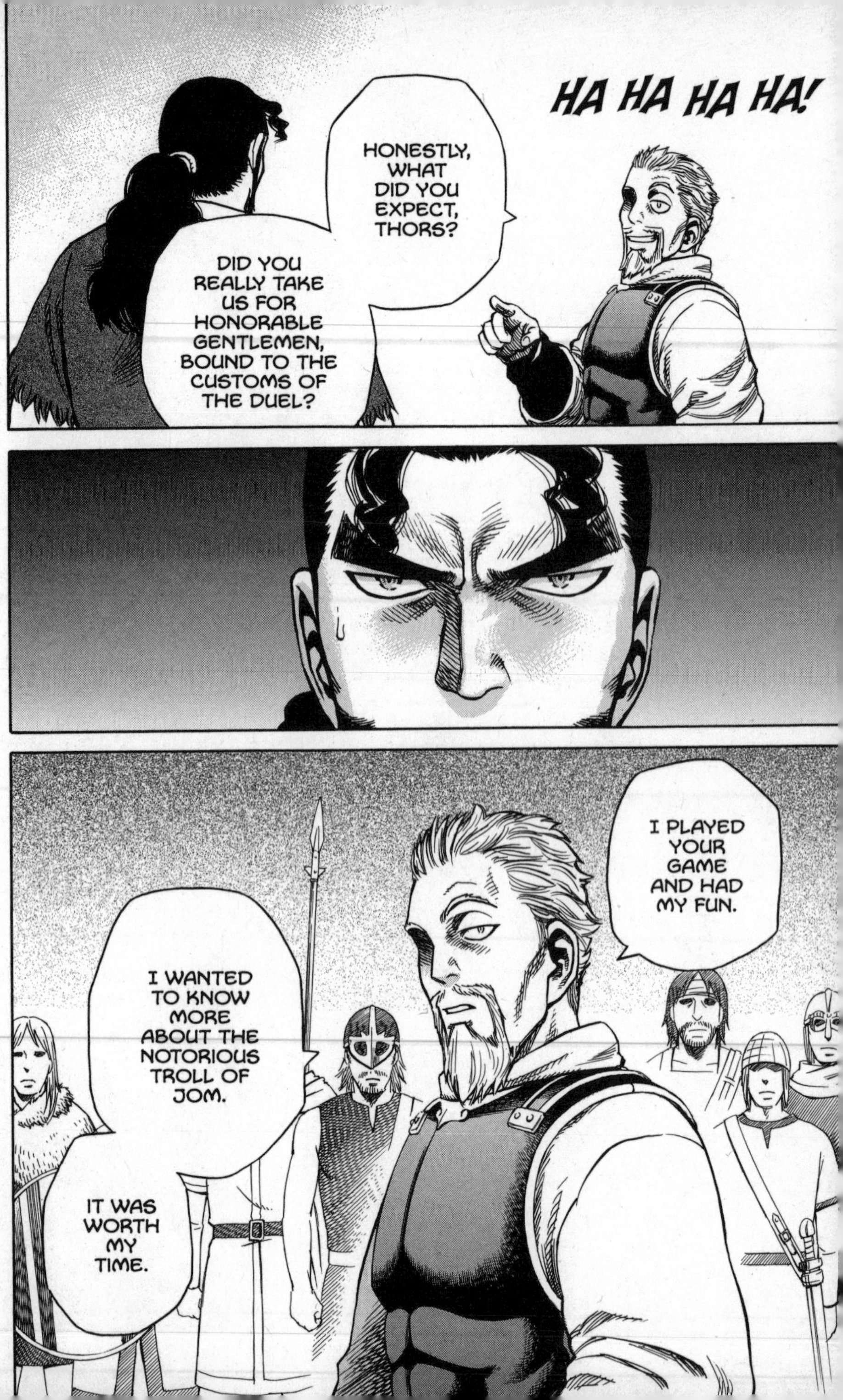
HA HA HA HA!
HONESTLY, WHAT DID YOU EXPECT, THORS?
DID YOU REALLY TAKE US FOR HONORABLE GENTLEMEN, BOUND TO THE CUSTOMS OF THE DUEL?
I PLAYED YOUR GAME AND HAD MY FUN.
I WANTED TO KNOW MORE ABOUT THE NOTORIOUS TROLL OF JOM.
IT WAS WORTH MY TIME.

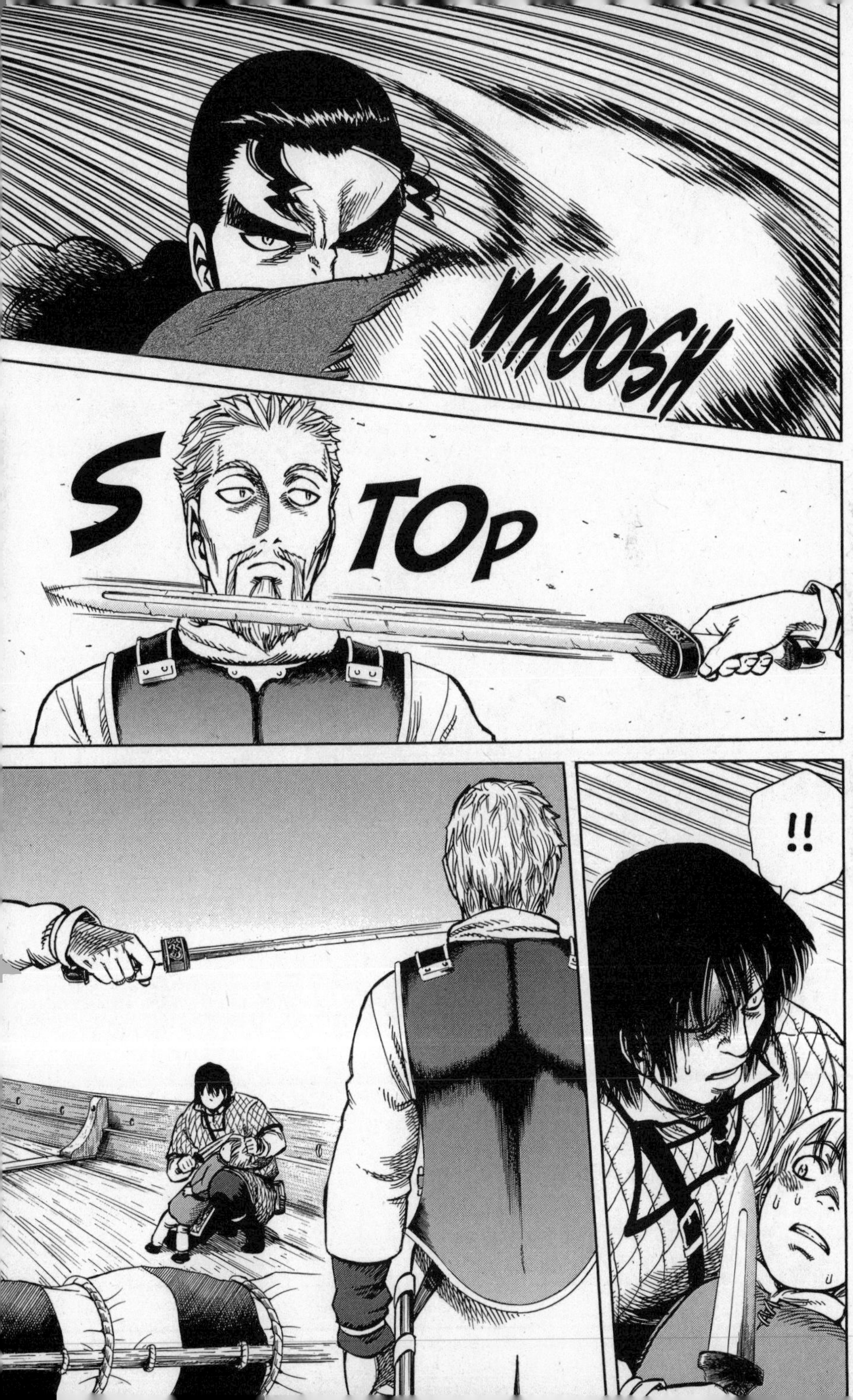
WHOOSH
STOP
!!

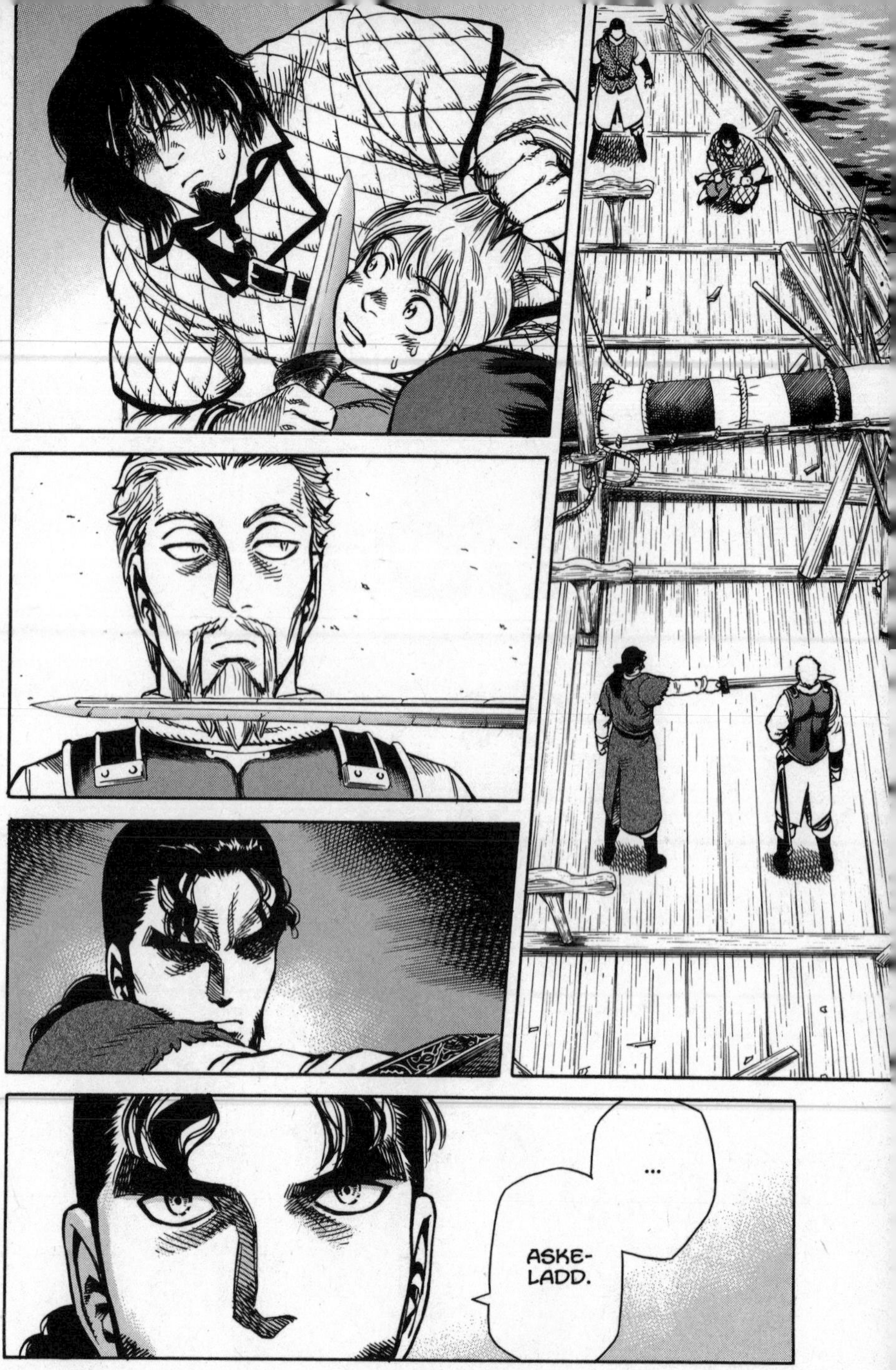
...
ASKE-
LADD.

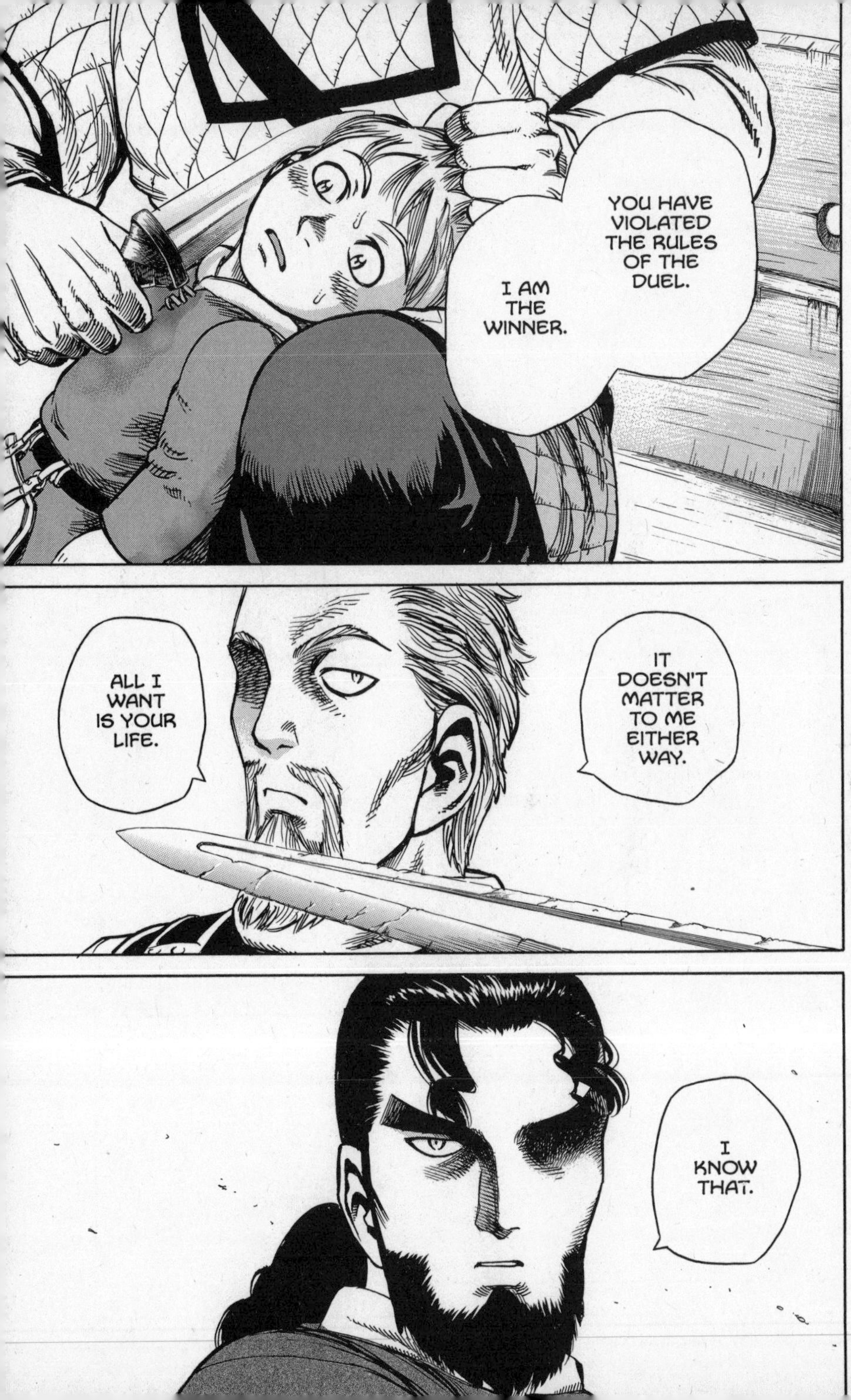
YOU HAVE VIOLATED THE RULES OF THE DUEL.
I AM THE WINNER.
IT DOESN'T MATTER TO ME EITHER WAY.
ALL I WANT IS YOUR LIFE.
I KNOW THAT.

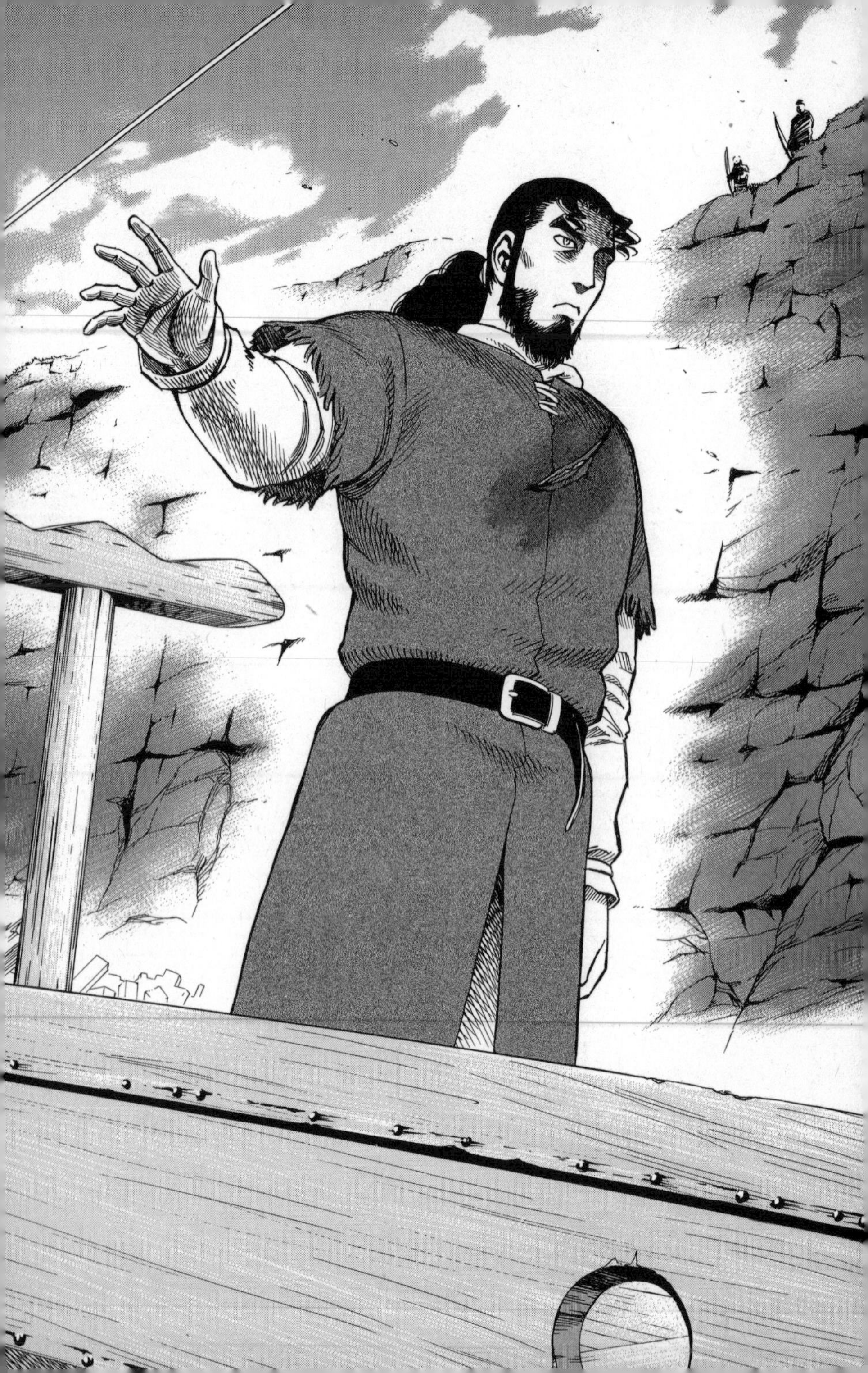

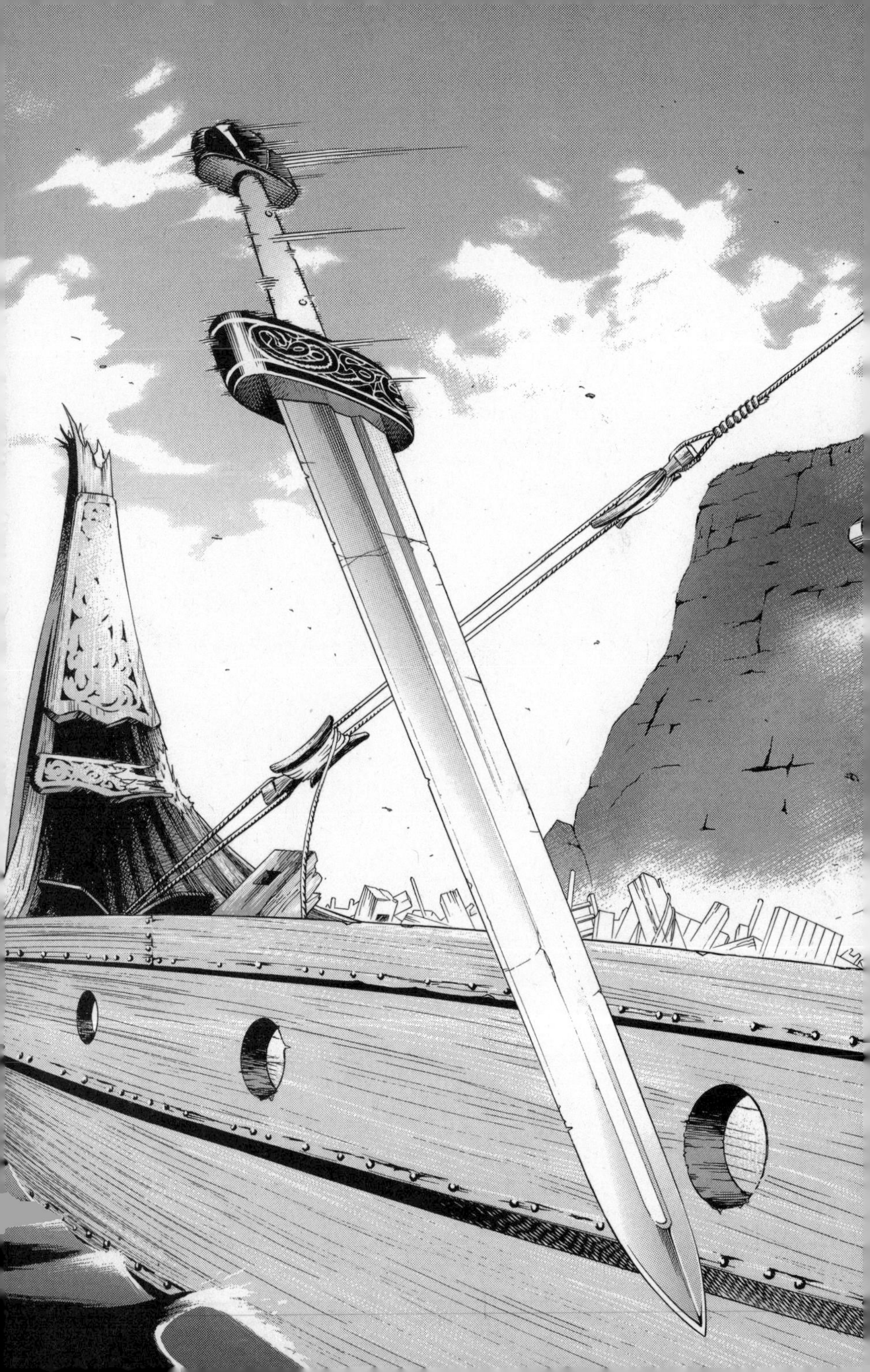

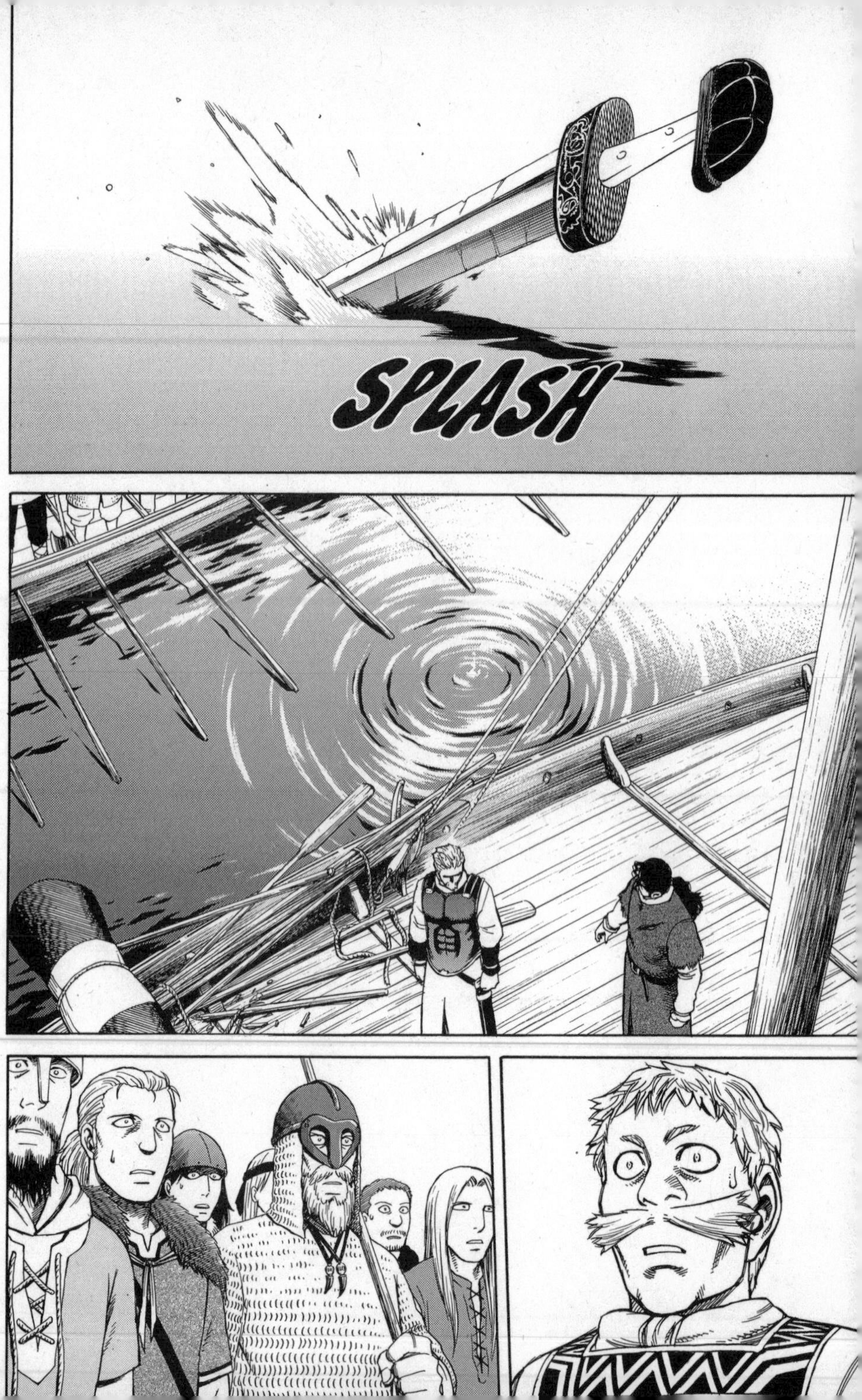
SPLASH

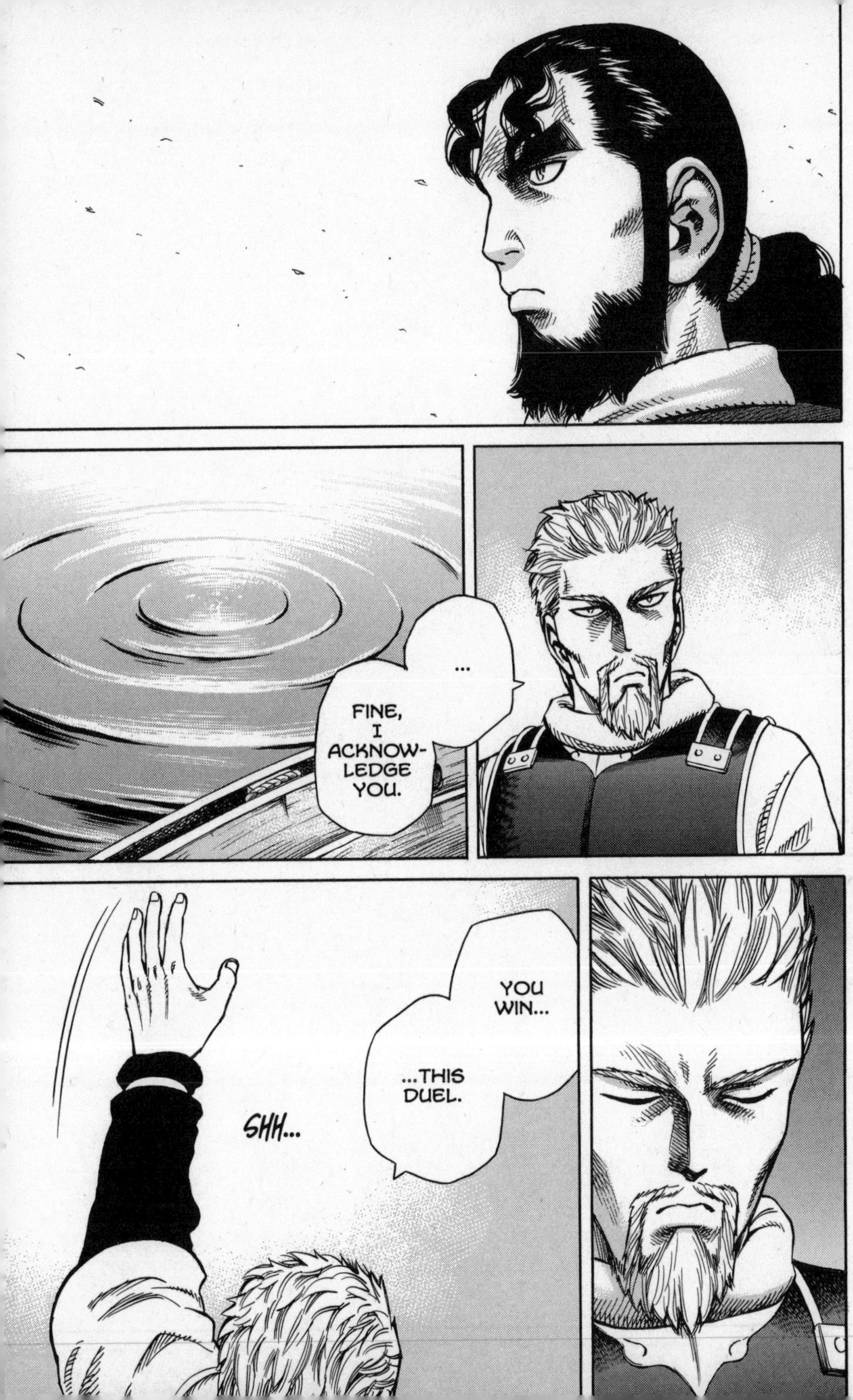
...
FINE, I ACKNOW-LEDGE YOU.
YOU WIN...
...THIS DUEL.
SHH...

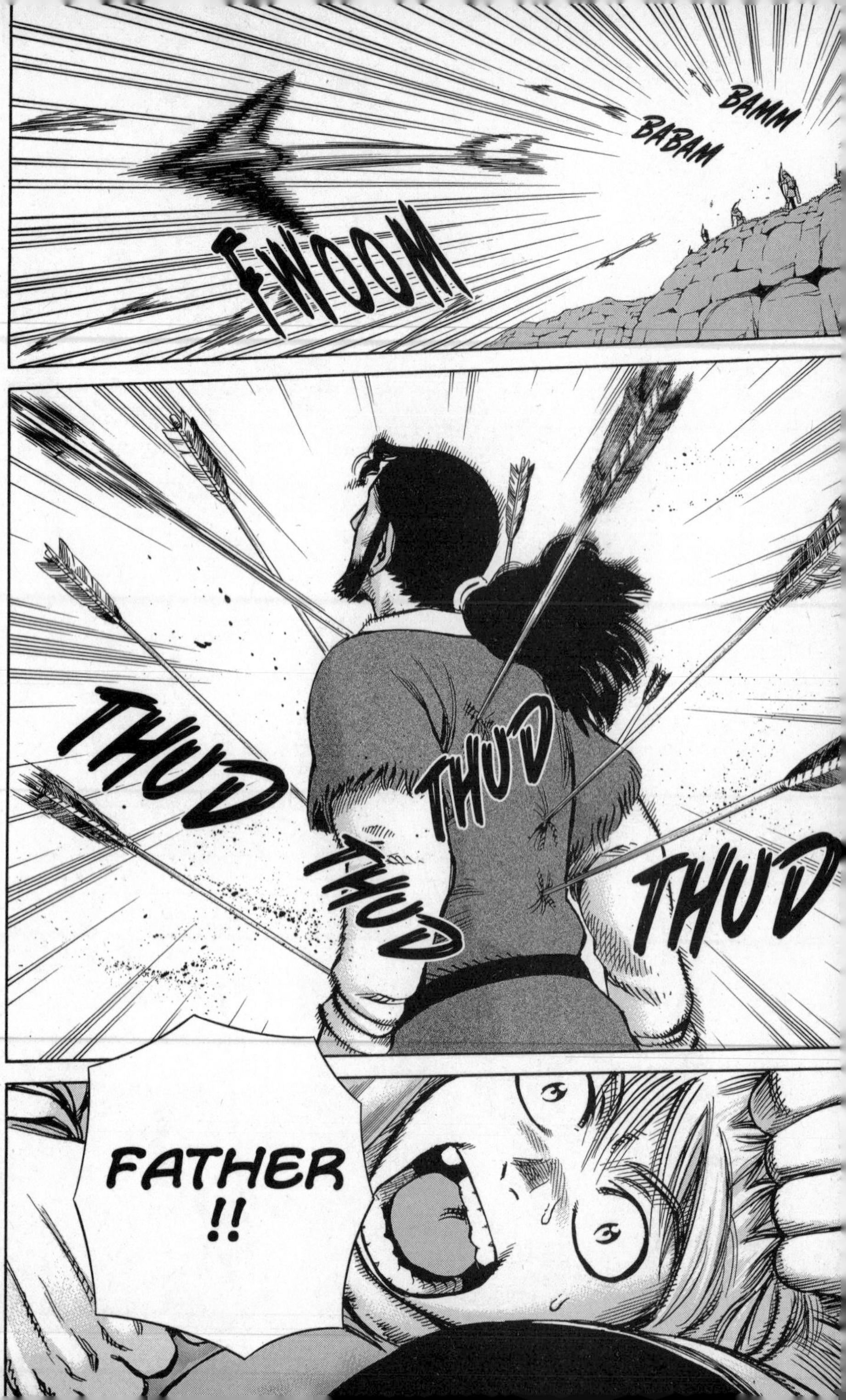
BAMM
BABAM
FWOOM
THUD
THUD
THUD
THUD
FATHER !!

CHAPTER 15 - END

CHAPTER 16: THE DEATH OF THORS

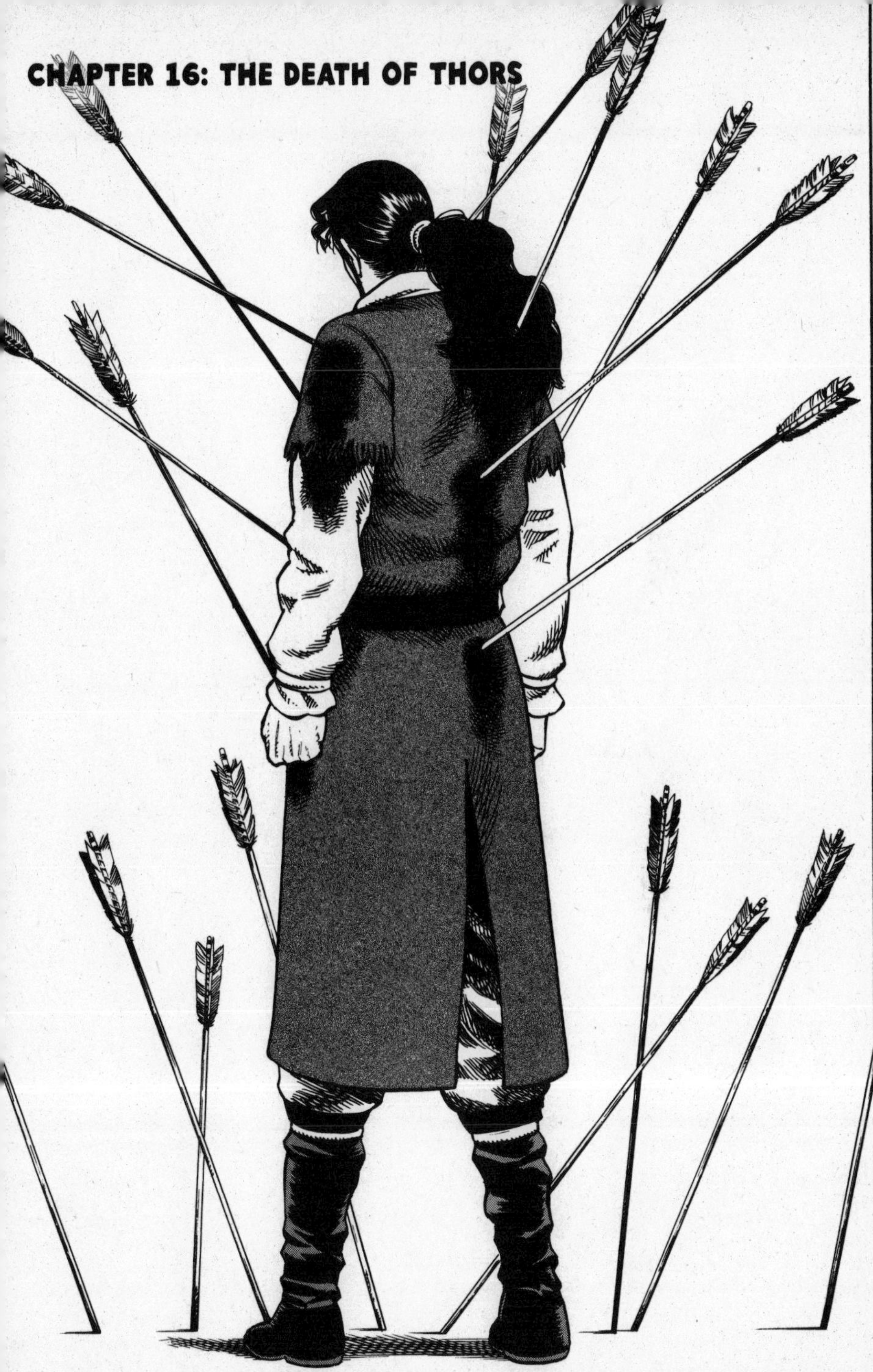

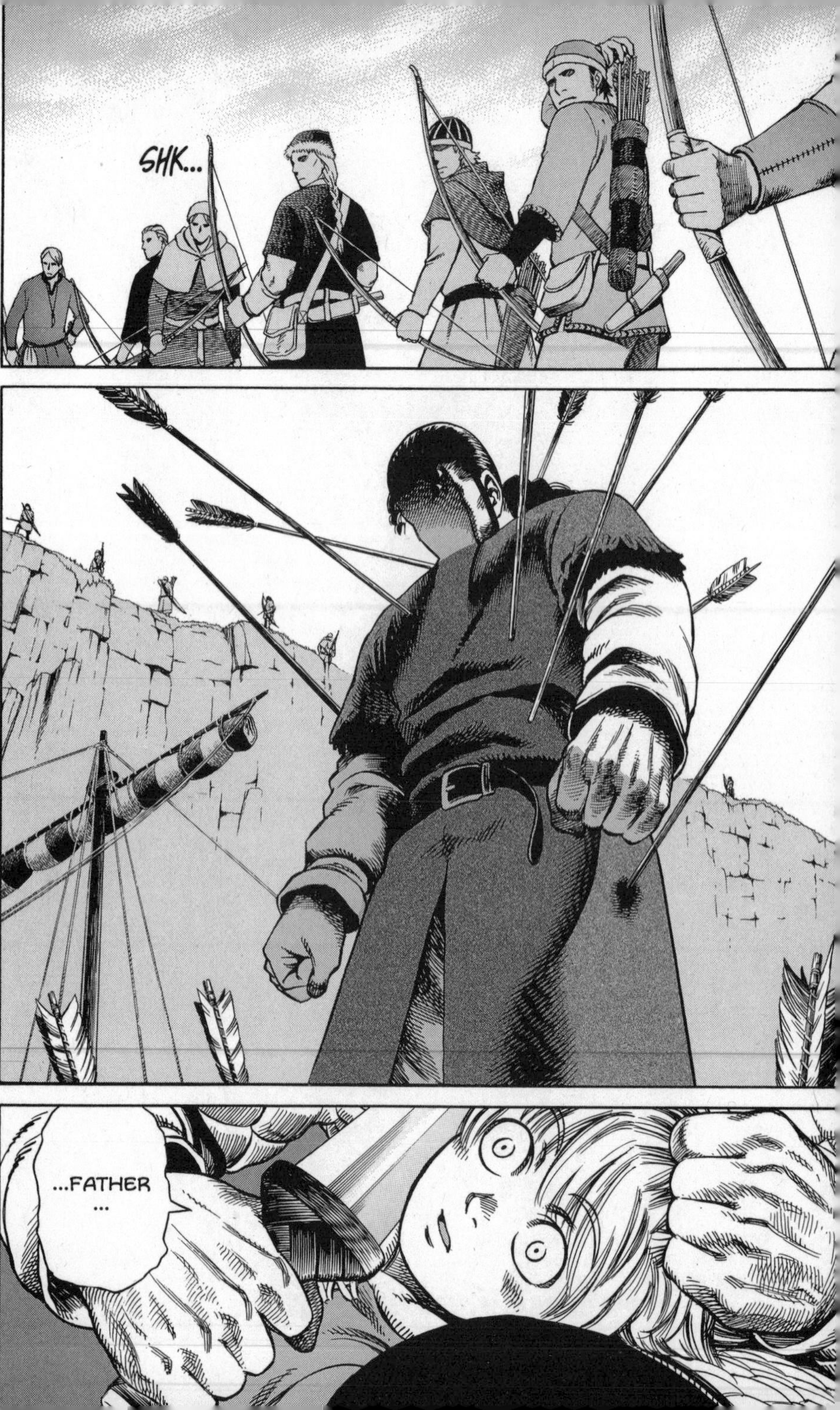
SHK...
...FATHER ...

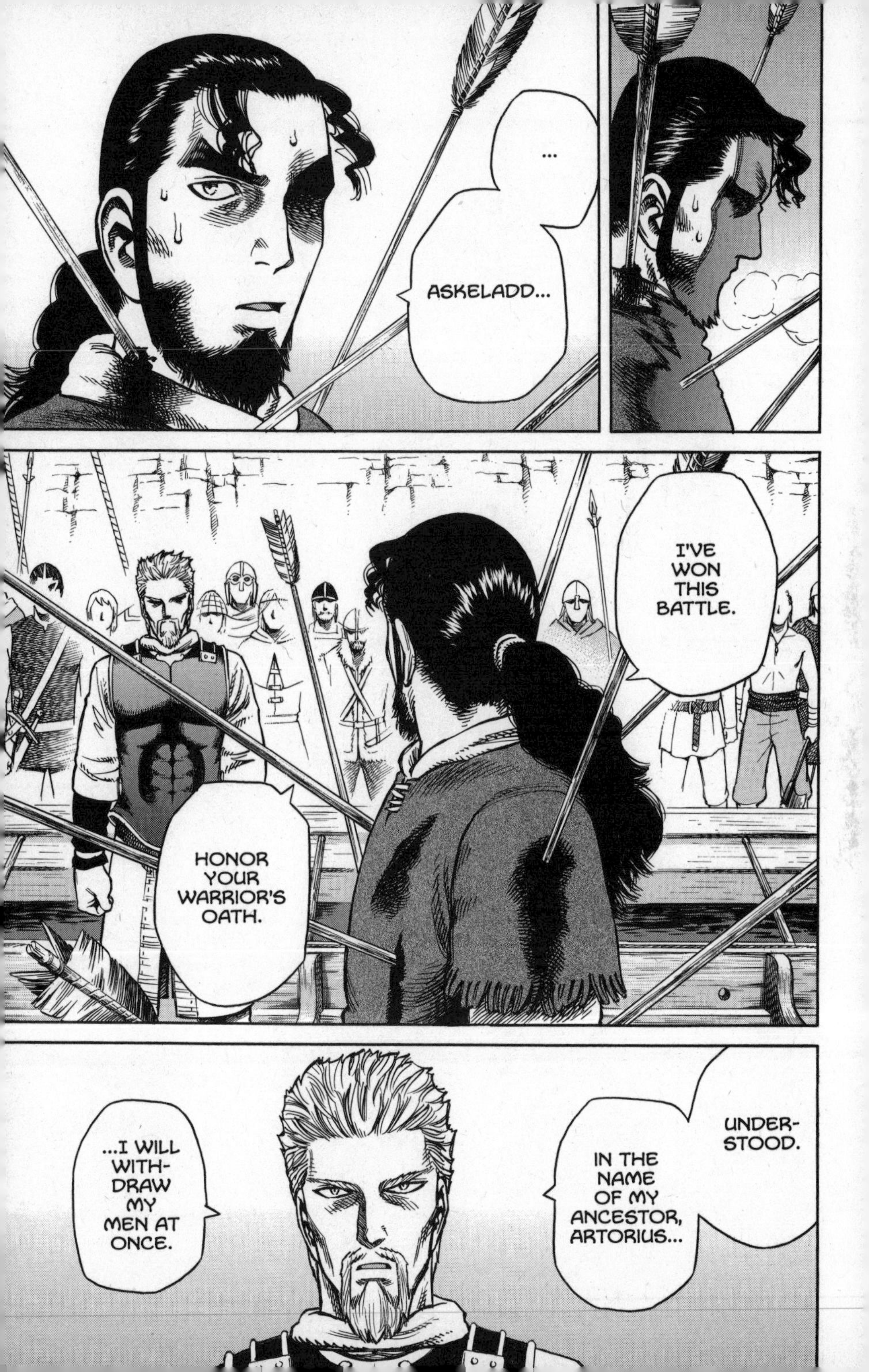
...
ASKELADD...
I'VE WON THIS BATTLE.
HONOR YOUR WARRIOR'S OATH.
UNDER-STOOD.
IN THE NAME OF MY ANCESTOR, ARTORIUS...
...I WILL WITH-DRAW MY MEN AT ONCE.

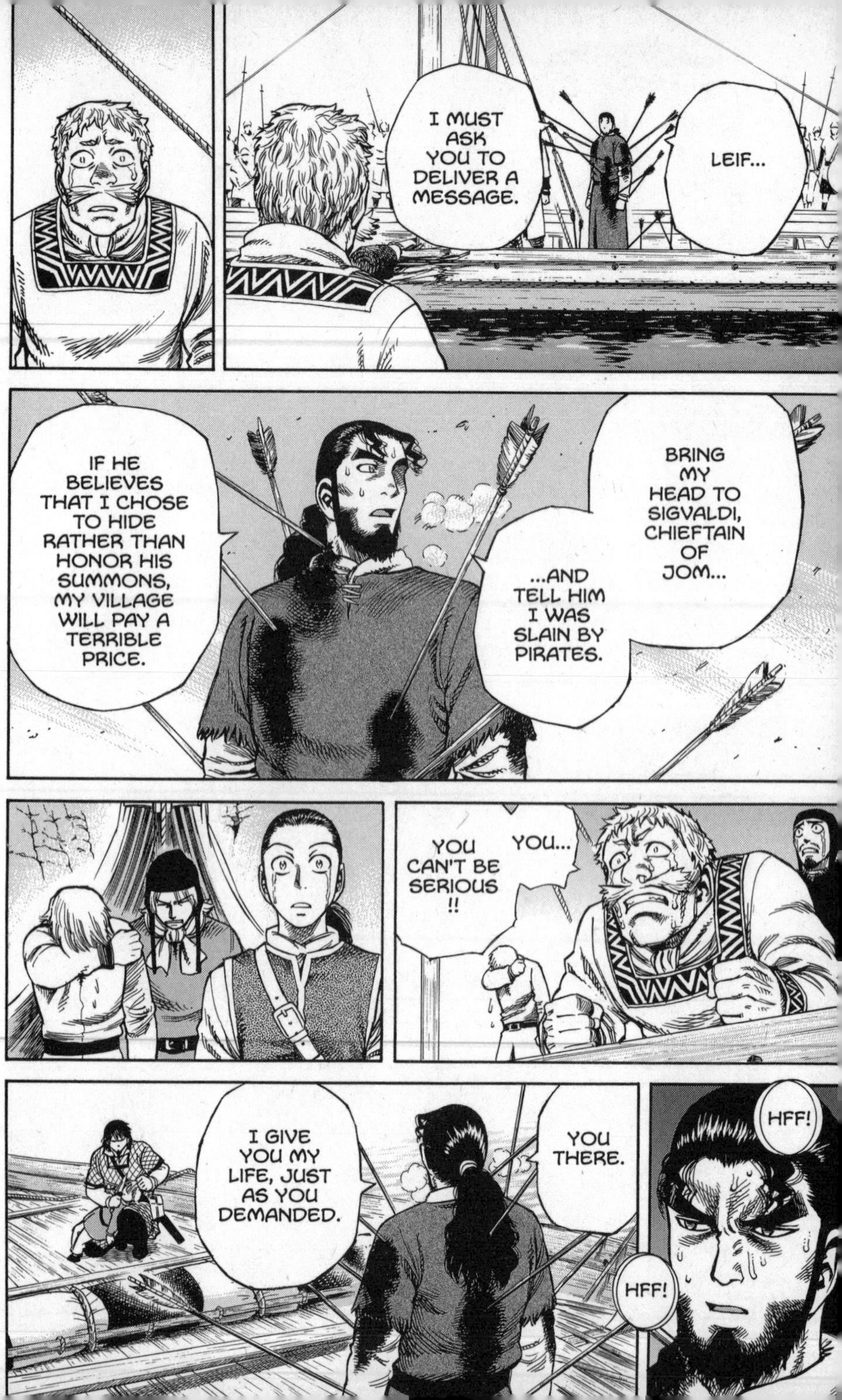
LEIF...
I MUST ASK YOU TO DELIVER A MESSAGE.
BRING MY HEAD TO SIGVALDI, CHIEFTAIN OF JOM...
...AND TELL HIM I WAS SLAIN BY PIRATES.
IF HE BELIEVES THAT I CHOSE TO HIDE RATHER THAN HONOR HIS SUMMONS, MY VILLAGE WILL PAY A TERRIBLE PRICE.
YOU...
YOU CAN'T BE SERIOUS !!
HFF!
HFF!
YOU THERE.
I GIVE YOU MY LIFE, JUST AS YOU DEMANDED.

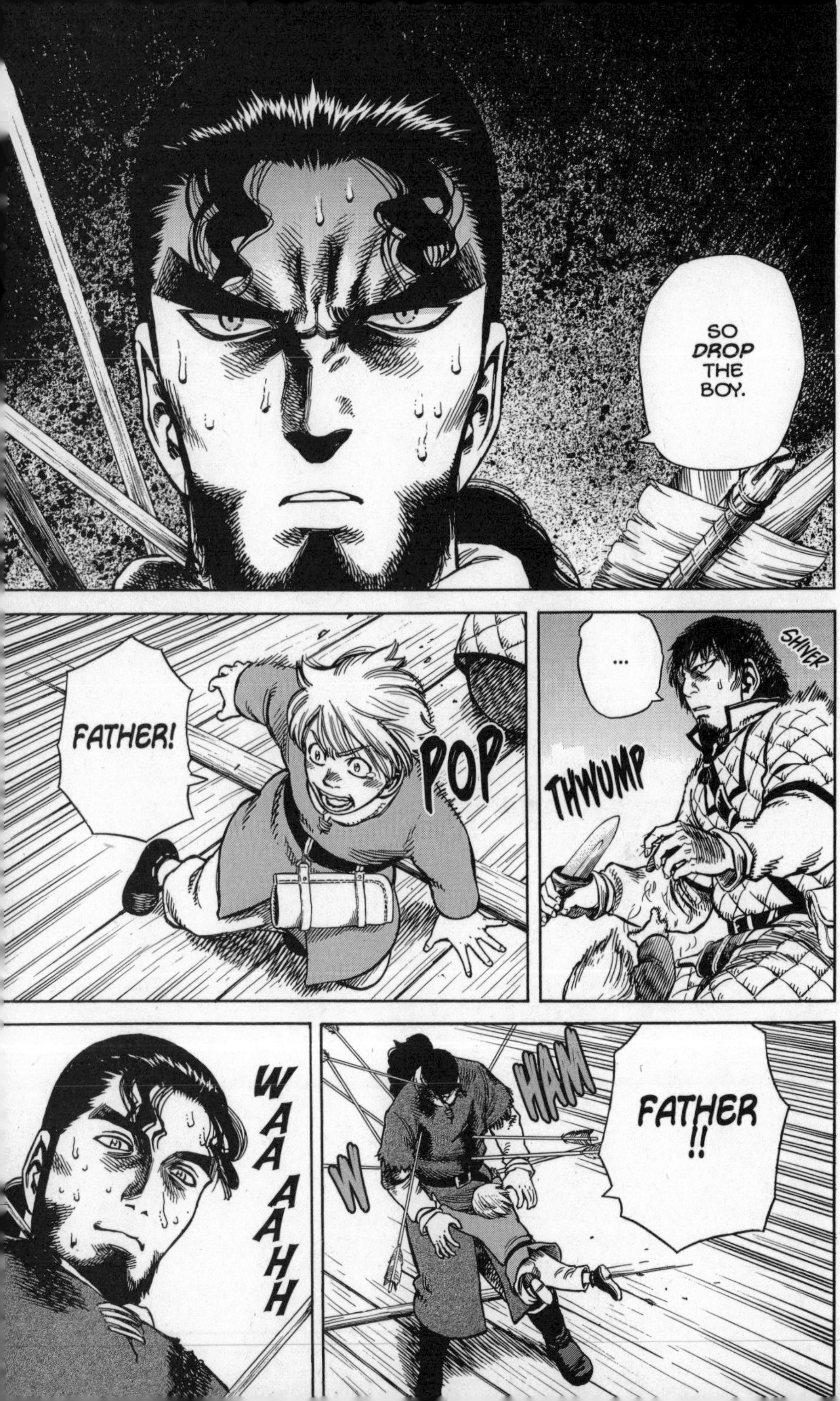
SO DROP THE BOY.
...
SHIVER
THWUMP
FATHER!
POP
FATHER !!
WHAM
W
WAAAAAHH

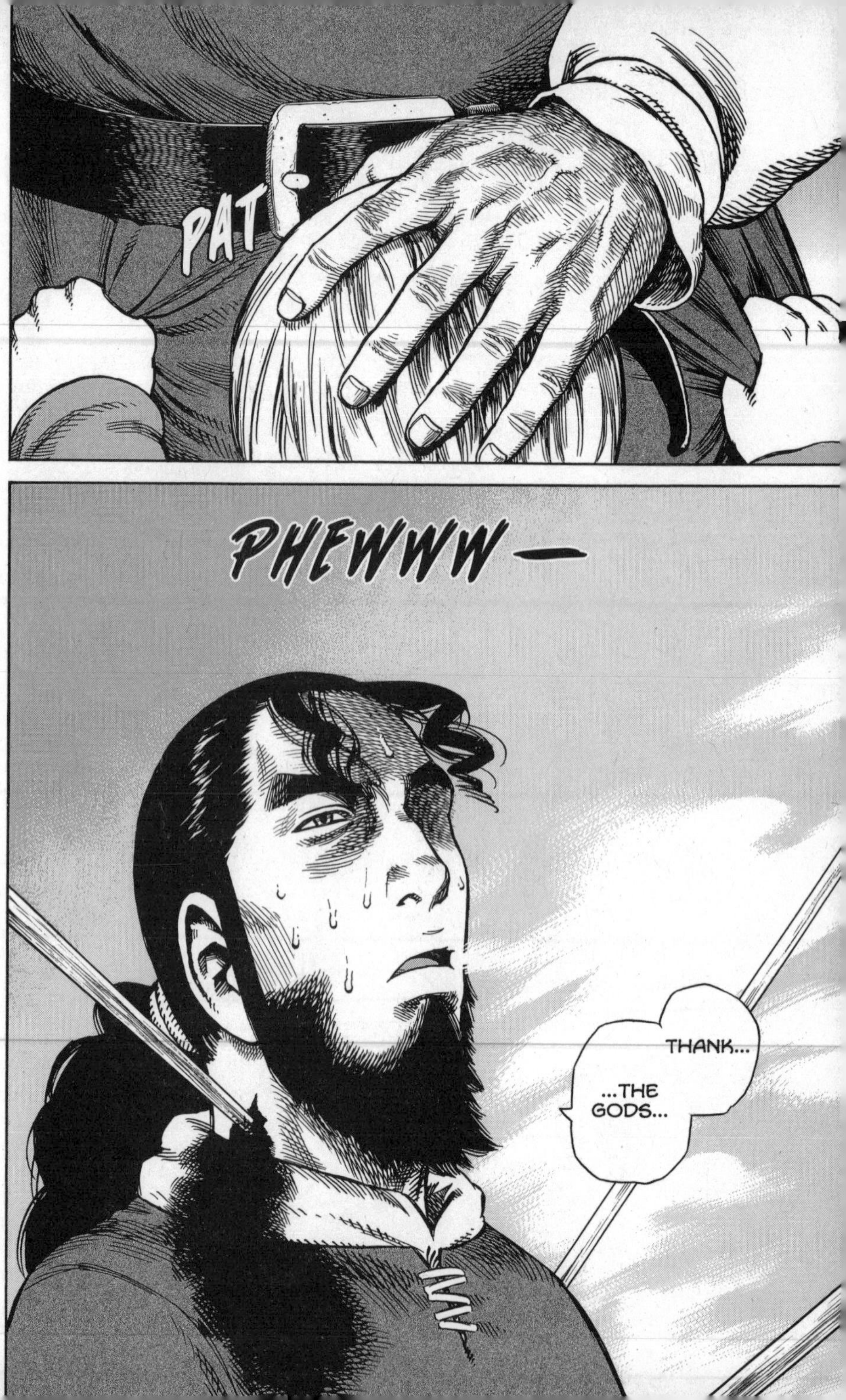
PAT
PHEWWW—
THANK... ...THE GODS...

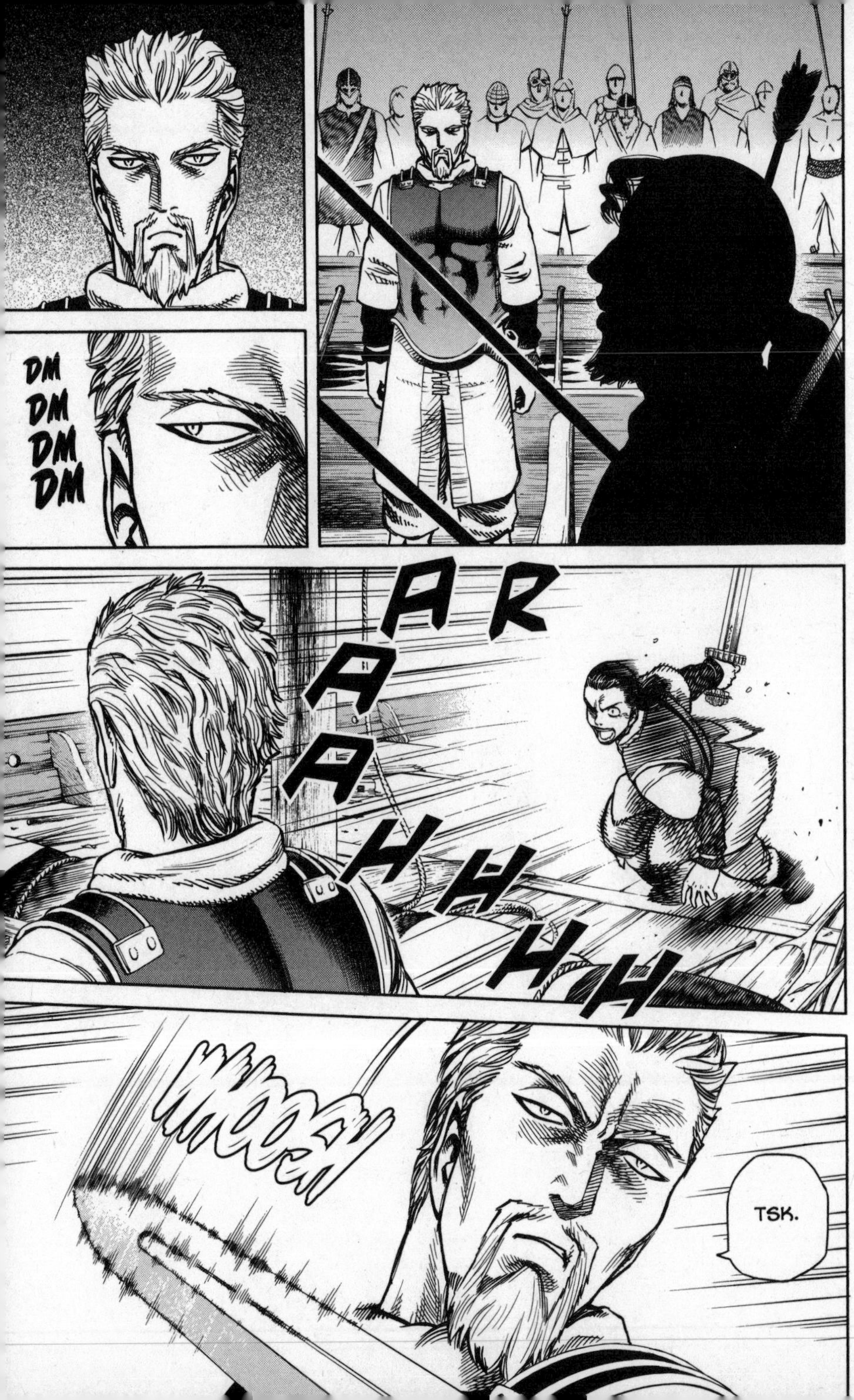
DM DM DM DM
ARAAHHHH
TSK.

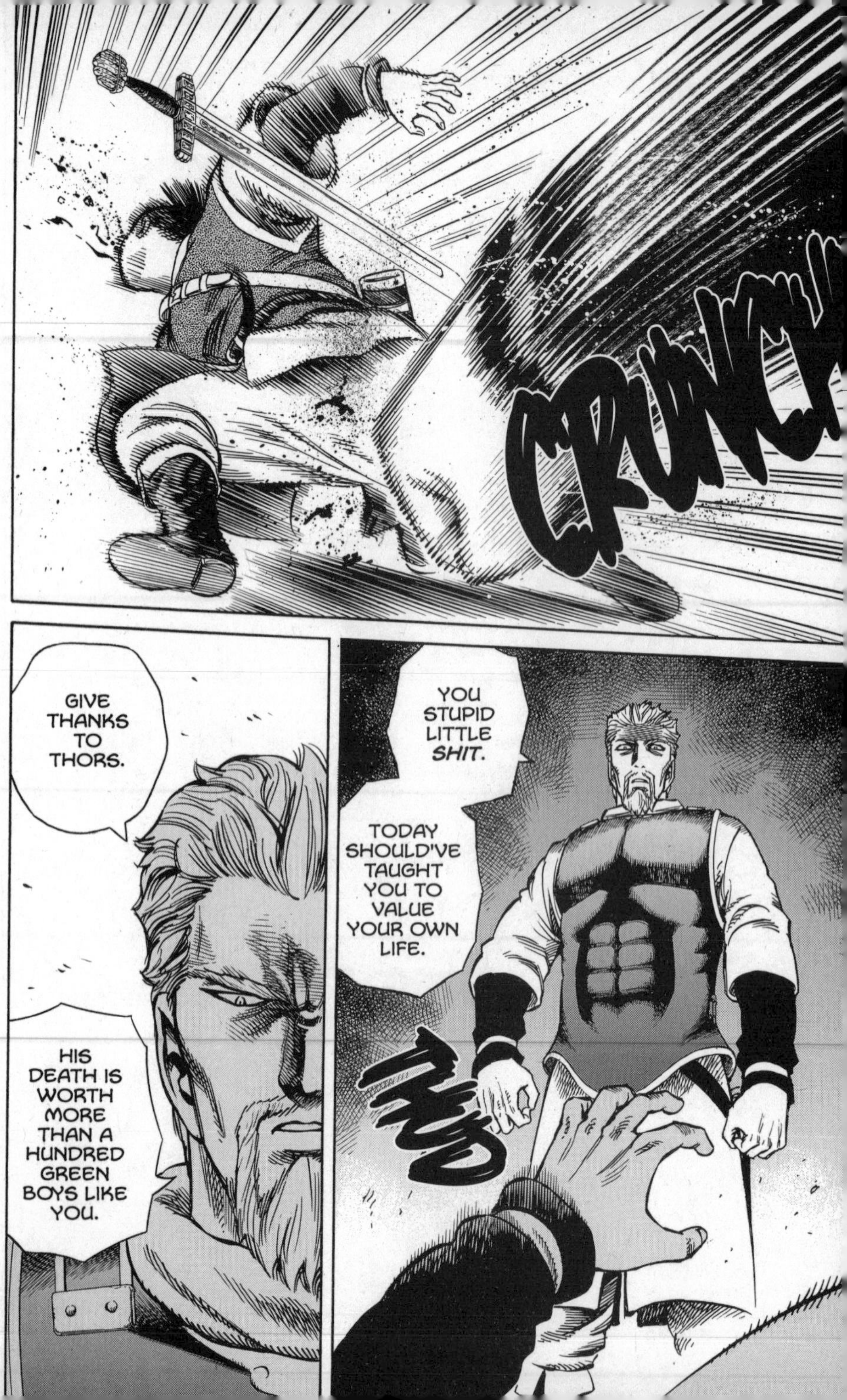
CRUNCH
YOU STUPID LITTLE *SHIT*.
TODAY SHOULD'VE TAUGHT YOU TO VALUE YOUR OWN LIFE.
GIVE THANKS TO THORS.
HIS DEATH IS WORTH MORE THAN A HUNDRED GREEN BOYS LIKE YOU.

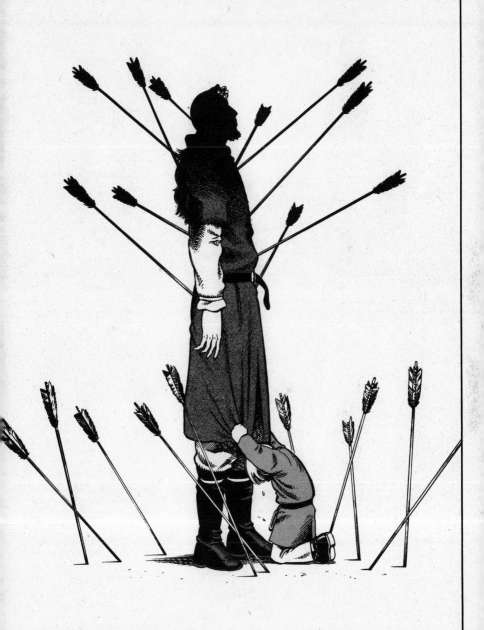

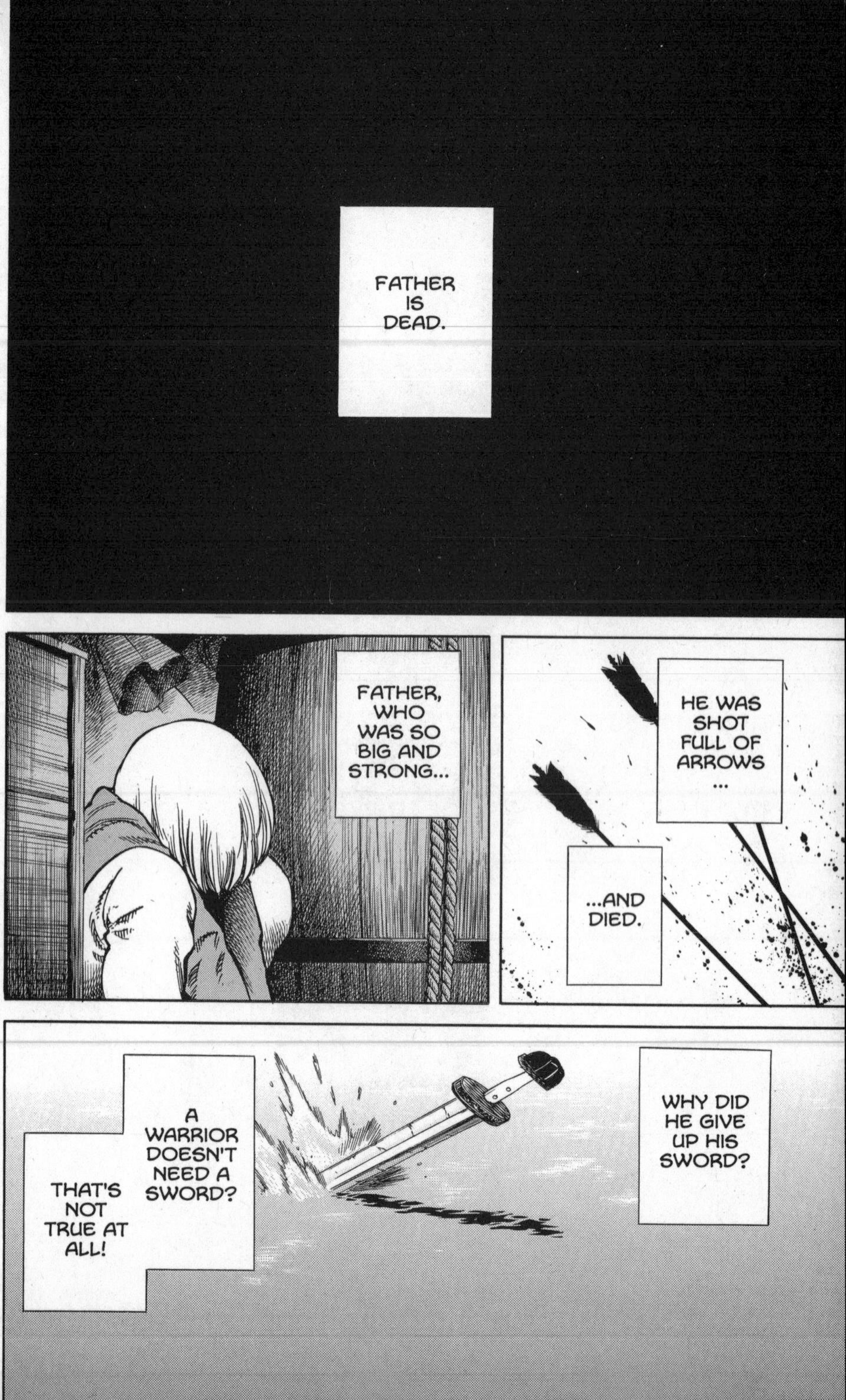
FATHER IS DEAD.
HE WAS SHOT FULL OF ARROWS ...
...AND DIED.
FATHER, WHO WAS SO BIG AND STRONG...
WHY DID HE GIVE UP HIS SWORD?
A WARRIOR DOESN'T NEED A SWORD?
THAT'S NOT TRUE AT ALL!

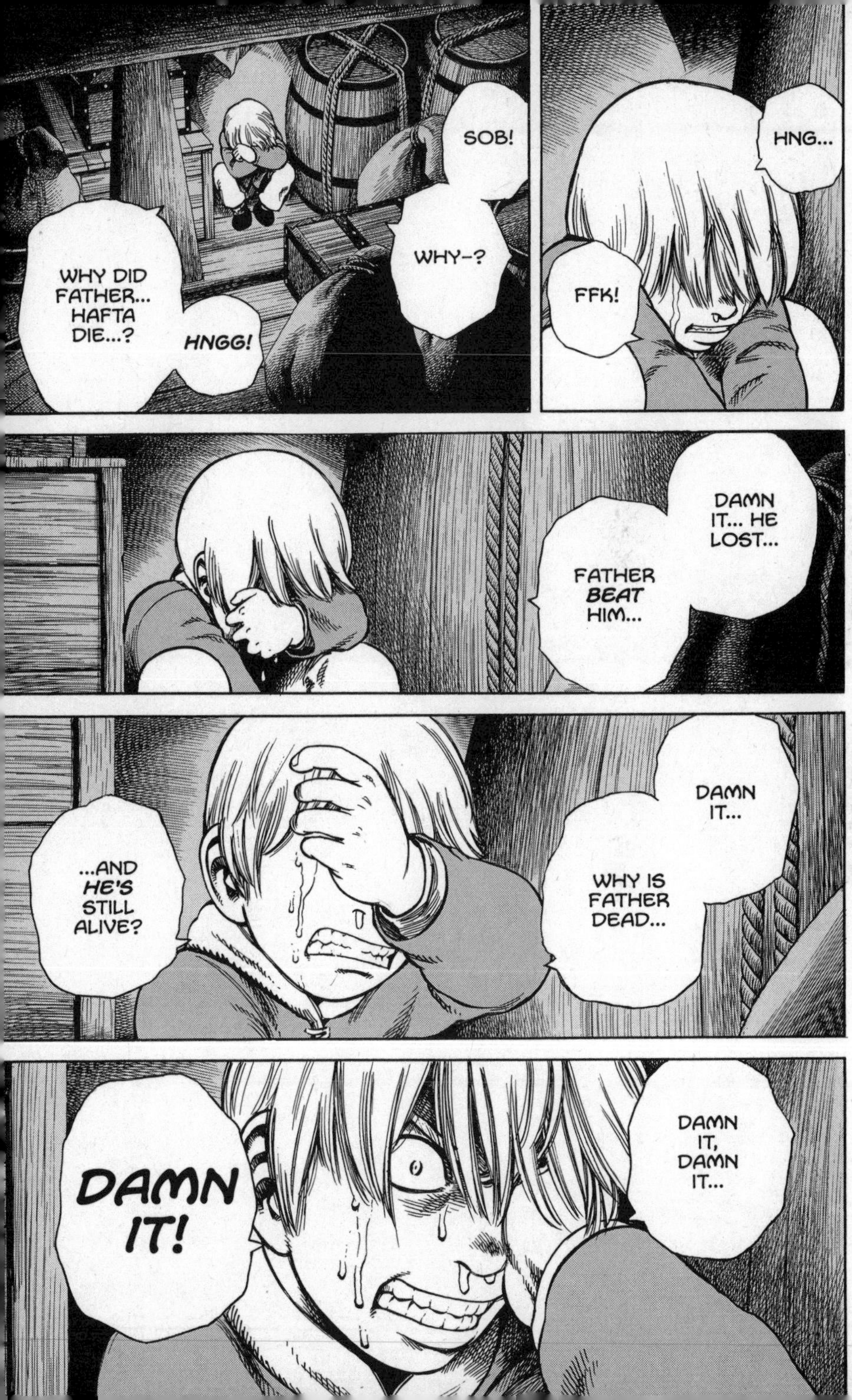
HNG...
FFK!
SOB!
WHY-?
WHY DID FATHER... HAFTA DIE...?
HNGG!
DAMN IT... HE LOST...
FATHER BEAT HIM...
DAMN IT...
WHY IS FATHER DEAD...
...AND HE'S STILL ALIVE?
DAMN IT, DAMN IT...
DAMN IT!

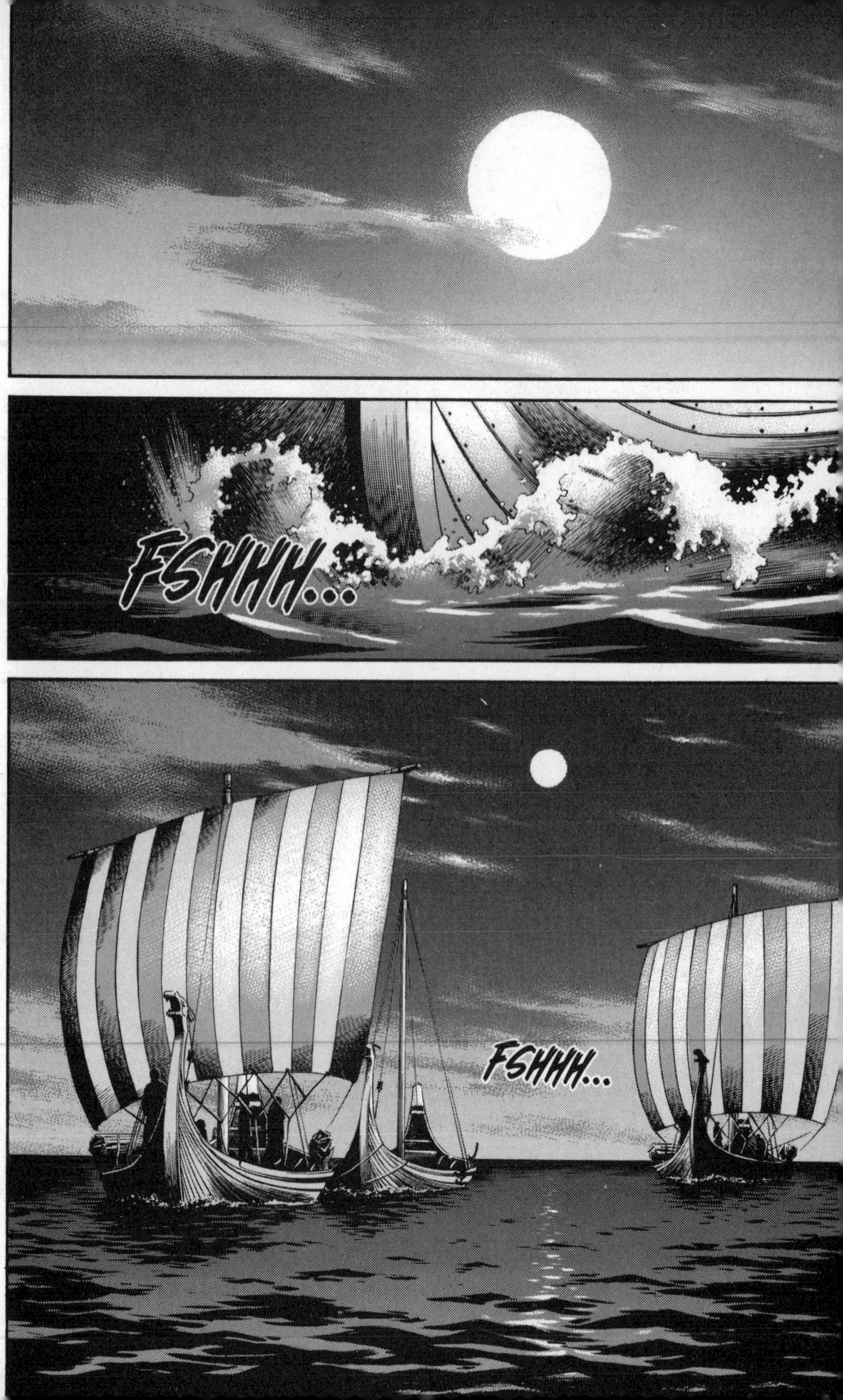
FSHHH...
FSHHH...

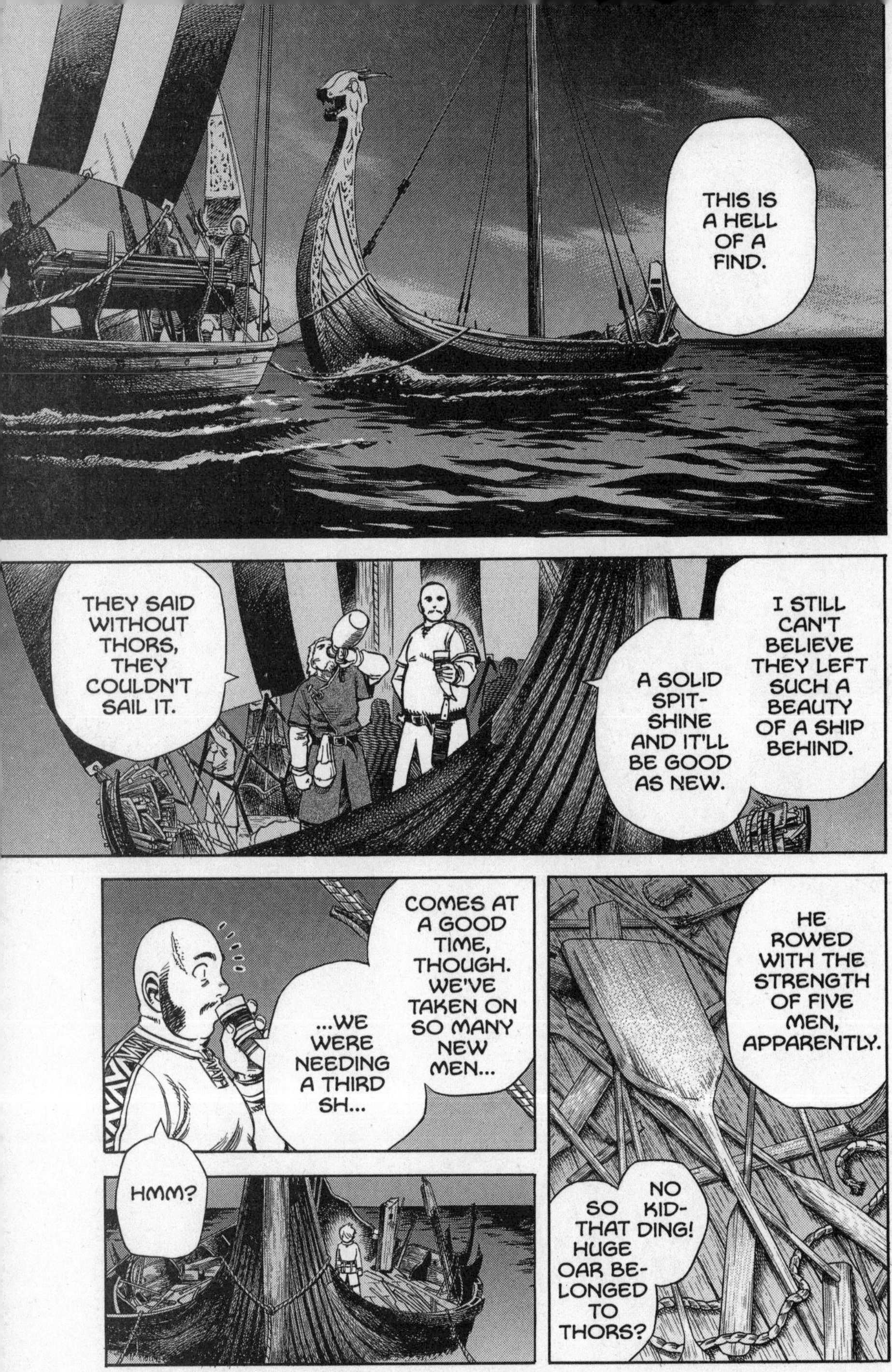
THIS IS A HELL OF A FIND.
I STILL CAN'T BELIEVE THEY LEFT SUCH A BEAUTY OF A SHIP BEHIND.
A SOLID SPIT-SHINE AND IT'LL BE GOOD AS NEW.
THEY SAID WITHOUT THORS, THEY COULDN'T SAIL IT.
HE ROWED WITH THE STRENGTH OF FIVE MEN, APPARENTLY.
NO KIDDING! SO THAT HUGE OAR BELONGED TO THORS?
COMES AT A GOOD TIME, THOUGH. WE'VE TAKEN ON SO MANY NEW MEN...
...WE WERE NEEDING A THIRD SH...
HMM?

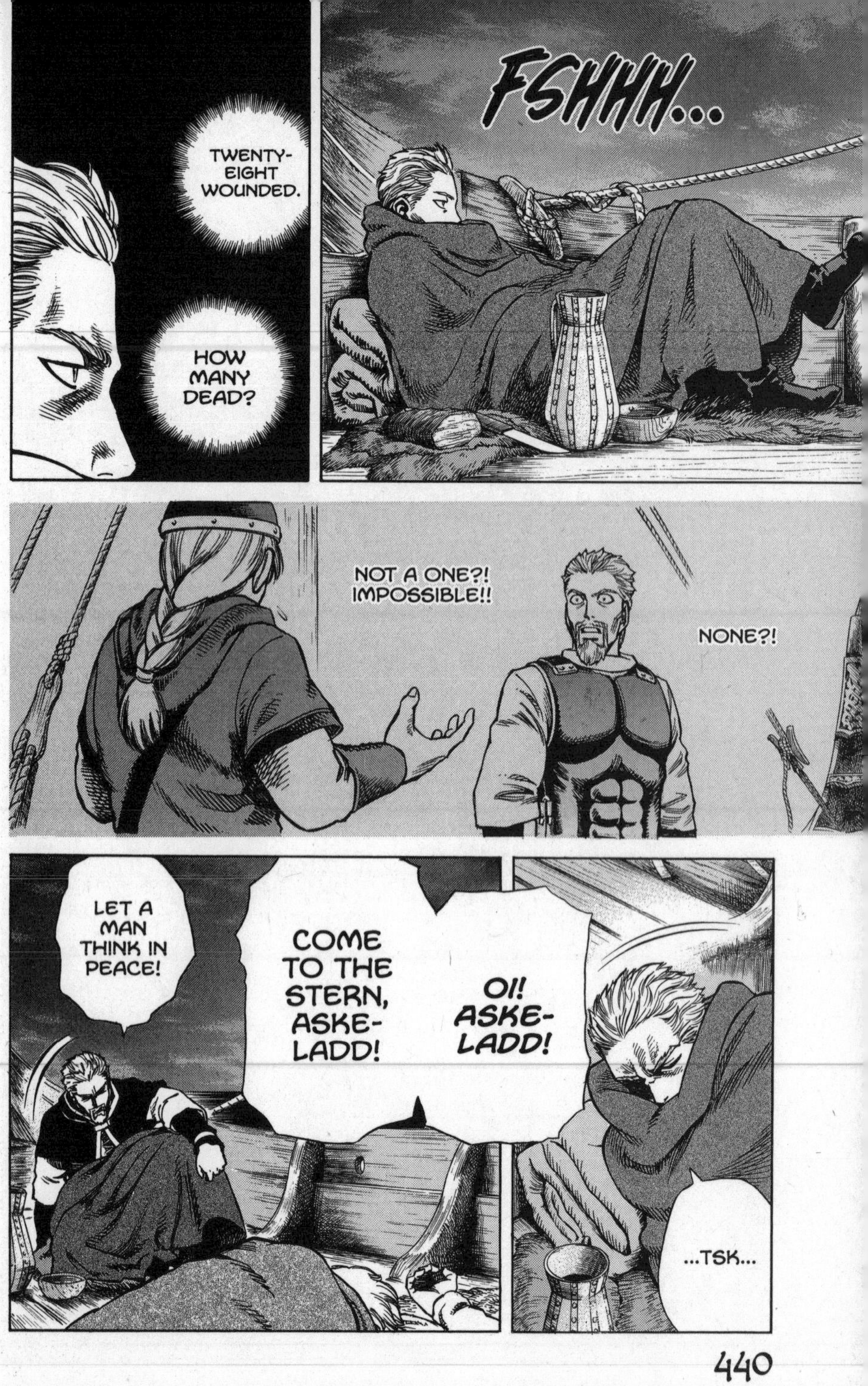
FSHHH...
TWENTY-EIGHT WOUNDED.
HOW MANY DEAD?
NONE?!
NOT A ONE?! IMPOSSIBLE!!
OI! ASKE-LADD!
COME TO THE STERN, ASKE-LADD!
...TSK...
LET A MAN THINK IN PEACE!

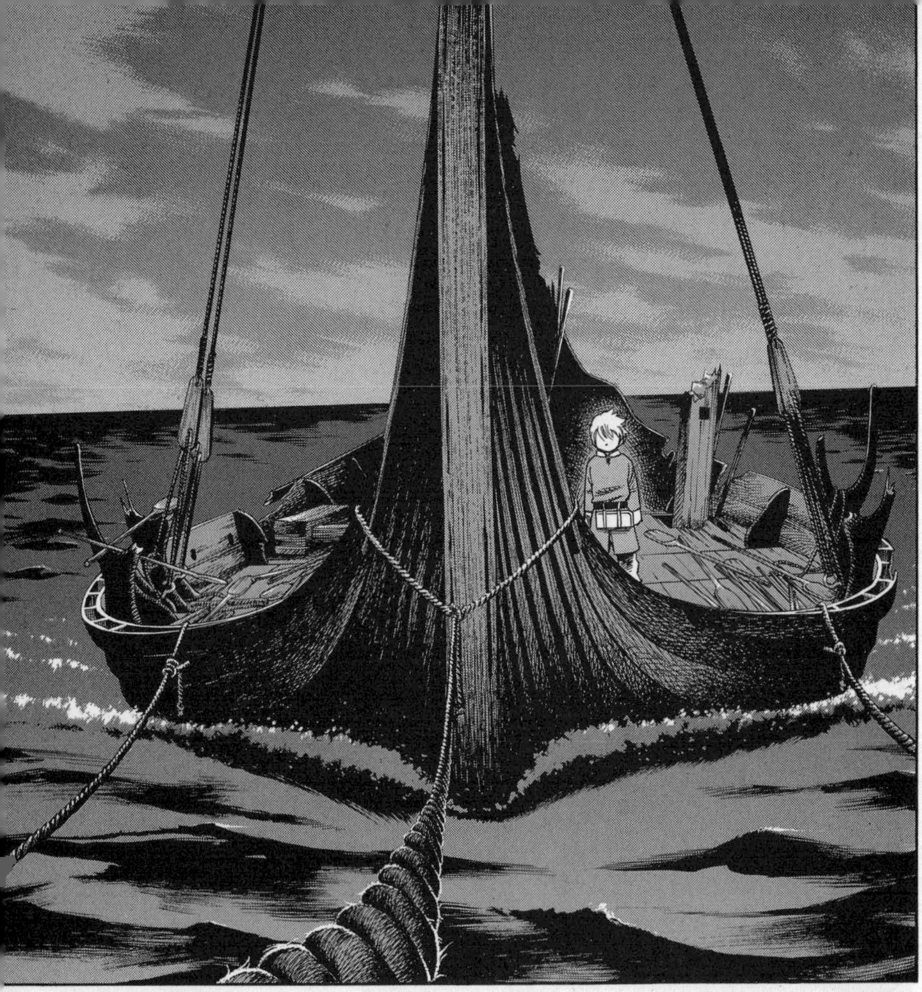
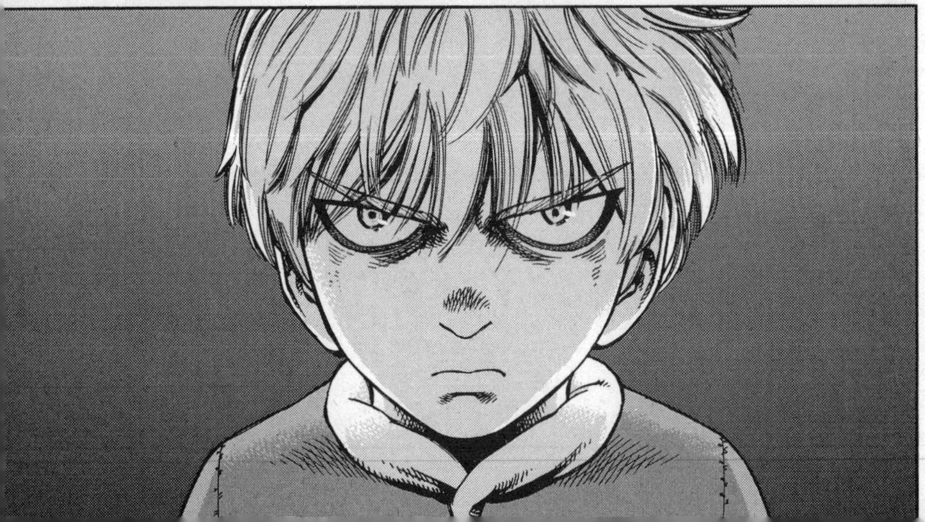

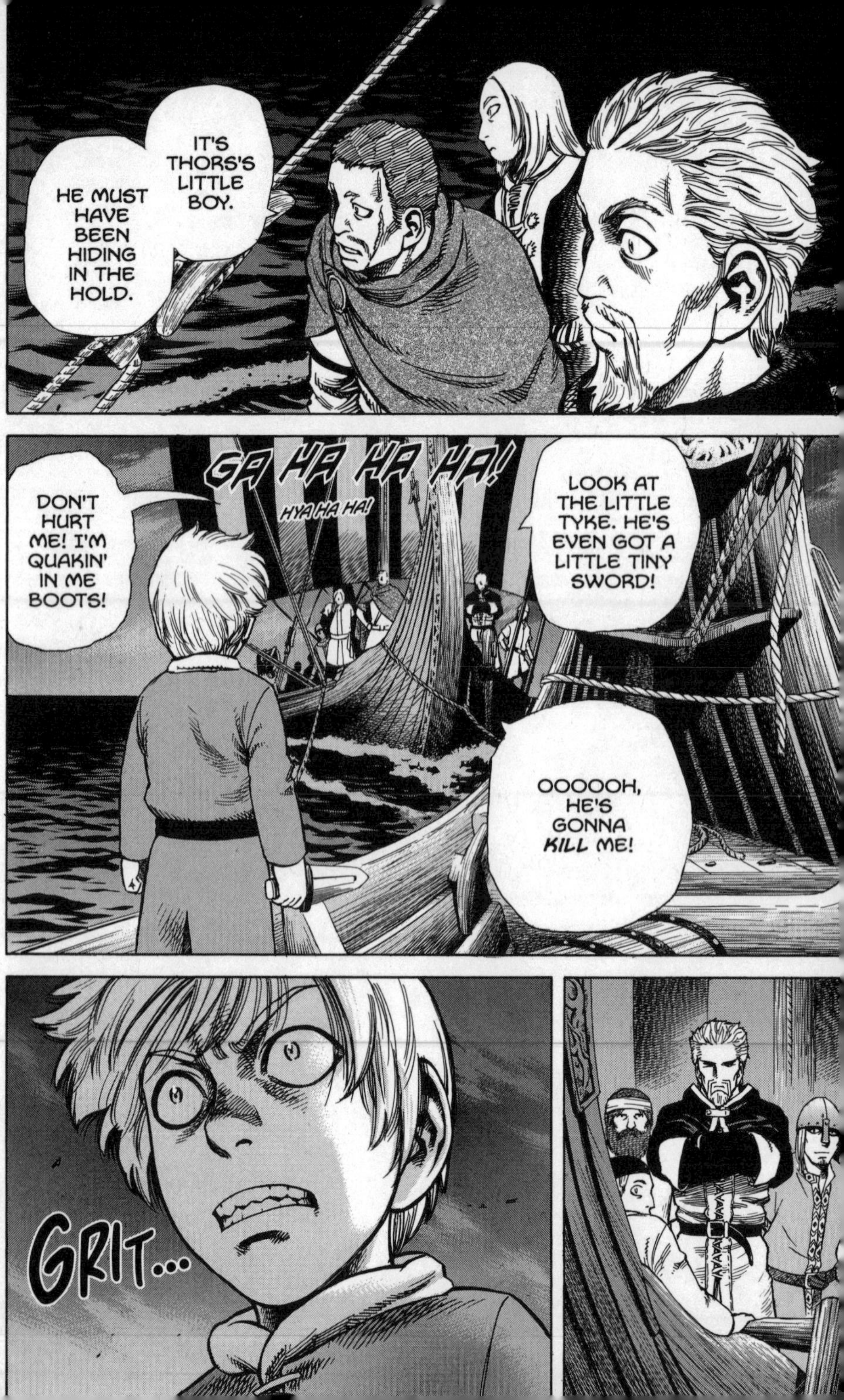
IT'S THORS'S LITTLE BOY.
HE MUST HAVE BEEN HIDING IN THE HOLD.
LOOK AT THE LITTLE TYKE. HE'S EVEN GOT A LITTLE TINY SWORD!
GA HA HA HA!
HYA HA HA!
DON'T HURT ME! I'M QUAKIN' IN ME BOOTS!
OOOOOH, HE'S GONNA *KILL* ME!
GRIT...

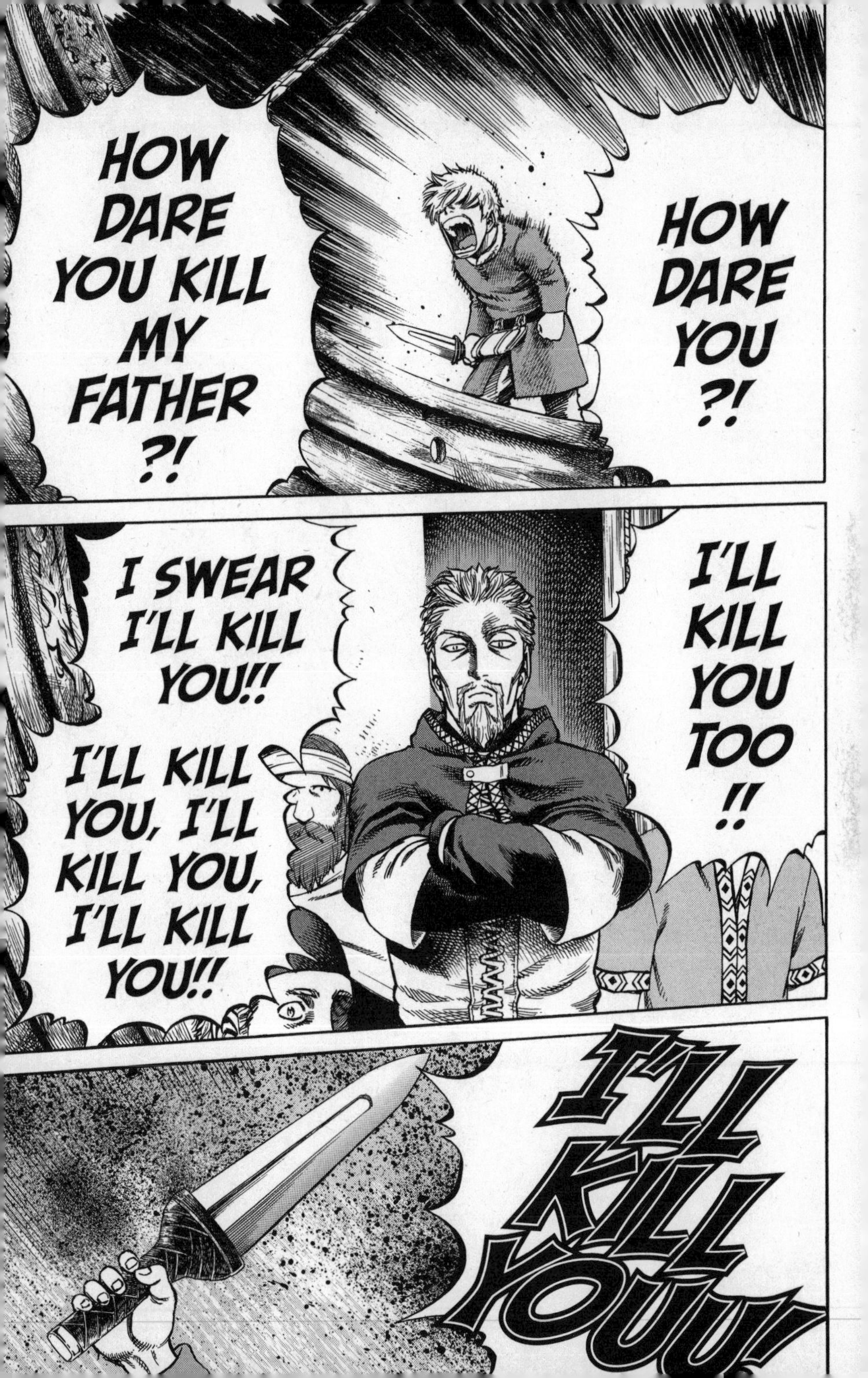
HOW DARE YOU ?!
HOW DARE YOU KILL MY FATHER ?!
I'LL KILL YOU TOO !!
I SWEAR I'LL KILL YOU!!
I'LL KILL YOU, I'LL KILL YOU, I'LL KILL YOU!!
I'LL KILL YOU!!

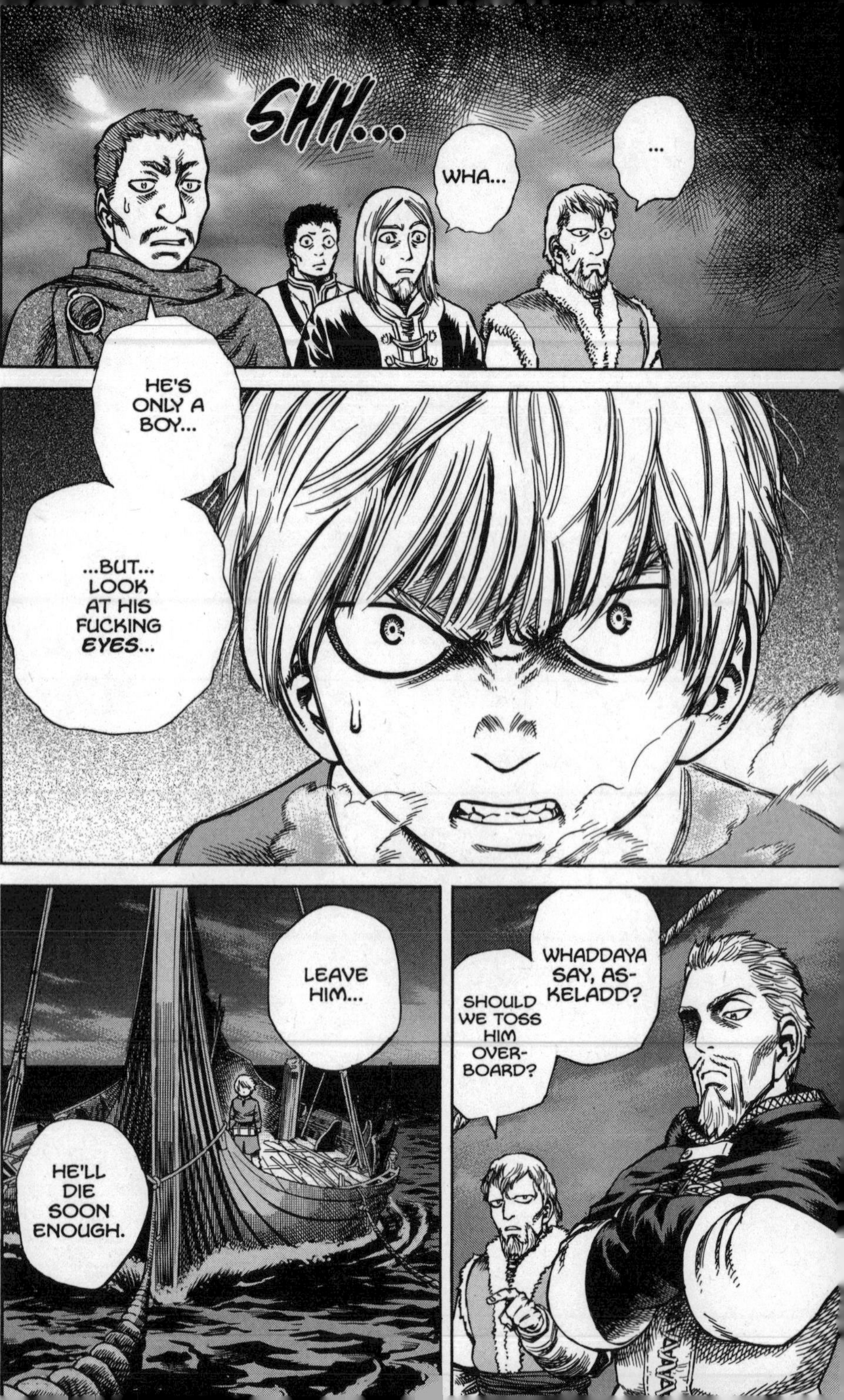
...
WHA...
SHH...
HE'S ONLY A BOY...
...BUT... LOOK AT HIS FUCKING EYES...
WHADDAYA SAY, AS-KELADD?
SHOULD WE TOSS HIM OVER-BOARD?
LEAVE HIM...
HE'LL DIE SOON ENOUGH.

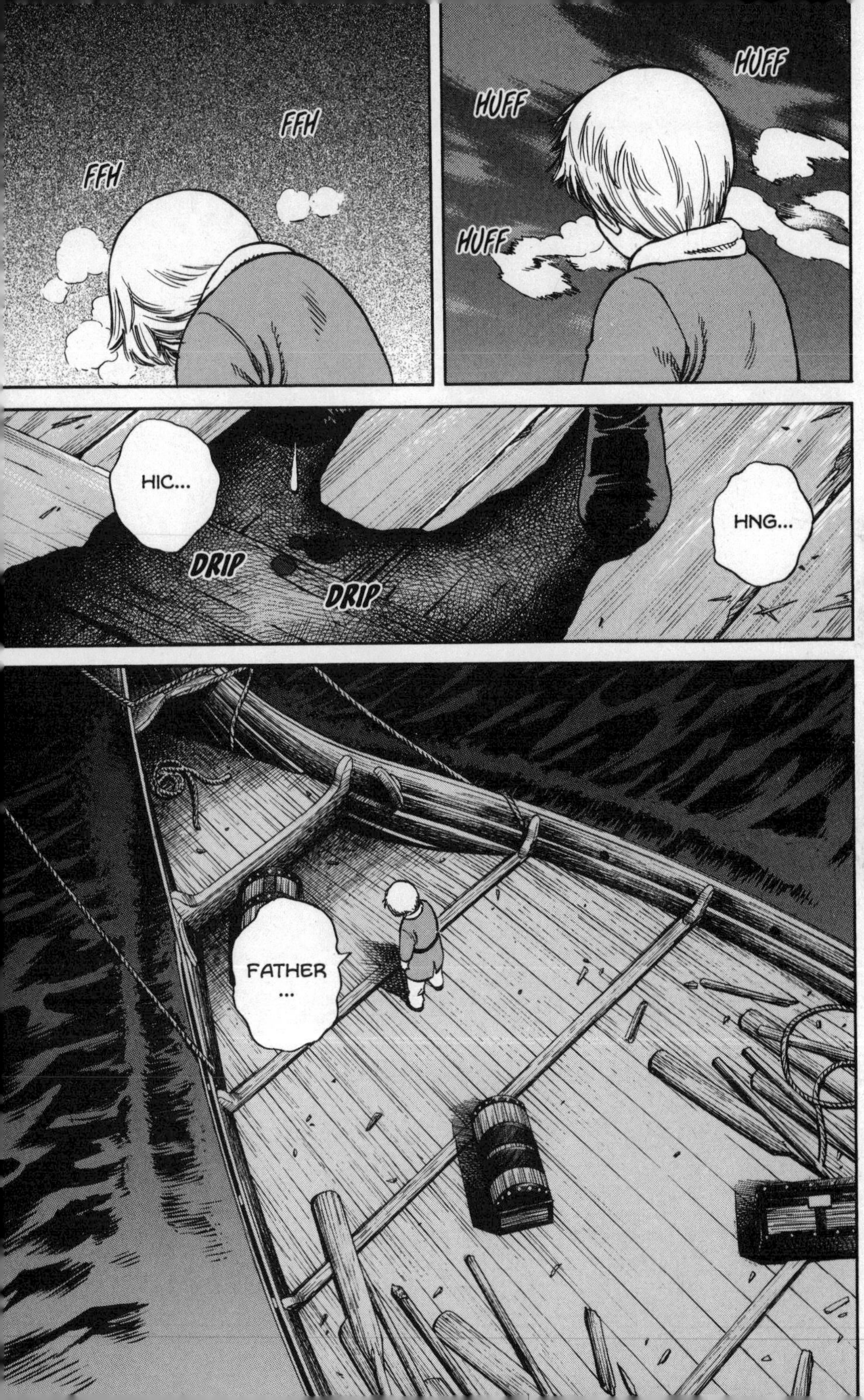
HUFF
HUFF
HUFF
FFH
FFH
HNG...
HIC...
DRIP
DRIP
FATHER ...

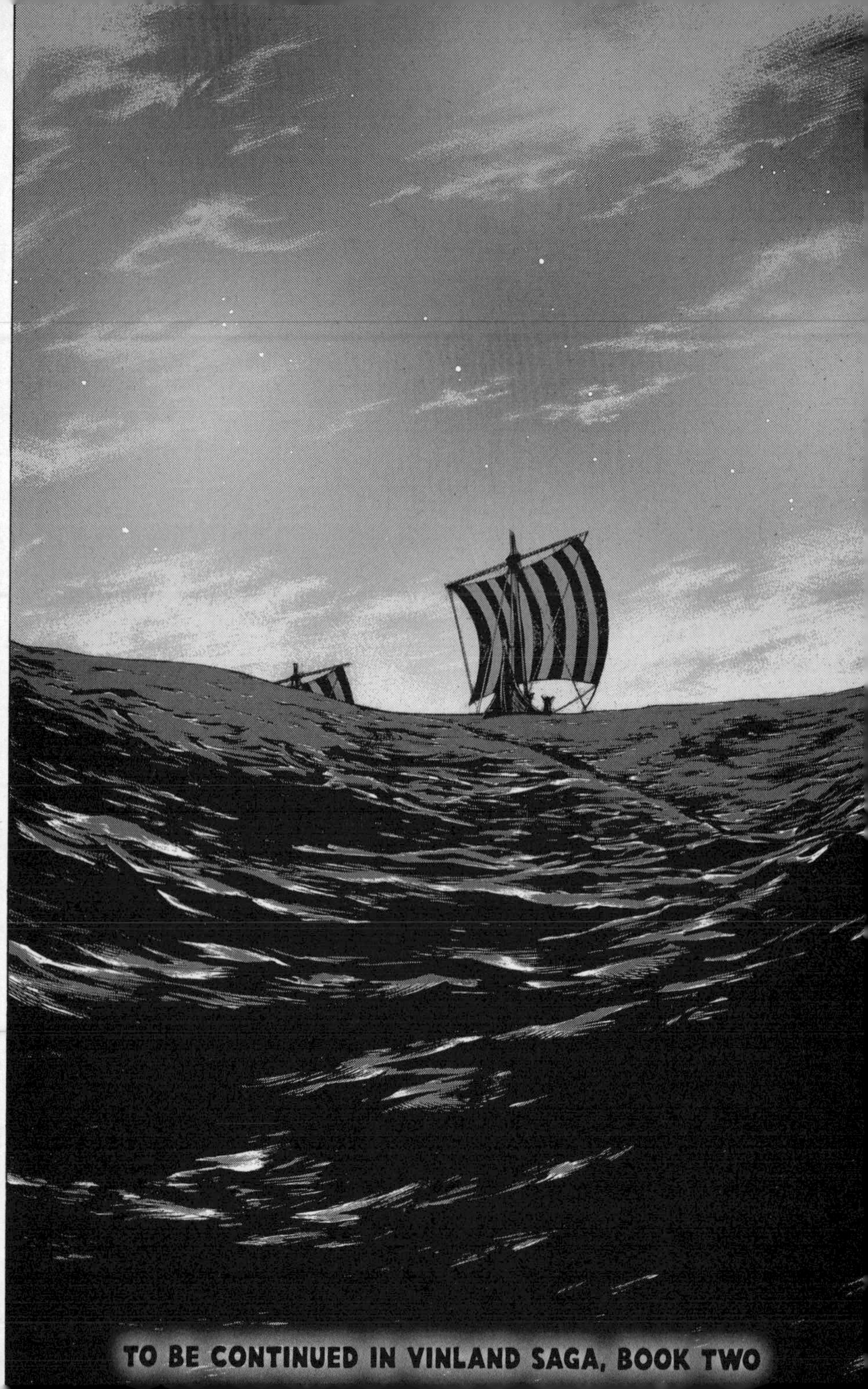
TO BE CONTINUED IN VINLAND SAGA, BOOK TWO

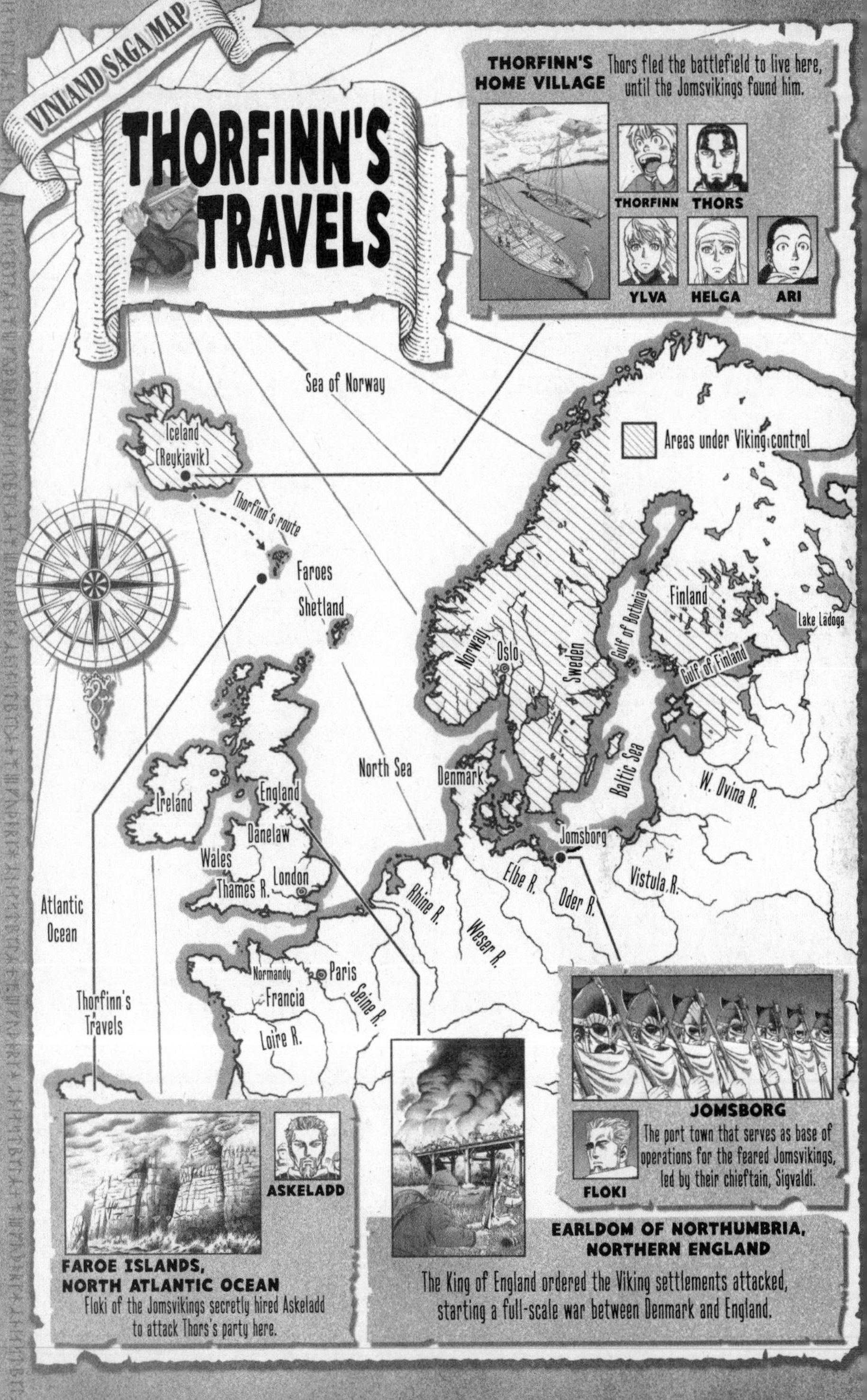
VINLAND SAGA MAP
THORFINN'S TRAVELS
THORFINN'S HOME VILLAGE
Thors fled the battlefield to live here, until the Jomsvikings found him.
THORFINN
THORS
YLVA
HELGA
ARI
Sea of Norway
Iceland (Reykjavik)
Areas under Viking control
Thorfinn's route
Faroes
Shetland
Finland
Lake Ladoga
Gulf of Bothnia
Norway
Oslo
Sweden
Gulf of Finland
North Sea
Denmark
Baltic Sea
W. Dvina R.
Ireland
England
Danelaw
Jomsborg
Wales
London
Thames R.
Elbe R.
Oder R.
Vistula R.
Rhine R.
Weser R.
Atlantic Ocean
Normandy
Paris
Francia
Seine R.
Thorfinn's Travels
Loire R.
JOMSBORG
The port town that serves as base of operations for the feared Jomsvikings, led by their chieftain, Sigvaldi.
FLOKI
ASKELADD
EARLDOM OF NORTHUMBRIA, NORTHERN ENGLAND
The King of England ordered the Viking settlements attacked, starting a full-scale war between Denmark and England.
FAROE ISLANDS, NORTH ATLANTIC OCEAN
Floki of the Jomsvikings secretly hired Askeladd to attack Thors's party here.

I RAN OUT OF IDEAS FOR YLVA, SO INSTEAD, HERE'S A SPECIAL REPORT

I WENT TO THE LAND OF AURORA BOREALIS

BY: MAKOTO YUKIMURA

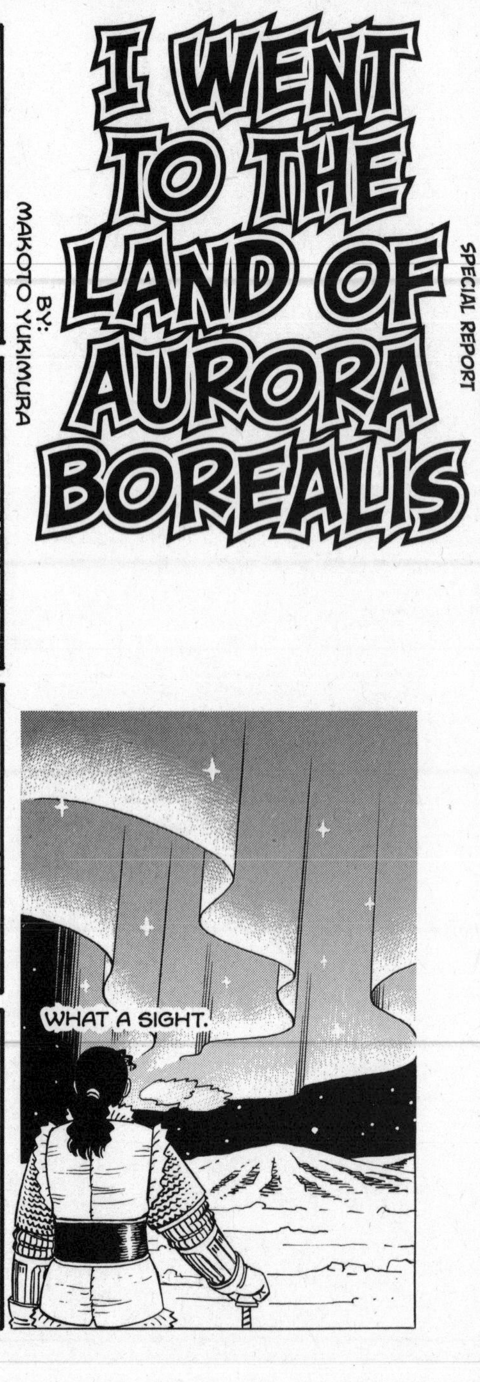
WHAT A SIGHT.

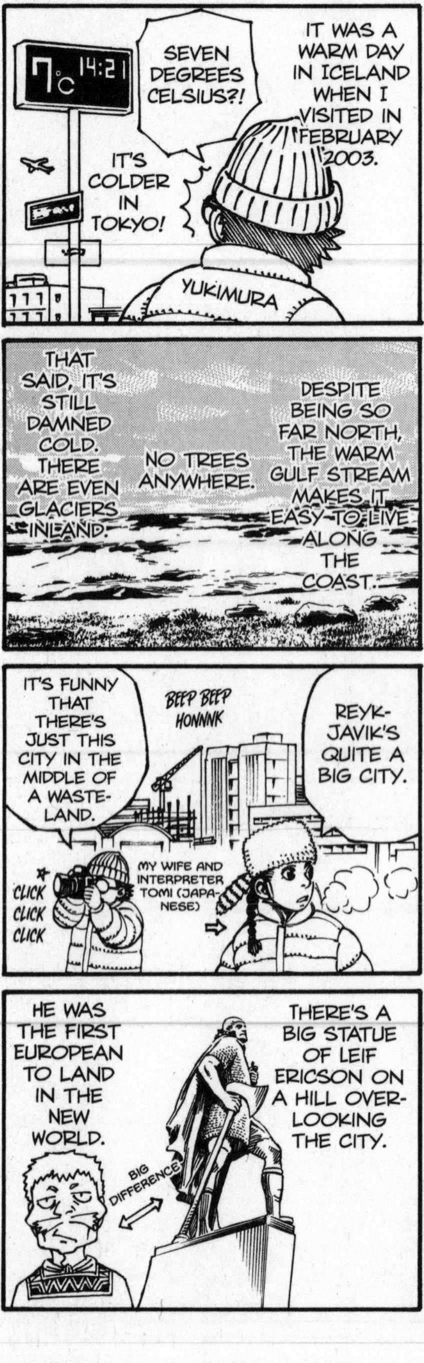
IT WAS A WARM DAY IN ICELAND WHEN I VISITED IN FEBRUARY 2003.
SEVEN DEGREES CELSIUS?!
7°C 14:21
IT'S COLDER IN TOKYO!
YUKIMURA
DESPITE BEING SO FAR NORTH, THE WARM GULF STREAM MAKES IT EASY TO LIVE ALONG THE COAST.
NO TREES ANYWHERE.
THAT SAID, IT'S STILL DAMNED COLD. THERE ARE EVEN GLACIERS INLAND.
REYK-JAVIK'S QUITE A BIG CITY.
BEEP BEEP HONNNK
IT'S FUNNY THAT THERE'S JUST THIS CITY IN THE MIDDLE OF A WASTE-LAND.
MY WIFE AND INTERPRETER TOMI (JAPA-NESE)
CLICK CLICK CLICK
THERE'S A BIG STATUE OF LEIF ERICSON ON A HILL OVER-LOOKING THE CITY.
HE WAS THE FIRST EUROPEAN TO LAND IN THE NEW WORLD.
BIG DIFFERENCE

* 45 DEGREES F

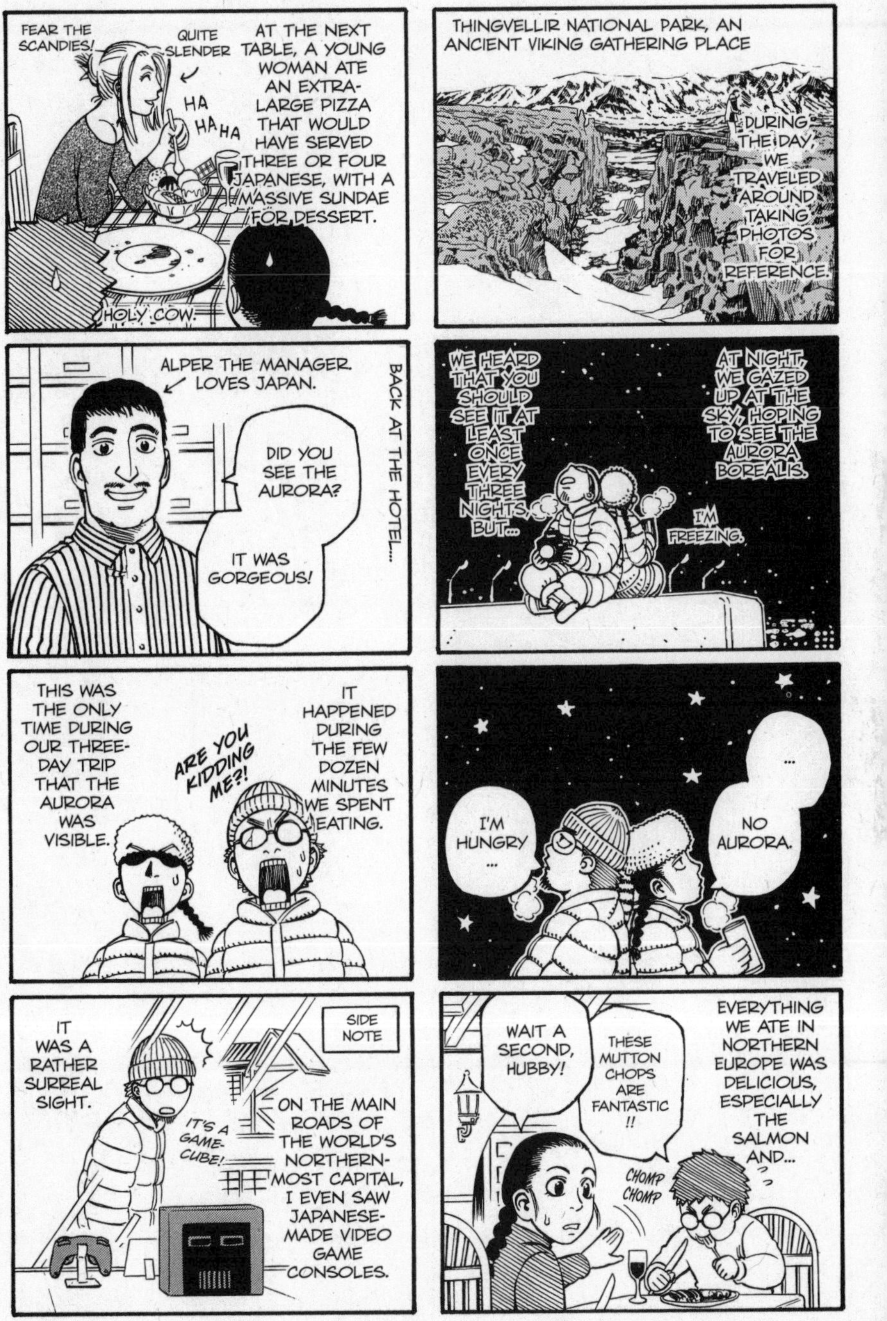
THINGVELLIR NATIONAL PARK, AN ANCIENT VIKING GATHERING PLACE
DURING THE DAY, WE TRAVELED AROUND TAKING PHOTOS FOR REFERENCE.
AT THE NEXT TABLE, A YOUNG WOMAN ATE AN EXTRA-LARGE PIZZA THAT WOULD HAVE SERVED THREE OR FOUR JAPANESE, WITH A MASSIVE SUNDAE FOR DESSERT.
QUITE SLENDER
FEAR THE SCANDIES!
HA HA HA HA
HOLY COW.
AT NIGHT, WE GAZED UP AT THE SKY, HOPING TO SEE THE AURORA BOREALIS.
WE HEARD THAT YOU SHOULD SEE IT AT LEAST ONCE EVERY THREE NIGHTS, BUT...
I'M FREEZING.
BACK AT THE HOTEL...
ALPER THE MANAGER. LOVES JAPAN.
DID YOU SEE THE AURORA?
IT WAS GORGEOUS!
...
NO AURORA.
I'M HUNGRY ...
IT HAPPENED DURING THE FEW DOZEN MINUTES WE SPENT EATING.
THIS WAS THE ONLY TIME DURING OUR THREE-DAY TRIP THAT THE AURORA WAS VISIBLE.
ARE YOU KIDDING ME?!
EVERYTHING WE ATE IN NORTHERN EUROPE WAS DELICIOUS, ESPECIALLY THE SALMON AND...
THESE MUTTON CHOPS ARE FANTASTIC !!
WAIT A SECOND, HUBBY!
CHOMP CHOMP
SIDE NOTE
ON THE MAIN ROADS OF THE WORLD'S NORTHERN-MOST CAPITAL, I EVEN SAW JAPANESE-MADE VIDEO GAME CONSOLES.
IT'S A GAME-CUBE!
IT WAS A RATHER SURREAL SIGHT.

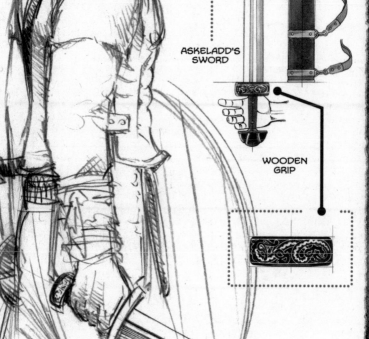

ASKELADD

ASKELADD'S
SWORD

WOODEN
GRIP

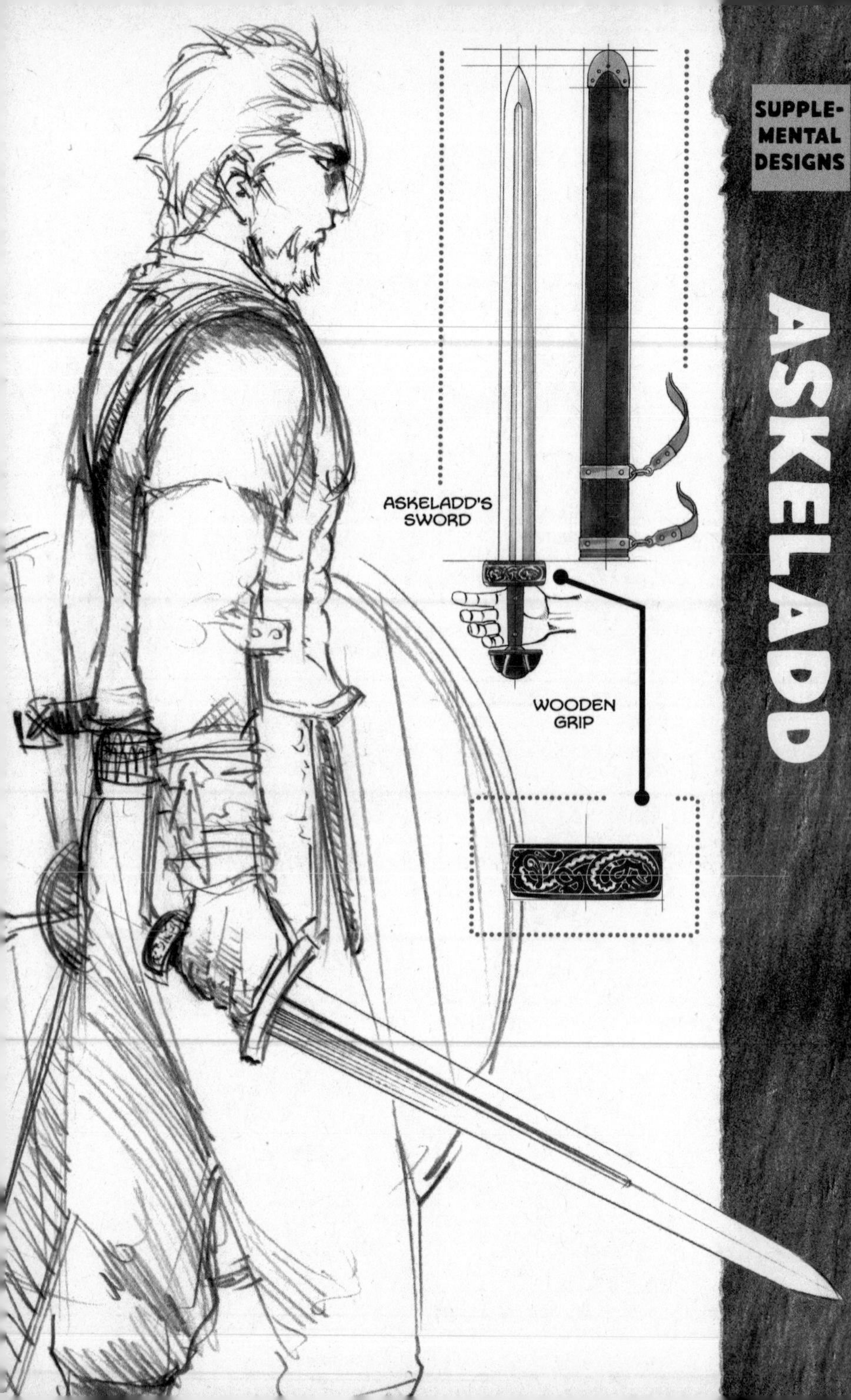

AFTERWORD

Despite its breezier appearance, all that chainmail the Vikings wear weighs about forty-five pounds. The swords and axes add six to eight pounds each, and once the iron helmets, wooden shields and short swords are added in, the entire equipment tops out at over sixty-five pounds. I tried to wear all that armor myself and I could barely walk, much less fight. I'm truly grateful that I wasn't born in the age of the Vikings. Those guys are monsters.

MAKOTO YUKIMURA

VINLAND SAGA

Translation Notes

Normanni, page 2

The Latin form for "men of the North," also known as Norsemen, Northmen, Normans, etc.

Frankish Kingdom, page 4

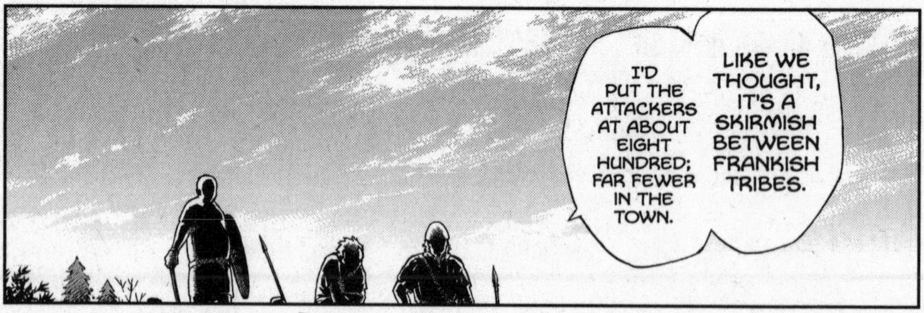
LIKE WE THOUGHT, IT'S A SKIRMISH BETWEEN FRANKISH TRIBES.
I'D PUT THE ATTACKERS AT ABOUT EIGHT HUNDRED; FAR FEWER IN THE TOWN.

Strictly speaking, the Frankish Kingdom as it is defined today — France under the Carolingian dynasty made notable by Charlesmagne — did not exist as a state in the 11th century. Rather, it was a decentralized period where princes and other lords held regional power, while the king was more of a religious figure. The key word here is "territory," i.e., land that was previously the realm of the Frankish Kingdom. The establishment of the Capet Dynasty in 987 created the first predecessor to what we define as France today.

Tyr, page 15

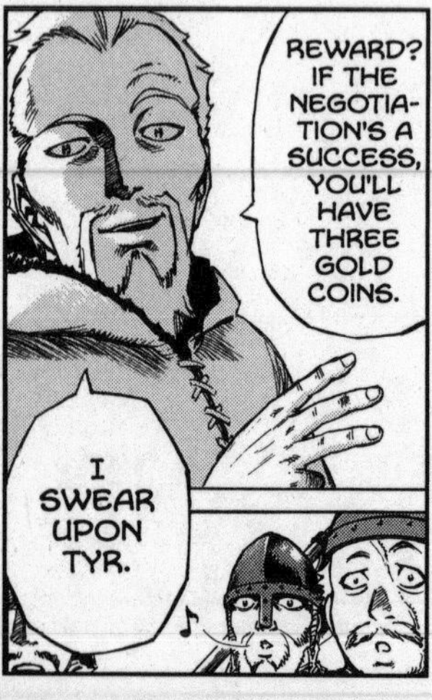
REWARD? IF THE NEGOTIA-TION'S A SUCCESS, YOU'LL HAVE THREE GOLD COINS.
I SWEAR UPON TYR.
♪

The Norse god of law, justice and war. By some accounts — the backgrounds, positions and importance of gods shift throughout history according to location and time period — Tyr is the son of Odin. He is invoked in this scene to emphasize the apparent truthfulness of the claim.

General Jabbathe, page 71

STILL...
...I HAVEN'T SEEN HIDE NOR HAIR OF THE NORMANNI FOR SOME TIME...
REPORTING TO GENERAL JABBATHE, SIR!!

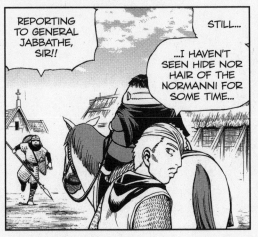

It should be noted that in the Japanese language, titles such as king, lord, president, and so on are always placed after the name rather than before. Thus, General Jabbathe appears as "Jabbathe-shogun," where shogun is the word for a military commander. I'll leave it to the reader's discretion to discern the meaning (or lack thereof) behind this particular choice.

Jörmungand, page 139

MY GRAND-PA TOLD ME...
...THAT THE GREAT SERPENT JÖRMUNGAND PROWLS THE SEAS TO THE WEST AND GOBBLES UP EVERY SHIP THAT VEN-TURES TOO CLOSE!
WRIGGLE

Also known as the Midgard Serpent, a variant on the Ouroboros theme of a snake eating its own tail. Jörmungand is a sea serpent that encircles the globe and served as a likely explanation for ships going lost at sea.

Knarr, page 153

A type of cargo ship used by Viking merchants. A knarr (plural knerrir) was wider and deeper than the famous longships used for raiding, which made it more suitable for ferrying goods, food and livestock.

Thing, page 174

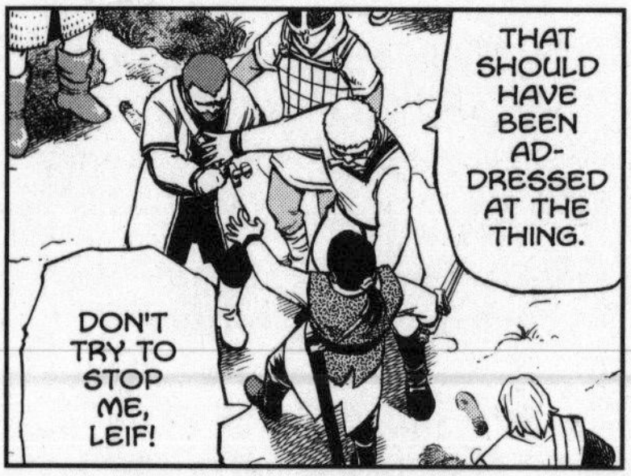
THAT SHOULD HAVE BEEN AD-DRESSED AT THE THING.
DON'T TRY TO STOP ME, LEIF!

Thing is the Norse/Icelandic word for "gathering." They were community meetings where legal grievances were addressed, among other things. The Althing was a national gathering of village representatives traditionally held at the Thingvellir plain starting in 930 A.D. with the founding of the Icelandic Commonwealth. This democratic structure was partly motivated by the desire to escape the authoritarian rule of King Harald of Norway. The Althing survived and is the official parliament of Iceland today, albeit in modern form.

Jomsvikings, page 207

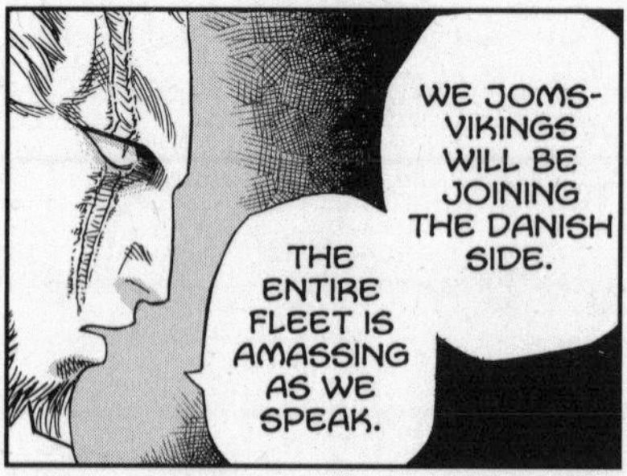
WE JOMS-VIKINGS WILL BE JOINING THE DANISH SIDE.
THE ENTIRE FLEET IS AMASSING AS WE SPEAK.

A legendary band of Viking mercenaries recounted in various Scandinavian epics. According to those legends, the Jomsvikings were active in the 10th and 11th centuries, but lack of primary evidence has led to debate over whether they truly existed or not.

Thingvellir National Park, page 229

The original home of the Althing, Iceland's historical meeting place in which matters of government were discussed and decided. The park, located in southwest Iceland, was officially founded in 1930 to preserve the historic site.

BONUS STORY: FOR OUR FAREWELL IS NEAR

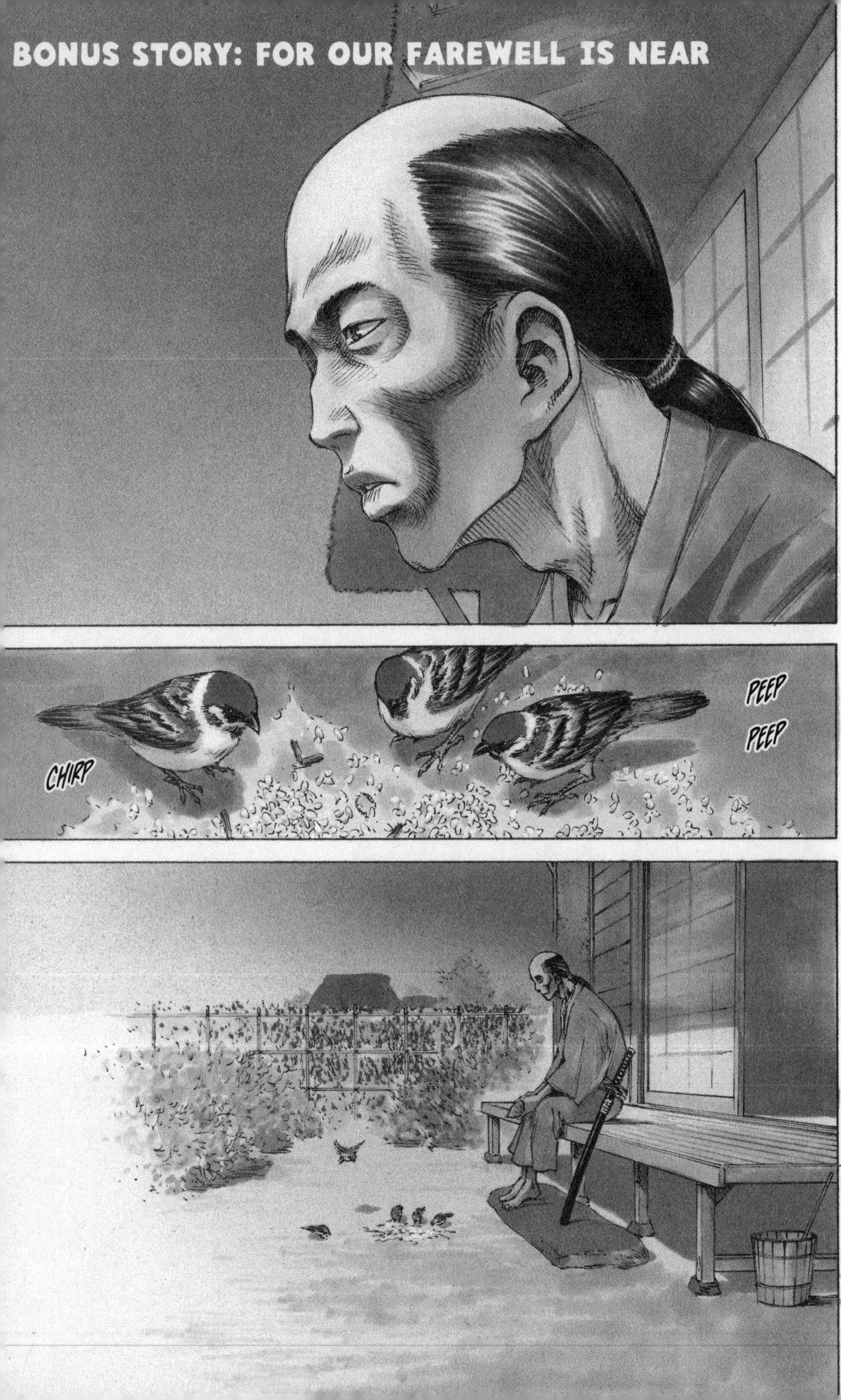
PEEP
PEEP
CHIRP

PEEP
PEEP
PEEP
PEEP
CHIRP
CHIP
CHIP
PEEP
CHIRP
CHIP
CHIRP

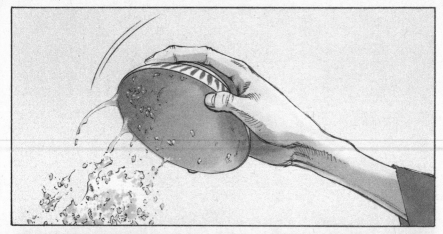

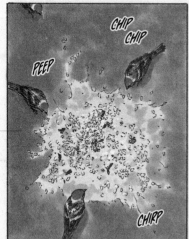

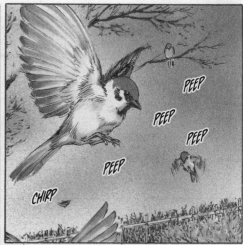

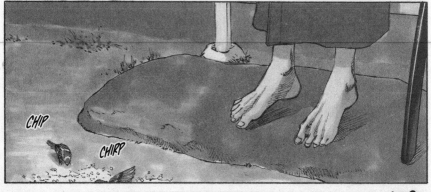

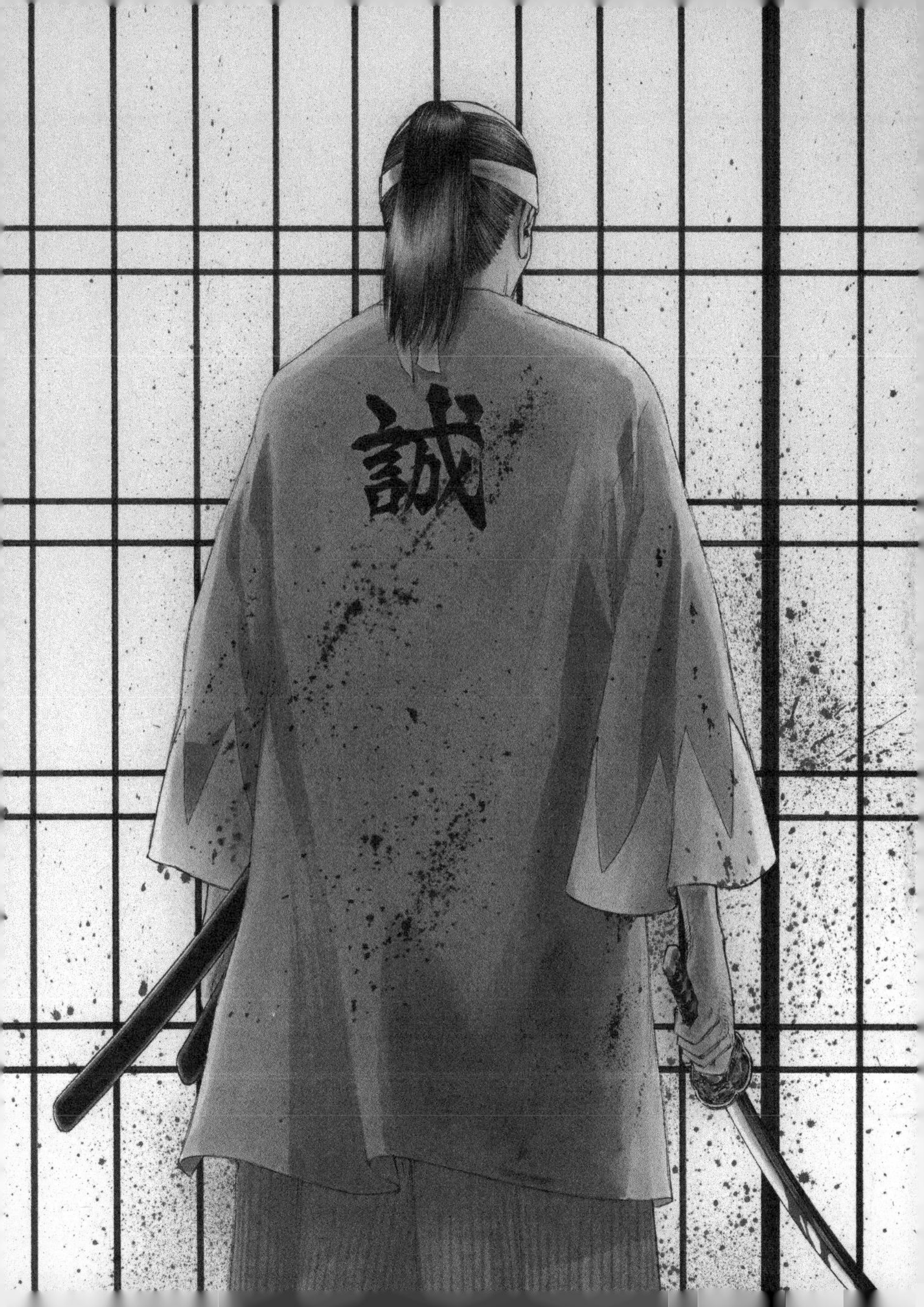
誠

For Our Farewell Is Near, Part 1
By Makoto Yukimura

Introduction

At the end of the Edo Period, the arrival of the "black ships" from abroad spelled the end of 260 years of isolation enforced by the shogunate. In response to the shogunate's desire to open the country's borders, disgruntled regional forces loyal to the emperor, such as the Choshu Domain, planned a rebellion. The imperial loyalists massed in Kyoto, where the emperor lived, growing increasingly bold until the city became, in effect, a lawless area. In an effort to restore order, the shogunate recruited ronin (masterless samurai) in Edo (now Tokyo) and sent them to Kyoto.

Among these men were Kondo Isami and Okita Soji, students at the Shieikan dojo in Tama. Upon reaching Kyoto, they formed the Shinsengumi under the orders of the daimyo of Aizu Domain, who had been charged with keeping the peace in the city. But, unable to reverse the tide of history, the shogunate lost power, and the Shinsengumi was defeated at the Battle of Toba-Fushimi. By 1868, Kondo and Okita had fled to Edo. Okita's body was already wracked with tuberculosis at this time.

Note:
This story first appeared in 2004 in Kodansha's Evening magazine. This is the first time it has been published in English.

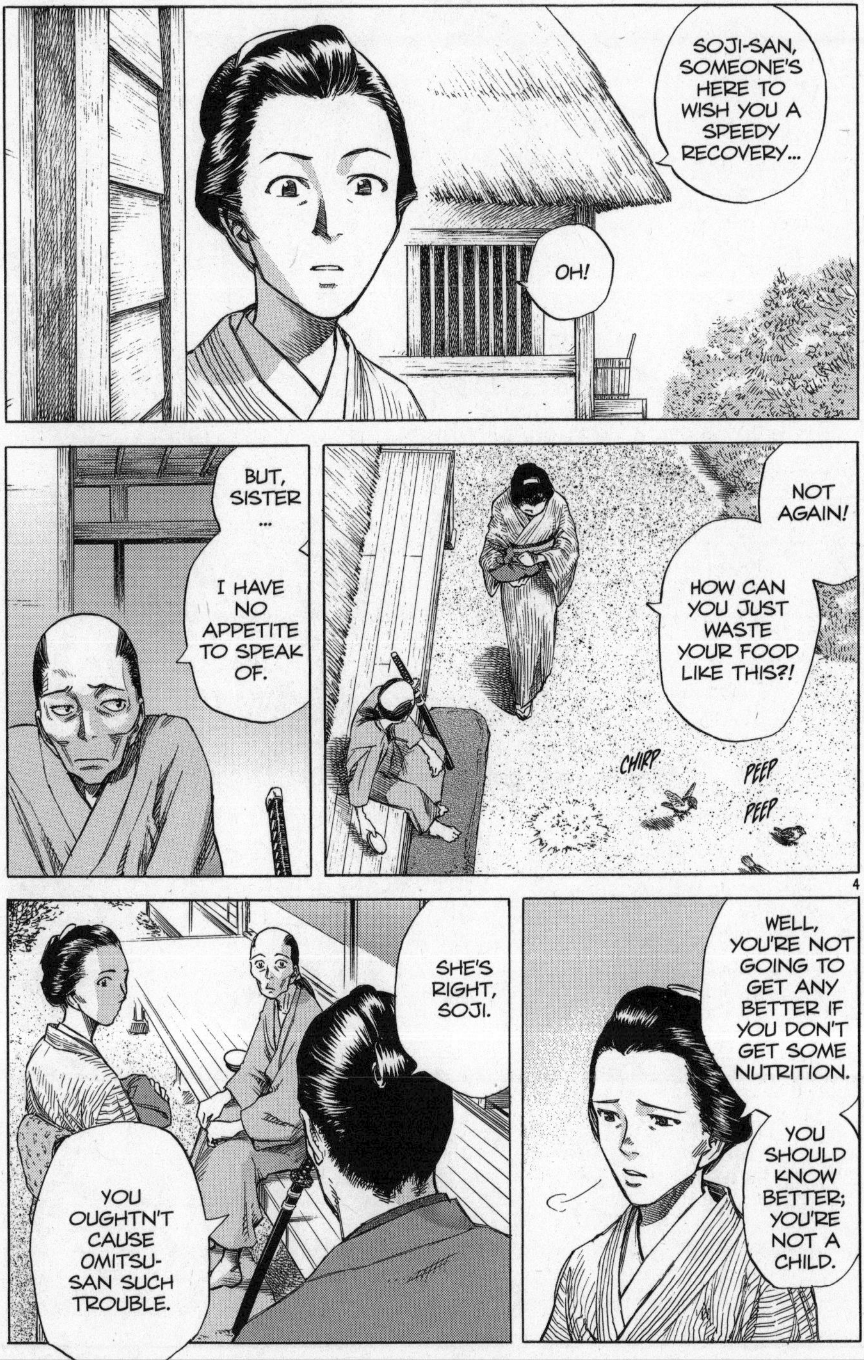
SOJI-SAN, SOMEONE'S HERE TO WISH YOU A SPEEDY RECOVERY...
OH!
NOT AGAIN!
HOW CAN YOU JUST WASTE YOUR FOOD LIKE THIS?!
PEEP
CHIRP
PEEP
BUT, SISTER ...
I HAVE NO APPETITE TO SPEAK OF.
WELL, YOU'RE NOT GOING TO GET ANY BETTER IF YOU DON'T GET SOME NUTRITION.
YOU SHOULD KNOW BETTER; YOU'RE NOT A CHILD.
SHE'S RIGHT, SOJI.
YOU OUGHTN'T CAUSE OMITSU-SAN SUCH TROUBLE.

4

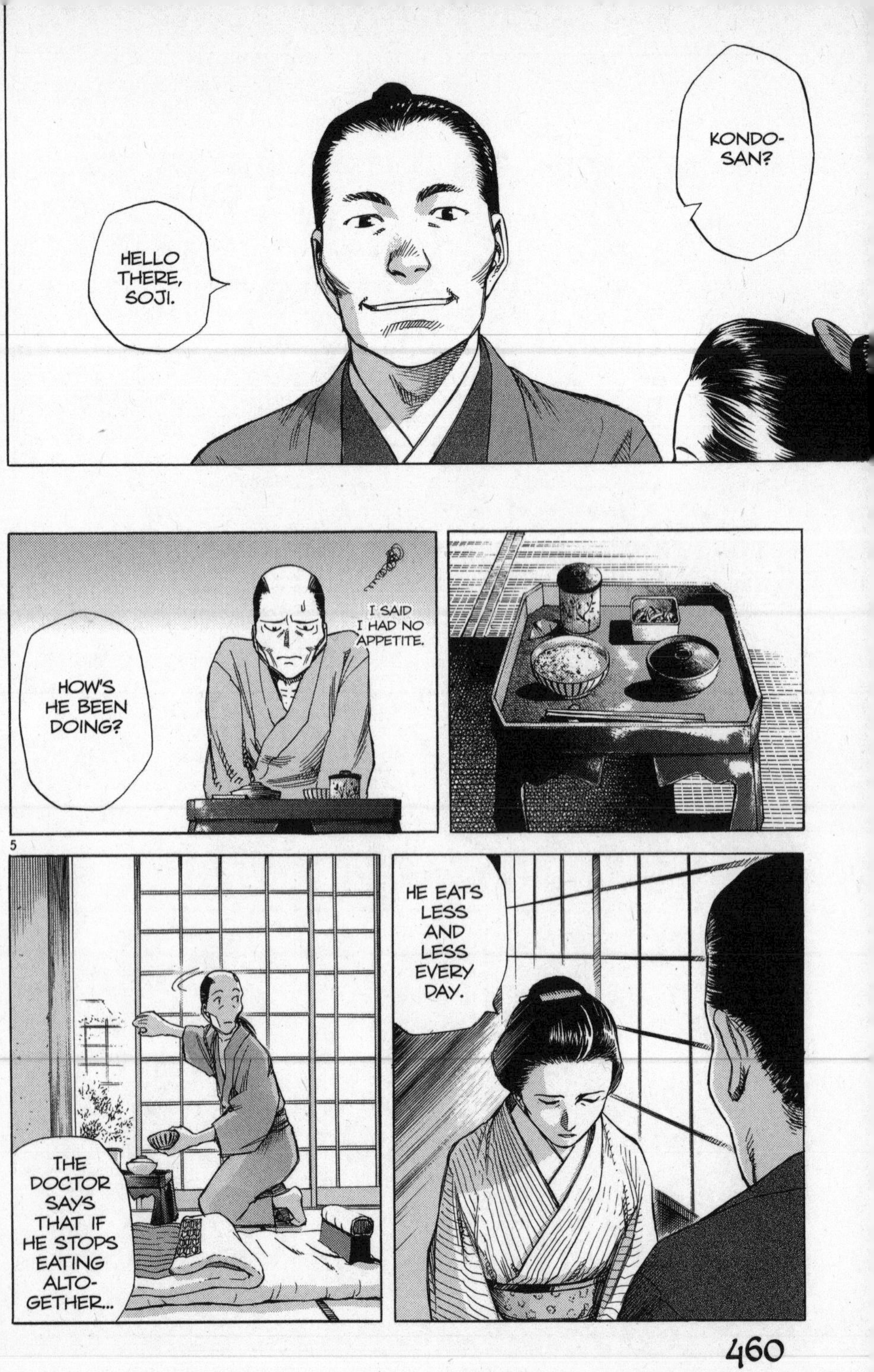
KONDO-SAN?
HELLO THERE, SOJI.
I SAID I HAD NO APPETITE.
HOW'S HE BEEN DOING?
HE EATS LESS AND LESS EVERY DAY.
THE DOCTOR SAYS THAT IF HE STOPS EATING ALTO-GETHER...

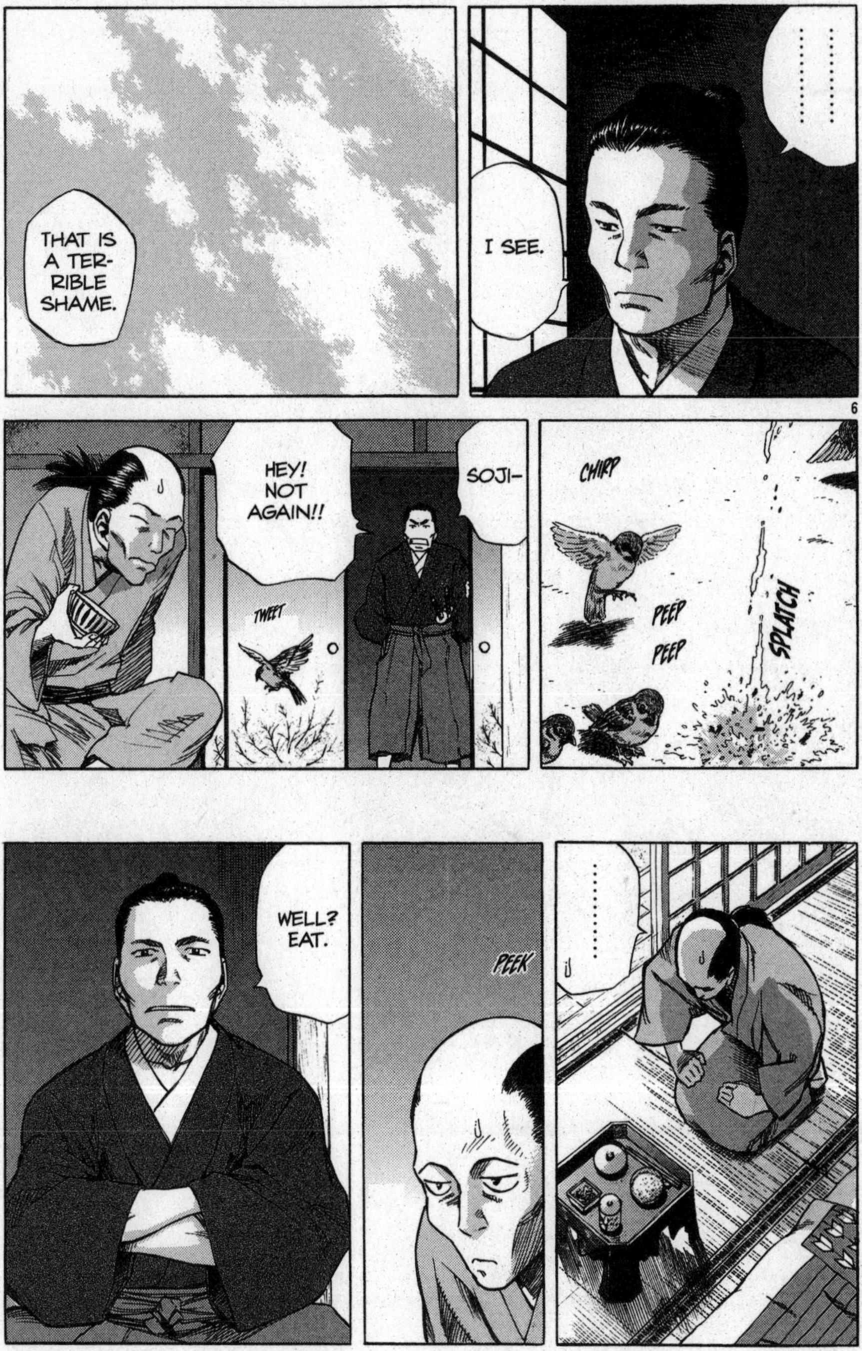
......
I SEE.
THAT IS A TERRIBLE SHAME.
CHIRP
PEEP
PEEP
SPLATCH
SOJI-
HEY! NOT AGAIN!!
TWEET
......
PEEK
WELL? EAT.

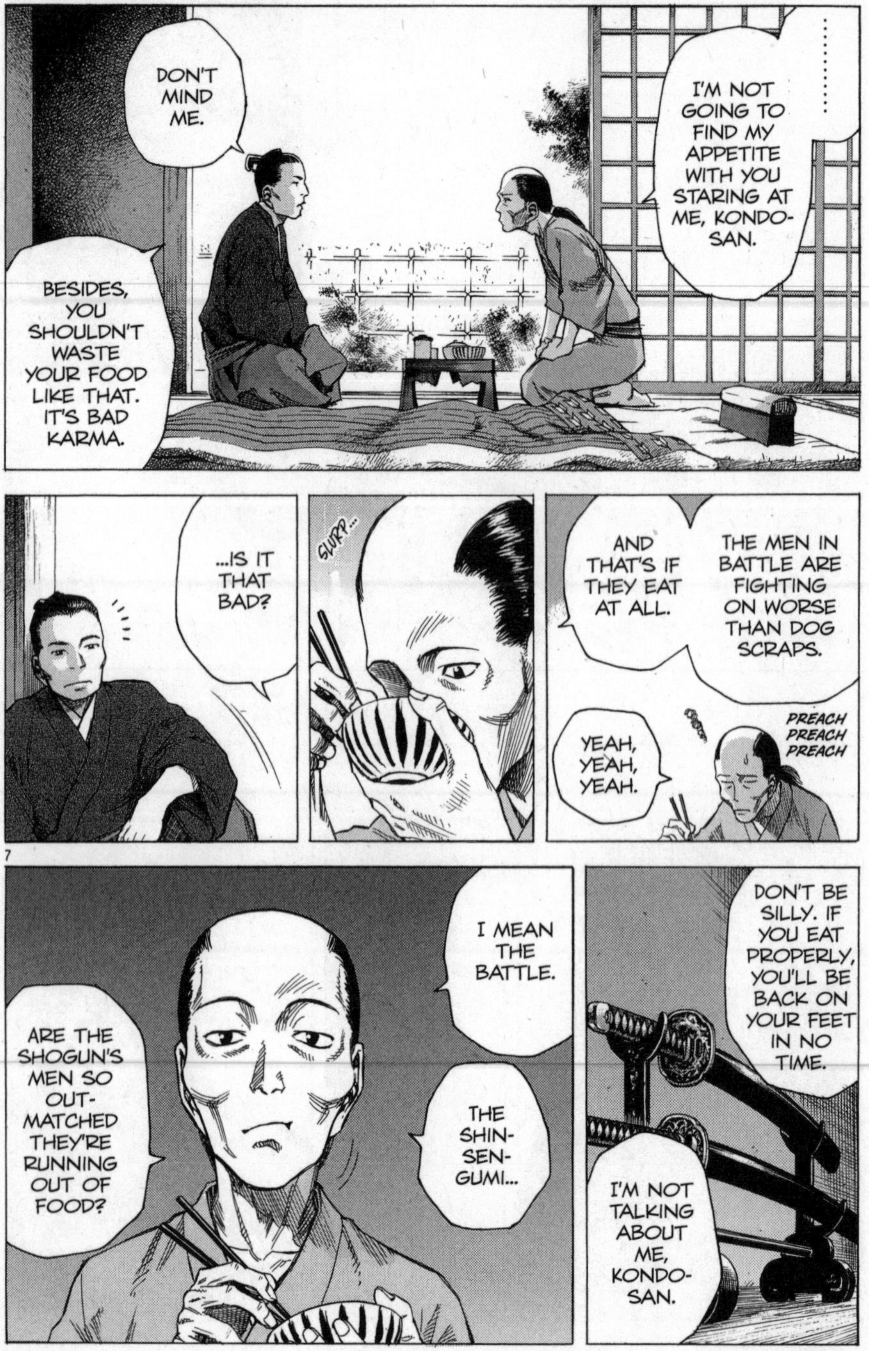
……
I'M NOT GOING TO FIND MY APPETITE WITH YOU STARING AT ME, KONDO-SAN.
DON'T MIND ME.
BESIDES, YOU SHOULDN'T WASTE YOUR FOOD LIKE THAT. IT'S BAD KARMA.
THE MEN IN BATTLE ARE FIGHTING ON WORSE THAN DOG SCRAPS.
AND THAT'S IF THEY EAT AT ALL.
PREACH PREACH PREACH
YEAH, YEAH, YEAH.
SLURP...
...IS IT THAT BAD?
DON'T BE SILLY. IF YOU EAT PROPERLY, YOU'LL BE BACK ON YOUR FEET IN NO TIME.
I'M NOT TALKING ABOUT ME, KONDO-SAN.
I MEAN THE BATTLE.
THE SHIN-SEN-GUMI...
ARE THE SHOGUN'S MEN SO OUT-MATCHED THEY'RE RUNNING OUT OF FOOD?

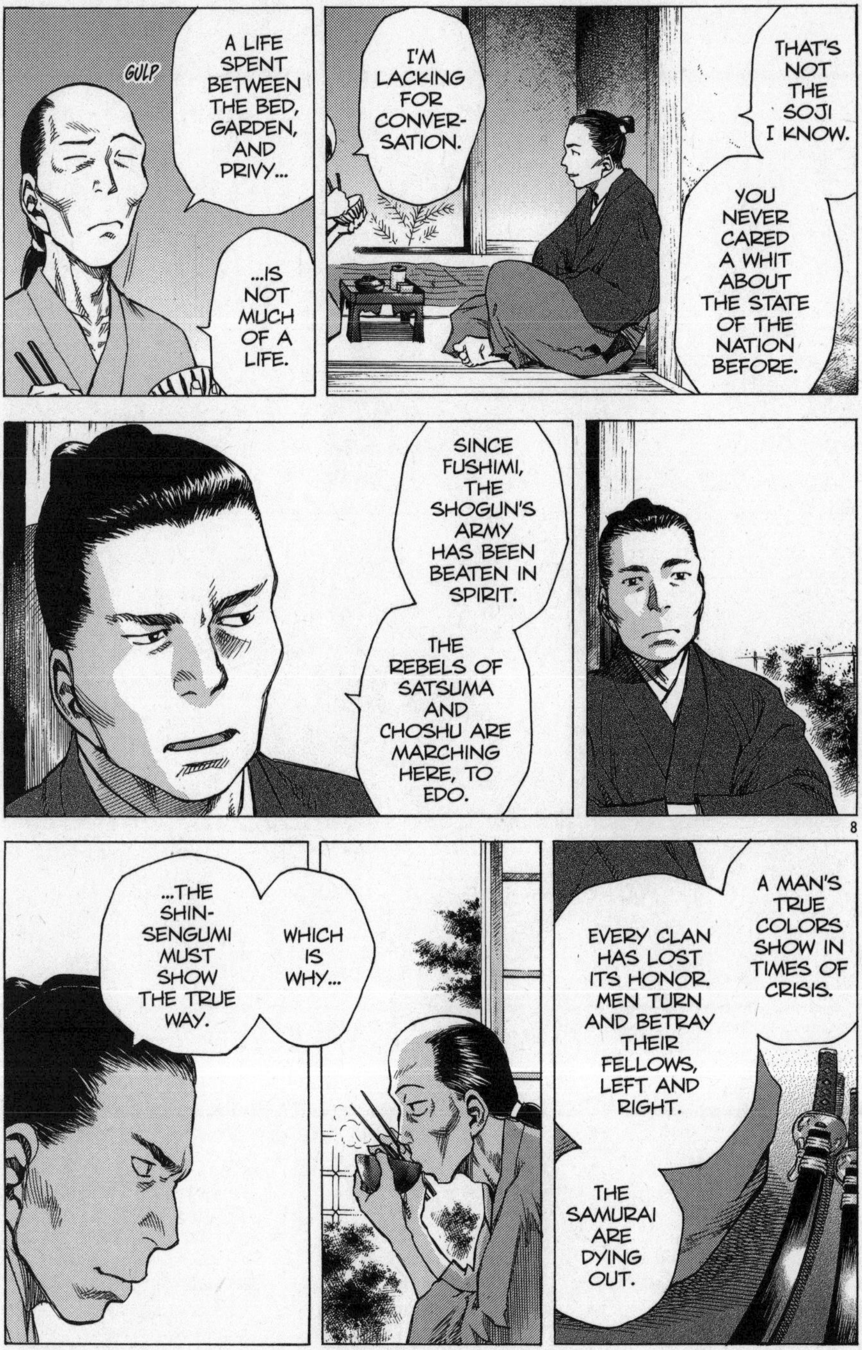
THAT'S NOT THE SOJI I KNOW.
YOU NEVER CARED A WHIT ABOUT THE STATE OF THE NATION BEFORE.
I'M LACKING FOR CONVER-SATION.
A LIFE SPENT BETWEEN THE BED, GARDEN, AND PRIVY...
GULP
...IS NOT MUCH OF A LIFE.
SINCE FUSHIMI, THE SHOGUN'S ARMY HAS BEEN BEATEN IN SPIRIT.
THE REBELS OF SATSUMA AND CHOSHU ARE MARCHING HERE, TO EDO.
8
A MAN'S TRUE COLORS SHOW IN TIMES OF CRISIS.
EVERY CLAN HAS LOST ITS HONOR. MEN TURN AND BETRAY THEIR FELLOWS, LEFT AND RIGHT.
THE SAMURAI ARE DYING OUT.
WHICH IS WHY...
...THE SHIN-SENGUMI MUST SHOW THE TRUE WAY.

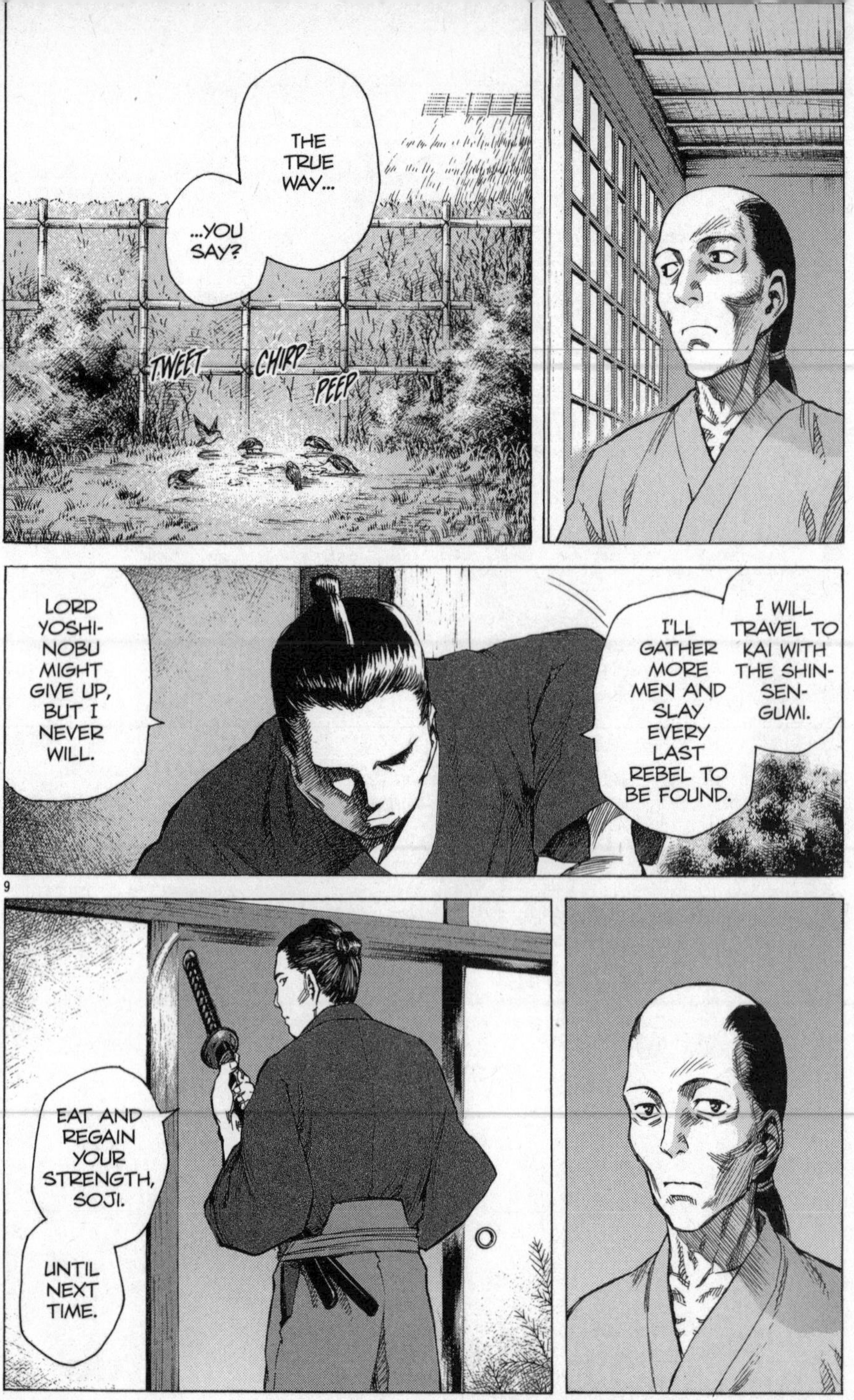
THE TRUE WAY...
...YOU SAY?
TWEET
CHIRP
PEEP
I WILL TRAVEL TO KAI WITH THE SHIN-SEN-GUMI.
I'LL GATHER MORE MEN AND SLAY EVERY LAST REBEL TO BE FOUND.
LORD YOSHI-NOBU MIGHT GIVE UP, BUT I NEVER WILL.
EAT AND REGAIN YOUR STRENGTH, SOJI.
UNTIL NEXT TIME.

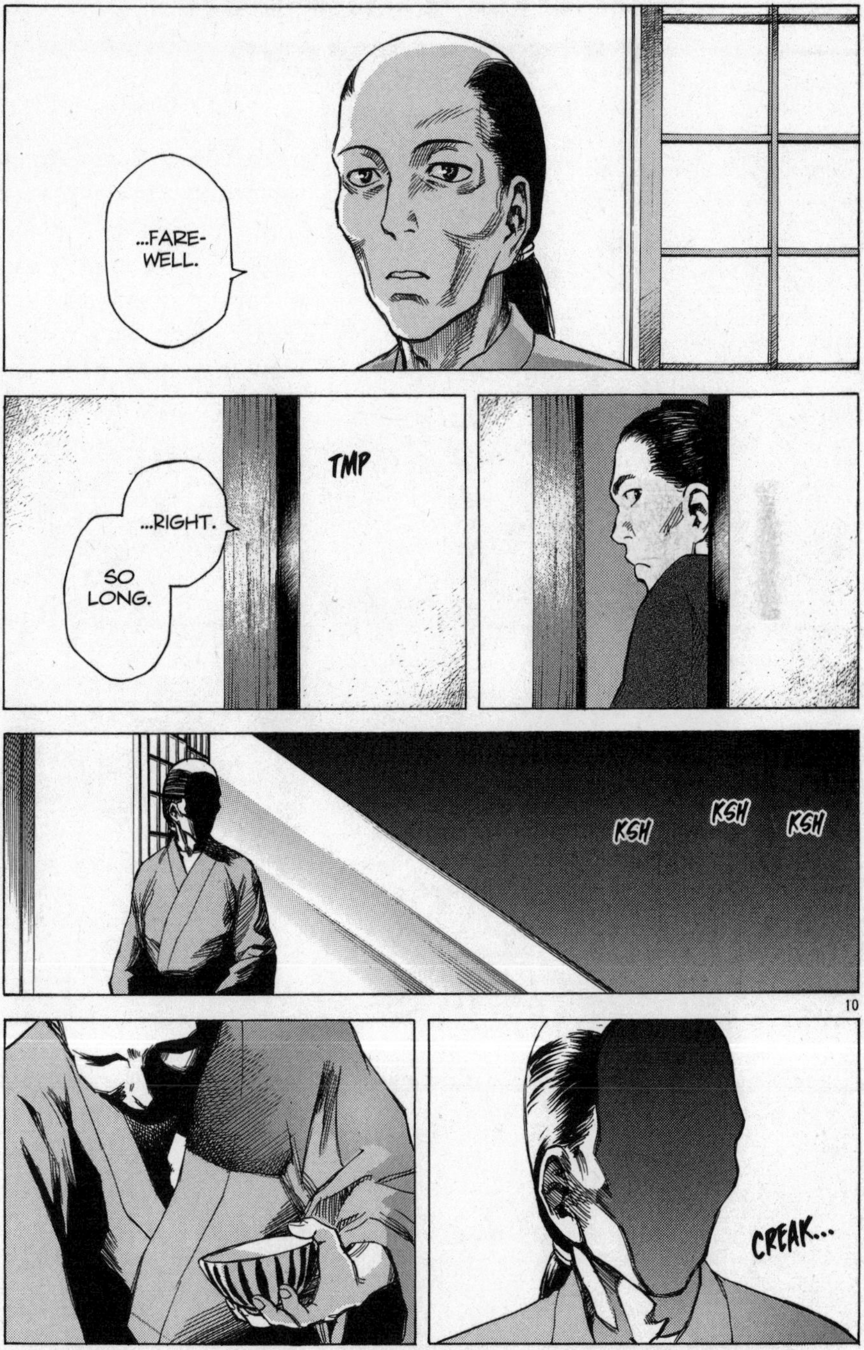
...FARE-WELL.
TMP
...RIGHT.
SO LONG.
KSH
KSH
KSH
CREAK...

TO BE CONTINUED IN VINLAND SAGA, BOOK TWO

MAKOTO YUKIMURA GETS AN AWARD

Creator Makoto Yukimura received a Kodansha Manga Award for "Vinland Saga." He decided to accept the award in style. On this page, we present a few snapshots from the awards ceremony.

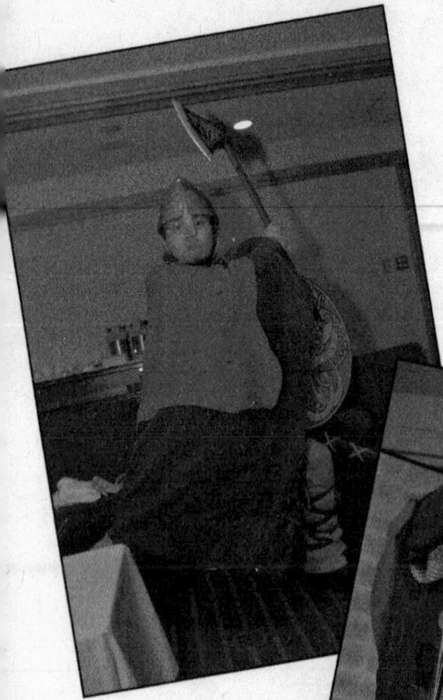

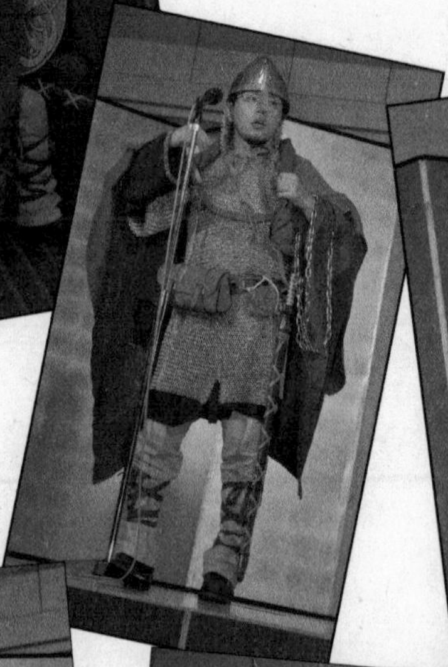

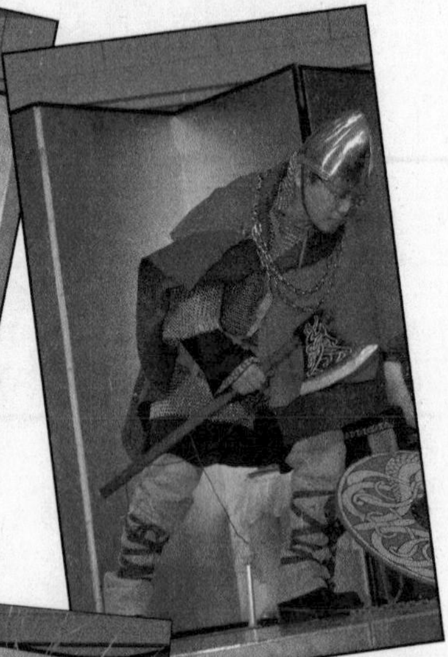

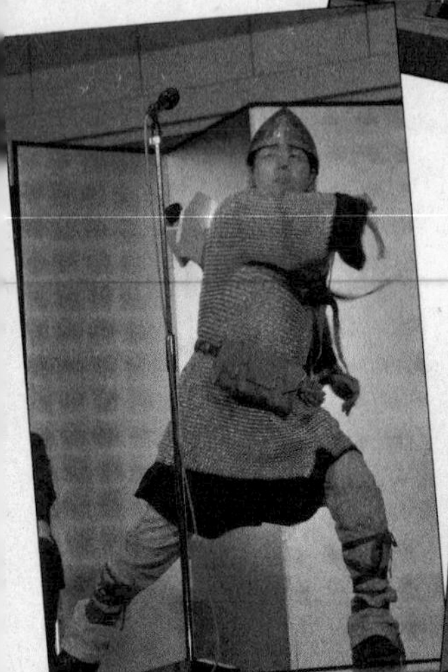

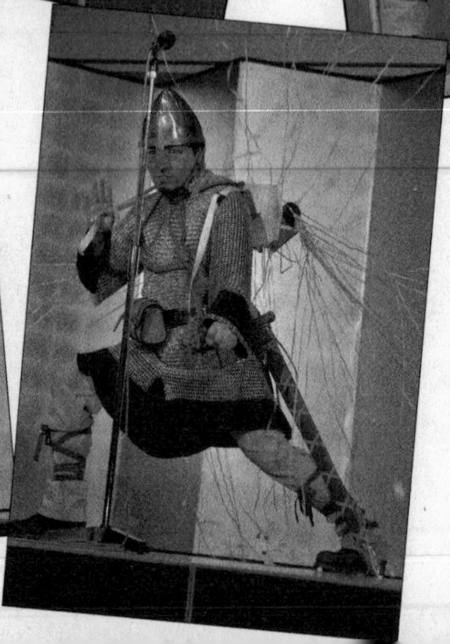